Volume I

The Humanities In Western Culture

Volume I

The Humanities In Western Culture
A Search For Human Values

Eighth Edition

Robert C. Lamm
Arizona State University

Neal M. Cross

with
Dale Davis
Texas Tech University

wcb
Wm. C. Brown Publishers
Dubuque, Iowa

Book Team
Developmental Editor *Raphael Kadushin*
Designer *Tara L. Bazata*
Production Editor *Barbara Rowe Day*
Photo Research Editor *Shirley Charley*
Permissions Editor *Mavis M. Oeth*
Visuals Processor *Joyce E. Watters*
Marketing Manager *Kathy Law Laube*

wcb group
Chairman of the Board *Wm. C. Brown*
President and Chief Executive Officer *Mark C. Falb*

wcb
Wm. C. Brown Publishers, College Division
President *G. Franklin Lewis*
Vice President, Editor-in-Chief *George Wm. Bergquist*
Vice President, Director of Production *Beverly Kolz*
National Sales Manager *Bob McLaughlin*
Director of Marketing *Thomas E. Doran*
Marketing Information Systems Manager *Craig S. Marty*
Executive Editor *John Woods*
Manager of Design *Marilyn A. Phelps*
Production Editorial Manager *Julie A. Kennedy*
Photo Research Manager *Faye M. Schilling*

Cover photo © Si Ch Ko/The Image Bank, Chicago

The credits section for this book begins on page C–1, and is considered an extension of the copyright page.

Unless otherwise credited, all photographs © Robert Lamm or © Kathryn S. Lamm.

Brief Contents

Volume II

Expanded Contents

Illustrations

Colorplates

Figures

Colormaps

Maps

Preface

This is the eighth edition of a text that first appeared forty years ago as *The Search for Personal Freedom*. The original title continued through the seventh edition, at which time I became the sole author of what is now *The Humanities in Western Culture*.

Longtime users of the book have always had a lively interest in its evolution. It is to them that the second section of the Preface is directed. The opening remarks are directed to those who are encountering the book for the first time.

The Humanities in Western Culture

This is a text for the integrated humanities: the arts of literature, painting, music, sculpture, photography, architecture, and film, and the discipline of philosophy. Though not an "art" in the strictest sense, philosophical ideas so consistently permeate each of the arts that theories of major philosophers are, of necessity, interwoven throughout the book. The components of the humanities—philosophy and the arts—are presented not as separate technical disciplines but as interrelated manifestations of human creativity. The arts and philosophy are not studied in isolation, however, but within the context of important developments in science, technology, economics, and politics. This is, in sum, a book about people and about "art's eternal victory over the human condition" (André Malraux).

In order to better understand why we are the way we are, our studies have been centered on our cultural heritage—from Mesopotamia, Egypt, Greece, and Rome to the present day. For a better comprehension of the great sweep of Western civilization, the text is divided into nine units (see the Brief Contents).

Throughout the book the accomplishments of the past are considered not as museum pieces but as living evidence of enduring responses to the perplexities of life. These achievements have become, in our day, a basic part of our attempts to make sense of the universe.

Because artists naturally respond to the issues of their own time, each unit is prefaced by an overview of the social, scientific, religious, and philosophical climate of the period. Forming the core of these volumes are the primary sources, the artworks themselves, many complete works rather than bits and pieces: plays, poetry, short stories, entire sections of large works, hundreds of art illustrations (many in color), and numerous musical examples. Introduced with appropriate commentary, the selections are followed by practical exercises and questions. Additionally, there are maps, graphs, time charts, and, at the end of each volume, there is a glossary of important terms in philosophy and the arts. An Instructor's Manual is available highlighting key points and including many suggestions for supplementary materials: slides, sound filmstrips, sound slidesets, and films. There is more than enough material for a two-semester course based entirely on the book, or the book can be used as a central text embellished by additional primary sources.

New in the Eighth Edition

There are many changes in both content and style, including new heads and subheads that clarify the text. There are new chapters on Mesopotamia and Egypt, expanded material on Islam, plus Shakespeare's *Tempest*, and Molière's *Tartuffe*. When added to *Agamemnon* and *Eumenides* by Aeschylus, *Oedipus* by Sophokles, and Euripides's *Trojan Women*, this brings the plays to a total of six.

There is a new unit on photography, new essays on everyday life in Egypt, Athens, Florence, and the like plus—for each chapter—a concluding essay on Culture and Human Values. Maps, graphs, time charts, exercises, black and white illustrations, and colorplates have all been increased.

The music chapters have been further simplified and illustrated with thirty-nine musical examples that are available on a tape made expressly for this book.

New literary selections include poetry by Gwendolyn Brooks and Susan Griffin, short stories by Eudora Welty and Flannery O'Connor, "If Shakespeare Had a Sister" by Virginia Woolf, and the "Letter from Birmingham Jail" by Martin Luther King, Jr. Also new is Mandelbaum's much-praised verse translation of Dante's *Divine Comedy*, a new translation of Machiavelli's *The Prince* by Bondanella and Musa, the translation of *Oedipus* by Fitts and Fitzgerald, and a selection from Fitzgerald's translation of the *Odyssey*. It was in his superb translations of the Homeric epics that Fitzgerald removed the "Latin screen" from Greek proper names by converting Ulysses to Odysseus, Achilles to Akhilleus, Hephaestus to Hephaistos, and so on. This long overdue reform—now advocated by many scholars—was adopted in the previous seventh edition of this book, mainly because the Greeks are entitled to their Greek names. The conversion from Latin to Greek spelling is still not total; no known authority uses the "correct" Alexandros for either Paris of Troy or Alexander the Great. In time, of course, that correction will also be made; after all, as late as the nineteenth century scholars still referred to the Parthenon as the Temple of Minerva.

The basic problem in writing a textbook (or teaching a humanities course) is determining not what to include, but what must be left out. A survey of Western culture in twenty volumes is less daunting than trying to cover the same material in only two volumes. As it is, some users say that there is too much material—literature in particular—for the standard two-semester humanities course. There is indeed too much material, except for the occasional class of brilliant overachievers—and these academic delights do exist. The instructor must evaluate the class and react accordingly; what should be abstracted or omitted is up to each instructor, which is just the way it should be. The key word is *selectivity;* the instructor may decide what to omit.

There are teachers who are concerned with in-depth studies and who prefer using additional complete works and fewer excerpts, selections, and the like. In terms of depth and breadth, this text holds to the middle ground with one hundred thirty nine complete works and thirty-three excerpts. Those who wish to be selective about omitting excerpts and adding complete novels, plays, essays, and the like are certainly at liberty to do so, and that is just the way it should be.

Robert C. Lamm

Acknowledgments

This book could not have been written without the diligence and expertise of a reference librarian, research and photographic associate, and in-house editor, namely, Katy Lamm.

I also wish to thank the following professors whose careful reading of the manuscript proved invaluable for this eighth edition.

J. Harly Chapman
William Rainey Harper College

Larry Dobbins
Missouri Western State College

Rose A. Doherty
Katherine Gibbs School

Debora A. Dreher
Florida Junior College

Clabourne Foster
Le Moyne-Owen College

Donna Karber Gardner
Mississippi County Community College

Ronald Ham
Ferris State College

David Hochstettler
Yavapai College

Leslie Huntress Hopkins
William Rainey Harper College

R. Harrison Kelton
Suffolk University

Scott J. Lowe
Pasco-Hernando Community College

Nancy McCollum
Pikes Peak Community College

James V. Mehl
Missouri Western State College

Jacob Opper
Frostburg State College

David C. Riede
University of Akron

Beverly A. Wallace
Carl Albert Junior College

Volume I

The Humanities In Western Culture

Prologue: An Introduction to Integrated Humanities

Today, all the normal mischances of living have been multiplied, a million-fold, by the potentialities for destruction, for an unthinking act of collective suicide, which man's very triumphs in science and invention have brought about. In this situation the artist has a special task and duty: the task of reminding men of their humanity and the promise of their creativity.[1]

Lewis Mumford

In Spain and in the modest mountains of southwestern France are numerous caves decorated with paintings that date from the late Old Stone (Paleolithic) Age (ca. 20,000–10,000 B.C.). In the caves of Lascaux there is, for example, a large chamber whose lofty ceiling is covered with paintings of antelope, horses, bulls, and other animals. Too deep and dark for human habitation, this may have been a sanctuary for religious rites or a setting for ritualistic magic to assure successful hunting, but no one knows for sure. No one knows the intentions of the people who created these images, but there is no question about what these people were. They were artists. Using intellect and imagination, late Paleolithic people had invented representation, a momentous step in the evolution of culture.

The invention of art symbolized major changes in the lives of people no longer at the mercy of the elements. Working together and planning ahead for seasonal changes, they hunted and gathered at optimum times and stored food for the long winters. It is now believed that they devoted as little as fifteen to twenty hours a week to the necessities of existence. There was time left over to make more efficient weapons and warmer clothing, to carve ivory and wood, to play, and to decorate cave sanctuaries. Late Paleolithic clans had created what every society must have if it is to advance its culture: free and unstructured time.

FIGURE P.1 *Bull, ceiling painting, 18' long, caves of Lascaux near Montignac, France, ca. 12,000 B.C.*

The creation of art also signified the emergence of individual artists. Lugging materials down through winding cave passages and erecting a scaffolding were undoubtedly communal efforts, but the artwork was done by an individual. That person, the artist, climbed atop the platform and painted a bull (figure P.1) in sweeping, confident lines, elegantly capturing a sense of life and communicating the illusion of powerful motion. In today's high-tech, nuclear-threatened world, the art of Lascaux is a poignant reminder of our kinship with Stone Age artists who, along with a multitude of successors, inspire us to recall our humanity, our intellect and imagination, our creative potential for a better life.

It is because everyone is capable of living a more rewarding life that we study the humanities. From cave art to the present, the arts and ideas of humans are beacons of hope, truth, and beauty for a world that needs to pay far more attention to the humanities, to the arts that teach us "nothing except the significance of life" (Henry Miller). In our integrated approach to the humanities,

---

1. Lewis Mumford, *In the Name of Sanity* (New York: Harcourt, Brace, 1954), p. 141.

we study literature, painting, music, sculpture, philosophy, and architecture not as separate disciplines but as interrelated manifestations of human creativity. Nor do we study the arts and artists in isolation. Artists are individuals, coping with the stress and strain of everyday life and, perhaps more than other people, influenced by the ideas and values of their society. "Artists are," observed composer Ned Rorem, "like everyone else, only more so."

The main focus of our study of the humanities is the idea that the quality of life can be enhanced and that this enrichment is available to all. Unlike Middle East oil reserves, the reservoir of Western culture is limitless; the more we draw from it the more there is to draw upon. The only deposits necessary are time and effort. The whole process amounts to addition or even multiplication. No one has to discard a collection of rock records to listen to Beethoven nor does Cowboy Art have to be traded in on Rembrandt.

This prologue is an introduction to the importance of the artist as an individual, the necessity of art, and the primacy of human values. The basic values that run through all cultures—the nature of truth, beauty, love, justice, faith—must be examined by each culture, each in its own way. Our study of how other cultures developed their value systems is chronological, a "return to the past" to see how the Egyptians, Greeks, and later civilizations handled their problems: the questions they asked and the solutions they tried. We examine earlier cultures from the vantage point of our own world, studying past achievements not as museum pieces but as living evidence of enduring responses to the perplexities of life. This priceless legacy becomes a basic part of our attempts to make sense of the world about us and of our own lives.

Why Study the Humanities?

We study the humanities not just to acquire facts about other cultures but to try to understand those cultures: their questions; their answers; what they valued. We can see the qualities they prized in their art and philosophy, and in their social and political institutions. We examine all of these areas to learn what they did; more importantly, we are concerned with *why* and *how* their cultures evolved in certain unique ways. Culture has sometimes been defined as that which remains after the civilization has vanished. What is left behind amounts to much more than artifacts; the creations of other cultures tell us of their visions, their hopes, their dreams.

This is a text for the integrated or interdisciplinary humanities, the interrelationships of the arts, philosophy, and social and political ideas and institutions. Life is itself interdisciplinary. We study the "lives" of other civilizations using the interdisciplinary approach to see how their values are manifested in just about everything they did or made or thought. Whatever understanding we gain from other cultures leads inevitably to a fuller understanding of culture in general and, in particular, our own culture, including our role in contemporary society.

Each person has the option of accepting value systems from other persons or institutions, or of developing a personal set of beliefs and values. Working to acquire an informed set of personal values is, of course, a lifelong project. The acquisition of knowledge and understanding about other cultures and about ourselves is certainly its own reward, but there are additional advantages. If "the unexamined life is not worth living," as Sokrates said, then self-knowledge would seem to be an acquired virtue. This would mean that the greater our understanding of what is going on in our lives, the more likely we are to be aware of our options and thus of opportunities to improve the quality of life.

We can acquire the freedom to objectively examine alternatives and possibly make better choices. This freedom is not conditioned absolutely by political, social, and economic considerations, although these factors can help or hinder our actions. One can imagine a political prisoner in Siberia whose knowledge and informed personal values allow a free and independent spirit in the most squalid of surroundings. The prisoner's goals, in this case, are not those of going somewhere or of acquiring material things, but of being a particular person. The movement of the person toward pure Being measures an approach toward the freedom we are discussing. Those who, in Thoreau's phrase, "live lives of quiet desperation" are at the mercy—intellectually and spiritually—of forces that are unknown to them and over which they have no control; with no knowledge, no understanding, there is no way to determine whether or not there are one, two, or more viable choices. All of us have to accept the "slings and arrows of outrageous fortune" (Shakespeare) when we have no alternative. The trick is to be so aware of what is going on in our society and in our lives that we can, at least some of the time, select viable options that will help improve the quality of life. It is worth our while—worth our lives in fact—to study cultures of the past and present, and to make conscious cultural choices on an ascending scale from good to the best.

The Culture-Epoch Theory

In order to study any culture, one should have some idea how that culture was built. In this book, we consider the historic past in terms of a simplified version of the *culture-epoch* theory of cultural formation. Except for possibly a smattering of political-military history, many of us are neither concerned nor knowledgeable about our cultural heritage. In attempting to help correct this deficiency, the culture-epoch theory has several virtues: the crucial fact of constant change is emphasized; cultural and intellectual history are incorporated into the historic tapestry; and evolutionary and revolutionary changes are better understood. The theory is neither more nor less "true" than any of a half-dozen other theories that attempt to account for cultural change. For our purposes, in an interdisciplinary context, the theory works.

According to the culture-epoch theory, a culture is founded upon whatever conception of reality is held by the great majority of people over a considerable period of time. This is true even though the majority may not be aware of any concept of reality or, more probably, take it so much for granted that they are not aware it is simply a human idea, held on faith. Thus, for most people at the time this is written, a typewriter is real, a physical tree is real, and all things which can be seen, heard, smelled, felt, or tasted are real.

As a matter of fact, a number of scientists, philosophers, and religious thinkers have given us different concepts of reality, which have also been widely held. These thinkers have contemplated the millions of forms of life, many of them bearing resemblances to others, yet each one different; they have examined the forms of earth, air, fire, and water; they have wondered about the processes of change by which a tree today may, at some time in the future, disintegrate into earth and reappear in some totally alien form. They have watched such nontangible things as sunlight and air becoming leaf and branch. Pondering these things, they come inevitably to the ultimate question: "What is the nature of reality?"

To reach an answer, they usually focus on a few profound inquiries, some of which may be given here. For example, they might say, "We see change all around us. We see grass eaten and turn into cow. We see cow eaten and turn into human. We see humans disintegrate and turn into earth. If all these changes can take place, what are the universal elements of which all things are composed?" Or they might say, "We see an individual human, John Doe, as baby, as youth, as adult, as senile old man, as corpse. From one moment to the next, he is never the same. Yet he is always the same, John Doe, a distinct being. Can it be that nothing is permanent, that reality is a process rather than a thing or group of things? If we have change, then, how does the process take place? And more important, we know that we live in a world of constant change, but what force directs the process?"

"Nonsense," retorts another group of thinkers. "That which is in a constant state of flow cannot be real. Only that which is permanent and unchanging can be real. What, then, in the universe is permanent, unchanging in itself, yet is able to transform itself, manifest itself, or produce from itself the countless forms we see around us?"

These are some of the basic questions the pure thinker contemplates. The answers are various concepts of reality.

Based upon the idea of reality accepted as "true," specialized thinkers build different thought-structures that underlie visible institutions. These include a philosophy of justice from which particular forms of law and government spring; a philosophy of education that dictates the nature of our schools and the material taught in them; a religious philosophy that becomes apparent in churches and creeds; and an economic philosophy that yields its particular ways of producing and distributing goods and services, including the token-systems used as money. Other philosophies and institutions could be named, but these are some that greatly affect our daily living.

When these are formed, we have a complete culture, but always by the time such a pattern is established, we have forces at work that tend to destroy it. The destroyers are new pure thinkers who note inconsistencies within the idea of reality itself, and who question postulates or find contradictions.

From these new thinkers (philosophers, scientists, theologians) comes a new idea of reality so convincing it cannot be brushed aside. It must be accepted. Suddenly the whole structure of the culture finds itself without foundation. The justice and the law appropriate in the old culture no longer fit on the new foundation; the old education is no longer appropriate; old religious beliefs no longer describe a person's position in relation to God; old ways of making things and distributing them no longer suffice.

Periods of Chaos

At this time people are plunged into a *period of chaos,* the first step in the formation of a new epoch.

The symptoms of the period of chaos lie around us now in such profusion that they scarcely need description. In the latter part of the twentieth century this is where we live. New and shocking ideas, moralities, and beliefs are introduced and discarded; terrorists attack established governments; civil strife and wars of conquest rage; everyone damages the environment; and over everything looms the menace of nuclear obliteration. At the mercy of events beyond their control, some people try to turn back the clock to better, more peaceful days; others seek refuge and security in fundamentalist beliefs; still others retreat to paramilitary armed camps; many just mindlessly camp in front of their television sets, perhaps hoping that all of the problems will somehow vanish. In other words, we see in the late twentieth century a period of chaos that, nevertheless, gives some evidence of resolution.

Periods of Adjustment

Out of the turmoil and confusion of chaotic periods of past cultures emerges the *period of adjustment.* At this point, notable artists—whether painters, writers, sculptors, composers, or creators in some other medium—make their important contributions to society. Pheidias and Sokrates of ancient Athens; the master builders of the celebrated Gothic churches; Michelangelo, Beethoven, Goethe—these innovators begin to suggest the new line, shape, and pattern for a new culture.

Two ideas need to be stressed about the role of the artist in the development of a cultural pattern. First, the artist does not necessarily know all about new ideas of reality. For example, the artist in our time does not necessarily know all about Einstein's theory. The artist is simply a person of greater sensitivity than others, and with great skill in one medium. As a sensitive person, the artist probably feels more keenly than the rest of us the tensions of the time—the pulls of this belief and the pulls of another contradictory one. An artist will not rest until he or she has explored this confusing experience and discovered some meaning, some significance, therein.

The great artist is always the composer (whether musician, writer, painter, choreographer, architect, or sculptor), the person who puts things together in new relationships and finds new meanings for experience.

A second idea about the artist's contribution to the formation of a cultural pattern is the important role of structure, rather than subject matter, conveying cultural meaning. For example, one may compare the structure of an Egyptian temple (see figure 2.5) with that of the Parthenon in Athens (see figure 7.23). The subject matter of both is roughly the same—they are temples built for the worship of a god. But what a difference! The Temple of Amon is enormous, both overpowering and intimidating, reflecting the total control of the populace by the pharaoh and a permanent priesthood. The temple of Athena, the Parthenon, is serene, rational, and exquisitely proportioned. Decorated with sculptured reliefs depicting gods *and* Greek citizens, it is a structure erected by the citizens of a democratic society in which there is no resident priesthood.

It comes down to this: styles in beauty change as the basic characteristics of people change. Or perhaps it works the other way; perhaps as new glimpses of beauty are caught by the artists, people themselves change to conform to the new beauty.

However it may happen, the artist, especially in the period of chaos and early in the period of adjustment within a culture-epoch, personally feels the stresses, tensions, and turmoil of the period. The artist explores conflicts within, which are the conflicts of the general population as well, and creates new structures, new designs, to synthesize the elements of conflict and to give new meaning to experience. Some works of art, probably depending upon the individual artist's breadth of vision and ability to compose insight into significance, are seized upon as symbols of new pattern and new truth in society. They express the new idea of beauty and truth.

At this point another element of the population—we may call them the *intellectuals*—enters the picture. They are people like ourselves, college students and faculty members, government officials, ministers, business executives, and many others who think seriously about things and who, like the artists, have been troubled by the conflict of their times. They still are working within the period of adjustment in an epoch. They become aware of new meanings and patterns produced by the artists, and they start reshaping these designs into new philosophies of justice, of economics, of religion, and the like, and begin to build concrete institutions out of the philosophies that they have created. Through their work, order slowly emerges out of chaos.

Periods of Balance

When their work is finished, we come to the third period within a culture-epoch, the *period of balance*. At this point, the idea of reality, the philosophies that underlie our basic institutions, and the institutions themselves are all in harmony. Early in a period of balance, life must be very satisfying; everyone must know the reason for getting up in the morning to face the day. But if balance lasts too long, life begins to get dull. The big jobs seem to be done, and decadence, boredom, and deterioration may set in. The long and painful decline of the Roman Empire was just such a period.

But change comes inevitably. At the beginning of the twentieth century, physicists were assuring young scientists that the great discoveries in physics had all been made and that only little tidying-up jobs remained. At the same time, Einstein was beginning his work, which was to supersede all our knowledge in physics. Just when people have been certain of everything in their periods of balance, new pure thinkers come along to upset the whole apple cart into a new epoch.

A word of caution should be appended here. This systematic description of an epoch makes it sound as if artists only function in a time of chaos or adjustment, or as if philosophers quit philosophizing until their proper time comes around. This, of course, is not true. While the epoch does divide itself into three rough periods, all of the functions occur with greater or lesser impact throughout the entire time period.

In this book, the various periods of history will be treated in the following way: The rise of Athenian democracy in the fifth century B.C. and its rapid decline will be treated as one culture-epoch. The Roman period from the time of the rule of Julius Caesar will be regarded as an attempt to maintain rationalistic Greek times, under law, and backed by strong military authority. It does not constitute an epoch of the type we have been describing. Because of their far-reaching importance, Judaism and Christianity will be treated separately, though inadequately because of limited space. Actually the teachings of Jesus represent the work of the pure thinker, and the Christian concept of God was a new concept of reality that served as the foundation for the Middle Ages. The Middle Ages, dating from about A.D. 450 to 1350 will be considered as a complete epoch. The time period from 1350 to the early twentieth century really constitutes another epoch, with the Renaissance as a large segment of the period of chaos within it. Because the Renaissance, using the approximate dates of 1350 to 1600, presents so much of interest for the student of humanities, however, it will be treated as a separate time period. Then, with the clash of rationalism and romanticism and the final emergence of the Faustian man, we will consider the period from about 1600 to the early twentieth century as a complete epoch. The last unit of this book will look as carefully as possible at the cultural changes with which we in the twentieth century are so deeply involved.

A Common Basis for Understanding the Arts

In the humanities we take art seriously because, as Aristotle observed, "art is a higher type of knowledge than experience." Earlier in this century the arts were regarded as "the finer things of life" and were respected as a sort of polish the upper classes received as a part of their education. Art was show-off stuff, valuable precisely because it was of no practical good. The upper middle-class child showed his status by wearing braces on his teeth and by taking piano lessons until he eventually learned to plunk out the *Moonlight Sonata* with little thought beyond the mechanical problem of getting the right fingers on the right notes. Another domestic status symbol was having a beautifully bound volume of the *Complete Works of Swinburne* (an "important" writer) resting casually on the coffee table, never opened let alone read, but advertising the good taste of the owner. As a matter of fact, this whole attitude towards art might well be called the coffee-table school of appreciation. The attitude still exists. But, as indicated in our description of a culture-epoch, we now recognize that eminent artists actually help create patterns for a way of life; "The object of art is to give life a shape" (Jean Anouilh).

One might ask what area of the universe is the darkest, the most unknown. The universe itself? Einstein once said that the most incomprehensible fact about the universe is that it is so comprehensible. No, the most bewildering portion of the universe is yourself. As a member of the human race, you are (or should be) asking yourself such questions as "Who am I?" "What am I?" "Why am I here?" It is the artist who persists in reacting to these questions, who seeks answers from within, and who discovers answers that strike responsive chords in the rest of us. As Henry Miller said, "art teaches nothing, except the significance of life."

A Shakespearean scholar once made the statement that in his plays Shakespeare had made discoveries as important as those made by any scientist. At first, such an assertion seems to be an overreaction to the dominance of science in the modern world. Consider, however, Shakespeare's treatment of love and hate in *Romeo and Juliet,* good and evil in *King Lear,* and murder and revenge in *Macbeth,* for example. These aspects of the human condition, as they are dramatized on the stage, are artistic truths. This idea of discoveries by Shakespeare or any other artist can give us a basis for understanding the arts. In this respect, as Jean Cocteau observed, "art is science in the flesh."

Generally we can think of scientific knowledge and artistic truth in this way: The physical sciences explore the world outside humankind; the social sciences make discoveries about the behavior and activities of people in various groups; and the arts and humanities probe the area of inner meaning: humanity's fears, hopes, loves, delights as the individual and society act and react within their world. "All art is social," as historian James Adams noted, "because it is the result of a relationship between an artist and his time." Art is also exploration, and the discoveries artists make are expressed as *concepts* and *percepts.* Concepts are ideas that cannot be seen, like friendship, beauty, and justice. Percepts are what we perceive with our senses: line, taste, color, aroma, volume, pitch, and so forth. Artists express concepts by the unique manner in which they choose to arrange the percepts, that is, the sense-apparent objects and materials. Obviously this kind of vivid creativity can never be done by committee: "Art is the most intense mode of individualism that the world has known" (Oscar Wilde).

Differences and Similarities

Because of differences in media and modes of expression, the arts differ from each other in many ways. Certainly a *time-art* such as music, which exists only as long as it is heard, differs from a *space-art* such as painting, which uses visual symbols as its means of expression. Both arts are separated from literature, a *word-art* that must be interpreted by the reader. The differences between Beethoven's Fifth Symphony, the *Mona Lisa,* and *Hamlet* are certainly obvious; what is not so obvious is their similarities. "Painting," wrote Emerson, "was called 'silent poetry,' and poetry 'speaking painting.' The laws of each art are convertible into the laws of any other." The common basis of all the arts is the exploration by means of sensory percepts into the emotion, the mind, the personality of humans; their common goal is to speak directly to our inner being. As Emerson also wrote: "Raphael paints wisdom; Handel sings it, Pheidias carves it, Shakespeare writes it." An examination of this common basis is the purpose of this chapter.

The artist deals subjectively with all materials as he or she draws upon a special store of personal experience. Moreover, artistic production depends as much upon the background and personality of the artist as it does upon the raw material of experience. It follows therefore that each artist is unique, an individual different from all other persons, and that the artist's production is equally unique. One might take, for example, the treatment two literary artists make of the same theme, the emptiness of the life of a woman who, in herself, is virtually a complete blank, but who moves from man to man, living only as a reflection of each man. Read Dorothy Parker's story, "Big Blonde," and Anton Chekhov's story, "The Darling" (filmed as *Darling,* starring Julie Christie). Although the experience is the "same" in both stories, the end result is quite different, and the experience of the reader is also very different, while reacting to the general idea in two different forms. The reader might protest, "But one of them must be right about this kind of person and one of them must be wrong." Actually both Parker and Chekhov are right; and any other artist who treated the same material with a different insight might also be right. The discovery of multiple truths is a personal matter and the corollary is that the realm of truth in personality, that prime area where the arts are focused, is inexhaustible. The person who understands any work of art grows with each facet of experience shared with the artist. In other words, our boundaries are expanded as we add the artist's experience to our own, thereby increasing the data in our own personal computer bank. Gabriel Marcel expressed a similar idea:

> Thanks to art, instead of seeing one world, our own, we see it multiplied and, as many original artists as there are, so many worlds are at our disposal.

The Creative Process

Not always recognized is the fact that the artists in literature, painting, sculpture, music, and the other arts have a method of investigation in their field of knowledge that we may call the method of intuition or insight. In much the same way that scientists start out, artists become aware of a problem in the realm of human experience, or they sense some aspect of the human personality that is dark and unknown. Put more simply, they feel the need to create, and this compulsion is the first step in the artistic process. As a second step, they begin to gather materials, both conceptual (idea-stuff) and perceptual (physical-stuff: visual images, sequences of sound, etc.). The third step is the appropriate arrangement of materials, which comes as an insight or an intuitive perception of new and varied relationships among the materials with which they are working. Since artists are dealing with a problem of relationships, the truth they seek takes the shape of arranging materials in proper order with respect to each other. In other words, the form (arrangement and relationship) is a very necessary part of artistic truth; this form involves the arrangement of incident, character, or images in literature, of visual elements in painting or sculpture, of sounds or themes in musical composition so that they arrive at the point that artists have felt by insight. In other words, this is the step we call *composition,* a term that is common to all of the arts. From this step the art-object emerges—a song, a pot, a picture, a poem—which has both an aesthetic and a utilitarian function in the world (and frequently the best of the utilitarian productions have a very high degree of aesthetic value).

Testing Artistic Truths

But how can artists check results of their exploration? That is the job of their audience. After the composition, artists turn their creations loose in the world. People examine these creations, both in terms of subject and explicit meaning, and in terms of the form in which they are presented. If an artwork is composed in such a way that the members of the audience *live through* the experience themselves and find that the artist has made a true statement of the experience in all of its relationships, then the discovery of the artist is accepted as a truth wrested from the dark ignorance of the human condition in the world. Two of the tests that might be applied are these: First, is it new? If the meaning (a combination of idea and formal structure) is old and trite, the artwork may be comfortable, but not of much artistic value. Second, is the emotional content proper for the subject? If the treatment is sentimentalized, then it is probable that the artist lacked either sincerity or a steady view of life.

One caution: The test of artistic truth cannot be made by the general public, although their criticism may be valuable. Scientists, for example, would not allow the validity of their conclusions to be tested by a plumber, a cab driver, and a meat cutter. They ask that these truths be tested by the experiments of scientists who are their equal in scientific knowledge. There is a little difference between scientists and artists, but the difference is not too marked. We could argue that since the butcher, the baker, and the candlestick maker are human personalities, they might be accepted as valid critics of the artist's discovery. To a certain extent this claim is true. On the other hand, certain people can read with more discernment than others. Some are excellent at understanding the language and symbolism of painting, sculpture, or music. Perhaps more important, some people are more sensitive than others to the problems of personality and experience. These people, those who can understand the medium of expression and who are sensitive to human problems, must constitute the group of judges for the validity of a work of art.

The Artist's Raw Materials

The next question for consideration is the nature of the raw materials for artistic investigation. These are sometimes hard to see. Most obvious are the many facets of such emotions as love, hatred, jealousy, contentment, sudden apprehension of the beauty in nature or people, and other emotional reactions. As a matter of fact, these materials from life are so common that it is probable that the great bulk of art is made from them, but there is much more material that has been explored in literature, art, and music. Artists present their explorations as experience that the members of the artistic audience may live through. Take, for example, the psychological experience confronting a young prince who has been humanely educated, who faces a problem of evil involving the murder of his father, the king, and the unfaithfulness, even incest, of his mother. (In other words, the problem Shakespeare explored in *Hamlet.*) The artist feels this problem within himself and composes its elements and its solution. Psychology and literature often run parallel to each other; the former gives facts, the latter gives truth-to-life. This truth is achieved because we become personally involved in the work of literature, live through the complexities of the problem with all their attendant, opposing emotions, and sense the logic, the rightness, and the freedom of the solution when it is reached.

Form

Perhaps one more consideration is necessary before we turn to examples of the explorations and discoveries of the artists. This consideration is that of the place and importance of form. Let us put it this way: human experience is seldom simple or direct. Rather, its importance is usually clouded with events of no importance, many of which are totally irrelevant. Perhaps the best illustration of this may be found in the artist who is painting a landscape. The artist's purpose is not to make a direct copy from nature—a camera might provide a more exact representation than a human being. Rather, the painter is seeking to interpret an experience with beauty. The natural scene, however, is cluttered with objects detracting from the impression the artist seeks. Consequently, the artist leaves many out, rearranges them mentally, and paints on canvas the objects that individual sees, so that the picture, when complete, is not a copy of nature, but a picture of beauty, with the natural objects selected and arranged to make the meaning clear. But no critic, nor commentator, perhaps not even the artist, could give us a definite, final statement as to what that "meaning" is. Perhaps it is a sense of the importance of peace, quiet, repose; perhaps it is the wonder of organization, order, design; perhaps it is the sheer joy of contrasting colors, the delight in appearances of objects, their texture and feel; perhaps the pleasure of a thing of beauty. If it could be expressed definitely in words, the picture would not be necessary, but since it cannot, it is the only means by which the artist can share a delight in the world. And the imperative need to share it, to get it "said," is the quality that makes artists; they not only do what they can, but what they must. Somehow, that creative urge, which everyone shares to some extent, is communicated to an audience; theorists of "aesthetic experience" do not agree on the "how," but something does happen. However little understood the process, the fact remains that people throughout the years have enjoyed (the word is too weak: they have *needed*) the making of pictures and the looking at them.

It is interesting that it is this element of form that all of the arts have in common, and it is this that gives them the "living-through" quality we have noted as distinctive of artistic truth. It is the process, not the end result, that is important. It is the form, not the final statement, that yields artistic truth, though this does not imply that the artist's final point is unimportant. The important thing is having gone through the experience with the artist and arriving at the discovery the artist wishes to communicate.

With this in mind, we are going to examine some examples of art in different media to see how the various artists have mined some truth from the darkness and chaos of the human experience. Every art form has much in common with other forms but each also has its own symbols, images, and materials, all used in ways that are unique for each medium. Written or spoken references to a painting, for example, are translations. If, as Gertrude Stein has written, "a rose is a rose is a rose," so also a painting is a painting is a painting. The mixture of paints on the canvas *is* the message; all else is translation in one way or another. "An artist cannot speak about his art," remarked Jean Cocteau, "any more than a plant can discuss horticulture." The literary arts resist translation just as obstinately as do the visual arts. Whether the poet, for example, uses familiar word sets ("Come live with me and be my love") or unconventional combinations ("love is more thicker than forget"), the exact arrangement of the precise words is what the poet has to say and nothing else, or the poet would have said that instead. In both arts a single work may have several levels of meaning, ranging deeper and deeper from the surface meaning, and lookers and readers can uncover greater depths of significance as they work through the symbols created by the artist. In both arts the interpretations are somewhat personal, depending upon the critical ability and background of the reader or the viewer. The response, however, *must be* within the limits set by the artist. In the arts, as in most other things, we can always arrive at some very mistaken interpretations.

Music

Music amounts to pure form and is not amenable to any one "story" interpretation. Many untutored listeners have one of two responses to music. When they think they are listening perceptively they arrive at some sort of story, which usually sounds something like this: This person is in love, and then his girl leaves him, and right at the end she comes back and everything is just dandy. The other listening attitude is simply to be submerged in the sound, to, in other words, take a tonal bath. The latter listeners usually find their attention wandering off in a thousand directions before a musical selection of any length is finished. In other words, they find themselves thinking about everything but the music.

But music, except for program music, which has a story to tell in sound and sometimes employs sounds heard in everyday life (and the composer's "story" is not necessarily that of the listener), is form in sound. It is a "time-art," which makes it particularly elusive, since by the time it is heard it is gone. Music makes greater demands on its audience, both in knowledge and attention, than do any of the other arts. The knowledgeable and attentive listener finds, however, that living through a musical selection yields as much meaning for life's experiences as do any of the other arts. In its structures one may find the grandeur of Bach, the elegance of Mozart, the serenity of Gregorian chant, or the sound of protest, which is sometimes characteristic of jazz. Whatever the significance of a piece of music, it is the composition that counts. As much as in any of the other arts, perhaps more, the composer must arrange materials so that the listener lives through an experience that lies deeper than words or the recognizable subject matter of painting. It is this process of composition that leads to "living through," our concern in this section, since it is the common basis for all the arts.

Music is sound moving in time, and therein lies its magical mystery. While listening to an unfamiliar piece of music, the listener does not know where the music is going until it gets there, that is, ceases to sound. From silence to sound to silence and what takes place in between is a mixture of sound and silence comprehended only in retrospect, after one musical section has followed upon another until silence reigns again. Readers can re-read difficult passages in a book and art lovers can study a painting for hours, but music listeners have one ride on a merry-go-round. There is no way to stop the music or freeze a beautiful sound, even though some critics are fond of referring to architecture as "frozen music." Nothing is ever that simple.

Music is a structural art built out of a multiplicity of materials by the composer, who picks and chooses tones, colors, textures, rhythms, and patterns just as a writer selects words and phrases that best suit the purpose and the painter chooses lines and colors. Rarely are these infinite choices deliberately calculated or contrived, except in so-called "bad" art. The artist, each in his own way, is seeking expression, to communicate some feeling, truth, or emotion about experience as it is perceived.

Music is the envy of many artists because it is so abstract that it can never pretend to represent anything specific, or exactly portray one iota of the sensible world in which we live. Music is *free,* truly free, to soar to the heights or descend to the depths of intellectual-emotional experiences. This unfettered freedom is the constant delight of all good musicians and experienced nonmusicians (listeners). It is also the cause of utter despair of teachers and students who have yet to learn the basic skills and thus the joys of listening to music with some degree of understanding. Only after understanding can there be any real "appreciation," and this appreciation need not include approbation; many experienced listeners can understand and even appreciate music that they really do not enjoy. But then, how can people who are illiterate know whether or not they dislike a novel?

Literacy in music is no more a common heritage of all humans than is the ability to read and write. To become a reasonably knowledgeable listener is not very difficult because the listener has only to learn to "read"; the "writing" is left to professional musicians. And what is there to read in music: notes, scales, intervals, keys, chords? Not at all; these are merely the "grammar" of music and not its content. The listener begins with the larger units of music, with its structure. In the fullness of time a certain minimal knowledge of musical grammar will fall into place within the overall picture of musical design. For example, the following musical phrase has a beginning and an incomplete and unsatisfying ending:

Ein feste Burg

However, when the next phrase is added we have the completion of a musical idea, even though it is something less than a complete composition:

The two phrases add up to a musical period or a relatively complete musical idea called, for convenience, letter *A*. Then, for purposes of balance, the period (or paired phrases) is repeated before proceeding to the next section (section *B*). This section retains the strong, stern character of the first section, but introduces several new ideas for contrast (phrases indicated by dotted lines):

Formal Structure: *Ein feste Burg*

Bar Form (A-A-B)

Literature

In order to see how this intricate interrelation of meaning and form is accomplished in literature, we can use some very simple illustrations for analysis. For example, a creative writing class once tried to make an "absolutely beautiful" line of poetry. This is what they came up with:

Rainy evening. Idle. Only music . . .

Most people would agree that this is a very pretty line. But what makes it so? You might ask yourself where the heavy accents fall. And then, what about the vowel sounds? Suddenly what appears at first to be only a nice lazy line begins to look like the work of a craftsman, for we discover that we are running down the long vowel sounds, exactly as they come in the alphabet *a, e, i, o, u,* and that these sounds occur exactly on the heavy accents. Now what about consonant sounds? The consonants are *r, n, v, ng, dl, l, m,* hard *c* (a *k* sound). We could have had *p, b, k, g,* and all the rest. Are the ones that appear in the line purely accidental choices? Not on your life. Except for the last *c,* all the consonants are *liquid* consonants. The term is self-explanatory; they flow along without creating much stoppage. Only the last one (the *c* in *music*) is of a different sort, and it is put there exactly because it *does* stop the line. We have here a line that doesn't "say" much in terms of making a declaration or asking a question, but it certainly creates a mood. And the mood is created because of a lot of hard work in choosing sounds carefully and distributing them in terms of accentuation.

As another example, a student in the same class wrote a five-line poem about the Cain and Abel story. Here are the first two lines:

Oh Cain, you slay in vain. You may not stay.
East of Eden, East of Eden, flee for. . . .

Notice not only the vowel music, but the change in rhythm between the first and second line. Using the same pattern, you might try to write the last three lines.

The examples given above are really only one-finger exercises in the craft of writing poetry. Now we can choose a complete poem for the same kind of analysis to see the intricate relationships of form that create a sum of meaning greater than the arithmetical addition of the meanings of the words themselves. We might choose A. E. Housman's deceptively simple, eight-line poem, "With Rue My Heart is Laden."

> With rue my heart is laden
>   For golden friends I had,
> For many a rose-lipt maiden
>   And many a light-foot lad.
> By brooks too broad for leaping
>   The lightfoot boys are laid;
> The rose-lipt girls are sleeping
>   In fields where roses fade.

Of course Housman is saying that he grieves for the friends of his youth, now dead. Where does one attack the *form* of a poem like this? You might ask yourself why he chose the word *boys* in the second stanza when he used *lads* in the first. Then examine the first line of the second stanza:

> By *b*rooks too *b*road for *l*eaping

Perhaps you begin to see that he chose *boys* in the second line to make an alliterative pattern with *brooks* and *broad*. What of the *l* in the first line of the second stanza? Suddenly one discovers that it forms a similar pattern with *lightfoot* and *laid* in the second line. In the first line of the second stanza we have two *b*s, one *l*; in the second line, two *l*s, one *b*. Is this purely accidental on the part of the composer? Try the last two lines of the first stanza, with its *m*s and *l*s. The same pattern reveals itself and, furthermore, the alliterative *l* of the first stanza carries over to repeat itself in the second stanza. In other words, the middle four lines of the poem form a unit by themselves, created by the alliterations.

But that's not all. Examine the rhymes: *laden, maiden; leaping, sleeping; had, lad; laid, fade.* The first four of the rhymes listed here (lines 1, 3, 5, 7 in the poem) are weak endings; that is, they end in a dropping-off syllable that gets almost no accent at all. The second group of rhymes (lines 2, 4, 6, 8 of the poem) are strong endings; they end sharply on the accented syllable. This is strengthened even further by Housman's use of end punctuation after the lines with strong endings. Reason? Look at the subject matter of the lines with weak endings and that of the lines with strong endings.

One more example, this time in prose, for it is easy to jump to the conclusion that poets take this much care with their sounds, but that prose writers do not have to. In a story by Wilbur Daniel Steele,[2] we find the following sentence:

Accept as he would with the top of his brain the fact of a spherical earth zooming through space, deep in his heart he knew that the world lay flat from modern Illinois to ancient Palestine, and that the sky above it, blue by day and by night festooned with guiding stars for wise men, was the nether side of a floor on which the resurrected trod.

An unskilled writer tried to communicate the "same" meaning with the following sentence:

Although he accepted in his mind the fact that the earth was a sphere travelling through space, yet in his deepest emotions he knew that it was flat and that the sky was the under-side of the floor of heaven.

Why, for example, does Steele say that the world "lay flat from modern Illinois to ancient Palestine" instead of simply saying that it was flat, as the other writer did? Perhaps he wanted to suggest an expanse of time, from the modern world back to the time of Christ, as well as an expanse of space. Why did he describe the sky as he did rather than plainly using the word *sky,* as the unskilled writer did? There is the possibility that while he was stating a fact about a person's belief concerning the physical structure of the earth he also wanted to suggest a religious significance to the belief. So he mentioned the stars and the wise men to flood our memories with the story of the birth of Christ. The two sentences differ in at least one more phase of meaning. The unskilled writer's sentence has no rhythm, while Steele's sentence reads in long undulations of sound. This kind of rhythm puts us in a philosophic frame of mind, which creates the kind of atmosphere he wanted. It is for such reasons that the author chose exactly the words he did, and arranged them as he did. For its purpose in the story it is a much better sentence than that of the unskilled writer.

Fine Arts

A common plaint among laypeople is that they cannot understand "modern art" and that they prefer "realistic" works, that is, painting and sculpture that tell a story, look like something, and are easy to understand. The sad truth is that most people have never learned to understand much of anything about any kind of art, are very vague as to what "realism" might be, do not know the story related in most figurative painting and sculpture (painting and sculpture presenting natural objects) and, if they do, are unaware that subject matter cannot make the art object beautiful, life-enhancing, or valuable by itself. Most painting, sculpture, and architecture *seem* to be easily understandable, but the qualities that make one work superior to another need to be learned, just as they must be learned in music and literature.

---

2. Wilbur Daniel Steele, "The Man Who Saw through Heaven," in *An Anthology of Famous American Stories,* ed. Angus Burrell and Bennett Cerf (New York: Modern Library, 1953).

Some people refuse to take art seriously, being convinced that it is all a matter of taste. They fall back on that old bromide "There is no disputing taste." We answer, "Nuts." Taste is a learned, not innate, ability and all statements to the contrary are delusive and established in self-defense to soothe the ego. The vocabulary, subject matter, materials, and techniques of the visual arts cannot be reduced to the confines of this book, which serves a broader purpose. Nevertheless, imparting basic knowledge of the visual arts, stimulating aesthetic response, and encouraging further investigation into the arts are part of that purpose.

It is regrettable that in this century the words *beauty* and *beautiful* have taken on a narrow meaning for the general public, a meaning of prettiness and niceness, which makes the words *beauty* and *beautiful* incomprehensible to many people when they are applied to a highly abstract painting by Picasso; a nonobjective orgy of bright, explosive, and intermingling colors by Kandinsky; miles of earthwork constructions in the wilderness, or mounds of earthworks on the parquet floors of distinguished museums; and sculpture that moves, screeches, or destroys itself. For the moment, then, let us discard these words and investigate a fundamental term, *aesthetics.* A survey of dictionaries to discover the meaning of the word *aesthetics* generally will only add to the confusion, for the word usually is defined as a sense of beauty, love of beauty, or philosophy of beauty. It would seem that we are on a merry-go-round until we realize that the opposite of aesthetic is anaesthetic, which is the diminution and/or loss of communication and excitement of ideas and emotions, irrespective of what these ideas and emotions might be. The quality of art is determined by how well the ideas and emotions have been communicated.

People by nature are sentient, communicative beings—creators, artists. Everyone creates, but few produce anything unique, life-enhancing, or enduring. In this book we are concerned with the fine arts of literature, music, painting, sculpture, and architecture. But we must be aware that there are many other arts, including the art of cooking, the art of dancing, the art of gardening, and the art of living.

The French painter Paul Gauguin (go–GAN; 1848–1903) never saw a scene such as he portrayed in *Where Do We Come From? What Are We? Where Are We Going?* (colorplate 1), nor has or will anyone else. Certainly he drew the images of the gentle islanders, their birds and dogs, the beautiful landscape, from the world about him. But these perceptions could have been captured by a camera, which would have given us a clearer, more detailed, visually accurate representation. Gauguin, however, produced a painting in which his perceptions were simplified, distorted, abstracted, to present his vision of humanity asking the eternal questions. Carefully observe in colorplate 1 that the bodies vary in color from gold to brown to red; that the trees are undulating patterns of blues and purples; that there is a systematic interweaving of shapes and colors. Patterns, shapes, lines, and colors are arranged so as to establish a mood of enduring silence, gentleness, and reflection. Although the title aids

us in understanding Gauguin's vision, it is not necessary for understanding the mood and the spirit of the painting. Obviously, this painting could not have been called *Joy and Celebration,* for it does not convey that mood. Likewise, *Natives on the Beach,* its elementary subject matter, fails to express the feeling this painting evokes. Of course philosophers, scientists, theologians, and historians have written books on the very questions Gauguin uses as his title and motif; this text will pursue these questions relentlessly. However, Gauguin painted instead of writing, because line, value, shape, form, color, and texture were his materials, which he used in repetition, opposition, dominance, and subordination, to produce a painting of unique rhythm and harmony.

How different, but equally challenging, is the *Return of the Hunters* (colorplate 2) by the Flemish painter Pieter Bruegel (BROO–gull; 1525–1569). Two moods are conveyed in this painting: the coldness and bleakness of nature, and the warmth and activity of humans. This painting is a wonderful study in linear and aerial perspective, for Bruegel was a master of illusion, convincingly conveying on a two-dimensional surface the illusion of the third dimension. Linear perspective is based on our visual memory, which tells us that two parallel lines eventually seem to meet in the distance; aerial perspective relies again on a visual memory, which tells us that objects seem to become obscure, faint, as we increase our distance from them. Our eyes tell us lies and Bruegel repeated the lies of visual memory. In this painting, which also is called *Winter,* our eyes are directed to the distant snow-covered mountains by strong diagonal lines, which lead away from the picture plane; likewise, people, buildings, even the mountains decrease in size and clarity as we move away from the returning hunters at the lower left-hand side of the painting. We have been brought up to understand perspective and proportion and thus appreciate Bruegel's mastery accordingly. An ancient Egyptian would not have understood this painting, since Egyptian art did not use these principles of perspective, and proportion was determined by the importance of the personages represented. Different cultures see and express themselves with different conventions.

Bruegel's work is considered a masterpiece not only because of his technical virtuosity, but also because the artist presented an image of his time, of life as he saw it. The day may be cold, the hunters and their dogs bent with fatigue after a long and arduous hunt, but within this little hamlet there is a variety of activity that shows the warmth and delights of human life. Bruegel presents a microcosm under the guise of a deceptively simple genre scene.

The Dutch painter Meindert Hobbema (MINE–dirt HOB–a–moh; 1639–1709) records a gentler nature in *The Watermill with the Great Red Roof* (colorplate 3). This scene of a countryside with soft, downy clouds in a baby-blue sky, gnarled trees with fuzzy foliage, sparkling water falling gently into the still pond, has a lyric quality that is enhanced by backlighting the scene. There is a gentle gradation from dark to light from foreground to background. Hobbema refined his work so that we can hardly see the brush strokes. The artist disappears in the image he creates. The artist is concerned with the beauty of domesticated nature as revealed by light. The scene is calm, quiet, and peaceful—a scene such as Wordsworth recounted in many poems.

The Dutch artist Vincent van Gogh (van–GO; 1853–1890) was no pastoral lyricist. He wanted to paint the world, people, and nature, with all the love, passion, and excitement that he failed to convey in personal relationships. In *Starry Night* (colorplate 4), nature is shown to be violent: the moon and stars of brilliant oranges and yellows are glowing, burning whirligigs that leave trails of golden streaks as they speed through the sky, which also moves in dashes, spots, and streaks of a variety of assertive blues. In the foreground the top branches of a cypress shoot into the sky like flames seeking to reach the highest heavens, devouring the very air in their pursuit. No camera could ever reproduce this scene; all knowledge of perspective and of natural color is disregarded; optical illusions and visual truths are forsaken. Van Gogh painted the scene not as he saw it, but as he felt it. And he painted it in heavy pigment (impasto) into which he gouged and scratched, so that in addition to the strength of color and violence of lines, the painting is rich in animated surface texture. Even cursory observation makes us keenly aware of the artist's physical activity in creating the work, and thus heightens our emotional response. Not for a moment, however, should we think of van Gogh as a madman, the popular conception of this great artist. Van Gogh was a driven man, indeed, but he planned his paintings in great detail, as his writings prove; and in this case he purposely established the small hamlet with its buildings composed of quiet squares and rectangles in the lower foreground to contrast with the turbulence of the heavens and the cypress. This painting relies very little on perception, very much on conception, in this case through very personalized abstractions.

What Is "Abstract"?

The word *abstract* in relation to art is greatly misunderstood and commonly misused. All art is abstract—even the most naturalistic. Take a photo of a friend from your wallet and ask yourself how realistic it is. Quite obviously, your friend's body or head is not flat, not small enough to put in a wallet, and is not black, white, and gray. This photographic likeness is just that: a likeness or an abstraction of your friend. Painters or sculptors have always used abstractions in art; and society, as a group or as individuals, determines the degree to which it will accept these abstractions. Therefore, there are many degrees of abstractions, just as there are many languages, which are oral and written abstractions. Among some primitive tribes a high degree of abstraction from visual reality is so accepted that the primitives cannot recognize photographs of themselves or friends, but do "see" themselves and others in geometric signs and symbols. Some critics persist in claiming that the greatest art is that which is most illusionistic, that is, art that conveys the most convincing illusions of physical bulk and texture, visual recognition, and sense of three-dimensional space.

Some of the greatest painters and sculptors in history have been superb illusionists, but illusionism by itself has little merit. There is no art form more illusionistic than the sculptured figures in a wax museum, but these figures lack vitality in that they resemble corpses rather than human beings.

When a painter chooses to forsake the perceptual world completely and paints on canvas with shapes, lines, and colors that draw upon no natural counterpart, the painting is called nonobjective. Wassily Kandinsky (va–SILL–ee can–DIN–ski; 1866–1944), a Russian painter, is often heralded as the first nonobjective artist. Without disclaiming his brilliance and importance to the development of modern art, it is important to note that the pottery painters of the geometric period of ancient Greece, the monks responsible for the medieval *Book of Kells,* the mosaicists who designed and executed the beautifully patterned floors of the public buildings of Byzantium, weavers from all periods of history, and your grandmothers who made patchwork crazy quilts were among the many thousands of artists who worked nonobjectively long before Kandinsky appeared upon the scene.

How Can We Look at Art?

It was Kandinsky and the Dutch painter Piet Mondrian (Pete MOAN–dree–ahn; 1872–1944) who were the great pioneers of modern nonobjective art. Mondrian became the forerunner of the geometric nonobjective school and Kandinsky of expressionistic nonobjective art, both styles being carried to new and further directions by avant-garde artists today. Kandinsky's *Panel* (3) (colorplate 5) has all the turbulence of van Gogh's *Starry Night* without the subject matter drawn from nature. Colors and shapes move, impinge upon, and obliterate each other in this dynamic composition. For those who say, "I can't understand this kind of painting," here are a few questions: (1) Is this painting quiet or lively? (2) Is this painting somber or gay in mood? (3) Is this painting dull or bright? If your answers are (1) lively, (2) gay in mood, and (3) bright, you do understand the basic nature and elements of this painting. Keep asking questions of this type about any painting or work of art and you will learn a great deal. All that is needed is time and perseverance. One note of caution: whether or not you understand a work of art has little if any bearing on whether it is a good work.

We are brought to the problem, then, of how does one look at and judge a work of art? Just as with music and literature, there is no easy answer, but perhaps the following guidelines will be of some assistance.

First, look at the work and ask yourself what you *see.* Inventory the painting, not just for the figurative parts but also for all the shapes, colors, lines, textures, and spaces, and notice the manner in which these elements are put together, that is, the composition.

Second, almost at the same time you are asking yourself what you see, ask yourself what you *know.* There is an immense difference between seeing and knowing. For example, you might *see* a figure of a haloed man with a white beard carrying a key, but you might *know,* also, that the halo represents sainthood and that the key is the attribute (or symbol) through which we recognize St. Peter. You might see a tree form, but only special knowledge will define that particular tree as an oak, aspen, or willow.

Third, ask yourself what the artist was attempting to do. It is at this point that most amateurs falter, quite naturally. But the artist sets a mood for a painting, describes items in certain ways through color, shapes, lines, arrangements of many elements to create certain effects. For example, Bruegel bent the backs of his hunters to indicate their weariness, van Gogh painted stars in bright colors to make them seem like glowing orbs, and Kandinsky used white extensively to set off the bright reds, blues, and yellows of his painting. Each artwork, be it painting, sculpture, architecture, or craft item, has a composition that should function to make all parts work together in rhythm and harmony. The rules for judging any work are implicit in the work itself.

Fourth, judge how well the artist solves self-imposed problems. Remember that even the "Divine Michelangelo" goofed sometimes and that some tenth-rate artists turned out single works of inestimable merit. Do not hesitate to be critical. Do Bruegel's hunters give a convincing impression of weariness? Does the little and quiet hamlet afford a balancing contrast for the *Starry Night?* At this point you are evaluating or appreciating the painting, making a judgment on the basis of all that you *see* and *know,* and an analysis of how well the artist resolved the problems.

You have just received an elementary lesson in criticism. Try it often; you'll improve with practice.

Do not be discouraged or embarrassed if some of the world's greatest masterpieces leave you cold. If you can recognize the obvious merit of a work of art but find in it qualities distasteful to your temperament, you are developing discriminating personal taste. It is altogether possible to recognize the greatness of Raphael and van Gogh and at the same time dislike them because Raphael's figures are too saccharine for you and van Gogh's paintings are much too wild for you to live with comfortably. If you find, also, that you like paintings that have little artistic merit but are predominately orange (your favorite color) or whose subject matter is cats (and you love cats), recognize that there often are factors in a work of art that you value over the purely artistic values. In any case, you should begin to know how and why a work moves you. This is part of the process of learning how to judge a painting and yourself. Aesthetic understanding and appreciation is a give-and-take process involving you and the work of art. In undertaking the problem of criticism you should become a more knowledgeable, humanized individual.

Only a historian would know that the portrait (colorplate 6) by Hyacinthe Rigaud (REE–go; 1659–1743) of the imposing old man with the flowing wig, sumptuous robe, and red-heeled and red-ribboned shoes was the famous Louis XIV of France. Still, practically anyone would know that this gentleman was an overdressed, important personage posing in an elaborate setting. The French artist wanted to impress the viewer with the magnificence of the "Sun King," the elegance of his costume, and the majesty of his pose. Observe the artist's mastery in describing the fabrics, which are masterpieces of illusion. This is a beautiful painting of a homely old man, although the artist used every trick in the trade to deemphasize the face. It is relatively easy to appreciate the quality of this painting, but it is difficult to like it because contemporary taste rejects the overblown extravagance of garb and ceremonial authoritarian poses. Remember that this painting was produced for a palace and now resides in a palace museum. It was not meant to hang over a television set and, despite its beauty as a painting, would have little relevance in most homes.

The Spanish artist Pablo Picasso (PAB–lo pea–KAH–so; 1881–1973) painted the *Girl Before a Mirror* (colorplate 7) in 1932. Like most of his works, it is a very controversial painting, which most people find difficult to understand; and even today it is seldom called beautiful. A cursory examination reveals only a series of circles and triangles in bright colors and patterns working on the picture plane. Perhaps you need to be told that the girl on the left is shown both in full-face and profile. Look carefully and you will see a profile view in pink and then its merging with a yellow side to describe a face frontally, a device now used by many comic strip artists. Picasso told us that he *knew* that each individual has profile views as well as a frontal view, that he painted not only what he actually saw but what he knew exists in a combination or "Picasso-view." That the colors of these sections do not coincide and are different again from the profile reflection in the mirror made no difference to Picasso because, in the last analysis, this painting is a highly abstracted study of a woman presented from many viewpoints and brightly colored and patterned to achieve a complex decorative composition. Pattern and color are the keys to this painting, but the psychological interpretations that may be made are numerous. This painting still seems new, unique, and very intriguing; Picasso created new forms, a new way of seeing and presenting. Those of us who have been brought up with Picasso's works find them easy to understand, and we enjoy this painting for its decorative qualities, mystery of interpretation, and bold innovations. Art styles change as people's basic ideas and characteristics change. Picasso was one of the great artists of our century who not only reflected but produced these changes. All innovations seem heretical, sometimes even crazy, but often they become part of the mainstream of life, and inevitably are superseded by new and seemingly wilder innovations.

All the works illustrated and discussed were composed to communicate ideas and emotions; all differ from each other in style, degree of abstraction, and perceptual and conceptual understanding of people and nature. It is hoped, even anticipated, that you will appreciate or learn to appreciate each of these works, but it is unlikely you will like each of them. Remember, nevertheless, that each artist is sharing with you a vision of the world, a way of seeing, and in so doing communicates artistic truth.

Exercises

1. George Meredith's poem "Dirge in Woods" is given here together with two other versions, which attempt to say the same thing. What differences in the meaning do the differences in form create?

DIRGE IN WOODS

George Meredith

A wind sways the pines
    And below
Not a breath of wild air:
Still as the mosses that glow
On the flooring and over the lines
Of the roots here and there.
The pine-tree drops its dead:
They are quiet as under the sea.
    Overhead, overhead
Rushes life in a race
As the clouds the clouds chase:
    And we go,
And we drop like the fruits of the tree,
    Even we,
    Even so.

A SECOND VERSION

Pines in the wind are swaying.
    It is quiet down below;
Not one wild breath is straying
    Above the mosses that glow
Among the roots in wandering lines
    Upon the forest floor.
The needles quietly fall from the pines,
    Fall, and are no more.
As darkly green, as stilly quiet
    As under the sea, this place.
Look! overhead, in restless riot,
    The rushing clouds' wild chase!
But like the needles we shall fall,
    Nor run in life's swift race;
We all shall die—all, all.

A THIRD VERSION

Above, wind in the pines;
below, stillness—
quiet as the mosses
creeping over roots.
    The pine needles drop, drop,
quiet, dead.
Overhead, the rushing clouds
chasing each other.
    We too die and become
quiet: drop like dead leaves,
like a dying wind
vanish into silence.

Here are three ways of saying the same thing, or nearly the same thing. Yet two of these ways are definitely inferior, although the words repeat, the ideas are like, and the "meaning" is similar. What makes the difference?

Perhaps a fourth way of straight prose without versification, could convey the "meaning" more clearly, if by "meaning" we understand only the words and what they refer to; but there is—or should be—more to a poem than the words and their immediate, surface significance. For part of the stuff of the poem is its pattern, arrangement, and design; the form is significant as well as the meanings of the words. In order to see better the effective form of one, we look at the other poorer versions.

Which one sounds most like a sermon, a teaching with a moral rather than like a poem? Which one is singsong, so monotonous that your ear is distracted from meaning by the regularity of expected sound? Which one most effectively presents the three successive ideas: trees, clouds, ourselves?

In the first version, what is gained by the short second line?
What is the effect of the succession of vowel sounds in "st*I*ll *A*s th*E* m*O*sses that gl*O*w"? (*the* is *thuh,* not *thee*)
What is the effect of repeated sounds in "glow . . . flooring . . . over"?
Why is "overhead" repeated, and "clouds" (in the eleventh line)? Also the *r* sounds, and the sibilant *s*'s?
What is gained by the short line, "and we go"?
What is the effect of the near repetition in the last two lines?

Again one might ask, what does the poem gain by being a *poem?* It is not merely by the dictionary meanings of the words employed, but by the patterns of sound and arrangement, that the poet has achieved a meaning.

2. Here, again, we might compare the writing of an expert and a rank amateur in terms of meanings that lie beyond pure sense meaning. Both the stanza from Matthew Arnold's "Dover Beach" and the paraphrase of it "mean" the same thing in that they deplore the loss of faith in the world. But what additional overtones and undertones of meaning does Arnold get? In what specific ways does he achieve them?

The Sea of Faith
Was once, too, at the full, and round earth's shore
Lay like the folds of a bright girdle furled.
But now I only hear
Its melancholy, long, withdrawing roar,
Retreating, to the breath
Of the night wind, down the vast edges drear
And naked shingles of the world.

Paraphrase

Once men the world around believed
In other men and God.
But faith's now lost, men are deceived,
And earth's a dusty clod.

3. Here is Robert Frost's lovely poem "Stopping by Woods on a Snowy Evening."

Whose woods these are I think I know.
His house is in the village, though;
He will not see me stopping here
To watch his woods fill up with snow.

My little horse must think it queer
To stop without a farmhouse near
Between the woods and frozen lake
The darkest evening of the year.

He gives the harness bells a shake
To ask if there is some mistake.
The only other sound's the sweep
Of easy wind and downy flake.

The woods are lovely, dark, and deep,
But I have promises to keep,
And miles to go before I sleep,
And miles to go before I sleep.

Notice how the choice of words in a poem, once it is done, seems right, almost inevitable. In the twelfth line one accepts the word *easy* as an adjective describing the wind. What other adjectives could Frost have chosen? Why do you suppose he selected the rather unusual word *easy?*

In answering these questions, you might notice some of the music of the poem. For example, look at lines three and four. In line three we find the words *will* and *stopping;* in line four, the words *watch* and *fill.* Do you notice the cross-rhyme: *stop* and *watch, will* and *fill?* In lines seven and eight we have something of the same thing with the words *between* and *evening.* Now look at lines eleven and twelve to see why the choice of the word *easy.* You might notice the pattern of end-rhymes, too. Where does the word that ends line three of each

stanza find its rhyme? What is the effect, and the author's purpose, of having all four lines of the last stanza rhyme? As one begins to discover these rather hidden elements, a simple-seeming poem becomes a complicated fabric of rhyme and music, most of which has its effect, even though the reader is not conscious of it.

4. Raphael painted *Madonna della Seggiola* within a circle: why he did so does not especially matter—probably because he wanted to! But the decision once made, the problem of the arrangement within that circle was his to solve. (How he did, the picture shows.) Suppose that he had chosen some other arrangement of the mother and child: suppose he had (like Cimabue) presented her and the infant face-on. Suppose he had turned the child the other way. Being Raphael, he probably would have made a better design of it than the following sketches would indicate!—but whatever the design he might have effected, the new picture would not have done what the present one does; it might have been better or worse; it would certainly have been different. The "Madonna of the Chair" is what it is because it was designed the way it is; the flowing curves fitted together with their interweave of movement give the painting its quality of "coziness" (if the word may be forgiven), its intimately human appeal. The mother is not the "Virgin Enthroned," the baby is not God Incarnate, in this picture; the majesty and awe of the subsequent story are foregone to portray the most understandable, the most appealing of human relationships— simply mother and child.

Consider some other possible arrangements, not with a view of bettering or worsening Raphael's design, but in the hope of understanding more fully what this form, this arrangement, accomplishes. (There's even a circle for you to try your hand in.)

Summary

The humanities are the arts of literature, painting, music, sculpture, architecture, and dance, and the discipline of philosophy that permeates all of the arts and finally unites them all. As set forth in unit 2, the arts, taken together, are a separate field of human knowledge with their own area of exploration and discovery, and with a method of their own. So these volumes will concentrate on the great artistic production of each of the time periods outlined above. Each unit is planned to give a chapter or two to the social, scientific, religious, and philosophic climate of the period in which the artists were working, for the artists usually accept the scientific and social world-picture of their time. Following these introductory discussions, direct attention is given to the arts themselves, with enough examples of each to reveal new answers to the great questions of mankind, new patterns, structures, and meaning the artists found for life in their time. By this treatment, the student will be able to trace the development and changes through history of the problems that plague us so sorely in our own time. Equipped with knowledge of the great answers found in the past that shape the way we live today, having come to know the exalted expressions of humanity revealed at their fullest, each individual can work to develop an informed set of values and a freedom to be the person he or she wants to be.

In such fashions as those illustrated, artists, whatever their medium—music, painting, literature—have made form the vehicle of idea, have made the raw materials of art acquire significance by arrangement and handling. It is a different kind of meaning from that of scientists, which can be perceived and measured in an objective world, for this sort of meaning can be known only by the individual who can see the relationships the artists have formulated, and who can find them valid in terms of personal experience. It is not an easy process, sometimes; and just as the effectiveness of the scientist depends upon two things—the validity of the discovery, and the ability of the beholder to understand or comprehend it—so the effectiveness of the artist depends upon the validity of the discovery, and the sensitivity of the beholder to apprehend it. "I don't get it" is no refutation of either Einstein or Bach.

Not everyone will derive the same kind or degree of satisfaction from a particular art form, obviously; but the educated person is obligated to know that "there is something in it," even if that "something" does not deeply move that individual. And perhaps, with deeper acquaintance and wider knowledge, that "something" will become clearer and of greater value than before.

In this chapter we have made the assertion that the artist is an explorer and discoverer in the realm of the human personality. The artist uses the method of intuition and composition. The artist's raw material lies in the human personality and in human experience, with their vast and unknown reaches, their disrupting conflicts. The artist gives form to the component elements of personality and experience, and in so doing yields an artistic truth. No matter whether we speak of literature, painting, sculpture, music, or any of the other arts, this concept of creating form out of chaos is the single common basis and foundation for all aesthetics.

Annotated Bibliography

Bennett, William J. *To Reclaim a Legacy: A Report on the Humanities in Higher Education.* Washington, D.C.: Government Printing Office, 1984. Bennett bewails the current lack of emphasis on our past cultural creations and argues for their centrality in education and for understanding our own civilization.

Boorstein, Daniel J. *The Discoverers: A History of Man's Search to Know His World and Himself.* New York: Random House, 1983. An exciting introduction to cultural and intellectual history. Very highly recommended.

Hassan, Ihab, and Hassan, Sally, eds. *Innovation/ Renovation: New Perspectives on the Humanities.* Madison: The University of Wisconsin Press, 1982. Innovative approaches to furthering our understanding of the humanities.

Lockspeiser, Edward. *Music and Painting: A Study in Comparative Ideas from Turner to Schoenberg.* New York: Harper & Row, Publishers, 1973. Using what the author calls the humanities approach, the "why" rather than the "how," this is an interdisciplinary study of some interesting relationships between visual and musical arts.

Munro, Thomas. *The Arts—Their Interrelations.* Western Reserve University Press, 1967. An unusual and fascinating approach to comparative aesthetics by a man who is both a professor of philosophy and professor of art.

Post, Gaines, Jr. *The Humanities in American Life.* Berkeley: The University of California Press, 1980. Supported by the Rockefeller Foundation, this report of a special commission notes deficiencies in current education and recommends a better integration of the humanities into the curriculum.

Rader, Melvin, and Jessup, Bertram. *Art and Human Values.* Englewood Cliffs, N.J.: Prentice-Hall, 1976. The role of art in formulating and communicating values.

Read, Herbert. *Education Through Art.* New York: Pantheon Books, 1974. The author bases his approach to aesthetic education on Plato's thesis that art should be the basis of education.

Ronning, Ronald H., and Reedy, Jeremiah. *Articulating the Ineffable: Approaches to the Teaching of the Humanities.* St. Paul: Minnesota State Department of Education, 1979. A helpful collection of articles on effectively teaching the interdisciplinary humanities. Highly recommended.

Toynbee, Arnold. *A Study of History.* In several editions (preferably the one-volume abridgement). This classic study articulates and documents one of the most impressive culture-epoch theories of the rise and fall of civilizations.

UNIT 1

ANCIENT RIVER-VALLEY
CIVILIZATIONS

MESOPOTAMIA

EGYPT

(most dates approximate)

	MESOPOTAMIA	EGYPT
PALEOLITHIC AGE **8000** B.C.	**Domestication of animals and development of agriculture, pottery, weaving, permanent houses and settlements, fortifications, warfare**	
NEOLITHIC AGE **5000** B.C.	**5000** Infiltration of Semites from west and north, non-Semites from east; fusion **3500–3000** Sumerian Protoliterate Period. Infiltration of Sumerians (origin?) and fusion with resident population. Invention of written language	**5000–3100** Pre-Dynastic Period **4200** Invention of solar calendar **3500** Development of religion: sunworship **3100–2700** Dynasties I and II. Development of hieroglyphics and central administration
BRONZE AGE **3000** B.C.	**3000–2350** Sumerian dynasties **2700** Reign of Gilgamesh, king of Uruk **2500** First dynasty of Ur **2350–2100** Akkadian Period **2350** Sargon the Great **2050–1900** Third dynasty of Ur (Neo-Sumerian Period) Gudea of Lagash	**2686–2181** Old Kingdom, dynasties III–VI. Highly centralized political theocracy; strong artistic development **2590–2514** Pyramid Age **2260–2130** First Intermediate Period, dynasties VII–X **2134–1786** Middle Kingdom, dynasties XI–XII. Expansion and prosperity; refinement of arts
2000 B.C.	**2000** *Epic of Gilgamesh* **1900–1500** First dynasty of Babylonia **1792–1750** Hammurabi and Law Code **1500–1100** Kassite Period, status quo **1076–612** Assyrian Empire **884–859** Assurnasirpal II, capital at Nimrud **722–709** Sargon II, capital at Khorsabad **669–626** Ashurbanipal, capital at Nineveh	**1780–1550** Second Intermediate Period: Hyksos, dynasties XIII–XVII **1570–1085** New Kingdom (Empire), dynasties XVIII–XX **1379–1362** Akhenaton (Amarna Period) **1085–664** Post-Empire Period, dynasties XXI–XXV
IRON AGE **1000** B.C.	**625–539** Chaldean (Neo-Babylonian) Empire **604–562** Nebuchadnezzar II **586–539** Babylonian Captivity of Israelites **539–331** Persian Empire **539–530** Cyrus the Great **521–485** Darius I **(490–479** Persian invasions of Greece) **485–465** Xerxes I **331** Alexander the Great conquers Persian Empire	**670** Assyrian conquest of Egypt **663–525** Saite Period, dynasty XXVI; cultural renaissance **525** Persia conquers Egypt **525–343** Persian kings, Egyptian dynasties XXVII–XXX **343–332** Persian kings **332** Alexander the Great conquers Egypt **332–311** Macedonian kings **311–30** The Ptolemies **51–30** Cleopatra VII
1 B.C.		

1

Mesopotamia

The history of Western civilization began in Sumer. A new way of life developed in southern Mesopotamia (Gk., "Land between the Rivers") in the fertile valley of the Tigris and Euphrates rivers. Sometime after 8000 B.C. a series of innovations slowly emerged: pottery, weaving, permanent houses, organized communities, the buying and selling of crops and goods, calendar making, mathematics, and most importantly, writing. What prompted this startling surge of new ideas?

Culture: Cultivation

The answer, in a word, is *agriculture*. For hundreds of thousands of years nomadic tribes had followed the seasons, gathering edible plants and hunting wild animals. About ten thousand years ago someone, possibly a woman who noticed sprouting seeds in garbage, discovered that several edible plants could be cultivated. This marked the beginning of "culture," which originally meant cultivating the soil. As the Mesopotamian communities flourished they evolved a higher civilization than that of

MAP 1.1 *Ancient Near East.*

Neolithic nomads, a culture as we understand the meaning of the term: socially transmitted behavior patterns, beliefs, institutions, arts, and other human creations. All this as a direct consequence of dropping seeds in a trench and watering them.

Consider the ramifications of a newly established agricultural community. Permanent dwellings become necessary for a population no longer on the move (domestic architecture, pottery, and other household items). Cultivated land was divided into "your land" and "my land," and properly identified, measured, and recorded (surveying, maps, mathematics, and writing). Because privately owned lands were now at stake, villages had to be organized for defense against those who chose to steal rather than plant (community organization, village fortification and defense). The spring floods upon which agriculture depended had to be anticipated, measured, recorded, and in time, somehow controlled and exploited (development of a calendar, study of the heavens to determine the wishes of the gods, invention of dams and the water wheel, development of irrigation, and ever more writing and recording).

Inevitably, farmers grew too much of one crop and not enough of something else; this led to bartering grain and later, to full-fledged commerce as not only crops but animals and household goods were bought and sold. This commercial activity necessitated a legal system to stabilize the new world of agriculture, manufacturing, and trade. Further, the buying and selling of goods works most efficiently when concentrated in financial centers; this stimulates the development of commercial hubs that, in turn, help promote commerce. As commerce increases villages grow into towns that become cities and then city-states as urban developments interact with the countryside around them.

It was in Sumer that a loose confederation of city-states became the first to consolidate political and economic power into history's first ruling dynasties. The roots of Western civilization can be traced directly back to Sumer which, in our own time, has been characterized as the Cradle of Civilization. Sumer lay in the eastern arc of the Fertile Crescent, that wide belt of productive land extending northwestward from the Persian Gulf and curving down the Mediterranean coast almost to Egypt. This was not only a settlement zone but also one of transit in which the ebb and flow of people and ideas enriched—and disrupted—the evolution of civilization.

Sumerian Period, 3000–2350 B.C.

No one knows why a high civilization began in Sumer and, maybe slightly later, in Egypt. In prehistoric times both centers formed part of a larger cultural province: Mesopotamia was at first indistinguishable from northern

MAP 1.2 *The Fertile Crescent.*

Syria and southern Mesopotamia (Sumer) was linked with Persia; Egypt shared its early pre-dynastic culture with Libya, Nubia, and possibly the Sudan. And then came the unprecedented development (discussed in this and the next chapter) that differentiated Sumer and Egypt from their surroundings, as it also established their unique niche in history.

The mystery is further compounded because the origin of the Sumerians is also unknown. Migrating into the river valley during the fifth millenium (4999–4000 B.C.), they amalgamated with the resident population and by about 3000 B.C. had established themselves as the dominant class. Until recently they had been credited with inventing the first written language, a system called cuneiform (KYOO–nay–uh–FORM, "wedge") writing. It now appears that a tribe from the north, the Subarians, actually invented writing. In any event, the original purpose of written accounts was to record the behavior of the rivers and the astronomical events that provided clues to the return of the life-giving floods.

Early Religion

Annual inundations were only one of the reasons for studying the stars. Primitive religions attribute natural phenomena—floods, storms, earthquakes—to unseen gods; more sophisticated cultures study the heavens for clues to superhuman powers involved with the creation and governance of the universe. Scholars of religion believe, moreover, that societies tend to develop religions to deal with problems both in their culture and in their more immediate spiritual lives. Sumerian beliefs reflected the considerable concerns of everyday life: storms, catastrophic floods, earthquakes, and endless raids by hostile neighbors. Consequently, their religion tended to be self-centered and practical, with the emphasis upon sheer survival in a dangerous world. As we shall see in more detail in the next chapter, religion in Egypt was totally different from that of Sumer. The Egyptians led rather serene and happy lives in a prosperous and unified land. They assumed, quite naturally, that life would continue blissfully into a hereafter much like the here and now. The Eygptian view of death was one of cheerful resignation, but the average Mesopotamian lived for the present and cherished few hopes for a fate beyond the grave.

For the Mesopotamians the gods were powerful and immortal but otherwise much like human beings writ large: frivolous, selfish, quarrelsome, sometimes petty, often childish. The gods were arranged in a hierarchy, making this the first systematic polytheistic religion. *An* (or *Anu*) was a sky god and head of the pantheon (Gk., "all the gods"). *Enlil* was "Lord Breath," god of the atmosphere. *Inanna* (or *Inini*) was "Queen of Heaven," the planet Venus, daughter of the moon god, and spouse of Anu; later her name was changed to the more familiar *Ishtar.*

Determining the will of these fractious gods was an overriding concern of the believers and thus was born astrology, later to be transformed into the science of astronomy. Through prayer, incantations, and magic the Sumerians attempted to keep the gods happy or at least tolerant and forgiving. Pleasing the gods was more desirable than leading a good life—a pragmatic point of view that did little to improve ethical behavior.

The king was chief servant of the gods; as their earthly representative he headed a government that can be described as theocratic socialism, meaning that the gods were presumed to be in charge and that large areas of the city were set aside as sacred communities. Collective labor was employed on temple lands but the rest of the city was divided into private properties, thus limiting state socialism. Because sky gods made up the pantheon, their worship should be from temples atop hills or, preferably, mountains; the closer the temples were to the gods the more likely were the deities to be content—and less likely to torment helpless humans.

Sumerian Art and Architecture

With no hills, much less mountains, in the vast and flat deserts surrounding the river valleys, the Sumerians had no natural building sites nor were there any practical building stones. The problem was solved by building massive artificial hills out of sun-dried mud bricks. These *ziggurats* were temple towers constructed as terraced pyramids with inclined walkways connecting each terrace. The ziggurat at Ur (figure 1.1) dates from the Neo-Sumerian Period and represents a refined version of the earliest ziggurat erected at Uruk a thousand years earlier.

■ **FIGURE 1.1** *Ziggurat at Ur (partially reconstructed), ca. 2150–2050* B.C., *Third Dynasty of Ur, Iraq. Photo © Hirmer Fotoarchiv.*

FIGURE 1.2 *Statuettes of worshippers from Tell Asmar, ca. 2700–2600 B.C. Marble and black shell inlay. Height of tallest figure ca. 30". Iraq Institute, Baghdad and Oriental Institute, Chicago.*

The Ur ziggurat has three stairways, a hundred steps each, that converge on the first platform; other stairways ascended to the second and then to a third level on which stood the temple of the god.

Dating from around the reign of the legendary Gilgamesh, an assemblage of marble statuettes depicts, probably, common people, priests, and a king and queen as they await the descent of Dumuzi, another legendary king of Uruk who became a god called the "shepherd" (figure 1.2). After deification Dumuzi personified the annual vegetation that dies in the summer. He was the spouse of Inanna, who was held responsible for his demise. His death occurred annually, of course, reflecting the cycle of flowering spring and summer (or fall) desiccation that characterized all agricultural societies. The cylindrical shapes of these statuettes is typically Mesopotamian, totally different from Egyptian sculptures that are uniformly rectangular.

The strange and fascinating *He-Goat and Flowering Tree* (colorplate 8) is a masterful example of sculpture that is created by adding elements instead of subtracting them. Marvelously alive and alert, the animal peers intently through the decorative branches of a symbolic tree. A symbol himself, the goat is an age-old emblem of masculinity, mainly that associated with sex; thus the sculpture is very likely a fertility symbol.

In addition to their distinctive art and architecture, the Sumerians made important contributions to writing, law, and religion. They also established the foundations of mathematics, science, and engineering. In arithmetic they created multiplication, division, and square and cube roots. They used a 10-base (decimal) system of mathematics plus a 60-base system from which they were the first to derive 60 seconds to a minute and 60 minutes to an hour. In geometry they used the 60-base system to mark out a circle of 360 degrees.

The Epic of Gilgamesh

Their most significant literary work was *The Epic of Gilgamesh,* the story of the first individual in world literature, the first protagonist with a name and a personality. This was also the first written record of the discovery of death, which Gilgamesh strongly suspected meant total extinction but which his contemporaries, still rooted in primitive notions, assumed to be another form of existence. Originally sketched by the Sumerians, reworked by the Akkadians, and shaped into final form by the Babylonians, *The Epic of Gilgamesh* is the story of a debauched half-historical, half-legendary king whom the gods propose to chastise. To humble the arrogant monarch they create a foil: Enkidu of the strong limbs and simple heart. Before he encounters Gilgamesh the gods make sure that Enkidu is civilized by providing him with a courtesan who instructs him in the arts of erotic love. This humanizing process enables Enkidu to overcome his brutish nature and gain worldly wisdom. Inevitably Enkidu and Gilgamesh meet in combat (as the gods intended), the battle ends in a draw, and a chastened Gilgamesh joins forces with his new-found friend in a series of exciting adventures. An unfortunate misadventure brings down the wrath of the gods, equally inevitably, and Enkidu dies in the arms of a bereft Gilgamesh, who is left alone to face the meaning of life—and death.

But the story does not end there. Learning that Utnapishtim, the legendary hero of the great flood, possesses the secret of eternal life, Gilgamesh finally tracks him down and, after many more adventures, finds the thorny plant that restores life and guarantees immortality, exactly as revealed to him by the hero. Ecstatic over his precious discovery, Gilgamesh celebrates by bathing in a nearby pool. At that moment "a serpent snuffed the fragrance of the plant; it came up from the water and carried off the plant. Going back it shed its slough." Considered immortal because of its annual sloughing off of skin, the snake steals immortality from Gilgamesh. "Thereupon Gilgamesh sits down and weeps, His tears running down over his face." This is the truly final loss, confirming the dark Mesopotamian suspicion that life only appears to be hopeful, happy, and bright. Ultimately the truth is learned and generally learned the hard way: life ends in nothingness.

Given below are selections from the epic about a great flood, which may have been the famous deluge that inundated Mesopotamia around 2900 B.C. The story may, on the other hand, relate what amounts to a creation myth. Whatever the intention, there are interesting parallels with the flood described in Genesis, chapters 6–8. This is understandable for "The biblical accounts are themselves based on some form of the *Gilgamesh* epic: Sumerian, Babylonian, or Assyrian, either brought in by Abraham from Ur of the Chaldees or experienced in Jewish exile in Babylonia."[1]

---

1. Wiener, Philip R., editor in chief. *Dictionary of the History of Ideas,* Volume III. New York: Charles Scribner's Sons, 1973, pp. 279–80. Source: Pritchard, James B., editor. *Ancient Near Eastern Texts Relating to the Old Testament.* Princeton: Princeton University Press, 1950, pp. 42, 72, 109.

THE EPIC OF GILGAMESH

From Tablet XI
The story is told to Gilgamesh by Utnapishtim, who relates how he was instructed by the gods to:

Tear down this house, build a ship!
Give up possessions, seek thou life.
Forswear worldly goods and keep the soul alive!
Aboard the ship take thou the seed of all living things.
The ship that thou shalt build,
Her dimensions shall be to measure.
Equal shall be her width and length.
On the fifth day I laid her framework.
One whole acre was her floor space,
Ten dozen cubits the height of each of her walls,
Ten dozen cubits each edge of the square deck.
I laid out the contours and joined her together.
I provided her with six decks,
Dividing her thus into seven parts.
Her floor plan I divided into nine parts.
I hammered water-plugs into her.
I saw to the punting poles and laid in supplies.
Bullocks I slaughtered for the people,
And I killed sheep every day.
Must, red wine, oil, and white wine
I gave the workmen to drink, as though river water,
That they might feast as on New Year's Day.
On the seventh day the ship was completed.
The launching was very difficult,
So that they had to shift the floor planks above and below,
Until two-thirds of the structure had gone into the water.
Whatever I had I laded upon her:
Whatever I had of silver I laded upon her;
Whatever I had of gold I laded upon her;
Whatever I had of all the living things I laded upon her.
All my family and kin I made go aboard the ship.
The beasts of the field, the wild creatures of the field,
        All the craftsmen I made go aboard.
I watched the appearance of the weather.
The weather was awesome to behold.
I boarded the ship and battened up the entrance.
With the first glow of dawn,
A black cloud rose up from the horizon.
For one day the south-storm blew,
Gathering speed as it blew, submerging the mountains,
Overtaking the people like a battle.
No one can see his fellow,
Nor can the people be recognized from heaven.
The gods were frightened by the deluge,
And, shrinking back, they ascended to the heaven of
        Anu.[2]

The gods cowered like dogs
        Crouched against the outer wall.
Ishtar cried out like a woman in travail,
The sweet-voiced mistress of the gods moans aloud:
'The olden days are alas turned to clay,
Because I bespoke evil in the Assembly of the gods.
How could I bespeak evil in the Assembly of the gods,
Ordering battle for the destruction of my people,
When it is I myself who give birth to my people!'
Six days and six nights
Blows the flood wind, as the south-storm sweeps the land.
When the seventh day arrived,
        The flood-carrying south-storm subsided in the
            battle,
Which it had fought like an army.
The sea grew quiet, the tempest was still, the flood
        ceased.
I looked at the weather: stillness had set in,
And all of mankind had returned to clay.
The landscape was as level as a flat roof.
I opened a hatch, and light fell upon my face.
Bowing low, I sat and wept,
Tears running down my face.
I looked about for coast lines in the expanse of the sea:
In each of fourteen regions
        There emerged a region-mountain.
On Mount Nisir the ship came to a halt.
Mount Nisir held the ship fast,
        Allowing no motion.
One day, a second day, Mount Nisir held the ship fast,
        Allowing no motion.
A third day, a fourth day, Mount Nisir held the ship fast,
        Allowing no motion.
A fifth, and a sixth day, Mount Nisir held the ship fast,
        Allowing no motion.
When the seventh day arrived,
I sent forth and set free a dove.
The dove went forth, but came back;
Since no resting-place for it was visible, she turned round.
Then I sent forth and set free a swallow.
The swallow went forth, but came back;
Since no resting-place for it was visible, she turned round.
Then I sent forth and set free a raven.
The raven went forth and, seeing that the waters had
        diminished,
He eats, circles, caws, and turns not round.
Then I let out all to the four winds
        And offered a sacrifice.
I poured out a libation on the top of the mountain.

---

2. The highest heaven in the Mesopotamian conception of the cosmos.

■

FIGURE 1.3 *The 'Standard of Ur.' Early Dynastic II Period, ca. 2600–2400 B.C. Shell, red limestone, lapis lazuli inlaid in a bitumin base. Ht. 8" each panel. British Museum, London. Reproduced by courtesy of the Trustees of the British Museum.*

The "Standard of Ur"

The so-called "Standard of Ur" was found in one of the tombs of the royal cemetery (figure 1.3). Though these two panels form the front and back of a musical instrument they will be described as they appear here, i.e., as an upper and lower plate. The upper plate, called the "war" plate, shows, in the top register, the king alighting from his carriage in order to receive captives. In the center a line of lancers in heavy cloaks faces vanquished enemies on the right. In the bottom register four chariots drive across the bodies of fallen warriors.

The lower "peace" panel highlights a banquet scene: the court drinks with the king to the sound of apparently stirring music. In the center row servants are leading animals and holding fish, which may be a depiction of food preparation in a lower part of the palace. The bottom register very likely illustrates the spoils of war.

It should not be assumed that life in 2500 B.C. (or later) was generally as brutish as depicted in these panels. This was certainly the norm in Mesopotamia with a seemingly endless stream of natural and human-caused disasters. On the other hand, Egypt in this period was peaceful, prosperous, and remained so for centuries, as described in the next chapter.

Exercises

1. a. Imagine that you are living with a tribe of nomads and that everything you eat is either gathered or hunted. As you follow the seasons in search of food, what would you carry with you? What would constitute "excess baggage" (i.e., things neither useful nor needed)?

   b. Now, imagine that you are raising crops and breeding animals. In what ways will your life differ from that of the nomads? What possessions would you have that were previously impractical? How different will your relationships be with your neighbors and with your community?

2. The Latin poet Lucretius (see chapter 9) claimed that because early civilizations were unable to account for natural phenomena (particularly the more terrifying aspects) they ascribed such things to the gods. In those terms, what does the nature and behavior of the gods in the Sumerian pantheon suggest about the environment in Mesopotamia? (Environment would include climate, topography, and geography.)

3. Consider the environment in your own area and then devise an appropriate pantheon. Describe the nature and function of your newly created gods and goddesses.

4. What were the lasting contributions that the Sumerians made to civilization?

Akkadian Period, 2350–2150 B.C.

The rise of the Akkadians marked the second stage in the cycle of Mesopotamian dynasties. While the Sumerian city-states had a system supported by free peasants, Sumer remained dominant. But, in time, competition with, and the expansion of, large estates reduced the by then debt-ridden peasants to serfdom: the standard battle of the haves and have-nots. Sumer then fell to the Akkadians, barbarian tribesmen from the north, who had sampled the sweets of civilization and who had probably served (some of them) the Sumerians as mercenaries. The new rulers then settle down into the same pattern of inequalities; their peasants are broken down and the whole process starts all over again, leading to takeovers by the Babylonians, the Assyrians, and so forth.

The dynamic catalyst of the Semite Akkadians was Sargon the Great, the first notable military conqueror in history. The bronze head from Nineveh (figure 1.4), very likely representing Sargon, expresses a new idea in sculpture—a dignified, noble, and truly powerful monarch. Bound in the Sumerian fashion, the hair is plaited, wound around the head and gathered in a tight chignon. The impression is that of a ruler in total control.

The Akkadians refined and otherwise improved Sumerian art and the quality of life in general but they were never able to convince the Sumerians that they were sort of first cousins rather than rank outsiders. Sargon and his successors even took pains to call themselves kings of Sumer and Akkad but the Sumerians continued to chafe under "foreign" domination and eventually regained political control.

FIGURE 1.4 *Bronze head from Nineveh, Akkadian, ca. 2350–2150 B.C., ht. 14⅜". Iraq Museum, Baghdad.*

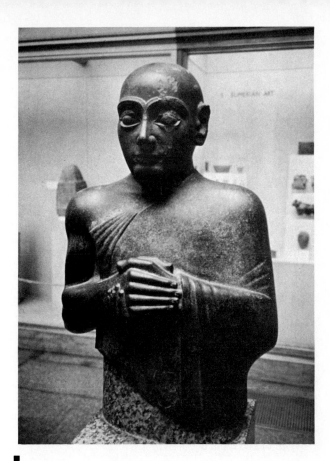

FIGURE 1.5 *Gudea of Lagash, Neo-Sumerian Period, ca. 2050 B.C., diorite. ht. 29". British Museum. Reproduced by courtesy of the Trustees of the British Museum.*

Neo-Sumerian Period, 2050–1900 B.C.

The Akkad dynasty fell in about 2100 B.C. and after a period of disunity and disorder, Gudea, ruler of the city of Lagash, united the Sumerians for a renaissance of Sumerian culture. About twenty statues of Gudea have survived, possibly indicating a popular king or an expert in public relations, or maybe even both. Like the statue illustrated here (figure 1.5), Sumerian sculptors used diorite, an exceptionally hard and intractable stone, thus at least partially accounting for the large number of surviving statues of the same king. All of the statues are similar to this one: the ruler is portrayed as both devout and wise. The impression is very similar to that produced fourteen centuries later in many statues of the Buddha: controlled and serene.

Old Babylonia, 1900–1500 B.C.

Though the Sumerians and Akkadians had managed to coexist through the revival of Sumer, the invading Babylonians found a weary and divided land so exhausted from constant friction that opposition was nonexistent. The Sumerians and Akkadians couldn't even get together long enough to fight off a truly foreign invader. Nomads from the Arabian desert, the Babylonians (also called Amorites) established a powerful state centered

on the royal city of Babylon. Excavations at Mari in the middle Euphrates valley have revealed an enormous palace of nearly 300 rooms containing thousands of tablets from the royal archives. Chief among the royal correspondents was Hammurabi (ca. 1792–1750 B.C.), who consolidated the territories of Sumer and Assad into a powerful Babylonian kingdom.[3]

One of the striking characteristics of all Mesopotamian cultures was the large number of land-owning merchants and farmers. This was a situation with a high potential for chaos unless restrained by some sort of legal system that regulated private property, trade, and other affairs of a flourishing commercial world. Various legal codes had been developed in the past but none so practical as that devised by Hammurabi, whose famous Code of Laws established the rule of law from the Persian Gulf

---

3. The reference to Old Babylonia is modern hindsight; there was a later kingdom called Neo-Babylonia.

FIGURE 1.6 *Stele of Hammurabi (upper portion), Babylonian, ca. 1760 B.C., basalt. Entire stele ca. 7'4" high. Louvre, Paris. The Code of Law is inscribed on the lower portion of the stele. Above the code the king is standing before a divinity who is probably Shamash, the sungod, regarded as the lawgiver.*

to the Mediterranean Sea (figure 1.6). Consisting of a rather poetic prologue and epilogue, the central section of the code listed 282 regulations dealing with perjury; theft; land tenure; licensed drinking; commerce; marriage and divorce; inheritance; adoption; medical treatment; construction; and the hire of livestock, laborers, and slaves. Oddly enough there is no reference to taxation. In common with earlier codes, the basic principle was "retaliation in kind" or, as expressed by the Hebrews, "an eye for an eye, a tooth for a tooth." As a combination of contemporary tribal practices and of more enlightened provisions for justice, the code did replace some (not all) "retaliation in kind" with fines and money compensation to aggrieved parties. Most importantly, it worked.

In the prologue Hammurabi summarized his contribution to the people after he "pronounced the majestic name of Babylon and decreed the extension of its power over the whole universe" so that he "might bring order to my people and so that I might free them from evil and wicked men, that I should defend the weak from the oppression of the mighty." Granted that these words are self-serving and verge on purple prose, they are, nevertheless, high-minded in intent. Establishing order, protecting society, and making all equal before the law are worthy goals in any society.

The Assyrian Empire, 1076–612 B.C.

After rather lackluster nomads from the East (Kassites from Iran) had ruled Babylonia in a reasonably benign manner from ca. 1500 to 1100 B.C., a far more warlike power emerged in the north. The first military state in history, Assyria was to become, in the words of one of its kings, "Lord of the World," the most powerful and ruthless of all Near Eastern empires.

Assyrian art and architecture was entirely in the service of the king, designed to glorify the image of the monarch as a mighty hunter and implacable warrior (figure 1.7). The intent was to intimidate any foes foolish enough to resist Assyrian military might. The enormous palace of Assurnasirpal II (uh–soor–NAS–ir–pall; 883–859 B.C.)[4] at Nimrud (ancient Kalkho), was the administrative center of a garrison state that extended from the Tigris to the Nile and from the Persian Gulf to Turkey. Erected in the Mesopotamian tradition of clusters of rooms surrounding courtyards, the palace walls were covered with elaborate reliefs of warring, hunting kings (much like the scene in figure 1.7), which were veritable symphonies of violence and death. The entrance to the palace was flanked by huge figures of human-headed, winged bulls carved in both relief and in the round (figure 1.8). Designed to ward off evil spirits, the bulls are depicted at rest (frontal view) and in motion (side view), an illusion furthered by the addition of a fifth leg.

---

4. These and subsequent royal dates are reigning dates.

MAP 1.3 *The Assyrian Empire, ca. 660 B.C.*

■
FIGURE 1.8 *Winged human-headed bull from Nimrud, Assyria, period of Assurnasirpal II, 883–859 B.C. Alabaster, height 10'4''. British Museum, London. Reproduced by courtesy of the Trustees of the British Museum.*

The combination of fine attention to detail, sweeping wings, and sheer intimidating size communicates an awesome vigor intended to symbolize the invincibility of the Assyrian military machine. Making certain that he and his army were feared, Assurnasirpal II followed a standard policy: after capturing an enemy town he would order his soldiers to round up all the inhabitants, cut off their hands and feet, and pile them in the town square to bleed and suffocate to death.

The Assyrian Empire reached the pinnacle of its power during the reign of Sargon II (722–705 B.C.). Because mass murder tended to stiffen enemy resistance, the Assyrians established an alternate policy: control dissent by removing entire populations from their homes and scattering them throughout the empire. It was Sargon II who, in 722 B.C., dispersed the population of Israel—the "ten lost tribes of Israel."

Shortly after the conquest of Israel, Assyrian power began gradually to wane. Sennacherib's (SEN–na–CHAIR–ib) sack of Babylon in 689 B.C. and the conquest of Egypt in 670 B.C. were the last major successes of the Assyrian juggernaut. A coordinated effort of Babylonians, Medes (from northern Persia), and Palestinians decisively defeated the Assyrians in 612 B.C. and led to the total destruction of all major cities, especially the royal city of Nineveh. The end was spectacular. No other ancient empire collapsed so swiftly; no other land was devastated so completely. Moreover, despite centuries of military domination and decades of imperial power, there is no trace of Assyrian influence on succeeding ages. In fact, the empire and the people simply disappeared, reinforcing the biblical saying that those who live by the sword shall perish by the sword.

Mesopotamia   **27**

Keeping in mind that Nahum was a Hebrew prophet and that Assyria was the hated enemy, the Old Testament account of the fall of Nineveh is appropriately impassioned:

Woe to the bloody city,
all full of lies and booty—
no end to the plunder!
The crack of whip, and rumble of wheel,
    galloping horse and bounding chariot!
Horsemen charging,
    flashing sword and glittering spear,
hosts of slain,
    heaps of corpses,
dead bodies without end—
    they stumble over the bodies!

Wasted is Nineveh; who will bemoan her?
    whence shall I seek comforters for her?

Your shepherds are asleep,
    O king of Assyria;
    your nobles slumber.
Your people are scattered on the mountains
    with none to gather them.
There is no assuaging your hurt,
    your wound is grievous.
All who hear the news of you
    clap their hands over you.
For upon whom has not come
    your unceasing evil?

Nahum 3:1–3, 7, 18–19

The Chaldean (Neo-Babylonian) Empire, 625–539 B.C.

The Chaldeans were a Semitic desert race from, perhaps, the Syrian area. Even before they allied themselves with the Medes to help destroy Assyria, they had settled in and around Babylon and rebuilt that ancient city on a grand scale. As the last upholder of Mesopotamian culture the new Babylon was actually little more than a sumptuous museum in which older traditions, especially those of Sumer, were collected and preserved. Innovation was virtually unknown in a Babylonia that had shut itself off from the outside world as it contemplated past glories.

With the accession of Nebuchadnezzar II (NEB–oo–kud–NEZ–ar, also spelled Nebuchadrezzar; 605–562 B.C.) to the kingship, the legendary might of Sumer and Assyria were recalled in a monumental architecture and in a series of military expeditions that consolidated Babylonian power. A vigorous and brilliant commander, Nebuchadnezzar drove the Egyptians from Palestine, conquered Jerusalem (in 586 B.C.), and exiled many Jews to Babylon. The Old Testament prophet, Jeremiah, had counseled cooperation with Babylon, reasoning that it was better to submit to a Semite foe than join a weak and faithless Egypt. His sensible counsel was ignored and the Jews revolted, with predictable results. The king of Judah was blinded, his children and nobles killed and

Nebuzaradan, the captain of the bodyguard who served the king of Babylon, entered Jerusalem.
And he burned the house of the Lord and the king's house and all the houses of Jerusalem.

Jeremiah 52:12–13

According to Jeremiah (52:27–30) 4,600 Jews were carried into what they called their Babylonian Captivity (586–516 B.C.). Though Jeremiah stated that "Judah was carried captive out of its land," this did not mean that the city was denuded of all its residents. Artisans and other workers were carted off but many, mostly of the poorer class, were left behind to continue the traditions of their people as best they could.

In Babylon, Nebuchadnezzar continued to design and build in the grand manner. The Hanging Gardens that he had constructed for his Median wife were rated among the wonders of the (ancient) world. He built an enormous ziggurat 295 feet high and named it Entemenanki ("Temple of the Foundation of Heaven and Earth"). This is the biblical Tower of Babel.

One of the more dazzling designs was for the glazed brick Ishtar Gate (colorplate 9). The Mesopotamians had a special talent for portraying animals, an ability especially notable in this monumental work. Embellished with figures of lions, bulls, and a kind of griffin, the gate stood at the end of the main processional entrance to the opulent capital city.

Despite its size and the splendor of its cities, the Babylonian Empire was basically fragile. After the death of Nebuchadnezzar in 562 B.C. the decline was quite swift, ending, according to the Bible, with the death of Belshazzar in 539 B.C. Biblical scholars have not been able to determine whether or not Belshazzar really existed or if that was indeed his name, but the Old Testament account of his demise effectively dramatizes royal decadence and the precipitous fall of Babylon.

King Belshazzar made a great feast for a thousand of his lords, and drank wine in front of the thousand.
Belshazzar, when he tasted the wine, commanded that the vessels of gold and of silver which Nebuchadnezzar his father had taken out of the temple in Jerusalem be brought, that the king and his lords, his wives, and his concubines might drink from them. Then they brought in the golden and silver vessels which had been taken out of the temple, the house of God in Jerusalem; and the king and his lords, his wives, and his concubines drank from them. They drank wine, and praised the gods of gold and silver, bronze, iron, wood, and stone.
Immediately the fingers of a man's hand appeared and wrote on the plaster of the wall of the king's palace. Then the king's color changed and his thoughts alarmed him; his limbs gave way and his knees knocked together.
Then Daniel was brought in [and] answered before the king "I will read the writing to the king and make known to him the interpretation.
"And this is the writing that was inscribed: MENE, MENE, TEKEL, and PARSIN. This is the interpretation of the matter: MENE, God has numbered the days of your kingdom and brought it to an end; TEKEL, you have been weighed in the balance and found wanting; PERES, your kingdom is divided and given to the Medes and Persians."
That very night Belshazzar the Chaldean king was slain.

Daniel 5:1–6, 13, 17, 25–28, 30

Internal strife, decadence, and degeneracy indeed took their toll; there was, in fact, no opposition to the conquering Persians. The Assyrian Empire had gone down fighting; Babylon, the last of twenty-five centuries of Mesopotamian kingdoms, expired with scarcely a whimper.

Exercises

1. Compare the portraits in figures 1.4 and 1.5. How do they differ and how are they similar? Based on the visual evidence, what can you deduce about the two rulers?

2. Why was Hammurabi's Code of Law so significant? Before responding to the question try to imagine what life would be like if you lived in an area in which each community had its own laws. How might this situation affect commerce, trade, and other intercommunity relations?

The Persian Empire, 539–330 B.C.

The Persians migrated from somewhere east of the Caspian Sea into the high plateau country north and east of the Persian Gulf. Apparently closely related to the Medes who lived farther north, both spoke an Indo-European language.[5] Under the remarkable leadership of Cyrus the Great (539–530 B.C.), the Persians first absorbed the Medes and then moved against the Lydian kingdom ruled by the legendary Croesus. Croesus had already formed alliances with Egypt and Sparta in anticipation of a preventive war against Persia, but he was uncertain about success until he took the precaution of consulting with the oracle at Delphi. According to the Greek historian, Herodotos (484–425 B.C.), the oracle predicted that a Lydian attack would destroy a great army. That did indeed happen but the defeated army was commanded by Croesus.

With the conquest of Egypt by Cyrus's son, Cambyses, in 525 B.C. the Persian Empire expanded rapidly, eventually extending from the Himalayas to Greece and from southern Russia to the Indian Ocean, the greatest empire the world had yet seen. Like the later Romans (with whom they had much in common), the Persians permitted subjugated peoples to retain their own customs, laws, and religion. The Hebrews, for example, were allowed to worship Jahweh (or Yahweh) and the Jews in Babylon were encouraged to return to Jerusalem, though few chose to do so. Such tolerance, for the practical Persians, was pragmatic, enabling the government to collect tribute from the far-flung empire without unduly riling the populace—just as Rome later collected taxes.

One of the major Persian achievements was an elaborate network of imperial roads, the best system prior to the Romans. The Royal Road, for example, covered some 1600 miles from the Persian Gulf to Asia Minor, connecting the principal cities of Susa and Sardis. Using a pony express of relay riders, the "king's messengers" could travel the entire Royal Road in a week. According to Herodotos "nothing mortal travels as fast as these Persian messengers. Not snow, nor rain, nor heat, nor gloom

■

FIGURE 1.9 *Audience Hall of Darius and Xerxes, Great Palace, ca. 500 B.C., Persepolis, Iran. Photo, Oriental Institute of Chicago.*

of night stays these couriers from the swift completion of their appointed rounds" (*Histories* VIII).[6]

Though the Persian king did not employ the terrorist tactics of the Assyrians, he was very much an absolute monarch with his authority tempered only by some power-sharing with his nobles. From the Greek point of view, admittedly biased, Cyrus, Darius, and Xerxes, among others, were oriental despots and the Persian army a mindless but mighty machine. Though some contemporary scholars contend that the Persian Empire was fairly liberal and humane, the fact that there were numerous insurrections throughout imperial history testifies to the heavy yoke of the man the Persians called the King of Kings.

Persian culture was as derivative and eclectic as that of Rome. With nothing original to contribute, their art and architecture was adapted from Mesopotamian, Egyptian, Lydian, Palestinian, and Greek models. Possibly the most positive (i.e., Persian) expression of the culture was their architecture. They copied the raised platform and terraced building style of Babylon and Assyria, adding winged Assyrian bulls and glazed Babylonian bricks. Rather than the Mesopotamian arch and vault they chose columns and colonnades in the Egyptian style but with Greek fluting and capitals. The only unique aspect of their architecture was that it was wholly secular. Because their new religion of Zoroastrianism (discussed shortly) required no priests, rituals, statues, or temples, the Persians concentrated on building elaborate palaces.

The Great Palace of Darius and Xerxes at Persepolis (figure 1.9) was destroyed by Alexander but enough remains of this enormous complex to give some idea of its magnitude. The view shown is of the eastern stairway in front of the Audience Hall with the Gate of Xerxes on the left. The Great Hall originally had a hundred stone columns, each forty feet high and all brightly painted. This was the first use of interior columns in the Mesopotamian world. Though influenced by Egyptian examples, these columns are more closely patterned after

5. With only a few exceptions, all modern inhabitants of Europe speak languages derived from ancient tongues brought from Eurasia (Ukraine or east of there) by Bronze Age conquerors. The term Indo-European identifies various language branches as spoken in Europe, Iran, and northern India. These include Greek, Latin, Sanscrit, Persian, Celtic, and the Germanic languages. Iran (used after A.D. 600) means "land of the Aryan."

6. From which the U.S. Postal Service derived its motto.

Greek models and were probably designed and constructed by Greek artisans. The low reliefs show row upon row of Persian guards, a security guard in stone. The influence is clearly Assyrian but nowhere are there bloody scenes of kings at war or ruthlessly slaughtering helpless animals. Persian kings preferred tidy and efficient administration of their vast empire without blatant intimidation in the Assyrian manner.

Zoroastrianism

Perhaps the only original contribution of Persian culture was a new religion. A prophet named Zoroaster, in Greek, (Zarathrustra, in Persian) was both a reformer of traditional folk religion and the creator of a new faith. Born sometime in the seventh century B.C. (660?), he was the first exponent, according to some scholars, of an ethical monotheistic religion. Other scholars contend that Zoroastrianism was a dualistic religion, albeit ethical. Which was it? Which is it? An examination of the evidence may supply some answers but, as in most if not all religions, final interpretation must rest with each interpreter.

In the *Gathas,* his collected work, Zoroaster states that Ahura Mazda (also called Ormazd) is the principle of truth and also the Holy Spirit, the Creating Word that existed before the world was born, the Word that brought all forms of life into being, boding good for all species, particularly the human race. In order that people might, through struggle, appreciate the true meaning of goodness a twin of the Holy Spirit—Ahriman the Evil One—was created. It is unclear whether Ahriman was created by Ahura Mazda (Ormazd) or was created simultaneously as the evil twin of Ormazd, and thus the scholarly disagreement. In any event, all life became a contest between good and evil, truth and error, light and darkness.

In its original form, Zoroastrianism was a personal religion with no place for statues, elaborate rituals, or a priestly caste, and so no need to build temples. Any person seeking the good and the true could find them. Similarly, anyone could reject them or pervert them into evil, though it is not clear just why anyone would wish to do this.

There was an elaborate eschatology which looked forward to the coming of the Saoshyans or Savior, who would resurrect the dead for judgment. The righteous would then pass to heaven and the wicked to hell to suffer physically for their sins. In another passage Zoroaster described the just as residing in the House of Song while the unjust were doomed to the House of the Lie.

The dualism in Zoroastrianism was not an eternal conflict between good and evil; ultimately Ormazd would overcome Ahriman. Those condemned to the House of the Lie would not stay there forever. The final victory of Ormazd and the destruction of Ahriman would lead to the *Fraskart,* the ultimate "making excellent" or rehabilitation of the followers of Ahriman.

The new faith was so far beyond the capacity of the common people that changes were implemented both to minimize its abstractions and to emphasize its symbols, sacrifice, liturgy, and priestly mediation, the very paraphernalia Zoroastrianism attempted to eradicate. The ancient fertility goddess (Ishtar) returned to the pantheon as did Mithra, god of light. Thus, in time, a protest against polytheism and empty formalism took on some of the characteristics of the old beliefs it sought to supplant. Even so, there was so much that was new and vital in Zoroastrianism that some of its elements may be detected in subsequent religious movements.

Exercises

1. How would you explain the Persian conquest and rule of the largest empire prior to the Romans? What did they seem to learn (positive and negative) from earlier kingdoms and empires?
2. Compare Persian Zoroastrianism with the polytheism of Mesopotamia. What changed? Why?
3. What are the elements in Zoroastrianism that may have influenced Judaism, Christianity, and Islam?

Summary

The history of Western civilization begins in Mesopotamia with the invention of agriculture. When nomads settled down to farm, everything changed, with one invention following upon another: animal husbandry, pottery, weaving, permanent houses, communities, fortifications, mathematics, a calendar, and writing. In due course came trade, manufacturing, law, and all the other complexities of civilization—including warfare.

Sumer, in the Land between the Rivers, is generally called the Cradle of Civilization. The Sumerian Period (3000–2350 B.C.) saw the development of organized polytheism, ziggurats with temples on top; advances in mathematics, writing, and astronomy; and the first major literary work, *The Epic of Gilgamesh.*

Under Sargon the Great, the Akkadians assumed political control of Sumerian culture (2350–2150 B.C.) and refined and improved their art forms. Continually unhappy under Akkadian domination, the Sumerians regained control under Gudea of Lagash (Neo-Sumerian Period, 2050–1900 B.C.).

The incessant internecine strife of Sumerians and Akkadians left them vulnerable to the Amorites, opportunistic nomads from the Arabian desert, who established a Babylonian Empire (1900–1500 B.C.) centered on the royal city of Babylon. Chief among the royal rulers was Hammurabi, who was responsible for a code that established the rule of law throughout the empire.

Another tribe of desert nomads, the Kassites, established a rather benign rule in Babylon (1500–1100 B.C.), maintaining the culture but doing little to improve life or art. The Kassites were conquered in turn by Assyria, the first military state in history (1076–612 B.C.). Entirely at the service of the king, Assyrian art essentially had two subjects, both of them violent: war and hunting. Ruthless in their warring and ruling, the Assyrians actually bragged about their brutality, partly as a heavy warning to potential dissidents. When the end came, the enemies of the Assyrians were equally pitiless, totally destroying everything Assyrian; the empire and the people simply disappeared.

The Assyrians were destroyed mainly by the Medes and the Chaldeans, the latter a Semitic desert tribe that reestablished the Babylonian Empire, now known as the Chaldean (Neo-Babylonian) Empire (625–539 B.C.). Under Nebuchadnezzar II, Babylon bloomed briefly as a kind of museum of past glories, the final bastion of a Mesopotamian culture that had begun 2500 years before.

The last of the ancient Near Eastern powers, the Persian Empire (539–331 B.C.) was also the greatest that the world had yet seen. Though they made no original contributions to art or architecture—their culture was wholly eclectic—they did demonstrate an ability to govern efficiently. Their only original contribution, Zoroastrianism, was a significant and influential addition to world religions.

A culture that began in the Land between the Rivers in about 3000 B.C. succumbed, finally, to a European power in 331 B.C. Not until the expansion of Islam a thousand years later would the Near or Middle East again figure prominently in world affairs.

Culture and Human Values

For the average Mesopotamian, life was a matter of survival in the here and now. There was a bit of personal freedom but, in the final analysis, people were at the mercy of forces beyond their control, from raging rivers to warring kings. The gods were fractious, enemies seemed always to be at the gates, life was grim. Ultimate reality was only the visible world with all of its imperfections and terrors, no more, no less.

None of the Mesopotamian cultures seem to have achieved any appreciable period of balance. Each historical period was mainly one of adjustment, from Sumerians to Akkadians, to Sumerians, Babylonians, and all the rest. There was a chronic tendency to stagger from one crisis to another without falling totally into chaos but without rising to a plateau of stability.

Throughout Mesopotamia's long history there was not much concern about ideals such as the true, the good, or the beautiful. Neither the polytheistic religion nor the authoritarian government inspired any urge towards personal excellence. Pleasing the gods was more important than living the good life, a pragmatic attitude that added little to any value system. Pragmatism was also the name of the game in the individual's relationship to government. There were probably some local assemblies with some measure of limited authority but on the whole, citizens were helpless in the path of the monolithic state. A low profile and total submission were the prerequisites for political survival.

High cultural achievements, individually or collectively, are not likely in cultures in which little or no emphasis is placed upon truth, justice, love, and beauty. This explains why the Egyptians (and later the Greeks) felt that their civilization was superior to anything developed in Mesopotamia.

Annotated Bibliography

The bibliographies throughout this text were selected as particularly useful and interesting with a range from popular to scholarly works.

Amiet, Pierre. *Art of the Ancient Near East.* Translated by John Shepley and Claude Choquet. New York: Harry N. Abrams, 1980. Probably the best illustrated text now available.

Champdor, Albert. *Babylon.* New York: G. P. Putnam's Sons, 1958. A profusely illustrated overview of the two Babylonian kingdoms.

Fagan, Brian M. *Return to Babylon: Travelers, Archeologists, and Monuments in Mesopotamia.* Boston: Little, Brown, and Company, 1979. An engaging study with a wealth of information.

Ghirshman, Roman. *The Arts of Ancient Iran: From Its Origins to the Time of Alexander the Great.* Translated by Stuart Gilbert and James Emmons. New York: Golden Press, 1964. From the Arts of Mankind series edited by André Malraux and Georges Selles. Superbly done as with all volumes in the series.

Kostof, Spiro. *A History of Architecture: Settings and Rituals.* New York: Oxford University Press, 1985. From the first prehistoric environments on record to the most recent examples of architecture and urban design. A splendid one-volume survey.

Kramer, Samuel Noah. *Cradle of Civilization.* New York: Time, 1967. From the Great Ages of Man series. Excellent overview with the usual fine Time-Life illustrations.

Margueron, Jean-Claude. *Mesopotamia.* Translated by H. S. B. Harrison. Cleveland: The World Publishing Company, 1965. Traces the rediscovery of Sumer.

Moorthat, Anton. *The Art of Mesopotamia: The Classical Art of the Near East.* New York: Phaidon Publishers, 1969. Richly illustrated.

Oppenheim, A. Leo. *Ancient Mesopotamia: Portrait of a Dead Civilization.* Chicago: University of Chicago Press, 1977. A good portrait of ancient Mesopotamia.

Translation of Original Material

Grayson, A. Kirk, and Bedford, D. B., eds. *Papyrus and Tablet.* Englewood Cliffs, N.J.: Prentice-Hall, 1973. A good collection of Mesopotamian and Egyptian texts for the neophyte.

Herodotos of Halicarnassus. *The Persian Wars (Histories* in some translations). Translated by Aubrey de Selincourt. Baltimore: Penguin Books, 1972. The "Father of History" is more than a historian; he is an enthusiastic and fascinating storyteller. The first five of the nine books recount the growth of the Persian Empire and the beginnings of oriental aggression, following which he glowingly relates the Greek triumphs over the Persian invader.

McNeill, William H., and Sedlar, Jean W., ed. *The Ancient Near East.* New York: Oxford University Press, 1968. Includes both Mesopotamian and Egyptian texts with a brief historical background.

Pritchard, James B., ed. *The Ancient Near East: An Anthology of Texts and Pictures.* Princeton: Princeton University Press, 1958. A wide-ranging collection that includes *The Epic of Gilgamesh.*

2

Egypt

One People, One Language

As the first truly national state (one people, one language), Egypt had a far more consistent and unified development than did the quarreling, warring city-states of Mesopotamia. Egypt was, in fact, virtually the antithesis of Mesopotamia because of its geography and its climate. Mesopotamian cities lay exposed on the broad plain between the rivers with no naturally defensible sites. Egypt was protected on the north by the Mediterranean and by cataracts and mountains on the south. A 750-mile strip of richly fertile land averaging ten miles in width, it was further guarded on the east and west by the trackless Sahara Desert. For the Egyptians this stretch of lush land, so liberally blessed by nature, was the "gift of the Nile." It was no wonder that Herodotos defined Egypt as "all the country covered by inundations of the Nile" and Egyptians as "all men who drink Nile water" (*Histories,* II).

The Nile valley produced two crops a year, an agricultural prosperity unmatched in the ancient world. Herodotos put it quite succinctly: "They obtain the fruit of the field with less trouble than any other people in the world." The climate was healthy, very dry, and consistently sunny, with little likelihood of natural catastrophes such as the earthquakes, violent storms, and raging floods that so bedeviled Mesopotamian residents. No other area was so sedately stable as the land of the smoothly flowing Nile, with its life-giving and predictable patterns of flood and retreat. Naturally enough, the Egyptians viewed nature's laws and those of their living god, their king (later called pharaoh), as immutable and the afterlife as a continuation of the good life in their richly prosperous valley.

The God-Kings

Throughout its long history, Egypt was a theocracy. The pharaoh was the genesis of all, a living god on whom life, safety, and prosperity depended. Pharaoh was, after all, the source of the good life: he controlled the Nile. In addition to affluence and safety, the best kind of life should also include right actions. Proper ethical conduct was therefore supposed to prepare every citizen for a continuation of the good life beyond the grave. Death, the embalming of the body, and the tomb were fundamental concerns for every Egyptian. This would seem to indicate a morbid preoccupation with death but the exact opposite was true. Security, prosperity, a benign climate, with pharaoh on his throne and all right with the world made Egyptian life zestful and endlessly rewarding. Egyptians paid so much attention to death because they loved life. Their concern about embalming was based on the principle of the *ka,* the indestructible vital principle of each person. Though the ka left at death, it could return; proper mummification meant that the ka, on return, would find the properly intact body fully ready for the hereafter. And that next life would be even finer than the previous one.

In Mesopotamia, life was far more uncertain; the general inclination was to live for the present with dim hopes for anything beyond the grave. An afterlife seemed more like a threat (more of the same problems) than expectation of anything better. On the other hand, Egyptian life and religion were inseparable, with genuine concern about love and social equality plus a strong element of monotheism. Herodotos rated the Egyptians as "religious to excess, far beyond any other race of men." Mesopotamia's polytheistic religion was quite different: pragmatic, self-centered and self-serving. This results in part from the built-in problem of polytheism: if one of the gods is mad at me, which one is it and how can I satisfy him or her without offending any of the other gods?

Almost inevitably, this forces ethical conduct into a secondary position with self-interest and basic survival becoming primary. Egyptian culture was essentially ethical; that of Mesopotamia, legalistic.

A law code by Hammurabi or any other lawgiver was a natural consequence in a legalistic society. Egypt never had nor ever needed a code of law. On the other hand, there was more room in Mesopotamian kingdoms for individual initiative, and for social and economic mobility: the opportunity to rise higher—or fall lower.

The literature of the two areas was also quite different. Egyptian writing was limited in depth and in imagination: much was superficial and facile. There was nothing as serious as *The Epic of Gilgamesh* in the happier world of Egypt.

Mesopotamians built their ziggurats, temples, and palaces of sun-dried mud bricks and generally used art in the service of their kings. Egyptian tombs, temples, and sculptures of their god-kings were made of imperishable stone, symbolizing the timelessness of the Egyptian world. Pharaoh was the living god and the kingdom was an extension of him or her, eternal and unchanging. This was why so many animals were objects of worship; humans changed constantly while animals were part of the natural and changeless world. Art was massive and solemn because it was mainly sacramental, as were many of the rituals that formed the basis of everyday life. The main outlines of Egyptian religious belief remained constant for three thousand years; the arts themselves established canons of style and form that also endured down those long corridors of time.

No other people in the ancient world were as steadfastly consistent in their national characteristics. Herodotos stated that "the Egyptians adhere to their own national customs and adopt no foreign usages." Their sense of themselves and of their nation was exact and certain, for they were "the best skilled in history of any men that I have ever met" (Herodotos).

They were no less certain about their religion. The great sun god, giver of life, was *Re* (or *Ra*), usually called *Amon* or *Amon-Re*. The gods who personified the vegetative powers of nature were fused into a deity called *Osiris*, who was also—and fittingly—the god of the Nile. The cult of Osiris began as a nature religion but grew beyond that. According to the legend, Osiris was a benevolent ruler but he was slain by Set, his wicked brother, and his body chopped into pieces. His wife Isis, who was also his sister, put the pieces together and restored the body to life. The risen god regained his kingdom but eventually descended to the nether world as judge of the dead. Horus, his posthumous son, grew to manhood and avenged his father's murder by killing Set.

This nature myth first accounted for the inundation and recession of the Nile. Then it was broadened and deepened so that the death and resurrection of Osiris conveyed a promise of personal immortality; just as the god had risen, the individual could also triumph over the grave. Finally, the victory of Horus over Set symbolized the triumph of good over evil.

These and associated legends were communicated to each generation through what the Egyptians called "sacred carvings": a combination of pictographs and sound signs that the Greeks called hieroglyphs. "Signs

■
FIGURE 2.1 *Sphinx, ca. 2540–2514 B.C., 840' in length, original ht. 75'; top of the Great Pyramid of Khufu, ca. 2590–2568 B.C., original ht. 482'. Old Kingdom, Fourth Dynasty, Giza, Egypt.*

were not used only to denote the objects depicted, but also other words of like sound which were difficult or impossible to represent pictorially: thus the sledge and the mace signified respectively both these actual objects and the verbs 'be complete' and 'be bright.' "[1] (See figure 2.3 for an illustration of hieroglyphs.) The ability to read these sacred carvings was the key to the exalted position of the priestly class.

It was an Egyptian priest-historian, Manetho of Sebennytos, who in about 300 B.C. divided Egyptian history into thirty dynasties or periods of ruling houses. Though later information has altered some of the facts, Egyptologists still follow Manetho's scheme.

Old Kingdom, 2686–2181 B.C., Dynasties III–VI

Egyptian culture evolved very slowly during the Pre-Dynastic Period of ca. 5000–3100 B.C., possibly because there was no central government. By about 3100 B.C., with the beginning of the first dynasty, there were two kingdoms: Lower Egypt (Nile delta) and Upper Egypt (700 miles of river valley to the first cataract). The first unifier, the one who combined the two Egypts into one nation was the legendary—perhaps mythical—Menes, from whom scholars have dated the Old Kingdom, the first major division of Egyptian history. About a century after Menes, the pharaohs conceived the idea of enormous tombs and thus launched the short-lived but monumental Pyramid Age of the Old Kingdom.

When Herodotos gazed, in the fifth century B.C., upon the two-thousand-year-old Sphinx and the great pyramids he was as awed by their antiquity as by their overwhelming size (figure 2.1). Combining the body of a lion with the head of the Pharaoh Khafre, the Sphinx is the largest surviving colossus—a majestic symbol of royal power. It was not built; rather, it was carved out of the sedimentary bedrock. The prodigious amount of stone that was removed was apparently used to build a solar temple under the paws of the beast, with the rest

1. Edwards, I. E. E., et al., eds. *The Cambridge Ancient History,* 3d. ed., vol. 1, part 2, p. 43.

FIGURE 2.2 Mycerinus and His Queen, *ca. 2599–2571 B.C., Old Kingdom, Fourth Dynasty, from Giza. Slate schist, ht. 54½". Shaw Collection. Museum of Fine Arts, Boston.*

going into Khafre's pyramid. It is likely that the Sphinx represents Khafre as Horus, the god of kingship, and that the solar temple is the first evidence of a religious transition from Horus the hawk to Amon-Re the sun god.

The Great Pyramid of Khufu is about 775 feet square and covers over thirteen acres. The largest of the three major pyramids,[2] it contains about 250,000 stones, each weighing over two tons. The Pyramid Age was relatively brief, possibly because the basic idea was not a good one. The massiveness of each structure was intended to foil grave robbers searching for the treasure that each king required as an accompaniment to the afterlife. The pyramids were conspicuous targets, to put it mildly, and all were robbed. From then on, attempts were made to hide, disguise, or otherwise protect pharaonic tombs. However, only the treasure of Tutankhamon has survived; all other tombs were stripped clean.

With the exception of the pyramids, artists and architects established conventions of style and form that continued throughout Egypt's long history. What are stylistic conventions? An art 'convention' is a consistent way of seeing and depicting things in a manner that is generally accepted and understood. Conventions are, in other words, commonly held values that have been given form. The sum of all conventions of a given civilization can therefore be defined as its 'culture.' (This definition of culture can be compared with that given on p. 20.)

When depicting royalty, Egyptian sculpture displayed an impassive calm and enduring serenity that suggested their eternal existence. With pharaoh as the subject, the ongoing life of the State was intimately involved, for the Ruler and the State were one: calm, serene, and eternal. The statue of *Mycerinus and His Queen* (figure 2.2) shares qualities (conventions) that for about three millenia are common to every Egyptian sculpture depicting human figures.

Egyptian sculptors took a cubic view of the human form and prepared the statue by drawing its front and side views on the faces of a rectangular block, then working inward until the angular views met. The resultant image is one of startling clarity, but one that demands a 90 degree change of position every time the viewer desires another perspective. Egyptian statuary has a monumental frozen quality that can be best observed from directly in front, directly in back, or squarely from each side. Symbolizing the total control of the god-ruler, this immobility is a visual counterpart of Egyptian belief in immutable laws that govern people and nature. Also characteristic of Egyptian portraiture is the rectangularity of the figures, as if they were standing within a rectangular box, thus reinforcing the vivid impression of calmly composed immobility. The illusion of massiveness is heightened by leaving as much stone intact as possible as, for example, in the stone webbing that binds the rigid arms and clenched fists to the figure. By carving what amounted to very high reliefs, Egyptian sculptors consistently, and deliberately, avoided openings in the stone. Finally, the conventions of portraiture required formal depictions of persons of high rank, as here with the pharaoh, while less-exalted personages were portrayed more realistically. The queen's clasping of her husband's waist and the touching hand on his left arm symbolize, in a society in which property was inherited through the female line, the transfer of her power to the pharaoh.

Middle Kingdom, 2135–1786 B.C., Dynasties XI–XII

Between the Old and Middle Kingdom came what was later called the First Intermediate Period (2260–2130 B.C., dynasties VII–X). Apparently not even stable, conservative Egypt could tolerate more than five centuries of peace and prosperity. A constantly expanding bureaucracy, the growing power of priests, and rebellious local officials all weakened the power of the central authority. For over a century there was civil unrest, political instability (Manetho facetiously remarked that the seventh dynasty consisted of seventy kings in seventy days), and invasions by desert barbarians.[3] Nevertheless, the next four dynasties managed to stabilize the political situation and to eventually lead the country to renewed peace and prosperity.

---

2. There is a total of eighty pyramids.

3. Neither the First nor even the Second Intermediate Period was as chaotic and disruptive as most of the political turnovers in Mesopotamia. They were more like ripples on a calm sea but *seemed*, to the Egyptians, to be very troublesome just because the sea was usually so serene.

FIGURE 2.3 Sarcophagus of Queen Kawyt, *detail, white limestone, Eleventh Dynasty. From Deir-el Bahari (Thebes). Egyptian Museum, Cairo.*

Politically there was considerable local authority which, coupled with a weaker but stable central government, made the twelfth dynasty era the closest thing to a democratic state that the Egyptians ever achieved.

This was the affluent society of the Middle Kingdom with the highest standard of living in the ancient world. Even minor art forms reached new levels of craftsmanship and artistry. Jewelry, for example, though always impressive, became increasingly elegant and refined.

The major art forms of the age followed the canons of the Old Kingdom but with a refinement and mastery of the material that carried over into the New Kingdom, that last splendid period of Egyptian power and influence. In the scene from the *Sarcophagus of Queen Kawyt* (figure 2.3), the queen is seated on a throne holding a cup to her lips with her right hand and a mirror in her left. Behind her a maid ties the curls of her wig; in front, a manservant pours her a drink. The words he uses to wish her well appear in the hieroglyphs between them. The bas-relief is spacious in composition and sure in line, the latter as exemplified in the adroit curves of the hands of the woman dressing the wig. Egyptian painters and relief carvers almost invariably depicted the human body with a frontal view of the eyes and torso but with the face and legs in profile. This arrangement shows key body parts in their most telling and easily understood view: the way artists *know* (in their mind's eye) rather than how they actually *see* the parts. Further, by avoiding specific settings and placing boldly two-dimensional figures on a frontal plane, artists emphasize the timelessness that characterizes Egyptian art.

Exercises

1. What exactly does "gift of the Nile" mean? What did the Nile "give" that the Tigris and Euphrates rivers fail to provide? Why? NOTE: Some exercises in this text require the use of other sources, particularly those listed in the bibliographies.

2. If environment influences mythology, as it indeed does, how might this apply to the Egyptian pantheon? Why, for example, were Amon-Re and Osiris two of the most important gods?

3. What is a theocracy? Explain how Egyptian government functioned. Why was the Nile so crucial to the concept of a theocratic state?

4. What was the primary purpose of the pyramids and what, if anything, did sheer size contribute to this function? If you were a pharaoh, would you order the world's largest pyramid? For what reason? Insurance? Vanity? None of the above?

5. Explain the artistic conventions endemic to portraits of the pharaohs. Could a pharaoh display any human weaknesses or imperfections? What qualities should he have?

New Kingdom (Empire), 1570–1085 B.C., Dynasties XVIII–XX

The disruption that ended the Middle Kingdom was more serious and longlasting than the disruption of the earlier Intermediate Period. This was the Second Intermediate Period (1780–1550 B.C., dynasties XIII–XVII), the invasion of the Hyksos (Egyptian, "rulers of foreign lands"). Originally from western Asia (possibly Syria), these foreign conquerors unwittingly set the stage for the emergence of the Egyptian Empire. Though very little is known about the Hyksos domination, it appears that they introduced the horse and the war chariot to their hostile hosts and that the culture neither flourished nor declined, despite the negative Egyptian view of the entire period. The most important thing that happened to the Egyptians was psychological.

By Egyptian standards, the Hyksos were representatives of a vastly inferior culture. The barbarian conquest was a mighty blow to Egyptian pride and one from which they were painfully slow to recover. In the long run, the Asian occupation acted as a catalyst, spurring Egyptian rulers of the eighteenth dynasty to imperial conquests.

At first the New Kingdom pharaohs were neither land hungry nor bound for glory. They so detested anything foreign, let alone foreign domination, that they embarked on crusades solely (at first) to conquer and occupy adjoining states that could serve as buffers against foreign incursions. Later on, with human nature being what it is, conquests inevitably came to mean more power, more taxes, and more glory.

Government in the New Kingdom was more absolute than even in the Old Kingdom, with military power rather than national unity forming the basis for the rule of the pharaoh, a title now associated with the person of the ruler. ('Pharaoh' means 'great house,' a term originally applied to the king's residence and to his court.) Local authority declined to its lowest level, leaving the pharaoh with a consolidated royal control roughly comparable to that of Louis XIV, the sun-king of seventeenth century France.

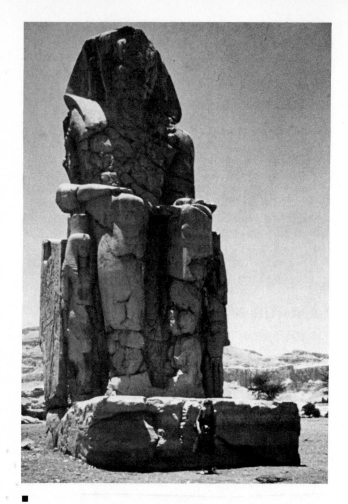

The exalted position of the pharaoh is symbolized by the statue (one of two remaining) of Amenhotep III (figure 2.4) that once flanked his mortuary temple, a grandiose structure now totally vanished. Necessitated perhaps by the vastness of the desert landscape, the giant figure remains as an awesome reminder of the magnificence of the pharaoh.

Temples and Worship

Egyptian temples were the first structures in the ancient world built entirely of stone, and that was not the only innovation. Post and lintel construction (see the glossary) has been used by a number of cultures but the Egyptians were the very first to conceive of the basic principle of supporting a beam with upright posts.

Their imposing, thickly columned temples were visual symbols of the wealth of the pharaohs and the power of the gods, not to mention the authority of the priests who served the gods. The Temple of Amon at Karnak (figure 2.5) was the seat of the throne of Amon and the center of religious administration. The view shown is of the main entrance. The entry was made from the Nile and through the avenue of ram-headed sphinxes to Pylon I, thus following the solar path of Amon-Re. This was the most extensive temple in Egypt and one of the largest sanctuaries in the ancient world, containing 134 massive columns in the Great Hall alone.

For symbolic reasons, Egyptian temples were located on flat banks bordering the Nile, the eternal source of Egyptian power. Placing the temple in a setting that enhanced its visual appearance was usually not a consideration. The Greeks, on the other hand, placed their temples so that the environment contributed substantially to the overall effect. See, for example, figures 7.36 and 7.40.

FIGURE 2.4 *Colossus of Memnon, ca. 1400 B.C., New Kingdom, Eighteenth Dynasty. Quartzite originally 68' high, Thebes.*

FIGURE 2.5 *Avenue of the Rams and Temple of Amon, New Kingdom, dating from the twentieth century B.C. but constructed mainly from the sixteenth to twelfth centuries B.C., Karnak.*

■
FIGURE 2.6 *Mortuary Temple of Queen Hatshepsut, ca. 1480 B.C., New Kingdom, Eighteenth Dynasty, Deir el-Babari.*

■
FIGURE 2.7 *Temple of Amon-Mut-Khonsu, ca. 1390–1260 B.C., New Kingdom, Eighteenth Dynasty, Luxor.*

Constructed at the foot of sandstone cliffs on the western bank of the Nile at Thebes, the mortuary temple of Queen Hatshepsut (figure 2.6) is a brilliantly conceived complex and possibly the only Egyptian temple that was designed with an eye to its environment. It was planned as a memorial to the first woman (maybe the second or third) to rule Egypt, of whom there is any firm record. In order to make the structure more imposing, given the enormity of the setting, the architect, Senmet, has thrust the upper courtyard into the cliff face so that the towering mass can be seen as a kind of natural pyramid.

Even in its ruined condition, the Temple of Amon-Mut-Khonsu (figure 2.7) clearly illustrates the nature of Egyptian religious architecture. The temples were designed as a succession of spaces of increasing holiness

■ **FIGURE 2.8** *Floor plan of Temple of Amon-Mut-Khonsu: (1) entrance, (2) first court, (3) earlier sanctuaries, (4) great hall, (5) second court, and (6) sanctuaries of Amon, Mut, and Khonsu.*

entered through a main portal (number 1 in figure 2.8) flanked by ponderous masses of stone (called pylons) which led to the first inner court (number 2, figure 2.8). Passing through the 74 foot columns of the Great Hall (number 4, figure 2.8), ordinary worshippers assembled in the sequestered inner court (figure 2.7 and number 5, 2.8) but were forbidden to go any further. From here on they could only marvel at the mysterious forest of columns that darkened the inner recesses, the exclusive preserve of the priesthood (number 6, figure 2.8). There, the all-powerful clergy administered the temples of the deity Amon, his wife Mut, and their son Khonsu.

Amenhotep IV (Akhenaton)

The power of the priesthood was a grave concern of Amenhotep IV (reigned 1379–1362 B.C.), the son and, at first, co-regent of the pharaoh who constructed the Colossus of Memnon (figure 2.4), and there was ample reason for anxiety. Egyptian religion had reached its highest ethical level near the end of the Middle Kingdom and the beginning of the New Kingdom. By the time of Amenhotep, it had become seriously debased, its ethical foundation reduced as superstition and magic gained ascendancy. The result was a marked increase in the power of the priesthood, who preyed on the fears of the masses. Or, was the debasing of the religion a means of increasing priestly power? In any case, priests began selling magical charms that supposedly prevented the heart of the deceased from alerting Osiris to his or her true character. The priests also sold formulas which, inscribed on papyrus and placed in the tomb, supposedly facilitated the passage of the dead to celestial realms. The aggregate of these formulas constituted the *Book of the Dead.* This was not an Egyptian Bible, just mortuary inscriptions, all of which were bought in the belief that they guaranteed an entrance into the kingdom of Amon-Re. Good deeds and a clear conscience had become passé.

Amenhotep met the problem head on by driving the priests from their temples and confiscating their property and possessions. He followed that up by ordering the names of the traditional gods removed from everything in the land.

The pharaoh then commanded all his people to worship a new god called Aton, an ancient designation for the sun. The pharaoh further stipulated that all worship must be directed to him personally, for only he could

■ **FIGURE 2.9** *Portrait head of Queen Nefertiti, ca. 1370 B.C., New Kingdom, Eighteenth Dynasty. Painted limestone, ht. 20''. State Museums West Berlin.*

communicate with the Aton. Changing his name from Amenhotep ("Amon is satisfied") to Akhenaton (ah-kun-AH-tun; "beneficial to the Aton"), he ordered the construction of his capital, Akhetaton ("the horizon of Aton"), on a totally new site at Tell el-Amarna. During this period the traditional artistic style was temporarily replaced by a new lightness and naturalism known as the Amarna style. Perhaps the best-known Egyptian sculpture, the portrait of Akhenaton's wife, Queen Nefertiti (figure 2.9), portrays an elegantly beautiful young woman. There is no way of knowing whether or not this is an idealized portrait, but it is certainly an excellent example of the Amarna style.

A Day in Ancient Egypt

Arising at dawn, the Egyptian nobleman, Senemut, begins his day with a bath of cold water and soda (for soap). After a barber trims his hair and shaves him, his valet massages him with ointments and perfumes. To dress his master, the valet first binds on his loincloth and then slips on his fine, white, pleated, linen kilt. Next he drapes several gold necklaces and some jasper beads around his master's neck and hands him his gold signet ring. Normally barefoot, Senemut today wears sandals because he is going out.

In the dining room he bids good morning to his wife, Nefertiry, the overseer of the household. He never violates his father's wise advice: "Do not supervise your wife in her house." Because he has housed, clothed, and adorned her beauty with fine jewelry, he observes her with pride and contentment. Dressed in a white, sleeveless, form-fitting sheath that hangs gracefully to her bare feet, she wears a black, pleated wig. Her eyes are outlined in black kohl and surrounded by green paint in an almond shape. She tints her fingernails and toenails with red juice from a henna plant and colors her lips with a mixture of red ocher and tallow. Besides gold necklaces, she wears gold bracelets and anklets.

Eating at separate tables, Senemut and Nefertiry enjoy a simple breakfast of dates, figs, bread, and beer. Murals adorn the white-washed mud-brick walls. She talks lovingly of the children, who will soon be up and about, playing games in the yard—"tug of war," "leap frog," or "pressing grapes."

His eldest son, Anen, bids his father good day before leaving for school, where he is studying literature, geography, history, arithmetic, and hieroglyphs (his hardest subject). Having been promoted to the higher school, he now writes with ink on papyrus. He takes no lunch to school, knowing that his mother will bring him bread and beer.

Waiting for his steward, Senemut surveys his garden, where lotus and papyrus plants surround the pool and stately palm trees line the walks. Beyond his garden he senses the flurry of the day's activities among his servants. Soon he will smell breads baking in the ovens and barley beer brewing in the brewery, both being dietary staples for all Egyptians. Noisy Nile geese, the family pets, roam the courtyards and garden.

With his steward he begins a tour of his estate. His vineyards on the Nile delta look almost ready to harvest. From the good moisture and rich silt of the Nile overflow this year, the fields of barley, wheat, flax, and cotton promise fine crops. Even after the Pharaoh's taxes there should be plenty left—all accounted for by meticulous scribes' records.

Senemut notices that, since the itinerant barber came yesterday, the peasants all had their heads shaved for convenience and cleanliness. Dressed only in loincloths, they work diligently in their barefeet. As free tenants, they will get a small portion of the crops, enough to amply feed their families. Their wheat bread and barley beer will be made by their wives in their own small mud-brick dwellings. Good-natured and cheerful, they spend much time outdoors in the bright sunshine, singing of the beauty of land and sky as they work or of some adventure such as rescuing cattle from the swamp.

While touring his estate, Senemut plans a future family outing: fowling among the tall papyrus reeds along the Nile bank, killing the birds with boomerangs. By next summer he hopes to take Anen on a trip into the desert to hunt gazelle and antelope with his pack of trained hounds. He must see that his chariot is in good condition for the trip.

Returning homeward, he admires the heavy gate and high brick wall around his house that ensure privacy for the indoor-outdoor life his family enjoys. Passing the massive porch columns of brightly painted wood on stone bases, he looks forward to the main meal of the day, the evening meal with the whole family. Would the meat be beef, oxen, duck, goose, or pigeon today? Would the vegetables include peas, beans, lettuce, onions, leeks, or garlic? The fruit could be dates, figs, grapes, or pomegranates. Whatever the menu, the tables would be piled with food served in gold and silver dishes.

At twilight, after the meal, Senemut and Nefertiry climb the stairs to the roof, where they play a board game called "Hounds and Jackals" while the children play with their dolls and balls, and a servant girl plays melodious music on a small harp. It is his favorite time of day.

At full dusk, as darkness deepens, he lies down on his bed—a mattress supported by a mesh of cord attached to a wooden frame. His pillow is a carved wooden headrest. Before leaving, his servant lets down a mosquito netting over his master's bed.

So ends a typical day in the life of a nobleman along the ancient Nile.

Was the worship of Aton history's first monotheistic religion? Aton was indeed the only god but it should be pointed out that Amon-Re was already regarded as the god of the whole earth, an attitude that was well-established during the reign of Akhenaton's father, Amenhotep III. This makes Akhenaton's reform less drastic than it might appear to be.

What were Akhenaton's motives? Was he trying primarily to establish a new religion or attempting to regain religious control of the country? He certainly put the priests of Amon-Re out of business and exercised total control through his claim that only he spoke for and to the Aton. All prayers had to be directed to the pharaoh, "the beautiful child of the Aton." All depictions of the sun disk showed the rays descending to the pharaoh and his queen and to no one else. This was, in effect, a return to the Old Kingdom idea that the king was identified with the sun god, the only difference being the name change.

The Egyptian fiscal system of past centuries that had divided income between local shrines, the larger temples, and the needs of the palace without being too burdensome now gave way to the all-powerful pharaoh and his new religion, and his new city. Designed for shrines to the Aton and for the royal court, Akhetaton was built with incredible haste, not to mention expense. Financing was made possible only by pouring "all the nation's resources into the coffers of the king and his god."[4]

Shortly after Akhenaton's death, his god was quickly replaced by the traditional religion. What prompted this to happen so rapidly

> was doubtless the chaos caused by the economic consequences of Akhenaton's religious reforms that brought about a complete reversal to the old order as soon as he was dead. The recollection of the misery of such times was strong enough to bring upon him the odium of later generations.[5]

The naturalistic Amarna style ended with the reign of Akhenaton's son-in-law Tutankhamon (toot-ahng-KAH-mun; 1347–1338 B.C.). Though he was a minor king, ruling about nine years and dying in his nineteenth year, his tomb contained a marvelous array of treasures. Discovered in 1922, the collection was relatively intact, making "King Tut" a household name. Colorplate 10 reveals a richly colored scene of the young king and his wife. The loose-limbed figures are portrayed in an intimate scene with a certain sweetness that was unusual in the Amarna style. The presence of the sun disk at the top is puzzling; Amon-Re had already been restored by this time.

---

4. Edwards et al., II, Part 2, p. 53.
5. Ibid.

The artistic backlash against the Amarna Period was strong and, given the unpopularity of Akhenaton, predictable. Rather than a direct return to the New Kingdom ornamental style, or even to the classic style of the Middle Kingdom, the reaction thrust Egyptian art back about twelve centuries to the static formal style of the Old Kingdom. The style then remained about the same until the gradual decline of Egyptian power after 1085 B.C. Both the country and its art became ever more feeble. To be fair, however, that last term is appropriate only when the art of the decline is compared with the magnificent achievements in art and architecture over an incredible span of sixteen hundred years. No other nation has had a longer or more distinguished record.

Exercises

1. Explain the forces at work that impel a military state to ever more conquests. You should expand your discussion beyond the army and officer corps to include merchants, contractors, those who needed workers, patriots, and so on.
2. For a fascinating term project, see what different historians have to say about Akhenaton and his innovations.
3. How does "A Day in Ancient Egypt" compare with a typical day with your own family? What is different? What do you and your family seem to have in common with people who lived four or five thousand years ago?
4. What were the outstanding achievements of Egyptian civilization? What seems admirable? Incomprehensible? What do we owe to their culture?

Summary

Egypt was the first national state, the most homogeneous country of the ancient world. With only two significant interruptions, her history extended from the first dynasty of about 3100 B.C. until a final slow decline began after the fall of the New Kingdom in 1085 B.C. This power, prosperity, and continuity was a direct result of the relative security and consistent agricultural affluence of this "gift of the Nile." Though there was some evolution in styles of art and architecture, the basic artistic conventions remained the same throughout Egyptian history, prompting Plato to remark that Egyptian art had not changed "in ten thousand years" (*Laws*, 656D-E).

It was during the Old Kingdom (2686–2181 B.C.) that the artistic conventions were perfected: a cubic view of standing or seated human figures that conveyed immutability. This was an expression of the theology that the ruler and the state were one: divine and indivisible.

After an era of instability (First Intermediate Period, 2260–2130 B.C.) the eleventh dynasty established the less autocratic Middle Kingdom (2135–1786 B.C.). This was the classical period of an Egyptian civilization that reached new levels of affluence and artistic achievement, possibly indicating that achievement and affluence are symbiotically related. Artists continued and refined the creation of fine jewelry, furniture, pottery, and other household items. In their reliefs and paintings, artists pictured their subjects not as they *saw* them but as they *knew* them: the eyes and torso as viewed from the front but with the face and legs in profile. The emphasis was still upon the timelessness that characterized Egyptian art but with a new mastery of elegant line and spacious composition.

The invasion of the Asiatic Hyksos was a serious and long-lasting blow to Egyptian pride (Second Intermediate Period, 1780–1550 B.C.). After the seventeenth dynasty finally conquered and expelled the invaders, the eighteenth dynasty of the New Kingdom (1570–1085 B.C.) began a series of military campaigns designed to remove any subsequent foreign menace. This was the imperial period in which pharaohs, at first, conquered and occupied only adjoining states as buffers against further invasions. Inevitably, a military state becomes its own reason for being and this happened to the pharaoh-generals of the Egyptian Empire: conquest became a necessary adjunct to pharaonic prestige.

Some of the justly famous surviving buildings were constructed during the imperial (New Kingdom) period: the mortuary temple of Queen Hatshepsut, the Temple of Amon at Karnak, the Temple of Amon-Mut-Khonsu at Luxor.

It was a pharaoh of the eighteenth dynasty who introduced a new religion and then launched systematic attacks on the traditional religion and its priests. Egyptologists still debate the motives of Amenhotep IV, who changed his name to Akhenaton and decreed that the nation would worship one God, Aton the sun disk, whose sole earthly representative was the pharaoh himself. The powerful priesthoods of Amon were disbanded and their treasuries and temples confiscated by the crown. This was the Amarna period, when artistic styles became more naturalistic than at any other time in Egyptian history.

With all revenues funneled into the royal treasury for maintaining the pharaoh and his god and for building the new capital of Akhetaton at el-Amarna, the economic consequences were disastrous. Following the death of Akhenaton, the new city was immediately abandoned and the nation returned to its traditional religion. A strong effort to totally eradicate Akhenaton and Aton from Egyptian history had no more success than Akhenaton had in trying to wipe out the religion and clergy of Amon-Re.

When Alexander the Great conquered Egypt in 332 B.C. he put an end, finally, to several millenia of Egyptian cultural achievements—accomplishments that remain unique in the annals of humankind.

Culture and Human Values

Each major division of Egyptian history—the Three Kingdoms—can be seen as an extended period of balance. There seem to be just two periods of adjustment: before the Old Kingdom and between the Old and Middle Kingdoms. Once the nation had a central government, the society was so structured and stable that periods of chaos were not experienced, at least not until the arrival of Alexander.

Human life was apparently valued no more in Egypt than in Mesopotamia. Egyptian life was generally safer and more pleasant, but the great mass of people functioned as cogs in the splendid state machine. A rigid class structure allowed virtually no social mobility but, under the law, there was some equality of treatment despite the differences in class.

There was no Egyptian contribution to civilization comparable to Roman law, Greek philosophy, or Hebrew ethics. Nevertheless, religion did have a significant ethical component called *maat*. Perhaps the best way to translate this is to call it a synthesis of four ideas: order, truth, justice, righteousness. Not a quality of people but of the world, maat symbolized the established moral order of the universe that represented the will of the gods. Acting in accordance with that will meant that one achieved harmony with the gods. For peasants this mainly meant working hard and honestly, and for officials it meant dealing justly. A concern for maat coupled with the highest standard of living in the ancient world helped make Egyptian life cheerful and certain for all and—for the wealthy—wonderfully elegant.

Annotated Bibliography

Aldred, Cyril. *The Egyptians*. New York: Thames Hudson, 1984. An overview of cultural and political history.

Casson, Lionel. *Ancient Egypt*. Alexandria, Va.: Time-Life Books, 1965. An excellent account from the Great Ages of Man series.

Edwards, I. E. S. *The Pyramids of Egypt*. Baltimore: Penguin, 1975. The development of the pyramids with speculation on their meaning.

Frankfort, Henri. *Ancient Egyptian Religion: An Interpretation*. New York: Harper-Row, 1961. Good coverage of a complicated religion.

Hayes, William C. *The Sceptor of Egypt*, 2 volumes. New York: Metropolitan Museum of Art, 1953, 1959. A cultural history based on art in the Metropolitan Museum of Art.

Romer, John. *Ancient Lives: Daily Life in Egypt of the Pharaohs*. New York: Holt, Rinehart and Winston, 1984. Fascinating study of a New Kingdom village based on recent excavations.

Samson, Julia. *Amarna: City of Akhenaton and Nefertiti*. London: Biddles Limited, 1972. Discussion, with many illustrations, of one of the finest collections of Amarna art.

Smith, W. Stevenson. *Art and Architecture of Ancient Egypt*. Baltimore: Penguin, 1958. One of the finest general studies.

Steindorff, George, and Seele, Keith C. *When Egypt Ruled the East*. Chicago: University of Chicago Press, 1963. Admirable study of the New Kingdom.

Wilson, John A. *The Culture of Ancient Egypt*. Chicago: University of Chicago Press, 1956. Acclaimed as the one book not to miss.

Translations of Original Material

Erman, A., ed. *The Ancient Egyptians: A Sourcebook of Their Writings*. New York: Harper Torchbooks, 1966. Fine collection.

Faulkner, R. O. *The Ancient Egyptian Pyramid Texts*. Oxford: Clarendon Press, 1969. Translations with commentary.

Also see the Bibliography (Translations of Original Material) for chapter 1.

GREECE: BIRTHPLACE OF WESTERN CIVILIZATION

	People and Events	Art and Architecture	Literature	Philosophy and Science
BRONZE AGE 3000–1100 B.C.	**3000–2000** Early Helladic (mainland) culture Early Cycladic culture in Aegean **2000–1700** Mycenaeans enter Greece **2000–1100** Minoan civilization on Crete **1550–1100** Mycenaean civilization **1200** Trojan War	**3000–2000** Helladic and Cycladic figurines **1700–1380** Minoan Late Palace Period: frescoes, pottery, jewelry	**1750–1500** Minoan Linear A script **1500–1100** Minoan-Mycenaean Linear B script	
DARK AGE 1100–900 B.C.	**1100–800** Dorian invasions of mainland **1100–950** Ionian migrations to Asia Minor **900–** Dorian migrations to Aegean islands and Asia Minor		**1100–900** Loss of writing	
GEOMETRIC PERIOD 900–750 B.C.	**800** Aristocracies begin to replace kingships **776** First Olympic Games	**900–750** Furniture, textiles, glassware, figurines, but mostly pottery		
ARCHAIC PERIOD 750–480 B.C.	**750–550** Colonization by city-states **621** Draco's law code, Athens **600** Coinage introduced **594** Constitutional and economic reforms by Solon of Athens **546–527** Pisistratus third great reformer in Athens **546** Persian conquest of Greeks in Asia Minor **507** Democratic constitution of Kleisthenes **490** First Persian invasions; Battle of Marathon	**660** First life-sized statues **620–500** Attic black-figured pottery **600** Early Doric temples **580–500** *Kouros* and *Kore* figures **530–400** Attic red-figured pottery	**750–700** Homer composes *Iliad* and *Odyssey* **700** *Theogony* by Hesiod **600** Sappho: lyric poet Fables by Aesop **Herakleitos of Ephesus** 535–475 Ionian philosopher	**Thales** 636–546 Ionian philosopher **Anaximandros** 610–546 Ionian philosopher **Pythagoras** 582–507 philosopher and mathematician
CLASSICAL PERIOD 480–400 B.C.	**480–479** Second Persian invasion; Battles of Thermopylae, Salamis, and Plataea **460–430** Golden Age of Athens (Age of Perikles) **431–404** Peloponnesian War	**Pheidias** 490–430 sculptor Parthenon frieze and metopes **480–470** Severe Style of early classicism: *Kritios Boy* and *Delphi Charioteer* **Myron** 480–407 *Discobolus* **460** Bronze sculpture of *Poseidon* **447–405** Buildings on Akropolis: *Parthenon, Propylaea, Temple of Athena Nike, Erechtheion* **fl. 430** Polykleitos: sculptor and initiator of the ''canon''	**Aeschylus** 525–456 dramatist *Oresteia* **Sophokles** 496–406 dramatist *Antigone, Oedipus* **Herodotos** 484–425 ''father of history'' **Euripides** 480–406 dramatist, *Medea, Trojan Women* **471–399** Thucydides: *History of the Peloponnesian War* **Aristophanes** 448–380 dramatist (Old Comedy), *Lysistrata*	**Empedokles** 495–435 philosopher and scientist **Protagoras** 481–411 sophist **Sokrates** 469–399 philosopher and ''gadfly of Athens'' **Hippokrates** 460–377 physician **Demokritos** 460–362 atomic theory **Plato** 427–347 philosopher, writer, and teacher
LATE CLASSICAL 400–323 B.C.	**395–340** Warfare among Greek leagues **Demosthenes** 384–322 Athenian orator and statesman **338** Battle of Chaeronea; Philip of Macedon controls city-states **336–323** Reign and conquests of Alexander the Great	**350** Theatre at Epidauros by Polykleitos the Younger **fl. 340** Praxiteles of Athens: sculptor **4th c.** Lysippus: sculptor	**Xenophon** 434–355 historian and general	**399** Trial and death of Sokrates **387** Plato founds Academy near Athens **Aristotle** 384–322 philosopher and teacher, founded Lyceum in Athens in 335
HELLENISTIC AGE 323–30 B.C.	**323–30** Despotism dominant form of government **148** Macedonia becomes Roman province **146** Romans level Corinth **86** Sulla sacks Athens	**230–220** *The Dying Gaul* **190** *Nike of Samothrace* **180** Altar of Zeus at Pergamon **174** Work begun on Temple of the Olympian Zeus **120** *Aphrodite of Melos*	**Menander** 342–291 New Comedy dramatist **300** Founding of library at Alexandria **3rd c.** Eratosthenes: mathematician and astronomer	**Epicurus** 342–270 philosopher **Zeno the Stoic** 335–263 **fl. 300** Euclid: mathematician and physicist

■ **COLORPLATE 1** *Paul Gauguin,* Where Do We Come From? What Are We? Where Are We Going? *signed and dated 1897. Oil, on canvas, 54¾" × 147½". Tompkins Collection. Arthur Gordon Tompkins Fund. Courtesy, Museum of Fine Arts, Boston.*

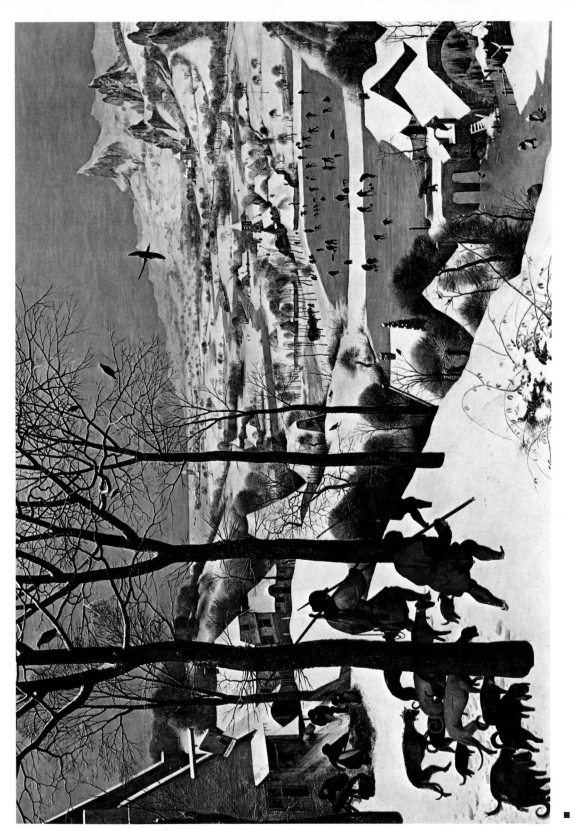

■ **COLORPLATE 2** *Pieter Bruegel the Elder,* Winter (Return of the Hunters), *1565. Oil on panel, 46" × 63¾".*
Kunsthistorisches Museum, Vienna.

■
COLORPLATE 3 *Meindert Hobbema,* The Watermill with the Great Red Roof, *ca. 1670.*
Oil on canvas, 32" × 43⅛". Collection of the Art Institute of Chicago.

■
COLORPLATE 4 *Vincent van Gogh,* The Starry Night *(1889). Oil on canvas,*
29" × 36¼". Collection, The Museum of Modern Art, New York.
Acquired through the Lillie P. Bliss Bequest.

■
COLORPLATE 5 *Wassily Kandinsky,* Painting no. 198, *1914. Oil on canvas, 64" × 36¼". Collection, The Museum of Modern Art, New York. Mrs. Simon Guggenheim Fund.*

COLORPLATE 6 *Hyacinthe Rigaud,* Portrait of Louis XIV, *1701. Oil on canvas, 9'1½" × 6'2⅜".*
The Louvre, Paris.

COLORPLATE 7 *Pablo Picasso,* Girl Before a Mirror, *1932, March 14. Oil on canvas, 64" × 51¼". Collection, The Museum of Modern Art, New York. Gift of Mrs. Simon Guggenheim.*

COLORMAP 1 *Early Mesopotamia.*

■
COLORPLATE 8 He-Goat and Flowering Tree *(offering stand), Sumerian, from Ur, ca. 2500 B.C. Wood overlaid with gold, silver, lapis lazuli, shell, and red limestone. Height 20". British Museum, London. Reproduced by courtesy of the Trustees of the British Museum.*

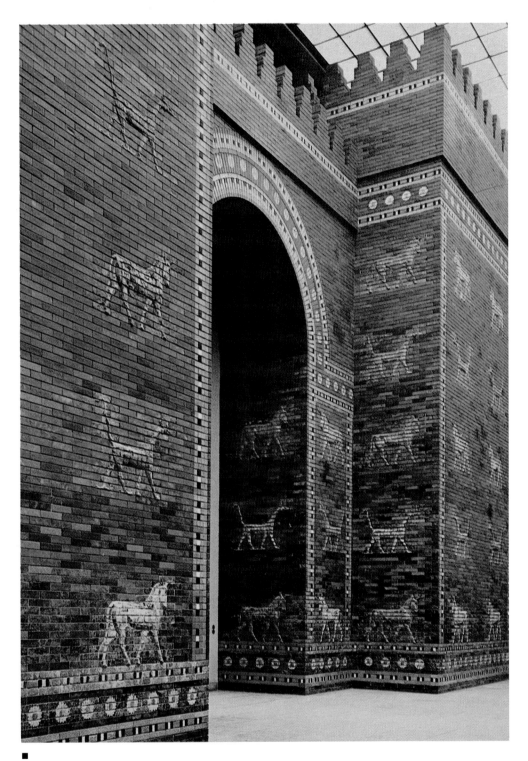

COLORPLATE 9 The Ishtar Gate *(restored), Babylon, reign of Nebuchadnezzar II (604–562 B.C.), glazed brick, height 48'. Staatliche Museum zu Berlin.*

THRACE

MACEDON

BLACK SEA

CAUCASUS MTS.

ARAL SEA

CASPIAN SEA

Oxus R.

Hellespont

Halys R.

Araxes R.

BACTRIA

Athens

AEGEAN SEA

Sparta

Sardis

LYDIA

ARMENIA

PARTHIA

IONIA

CILICIA

SYRIA

Nineveh

Ecbatana

Euphrates R.

Tigris R.

MEDIA

MEDITERRANEAN SEA

CRETE

CYPRUS

Sidon

Damascus

Tyre

Susa

Babylon

Jerusalem

PERSIA

Persepolis

Memphis

PALESTINE

EGYPT

Nile R.

ARABIA

PERSIAN GULF

INDUS R.

Thebes

RED SEA

ARABIAN SEA

The Empire

Royal Road

Scale of Miles

0   1000

COLORMAP 2 *The Persian Empire, ca. 500 B.C.*

■ COLORPLATE 10 Throne with Tutankhamon and Queen, *detail of the back, late Amarna period, New Kingdom, Eighteenth Dynasty. Wood plated with gold and silver, inlays of glass paste, ca. 12″ × 12″, Egyptian Museum, Cairo.*

■ COLORMAP 3 *Ancient Egypt.*

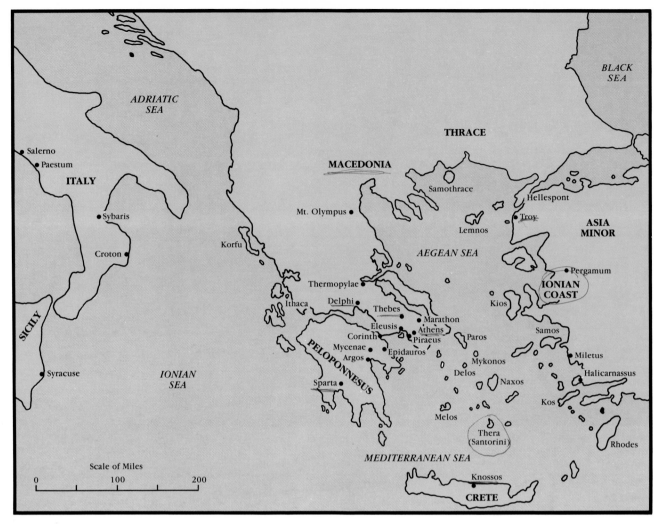

■Ancient Greece
COLORMAP 4 *Ancient Greece.*

3

The Aegean Heritage, ca. 3000–1100 B.C.

The emergence of Greek civilization divided the ancient world into East and West. In the East, in Mesopotamia and Egypt, the stamp was the same everywhere: Oriental despotism, powerful priestly organizations, a thoroughly subjugated populace; in essence there were two classes—the elite and the rest—and virtually no middle class. In the West, in the Greek world, a new civilization arose that was utterly unlike any Eastern civilization.

Historians sometimes refer to the great leap forward that launched Western culture as the "miracle of Greece." "Miracle" implies something that can't be explained, but the Greeks valued individualism, rationalism, justice, beauty, and the pursuit of excellence—and those values helped them create a remarkable civilization.

As we have seen in Egypt and Mesopotamia, climate, topography, and geography tend to shape cultures in particular ways, and Greece is no exception. Further, there is the Aegean heritage that furnished some basic ingredients. These early cultures were important in and of themselves; they also seem to have been a critical prelude to the rise of classical Greece.

Prior to Greek civilization there were three Aegean cultures: the Cycladic (KYE-kla-deek) of the Aegean Islands; the Minoan (mi-NO-un) of Crete; and the Late Helladic of the Mycenaeans (my-se-NEE-uns) on the Greek mainland. All three cultures enjoyed a climate and geography that were apparently more energizing than that of the land-locked agricultural lands of the East. Whether living on the islands or on the mainland, the Aegean peoples had some solid assets: adequate agricultural resources, a temperate maritime climate, and, most important, ready access to the sea. With about one thousand islands dotting the Aegean, sailors were never out of sight of land (a vital factor in the days of primitive navigation); even on the mainland no one was more than hours from the Aegean. Homer's "wine-dark sea" was instrumental in shaping the destinies of the Aegean cultures and, later, that of classical Greece.

The Greek lands consisted of narrow valleys guarded by steep mountains, narrow coastal plains, plus the multitude of islands studding the Aegean Sea. There was no single land mass that could be controlled as pharaoh ruled the Nile valley nor were the Aegean lands subject to the extremes of continental weather that so frequently plagued Mesopotamia. For the inhabitants of the Aegean world, the sea was a kind of golden bowl that supported and nourished the development of their civilizations. A temperate climate, security against invasion, rich fishing grounds, and multiple highways for trade and travel—the sea provided it all. The constant voyages to foreign ports exposed sailors, merchants, and tourists to a wide world of different ideas and customs—making the travelers considerably more cosmopolitan than the more provincial people in the East, most of whom never left home.

There appear to be several constants that run through all cultures: seaports are, by their nature, urban centers, cities that are more receptive to change than are rural areas; those who travel are generally more open to innovative ideas and foreign customs than those who habitually stay home, especially farmers. In many cases there seems to be a consistent equation: the farther a person is from a seacoast, the more resistant that person will be to change and new ideas. Maritime cultures are generally more vigorous and adventuresome than land-locked agricultural societies.

Throughout history, civilizations have evolved to levels that were largely determined by their developments in urban living, commerce, trade, and travel. Considering all these factors, it is hardly surprising—much less miraculous—that civilizations in the Aegean reached such high levels.

FIGURE 3.1 *Cycladic figurine, 2400–2000 B.C. Marble, height 30¼". British Museum, London. Reproduced by courtesy of the Trustees of the British Museum.*

Cycladic Civilization, ca. 3000–2000 B.C.

In the Aegean Sea north of Crete lies a group of islands called the Cyclades because they "cycle" around the hub of the sacred island of Delos, birthplace of Apollo and his twin sister Artemis. A late Neolithic culture flourished here, but little remains of it beyond some remarkable marble idols, if that is what these figures were. Strangely modern, the figurines are characterized by a rectangular angularity and an abstract simplicity. They include heads and, primarily, standing nude female figures, all carved of pristine white Parian marble. Ranging in height from several inches to one-half life size, most female figurines have been found in tombs throughout the Aegean.

The earliest Neolithic sculptures were rather standard bulbous figures with the large belly and swollen breasts of a fertility goddess. The Cycladic figures evolved, however, into slim, almost virginal figurines with subtle sexual characteristics (figure 3.1). This, like all Cycladic sculpture, can be favorably compared with the work of modern abstract sculptors. Here we have an artistic verity: all figurative art is essentially abstract, a restatement of what the artist actually saw. Moreover, because all Cycladic sculptures are similar in style, we can easily see certain artistic conventions at work. All of the sculptures

have sharply defined noses and there are traces of pigment outlining the eyes and mouths. The female figurines are all delicately made with the arms folded across the midriff. Since there is still no trace of Cycladic writing, there is no way to determine what the conventions may mean. Certainly the figures are abstracted versions of the artist's perception; they are not portraits, but images of women, which may indicate their possible function as idols that had something to do with death or maybe even an afterlife.

Because the Cycladic figures as well as the entire Minoan and Mycenaean civilizations were all discovered during the past century or so, we still have no way of knowing the full extent of their influence on ancient Greek culture. We can only suggest that because of their proximity, the intensely curious Greeks knew more about the three early Aegean civilizations than is indicated by current evidence.

Minoan Civilization, ca. 2600–1100 B.C.

The first people who dwelt in Greek lands about whom we have much information were the Minoans, named after the fabled King Minos (MY-nus) who lived on the island of Crete. These were probably not "Greek" people in that their language, as far as one can tell, does not seem to be related to the Indo-European family. (Of this language, we have only clay tablets in the "Linear A" script, which has not yet been deciphered.) Minoan culture existed from about 2600 to around 1100 B.C., and reached its peak around the year 2000 with the building of the splendid palaces at Knossos (KNAWS-us), Phaistos (FEST-os), Mallia (MAH-ya), and Zakro (ZAW-kro).

Despite the continuing mystery of Linear A we know a great deal about this culture because of the excavations by Sir Arthur Evans and others. (There are active excavations at all four palaces plus a number of other interesting sites in Crete.) From Evans's excavations and reconstructions at Knossos, we see that this rich and sophisticated culture prospered because of a combination of factors in addition to a semi-tropical maritime climate and productive agricultural areas. The Minoans had no traditional enemies nor were they concerned about invading barbarians; their unfortified shores were guarded by the greatest seapower of the age. Their ships carried agricultural and manufactured products all over the eastern Mediterranean and returned to Crete bringing products from many cultures. The Minoans were, in short, the greatest traders in the Mediterranean Sea prior to the Greeks and Phoenicians.

Religion

Minoan religion seems to have been a fertility cult connected with the worship of an earth goddess. This, in turn, led to a matriarchal form of government, with the essential power lying with the queen as the earthly representative, indeed the incarnation of the earth mother. A part of this worship was a tradition that the king marry the queen for a specified time—a year, four years, or more years—after which he was killed and the queen took another husband. This custom related to the concept that the earth (the queen) must be refertilized to maintain the prosperity of the Minoan city-states.

FIGURE 3.2 *Custom House, Palace of Minos, Knossos, 1650–1450* B.C.

A noted architectural historian[1] is convinced that the consistency of palace orientations and settings confirms the matriarchal nature of Minoan society. All major palaces are set in enclosed valleys with the north-south axis pointing towards a nearby conical or mounded hill and a more distant notched cleft (saddleback) or a set of double peaks. The paired mountains can be seen as breasts and the saddleback as the female cleft. This orientation is particularly noticeable at Knossos and Mallia.

Palaces

Remarkably different from other civilizations, the Minoans built no showplace palaces for divine monarchs, no temples (as far as we now know), and no fortifications because, as noted above, there was no need for land defenses. Minoan palaces were designed for comfort and pleasure. They had hundreds of small rooms, rambling corridors and staircases, walls gaily decorated with colorful murals, running water, bathtubs, flush toilets, a sewage system, terraces, open galleries, and numerous light wells to convey natural illumination to lower levels of the three- to five-story structures. The palaces also functioned as administrative centers for the far-flung trade empire, which provides a clue to the business orientation of the Minoans.

Probably the most important of the palaces on Crete (considered the first among equals) was that of King Minos at Knossos (figure 3.2), the vastness of which can only be hinted at in the partial reconstruction by Sir Arthur Evans. The building illustrated stands at the northern end of the palace and was labeled a Customs House by Evans because it was apparently the main checkpoint for visitors arriving by sea several kilometers to the north. The flaring columns are of wood and apparently were symbols of tree trunks. The multiple levels, wandering corridors, and countless rooms (figure 3.3) probably inspired the Greek legend of the labyrinth of Minos that was guarded by a fearful Minotaur (half man, half bull).

FIGURE 3.3 *Floor plan of the Palace at Knossos (after Reynold Higgins).*

---

1. Scully, Vincent. *The Earth, the Temple, and the Gods.* New Haven, Conn.: Yale University Press, 1979.

FIGURE 3.4 *Throne Room, Palace of Minos, Knossos.*

FIGURE 3.5 *Queen's Megaron, Palace of Minos, Knossos.*

FIGURE 3.6 *Snake Goddess, ca. 1600 B.C., faience, height 17½". Archaelogical Museum, Heraklion, Crete.*

After his wife gave birth to the monster, Minos had it imprisoned in the basement of the palace. The earth-shaking roars attributed to the awesome beast can undoubtedly be linked to the earthquakes that periodically wracked Crete.

Totally unlike that of an Egyptian king's, for instance, the Throne Room (figure 3.4) is a small chamber at ground level containing a simple, high-backed alabaster throne with stone benches around three walls, including the wall with the throne. The fanciful griffin mural (white on red) is a modern reconstruction based on fragments found in the ruins. Opposite the throne is a colonnade separating the throne room from an open atrium, which adds air and light to an intimate and unpretentious setting.

Legendary friends to all sailors, five dolphins frolic contentedly in a seascape mural in the Queen's Megaron (figure 3.5). The queen's apartment, which is illuminated by a light well, also features ornamental floral designs on the door frames and an adjoining bathroom complete with bathtub. Even now there is an air of understated elegance, an ambience of good taste.

Minoan Art

Whether she was a priestess, goddess, or queen, the so-called *Snake Goddess* (figure 3.6) is typical of diminutive Minoan sculpture. A culture with neither divine monarch nor priesthood has no compelling need for monumental sculpture, and indeed none has been found. Though the rigid frontal pose of this small figure indicates an Egyptian influence, the raised arms plus the small animal on her head (panther?) lighten the mood to one akin to playfulness. Characteristic of feminine attire at the time, the colorful tiered skirt, tight bodice, and bared breasts are very stylish for a cult figure. Whatever her position or function was, she is a delightful work of art.

Sometime after 1450 B.C. Crete was conquered by the Mycenaeans, a rugged warrior race from the mainland. The conquest was not difficult because Minoan culture had apparently been already devastated by a volcano on an Aegean island to the north. A persistent legend and mounting archeological evidence, particularly at Akrotiri on the island of Thera (named Santorini until 1945), suggest that the decline of Crete resulted from a cataclysmic eruption of the volcano on Thera in about 1450 B.C. After the volcano's final mighty convulsion, it collapsed into the sea and caused tidal waves possibly four- or five-hundred feet in height to spread throughout the Aegean, fatally damaging, among other things, the entire Minoan culture. The ongoing excavations at Akrotiri (the Minoan Pompeii, discovered in 1967) indicate that this was a wealthy Minoan city with a standard of living just as high as that enjoyed at Knossos. The fresco of the *Antelopes* (figure 3.7) is comparable in style and quality to frescoes found at Knossos. The broad sinuous ribbons that outline the bodies give the illusion of being enameled areas in an elegant cloisonné. The contrast of rhythmic curves with open interior space sets up a masterful mobile tension that is both fluid and artful.

FIGURE 3.7 Antelopes, *from Thera, ca. 1500* B.C. *Fresco, height 98½". National Archaelogical Museum, Athens.*

The excavations on Thera also tend to support the theory that this island was the legendary Atlantis; most of the island did indeed sink into the sea, carrying with it an advanced civilization. Also, there are partially substantiated theories that the Thera catastrophe caused gases and dust clouds to reach Egypt, resulting in the plagues described in the Bible. The parting of the Red Sea (actually Reed Sea) has been explained by the tidal waves generated by the eruption. Whatever the cause, the power of Crete was broken and the Mycenaean Greeks became the overlords of the Aegean world.

Mycenaean Civilization, ca. 1600–1110 B.C.

From about 1900 B.C. tribes from northern Europe had been slowly infiltrating Greece. By about 1600, the invaders had occupied all of the Greek mainland, including the Pelopennesus where, at Mycenae, their Great King established his fortified palace. These were warlike people who, inevitably, came into contact and conflict with the Minoans. Their conquest of Crete put an end to the Minoan script that we know as Linear A, replacing it with Linear B. The deciphering of clay tablets in the

Linear B script in 1953 showed that the Mycenaeans were true Greeks who not only spoke a Greek language, but also worshipped the Greek pantheon of sky gods. They created the heritage that united the Hellenes (as the Greeks called themselves) for the Mycenaeans fought the Trojan War that centuries later was to become the subject of the Homeric poems and the core of the Hellenic tradition.

Homeric Poems

Until little more than a century ago, all anyone knew of the Aegean world was contained in some Greek myths about Crete and in Homer's supposedly fictional *Iliad* and *Odyssey.* Helen of Troy, Akhilleus, Hektor, and Agamemnon were, according to the experts, figments of Homer's fertile imagination, and Troy and Mycenae were apparently equally fictitious. Heinrich Schliemann, a wealthy German merchant-cum-archeologist, startled the world when, in 1871, he announced the discovery of Troy in northwest Turkey, just where his careful study of the *Iliad* indicated it should be. A few years later he located the palace of Agamemnon at Mycenae and uncovered a wealth of art treasures in and near Mycenae.

The Mycenaeans established themselves in small in-dependent kingdoms and their kings lived in strongly fortified but richly decorated palaces. Each king was independent, administering his rule through a group of officials who supervised the farmlands, collected taxes in produce, managed religious celebrations, and otherwise handled all of the delegated affairs of government. Although each king was independent, each owed some allegiance to the high king at Mycenae. As seen in the *Iliad,* a local ruler could disobey the high king—as Akhilleus (ah-KILL-eoos) did with Agamemnon (ag-a-MEM-non)—and not be disciplined or forced to follow the ruler. Each king had a force of well-armed troops; the nobles rode chariots into battle but most of the fighting was done on foot, again as described in the *Iliad.*

These people carried on extensive trade, mostly among the islands and Asia Minor, although their influence extended throughout the Mediterranean world. Gold, ivory, textiles, and spices were bartered for the local products, and the number of gold ornaments and cups found in the royal tombs at Mycenae and at other great palaces attests to the rather barbaric wealth of these kings. In general their prosperity seems to have depended upon trade, commerce, and barter, which is to be remembered as we see this civilization decline in later years.

This was a society in which the masculine virtues were honored, as evidenced in the Homeric poems. Although Homer wrote his epic poems around 750–700 B.C., his poetry seems to reflect with considerable accuracy the knowledge we can piece together about the Mycenaeans.

The chief virtues of the early Greeks were physical courage and the preservation of individual honor. These qualities are shown time and time again in the *Iliad,* as when Diomedes (di-uh-MEED-eez) broke from the ranks of his troops and ranged through the Trojan forces risking everything in individual combat. Or by Akhilleus, who by twentieth-century standards appears to be a pouting boy when Agamemnon takes his girl, Briseis (bri-SEE-us), from him, but was in reality the Greek hero whose personal honor had been affronted. He refused to fight, not from cowardice or pique, but simply because Agamemnon had insulted his pride and belittled him in front of the entire Argive army (the Greeks, led by the king from Argos). The hero must retaliate, and he did so by refusing to fight until he was moved, not by loyalty to his cause or to his king, but by the grief he felt at the loss of his friend Patroklos (Pa-TRO-kloss). The greatest example of all is the death of Hektor in Book XXII of the *Iliad.* Here was a man, the greatest and strongest of the Trojan warriors, who could easily have shirked this last individual battle. His aged father pled with him to stay within the city walls; earlier, in a touching scene with his wife and his little child he admitted he knew that he and his city were doomed. Yet, when the time came, he had to assert himself in a glorious action that would test all of his powers to the utmost, fulfill all of his capacities, and finally bring him immortality, not in heaven, but in the minds of men. For these Greeks, human worth and

dignity lay in total self-fulfillment, usually on the battlefield where their exploits would bring death, perhaps, but certainly fame among their fellows and among people to come after them as their deeds were recounted in song and story.

Another aspect of the Greek character, much admired throughout their history, was the use of a wily and tricky intelligence. For this quality, Odysseus (o-DIS-yews) stands as the supreme example. Thus, when Odysseus finally won his way home to his kingdom of Ithaka he was put ashore disguised as a beggar. Here Athena (uh-THEE-nuh) met him and heard his lying tale. Her response was typical of the Greek attitude:

> ''What a cunning knave it would take,'' she said, ''to beat you at your tricks! Even a god would be hard put to it.''
>
> ''And so my stubborn friend, Odysseus the archdeceiver, with his craving for intrigue, does not propose even in his own country to drop his sharp practice and the lying tales that he loves from the bottom of his heart. But no more of this: we are both adepts at chicane. For in the world of men you have no rival as a statesman and orator, while I am preeminent among the gods for invention and resource.''

And a few lines later:

> ''How like you to be so wary!'' said Athena. ''And this is why I cannot desert you in your misfortunes: you are so civilized, so intelligent, so self-possessed.''

Perhaps in our time we cannot so admire the man who was so smoothly deceitful to gain his own ends; even in classic Greece Sophokles (SOF-o-kleez) despised these qualities, as he pictured a rather despicable Odysseus in the drama *Philoktetes* (fil-OK-ti-teez). But for the Greek of heroic age, this was simply another example of the idea of self-fulfillment. Odysseus had been given the quality and the capacity for sharp intelligence, and it was his purpose, a purpose of all people, to utilize all of his capacities to their utmost. He would be a fool, shirking his own fate, not to use this ability. (A selection from the *Odyssey* appears at the end of chapter 4.)

The armies of Odysseus, Akhilleus, and other kings had assembled at the palace of Agamemnon at Mycenae and then marched north to their waiting ships in the Gulf of Patrai. Everyone knew that some would never see Mycenae again; no one would have believed that it would take ten years to conquer Troy or that so many valiant warriors would fall in a foreign land.

The King's Citadel

The citadel of the Great King at Mycenae, which is today in ruins, is a massive structure whose gigantic stones were placed, according to legend, by the Cyclopes (ky-KLO-peas), a mythical race of one-eyed giants. Located on a broad hilltop site backed by a rugged mountain, what remains of the palace is immediately below the mountain peak. Continuous waves of Proto-Greeks, the invading Dorians, made fortress architecture a necessity on the Greek mainland.

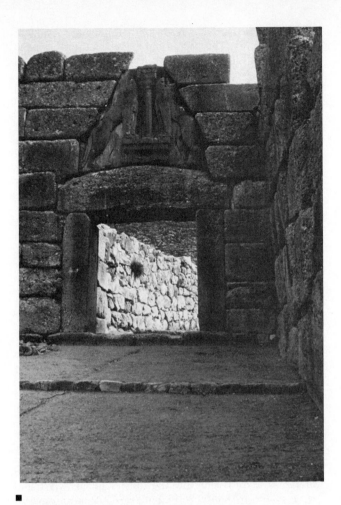

FIGURE 3.8 *Lion Gate, citadel at Mycenae, ca. 1250 B.C. Limestone, height of relief 9'6".*

This highly efficient citadel has a single entrance protected by high walls on three sides (figure 3.8). The lintel of the ponderous gate is topped by a stone relief of two lions, now headless, flanking a Minoan column symbolizing Mycenaean hegemony in Crete.

After astounding archeologists with his discovery of Mycenaean civilization, Schliemann excavated the royal tombs at Mycenae. They were full of precious jewelry, elaborately decorated weapons, and gold death masks, one of which Schliemann attributed to Agamemnon himself (figure 3.9). It was soon determined, however, that this Mycenae predated the Homeric king; the remains of "Agamemnon" were of some personage from an earlier period. The undaunted German, realizing that argument was futile and acknowledging the lack of positive identification, jokingly renamed his Agamemnon "Schulze." Regardless of the appropriate name, the Mask from Mycenae is a superb example of the highly developed metal craftsmanship called toreutics (tuh-RUE-tiks), the hammering of metals into representational form. The death mask (plus weapons and jewelry) represents a Mycenaean adaptation of the Egyptian funeral practice of burying the illustrious dead with items that were commensurate with their status in life.

FIGURE 3.9 *Mask from Mycenae, ca. 1500 B.C. Funeral mask from the royal tombs. Beaten gold, ca. 12" high. National Archeological Museums, Athens.*

During the period of about 1200 to around 1100 B.C. the Dorians became ever more numerous. Eventually they overwhelmed the Mycenaean fortresses, bringing the civilization to an end. They had completed their turn on the stage of history but were later immortalized in the Homeric sagas of the *Iliad* and the *Odyssey,* perhaps the two greatest epic poems in Western history.

Exercises

1. a. Consider the cultures that developed in ancient Mesopotamia, Egypt, and the Greek lands in the Aegean area. (1) In what ways did climate, topography, and geography affect or condition cultural development in each major area? (2) How and why did agricultural (rural) areas react differently from urban areas? (3) How and why did seaports differ from inland cities? (4) What conclusions can you draw about the three areas?
    b. Consider the cultures that developed in New England and in the Deep South during the eighteenth and nineteenth centuries. Then, answer questions (1)–(4) as posed above. What are the similarities between American cultural development and that in the ancient world? Are there any differences? Why or why not?

2. Consult three or four art history texts for additional illustrations of Cycladic art. Are all of the sculptures absolutely identical in style? What are the differences, if any?

3. Consider the peaceful Minoan trade empire as compared with a trade network based on conquest. Which territory will be more productive for all concerned? Why? Consider psychological factors, motivation, efficiency of production, transportation, and merchandising.

4. Assume that our world has miraculously grown so peaceful that no nation need maintain any armed forces. What might the total Pentagon budget be spent on and how might this affect American society? Be sure to also consider the short- and long-term effects of the elimination of defense contracts.

5. As a general in Agamemnon's army, Akhilleus was highly visible. Imagine that you are a soldier in the rear ranks of the same army. How might your attitude about heroic ideals differ from that of Akhilleus? Why or why not? What if you were also a general?

6. Has there ever been a book in this country with the status of Homer's epics in ancient Greece? Why or why not?

Summary

The rise of Greek Civilization divided the known world into East and West. The East was consistently despotic while Greece led the West to the world's first democracy.

The Greeks absorbed much of the cultural heritage of Mesopotamia and Egypt while also drawing upon the indigenous culture of the Aegean civilizations: the Cycladic, Minoan, and Mycenaean. Except for their abstract sculptures, little is known about the Cycladic civilization. The Minoans, however, have been extensively documented as a prosperous and peaceful people who operated the greatest trade empire of the age. Elegant and refined, their culture was more European than Oriental and formed a firm basis for the flowering of Western culture.

The Mycenaeans, conquerors of the Minoans, were a warrior race descended from migrating Dorian tribes that infiltrated from the north. The apex of their civilization was reached with the Trojan expedition of about 1200 B.C. Further Dorian invasions brought down the Great King and his subordinate rulers, leaving for posterity the remains of their culture and, most especially, their Heroic Age as immortalized by Homer.

Culture and Human Values

Not enough is known of Cycladic culture to justify any speculation about cultural evolution, nor do we know what their view of reality was or what they particularly valued in life. Such knowledge may still come to light.

The Minoans have been studied in great detail for nearly a century. The period of balance of their high civilization lasted, it would appear, from about 2000 through about 1450 B.C., when a volcanic eruption effectively destroyed the civilization. From then on there was a period of adjustment as the Minoans tried to adapt to the rule of the invading Mycenaeans.

The overriding reality of Minoan culture was that a good life of security, peace, and possessions was available to much of the population. The Minoan economy supported a high standard of living, partly because funds did not have to be diverted to support a standing army or a priestly hierarchy. A stable empire was built based not on military conquest but on peaceful commerce and trade. Vigorous trade also helped in the development of a middle class of artisans and merchants, thus reinforcing political and economic stability.

Not enough can be said about the higher quality of life in a society that did not consider warfare a necessary instrument of national policy. The history of the Assyrian Empire, in comparison, presents a picture of unrelieved pillage, brutality, and death, the usual fate of conquered nations under the heel of a military state.

It appears that the period of balance of Mycenaean civilization began shortly after their conquest of Crete in about 1450 B.C., and concluded sometime after the taking of Troy in about 1200 B.C. The fall of Troy marked the high point of Mycenaean civilization and, ironically, the beginning of its decline and fall. Integrity and honor had been compromised in the quest for victory over the Trojans. The price was too high. (See *The Trojan Women* by Euripides in chapter 5 to better comprehend the price of victory.)

For the inhabitants of the Mycenaean city-states ultimate reality was the heroic life—and death—of the noble warrior. An ethical man told the truth, kept his word, and kept the faith with king and comrades. First and foremost, he was prepared at all times to make the ultimate sacrifice, to die fighting for a noble cause, as did Akhilleus, Hektor, and many another warrior.

There are at least three ways to view the Heroic Age: the actual time period; the Homeric view; the view from the Golden Age of Athens. For most of the men and women and children of Mycenae, it would seem that the heroic ideal was something espoused by a noble warrior who was also an aristocrat. What about the common soldiers? An incredible number of nameless victims fell to the swords of Agamemnon, Odysseus, and the like. In a later age these anonymous soldiers who were sacrificed to the ambitions of a conquering hero would be called "cannon fodder." Akhilleus (with all his faults) was unquestionably the personification of the heroic ideal, but what of the victims of all wars whether victors or vanquished? Euripides makes a clear judgement about those who "win" and "lose" wars (see *The Trojan Women* in chapter 5).

Homer composed the *Iliad* between 750 and 700 B.C., nearly four centuries after the Trojan campaign. As with many long-ago events, time heals, and violence is often romanticized as necessary in the service of a noble cause. (American Civil War buffs, for example, seem to revel in romantic fantasies about Antietam, Shiloh, or other bloody battlegrounds.) The pain and horror of the Trojan War had faded away; only the heroic ideals were left and no one could extol the fighting virtues better than the blind poet.

By the time of the Athenian Golden Age—centering around 450 B.C.—another four centuries had passed and the Trojan adventure was twice removed. Homer and the *Iliad* had become romanticized. Small wonder that nineteenth-century scholars considered the Trojan campaign the stuff of dreams. The Athenians accorded the Mycenaean heroes their just dues without, however, endorsing war (Ares, the god of war, was never treated as anything other than an in-human outcast). Odysseus and his comrades were, in other words, great figures of the Hellenic past; they had earned admiration but no one expected emulation.

Annotated Bibliography

Alsop, Joseph. *From the Silent Earth: A Report on the Greek Bronze Age.* New York: Greenwood, 1964. A popular account of the Minoan and Mycenaean archeological finds.

Getz-Preziosi, Pat. *Sculptors of the Cyclades: Individual and Tradition in the Third Millenium* B.C. Ann Arbor: University of Michigan Press, 1985. A basic introduction carefully noting individual artistic features in a highly stylized tradition of primitive art.

Higgins, Reynold. *Minoan and Mycenaean Art.* World of Arts series. New York: Oxford University Press, 1981. A finely illustrated survey.

Hood, Sinclair. *The Arts in Prehistoric Greece.* Pelican History of Art series. New York: Penguin Books, 1979. By a noted authority.

Nilsson, Martin P. *The Mycenaean Origins of Greek Mythology.* Berkeley: University of California Press, 1983. As the title says.

Palmer, Leonard R. *Mycenaeans and Minoans: Aegean Prehistory in the Light of the Linear B Tablets.* New York: Greenwood, 1980. Interpretations of their probable relationships.

Renault, Mary. *The Bull from the Sea.* New York: Random House, 1962. Fine historical fiction that brings ancient Crete to life.

———. *The King Must Die.* New York: Bantam Books, 1964.

Verneule, Emily. *Greece in the Bronze Age.* Chicago: University of Chicago Press, 1964. Still one of the finest works on the subject.

4

Early Greece: Preparation for the Good Life

As nearly everyone knows, it was in Greece, particularly in Athens for a short time in the fifth century (ca. 500–400 B.C.), that human life developed a quality that has seldom if ever been equaled. Here for the first time—and most gloriously—personal freedom was achieved for a large percentage of the population, with a sense of justice embodied in laws and a political system that gave individuals the greatest possible freedom compatible with the coherence of the social group. Here, too, there was a sufficient amount of wealth and leisure to allow individuals to develop their capabilities to the fullest. A sufficient challenge in the differences between the various city-states and between the individuals within them kept many persons keenly alive in the development of their full selves.

It would be convenient for the reader, and certainly for the authors, if the development to the apex of culture had proceeded in some sort of regular progression from the beginning of our knowledge about the Greeks until its culmination during the reign of Perikles[1] (PAIR-i-kleez) in Athens or if all of the statesmen who brought change to the Greek social structure had been high-minded men with a clear vision of the ultimate goal of human values. Unfortunately this is not the case. Greek history—even Greek geography—represents the ultimate in confusion, and even the statesmen who made the greatest contributions in the development of the social structure were often self-seeking politicians, not above taking bribes or committing treason to accomplish their purposes. Out of all of this confusing history the evolution of a society devoted, even for a brief time, to human values becomes a tribute to the toughness of the human spirit.

This chapter traces the development of Greek society from its early beginnings to the fifth century (499–400 B.C.). Inevitably the focus will be on Athens, where the highest developments took place and where ideas that were generated throughout Greece came into the marketplace to be vigorously discussed and just as vigorously disputed. This was a lively, highly verbal, even a brawling culture in which the seeds—and some of the finest flowers—of all Western art and philosophy revealed themselves.

In the first place, let it be made clear that there never was a nation called Greece. Instead, we find a group of people who called themselves Hellenes (HEL-e-neez), united by a common language, with several dialects; by a common though diversified religion; and a common heritage. Politically these people lived in independent city-states, each with its own form of government. Frequently there were alliances between these small states, and in the fifth century Athens put together a very loose Athenian Empire, opposing a strong coalition of city-states whose allegiance was to Sparta. Greece was not even confined to a single geographical location. The map shows that the mainland of Greece is the tip of the Balkan Peninsula, joined by a narrow isthmus to a fairly large land mass known as the Peloponnesus (pel-uh-puh-NEES-us). This is the heartland. But Greece was invaded from the north by Dorian tribes from about 1100–800 B.C. during which time many Ionians of the mainland fled to the Asiatic coast of the Aegean Sea and the islands off the Asian coast to form a flourishing Greek cultural center. This was the Ionian Coast that eventually caused so much trouble for the Persian Empire. Later, in the seventh and sixth centuries (699–500 B.C.), land poverty on the mainland encouraged many of the city-states to send out colonies to occupy new land. As a result, a great number of Greek cities were formed all the way from Byzantium (bi-ZANT-e-um), now Istanbul, along both shores of the Mediterranean Sea, in Sicily, and in Italy. For example, Syracuse in Sicily, and Sybaris and Paestum in Italy were important Greek cities. Although these cities were widely dispersed and frequently at war with each other, their common culture, heritage, religion, and language gave

---

1. Greek spelling is used throughout, removing what Robert Fitzgerald, translator of Homer, has called a "Roman screen." Some Latinized spellings have been retained (Helen, Priam, Troy, Crete); other inconsistencies are, we trust, equally deliberate. Rather than include Greek accent marks we have provided phonetic pronunciations, e.g., Hêphaistos = Hephaistos (Hay-FYCE-toss). As Fitzgerald suggests, "Pronounce it slowly and boldly, and savor every syllable."

them a sense of kinship as Hellenes, while all other people were regarded as barbarians or strangers. The Hellenes felt that they were different from and better than the "barbarians" (which means non-Greek), a sense that created unity amid the vast diversity and a pride that led to the remarkable accomplishments of the people we know as the Greeks.

The Geography of Mainland Greece

The Aegean Islands had a relatively benign climate but the mainland was a harder country in which to live, a challenging countryside that seems to have added something critical to the Greek character. Ranges of mountains divided the area so that communication across the countryside was extremely difficult. Furthermore, the mountains were so eroded that little farmland was available. Only in the north were there any broad and fertile plains. For the remainder, sheep and goats grazed on the mountain slopes and bee-culture was common. The valleys between the mountains offered small plots of arable land on which olives and grapes were the chief crops. It was in these valleys that the first villages appeared that would later unite to become city-states.

Nor was the climate conducive to easy living. In the winter great storms blew down from the north bringing torrential rains and, on the mountain peaks, a good deal of snow. The summers were extremely hot and dry.

As with the islands, the sea was basic to Greek life. Major cities (Athens, Argos, Corinth) were located adjacent to the sea and no city, not even Sparta, was far from the sea.

All of these factors contributed to the Greek character. In a hard land, people must be ingenious and clever to survive. In a land where nature yields little, people must turn to manufacturing objects in order to make a living. As compared to other early civilizations, the Greek population contained many more artisans and artists than peasants. Finally, the proximity of the sea always offered the possibility of trade and commerce (and piracy) as a source of livelihood. Such commerce always broadens horizons; in addition to the bartering of goods, the traders barter ideas and bring them home. It is never possible to attribute the character of a people to geography and climate alone, yet the factors mentioned here must have done much to shape the personality of the Hellenes.

Greek Religion in the Heroic Age

The worship of the Olympian gods forms one of the most complex and fascinating of all religions. At its most straightforward, the religion explains various natural forces in terms of mythical gods and goddesses (e.g., Poseidon, who controls the storms that stir the seas and the quakes that shake the land). At a higher level, the Olympians symbolized the most complex of human drives and aspirations (e.g., Athena, who represents all that is vital in living one's life as an art form).

Their religion illustrates one of the prime characteristics of the Greeks: their special ability to deal with information on both a literal and an abstract level. It is probable, for example, that Pythagoras discovered his theorem[2] empirically. He went beyond empirical data, however, to the world of ideas, soaring to heights that Plato was later to explore more fully.

This religion had no "revealer," divine or mortal; no Christ, no Mohammed, no Buddha. Nor did it have any sacred book such as the Talmud, Bible, or Koran. The religion grew primarily as a collection of myths that were honored in various ways throughout the Greek world. The myths were consistently imaginative and varied greatly, so that no single version of the history and nature of the gods exists. Hesiod (HEE-see-ud) in his *Theogony* (thee-OG-uh-nee), and other writers as well, attempted to systematize the story of the gods, but only with limited success. The truth of the matter is that Greek religion—all Greek mythology, in fact—was probably the most creative collection of mythic literature that the world has ever known.

Vastly simplified, the geneology of the gods can be presented in the following way:

In the beginning was Chaos, composed of void, mass, and darkness. From Chaos emerged a male god, Ouranos (YOOR-uh-noss), who represented the heavens, and a female god, Gaea (JEE-ah), who represented earth. These gods had three types of offspring, one of which was the Titans, who represented earthquakes and other cataclysms of the earth. Kronos (KRO-nos), one of the Titans, led a revolt against his father and overthrew him. (It is interesting that from the drops of blood of Ouranos sprang the fearful hags known as the Furies, whose duty it was to pursue anyone who had shed the blood of his kindred; this type of belief was important because it helped hold the clans together.) Kronos took his sister Rhea (REE-uh), another representation of the earth goddess, as his wife, and from this union, although not without some difficulty, came the Olympian gods. The difficulty alluded to was the fact that Kronos had a prophecy that one of his children would overthrow him; to prevent this, he swallowed all his children at birth (Kronos, of course, may be thought of as Time, which swallows all things). By a trick, Rhea saved Zeus from being swallowed and spirited him away to Crete where he grew to manhood. Then Zeus led the prophesied revolt and, aided by some of the Titans, managed to imprison his father in the dark cave of Tartarus, but not before Kronos had regurgitated the other children, Demeter (di-MEET-er), Hera (HAY-ra), Hades (also called Pluto), Poseidon (po-SIDE-on), and Hestia. Zeus then took Hera as his wife and from this union came such gods and goddesses as Apollo, Aphrodite, Artemis, and others. (See box 4.1.)

---

2. In right-angle triangles, the square of the hypotenuse equals the sum of the squares of the other two sides. Also see p. 64.

Box 4.1 *The Greek Pantheon*

Zeus and his two brothers seized power from Kronos (Saturn) to originate "The Twelve," the Olympians who figure most prominently in Greek life. (The names in parentheses are Roman but these represent only approximations since Greeks and Romans had entirely different attitudes towards their respective gods, and towards most everything else for that matter.)

Zeus (Jupiter, Jove). Leader, god of the thunderbolt, representative of the power principle and chaser of women.

Hera (Juno). Long-suffering wife of Zeus, goddess of marriage and domestic stability.

Poseidon (Neptune). God of the sea and earthshaker (earthquakes).

Demeter (Ceres). Sister of Zeus and goddess of agriculture. Mother of *Persephone* and symbol of fertility.

Hades (Pluto, Dis). God of the underworld. Connected with nature myth by his marriage to Persephone who spends half her time on earth (the growing season) and half in the underworld (fall and winter). *Thanatos* represents death itself.

Pallas Athena (Minerva). Goddess of wisdom, warfare, arts and crafts. Sprang full-armed from the brow of Zeus. Patron goddess of Athens, representing the art of civilized living.

Phoibos Apollo (Sol). Son of Zeus and *Leto*, daughter of the Titans Krios and Phoebe. Sun god, archer, musician, god of truth, light, and healing. Represents principle of intellectual beauty.

Artemis (Diana, Cynthia). Sister of Apollo; virgin goddess of the moon and the hunt.

Aphrodite (Venus). Goddess of love and physical beauty. According to one version she was the daughter of Zeus and Dione; an alternate mythic version has her rising from the waves a la Botticelli.

Hephaistos (Vulcan). Lame blacksmith god who made armor for heroes, forged the thunderbolts of Zeus. Much-deceived husband of Aphrodite.

Hermes (Mercury). Son of Zeus and Maia, daughter of Atlas. Messenger and general handyman of Zeus. God of commerce, traders, travelers, and thieves.

Ares (Mars). Son of Zeus and Hera. God of war.

Hestia (Vesta). Virgin sister of Zeus and goddess of hearth and home. Later replaced among the Twelve by Dionysos.

Dionysos (Bacchus). Son of Zeus and mortal woman Semele. Like Demeter, connected with the principle of fertility and, like Persephone, represented the nature myth by dying in the autumn and being reborn in the spring. The Eleusinian Mysteries were dedicated to all three fertility deities and the festivals of Dionysos were periods of wild, Bacchic rejoicing, scheduled orgies so to speak. Since plays were usually performed at these festivals Dionysos also became god of the theatre. He represents the ecstatic principle as contrasted with the intellectual principle represented by Apollo.

LESSER OLYMPIANS

Eros (Cupid). Eternal child of Aphrodite and Hephaistos. Spirit of love with darts.

Pan (Pan). Son of Hermes, woodland god with goatlike horns and hoofs. Player of the pipes (panpipes).

Nemesis. Avenging goddess, the principle of retribution.

Hebe. Goddess of youth and cupbearer to the gods.

Iris. Goddess of the rainbow and sometimes messenger of the gods.

Hymen. Son of Aphrodite and Dionysos; god of the marriage festival.

The Three Graces: Aglaia (Splendor), *Euphrosyne* (Mirth), and *Thalia* (Good Cheer). Represented the principle of the happy life and always represented as a unit, which is a clear indication of the Greek version of the happy life.

The Nine Muses. Spirits of learning and of the arts. *Clio* (History), *Ourania* (Astronomy), *Melpomene* (Tragedy), *Thalia* (Comedy), *Terpsichore* (Dance), *Calliope* (Epic Poetry), *Erato* (Love Poetry), *Polyhymnia* (Sacred Poetry), and *Euterpe* (Lyric Poetry).

The Erinyes (Furies). *Tisiphone, Megaera,* and *Alecto.* Represented pangs of conscience; relentlessly hounded wrongdoers.

The Three Fates allotted to each man his destiny. *Clotho* spun the thread of life. *Lachesis* wove it into a pattern that determined the kind of life that would be led. *Atropos* cut the thread, terminating existence.

The stories of the actions of the gods offer a fascinating range of subjects; we see Zeus almost constantly pursuing (and seducing) an infinite variety of mortal girls; all of the gods quarreled constantly among themselves; all had favorites among the mortals, as we saw Athena protecting Odysseus; and all used all sorts of trickery to foil each other's designs for the success of their favorite mortals. How could such a group possibly be revered and worshipped?

If we can understand this worship, even faintly, then we may come to know something of the Greek character, and particularly some of their love for the very process of living, and living life to the fullest.

The Greeks created the gods in their own image. Emphasizing this, Xenophanes of Colophon (zuh-NOFF-uh-neas; 6th century B.C.) went on to state that if oxen, horses, and lions had hands and could paint like men, they would paint their gods as, respectively, oxen, horses, and lions. Black people would worship black gods and Thracians would believe in gods with blue eyes and red hair.

The gods were regarded as a race infinitely superior to human beings in that they were completely powerful, immortal, and always young and beautiful; they had the same characteristics as humans, but in a higher category. If people sometimes showed wisdom and nobility, so did Athena or Apollo (uh-POL-o), but to a vastly superior degree. If mortals were sometimes lustful, Zeus was much more so, and in his power, much more successful. If people were skilled artisans, so was Hephaistos (hay-FYCE-toss); if humans were crafty and skillful, so was Prometheus (pro-MEE-thee-us)—but the skill, wisdom, lust, or whatever quality one may choose of the gods was infinitely beyond that of mortals. For Greeks, death was a sort of dark oblivion, but the gods had life forever, and life in full beauty, full youth, and complete power.

The Gods' Symbolic Roles

Before reviewing actual religious practices, the symbolic roles of the gods should be considered. Representing the power principle, Zeus is of course amoral, just as power is amoral. At the opposite extreme is Hera, goddess of marriage and domestic order, constantly striving to control and civilize a force dealing in thunderbolts. Athena and Apollo represent the Greek ideals of the arts of civilization and the beauty of intellect. Aphrodite was enthusiastically worshipped by a civilization that viewed the erotic arts as good, necessary, and proper. Superior craftsmanship was also highly valued as attested to by the importance of Hephaistos, an artisan elevated to the status of a god. The Greeks even had a god—Hermes—for their peripatetic world of travel, commerce, and trade (and thievery).

Throughout Greek history, Ares never received a kind word. He represented the principle of violence and destruction and, thus, had no redeeming virtues.

Dionysos is particularly important and peculiarly Greek. Espousing the virtues of rationality and the life of reason, the Greeks were acutely aware and deeply respectful of the nonrational aspect of humankind. These deep, surging drives had to be understood and treated with respect.

The worship of these gods during Mycenaean times and later may illustrate the point, for the formal ceremonies were always feasts. Animals were sacrificed, and a portion of the meat was burnt upon the fire. The rest was roasted and eaten by those performing the sacrifice. Wine was drunk, with a certain amount poured out first as a libation to the gods. Then the feast proceeded, with the assumption that the god was present as a guest at the meal, and that he or she enjoyed such things as well as the mortals did.

A Humanistic Culture

In what must seem to be a very diverse religious practice, one aspect of the life with the gods is of great importance. The Hellenes were never a priest-ridden group of people, as were the Egyptians. To us their religious practices seem relatively unstructured, almost casual; there was certainly plenty of room for freedom of thought. We will see later that in political organization the Greeks were not oppressed by despots, or at least not for very long. The Persians were, and culturally they produced only the monuments of an authoritarian state. In both religion and politics, the Greeks maintained the widest possible latitude for thought, questioning, and experimentation, which though turbulent and unstable, produced a great humanistic value system.

Such, greatly simplified, was the Olympian religion that existed from the fifteenth century throughout all of Greek history. During classical times and later, doubt may have existed about the nature and the presence of the gods but most people, excluding some of the intellectuals, believed in the gods, and for almost every important state decision one of the oracles was consulted, usually the oracle at Delphi. That the answers given by the oracles were frequently riddles that could be interpreted in any of several ways did not shake the faith of the people in the oracles themselves.

In this bewildering complexity of gods and people, what determined the events and the fate, or doom, of any individual? Here as before, we must rely on Homer, who wrote centuries after the heroic age and was none too certain himself of the answer to the question we have posed. In the first place, they had a vague belief that each of the people, or each of the heroes, had their own *moira* (MOY-ruh), or pattern of life, which they would fulfill. This may be illustrated as a sort of jigsaw puzzle that the hero's life would fill in—with the added complexity that the individual never knew what the picture would be when it was finished nor when it was completed. Within the individual's life we have the three forces of free will as determined by character, accident, and the intervention of the gods. These worked together, and sometimes in opposition, to determine the course of a person's life, and nothing could be counted on as certain until death finished the picture. This problem is considered in greater depth in *Oedipus the King* by Sophokles (see complete work in this volume). Frequently the gods intervened and brought tragedy to a person who overstepped the limits of human action and, out of pride, attempted to act in the realm of the gods. Such action almost certainly brought about a doom. But for the most part it seems that in the heroic age a person's character *was* fate. The people did the things they did, receiving their attendant consequences, because of the kind of person they were. Thus Akhilleus, in spite of all sorts of ruses to outwit his predicted fate, had his short and glorious life just because he was the kind of person to whom personal honor was all important, because he took great risks in the hope of winning great fame. Odysseus, on the other hand, lived a long life not only because of his heroic strength, but also because of his ability to talk, to deceive, and to plan ahead for survival.

Such, then, is at least a suggestion of the nature of the Mycenaean civilization, the culture in which the Trojan War occurred, in which Agamemnon, Menelaos (men-uh-LAY-us), Helen, and the other fabled Greeks actually lived.

This Mycenaean culture began its decline in the twelfth century (the 1100s) as a result of many factors: a forced closing of trade with the Middle East; a series of wars between the kingdoms within the Mycenaean groups; and, most importantly, an invasion from the north by a group called the Dorians. These last were a people of the same racial stock as the Mycenaeans, but who were just now forced to migrate south because of the complicated folk movements of the time. They slowly occupied the mainland of Greece during the twelfth to the tenth centuries, overcoming the already spent civilization they found there. Two important consequences followed. First, a long "dark ages" descended upon Greece in which there was little cultural or artistic creation. Second, while retreating from the Dorians, the inhabitants of the Greek mainland emigrated to the Asiatic coast of the Aegean Sea where in the course of time, they developed a number of Greek cities in an advanced state of civilization. Because these last people spoke the Ionian dialect of Greek, this region became known as the Ionian coast and was later to become the center of the earliest Greek philosopher-scientists, as well as a land that was a sort of military football between the kingdoms of Lydia and Persia (the great Asiatic powers) and the city-states of Greece.

The Archaic Period, ca. 750–500 B.C.

These dark ages move almost imperceptibly into the Archaic (ar-KAY-ic) times of historic Greece. We know quite a bit about the life of the period through the poems of Hesiod (HEE-see-ud), *Works and Days.* Hesiod was a farmer in Boeotia who, except for once winning a poetry contest, seems to have known nothing but bad luck. He gives us a picture of a landed aristocracy whose chief occupation was to squeeze the small farmer. Life was a continual round of jobs to be done with little or no reward or future in the work. Justice lay in the hands of the aristocrats who rendered their decisions almost entirely in terms of who could offer the largest bribe. Hesiod was always reverent towards the gods, but he neither expected nor received any reward in this life except for continuous toil, and Hesiod's plight was the common lot of most of the Greeks of his time.

■

FIGURE 4.1 *Portrait bust of Homer, marble, Roman copy of ca. 150 B.C. Certainly not a likeness, this is an idealized version of how a divinely inspired blind poet should look. National Archeological Museum, Naples.*

Of course the latter part of the eighth century was also the time when Homer wrote. While Hesiod was describing the life of his own time, Homer's work describes the departed glories of the heroic or Mycenaean period, which has already been discussed. We know little about Homer; computer analysis has shown that a single person, whom we call Homer, composed the tragedy of the *Iliad.* Analysis of the adventure tale that is the *Odyssey* is less conclusive, though Homer is the probable poet. However, precise knowledge about authorship is not as important as the fact that the *Iliad* and the *Odyssey* are at the very heart of the Greek heritage (see the selection from the *Odyssey* at the end of this chapter). Greek ideals, the idea of Greek superiority over the barbarians, and the overwhelming desire for personal honor were embodied in these works, and they became as close to a central religious book as the Greeks ever possessed. The works of Homer were memorized by every Greek student; they were recited at all of the great Greek festivals and games throughout the Hellenic world. Homer, of course, did not make up the stories he wrote. The poems were a collection of the legends that had their origins from time out of mind sung or recited by bards in the palaces. But they were brought together by the sure hand of a literary genius and transformed into the works that inspired the Greek mind from the time of their composition (figure 4.1).

A Day in Ancient Athens

Waking at dawn, Dimitrios, an Athenian citizen, throws back the embroidered cover that his wife had recently completed. His bed is a framed couch of leather thongs with pallet and pillow. Stepping onto a floor of hard-packed earth covered with rush mats he glances at the white-washed bedroom walls. Used mainly for sleeping and eating, his house is simple. Made of sun-dried bricks and hardened clay, it is sparsely furnished with a few chairs and some plain couches for reclining at meals. In his bedroom a small cabinet (made in his own shop) serves both as chair and chest. A large marble water basin stands in the corner, but today he simply rubs his body with perfumed oil and wipes it off for a quick bath. Slipping into sandals, he dons his *peplos*—two rectangular strips of linen (bleached white), pinned at the shoulders and belted at the waist. Then, wrapping himself in a larger linen sheet (*himation*) as cloak, he sallies forth, eager to begin another day in the sparkling sunlight of his native Athens.

Stopping by his barber, Dimitrios has his beard trimmed and his hair curled today rather than braided. As he reaches the *agora* (the central marketplace/business district), he smiles in anticipation. Athens is all abustle! People swarm in the streets and in the many shops—lampmakers, locksmiths, millers, swordmakers, lyretuners, bakers, shipbuilding crafts. From perfumes to octopus, the odors of the marketplace mingle in the air. Because most women do not leave their homes even to shop, the people are mainly men—citizens, resident aliens, sailors from near and far, and slaves. Strolling along the *stoa* (covered walks) he greets his friends. Passing the imports from the busy harbor, he notes the usual variety of goods: cheese and salted pork from Sicily, rugs from Carthage, ivory from Ethiopia, glass from Egypt, perfumes from the Far East.

After gazing up at the *akropolis* where the civic goddess Athena has her incomparable temple (the Parthenon), he enters his own small furniture shop. There he spends the remainder of the morning, inspecting the work of his two slaves (whom he has trained in woodcraft) and putting the finishing touches on a cabinet order of a Syrian importer.

Later, heading home for his first meal of the day he buys a bouquet from a girl peddling violets, roses, irises, and crocuses. (All Greeks love flowers!) Soon he passes some of the private schools that Athenian boys attend from ages six to sixteen. The younger boys are accompanied to school by a *paidagogos,* an elderly slave. Seated in front of the teacher with a scroll in his lap, each boy learns reading, writing, arithmetic, poetry, drawing, and music. Ever handy is a sandal used for flogging reluctant scholars; educating citizens is a serious business in a democracy.

At home Dimitrios is greeted by his wife Kastalia. Over a long, loose-hanging skirt she wears a red linen *peplos.* Her hair is curled and tied with bright ribbons. With minium sticks and alkanet root, she tints her cheeks and lips a reddish hue. Her eye makeup is dramatic: eyebrows darkened with lampblack, eyelids shaded with kohl, eyelashes set with eggwhite. She is further adorned with bracelets, necklaces, and earrings. In his absence she has been busy directing the household slaves in their tasks: grinding grain, baking bread, weaving clothing, making bedding. As a proper mother Kastalia provides her husband's children with the comfort and security of a well-organized household. As the children turn six, the boys are sent to school while the girls are taught to sing, dance, and manage household affairs as well as their mother. Today, since Dimitrios brought no friends home with him, Kastalia stays to share the simple midday meal with him—barley cakes, cheese, olives, leeks, fish.

After lunch Dimitrios goes to the public gymnasium to exercise, bathe, and, especially, to talk. With the other men he discusses the next election, the plays in the last drama festival, and sports. They speculate about who will win the olive wreaths for running, broad jumping, wrestling, and hurling the javelin or throwing the discus in the upcoming Olympic Games.

In the evening Dimitrios attends a banquet at a wealthy merchant's home, a lavish residence with murals and marble walls. As the guests arrive attendants remove their sandals, wash their feet, anoint their heads with oil, and pour water for hand washing. Reclining on couches, they enjoy a rich array of foods: pork, fish, shark, or eel with many breads and cakes. Vegetables include beans, peas, cabbage, lentils, lettuce, onions, and garlic, all bathed in olive oil. Desserts include cheeses, honey, sweetmeats, and cheesecake. A drinking session (*symposium*) follows dinner. As they drink wine diluted with water they are entertained by magicians, acrobats, singers, and dancers. Lyric poetry is sung to the accompaniment of the soothing lyre, after which the dancing girls weave their spell to the sound of the exotic aulos. Later, the dancing girls may be auctioned off to guests to be their companions for the remainder of the evening. (As Demosthenes once said, "We have courtesans for cultivated pleasure, concubines for the daily health of our bodies, and wives to bear us lawful offspring"—not to mention the common adolescent phase of infatuation with male companions.)

Meanwhile, Kastalia has retired to the women's quarters of her house to bathe in a terra-cotta tub and to anoint her body with oil. After dreamily reading some poetry (her mother taught her to read and write) she sleepily goes to bed. Much later, Dimitrios confirms the old Athenian adage: the man of the house returns home when he has no place left to go. He plops into the bed Kastalia has prepared for him and drops immediately into deep slumber. The waiting slave girl extinguishes the olive-oil lamp and retires soundlessly to her quarters.

Economic and Political Changes

But to return to the times of Hesiod. We witness first the rise of a landed aristocracy who, by force and guile, seized most of the land from the poor farmers. Not the least of the ways of acquiring land by the aristocrat was to lend money to the farmer, who used his own person as security for the loan. When he was unable to pay his debt, his land became the property of the aristocrat and the farmer became a slave. Numerous forms of governments arose at this time. Frequently the most powerful landowner became king; at other times the city-state was ruled by a committee of landowners, constituting an oligarchy. It was during this time that land poverty, simply the fact that there was not enough land to support the population, became painfully evident.

As a result of this land poverty the colonizing process that was mentioned earlier began to take place. Many city-states simply exported fairly large bands of adventurers to found colonies throughout the Aegean and Mediterranean world. Many colonies were established in northern Greece, including Byzantium, and a number of cities on the shores of the Black Sea. The present city of Marseilles in France was originally a Greek colony, as were a number of the cities of Sicily and Italy. The Greek world expanded greatly, and with the expansion came the development of trade and commerce among all of the Hellenic cities and an increasing flow of wealth into the original Greek cities. A large, important, and wealthy commercial class of people also began to form a part of the population of the cities, different from the landed aristocracy and opposed to them and different from the small-farmer group. This new group was to become a political faction to reckon with in the development of new governmental forms.

The first of the political changes came with the rise of *tyrants*. For us in the twentieth century, the term suggests a harsh military dictator, but at first, among the Hellenic cities, it was just another word meaning "king." The tyrant was simply a man, sometimes chosen by the people, more usually a man who seized power and established himself as absolute ruler as long as he could hold office. Sometimes he came from the members of the old landowning families, a man who discerned the "wave of the future" and grabbed power either by allying himself with the merchant class or the farming class and promising political reforms, which would bring help to his political allies. Sometimes he rose from the merchant group; sometimes he was an outsider who came in to take over the rule of a city-state. No matter what his origin, he had to win over a good part of the population in order to try to hold his position, and he did this by effecting political, judicial, or economic reforms that would make him popular with a fairly large segment of the population. From this movement toward tyranny came the earliest reforms that were to lead, in Athens and some other cities, toward eventual democracy. None of this development was uniform through the cities of the Hellenic world; in none of them was progress a steady evolutionary process.

From this point on in our discussion, we shall focus our attention on governmental changes in the city of Athens, which in most ways was to become the most glorious of the Greek cities. For our purposes in this chapter, we shall consider only the changes made under the rule of four leaders: Draco (DRAY-ko), Solon (SO-lon), Pisistratus (pi-SIS-truh-tus), and Kleisthenes (KLICE-the-neez). They will seem to have appeared in orderly succession but this did not happen. For example, two of Pisistratus's sons attempted to follow their father in the corridors of power but one was assassinated in 514 and the other was exiled in 510. The course of leadership never seems to run smoothly.

The Rise of Athens

In considering the political and economic development of Athens from the sixth century on, it is well to bear in mind a rather curious power structure. Three political factions, largely determined by economic status, struggled for power. They were the old landed aristocracy, the poor farmers who eked out a living on marginal land, and the growing commercial class. In addition to these economic groups, Athenian life was dominated by four family-clans, originally of the aristocracy, who controlled the individual lives of their members, and in a fairly large measure controlled as well the political developments within the city. As long as these four tribes remained powerful, political and economic advances would always be dominated by the traditions of the tribes.

The Reformers

The first of the reformers in the seventh century was an almost legendary figure, Draco (fl. 621 B.C.), one of the early tyrants. His great contribution was to publish a code of laws. This simple act was a great step toward freedom. Hesiod, for example, had complained that the aristocrats who were the judges of his time were the only ones who knew the laws, and it appears that they made up the rules as they went along. An ordinary citizen involved in a legal suit about land or homicide really cast himself on the mercy of the judges who rendered decisions as they saw fit; decisions that depended upon the economic status of the litigants, their family connections, and the size of the bribe that could be offered. Obviously justice cannot prevail in such a system. Draco's Code, although it is reputed to have been very severe, did offer a single standard of justice for *all* people, and since the law was published, individuals within the state could know their legal rights. No matter how harsh the laws may have been, the publication of the laws became a step forward in developing a *rational* system of justice rather than one based upon tradition, privilege, and wealth.

The second of the great reformers was Solon (ca. 640–558 B.C.), a man whose name has come down to us as the synonym for a wise lawgiver. Like Draco, he was a member of the nobility, but evidently in his youth he had travelled extensively and had developed interests in the possibilities of trade and commerce, and he also became aware of the injustice of land distribution in his native state of Attica. Perhaps his most important reform was to free all slaves who had reached that condition because of debt, and to abolish the custom that made debt-slavery possible. A man who sought moderation in all things, he was evidently pressured to break up the great estates and to distribute the land to the farmers, but he did not have sufficient faith in the poor and uneducated masses to take this step. He did, however, allow all people to become involved to some extent with the government. He limited the magistracies and important governmental offices to the upper classes, but he allowed members of the lowest class, even, to serve as jurors, and thus he began a process of educating all people in the processes of social action and social change. In running the day-to-day affairs of Athens he established an administrative council of four hundred members, and thus greatly broadened the civic responsibilities of the citizens. Shrewdly anticipating conservative resistance to change and liberal proclivities for tinkering with reforms, Solon stipulated that all reforms had to remain in force and unchanged for ten years.

In order to encourage trade and commerce, Solon adopted a much lighter coinage than Athens had used in the past, and also he imported many artisans, particularly potters, since pottery manufacture was one of the chief industries of Athens and one of its main exports. These last reforms began a series of developments that were to break Athens away from an economic dependence upon agriculture and land and to establish it as a city whose wealth depended upon manufactured objects that were more or less independent of the uncontrollable forces of nature.

The third great reformer was Pisistratus (ca. 605–527 B.C.), who governed Athens from 546 till his death. In his economic reforms he was to follow the precedent that had already been set by Solon in that he broke up the large estates and distributed the land to the almost landless peasants. Since voting privileges and participation in the government were determined largely by economic status, this single reform did much to broaden the base for government, and it allowed the people who had already been somewhat educated in social action by Solon's changes to take a more important role than before in the actual government of the state. He and his sons further increased employment by starting a number of great public works within the city. Perhaps the most important of Pisistratus's contributions to the city lay in the development of its art. Two of the greatest Hellenic poets of the time, Simonides and Anakreon, were brought to Athens, and Pisistratus and his sons also commissioned the preparation of the first careful edition of Homer's poems, which were later sung and recited at all of the important festivals and sacrifices within the city. This last step may not seem to be of great importance, but its significance is apparent when one realizes that the learning of these poems by most of the citizens and their recitation at public functions gave the people a sense of common heritage and a feeling of unity *as citizens of Athens,* not as members of a particular family clan. These tyrants of Athens, consciously or unconsciously, were leading the people toward democracy and, by educating them through increased responsibility, made them ready for active participation in a truly democratic government.

A Democratic Government

This government came into being with the reforms of Kleisthenes (fl. 507 B.C.) who attempted to abolish the influence of the four old aristocratic tribes whose power had, for years, been the dominant political influence in Athens. To accomplish this he instituted ten new "tribes" whose membership was based simply on place of residence rather than upon heredity. In order to do this he first divided the city into "demes" or neighborhoods. These purely artificial units furnished the basis for the political structure. Then a number of demes were combined to form a tribe, of which there were ten within the city-state. Furthermore, the demes for any single tribe were selected at random, so that within any tribe one found neighborhoods composed of the shore (people connected with shipping and seafaring trades), the city itself, and the rural areas. Thus no tribe was dominated by any single economic group. To make a not-too-exact analogy, we might think of the city of Detroit as divided into ten political groups but within each group one would find neighborhoods from the inner city, neighborhoods from the regularly employed working class, and neighborhoods from suburbs like Grosse Pointe.

Kleisthenes abolished the old Council of Four Hundred, which had come into being with the reforms of Solon, and substituted a Council of Five Hundred, with fifty members representing each of the new political tribes. He did this since the old council had come to be simply the voice of the four traditional tribes, and Kleisthenes wished to break their hold upon political and judicial matters. In the new government, each artificial political tribe nominated a large slate of candidates for the Council, from which fifty were selected by lot, on the theory that any citizen who was nominated (the nomination process eliminated the obviously unfit) was just as capable as any other citizen to administer the affairs of the state, so that actual membership could be left to chance.

The executive branch of the government was placed in the hands of a committee of ten generals who were elected yearly by the Council, and in turn this committee-of-ten was headed by a commander-in-chief whose term was also for a single year.

Political freedom was something that the Athenians had to get used to. When ruled by a despot, people tend to adjust, turn inward, just survive. One of the greatest defects of any tyranny (out of a very long list) is that it stifles not only dissent but productivity and creativity as well. Freedom offers challenge and opportunity; despotism is denial. What happened in a democratic Athens was succinctly described by Herodotos:

> And it is plain enough that freedom is an excellent thing; since even the Athenians, who, while they continued under the rule of tyrants, were not a whit more valiant than any of their neighbors, no sooner shook off the yoke than they became decidedly the first of all.
>
> *Histories,* V

Persian Invasions

While Athens was developing its political institutions, the mighty Persian Empire was becoming increasingly irritated with the rebellious Greek cities in Asia Minor. Athens supported the Ionian Greeks in their refusal to pay tribute to Darius (da-RYE-us), the Persian King, which gave him all the excuse a despot needs to give rebels a lesson in power, and the free city-state of Athens some instruction in humility. The Persians invaded mainland Greece in 490 B.C., a date that became pivotal for the future of Western culture. North of Athens, on the plain of Marathon, the mighty army of a totalitarian state was confronted by a badly outnumbered Athenian force. Led by General Miltiades (mil-TIE-uh-deez), the Greeks, like the wily Odysseus, plotted to outwit the Persians and in a swift and stunning dawn attack drove the Persians back into their ships. According to the historian, Herodotos, the Persians lost more than six thousand men, while Greek casualties were minimal. Free people had turned back the Asian hordes and changed the course of history. The messenger who ran the twenty-six plus miles from Marathon to Athens symbolized more than news of an incredible victory. Greek pride in Hellenism, in the superiority of their culture over that of the barbarians, was fully vindicated.

The Persians were not to give up easily, and a second invasion was planned, but held up for ten years while the Persians put down a revolt in Egypt. In 480, however, they effected their second invasion. In the meantime the Athenians had discovered rich silver deposits at Mount Laurium in Attica, and had achieved a fairly high degree of wealth. Themistokles (the-MIS-tuh-kleez), the commander-in-chief in Athens, sent a delegation to Delphi to ask how best to meet the Persians in their second invasion, and was told that they should protect themselves with "wooden walls." Themistokles, with the usual Greek intellectual twist, believed that the Athenians could best protect themselves with a strong navy, and convinced his fellow citizens that the "wooden walls" were ships. Consequently, the money from the silver mines was used to build a strong Athenian navy, which proved to be not only a military force but also the determining factor in establishing Athens as a great commercial center. The Persian invasion of 480 was conducted on an even larger scale than the earlier war, for Herodotos estimated the Persian forces at five million men—an obvious exaggeration—but indicative of the size of the invading army. This army crossed the Aegean Sea far in the north and marched down the Greek peninsula, closely attended by the great Persian navy. The first of the great battles was a Persian victory, but a glorious episode in the history of Greece. This was the battle at the pass of Thermopylai (Ther-MOP-a-lye).

Here, at a narrow pass between the mountains and the sea, three hundred Spartans (now actually allied with Athens as a part of the fighting force) under their king, Leonidas (lee-ON-uh-dus), faced the entire Persian army and fought magnificently. When the Spartans were told to surrender or the sky would be darkened with arrows, Leonidas calmly replied that the Spartans would therefore fight in the shade. As usual in Greek wars, they were betrayed by a traitor who showed the Persians an alternative route through the mountains so that the Spartans were surrounded, but even in the face of such odds, they kept on fighting until they were all killed. The inscription later carved on the tomb of the heroic Spartans, in tremendous understatement and compression of meaning, gives testimony to the spirit of the encounter:

> Go tell the Spartans, thou that passest by,
> That here, obedient to their laws, we lie.

In the meantime the Persian fleet sailing down the coast in support of the army had suffered defeats from the Greeks and from the storms, but it still overwhelmingly outnumbered the ships of Athens and its allies. Eventually this fleet reached the sea just off Athens near the bay of Salamis (SAL-a-mus), while the land army moved inexorably toward its goal. Themistokles abandoned the city and all of Attica, moved the population to the island of Salamis, and prepared to gamble everything on a single naval battle. By trickery he enticed the Persian fleet into the Bay of Salamis, where the fleet's very size was a disadvantage, since in the narrow waters it was impossible to maneuver so many ships, and the Greek fleet attacked around the edges of the Persian ships and destroyed the Persians. The war continued for a year more on land, but the Persian army was finally defeated by the Spartans at the Battle of Plataea (pla-TEE-uh), and the Persian threat was broken.

It is almost impossible to overestimate the feeling of pride the Greeks felt as a result of these victories. Persia controlled Egypt, the entire eastern end of the Mediterranean Sea, and all of the land as far east as India. The wealth of the Persian kings and their satraps is impossible to estimate. Yet a relatively few Greek men, poverty-stricken in comparison to the Persians, had beaten off the totalitarian enemy. The Greeks rightly felt that their tradition of personal freedom, their pride in personal honor, and the love they felt for their cities had been the decisive factor. As indeed it was. Although the old aristocratic, oligarchical party continued in Athens, the years following the Persian wars marked the complete triumph of democracy in Athens. Suddenly the idea of freedom had worked.

For us in the Western world in the twentieth century, these far-off wars are of equal importance, for the Greek tradition—principally the concept of the worth of the individual person—survived and has given form to the ideas we now hold as of greatest worth. If the Greeks had failed, that tradition might have been snuffed out.

Another Quest for Freedom: The Philosophers

Developments in Greece during these preclassical times were not only political, economic, and military. One important phase of individual freedom is always the liberation of the human mind, allowing the individual to ask all the important questions of the gods and the universe and to formulate new and original answers. This, too, had been going on during the time of more tangible and material progress of which we have been taking note. Curiously, the abstract speculation about the nature of the universe was a Greek phenomenon, one not found in other parts of the Western world. The Egyptians had made astronomical observations, but always for such practical purposes as the prediction of the flooding of the Nile upon which their agriculture depended. So, too, in Babylon a number of astrologers had observed the stars, largely for use in making practical predictions about the affairs of the earth. But pure thought about the nature of things was uniquely Greek; Edith Hamilton attributes it to the loose, nonauthoritarian nature of Greek religion, which was never dominated by a priestly class. For whatever reason, the Greek philosopher-scientists were the first true philosophers (pure thinkers) in Western civilization.

The Ionian Philosophers

The first philosopher-scientists lived in the Ionian city of Miletus (my-LEET-us) with Thales (THAY-leez; ca. 636–546 B.C.) as their leading thinker. The *questions* they asked are always more important than the answers they found, for the questions are those that constantly return to challenge people's minds. The answers change as our knowledge of the universe becomes more varied.

One problem consistently bothered the philosophers of the Ionian (or Milesian) School. They were intrigued by the constant change of all the things they could see around them. Earth changed to plant life; plant life changed to animal; wherever one turned, one observed movement from one form of existence to another. They postulated that there must be one single basic substance of which all the forms of being are made, so that the process of change is simply the transformation of the basic element. The first question Thales asked, then, is *What is the single element, the basic stuff, of which the universe is composed?*

His answer was that this basic element is water, for all things need water for their existence, and water itself changes when heated or cooled to a gaseous nature—steam—or to a solid state—ice. These things being true and observable by our relatively coarse sensory equipment, all sorts of other changes and transformations that are not sense-apparent, could take place in water. Other philosophers, following the line of thought first explored by Thales, argued for earth or air as the basic world-stuff. But, as we have said before, the questions are important, not necessarily the answers.

The key point is that the Greeks, beginning with Thales, made informed guesses that were completely naturalistic without reference to supernatural powers. One of the Babylonian creation myths, for example, stated that the world was once all water and that the god Marduk then made a rush mat and piled dirt beside it to construct the dry lands.

> What Thales did was to leave Marduk out. He, too, said that everything was once water. But he thought that the earth and everything else had been formed out of water by a natural process, like the silting up of the Delta of the Nile. It is an admirable beginning, the whole point of which is that it gathers together into a coherent picture a number of observed facts *without letting Marduk in.*[3]

One of the followers of Hippokrates (hy-POK-ra-teas; 460–377 B.C.), the Greek physician, wrote of the mysterious ailment epilepsy (then called the divine malady):

> It seems to me that the disease is no more divine than any other. It has a natural cause, just as other diseases have. Men think it divine merely because they do not understand it. But if they called everything divine which they do not understand, why, there would be no end of divine things.[4]

A second of the Ionians, Anaximandros (a-NAKS-uh-man-dros; ca. 611–547 B.C.), a student of Thales, came up with the second question of importance, *How do specific things emerge from the basic element?* His answer, while it may seem unsatisfactory and vague, is probably more scientifically accurate than those of many of his contemporaries or successors. In the first place, he rejected the idea of a physical element such as water, earth, or air, and simply called his basic stuff "the Boundless." This, he suggested, was a form of being we cannot perceive with our senses; that is, it permeates everything and surrounds everything. In specific answer to the question he raised, he simply said that all forms that we can see—trees, living animal bodies, all specific things—are formed by "separating out" of this boundless element. Thus all forms that our senses can know, all physical things, simply coagulate out of the non-sense-apparent boundless and eventually lose their form and disappear back into it.

A later philosopher-scientist, not strictly a Milesian, since his native city was Ephesos on the Ionian coast and since he was doing most of his work right at the end of the sixth century (500 B.C.), was the philosopher Herakleitos (Hair-uh-KLY-toss; ca. 535–475 B.C.). Following the same line of thought as Thales and Anaximandros, he raised a third important question, *What guides the process of change?* He would grant a basic element from which all particular forms emerged, but he felt there must be some sort of controlling force to keep the process of universal change in order so that, let us say, an elm tree always produces elm trees rather than hippopotamuses.

Herakleitos denied the possibility of *being,* for he felt that the universe was in a process of flow, not fixed. His basic belief is that nothing *is;* everything is *becoming.* Thus his famous statement that one can never step into the same river twice. The appearance of the river may be the "same," whatever that may mean, but by the time one has taken a foot out of the river and put it back, the water has changed, the bank has changed, nothing is exactly the same. The universe is in the same condition. Between *now* and *now* it has flowed, changed, varied; it is no longer the same even though its appearance may seem to remain.

Perhaps to illustrate this contention, he chose fire as his basic element. Thus one may watch a flame in a fireplace for half an hour and say to one's companion, "I have been watching that same flame for thirty minutes." Actually, though the shape of the flame may remain fairly constant, the burning gas that is the flame is never the same, even for the smallest fraction of a second. Thus is the universe envisioned by Herakleitos.

3. Farrington, Benjamin. *Greek Science.* Baltimore: Penguin Books, 1961, p. 37.

4. Op. cit., p. 81.

But such a universe needs a guiding force, for the human mind finds it hard to live with a picture of a changing world without some order and direction. So Herakleitos proposed a great *Logos* as the direct answer to his question of the guiding force. Now *logos* in Greek means *word*. Thus, the Gospel according to John, originally written in Greek, starts with the sentence, "In the beginning was the Word"—*logos* in Greek. But with John, as with Herakleitos, it obviously has a much more important significance than our word, *word*. For Herakleitos it meant a great *Intelligence,* which permeated the world and somehow guided the constant change of its flamelike element of which all things were composed. This sense of all things "knowing" what shapes they should take, what forms they should assume, is one of the great mysteries of the universe. (How does each maple leaf differ from every other maple leaf in the world, yet take a characteristic shape so that we can identify it at a glance? How does it "know" the form it must fulfill?) Herakleitos's assumption of a great Logos or Intelligence is not far from the assumption of a single God as an intellectual Principle in the universe.

The line of thought of these Ionian philosophers seems reasonable enough in their attempt to explain the element that is One and yet so many, which seems to be always the same and yet so varied. However, the basic assumption here is one of constant change, and furthermore, all of the conclusions these thinkers reached are based on the testimony of the human senses. We see, hear, taste, feel, or smell the phenomena of the world and the changing nature of all things. The search for a basic element from which it is all made is essentially a quest for "That Which is Real."

But the human mind can take an entirely different tack in this same quest. For example, our mind can simply say that whatever is *real* cannot always be changing. The mind can equate *permanence* with reality and say that only the things, or thing, that are absolutely permanent and unchanging are real. Furthermore, it can easily be proven that our senses cannot be trusted. We know they give us varying reports about the "same" thing. For example, water at the same temperature as measured by a thermometer will be either "hot" or "cold," depending on the temperature of our hands as we feel the water. Perhaps only the "thought process," independent of the senses, can be trusted as a guide to truth. Here we have the difference between scientists—people who trust their senses as they can be refined through such instruments as they can make—and pure philosophers, those who trust their minds alone to lead them to truth. This distinction appeared early in Greek thought.

Pythagoras

Pythagoras (ca. 582–507 B.C.) was one of the most original, interesting, and least-understood Greek philosophers. He was an Ionian Greek from the Aegean Island of Samos but he was most influential in southern Italy (Magna Graecia), where he established a religious brotherhood in Krotona (figure 4.2).

FIGURE 4.2 *Marble bust identified as a portrait of Pythagoras and placed in the Roman Forum in 343 B.C. The identification is probably correct, for what we see here is a religious mystic. Museum, Ostia.*

Pythagoras taught that number was the essence of all things, in the same sense that his predecessors saw ultimate reality as water or the boundless or fire. He believed that number was more than a symbolic construction, that all matter was essentially numerical, and that all relationships in the universe could be expressed through number. Pythagoras was the first Greek philosopher to reject the geocentric theory that the sun revolved around the earth. He reduced the earth to the status of a planet that revolved around the fixed point of a central fire; he also saw the sun revolving around what he called the hearth of the universe.

In his search for *that-which-is-most-real,* Pythagoras kept returning to the universality of mathematical relationships. For example, most of us know the formula in plane geometry called the Pythagorean theorem: In right-angle triangles the square of the hypotenuse is equal to the sum of the square of the other two sides. There are three such triangles on page 65.

Although the triangles are dissimilar in appearance, one fact about them is true: $AB^2 + AC^2 = BC^2$. In Euclidean geometry this relationship was true before it was ever discovered, and it will remain true when there is no one on earth to be aware of it. Furthermore, it is true no matter what sensory conditions surround it. In the hottest furnace or the coldest refrigerator it is true. Here is an "idea" that has no substance, that exists entirely apart from people's minds; yet any shape that fulfills the equation is inevitably a right triangle. In this numerical relationship we have the pattern for a physical thing. Pythagoras is therefore credited with the discovery of pure

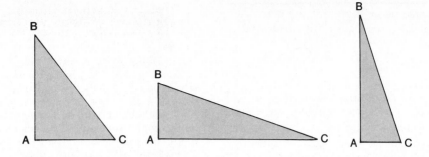

mathematics, with the development of mathematical proofs, and with the awareness that form and structure give objects individual identities. These monumental achievements provide the framework for the Eleatic philosophers and particularly Plato (see chapter 6), upon whom Pythagoras was the single most important influence.

Pythagoras was the first to prove a relationship between mathematics and the harmonies of music. He discovered, through experimentation, that vibrating strings had certain relationships that were dependent on the relative lengths of the strings. Based on these musical relationships, Pythagoras developed his theory of the relationships of the planets. He pictured the heavenly bodies as revolving from east to west in orderly circular orbits around a central fire. There was, he said, an agreement between nature (the planets) and number (the musical intervals). The predictability of nature, like the musical intervals on a vibrating string, was therefore musical and the wheeling arcs of the celestial globes formed the *harmonia* of the *kosmos:* the music of the spheres.

Pythagoras was both a speculative and a practical philosopher, applying his ideas to the religious order that he founded in Italy at Krotona. In the Pythagorean Order, philosophy was a central part of a religious way of life, a life-style that was intellectual, political, religious, and ethical. Small communities functioned within the larger community, each a social and religious unit as well as a scientific study group. Property was held in common, there was no discrimination based on sex, and music and mathematics were a regular part of social life.

The Pythagoreans are known especially for their doctrine of the transmigration of souls. They believed that souls were reincarnated in a series of lives as they tried to ascend to an ideal existence in a life of divine bliss. The ideal could be approached only through purification, emphasis upon intellectual activity, and renunciation of worldly sensuality. Salvation could be attained only after a final escape from the cycle of intermediate births.

The Pythagoreans were vegetarians who believed in the brotherhood of all living things. They believed in spiritual purification through music and science and physical purification through medicine and gymnastics. They advocated a humane society in which people would live always in harmony and friendship. Eventually they were either killed or forced to flee their communes by neighboring tribes who considered the Pythagoreans a threat to established religious practices.

Exercises

1. For a culture as rich as that of Greece, a time line is both useful and instructive. Each of the following topics can be assigned a date (sometimes approximate) or bracket of dates. Then they should be arranged in chronological order. This will provide an outline of Greek history up to the beginning of the Classical Period (480 B.C.). Finally, the significance of each topic should be explained as contributing in some way to the development of Greek civilization.
   a. Reforms of Kleisthenes 507 B.C. p.60
   b. Dorian invasions p.50
   c. Persian wars p.49
   d. Mycenaean culture p.49
   e. Traditional date of the Trojan War
   f. Peak of Minoan culture p.47
   g. Homer and Hesiod active p.50
   h. Volcanic eruption on Thera p.48
   i. Solon's reforms 61
   j. Linear B script 49
   k. Early Cycladic culture in the Aegean 45
   l. First Olympic Games
   m. Introduction of coinage 61
2. Greek religion functioned at about four levels of belief/disbelief:
   a. Olympians subject to literal belief at face value
   b. Gods/goddesses represent aspects of the forces of nature
   c. Gods/goddesses symbolize abstract ideas such as power, love, intellectuality, civilized living, fine craftsmanship, and so forth
   d. The gods/goddesses were created by people and usually in their own image

Explain each level and what each may imply about religious beliefs. Then, consider other religions and whether or not these same levels are appropriate. Other religions can include Christianity, Islam, Judaism, Hinduism, and Buddhism.

Literary Selections

THE ODYSSEY

Homer (fl. 9th c. B.C.)

"An epic," said Aristotle, "is a poem about men in action." The action in the *Odyssey* is concerned with getting a husband back to his wife and son, and a king back to his kingdom. The wife is Penelope, the son Telemakhos (tuh-LEM-uh-koss), and the kingdom is the island of Ithaka off the west coast of the mainland.

Odysseus spent ten years fighting at Troy and another ten trying to get home. The story of the wanderer's return is divided, as was the *Iliad,* into twenty-four books, which happens to be one for each letter of the Greek alphabet. There are four interior divisions: (1) The Adventures of Telemakhos, (2) The Homecoming of Odysseus, (3) The Great Wanderings, and (4) Odysseus in Ithaka.

Odysseus is the narrator in the third section as he relates, in Book XI, his hazardous journey to the underworld. This account is probably based on the oldest story that Homer collected; it has much in common with the underworld story in *The Epic of Gilgamesh.*

Just how Odysseus manages to sail to Hades is deliberately vague but, once there, his encounters with the shades are among the most dramatic in this consistently engrossing epic. Much of the poem is about sailing the seas to faraway lands; Book XI, on the other hand, represents movement in time: figures from the past—Elpenor, Teiresias, his mother (recently dead), heroic mothers and grandmothers, famous heroes—Odysseus in the present; Odysseus as he envisions himself in Hades with Herakles, the hero he most resembles.[5] The translation is by Robert Fitzgerald.

Book Eleven

A Gathering of Shades

We bore down on the ship at the sea's edge
and launched her on the salt immortal sea,
stepping our mast and spar in the black ship;
embarked the ram and ewe and went aboard
in tears, with bitter and sore dread upon us.
But now a breeze came up for us astern—
a canvas-bellying landbreeze, hale shipmate
sent by the singing nymph with sun-bright hair;
so we made fast the braces, took our thwarts,
and let the wind and steersman work the ship
with full sail spread all day above our coursing,
till the sun dipped, and all the ways grew dark
upon the fathomless unresting sea.

---

5. The *Aeneid* of Virgil, the great Roman epic, is consciously based on Homer's poems. In Book VI of the *Aeneid,* Virgil has Aeneas visit the underworld as a kind of sequel to the visit of Odysseus (see chapter 9).

our ship ran onward toward the Ocean's bourne,
the realm and region of the Men of Winter,
hidden in mist and cloud. Never the flaming
eye of Hêlios lights on those men
at morning, when he climbs the sky of stars,
nor in descending earthward out of heaven;
ruinous night being rove over those wretches.
We made the land, put ram and ewe ashore,
and took our way along the Ocean stream
to find the place foretold for us by Kirkê.
There Perimêdês and Eurýlokhos
pinioned the sacred beasts. With my drawn blade
I spaded up the votive pit, and poured
libations round it to the unnumbered dead:
sweet milk and honey, then sweet wine, and last
clear water; and I scattered barley down.
Then I addressed the blurred and breathless dead,
vowing to slaughter my best heifer for them
before she calved, at home in Ithaka,
and burn the choice bits on the altar fire;
as for Teirêsias, I swore to sacrifice
a black lamb, handsomest of all our flock.
Thus to assuage the nations of the dead
I pledged these rites, then slashed the lamb and ewe,
letting their black blood stream into the wellpit.
Now the souls gathered, stirring out of Erebos,
brides and young men, and men grown old in pain,
and tender girls whose hearts were new to grief;
many were there, too, torn by brazen lanceheads,
battle-slain, bearing still their bloody gear.
From every side they came and sought the pit
with rustling cries; and I grew sick with fear.
But presently I gave command to my officers
to flay those sheep the bronze cut down, and make
burnt offerings of flesh to the gods below—
to sovereign Death, to pale Perséphonê.
Meanwhile I crouched with my drawn sword to keep
the surging phantoms from the bloody pit
till I should know the presence of Teirêsias.

One shade came first—Elpênor, of our company,
who lay unburied still on the wide earth
as we had left him—dead in Kirkê's hall,
untouched, unmourned, when other cares compelled us.
Now when I saw him there I wept for pity
and called out to him:

                              'How is this, Elpênor,
how could you journey to the western gloom
swifter afoot than I in the black lugger?'

He sighed, and answered:

                              'Son of great Laërtês,
Odysseus, master mariner and soldier,
bad luck shadowed me, and no kindly power;
ignoble death I drank with so much wine.
I slept on Kirkê's roof, then could not see
the long steep backward ladder, coming down,
and fell that height. My neck bone, buckled under,
snapped, and my spirit found this well of dark.
Now hear the grace I pray for, in the name
of those back in the world, not here—your wife
and father, he who gave you bread in childhood,
and your own child, your only son, Telémakhos,
long ago left at home.

When you make sail
and put these lodgings of dim Death behind,
you will moor ship, I know, upon Aiaia Island;
there, O my lord, remember me, I pray,
do not abandon me unwept, unburied,
to tempt the gods' wrath, while you sail for home;
but fire my corpse, and all the gear I had,
and build a cairn for me above the breakers—
an unknown sailor's mark for men to come.
Heap up the mound there, and implant upon it
the oar I pulled in life with my companions.'

He ceased, and I replied:

'Unhappy spirit,
I promise you the barrow and the burial.'

So we conversed, and grimly, at a distance,
with my long sword between, guarding the blood,
while the faint image of the lad spoke on.
Now came the soul of Antikleía, dead,
my mother, daughter of Autólykos,
dead now, though living still when I took ship
for holy Troy. Seeing this ghost I grieved,
but held her off, through pang on pang of tears,
till I should know the presence of Teirêsias.
Soon from the dark that prince of Thebes came forward
bearing a golden staff; and he addressed me:

'Son of Laërtês and the gods of old,
Odysseus, master of land ways and sea ways,
why leave the blazing sun, O man of woe,
to see the cold dead and the joyless region?
Stand clear, put up your sword;
let me but taste of blood, I shall speak true.'

At this I stepped aside, and in the scabbard
let my long sword ring home to the pommel silver,
as he bent down to the sombre blood. Then spoke
the prince of those with gift of speech:
'Great captain,
a fair wind and the honey lights of home
are all you seek. But anguish lies ahead;
the god who thunders on the land prepares it,
not to be shaken from your track, implacable,
in rancor for the son whose eye you blinded.
One narrow strait may take you through his blows:
denial of yourself, restraint of shipmates.
When you make landfall on Thrinakia first
and quit the violet sea, dark on the land
you'll find the grazing herds of Hêlios
by whom all things are seen, all speech is known.
Avoid those kine, hold fast to your intent,
and hard seafaring brings you all to Ithaka.
But if you raid the beeves, I see destruction
for ship and crew. Though you survive alone,
bereft of all companions, lost for years,
under strange sail shall you come home, to find
your own house filled with trouble: insolent men
eating your livestock as they court your lady.
Aye, you shall make those men atone in blood!
But after you have dealt out death—in open
combat or by stealth—to all the suitors,
go overland on foot, and take an oar,
until one day you come where men have lived

with meat unsalted, never known the sea,
nor seen seagoing ships, with crimson bows
and oars that fledge light hulls for dipping flight.
The spot will soon be plain to you, and I
can tell you how: some passerby will say,
"What winnowing fan is that upon your shoulder?"
Halt, and implant your smooth oar in the turf
and make fair sacrifice to Lord Poseidon:
a ram, a bull, a great buck boar; turn back,
and carry out pure hekatombs at home
to all wide heaven's lords, the undying gods,
to each in order. Then a seaborne death
soft as this hand of mist will come upon you
when you are wearied out with rich old age,
your country folk in blessed peace around you.
And all this shall be just as I foretell.'

When he had done, I said at once,

'Teirêsias,
my life runs on then as the gods have spun it.
But come, now, tell me this; make this thing clear:
I see my mother's ghost among the dead
sitting in silence near the blood. Not once
has she glanced this way toward her son, nor spoken.
Tell me, my lord,
may she in some way come to know my presence?'

To this he answered:

'I shall make it clear
in a few words and simply. Any dead man
whom you allow to enter where the blood is
will speak to you, and speak the truth; but those
deprived will grow remote again and fade.'

When he had prophesied, Teirêsias' shade
retired lordly to the halls of Death;
but I stood fast until my mother stirred,
moving to sip the black blood; then she knew me
and called out sorrowfully to me:

'Child,
how could you cross alive into this gloom
at the world's end?—No sight for living eyes;
great currents run between, desolate waters,
the Ocean first, where no man goes a journey
without ship's timber under him.

Say, now,
is it from Troy, still wandering, after years,
that you come here with ship and company?
Have you not gone at all to Ithaka?
Have you not seen your lady in your hall?'

She put these questions, and I answered her:

'Mother, I came here, driven to the land of death
in want of prophecy from Teirêsias' shade;
nor have I yet coasted Akhaia's hills

nor touched my own land, but have had hard roving
since first I joined Lord Agamémnon's host
by sea for Ilion, the wild horse country,
to fight the men of Troy.
But come now, tell me this, and tell me clearly,
what was the bane that pinned you down in Death?
Some ravaging long illness, or mild arrows
a-flying down one day from Artemis?
Tell me of Father, tell me of the son
I left behind me; have they still my place,
my honors, or have other men assumed them?
Do they not say that I shall come no more?
And tell me of my wife: how runs her thought,
still with her child, still keeping our domains,
or bride again to the best of the Akhaians?'

To this my noble mother quickly answered:

'Still with her child indeed she is, poor heart,
still in your palace hall. Forlorn her nights
and days go by, her life used up in weeping.
But no man takes your honored place. Telémakhos
has care of all your garden plots and fields,
and holds the public honor of a magistrate,
feasting and being feasted. But your father
is country bound and comes to town no more.
He owns no bedding, rugs, or fleecy mantles,
but lies down, winter nights, among the slaves,
rolled in old cloaks for cover, near the embers.
Or when the heat comes at the end of summer,
the fallen leaves, all round his vineyard plot,
heaped into windrows, make his lowly bed.
He lies now even so, with aching heart,
and longs for your return, while age comes on him.
So I, too, pined away, so doom befell me, not
that the keen-eyed huntress with her shafts
had marked me down and shot to kill me; not
that illness overtook me—no true illness
wasting the body to undo the spirit;
only my loneliness for you, Odysseus,
for your kind heart and counsel, gentle Odysseus,
took my own life away.'

                                        I bit my lip,
rising perplexed, with longing to embrace her,
and tried three times, putting my arms around her,
but she went sifting through my hands, impalpable
as shadows are, and wavering like a dream.
Now this embittered all the pain I bore,
and I cried in the darkness:

                                        'O my mother,
will you not stay, be still, here in my arms,
may we not, in this place of Death, as well,
hold one another, touch with love, and taste
salt tears' relief, the twinge of welling tears?
Or is this all hallucination, sent
against me by the iron queen, Perséphonê,
to make me groan again?'

                                        My noble mother
answered quickly:

                                        'O my child—alas,
most sorely tried of men—great Zeus's daughter,
Perséphonê, knits no illusion for you.
All mortals meet this judgment when they die.
No flesh and bone are here, none bound by sinew,
since the bright-hearted pyre consumed them down—
the white bones long exanimate—to ash;
dreamlike the soul flies, insubstantial.

You must crave sunlight soon.

                                        Note all things strange
seen here, to tell your lady in after days.'

So went our talk; then other shadows came,
ladies in company, sent by Perséphonê—
consorts or daughters of illustrious men—
crowding about the black blood.

                                        I took thought
how best to separate and question them,
and saw no help for it, but drew once more
the long bright edge of broadsword from my hip,
that none should sip the blood in company
but one by one, in order; so it fell
that each declared her lineage and name.

Here was great loveliness of ghosts! I saw
before them all, that princess of great ladies,
Tyro, Salmoneus' daughter, as she told me,
and queen to Krêtheus, a son of Aiolos.
She had gone daft for the river Enipeus,
most graceful of all running streams, and ranged
all day by Enipeus' limpid side,
whose form the foaming girdler of the islands,
the god who makes earth tremble, took and so
lay down with her where he went flooding seaward,
their bower a purple billow, arching round
to hide them in a sea-vale, god and lady.
Now when his pleasure was complete, the god
spoke to her softly, holding fast her hand:

'Dear mortal, go in joy! At the turn of seasons,
winter to summer, you shall bear me sons;
no lovemaking of gods can be in vain.
Nurse our sweet children tenderly, and rear them.
Home with you now, and hold your tongue, and tell
no one your lover's name—though I am yours,
Poseidon, lord of surf that makes earth tremble.'

He plunged away into the deep sea swell,
and she grew big with Pelias and Neleus,
powerful vassals, in their time, of Zeus.
Pelias lived on broad Iolkos seaboard
rich in flocks, and Neleus at Pylos.
As for the sons borne by that queen of women
to Krêtheus, their names were Aison, Pherês,
and Amytháon, expert charioteer.

Next after her I saw Antiopê,
daughter of Asopos. She too could boast
a god for lover, having lain with Zeus
and borne two sons to him: Amphion and
Zêthos, who founded Thebes, the upper city,
and built the ancient citadel. They sheltered
no life upon that plain, for all their power,
without a fortress wall.

Amphitrion's true wife, Alkmênê, mother,
as all men know, of lionish Heraklês,
conceived when she lay close in Zeus's arms;
and Megarê, high-hearted Kreon's daughter,
wife of Amphitrion's unwearying son.

I saw the mother of Oidipous, Epikastê,
whose great unwitting deed it was
to marry her own son. He took that prize
from a slain father; presently the gods
brought all to light that made the famous story.
But by their fearsome wills he kept his throne
in dearest Thebes, all through his evil days,
while she descended to the place of Death,
god of the locked and iron door. Steep down
from a high rafter, throttled in her noose,
she swung, carried away by pain, and left him
endless agony from a mother's Furies.

And I saw Khloris, that most lovely lady,
whom for her beauty in the olden time
Neleus wooed with countless gifts, and married.
She was the youngest daughter of Amphion,
son of Iasos. In those days he held
power at Orkhómenos, over the Minyai.
At Pylos then as queen she bore her children—
Nestor, Khromios, Periklýmenos,
and Pêro, too, who turned the heads of men
with her magnificence. A host of princes
from nearby lands came courting her; but Neleus
would hear of no one, not unless the suitor
could drive the steers of giant Iphiklos
from Phylakê—longhorns, broad in the brow,
so fierce that one man only, a diviner,
offered to round them up. But bitter fate
saw him bound hand and foot by savage herdsmen.
Then days and months grew full and waned, the year
went wheeling round, the seasons came again,
before at last the power of Iphiklos,
relenting, freed the prisoner, who foretold
all things to him. So Zeus's will was done.

And I saw Lêda, wife of Tyndareus,
upon whom Tyndareus had sired twins
indomitable: Kastor, tamer of horses,
and Polydeukês, best in the boxing ring.
Those two live still, though life-creating earth
embraces them: even in the underworld
honored as gods by Zeus, each day in turn
one comes alive, the other dies again.
Then after Lêda to my vision came
the wife of Aloeus, Iphimedeia,
proud that she once had held the flowing sea
and borne him sons, thunderers for a day,
the world-renowned Otos and Ephialtês.
Never were men on such a scale
bred on the plowlands and the grainlands, never
so magnificent any, after Orion.
At nine years old they towered nine fathoms tall,
nine cubits in the shoulders, and they promised
furor upon Olympos, heaven broken by battle cries,
the day they met the gods in arms.

mountain peak they meant to crown Olympos
and over Ossa Pelion's forest pile
for footholds up the sky. As giants grown
they might have done it, but the bright son of Zeus
by Lêto of the smooth braid shot them down
while they were boys unbearded; no dark curls
clustered yet from temples to the chin.

Then I saw Phaidra, Prokris; and Ariadnê,
daughter of Minos, the grim king. Theseus took her
aboard with him from Krete for the terraced land
of ancient Athens; but he had no joy of her.
Artemis killed her on the Isle of Dia
at a word from Dionysos.

                                    Maira, then,
and Klymênê, and that detested queen,
Eríphylê, who betrayed her lord for gold . . .
but how name all the women I beheld there,
daughters and wives of kings? The starry night
wanes long before I close.

                              Here, or aboard ship,
amid the crew, the hour for sleep has come.
Our sailing is the gods' affair and yours."

Homer speaking

Then he fell silent. Down the shadowy hall
the enchanted banqueters were still. Only
the queen with ivory pale arms, Arêtê, spoke,
saying to all the silent men:

                                    "Phaiákians,
how does he stand, now, in your eyes, this captain,
the look and bulk of him, the inward poise?
He is my guest, but each one shares that honor.
Be in no haste to send him on his way
or scant your bounty in his need. Remember
how rich, by heaven's will, your possessions are."

Then Ekheneôs, the old soldier, eldest
of all Phaiákians, added his word:

"Friends, here was nothing but our own thought spoken,
the mark hit square. Our duties to her majesty.
For what is to be said and done,
we wait upon Alkínoös' command."

At this the king's voice rang:

                                    "I so command—
as sure as it is I who, while I live,
rule the sea rovers of Phaiákia. Our friend
longs to put out for home, but let him be
content to rest here one more day, until
I see all gifts bestowed. And every man
will take thought for his launching and his voyage,
I most of all, for I am master here."

Odysseus, the great tactician, answered:

"Alkínoös, king and admiration of men,
even a year's delay, if you should urge it,
in loading gifts and furnishing for sea—
I too could wish it; better far that I
return with some largesse of wealth about me—
I shall be thought more worthy of love and courtesy
by every man who greets me home in Ithaka."

The king said:

                    "As to that, one word, Odysseus:
from all we see, we take you for no swindler—
though the dark earth be patient of so many,
scattered everywhere, baiting their traps with lies
of old times and of places no one knows.
You speak with art, but your intent is honest.
The Argive troubles, and your own troubles,
you told as a poet would, a man who knows the world.
But now come tell me this: among the dead
did you meet any of your peers, companions
who sailed with you and met their doom at Troy?
Here's a long night—an endless night—before us,
and no time yet for sleep, not in this hall.
Recall the past deeds and the strange adventures.
I could stay up until the sacred Dawn
as long as you might wish to tell your story."

Odysseus the great tactician answered:

"Alkínoös, king and admiration of men,
there is a time for story telling; there is
also a time for sleep. But even so,
if, indeed, listening be still your pleasure,
I must not grudge my part. Other and sadder
tales there are to tell, of my companions,
of some who came through all the Trojan spears,
clangor and groan of war,
only to find a brutal death at home—
and a bad wife behind it.

                    After Perséphonê,
icy and pale, dispersed the shades of women,
the soul of Agamémnon, son of Atreus,
came before me, sombre in the gloom,
and others gathered round, all who were with him
when death and doom struck in Aegísthos' hall.
Sipping the black blood, the tall shade perceived me,
and cried out sharply, breaking into tears;
then tried to stretch his hands toward me, but could not,
being bereft of all the reach and power
he once felt in the great torque of his arms.
Gazing at him, and stirred, I wept for pity,
and spoke across to him:

                    'O son of Atreus,
illustrious Lord Marshal, Agamémnon,
what was the doom that brought you low in death?
Were you at sea, aboard ship, and Poseidon
blew up a wicked squall to send you under,
or were you cattle-raiding on the mainland
or in a fight for some strongpoint, or women,
when the foe hit you to your mortal hurt?'

But he replied at once:

                                        'Son of Laërtês,
Odysseus, master of land ways and sea ways,
neither did I go down with some good ship
in any gale Poseidon blew, nor die
upon the mainland, hurt by foes in battle.
It was Aigísthos who designed my death,
he and my heartless wife, and killed me, after
feeding me, like an ox felled at the trough.
That was my miserable end—and with me
my fellows butchered, like so many swine
killed for some troop, or feast, or wedding banquet
in a great landholder's household. In your day
you have seen men, and hundreds, die in war,
in the bloody press, or downed in single combat,
but these were murders you would catch your breath at:
think of us fallen, all our throats cut, winebowl
brimming, tables laden on every side,
while blood ran smoking over the whole floor.
In my extremity I heard Kassandra,
Priam's daughter, piteously crying
as the traitress Klytaïmnestra made to kill her
along with me. I heaved up from the ground
and got my hands around the blade, but she
eluded me, that whore. Now would she close
my two eyes as my soul swam to the underworld
or shut my lips. There is no being more fell,
more bestial than a wife in such an action,
and what an action that one planned!
The murder of her husband and her lord.
Great god, I thought my children and my slaves
at least would give me welcome. But that woman,
plotting a thing so low, defiled herself
and all her sex, all women yet to come,
even those few who may be virtuous.'

He paused then, and I answered:

                                        'Foul and dreadful.
That was the way that Zeus who views the wide world
vented his hatred on the sons of Atreus—
intrigues of women, even from the start.

                                        Myriads
died by Helen's fault, and Klytaïmnestra
plotted against you half the world away.'

And he at once said:

                                        'Let it be a warning
even to you. Indulge a woman never,
and never tell her all you know. Some things
a man may tell, some he should cover up.
Not that I see a risk for you, Odysseus,
of death at your wife's hands. She is too wise,
too clear-eyed, sees alternatives too well,
Penélopê, Ikários' daughter—
that young bride whom we left behind—think of it!—
when we sailed off to war. The baby boy
still cradled at her breast—now he must be
a grown man, and a lucky one. By heaven,
you'll see him yet, and he'll embrace his father
with old fashioned respect, and rightly.

                                        My own
lady never let me glut my eyes
on my own son, but bled me to death first.
One thing I will advise, on second thought;
stow it away and ponder it.

                                        Land your ship
in secret on your island; give no warning.
The day of faithful wives is gone forever.

But tell me, have you any word at all
about my son's life? Gone to Orkhómenos
or sandy Pylos, can he be? Or waiting
with Meneláos in the plain of Sparta?
Death on earth has not yet taken Orestês.'

But I could only answer:

'Son of Atreus,
why do you ask these questions of me? Neither
news of home have I, nor news of him,
alive or dead. And empty words are evil.'

So we exchanged our speech, in bitterness,
weighed down by grief, and tears welled in our eyes,
when there appeared the spirit of Akhilleus,
son of Peleus; then Patróklos' shade,
and then Antílokhos, and then Aías,
first among all the Danaans in strength
and bodily beauty, next to prince Akhilleus.
Now that great runner, grandson of Aíakhos,
recognized me and called across to me:

'Son of Laërtês and the gods of old,
Odysseus, master mariner and soldier,
old knife, what next? What greater feat remains
for you to put your mind on, after this?
How did you find your way down to the dark
where these dimwitted dead are camped forever,
the after images of used-up men?'

I answered:
'Akhilleus, Peleus' son, strongest of all
among the Akhaians, I had need of foresight
such as Teirêsias alone could give
to help me, homeward bound for the crags of Ithaka.
I have not yet coasted Akhaia, not yet
touched my land; my life is all adversity.
But was there ever a man more blest by fortune
than you, Akhilleus? Can there ever be?
We ranked you with immortals in your lifetime,
we Argives did, and here your power is royal
among the dead men's shades. Think, then, Akhilleus:
you need not be so pained by death.'

To this
he answered swiftly:

'Let me hear no smooth talk
of death from you, Odysseus, light of councils.
Better, I say, to break sod as a farm hand
for some poor country man, on iron rations,
than lord it over all the exhausted dead.
Tell me, what news of the prince my son: did he
come after me to make a name in battle
or could it be he did not? Do you know
if rank and honor still belong to Peleus
in the towns of the Myrmidons? Or now, may be,
Hellas and Phthia spurn him, seeing old age
fetters him, hand and foot. I cannot help him
under the sun's rays, cannot be that man
I was on Troy's wide seaboard, in those days
when I made bastion for the Argives
and put an army's best men in the dust.
Were I but whole again, could I go now
to my father's house, one hour would do to make
my passion and my hands no man could hold
hateful to any who shoulder him aside.'

Now when he paused I answered:

'Of all that—
of Peleus' life, that is—I know nothing;
but happily I can tell you the whole story
of Neoptólemos, as you require.
In my own ship I brought him out from Skyros
to join the Akhaians under arms.

And I can tell you,
in every council before Troy thereafter
your son spoke first and always to the point;
no one but Nestor and I could out-debate him.
And when we formed against the Trojan line
he never hung back in the mass, but ranged
far forward of his troops—no man could touch him
for gallantry. Aye, scores went down before him
in hard fights man to man. I shall not tell
all about each, or name them all—the long
roster of enemies he put out of action,
taking the shock of charges on the Argives.
But what a champion his lance ran through
in Eurýpulos the son of Télephos! Keteians
in throngs around that captain also died—
all because Priam's gifts had won his mother
to send the lad to battle; and I thought
Memnon alone in splendor ever outshone him.

But one fact more: while our picked Argive crew
still rode that hollow horse Epeios built,
and when the whole thing lay with me, to open
the trapdoor of the ambuscade or not,
at that point our Danaan lords and soldiers
wiped their eyes, and their knees began to quake,
all but Neoptólemos. I never saw
his tanned cheek change color or his hand
brush one tear away. Rather he prayed me,
hand on hilt, to sortie, and he gripped
his tough spear, bent on havoc for the Trojans.
And when we had pierced and sacked Priam's tall city
he loaded his choice plunder and embarked
with no scar on him; not a spear had grazed him
nor the sword's edge in close work—common wounds
one gets in war. Arês in his mad fits
knows no favorites.'

But I said no more,
for he had gone off striding the field of asphodel,
the ghost of our great runner, Akhilleus Aiákidês,
glorying in what I told him of his son.

Now other souls of mournful dead stood by,
each with his troubled questioning, but one
remained alone, apart: the son of Télamon,
Aîas, it was—the great shade burning still
because I had won favor on the beachhead
in rivalry over Akhilleus' arms.
The Lady Thetis, mother of Akhilleus,
laid out for us the dead man's battle gear,
and Trojan children, with Athena,
named the Danaan fittest to own them. Would
god I had not borne the palm that day!
For earth took Aîas then to hold forever,
the handsomest and, in all feats of war,
noblest of the Danaans after Akhilleus.
Gently therefore I called across to him:

'Aîas, dear son of royal Télamon,
you would not then forget, even in death,
your fury with me over those accurst
calamitous arms?—and so they were, a bane
sent by the gods upon the Argive host.
For when you died by your own hand we lost
a tower, formidable in war. All we Akhaians
mourn you forever, as we do Akhilleus;
and no one bears the blame but Zeus.
He fixed that doom for you because he frowned
on the whole expedition of our spearmen.
My lord, come nearer, listen to our story!
Conquer your indignation and your pride.'

But he gave no reply, and turned away,
following other ghosts toward Erebos.
Who knows if in that darkness he might still
have spoken, and I answered?

                                But my heart
longed, after this, to see the dead elsewhere.

And now there came before my eyes Minos,
the son of Zeus, enthroned, holding a golden staff,
dealing out justice among ghostly pleaders
arrayed about the broad doorways of Death.

And then I glimpsed Orion, the huge hunter,
gripping his club, studded with bronze, unbreakable,
with wild beasts he had overpowered in life
on lonely mountainsides, now brought to bay
on fields of asphodel.

                           And I saw Títyos,
the son of Gaia, lying
abandoned over nine square rods of plain.
Vultures, hunched above him, left and right,
rifling his belly, stabbed into the liver,
and he could never push them off.

                              This hulk
had once committed rape of Zeus's mistress,
Lêto, in her glory, when she crossed
the open grass of Panopeus toward Pytho.

Then I saw Tántalos put to the torture:
in a cool pond he stood, lapped round by water
clear to the chin, and being athirst he burned
to slake his dry weasand with drink, though drink
he would not ever again. For when the old man
put his lips down to the sheet of water
it vanished round his feet, gulped underground,
and black mud baked there in a wind from hell.
Boughs, too, drooped low above him, big with fruit,
pear trees, pomegranates, brilliant apples,
luscious figs, and olives ripe and dark;
but if he stretched his hand for one, the wind
under the dark sky tossed the bough beyond him.

Then Sísyphos in torment I beheld
being roustabout to a tremendous boulder.
Leaning with both arms braced and legs driving,
he heaved it toward a height, and almost over,

but then a Power spun him round and sent
the cruel boulder bounding again to the plain.
Whereon the man bent down again to toil,
dripping sweat, and the dust rose overhead.
Next I saw manifest the power of Heraklês—
a phantom, this, for he himself has gone
feasting amid the gods, reclining soft
with Hêbê of the ravishing pale ankles,
daughter of Zeus and Hêra, shod in gold.
But, in my vision, all the dead around him
cried like affrighted birds; like Night itself
he loomed with naked bow and nocked arrow
and glances terrible as continual archery.
My hackles rose at the gold swordbelt he wore
sweeping across him: gorgeous intaglio
of savage bears, boars, lions with wildfire eyes,
swordfights, battle, slaughter, and sudden death—
the smith who had that belt in him, I hope
he never made, and never will make, another.
The eyes of the vast figure rested on me,
and of a sudden he said in kindly tones:

'Son of Laërtês and the gods of old,
Odysseus, master mariner and soldier,
under a cloud, you too? Destined to grinding
labors like my own in the sunny world?
Son of Kroníon Zeus or not, how many
days I sweated out, being bound in servitude
to a man far worse than I, a rough master!
He made me hunt this place one time
to get the watchdog of the dead: no more
perilous task, he thought, could be; but I
brought back that beast, up from the underworld;
Hermês and grey-eyed Athena showed the way.'

And Heraklês, down the vistas of the dead,
faded from sight; but I stood fast, awaiting
other great souls who perished in times past.
I should have met, then, god-begotten Theseus
and Peirithoös, whom both I longed to see,
but first came shades in thousands, rustling
in a pandemonium of whispers, blown together,
and the horror took me that Perséphonê
had brought from darker hell some saurian death's head.
I whirled then, made for the ship, shouted to crewmen
to get aboard and cast off the stern hawsers,
an order soon obeyed. They took their thwarts,
and the ship went leaping toward the stream of Ocean
first under oars, then with a following wind.

    The *Odyssey* is the first novel in Western literature and, according to many authorities, still the greatest. Adventure, romance, fidelity, treachery, sorcery, revenge, love—the range of themes is remarkable. Included are some of the memorable characters in literature: a nymph, sorceress, giants, sirens, cannibals, heroes, dupes, traitors, collaborators, the noble and ignoble. Many events are on a heroic scale but some are very personal and intimate. In one of the most touching little scenes in literature, Odysseus, disguised as a beggar, has finally returned to his palace. Accompanied by a loyal swineherd, Odysseus suggests that Eumaios the swineherd enter the palace first.

                                              While he spoke
an old hound, lying near, pricked up his ears
and lifted up his muzzle. This was Argos,
trained as a puppy by Odysseus,
but never taken on a hunt before
his master sailed for Troy. The young men, afterward,
hunted wild goats with him, and hare, and deer,
but he had grown old in his master's absence.
Treated as rubbish now, he lay at last
upon a mass of dung before the gates—
manure of mules and cows, piled there until
fieldhands could spread it on the king's estate.
Abandoned there, and half destroyed with flies,
old Argos lay.

                                        But when he knew he heard
Odysseus' voice nearby, he did his best
to wag his tail, nose down, with flattened ears,
having no strength to move nearer his master.
And the man looked away,
wiping a salt tear from his cheek; but he
hid this from Eumaios.

                                        ———Book XVII

Exercises

1. Not even a warrior as daring as Odysseus would visit the underworld just for a new experience. Why does he wish to visit Hades? Who does he want to meet and what does he expect to learn? What, in fact, does he learn that is useful and practical when he returns to the realm of the living?
2. Until he met Akhilleus, Odysseus had assumed that the afterlife was to be envied. What, according to Akhilleus and others was the true situation? What was lacking that frustrated those who were called the "dimwitted dead" (line 548)?
3. How does the Greek view of existence after death differ from the Mesopotamian version as expressed in the *Epic of Gilgamesh?*
4. If an epic "is a poem about men in action" (Aristotle), why does Homer include the episode of the old dog?

Summary

Introduced in this background chapter were some of the threads that were later woven into the glorious tapestry known as the Athenian Golden Age. The basic strand was the mainland geography that had so much to do with the development of Greek character and the expansion of commerce and trade.

Individualistic to the extreme, the Greeks had no organized religion and, consequently, no hierarchy of priests. Their pantheon of Olympian gods can be viewed as highly imaginative explanations of natural phenomena, as symbols of power, love, intellect, and so forth, and as the Greeks themselves, writ large.

*Control nature → anger)
love, power etc.
how Greeks would like
to be*

Our knowledge of early Greece has been obtained in large part from Hesiod and Homer. A commentator on the Archaic Period, Hesiod spoke as a farmer in, at the time, a losing battle with the aristocracy. Homer wrote, of course, of the Mycenaeans and the Heroic Age, but he spoke to Greeks of all periods.

The Greeks were highly competitive and this drive seems to partially explain the upward mobility of the land-poor farmer who migrated to a colony to improve his opportunities to get ahead. The rise of trade, a natural consequence of home cities and overseas colonies, was very competitive in the quality of goods and the expansion of markets. The key factor in the upward movement of the lower classes was the surplus value created by Greek artisans.

A society that labors from dawn to dusk just to make ends meet cannot expand its economy or find time for leisure activities. By producing more goods than they needed, the Greeks both expanded the economy and gained the leisure time they needed for other pursuits: education, gymnastics, philosophic–scientific investigations, politics.

Athens achieved dominance in large part because of a series of political reforms inaugurated, in turn, by Draco, Solon, Pisistratus, and Kleisthenes. The movement from tyranny to oligarchy to democracy was not smooth by any means but it was generally headed in the right direction.

Actually, the evolution of Athenian democracy was a natural consequence of the individual drive and initiative of a growing middle class of artisans, traders, and businessmen. A good income and some discretionary time made the middle class avid for more of each. To accomplish this they had to get involved in politics, to become part of the government that made and administered laws on coinage, trade, and taxes. Of course the four tribes did not meekly submit to political reforms but, given the clout of the new monied class, they had no alternative.

With the reforms of Kleisthenes, democratic government was well established, and Athens had convincingly demonstrated her capabilities as a political and economic power. Her military power, however, was put to the test by the Persians.

It is difficult today to even imagine the situation in Athens just before the Battle of Marathon. The might of the Persian armies was unquestioned. Fielded by a powerful totalitarian state and led by skilled professional soldiers, the Persian hordes overran and destroyed everything they attacked. Their strength lay in their overpowering numbers and the merciless discipline enforced by their officers. Individual action was inconceivable; mass assaults were the rule; heavy casualties were expected and were of no consequence. More cannon fodder could always be pressed into service.

The Athenians felt that they could do little more than slow the Persian juggernaut. No one, it seems, believed the Persians could be defeated. Even though the coming battlefield was on home ground, only a few miles outside the city, the odds were enormous.

The defeat at Marathon was totally unexpected; it profoundly shocked and enraged the Persians. Consequently, the second invasion of Greece—some ten years later—was supposed to teach the Greeks a lesson for the loss of face at Marathon. The army and navy would sweep the land and the sea and the arrogant Greeks would be humiliated. By this time the Greeks were, if anything, even prouder and their military power was considerably greater. The battle at Thermopylai was lost against overwhelming odds but, from then on, the Greeks outsmarted and outfought the enemy and profoundly changed the course of history.

In one form or another the questions posed by the Ionian philosophers are still being asked today. If the Greeks had made only one contribution to Western civilization, the search for *what is* and the introduction of speculative philosophy are more than sufficient to earn the gratitude of all humankind.

Culture and Human Values

During the Dorian in-migrations of ca. 1100–800 B.C. there was a major step backward into the Greek Dark Ages. In every sense of the term it was a period of chaos. Sometime after 850 B.C. or so there began a long period of adjustment as a new, more stable society began to take shape. Just where the adjustment matured into the balance of the Golden Age is difficult to say. From 490 to 480 was very likely the final decade of adjustment, from the victory at Marathon to the triumph at Salamis. Defeating the Persians seemed to provide the inspiration necessary to take the confident stride into classical Greek civilization.

Annotated Bibliography

Andrews, Antony. *The Greek Tyrants*. Dover, N.H.: Hutchinson University Library, 1956. Excellent short account.

Boardman, John. *The Greeks Overseas: Their Early Colonies and Trade*. New York: Thames and Hudson, 1982. An authoritative study.

Burn, A. R. *Persia and the Greeks: The Defense of the West*. Stanford, Calif.: Stanford University Press, 1984. A stirring account of the heroic battles that set the stage for the Greek Golden Age.

Creasy, E., and Mitchell, J. P. *Twenty Decisive Battles of the World*. New York: Macmillan, 1964. Colonel Mitchell added five battles to Creasy's 1851 classic.

Desborough, Vincent R. *The Greek Dark Ages*. New York: St. Martin's Press, 1972. A highly recommended survey.

Ehrenberg, Victor. *From Solon to Sokrates: Greek History During the 6th and 5th Centuries B.C.* New York: Methuen, 1973. An excellent study of the evolution of Athens towards its Golden Age.

Finley, M. I. *Early Greece: The Bronze and Archaic Ages*. New York: W. W. Norton & Co., 1982. Fine survey.

———. *The World of Odysseus*. New York: Pelican Books, 1979. Good orientation by a recognized scholar.

Forrest, William G. *The Emergence of Greek Democracy: 800–400 B.C.* New York: McGraw-Hill, 1966. Brief, thoughtful introduction.

Huxley, George L. *The Early Ionians*. Atlantic Highlands, N.J.: Humanities Press, 1966. A perspective on the emergence of philosophy.

Schein, Seth L. *The Mortal Hero: An Introduction to Homer's ILIAD*. Berkeley: University of California Press, 1984. A clear presentation for nonspecialists.

Vivante, Paolo. *Homer*. New Haven: Yale University Press, 1985. An enthusiastic introduction for the general reader.

General Studies of Greek Culture. These works cover the whole period through the Hellenistic Age and will not be listed again.

Asimov, Isaac. *The Greeks: A Great Adventure*. Boston: Houghton Mifflin, 1965. Informal and lively.

Barr, Stringfellow. *The Will of Zeus; A History of Greece from the Origins of Hellenic Culture to the Death of Alexander*. Philadelphia: J. B. Lippincott, 1961. Whenever possible Barr lets the Greeks tell their own tale. No one can tell it better.

Beye, Charles Rowan. *Ancient Greek Literature and Society*. Anchor Press, 1975. An interesting and sometimes pungent analysis of the beauty of classical Greek and the deficiencies of Latin.

Bullfinch, Thomas. *Mythology*. New York: The New American Library, n.d. The recognized standard work.

Bury, J. B. *History of Greece*. New York: St. Martin's Press, 1975. Still the standard history and for all the right reasons.

Chamoux, Francois. *The Civilization of Greece*. New York: Simon & Schuster, 1965. A handsome cultural history with fine illustrations.

de Romilly, Jacqueline. *A Short History of Greek Literature*. Trans. Lillian Doherty. Chicago: University of Chicago Press, 1985. Illuminating discussions of all the significant figures.

Eliot, Alexander. *The Horizon Concise History of Greece*. New York: Horizon Press, 1973. Packed with information; fascinating reading.

Finley, M. I., *The Legacy of Greece: A New Appraisal*. New York: Oxford University Press, 1981. After a lifetime of study a noted classicist offers his mature assessment of the Greek achievement.

Marrou, H. I. *A History of Education in Antiquity*. Madison: University of Wisconsin Press, 1982. A classic modern study that covers the entire ancient world.

Translations of Original Material

Fitzgerald, Robert. *The Iliad of Homer*. Garden City, N.Y.: Doubleday & Company, 1975. And *The Odyssey of Homer*. Garden City, N.Y.: Doubleday & Company, 1961. Each generation should have its own translation of Homer and these are superb. See also Hogan, James C. *A Guide to the Iliad; based on the translation by Robert Fitzgerald*. Garden City, N.Y.: Doubleday & Company, 1979.

NOTE: New archeological evidence about Aegean civilizations can be found in periodicals such as: *National Geographic, Smithsonian, Science News, Archeology*.

5

Hellenic Athens: The Fulfillment of the Good Life

Athens: A City of Hope

The city of Athens in 461 B.C. must have been an exciting place in which to live. It was prosperous and strong and, though no one knew it at the time, about to enter its Golden Age, that incredible era (ca. 460–430 B.C.) during which the resident artists, writers, statesmen, and philosophers would establish a society based on human values and on a commitment to truth, beauty, and justice. It was not a perfect society—far from it—but it did aspire to perfection. For a fleeting moment life was enveloped in the lusty embrace of a society that dared to compete with the gods.

Athenian Greeks may have been the most verbal people in the ancient world. Blessed with a sophisticated language rich in vocabulary and capable of infinite subtleties, they talked, discussed, argued, and debated everything under the sun: politics, society, love, and especially philosophy, because the intellectuals of the city were fascinated by the world of ideas. Herakleitean belief in constant change had its supporters, while others contended that reality could be expressed through numerical relationships, as Pythagoras had said. Entering into the debate came new ideas from Elea, the prosperous Greek colony in southern Italy. Led by Parmenides (par-MEN-uh-deez; born ca. 514 B.C.), the Eleatic School refused to accept the Herakleitean idea that nothing *is,* that the universe was in a constant state of *becoming.*

As the very basis of their thought they stated that whatever is *real* must be permanent and unchanging. If one turns the statement around, it may seem more logical: anything that constantly changes its state of Being cannot be real. Furthermore, they attacked the method of the Ionian philosophers by pointing out that the Ionians depended entirely upon their senses for the discovery of truth, trusting their sight, their sense of feeling, their hearing, the senses of smell and taste to lead them to valid conclusions. The Eleatics were quick to point out that the senses cannot be trusted. Of course this contention is easy to support; the sense impression that one receives depends quite as much on the state of the receiving sense organ as upon the thing itself. (The color-blind person sees a green traffic light as a sort of neutral gray; the person with "normal" sight sees it as green. Which is it really? For that matter, when one person sees "green" and another person agrees, are they really seeing the same color?) If the senses cannot be trusted as a guide to truth, what can? The Eleatic philosophers asserted that only the mind is a sure guide, and they could point to such truths as those found by the geometers like Pythagoras to support their theory that the mind, without the aid of the senses, can arrive at truth. As a matter of fact, these thinkers were much like the Pythagoreans, and form a sort of bridge between Pythagoras and Plato, who will be discussed later. In the middle of the fifth century, Parmenides visited Athens at a time when Sokrates would have been about twenty years old. The two men could have met at that time.

The development of material philosophy reached its high point with the Athenian Leucippus, and his student, Demokritos (Di-MOK-ruh-toss; ca. 460–370 B.C.). Demokritos synthesized the attempts of the Milesians to understand the physical world and developed a theory of the material world that could not be verified until the twentieth century. He postulated Greek atomic theory, apparently using no more and no less than the power of his mind. According to Demokritos all matter consists of minute particles called *atoma* (unable to be cut). These atoms exist in space, combine and separate because of "necessity," and represent a strict conservation of matter and energy, i.e., the same number of atoms always exists; only the combinations differ. Contemporary nuclear physics confirms a strict conservation of matter and energy when taken together but identifies probability rather than necessity in terms of causality. As everyone knows, atoms do exist and some of them can be divided.

FIGURE 5.1 *Stone carving of theatrical mask at Epbesos, Turkey, where the Graeco-Roman theatre seated 25,000 spectators.*

Following the Persian wars, Athens was optimistic and hopeful, filled with democratic pride and a confusion of ideas. Furthermore, the entire city had been burned by the Persians and needed to be rebuilt. The possibilities for growth and progress lay everywhere, but direction for human growth was needed. In terms of the development of the spirit, Aeschylus (ESK-i-lus), the playwright-artist in a time of chaos and early adjustment, was to point the way.

The Drama and Aeschylus

Before speaking specifically of the plays of Aeschylus, it might be well to mention something about the history of the drama. It began in Greece, as it was to do later in the Middle Ages in Europe, as a part of the worship service. Originally the priest spoke individual parts, while a chorus chanted responses. An original and almost mythical dramatist, Thespis (THES-pis), began to transform this rite into secular drama during the Archaic period.

Theatres and Festivals

The theatres were always in the open air, with the seats for spectators ascending the side of a hill. At the bottom of the hill a round flat area (the orchestra) provided a space in which the chorus danced and sang and chanted, and which had as its center the statue or altar of the god. Back of this and facing the audience was a long low building (the skene) with a room at either end and a platform between the two rooms. The rooms were for dressing and storage and the chief actors performed on the platform above and behind the chorus. (See figure 8.7.)

Since they functioned as places of education and entertainment for most of the populace of a city-state, theatres were very large; seating was for 13,000 at Epidauros and 18,000 in Athens. These semicircular stadiums featured acoustics so fine that the actors could be understood fifty rows above the stage; however, because facial expressions could not be seen from this distance, performers wore large masks of easily recognizable character types (figure 5.1). To compensate for distortions when viewed from high above, actors wore clog shoes that were about eight inches high, a convention that also contributed to the larger-than-life image of the subjects. Violence always took place offstage and was reported either by a messenger or another character. One stage set served throughout the play, and the only stage machinery was the *mechane,* a crane that transported the actors who played gods. This was the celebrated *deus ex machina,* or "god from a machine." Permanent stage sets, masks, clogs, offstage violence, dance, and music all challenged spectators to use their imaginations. (See also chapter 8.)

Drama festivals were held throughout Greece, but the one at Athens in honor of the god Dionysos (Di-uh-NYE-sos, and several other pronunciations) was the most important. Before the festival a number of playwrights would submit their plays to a board of judges, and the plays of four dramatists would be chosen for presentation, each one on a different day. In Aeschylus's time, each dramatist submitted a trilogy (a series of three plays on one theme) and a satyr play, which was a bawdy comedy presented at the end of the trilogy. A wealthy citizen paid the production costs for a playwright in the hope that his dramatist would win the first prize. A slight charge was made for seats at the drama, but in the fifth century the city paid for the admission of any citizens who could not afford it. Thus, if a writer had a message he wished to give to the entire population of his city, the drama was an almost perfect vehicle.

Aeschylus

Aeschylus lived from 525 to 456 B.C. and was, therefore, a part of the great development of Greece as a whole, and Athens in particular. He was a soldier at the Battle of Marathon, a fact he had recorded on his tomb rather than that he was a dramatist. An aristocrat by birth, his drama presents a synthesis between the old ideas and those of the most enthusiastic democrats. Aeschylus has sometimes been accused of being much more of a preacher than a dramatist, for all of his plays carry a clearly stated message; yet Edith Hamilton points out that he was so much a dramatist that when the dramatic form did not exist, he invented it. Certainly before his time the cast contained only one speaking actor and the chorus. Aeschylus introduced a second speaking actor so that we could have the possibility of dialogue, real conflict, and resolution between two people and two ideas.

Aeschylus wrote about ninety plays, of which seven survive. Of these, only the trilogy called the *Oresteia* (O-res-TYE-ya), the story of Orestes, son of Agamemnon, will be discussed here. The trilogy consists of *Agamemnon,* the *Libation Bearers,* and the *Eumenides* (you-MEN-i-deez). The first and third plays are included in this

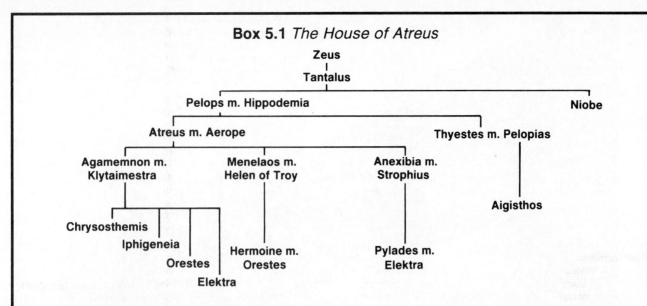

Box 5.1 *The House of Atreus*

Zeus
|
Tantalus

Pelops m. Hippodemia — Niobe

Atreus m. Aerope — Thyestes m. Pelopias

Agamemnon m. Klytaimestra — Menelaos m. Helen of Troy — Anexibia m. Strophius

Aigisthos

Chrysosthemis
Iphigeneia
Orestes
Elektra

Hermoine m. Orestes

Pylades m. Elektra

Like most old Greek families the roots go back to Zeus, in this case through Tantalus, a mortal who was permitted nectar and ambrosia at the table of the gods. In order to trick the gods and show them as fallible Tantalus hosted a banquet and served them a stew made of his son Pelops. The furious immortals dispatched Tantalus to Hades to suffer eternal hunger and thirst for he was guilty of *hubris* (overbearing pride), the worst of all sins. The family curse continued with the sons of Pelops. Thyestes (thigh-ES-teez) seduced Aerope, his brother's wife; Atreus, in revenge, killed three of Thyestes' four sons (Aigisthos survived) and served them to their father as a meat course. In his *Oresteia* trilogy Aeschylus dramatizes the working out of the curse.

chapter, but all three will be considered here as if they were three acts of a single drama. They relate the story of the evolution of a system of justice dominated by tradition, fear, and personal revenge into a new justice administered by the law courts of a free society.

Agamemnon

Agamemnon begins in what Aeschylus must have regarded as the rural district of Argos, in front of the palace of Agamemnon, on what should be the most joyous day in ten years, for word has just been received that Troy has fallen, the ten-year Trojan War is over, the Greeks have been victorious, and Agamemnon, the great king, is returning. It should be a day of rejoicing, but the watchman on the palace who first sees the signal fires announcing the victory mutters darkly about the evil deeds that have been going on within the palace; the chorus refuses to believe in the message of the signal fires and spends much of the first part of the play recounting the sacrifice that was a part of the beginning of the war.

Their particular concern is with the death of Iphigeneia (If-i-je-NY-ya), the daughter of Agamemnon and Klytaïmnestra (Kly-tem-NES-tra) at Aulis (AW-lis) ten years before. The myth tells us that at the beginning of the war the brother kings, Agamemnon and Menelaos (Men-uh-LAY-os), had assembled the Greek army at the port of Aulis for embarkation to Troy, but after the troops were gathered Agamemnon had offended the goddess Artemis (ART-uh-mis) by violating her injunction against hunting. In retaliation she refused to grant favorable

winds to the fleet unless Agamemnon offered his daughter as a sacrifice. Faced with a choice of standing firm against restless troops anxious for battle or sacrificing his daughter, Agamemnon, truly the son of his father, made the worst choice. He compounded the evil by sending for Iphigeneia on the pretext that she was to be married. (See box 5.1.)

The chorus also calls our attention to Agamemnon's cousin, Aigisthos (i-JIS-thos), who now occupies the bed of the warring king. Moreover, Klytaïmnestra has not only taken a lover, she has dared to act as a man, to govern with a firm hand as a man would govern. What should be a day of rejoicing at the return of the victorious king starts as a day when all the dark collective guilt of the past is forced on the awareness of the chorus and the audience.

Finally Agamemnon himself returns (figure 5.2), accompanied by Kassandra (ka-SAN-druh), a princess from Troy who has received the unfortunate gift from Apollo that she can prophesy the future, but that no one will believe her prophesies. The last is not of immediate concern, though it will become important later in the play. What is of importance is that she has come on the same ship with the king, and now appears with him in his chariot. Of course Greek heroes were expected to take captive maidens as their mistresses, but the custom was that they would be brought home in a ship with the rest of the captured booty, and would serve as slaves in the household of their new master. Kassandra's appearance in Agamemnon's chariot is another act that will anger Klytaïmnestra.

FIGURE 5.2 *Entrance to the Palace of Agamemnon at Mycenae. In the right background is the Argive plain across which Agamemnon marched after landing at Tiryns. To the left is the entrance way to the Lion Gate (see figure 3.9) where Klytaïmnestra awaits the king.*

Upon his arrival at the palace, Klytaïmnestra greets her husband so effusively that one recognizes this as a set speech, the sort of thing that is said when a returning hero is presented the keys to the city on the courthouse steps. Symbolically there follows one of the most important events of the drama, for the wife asks Agamemnon to enter the palace on a carpet dyed with a crimson (or purple) dye, which is so costly that it is reserved for the gods. Agamemnon refuses at first, but is persuaded by his wife. The act shows a pride too great for men; this mortal is stepping out of his proper zone and into the area reserved for the gods. Quite aside from his human errors, which angered his wife, this prideful act alone is sufficient to mark him for death.

After he has gone into the palace, we have one of the most interesting scenes of the play, for Kassandra tries to tell the chorus that Agamemnon is to be killed. Raging back and forth in an almost animal fury, probably in opposition to the strophe and antistrophe of the chorus, she tries to tell them of the murder being committed and urges them to break down the palace doors and prevent the deed. Casting aside all of her prophetic regalia, she finally shouts, "I say you shall see Agamemnon dead!" The chorus remains dumb and stupid, refusing to act. Then Kassandra, knowing she is to be murdered, meekly goes into the palace, hoping only that her death blow will be sure and swift.

Only when they hear Agamemnon cry out that he has been struck does the chorus nearly rouse itself to action. For the first time in Greek drama the members of the chorus speak as individuals, each with a short solo speech. The mood reaches a crescendo in the middle of this brief section when they are almost ready to break in and catch the murderers red-handed. Then apathy takes over, and at the end of the sequence they agree to wait until they really know what has happened. They do not have long to wait.

The palace doors are flung open, revealing the bodies of Agamemnon and Kassandra, with Klytaïmnestra proudly announcing that she has done this deed. The chorus mutters its protest, and Klytaïmnestra tries to calm them by suggesting that she is only the instrument of fate and the ancient curse on the house. Finally Aigisthos appears, rattles his sword a bit, and tells them to go home. The play closes as the chorus rather childishly tells the murderers just to wait until Orestes comes home to take his vengeance.

What does all this mean? It is interesting that the image most often presented in the play is that of a net or web. The purple carpet is referred to as a web, and Agamemnon has a net thrown over him in his bath so that he cannot resist while the murderous blows are being struck. Perhaps Aeschylus felt that this net was the old traditionalism, the belief in fate, and the idea of justice as revenge. Certainly the chorus is bound up in this web, since many of their speeches warn against pride, against wealth that breeds pride, and against any sort of innovation. Their wisdom follows the ancestral traditions hindering action. If they had acted by breaking down the door of the palace, they might have done more than merely break through a door; they might have broken the barrier between themselves and freedom. Curiously, Kassandra tries to inspire them to act, but she cannot do it. She, too, is caught in the net. The key to this lies in her entrance into the palace to meet her known fate. Even the chorus admonishes her that to delay her death even by a short time is to gain a small victory, but she answers that the time of her doom has arrived. She, too, is enmeshed by a belief in a fate that rules her life. Of all the characters in the play, only Klytaïmnestra seems free to act as a human being. True, she falls back upon the curse on the House of Atreus at the end, but this is only to placate the chorus in terms that they can understand. But her action is murderous and destructive, a type of freedom that cannot be permitted in a community of human beings. So, at the end of the first play we have two conditions of human existence: that of the chorus, which is always looking backward to tradition for guidance in their lives, and that of Klytaïmnestra, whose wild destructive freedom will destroy human society. Aeschylus's job in the remaining two plays of the trilogy is to free one segment of society and restrict the other.

Libation Bearers

The second play in the trilogy, the *Libation Bearers,* is principally a transition play designed to bring the problem to a head. Orestes as a young man returns from Phocis (rhymes with *focus*) where he has been reared. He bears with him the command of Apollo to kill his mother and Aigisthos to avenge the murder of his father. It is interesting that this is the command of Apollo, a member of the new generation of progressive gods. On the other hand, we have the old tradition coming from clan and tribal governments that anyone who spills kindred blood will be hounded to his death by the Furies. Orestes is caught between two seemingly equally forceful commands; in his killing of his mother, he is damned if he does, and damned if he doesn't. But he does return, and in what must be the most awkwardly handled recognition scene in the history of drama, he is reunited with his sister Elektra (i-LEK-tra) and finally commits the murder. As the play ends he is set upon by the Furies and driven from the stage.

Eumenides

The word *Eumenides* may be translated as the *Gracious Ones,* and the change of the Furies (the Erinyes [i-RIN-e-eez]) to the Eumenides is the point of the third play in the series. The scene opens in Delphi at the shrine of Apollo, with the Furies temporarily sleeping, and with Orestes as a suppliant to the god having performed all the rites for the cleansing of guilt. He is told to go to the Temple of Athena on the Akropolis in Athens where he will receive justice. The movement in the trilogy is interesting to note at this point. *Agamemnon* started in the darkness with the gloomy mutterings of the watchman and the chorus in rural Argos. Now, in *Eumenides* we come to full light in the city of Athens. Because of the clash of ideas, the city is the place where new thought is generated, and Athens is chosen not only because it was the leading city of Greece, but also because it was Aeschylus's own city. The patriotic gesture is the appropriate one.

In Athens the chorus of Furies lament that they, the older gods, are being shamed and dishonored, and predict that if Orestes is allowed to go free, children will murder their parents at will, and that they, the Furies, will bring a blight upon the land. At this point Athena arrives and, after hearing the preliminaries of the case, asserts that the cause is too grave for a god to decide, and too grave, also, for a mortal man. She then sends out for a jury of twelve citizens of Athens to hear the case and render a verdict. What appears to be contradiction may be resolved in this way. A trial by a jury transcends the judgment of a mortal man since, in the course of time, a jury will build up a body of law that will provide a rational basis for judgment, and thus go beyond the limits of on-the-spot mortal judgment.

With the jury selected and sworn in, the evidence in the case is presented, with Apollo acting as attorney for the defense. A modern reader must admit that his case—that the mother is not related to the child, but is only a sort of animated baby carriage—sounds pretty flimsy, but fortunately that is almost beside the point. After the presentation of evidence, Athena establishes the court, the Areopagus (are-ee-OP-uh-gus; located at the foot of the Akropolis), and charges it with its duties as the highest court of justice. Her speech, given elsewhere in context, cannot be quoted often enough:

> Here reverence
> For law and inbred fear among my people
> Shall hold their hands from evil night and day,
> Only let them not tamper with the laws,
> But keep the fountain pure and sweet to drink.
> I warn you not to banish from your lives
> All terror but to seek the mean between
> Autocracy and anarchy; and in this way
> You shall possess in ages yet unborn
> An impregnable fortress of liberty
> Such as no people has throughout the world.

The tied vote of the jury follows, with Athena casting her vote for the acquittal of Orestes. There is, however, another interpretation of the voting process that is more closely attuned to the situation, more subtle, more Greek. This second version posits a jury of eleven persons and a vote of six to five for conviction. When Athena casts her vote for acquittal the result is a six–six division, which is, of course, a hung jury. Orestes is acquitted in either case but a hung jury, in a case of matricide, is as close as Orestes can come and still walk out of the court vowing a perpetual alliance between Argos and Athens. We must also consider the curious dramatic structure here when the hero of the drama can walk out with only two-thirds of the play finished. The reader must realize that Orestes is not the hero; *the real hero is an idea of justice*—of people getting along with people in such a way as to promote freedom and happiness for all.

The last third of the play deals with the conversion of the Erinyes to the Eumenides. These ancient and immortal hag-goddesses have real power, which cannot simply be taken from them by force; and they start the dialogue with their usual threats of civil violence and sterility in the city of Athens. But Athena, the goddess not only of wisdom but also of persuasion, slowly reveals to the Furies the role they can play and the worship they will receive as defenders of the city. Finally the Eumenides agree to accept their new role, and the drama closes with a procession, probably including the citizens of Athens, to the altar of the Eumenides on the site of the Areopagus.

As far as the significance of the play is concerned, Aeschylus probably had several specific messages for the Athens of his time. The court Athena founds is the old Areopagus, which represented the conservative element of the city as opposed to the more democratic Council. Four years before the production of the play, the Areopagus had been stripped of much of its authority, and perhaps Aeschylus is protesting this action. On the other hand, he may be considering the development of the Areopagus as the real birth of the polis (PO-lis), the city–state that through law was to give people freedom under a democratic government. For us, this latter is the significant interpretation.

In terms of the problem we noticed at the end of the discussion of *Agamemnon,* we have a much broader and more relevant meaning than the local Athenian one. The problem was that of bringing all the people out of the net of bondage to tradition and fate and, at the same time, limiting the freedom of such a person as Klytaïmnestra. The universal significance, which is our chief concern, may be described in the following way:

The people, as represented by the old chorus in *Agamemnon,* are set free simply because their eyes are turned forward rather than backward. No longer do they act under the shadow of old tradition and old superstition, since each case is tried in terms of its own evidence, and decided in terms of a law that has been made by human beings. In *Eumenides,* Aeschylus is setting forth the idea that people are to establish the limits for their own zone of action, limits determined by the amount of freedom each person can have while still maintaining the freedom of others. The same thing applies to the Klytaïmnestras of this new world. Their acts will also be brought to this tribunal to be checked by the same standard. Humanity—at least humanity in Athens—is now free for individual action for the best interests of the person and the state.

One more point is of interest here. The Furies insisted on rule by fear, and one is tempted to discard the element of fear in this new order toward which Aeschylus is pointing. But Athena insists that a certain amount of fear is still necessary. While Aeschylus was optimistic about human nature and human behavior in an atmosphere of freedom, he was not willing to go completely overboard with his hope. He knew that in spite of laws and courts there is in human nature a tendency to act completely selfishly, without any consideration for others. To curb this tendency an inbred fear must remain, more deeply felt than the purely intellectual respect for law. A number of critics have seen in the

■
FIGURE 5.3 *Marble bust from Tivoli inscribed with the name of Perikles. Roman copy after a bronze original of 450–425 B.C. The bronze original was possibly by Kresilas and placed on the Akropolis after the death of Perikles. Though the original work was probably a full figure this copy conforms to the Roman tradition of portrait busts, thus accounting for the feeling that this is an incomplete composition. British Museum, London. Reproduced by permission of the Trustees of the British Museum.*

conversion of the Furies to the Gracious Ones a sort of birth of conscience. If this is true, the conversion must be to a very sophisticated conscience rather than the old primordial cultural fear. This must be an ethical conscience that while incorporating some element of fear, is chiefly concerned with the safety, even the total welfare, of the group. Conscience, of course, is the internal regulating force within each individual by which the morality of the culture is maintained. This may be the type of "fear" Athena maintains; perhaps we do not stretch the meaning of the play to think of the conversion of the old superstitious fears into household gods as the beginning of ethical conscience. At least it is a point to think about.

The Athens of Perikles

After such leaders as Cimon and Ephialtes made the laws of Kleisthenes ever more democratic, we come to the long and glorious rule of Perikles (PAIR-i-kleez). Perikles was first elected as general-in-chief in 461 and, with the exception of two years when he was voted out of office, directed Athenian affairs until his death in 429 (figure 5.3).

One historian has estimated the population of Attica (the city of Athens and the surrounding territory it governed) at about 230,000 people. Of these, 40,000 were free male citizens, the actual voting population that participated in the democracy; 40,000 were women who, at best, were second-class citizens; 50,000 were foreign-born; and 100,000 were slaves. One must remember that in all of our discussion of the glories of Athenian democracy, we are talking about only the 40,000 free men. The rest of the free people participated only on the periphery, and the slaves had no voice at all. Nevertheless it is a miracle of history that a small group of less than a quarter of a million people, in about a single century starting with the second defeat of the Persians, could have produced three of the great writers of tragic drama and one of the great comedy writers in the history of literature, and two or more of the philosophers whose ideas still give shape to our lives, great architecture, and magnificent sculpture. The music and the painting of the time are lost, but in the contemporary writings music is regarded as the highest and the best developed of the arts, and sculpture was considered as a secondary art in comparison with painting.

Finally, and most significant of all, the people, at least in the first generation of this century, produced a life-style that in its freedom for the individual, coupled with a concern for the welfare of the state as a whole, has been envied and emulated by the Western world ever since. This was the life-style toward which the plays of Aeschylus pointed. The ideal of this life-style is nowhere better stated than by C. M. Bowra (*The Greek Experience*), who writes, "A man served his state best by being himself in the full range of his nobility, and not by sacrificing it to some abstract notion of political power or expediency."

Life at this time was largely out-of-doors. The courts and the council met on the Pynx Hill opposite the Akropolis and heard matters of state argued. The town assembly met also on the Pynx, which could seat up to 18,000 people. Life was vigorous in the Agora (AG-uh-ruh), a level area at the foot of the Akropolis, the marketplace for the city and also the place where the men went to meet each other and to argue politics and philosophy. Here visiting teachers would lecture to any audience they could attract, and one assumes that they did a thriving business. The Greeks were a dynamic and talkative people, and the issues of the day were thrashed out in the Agora with most of the free men listening and joining in the debate.

When not in the Agora, many men spent their time in the gymnasia. These were parks set aside for physical exercise not far from the city limits of Athens. These provided a running-track, a wrestling-ground, and other facilities for exercise, and provided, as well, for shady walks and places for discussion, since the ideal was the development of the whole man, with full development of both mind and body. Later, Plato's Academy and Aristotle's Lyceum were to be founded in surroundings like those of the gymnasia.

FIGURE 5.4 *Athenian silver drachma, ca. 450 B.C. Diameter 15.5 mm., weight 4.26 gm. Obverse (heads): Archaic head of Athena wearing a crested helmet with three upright olive leaves. Reverse: Owl with olive spray at the left and A θ E at the right, standing for Athens. Known as the "owls of Athena," these coins dominated the Eastern Mediterranean for six hundred years. Museum of Fine Arts, Boston. Theodora Wilbour Fund No. 1.*

Home was the place where the Greek man went when there was no place else to go, and it is interesting that in all of the archeological remains, we have little indication of the nature of the private houses. Public buildings and palaces were built to last, while individual homes were not. We do know that Greek homes were built in the standard Mediterranean pattern of windowless walls adjoining the street with inner courts for coolness and privacy. The homes to which Greek men retired were, in effect, not their houses but those of their wives. Wives were not citizens and could not vote but they did run the household: raising children, supervising servants, going to market, and keeping household accounts.

Perikles did not make many great changes in the government of the city. His role, instead, was to maintain the democratic values and the human values that had already come into being. In order to do this, he rebuilt the city as a proper home for these ideals. Probably the Agora was first rebuilt, since it formed a marketplace for ideas as well as things, and later he commissioned the building of the Parthenon (447–438 B.C.) and other temples on the Akropolis. The care with which the architect shaped the building to conform to human standards rather than rigid mathematical and physical rules suggests the complete devotion of the Athenians to the standard of human values.

The balance the Athenians maintained between individualism and the welfare of the state was a most delicate one. During the Age of Perikles there was a shift towards individuality and away from the general, especially in the welfare of other city–states. This was first noticeable in the international relations of the city, for it converted the Delian League into what was really an Athenian empire, and moved the treasury from the island of Delos to Athens. As a matter of fact, the Parthenon and other buildings were constructed with money that belonged to this treasury. When member cities objected, they were simply told that if Athens were to assume the burden of protection for the league as a whole, Athens alone should be able to decide what to do with the money that was paid into the treasury (figure 5.4).

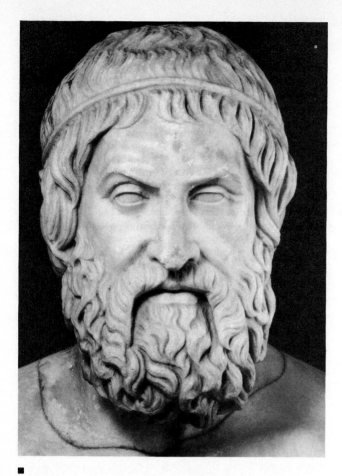

■

FIGURE 5.5 *Portrait bust of Sophokles. Marble, ca. 340 B.C. British Museum, London. Reproduced by courtesy of the Trustees of the British Museum.*

As an international power, Athens became autocratic, and within the city the older values of reverence to the gods and to the state, ideas that had been triumphant at Marathon and that Aeschylus had preached in his plays, moved toward self-centered individuality. This metamorphosis probably had its start with the teachings of the atomists like Demokritos, who argued for complete materialism, even with the gods, and ascribed all change to accident. In such a world, the only human goal can be material pleasure, since with accident as the ruling force, nothing about the future can be predicted, and the gods who are material and subject to chance offer no guidance or inspiration.

Probably taking their cue from the atomists, leading teachers of Athens became the sophists (sof [o as in *hot*]-ists). This group had a leader in Protagoras (pro-TAG-uh-rus; ca. 481–411 B.C.), a high-minded thinker and teacher whose chief pronouncement was that *man is the measure of all things*. Taken by itself, this is simply a slogan-like reassertion of the idea of human values we have already praised so highly in this Greek state. But dangers also appear. If humankind is the measure, then all may be well; if the individual is the measure of all, then whatever the individual person may choose to do or believe

is proper. The later sophists moved toward this last position, teaching, for example, that the laws were merely a set of people's opinions, so that if any people hold a different opinion, their conviction is as valid for them as are the laws. Moreover, Protagoras said, "about the gods I can have no knowledge either that they are or that they are not or what is their nature."

Much can be said in favor of the sophists' teachings, for they introduced a healthy questioning of the old traditions and the veneration of the gods. On the other hand, their complete relativism, if taken seriously, undermined any coherence within the group and all thought or action became merely a matter of expediency.

Into this new and changing atmosphere came two of the great tragic writers to direct Athenian thought and feeling: Sophokles (SOF [as in hot]-uh-kleez; 496–406 B.C.) and his younger contemporary, Euripides (you-RIP-uh-deez; 484–406 B.C.).

Sophokles

Sophokles was a general, a priest, and the most popular dramatist in Athenian history (figure 5.5). He is reputed to have written 123 plays and to have won first prize more than twenty times; he never placed lower than second. Of the seven complete plays that have survived, only *Oedipus the King* (ED-uh-pus, or EED-uh-pus; see complete text in this chapter) will be discussed here.

The plot of *Oedipus the King* concerns a plague in the city of Thebes, which the Delphic oracle says will be lifted only when the murderer of Laïos (LYE-us), the former king, is discovered and punished. Oedipus, the new king, who has according to custom married the widowed queen, Iocaste (yoe-KAS-ta), swears to find this murderer in order to save the city. This is done in the face of two prophecies. One was known to Iocaste and Laïos, that their son would kill his father and marry his mother (see box 5.2). Accordingly, when a son was born to them, Laïos (without Iocaste's consent) had the baby exposed to die on the slopes of Mount Kithaeron (kee-the-RON). The second prophecy, known to Oedipus when he grew up in Corinth as the son of the king and queen there, was that he would kill his father and marry his mother. To avert this, he had fled the city of Corinth. On his flight he had an altercation with an old man and his bodyguard at the place where three roads come together, and in a fit of rage Oedipus had killed the whole group. He had then proceeded to Thebes where he solved the riddle of the Sphinx, was chosen king by the populace, and married Iocaste. The play is riddled with irony, for the audience and the readers know that in the search for the murderer, Oedipus is searching for himself, and that the curse he has pronounced on the killer of King Laïos will fulfill itself on him. This expected event comes to pass; Iocaste commits suicide, and Oedipus blinds himself and exiles himself from the city. With these events the play of Oedipus ends.

The play is, of course, subject to a number of interpretations. It can be viewed as an exploration of man's fate; whether Oedipus because of a "fatal flaw" (see Aristotle's *Poetics* in chapter 6) brought disaster upon himself, whether he was just a pawn of the gods, or whether the answer lies somewhere in between.

Box 5.2 House of Kadmus, founder of Thebes

Kadmos m. Harmonia

Semele m. Zeus	Ino (Lencothes) m. Mehcertes (Palaemon)	Agave	Antonoe	Polydorus
Dionysos		Pentheus	Actaeon	Labdacus

Laius m. Iocasta

Oedipus m. Iocasta

Eteokles	Polynices	Antigone	Ismene

The King of Sidon had a daughter, Europa, who was abducted by Zeus in the form of a bull and carried quite willingly to Crete, where she became the mother of Minos and Rhadamanthys. The King of Sidon sent his sons to search for her; one of them, Kadmus, consulted the oracle at Delphi, who told him to found his own city and forget Europa. He was told to follow a heifer and to build his city of Thebes on the heifer's first resting place. First, however, he had to kill a dragon, whose teeth Athena ordered him to sow; armed warriors sprang up, killing each other until five survived. With the five Kadmus built Thebes and had five daughters and a son. Though Kadmus was a good man misfortune tormented his descendents and none more than Oedipus and Antigone.

Professor Bernard Knox sees the play as an example of the power of the gods presented to the Athenians to stop them in their progress toward skepticism and atheism, and certainly this does constitute one level of meaning. Oedipus first quarrels with the ancient prophet, Teiresias (tie-REE-see-us), and ends up shouting angrily that all prophets are cheats. Several times Iocaste entreats Oedipus to put no faith in oracles, each time trying to show him how the oracles have lied. The final statement of her belief is given in the lines:

Why should anyone in the world be afraid,
Since Fate rules us and nothing can be foreseen?
A man should live only for the present day.

The thought here is almost exactly the day-to-day philosophy of the atomic materialists, but each time Iocaste attempts to prove that the oracles are useless, Oedipus receives a new jolt that points to the fact that he is the murderer whom he is seeking.

This scoffing at the prophecies from the gods has an interesting effect on the populace as represented by the chorus of Thebans. One of their odes is a plea for reverence to the gods, ending with these lines:

Shall we lose faith in Delphi's obscurities,
We who have heard the world's core
Discredited, and the sacred wood
Of Zeus at Elis praised no more?
The deeds and the strange prophecies
Must make a pattern yet to be understood.
Zeus, if indeed you are lord of all,
Throned in light over night and day,
Mirror this in your endless mind:
Our masters call the oracle
Words on the wind, and the Delphic vision blind!
Their hearts no longer know Apollo,
And reverence for the gods has died away.

But the oracles are upheld; faith is restored. From the moment of Oedipus's highest hope when the messenger brings news that the king of Corinth has died and that the citizens there have chosen *him* king, he is dashed to the bottom of despair as he finally learns that he was the baby who was exposed to die, and that the old man he killed was his true father. Strained beyond endurance by her burden of knowledge, Iocaste commits suicide, and Oedipus, who has seen external things throughout his life, blinds himself as he comes to see himself and, with clear vision, sees truths that lie beyond the externals. He and the blind Teiresias, also one of the clear-sighted ones, reach equality at the end of the play. On this level of meaning this drama is a clear admonition that the gods are powerful and should receive worship and honor.

Euripides

The third great tragedian of Athens, Euripides (484–406 B.C.), directed his tragic vision towards psychological drama with plots revolving around the plight of the underdog: the inferior status of women, the exploitation of peasants, the rejected wife, the exploited wife, those who lose wars. Aristotle said that Aeschylus composed properly without knowing it, that Sophokles painted men as they should be, and that Euripides painted men as they were. Euripides exposed the reality of suffering and suffered the usual fate of the artist who deals with unpopular truths. Euripides wrote ninety-two plays but won only

FIGURE 5.6 *Portrait bust of Euripides. Marble, Roman copy, ca. 320 B.C. Portraits of Euripides survived about as well as his plays; this is one of twenty-five replicas. National Museum, Naples.*

four first prizes; the fourth one was awarded after Sophokles made an issue of the case. However, nineteen plays have survived, more than the combined extant dramas of Aeschylus and Sophokles, an ironic twist Euripides would have appreciated (figure 5.6).

Elektra provides a good example of the different styles of the three dramatists. Aeschylus portrays Orestes and Elektra as vehicles for developing an idea of justice; Sophokles writes a classic study of a woman possessed and driven almost mad by the indignities that have been heaped upon her; Euripides presents Elektra and Orestes as cold-blooded butchers bent solely on revenge. Orestes craftily insists upon staying close to the borders of Argos so he can escape should anything go wrong. Elektra is a proud, disdainful aristocrat who looks down upon Pylades, her peasant husband. The nobility of the poor is another of Euripides' themes; the peasant is as good a man as one can find, stoically suffering his wife's scorn.

In *Medea,* two more of Euripides' great themes appear: the strength and greatness of a woman, and the hypocrisy and shabby ethics found so often in highly developed cultures. Medea is a raging woman, consumed by love turned to hate because of the sniveling opportunism of her civilized Greek husband. As she arranges for the murder of Kreusa, Jason's intended bride, and then murders her own sons in order to wipe out Jason's line, she is the magnificent Medea, destroyer of a decadent, materialistic civilization.

In *The Trojan Women,* Euripides shows us war as it really is. He does not treat the Trojan War as a glorious victory for the good Greeks; instead, he selects the time immediately after the victory and shows the misery of the women of Troy as they are parceled out to the conquerors and their heartbreak as they see their children murdered by the ''heroic'' victors (see the complete text near the end of this chapter.)

During the last two years of his life, Euripides exiled himself from civilized Athens and went to live in primitive Macedonia, where he died. There he wrote *The Bacchae* (BOCK-ee), in which he repudiates the rationalistic civilization he had known—a civilization that had rejected him and that he had, in turn, rejected. Though Euripides did not live to see the play produced, Sophokles used his immense prestige to see that the play received the production it merited in the city that deserved it.

Athenian Background after Perikles

Throughout the times of these dramatists, the cities of Athens and Sparta had each been growing in power until a confrontation between the two for dominance throughout the Hellenic world was inevitable. In 445 the two city-states signed a pact for a thirty-year truce, which was observed, more or less, for fourteen years. In 431 the Peloponnesian War broke out; it ended in 404 with Sparta's total conquest of Athens. Perikles believed that this would be a long war of attrition, and decided to abandon the land to Sparta, bringing all the people of Attica inside the walls of Athens, and trusting the Athenian navy to attack Sparta and her allies wherever a hit-and-run attack would do the most damage. Athens was almost immediately crippled when, in 430, plague broke out in the city and a third of the population died. Perikles himself died of the disease in 429. The conflict that followed furnishes almost a classic example of the stupidity of war. On two or three occasions Athens obtained the upper hand and could have made peace with Sparta without serious loss of honor, but the hawks within the government demanded total victory.

A number of Athenian acts during the war demonstrate the temper of the times. For example, in 416 the Athenians attacked the neutral island of Melos on the general principle that if you aren't for us, you are against us. The battle lasted a single day, with Athens winning, killing all the men on the island, and selling the women and children into slavery.

In the following year Athens mounted a great attack on the city of Syracuse in Sicily, an attack that was foolhardy and doomed to failure. Of the three generals in command, one of them, Alkibiades (Al-ki-BY-uh-deez), represents an extreme example of the new egocentric individualism that was becoming so prevalent in Athens. His self-indulgent actions and ethical relativism could be construed by the sophists of the city as proper (successful) behavior. In the first place, Alkibiades left Athens under a cloud, for after a series of farewell parties a number of the sacred shrines in the city were defaced, and it was generally supposed that Alkibiades and his followers committed this sacrilege. Before reaching Sicily, he defected to Sparta, and in Sparta became a leading citizen and military adviser. When he felt that his good fortune in Sparta was running out, he deserted to Persia, and even later he returned to Athens where he was greeted as a national hero and reelected to a generalship. This, as we have said, is an extreme case, but when such conduct could be tolerated, the moral fiber of the city must have been extremely weak. After the Sicilian disaster in which the navy and most of the army were lost, the war dragged on to what had become an inevitable victory for Sparta. Then, during the fourth century, the government vacillated between the strong antidemocratic element in the population, the democrats, and a moderate element, which sought to limit the voting power to a few thousand of the upper classes but still maintain some sort of democratic voice.

The Critics of Athens: Sokrates and Aristophanes

Probably the greatest questioner of the new value system in Athens was the philosopher, Sokrates, of whom we know little, since he never wrote and the only reports we have about him are from his pupils, principally Plato and Xenophon (ZEN-oh-fun). It is apparent, however, that he spent most of his life raising embarrassing questions and demanding that the Athenians examine their motives for their way of life. He was an extremely popular teacher for a group of the intellectual young men who shared his views about the decay of the old value systems, but he was certainly not popular with those whose motives were totally selfish. This last group finally had him arrested on the charge of corrupting the youth of Athens; in 399, a jury of his peers found him guilty of impiety and corrupting the youth and sentenced him to death. At his trial he described himself as the gadfly of Athens, and the description is probably very exact. He insisted that the only good life was the well-examined life, and he sought to help others by causing them to examine themselves by asking them what they meant by the words they used—what do you mean, "justice"?—and then by a series of other questions finally revealing to the individuals that they simply didn't know what they were talking about. His method was always the same: to ask a question and arrive at an answer that seemed to be true. Then, by further questions he would test each part of the original answer, paring away those parts that proved themselves to be false, until the original answer was refined to truth by the clear process of thought.

For Sokrates, the end of the good life is happiness, which is not only the avoidance of ignorance and its fruits, but the virtue that comes from knowledge. To know rightly, to make right choices, is virtue, for it alone can satisfy reason. Knowledge and virtue are inseparable. And happiness is the result of worthiness that comes when enlightenment and knowledge result, as necessarily they must in this highest good, which we call virtue.

The other great critic of late fifth-century Athens was Aristophanes (air-i-STOF-uh-neez; ca. 448–388 B.C.), the great writer of Greek Old Comedy. An aristocrat and a conservative, he sought to make Athens aware of its faults through the biting wit of his satires. In *The Clouds* he depicted Sokrates as a sophist who, for a fee, taught either right logic or wrong logic, which did not help matters at the trial of Sokrates. *The Wasps* poked fun at the Athenian passion for litigation and *The Frogs* was a literary satire involving Aeschylus and Euripides; he was sharply critical of Euripides. Perhaps his greatest play was *Lysistrata* (LIS-i-stra-ta or li-SIS-tra-ta) in which the war between Athens and Sparta, or any war for that matter, was satirized. The Athenian woman Lysistrata enlists the cooperation of all the Greek women in a simple and wonderfully effective plan to stop warfare: no sex until all fighting stops. Given a choice between making love and making war, the men, after considerable controversy and much pleading, opt for the former.

Thus was the great fifth century in Athens. It had started with the pride of victory over the Persians, with the triumph of democracy, and with the promise of the great life in the plays of Aeschylus. Within the early years of the leadership of Perikles that good life had been realized about as much as it ever can be. It ended in a time of military defeat; a time when selfish individualism was the dominant mood; a time when Athens could no longer listen to the voice of its best critic, and when even criticism-through-comedy turned from biting satire to simple comedy-for-amusement, which we see in the later plays of Aristophanes.

The highest assertion of the human spirit in these exhausted times came at the very end with the trial of Sokrates and a glimpse of the philosopher as hero. In his *Apology* (see chapter 6 for the complete text) he spoke to his jury as a highly urbane and civilized man, disdaining high-flown rhetoric on the one hand, and sentiment on the other. Instead, he speaks almost in a conversational tone about his own life and his devotion to his own highest ideals for human conduct. Perhaps the highest statement comes after the vote has been taken that condemned him to death:

> . . . And there are many other ways of avoiding death in every danger if a man is willing to say and to do anything. But, my friends, I think that it is a much harder thing to escape from wickedness than from death, for wickedness is swifter than death. And now I, who am old and slow, have been overtaken by the slower pursuer: and my accusers, who are clever and swift, have been overtaken by the swifter pursuer—wickedness. And now I shall go away, sentenced by you to death; and they will go away, sentenced by truth to wickedness and injustice. I abide by my penalty, they by theirs.

Literary Selections

AGAMEMNON

Aeschylus (525–456 B.C.)

This is the first of a series of three plays by Aeschylus, called the *Oresteia*. He investigates in these plays the question of man's relation to other men. He is asking the question, "What is justice?" In the first of the plays he presents the old idea of justice and the individual's freedom of choice as it probably existed in the period of chaos. In the second of the plays (omitted here) he carries the question further. In the last of the series he presents a new idea of justice and explains the meaning of it to his Athenian audience as they approached the period of balance in their epoch. To understand this series of plays, one needs to know a little about the history of the dynasty of the kings who ruled in the land of Argos. Since Atreus (A-tree-us) was one of the early kings in this dynasty, the family line is called the House of Atreus. (See box 5.1.)

The sons of Atreus, Agamemnon and Menelaos, married the sisters, Klytaïmnestra and Helen, daughters of the King of Lacedaemon. Helen left her husband, fleeing to Troy with Paris, and Agamemnon rallied all the forces of Greece to help his brother win her back. The fleet could not leave from Aulis because of adverse winds; the seer, Kalchas (KAL-kus), interpreted omens to mean that the winds would change when Agamemnon sacrificed his daughter, Iphigeneia. That sacrifice was made.

While the war was in progress and Agamemnon fighting before Troy, Aigisthos returned to Argos and became Klytaïmnestra's lover. He roused discontent among the people and became powerful.

These plays, then, develop a new idea of justice and freedom in the period in which Aeschylus lived. The first one presents the old ideas that made the tragedy of Agamemnon possible. Watch for those ideas.

The Greeks had arranged a series of beacons stretching from Troy to the Grecian mainland to be kindled as a token of victory over Troy. It is with their imminent flaming that the play opens.

The translations of the *Oresteia* are by the twentieth-century scholar George Thomson.

CHARACTERS

Watchman
Chorus of Old Men
Klytaïmnestra → queen
Herald
Agamemnon → king
Kassandra
Aigisthos
Captain of the Guard

The scene is the entrance to the palace of the Atreidae. Before the doors stand shrines of the gods.
   [*A WATCHMAN is posted on the roof.*]
Watchman: I've prayed God to release me from sentry duty
All through this long year's vigil, like a dog
Couched on the roof of Atreus, where I study
Night after night the pageantry of this vast
Concourse of stars, and moving among them like
Noblemen the constellations that bring

Summer and winter as they rise and fall.
And I am still watching for the beacon signal
All set to flash over the sea the radiant
News of the fall of Troy. So confident
Is a woman's spirit, whose purpose is a man's.
Every night, as I turn in to my stony bed,
Quilted with dew, not visited by dreams,
Not mine—no sleep, fear stands at my pillow
Keeping tired eyes from closing once too often;
And whenever I start to sing or hum a tune,
Mixing from music an antidote to sleep,
It always turns to mourning for the royal house,
Which is not in such good shape as it used to be.
But now at last may the good news in a flash
Scatter the darkness and deliver us.
   [*The beacon flashes.*]
O light of joy, whose gleam turns night to day,
O radiant signal for innumerable
Dances of victory! Ho there! I call the queen,
Agamemnon's wife, to raise with all the women
Alleluias of thanksgiving through the palace
Saluting the good news, if it is true
That Troy has fallen, as this blaze portends:
Yes, and I'll dance an overture myself.
My master's dice have fallen out well, and I
Shall score three sixes for this nightwatching.
   [*A pause.*]
Well, come what will, may it soon be mine to grasp
In this right hand my master's, home again!
   [*Another pause.*]
The rest is secret. A heavy ox has trodden
Across my tongue. These walls would have tales to tell
If they had mouths. I speak only to those
Who are in the know, to others—I know nothing.
   [*The WATCHMAN goes into the palace. Women's cries are heard. Enter CHORUS OF OLD MEN.*]
Chorus: It is ten years since those armed prosecutors of Justice, Menelaos and Agamemnon, twin-sceptred in God-given sovereignty, embarked in the thousand ships crying war, like eagles with long wings beating the air over a robbed mountain nest, wheeling and screaming for their lost children. Yet above them some god, maybe Apollo or Zeus, overhears the sky-dweller's cry and sends after the robber a Fury.
   [*KLYTAIMNESTRA comes out of the palace and unseen by the elders places offerings before the shrines.*]
Just so the two kings were sent by the greater king, Zeus, for the sake of a promiscuous woman to fight Paris, Greek and Trojan locked fast together in the dusty betrothals of battle. And however it stands with them now, the end is unalterable; no flesh, no wine can appease God's fixed indignation.

As for us, with all the able-bodied men enlisted and gone, we are left here leaning our strength on a staff; for, just as in infancy, when the marrow is still unformed, the War-god is not at his post, so it is in extreme old age, as the leaves fall fast, we walk on three feet, like dreams in the daylight.
   [*They see KLYTAIMNESTRA.*]
O Queen, what news? what message sets light to the altars? All over the town the shrines are ablaze with unguents drawn from the royal stores and the flames shoot up into the night sky. Speak, let us hear all that may be made public, so healing the anxieties that have gathered thick in our hearts; let the gleam of good news scatter them!
   [*KLYTAIMNESTRA goes out to tend the other altars of the city.*]

Strength have I still to recall that sign which greeted the
  two kings
Taking the road, for the prowess of song is not yet spent.
I sing of two kings united in sovereignty, leading
Armies to battle, who saw two eagles
Beside the palace
Wheel into sight, one black, and the other was white-
  tailed,
Tearing a hare with her unborn litter.
Cry Sorrow cry, but let good conquer!
Shrewdly the priest took note and compared each eagle
  with each king.
Then spoke out and prefigured the future in these words:
"In time the Greek arms shall demolish the fortress of
  Priam;
Only let no jealous God, as they fasten
On Troy the slave's yoke,
Strike them in anger; for Artemis[1] loathes the rapacious
Eagles of Zeus that have slaughtered the frail hare.
Cry Sorrow cry, but let good conquer!
O Goddess, gentle to the tender whelp of fierce lions
As to all young life of the wild,
So now fulfil what is good in the omen and mend what is
  faulty.
And I appeal unto the Lord Apollo,
Let not the north wind hold the fleet storm-bound,
Driving them on to repay that feast with another,
Inborn builder of strife, feud that fears no man, it is still
  there,
Treachery keeping the house, it remembers, revenges, a
  child's death!"
Such, as the kings left home, was the seer's revelation.
Cry Sorrow cry, but let good conquer!
Zeus, whoe'er he be, if so it best
Please his ear to be addressed,
So shall he be named by me.
All things have I measured, yet
None have found save him alone,
Zeus, if a man from a heart heavy-laden
Seek to cast his cares aside.
Long since lived a ruler of the world,[2]
Puffed with martial pride, of whom
None shall tell, his day is done;
Also, he who followed him
Met his master and is gone.
Zeus the victorious, gladly acclaim him;
Perfect wisdom shall be yours;
Zeus, who laid it down that man
Must in sorrow learn and through
Pain to wisdom find his way.
When deep slumber falls, remembered wrongs
Chafe the bruised heart with fresh pangs, and no
Welcome wisdom meets within.
Harsh the grace dispensed by powers immortal,
Pilots of the human soul.
Even so the elder prince,[3]

learn hard way

Marshal of the thousand ships,
Rather than distrust a priest,
Torn with doubt to see his men
Harbor-locked, hunger-pinched, hard-oppressed,
Strained beyond endurance, still
Watching, waiting, where the never-tiring
Tides of Aulis ebb and flow:
And still the storm blew from mountains far north,
With moorings windswept and hungry crews pent
In rotting hulks,
With tackling all torn and seeping timbers,
Till Time's slow-paced, enforced inaction
Had all but stripped bare the bloom of Greek manhood.
And then was found but one
Cure to allay the tempest—never a blast so bitter—
Shrieked in a loud voice by the priest, "Artemis!" striking
  the Atreidae with dismay, each with his staff smiting
  the ground and weeping.
And then the king spoke, the elder, saying:
"The choice is hard—hard to disobey him,
And harder still
To kill my own child, my palace jewel,
With unclean hands before the altar
Myself, her own father, spill a maid's pure blood.
I have no choice but wrong.
How shall I fail my thousand ships and betray my
  comrades?
So shall the storm cease, and the men eager for war
  clamor for that virginal blood righteously! So pray for
  a happy outcome!"
And when he bowed down beneath the harness
Of cruel coercion, his spirit veering
With sudden sacrilegious change,
He gave his whole mind to evil counsel.
For man is made bold with base-contriving
Impetuous madness, first cause of much grief.
And so then he slew his own child
For a war to win a woman
And to speed the storm-bound fleet from the shore to
  battle.
She cried aloud "Father!" yet they heard not;
A girl in first flower, yet they cared not,
The lords who gave the word for war.
Her father prayed, then he bade his vassals
To seize her where swathed in folds of saffron
She lay, and lift her up like a yearling
With bold heart above the altar,
And her lovely lips to bridle
That they might not cry out, cursing the House of Atreus,
With gags, her voice sealed with brute force and crushed.
And then she let fall her cloak
And cast at each face a glance that dumbly craved
  compassion;
And like a picture she would but could not greet
Her father's guests, who at home
Had often sat when the meal was over,
The cups replenished, with all hearts enraptured
To hear her sing grace with clear unsullied voice for her
  loving father.
The end was unseen and unspeakable.
The task of priestcraft was done.
For Justice first chastens, then she presses home her
  lesson.

anti-religion

---

1. Artemis is the goddess of the hunt and all wild things. In this context, the hare is the city of Troy.

2. The reference here is Ouranus and Kronos, both kings of the gods. Zeus led a successful revolt against Kronos so that Zeus could become king.

3. This refers to the beginning of the Trojan War when the Greek fleet was delayed in the harbor of Aulis. In order to appease Artemis and secure favorable winds, Agamemnon, "the elder prince," followed the prophecy of the seer, Kalkhas, and sacrificed his daughter, Iphigeneia.

this story justifies Queen's attitude

The morrow must come, its grief will soon be here,
So let us not weep today.
It shall be made known as clear as daybreak.
And so may all this at last end in good news,
For which the queen prays, the next of kin and stay of the
    land of Argos.
        [KLYTAÏMNESTRA *appears at the door of the palace.*]
Our humble salutations to the queen!
Hers is our homage, while our master's throne
Stands empty. We are still longing to hear
The meaning of your sacrifice. Is it good news?

Klytaïmnestra: Good news! With good news may the
    morning rise
Out of the night—good news beyond all hope!
My news is this: The Greeks have taken Troy.

Chorus: What? No, it cannot be true! I cannot grasp it.

Klytaïmnestra: The Greeks hold Troy—is not that plain
    enough?

Chorus: Joy steals upon me and fills my eyes with tears.

Klytaïmnestra: Indeed, your looks betray your loyalty.

Chorus: What is the proof? Have you any evidence?

Klytaïmnestra: Of course I have, or else the Gods have
    cheated me.

Chrous: You have given ear to some beguiling dream.

Klytaïmnestra: I would not come screaming fancies out
    of my sleep.

Chorus: Rumors have wings—on these your heart has
    fed.

Klytaïmnestra: You mock my intelligence as though I
    were a girl.

Chorus: When was it? How long is it since the city fell?

Klytaïmnestra: In the night that gave birth to this
    dawning day.

Chorus: What messenger could bring the news so fast?

Klytaïmnestra: The God of Fire, who from Ida sent
    forth light
And beacon by beacon passed the flame to me.
From the peak of Ida first to the cliff of Hermes
On Lemnos, and from there a third great lamp
Was flashed to Athos, the pinnacle of Zeus;
Up, up it soared, luring the dancing fish
To break surface in rapture at the light;
A golden courier, like the sun, it sped
Post-haste its message to Macistus, thence
Across Euripus, till the flaming sign
Was marked by the watchers on Messapium,
And thence with strength renewed from piles of heath
Like moonrise over the valley of Asopus,
Relayed in glory to Kithairon's heights,
And still flashed on, not slow the sentinels,
Leaping across the lake from peak to peak,
It passed the word to burn and burn, and flung
A comet to the promontory that stands
Over the Gulf of Saron, there it swooped
Down to the Spider's Crag above the city,
Then found its mark on the roof of this house of Atreus,
That beacon fathered by Ida's far off fires.
Such were the stages of our torch relay,
And the last to run is the first to reach the goal.
That is my evidence, the testimony which
My lord has signaled to me out of Troy.

Chorus: Lady, there will be time later to thank the Gods.
Now I ask only to listen: speak on and on.

Klytaïmnestra: Today the Greeks have occupied Troy.
I seem to hear there a very strange street-music.
Pour oil and vinegar into one cup, you will see
They do not make friends. So there two tunes are heard.
Slaves now, the Trojans, brothers and aged fathers,
Prostrate, sing for their dearest the last dirge.
The others, tired out and famished after the night's
    looting.
Grab what meal chance provides, lodgers now
In Trojan houses, sheltered from the night frosts,
From the damp dews delivered, free to sleep
Off guard, off duty, a blissful night's repose.
Therefore, provided that they show due respect
To the altars of the plundered town and are not
Tempted to lay coarse hands on sanctities,
Remembering that the last lap—the voyage home—
Lies still ahead of them, then, if they should return
Guiltless before God, the curses of the bereaved
Might be placated—barring accidents.
That is my announcement—a message from my master.
May all end well, and may I reap the fruit of it!

Chorus: Lady, you have spoken with a wise man's
    judgment.
Now it is time to address the gods once more
After this happy outcome of our cares.
Thanks be to Zeus and to gracious Night, housekeeper of
heaven's embroidery, who has cast over the towers of Troy
a net so fine as to leave no escape for old or young, all
caught in the snare! All praise to Zeus, who with a shaft
from his outstretched bow has at last brought down the
transgressor!
"By Zeus struck down!" The truth is all clear
With each step plainly marked. He said, Be
It so, and so it was. A man denied once
That heaven pays heed to those who trample
Beneath the feet holy sanctities. He lied wickedly;
For God's wrath soon or late destroys all sinners filled
With pride, puffed up with vain presumption,
And great men's houses stocked with silver
And gold beyond measure. Far best to live
Free of want, without grief, rich in the gift of wisdom.
Glutted with gold, the sinner kicks
Justice out of his sight, yet
She sees *him* and remembers.
As sweet temptation lures him onwards
With childlike smile into the death-trap
He cannot help himself. His curse is lit up
Against the darkness, a bright baleful light.
And just as false bronze in battle hammered turns black
    and shows
Its true worth, so the sinner time-tried stands condemned.
His hopes take wing, and still he gives chase, with foul
    crimes branding all his people.
He cries to deaf heaven, none hear his prayers.
Justice drags him down to hell as he calls for succor.
Such was the sinner Paris, who
Rendered thanks to a gracious
Host by stealing a woman.
She left behind her the ports all astir
With throngs of men under arms filing onto shipboard;
She took to Troy in lieu of dowry death.
A light foot passed through the gates and fled,
And then a cry of lamentation rose.

The seers, the king's prophets, muttered darkly:
"Bewail the king's house that now is desolate,
Bewail the bed marked with print of love that fled!"
Behold, in silence, without praise, without reproach,
They sit upon the ground and weep.
Beyond the wave lies their love;
Here a ghost seems to rule the palace!
Shapely the grace of statues.
Yet they can bring no comfort,
Eyeless, lifeless and loveless.
Delusive dream shapes that float through the night
Beguile him, bringing delight sweet but unsubstantial;
For, while the eye beholds the heart's desire,
The arms clasp empty air, and then
The fleeting vision fades and glides away
On silent wing down the paths of slumber.
The royal hearth is chilled with sorrows such as these,
And more; in each house from end to end of Greece
That sent its dearest to wage war in foreign lands
The stout heart is called to steel itself
In mute endurance against
Blows that strike deep into the heart's core:
Those that they sent from home they
Knew, but now they receive back
Only a heap of ashes.
The God of War holds the twin scales of strife,
Heartless gold-changer trafficking in men,
Consigning homeward from Troy a jar of dust fire-refined,
Making up the weight with grief,
Shapely vessels laden each
With the ashes of their kin.
They mourn and praise them saying, "He
Was practiced well in sword and spear,
And he, who fell so gallantly—
All to avenge another man's wife":
It is muttered in a whisper
And resentment spreads against each of the royal
    warlords.
They lie sleeping, perpetual
Owners each of a small
Holding far from their homeland.
The sullen rumors that pass mouth to mouth
Bring the same danger as a people's curse.
And brooding hearts wait to hear of what the night holds
    from sight.
Watchful are the Gods of all
Hands with slaughter stained. The black
Furies wait, and when a man
Has grown by luck, not justice, great,
With sudden turn of circumstance
He wastes away to nothing, dragged
Down to be food in hell for demons.
For the heights of fame are perilous.
With a jealous bolt the Lord Zeus in a flash shall blast
    them.
Best to pray for a tranquil
Span of life and to be
Neither victor nor vanquished.
—The news has set the whole town aflame.
Can it be true? Perhaps it is a trick.
—Only a child would let such fiery words
Kindle his hopes, then fade and flicker out.
—It is just like a woman
To accept good news without the evidence.
—An old wives' tale, winged with a woman's wishes,
Spreads like wildfire, then sinks and is forgotten.
We shall soon know what the beacon signifies,
Whether it is true or whether this joyful daybreak
Is only a dream sent to deceive us all.

Here comes a messenger breathless from the shore,
Wearing a garland and covered in a cloud
Of dust, which shows that he has news to tell,
And not in soaring rhetoric of smoke and flame,
But either he brings cause for yet greater joy,
Or else—no, let us abjure the alternative.
Glad shone the light, as gladly break the day!
    [*Enter* HERALD]
Herald: O joy! Argos, I greet you, my fatherland!
Joy brings me home after ten years of war.
Many the shattered hopes, but this has held.
Now I can say that when I die my bones
Will lie at rest here in my native soil.
I greet you joyfully, I greet the Sun,
Zeus the All-Highest, and the Pythian King,
Bending no more against us his fatal shafts,
As he did beside Scamander—that was enough,
And now defend us, Savior Apollo; all
The Gods I greet, among them Hermes, too,
Patron of messengers, and the spirits of our dead,
Who sent their sons forth, may they now prepare
A joyful welcome for those whom war has spared.
Joy to the palace and to these images
Whose faces catch the sun, now, as of old,
With radiant smiles greet your sovereign lord,
Agamemnon, who brings a lamp to lighten you
And all here present, after having leveled
Troy with the mattock of just-dealing Zeus,
Great son of Atreus, master and monarch, blest
Above all living men. The brigand Paris
Has lost his booty and brought down the house of Priam.
Chorus: Joy to you, Herald, welcome home again!
Herald: Let me die, having lived to see this day!
Chorus: Your yearning for your country has worn you
    out.
Herald: So much that tears spring to the eyes for joy.
Chorus: Well, those you longed for longed equally for
    you.
Herald: Ah yes, our loved ones longed for our safe
    return.
Chorus: We have had many anxieties here at home.
Herald: What do you mean? Has there been disaffection?
Chorus: Never mind now. Say nothing and cure all.
Herald: Is it possible there was trouble in our absence?
Chorus: Now, as you said yourself, it would be a joy to
    die.
Herald: Yes, all has ended well. Our expedition
Has been successfully concluded, even though in part
The issue may be found wanting. Only the Gods
Prosper in everything. If I should tell you all
That we endured on shipboard in the night watches,
Our lodging the bare benches, and even worse
Ashore beneath the walls of Troy, the rains
From heaven and the dews that seeped
Out of the soil into lice-infested blankets;
If I should tell of those winters, when the birds
Dropped dead and Ida heaped on us her snows;
Those summers, when unruffled by wind or wave
The sea slept breathless under the glare of noon—
But why recall that now? It is all past,
Yes, for the dead past never to stir again.
Ah, they are all gone. Why count our losses? Why
Should we vex the living with grievance for the dead?
Goodbye to all that for us who have come back!

Victory has turned the scale, and so before
This rising sun let the good news be proclaimed
And carried all over the world on wings of fame:
"These spoils were brought by the conquerors of Troy
And dedicated to the Gods of Greece."
And praise to our country and to Zeus the giver
And thanks be given. That is all my news.

[KLYTAÏMNESTRA *appears at the palace door.*]

Chorus: Thank God that I have lived to see this day!
This news concerns all, and most of all the queen.

Klytaïmnestra: I raised my alleluia hours ago,
When the first messenger lit up the night,
And people mocked me saying, "Has a beacon
Persuaded you that the Greeks have captured Troy?
Truly a woman's hopes are lighter than air."
But I still sacrificed, and at a hundred
Shrines throughout the town the women chanted
Their endless alleluias on and on,
Singing to sleep the sacramental flames,
And now what confirmation do I need from you?
I wait to hear all from my lord, for whom
A welcome is long ready. What day is so sweet
In a woman's life as when she opens the door
To her beloved, safe home from war? Go and tell him
That he will find, guarding his property,
A wife as loyal as he left her, one
Who in all these years has kept his treasuries sealed,
Unkind only to enemies, and knows no more
Of other men's company than of tempering steel.

[*Exit*]

Herald: Such a protestation, even though entirely true,
Is it not unseemly on a lady's lips?

Chorus: Such is her message, as you understand,
Full of fine phrases plain to those who know.
But tell us now, what news have you of the king's
Co-regent, Menelaos? Is he too home again?

Herald: Lies cannot last, even though sweet to hear.

Chorus: Can you not make your news both sweet and
true?

Herald: He and his ships have vanished. They are
missing.

Chorus: What, was it a storm that struck the fleet at sea?

Herald: You have told a long disaster in a word.

Chorus: Has no one news whether he is alive or dead?

Herald: Only the Sun, from whom the whole earth draws
life.

Chorus: Tell us about the storm. How did it fall?

Herald: A day of national rejoicing must not be marred
By any jarring tongue. A messenger who comes
With black looks bringing the long prayed-against
Report of total rout, which both afflicts
The state in general and in every household leaves
The inmates prostrate under the scourge of war—
With such a load upon his lips he may fitly
Sing anthems to the Furies down in hell;
But when he greets a prospering people with
News of the war's victorious end—how then
Shall I mix foul with fair and find words to tell you
Of the blow that struck us out of that angry heaven?
Water and Fire, those age-old enemies,
Made common cause against the homebound fleet.
Darkness had fallen, and a northerly gale
Blew up and in a blinding thunderstorm
Our ships were tossed and buffeted hull against hull
In a wild stampede and herded out of sight;
Then, at daybreak, we saw the Aegean in blossom
With a waving crop of corpses and scattered timbers.

Our ship came through, saved by some spirit, it seems,
Who took the helm and piloted her, until
She slipped under the cliffs into a cove.
There, safe at last, incredulous of our luck,
We brooded all day, stunned by the night's disaster.
And so, if any of the others have survived,
They must be speaking of us as dead and gone.
May all yet end well! Though it is most to be expected
That Menelaos is in some great distress.
Yet, should some shaft of sunlight spy him out
Somewhere among the living, rescued by Zeus,
Lest the whole house should perish, there is hope
That he may yet come home. There you have the truth.

Chorus: Tell us who invented that
Name so deadly accurate?
Was it one who presaging
Things to come divined a word
Deftly tuned to destiny?
Helen—hell indeed she carried
To men, to ships, to a proud city, stealing
From the silk veils of her chamber, sailing seaward
With the Zephyr's breath behind her;
And they set forth in a thousand ships to hunt her
On the path that leaves no imprint,
Bringers of endless bloodshed.
So, as Fate decreed, in Troy,
Turning into keeners kin,
Furies, instruments of God's
Wrath, at last demanded full
Payment for the stolen wife;
And the wedding song that rang out
To greet the bride from beyond the broad Aegean
Was in time turned into howls of imprecation
From the countless women wailing
For the loved ones they had lost in war for her sake,
And they curse the day they gave that
Welcome to war and bloodshed.
An old story is told of an oxherd who reared at his hearth
        a lion-cub, a pet for his children,
Pampered fondly by young and old with dainty morsels
        begged at each meal from his master's table.
But Time showed him up in his true nature after his
        kind—a beast savaging sheep and oxen,
Mad for the taste of blood, and only then they knew what
        they had long nursed was a curse from heaven.
And so it seemed then there came to rest in Troy
A sweet-smiling calm, a clear sky, seductive,
A rare pearl set in gold and silver,
Shaft of love from a glancing eye.
She is seen now as an agent
Of death sent from Zeus, a Fury
Demanding a bloody bride-price.

[*Enter* KLYTAÏMNESTRA]

From ancient times people have believed that when
A man's wealth has come to full growth it breeds
And brings forth tares and tears in plenty.
No, I say, it is only wicked deeds
That increase, fruitful in evil.
The house built on justice always
Is blest with a happy offspring.
And yet the pride bred of wealth often burgeons anew
In evil times, a cloud of deep night,
Spectre of ancient crimes that still
Walks within the palace walls,
True to the dam that bore it.
But where is Justice? She lights up the smoke-darkened
        hut.

From mansions built by hands polluted
Turning to greet the pure in heart,
Proof against false praise, she guides
All to its consummation.

[*Enter* AGAMEMNON *in a chariot followed by another chariot carrying* KASSANDRA *and spoils of war.*]

Agamemnon, conqueror, joy to our king! How shall my greeting neither fall short nor shoot too high? Some men feign rejoicing or sorrow with hearts untouched; but those who can read man's nature in the book of the eyes will not be deceived by dissembled fidelity. I declare that, when you left these shores ten years ago to recover with thousands of lives one woman, who eloped of her own free will, I deemed your judgment misguided; but now in all sincerity I salute you with joy. Toil happily ended brings pleasure at last, and in time you shall learn to distinguish the just from the unjust steward. *[honest vs. dishonest — some remain loyal]*

Agamemnon: First, it is just that I should pay my respects
To the land of Argos and her presiding Gods,
My partners in this homecoming as also
In the just penalty which I have inflicted on
The city of Troy. When the supreme court of heaven
Adjudicated on our cause, they cast
Their votes unanimously against her, though not
Immediately, and so on the other side
Hope hovered hesitantly before it vanished.
The fires of pillage are still burning there
Like sacrificial offerings. Her ashes
Redolent with riches breathe their last and die.
For all this it is our duty to render thanks *[Justice]*
To the celestial powers, with whose assistance
We have exacted payment and struck down
A city for one woman, forcing our entry
Within the Wooden Horse, which at the setting
Of the Pleiads like a hungry lion leapt
Out and slaked its thirst in royal blood.
As to your sentiments, I take due note
And find that they accord with mine. Too few
Rejoice at a friend's good fortune. I have known
Many dissemblers swearing false allegiance.
One only, though he joined me against his will,
Once in the harness, proved himself a staunch
Support, Odysseus, be he now alive or dead.
All public questions and such as concern the Gods
I shall discuss in council and take steps
To make this triumph lasting; and if here or there
Some malady comes to light, appropriate *[problem]*
Remedies will be applied to set it right. *[find out disloyal & take care of them]*
Meanwhile, returning to my royal palace,
My first duty is to salute the Gods
Who led me overseas and home again.
Victory attends me; may she remain with me!

Klytaïmnestra: Citizens of Argos, councillors and elders,
I shall declare without shame in your presence
My feelings for my husband. Diffidence
Dies in us all with time. I shall speak of what
I suffered here, while he was away at the war,
Sitting at home, with no man's company, *[→ keeps denying]*
Waiting for news, listening to one
Messenger after another, each bringing worse
Disasters. If all his rumored wounds were real,
His body was in shreds, shot through and through.
If he had died—the predominant report—
He was a second Geryon, an outstretched giant
With three corpses and one death for each,
While I, distraught, with a knot pressing my throat,
Was rescued forcibly, to endure still more.

And that is why our child is not present here, *[Son gone so doesn't tell she's unfaithful]*
As he should be, pledge of our marriage vows,
Orestes. Let me reassure you. He lives
Safe with an old friend, Strophius, who warned me
Of various dangers—your life at stake in Troy
And here a restive populace, which might perhaps
Be urged to kick a man when he is down.
As for myself, the fountains of my tears
Have long ago run dry. My eyes are sore
After so many nights watching the lamp
That burnt at my bedside always for you.
If I should sleep, a gnat's faint whine would shatter
The dreams that were my only company.
But now, all pain endured, all sorrow past,
I salute this man as the watchdog of the fold,
The stay that saves the ship, the sturdy oak
That holds the roof up, the longed-for only child,
The shore despaired-of sighted far out at sea.
God keep us from all harm! And now, dearest,
Dismount, but not on the bare ground! Servants,
Spread out beneath those feet that have trampled Troy
A road of royal purple, which shall lead him
By the hand of Justice into a home unhoped-for,
And there, when he has entered, our vigilant care
Shall dispose of everything as the Gods have ordained.

Agamemnon: Lady, royal consort and guardian of our home, *[Shouldn't walk on purple color carpet]*
I thank you for your words of welcome, extended
To fit my lengthy absence; but due praise
Should rather come from others; and besides,
I would not have effeminate graces unman me
With barbarous salaams and beneath my feet
Purple embroideries designed for sacred use.[4] *[She wants gods angry]*
Honor me as a mortal, not as a god.
Heaven's greatest gift is wisdom. Count him blest
Who has brought a long life to a happy end.
I shall do as I have said, with a clear conscience.

Klytaïmnestra: Yet tell me frankly, according to your judgment.

Agamemnon: My judgment stands. Make no mistake about that.

Klytaïmnestra: Would you not in time of danger have vowed such an act?

Agamemnon: Yes, if the priests had recommended it.

Klytaïmnestra: And what would Priam have done, if he had won?

Agamemnon: Oh, he would have trod the purple without a doubt.

Klytaïmnestra: Then you have nothing to fear from wagging tongues.

Agamemnon: Popular censure is a potent force.

Klytaïmnestra: Men must risk envy in order to be admired.

Agamemnon: A contentious spirit is unseemly in a woman.

Klytaïmnestra: Well may the victor yield a victory.

Agamemnon: Do you set so much store by your victory?

Klytaïmnestra: Be tempted, freely vanquished, victor still!

Agamemnon: Well, if you will have it, let someone unlace
These shoes, and, as I tread the purple, may
No far-off god cast at me an envious glance
At the prodigal desecration of all this wealth! *[✓ gives in because really wanted to]*

---

4. The purple dye was extracted from seaweed. It was very rare, therefore very expensive; a color reserved for the gods.

Meanwhile, extend your welcome to this stranger.
Power tempered with gentleness wins God's favor.
No one is glad to be enslaved, and she
Is a princess presented to me by the army,
The choicest flower culled from a host of captives.
And now, constrained to obey you, setting foot
On the sacred purple, I pass into my home.

Klytaïmnestra: The sea is still there, nothing can dry it
    up,
Renewing out of its infinite abundance
Unfailing streams of purple and blood-red dyes.
So too this house, the Gods be praised, my lord,
Has riches inexhaustible. There is no counting
The robes *I* would have vowed to trample on,
Had some oracle so instructed, if by such means
I could have made good the loss of one dear soul.[5]
So now your entry to your hearth and home
Is like a warm spell in the long winter's cold,
Or when Zeus from the virgin grape at last
Draws wine, coolness descends upon the house
(For there from the living root the new leaves raise
A welcome shelter against the burning Dog-Star)
As man made perfect moves about his home.
    [*Exit* AGAMEMNON]
Zeus, perfector of all things, fulfil my prayers
And fulfil also your own purposes!
    [*Exit*]

Chorus: What is this delirious dread,
Ominous, oracular,
Droning through my brain with unrelenting
Beat, irrepressible prophet of evil?
Why can I not cast it out
Planting good courage firm
On my spirit's empty throne?
In time the day came
When the Greeks with anchors plunged
Moored the sloops of war, and troops
Thronged the sandy beach of Troy.
So today my eyes have seen
Safe at last the men come home.
Still I hear the strain of stringless music,
Dirge of the Furies, a choir uninvited
Chanting in my heart of hearts.
Mortal souls stirred by God
In tune with fate divine the shape
Of things to come; yet
Grant that these forebodings prove
False and bring my fears to naught.
If a man's health be advanced over the due mean,
It will trespass soon upon sickness, who stands
Next neighbor, between them a thin wall.
So does the vessel of life
Launched with a favoring breeze
Suddenly founder on reefs of destruction.
Caution seated at the helm
Casts a portion of the freight
Overboard with measured throw;
So the ship may ride the storm.
Furrows enriched each season with showers from heaven
Banish hunger from the door.
But if the red blood of a man spatters the ground,
    dripping and deadly, then who
Has the magical power to recall it?
Even the healer who knew
Spells to awaken the dead,
Zeus put an end to his necromancy.

Portions are there preordained,
Each supreme within its own
Province fixed eternally.
That is why my spirit groans
Brooding in fear, and no longer it hopes to unravel
Mazes of a fevered mind.
    [*Enter* KLYTAÏMNESTRA]

Klytaïmnestra: You, too, Kassandra, come inside! The
    merciful
Zeus gives you the privilege to take part
In our domestic sacrifice and stand
Before his altar among the other slaves there.
Put by your pride and step down. Even Heracles
Submitted once to slavery, and be consoled
In serving a house whose wealth has been inherited
Over so many generations. The harshest masters
Are those who have snatched their harvest out of hand.
You shall receive here what custom prescribes.

Chorus: She is speaking to you. Caught in the net,
    surrender.

Klytaïmnestra: If she knows Greek and not some
    barbarous language,
My mystic words shall fill the soul within her.

Chorus: You have no choice. Step down and do her will.

Klytaïmnestra: There is no time to waste. The victims
    are
All ready for the knife to render thanks
For this unhoped-for joy. If you wish to take part,
Make haste, but, if you lack the sense to understand,—
    [*To the* CHORUS]
Speak to her with your hands and drag her down.

Chorus: She is like a wild animal just trapped.

Klytaïmnestra: She is mad, the foolish girl. Her city
    captured,
I'll waste no words on her to demean myself.
    [*Exit*]

Kassandra: Oh! oh! Apollo!

Chorus: What blasphemy, to wail in Apollo's name!

Kassandra: Oh! oh! Apollo!

Chorus: Again she cries in grief to the god of joy!

Kassandra: Apollo, my destroyer! a second time!

Chorus: Ah, she foresees what is in store for her. She is
    now a slave, and yet God's gift remains.

Kassandra: Apollo, my destroyer! What house is this?

Chorus: Do you not know where you have come, poor
    girl?
Then let us tell you. This is the House of Atreus.

Kassandra: Yes, for its very walls smell of iniquity,
A charnel house that drips with children's blood.[6]

Chorus: How keen her scent to seize upon the trail!

Kassandra: Listen to them as they bewail the foul
Repast of roast meat for a father's mouth!

Chorus: Enough! Reveal no more! We know it all.

Kassandra: What is it plotted next? Horror unspeakable.
A hard cross for kinsfolk.
The hoped-for savior is far away.

Chorus: What does she say? This must be something
    new.

Kassandra: Can it be so—to bathe one who is travel-
    tired,
And then smiling stretch out
A hand followed by a stealthy hand!

Chorus: She speaks in riddles, and I cannot read them.

Kassandra: What do I see? A net!
Yes, it is she, his mate and murderess!
Cry alleluia, cry, angels of hell, rejoice,
Fat with blood, dance and sing!

---

5. Iphigeneia

6. She refers to Thyestes' banquet. See introduction.

Chorus: What is the Fury you have called upon?
Helpless the heart faints with the sinking sun.
Closer still draws the stroke.
Kassandra: Ah, let the bull[7] beware!
It is a robe she wraps him in, and strikes!
Into the bath he slumps heavily, drowned in blood.
Such her skilled handicraft.
Chorus: It is not hard to read her meaning now.
Why does the prophet's voice never have good to tell,
Only cry woes to come?
Kassandra: Oh, pitiful destiny! Having lamented his,
Now I lament my own passion to fill the bowl.
Where have you brought me? Must I with him die?
Chorus: You sing your own dirge, like the red-brown
bird
That pours out her grief-stricken soul,
Itys, Itys! she cries, the sad nightingale.
Kassandra: It is not so; for she, having become a bird,
Forgot her tears and sings her happy lot,
While I must face the stroke of two-edged steel.
Chorus: From whence does this cascade of harsh
discords
Issue, and where will it at last be calmed?
Calamity you cry—O where must it end?
Kassandra: O wedding day, Paris accurst of all!
Scamander,[8] whose clear waters I grew beside!
Now I must walk weeping by Akheron.
Chorus: Even a child could understand.
The heart breaks, as these pitiful cries
Shatter the listening soul.
Kassandra: O fall of Troy, city of Troy destroyed!
The king's rich gifts little availed her so
That she might not have been what she is now.
Chorus: What evil spirit has possessed
Your soul, strumming such music upon your lips
As on a harp in hell?
Kassandra: Listen! My prophecy shall glance no longer
As through a veil like a bride newly-wed,
But bursting towards the sunrise shall engulf
The whole world in calamities far greater
Than these. No more riddles, I shall instruct,
While you shall verify each step, as I
Nose out from the beginning this bloody trail.
Upon this roof—do you see them?—stands a choir—
It has been there for generations—a gallery
Of unmelodious minstrels, a merry troop
Of wassailers drunk with human blood, reeling
And retching in horror at a brother's outraged bed.
Well, have I missed? Am I not well-read in
Your royal family's catalogue of crime?
Chorus: You come from a far country and recite
Our ancient annals as though you had been present.
Kassandra: The Lord Apollo bestowed this gift on me.
Chorus: Was it because he had fallen in love with you?
Kassandra: I was ashamed to speak of this till now.
Chorus: Ah yes, adversity is less fastidious.
Kassandra: Oh, but he wrestled strenuously for my love.
Chorus: Did you come, then, to the act of getting child?
Kassandra: At first I consented, and then I cheated him.
Chorus: Already filled with his gift of prophecy?
Kassandra: Yes, I forewarned my people of their destiny.
Chorus: Did your divine lover show no displeasure?
Kassandra: Yes, the price I paid was that no one
listened to me.

Chorus: Your prophecies seem credible enough to us.
Kassandra: Oh!
Again the travail of the prophetic trance
Runs riot in my soul. Do you not see them
There, on the roof, those apparitions—children
Murdered by their own kin, in their hands
The innards of which their father ate—oh
What a pitiable load they carry! For that crime
Revenge is plotted by the fainthearted lion,[9]
The stay-at-home, stretched in my master's bed
(Being his slave, I must needs call him so),
Lying in wait for Troy's great conqueror.
Little he knows what that foul bitch with ears
Laid back and rolling tongue intends for him
With a vicious snap, her husband's murderess.
What abominable monster shall I call her—
A two-faced amphisbaene or Scylla that skulks
Among the rocks to waylay mariners,
Infernal sea-squib locked in internecine
Strife—did you not hear her alleluias
Of false rejoicing at his safe return?
Believe me or not, what must be will be, and then
You will pity me and say, She spoke the truth.
Chorus: The feast of Thyestes I recognized, and
shuddered,
But for the rest my wits are still astray.
Kassandra: Your eyes shall see the death of
Agamemnon.
Chorus: No, hush those ill-omened lips, unhappy girl!
Kassandra: There is no Apollo present, and so no cure.
Chorus: None, if you speak the truth; yet God forbid!
Kassandra: Pray God forbid, while they close in for the
kill!
Chorus: What man is there who would plot so foul a
crime?
Kassandra: Ah, you have altogether misunderstood.
Chorus: But how will he do it? That escapes me still.
Kassandra: And yet I can speak Greek only too well.
Chorus: So does Apollo, but his oracles are obscure.
Kassandra: Ah, how it burns me up! Apollo! Now
That lioness[10] on two feet pours in the cup
My wages too, and while she whets the blade
For him promises to repay my passage money
In my own blood. Why wear these mockeries,
This staff and wreath, if I must die, then you
Shall perish first and be damned. Now we are quits!
Apollo himself has stripped me, looking upon me
A public laughingstock, who has endured
The name of witch, waif, beggar, castaway.
So now the god who gave me second sight
Takes back his gift and dismisses his servant,
Ready for the slaughter at a dead man's grave.
Yet we shall be avenged. Now far away,
The exile[11] shall return, called by his father's
Unburied corpse to come and kill his mother.
Why weep at all this? Have I not seen Troy fall,
And those who conquered her are thus discharged.
I name this door the gate of Hades: now
I will go and knock, I will take heart to die.

---

9. Aigisthos.
10. Klytaïmnestra
11. Orestes.

---

7. Agamemnon.
8. Scamander is a river near Troy; Akheron (AK-e-ron) is the
river of the underworld.

I only pray that the blow may be mortal,
Closing these eyes in sleep without a struggle,
While my life blood ebbs quietly away.

Chorus: O woman, in whose wisdom is so much grief,
How, if you know the end, can you approach it
So gently, like an ox that goes to the slaughter?

Kassandra: What help would it be if I should put it off?

Chorus: Yet, while there is life there's hope—so people say.

Kassandra: For me no hope, no help. My hour has come.

Chorus: You face your end with a courageous heart.

Kassandra: Yes, so they console those whom life has crossed.

Chorus: Is there no comfort in an honorable death?

Kassandra: O Priam, father, and all your noble sons!
[*She approaches the door, then draws back.*]

Chorus: What is it? Why do you turn back, sick at heart?

Kassandra: Inside there is a stench of dripping blood.

Chorus: It is only the blood of their fireside sacrifice.

Kassandra: It is the sort of vapor that issues from a tomb.
I will go now and finish my lament
Inside the house. Enough of life! O friends!
I am not scared. I beg of you only this:
When the day comes for them to die, a man
For a man, woman for woman, remember me!

Chorus: Poor soul condemned to death, I pity you.

Kassandra: Yet one word more, my own dirge for myself.
I pray the Sun, on whom I now look my last,
That he may grant to my master's avengers
A fair price for the slave-girl slain at his side.
O sad mortality! when fortune smiles,
A painted image; and when trouble comes,
One touch of a wet sponge wipes it away. [*Exit*]

Chorus: And her case is even more pitiable than his.
Human prosperity never rests but always craves more, till blown up with pride it totters and falls. From the opulent mansions pointed at by all passersby none warns it away, none cries. "Let no more riches enter!" To him was granted the capture of Troy, and he has entered his home as a god, but now, if the blood of the past is on him, if he must pay with his own death for the crimes of bygone generations, then who is assured of a life without sorrow?

Agamemnon: Oh me!

Chorus: Did you hear?

Agamemnon: Oh me, again!

Chorus:[12] It is the King. Let us take counsel!
  1 I say, raise a hue and cry!
  2 Break in at once!
  3 Yes, we must act.
  4 *They* spurn delay.
  5 They plot a tyranny.
  6 Must we live their slaves?
  7 Better to die.
  8 Old men, what can we do?
  9 We cannot raise the dead.
  10 His death is not yet proved.
  11 We are only guessing.
  12 Let us break in and learn the truth!

[handwritten: Speak as individuals — don't all agree]

---

12. To the best of our knowledge, this is the first time in any Greek play when the chorus-members have spoken as individuals. Some translations show the passage as a crescendo through the seventh speech; then a lapse into a do-nothing attitude. What does this movement show about the relation of the chorus to the tradition-ridden, fatalistic society?

[*The doors are thrown open and* KLYTAÏMNESTRA *is seen standing over the bodies of* AGAMEMNON *and* KASSANDRA, *which are laid out on a purple robe.*]

Klytaïmnestra: All that I said before to bide my time
Without any shame I shall now unsay. How else
Could I have plotted against an enemy
So near and seeming dear and strung the snare
So high that he could not jump it? Now the feud
On which I have pondered all these years has been
Fought out to its conclusion. Here I stand
Over my work, and it was so contrived
As to leave no loophole. With this vast dragnet
I enveloped him in purple folds, then struck
Twice, and with two groans he stretched his legs,
Then on his outspread body I struck a third blow,
A drink for Zeus the Deliverer of the dead.
There he lay gasping out his soul and drenched me
In these deathly dew-drops, at which I cried
In sheer delight like newly-budding corn
That tastes the first spring showers. And so,
Venerable elders, you see how the matter stands.
Rejoice, if you are so minded. I glory in it.
With bitter tears he filled the household bowl;
Now he has drained it to the dregs and gone.

Chorus: How can you speak so of your murdered king?

Klytaïmnestra: You treat me like an empty-headed woman.
Again, undaunted, to such as understand
I say—commend or censure, as you please—
It makes no difference—here is Agamemnon,
My husband, dead, the work of this right hand,
Which acted justly. There you have the truth.

Chorus: Woman, what evil brew have you devoured to take
On you a crime that cries out for a public curse?
Yours was the fatal blow, banishment shall be yours,
Hissed and hated of all men.

Klytaïmnestra: Your sentence now for me is banishment,
But what did you do then to contravene
As though picking a ewe-lamb from his flocks,
Whose wealth of snowy fleeces never fails
To increase and multiply, he killed his own
Child, born to me in pain, my best-beloved?
Why did you not drive *him* from hearth and home?
I bid you cast at me such menaces
As make for mastery in equal combat
With one prepared to meet them, and if, please God,
The issue goes against you, suffering
Shall school those grey hairs in humility.

Chorus: You are possessed by some spirit of sin that stares
Out of your bloodshot eyes matching your bloody hands.
Dishonored and deserted of your kind, for this
Stroke you too shall be struck down.

Klytaïmnestra: Listen! By Justice, who avenged my child,
By the Fury to whom I vowed this sacrament,
So long as the hearth within is kindled by
Aigisthos, faithful to me now as always.
Low lies the man who insulted his wedded wife,
The darling of the Khryseids at Troy,
And stretched beside him this visionary seer,
Whom he fondled on shipboard, both now rewarded,
He as you see, and she swanlike has sung
Her dying ditty, his tasty side dish, for me
A rare spice to add relish to my joy.

Chorus: Oh, for the gift of death
To bring the long sleep that knows no waking,
Now that my lord and loyal protector
Breathes his last. For woman's sake
Long he fought overseas,
Now at home falls beneath a woman's hand
    Helen, the folly-beguiled, having ravaged the city of
    Troy,
    She has set on the curse of Atreus
    A crown of blood beyond ablution.
Klytaïmnestra: Do not pray for death nor turn your
    anger against one woman as the slayer of thousands!
Chorus: Demon of blood and tears
Inbred in two women single-hearted!
Perched on the roof he stands and preens his
Sable wings, a carrion-crow
Loud he croaks, looking down
Upon the feast spread before him here below.
Klytaïmnestra: Ah now you speak truth, naming the
    thrice-fed demon, who, glutted with blood, craves
    more, still young in his hunger.
Chorus: When will the feast be done?
Alas, it is the will of Zeus,
Who caused and brought it all to pass.
Nothing is here but was decreed in heaven.
Klytaïmnestra: It was not my doing, nor am I
    Agamemnon's wife, but a ghost in woman's guise,
    the shade of the banqueter whom Atreus fed.
Chorus: How is the guilt not yours?
And yet the crimes of old may well
Have had a hand, and so it drives
On, the trail of internecine murder.
Klytaïmnestra: What of *him?* Was the guilt not his,
    when he killed the child that I bore him? And so by
    the sword he has fallen.
Chorus: Alas, the mind strays. The house is falling.
A storm of blood lays the walls in ruins.
Another mortal stroke for Justice's hand
Will soon be sharpened.
    Oh me, who shall bury him, who sing the dirge?
    Who shall intone at the tomb of a blessed spirit
    A tribute pure in heart and truthful?
Klytaïmnestra: No, I'll bury him, but without mourners.
    By the waters of Akheron Iphigeneia is waiting for
    him with a kiss.
Chorus: The charge is answered with countercharges.
The sinner must suffer: such is God's will.
The ancient curse is bringing down the house
In self-destruction.
Klytaïmnestra: That is the truth, and I would be
    content that the spirit of vengeance should rest,
    having absolved the house from its madness.
    [*Enter* AIGISTHOS *with a bodyguard*]
Aigisthos: Now I have proof that there are Gods in
    heaven,
As I gaze on this purple mesh in which
My enemy lies, son of a treacherous father,
His father, Atreus, monarch of this realm,
Was challenged in his sovereign rights by mine,
Thyestes, his own brother, and banished him
From hearth and home. Later he returned
A suppliant and found sanctuary, indeed
A welcome; for his brother entertained him
To a feast of his own children's flesh, of which
My father unsuspecting took and ate.
Then, when he knew what he had done, he fell
Back spewing out the slaughtered flesh and, kicking
The table to the floor, with a loud cry
He cursed the House of Pelops. That is the crime

For which the son lies here. And fitly too
The plot was spun by me; for as a child
I was banished with my father, until Justice
Summoned me home. Now let me die, for never
Shall I live to another sight so sweet.
Chorus: Aigisthos, if it was you who planned this
    murder,
Then be assured, the people will stone you for it.
Aigisthos: Such talk from the lower benches! Even in
    dotage
Prison can teach a salutary lesson.
Better submit, or else you shall smart for it.
Chorus: You woman, who stayed at home and wallowed
    in
His bed, you plotted our great commander's death!
Aigisthos: Orpheus led all in rapture after him.[13]
Your senseless bark will be snuffed out in prison.
Chorus: You say the plot was yours, yet lacked the
    courage
To raise a hand but left it to a woman!
Aigisthos: As his old enemy, I was suspect.
Temptation was the woman's part. But now
I'll try my hand at monarchy, and all
Who disobey me shall be put in irons
And starved of food and light till they submit.
Chorus: Oh, if Orestes yet beholds the sun,
May he come home and execute them both!
Aigisthos: Ho, my guards, come forward, you have work
    to do.
Captain of the Guard: Stand by, draw your swords!
Chorus: We are not afraid to die.
Aigisthos: Die! We'll take you at your word.
Klytaïmnestra: Peace, my lord, and let no further wrong
    be done.
Captain, sheathe your swords. And you, old men,
Go home quietly. What has been, it had to be.
Scars enough we bear, now let us rest.
Aigisthos: Must I stand and listen to their threats?
Chorus: Men of Argos never cringed before a rogue.
Aigisthos: I shall overtake you yet—the day is near.
Chorus: Not if Orestes should come home again.
Aigisthos: Vain hope, the only food of castaways.
Chorus: Gloat and grow fat, blacken justice while you
    dare!
Aigisthos: All this foolish talk will cost you dear.
Chorus: Flaunt your gaudy plumes and strut beside your
    hen!
Klytaïmnestra: Pay no heed to idle clamor. You and I,
Masters of the house, shall now direct it well.

---

13. That is: You are not Orpheus, whose music caused people to
follow him.

1. Book Eleven of Homer's *Odyssey* is given in chapter 4. In this excerpt, Odysseus visits the underworld and, among others, meets the shade of Agamemnon, who found "a brutal death at home—and a bad wife behind it" (line 361 ff.). Compare Homer's story—presumably the accepted version—with the *Agamemnon* by Aeschylus. Homer portrays Agamemnon as a blameless hero who was done in by Aigisthos with the assistance of the "bad wife." Aeschylus, however, depicts Agamemnon as a weak and vain ruler and, rather than just a "bad wife," Klytaïmnestra becomes the avenging mother of a murdered daughter. Why were these changes made? Did they strengthen the plot? How?

2. It might be interesting to read through the speeches of the Chorus without any reference to the other speeches or action of the play. What is your impression of their attitude toward life in general? Do you find many examples of them speaking proverbial wisdom? It is one theme of this discussion of the Greeks that in their early cultural development they were bound by tradition and nature. Does this speaking in proverbs have any relation to this theme?

3. Kassandra, of course, is trying to arouse the Chorus to action. Quite aside from the mythical problem of the curse of Apollo, which caused everyone to disbelieve her prophecies, can you see any other reason why she cannot get these men to act? For example, why, when she was left alone in the chariot, knowing that she faced death as soon as she entered the palace, did she not run away? Certainly the members of the Chorus would not stop her.

4. Below is given a chart dealing with the levels of human freedom of action. It might be interesting to place the characters somewhere above or below the dividing line. Where would you place the Chorus throughout the play? Do they stand still, or does their position fluctuate? Where would you place Kassandra? Agamemnon? Klytaïmnestra?

The area of conduct
in which people are free
to accomplish their
purposes and desires.

The Dividing Line ——————

A not-quite-human
level where the ideas
of justice are bound by
tradition and nature.

5. When the chorus is telling of the death of Iphigeneia, they speak of her "swathed in folds of saffron." Later they say, "Night . . . who has cast over the towers of Troy a net so fine." Still later, Agamemnon walks on a purple "web," or "net." Why did Aeschylus use this image throughout the play? Does it have any significance beyond its literal meaning?

6. Notice that *Agamemnon* has its beginning in the darkness in the country town of Mycenae. The *Eumenides,* the third play of the trilogy, ends in the bright sunlight of Athens. Does this symbolism have any significance?

EUMENIDES

Aeschylus

This is the third play of the *Oresteia*. In the second one (*Choephori* or *The Libation Bearers*), Orestes has returned to Argos, recognized his sister, Elektra, and the two of them have planned and carried out the murder of Aigisthos and Klytaïmnestra. In the second play, the two ideas of justice became more apparent, for Orestes felt qualms about the murder of his mother. His sense of filial duty in carrying out revenge, as well as the fact that Apollo had commanded him to the deed, triumphed over his own conscience. Immediately after the murder he was set upon by the old hags, goddesses descended from the blood of Ouranos, whose duty it was to pursue those who had killed their own kindred.

The old idea of justice, revenge or retaliation, was presented in *Agamemnon;* we see in *Eumenides* the development of a new idea of justice and freedom for the city of Athens. As the play opens Orestes has taken refuge in the temple of Apollo at Delphi where he lies in exhausted sleep surrounded by the slumbering Furies. Apollo appears and sends him to Athens for trial. Meanwhile, the ghost of Klytaïmnestra appears before the Chorus (the Furies) and demands revenge. At this point Apollo and Athena together protect Orestes. Though the Furies demand revenge, Athena counters with a plea for justice. The scene then shifts to Athens where Athena has convened a court to sit in judgment on Orestes.

[*Enter* ATHENA *with the* JUDGES, *followed by citizens of Athens.*]
Athena: Herald, give orders to hold the people back,
Then sound the trumpet and proclaim silence.
For while this new tribunal is being enrolled,
It is right that all should ponder on its laws,
Both the litigants here whose case is to be judged,
And my whole people for all generations.
[*Enter* APOLLO]
Chorus: Apollo, what is there here that concerns you?
We say you have no authority in this matter.
Apollo: I come both as a witness, the accused
Having been a suppliant at my sanctuary
And purified of homicide at my hands,
And also to be tried with him, for I too
Must answer for the murder of his mother.
Open the case, and judge as you know how.
Athena: The case is open. You shall be first to speak.
[*To the* CHORUS]
The prosecutors shall take precedence
And first inform us truthfully of the facts.

Chorus: Many in number, we shall be brief in speech.
We beg you to answer our questions one by one.
First, is it true that you killed your mother?
Orestes: I killed her. That is true, and not denied.
Chorus: So then the first of the three rounds is ours.
Orestes: You should not boast that you have thrown me
yet.
Chorus: Next, since you killed her, you must tell us how.
Orestes: Yes, with a drawn sword leveled at the throat.
Chorus: Who was it who impelled or moved you to it?
Orestes: The oracle of this God who is my witness.
Chorus: The God of prophecy ordered matricide?
Orestes: Yes, and I have not repented it to this day.
Chorus: You *will* repent it, when you have been
condemned.
Orestes: My father shall defend me from the grave.
Chorus: Having killed your mother, you may well trust
the dead!
Orestes: She was polluted by a double crime.
Chorus: How so? Explain your meaning to the judges.
Orestes: She killed her husband and she killed my
father.
Chorus: She died without bloodguilt, and you still live.
Orestes: Why did you not hunt her when she was alive?
Chorus: She was not bound by blood to the man she
killed.
Orestes: And am I then bound by blood to my mother?
Chorus: Abandoned wretch, how did she nourish you
Within the womb? Do you repudiate
The nearest and dearest tie of motherhood?
Orestes: Apollo, give your evidence. I confess
That I did this deed as I have said.
Pronounce your judgment: was it justly done?
Apollo: Athena's appointed judges, I say to you,
Justly, and I, as prophet, cannot lie.
Never from my prophetic shrine have I
Said anything of city, man or woman
But what my father Zeus has commanded me.
This plea of mine must override all others,
Since it accords with our great father's will.
Chorus: Your argument is, then, that Zeus commanded
you
To charge Orestes with this criminal act
Regardless of the bond between son and mother?
Apollo: It is not the same, to murder a great king,
A woman too to do it, and not in open
Fight like some brave Amazon, but in such
Manner as I shall now inform this court.
On his return from battle, bringing home
A balance for the greater part of good,
She welcomed him with fine words and then, while
He bathed, pavilioned him in a purple robe
And struck him down and killed him—a man and king
Whom the whole world had honored. Such was the crime
For which she paid. Let the judges take note.
Chorus: According to your argument Zeus gives
Precedence to the father; yet Zeus it was
Who cast into prison his own father Kronos.
Judges, take note, and ask him to explain.
Apollo: Abominable monsters, loathed by gods
And men, do you not understand that chains
Can be unfastened and prison doors unlocked?
But once the dust has drunk a dead man's blood,
He can never rise again—for that no remedy
Has been appointed by our almighty Father,
Although all else he can overturn at will
Without so much effort as a single breath.

[handwritten, rotated in bottom margin:] Chorus not people
[handwritten, rotated in bottom margin:] Change of scene

Chorus: See what your plea for the defendant means.
Is this not what he did—to spill his mother's
Blood on the ground? And shall he then be allowed
To live on in his father's house? What public
Altar can he approach and where find fellowship?
Apollo: The mother is not a parent, only the nurse
Of the seed which the true parent, the father,
Commits to her as to a stranger to
Keep it with God's help safe from harm. And I
Have proof of this. There can be a father
Without a mother. We have a witness here,
This daughter of Olympian Zeus, who sprang
Armed from her father's head, a goddess whom
No goddess could have brought to birth. Therefore,
Out of goodwill to your country and your people
I sent this suppliant to seek refuge with you,
That you, Athena, may find in him and his
A faithful ally for all time to come.
Athena: Enough has now been spoken. Are you agreed
That I call on the judges to record
Their votes justly according to their conscience?
Apollo: Our quiver is empty, every arrow spent.
We wait to hear the issue of the trial.
Athena: And has my ruling your approval too?
Chorus: Sirs, you have heard the case, and now declare
Judgment according to your solemn oath.
Athena: Citizens of Athens, hear my declaration
At this first trial in the history of man.
This great tribunal shall remain in power
Meeting in solemn session on this hill,
Where long ago the Amazons encamped
When they made war on Theseus, and sacrificed
To Ares—hence its name:[14] Here reverence
For law and inbred fear among my people
Shall hold their hands from evil night and day,
Only let them not tamper with the laws,
But keep the fountain pure and sweet to drink.
<u>I warn you not to banish from your lives
All terror but to seek the mean between
Autocracy and anarchy</u>; and in this way
You shall possess in ages yet unborn
An impregnable fortress of liberty
Such as no people has throughout the world.
With these words I establish this tribunal
Grave, quick to anger, incorruptible,
And always vigilant over those that sleep.
Let the judges now rise and cast their votes.[15]

[handwritten, right margin:] don't go from one extreme to another

Chorus: We charge you to remember that we have
Great power to harm, and vote accordingly.
Apollo: I charge you to respect the oracles
Sanctioned by Zeus and see that they are fulfilled.
Chorus: By interfering in what is not your office
You have desecrated your prophetic shrine.
Apollo: Then was my Father also at fault when he
Absolved Ixion, the first murderer?
Chorus: Keep up your chatter, but if our cause should
fail,
We shall lay on this people a heavy hand.

---

14. The hill and the court which met on it were called the
Areopagus.

15. It is understood that the members of the jury are dropping
their votes into an urn during the next eight speeches.

Apollo: Yes, you will lose your case, and then you may
Spit out your poison, but it will do no harm.
Chorus: Insolent youth mocks venerable age.
We await the verdict, ready to let loose
Against this city our destructive rage.
Athena: The final judgment rests with me, and I
Announce that my vote shall be given to Orestes.
No mother gave me birth, and in all things
Save marriage I commend with all my heart
The masculine, my father's child indeed.
Therefore I cannot hold in higher esteem
A woman killed because she killed her husband.
If the votes are equal, Orestes wins.
Let the appointed officers proceed
To empty the urns and count the votes.
Orestes: O bright Apollo, how shall the judgment go?
Chorus: O black mother Night, are you watching this?
Orestes: My hour has come—the halter or the light.
Chorus: And ours—to exercise our powers or perish.
Apollo: Sirs, I adjure you to count carefully.
If judgment errs, great harm will come of it,
Whereas one vote may raise a fallen house.
Athena: He stands acquitted on the charge of
bloodshed,
The human votes being equally divided.
Orestes: Lady Athena, my deliverer,
I was an outcast from my country, now
I can go home again and live once more
In my paternal heritage, thanks to you
And to Apollo and to the third, Zeus,
Who governs the whole world. Before I go
I give my word to you and to your people
For all posterity that no commander
Shall lead an Argive army in war against
This city. If any should violate this pledge,
Out of the graves which shall then cover us
We would arise with adverse omens to
Obstruct and turn them back. If, however,
They keep this covenant and stand by your side,
They shall always have our blessing. And so farewell!
May you and your people always prevail
Against the assaults of all your enemies!
[*Exit*]
Chorus: Oho, you junior gods, since you have trod
under foot
The laws of old and robbed us of our powers,
We shall afflict this country
With damp contagion, bleak and barren, withering up the
soil,
Mildew on bud and birth abortive. Venomous pestilence
Shall sweep your cornlands with infectious death.
To weep—No! To work? Yes! To work ill and lay low the
people!
So will the maids of Night mourn for their stolen honors.
Athena: Let me persuade you to forget your grief!
You are not defeated. The issue of the trial
Has been determined by an equal vote.
It was Zeus himself who plainly testified
That Orestes must not suffer for what he did.
I beg you, therefore, do not harm my country,
Blasting her crops with drops of rank decay
And biting cankers in the early buds.
Rather accept my offer to stay and live
In a cavern on this hill and there receive
The adoration of my citizens.
Chorus: Oho, you junior gods, etc.

Athena: No, *not* dishonored, and therefore spare my
people!
I too confide in Zeus—why speak of that?—
And I alone of all the Olympian gods
Know of the keys which guard the treasury
Of heaven's thunder. But there is no need of that.
Let my persuasion serve to calm your rage.
Reside with me and share my majesty;
And when from these wide acres you enjoy
Year after year the harvest offerings
From couples newly-wed praying for children,
Then you will thank me for my intercession.
Chorus: How can you treat us so?
Here to dwell, ever debased, defiled!
Hear our passion, hear, black Night!
For the powers once ours, sealed long, long ago
Have by the junior gods been all snatched away.
Athena: You are my elders, and therefore I indulge
Your passion. And yet, though not so wise as you,
To me too Zeus has granted understanding.
If you refuse me and depart, believe me,
This country will yet prove your heart's desire,
For as the centuries pass so there will flow
Such glory to my people as will assure
To all divinities worshipped here by men
And women gathered on festive holidays
More honors than could be yours in any other
City throughout the world. And so, I beg you,
Keep from my citizens the vicious spur
Of internecine strife, which pricks the breast
Of manhood flown with passion as with wine!
Abroad let battle rage for every heart
That is fired with love of glory—that shall be theirs
In plenty. So this is my offer to you—
To give honor and receive it and to share
My glory in this country loved by heaven.
Chorus: How can you, etc.
Athena: I will not weary in my benedictions,
Lest it should ever be said that you, so ancient
In your divinity, were driven away
By me and by my mortal citizens.
No, if Persuasion's holy majesty,
The sweet enchantment of these lips divine,
Has power to move you, please, reside with me.
But, if you still refuse, then, since we have made
This offer to you, it would be wrong to lay
Your hands upon us in such bitter rage.
Again, I tell you, it is in your power to own
This land attended with the highest honors.
Chorus: Lady Athena, what do you offer us?
Athena: A dwelling free of sorrow. Pray accept.
Chorus: Say we accept, what privileges shall we have?
Athena: No family shall prosper without your grace.
Chorus: Will you ensure us this prerogative?
Athena: I will, and bless all those that worship you.
Chorus: And pledge that assurance for all time to come?
Athena: I need not promise what I will not perform.
Chorus: Your charms are working, and our rage
subsides.
Athena: Here make your dwelling, where you shall win
friends.
Chorus: What song then shall we chant in salutation?
Athena: A song of faultless victory—from land and sea,
From skies above let gentle breezes blow
And breathing sunshine float from shore to shore;
Let crops and cattle increase and multiply
And children grow in health and happiness,

And let the righteous prosper; for I, as one
Who tends flowers in a garden, cherish fondly
The seed that bears no sorrow. That is your part,
While I in many a battle shall strive until
This city stands victorious against all
Its enemies and renowned throughout the world.

Chorus: We accept; we agree to dwell with you
Here in Athens, which by grace of Zeus
Stands a fortress for the gods,
Jeweled crown of Hellas. So
With you now we join in prayer
That smiling suns and fruitful soils unite to yield
Lifelong joy, fortune fair,
Light and darkness reconciled.

Athena: For the good of my people I have given homes
in the city to these deities,[16] whose power is so great and
so slowly appeased; and, whenever a man falls foul of
them, apprehended to answer for the sins of his fathers,
he shall be brought to judgment before them, and the
dust shall stifle his proud boast.

Chorus: Free from blight may the early blossom deck
Budding trees, and may no parching drought
Spread across the waving fields.
Rather Pan in season grant
From the flocks and herds a full
Return from year to year, and from the rich
Store which these gods vouchsafe
May the Earth repay them well!

Athena: Guardians of my city, listen to the blessings they
bring, and remember that their power is great in heaven
and hell, and on earth too they bring to some glad
music and to some lives darkened with weeping.

Chorus: Free from sudden death that cuts
Short the prime of manhood, blest
In your daughters too, to whom
Be granted husband and home, and may the dread Fates
Keep them safe, present in every household,
Praised and magnified in every place!

Athena: Fair blessings indeed from powers that so
lately were averted in anger, and I thank Zeus and the
spirit of persuasion that at last there is no strife left
between us, except that they vie with me in blessing my
people.

Chorus: Peace to all, free from that
Root of evil, civil strife!
May they live in unity,
And never more may the blood of kin be let flow!
Rather may all of them bonded together
Feel and act as one in love and hate!

Athena: From these dread shapes, so quick to learn a
new music, I foresee great good for my people, who, if
only they repay their favors with the reverence due, shall
surely establish the reign of justice in a city that will
shine as a light for all mankind.
[*Enter* ESCORT OF WOMEN, *carrying crimson robes
and torches.*]

Chorus: Joy to you all in your justly appointed riches,
Joy to all the people blest
With the Virgin's love, who stands
Next beside her Father's throne!
Wisdom man has learnt at last.
Under her protection this
Land enjoys the grace of Zeus.

---

16. This is the transition of the awful goddesses from the *Erinyes*
(the Furies) to the *Eumenides* (the Gracious Ones).

Athena: Joy to you also, and now let me lead you in
torchlight to your new dwelling place! Let solemn
oblations speed you in joy to your home beneath the
earth, and there imprison all harm while still letting flow
your blessings!

Chorus: Joy to you, joy, yet again we pronounce our
blessing,
Joy to all the citizens,
Gods and mortals both alike.
While you hold this land and pay
Homage to our residence,
You shall have no cause to blame
Chance and change in human life.

Athena: I thank you for your gracious salutations,
And now you shall be escorted in the light
Of torches to your subterranean dwelling,
Attended by the sacristans of my temple
Together with this company of girls
And married women and others bowed with years.
Women, let them put on these robes of crimson,
And let these blazing torches light the way,
That the goodwill of our new co-residents
Be shown in the manly prowess of your sons!
[*The* CHORUS *put on the crimson robes and a
procession is formed led by young men in armor,
with the* CHORUS *and the escort following, and
behind them the citizens of Athens. The rest is sung
as the procession moves away.*]

Chorus of the Escort: Pass on your way, O powers
majestic,
Daughters of darkness in happy procession!
People of Athens, hush, speak fair!
Pass to the caverns of earth immemorial
There to be worshipped in honor and glory!
People of Athens, hush, speak fair!
Gracious and kindly of heart to our people,
Come with us, holy ones, hither in gladness,
Follow the lamps that illumine the way!
O sing at the end alleluia!
Peace to you, peace of a happy community,
People of Athens! Zeus who beholds all
Watches, himself with the Fates reconciled.
O sing at the end alleluia!

Exercises due

1. Of course all that one has to do to understand
this play almost completely is to understand the
difference in the meaning of the word *justice* as
it is first used in the play by the Furies and as it
is used by Athena in her last speech of the play.
That difference in meaning is worth analyzing
in class. To do so, here are some questions that
may guide your discussion:
a. Insofar as the structure of the play is
concerned—and its significance—why can
Orestes leave when two-thirds of the play is
over?

*he is not real hero —
justice is*

POLITICAL & SOCIAL PLAY

b. The Furies insist that *fear* is a necessary part of the idea of justice that people hold. How right are they?
c. The real turning point of the play probably comes when Athena gives her final instructions to the jury:

> Here reverence
> For law and inbred fear among my people
> Shall hold their hands from evil night and day,
> Only let them not tamper with the laws,
> But keep the fountain pure and sweet to drink.
> I warn you not to banish from your lives
> All terror but to seek the mean between
> Autocracy and anarchy; and in this way
> You shall possess in ages yet unborn
> An impregnable fortress of liberty . . .

What principles are involved in this statement?
d. The actual role of the Eumenides (as they are changed from the Furies) is never made entirely clear. From the evidence in the play itself, what seems to be their role in the maintenance of a new type of justice?

2. What difference will be found in the lives of the people of Athens as they change from the old idea of justice to the new? In what way will the new idea allow for personal freedom?
3. Refer back to question 1 of the Exercises following the *Agamemnon*. Could the *Eumenides* have been written if Aeschylus had stuck to Homer's version of the plot? Why or why not?

MEMORIAL ORATION

Perikles (?–429 B.C.)

This portion of Perikles' famous oration is taken from the history of the Peloponnesian War as written by Thucydides (thoo-SID-i-deez). Perikles made this address at the public funeral of a group of Athenian young men who had been killed in the war.

Some scholars contend that Aspasia exerted considerable influence not only on this notable speech but also on the political strategies of Perikles in general. An intelligent and highly educated foreigner from Ionia, Aspasia was a former hetaera (Gk., *hetaira,* female companion), Perikles' concubine (in effect, common-law wife), and the mother of his son Perikles, who was legitimized by vote of the people. The hetaerae of ancient Greece were companions—physically, intellectually, and emotionally—to influential men in Athenian society. Well-educated and adept in music, dancing, conversation, and other social graces, they fulfilled a role generally denied to Greek wives who, though undisputed mistresses of their households, were not permitted to partake fully in life outside the home.

Though criticized by some because of her former profession and her political influence, Aspasia established in the home of Perikles what might be called the first salon. Here she entertained notable artists, philosophers, and political leaders, including the more liberated women of Athens. Breaking with tradition, some men brought their wives to Aspasia's dinner parties to participate in discussions about the need for wives to be better educated and thus better able to be fit companions for their husbands. Since she was credited by Sokrates with teaching Perikles the art of rhetoric, it is likely that the brilliant Aspasia assisted Perikles in the composition of some of his speeches, most especially the Memorial Oration. (In his *Menexenus* Plato credited Aspasia with the composition of the Funeral Oration.)

As you read this eloquent address, you should remind yourself of the questions about human aspirations that had been raised in the plays of Aeschylus. In the *Agamemnon* the chorus railed against great wealth, insisting that the most humble life was the best. In *Eumenides* we observed the question of whether justice should be by reason or by stern revenge within the family. The question of the conflict between maturing man and an absolute god who ruled through fear had been raised. Other questions we have not yet seen in the literature, but which were present in the Greek mind (and in our own) are whether the state needs to protect itself by universal military training or not, and whether a life of cultural pursuits does not enfeeble people in a nation. Perhaps the greatest question for our time and theirs is whether a democracy can really function. The argument on the one side is that an absolute government gets things done quickly and efficiently, while in a democracy, people talk so much that they have no time for action.

You will find some of the answers in which the Athenians believed in the following selection.

. . . Before I praise the dead, I should like to point out by what principles of action we rose to power, and under what institutions and through what manner of life our empire became great. For I conceive that such thoughts are not unsuited to the occasion, and that this numerous assembly of citizens and strangers may profitably listen to them.

Our form of government does not enter into rivalry with the institutions of others. We do not copy our neighbors, but are an example to them. It is true that we are called a democracy; for the administration is in the hands of the many and not of the few. But while the law secures equal justice to all alike in their private disputes, the claim of excellence is also recognized; and when a citizen is in any way distinguished, he is preferred to the public service, not as a matter of privilege, but as the reward of merit. Neither is poverty a bar, but a man may benefit his country whatever be the obscurity of his condition. There is no exclusiveness in our public life, and in our private intercourse we are not suspicious of one another, nor angry with our neighbor if he does what he likes; we do not put on sour looks at him, which though harmless are not pleasant. While we are thus unconstrained in our private intercourse, a spirit of reverence pervades our public acts: we are prevented from doing wrong by respect for authority and for the laws; having an especial regard to those which are ordained for the protection of the injured, as well as to these unwritten laws which bring upon the transgressor of them the reprobation of the general sentiment.

And we have not forgotten to provide for our weary spirits many relaxations from toil; we have regular games and sacrifices throughout the year; at home the style of our life is refined; and the delight which we daily feel in all these things helps to banish melancholy. Because of the greatness of our city the fruits of the whole earth flow in upon us; so that we enjoy the goods of other countries as freely as of our own.

Then again, our military training is in many respects superior to that of our adversaries. Our city is thrown open to the world; and we never expel a foreigner, or prevent him from seeing or learning anything of which the secret, if revealed to an enemy, might profit him. We rely not upon management of trickery, but upon our own hearts and hands. And in the matter of education whereas they from early youth are always undergoing laborious exercises which are to make them brave, we live at ease, and yet are equally ready to face the perils which they face. . . .

If, then, we prefer to meet danger with a light heart but without laborious training, and with a courage which is gained by habit and not enforced by law, are we not greatly the gainers? Since we do not anticipate the pain, although, when the hour comes, we can be as brave as those who never allow themselves to rest; and thus too our city is equally admirable in peace and in war. For we are lovers of the beautiful, yet simple in our tastes, and we cultivate the mind without loss of manliness. Wealth we employ, not for talk and ostentation, but when there is a real use for it. To avow poverty with us is no disgrace; the true disgrace is in doing nothing to avoid it. An Athenian citizen does not neglect the State because he takes care of his own household; and even those of us who are engaged in business have a very fair idea of politics. We alone regard a man who takes no interest in public affairs, not as a harmless but as a useless character; and if few of us are originators, we are all sound judges, of a policy. The great impediment to action is, in our opinion, not discussion, but the want of that knowledge which is gained by discussion preparatory to action. For we have a peculiar power of thinking before we act, and of acting too; whereas other men are courageous from ignorance but hesitate upon reflection. And they are surely to be esteemed the bravest spirits, who, having the clearest sense both of the pains and the pleasures of life, do not on that account shrink from danger. In doing good, again we are unlike others; we make our friends by conferring, not by receiving favors. Now he who confers a favor is the firmer friend, because he would fain by kindness keep alive the memory of an obligation; but the recipient is colder in his feelings, because he knows that in requiting another's generosity he will not be winning gratitude, but only paying a debt. We alone do good to our neighbors not upon a calculation of interest, but in the confidence of freedom and in a frank and fearless spirit.

To sum up: I say that Athens is the school of Hellas, and that the individual Athenian in his own person seems to have the power of adapting himself to the most varied forms of action with the utmost versatility and grace. This is no passing and idle word, but truth and fact; and the assertion is verified by the position to which these qualities have raised the State. For in the hour of trial, Athens alone among her contemporaries is superior to the report of her. No enemy who comes against her is indignant at the reverses which he sustains at the hands of such a city; no subject complains that his masters are unworthy of him. And we shall assuredly not be without witnesses: there are mighty monuments of our power, which will make us the wonder of this and of succeeding ages; we shall not need the praises of Homer or of any other panegyrist, whose poetry may please for the moment although his representation of the facts will not bear the light of day. For we have compelled every land and every sea to open a path for our valor, and have everywhere planted eternal memorials of our friendship and of our enmity. Such is the city for whose sake these men nobly fought and died: they could not bear the thought that she might be taken from them; and every one of us who survive should gladly toil on her behalf.

Exercises

1. The chorus of *Agamemnon* cautions against the evils of wealth. We, too, have a proverb about money and evil. How have the Greeks grown since Aeschylus wrote of the earlier populace? How would Perikles argue with our own proverb?
2. What similarities in terms of purpose and ideals do you see between this oration and Lincoln's "Gettysburg Address" (delivered when our own nation was undergoing the ordeal of a Civil War)? Are the ideals of both any less relevant today?
3. Here is raised an old question about men of words and men of action. It is frequently said that the democratic ways are terribly slow because people spend their time talking and never act. Is a compromise between words and action possible?
4. Why does Perikles speak of the individual Athenian when he is making a summary of the government?

OEDIPUS THE KING

Sophokles (496–406 B.C.)

This play is perhaps the best known of all the Greek tragedies, since it was taken by Aristotle in his treatise, *Poetics* (see chapter 6), as a model for this form of drama. All of the classic elements of tragedy are here: a man of great stature who falls from high station to low because of a fatal flaw in his personality; the unity of time (one day) and of place (the exterior of the royal palace at Thebes); the calling forth of the emotions of pity and fear in the spectator; and the final sense of catharsis. This last might be defined as the sense that the action has worked itself out to its one inevitable conclusion. In doing so, the emotions of pity and fear are purged in the spectator, who is left at peace. We feel that the ending, though tragic, is right, and that there is no more to be said or done.

In order to understand the play, one should know some of the mythology that lies in its background. The city of Thebes was founded by Kadmos, as we are reminded frequently in the speeches. The history that follows is not of immediate concern until we come to the reign of King Laïos and his queen, Iocaste. Two things happened at that time. First, Laïos set out on a journey and was murdered on the road by unknown assailants. In the meantime a fearful monster known as the Sphinx (to whom frequent references are made in the play) established itself outside the gate of Thebes and demanded a yearly tribute from the city. This was to continue until someone could solve the riddle the Sphinx proposed to every passer-by. The riddle, we might think, is a simple one, for it was the old one, "What goes on four legs in the morning, on two legs at noon, and on three legs in the evening?" The answer, of course, is *Man.* The riddle and its answer in this play are symbolic of the idea that the one who could solve the riddle knew the nature of man.

To the city at this time came a young man, Oedipus, supposedly the son of the king and queen of Corinth. The Sphinx posed her riddle and he gave the right answer readily, thus freeing the city of the monster and the tribute she demanded. The king being dead, the people of the city chose Oedipus as their king. As was the custom, he married Iocaste, who bore him two sons and two daughters. It is several years after this when the play begins.

One question this play might bring up in the mind of a spectator is whether Oedipus is the victim of fate, or whether he is a man with free will whose character is his fate and produces his doom. Probably one will not find a clear answer to this question. In this connection one might ask what is the fatal flaw in Oedipus's character. Is it his sudden anger? Is it his impulsiveness in all of his actions, an impulsiveness that might be of great value to a ruler who must make quick decisions? Or is it his search for truth that will not be turned aside even when his wife and the chorus suggest that he should leave well enough alone?

Is this an admirable trait or a sign of plain stubbornness? Another question is about the clarity of vision: Oedipus thinks he sees clearly but the blind Teiresias perceives the truth with a kind of inner vision. Which one beholds more clearly? And why is the wound Oedipus inflicts upon himself not only *an* appropriate one but *the* appropriate one? The translation is by Dudley Fitts and Robert Fitzgerald.

Below is an outline of the formal structure of the play followed by a brief explanation:

Prologue; Parodos	exposition
Scene I; Ode I	
Scene II; Ode II	
Scene III; Ode III	complication
Scene IV; Ode IV	
Exodos	resolution

In the Prologue, the background to the coming action is supplied by Oedipus, Priest, and Creon. Next, the chorus enters in the Parados, singing, dancing, and commenting on the situation. The combination of Prologue and Parados presents the dramatic exposition, the explanation of the coming conflict (Theban woes and Oedipus's search for the cause).

In the body of the play (the dramatic complication), there are four scenes alternating with four choral odes. The scenes involve dialogue between two or more characters including, sometimes, Choragos, the leader of the chorus and a representative Theban citizen. During the odes, the chorus sings and dances to paired stanzas (strophes and antistrophes); for the strophe they dance up one side of the stage and down the other side during the antistrophe.

Finally, in the Exodos, the complications are resolved, the consequences revealed, and the characters make their exit.

CHARACTERS

Oedipus
A Priest
Creon
Teiresias
Iocaste
Messenger
Shepherd of Laïos
Second Messenger
Chorus of Theban Elders

The scene. Before the palace of Oedipus, King of Thebes. A central door and two lateral doors open onto a platform which runs the length of the facade. On the platform, right and left, are altars; and three steps lead down into the "orchestra," or chorus-ground. At the beginning of the action these steps are crowded by suppliants who have brought branches and chaplets of olive leaves and who lie in various attitudes of despair. OEDIPUS enters.

PROLOGUE

Oedipus:
My children, generations of the living
In the line of *Kadmos,* nursed at his ancient hearth:
Why have you strewn yourselves before these altars
In supplication, with your boughs and garlands?
The breath of incense rises from the city
With a sound of prayer and lamentation.

Children,
I would not have you speak through messengers,
And therefore I have come myself to hear you—
I, Oedipus, who bear the famous name.

[*To a* Priest:

You, there, since you are eldest in the company,
Speak for them all, tell me what preys upon you,
Whether you come in dread, or crave some blessing:
Tell me, and never doubt that I will help you
In every way I can; I should be heartless
Were I not moved to find you suppliant here.

Priest:
Great Oedipus, O powerful King of Thebes!
You see how all the ages of our people
Cling to your altar steps: here are boys
Who can barely stand alone, and here are priests
By weight of age, as I am a priest of God,
And young men chosen from those yet unmarried;
As for the others, all that multitude,
They wait with olive chaplets in the squares,
At the two shrines of Pallas, and where Apollo
Speaks in the glowing embers.

Your own eyes

Must tell you: Thebes is tossed on a murdering sea
And can not lift her head from the death surge.
A rust consumes the buds and fruits of the earth;
The herds are sick; children die unborn,
And labor is vain. The god of plague and pyre
Raids like detestable lightning through the city,
And all the house of Kadmos is laid waste,
All emptied, and all darkened: Death alone
Battens upon the misery of Thebes.

You are not one of the immortal gods, we know;
Yet we have come to you to make our prayer
As to the man surest in mortal ways
And wisest in the ways of God. You saved us
From the Sphinx, that flinty singer, and the tribute
We paid to her so long; yet you were never
Better informed than we, nor could we teach you:
It was some god breathed in you to set us free.

Therefore, O mighty King, we turn to you:
Find us our safety, find us a remedy,
Whether by counsel of the gods or men.
A king of wisdom tested in the past
Can act in a time of troubles, and act well.
Noblest of men, restore
Life to your city! Think how all men call you
Liberator for your triumph long ago;
Ah, when your years of kingship are remembered,
Let them not say *We rose, but later fell*—
Keep the State from going down in the storm!
Once, years ago, with happy augury,
You brought us fortune; be the same again!
No man questions your power to rule the land:
But rule over men, not over a dead city!
Ships are only hulls, citadels are nothing,
When no life moves in the empty passageways.

Oedipus:
Poor children! You may be sure I know
All that you longed for in your coming here.
I know that you are deathly sick; and yet,
Sick as you are, not one is as sick as I.
Each of you suffers in himself alone
His anguish, not another's; but my spirit
Groans for the city, for myself, for you.

I was not sleeping, you are not waking me.
No, I have been in tears for a long while
And in my restless thought walked many ways.
In all my search, I found one helpful course,
And that I have taken: I have sent Creon,
Son of Menoikeus, brother of the Queen,
To Delphi, Apollo's place of revelation,
To learn there, if he can,
What act or pledge of mine may save the city.
I have counted the days, and now, this very day,
I am troubled, for he has overstayed his time.
What is he doing? He has been gone too long.
Yet whenever he comes back, I should do ill
To scant whatever duty God reveals.

Priest:
It is a timely promise. At this instant
They tell me Creon is here.

Oedipus:

O Lord Apollo!

May his news be fair as his face is radiant!

Priest:
It could not be otherwise: he is crowned with bay,
The chaplet is thick with berries.

Oedipus:

We shall soon know;

He is near enough to hear us now.

[*Enter* Creon

O Prince:

Brother: son of Menoikeus:
What answer do you bring us from the god?

Creon:
A strong one. I can tell you, great afflictions
Will turn out well, if they are taken well.

Oedipus:
What was the oracle? These vague words
Leave me still hanging between hope and fear.

Creon:
Is it your pleasure to hear me with all these
Gathered around us? I am prepared to speak,
But should we not go in?

Oedipus:

Let them all hear it.

It is for them I suffer, more than for myself.

Creon:
Then I will tell you what I heard at Delphi.

In plain words
The god commands us to expel from the land of Thebes
An old defilement we are sheltering.
It is a deathly thing, beyond cure;
We must not let it feed upon us longer.

Oedipus:
What defilement? How shall we rid ourselves of it?

Creon:
By exile or death, blood for blood. It was
Murder that brought the plague-wind on the city.

Oedipus:
Murder of whom? Surely the god has named him?

Creon:
My lord, long ago Laïos was our king,
Before you came to govern us.

Oedipus:

I know;

I learned of him from others; I never saw him.

Creon:
He was murdered; and Apollo commands us now
To take revenge upon whoever killed him.

Oedipus:
Upon whom? Where are they? Where shall we find a clue
To solve that crime, after so many years?
Creon:
Here in this land, he said.
                                        If we make enquiry,
We may touch things that otherwise escape us.
Oedipus:
Tell me: Was Laïos murdered in his house,
Or in the fields, or in some foreign country?
Creon:
He said he planned to make a pilgrimage.
He did not come home again.
Oedipus:
                                        And was there no one,
No witness, no companion, to tell what happened?
Creon:
They were all killed but one, and he got away
So frightened that he could remember one thing only.
Oedipus:
What was that one thing? One may be the key
To everything, if we resolve to use it.
Creon:
He said that a band of highwaymen attacked them,
Outnumbered them, and overwhelmed the King.
Oedipus:
Strange, that a highwayman should be so daring—
Unless some faction here bribed him to do it.
Creon:
We thought of that. But after Laïos' death
New troubles arose and we had no avenger.
Oedipus:
What troubles could prevent your hunting down the
        killers?
Creon:
The riddling Sphinx's song
Made us deaf to all mysteries but her own.
Oedipus:
Then once more I must bring what is dark to light.
It is most fitting that Apollo shows,
As you do, this compunction for the dead.
You shall see how I stand by you, as I should,
To avenge the city and the city's god,
And not as though it were for some distant friend,
But for my own sake, to be rid of evil.
Whoever killed King Laïos might—who knows?—
Decide at any moment to kill me as well.
By avenging the murdered king I protect myself.

Come, then, my children: leave the altar steps,
Lift up your olive boughs!
                                        One of you go.
And summon the people of Kadmos to gather here.
I will do all that I can; you may tell them that.
                                        [*Exit a* Page
So, with the help of God,
We shall be saved—or else indeed we are lost.
Priest:
Let us rise, children. It was for this we came,
And now the King has promised it himself.
Phoibos has sent us an oracle; may he descend
Himself to save us and drive out the plague.

[*Exeunt* OEDIPUS *and* CREON *into the palace by the central door. The* PRIEST *and the* SUPPLIANTS *disperse R and L. After a short pause the* CHORUS *enters the orchestra.*

PARODOS

Chorus:

[Strophe 1

What is God singing in his profound
Delphi of gold and shadow?
What oracle for Thebes, the sunwhipped city?

Fear unjoints me, the roots of my heart tremble.

Now I remember, O Healer, your power, and wonder:
Will you send doom like a sudden cloud, or weave it
Like nightfall of the past?

Speak, speak to us, issue of holy sound:
Dearest to our expectancy: be tender!

[Antistrophe 1

Let me pray to Athenê, the immortal daughter of Zeus,
And to Artemis her sister
Who keeps her famous throne in the market ring,
And to Apollo, bowman at the far butts of heaven—

O gods, descend! Like three streams leap against
The fires of our grief, the fires of darkness;
Be swift to bring us rest!

As in the old time from the brilliant house
Of air you stepped to save us, come again!

Now our afflictions have no end,   [Strophe 2
Now all our stricken host lies down
And no man fights off death with his mind;

The noble plowland bears no grain,
And groaning mothers can not bear—

See, how our lives like birds take wing,
Like sparks that fly when a fire soars,
To the shore of the god of evening.

The plague burns on, it is pitiless,   [Antistrophe 2
Though pallid children laden with death
Lie unwept in the stony ways,

And old gray women by every path
Flock to the strand about the altars
There to strike their breasts and cry
Worship of Phoibos in wailing prayers:
Be kind, God's golden child!

                                                    [Strophe 3
There are no swords in this attack by fire,
No shields, but we are ringed with cries.
Send the besieger plunging from our homes
Into the vast sea-room of the Atlantic
Or into the waves that foam eastward of Thrace—

For the day ravages what the night spares—

Destroy our enemy, lord of the thunder!
Let him be riven by lightning from heaven!

                                                    [Antistrophe 3
Phoibos Apollo, stretch the sun's bowstring,
That golden cord, until it sing for us,
Flashing arrows in heaven!
                                        Artemis, Huntress,
Race with flaring lights upon our mountains!

O scarlet god, O golden-banded brow,
O Theban Bacchos in a storm of Maenads,

[*Enter* Oedipus, C.

Whirl upon Death, that all the Undying hate!
Come with blinding torches, come in joy!

SCENE I

Oedipus:
Is this your prayer? It may be answered. Come,
Listen to me, act as the crisis demands,
And you shall have relief from all these evils.

Until now I was a stranger to this tale,
As I had been a stranger to the crime.
Could I track down the murderer without a clue?
But now, friends,
As one who became a citizen after the murder,
I make this proclamation to all Thebans:
If any man knows by whose hand Laïos, son of Labdakos,
Met his death, I direct that man to tell me everything,
No matter what he fears for having so long withheld it.
Let it stand as promised that no further trouble
Will come to him, but he may leave the land in safety.

Moreover: If anyone knows the murderer to be foreign,
Let him not keep silent: he shall have his reward from
      me.
However, if he does conceal it; if any man
Fearing for his friend or for himself disobeys this edict,
Hear what I propose to do:

I solemnly forbid the people of this country,
Where power and throne are mine, ever to receive that
      man
Or speak to him, no matter who he is, or let him
Join in sacrifice, lustration, or in prayer.
I decree that he be driven from every house,
Being, as he is, corruption itself to us: the Delphic
Voice of Zeus has pronounced this revelation.
Thus I associate myself with the oracle
And take the side of the murdered king.

As for the criminal, I pray to God—
Whether it be a lurking thief, or one of a number—
I pray that that man's life be consumed in evil and
      wretchedness.
And as for me, this curse applies no less
If it should turn out that the culprit is my guest here,
Sharing my hearth.
                    You have heard the penalty.
I lay it on you now to attend to this
For my sake, for Apollo's, for the sick
Sterile city that heaven has abandoned.
Suppose the oracle had given you no command:
Should this defilement go uncleansed for ever?
You should have found the murderer: your king,
A noble king, had been destroyed!
                              Now I,
Having the power that he held before me,
Having his bed, begetting children there
Upon his wife, as he would have, had he lived—
Their son would have been my children's brother,
If Laïos had had luck in fatherhood!
(But surely ill luck rushed upon his reign)—
I say I take the son's part, just as though
I were his son, to press the fight for him
And see it won! I'll find the hand that brought
Death to Labdakos' and Polydoros' child,
Heir of Kadmos' and Agenor's line.

And as for those who fail me,
May the gods deny them the fruit of the earth,
Fruit of the womb, and may they rot utterly!
Let them be wretched as we are wretched, and worse!

For you, for loyal Thebans, and for all
Who find my actions right, I pray the favor
Of justice, and of all the immortal gods.
Choragos:
Since I am under oath, my lord, I swear
I did not do the murder, I can not name
The murderer. Might not the oracle
That has ordained the search tell where to find him?
Oedipus:
An honest question. But no man in the world
Can make the gods do more than the gods will.
Choragos:
There is one last expedient—
Oedipus:
                              Tell me what it is.
Though it seem slight, you must not hold it back.
Choragos:
A lord clairvoyant to the lord Apollo,
As we all know, is the skilled Teiresias.
One might learn much about this from him, Oedipus.
Oedipus:
I am not wasting time:
Creon spoke of this, and I have sent for him—
Twice, in fact; it is strange that he is not here.
Choragos:
The other matter—that old report—seems useless.
Oedipus:
Tell me. I am interested in all reports.
Choragos:
The King was said to have been killed by highwaymen.
Oedipus:
I know. But we have no witnesses to that.
Choragos:
If the killer can feel a particle of dread,
Your curse will bring him out of hiding!
Oedipus:
                              No.
The man who dared that act will fear no curse.

[*Enter the blind seer* Teiresias, *led by a* Page

Choragos:
But there is one man who may detect the criminal.
This is Teiresias, this is the holy prophet
In whom, alone of all men, truth was born.
Oedipus:
Teiresias: seer: student of mysteries,
Of all that's taught and all that no man tells,
Secrets of Heaven and secrets of the earth:
Blind though you are, you know the city lies
Sick with plague; and from this plague, my lord,
We find that you alone can guard or save us.

Possibly you did not hear the messengers?
Apollo, when we sent to him,
Sent us back word that this great pestilence
Would lift, but only if we established clearly
The identity of those who murdered Laïos.
They must be killed or exiled.
                              Can you use
Birdflight or any art of divination
To purify yourself, and Thebes, and me
From this contagion? We are in your hands.
There is no fairer duty
Than that of helping others in distress.

Teiresias:
How dreadful knowledge of the truth can be
When there's no help in truth! I knew this well,
But made myself forget. I should not have come.

Oedipus:
What is troubling you? Why are your eyes so cold?

Teiresias:
Let me go home. Bear your own fate, and I'll
Bear mine. It is better so: trust what I say.

Oedipus:
What you say is ungracious and unhelpful
To your native country. Do not refuse to speak.

Teiresias:
When it comes to speech, your own is neither temperate
Nor opportune. I wish to be more prudent.

Oedipus:
In God's name, we all beg you—

Teiresias:
                              You are all ignorant.
No; I will never tell you what I know.
Now it is my misery; then, it would be yours.

Oedipus:
What! You do know something, and will not tell us?
You would betray us all and wreck the State?

Teiresias:
I do not intend to torture myself, or you.
Why persist in asking? You will not persuade me.

Oedipus:
What a wicked old man you are! You'd try a stone's
Patience! Out with it! Have you no feeling at all?

Teiresias:
You call me unfeeling. If you could only see
The nature of your own feelings . . .

Oedipus:
                                      Why,
Who would not feel as I do? Who could endure
Your arrogance toward the city?

Teiresias:
                         What does it matter!
Whether I speak or not, it is bound to come.

Oedipus:
Then, if "it" is bound to come, you are bound to tell me.

Teiresias:
No, I will not go on. Rage as you please.

Oedipus:
Rage? Why not!
                  And I'll tell you what I think:
You planned it, you had it done, you all but
Killed him with your own hands: if you had eyes,
I'd say the crime was yours, and yours alone.

Teiresias:
So? I charge you, then,
Abide by the proclamation you have made:
From this day forth
Never speak again to these men or to me;
You yourself are the pollution of this country.

Oedipus:
You dare say that! Can you possibly think you have
Some way of going free, after such insolence?

Teiresias:
I have gone free. It is the truth sustains me.

Oedipus:
Who taught you shamelessness? It was not your craft.

Teiresias:
You did. You made me speak. I did not want to.

Oedipus:
Speak what? Let me hear it again more clearly.

Teiresias:
Was it not clear before? Are you tempting me?

Oedipus
I did not understand it. Say it again.

Teiresias:
I say that you are the murderer whom you seek.

Oedipus
Now twice you have spat out infamy. You'll pay for it!

Teiresias:
Would you care for more? Do you wish to be really angry?

Oedipus:
Say what you will. Whatever you say is worthless.

Teiresias:
I say you live in hideous shame with those
Most dear to you. You can not see the evil.

Oedipus:
It seems you can go on mouthing like this for ever.

Teiresias:
I can, if there is power in truth.

Oedipus:
                              There is:
But not for you, not for you,
You sightless, witless, senseless, mad old man!

Teiresias:
You are the madman. There is no one here
Who will not curse you soon, as you curse me.

Oedipus:
You child of endless night! You can not hurt me
Or any other man who sees the sun.

Teiresias:
True: it is not from me your fate will come.
That lies within Apollo's competence,
As it is his concern.

Oedipus:
                  Tell me:
Are you speaking for Creon, or for yourself?

Teiresias:
Creon is no threat. You weave your own doom.

Oedipus:
Wealth, power, craft of statesmanship!
Kingly position, everywhere admired!
What savage envy is stored up against these,
If Creon, whom I trusted, Creon my friend,
For this great office which the city once
Put in my hands unsought—if for this power
Creon desires in secret to destroy me!

He has bought this decrepit fortune-teller, this
Collector of dirty pennies, this prophet fraud—
Why, he is no more clairvoyant than I am!
                                          Tell us:
Has your mystic mummery ever approached the truth?
When that hellcat the Sphinx was performing here,
What help were you to these people?
Her magic was not for the first man who came along:
It demanded a real exorcist. Your birds—
What good were they? or the gods, for the matter of that?
But I came by,
Oedipus, the simple man, who knows nothing—
I thought it out for myself, no birds helped me!
And this is the man you think you can destroy,
That you may be close to Creon when he's king!
Well, you and your friend Creon, it seems to me,
Will suffer most. If you were not an old man,
You would have paid already for your plot.

Choragos:
We can not see that his words or yours
Have been spoken except in anger, Oedipus,
And of anger we have no need. How can God's will
Be accomplished best? That is what most concerns us.

Teiresias:
You are a king. But where argument's concerned
I am your man, as much a king as you.
I am not your servant, but Apollo's.
I have no need of Creon to speak for me.

Listen to me. You mock my blindness, do you?
But I say that you, with both your eyes, are blind:
You can not see the wretchedness of your life,
Nor in whose house you live, no, nor with whom.
Who are your father and mother? Can you tell me?
You do not even know the blind wrongs
That you have done them, on earth and in the world
   below.
But the double lash of your parents' curse will whip you
Out of this land some day, with only night
Upon your precious eyes.
Your cries then—where will they not be heard?
What fastness of Kithairon will not echo them?
And that bridal-descant of yours—you'll know it then,
The song they sang when you came here to Thebes
And found your misguided berthing.
All this, and more, that you can not guess at now,
Will bring you to yourself among your children.

Be angry, then. Curse Creon. Curse my words.
I tell you, no man that walks upon the earth
Shall be rooted out more horribly than you.
Oedipus:
Am I to bear this from him?—Damnation
Take you! Out of this place! Out of my sight!
Teiresias:
I would not have come at all if you had not asked me.
Oedipus:
Could I have told that you'd talk nonsense, that
You'd come here to make a fool of yourself, and of me?
Teiresias:
A fool? Your parents thought me sane enough.
Oedipus:
My parents again!—Wait: who were my parents?
Teiresias:
This day will give you a father, and break your heart.
Oedipus:
Your infantile riddles! Your damned abracadabra!
Teiresias:
You were a great man once at solving riddles.
Oedipus:
Mock me with that if you like; you will find it true.
Teiresias:
It was true enough. It brought about your ruin.
Oedipus:
But if it saved this town?
Teiresias:

[*To the* Page:
Boy, give me your hand.
Oedipus:
Yes, boy; lead him away.
—While you are here
We can do nothing. Go; leave us in peace.
Teiresias:
I will go when I have said what I have to say.
How can you hurt me? And I tell you again:
The man you have been looking for all this time,
The damned man, the murderer of Laïos,
That man is in Thebes. To your mind he is foreign-born,
But it will soon be shown that he is a Theban,
A revelation that will fail to please.

A blind man,
Who has his eyes now; a penniless man, who is rich now;
And he will go tapping the strange earth with his staff
To the children with whom he lives now he will be
Brother and father—the very same; to her
Who bore him, son and husband—the very same
Who came to his father's bed, wet with his father's blood.
Enough. Go think that over.
If later you find error in what I have said,
You may say that I have no skill in prophecy.

   [*Exit* Teiresias, *led by his* Page. Oedipus *goes
   into the palace.*

ODE I

Chorus:
The Delphic stone of prophecies   [Strophe 1
Remembers ancient regicide
And a still bloody hand.
That killer's hour of flight has come.
He must be stronger than riderless
Coursers of untiring wind,
For the son of Zeus armed with his father's thunder
Leaps in lightning after him;
And the Furies follow him, the sad Furies.

Holy Parnassos' peak of snow   [Antistrophe 1
Flashes and blinds that secret man,
That all shall hunt him down:
Though he may roam the forest shade
Like a bull gone wild from pasture
To rage through glooms of stone.
Doom comes down on him; flight will not avail him;
For the world's heart calls him desolate,
And the immortal Furies follow, for ever follow.

But now a wilder thing is heard   [Strophe 2
From the old man skilled at hearing Fate in the wing-beat
   of a bird.
Bewildered as a blown bird, my soul hovers and can not
   find
Foothold in this debate, or any reason or rest of mind.
But no man ever brought—none can bring
Proof of strife between Thebes' royal house,
Labdakos' line, and the son of Polybos;
And never until now has any man brought word
Of Laïos' dark death staining Oedipus the King.

Divine Zeus and Apollo hold   [Antistrophe 2
Perfect intelligence alone of all tales ever told;
And well though this diviner works, he works in his own
   night;
No man can judge that rough unknown or trust in second
   sight,
For wisdom changes hands among the wise.
Shall I believe my great lord criminal
At a raging word that a blind old man let fall?
I saw him, when the carrion woman faced him of old,
Prove his heroic mind! These evil words are lies.

SCENE II

Creon:
Men of Thebes:
I am told that heavy accusations
Have been brought against me by King Oedipus.

I am not the kind of man to bear this tamely.

If in these present difficulties
He holds me accountable for any harm to him
Through anything I have said or done—why, then,
I do not value life in this dishonor.
It is not as though this rumor touched upon
Some private indiscretion. The matter is grave.
The fact is that I am being called disloyal
To the State, to my fellow citizens, to my friends.

Choragos:
He may have spoken in anger, not from his mind.

Creon:
But did you not hear him say I was the one
Who seduced the old prophet into lying?

Choragos:
The thing was said; I do not know how seriously.

Creon:
But you were watching him! Were his eyes steady?
Did he look like a man in his right mind?

Choragos:
                                    I do not know.
I can not judge the behavior of great men.
But here is the King himself.

                                    [*Enter* Oedipus

Oedipus:
                          So you dared come back.
Why? How brazen of you to come to my house,
You murderer!
          Do you think I do not know
That you plotted to kill me, plotted to steal my throne?
Tell me, in God's name: am I coward, a fool,
That you should dream you could accomplish this?
A fool who could not see your slippery game?
A coward, not to fight back when I saw it?
You are the fool, Creon, are you not? hoping
Without support or friends to get a throne?
Thrones may be won or bought: you could do neither.

Creon:
Now listen to me. You have talked; let me talk, too.
You can not judge unless you know the facts.

Oedipus:
You speak well: there is one fact; but I find it hard
To learn from the deadliest enemy I have.

Creon:
That above all I must dispute with you.

Oedipus:
That above all I will not hear you deny.

Creon:
If you think there is anything good in being stubborn
Against all reason, then I say you are wrong.

Oedipus:
If you think a man can sin against his own kind
And not be punished for it, I say you are mad.

Creon:
I agree. But tell me: what have I done to you?

Oedipus:
You advised me to send for that wizard, did you not?

Creon:
I did. I should do it again.

Oedipus:
                          Very well. Now tell me:
How long has it been since Laïos—

Creon:
                                    What of Laïos?

Oedipus:
Since he vanished in that onset by the road?

Creon:
It was long ago, a long time.

Oedipus:
                          And this prophet,
Was he practicing here then?

Creon:
                          He was; and with honor, as now.

Oedipus:
Did he speak of me at that time?

Creon:
                                    He never did;
At least, not when I was present.

Oedipus:
                          But . . . the enquiry?
I suppose you held one?

Creon:
                          We did, but we learned nothing.

Oedipus:
Why did the prophet not speak against me then?

Creon:
I do not know; and I am the kind of man
Who holds his tongue when he has no facts to go on.

Oedipus:
There's one fact that you know, and you could tell it.

Creon:
What fact is that? If I know it, you shall have it.

Oedipus:
If he were not involved with you, he could not say
That it was I who murdered Laïos.

Creon:
If he says that, you are the one that knows it!—
But now it is my turn to question you.

Oedipus:
Put your questions. I am no murderer.

Creon:
First, then: You married my sister?

Oedipus:
                          I married your sister.

Creon:
And you rule the kingdom equally with her?

Oedipus:
Everything that she wants she has from me.

Creon:
And I am the third, equal to both of you?

Oedipus:
That is why I call you a bad friend.

Creon:
No. Reason it out, as I have done.
Think of this first: Would any sane man prefer
Power, with all a king's anxieties,
To that same power and the grace of sleep?
Certainly not I.
I have never longed for the king's power—only his rights.
Would any wise man differ from me in this?
As matters stand, I have my way in everything
With your consent, and no responsibilities.
If I were king, I should be a slave to policy.

How could I desire a scepter more
Than what is now mine—untroubled influence?
No, I have not gone mad; I need no honors,
Except those with the perquisites I have now.
I am welcome everywhere; every man salutes me,
And those who want your favor seek my ear,
Since I know how to manage what they ask.
Should I exchange this ease for that anxiety?
Besides, no sober mind is treasonable.
I hate anarchy
And never would deal with any man who likes it.

Test what I have said. Go to the priestess
At Delphi, ask if I quoted her correctly.
And as for this other thing: if I am found
Guilty of treason with Teiresias,
Then sentence me to death! You have my word
It is a sentence I should cast my vote for—
But not without evidence!
                                    You do wrong
When you take good men for bad, bad men for good.
A true friend thrown aside—why, life itself
Is not more precious!
                            In time you will know this well:
For time, and time alone, will show the just man,
Though scoundrels are discovered in a day.
Choragos:
This is well said, and a prudent man would ponder it.
Judgments too quickly formed are dangerous.
Oedipus:
But is he not quick in his duplicity?
And shall I not be quick to parry him?
Would you have me stand still, hold my peace, and let
This man win everything, through my inaction?
Creon:
And you want—what is it, then? To banish me?
Oedipus:
No, not exile. It is your death I want,
So that all the world may see what treason means.
Creon:
You will persist, then? You will not believe me?
Oedipus:
How can I believe you?
Creon:
                            Then you are a fool.
Oedipus:
To save myself?
Creon:
                            In justice, think of me.
Oedipus:
You are evil incarnate.
Creon:
                            But suppose that you are wrong?
Oedipus:
Still I must rule.
Creon:
                            But not if you rule badly.
Oedipus:
O city, city!
Creon:
                            It is my city, too!
Choragos:
Now, my lords, be still. I see the Queen,
Iocastê, coming from her palace chambers;
And it is time she came, for the sake of you both.
This dreadful quarrel can be resolved through her.
                            [*Enter* Iocaste

Iocaste:
Poor foolish men, what wicked din is this?
With Thebes sick to death, is it not shameful
That you should rake some private quarrel up?
                            [*To* Oedipus
Come into the house.

                    —And you, Creon, go now:
Let us have no more of this tumult over nothing.
Creon:
Nothing? No, sister: what your husband plans for me
Is one of two great evils: exile or death.
Oedipus:
He is right.
                    Why, woman I have caught him squarely
Plotting against my life.
Creon:
                            No! Let me die
Accurst if ever I have wished you harm!
Iocaste:
Ah, believe it, Oedipus!
In the name of the gods, respect this oath of his
For my sake, for the sake of these people here!
Choragos: [Strophe 1
Open your mind to her, my lord. Be ruled by her, I beg
        you!
Oedipus:
What would you have me do?
Choragos:
Respect Creon's word. He has never spoken like a fool,
And now he has sworn an oath.
Oedipus:
                    You know what you ask?
Choragos:
                                            I do.
Oedipus:
                                    Speak on, then.
Choragos:
A friend so sworn should not be baited so,
In blind malice, and without final proof.
Oedipus:
You are aware, I hope, that what you say
Means death for me, or exile at the least.
Choragos: [Strophe 2
No, I swear by Helios, first in Heaven!
    May I die friendless and accurst,
The worst of deaths, if ever I meant that!
        It is the withering fields
            That hurt my sick heart:
        Must we bear all these ills,
            And now your bad blood as well?
Oedipus:
Then let him go. And let me die, if I must,
Or be driven by him in shame from the land of Thebes.
It is your unhappiness, and not his talk,
That touches me.
                    As for him—
Wherever he goes, hatred will follow him.
Creon:
Ugly in yielding, as you were ugly in rage!
Natures like yours chiefly torment themselves.
Oedipus:
Can you not go? Can you not leave me?

Creon:

I can.

You do not know me; but the city knows me,
And in its eyes I am just, if not in yours.

[*Exit* Creon

[Antistrophe 1
Choragos:
Lady Iocastê, did you not ask the King to go to his
        chambers?
Iocaste:
First tell me what has happened.
Choragos:
There was suspicion without evidence; yet it rankled
As even false charges will.
Iocaste:

On both sides?

Choragos:

On both.

Iocaste:

But what was said?

Choragos:
Oh let it rest, let it be done with!
Have we not suffered enough?
Oedipus:
You see to what your decency has brought you:
You have made difficulties where my heart saw none.
Choragos: [Antistrophe 2
Oedipus, it is not once only I have told you—
    You must know I should count myself unwise
To the point of madness, should I now forsake you—
        You, under whose hand,
          In the storm of another time,
          Our dear land sailed out free.
          But now stand fast at the helm!
Iocaste:
In God's name, Oedipus, inform your wife as well:
Why are you so set in this hard anger?
Oedipus:
I will tell you, for none of these men deserves
My confidence as you do. It is Creon's work,
His treachery, his plotting against me.
Iocaste:
Go on, if you can make this clear to me.
Oedipus:
He charges me with the murder of Laïos.
Iocaste:
Has he some knowledge? Or does he speak from hear-say?
Oedipus:
He would not commit himself to such a charge,
But he has brought in that damnable soothsayer
To tell his story.
Iocaste:
            Set your mind at rest.
If it is a question of soothsayers, I tell you
That you will find no man whose craft gives knowledge
Of the unknowable.

            Here is my proof:

An oracle was reported to Laïos once
(I will not say from Phoibos himself, but from
His appointed ministers, at any rate)
That his doom would be death at the hands of his own
        son—
His son, born of his flesh and of mine!

Now, you remember the story: Laïos was killed
By marauding strangers where three highways meet,
But his child had not been three days in this world
Before the King had pierced the baby's ankles
And left him to die on a lonely mountainside.

Thus, Apollo never caused that child
To kill his father, and it was not Laïos' fate
To die at the hands of his son, as he had feared.
This is what prophets and prophecies are worth!
Have no dread of them.
                        It is God himself
Who can show us what he wills, in his own way.
Oedipus:
How strange a shadowy memory crossed my mind,
Just now while you were speaking; it chilled my heart.
Iocaste:
What do you mean? What memory do you speak of?
Oedipus:
If I understand you, Laïos was killed
At a place where three roads meet.
Iocaste:
                        So it was said;
We have no later story.
Oedipus:
                        Where did it happen?
Iocaste:
Phokis, it is called: at a place where the Theban Way
Divides into the roads toward Delphi and Daulia.
Oedipus:
When?
Iocaste:
        We had the news not long before you came
And proved the right to your succession here.
Oedipus:
Ah, what net has God been weaving for me?
Iocaste:
Oedipus! Why does this trouble you?
Oedipus:
                        Do not ask me yet.
First, tell me how Laïos looked, and tell me
How old he was.
Iocaste:
                He was tall, his hair just touched
With white; his form was not unlike your own.
Oedipus:
I think that I myself may be accurst
By my own ignorant edict.
Iocaste:
                You speak strangely.
It makes me tremble to look at you, my King.
Oedipus:
I am not sure that the blind man can not see.
But I should know better if you were to tell me—
Iocaste:
Anything—though I dread to hear you ask it.
Oedipus:
Was the King lightly escorted, or did he ride
With a large company, as a ruler should?
Iocaste:
There were five men with him in all: one was a herald,
And a single chariot, which he was driving.
Oedipus:
Alas, that makes it plain enough!
                        But who—
Who told you how it happened?

Iocaste:
                              A household servant,
The only one to escape.
Oedipus:
                              And is he still
A servant of ours?
Iocaste:
                              No; for when he came back at last
And found you enthroned in the place of the dead king,
He came to me, touched my hand with his, and begged
That I would send him away to the frontier district
Where only the shepherds go—
As far away from the city as I could send him.
I granted his prayer; for although the man was a slave,
He had earned more than this favor at my hands.
Oedipus:
Can he be called back quickly?
Iocaste:
                              Easily.
But why?
Oedipus:
              I have taken too much upon myself
Without enquiry; therefore I wish to consult him.
Iocaste:
Then he shall come.
                              But am I not one also
To whom you might confide these fears of yours?
Oedipus:
That is your right; it will not be denied you,
Now least of all; for I have reached a pitch
Of wild foreboding. Is there anyone
To whom I should sooner speak?

Polybos of Corinth is my father.
My mother is a Dorian: Meropê.
I grew up chief among the men of Corinth
Until a strange thing happened—
Not worth my passion, it may be, but strange.

At a feast, a drunken man maundering in his cups
Cries out that I am not my father's son!

I contained myself that night, though I felt anger
And a sinking heart. The next day I visited
My father and mother, and questioned them. They
     stormed,
Calling it all the slanderous rant of a fool;
And this relieved me. Yet the suspicion
Remained always aching in my mind;
I knew there was talk; I could not rest;
And finally, saying nothing to my parents,
I went to the shrine at Delphi.
The god dismissed my question without reply;
He spoke of other things.
                              Some were clear,
Full of wretchedness, dreadful, unbearable:
As, that I should lie with my own mother, breed
Children from whom all men would turn their eyes;
And that I should be my father's murderer.

I heard all this, and fled. And from that day
Corinth to me was only in the stars
Descending in that quarter of the sky,
As I wandered farther and farther on my way
To a land where I should never see the evil
Sung by the oracle. And I came to this country
Where, so you say, King Laïos was killed.

I will tell you all that happened there, my lady.

There were three highways
Coming together at a place I passed;
And there a herald came towards me, and a chariot
Drawn by horses, with a man such as you describe
Seated in it. The groom leading the horses
Forced me off the road at his lord's command;
But as this charioteer lurched over towards me
I struck him in my rage. The old man saw me
And brought his double goad down upon my head
As I came abreast.
                              He was paid back, and more!
Swinging my club in this right hand I knocked him
Out of his car, and he rolled on the ground.
                              I killed him.
I killed them all.
Now if that stranger and Laïos were—kin,
Where is a man more miserable than I?
More hated by the gods? Citizen and alien alike
Must never shelter me or speak to me—
I must be shunned by all.
                              And I myself
Pronounced this malediction upon myself!

Think of it: I have touched you with these hands,
These hands that killed your husband. What defilement!

Am I all evil, then? It must be so,
Since I must flee from Thebes, yet never again
See my own countrymen, my own country,
For fear of joining my mother in marriage
And killing Polybos, my father.
                              Ah,
If I was created so, born to this fate,
Who could deny the savagery of God?

O holy majesty of heavenly powers!
May I never see that day! Never!
Rather let me vanish from the race of men
Than know the abomination destined me!

Choragos:
We too, my lord, have felt dismay at this.
But there is hope: you have yet to hear the shepherd.
Oedipus:
Indeed, I fear no other hope is left me.
Iocaste:
What do you hope from him when he comes?
Oedipus:
                              This much:
If his account of the murder tallies with yours,
Then I am cleared.
Iocaste:
                              What was it that I said
Of such importance?
Oedipus:
                              Why, "marauders," you said,
Killed the King, according to this man's story.
If he maintains that still, if there were several,
Clearly the guilt is not mine: I was alone.
But if he says one man, singlehanded, did it,
Then the evidence all points to me.

Iocaste:
You may be sure that he said there were several;
And can he call back that story now? He cán not.
The whole city heard it as plainly as I.
But suppose he alters some detail of it:
He can not ever show that Laïos' death
Fulfilled the oracle: for Apollo said
My child was doomed to kill him; and my child—
Poor baby!—it was my child that died first.

No. From now on, where oracles are concerned,
I would not waste a second thought on any.
Oedipus:
You may be right.
           But come: let someone go
For the shepherd at once. This matter must be settled.
Iocaste:
I will send for him.
I would not wish to cross you in anything,
And surely not in this.—Let us go in.
           [Exeunt into the palace

ODE II

Chorus: [Strophe 1
Let me be reverent in the ways of right,
Lowly the paths I journey on;
Let all my words and actions keep
The laws of the pure universe
From highest Heaven handed down.
For Heaven is their bright nurse,
Those generations of the realms of light;
Ah, never of mortal kind were they begot,
Nor are they slaves of memory, lost in sleep:
Their Father is greater than Time, and ages not.

The tyrant is a child of Pride   [Antistrophe 1
Who drinks from his great sickening cup
Recklessness and vanity,
Until from his high crest headlong
He plummets to the dust of hope.
That strong man is not strong.
But let no fair ambition be denied;
May God protect the wrestler for the State
In government, in comely policy,
Who will fear God, and on His ordinance wait.

                            [Strophe 2
Haughtiness and the high hand of disdain
Tempt and outrage God's holy law;
And any mortal who dares hold
No immortal Power in awe
Will be caught up in a net of pain:
The price for which his levity is sold.
Let each man take due earnings, then,
And keep his hands from holy things,
And from blasphemy stand apart—
Else the crackling blast of heaven
Blows on his head, and on his desperate heart;
Though fools will honor impious men,
In their cities no tragic poet sings.

                            [Antistrophe 2
Shall we lose faith in Delphi's obscurities,
We who have heard the world's core
Discredited, and the sacred wood
Of Zeus at Elis praised no more?
The deeds and the strange prophecies
Must make a pattern yet to be understood.
Zeus, if indeed you are lord of all,
Throned in light over night and day,
Mirror this in your endless mind:
Our masters call the oracle
Words on the wind, and the Delphic vision blind!
Their hearts no longer know Apollo,
And reverence for the gods has died away.

SCENE III

                           [Enter Iocaste
Iocaste:
Princes of Thebes, it has occurred to me
To visit the altars of the gods, bearing
These branches as a suppliant, and this incense.
Our King is not himself: his noble soul
Is overwrought with fantasies of dread,
Else he would consider
The new prophecies in the light of the old.
He will listen to any voice that speaks disaster,
And my advice goes for nothing.
       [She approaches the altar, R.
           To you, then, Apollo,
Lycean lord, since you are nearest, I turn in prayer.
Receive these offerings, and grant us deliverance
From defilement. Our hearts are heavy with fear
When we see our leader distracted, as helpless sailors
Are terrified by the confusion of their helmsman.
                     [Enter Messenger

Messenger:
Friends, no doubt you can direct me:
Where shall I find the house of Oedipus,
Or, better still, where is the King himself?
Choragos:
It is this very place, stranger; he is inside.
This is his wife and mother of his children.
Messenger:
I wish her happiness in a happy house,
Blest in all the fulfillment of her marriage.
Iocaste:
I wish as much for you: your courtesy
Deserves a like good fortune. But now, tell me:
Why have you come? What have you to say to us?
Messenger:
Good news, my lady, for your house and your husband.
Iocaste:
What news? Who sent you here?
Messenger:
                      I am from Corinth.
The news I bring ought to mean joy for you,
Though it may be you will find some grief in it.
Iocaste:
What is it? How can it touch us in both ways?
Messenger:
The word is that the people of the Isthmus
Intend to call Oedipus to be their king.
Iocaste:
But old King Polybos—is he not reigning still?

Messenger:
No. Death holds him in his sepulchre.

Iocaste:
What are you saying? Polybos is dead?

Messenger:
If I am not telling the truth, may I die myself.

Iocaste:
                                          [*To a* Maidservant:
Go in, go quickly; tell this to your master.
O riddlers of God's will, where are you now!
This was the man whom Oedipus, long ago,
Feared so, fled so, in dread of destroying him—
But it was another fate by which he died.

                                    [*Enter* Oedipus, C.

Oedipus:
Dearest Iocastê, why have you sent for me?

Iocaste:
Listen to what this man says, and then tell me
What has become of the solemn prophecies.

Oedipus:
Who is this man? What is his news for me?

Iocaste:
He has come from Corinth to announce your father's
    death!

Oedipus:
Is it true, stranger? Tell me in your own words.

Messenger:
I can not say it more clearly: the King is dead.

Oedipus:
Was it by treason? Or by an attack of illness?

Messenger:
A little thing brings old men to their rest.

Oedipus:
It was sickness, then?

Messenger:
                    Yes, and his many years.

Oedipus:
Ah!
Why should a man respect the Pythian hearth, or
Give heed to the birds that jangle above his head?
They prophesied that I should kill Polybos,
Kill my own father; but he is dead and buried,
And I am here—I never touched him, never,
Unless he died of grief for my departure,
And thus, in a sense, through me. No. Polybos
Has packed the oracles off with him underground.
They are empty words.

Iocaste:
                   Had I not told you so?

Oedipus:
You had; it was my faint heart that betrayed me.

Iocaste:
From now on never think of those things again.

Oedipus:
And yet—must I not fear my mother's bed?

Iocaste:
Why should anyone in this world be afraid,
Since Fate rules us and nothing can be foreseen?
A man should live only for the present day.

Have no more fear of sleeping with your mother:
How many men, in dreams, have lain with their mothers!
No reasonable man is troubled by such things.

Oedipus:
That is true; only—
If only my mother were not still alive!
But she is alive. I can not help my dread.

Iocaste:
Yet this news of your father's death is wonderful.

Oedipus:
Wonderful. But I fear the living woman.

Messenger:
Tell me, who is this woman that you fear?

Oedipus:
It is Meropê, man; the wife of King Polybos.

Messenger:
Meropê? Why should you be afraid of her?

Oedipus:
An oracle of the gods, a dreadful saying.

Messenger:
Can you tell me about it or are you sworn to silence?

Oedipus:
I can tell you, and I will.
Apollo said through his prophet that I was the man
Who should marry his own mother, shed his father's
    blood
With his own hands. And so, for all these years
I have kept clear of Corinth, and no harm has come—
Though it would have been sweet to see my parents
    again.

Messenger:
And is this the fear that drove you out of Corinth?

Oedipus:
Would you have me kill my father?

Messenger:
                        As for that
You must be reassured by the news I gave you.

Oedipus:
If you could reassure me, I would reward you.

Messenger:
I had that in mind, I will confess: I thought
I could count on you when you returned to Corinth.

Oedipus:
No: I will never go near my parents again.

Messenger:
Ah, son, you still do not know what you are doing—

Oedipus:
What do you mean? In the name of God tell me!

Messenger:
—If these are your reasons for not going home.

Oedipus:
I tell you, I fear the oracle may come true.

Messenger:
And guilt may come upon you through your parents?

Oedipus:
That is the dread that is always in my heart.

Messenger:
Can you not see that all your fears are groundless?

Oedipus:
How can you say that? They are my parents, surely?

Messenger:
Polybos was not your father.

Oedipus:
                     Not my father?

Messenger:
No more your father than the man speaking to you.

Oedipus:
But you are nothing to me!

Messenger:
                    Neither was he.

Oedipus:
Then why did he call me son?

Messenger:
                        I will tell you:
Long ago he had you from my hands, as a gift.

wife readings didn't change fate afterall

Oedipus:
Then how could he love me so, if I was not his?
Messenger:
He had no children, and his heart turned to you.
Oedipus:
What of you? Did you buy me? Did you find me by
    chance?
Messenger:
I came upon you in the crooked pass of Kithairon.
Oedipus:
And what were you doing there?
Messenger:
                        Tending my flocks.
Oedipus:
A wandering shepherd?
Messenger:
                But your savior, son, that day.
Oedipus:
From what did you save me?
Messenger:
            Your ankles should tell you that.
Oedipus:
Ah, stranger, why do you speak of that childhood pain?
Messenger:
I cut the bonds that tied your ankles together.
Oedipus:
I have had the mark as long as I can remember.
Messenger:
That was why you were given the name you bear.
Oedipus:
God! Was it my father or my mother who did it?
Tell me!
Messenger:
       I do not know. The man who gave you to me
Can tell you better than I.
Oedipus:
It was not you that found me, but another?
Messenger:
It was another shepherd gave you to me.
Oedipus:
Who was he? Can you tell me who he was?
Messenger:
I think he was said to be one of Laïos' people.
Oedipus:
You mean the Laïos who was king here years ago?
Messenger:
Yes; King Laïos; and the man was one of his herdsmen.
Oedipus:
Is he still alive? Can I see him?
Messenger:
                  These men here
Know best about such things.
Oedipus:
                Does anyone here
Know this shepherd that he is talking about?
Have you seen him in the fields, or in the town?
If you have, tell me. It is time things were made plain.
Choragos:
I think the man he means is that same shepherd
You have already asked to see. Iocastê perhaps
Could tell you something.
Oedipus:
              Do you know anything
About him, Lady? Is he the man we have summoned?
Is that the man this shepherd means?

Iocaste:
                    Why think of him?
Forget this herdsman. Forget it all.
This talk is a waste of time.
Oedipus:
                 How can you say that,
When the clues to my true birth are in my hands?
Iocaste:
For God's love, let us have no more questioning!
Is your life nothing to you?
My own is pain enough for me to bear.
Oedipus:
You need not worry. Suppose my mother a slave,
And born of slaves: no baseness can touch you.
Iocaste:
Listen to me, I beg you: do not do this thing!
Oedipus:
I will not listen; the truth must be made known.
Iocaste:
Everything that I say is for your own good!
Oedipus:
                  My own good
Snaps my patience, then; I want none of it.
Iocaste:
You are fatally wrong! May you never learn who you are!
Oedipus:
Go, one of you, and bring the shepherd here.
Let us leave this woman to brag of her royal name.
Iocaste:
Ah, miserable!
That is the only word I have for you now.
That is the only word I can ever have.

                             [Exit into the palace
Choragos:
Why has she left us, Oedipus? Why has she gone
In such a passion of sorrow? I fear this silence:
Something dreadful may come of it.
Oedipus:
                  Let it come!
However base my birth, I must know about it.
The Queen, like a woman, is perhaps ashamed
To think of my low origin. But I
Am a child of Luck; I can not be dishonored.
Luck is my mother; the passing months, my brothers,
Have seen me rich and poor.
                If this is so,
How could I wish that I were someone else?
How could I not be glad to know my birth?

        ODE III
Chorus:
If ever the coming time were known   *[Strophe*
To my heart's pondering,
Kithairon, now by Heaven I see the torches
At the festival of the next full moon,
And see the dance, and hear the choir sing
A grace to your gentle shade:
Mountain where Oedipus was found,
O mountain guard of a noble race!
May the god who heals us lend his aid,
And let that glory come to pass
For our king's cradling-ground.

                            [Antistrophe
Of the nymphs that flower beyond the years,
Who bore you, royal child,
To Pan of the hills or the timberline Apollo,
Cold in delight where the upland clears,
Or Hermês for whom Kyllenê's heights are piled?

Or flushed as evening cloud,
Great Dionysos, roamer of mountains,
He—was it he who found you there,
And caught you up in his own proud
Arms from the sweet god-ravisher
Who laughed by the Muses' fountains?

SCENE IV

Oedipus:
Sirs: though I do not know the man,
I think I see him coming, this shepherd we want:
He is old, like our friend here, and the men
Bringing him seem to be servants of my house.
But you can tell, if you have ever seen him.

[*Enter* Shepherd *escorted by servants*

Choragos:
I know him, he was Laïos' man. You can trust him.
Oedipus:
Tell me first, you from Corinth: is this the shepherd
We were discussing?
Messenger:
                    This is the very man.
Oedipus: [*To* Shepherd
Come here. No, look at me. You must answer
Everything I ask.—You belonged to Laïos?
Shepherd:
Yes: born his slave, brought up in his house.
Oedipus:
Tell me: what kind of work did you do for him?
Shepherd:
I was a shepherd of his, most of my life.
Oedipus:
Where mainly did you go for pasturage?
Shepherd:
Sometimes Kithairon, sometimes the hills near-by.
Oedipus:
Do you remember ever seeing this man out there?
Shepherd:
What would he be doing there? This man?
Oedipus:
This man standing here. Have you ever seen him before?
Shepherd:
No. At least, not to my recollection.
Messenger:
And that is not strange, my lord. But I'll refresh
His memory: he must remember when we two
Spent three whole seasons together, March to September,
On Kithairon or thereabouts. He had two flocks;
I had one. Each autumn I'd drive mine home
And he would go back with his to Laïos' sheepfold.—
Is this not true, just as I have described it?
Shepherd:
True, yes; but it was all so long ago.
Messenger:
Well, then: do you remember, back in those days,
That you gave me a baby boy to bring up as my own?
Shepherd:
What if I did? What are you trying to say?
Messenger:
King Oedipus was once that little child.
Shepherd:
Damn you, hold your tongue!
Oedipus:
                        No more of that!
It is your tongue needs watching, not this man's.
Shepherd:
My King, my Master, what is it I have done wrong?

Oedipus:
You have not answered his question about the boy.
Shepherd:
He does not know . . . He is only making trouble . . .
Oedipus:
Come, speak plainly, or it will go hard with you.
Shepherd:
In God's name, do not torture an old man!
Oedipus:
Come here, one of you; bind his arms behind him.
Shepherd:
Unhappy king! What more do you wish to learn?
Oedipus:
Did you give this man the child he speaks of?
Shepherd:
                                        I did.
And I would to God I had died that very day.
Oedipus:
You will die now unless you speak the truth.
Shepherd:
Yet if I speak the truth, I am worse than dead.
Oedipus:
Very well; since you insist upon delaying—
Shepherd:
No! I have told you already that I gave him the boy.
Oedipus:
Where did you get him? From your house? From
        somewhere else?
Shepherd:
Not from mine, no. A man gave him to me.
Oedipus:
Is that man here? Do you know whose slave he was?
Shepherd:
For God's love, my King, do not ask me any more!
Oedipus:
You are a dead man if I have to ask you again.
Shepherd:
Then . . . Then the child was from the palace of Laïos.
Oedipus:
A slave child? or a child of his own line?
Shepherd:
Ah, I am on the brink of dreadful speech!
Oedipus:
And I of dreadful hearing. Yet I must hear.
Shepherd:
If you must be told, then . . .
                                They said it was Laïos' child;
But it is your wife who can tell you about that.
Oedipus:
My wife!—Did she give it to you?
Shepherd:
                                My lord, she did.
Oedipus:
Do you know why?
Shepherd:
                        I was told to get rid of it.
Oedipus:
An unspeakable mother!
Shepherd:
                        There had been prophecies . . .
Oedipus:
Tell me.
Shepherd:
It was said that the boy would kill his own father.
Oedipus:
Then why did you give him over to this old man?

Shepherd:
I pitied the baby, my King,
And I thought that this man would take him far away
To his own country.
                    He saved him—but for what a fate!
For if you are what this man says you are,
No man living is more wretched than Oedipus.
Oedipus:
Ah God!
It was true!
            All the prophecies!
                                —Now,
O Light, may I look on you for the last time!
I, Oedipus,
Oedipus, damned in his birth, in his marriage damned,
Damned in the blood he shed with his own hand!
                            [*He rushes into the palace*

        ODE IV
Chorus:
Alas for the seed of men.   [Strophe 1

What measure shall I give these generations
That breathe on the void and are void
And exist and do not exist?

Who bears more weight of joy
Than mass of sunlight shifting in images,
Or who shall make his thought stay on
That down time drifts away?

Your splendor is all fallen.
O naked brow of wrath and tears,
O change of Oedipus!
I who saw your days call no man blest—
Your great days like ghósts góne.

That mind was a strong bow.   [Antistrophe 1

Deep, how deep you drew it then, hard archer,
At a dim fearful range,
And brought dear glory down!

You overcame the stranger—
The virgin with her hooking lion claws—
And though death sang, stood like a tower
To make pale Thebes take heart.

Fortress against our sorrow!

True king, giver of laws,
Majestic Oedipus!
No prince in Thebes had ever such renown,
No prince won such grace of power.

And now of all men ever known   [Strophe 2
Most pitiful is this man's story:
His fortunes are most changed, his state
Fallen to a low slave's
Ground under bitter fate.

O Oedipus, most royal one!
The great door that expelled you to the light
Gave at night—ah, gave night to your glory:
As to the father, to the fathering son.

All understood too late.

How could that queen whom Laïos won,
The garden that he harrowed at his height,
Be silent when that act was done?

But all eyes fail before time's eye,   [Antistrophe 2
All actions come to justice there.
Though never willed, though far down the deep past,
Your bed, your dread sirings,
Are brought to book at last.
Child by Laïos doomed to die,
Then doomed to lose that fortunate little death,
Would God you never took breath in this air
That with my wailing lips I take to cry:

For I weep the world's outcast.

I was blind, and now I can tell why:
Asleep, for you had given ease of breath
To Thebes, while the false years went by.

        EXODOS
                    [*Enter, from the palace,* Second Messenger
Second Messenger:
Elders of Thebes, most honored in this land,
What horrors are yours to see and hear, what weight
Of sorrow to be endured, if, true to your birth,
You venerate the line of Labdakos!
I think neither Istros nor Phasis, those great rivers,
Could purify this place of the corruption
It shelters now, or soon must bring to light—
Evil not done unconsciously, but willed.

The greatest griefs are those we cause ourselves.
Choragos:
Surely, friend, we have grief enough already;
What new sorrow do you mean?
Second Messenger:
                                The Queen is dead.

Choragos:
Iocastê? Dead? But at whose hand?
Second Messenger:
                                Her own.
The full horror of what happened you can not know,
For you did not see it; but I, who did, will tell you
As clearly as I can how she met her death.

When she had left us,
In passionate silence, passing through the court,
She ran to her apartment in the house,
Her hair clutched by the fingers of both hands.
She closed the doors behind her; then, by that bed
Where long ago the fatal son was conceived—
That son who should bring about his father's death—
We heard her call upon Laïos, dead so many years,
And heard her wail for the double fruit of her marriage,
A husband by her husband, children by her child.

Exactly how she died I do not know:
For Oedipus burst in moaning and would not let us
Keep vigil to the end: it was by him
As he stormed about the room that our eyes were caught.
From one to another of us he went, begging a sword,
Cursing the wife who was not his wife, the mother
Whose womb had carried his own children and himself.
I do not know: it was none of us aided him,
But surely one of the gods was in control!
For with a dreadful cry
He hurled his weight, as though wrenched out of himself,
At the twin doors: the bolts gave, and he rushed in.

And there we saw her hanging, her body swaying
From the cruel cord she had noosed about her neck.
A great sob broke from him, heartbreaking to hear,
As he loosed the rope and lowered her to the ground.

I would blot out from my mind what happened next!
For the King ripped from her gown the golden brooches
That were her ornament, and raised them, and plunged
    them down
Straight into his own eyeballs, crying, "No more,
No more shall you look on the misery about me,
The horrors of my own doing! Too long you have known
The faces of those whom I should never have seen,
Too long been blind to those for whom I was searching!
From this hour, go in darkness!" And as he spoke,
He struck at his eyes—not once, but many times;
And the blood spattered his beard,
Bursting from his ruined sockets like red hail.

So from the unhappiness of two this evil has sprung,
A curse on the man and woman alike. The old
Happiness of the house of Labdakos
Was happiness enough: where is it today?
It is all wailing and ruin, disgrace, death—all
The misery of mankind that has a name—
And it is wholly and for ever theirs.

Choragos:
Is he in agony still? Is there no rest for him?

Second Messenger:
He is calling for someone to lead him to the gates
So that all the children of Kadmos may look upon
His father's murderer, his mother's—no,
I can not say it!
          And then he will leave Thebes,
Self-exiled, in order that the curse
Which he himself pronounced may depart from the
    house.
He is weak, and there is none to lead him,
So terrible is his suffering.
          But you will see:
Look, the doors are opening; in a moment
You will see a thing that would crush a heart of stone.
[*The central door is opened;* Oedipus, *blinded, is led in*

Choragos:
Dreadful indeed for men to see.
Never have my own eyes
Looked on a sight so full of fear.

Oedipus!
What madness came upon you, what daemon
Leaped on your life with heavier
Punishment than a mortal man can bear?
No: I can not even
Look at you, poor ruined one.
And I would speak, question, ponder,
If I were able. No.
You make me shudder.

Oedipus:
God.   God.
Is there a sorrow greater?
Where shall I find harbor in this world?
My voice is hurled far on a dark wind.
What has God done to me?

Choragos:
Too terrible to think of, or to see.

Oedipus:
O cloud of night,   [Strophe 1
Never to be turned away: night coming on,
I can not tell how: night like a shroud!

My fair winds brought me here.
                    O God. Again
The pain of the spikes where I had sight,
The flooding pain
Of memory, never to be gouged out.

Choragos:
This is not strange.
You suffer it all twice over, remorse in pain,
Pain in remorse.

Oedipus:
Ah dear friend   [Antistrophe 1
Are you faithful even yet, you alone?
Are you still standing near me, will you stay here,
Patient, to care for the blind?
                 The blind man!
Yet even blind I know who it is attends me,
By the voice's tone—
Though my new darkness hide the comforter.

Choragos:
Oh fearful act!
What god was it drove you to rake black
Night across your eyes?

Oedipus:
Apollo. Apollo. Dear   [Strophe 2
Children, the god was Apollo.
He brought my sick, sick fate upon me.
But the blinding hand was my own!
How could I bear to see
When all my sight was horror everywhere?

Choragos:
Everywhere; that is true.

Oedipus:
And now what is left?
Images? Love? A greeting even,
Sweet to the senses? Is there anything?
Ah, no, friends: lead me away.
Lead me away from Thebes.
                Lead the great wreck
And hell of Oedipus, whom the gods hate.

Choragos:
Your fate is clear, you are not blind to that.
Would God you had never found it out!

Oedipus: [Antistrophe 2
Death take the man who unbound
My feet on that hillside
And delivered me from death to life! What life?
If only I had died,
This weight of monstrous doom
Could not have dragged me and my darlings down.

Choragos:
I would have wished the same.

Oedipus:
Oh never to have come here
With my father's blood upon me! Never
To have been the man they call his mother's husband!
Oh accurst! Oh child of evil,
To have entered that wretched bed—
                the selfsame one!
More primal than sin itself, this fell to me.

Choragos:
I do not know how I can answer you.
You were better dead than alive and blind.
Oedipus:
Do not counsel me any more. This punishment
That I have laid upon myself is just.
If I had eyes,
I do not know how I could bear the sight
Of my father, when I came to the house of Death,
Or my mother: for I have sinned against them both
So vilely that I could not make my peace
By strangling my own life.

          Or do you think my children,
Born as they were born, would be sweet to my eyes?
Ah never, never! Nor this town with its high walls,
Nor the holy images of the gods.

              For I,
Thrice miserable!—Oedipus, noblest of all the line
Of Kadmos, have condemned myself to enjoy
These things no more, by my own malediction
Expelling that man whom the gods declared
To be a defilement in the house of Laïos.
After exposing the rankness of my own guilt,
How could I look men frankly in the eyes?
No, I swear it,
If I could have stifled my hearing at its source,
I would have done it and made all this body
A tight cell of misery, blank to light and sound:
So I should have been safe in a dark agony
Beyond all recollection.

              Ah Kithairon!
Why did you shelter me? When I was cast upon you,
Why did I not die? Then I should never
Have shown the world my execrable birth.

Ah Polybos! Corinth, city that I believed
The ancient seat of my ancestors: how fair
I seemed, your child! And all the while this evil
Was cancerous within me!

            For I am sick
In my daily life, sick in my origin.

O three roads, dark ravine, woodland and way
Where three roads met: you, drinking my father's blood,
My own blood, spilled by my own hand: can you
    remember
The unspeakable things I did there, and the things
I went on from there to do?

           O marriage, marriage!
The act that engendered me, and again the act
Performed by the son in the same bed—

              Ah, the net
Of incest, mingling fathers, brothers, sons,
With brides, wives, mothers: the last evil
That can be known by men: no tongue can say
How evil!

      No. For the love of God, conceal me
Somewhere far from Thebes; or kill me; or hurl me
Into the sea, away from men's eyes for ever.

Come, lead me. You need not fear to touch me.
Of all men, I alone can bear this guilt.

               [*Enter* Creon
Choragos:
We are not the ones to decide; but Creon here
May fitly judge of what you ask. He only
Is left to protect the city in your place.

Oedipus:
Alas, how can I speak to him? What right have I
To beg his courtesy whom I have deeply wronged?
Creon:
I have not come to mock you, Oedipus,
Or to reproach you, either.

              [*To* Attendants:
         —You, standing there:
If you have lost all respect for man's dignity,
At least respect the flame of Lord Helios:
Do not allow this pollution to show itself
Openly here, an affront to the earth
And Heaven's rain and the light of day. No, take him
Into the house as quickly as you can.
For it is proper
That only the close kindred see his grief.
Oedipus:
I pray you in God's name, since your courtesy
Ignores my dark expectation, visiting
With mercy this man of all men most execrable:
Give me what I ask—for your good, not for mine.
Creon:
And what is it that you would have me do?
Oedipus:
Drive me out of this country as quickly as may be
To a place where no human voice can ever greet me.
Creon:
I should have done that before now—only,
God's will had not been wholly revealed to me.
Oedipus:
But his command is plain: the parricide
Must be destroyed. I am that evil man.
Creon:
That is the sense of it, yes; but as things are,
We had best discover clearly what is to be done.
Oedipus:
You would learn more about a man like me?
Creon:
You are ready now to listen to the god.
Oedipus:
I will listen. But it is to you
That I must turn for help. I beg you, hear me.

The woman in there—
Give her whatever funeral you think proper:
She is your sister.

          —But let me go, Creon!
Let me purge my father's Thebes of the pollution
Of my living here, and go out to the wild hills,
To Kithairon, that has won such fame with me,
The tomb my mother and father appointed for me,
And let me die there, as they willed I should.
And yet I know
Death will not ever come to me through sickness
Or in any natural way: I have been preserved
For some unthinkable fate. But let that be.

As for my sons, you need not care for them.
They are men, they will find some way to live.
But my poor daughters, who have shared my table,
Who never before have been parted from their father—
Take care of them, Creon; do this for me.
And will you let me touch them with my hands
A last time, and let us weep together?
Be kind, my lord,
Great prince, be kind!

           Could I but touch them,
They would be mine again, as when I had my eyes.

[*Enter* Antigone *and* Ismene, *attended*

Ah, God!
Is it my dearest children I hear weeping?
Has Creon pitied me and sent my daughters?
Creon:
Yes, Oedipus: I knew that they were dear to you
In the old days, and know you must love them still.
Oedipus:
May God bless you for this—and be a friendlier
Guardian to you than he has been to me!

Children, where are you?
Come quickly to my hands: they are your brother's—
Hands that have brought your father's once clear eyes
To this way of seeing—
                                        Ah dearest ones,
I had neither sight nor knowledge then, your father
By the woman who was the source of his own life!
And I weep for you—having no strength to see you—,
I weep for you when I think of the bitterness
That men will visit upon you all your lives.
What homes, what festivals can you attend
Without being forced to depart again in tears?
And when you come to marriageable age,
Where is the man, my daughters, who would dare
Risk the bane that lies on all my children?
Is there any evil wanting? Your father killed
His father; sowed the womb of her who bore him;
Engendered you at the fount of his own existence!
That is what they will say of you.

                                Then, whom
Can you ever marry? There are no bridegrooms for you,
And your lives must wither away in sterile dreaming.

O Creon, son of Menoikeus!
You are the only father my daughters have,
Since we, their parents, are both of us gone for ever.
They are your own blood: you will not let them
Fall into beggary and loneliness;
You will keep them from the miseries that are mine!
Take pity on them; see, they are only children,
Friendless except for you. Promise me this,
Great Prince, and give me your hand in token of it.
                                [Creon *clasps his right hand*
Children:
I could say much, if you could understand me,
But as it is, I have only this prayer for you:
Live where you can, be as happy as you can—
Happier, please God, than God has made your father!
Creon:
Enough. You have wept enough. Now go within.
Oedipus:
I must; but it is hard.
Creon:
                        Time eases all things.
Oedipus:
But you must promise—
Creon:
                                Say what you desire.
Oedipus:
Send me from Thebes!
Creon:
                                God grant that I may!
Oedipus:
But since God hates me . . .
Creon:
                                No, he will grant your wish.
Oedipus:
You promise?

Creon:
                I can not speak beyond my knowledge.
Oedipus:
Then lead me in.
Creon:
                        Come now, and leave your children.
Oedipus:
No! Do not take them from me!
Creon:
                                        Think no longer
That you are in command here, but rather think
How, when you were, you served your own destruction.
[*Exeunt into the house all but the* Chorus; *the* Choragos
                chants directly to the audience:
Choragos:
Men of Thebes: look upon Oedipus.

This is the king who solved the famous riddle
And towered up, most powerful of men.
No mortal eyes but looked on him with envy,
Yet in the end ruin swept over him.

Let every man in mankind's frailty
Consider his last day; and let none
Presume on his good fortune until he find
Life, at his death, a memory without pain.

Exercises

1. *Oedipus* is sometimes cited as a forerunner of the detective story. Though most everyone in the original audience knew "who done it," the suspense concerns when and how the murderer (Oedipus) will be revealed while the detective (Oedipus) puts the clues together. Step by step, what were the clues that led inevitably to the terrible truth?
2. Did the murder of Laïos reveal a character flaw of both Laïos and Oedipus? Consider Oedipus' description in Ode II of the encounter on the road. What was the mutual flaw and how did it contribute to the killing?
3. Describe how the motif of blindness functions ironically in the play. When does the king truly see what the blind prophet saw so clearly early in the play?
4. There are at least three different interpretations of *Oedipus:*
    a. The theory that this is a story of a man's discovery of his own identity and a consideration of the interrelationship of free will and predestination (a man's character is his fate, in other words, he chooses his character and thus his fate).
    b. The theory that Oedipus, Creon, Teiresias, and Iocaste knew the true identity of Oedipus ever since he began ruling in Thebes. This interpretation need not contradict the theory outlined above but it will change the point of view.

c. A few critics feel that the play is a presentation of the power of divine authority—the will of the gods—to a population that was less and less concerned about traditional religion.

Using evidence from the play, support each of these theories as best you can. Then select the theory that seems most logical based on the evidence.

THE TROJAN WOMEN

Euripides (484–406 B.C.)

In his *History of the Peloponnesian War*, Thucydides relates the mournful story of the unprovoked Athenian attack of 416 B.C. on the neutral island of Melos, during which all the men were killed and the women and children enslaved. The only horrified reaction to this terrible deed that has come down to us is *The Trojan Women*, apparently written shortly after the slaughter. *The Trojan Women* is Euripides' passionate protest against this brutal action and against the whole sickening business of war. With no plot and little action, the play is set in the aftermath of the fall of Troy. Except for two subordinate roles, all the characters are women who are also, except for Helen, sorrowing, bereft widows. Waiting on the beach for the victors to divide the spoils of war, including themselves and their children, their situation is hopeless. The ultimate irony, however, is that victors and vanquished suffer equally; those who destroyed the city will themselves be given, in the words of Athena, "a bitter home-coming." Euripides, the "poet of the world's grief," saw clearly that the great god War destroys everything and solves nothing.

This translation is by the noted classical scholar Edith Hamilton.

[*The scene is a space of waste ground except for a few huts to right and left, where the women selected for the Greek leaders are housed. Far in the background Troy, the wall in ruins, is slowly burning, as yet more smoke than flame. In front a woman with white hair lies on the ground. It is just before dawn. A tall dim figure is seen, back of the woman.*]

Poseidon: I am the sea god. I have come
up from the salt sea depths of the Aegean,
from where the sea nymphs' footsteps fall,
weaving the lovely measures of the dance.
For since that day I built the towers of stone
around this town of Troy, Apollo with me,
—and straight we raised them, true by line and
        plummet—
good will for them has never left my heart,
my Trojans and their city.
City? Smoke only—all is gone,
perished beneath Greek spears.
A horse was fashioned, big with arms.
Parnassus was the workman's home,
in Phocia, and his name Epeius.
The skill he had Athena gave him.
He sent it through the walls—it carried death.
The wooden horse, so men will call it always,
which held and hid those spears.

A desert now where groves were. Blood drips down
from the gods' shrines. Beside his hearth
Priam lies dead upon the altar steps
of Zeus, the hearth's protector.
While to the Greek ships pass the Trojan treasure,
gold, gold in masses, armor, clothing,
stripped from the dead.
The Greeks who long since brought war to the town,
—ten times the seed was sown before Troy fell—
wait now for a fair wind for home,
the joyful sight of wife and child again.
Myself defeated by the Argive goddess
Hera and by Athena, both in league together—
I too must take my leave of glorious Troy,
forsake my altars. When a town is turned
into a desert, things divine fall sick.
Not one to do them honor.
Scamander's stream is loud with lamentation,
so many captive women weeping.
Their masters drew lots for them. Some will go
to Arcady and some to Thessaly.
Some to the lords of Athens, Theseus' sons.
Huts here hold others spared the lot, but chosen
for the great captains.
With them, like them a captive of the spear,
the Spartan woman, Helen.
But if a man would look on misery,
it is here to see—Hecuba lies there
before the gates. She weeps.
Many tears for many griefs.
And one still hidden from her.
But now upon Akhilleus' grave her daughter
was killed—Polyxena. So patiently she died.
Gone is her husband, gone her sons, all dead.
One daughter whom the Lord Apollo loved,
yet spared her wild virginity, Kassandra,
Agamemnon, in the dark, will force upon his bed.
No thought for what was holy and was God's.
O city happy once, farewell.
O shining towers, crumbling now
beneath Athena's hand, the child of God,
or you would still stand firm on deep foundations.

[*As he turns to go the goddess* PALLAS ATHENA *enters.*]

Athena: Am I allowed to speak to one who is
my father's nearest kinsman,
a god among gods honored, powerful?
If I put enmity aside, will he?

Poseidon: He will, most high Athena. We are kin,
old comrades too, and these have magic power.

Athena: Thanks for your gentleness. What I would say
        touches us both, great king.

Poseidon: A message from the gods? A word from Zeus?
        Some spirit, surely?

Athena: No, but for Troy's sake, where we stand, I seek
        your power to join my own with it.

Poseidon: What! Now—at last? Has that long hatred left
        you?
Pity—when all is ashes—burned to ashes?

Athena: The point first, please. Will you make common
        cause
with me? What I wish done will you wish, too?

Poseidon: Gladly. But what you wish I first must know.
You come to me for Troy's sake or for Greece?

Athena: I wish to make my Trojan foes rejoice, and give
        the Greeks a bitter home-coming.

Poseidon: The way you change! Here—there—then back
        again.
Now hate, now love—no limit ever.

Athena: You know how I was outraged and my temple.

Poseidon: Oh that—when Ajax dragged Kassandra out?

Athena: And not one Greek to punish him—not one to blame him.

Poseidon: Even though your power ruined Troy for them.

Athena: Therefore with you I mean to hurt them.

Poseidon: Ready for all you wish. But—hurt them? How?

Athena: Give them affliction for their coming home.

Poseidon: Held here, you mean? Or out on the salt sea?

Athena: Whenever the ships sail.
Zeus shall send rain, unending rain, and sleet, and darkness blown from heaven.
He will give me—he has promised—his thunderbolt,
to strike the ships with fire. They shall burn.
Your part, to make your sea-roads roar—
wild waves and whirlwinds,
while dead men choke the winding bay.
So Greeks shall learn to reverence my house
and dread all gods.

Poseidon: These things shall be. No need of many words
to grant a favor. I will stir the sea,
the wide Aegean. Shores and reefs and cliffs
will hold dead men, bodies of many dead.
Off to Olympus with you now, and get
those fiery arrows from the hand of Zeus.
Then when a fair wind sends the Greeks to sea,
watch the ships sail.

[*Exit* ATHENA]

Oh, fools, the men who lay a city waste,
giving to desolation temples, tombs,
the sanctuaries of the dead—so soon
to die themselves.

[*Exit* POSEIDON]

[*The two gods have been talking before daylight, but now the day begins to dawn and the woman lying on the ground in front moves. She is* HECUBA, *the aged queen of Troy.*]

Hecuba: Up from the ground—O weary head, O breaking neck.
This is no longer Troy. And we are not
the lords of Troy.
Endure. The ways of fate are the ways of the wind.
Drift with the stream—drift with fate.
No use to turn the prow to breast the waves.
Let the boat go as it chances.
Sorrow, my sorrow.
What sorrow is there that is not mine,
grief to weep for.
Country lost and children and husband.
Glory of all my house brought low.
All was nothing—nothing, always.
Keep silent? Speak?
Weep then? Why? For what?

[*She begins to get up.*]

Oh, this aching body—this bed—
it is very hard. My back pressed to it—
Oh, my side, my brow, my temples.
Up! Quick, quick. I must move.
Oh, I'll rock myself this way, that way,
to the sound of weeping, the song of tears,
dropping down forever.
The song no feet will dance to ever,
for the wretched, the ruined.
O ships, O prows, swift oars,
out from the fair Greek bays and harbors,
over the dark shining sea,

you found your way to our holy city,
and the fearful music of war was heard,
the war song sung to flute and pipe,
as you cast on the shore your cables,
ropes the Nile dwellers twisted and coiled,
and you swung, oh, my grief, in Troy's waters.
What did you come for? A woman?
A thing of loathing, of shame,
to husband, to brother, to home.
She slew Priam, the king,
father of fifty sons,
she wrecked me upon
the reef of destruction.
Who am I that I wait[17]
here at a Greek king's door?
A slave that men drive on,
an old gray woman that has no home.
Shaven head brought low in dishonor.
O wives of the bronze-armored men who fought,
and maidens, sorrowing maidens,
plighted to shame,
see—only smoke left where was Troy.
Let us weep for her.
As a mother bird cries to her feathered brood,
so will I cry.
Once another song I sang
when I leaned on Priam's scepter,
and the beat of dancing feet
marked the music's measure.
Up to the gods
the song of Troy rose at my signal.

[*The door of one of the huts opens and a woman steals out, then another, and another.*]

First Woman: Your cry, O Hecuba—oh, such a cry—
What does it mean? There in the tent
we heard you call so piteously,
and through our hearts flashed fear.
In the tent we were weeping, too,
for we are slaves.

Hecuba: Look, child, there where the Greek ships lie—

Another Woman: They are moving. The men hold oars.

Another: O God, what will they do? Carry me off over
the sea in a ship far from home?

Hecuba: You ask and I know nothing, but I think ruin is
here.

Another Woman: Oh, we are wretched. We shall hear
the summons.
Women of Troy, go forth from your home,
for the Greeks set sail.

Hecuba: But not Kassandra, oh, not her.
She is mad—she has been driven mad. Leave her within.
Not shamed before the Greeks—not that grief too.
I have enough.
        O Troy, unhappy Troy, you are gone
and we, the unhappy, leave you,
we who are living and we who are dead.

---

17. This is the way Professor Murray translates the line and the one following. The translation is so simple and beautiful, I cannot bear to give it up for a poorer one of my own.

[*More women now come out from a second hut.*]
A Woman: Out of the Greek king's tent
trembling I come, O Queen,
to hear my fate from you.
Not death—They would not think of death
for a poor woman.
Another: The sailors—they are standing on the prow.
Already they are running out the oars.
Another: [*She comes out of a third hut and several
      follow her.*]
It is so early—but a terror woke me.
      My heart beats so.
Another: Has a herald come from the Greek camp?
Whose slave shall I be? I—bear that?
Hecuba: Wait for the lot drawing. It is near.
Another: Argos shall it be, or Phthia? or an island of the
      sea?
      A Greek soldier lead me there,
far, far from Troy?
Hecuba: And I a slave—to whom—where—how?
You old gray woman, patient to endure,
you bee without a sting,
only an image of what was alive, or the ghost of one dead.
I watch a master's door?
      I nurse his children?
      Once I was queen in Troy.
One Woman to Another: Poor thing. What are your
      tears
to the shame before you?
The Other: The shuttle will still pass through my hands,
      but the loom will not be in Troy.
Another: My dead sons. I would look at them once
      more.
Never again.
Another: Worse to come.
A Greek's bed—and I—
Another: A night like that? Oh, never—
oh, no—not that for me.
Another: I see myself a water carrier,
dipping my pitcher in the great Pierian spring.
Another: The land of Theseus, Athens, it is known
to be a happy place. I wish I could go there.
Another: But not to the Eurotas, hateful river,
where Helen lived. Not there, to be a slave
to Menelaos who sacked Troy.
Another: Oh, look. A man from the Greek army—
a herald. Something strange has happened,
he comes so fast. To tell us—what?
What will he say? Only Greek slaves are here,
waiting for orders.
[*Enter* TALTHYBIUS *with soldiers.*]
Talthybius: You know me, Hecuba. I have often come
with messages to Troy from the Greek camp.
Talthybius—these many years you've known me.
I bring you news.
Hecuba: It has come, women of Troy. Once we only
      feared it.
Talthybius: The lots are drawn, if that is what you
      feared.
Hecuba: Who—where? Thessaly? Phthia? Thebes?
Talthybius: A different man takes each. You're not to go
      together.
Hecuba: Then which takes which? Has any one good
      fortune?
Talthybius: I know, but ask about each one, not all at
      once.
Hecuba: My daughter, who—who drew her? Tell me—
      Kassandra. She has had so much to bear

Talthybius: King Agamemnon chose her out from all.
Hecuba: Oh! but—of course—to serve his Spartan wife?
Talthybius: No, no—but for the king's own bed at night.
Hecuba: Oh, never. She is God's, a virgin, always.
That was God's gift to her for all her life.
Talthybius: He loved her for that same strange purity.[18]
Hecuba: Throw away, daughter, the keys of the temple.
Take off the wreath and the sacred stole.
Talthybius: Well, now—a king's bed is not so bad.
Hecuba: My other child you took from me just now?
Talthybius: [*Speaking with constraint*]
Polyxena, you mean? Or someone else?
Hecuba: Her. Who drew her?
Talthybius: They told her to watch Akhilleus' tomb.
Hecuba: To watch a tomb? My daughter?
That a Greek custom?
What strange ritual is that, my friend?
Talthybius: [*Speaking fast and trying to put her off*]
Just think of her as happy—all well with her.
Hecuba: Those words—Why do you speak like that?
She is alive?
Talthybius: [*Determined not to tell her*]
What happened was—well, she is free from trouble.
Hecuba: [*Wearily giving the riddle up*]
Then Hektor's wife—my Hektor, wise in war—
Where does she go, poor thing—Andromache?
Talthybius: Akhilleus' son took her. He chose her out.
Hecuba: And I, old gray head, whose slave am I,
creeping along with my crutch?
Talthybius: Slave of the king of Ithaca, Odysseus.
Hecuba: Beat, beat my shorn head! Tear, tear my cheek!
His slave—vile lying man. I have come to this—
There is nothing good he does not hurt—a lawless beast.
He twists and turns, this way and that, and back again.
A double tongue, as false in hate as false in love.
Pity me, women of Troy,
I have gone. I am lost—oh, wretched.
An evil fate fell on me,
a lot the hardest of all.
A Woman: You know what lies before you, Queen,
      but I—
What man among the Greeks owns me?
Talthybius: [*To the soldiers*]
Off with you. Bring Kassandra here. Be quick,
you fellows. We must give her to the chief,
into his very hand. And then these here
to all the other generals. But what's that—
that flash of light inside there?
[*Light shines through the crevices of one of the huts.*]
Set fire to the huts—is that their plan,
these Trojan women? Burn themselves to death
rather than sail to Greece. Choosing to die instead.
How savagely these days the yoke bears down
on necks so lately free.
Open there, open the door. [*Aside*] As well for them
      perhaps,
but for the Greeks—they'd put the blame on me.
Hecuba: No, no, there is nothing burning. It is my
      daughter,
Kassandra. She is mad.
[KASSANDRA *enters from the hut dressed like a priestess,
a wreath in her hair, a torch in her hand. She does not
seem to see anyone.*]

---

18. This line, too, is Professor Murray's, and retained here for the
reason given in footnote 17.

Kassandra: Lift it high—in my hand—light to bring.
    I praise him. I bear a flame.
    With my torch I touch to fire this holy place.
    Hymen, O Hymen.
    Blessed the bridegroom, blessed am I
to lie with a king in a king's bed in Argos.
    Hymen, O Hymen.
Mother, you weep
tears for my father dead,
mourning for the beloved country lost.
I for my bridal here
lift up the fire's flame
to the dawn, to the splendor,
to you, O Hymen.
Queen of night,
give your starlight
to a virgin bed,
as of old you did.
Fly, dancing feet.
Up with the dance.
    Oh, joy, oh, joy!
Dance for my father dead, most blest to die.
Oh, holy dance!
Apollo—you?
Lead on then.
There in the laurel grove
I served your altar.
    Dance, Mother, come. Keep step with me.
Dear feet with my feet tracing the measure this way and
    that.
Sing to the Marriage god,
oh, joyful song.
Sing for the bride, too,
joyously all.
Maidens of Troy,
dressed in your best,
honor my marriage.
Honor too him
whose bed fate drives me to share.

A Woman: Hold her fast, Queen, poor frenzied girl.
She might rush straight to the Greek camp.

Hecuba: O fire, fire, when men make marriages
you light the torch, but this flame flashing here
is for grief only. Child, such great hopes once I had.
I never thought that to your bridal bed
Greek spears would drive you.
Give me your torch. You do not hold it straight,
you move so wildly. Your sufferings, my child,
have never taught you wisdom.
You never change. Here! someone take the torch
into the hut. This marriage needs no songs,
but only tears.

Kassandra: O Mother, crown my triumph with a wreath.
Be glad, for I am married to a king.
Send me to him, and if I shrink away,
drive me with violence. If Apollo lives,
my marriage shall be bloodier than Helen's.
Agamemnon, the great, the glorious lord of Greece—
I shall kill him, Mother, lay his house as low
as he laid ours, make him pay for all
he made my father suffer, brothers, and—
But no. I must not speak of that—that axe
which on my neck—on others' too—
nor of that murder of a mother.
All, all because he married me and so
pulled his own house down.
But I will show you. This town now, yes, Mother,
is happier than the Greeks. I know that I am mad,
but Mother, dearest, now, for this one time
I do not rave.

One woman they came hunting, and one love,
Helen, and men by tens of thousands died.
Their king, so wise, to get what most he hated
destroyed what most he loved,
his joy at home, his daughter, killing her
for a brother's sake, to get him back a woman
who had fled because she wished—not forced to go.
And when they came to the banks of the Scamander
those thousands died. And why?
No man had moved their landmarks
or laid siege to their high-walled towns.
But those whom war took never saw their children.
No wife with gentle hands shrouded them for their grave.
They lie in a strange land. And in their homes
are sorrows, too, the very same.
Lonely women who died, old men who waited
for sons that never came—no son left to them
to make the offering at their graves.
That was the glorious victory they won.
But we—we Trojans died to save our people,
no glory greater. All those the spear slew,
friends bore them home and wrapped them in their
    shroud
with dutiful hands. The earth of their own land
covered them. The rest, through the long days they
    fought,
had wife and child at hand, not like the Greeks,
whose joys were far away.
And Hektor's pain—your Hektor. Mother, hear me.
This is the truth: he died, the best, a hero.
Because the Greeks came, he died thus.
Had they stayed home, we never would have known him.
This truth stands firm: the wise will fly from war.
But if war comes, to die well is to win
the victor's crown.
The only shame is not to die like that.
So, Mother, do not pity Troy,
or me upon my bridal bed.

Talthybius: [*Has been held awestruck through all this,
but can bear no more*]
Now if Apollo had not made you mad
I would have paid you for those evil words,
bad omens, and my general sailing soon.
[*Grumbles to himself*]
The great, who seem so wise, have no more sense
than those who rank as nothing.
Our king, the first in Greece, bows down
before this mad girl, loves her, chooses her
out of them all. Well, I am a poor man,
but I'd not go to bed with her.
[*Turns to* KASSANDRA]
Now you—you know your mind is not quite right.
So all you said against Greece and for Troy,
I never heard—the wind blew it away.
Come with me to the ship now.
[*Aside*]
A grand match for our general, she is.
[*To* HECUBA, *gently*]
And you, do follow quietly when Odysseus' men come.
His wife's a good, wise woman, so they say.

Kassandra: [*Seeming to see* TALTHYBIUS *for the first
time and looking him over haughtily*]
A strange sort of slave, surely.
Heralds such men are called,
hated by all, for they are tyrants' tools.

You say my mother goes to serve Odysseus?
[*She turns away and speaks to herself.*]
But where then is Apollo's word, made clear
to me, that death will find her here?
And—no, that shame I will not speak of.
Odysseus! wretched—but he does not know.
	Soon all these sorrows, mine and Troy's, will seem
compared to his like golden hours.
Ten years behind him here, ten years before him.
Then only, all alone, will he come home,
and there find untold trouble has come first.
But his cares—why let fly one word at him?
Come, let us hasten to my marriage.
We two shall rest, the bridegroom and the bride,
within the house of death.
O Greek king, with your dreams of grandeur yet to come,
vile as you are, so shall your end be,
in darkness—all light gone.
And me—a cleft in the hills,
washed by winter rains,
his tomb near by.
There—dead—cast out—naked—
and wild beasts seeking food—
It is I there—I myself—Apollo's servant.
O flowers of the God I love, mysterious wreaths,
away. I have forgotten temple festival,
I have forgotten joy.
Off. I tear them from my neck.
Swift winds will carry them
up to you, O God of truth.
My flesh still clean, I give them back to you.
Where is the ship? How do I go on board?
Spread the sail—the wind comes swift.
Those who bring vengeance—three are they,
And one of them goes with you on the sea.
Mother, my Mother, do not weep. Farewell,
dear City. Brothers, in Troy's earth laid, my father,
a little time and I am with you.
You dead, I shall come to you a victor.
Those ruined by my hand who ruined us.
[*She goes out with* TALTHYBIUS *and the soldiers.*
HECUBA, *motionless for a moment, falls.*]
A Woman: The Queen! See—see—she is falling.
Oh, help! She cannot speak.
Miserable slaves, will you leave her on the ground,
old as she is. Up—lift her up.
Hecuba: Let me be. Kindness not wanted is unkindness.
I cannot stand. Too much is on me.
Anguish here and long since and to come—
O God—Do I call to you? You did not help.
But there is something that cries out for God
when trouble comes.
Oh, I will think of good days gone,
days to make a song of,
crowning my sorrow by remembering.
We were kings and a king I married.
Sons I bore him, many sons.
That means little—but fine, brave lads.
They were the best in all Troy.
No woman, Trojan, Greek, or stranger,
had sons like mine to be proud of.
I saw them fall beneath Greek spears.
My hair I shore at the grave of the dead.
Their father—I did not learn from others
that I must weep for him—these eyes beheld him.
I, my own self, saw him fall murdered
upon the altar, when his town was lost.

My daughters, maidens reared to marry kings,
are torn from me. For the Greeks I reared them.
All gone—no hope that I shall look upon
their faces any more, or they on mine.
And now the end—no more can lie beyond—
an old gray slave woman I go to Greece.
The tasks they know for my age hardest, mine.
The door to shut and open, bowing low
—I who bore Hektor—meal to grind; upon
the ground lay this old body down that once
slept in a royal bed; torn rags around me,
torn flesh beneath.
And all this misery and all to come
because a man desired a woman.
Daughter, who knew God's mystery and joy,
what strange chance lost you your virginity?
And you, Polyxena—where are you gone?
No son, no daughter, left to help my need,
and I had many, many—
Why lift me up? What hope is there to hold to?
	This slave that once went delicately in Troy,
take her and cast her on her bed of clay,
rocks for her pillow, there to fall and die,
wasted with tears. Count no one happy,
however fortunate, before he dies.
Chorus: Sing me, O Muse, a song for Troy,
a strange song sung to tears,
a music for the grave.
O lips, sound forth a melody for Troy.
A four-wheeled cart brought the horse to the gates,
brought ruin to me, captured, enslaved me.
Gold was the rein and the bridle,
deadly the arms within,
and they clashed loud to heaven as the threshold was
	passed.
High on Troy's rock the people cried,
"Rest at last, trouble ended.
Bring the carven image in.
Bear it to Athena,
fit gift for the child of God."
Who of the young but hurried forth?
Who of the old would stay at home?
With song and rejoicing they brought death in,
treachery and destruction.
All that were in Troy,
hastening to the gate,
drew that smooth-planed horse of wood
carven from a mountain pine,
where the Greeks were hiding,
where was Troy's destruction,
gave it to the goddess,
gift for her, the virgin,
driver of the steeds that never die.
With ropes of twisted flax,
as a ship's dark hull is drawn to land,
they brought it to her temple of stone,
to her floor that soon would run with blood, to Pallas
	Athena.
	On their toil and their joy
the dark of evening fell,
but the lutes of Egypt still rang out to the songs of Troy.
And girls with feet light as air
dancing, sang happy songs.
The houses blazed with light
through the dark splendor, and sleep was not.
A Girl: I was among the dancers.
I was singing to the maiden of Zeus,
the goddess of the hills.

A shout rang out in the town,
a cry of blood through the houses,
and a frightened child caught his mother's skirt
and hid himself in her cloak.
Then War came forth from his hiding place—
Athena, the virgin, devised it.
Around the altars they slaughtered us.
Within on their beds lay headless men,
young men cut down in their prime.
This was the triumph-crown of Greece.
We shall bear children for her to rear,
grief and shame to our country.

[*A chariot approaches, loaded with spoils. In it sits a woman and a child.*]

A Woman: Look, Hecuba, it is Andromache.
See, in the Greek car yonder.
Her breast heaves with her sobs and yet
the baby sleeps there, dear Astyanax, the son of Hektor.
Another: Most sorrowful of women, where do you go?
Beside you the bronze armor that was Hektor's,
the spoil of the Greek spear, stripped from the dead.
Will Akhilleus' son use it to deck his temples?
Andromache: I go where my Greek masters take me.
Hecuba: Oh, our sorrow—our sorrow.
Andromache: Why should you weep? This sorrow is
      mine.
Hecuba: O God—
Andromache: What has come to me is mine.
Hecuba: My children—
Andromache: Once we lived, not now.
Hecuba: Gone—gone—happiness—Troy—
Andromache: And you bear it.
Hecuba: Sons, noble sons, all lost.
Andromache: Oh, sorrow is here.
Hecuba: For me—for me.
Andromache: For the city, in its shroud of smoke.
Come to me, O my husband.
Hecuba: What you cry to lies in the grave.
My son, wretched woman, mine.
Andromache: Defend me—me, your wife.
Hecuba: My son, my eldest son,
whom I bore to Priam,
whom the Greeks used shamefully,
come to me, lead me to death.
Andromache: Death—oh, how deep a desire.
Hecuba: Such is our pain—
Andromache: For a city that has fallen, fallen.
Hecuba: For anguish heaped upon anguish.
Andromache: For the anger of God against Paris,
your son, who fled from death,
who laid Troy's towers low to win an evil love.
Dead men—bodies—blood—
vultures hovering—
Oh, Athena the goddess is there, be sure,
and the slave's yoke is laid upon Troy.
Hecuba: O country, desolate, empty.
Andromache: My tears fall for you.
Hecuba: Look and see the end—
Andromache: Of the house where I bore my children.
Hecuba: O children, your mother has lost her city,
and you—you have left her alone.
Only grief is mine and mourning.
Tears and more tears, falling, falling.
The dead—they have forgotten their pain.
They weep no more.
A Woman: [*Aside to another*]
Tears are sweet in bitter grief,
and sorrow's song is lamentation.

Andromache: Mother of him whose spear of old
      brought death
to Greeks unnumbered, you see what is here.
Hecuba: I see God's hand that casts the mighty down
and sets on high the lowly.
Andromache: Driven like cattle captured in a raid,
my child and I—the free changed to a slave.
Oh, changed indeed.
Hecuba: It is fearful to be helpless. Men just now
have taken Kassandra—forced her from me.
Andromache: And still more for you—more than
      that—
Hecuba: Number my sorrows, will you? Measure them?
One comes—the next one rivals it.
Andromache: Polyxena lies dead upon Akhilleus' tomb,
a gift to a corpse, to a lifeless thing.
Hecuba: My sorrow! That is what Talthybius meant—
I could not read his riddle. Oh, too plain.
Andromache: I saw her there and left the chariot
and covered her dead body with my cloak,
and beat my breast.
Hecuba: Murdered—my child. Oh, wickedly!
Again I cry to you. Oh, cruelly slain!
Andromache: She has died her death, and happier by
      far
dying than I alive.
Hecuba: Life cannot be what death is, child.
Death is empty—life has hope.
Andromache: Mother, O Mother, hear a truer word.
Now let me bring joy to your heart.
I say to die is only not to be,
and rather death than life with bitter grief.
They have no pain, they do not feel their wrongs.
But the happy who has come to wretchedness,
his soul is a lost wanderer,
the old joys that were once, left far behind.
She is dead, your daughter—to her the same
as if she never had been born.
She does not know the wickedness that killed her.
While I—I aimed my shaft at good repute.
I gained full measure—then missed happiness.
For all that is called virtuous in a woman
I strove for and I won in Hektor's house.
Always, because we women, whether right or wrong,
are spoken ill of
unless we stay within our homes, my longing
I set aside and kept the house.
Light talk, glib women's words,
could never gain an entrance there.
My own thoughts were enough for me,
best of all teachers to me in my home.
Silence, a tranquil eye, I brought my husband,
knew well in what I should rule him,
and when give him obedience.
And this report of me came to the Greeks
for my destruction. When they captured me
Akhilleus' son would have me.
I shall be a slave to those who murdered—
O Hektor, my beloved—shall I thrust him aside,
open my heart to the man that comes to me,
and be a traitor to the dead?
And yet to shrink in loathing from him
and make my masters hate me—
One night, men say, one night in a man's bed
will make a woman tame—
Oh, shame! A woman throw her husband off
and in a new bed love another—

Why, a young colt will not run in the yoke
with any but her mate—not a dumb beast
that has no reason, of a lower nature.
O Hektor, my beloved, you were all to me,
wise, noble, mighty, in wealth, in manhood, both.
No man had touched me when you took me,
took me from out my father's home
and yoked a girl fast to you.
And you are dead, and I, with other plunder,
am sent by sea to Greece. A slave's yoke there.
Your dead Polyxena you weep for,
what does she know of pain like mine?
The living must have hope. Not I, not any more.
I will not lie to my own heart. No good will ever come.
But oh, to think it would be sweet.

A Woman: We stand at the same point of pain. You
    mourn your ruin,
and in your words I hear my own calamity.

Hecuba: Those ships—I never have set foot on one,
but I have heard of them, seen pictures of them.
I know that when a storm comes which they think
they can ride out, the sailors do their best,
one by the sail, another at the helm,
and others bailing.
But if great ocean's raging overwhelms them,
they yield to fate.
They give themselves up to the racing waves.
So in my many sorrows I am dumb.
I yield, I cannot speak.
The great wave from God has conquered me.
But, O dear child, let Hektor be,
and let be what has come to him.
Your tears will never call him back.
Give honor now to him who is your master.
Your sweet ways—use them to allure him.
So doing you will give cheer to your friends.
Perhaps this child, my own child's son,
you may rear to manhood and great aid for Troy,
and if ever you should have more children,
they might build her again. Troy once more be a city!
Oh—one thought leads another on.
But why again that servant of the Greeks?
I see him coming. Some new plan is here.

[*Enter* TALTHYBIUS *with soldiers. He is troubled and
advances hesitatingly.*]

Talthybius: Wife of the noblest man that was in Troy,
O wife of Hektor, do not hate me.
Against my will I come to tell you.
The people and the kings have all resolved—

Andromache: What is it? Evil follows words like those.

Talthybius: This child they order—Oh, how can I say
    it—

Andromache: Not that he does not go with me to the
    same master—

Talthybius: No man in Greece shall ever be his master.

Andromache: But—leave him here—all that is left of
    Troy?

Talthybius: I don't know how to tell you. What is bad,
words can't make better—

Andromache: I feel you kind. But you have not good
    news.

Talthybius: Your child must die. There, now you know
    the whole, bad as it is.

Andromache: Oh, I have heard an evil worse than a
    slave in her master's bed.

Talthybius: It was Odysseus had his way. He spoke to all
    the Greeks.

Andromache: O God. There is no measure to my pain.

Talthybius: He said a hero's son must not grow up—

Andromache: God, on his own sons may that counsel
    fall.

Talthybius: —but from the towering wall of Troy be
    thrown.
Now, now—let it be done—that's wiser.
Don't cling so to him. Bear your pain
the way a brave woman suffers.
You have no strength—don't look to any help.
There's no help for you anywhere. Think—think.
The city gone—your husband too. And you
a captive and alone, one woman—how
can you do battle with us? For your own good
I would not have you try, and draw
hatred down on you and be shamed.
Oh, hush—never a curse upon the Greeks.
If you say words that make the army angry
the child will have no burial, and without pity—
Silence now. Bear your fate as best you can.
So then you need not leave him dead without a grave,
and you will find the Greeks more kind.

Andromache: Go die, my best beloved, my own, my
    treasure,
in cruel hands, leaving your mother comfortless.
Your father was too noble. That is why
they kill you. He could save others,
he could not save you for his nobleness.
My bed, my bridal—all for misery—
when long ago I came to Hektor's halls
to bear my son—oh, not for Greeks to slay,
but for a ruler over teeming Asia.
Weeping, my little one? There, there.
You cannot know what waits for you.
Why hold me with your hands so fast, cling so fast to me?
You little bird, flying to hide beneath my wings.
And Hektor will not come—he will not come,
up from the tomb, great spear in hand, to save you.
Not one of all his kin, of all the Trojan might.
How will it be? Falling down—down—oh, horrible.
And his neck—his breath—all broken.
And none to pity. You little thing,
curled in my arms, you dearest to your mother,
how sweet the fragrance of you.
All nothing then—this breast from where
your baby mouth drew milk, my travail too,
my cares, when I grew wasted watching you.
Kiss me—Never again. Come, closer, closer.
Your mother who bore you—put your arms around my
    neck.
Now kiss me, lips to lips.
O Greeks, you have found out ways to torture
that are not Greek.
A little child, all innocent of wrong—
you wish to kill him.
O Helen, evil growth, that was sown by Tyndareus,
you are no child of Zeus, as people say.
Many the fathers you were born of,
Madness, Hatred, Red Death, whatever poison
the earth brings forth—no child of Zeus,
but Greece's curse and all the world's.
God curse you, with those beautiful eyes
that brought to shame and ruin
Troy's far-famed plains.
Quick! take him—seize him—cast him down—
if so you will. Feast on his flesh.
God has destroyed me, and I cannot—
I cannot save my child from death.
Oh hide my head for shame and fling me into the ship.

[*She falls, then struggles to her knees.*]

My fair bridal—I am coming—
Oh, I have lost my child, my own.

A Woman: O wretched Troy, tens of thousands lost
for a woman's sake, a hateful marriage bed.
Talthybius: [*Drawing the child away*]
Come, boy, let go. Unclasp those loving hands,
poor mother.
Come now, up, up, to the very height,
where the towers of your fathers crown the wall,
and where it is decreed that you must die.
[*To the soldiers*]
Take him away.
A herald who must bring such orders
should be a man who feels no pity,
and no shame either—not like me.
Hecuba: Child, son of my poor son, whose toil was all
    in vain,
we are robbed, your mother and I, oh, cruelly—
robbed of your life. How bear it?
What can I do for you, poor piteous child?
Beat my head, my breast—all I can give you.
Troy lost, now you—all lost.
The cup is full. Why wait? For what?
Hasten on—swiftly on to death.
[*The soldiers, who have waited while* HECUBA *speaks, go
out with the child and* TALTHYBIUS. *One of them takes*
ANDROMACHE *to the chariot and drives off with her.*]
Chorus: The waves make a ring around Salamis.
The bees are loud in the island.
King Telamon built him a dwelling.
It fronted the holy hills,
where first the gray gleaming olive
Athena showed to men,
the glory of shining Athens,
her crown from the sky.
He joined himself to the bowman,
the son of Alcmena, for valorous deeds.
Troy, Troy he laid waste, my city,
long ago when he went forth from Greece.
When he led forth from Greece the bravest
in his wrath for the steeds[19] withheld,
and by fair-flowing Simois stayed his oar
that had brought him over the sea.
Cables there made the ship fast.
In his hand was the bow that never missed.
It brought the king to his death.
Walls of stone that Phoebus had built
he wrecked with the red breath of fire.
He wasted the plain of Troy.
Twice her walls have fallen. Twice
a blood-stained spear struck her down, laid her in ruin.

In vain, O you who move
with delicate feet where the wine-cups are gold,
son of that old dead king,
who fill with wine the cup Zeus holds,
service most fair—
she who gave you birth is afire.
The shores of the sea are wailing for her.
As a bird cries over her young,
women weep for husbands, for children,
for the old, too, who gave them birth.
Your dewy baths are gone,
and the race-course where you ran.

Yet your young face keeps the beauty of peace
in joy, by the throne of Zeus.
While Priam's land
lies ruined by Greek spearsmen.

Love, O Love,
once you came to the halls of Troy,
and your song rose up to the dwellers in heaven.
How did you then exalt Troy high,
binding her fast to the gods, by a union—
No—I will not speak blame of Zeus.
But the light of white-winged Dawn, dear to men,
is deadly over the land this day,
shining on fallen towers.
And yet Dawn keeps in her bridal bower
her children's father, a son of Troy.
Her chariot bore him away to the sky.
It was gold, and four stars drew it.
Hope was high then for our town.
But the magic that brought her the love of the gods
has gone from Troy.
[*As the song ends* MENELAOS *enters with a bodyguard of
soldiers.*]
Menelaos: How bright the sunlight is today—
this day, when I shall get into my power
Helen, my wife. For I am Menelaos,
the man of many wrongs.
I came to Troy and brought with me my army,
not for that woman's sake, as people say,
but for the man who from my house,
and he a guest there, stole away my wife.
Ah, well, with God's help he has paid the price,
he and his country, fallen beneath Greek spears.
I am come to get her—wretch—I cannot speak her name
who was my wife once.
In a hut here, where they house the captives,
she is numbered with the other Trojan women.
The men who fought and toiled to win her back,
have given her to me—to kill, or else,
if it pleases me, to take her back to Argos.
And it has seemed to me her death in Troy
is not the way. I will take her overseas,
with swift oars speeding on the ship,
and there in Greece give her to those to kill
whose dearest died because of her.
[*To his men*]
Attention! Forward to the huts.
Seize her and drag her out by that long blood-drenched
    hair—
[*Stops suddenly and controls himself*]
And when fair winds come, home with her to Greece.
[*Soldiers begin to force the door of one of the huts.*]
Hecuba: [*Comes slowly forward*]
O thou who dost uphold the world,
whose throne is high above the world,
thou, past our seeking hard to find, who art thou?
God, or Necessity of what must be,
or Reason of our reason?
Whate'er thou art, I pray to thee,
seeing the silent road by which
all mortal things are led by thee to justice.
Menelaos: What have we here? A queer prayer that.

---

19. When Troy was destroyed the first time, the reason was that
the Trojan king had promised two immortal horses to Herakles
("the son of Alcmena") but did not give them to him. Herakles
in revenge ruined the city. The son of this king was Ganymede,
cup-bearer to Zeus.

Hecuba: [*She comes still nearer to him and he recognizes her.*]
Kill her, Menelaos? You will? Oh, blessings on you!
But—shun her, do not look at her.
Desire for her will seize you, conquer you.
For through men's eyes she gets them in her power.
She ruins them and ruins cities too.
Fire comes from her to burn homes,
magic for death. I know her—so do you,
and all these who have suffered.
[HELEN *enters from the hut. The soldiers do not touch her. She is very gentle and undisturbed.*]
Helen: [*With sweet, injured dignity. Not angry at all.*]
Menelaos, these things might well make a woman fear.
Your men with violence have driven me from my room,
have laid their hands upon me.
Of course, I know—almost I know—you hate me,
but yet I ask you, what is your decision,
yours and the Greeks? Am I to live or not?
Menelaos: Nothing more clear. Unanimous, in fact.
Not one who did not vote you should be given me,
whom you have wronged, to kill you.
Helen: Am I allowed to speak against the charge?
To show you if I die that I shall die
most wronged and innocent?
Menelaos: I have come to kill you, not to argue with
   you.
Hecuba: Oh, hear her. She must never die unheard.
Then, Menelaos, let me answer her.
The evil that she did in Troy, you do not know.
But I will tell the story. She will die.
She never can escape.
Menelaos: That means delay. Still—if she wants to
   speak,
she can. I grant her this because of what you say,
not for her sake. She can be sure of that.
Helen: And perhaps, no matter if you think I speak
the truth or not, you will not talk to me,
since you believe I am your enemy.
Still, I will try to answer what I think
you would say if you spoke your mind,
and my wrongs shall be heard as well as yours.
First: who began these evils? She, the day
when she gave birth to Paris. Who next was guilty?
The old king who decreed the child should live,
and ruined Troy and me—Paris, the hateful,
the firebrand.
What happened then? Listen and learn.
This Paris—he was made the judge for three,
all yoked together in a quarrel—goddesses.
Athena promised he should lead the Trojans
to victory and lay all Greece in ruins.
And Hera said if he thought her the fairest
she would make him lord of Europe and of Asia.
But Aphrodite—well, she praised my beauty—
astonishing, she said—and promised him
that she would give me to him if he judged
that she was loveliest. Then, see what happened.
She won, and so my bridal brought all Greece
great good. No strangers rule you,
no foreign spears, no tyrant.
Oh, it was well for Greece, but not for me,
sold for my beauty and reproached besides
when I deserved a crown.
But—to the point. Is that what you are thinking?
Why did I go—steal from your house in secret?
That man, Paris, or any name you like to call him,
his mother's curse—oh, when he came to me
a mighty goddess walked beside him.

And you, poor fool, you spread your sails for Crete,
left Sparta—left him in your house.
Ah well—Not you, but my own self I ask,
what was there in my heart that I went with him,
a strange man, and forgot my home and country?
Not I, but Aphrodite. Punish her,
be mightier than Zeus who rules
the other gods, but is her slave.
She is my absolution—
One thing with seeming justice you might say.
When Paris died and went down to the grave,
and when no god cared who was in my bed,
I should have left his house—gone to the Greeks.
Just what I tried to do—oh, many times.
I have witnesses—the men who kept the gates,
the watchmen on the walls. Not once, but often
they found me swinging from a parapet,
a rope around this body, stealthily
feeling my way down.
The Trojans then no longer wanted me,
but the man who next took me—and by force—
would never let me go.
My husband, must I die, and at your hands?
You think that right? Is that your justice?
I was forced—by violence. I lived a life
that had no joy, no triumph. In bitterness
I lived a slave.
Do you wish to set yourself above the gods?
Oh, stupid, senseless wish!
A Woman: O Queen, defend your children and your
   country.
Her soft persuasive words are deadly.
She speaks so fair and is so vile.
A fearful thing.
Hecuba: Her goddesses will fight on my side while
I show her for the liar that she is.
Not Hera, not virgin Athena, do I think
would ever stoop to folly great enough
to sell their cities. Hera sell her Argos,
Athena Athens, to be the Trojan's slave!
playing like silly children there on Ida,
and each one in her insolence demanding
the prize for beauty. Beauty—why was Hera
so hot for it? That she might get herself
a better mate than Zeus?
Athena—who so fled from marriage that she begged
one gift from Zeus, virginity.
But she would have the prize, you say. And why?
To help her hunt some god to marry her?
Never make gods out fools to whitewash your own evil.
No one with sense will listen to you.
And Aphrodite, did you say—who would not laugh?
—must take my son to Menelaos' house?
Why? Could she not stay quietly in heaven
and send you on—and all your town—to Troy?
My son was beautiful exceedingly.
You saw him—your own desire was enough.
No need of any goddess.
Men's follies—they are Aphrodite.
She rose up from the sea-foam; where the froth
and foam of life are, there she is.
It was my son. You saw him in his Eastern dress
all bright with gold, and you were mad with love.
Such little things had filled your mind in Argos,
busied with this and that.
Once free of Sparta and in Troy where gold,
you thought, flowed like a river, you would spend
and spend, until your spendthrift hand
had drowned the town.

Your luxuries, your insolent excesses,
Menelaos' halls had grown too small for them.
Enough of that. By force you say he took you?
You cried out? Where? No one in Sparta heard you.
Young Castor was there and his brother too,
not yet among the stars.
And when you came to Troy and on your track the Greeks,
and death and agony in battle,
if they would tell you, "Greece has won today,"
you would praise this man here, Menelaos,
to vex my son, who feared him as a rival.
Then Troy had victories, and Menelaos
was nothing to you.
Looking to the successful side—oh yes,
you always followed there.
There was no right or wrong side in your eyes.
And now you talk of ropes—letting your body down
in secret from the wall, longing to go.
Who found you so?
Was there a noose around your neck?
A sharp knife in your hand? Such ways
as any honest woman would have found,
who loved the husband she had lost?
Often and often I would tell you, Go,
my daughter. My sons will find them other wives.
I will help you. I will send you past the lines
to the Greek ships. Oh, end this war
between our foes and us. But this was bitter to you.
In Paris' house you had your insolent way.
You liked to see the Eastern men fall at your feet.
These were great things to you.
Look at the dress you wear, your ornaments.
Is that the way to meet your husband?
You should not dare to breathe the same air with him.
Oh, men should spit upon you.
Humbly, in rags, trembling and shivering,
with shaven head—so you should come,
with shame at last, instead of shamelessness,
for all the wickedness you did.
King, one word more and I am done.
Give Greece a crown, be worthy of yourself.
Kill her. So shall the law stand for all women,
that she who plays false to her husband's bed,
shall die.
A Woman: O son of an ancient house, O King, now show
that you are worthy of your fathers.
The Greeks called you a woman, shamed you
with that reproach. Be strong. Be noble. Punish her.
Menelaos: [*Impatiently*]
I see it all as you do. We agree.
She left my house because she wanted to—
went to a stranger's bed. Her talk of Aphrodite—
big words, no more. [*Turns to* HELEN] Go. Death is near.
Men there are waiting for you. In their hands are stones.
Die—a small price for the Greeks' long suffering.
You shall not any more dishonor me.
Helen: [*Kneeling and clinging to him*]
No! No! Upon my knees—see, I am praying to you.
It was the gods, not me. Oh, do not kill me.
Forgive.
Hecuba: The men she murdered. Think of those
who fought beside you—of their children too.
Never betray them. Hear that prayer.
Menelaos: [*Roughly*]
Enough, old woman. She is nothing to me.
Men, take her to the ships and keep her safe
until she sails.
Hecuba: But not with you! She must not set foot on
your ship.

Menelaos: [*Bitterly*]
And why? Her weight too heavy for it?
Hecuba: A lover once, a lover always.
Menelaos: [*Pauses a moment to think*]
Not so when what he loved has gone.
But it shall be as you would have it.
Not on the same ship with me. The advice is good.
And when she gets to Argos she shall die
a death hard as her heart.
So in the end she will become a teacher,
teach women chastity—no easy thing,
but yet her utter ruin will strike terror
into their silly hearts,
even women worse than she.
Chorus: And so your temple in Ilium,
your altar of frankincense,
are given to the Greek,
the flame from the honey, the corn and the oil,
the smoke from the myrrh floating upward,
the holy citadel.
And Ida, the mountain where the ivy grows,
and rivers from the snows rush through the glens,
and the boundary wall of the world
where the first sunlight falls,
the blessed home of the dawn.

The sacrifice is gone, and the glad call
of dancers, and the prayers at evening to the gods
that last the whole night long.
Gone too the golden images,
and the twelve Moons, to Trojans holy.
Do you care, do you care, do you heed these things,
O God, from your throne in high heaven?
My city is perishing,
ending in fire and onrushing flame.
A Woman: O dear one, O my husband,
you are dead, and you wander
unburied, uncared for, while over-seas
the ships shall carry me,
swift-winged ships darting onward,
on to the land the riders love,
Argos, where the towers of stone
built by giants reach the sky.
Another: Children, our children.
At the gate they are crying, crying,
calling to us with tears,
Mother, I am all alone.
They are driving me away
to a black ship, and I cannot see you.
Another: Where, oh where? To holy Salamis,
with swift oars dipping?
Or to the crest of Corinth,
the city of two seas,
where the gates King Pelops built
for his dwelling stand?
Another: Oh, if only, far out to sea,
the crashing thunder of God
would fall down, down on Menelaos' ship,
crashing down upon her oars,
the Aegean's wild-fire light.
He it was drove me from Troy.
He is driving me in tears
over to Greece to slavery.
Another: And Helen, too, with her mirrors of gold,
looking and wondering at herself,
as pleased as a girl.
May she never come to the land of her fathers,
never see the hearth of her home,
her city, the temple with brazen doors
of goddess Athena.

Oh, evil marriage that brought
shame to Greece, the great,
and to the waters of Simois
sorrow and suffering.
[*TALTHYBIUS approaches with a few soldiers. He is
carrying the dead child.*]
Another Woman: Before new sufferings are grown old
come other new.
Look, unhappy wives of Troy,
the dead Astyanax.
They threw him from the tower as one might pitch a ball.
Oh, bitter killing.
And now they have him there.
Talthybius: [*He gives the body into* HECUBA'S *arms.*]
One ship is waiting, Hecuba, to take aboard
the last of all the spoil Akhilleus' son was given,
and bear it with the measured beat of oars
to Thessaly's high headlands.
The chief himself has sailed because of news
he heard, his father's father
driven from his land by his own son.
So, more for haste even than before,
he went and with him went Andromache.
She drew tears from me there upon the ship
mourning her country, speaking to Hektor's grave,
begging a burial for her child, your Hektor's son,
who thrown down from the tower lost his life.
And this bronze-fronted shield, the dread of many a
    Greek,
which Hektor used in battle,
that it should never, so she prayed,
hang in strange halls, her grief before her eyes,
nor in that bridal chamber where she must be a wife,
Andromache, this dead boy's mother.
She begged that he might lie upon it in his grave,
instead of cedar wood or vault of stone.
And in your arms she told me I must lay him,
for you to cover the body, if you still
have anything, a cloak left—
And to put flowers on him if you could,
since she has gone. Her master's haste
kept her from burying her child.
So now, whenever you have laid him out,
we'll heap the earth above him, then
up with the sails!
Do all as quickly as you can. One trouble
I saved you. When we passed Scamander's stream
I let the water run on him and washed his wounds.
I am off to dig his grave now, break up the hard earth.
Working together, you and I,
will hurry to the goal, oars swift for home.
Hecuba: Set the shield down—the great round shield
    of Hektor.
I wish I need not look at it.
[*TALTHYBIUS goes out with the soldiers.*]
You Greeks, your spears are sharp but not your wits.
You feared a child. You murdered him.
Strange murder. You were frightened, then? You thought
he might build up our ruined Troy? And yet
when Hektor fought and thousands at his side,
we fell beneath you. Now, when all is lost,
the city captured and the Trojans dead,
a little child like this made you afraid.
The fear that comes when reason goes away—
Myself, I do not wish to share it.
[*She dismisses the Greeks and their ways.*]
Beloved, what a death has come to you.

If you had fallen fighting for the city,
if you had known strong youth and love
and godlike power, if we could think
you had known happiness—if there is
happiness anywhere—
But now—you saw and knew, but with your soul
you did not know, and what was in your house
you could not use.
Poor little one. How savagely our ancient walls,
Apollo's towers, have torn away the curls
your mother's fingers wound and where she pressed
her kisses—here where the broken bone grins white—
Oh no—I cannot—
Dear hands, the same dear shape your father's had,
how loosely now you fall. And dear proud lips
forever closed. False words you spoke to me
when you would jump into my bed, call me sweet names
and tell me, Grandmother, when you are dead,
I'll cut off a great lock of hair and lead my soldiers all
to ride out past your tomb.
Not you, but I, old, homeless, childless,
must lay you in your grave, so young,
so miserably dead.
Dear God. How you would run to greet me.
And I would nurse you in my arms, and oh,
so sweet to watch you sleep. All gone.
What could a poet carve upon your tomb?
"A child lies here whom the Greeks feared and slew."
Ah, Greece should boast of that.
Child, they have taken all that was your father's,
but one thing, for your burying, you shall have,
the bronze-barred shield.
It kept safe Hektor's mighty arm, but now
it has lost its master.
The grip of his own hand has marked it—dear to me
    then—
His sweat has stained the rim. Often and often
in battle it rolled down from brows and beard
while Hektor held the shield close.
Come, bring such covering for the pitiful dead body
as we still have. God has not left us much
to make a show with. Everything I have
I give you, child.
    O men, secure when once good fortune comes—
fools, fools. Fortune's ways—
here now, there now. She springs
away—back—and away, an idiot's dance.
No one is ever always fortunate.
[*The women have come in with coverings and garlands.*]
A Woman: Here, for your hands, they bring you
        clothing for the dead,
got from the spoils of Troy.
Hecuba: [*Shrouding the body and putting garlands
beside it*]
Oh, not because you conquered when the horses raced,
or with the bow outdid your comrades,
your father's mother lays these wreaths beside you,
and of all that was yours, gives you this covering.
A woman whom God hates has robbed you,
taken your life, when she had taken your treasure
and ruined all your house.
A Woman: Oh, my heart! As if you touched it—touched
        it.
Oh, this was once our prince, great in the city.
Hecuba: So on your wedding day I would have dressed
        you,
the highest princess of the East your bride.
Now on your body I must lay the raiment,
all that is left of the splendor that was Troy's.

And the dear shield of Hektor, glorious in battle,
mother of ten thousand triumphs won,
it too shall have its wreath of honor,
undying it will lie beside the dead.
More honorable by far than all the armor
Odysseus won, the wicked and the wise.

A Woman: You, O child, our bitter sorrow,
earth will now receive.
Mourn, O Mother.

Hecuba: Mourn, indeed.

A Woman: Weeping for all the dead.

Hecuba: Bitter tears.

A Woman: Your sorrows that can never be forgotten.

[*The funeral rite is now begun,* HECUBA *symbolically healing the wounds.*]

Hecuba: I heal your wounds; with linen I bind them.
Ah, in words only, not in truth—
a poor physician.
But soon among the dead your father
will care for you.

A Woman: Beat, beat your head.
Lift your hands and let them fall,
moving in measure.

Hecuba: O Women. Dearest—

A Woman: Oh, speak to us. Your cry—what does it
mean?

Hecuba: Only this the gods would have,
pain for me and pain for Troy,
those they hated bitterly.
Vain, vain, the bulls we slew.
And yet—had God not bowed us down,
not laid us low in dust,
none would have sung of us or told our wrongs
in stories men will listen to forever.
Go: lay our dead in his poor grave,
with these last gifts of death given to him.
I think those that are gone care little
how they are buried. It is we, the living,
our vanity.

[*Women lift the shield with the body on it and carry it out.*]

A Woman: Poor mother—her high hopes were stayed
on you
and they are broken.
They called you happy at your birth,
a good man's son.
Your death was miserable exceedingly.

Another: Oh, see, see—
On the crested height of Troy
fiery hands. They are flinging torches.
Can it be
some new evil?
Something still unknown?

Talthybius: [*Stops as he enters and speaks off stage*]
Captains, attention. You have been given charge
to burn this city. Do not let your torches sleep.
Hurry the fire on.
When once the town is level with the ground
then off for home and glad goodbye to Troy.
And you, you Women—I will arrange for you
as well, one speech for everything—
whenever a loud trumpet-call is sounded,
go to the Greek ships, to embark.
Old woman, I am sorriest for you,
follow. Odysseus' men are here to get you.
He drew you—you must leave here as his slave.

Hecuba: The end then. Well—the height of sorrow, I
stand there.
Troy is burning—I am going.
But—hurry, old feet, if you can,
a little nearer—here, where I can see
my poor town, say goodbye to her.
You were so proud a city, in all the East
the proudest. Soon your name the whole world knew,
will be taken from you. They are burning you
and leading us away, their slaves.
O God—What makes me say that word?
The gods—I prayed, they never listened.
Quick, into the fire—Troy, I will die with you.
Death then—oh, beautiful.

Talthybius: Out of your head, poor thing, with all
you've suffered.
Lead her away—Hold her, don't be too gentle.
She must be taken to Odysseus.
Give her into his hands. She is his—
[*Shakes his head*]
his prize.

[*It grows darker.*]

A Woman: Ancient of days, our country's Lord,
Father, who made us,
You see your children's sufferings.
Have we deserved them?

Another: He sees—but Troy has perished, the great
city.
No city now, never again.

Another: Oh, terrible!
The fire lights the whole town up.
The inside rooms are burning.
The citadel—it is all flame now.

Another: Troy is vanishing.
War first ruined her.
And what was left is rushing up in smoke,
the glorious houses fallen.
First the spear and then the fire.

Hecuba: [*She stands up and seems to be calling to someone far away.*]
Children, hear, your mother is calling.

A Woman: [*Gently*]
They are dead, those you are speaking to.

Hecuba: My knees are stiff, but I must kneel.
Now, strike the ground with both my hands—

A Woman: I too, I kneel upon the ground.
I call to mine down there.
Husband, poor husband.

Hecuba: They are driving us like cattle—taking us
away.

A Woman: Pain, all pain.

Another: To a slave's house, from my country.

Hecuba: Priam, Priam, you are dead,
and not a friend to bury you.
The evil that has found me—
do you know?

A Woman: No. Death has darkened his eyes.
He was good and the wicked killed him.

Hecuba: O dwellings of the gods and O dear city,
the spear came first and now
only the red flame lives there.

A Woman: Fall and be forgotten. Earth is kind.

Another: The dust is rising, spreading out like a great
wing of smoke.
I cannot see my house.

Another: The name has vanished from the land,
and we are gone, one here, one there.
And Troy is gone forever.
[*A great crash is heard.*]
Hecuba: Did you hear? Did you know—
A Woman: The fall of Troy—
Another: Earthquake and flood and the city's end—
Hecuba: Trembling body—old weak limbs,
you must carry me on to the new day of slavery.
[*A trumpet sounds.*]
A Woman: Farewell, dear city.
Farewell, my country, where once my children lived.
On to the ships—
There below, the Greek ships wait.
[*The trumpet sounds again and the women pass out.*]

Exercises

1. Why did Euripides stage an argument between Hecuba and Andromache about who had the greater grief? What does this scene tell us about each woman? About human nature?

2. All the women are tear-stained and disheveled, except Helen; Euripides implies that Helen has tidied up before making her grand entrance. Why did Euripides do this? Is he sympathetic to Helen? How does Helen come off when compared with the vindictive women? When compared with Menelaos?

3. What is implied when Helen says to Menelaos, "And you, poor fool, you spread your sails for Crete, left Sparta—left him in your house"? What kind of a husband was Menelaos? What kind of a marriage was this?

4. Of all ancient playwrights, Euripides is considered the most "modern" or "contemporary." Is his treatment of war and the subordination of women "modern"? Why?

5. You are going to produce *The Trojan Women* as a movie and can have your pick of any actor (stage, screen, or TV). Cast the following roles: Helen, Menelaos, Hecuba, Andromache, Kassandra, Talthybius. Explain why you chose these particular people.

Summary

The Athenian Golden Age lasted only one generation (ca. 460–430 B.C.) and yet its achievements are, after twenty-five centuries, still among the most significant in human history. Why was this brief period so spectacular? The answer seems to lie in a combination of factors that were paramount in Athenian life: optimism, freedom, individuality and competition, the pursuit of excellence, and pride.

Optimism

The upstart Greeks, led by the Athenians, had within a ten-year period twice defeated the mighty Persian Empire. For a loose confederation of highly individualistic city-states, this was an incredible accomplishment, after which just about anything seemed possible.

Freedom

The progressive political reforms of Solon, Pisistratus, and Kleisthenes were carried out at the highest effective level by the inspired leadership of Perikles. Political freedom provided the necessary framework for the pursuit of truth and justice. Moreover, the citizens optimistically assumed that a free society best served the interests of all the people (just as the American Founding Fathers assumed that a free society naturally encouraged life, liberty, and the pursuit of happiness).

The critical freedom was the unrestrained pursuit of knowledge in a society that valued knowledge for its own sake. With neither an organized religion nor a priestly caste with vested interests in the status quo, individuals were free to seek answers wherever they might be found. Ignorance and superstition were still very much in evidence but they were no real threat because they were not institutionalized by creeds and dogmas.

Individuality and Competition

That we know so many Greeks by name is not surprising for a society in which *reality was the individual*. Little is known about who made what in the Middle Ages nor do we have much real knowledge of more than a comparatively few Romans. God was the ultimate reality during the Middle Ages and, in Rome, reality was the State. The individual was paramount in Greece because individual achievements were the measure of all things.

It was the emphasis upon individuality that characterized the Greek city-states. Athens, for example, was an Ionian city in which life was sophisticated and elegant. Sparta was Dorian and life was lean and "Spartan." Athens was a cosmopolitan seaport; Sparta was landlocked and provincial. Athenians loved to joke about Sparta. The reason, they said, that the Spartans fought to the death on the battlefield was so they would not have to return to Sparta. Spartans did not make jokes; life was a serious business. Athens and Sparta were not only different but, as might be expected, very competitive. Each thought its life-style superior to that of the other, leading, perhaps inevitably, to the Peloponnesian War, a conflict that ultimately drained the vitality of all combatants.

The Pursuit of Excellence

The Greek word for skill is *arete* (ARE-uh-tay), which can best be translated as "diligence in the pursuit of excellence." Whether an artist, politician, or athlete, each Greek generally assumed that he could be the best at whatever he chose to do and that, moreover, what he accomplished would be rated among the best in its field. Greek artists, for example, competed against each other for pride of place but they also competed against an unspoken standard of excellence known only to each artist.

Pride

A justifiable pride in superior accomplishments was the hallmark of the Greek drive for excellence. Contrary to later Christian doctrine, pride was not a vice but a virtue. The virtue of pride should not be confused, however, with the vice of *hubris,* which identified an excessive pride that could harm another human being. The proper balance was struck by observing the Greek motto: "Nothing in Excess." For Pythagoras the standard was defined as the "middle way" and by Aristotle as the "Golden Mean." However stated, it was the rational Greek approach to moderation in all things.

The achievements of the individuals discussed in this chapter can now be viewed against a backdrop of the freedom to excel in a society that valued excellence. The Eleatics, particularly Parmenides, saw that whatever was real must be permanent and unchanging, a position that contradicted the idea of the individual as the working definition of reality. Demokritos, on the other hand, postulated an atomic theory that confirmed the materialistic view of reality and the individual.

In his *Oresteia,* Aeschylus presented the Athenians with a model of how true justice should work in a court of law. Sophokles warned, in no uncertain terms, of the danger of overweening pride (*hubris*) as demonstrated by Oedipus. In *The Trojan Women,* written and produced after the Golden Age, Euripides exposed the ethical degeneration of the heroic Greeks, who sacrificed their integrity in the service of expediency. The decline had begun after the death of Perikles in 429 B.C. and continued in increasing degree as the Peloponnesian War dragged on.

The Post-Periklean decline was identified and satirized by Aristophanes, whose sharply satiric plays eventually degenerated into amusing and popular comedies designed only to entertain. The trial and execution of Sokrates in 399 B.C. signified the end of the epilogue to the Golden Age and the beginning of a world less and less interested in liberty, truth, and justice.

Culture and Human Values

In terms of the culture-epoch theory the Periklean Age was the golden moment of a period of balance that extended from the Greek Classical Period to the beginning of the long decline of the Roman Empire (ca. 480 B.C.–A.D. 180). Whatever its flaws, and they were abundant, this Graeco-Roman epoch was distinguished, generally speaking, by a rational approach to civilized living in the secular world of the here and now. That view is reinforced when one considers what followed Classical civilization, namely the decline and fall of Rome and the Dark Ages.

A balance was struck during the Periklean Age between the rights of the individual and the welfare of the group. An idealistic society that firmly believed in what people *should* be, the Athenians advocated Freedom, Beauty, Truth, and Justice as the necessary foundation for the art of civilized, elegant living. From that time to ours Athenian achievements in the arts, government, and philosophy testify to the high goals these remarkable people set for themselves. This high-mindedness can be compared with the stated ideals of our own Founding Fathers, who were convinced that the birthright of every American was life, liberty, and the pursuit of happiness.

Annotated Bibliography

Bowra, C. M. *Classical Greece.* Great Ages of Man series. Alexandria, Va.: Time-Life Books, 1965. A fine popular treatment.

Dodd, E. R. *The Greeks and the Irrational.* Berkeley: University of California Press, 1973. An exploration of another side of Greek culture.

Fontenrose, Joseph. *The Delphic Oracle: Its Responses and Operations with a Catalog of Responses.* Berkeley: University of California Press, 1979. Interesting demythification of the fascinating oracle.

Hadas, Moses. *History of Greek Literature.* New York: Columbia University Press, 1950. Useful survey.

Hamilton, Edith. *The Greek Way.* New York: W. W. Norton, 1948. Enthusiastic survey once considered minor classic but marred by bias towards Greeks and against other cultures.

Hill, Donald. *A History of Engineering in Classical and Medieval Times.* La Salle, Ill.: Open Court Publishing Co., 1984. Includes an important reevaluation of the role of technology in ancient Greece.

Meiggs, R. *The Athenian Empire.* New York: Oxford University Press, 1972. Major study of Athenian imperialism.

Pomeroy, Sarah. *Goddesses, Whores, Wives and Slaves: Women in Classical Antiquity.* New York: Schocken Books, 1975. Valuable study.

Robertson, Charles A., Jr. *Athens in the Days of Perikles.* Norman, Okla.: University of Oklahoma Press, 1971. Fine study of the great leader.

Rose, H. J. *A Handbook of Greek Literature.* London: Methuen, 1948. A standard reference work in the field.

Thucydides. *History of the Peloponnesian War.* Translated by Richard Crawley. New York: Random House, 1981. Objective, thorough, a highly readable book by one of the great ancient Greek historians.

Translations and Studies of Greek Drama

Bates, William N. *Euripides: A Student of Human Nature.* New York: Russell & Russell, Publishers, 1969. The dramatist as a realist.

Cook, Albert. *Oedipus Rex: A Mirror for Greek Drama.* Belmont, Calif.: Wadsworth Publishing Company, 1964. A broad, general approach to Greek drama and highly recommended.

Fitts, Dudley, and Fitzgerald, Robert. *The Oedipus Cycle.* New York: Harcourt, Brace, Jovanovich, 1967. Brilliant translations that are both faithful and poetic.

Grene, David, and Lattimore, Richard. *Greek Tragedies.* 3 vols. Chicago: University of Chicago Press, 1960. Excellent modern translations of the more important plays of Aeschylus, Sophokles, and Euripides.

Herington, John. *Aeschylus.* New Haven: Yale University Press, 1986. A general reader's guide to Aeschylus' majestic achievement plus a discussion of the evolution of Athenian theatre.

Hogan, James C. *Aeschylus: A Commentary on the Complete Greek Tragedies.* Chicago: University of Chicago Press, 1985. General introduction to Aeschylean drama plus detailed discussion of the seven surviving plays.

O'Brien, Michael J., ed. *Twentieth Century Interpretations of Oedipus Rex: A Collection of Critical Essays.* Englewood Cliffs, N.J.: Prentice-Hall, 1968. Contemporary scholars present varied views of this inexhaustibly challenging play.

Segal, Erich, ed. *Euripides: A Collection of Critical Essays.* Englewood Cliffs, N.J.: Prentice-Hall, 1968. Interesting and useful.

Whitman, Cedric H. *Euripides and the Full Circle of Myth.* Cambridge: Harvard University Press, 1974. How the dramatist used and adapted the ancient myths.

6

Greece: From Hellenic to Hellenistic World

"The name Greek is no longer a mark of race, but of outlook, and is accorded to those who share our culture rather than our blood," said the Athenian orator Isokrates in 380 B.C. By then the Greek city-states no longer exercised political and military dominance in the Hellenic world of the eastern Mediterranean; Greek culture, however, continued to spread throughout the Mediterranean, into Egypt, and even into the vast Persian empire. What caused the decline of the Greek city-states? Their contentious fervor and pride had enabled them to soundly defeat the much larger forces of the Persian empire.

However, this was because they were, for the first and last time, united against a common foe. Afterwards their pride and aggressive independence caused endless squabbles with each other, culminating in the disastrous war between Athens and Sparta and assorted allies on both sides. The Persian Wars (490–479 B.C.) inspired confidence but the internecine Peloponnesian War (431–404 B.C.) left despair and decay in its wake. Not one city-state was strong enough to take control, so a federation was impossible. Sparta dominated for a time, followed by

■

MAP 6.1 *Alexander's Empire 323* B.C.

Thebes, Athens,[1] and Corinth, but always with the tireless Persians in the background manipulating events through bribery and coercion.

By the middle of the fourth century in a backwater of Greek civilization, King Philip of Macedonia began to move toward an empire that united all of Greece. Some purposes were gained by military strategy; however, most were through a series of wily political and diplomatic moves, accomplished despite repeated warnings by the Athenian orator Demosthanes (figure 6.1). Upon Philip's assassination in 336, his brilliant young son, Alexander (figure 6.2), who was a student of Aristotle, became king. In one remarkable campaign Alexander brought all of Persia (including the territory of modern Turkey) as far east as India, Egypt, and all of Greece into one vast empire. In doing so, he carried Greek culture as it had been influenced by many foreign sources throughout that vast territory. Significantly, he established at least a half-dozen new cities named Alexandria throughout the empire, and in these he built libraries and other centers of culture. The Alexandria he built in Egypt was to supplant Athens as the cultural center of the world for centuries. Remnants of Alexander's empire survived until 146 B.C., when Rome finally conquered the last Achaean League, but the influence of Hellenistic art and thought was to flourish throughout most of the Roman period.

---

1. After ineffectual Spartan rule, Athens underwent a reign of terror under Kritias and the Thirty Tyrants, followed by a brief civil war. Democracy was restored in 401 B.C. It was the insecure government of a reestablished Athens that tried and condemned Sokrates in 399 B.C. (See the *Apology* on p. 140 for Plato's account of the trial.)

Our concern during this time must limit itself to the developments in art, which are discussed in chapter 7, and to the contributions of two philosophers, Plato and Aristotle.

Plato, 427–347 B.C.

Born two years after the death of Perikles, Plato (figure 6.3) was a young man at the time of the Athenian defeat in the Peloponnesian War and an ardent student of Sokrates. It is impossible to distinguish between the thought of Plato and Sokrates in the early writings of Plato, for most of these are dialogues in which Sokrates is the principal speaker. It is probable that Plato included much of his own thought in these dialogues, or certainly he reported the ideas of Sokrates with which he was in agreement. Only in the latter part of his life did he speak entirely for himself, as in the *Laws*.

Plato's thought about that-which-is-real is perhaps his most significant contribution to modern thought. In developing this he started with the work of Pythagoras and the Eleatic philosophers in that he accepted permanence and unchangeability as the basic criteria for reality, and he accepted the mind as the only way to approach a knowledge of the real. In so doing, he denied the reality of all the sense-apparent objects around us, whether they be trees, animals, humans, or even such abstract concepts as the various manifestations of love or justice. All sense-apparent things he regarded as shadows of the Real, made imperfect by an alliance with material stuff. (See his illustration of this in "The Allegory of the Cave" in the excerpts from the *Republic* later in this chapter.)

FIGURE 6.1 *Portrait bust of Demosthanes. Roman marble copy, probably after a original bronze of 280/ 279 B.C. Ashmolean Museum, Oxford. This last great champion of Athenian liberty lived to see Athens free itself from Macedonia after Alexander's death in 323 B.C.*

FIGURE 6.2 *Portrait bust of Alexander the Great (356– 323 B.C.) by Leochares (?). Original marble of 450–425 B.C., Akropolis Museum, Athens. The greatest military genius in history, Alexander conquered and Hellenized the then-known world in just twelve years.*

■
FIGURE 6.3 *Portrait bust of Plato. Boeringer Collection, Geneva. Roman copy (one of eighteen) of a bronze probably created by Silanion. Apparently the original was dedicated in the Academy after Plato's death in 347 B.C. Though his real name was Aristokles, Plato has always been known by his nickname, which means "the Broad."*

Reality

Reality, for Plato, consisted of Ideas (or Forms) of all basic things, Forms that existed beyond the grasp of human senses or even of the human mind. These Ideas had no physical attributes, no material substance; they were the "pure form" of all things we see and know in our earthly existence. One must bear in mind that these Forms are not ideas-in-the-minds-of-people. One can imagine—or try to imagine—the perfect tree or the perfect human being but that has nothing to do with Plato's Forms. His Ideas[2] had existence, they were unchanging, and they were the source of all things. They were the eternal Forms of all material things in the universe. But the individual thing—that which we perceive—is always a distorted or impure shadow of its Form; because it is involved with matter the thing is at least once removed from its Idea.

At this point a homely illustration might be in order. Let us imagine that an architect has been commissioned to design a building. It may not happen just this way but assume that one morning, after wrestling with design problems for quite some time, the architect suddenly has a mental image of the completed structure, exactly as it

should be. "Eureka!" is the cry. "This is *it!*" So she (or he) dashes off to the drawing board. However, in drawing the plans changes have to be made that affect the original conception: practical problems involving heating, cooling, lights, and service areas. By the time the blueprints are finished the building is no longer the same as it was when it was pure idea. Then comes the construction. First, there is a strike and one material has to be substituted for another that is not available. Costs go over budget necessitating cutbacks in space; some less expensive finishing materials have to be used. But finally the building is complete, existing in its material form for people to use.

When was the structure most real? A good argument can be made that it was most real when it was pure idea and that the building has become less real each time it was compromised in substance or material. One suspects that the architect, at least, when looking at the final product, will see it as only a shadow of what she originally had in mind. To avoid argument, let us accept this last statement as true; the physical building is but a rather clumsy manifestation of the "real" idea.

Can we take another step now? Assume that the architect is God and that the building is the universe. The ideas for all things existed in God's mind and these Forms exist forever. But, as they are mixed with material substance—animal, vegetable, mineral—they become changed and distorted. Now, perhaps, we have Plato's belief about true reality but with one more step needed. Subtract the picture of God. Though Plato spoke of the gods—and sometimes of God—he did not believe that the Forms had been brought into existence by a creator; they had existed eternally.

For a further illustration of this concept of reality one can turn to Plato's dialogue *The Symposium,* in which the primary discussion is about the nature of love. At one point the discussion turns on the thought that in the realm of Ideas there is one that is Beauty—not a beautiful sunset or a beautiful song, just pure Beauty. Many physical things can reflect this idea, among them a person. When someone says, "I am in love with Isabella (or Henry) what he (or she) could mean is, "I am attracted by Beauty, and Henry (or Isabella) reflects that Idea to me."

There are a great many important philosophic repercussions from this Platonic belief about reality. One of the most important is the separation of the soul from the body, and the belief that soul was related to the realm of the essences, and that body was evil because it imprisoned and distracted the soul. This has been a major bone of contention in all Christian religion, for St. Augustine, in formulating the first unified Christian theology, borrowed a great deal from Platonism. Specifically, Plato believed that in the realm of ideas a hierarchy existed, starting at the bottom with the essences of plants and animals, and ending at the top with the idea of the Good (the light or fire one encounters in "The Allegory of the Cave"). This Good was transmuted in early Christian theology into a concept of God as the highest and best pattern for all things and the goal toward which all Christians should strive.

---

2. Ideas and Forms are used interchangeably because it takes both words to approximate Plato's conception.

The Republic

The dialogue called the *Republic* provides a comprehensive view of the Sokratic–Platonic idea of the nature of people on earth and the nature of their government. A much later dialogue, the *Laws,* differs from the *Republic* in some significant ways, presenting a purely Platonic view of the same subject matter (see chapter 8). The *Republic,* it should be emphasized, is not Plato's formation of an ideal state (or Utopia as Sir Thomas More was later to call it). Instead, the *Republic* is an extended dialogue between Sokrates and his students concerning the nature of justice. Though not a problem when a person lives alone on a desert island, justice and the administration of justice becomes a critical issue in a populous city-state composed of rich and poor, saints and scoundrels, masters and slaves. So in the *Republic,* discussants formulate a picture of the luxurious city-state (one that goes beyond minimal human needs) in order to seek out the elusive quality—justice—that exists to a greater or lesser degree in the interrelationships of human beings.

In regard to men and women themselves, Plato felt that they were dominated by one of three qualities: appetite, spirit, or intellect. For this reason he divided people into three classes: those of iron (or brass), those of silver, and those of gold. Those who were essentially people of appetite, iron, were to be the workers, including all who followed commercial pursuits. The silver, people of spirit, were to form the auxiliaries or soldier class, who had no property or money to distract them from their duty—the maintenance of order at home and protection from foreign enemies. The men or women of intellect, or the people of gold, were to be carefully educated to become the guardians of the state, the rulers, the philosopher–kings.

Education was to be the force that gave form to this state. The lowest class was to receive little or no education. The soldier or auxiliary group was to be taught gymnastics (to give them strong bodies, fit for their duties at all times), and music to make their personalities sensitive and considerate (see also chapter 8). Sokrates used the example of the good watchdog to illustrate his point, for such an animal is gentle toward the master and known friends but fierce toward enemies. The soldier class should have such a nature, with their spirit tempered by the study of music. The guardian class would have all of the education of the soldiers (and police men and women) plus studies in reasoning—emphasizing mathematics—and philosophy. After their long years of formal education, those of the guardian class were to be subjected to a series of trials and temptations to test their strength of character and their ability to make decisions that contributed to the general good of the state. Later, at about the age of fifty, the guardians would be called upon to govern the city, to become philosopher–kings. Selected from the best specimens of men and women, these educated executives were to be highly original scientific thinkers and persons of impeccable integrity.

Sokrates advocates strict censorship of the arts, particularly stories, poetry, and music, so that boys and girls may be educated in an environment of beauty. They were to be exposed to only the best and most morally uplifting of the arts so that only the highest good could enter into their souls. (That the state should control [censor] the arts in the interest of maintaining high moral standards has provoked arguments on both sides that continue, without resolution, to this day.)

Neither the soldiers nor the guardians were to be encumbered or influenced by material possessions. Wealth was banished as was poverty. Sokrates was convinced that a person's character could be spoiled by wealth and his or her judgment influenced by vested interests. On the other hand, poverty could break the human spirit and render men and women unfit to be servants of the public as soldiers and guardians.

By far the largest class, the men and women of iron, included workers, farmers, sailors, artisans, merchants, professionals, and entrepreneurs. Their properties were expressly their own; property held in common was explicitly forbidden. Despite some current opinions to the contrary, Plato's *Republic* was basically neither socialistic nor communistic. The two small classes of guardians and soldiers—servants of the state—were denied the ownership of property for economic reasons: to eliminate conflicts between self-interest and public duty. The intent was to put a chasm between political power and financial influence. Everyone who did not serve the state (the bulk of the population) worked as individuals of varying degrees of wealth, from a farmer or worker to the owner of a merchant fleet.

At first glance the iron-silver-gold classes of the *Republic* seem as structured as the caste system still prevalent in modern India. But "caste" means something people are born into above which they can never rise. Most societies have class structures in which the ease or difficulty of vertical movement depends on the rigidity of the society or nation in question. The opportunity for moving across class lines—up or down—was considerably greater in the *Republic* than in, say, modern England.

Sokrates believed that heredity was a powerful force in shaping a person's character and abilities. He also believed, therefore, that a person would normally find his or her rightful place in the class of the parents. Some would be unfit for the class in which they were born while others had the ambition and ability to rise above their class origins, even from iron to gold. The possibility of class mobility was a fundamental necessity for a state that depended upon an elite class of philosopher–kings. Absolutely any boy or girl could be identified by the authorities as worthy of an education that could lead to the highest responsibilities of government.

And where does justice come in? Each citizen, regardless of class, has theoretically found a proper niche in society with little inclination or opportunity to interfere with the rights of others. Potters make pots and merchants make profits, police keep the peace, soldiers guard the state, the rulers govern fairly and, therefore, justly. Citizens are guaranteed equality of educational opportunities regardless of class or sex. The people of iron may indulge their appetite for money and possessions, those of silver may gratify their spirit with honor and glory, and the men and women of gold may exercise their intellect to the fullest in the responsible governance of the state. Based on the principle of specialization of function according to vocation, justice has been established on a grand scale.

Did Plato believe that his theoretical city-state could really work? Think back to the illustration about the architect and the commissioned building. Plato's *Republic* and the completed blueprints for the structure are roughly analogous but both are already one step removed from the original conceptions of perfect justice and a perfect building. If constructing the building requires compromises in materials and design, what might the problems be if we tried to construct a complex human society? Plato had no illusions. At one point in the *Republic,* Plato introduces the story of a young shepherd boy: "The Ring of Gyges." After Gyges had discovered a ring that made him invisible (and, thus, not accountable for his actions), he embarked on a successful career of robbery and murder that led him to the highest and richest position in his native land.

Though the "Ring of Gyges" may (or may not) be an extreme example, Plato was convinced that no human being could maintain an intact virtue when guaranteed immunity from detection. If no one knew what we were doing, would we lower our standards? Do we ever act out of self-interest rather than out of duty? There is no need to beg the question; Plato saw that narrow self-interest, greed, envy, and other human failings would tend to destroy any republic, no matter how perfectly constructed.

Insofar as the ultimate question of the nature of justice is concerned, Plato and Sokrates take the middle ground, the Golden Mean, which was ever a Greek ideal. In the qualities of men and women, wisdom should control the other qualities, so that appetite would be curbed to the point of temperance, spirit should be limited to the point of courage, and intellect should become wisdom. When these conditions are met, justice emerges. These—temperance, courage, wisdom, and justice—were the great Platonic virtues. Later on, the Christians were to add faith, hope, and love to these to establish the seven cardinal virtues. The difference between the Platonic intellectual virtues and the Christian emotional and spiritual virtues illustrates a fundamental difference between the hopes and aspirations of the two cultures.

Aristotle 384–322 B.C.

Aristotle came from a very different background than that of Plato, and although he studied with Plato at the academy, his answers to the important questions are quite different, perhaps because of the difference in youthful experience. Aristotle's father was a physician in northern Greece and early in Aristotle's life was called to the city of Pella to serve as a physician in the court of King Philip. Perhaps Aristotle's inquiring mind about sense-apparent things, his interest in experimentation, his concern in change rather than permanence, and his inability to accept the mind alone as a guide to truth came from his father's interest in similar things. As a matter of fact, exactly as Plato's thought had its source in the Eleatics and Pythagoras, Aristotle's mature conclusions have their roots in the Ionians.

Aristotle is one of the most extraordinary minds of all time; the keenness of his intellect, the range of his interests and studies, and the staggering amount of information and speculation in his enormous collection of writings, rouse the admiration and awe of any who read his work. Not the least of his distinctions is the fact that he served as tutor to the youthful Prince Alexander, and must have had a great influence on the brilliant career of that monarch. After this period of tutoring, Aristotle went to Athens and founded his own school, the Lyceum. With Plato, he was to shape the course of Western thought: these two men are probably the most powerful influences from our Greek heritage.

As we have seen, Plato's quest for the permanent, the Idea or Form, rather than the actuality of experience, led him into a dualism that separates form from substance, soul from body. Aristotle, profoundly interested in the changing life about him, tried to reconcile the two. Perhaps the difference could be expressed in this way: when Plato wished to discuss his ideas of the state, he wrote the *Republic,* and later the *Laws,* theoretical speculations that construct the wholly imaginary idea of a state. When Aristotle wished to discuss his ideas of the state, he and his students collected and studied the constitutions of 158 Greek city-states as a prelude to the work known as *Politics.*

It is an impossible task, and not to the present purpose, to even mention the multitude of Aristotle's writings. His speculations ranged all the way from his logic, the proper process of thought, through biology, physics, metaphysics, ethics, law and politics, and literary criticism (see his *Poetics* at the end of this chapter). Only two of his ideas concern us here: one is his view of the nature of reality; the other is his idea of the conduct of life in the light of that view. These last are drawn from the *Nicomachean Ethics* and the *Eudemian Ethics,* summaries of his thought about the proper conduct of life as written by his son and one of his students.

For Aristotle, the abstract idea or form of Plato's teaching could not be separated from the matter or substance by which it was known; the two must somehow come together as different aspects of the same thing. Thus Plato's "ideal" chair did not exist for Aristotle apart from the actual wood and metal that composed it. A brick is a brick only when the "idea" brick and the clay composing it come together; then the brick is "real." The brick then may become the matter or substance of another "idea," and become house; and the house, in turn, may be substance to the idea of town or city. At every stage, the union of substance and form, of matter and idea, is necessary to constitute "reality"; but there is a progression, upwards or downwards. The substance that Plato is not concerned with becomes for Aristotle the basis for higher, more complex realities when it is informed by idea or form. Such, at least, is the direction of the difference between the two men; Plato's static view becomes more dynamic in Aristotle's teaching.

The process of change (which Plato never satisfactorily explains) is accounted for, by Aristotle, in his theory of enteleche (en-TEL-uh-kee; the Greek word is made of the particles *en,* "within"; *telos,* "purpose or end"; and *echaia,* "having, possessing"). That is to say, it is in the nature of things that they have within them a goal, a destiny, to fulfill: the seed becomes the plant, for that is its "enteleche"; the clay becomes the brick, for that is its "enteleche." The movement upward through increasing complexity is the "enteleche" of the universe; and the cause of the process, drawing all things toward their own perfection, is God, the First Cause, who moved all things without being moved: the "Unmoved Mover," in Aristotle's phrase.

The motive power of Aristotle's God is apparently not love, as Christianity might contend, nor will, as Judaism might argue; it is rather that there seems to be a cosmic yearning toward perfection, and that perfection is, by definition, God. Aristotle's customary view of the necessity for the union of both form and matter to constitute reality here breaks down (or more kindly, "transcends itself"?) for such a God must be pure form, with none of the inherent weakness or imperfection of the material.[3] God is the only instance where pure form is separated from matter.

How does one lead the good life? It is interesting to note that Aristotle makes no apology for thinking that it must begin with sufficient means; he holds no ascetic views on the matter, and quite matter-of-factly begins with an assumption of enough material possessions to allow each person to choose among reasonable alternatives. Given adequate wealth, what does one do? The enteleche of which Aristotle speaks implies that there is a goal, or end, reached when the person or thing is functioning properly—that is, in accord with its inner purposes; when conditions permit such functioning there is a highest good, a summum bonum, attained. The enteleche of humans, then, would lead them to their own summum bonum, their own best functioning, the worthy and proper fulfillment of their humanity. And since humans are for Aristotle the "rational animal," that fulfillment would be the life of reason. When they are living harmoniously, using their minds, functioning in family and state (for Aristotle also calls humans a "political," i.e., social animal), they have achieved their greatest good. Such a life has two implications, among many others, that concern us here.

One is that such a life will be a life of virtue, or excellence. But virtues may fail by being deficient, or by being carried to excess; the middle ground between is what is to be desired. Courage, for instance, is a virtue; but it may be perverted through deficiency into cowardice, or no less perverted by being carried to the excess of foolhardiness or rashness. Generosity is a virtue, but it can be carried to the excess of prodigality and wastefulness, or perverted through deficiency to stinginess. To mediate between extremes, to discover the "Golden Mean"—which it is to be noted is a relative and not an absolute matter—that is to achieve virtue.

The other implication, then, is that people's best use of reason is in the life of contemplation. They must have time to read, to talk, to think about the whole idea of excellence, that they may achieve the high-mindedness that is their summum bonum; the word that Aristotle uses is "magnanimity." Such a quality is not to be won in the heat and dust of the marketplace; though good persons will perform their duties as members of society, the life of action is not as good as the life of contemplation.

---

3. "Such then is the principle upon which depend the heavens and the world of nature. And its life (i.e., the principle, or God) is like the best that we enjoy, and enjoy but for a short time; for it is ever in this state, which we cannot be. And if then God is always in that good state in which we sometimes are, this compels our wonder; and if in a better state, then this compels it yet more. And God is in a better state. We say therefore, that God is a living being, eternal, most good; so that life and a continual eternal existence belong to God; for this is God." (Aristotle, *Metaphysics,* XII, 7.)

The Greek Legacy

Plato and Aristotle are generally considered the most influential philosophers in the history of Western culture. Plato's search for knowledge had an incredible range and depth: physics, metaphysics, mathematics, ethics, politics, religion, literature, music, and art. His influence on Aristotle is incalculable; surely this is the most remarkable teacher–student combination in human history.

Their answers might vary, sometimes considerably, but Plato and Aristotle asked many of the same questions: What are the moral, ethical, and legal bases of life? How, in a democracy, can we define the public good? Where is the line between protecting the individual and guarding the community? What is the good life and how may it be achieved?

Aristotle's influence has perhaps been greatest in the field of logic, particularly his invention of the syllogism as a tool for deductive reasoning. That the syllogism was a less than perfect tool for logical deduction was not the fault of Aristotle. As Plato's greatest student, he stood alone at the end of the golden age of Greek philosophy. Plato was followed by Aristotle (and many other students), but not for two thousand years did anyone follow Aristotle, who for centuries stood as the unquestioned authority—*the philosopher*—of medieval scholars, especially the scholastic philosophers of the High Middle Ages.

Plato's influence was particularly strong during the formation of the theology of the early Christian church. There were revivals of Platonism during the Italian Renaissance, throughout the Age of Reason, and into our own century. That he was also one of the finest literary artists of Western civilization is a whole other topic. Perhaps Alfred North Whitehead (1861–1947), the British philosopher and mathematician, best summarized Plato's contributions with his oft-quoted remark: "The safest general characterization of the European philosophical tradition is that it consists of a series of footnotes to Plato."

Exercises

1. Identify the essential differences between Hellenic and Hellenistic culture. Then, explain how and why these differences developed.
2. In your own words explain what Plato means by his Ideas (his Pure Forms).
3. Plato's concept of reality leads to a static universe while Aristotle's thinking leads to an ever-changing universe (essentially the difference between the ideas of the Eleatics and the Ionians).
   a. Explain the differences between the ideas of the two philosophers about the nature of reality.
   b. With both Plato and Aristotle, how much can one know of reality?
   c. What, for Aristotle, guides the process of change?
   d. It appears that Plato sought permanence while Aristotle was prepared to cope with change. If, as has been frequently said, everyone is either a Platonist or an Aristotelian, which are you?

■

FIGURE 6.4 *Portrait bust of Sokrates. Roman marble copy of an original bronze supposedly created by Lysippos in ca. 350 B.C. Museo della Terme, Rome.*

Literary Selections

APOLOGY

*Plato (427–347 **B.C.**)*

Sokrates was tried in 399 B.C. before a generally hostile jury of 501 citizens on vague charges of impropriety towards the gods and corruption of the young. Long regarded as a suspicious character because of his relentless questioning of fellow Athenians, Sokrates, due to a general amnesty, could not be charged for any offenses prior to the defeat of Athens in 404 B.C. The unspoken charges were: (1) being the teacher of Alkibiades the traitor (interpreted as a corruptor of the young), (2) associating with the Thirty Tyrants (viewed as possible collaboration), (3) accepting money for teaching argumentation (mistakenly taking him for a Sophist), and (4) causing general intellectual unrest. Sokrates (figure 6.4) cheerfully admits to causing unrest, contending that the gods had commanded him to search into himself and other men to find the truth. This trial is his apology (or "defense") for his philosophical life. The translation is by F. J. Church and R. D. Cummings.

CHARACTERS

Sokrates
Meletus

SCENE: *The Court of Justice*

Sokrates: I cannot tell what impression my accusers have made upon you, Athenians. For my own part, I know that they nearly made me forget who I was, so persuasive were they; and yet they have scarcely uttered one single word of truth. But of all their many falsehoods, the one which astonished me most was when they said that I was a clever speaker, and that you must be careful not to let me deceive you. I thought that it was most shameless of them not to be ashamed to talk in that way; for as soon as I open my mouth they will be refuted, and I shall prove that I am not a clever speaker in any way at all—unless, indeed, by a clever speaker they mean a man who speaks the truth. If that is their meaning, I agree with them that I am an orator not to be compared with them. My accusers, then I repeat, have said little or nothing that is true; but from me you shall hear the whole truth. Certainly you will not hear an elaborate speech, Athenians, dressed up, like theirs, with words and phrases. I will say to you what I have to say, without preparation, and in the words which come first, for I believe that my cause is just; so let none of you expect anything else. Indeed, my friends, it would hardly be seemly for me, at my age, to come before you like a young man with his specious phrases. But there is one thing, Athenians, which I do most earnestly beg and entreat of you. Do not be surprised and do not interrupt with shouts if in my defense I speak in the same way that I am accustomed to speak in the market-place, at the tables of the money-changers, where many of you have heard me, and elsewhere. The truth is this. I am more than seventy years old, and this is the first time that I have ever come before a law-court; so your manner of speech here is quite strange to me. If I had been really a stranger, you would have forgiven me for speaking in the language and the manner of my native country; and so now I ask you to grant me what I think I have a right to claim. Never mind the manner of my speech—it may be better or it may be worse—give your whole attention to the question, Is what I say just, or is it not? That is what makes a good judge, as speaking the truth makes a good orator.

I have to defend myself, Athenians, first against the old false accusations of my old accusers, and then against the later ones of my present accusers. For many men have been accusing me to you, and for very many years, who have not uttered a word of truth; and I fear them more than I fear Anytus and his associates, formidable as they are. But, my friends, those others are still more formidable; for they got hold of most of you when you were children, and they have been more persistent in accusing me untruthfully and have persuaded you that there is a certain Sokrates, a wise man, who speculates about the heavens, and who investigates things that are beneath the earth, and who can make the worse argument appear the stronger. These men, Athenians, who spread abroad this report are the accusers whom I fear; for their hearers think that persons who pursue such inquiries never believe in the gods. Then they are many, and their attacks have been going on for a long time, and they spoke to you when you were at the age most readily to believe them, for you were all young, and many of you were children, and there was no one to answer them when they attacked me. And the most unreasonable thing of all is that I do not even know their names: I cannot tell you who they are except when one happens to be a comic poet. But all the rest who have persuaded you, from motives of resentment and prejudice, and sometimes, it may be, from conviction, are hardest to cope with. For I cannot call any one of them forward in court to cross-examine him. I have, as it were, simply to spar with shadows in my defense, and to put questions which there is no one to answer. I ask you, therefore, to believe that, as I say, I have been attacked by two kinds of accusers—first, by Meletus and his associates, and, then, by those older ones of whom I have spoken. And, with your leave, I will defend myself first against my old accusers; for you heard their accusations first, and they were much more forceful than my present accusers are.

Well, I must make my defense, Athenians, and try in the short time allowed me to remove the prejudice which you have been so long a time acquiring. I hope that I may manage to do this, if it be good for you and for me, and that my defense may be successful; but I am quite aware of the nature of my task, and I know that it is a difficult one. Be the outcome, however, as is pleasing to God, I must obey the law and make my defense.

Let us begin from the beginning, then, and ask what is the accusation which has given rise to the prejudice against me, which was what Meletus relied on when he brought his indictment. What is the prejudice which my enemies have been spreading about me? I must assume that they are formally accusing me, and read their indictment. It would run somewhat in this fashion: "Sokrates is a wrongdoer, who meddles with inquiries into things beneath the earth and in the heavens, and who makes the worse argument appear the stronger, and who teaches others these same things." That is what they say; and in the comedy of Aristophanes[4] you yourselves saw a man called Sokrates swinging round in a basket and saying that he walked the air, and sputtering a great deal of nonsense about matters of which I understand nothing, either more or less. I do not mean to disparage that kind of knowledge if there is any one who is wise about these matters. I trust Meletus may never be able to prosecute me for that. But the truth is, Athenians, I have nothing to do with these matters, and almost all of you are yourselves my witnesses of this. I beg all of you who have ever heard me discussing, and they are many, to inform your neighbors and tell them if any of you have ever heard me discussing such matters, either more or less. That will show you that the other common statements about me are as false as this one.

But the fact is that not one of these is true. And if you have heard that I undertake to educate men, and make money by so doing, that is not true either, though I think that it would be a fine thing to be able to educate men, as Gorgias of Leontini, and Prodicus of Keos, and Hippias of Elis do. For each of them, my friends, can go into any city, and persuade the young men to leave the society of their fellow citizens, with any of whom they might associate for nothing, and to be only too glad to be allowed to pay money for the privilege of associating with themselves. And I believe that there is another wise man from Paros residing in Athens at this moment. I happened to meet Kallias, the son of Hipponicus, a man who has spent more money on sophists than every one else put together. So I said to him (he has two sons), Kallias, if your two sons had been foals or calves, we could have hired a trainer for them who would have made them perfect in the virtue which belongs to their nature. He would have been either a groom or a farmer. But whom do you intend to take to train them, seeing that they are men? Who understands the virtue which belongs to men and to citizens? I suppose that you must have thought of this, because of your sons. Is there such a person, said I, or not? Certainly there is, he replied. Who is he, said I, and where does he come from, and what is his fee?

Evenus, Sokrates, he replied, from Paros, five minae. Then I thought that Evenus was a fortunate person if he really understood this art and could teach so cleverly. If I had possessed knowledge of that kind, I should have been conceited and disdainful. But, Athenians, the truth is that I do not possess it.

Perhaps some of you may reply: But, Sokrates, what is the trouble with you? What has given rise to these prejudices against you? You must have been doing something out of the ordinary. All these rumors and reports of you would never have arisen if you had not been doing something different from other men. So tell us what it is, that we may not give our verdict in the dark. I think that that is a fair question, and I will try to explain to you what it is that has raised these prejudices against me and given me this reputation. Listen, then. Some of you, perhaps, will think that I am joking, but I assure you that I will tell you the whole truth. I have gained this reputation, Athenians, simply by reason of a certain wisdom. But by what kind of wisdom? It is by just that wisdom which is perhaps human wisdom. In that, it may be, I am really wise. But the men of whom I was speaking just now must be wise in a wisdom which is greater than human wisdom, or else I cannot describe it, for certainly I know nothing of it myself, and if any man says that I do, he lies and speaks to arouse prejudice against me. Do not interrupt me with shouts, Athenians, even if you think that I am boasting. What I am going to say is not my own. I will tell you who says it, and he is worthy of your respect. I will bring the god of Delphi to be the witness of my wisdom, if it is wisdom at all, and of its nature. You remember Khaerephon. From youth upwards he was my comrade; and also a partisan of your democracy, sharing your recent exile[5] and returning with you. You remember, too, Khaerephon's character—how impulsive he was in carrying through whatever he took in hand. Once he went to Delphi and ventured to put this question to the oracle—I entreat you again, my friends, not to interrupt me with your shouts—he asked if there was any one who was wiser than I. The priestess answered that there was no one. Khaerephon himself is dead, but his brother here will witness to what I say.

Now see why I tell you this. I am going to explain to you how the prejudice against me has arisen. When I heard of the oracle I began to reflect: What can the god mean by this riddle? I know very well that I am not wise, even in the smallest degree. Then what can he mean by saying that I am the wisest of men? It cannot be that he is speaking falsely, for he is a god and cannot lie. For a long time I was at a loss to understand his meaning. Then, very reluctantly, I turned to investigate it in this manner: I went to a man who was reputed to be wise, thinking that there, if anywhere, I should prove the answer wrong, and meaning to point out to the oracle its mistake, and to say, "You said that I was the wisest of men, but this man is wiser than I am." So I examined the man—I need not tell you his name, he was a politician—but this was the result, Athenians. When I conversed with him I came to see that, though a great many persons, and most of all he himself, thought that he was wise, yet he was not wise. Then I tried to prove to him that he was not wise, though he fancied that he was; and by so doing I made him indignant, and many of the bystanders. So when I went away, I thought to myself, "I am wiser than this man: neither of us knows anything that is really worthwhile,

---

4. *The Clouds.* The basket was satirically assumed to facilitate Sokrates' inquiries into things in the heavens.

5. During the totalitarian regime of *The Thirty* which remained in power for eight months (404 B.C.), five years before the trial.

but he thinks that he has knowledge when he has not, while I, having no knowledge, do not think that I have. I seem, at any rate, to be a little wiser than he is on this point: I do not think that I know what I do not know." Next I went to another man who was reputed to be still wiser than the last, with exactly the same result. And there again I made him, and many other men, indignant.

Then I went on to one man after another, seeing that I was arousing indignation every day, which caused me much grief and anxiety. Still I thought that I must set the god's command above everything. So I had to go to every man who seemed to possess any knowledge, and investigate the meaning of the oracle. Athenians, I must tell you the truth; by the dog, this was the result of the investigation which I made at the god's bidding: I found that the men whose reputation for wisdom stood highest were nearly the most lacking in it, while others who were looked down on as common people were much more intelligent. Now I must describe to you the wanderings which I undertook, like Heraklean labors, to prove the oracle irrefutable. After the politicians, I went to the poets, tragic, dithyrambic, and others, thinking that there I should find myself manifestly more ignorant than they. So I took up the poems on which I thought that they had spend most pains, and asked them what they meant, hoping at the same time to learn something from them. I am ashamed to tell you the truth, my friends, but I must say it. Almost any one of the bystanders could have talked about the works of these poets better than the poets themselves. So I soon found that it is not by wisdom that the poets create their works, but by a certain natural power and by inspiration, like soothsayers and prophets, who say many fine things, but who understand nothing of what they say. The poets seemed to me to be in a similar situation. And at the same time I perceived that, because of their poetry, they thought that they were the wisest of men in other matters, too, which they were not. So I went away again, thinking that I had the same advantage over the poets that I had over the politicians.

Finally, I went to the artisans, for I knew very well that I possessed no knowledge at all worth speaking of, and I was sure that I should find that they knew many fine things. And in that I was not mistaken. They knew what I did not know, and so far they were wiser than I. But, Athenians, it seemed to me that the skilled artisans had the same failing as the poets. Each of them believed himself to be extremely wise in matters of the greatest importance because he was skillful in his own art: and this presumption of theirs obscured their real wisdom. So I asked myself, on behalf of the oracle, whether I would choose to remain as I was, without either their wisdom or their ignorance, or to possess both, as they did. And I answered to myself and to the oracle that it was better for me to remain as I was.

From this examination, Athenians, has arisen much fierce and bitter indignation, and from this a great many prejudices about me, and people say that I am "a wise man." For the bystanders always think that I am wise myself in any matter wherein I refute another. But, gentlemen, I believe that the god is really wise, and that by this oracle he meant that human wisdom is worth little or nothing. I do not think that he meant that Sokrates was wise. He only made use of my name, and took me as an example, as though he would say to men, "He among you is the wisest who, like Sokrates, knows that in truth his wisdom is worth nothing at all." Therefore I still go about testing and examining every man whom I think wise, whether he be a citizen or a stranger, as the god has commanded me; and whenever I find that he is not wise, I point out to him, on the god's behalf, that he is not wise. I am so busy in this pursuit that I have never had leisure to take any part worth mentioning in public matters or to look after my private affairs. I am in great poverty as the result of my service to the god.

Besides this, the young men who follow me about, who are the sons of wealthy persons and have the most leisure, take pleasure in hearing men cross-examined. They often imitate me among themselves; then they try their hands at cross-examining other people. And, I imagine, they find plenty of men who think that they know a great deal when in fact they know little or nothing. Then the persons who are cross-examined get angry with me instead of with themselves, and say that Sokrates is an abomination and corrupts the young. When they are asked, "Why, what does he do? what does he teach?" they do not know what to say; but, not to seem at a loss, they repeat the stock charges against all philosophers, and allege that he investigates things in the air and under the earth, and that he teaches people to disbelieve in the gods, and to make the worse argument appear the stronger. For, I suppose, they would not like to confess the truth, which is that they are shown up as ignorant pretenders to knowledge that they do not possess. So they have been filling your ears with their bitter prejudices for a long time, for they are ambitious, energetic, and numerous; and they speak vigorously and persuasively against me. Relying on this, Meletus, Anytus, and Lykon have attacked me. Meletus is indignant with me on the part of the poets, Anytus on the part of the artisans and politicians, and Lykon on the part of the orators. And so, as I said at the beginning, I shall be surprised if I am able, in the short time allowed me for my defense, to remove from your minds this prejudice which has grown so strong. What I have told you, Athenians, is the truth: I neither conceal nor do I suppress anything, small or great. Yet I know that it is just this plainness of speech which rouses indignation. But that is only a proof that my words are true, and that the prejudice against me, and the causes of it, are what I have said. And whether you investigate them now or hereafter, you will find that they are so.

What I have said must suffice as my defense against the charges of my first accusers. I will try next to defend myself against Meletus, that "good patriot," as he calls himself, and my later accusers. Let us assume that they are a new set of accusers, and read their indictment, as we did in the case of the others. It runs thus. He says that Sokrates is a wrongdoer who corrupts the youth, and who does not believe in the gods whom the state believes in, but in other new divinities. Such is the accusation. Let us examine each point in it separately. Meletus says that I do wrong by corrupting the youth. But I say, Athenians, that he is doing wrong, for he is playing a solemn joke by casually bringing men to trial, and pretending to have a solemn interest in matters to which he has never given a moment's thought. Now I will try to prove to you that it is so.

Come here, Meletus. Is it not a fact that you think it very important that the young should be as good as possible?

Meletus: It is.

Sokrates: Come then, tell the judges who is it who improves them? You care so much,[6] you must know. You are accusing me, and bringing me to trial, because, as you say, you have discovered that I am the corrupter of the youth. Come now, reveal to the gentlemen who improves them. You see, Meletus, you have nothing to say; you are silent. But don't you think that this is shameful? Is not your silence a conclusive proof of what I say—that you have never cared. Come, tell us, my good man, who makes the young better?

Mel: The laws.

Sokr: That, my friend, is not my question. What man improves the young, who starts with the knowledge of the laws?

Mel: The judges here, Sokrates.

Sokr: What do you mean, Meletus? Can they educate the young and improve them?

Mel: Certainly.

Sokr: All of them? or only some of them?

Mel: All of them.

Sokr: By Hera, that is good news! Such a large supply of benefactors! And do the listeners here improve them, or not?

Mel: They do.

Sokr: And do the senators?

Mel: Yes.

Sokr: Well then, Meletus, do the members of the assembly corrupt the young or do they again all improve them?

Mel: They, too, improve them.

Sokr: Then all the Athenians, apparently, make the young into good men except me, and I alone corrupt them. Is that your meaning?

Mel: Most certainly; that is my meaning.

Sokr: You have discovered me to be most unfortunate. Now tell me: do you think that the same holds good in the case of horses? Does one man do them harm and every one else improve them? On the contrary, is it not one man only, or a very few—namely, those who are skilled with horses—who can improve them, while the majority of men harm them if they use them and have anything to do with them? Is it not so, Meletus, both with horses and with every other animal? Of course it is, whether you and Anytus say yes or no. The young would certainly be very fortunate if only one man corrupted them, and every one else did them good. The truth is, Meletus, you prove conclusively that you have never thought about the youth in your life. You exhibit your carelessness in not caring for the very matters about which you are prosecuting me.

Now be so good as to tell us, Meletus, is it better to live among good citizens or bad ones? Answer, my friend. I am not asking you a difficult question. Do not the bad harm their associates and the good, good?

Mel: Yes.

Sokr: Is there any one who would rather be injured than benefited by his companions? Answer, my good sir; you are obliged by the law to answer. Does any one like to be injured?

Mel: Certainly not.

Sokr: Well then, are you prosecuting me for corrupting the young and making them worse, voluntarily or involuntarily?

Mel: For doing it voluntarily.

---

6. Throughout the following passage Sokrates plays on the etymology of the name "Meletus" as meaning "the man who cares."

Sokr: What, Meletus? Do you mean to say that you, who are so much younger than I, are yet so much wiser than I that you know that bad citizens always do evil, and that good citizens do good, to those with whom they come in contact, while I am so extraordinarily ignorant as not to know that, if I make any of my companions evil, he will probably injure me in some way, and as to commit this great evil, as you allege, voluntarily? You will not make me believe that, nor anyone else either, I should think. Either I do not corrupt the young at all or if I do I do so involuntarily: so that you are lying in either case. And if I corrupt them involuntarily, the law does not call upon you to prosecute me for an error which is involuntary, but to take me aside privately and reprove and educate me. For, of course, I shall cease from doing wrong involuntarily, as soon as I know that I have been doing wrong. But you avoided associating with me and educating me; instead you bring me up before the court, where the law sends persons, not for education, but for punishment.

The truth is, Athenians, as I said, it is quite clear that Meletus has never cared at all about these matters. However, now tell us, Meletus, how do you say that I corrupt the young? Clearly, according to your indictment, by teaching them not to believe in the gods the state believes in, but other new divinities instead. You mean that I corrupt the young by that teaching, do you not?

Mel: Yes, most certainly I mean that.

Sokr: Then in the name of these gods of whom we are speaking, explain yourself a little more clearly to me and to these gentlemen here. I cannot understand what you mean. Do you mean that I teach the young to believe in some gods, but not in the gods of the state? Do you accuse me of teaching them to believe in strange gods? If that is your meaning, I myself believe in some gods, and my crime is not that of complete atheism. Or do you mean that I do not believe in the gods at all myself, and that I teach other people not to believe in them either?

Mel: I mean that you do not believe in the gods in any way whatever.

Sokr: You amaze me, Meletus! Why do you say that? Do you mean that I believe neither the sun nor the moon to be gods, like other men?

Mel: I swear he does not, judges; he says that the sun is a stone, and the moon earth.

Sokr: My dear Meletus, do you think that you are prosecuting Anaxagoras? You must have a very poor opinion of these men, and think them illiterate, if you imagine that they do not know that the works of Anaxagoras of Klazomenae are full of these doctrines. And so young men learn these things from me, when they can often buy them in the theatre for a drachma at most, and laugh at Sokrates were he to pretend that these doctrines, which are very peculiar doctrines, too, were his own. But please tell me, do you really think that I do not believe in the gods at all?

Mel: Most certainly I do. You are a complete atheist.

Sokr: No one believes that, Meletus, not even you yourself. It seems to me, Athenians, that Meletus is very insolent and reckless, and that he is prosecuting me simply out of insolence, recklessness and youthful bravado. For he seems to be testing me, by asking me a riddle that has no answer. "Will this wise Sokrates," he says to himself, "see that I am joking and contradicting myself? or shall I deceive him and every one else who hears me?" Meletus seems to me to contradict himself in his indictment: it is as if he were to say, "Sokrates is a wrongdoer who does not believe in the gods, but who believes in the gods." But this is joking.

Now, my friends, let us see why I think that this is his meaning. Do you answer me, Meletus; and do you, Athenians, remember the request which I made to you at the start, and do not interrupt me with shouts if I talk in my customary manner.

Is there any man, Meletus, who believes in the existence of things pertaining to men and not in the existence of men? Make him answer the question, gentlemen, without these interruptions. Is there any man who believes in the existence of horsemanship and not in the existence of horses? or in flute-playing and not in flute-players? There is not, my friend. If you will not answer, I will tell both you and the judges. But you must answer my next question. Is there any man who believes in the existence of divine things and not in the existence of divinities?

Mel: There is not.

Sokr: I am very glad that these gentlemen have managed to extract an answer from you. Well then,you say that I believe in divine things, whether they be old or new ones, and that I teach others to believe in them; at any rate, according to your statement, I believe in divine things. That you have sworn in your indictment. But if I believe in divine things, I suppose it follows necessarily that I believe in divinities. Is it not so? It is. I assume that you grant that, as you do not answer. But do we not believe that divinities are either gods themselves or the children of the gods? Do you admit that?

Mel: I do.

Sokr: Then you admit that I believe in divinities. Now, if these divinities are gods, then, as I say, you are joking and asking a riddle, and asserting that I do not believe in the gods, and at the same time that I do, since I believe in divinities. But if these divinities are the illegitimate children of the gods, either by the nymphs or by other mothers, as they are said to be, then, I ask, what man could believe in the existence of the children of the gods, and not in the existence of the gods? That would be as absurd as believing in the existence of the offspring of horses and asses, and not in the existence of horses and asses. You must have indicted me in this manner, Meletus, either to test me or because you could not find any crime that you could accuse me of with truth. But you will never contrive to persuade any man with any sense at all that a belief in divine things and things of the gods does not necessarily involve a belief in divinities, and in the gods, and in heroes.

But in truth, Athenians, I do not think that I need say very much to prove that I have not committed the crime for which Meletus is prosecuting me. What I have said is enough to prove that. But I repeat it is certainly true, as I have already told you, that I have aroused much indignation. That is what will cause my condemnation if I am condemned; not Meletus nor Anytus either, but that prejudice and resentment of the multitude which have been the destruction of many good men before me, and I think will be so again. There is no fear that I shall be the last victim.

Perhaps some one will say: "Are you not ashamed, Sokrates, of leading a life which is very likely now to cause your death?" I should answer him with justice, and say: "My friend, if you think that a man of any worth at all ought to reckon the chances of life and death when he acts, or that he ought to think of anything but whether he is acting rightly or wrongly, and as a good or bad man would act, you are mistaken. According to you, the demigods who died at Troy would be foolish, and among them the son of Thetis, who thought nothing of danger when the alternative was disgrace. For when his mother—and she was a goddess—addressed him, when he was resolved to slay Hektor, in this fashion, "My son, if you avenge the death of your comrade Patroklos and slay Hektor, you will die yourself, for 'fate awaits you straightway after Hektor's death' "; when he heard this, he scorned danger and death; he feared much more to live a coward and not to avenge his friend. "Let me punish the evildoer and straightway die," he said, "that I may not remain here by the beaked ships jeered at, encumbering the earth."[7] Do you suppose that he thought of danger or of death? For this, Athenians, I believe to be the truth. Wherever a man's station is, whether he has chosen it of his own will, or whether he has been placed at it by his commander, there it is his duty to remain and face the danger without thinking of death or of any other thing except disgrace.

When the generals whom you chose to command me, Athenians, assigned me my station at Potidaea and at Amphipolis and at Delium, I remained where they stationed me and ran the risk of death, like other men. It would be very strange conduct on my part if I were to desert my station now from fear of death or of any other thing when God has commanded me—as I am persuaded that he has done—to spend my life in searching for wisdom, and in examining myself and others. That would indeed be a very strange thing. Then certainly I might with justice be brought to trial for not believing in the gods, for I should be disobeying the oracle, and fearing death and thinking myself wise when I was not wise. For to fear death, my friends, is only to think ourselves wise without really being wise, for it is to think that we know what we do not know. For no one knows whether death may not be the greatest good that can happen to man. But men fear it as if they knew quite well that it was the greatest of evils. And what is this but that shameful ignorance of thinking that we know what we do not know? In this matter, too, my friends, perhaps I am different from the multitude; and if I were to claim to be at all wiser than others, it would be because, not knowing very much about the other world, I do not think I know. But I do know very well that it is evil and disgraceful to do wrong, and not to be persuaded by my superior, whether man or god. I will never do what I know to be evil, and shrink in fear from what I do not know to be good or evil. Even if you acquit me now, and do not listen to Anytus' argument that, if I am to be acquitted, I ought never to have been brought to trial at all, and that, as it is, you are bound to put me to death because, as he said, if I escape, all your sons will be utterly corrupted by practicing what Sokrates teaches. If you were therefore to say to me, "Sokrates, this time we will not listen to Anytus; we will let you go, but on this condition that you give up this investigation of yours, and philosophy; if you are found following those pursuits again, you shall die." I say, if you offered to let me go on these terms, I should reply: "Athenians, I hold you in the highest regard and affection, but I will be persuaded by the god rather than you; and as long as I have breath and strength I will not give up philosophy and exhorting you and declaring the truth to every one of you whom I meet, saying, as I am accustomed, "My good friend, you are a citizen of Athens, a city which is very great and very famous for its wisdom and power—are you not ashamed of caring so much for

---

7. Homer, Iliad, xviii, 96, 98.

the making of money and for fame and prestige, when you neither think nor care about wisdom and truth and the improvement of your soul?'' And if he disputes my words and says that he does care about these things, I shall not at once release him and go away: I shall question him and cross-examine him and test him. If I think that he does not possess virtue, though he says that he does, I shall reproach him for under-valuing the most valuable things, and over-valuing those that are less valuable. This I shall do to every one whom I meet, young or old, citizen or stranger, but especially to citizens, for they are more closely related to me. For know that the god has commanded me to do so. And I think that no greater good has ever befallen you in the state than my service to the god. For I spend my whole life in going about and persuading you all to give your first and greatest care to the improvement of your souls, and not till you have done that to think of your bodies or your wealth; and telling you that virtue does not come from wealth, but that wealth, and every other good thing which men have, whether in public or in private, comes from virtue. If then I corrupt the youth by this teaching, these things must be harmful; but if any man says that I teach anything else, there is nothing in what he says. And therefore, Athenians, I say, whether you are persuaded by Anytus or not, whether you acquit me or not, I shall not change my way of life: no, not if I have to die for it many times.

Do not interrupt me, Athenians, with your shouts. Remember the request which I made to you, and do not interrupt my words. I think that it will profit you to hear them. I am going to say something more to you, at which you may be inclined to protest, but do not do that. Be sure that if you put me to death, who am what I have told you that I am, you will do yourselves more harm than me. Meletus and Anytus can do me no harm: that is impossible, for I am sure it is not allowed that a good man be injured by a worse. He may indeed kill me, or drive me into exile, or deprive me to my civil rights; and perhaps Meletus and others think those things great evils. But I do not think so: I think it is a much greater evil to do what he is doing now, and to try to put a man to death unjustly. And now, Athenians, I am not arguing in my own defense at all, as you might expect me to do, but rather in yours in order you may not make a mistake about the gift of the god to you by condemning me. For if you put me to death, you will not easily find another who, if I may use a ludicrous comparison, clings to the state as a sort of gadfly to a horse that is large and well-bred but rather sluggish from its size, and needing to be aroused. It seems to me that the god has attached me like that to the state, for I am constantly alighting upon you at every point to rouse, persuade, and reproach each of you all day long. You will not easily find anyone else, my friends, to fill my place; and if you are persuaded by me, you will spare my life. You are indignant, as drowsy persons are, when they are awakened, and, of course, if you are persuaded by Anytus, you could easily kill me with a single blow, and then sleep on undisturbed for the rest of your lives unless the god in his care for you sends another to arouse you. And you may easily see that it is the god who has given me to your city; for it is not human the way in which I have neglected all my own interests and endured seeing my private affairs neglected now for so many years, while occupying myself unceasingly in your interests, going to each of you privately, like a father or an elder brother, trying to persuade him to care for virtue. There would have been a reason for it, if I had gained any advantage by this, or if I had been paid for my exhortations; but you see yourselves that my accusers, though they accuse me of everything else without shame, have not had the shamelessness to say that I ever either exacted or demanded payment. To that they have no witness. And I think that I have sufficient witness to the truth of what I say—my poverty.

Perhaps it may seem strange to you that, though I go about giving this advice privately and meddling in others' affairs, yet I do not venture to come forward in the assembly and advise the state. You have often heard me speak of my reason for this, and in many places: it is that I have a certain divine sign, which is what Meletus has caricatured in his indictment. I have had it from childhood. It is a kind of voice which, whenever I hear it, always turns me back from something which I was going to do, but never urges me to act. It is this which forbids me to take part in politics. And I think it does well to forbid me. For, Athenians, it is quite certain that, if I had attempted to take part in politics, I should have perished at once and long ago without doing any good either to you or to myself. And do not be indignant with me for telling the truth. There is no man who will preserve his life for long, either in Athens or elsewhere, if he firmly opposes the multitude, and tries to prevent the commission of much injustice and illegality in the state. He who would really fight for justice must do so as a private citizen, not as an office-holder, if he is to preserve his life, even for a short time.

I will prove to you that this is so by very strong evidence, not by mere words, but by what you value more—actions. Listen then to what has happened to me, that you may know that there is no man who could make me consent to do wrong from the fear of death, but that I would perish at once rather than give way. What I am going to tell you may be a commonplace in the lawcourt; nevertheless it is true. The only office that I ever held in the state, Athenians, was that of Senator. When you wished to try the ten generals who did not rescue their men after the battle of Arginusae, as a group, which was illegal, as you all came to think afterwards, the tribe Antiokhis, to which I belong, held the presidency. On that occasion I alone of all the presidents opposed your illegal action and gave my vote against you. The orators were ready to impeach me and arrest me; and you were clamoring against me, and crying out to me to submit. But I thought that I ought to face the danger, with law and justice on my side, rather than join with you in your unjust proposal, from fear of imprisonment or death. That was when the state was democratic. When the oligarchy came in, the Thirty sent for me, with four others, to the council-chamber, and ordered us to bring Leon the Salaminian from Salamis, that they might put him to death. They were in the habit of frequently giving similar orders to many others, wishing to implicate as many as possible in their crimes. But, then, I again proved, not by mere words, but by my actions, that, if I may speak bluntly, I do not care a straw for death; but that I do care very much indeed about not doing anything unjust or impious. That government with all its power did not terrify me into doing anything unjust; but when we left the council-chamber, the other four went over to Salamis and brought Leon across to Athens; and I went home. And if the rule of the Thirty had not been overthrown soon afterwards, I should very likely have been put to death for what I did then. Many of you will be my witnesses in this matter.

Now do you think that I could have remained alive all these years if I had taken part in public affairs, and had always maintained the cause of justice like a good man, and had held it a paramount duty, as it is, to do so? Certainly not, Athenians, nor could any other man. But throughout my whole life, both in private and in public, whenever I have had to take part in public affairs, you will find I have always been the same and have never yielded unjustly to anyone; no, not to those whom my enemies falsely assert to have been my pupils.[8] But I was never anyone's teacher. I have never withheld myself from anyone, young or old, who was anxious to hear me discuss while I was making my investigation; neither do I discuss for payment, and refuse to discuss without payment. I am ready to ask questions of rich and poor alike, and if any man wishes to answer me, and then listen to what I have to say, he may. And I cannot justly be charged with causing these men to turn out good or bad, for I never either taught or professed to teach any of them any knowledge whatever. And if any man asserts that he ever learned or heard anything from me in private which everyone else did not hear as well as he, be sure that he does not speak the truth.

Why is it, then, that people delight in spending so much time in my company? You have heard why, Athenians. I told you the whole truth when I said that they delight in hearing me examine persons who think that they are wise when they are not wise. It is certainly very amusing to listen to that. And, I say, the god has commanded me to examine men, in oracles and in dreams and in every way in which the divine will was ever declared to man. This is the truth, Athenians, and if it were not the truth, it would be easily refuted. For if it were really the case that I have already corrupted some of the young men, and am now corrupting others, surely some of them, finding as they grew older that I had given them bad advice in their youth, would have come forward today to accuse me and take their revenge. Or if they were unwilling to do so themselves, surely their relatives, their fathers or brothers, or others, would, if I had done them any harm, have remembered it and taken their revenge. Certainly I see many of them in Court. Here is Crito, of my own deme and of my own age, the father of Critobulus; here is Lysanias of Sphettus, the father of Aeschines; here is also Antiphon of Cephisus, the father of Epigenes. Then here are others whose brothers have spent their time in my company—Nicostratus, the son of Theozotides and brother of Theodotus—and Theodotus is dead, so he at least cannot entreat his brother to be silent; here is Paralus, the son of Demodocus and the brother of Theages; here is Adeimantus, the son of Ariston, whose brother is Plato here; and Aeantodorus, whose brother is Aristodorus. And I can name many others to you, some of whom Meletus ought to have called as witnesses in the course of his own speech; but if he forgot to call them then, let him call them now—I will yield the floor to him—and tell us if he has any such evidence. No, on the contrary, my friends, you will find all these men ready to support me, the corrupter, the injurer, of their relatives, as Meletus and Anytus call me. Those of them who have been already corrupted might perhaps have some reason for supporting me, but what reason can their relatives have who are grown up, and who are uncorrupted, except the reason of truth and justice—that they know very well that Meletus is lying, and that I am speaking the truth?

Well, my friends, this, and perhaps more like this, is pretty much all I have to offer in my defense. There may be some one among you who will be indignant when he remembers how, even in a less important trial than this, he begged and entreated the judges, with many tears, to acquit him, and brought forward his children and many of his friends and relatives in Court in order to appeal to your feelings; and then finds that I shall do none of these things, though I am in what he would think the supreme danger. Perhaps he will harden himself against me when he notices this: it may make him angry, and he may cast his vote in anger. If it is so with any of you—I do not suppose that it is, but in case it should be so—I think that I should answer him reasonably if I said: "My friend, I have relatives, too, for, in the words of Homer,[9] "I am not born of an oak or a rock but of flesh and blood"; and so, Athenians, I have relatives, and I have three sons, one of them a lad, and the other two still children. Yet I will not bring any of them forward before you and implore you to acquit me. And why will I do none of these things? It is not from arrogance, Athenians, nor because I lack respect for you—whether or not I can face death bravely is another question—but for my own good name, and for your good name, and for the good name of the whole state. I do not think it right, at my age and with my reputation, to do anything of that kind. Rightly or wrongly, men have made up their minds that in some way Sokrates is different from the multitude of men. And it will be shameful if those of you who are thought to excel in wisdom, or in bravery, or in any other virtue, are going to act in this fashion. I have often seen men of reputation behaving in an extraordinary way at their trial, as if they thought it a terrible fate to be killed, and as though they expected to live for ever if you did not put them to death. Such men seem to me to bring shame upon the state, for any stranger would suppose that the best and most eminent Athenians, who are selected by their fellow citizens to hold office, and for other honors, are no better than women. Those of you, Athenians, who have any reputation at all ought not to do these things, and you ought not to allow us to do them; you should show that you will be much more ready to condemn men who make the state ridiculous by these pitiful pieces of acting, than to men who remain quiet.

But apart from the question of reputation, my friends, I do not think that it is right to entreat the judge to acquit us, or to escape condemnation in that way. It is our duty to teach and persuade him. He does not sit to give away justice as a favor, but to pronounce judgment; and he has sworn, not to favor any man whom he would like to favor, but to judge according to law. And, therefore, we ought not to encourage you in the habits of breaking your oaths; and you ought not to allow yourselves to fall into this habit, for then neither you nor we would be acting piously. Therefore, Athenians, do not require me to do these things, for I believe them to be neither good nor just nor pious; and, more especially, do not ask me to do them today when Meletus is prosecuting me for impiety. For were I to be successful and persuade you by my entreaties to break your oaths, I should be clearly teaching you to believe that there are no gods, and I should be simply accusing myself by my defense of not believing in them. But, Athenians, that is very far from the truth. I do believe in the gods as no one of my accusers believes in them: and to you and to god I commit my cause to be decided as is best for you and for me.

(He is found guilty by 281 votes to 220.)

---

8. E.g. Kritias, a leader of The Thirty, and Alkibiades.

9. Homer, Odyssey, xix, 163.

I am not indignant at the verdict which you have given, Athenians, for many reasons. I expected that you would find me guilty; and I am not so much surprised at that as at the numbers of the votes. I certainly never thought that the majority against me would have been so narrow. But now it seems that if only thirty votes had changed sides, I should have escaped. So I think that I have escaped Meletus, as it is; and not only have I escaped him, for it is perfectly clear that if Anytus and Lycon had not come forward to accuse me, too, he would not have obtained the fifth part of the votes, and would have had to pay a fine of a thousand drachmae.

So he proposes death as the penalty. Be it so. And what alternative penalty shall I propose to you, Athenians?[10] What I deserve, of course, must I not? What then do I deserve to pay or to suffer for having determined not to spend my life in ease? I neglected the things which most men value, such as wealth, and family interests, and military commands, and popular oratory, and all the political appointments, and clubs, and factions, that there are in Athens; for I thought that I was really too honest a man to preserve my life if I engaged in these matters. So I did not go where I should have done no good either to you or to myself. I went, instead, to each one of you privately to do him, as I say, the greatest of benefits, and tried to persuade him not to think of his affairs until he had thought of himself and tried to make himself as good and wise as possible, nor to think of the affairs of Athens until he had thought of Athens herself; and to care for other things in the same manner. Then what do I deserve for such a life? Something good, Athenians, if I am really to propose what I deserve; and something good which it would be suitable to me to receive. Then what is a suitable reward to be given to a poor benefactor who requires leisure to exhort you? There is no reward, Athenians, so suitable for him as a public maintenance in the prytaneum. It is a much more suitable reward for him than for any of you who has won a victory at the Olympic games with his horse or his chariots. Such a man only makes you seem happy, but I make you really happy; and he is not in want, and I am. So if I am to propose the penalty which I really deserve, I propose this—a public maintenance in the prytaneum [town hall].

Perhaps you think me stubborn and arrogant in what I am saying now, as in what I said about the entreaties and tears. It is not so, Athenians; it is rather that I am convinced that I never wronged any man voluntarily, though I cannot persuade you of that, for we have discussed together only a little time. If there were a law at Athens, as there is elsewhere, not to finish a trial of life and death in a single day, I think that I could have persuaded you; but now it is not easy in so short a time to clear myself of great prejudices. But when I am persuaded that I have never wronged any man, I shall certainly not wrong myself, or admit that I deserve to suffer any evil, or propose any evil for myself as a penalty. Why should I? Lest I should suffer the penalty which Meletus proposes when I say that I do not know whether it is a good or an evil? Shall I choose instead of it something which I know to be an evil, and propose that as a penalty? Shall I propose imprisonment? And why should I pass the rest of my days in prison, the slave of successive officials? Or shall I propose a fine, with imprisonment until it is paid?

I have told you why I will not do that. I should have to remain in prison, for I have no money to pay a fine with. Shall I then propose exile? Perhaps you would agree to that. Life would indeed be very dear to me if I were unreasonable enough to expect that strangers would cheerfully tolerate my discussions and arguments when you who are my fellow citizens cannot endure them, and have found them so irksome and odious to you that you are seeking now to be relieved of them. No, indeed, Athenians, that is not likely. A fine life I should lead for an old man if I were to withdraw from Athens and pass the rest of my days in wandering from city to city, and continually being expelled. For I know very well that the young men will listen to me wherever I go, as they do here; and if I drive them away, they will persuade their elders to expel me; and if I do not drive them away, their fathers and kinsmen will expel me for their sakes.

Perhaps some one will say, "Why cannot you withdraw from Athens, Sokrates, and hold your peace?" It is the most difficult thing in the world to make you understand why I cannot do that. If I say that I cannot hold my peace because that would be to disobey the god, you will think that I am not in earnest and will not believe me. And if I tell you that no greater good can happen to a man than to discuss virtue every day and the other matters about which you have heard me arguing and examining myself and others, and that an unexamined life is not worth living, then you will believe me still less. But that is so, my friends, though it is not easy to persuade you. And, what is more, I am not accustomed to think that I deserve anything evil. If I had been rich, I would have proposed as large a fine as I could pay: that would have done me no harm. But I am not rich enough to pay a fine unless you are willing to fix it at a sum within my means. Perhaps I could pay you a mina, so I propose that. Plato here, Athenians, and Crito, and Critobulus, and Apollodorus bid me propose thirty minae, and they will be sureties for me. So I propose thirty minae.[11] They will be sufficient sureties to you for the money.

(He is condemned to death.)

You have not gained very much time, Athenians, and, as the price of it, you will have an evil name for all who wish to revile the state, and they will say that you put Sokrates, a wise man, to death. For they will certainly call me wise, whether I am wise or not, when they want to reproach you. If you would have waited for a little while, your wishes would have been fulfilled in the course of nature; for you see that I am an old man, far advanced in years, and near to death. I am saying this not to all of you, only to those who have voted for my death. And to them I have something else to say. Perhaps, my friends, you think that I have been convicted because I was wanting in the arguments by which I could have persuaded you to acquit me, if, that is, I had thought it right to do or to say anything to escape punishment. It is not so. I have been convicted because I was wanting, not in arguments, but in impudence and shamelessness—because I would not plead before you as you would have liked to hear me plead, or appeal to you with weeping and wailing, or say and do many other things which I maintain are unworthy

---

10. For certain crimes no penalty was fixed by Athenian law, and, having reached a verdict of guilty, the court had still to decide between the alternative penalties proposed by the prosecution and the defense.

11. [One mina was a trifling sum, Sokrates's honest opinion of his just deserts but insulting to the court. A thirty minae fine was comparable to the dowry of a moderately rich man's daughter, as Plato later mentioned, but, by this time, totally unacceptable to the court.]

of me, but which you have been accustomed to from other men. But when I was defending myself, I thought that I ought not to do anything unworthy of a free man because of the danger which I ran, and I have not changed my mind now. I would very much rather defend myself as I did, and die, than as you would have had me do, and live. Both in a lawsuit and in war, there are some things which neither I nor any other man may do in order to escape from death. In battle, a man often sees that he may at least escape from death by throwing down his arms and falling on his knees before the pursuer to beg for his life. And there are many other ways of avoiding death in every danger if a man is willing to say and to do anything. But, my friends, I think that it is a much harder thing to escape from wickedness than from death, for wickedness is swifter than death. And now I, who am old and slow, have been overtaken by the slower pursuer: and my accusers, who are clever and swift, have been overtaken by the swifter pursuer—wickedness. And now I shall go away, sentenced by you to death; and they will go away, sentenced by truth to wickedness and injustice. And I abide by this award as well as they. Perhaps it was right for these things to be so; and I think that they are fairly balanced.

And now I wish to prophesy to you, Athenians, who have condemned me. For I am going to die, and that is the time when men have most prophetic power. And I prophesy to you who have sentenced me to death that a far more severe punishment than you have inflicted on me will surely overtake you as soon as I am dead. You have done this thing, thinking that you will be relieved from having to give an account of your lives. But I say that the result will be very different. There will be more men who will call you to account, whom I have held back, though you did not recognize it. And they will be harsher toward you than I have been, for they will be younger, and you will be more indignant with them. For if you think that you will restrain men from reproaching you for not living as you should, by putting them to death, you are very much mistaken. That way of escape is neither possible nor honorable. It is much more honorable and much easier not to suppress others, but to make yourselves as good as you can. This is my parting prophecy to you who have condemned me.

With you who have acquitted me I should like to discuss this thing that has happened, while the authorities are busy, and before I go to the place where I have to die. So, remain with me until I go: there is no reason why we should not talk with each other while it is possible. I wish to explain to you, as my friends, the meaning of what has happened to me. An amazing thing has happened to me, judges—for you I am right in calling judges.[12] The prophetic sign has been constantly with me all through my life till now, opposing me in quite small matters if I were not going to act rightly. And now you yourselves see what has happened to me—a thing which might be thought, and which is sometimes actually reckoned, the supreme evil. But the divine sign did not oppose me when I was leaving my house in the morning, nor when I was coming up here to the court, nor at any point in my speech when I was going to say anything; though at other times it has often stopped me in the very act of speaking. But now, in this matter, it has never once opposed me, either in my words or my actions. I will tell you what I believe to be the reason. This thing that has come upon me must be a good; and those of us who think that death is an evil must needs be mistaken. I have a clear proof that that is so; for my accustomed sign would certainly have opposed me if I had not been going to meet with something good.

And if we reflect in another way, we shall see that we may well hope that death is a good. For the state of death is one of two things: either the dead man wholly ceases to be and loses all consciousness or, as we are told, it is a change and a migration of the soul to another place. And if death is the absence of all consciousness, and like the sleep of one whose slumbers are unbroken by any dreams, it will be a wonderful gain. For if a man had to select that night in which he slept so soundly that he did not even dream, and had to compare with it all the other nights and days of his life, and then had to say how many days and nights in his life he had spent better and more pleasantly than this night, I think that a private person, nay, even the great King[13] himself, would find them easy to count, compared with the others. If that is the nature of death, I for one count it a gain. For then it appears that all time is nothing more than a single night. But if death is a journey to another place, and what we are told is true— that there are all who have died—what good could be greater than this, my judges? Would a journey not be worth taking, at the end of which, in the other world, we should be delivered from the pretended judges here and should find the true judges who are said to sit in judgment below, such as Minos and Rhadamanthus and Aeacus and Triptolemus, and the other demigods who were just in their own lives? Or what would you not give to discuss with Orpheus and Musaeus and Hesiod and Homer? I am willing to die many times if this be true. And for my own part I should find it wonderful to meet there Palamedes, and Aias, the son of Telamon, and the other men of old who have died through an unjust judgment, and in comparing my experiences with theirs. That I think would be no small pleasure. And, above all, I could spend my time in examining those who are there, as I examine men here, and in finding out which of them is wise, and which of them thinks himself wise when he is not wise. What would we not give, my judges, to be able to examine the leader of the great expedition against Troy, or Odysseus, or Sisyphus, or countless other men and women whom we could name? It would be an infinite happiness to discuss with them and to live with them and to examine them. Assuredly there they do not put men to death for doing that. For besides the other ways in which they are happier than we are, they are immortal, at least if what we are told is true.

And you, too, judges, must face death hopefully, and believe this as a truth that no evil can happen to a good man, either in life or after death. His fortunes are not neglected by the gods; and what has happened to me today has not happened by chance. I am persuaded that it was better for me to die now, and to be released from trouble; and that was the reason why the sign never turned me back. And so I am not at all angry with my accusers or with those who have condemned me to die. Yet it was not with this in mind that they accused me and condemned me, but meaning to do me an injury. So far I may blame them.

---

12. The form of address hitherto has always been "Athenians," or "my friends."

13. Of Persia.

Yet I have one request to make of them. When my sons grow up, punish them, my friends, and harass them in the same way that I have harassed you, if they seem to you to care for riches or for any other thing more than virtue; and if they think that they are something when they are really nothing, reproach them, as I have reproached you, for not caring for what they should, and for thinking that they are something when really they are nothing. And if you will do this, I myself and my sons will have received justice from you.

But now the time has come, and we must go away—I to die, and you to live. Which is better is known to god alone.

Exercises

1. The so-called offenses of Sokrates were, as mentioned in the text, committed under the old democracy. An amnesty (the Act of Oblivion) forbade any reference to the past, which set up a tension of unspoken thoughts throughout the trial. The charge of "corruption of the young" was therefore particularly weak, but its origins can be detected by carefully reading between the lines of the defense. What are some examples of Sokrates's oblique references to his past actions?
2. Another charge, that of not respecting the gods, was equally vague. What are some of the indications that Meletus, or anyone else, did not know what "impiety" really meant? To what extent was the charge a cover-up for the attacks of Sokrates upon traditional morality and conventional behavior? What, in essence, were the *real* charges and why was Sokrates such a problem for the new democracy?
3. Sokrates could have saved his life by paying a moderate fine. Why didn't he do this? What is implied if he pays a fine?
4. Refusing to pay a reasonable rather than a token fine is one thing, but proposing lifetime maintenance at public expense is another matter. Why did Sokrates antagonize the court with this proposal? Was he serious?
5. Would Sokrates have taken this uncompromising position had he been, say, twenty years younger?

REPUBLIC

Plato

The *Republic* is discussed on page 137. At this point in the dialogue the conversation is mainly between the narrator, Sokrates, and Plato's brother, Glaucon. The translation is by F. M. Cornford.

Book IV

For the moment, we had better finish the inquiry which we began with the idea that it would be easier to make out the nature of justice in the individual if we first tried to study it in something on a larger scale. That larger thing we took to be a state, and so we set about constructing the best one we could, being sure of finding justice in a state that was good. The discovery we made there must now be applied to the individual. If it is confirmed, all will be well; but if we find that justice in the individual is something different, we must go back to the state and test our new result. Perhaps if we brought the two cases into contact like flint and steel, we might strike out between them the spark of justice, and in its light confirm the conception in our own minds.

A good method. Let us follow it.

Now, I continued, if two things, one large, the other small, are called by the same name, they will be alike in that respect to which the common name applies. Accordingly, in so far as the quality of justice is concerned, there will be no difference between a just man and a just society.

No.

Well, but we decided that a society was just when each of the three types of human character it contained performed its own function; and again, it was temperate and brave and wise by virtue of certain other affections and states of mind of those same types.

True.

Accordingly, my friend, if we are to be justified in attributing those same virtues to the individual, we shall expect to find that the individual soul contains the same three elements and that they are affected in the same way as are the corresponding types in society.

That follows.

Here, then, we have stumbled upon another little problem: Does the soul contain these three elements or not?

Not such a very little one, I think. It may be a true saying, Sokrates, that what is worth while is seldom easy.

Apparently; and let me tell you, Glaucon, it is my belief that we shall never reach the exact truth in this matter by following our present methods of discussion; the road leading to that goal is longer and more laborious. However, perhaps we can find an answer that will be up to the standard we have so far maintained in our speculations.

Is not that enough? I should be satisfied for the moment.

Well, it will more than satisfy me.

Don't be disheartened, then, but go on.

Surely, we must admit that the same elements and characters that appear in the state must exist in every one of us; where else could they have come from? It would be absurd to imagine that among peoples with a reputation for a high-spirited character, like the Thracians and Scythians and northerners generally, the states have not derived that character from their individual members; or that it is otherwise with the love of knowledge, which would be ascribed chiefly to our own part of the world, or with the love of money, which one would specially connect with Phoenicia and Egypt.

Certainly.

So far, then, we have a fact which is easily recognized. But here the difficulty begins. Are we using the same part of ourselves in all these three experiences, or a different part in each? Do we gain knowledge with one part, feel anger with another, and with yet a third desire the pleasures of food, sex, and so on? Or is the whole soul at work in every impulse and in all these forms of behavior? The difficulty is to answer that question satisfactorily.

I quite agree.

Let us approach the problem whether these elements are distinct or identical in this way. It is clear that the same thing cannot act in two opposite ways or be in two opposite states at the same time, with respect to the same part of itself, and in relation to the same object. So if we find such contradictory actions or states among the elements concerned, we shall know that more than one must have been involved.

Very well.

Consider this proposition for mine, then. Can the same thing, at the same time and with respect to the same part of itself, be at rest and in motion?

Certainly not.

We had better state this principle in still more precise terms, to guard against misunderstanding later on. Suppose a man is standing still, but moving his head and arms. We should not allow anyone to say that the same man was both at rest and in motion at the same time, but only that part of him was at rest, part in motion. Isn't that so?

Yes.

An ingenious objector might refine still further and argue that a peg-top, spinning with its peg fixed at the same spot, or indeed any body that revolves in the same place, is both at rest and in motion as a whole. But we should not agree, because the parts in respect of which such a body is moving and at rest are not the same. It contains an axis and a circumference; and in respect of the axis it is at rest inasmuch as the axis is not inclined in any direction, while in respect of the circumference it revolves; and if, while it is spinning, the axis does lean out of the perpendicular in all directions, then it is in no way at rest.

That is true.

No objection of that sort, then, will disconcert us or make us believe that the same thing can ever act or be acted upon in two opposite ways, or be two opposite things, at the same time, in respect of the same part of itself, and in relation to the same object.

I can answer for myself at any rate.

Well, anyhow, as we do not want to spend time in reviewing all such objections to make sure that they are unsound, let us proceed on this assumption, with the understanding that, if we ever come to think otherwise, all the consequences based upon it will fall to the ground.

Yes, that is a good plan.

Now, would you class such things as assent and dissent, striving after something and refusing it, attraction and repulsion, as pairs of opposite actions or states of mind—no matter which?

Yes, they are opposites.

And would you not class all appetites such as hunger and thirst, and again willing and wishing, with the affirmative members of those pairs I have just mentioned? For instance, you would say that the soul of a man who desires something is striving after it, or trying to draw to itself the thing it wishes to possess, or again, in so far as it is willing to have its want satisfied, it is giving its assent to its own longing, as if to an inward question.

Yes.

And, on the other hand, disinclination, unwillingness, and dislike, we should class on the negative side with acts of rejection or repulsion.

Of course.

That being so, shall we say that appetites form one class, the most conspicuous being those we call thirst and hunger?

Yes.

Thirst being desire for drink, hunger for food?

Yes.

Now, is thirst, just in so far as it is thirst, a desire in the soul for anything more than simply drink? Is it, for instance, thirst for hot drink or for cold, for much drink or for little, or in a word for drink of any particular kind? Is it not rather true that you will have a desire for cold drink only if you are feeling hot as well as thirsty, and for hot drink only if you are feeling cold; and if you want much drink or little, that will be because your thirst is a great thirst or a little one? But, just in itself, thirst or hunger is a desire for nothing more than its natural object, drink or food, pure and simple.

Yes, he agreed, each desire, just in itself, is simply for its own natural object. When the object is of such and such a particular kind, the desire will be correspondingly qualified.[14]

We must be careful here, or we might be troubled by the objection that no one desires mere food and drink, but always wholesome food and drink. We shall be told that what we desire is always something that is good; so if thirst is a desire, its object must be, like that of any other desire, something—drink or whatever it may be—that will be good for one.[15]

Yes, there might seem to be something in that objection.

But surely, wherever you have two correlative terms, if one is qualified, the other must always be qualified too; whereas if one is unqualified, so is the other.

I don't understand.

Well, "greater" is a relative term; and the greater is greater than the less; if it is much greater, then the less is much less; if it is greater at some moment, past or future, then the less is less at that same moment. The same principle applies to all such correlatives, like "more" and "fewer," "double" and "half"; and again to terms like "heavier" and "lighter," "quicker" and "slower," and to things like hot and cold.

Yes.

Or take the various branches of knowledge: is it not the same there? The object of knowledge pure and simple is the knowable—if that is the right word—without any qualification; whereas a particular kind of knowledge has an object of a particular kind. For example, as soon as men learnt how to build houses, their craft was distinguished from others under the name of architecture, because it had a unique character, which was itself due to the character of its object; and all other branches of craft and knowledge were distinguished in the same way.

True.

This, then, if you understand me now, is what I meant by saying that, where there are two correlatives, the one is qualified if, and only if, the other is so. I am not saying that the one must have the same quality as the other—that the science of health and disease is itself healthy and diseased, or the knowledge of good and evil

---

14. The object of the following subtle argument about relative terms is to distinguish thirst as a mere blind craving for drink from a more complex desire whose object includes the pleasure or health expected to result from drinking. We thus forestall the objection that all desires have "the good" (apparent or real) for their object and include an intellectual or rational element, so that the conflict of motives might be reduced to an intellectual debate, in the same "part" of the soul, on the comparative values of two incompatible ends.

15. If this objection were admitted, it would follow that the desire would always be correspondingly qualified. It is necessary to insist that we do experience blind cravings which can be isolated from any judgment about the goodness of their object.

is itself good and evil—but only that, as soon as you have a knowledge that is restricted to a particular kind of object, namely health and disease, the knowledge itself becomes a particular kind of knowledge. Hence we no longer call it merely knowledge, which would have for its object whatever can be known, but we add the qualification and call it medical science.

I understand now and I agree.

Now, to go back to thirst: is not that one of these relative terms? It is essentially thirst for something.

Yes, for drink.

And if the drink desired is of a certain kind, the thirst will be correspondingly qualified. But thirst which is just simply thirst is not for drink of any particular sort—much or little, good or bad—but for drink pure and simple.

Quite so.

We conclude, then, that the soul of a thirsty man, just in so far as he is thirsty, has no other wish than to drink. That is the object of its craving, and towards that it is impelled.

That is clear.

Now if there is ever something which at the same time pulls it the opposite way, that something must be an element in the soul other than the one which is thirsting and driving it like a beast to drink; in accordance with our principle that the same thing cannot behave in two opposite ways at the same time and towards the same object with the same part of itself. It is like an archer drawing the bow: it is not accurate to say that his hands are at the same time both pushing and pulling it. One hand does the pushing, the other the pulling.

Exactly.

Now, is it sometimes true that people are thirsty and yet unwilling to drink?

Yes, often.

What, then, can one say of them, if not that their soul contains something which urges them to drink and something which holds them back, and that this latter is a distinct thing and overpowers the other?

I agree.

And is it not true that the intervention of this inhibiting principle in such cases always has its origin in reflection; whereas the impulses driving and dragging the soul are engendered by external influences and abnormal conditions.[16]

Evidently.

We shall have good reason, then, to assert that they are two distinct principles. We may call that part of the soul whereby it reflects, rational; and the other, with which it feels hunger and thirst and is distracted by sexual passion and all the other desires, we will call irrational appetite, associated with pleasure in the replenishment of certain wants.

Yes, there is good ground for that view.

Let us take it, then, that we have now distinguished two elements in the soul. What of that passionate element which makes us feel angry and indignant? Is that a third, or identical in nature with one of those two?

It might perhaps be identified with appetite.

I am more inclined to put my faith in a story I once heard about Leontius, son of Aglaion. On his way up from the Piraeus outside the north wall, he noticed the bodies of some criminals lying on the ground, with the executioner standing by them. He wanted to go and look at them, but at the same time he was disgusted and tried to turn away. He struggled for some time and covered his eyes, but at last the desire was too much for him. Opening his eyes wide, he ran up to the bodies and cried, "There you are, curse you; feast yourselves on this lovely sight!"

Yes, I have heard that story too.

The point of it surely is that anger is sometimes in conflict with appetite, as if they were two distinct principles. Do we not often find a man whose desires would force him to go against his reason, reviling himself and indignant with this part of his nature which is trying to put constraint on him? It is like a struggle between two factions, in which indignation takes the side of reason. But I believe you have never observed, in yourself or anyone else, indignation make common cause with appetite in behavior which reason decides to be wrong.

No, I am sure I have not.

Again, take a man who feels he is in the wrong. The more generous his nature, the less can he be indignant at any suffering, such as hunger and cold, inflicted by the man he has injured. He recognizes such treatment as just, and, as I say, his spirit refuses to be roused against it.

This is true.

But now contrast one who thinks it is he that is being wronged. His spirit boils with resentment and sides with the right as he conceives it. Persevering all the more for the hunger and cold and other pains he suffers, it triumphs and will not give in until its gallant struggle has ended in success or death; or until the restraining voice of reason, like a shepherd calling off his dog, makes it relent.

As apt comparison, he said; and in fact it fits the relation of our Auxiliaries to the Rulers: they were to be like watch-dogs obeying the shepherds of the commonwealth.

Yes, you understand very well what I have in mind. But do you see how we have changed our view? A moment ago we were supposing this spirited element to be something of the nature of appetite; but now it appears that, when the soul is divided into factions, it is far more ready to be up in arms on the side of reason.

Quite true.

Is it, then, distinct from the rational element or only a particular form of it, so that the soul will contain no more than two elements, reason and appetite? Or is the soul like the state, which had three orders to hold it together, traders, Auxiliaries, and counsellors? Does the spirited element make a third, the natural auxiliary of reason, when not corrupted by bad upbringing?

It must be a third.

Yes, I said, provided it can be shown to be distinct for reason, as we saw it was from appetite.

That is easily proved. You can see that much in children: they are full of passionate feelings from their very birth; but some, I should say, never become rational, and most of them only late in life.

A very sound observation, said I, the truth of which may also be seen in animals. And besides, there is the witness of Homer in that line I quoted before: "He smote his breast and spoke, chiding his heart." The poet is plainly thinking of the two elements as distinct, when he makes the one which has chosen the better course after reflection rebuke the other for its unreasoning passion.

---

16. Some of the most intense bodily desires are due to morbid conditions, e.g. thirst in fever, and even milder desires are caused by a departure from the normal state, which demands "replenishment."

I entirely agree.

The Equality of Women

What I see is that, whereas there is only one form of excellence, imperfection exists in innumerable shapes, of which there are four that specially deserve notice.

What do you mean?

It looks as if there were as many types of character as there are distinct varieties of political constitution.

How many?

Five of each.

Will you define them?

Yes, I said. One form of constitution will be the form we have been describing, though it may be called by two names: monarchy, when there is one man who stands out above the rest of the Rulers; aristocracy, when there are more than one.[17]

True.

That, then, I regard as a single form; for, so long as they observe our principles of upbringing and education, whether the Rulers be one or more, they will not subvert the important institutions in our commonwealth.

Naturally not.

Such, then, is the type of state or constitution that I call good and right, and the corresponding type of man. By this standard, the other forms in which a state or an individual character may be organized are depraved and wrong. There are four of these vicious forms.

What are they?

Here I was going on to describe these forms in the order in which, as I thought, they develop one from another, when Polemarchus, who was sitting a little way from Adeimantus, reached out his hand and took hold of his garment by the shoulder. Leaning forward and drawing Adeimantus towards him, he whispered something in his ear, of which I only caught the words: What shall we do? Shall we leave it alone?

Certainly not, said Adeimantus, raising his voice.

What is this, I asked, that you are not going to leave alone?

You, he replied.

Why, in particular? I inquired.

Because we think you are shirking the discussion of a very important part of the subject and trying to cheat us out of an explanation. Everyone, you said, must of course see that the maxim "friends have all things in common" applies to women and children. You thought we should pass over such a casual remark!

But wasn't that right, Adeimantus? said I.

Yes, he said, but "right" in this case, as in others, needs to be defined. There may be many ways of having things in common, and you must tell us which you mean. We have been waiting a long time for you to say something about the conditions in which children are to be born and brought up and your whole plan of having wives and children held in common. This seems to us a matter in which right or wrong management will make all the difference to society; and now, instead of going into it thoroughly, you are passing on to some other form of constitution. So we came to the resolution which you overheard, not to let you off discussing it as fully as all the other institutions.

I will vote for your resolution too, said Glaucon.

In fact, Sokrates, Thrasymachus added, you may take it as carried unanimously.

You don't know what you are doing, I said, in holding me up like this. You want to start, all over again, on an enormous subject, just as I was rejoicing at the idea that we had done with this form of constitution. I was only too glad that my casual remark should be allowed to pass. And now, when you demand an explanation, you little know what a swarm of questions you are stirring up. I let it alone, because I foresaw no end of trouble.

Well, said Thrasymachus, what do you think we came here for—to play pitch-and-toss or to listen to a discussion?

A discussion, no doubt, I replied; but within limits.

No man of sense, said Glaucon, would think the whole of life too long to spend on questions of this importance. But never mind about us; don't be faint-hearted yourself. Tell us what you think about this question: how our Guardians are to have wives and children in common, and how they will bring up the young in the interval between their birth and education, which is thought to be the most difficult time of all. Do try to explain how all this is to be arranged.

I wish it were as easy as you seem to think, I replied. These arrangements are even more open to doubt than any we have so far discussed. It may be questioned whether the plan is feasible, and even if entirely feasible, whether it would be for the best. So I have some hesitation in touching on what may seem to be an idle dream.

You need not hesitate, he replied. This is not an unsympathetic audience; we are neither incredulous nor hostile.

Thank you, I said; I suppose that remark is meant to be encouraging.

Certainly it is.

Well, I said, it has just the opposite effect. You would do well to encourage me, if I had any faith in my own understanding of these matters. If one knows the truth, there is no risk to be feared in speaking about the things one has most at heart among intelligent friends; but if one is still in the position of a doubting inquirer, as I am now, talking becomes a slippery venture. Not that I am afraid of being laughed at—that would be childish—but I am afraid I may miss my footing just where a false step is most to be dreaded and drag my friends down with me in my fall. I devoutly hope, Glaucon, that no nemesis will overtake me for what I am going to say; for I really believe that to kill a man unintentionally is a lighter offense than to mislead him concerning the goodness and justice of social institutions. Better to run that risk among enemies than among friends; so your encouragement is out of place.

Glaucon laughed at this. No, Sokrates, he said, if your theory has any untoward effect on us, our blood shall not be on your head; we absolve you of any intention to mislead us. So have no fear.

Well, said I, when a homicide is absolved of all intention, the law holds him clear of guilt; and the same principle may apply to my case.

Yes, so far as that goes, you may speak freely.

We must go back, then, to a subject which ought, perhaps, to have been treated earlier in its proper place; though, after all, it may be suitable that the women should have their turn on the stage when the men have quite finished their performance, especially since you are so insistent. In my judgment, then, the question under what conditions people born and educated as we have described should possess wives and children, and how

17. The question whether wisdom rules in the person of one man or of several is unimportant. In the sequel the ideal constitution is called kingship or aristocracy (the rule of the best) indifferently.

they should treat them, can be rightly settled only by keeping to the course on which we started them at the outset. We undertook to put these men in the position of watch-dogs guarding a flock. Suppose we follow up the analogy and imagine them bred and reared in the same sort of way. We can then see if that plan will suit our purpose.

How will that be?

In this way. Which do we think right for watch-dogs: should the females guard the flock and hunt with the males and take a share in all they do, or should they be kept within doors as fit for no more than bearing and feeding their puppies, while all the hard work of looking after the flock is left to the males?

They are expected to take their full share, except that we treat them as not quite so strong.

Can you employ any creature for the same work as another, if you do not give them both the same upbringing and education?

No.

Then, if we are to set women to the same tasks as men, we must teach them the same things. They must have the same two branches of training for mind and body and also be taught the art of war, and they must receive the same treatment.

That seems to follow.

Possibly, if these proposals were carried out, they might be ridiculed as involving a good many breaches of custom.

They might indeed.

The most ridiculous—don't you think?—being the notion of women exercising naked along with the men in the wrestling-schools; some of them elderly women too, like the old men who still have a passion for exercise when they are wrinkled and not very agreeable to look at.

Yes, that would be thought laughable, according to our present notions.

Now we have started on this subject, we must not be frightened of the many witticisms that might be aimed at such a revolution, not only in the matter of bodily exercise but in the training of women's minds, and not least when it comes to their bearing arms and riding on horseback. Having begun upon these rules, we must not draw back from the harsher provisions. The wits may be asked to stop being witty and try to be serious; and we may remind them that it is not so long since the Greeks, like most foreign nations of the present day, thought it ridiculous and shameful for men to be seen naked. When gymnastic exercises were first introduced in Crete and later at Sparta, the humorists had their chance to make fun of them; but when experience had shown that nakedness is better uncovered than muffled up, the laughter died down and a practice which the reason approved ceased to look ridiculous to the eye. This shows how idle it is to think anything ludicrous but what is base. One who tries to raise a laugh at any spectacle save that of baseness and folly will also, in his serious moments, set before himself some other standard than goodness of what deserves to be held in honour.

Most assuredly.

The first thing to be settled, then, is whether these proposals are feasible; and it must be open to anyone, whether a humorist or serious-minded, to raise the question whether a humorist or serious-minded, to raise question whether, in the case of mankind, the feminine nature is capable of taking part with the other sex in all occupations, or in none at all, or in some only; and in particular under which of these heads this business of military service falls. Well begun is half done, and would not this be the best way to begin?

Yes.

Shall we take the other side in this debate and argue against ourselves? We do not want the adversary's position to be taken by storm for lack of defenders.

I have no objection.

Let us state his case for him. "Sokrates and Glaucon," he will say, "there is no need for others to dispute your position; you yourselves, at the very outset of founding your commonwealth, agreed that everyone should do the one work for which nature fits him." Yes, of course; I suppose we did. "And isn't there a very great difference in nature between man and woman?" Yes, surely. "Does not that natural difference imply a corresponding difference in the work to be given to each?" Yes. "But if so, surely you must be mistaken now and contradicting yourselves when you say that men and women, having such widely divergent natures, should do the same things?" What is your answer to that, my ingenious friend?

It is not easy to find one at the moment. I can only appeal to you to state the case on our own side, whatever it may be.

This, Glaucon, is one of many alarming objections which I foresaw some time ago. That is why I shrank from touching upon these laws concerning the possession of wives and the rearing of children.

It looks like anything but an easy problem.

True, I said; but whether a man tumbles into a swimming-pool or into mid-ocean, he has to swim all the same. So must we, and try if we can reach the shore, hoping for some Arion's dolphin or other miraculous deliverance to bring us safe to land.[18]

I suppose so.

Come then, let us see if we can find the way out. We did agree that different natures should have different occupations, and that the natures of man and woman are different; and yet we are now saying that these different natures are to have the same occupations. Is that the charge against us?

Exactly.

It is extraordinary, Glaucon, what an effect the practice of debating has upon people.

Why do you say that?

Because they often seem to fall unconsciously into mere disputes which they mistake for reasonable argument, through being unable to draw the distinctions proper to their subject; and so, instead of a philosophical exchange of ideas, they go off in chase of contradictions which are purely verbal.

I know that happens to many people; but does it apply to us at this moment?

Absolutely. At least I am afraid we are slipping unconsciously into a dispute about words. We have been strenuously insisting on the letter of our principle that different natures should not have the same occupations, as if we were scoring a point in a debate; but we have altogether neglected to consider what sort of sameness or difference we meant and in what respect these natures and occupations were to be defined as different or the same. Consequently, we might very well be asking one another whether there is not an opposition in nature between bald and long-haired men, and, when that was admitted, forbid one set to be shoemakers, if the other were following that trade.

That would be absurd.

---

18. The musician Arion, to escape the treachery of Corinthian sailors, leapt into the sea and was carried ashore at Taenarum by a dolphin.

Yes, but only because we never meant any and every sort of sameness or difference in nature, but the sort that was relevant to the occupations in question. We meant, for instance, that a man and a woman have the same nature if both have a talent for medicine; whereas two men have different natures if one is a born physician, the other a born carpenter.

Yes, of course.

If, then, we find that either the male sex or the female is specially qualified for any particular form of occupation, then that occupation, we shall say, ought to be assigned to one sex or the other. But if the only difference appears to be that the male begets and the female brings forth, we shall conclude that no difference between man and woman has yet been produced that is relevant to our purpose. We shall continue to think it proper for our Guardians and their wives to share in the same pursuits.

And quite rightly.

The next thing will be to ask our opponent to name any profession or occupation in civic life for the purposes of which woman's nature is different from man's.

That is a fair question.

He might reply, as you did just now, that it is not easy to find a satisfactory answer on the spur of the moment, but that there would be no difficulty after a little reflection.

Perhaps.

Suppose, then, we invite him to follow us and see if we can convince him that there is no occupation concerned with the management of social affairs that is peculiar to women. We will confront him with a question: When you speak of a man having a natural talent for something, do you mean that he finds it easy to learn, and after a little instruction can find out much more for himself; whereas a man who is not so gifted learns with difficulty and no amount of instruction and practice will make him even remember what he has been taught? Is the talented man one whose bodily powers are readily at the service of his mind, instead of being a hindrance? Are not these the marks by which you distinguish the presence of a natural gift for any pursuit?

Yes, precisely.

Now do you know of any human occupation in which the male sex is not superior to the female in all these respects? Need I waste time over exceptions like weaving and watching over saucepans and batches of cakes, though women are supposed to be good at such things and get laughed at when a man does them better?

It is true, he replied, in almost everything one sex is easily beaten by the other. No doubt many women are better at many things than many men; but taking the sexes as a whole, it is as you say.

To conclude, then, there is no occupation concerned with the management of social affairs which belongs either to woman or to man, as such. Natural gifts are to be found here and there in both creatures alike; and every occupation is open to both, so far as their natures are concerned, though woman is for all purposes the weaker.

Certainly.

Is that a reason for making over all occupations to men only?

Of course not.

No, because one woman may have a natural gift for medicine or for music, another may not.

Surely.

Is it not also true that a woman may, or may not, be warlike or athletic?

I think so.

And again, one may love knowledge, another hate it; one may be high-spirited, another spiritless?

True again.

It follows that one woman will be fitted by nature to be a Guardian, another will not; because these were the qualities for which we selected our men Guardians. So for the purpose of keeping watch over the commonwealth, woman has the same nature as man, save in so far as she is weaker.

So it appears.

It follows that women of this type must be selected to share the life and duties of Guardians with men of the same type, since they are competent and of a like nature, and the same natures must be allowed the same pursuits.

Yes.

We come round, then, to our former position, that there is nothing contrary to nature in giving our Guardians' wives the same training for mind and body. The practice we proposed to establish was not impossible or visionary, since it was in accordance with nature. Rather, the contrary practice which now prevails turns out to be unnatural.

So it appears.

Well, we set out to inquire whether the plan we proposed was feasible and also the best. That it is feasible is now agreed; we must next settle whether it is the best.

Obviously.

Now, for the purpose of producing a woman fit to be a Guardian, we shall not have one education for men and another for women, precisely because the nature to be taken in hand is the same.

True.

What is your opinion on the question of one man being better than another? Do you think there is no such difference?

Certainly I do not.

And in this commonwealth of ours which will prove the better men—the Guardians who have received the education we described, or the shoemakers who have been trained to make shoes?[19]

It is absurd to ask such a question.

Very well. So these Guardians will be the best of all the citizens?

By far.

And these women the best of all the women?

Yes.

Can anything be better for a commonwealth than to produce in it men and women of the best possible type?

No.

And that result will be brought about by such a system of mental and bodily training as we have described?

Surely.

We may conclude that the institution we proposed was not only practicable, but also the best for the commonwealth.

Yes.

The wives of our Guardians, then, must strip for exercise, since they will be clothed with virtue, and they must take their share in war and in the other social duties of guardianship. They are to have no other occupation; and in these duties the lighter part must fall to the women, because of the weakness of their sex. The man who laughs at naked women, exercising their bodies for the best of reasons, is like one that "gathers fruit unripe,"

---

19. Elementary education will be open to all citizens, but presumably carried further (to the age of 17 or 18) in the case of those who show special promise.

for he does not know what it is that he is laughing at or what he is doing. There will never be a finer saying than the one which declares that whatever does good should be held in honour, and the only shame is in doing harm.

That is perfectly true.

Book V

Philosophers Must Be Kings

But really, Sokrates, Glaucon continued, if you are allowed to go on like this, I am afraid you will forget all about the question you thrust aside some time ago: whether a society so constituted can ever come into existence, and if so, how.

Well, said I, let me begin by reminding you that what brought us to this point was our inquiry into the nature of justice and injustice.

True; but what of that?

Merely this: suppose we do find out what justice is, are we going to demand that a man who is just shall have a character which exactly corresponds in every respect to the ideal of justice? Or shall we be satisfied if he comes as near to the ideal as possible and has in him a larger measure of that quality than the rest of the world?

That will satisfy me.

If so, when we set out to discover the essential nature of justice and injustice and what a perfectly just and perfectly unjust man would be like, supposing them to exist, our purpose was to use them as ideal patterns: we were to observe the degree of happiness or unhappiness that each exhibited, and to draw the necessary inference that our own destiny would be like that of the one we most resembled. We did not set out to show that these ideals could exist in fact.

That is true.

Then suppose a painter had drawn an ideally beautiful figure complete to the last touch, would you think any the worse of him, if he could not show that a person as beautiful as that could exist?

No, I should not.

Well, we have been constructing in discourse the pattern of an ideal state. Is our theory any the worse, if we cannot prove it possible that a state so organized should be actually founded?

Surely not.

That, then, is the truth of the matter. But if, for your satisfaction, I am to do my best to show under what conditions our ideal would have the best chance of being realized, I must ask you once more to admit that the same principle applies here. Can theory ever be fully realized in practice? Is it not in the nature of things that action should come less close to truth than thought? People may not think so; but do you agree or not?

I do.

Then you must not insist upon my showing that this construction we have traced in thought could be reproduced in fact down to the last detail. You must admit that we shall have found a way to meet your demand for realization, if we can discover how a state might be constituted in the closest accordance with our description. Will not that content you? It would be enough for me.

And for me too.

Then our next attempt, it seems, must be to point out what defect in the working of existing states prevents them from being so organized, and what is the least change that would effect a transformation into this type of government—a single change if possible, or perhaps two; at any rate let us make the changes as few and insignificant as may be.

By all means.

Well, there is one change which, as I believe we can show, would bring about this revolution—not a small change, certainly, nor an easy one, but possible.

What is it?

I have now to confront what we called the third and greatest wave. But I must state my paradox, even though the wave should break in laughter over my head and drown me in ignominy. Now mark what I am going to say.

Go on.

Unless either philosophers become kings in their countries or those who are now called kings and rulers come to be sufficiently inspired with a genuine desire for wisdom; unless, that is to say, political power and philosophy meet together, while the many natures who now go their several ways in the one or the other direction are forcibly debarred from doing so, there can be no rest from troubles, my dear Glaucon, for states, nor yet, as I believe, for all mankind; nor can this commonwealth which we have imagined ever till then see the light of day and grow to its full stature. This it was that I have so long hung back from saying; I knew what a paradox it would be, because it is hard to see that there is no other way of happiness either for the state or for the individual.

Book VII

The Allegory of the Cave

Next, said I, here is a parable to illustrate the degrees in which our nature may be enlightened or unenlightened. Imagine the condition of men living in a sort of cavernous chamber underground, with an entrance open to the light and a long passage all down the cave.[20] Here they have been from childhood, chained by the leg and also by the neck, so that they cannot move and can see only what is in front of them, because the chains will not let them turn their heads. At some distance higher up is the light of a fire burning behind them; and between the prisoners and the fire is a track[21] with a parapet built along it, like the screen at a puppet-show, which hides the performers while they show their puppets over the top.

I see, said he.

Now behind this parapet imagine persons carrying along various artificial objects, including figures of men and animals in wood or stone or other materials, which project above the parapet. Naturally, some of these persons will be talking, others silent.[22]

It is a strange picture, he said, and a strange sort of prisoners.

---

20. The *length* of the "way in" *(eisodos)* to the chamber where the prisoners sit is an essential feature, explaining why no daylight reaches them.

21. The track crosses the passage into the cave at right angles, and is *above* the parapet built along it.

22. A modern Plato would compare his Cave to an underground cinema, where the audience watch the play of shadows thrown by the film passing before a light at their backs. The film itself is only an image of "real" things and events in the world outside the cinema.

For the film Plato has to substitute the clumsier apparatus of a procession of artificial objects carried on their heads by persons who are merely part of the machinery, providing for the movement of the objects and the sounds whose echo the prisoners hear. The parapet prevents these persons' shadows from being cast on the wall of the Cave.

Like ourselves, I replied; for in the first place prisoners so confined would have seen nothing of themselves or of one another, except the shadows thrown by the fire-light on the wall of the Cave facing them, would they?

Not if all their lives they had been prevented from moving their heads.

And they would have seen as little of the objects carried past.

Of course.

Now, if they could talk to one another, would they not suppose that their words referred only to those passing shadows which they saw?[23]

Necessarily.

And suppose their prison had an echo from the wall facing them? When one of the people crossing behind them spoke, they could only suppose that the sound came from the shadow passing before their eyes.

No doubt.

In every way, then, such prisoners would recognize as reality nothing but the shadows of those artificial objects.

Inevitably.

Now consider what would happen if their release from the chains and the healing of their unwisdom should come about in this way. Suppose one of them set free and forced suddenly to stand up, turn his head, and walk with eyes lifted to the light; all these movements would be painful, and he would be too dazzled to make out the objects whose shadows he had been used to see. What do you think he would say, if someone told him that what he had formerly seen was meaningless illusion, but now, being somewhat nearer to reality and turned towards more real objects, he was getting a truer view? Suppose further that he were shown the various objects being carried by and were made to say, in reply to questions, what each of them was. Would he not be perplexed and believe the objects now shown him to be not so real as what he formerly saw?

Yes, not nearly so real.

And if he were forced to look at the fire-light itself, would not his eyes ache, so that he would try to escape and turn back to the things which he could see distinctly, convinced that they really were clearer than these other objects now being shown to him?

Yes.

And suppose someone were to drag him away forcibly up the steep and rugged ascent and not let him go until he had hauled him out into the sunlight, would he not suffer pain and vexation at such treatment, and, when he had come out into the light, find his eyes so full of its radiance that he could not see a single one of the things that he was now told were real?

Certainly he would not see them all at once.

He would need, then, to grow accustomed before he could see things in that upper world. At first it would be easiest to make out shadows, and then the images of men and things reflected in water, and later on the things themselves. After that, it would be easier to watch the heavenly bodies and the sky itself by night, looking at the light of the moon and stars rather than the Sun and the Sun's light in the day-time.

Yes, surely.

Last of all, he would be able to look at the Sun and contemplate its nature, not as it appears when reflected in water or any alien medium, but as it is in itself in its own domain.

No doubt.

And now he would begin to draw the conclusion that it is the Sun that produces the seasons and the course of the year and controls everything in the visible world, and moreover is in a way the cause of all that he and his companions used to see.

Clearly he would come at last to that conclusion.

Then if he called to mind his fellow prisoners and what passed for wisdom in his former dwelling-place, he would surely think himself happy in the change and be sorry for them. They may have had a practice of honouring and commending one another, with prizes for the man who had the keenest eye for the passing shadows and the best memory for he order in which they followed or accompanied one another, so that he could make a good guess as to which was going to come next. Would our released prisoner be likely to covet those prizes or to envy the men exalted to honour and power in the Cave? Would he not feel like Homer's Akhilleus, that he would far sooner "be on earth as a hired servant in the house of a landless man" or endure anything rather than go back to his old beliefs and live in the old way?

Yes, he would prefer any fate to such a life.

Now imagine what would happen if he went down again to take his former seat in the Cave. Coming suddenly out of the sunlight, his eyes would be filled with darkness. He might be required once more to deliver his opinion on those shadows, in competition with the prisoners who had never been released, while his eyesight was still dim and unsteady; and it might take some time to become used to the darkness. They would laugh at him and say that he had gone up only to come back with his sight ruined; it was worth no one's while even to attempt the ascent. If they could lay hands on the man who was trying to set them free and lead them up, they would kill him.[24]

Yes, they would.

Application of the Cave Allegory

Every feature in this parable, my dear Glaucon, is meant to fit our earlier analysis. The prison dwelling corresponds to the region revealed to us through the sense of sight, and the fire-light within it to the power of the Sun. The ascent to see the things in the upper world you may take as standing for the upward journey of the soul into the region of the intelligible; then you will be in possession of what I surmise, since that is what you wish to be told. Heaven knows whether it is true; but this, at any rate, is how it appears to me. In the world of knowledge, the last thing to be perceived and only with great difficulty is the essential Form of Goodness. Once it is perceived, the conclusion must follow that, for all things, this is the cause of whatever is right and good; in the visible world it gives birth to light and to the lord of light, while it is itself sovereign in the intelligible world and the parent of intelligence and truth. Without having had a vision of this Form no one can act with wisdom, either in his own life or in matters of state.

So far as I can understand, I share your belief.

Then you may also agree that it is no wonder if those who have reached this height are reluctant to manage the affairs of men. Their souls long to spend all their time in

---

23. Adam's text and interpretation. The prisoners, having seen nothing but shadows, cannot think their words refer to the objects carried past behind their backs. For them shadows (images) are the only realities.

---

24. An allusion to the fate of Sokrates.

that upper world—naturally enough, if here once more our parable holds true. Nor, again, is it at all strange that one who comes from the contemplation of divine things to the miseries of human life should appear awkward and ridiculous when, with eyes still dazed and not yet accustomed to the darkness, he is compelled, in a law-court or elsewhere, to dispute about the shadows of justice or the images that cast those shadows, and to wrangle over the notions of what is right in the minds of men who have never beheld Justice itself.

It is not at all strange.

No; a sensible man will remember that the eyes may be confused in two ways—by a change from light to darkness or from darkness to light; and he will recognize that the same thing happens to the soul. When he sees it troubled and unable to discern anything clearly, instead of laughing thoughtlessly, he will ask whether, coming from a brighter existence, its unaccustomed vision is obscured by the darkness, in which case he will think its condition enviable and its life a happy one; or whether, emerging from the depths of ignorance, it is dazzled by excess of light. If so, he will rather feel sorry for it; or, if he were inclined to laugh, that would be less ridiculous than to laugh at the soul which has come down from the light.

That is a fair statement.

If this is true, then, we must conclude that education is not what it is said to be by some, who profess to put knowledge into a soul which does not possess it, as if they could put sight into blind eyes. On the contrary, our own account signifies that the soul of every man does possess the power of learning the truth and the organ to see it with; and that, just as one might have to turn the whole body round in order that the eye should see light instead of darkness, so the entire soul must be turned away from this changing world, until its eye can bear to contemplate reality and that supreme splendour which we have called the Good. Hence there may well be an art whose aim would be to effect this very thing, the conversion of the soul, in the readiest way; not to put the power of sight into the soul's eye, which already has it, but to ensure that, instead of looking in the wrong direction, it is turned the way it ought to be.

Yes, it may well be so.

It looks, then, as though wisdom were different from those ordinary virtues, as they are called, which are not far removed from bodily qualities, in that they can be produced by habituation and exercise in a soul which has not possessed them from the first. Wisdom, it seems, is certainly the virtue of some diviner faculty, which never loses its power, though its use for good or harm depends on the direction towards which it is turned. You must have noticed in dishonest men with a reputation for sagacity the shrewd glance of a narrow intelligence piercing the objects to which it is directed. There is nothing wrong with their power of vision, but it has been forced into the service of evil, so that the keener its sight, the more harm it works.

Quite true.

And yet if the growth of a nature like this had been pruned from earliest childhood, cleared of those clinging overgrowths which come of gluttony and all luxurious pleasure and, like leaden weights charged with affinity to this mortal world, hang upon the soul, bending its vision downwards; if, freed from these, the soul were turned round towards true reality, then this same power in these very men would see the truth as keenly as the objects it is turned to now.

Yes, very likely.

Is it not also likely, or indeed certain after what has been said, that a state can never be properly governed either by the uneducated who know nothing of truth or by men who are allowed to spend all their days in the pursuit of culture? The ignorant have no single mark before their eyes at which they must aim in all the conduct of their own lives and of affairs of state; and the others will not engage in action if they can help it, dreaming that, while still alive, they have been translated to the Islands of the Blest.

Quite true.

It is for us, then, as founders of a commonwealth, to bring compulsion to bear on the noblest natures. They must be made to climb the ascent to the vision of Goodness, which we called the highest object of knowledge; and, when they have looked upon it long enough, they must not be allowed, as they now are, to remain on the heights, refusing to come down again to the prisoners or to take any part in their labours and rewards, however much or little these may be worth.

Shall we not be doing them an injustice, if we force on them a worse life than they might have?

You have forgotten again, my friend, that the law is not concerned to make any one class specially happy, but to ensure the welfare of the commonwealth as a whole. By persuasion or constraint it will unite the citizens in harmony, making them share whatever benefits each class can contribute to the common good; and its purpose in forming men of that spirit was not that each should be left to go his own way, but that they should be instrumental in binding the community into one.

True, I had forgotten.

You will see, then, Glaucon, that there will be no real injustice in compelling our philosophers to watch over and care for the other citizens. We can fairly tell them that their compeers in others states may quite reasonably refuse to collaborate: there they have sprung up, like a self-sown plant, in despite of their country's institutions; no one has fostered their growth, and they cannot be expected to show gratitude for a care they have never received. "But," we shall say, "it is not so with you. We have brought you into existence for your country's sake as well as for your own, to be like leaders and king-bees in a hive; you have been better and more thoroughly educated than those others and hence you are more capable of playing your part both as men of thought and as men of action. You must go down, then, each in his turn, to live with the rest and let your eyes grow accustomed to the darkness. You will then see a thousand times better than those who live there always; you will recognize every image for what it is and know what it represents, because you have seen justice, beauty, and goodness in their reality; and so you and we shall find life in our commonwealth no mere dream, as it is in most existing states, where men live fighting one another about shadows and quarrelling for power, as if that were a great prize; whereas in truth government can be at its best and free from dissension only where the destined rulers are least desirous of holding office."

Quite true.

Then will our pupils refuse to listen and to take their turns at sharing in the work of the community, though they may live together for most of their time in a purer air?

No; it is a fair demand, and they are fair-minded men. No doubt, unlike any ruler of the present day, they will think of holding power as an unavoidable necessity.

Yes, my friend; for the truth is that you can have a well-governed society only if you can discover for your future rulers a better way of life than being in office; then only will power be in the hands of men who are rich, not in gold, but in the wealth that brings happiness, a good and wise life. All goes wrong when, starved for lack of anything good in their own lives, men turn to public affairs hoping to snatch from thence the happiness they hunger for. They set about fighting for power, and this internecine conflict ruins them and their country. The life of true philosophy is the only one that looks down upon offices of state; and access to power must be confined to men who are not in love with it; otherwise rivals will start fighting. So whom else can you compel to undertake the guardianship of the commonwealth, if not those who, besides understanding best the principles of government, enjoy a nobler life than the politician's and look for rewards of a different kind?

There is indeed no other choice.

Exercises

1. Women in ancient Greece were generally considered inferior beings who were necessarily subordinate to men, and they are so treated in Plato's works except for the *Republic*. What changes has Plato made in his ideal state that gives women equality and equal opportunity to become guardians and philosopher-kings? What does this imply in regard to equal opportunity for women of today?

2. Are Plato's arguments for the equality of women convincing? Would they be persuasive today? How might leaders of NOW (National Organization for Women) state the issues?

3. How would the state function "if philosophers were kings"? What might the problems be? How might they be resolved?

4. In the history of Western civilization have there been any philosopher-kings? Who were they? To what extent were they selfless, wise, virtuous, and, most importantly, successful?

5. One way to visualize the situation in the Allegory of the Cave is to think of people chained in a movie theater with everyone facing the screen. In the allegory the pictures on the screen are the world of which our senses are aware. "Reality" is the series of moving images on the screen, complete with soundtrack, and the highest reality is the light that projects the images. Another, more depressing situation, would be people chained in front of a TV set in which the highest reality would be ABC, CBS, or NBC. Given, say, CBS as the ultimate reality, what are the implications? To what extent does Plato's allegory apply to modern life in the electronic age?

6. In the "Allegory of the Cave" why does Plato insist that the one who has come to know the true light *must* return to the cave, that he or she must partake of the labors and honors of the people in the cave, even though these are recognized as foolish?

POETICS

Aristotle (384–322 B.C.)

Aristotle's *Poetics*[25] is a critical examination of the nature of art and what constitutes good art. Specifically, the treatise is directed to the problems of poetry in the writing of tragedy, which Aristotle feels is the highest form of art. With no word for *fine art,* the Greek term for art is *techne,* which also translates as "craft" or "skill." Art is therefore the "making" of a thing that in its highest form is crafted with exceptional skill. The *Poetics* is the first clear statement in the history of aesthetics correlating the experience of a work of art with the skill of making the work itself.

For Aristotle, all art is an imitation of nature, and tragedy is

the imitation of an action that is serious and also, as having magnitude, complete in itself; in language with pleasurable accessories, each kind brought in separately in the parts of the work; in a dramatic, not a narrative form; with incidents arousing pity and fear, wherewith to accomplish a katharsis of such emotions.

The theoretical perfect plot of a tragedy must have a single issue, which should be resolved within a twenty-four-hour day. Further, a good man will be reduced from happiness to misery because of some great error on his part, his so-called "fatal flaw."

The six elements of a tragedy are:

Plot (Fable). The action, what happens.
Character. Moral qualities of the agents.
Diction. Metrical structure of the poetry as revealed in speech, recitation, chant, or song.
Thought. Implied themes and theses (universal truths) as exposed by all the elements together.
Spectacle. The stage appearance of set, costumes, movement, dance.
Melody. Aristotle takes this for granted, i.e., it is "too completely understood to require explanation." Melody refers to tunes played on the aulos (see p. 192) and the musical reciting, chanting, and singing of the actors and the chorus. With the statement that "melody is the greatest of the pleasurable accessories of tragedy," Aristotle acknowledges the sensual elements of tragedy.

The *Poetics* ends with the discussion of tragedy, although Aristotle had earlier stated that he would also deal with comedy and other kinds of poetry. Even as an incomplete work, this has been one of the most influential of Aristotle's treatises.

The objects the imitator represents are actions, with agents who are necessarily either good men or bad—the diversities of human character being nearly always derivative from this primary distinction, since the line between virtue and vice is one dividing the whole of mankind. It follows, therefore, that the agents represented must be either above our own level of

---

25. Aristotle, *De Arte Poetika.* Translated by Ingram Bywater, 1911, with omissions.

goodness, or beneath it, or just such as we are. It is clear that each of the arts will admit of these differences, and that it will become a separate art by representing objects with this point of difference. Even in dancing, flute-playing, and lyre-playing such diversities are possible; and they are also possible in the nameless art that uses language, prose or verse without harmony, as its means. This difference it is that distinguishes Tragedy and Comedy also; the one would make its personages worse, and the other better, than the men of the present day.

A third difference in these arts is in the manner in which each kind of object is represented. Given both the same means and the same kind of object for imitation, one may either (1) speak at one moment in narrative and at another as an assumed character, as Homer does; or (2) one may remain the same throughout, without any such change; or (3) the imitators may represent the whole story dramatically, as though they were actually doing the things described. Therefore, the differences in the imitation of these arts comes under three heads, their means, their objects, and their manner.

It is clear that the general origin of poetry was due to two causes, each of them part of human nature. Imitation is natural to man since childhood, one of his advantages over the lower animals being this, that he is the most imitative creature in the world, and learns at first by imitation. And it is also natural for all to delight in works of imitation. The truth of this second point is shown by experience: though the objects themselves may be painful to see, we delight to view the most realistic representations of them in art, the forms for example of the lowest animals and of dead bodies. The explanation is to be found in a further fact: to be learning something is the greatest of pleasures not only to the philosopher but also to the rest of mankind, however small their capacity for it; the reason of the delight in seeing the picture is that one is at the same time learning—gathering the meaning of things, e.g. that the man there is so-and-so; for if one has not seen the things before, one's pleasure will not be in the picture as an imitation of it, but will be due to the execution or coloring or some similar cause. Imitation, then, being natural to us—as also the sense of harmony and rhythm, the meters being obviously species of rhythms—it was through their original aptitude, and by a series of improvements for the most part gradual on their first efforts, that they created poetry out of their improvisations.

Poetry, however, soon broke up into two kinds according to the differences of character in the individual poets; for the graver among them would represent noble actions, and those of noble personages; and the meaner sort the actions of the ignoble. The latter class produced invectives at first, just as others did hymns and panegyrics. We know of no such poem by any of the pre-Homeric poets, though there were probably many such writers among them; instances, however, may be found from Homer downwards, e.g. his *Margites,* and similar poems of others. In this poetry of invectives its natural fitness brought an iambic meter into use; hence our present term "iambic," because it was the meter of their "iambs" or invectives against one another. The result was that some of the old poets became writers of heroic and others of iambic verse. Homer's position, however, is peculiar: just as he was in the serious style the poet of poets, standing alone not only through the literary excellence, but also through the dramatic character of his imitations, so too he was the first to outline for us the general forms of Comedy

by producing not a dramatic invective, but a dramatic picture of the Ridiculous; his *Margites* in fact stands in the same relation to our comedies as the *Iliad* and the *Odyssey* to our tragedies. As soon, however, as Tragedy and Comedy appeared in the field, those naturally drawn to the one line of poetry became writers of comedies instead of iambs, and those naturally drawn to the other, writers of tragedies instead of epics, because these new modes of art were grander and of more esteem than the old. If it be asked whether Tragedy is now all that it need be in its formative elements, to consider that, and decide it theoretically and in relation to the theaters, is a matter for further inquiry.

It certainly began in improvisations—as did also Comedy; the one originating with the authors of the Dithyramb, the other with those of the phallic songs, which still survive as institutions in many of our cities. And its advance after that was little by little, through their improving on whatever they had before them at each stage. It was in fact only after a long series of changes that the movement of Tragedy stopped on attaining its natural form. (1) The number of actors was first increased to two by Aeschylus, who curtailed the business of the Chorus, and made the dialogue, or spoken portion, take the leading part in the play. (2) A third actor and scenery were due to Sophokles. (3) Tragedy acquired also its magnitude. Discarding short stories and a ludicrous diction, through its passing out of its satyric stage, it assumed, though only at a late point in its progress, a tone of dignity; and its meter changed from trochaic to iambic. The reason for their original use of the trochaic tetrameter was that their poetry was satyric and more connected with dancing than it now is. As soon, however, as a spoken part came in, nature herself found the appropriate meter. The iambic, we know, is the most speakable of meters, as is shown by the fact that we very often fall into it in conversation, whereas we rarely talk hexameters, and only when we do depart from the speaking tone of voice. (4) Another change was a plurality of episodes or acts.

As for Comedy, it is (as has been observed) an imitation of men worse than the average; worse, however, not as regards any and every sort of fault, but only as regards one particular kind, the Ridiculous, which is a species of the Ugly. The Ridiculous may be defined as a mistake or deformity not productive of pain or harm to others; the mask, for instance, that excites laughter , is something ugly and distorted without causing pain.

Though the successive changes in Tragedy and their authors are not unknown, we cannot say the same of Comedy; its early stages passed unnoticed, because it was not yet taken up in a serious way. It was only at a late point in its progress that a chorus of comedians was officially granted by the archon; they used to be mere volunteers. It had also already certain definite forms at the time when the record of those termed comic poets begins. Who it was who supplied it with masks, or prologues, or a plurality of actors and the like, has remained unknown.

Epic poetry has been seen to agree with Tragedy to this extent, that of being an imitation of serious subjects in a grand kind of verse. It differs from it, however, (1) in that it is in one kind of verse and in narrative form; and (2) in its length—which is due to its action having no fixed limit of time, whereas Tragedy endeavors to keep as far as possible within a single circuit of the sun, or something near that. This, I say, is another point of difference between them, though at first the practice in this respect was just the same in tragedies as in epic poems. They differ also (3) in their constituents, some being common to both and others peculiar to Tragedy—hence a judge of good and bad in Tragedy is a judge of that in epic poetry also. All of the parts of an epic are included in Tragedy; but those of Tragedy are not all of them to be found in the Epic.

Let us proceed now to the discussion of Tragedy; before doing so, however, we must gather up the definition resulting from what has been said. A tragedy, then, is the imitation of an action that is serious and also, as having magnitude, complete in itself; in language with pleasurable accessories, each kind brought in separately in the parts of the work; in a dramatic, not a narrative form; with incidents arousing pity and fear, wherewith to accomplish its katharsis of such emotions. Here by "language with pleasurable accessories" I mean that with rhythm and harmony or song superadded; and by "the kinds separately" I mean that some portions are worked out with verse only, and others in turn with song.

As they act the stories, it follows that in the first place the Spectacle (or stage-appearance of the actors) must be some part of the whole; and in the second Melody and Diction; these two being the means of their imitation. Here by "Diction" I mean merely this, the composition of the verses; and by "melody," what is too completely understood to require explanation. But further: the subject represented also is an action; and the action involves agents, who must necessarily have their distinctive qualities both of character and thought, since it is from these that we ascribe certain qualities to their actions. There are in the natural order of things, therefore, two causes, Thought and Character, of their actions, and consequently of their success or failure in their lives. Now the action (that which was done) is represented in the play by the Fable or Plot. The Fable, in our present sense of the term is simply this, the combination of the incidents, or things done in the story; whereas Character is what makes us ascribe certain moral qualities to the agents; and Thought is shown in all they say when proving a particular point or, it may be, enunciating a general truth. There are six parts consequently of every tragedy, as a whole (that is) of such or such quality, viz. a Fable or Plot, Characters, Diction, Thought, Spectacle, and Melody; two of them arising from the means, one from the manner, and three from the objects of the dramatic imitation; and there is nothing else besides these six. Of these, its formative elements, then, not a few of the dramatists have made due use, as every play, one may say, admits of Spectacle, Character, Fable, Diction, Melody, and Thought.

The most important of the six is the combination of the incidents of the story. Tragedy is essentially an imitation not of persons but of action and life, of happiness and misery. All human happiness or misery takes the form of action; the end for which we live is a certain kind of activity, not a quality. Character gives us qualities, but it is in our actions—what we do—that we are happy or the reverse. In a play accordingly they do not act in order to portray the Characters; they include the Characters for the sake of the action. So that it is the action in it, i.e. its Fable or Plot, that is the end and purpose of the tragedy; and the end is everywhere the chief thing. Besides this, a tragedy is impossible without action, but there may be one without Character.

The first essential, the life and soul, so to speak, of Tragedy is the Plot; the Characters come second—

compare the parallel in painting, where the most beautiful colors laid on without order will not give one the same pleasure as a simple black-and-white sketch of a portrait. We maintain that Tragedy is primarily an imitation of action, and that it is mainly for the sake of the action that it imitates the personal agents. Third comes the element of Thought, i.e. the power of saying whatever can be said, or what is appropriate to the occasion. One must not confuse it with Character. Character in a play is that which reveals the moral purpose of the agents, i.e. the sort of thing they seek or avoid, where that is not obvious—hence there is no room for Character in a speech on a purely indifferent subject. Thought, on the other hand, is shown in all they say when proving or disproving some particular point, or enunciating some universal proposition. Fourth among the literary elements is the Diction of the personages, the expression of their thoughts in words, which is practically the same thing with verse as with prose. As for the two remaining parts, the Melody is the greatest of the pleasurable accessories of Tragedy.The Spectacle, though an attraction, is the least artistic of all the parts, and has least to do with the art of poetry. The tragic effect is quite possible without a public performance and actors; and besides, the getting-up of the Spectacle is more a matter for the costumier than the poet.

Let us now consider the proper construction of the Fable or Plot, as that is at once the first and the most important thing in Tragedy. We have laid it down that a tragedy is an imitation of an action that is complete in itself, as a whole of some magnitude; for a whole may be of no magnitude to speak of. Now a whole is that which has beginning, middle, and end. A beginning is that which is naturally after something itself, either as its necessary or usual consequent, and with nothing else after it; and a middle, that which is by nature after one thing and has also another after it. A well-constructed Plot, therefore, cannot either begin or end at any point one likes; beginning and end in it must be of the forms just described. Again: to be beautiful, a living creature, and every whole made up of parts, must not only present a certain order in its arrangement of parts, but also be of a certain definite magnitude. Beauty is a matter of size and order, and therefore impossible either (1) in a very minute creature, since our perception becomes indistinct as it approaches instantaneity; or (2) in a creature of vast size, so large that its unity and wholeness is lost to the beholder. Just in the same way, then, as a beautiful whole made up of parts, or a beautiful living creature, must be of some size, but a size to be taken in by the eye, so a story or Plot must be of some length, but of a length to be taken in by the memory. The limit set by the actual nature of the thing is this: the longer the story, consistently with its being comprehensible as a whole, the finer it is by reason of its magnitude. As a rough general formula, a length which allows of the hero passing by a series of probable or necessary stages from misfortune to happiness, or from happiness to misfortune, may suffice as a limit for the magnitude of the story.

The Unity of a Plot does not consist, as some suppose, in its having one man as its subject. An infinity of things befall that one man, some of which it is impossible to reduce to unity; and in like manner there are many actions of one man which cannot be made to form one action. The truth is that, just as in the other imitative arts one imitation is always of one thing, so in poetry the story, as an imitation of action, must represent one action, a complete whole, with its several incidents so closely connected with the transposal or withdrawal of any one of them will disjoin and dislocate the whole. For that which makes no perceptible difference by its presence or absence is no real part of the whole.

From what we have said it will be seen that the poet's function is to describe, not the thing that has happened, but a kind of thing that might happen, i.e. what is possible as being probable or necessary. The distinction between historian and poet is not in the one writing prose and the other verse—you might put the work of Herodotos into verse, and it would still be a species of history; it consists really in this, that the one describes the thing that has been, and the other a kind of thing that might be. Hence poetry is something more philosophic and of graver import than history, since its statements are of the nature rather of universals, whereas those of history are singulars. By a universal statement I mean one as to what such or such a kind of man will probably or necessarily say or do—which is the aim of poetry, though it affixes proper names to the characters.

It is evident that the poet must be more the poet of his stories or Plots than of his verses, inasmuch as he is a poet by virtue of the imitative element in his work, and it is actions that he imitates. And if he should come to a subject from actual history, he is none the less a poet for that; since some historic occurrences may very well be in the probable and possible order of things; and it is in that aspect of them that he is their poet.

Tragedy is an imitation not only of a complete action but also of incidents arousing pity and fear. Such incidents have the very greatest effect on the mind when they occur unexpectedly and at the same time in consequence of one another; there is more of the marvelous in them then than if they happened of themselves or by mere chance. Even matters of chance seem most marvelous if there is an appearance of design as it were in them. A Plot, therefore, of this sort is necessarily finer than others.

The next points after what we have said above will be these: (1) What is the poet to aim at, and what is he to avoid, in constructing his Plots? and (2) What are the conditions on which the tragic effect depends?

We assume that, for the finest form of Tragedy, the Plot must be not simple but complex; and further, that it must imitate actions arousing fear and pity, since that is the distinctive function of this kind of imitation. It follows, therefore, that there are three forms of Plot to be avoided. ① A good man must not be seen passing from happiness to misery, or ② a bad man from misery to happiness. The first situation is not fear-inspiring or piteous, but simply odious to us. The second is the most untragic that can be; it has no one of the requisites of Tragedy; it does not appeal either to the human feeling in us, or to our pity, or to our fears. Nor, on the other hand, should ③ an extremely bad man be seen falling from happiness into misery. Such a story may arouse the human feeling in us, but it will not move us to either pity or fear; pity is occasioned by undeserved misfortune, and fear by that of one like ourselves; so that there will be nothing either piteous or fear-inspiring in the situation. There remains, then, the intermediate kind of personage, a man not pre-eminently virtuous and just, whose misfortune, however, is brought upon him not by vice or depravity but by some error of judgement, of the number of those in the enjoyment of great reputation and

prosperity, e.g.: Oedipus, Thyestes, and the men of note of similar families. The perfect Plot, accordingly, must have a single, and not (as some tell us) a double issue; the change in the hero's fortunes must be not from misery to happiness, but on the contrary from happiness to misery; and the cause of it must lie not in any depravity, but in some great error on his part; the man himself being either such as we have described, or better ,not worse than that. The theoretically best tragedy, then, has a Plot of this description. The critics, therefore, are wrong who blame Euripides for taking this line in his tragedies, and giving many of them an unhappy ending. It is, as we have said, the right line to take.

The tragic fear and pity may be aroused by the Spectacle; but they may also be aroused by the very structure and incidents of the play—which is the better way and shows the better poet. The Plot in fact should be so framed that, even without seeing the things take place, he who simply hears the account of them shall be filled with horror and pity at the incidents; which is just the effect that the mere recital of the story of *Oedipus* would have on one. To produce the same effect by means of the Spectacle is less artistic, and requires extraneous aid. Those, however, who make use of the Spectacle to put before us that which is merely monstrous and not productive of fear, are wholly out of touch with Tragedy; not every kind of pleasure should be required of a tragedy, but only its own proper pleasure.

The tragic pleasure is that of pity and fear, and the poet has to produce it by a work of imitation; it is clear, therefore, that the causes should be included in the incidents of his story. Let us see, then, what kinds of incident strike one as horrible, or rather as piteous. In a deed of this description the parties must necessarily be either friends, or enemies, or indifferent to one another. Now when enemy does it on enemy, there is nothing to move us to pity either in his doing or in his meditating the deed, except so far as the actual pain of the sufferer is concerned; and the same is true when the parties are indifferent to one another. Whenever the tragic deed, however, is done within the family—when murder or the like is done or meditated by brother on brother, by son on father, by mother on son, or son on mother—these are the situations the poet should seek after. The traditional stories, accordingly, must be kept as they are, e.g. the murder of Klytaïmnestra by Orestes.

In the Characters there are four points to aim at. First and foremost, that they shall be good. There will be an element of character in the play, if (as has been observed) what a personage says or does reveals a certain moral purpose; and a good element of character, if the purpose so revealed is good. Such goodness is possible in every type of personage, even in a woman or a slave, though the one is perhaps an inferior, and the other a wholly worthless being. The second point is to make them appropriate. The Character before us may be, say, manly; but it is not appropriate in a female Character to be manly, or clever. The third is to make them like the reality, which is not the same as their being good and appropriate, in our sense of the term. The fourth is to make them consistent and the same throughout; even if inconsistency be part of the man before one for imitation as presenting that form of character, he should still be consistently inconsistent.

There should be nothing improbable among the actual incidents. If it be unavoidable, however, it should be outside the tragedy, like the improbability in the *Oedipus* of Sophokles. But to return to the Characters. As

Tragedy is an imitation of personages better than the ordinary man, we in our way should follow the example of the good portrait-painters, who reproduce the distinctive features of a man, and at the same time, without losing the likeness, make him handsomer than he is. The poet in like manner, in portraying men quick or slow to anger, or with similar infirmities of character, must know how to represent them as such, and at the same time as good men, as Agathon and Homer have represented Akhilleus.

The Plot and Characters having been discussed, it remains to consider the Diction and the Thought. As for the Thought, we may assume what is said of it in our Art of Rhetoric, as it belongs more properly to that department of inquiry. The Thought of the personages is shown in everything to be effected by their language—in every effort to prove or disprove, to arouse emotion (pity, fear, anger, and the like) or to maximize or minimize things. It is clear, also, that their mental procedure must be on the same lines in their actions likewise, whenever they wish them to arouse pity or horror, or to have a look of importance or probability. The only difference is that with the act the impression has to be made without explanation; whereas with the spoken word it has to be produced by the speaker, and result from his language. What, indeed, would be the good of the speaker, if things appeared in the required light even apart from anything he says?

As regards the diction, one subject for inquiry under this head is the turns given to the language when spoken; e.g. the difference between command and prayer, simple statement and threat, question and answer, and so forth. The theory of such matters, however, belongs to Elocution and the professors of that art. Whether the poet knows these things or not, his art as a poet is never seriously criticized on that account. What fault can one see in Homer's "Sing of the wrath, Goddess"?—which Protagoras has criticized as being a command where a prayer was meant, since to bid one do or not do, he tells us, is a command. Let us pass over this, then, as appertaining to another art, and not to that of poetry.

Let this, then, suffice as an account of Tragedy, the art imitating by means of action on the stage.

Exercises

1. Aristotle contends that the ultimate aim of tragedy is to inspire pity and fear, which will be removed through a *katharsis* (Gk., to purify). Does he mean a kind of religious experience that will purge the soul? Or is the implication medical, like cleansing the body of poisons? Is there another explanation? Can the katharsis theory be applied to any one of the four tragedies that are included in chapter 5? Which ones? Why? Note: *Agamemnon* and the *Eumenides* should be considered as the beginning and end of a trilogy, with the katharsis theory applied to the *Eumenides*.
2. Review the six elements of tragedy and apply them to each of the four tragedies. Which play most closely resembles Aristotle's basic elements?
3. Consider *Oedipus* in terms of Aristotle's "unities." Is there a single, complete issue that is resolved? Does the time span conform to Aristotle's dictum?
4. What is the "fatal flaw" of Oedipus?
5. In the *Poetics* Aristotle uses the phrase "even in a woman or a slave, though one is perhaps an inferior, and the other a wholly worthless being." What does this say about the status of women (and slaves) in Athenian society? Why does he qualify the reference to women, i.e., "perhaps inferior"? Is there some doubt in his mind? Could this doubt have something to do with dramatic characters such as Klytaïmnestra, Antigone, Medea, and Lysistrata?
6. What is the "improbability" in *Oedipus* that Aristotle allows because it is outside the time frame of the play?

Summary

Greek civilization had started within the shadow of superstition and tradition in ancient times. Slowly those bondages had been cut away until a very delicate balance was achieved between the freedom of each individual person and the welfare of the group in Athens early in the reign of Perikles. The philosophers, the writers, and the artists of the time took an active interest in politics, and conducted their affairs in the bright sunlight of the Agora.

But change is inevitable. In Athens it would seem that the knife-edge between individuality and the welfare of the group was too thin, the balance on it too precarious, for a group of people to maintain an equilibrium for a long period of time. The skeptical sophists taught that complete individuality was the goal—violating Aeschylus's doctrine of the mean between autocracy and anarchy. The original strength of the city was sapped, but to give rise to a new and different kind of strength in the broadened horizons of Hellenistic culture. It is interesting that both Plato and Aristotle (except for their brief efforts to educate a king: Plato as tutor for the Syracusan Dionysius, Aristotle as Alexander's tutor) stood apart from politics and the vigorous life of the time; they deserted the active marketplace. They were contemplatives, aware that something had gone wrong, that the dream had somehow failed, and each in his own way, introspected into himself and his culture to discover what had failed. Probably nothing had really gone "wrong." Change had simply taken place in the cultural milieu, leading to new forms of life, new types of exploration into human existence, new forms of freedom.

What could have gone "right" was Alexander's dream of turning the ancient world into a kind of United Nations with Greek culture as its unifying and elevating core. Had he succeeded (had he lived) there would have been a functioning world federation over twenty-two centuries prior to two similar attempts in our own century. However, part of Alexander's vision—perhaps the crucial element—that did survive was the Greek cultural heritage, a bequest that still forms the core of Western civilization.

Annotated Bibliography

General Studies of the Hellenistic World

Burn, Andrew R. *Alexander the Great and the Hellenistic World*. New York: Macmillan, 1974. Alexander's role in spreading Greek culture.

Bury, J. B. *The Hellenistic Age*. New York: W. W. Norton and Co., 1970. A fine treatment by the eminent Greek historian.

Grant, Michael. *From Alexander to Cleopatra: The Hellenistic World*. New York: Charles Scribner's Sons, 1982. Comprehensive overview.

Hadas, Moses. *Hellenistic Culture: Fusion and Diffusion*. New York: W. W. Norton & Co., 1972. Synthesis and dissemination of Greek culture.

Hamilton, J. R. *Alexander the Great*. Pittsburgh: University of Pittsburgh Press, 1974. Excellent biographical study.

Walbank, R. W. *The Hellenistic World*. Cambridge: Harvard University Press, 1982. Updated treatment by a recognized authority.

Philosophy and Social Issues

Cornford, Francis. *Plato's Theory of Knowledge*. Atlantic Highlands, N.J.: Humanities Press, 1967. Exploration of a central Platonic doctrine.

Dover, K. J. *Aristophanic Comedy*. Berkeley: University of California Press, 1972. Form and technique within social/political context.

———. *Greek Homosexuality*. New York: Random House, 1980. Behavior and attitudes as revealed in vase paintings, poetry, Plato, lawcourt speeches, and the comedies of Aristophanes.

———. *Greek Popular Morality in the Time of Plato and Aristotle*. Berkeley: University of California Press, 1980. Social context for their ethical and political writings.

Huby, Patricia. *Plato and Modern Morality*. Atlantic Highlands, N. J.: Humanities Press, 1972. Assessment of Plato's enduring relevance.

Long, A. A. *Hellenistic Philosophy: Stoics, Epicureans, Sceptics*. New York: Charles Scribner's Sons, 1974. Important currents after Plato and Aristotle.

Randall, John Herman. *Aristotle*. New York: Columbia University Press, 1960. Authoritative study.

Taylor, A. E. *Plato: The Man and His Work*. New York: World Publishing Co., 1966. Outstanding and comprehensive.

———. *Sokrates*. Westport, Conn.: Greenwood Press, 1975. Notable effort to reconstruct the man and his thinking.

Translations of Original Material

Aristotle. *Aristotle: Selections from Seven Books*. Edited by Philip Wheelwright. Indianapolis: Odyssey Press, 1951. Significant selections.

———. *Aristotle's Poetics*. Trans. James Hutton. New York: W. W. Norton and Company, 1982. Includes helpful introduction and notes.

———. *The Ethics of Aristotle: The Nichomachean Ethics*. Edited by Hugh Tredennick, translated by J. A. Thompson. Baltimore: Penguin Books, 1977. The discussion of happiness is particularly accessible.

Plato. *Great Dialogues of Plato*. Translated by W. H. D. Rouse. New York: New American Library, 1956. The standard one-volume work.

Fiction

Renault, Mary. *Fire from Heaven*. New York: Pantheon Books, 1970. The first in her Alexandrian trilogy: Alexander's Youth. *The Persian Boy* (1972) recounts his life from age twenty-six to his death. *Funeral Games: The Combat of Alexander's Heirs* (1981) concludes the trilogy.

———. *The Mask of Apollo*. New York: Bantam Books, 1974. A lively picture of Plato's times.

7

Greek Art: Gods, Temples, and the Greeks

According to Greek mythology, Daidalos (DED-uh-los) was the first and greatest of artists, a legendary Minoan artificer who created amazing figures in wood, bronze, and stone, and who even invented the mysterious Minoan maze that housed the fabled Minotaur. Although the story is fascinating, it is immaterial whether or not Daidalos actually existed, because the central idea the myth celebrates is the Greek commitment to creative activity: to invent, design, sculpt, and build. Daidalean Greeks studied nature and used their discoveries to create dynamic new images and structures radiating the illusion of vitality and life. This urge to create is the hallmark of Greek genius.

While the story of Daidalos has an unhappy ending, it does point to a primary artistic consideration of Greek artists. According to the legend, Daidalos had an undisciplined son named Ikaros, who prevailed upon his father to invent wings made of wax and feathers that enabled the lad to soar birdlike in the air. Disregarding the sober advice of his father not to fly too near the sun, the reckless aviator soared so high that his wings melted, plummeting him to his death in a sea that now bears his name. A charming fabrication that reveals a higher truth, this myth symbolizes Greek respect for the laws of nature. Thus, through the story of Daidalos and his hubristic son, Ikaros, we see reflected the Greek search for freedom in the arts through the study of nature, invention, and obedience to reason.

Greek Civilization, ca. 900–30 B.C.

The complexity media and productivity of the Greek arts make it necessary to subdivide this chapter into the artistic periods (all dates approximate) in the Chronological Overview on this page. Following a fairly strict chronology, the different media (sculpture, architecture, pottery) will be examined as manifestations of the evolving artistic styles of ancient Greece.

CHRONOLOGICAL OVERVIEW

900–750 B.C.	Geometric Period
750–480 B.C.	Archaic Period
480–323 B.C.	Classical Period
	Early 480–450
	High 450–400
	Late 400–323
323–30 B.C.	Hellenistic Period

Geometric Period, ca. 900–750 B.C.

The invasions of Greek-speaking Dorians (ca. 1100–800 B.C.) not only abruptly terminated Mycenaean dominance and thoroughly disrupted the lives of all the Hellenes, but they also had a devastating effect on the arts of sculpture and architecture. Military invasions always disturb the arts, as political and economic turmoil is not conducive to the commissioning of such major works as temples and life-sized statues. While probably impoverishing many artists and interfering with the transmission of technology, the waves of Dorian invaders made relatively little impact upon the utilitarian arts of furniture, textiles, glassware, and, above all, pottery. Because most of the pottery produced during this chaotic period emphasized geometric decoration, this era is known as the Geometric period.

Pottery

Even though it had been practiced since the Stone Age, the craft of making pots made a great leap forward with the invention (probably in Sumer—Iran—ca. 3250 B.C.) of the potter's wheel. The wheel was introduced into Crete around 2000 B.C. and enabled Minoan potters to lead the Aegean world in transforming the craft of making utilitarian vessels into an art form that reached its apex with the classic Greek vase.

FIGURE 7.1 Amphora of the Dipylon, *ca. 750 B.C. Terra-cotta, height 61″ with base. National Archeological Museum, Athens.*

As early as the ninth century, geometric conventions of pottery decoration had evolved into a vocabulary of meanders, concentric circles, horizontal bands, wheel patterns, shaded triangles, swastikas, and zigzags. Abstract animal and figure patterns were used in a two-dimensional form in either full front or profile views. Sophisticated, aesthetically appealing, and utilitarian, the *Amphora of the Dipylon* (figure 7.1) is a masterwork of the potter's art. Because cremation had been abandoned, these monumental vases served as grave markers and also as receptacles for liquid offerings, which filtered down to the honored dead through openings in the base. The representational scene is a *prothesis* (PROTH-uh-sis), or lying-in-state of the deceased, flanked by triangulated geometric figures of mourners with their arms raised in grief. Alternating bands separate different versions of the meander[1] motif (also known as the Greek fret), with a

_____
1. From the name of a winding river in Asia Minor. In Greek decoration it is a mazelike pattern of lines that wind in and out or cross one another.

FIGURE 7.2 *Statuette of Youth, "Mantiklos dedicated me . . . , ca. 700–680 B.C. Bronze, height 8″. Francis Bartlett Donation. Courtesy, Museum of Fine Arts, Boston.*

band of grazing antelope highlighting the neck. Created about a quarter century after the inauguration of the Olympic Games in 776 B.C., this heroic vase can symbolically mark the beginning of the Homeric Age of ca. 750–700 B.C.

Temples

Though it achieved its final form during the Archaic Period (ca. 600 B.C.), it is apparent that the Greek temple was known to Homer (*Iliad,* I, 39). Fragmentary terracotta models from the eighth century display three of the elements of the temple canon: rectangular floor plan, enclosed inner shrine, and porch supported by columns. The "canon" (Gk., *kanon,* rule) of Greek temples refers to fundamental procedures that help convert a concept into reality, in this case, buildings that look precisely like what they are: temples for the gods.

Statuettes

Among the most popular products of the Greek artisans were statuettes, which were produced throughout Greek history. Though they were not as impressive as life-sized statuary, the very smallness of miniature figures enables one to hold and turn them around in one's hands—a very personal relationship. The statuette shown in figure 7.2

is a votive offering bearing on its thighs the inscription, "Mantiklos dedicated me to the Far Darter of the silver bow, as part of his tithe. Do thou, Phoibos, grant him gracious recompense." As obvious as the geometric elements are, the unknown artist also demonstrates a concern for volume, modeling, and some anatomical details, design elements that place this work on the borderline between the Geometric and Archaic periods.

Based on the surviving pottery and statuettes, the Geometric can be viewed as an interlude rather than a major artistic period. The fact that Homer's *Iliad* and *Odyssey* were the greatest achievements of this era makes one wonder, however. Did the visual arts lag behind epic poetry, or have some important artworks been lost? In any event, the Geometric was a period in which the Greeks began to see and think and create as a Greek, not as an Egyptian or a Minoan or a Mycenaean. Borrowings from these civilizations are evident, but the unique forms introduced during the Geometric period clearly indicate an elementary process of producing art forms not bound to traditional conventions but subject to experimentation and invention, and above all, art that was dynamic rather than static.

Archaic Period, 750–480 B.C.

Archaic is a term derived from a Greek word meaning *ancient* and is not to be confused with such contemporary definitions as antiquated, outdated, or old-fashioned. The sixth century saw Greek genius blossom with the production of brilliant works of art. This was one of the exalted periods in world art, a vigorous era that also produced the world's first democracy.

Sculpture

Throughout Greek art, beginning with the Archaic period, Greek sculptors evolved new representational modes that were different from all previous artistic conceptions. They were fascinated by the complex mechanics of the human body; this led to the creation of fully three-dimensional sculpture that more nearly represented the natural world. The ideal, as illustrated in the Pygmalion legend, was the creation of a marble figure that would step down from the platform and speak to its creator.

Two main subjects preoccupied sculptors throughout the sixth century: the standing nude male and the standing fully clothed female. Apparently serving as votive or commemorative statues, these figures were not personalized portraits but rather idealized representations placed somewhere between humankind and the gods. No one really knows why the men were always nude and the women fully clothed and, moreover, we can apply only vague and unsatisfactory names to these freestanding figures: *kouros* (KOO-rose; youth) and *kore* (KORE-ay; maiden). Probably adapted from Egypt and Mesopotamia, these two subjects were repeated again and again, never with the intention of exact repetition but rather with the competitive drive that leads to constant innovation. It is the degree of this ceaseless striving for something different, something better, that sets the Greeks apart from other cultures.

■

FIGURE 7.3 Kore of Auxerre, *ca. 630–600 B.C. Limestone with traces of paint, height 24". The Louvre, Paris.*

An early work, the *Kore of Auxerre* (figure 7.3) stands as stiffly as an Egyptian statue, but compared with Egyptian conventions shows some significant differences (see figure 2.2). Unlike his Egyptian predecessor, the sculptor has cut away some needless stone to outline the figure rather than encasing it. The hair is braided in the geometric manner, but a very human touch is conveyed by the way the waist is cinched by a wide belt. From the light shoulder covering to the swelling hips, there is a skillful contrast between curved and straight lines.

Compare the colossal statue of the *Kouros of Sounion* (figure 7.4) with the pharaoh (figure 2.2). We see that the Egyptian figure is "imprisoned" in stone in the manner of a very high relief, whereas the kouros statue has been liberated from unnecessary stone, with the exception of the hands. The pharaoh stands in repose with his weight on the back foot. The equal distribution of weight of the kouros figure gives the illusion that he is striding forward, an effect that is heightened by the taut thigh muscles. Vestiges of geometric ornamentation remain in the rosette hair with meticulous braids and, especially, in the scrolls (volutes) that serve as ears. The most critical difference between the Egyptian and Greek sculptures lies in the eyes and facial expression. Displaying the typical relaxed serenity of Egyptian portraiture, the pharaoh gazes dreamily into an undefined

FIGURE 7.4 Kouros of Sounion, *ca. 600 B.C. Marble, height 10'. National Archeological Museum, Athens.*

FIGURE 7.5 Calf-Bearer (Moschophoros), *ca. 575–550 B.C. Marble, height 66''. Akropolis Museum, Athens.*

distance. The *Kouros of Sounion* manifests the characteristic dynamism of Greek art, with tension present in every line of the face. Egyptian figures seem never to have known stress, whereas tension and striving are hallmarks of the restless Greeks.

Created shortly after the Greek triumphs over the Persians at Salamis and Plataea, the *Calf-Bearer* (figure 7.5) was something new in Greek art, a composition of two figures so unified that neither figure is conceivable without the other. A bearded man with a cloak draped over his upper body is gently balancing a bull calf on his shoulders as he strides confidently forward. With the corners of his mouth lifted slightly in the so-called Archaic smile, he stares ahead with hollow eyes that once contained inlays, probably making them quite realistic. Characteristic of the Archaic style, his braided hair and close-cropped beard are highly stylized, in contrast with the naturalistic depiction of the calf.

By the sixth century, Greek city-states had established colonies in North Africa and from Byzantium (Istanbul) westward to Italy, Sicily, France, and Spain. Magna Graecia (southern Italy) was particularly important, for it was here that Pythagoras founded his religious brotherhood (see chapter 4) and Parmenides and Empedokles established the Eleatic School of philosophy (see chapter 5). One of the better-preserved of the surviving Archaic temples is that of Hera at Paestum (figure 7.6), the site of two religious centers of Magna Graecia.

FIGURE 7.6 *Temple of Hera I, ca. 550 B.C. Paestum, Italy.*

Though employing an unusual nine-column front, this structure has all the elements of the basic Greek temple: rectangular floor plan, columns on four sides, three steps rising from the foundation to the top level on which the columns rest, and an enclosed inner shrine. (As far as we know the odd number of columns was never tried again. Regularity was an important Greek concept, as exemplified in the six- or eight-column fronts of classical temples; see figures 7.22 and 7.25.) Other archaic features are heavy, bulging columns that taper sharply as they near the oversize, pillowlike capitals. The whole effect is heavy because these features seem to create a sense of physical strain, unlike the Parthenon (see figure 7.25), which appears to be light and free of stress.

Black-Figure Pottery

Painting was, for the Greeks, one of the supreme art forms, and yet very little of it survives. We must focus instead on the superb achievements of Archaic vase painters, who raised that form of pictorial art to a level comparable to the best sculpture and architecture. That the Greeks themselves valued their vases is attested to by the number of painters (and potters) who signed their creations, which, incidentally, raised the value (and price) of the vase. They concentrated on lively interaction between individual gods, goddesses, and heroes; and using an incisive black-figure technique (silhouetted figures on a reddish background), vase painters like Exekias (e-ZEE-ki-as) set a standard that has not been surpassed (colorplate 11). In this quiet interlude during the Trojan War, we see Akhilleus (on the left) and Aias (Ajax) intent on a game of dice. From their mouths issue "balloons" with Akhilleus saying "four" (*tesara*) and Aias countering with "three" (*tria.*) (That does not tell us, however, who is winning the game.) The composition is sparse but elegant, with a sure line sustained by finely incised details in clothing and hair. The scene is quiet and dignified but thoroughly permeated with dramatic intensity. These warriors are just as determined to win a game as they were intent on defeating the Trojans. Exekias modeled and painted his own vases, eleven of which he signed but only two paintings. One wonders which he valued more. The vase shown is an amphora, which means "to carry on both sides." The reference is to the two handles of a large pot that was used to store wine, grain, or oil. The Greeks had several dozen differently shaped vases, each of a size and shape consistent with its function.

Clothing Styles—Peplos and Himation

By comparing the *Kore in Dorian Peplos* (figure 7.7) with the *Kore of Auxerre* (figure 7.3), one can observe a basic continuity while also noting significant changes. This is the last known archaic kore statue to wear the Dorian *peplos,* a heavy tunic reaching to the ground that was fastened at each shoulder and belted at the waist. It was commonly worn over a light, sleeved tunic called a

■
FIGURE 7.7 Kore in Dorian Peplos, *ca. 530 B.C. Marble with traces of paint, height 48". Akropolis Museum, Athens.*

chiton. Though there is still a rectangular frontality about this figure, there is no doubt about the presence of a young, nubile body beneath the woolen peplos. With its lovely natural smile and arched eyebrows, the softly rounded face exudes a serene kind of happiness. The remaining paint on the graceful braids indicates that the young woman was a redhead, a valued hue in ancient Athens.

The Ionian *himation* worn by the *Kore from Chios* (figure 7.8) contrasts sharply with the severe Dorian peplos. This elegant mantle, which was worn over the chiton, was of much lighter material than the peplos and could be draped over the body in a variety of graceful arrangements. Based on the number of surviving works, it is obvious that artists were entranced with the challenge of sculpting the sinuous lines of the garment. Moreover, the wholesale adoption by Athenian women of the stylish himation (see other styles in figure 8.6) symbolizes the individualistic, pleasure-loving Ionian orientation of Athenian society, as compared with the sober peplos and stolid, group-oriented society of the Dorian city of Sparta. As we have already seen (p. 84), the clash of these disparate cultures was apparently inevitable.

FIGURE 7.8 Kore from Chios *(?), ca. 520 B.C. Marble with traces of paint, ca. 22" high (lower part missing). Akropolis Museum, Athens.*

FIGURE 7.9 Anavyssos Kouros, *ca. 525 B.C. Marble with traces of paint, height 76". National Archeological Museum, Athens.*

Naturalism

The *Anavyssos Kouros* (figure 7.9), which was placed over the grave of a warrior named Kroisos, signals a major advance towards *naturalism,* fidelity to the actual appearance of the natural world. The revolutionary changes were already apparent in the *Kouros of Sounion* (see figure 7.4), but were realized in what is now more nearly a portrait of the finely tuned body of a youthful wrestler who had the misfortune to die on some unknown battlefield. Though the knees and calves are emphasized according to earlier conventions, the muscles of the powerful thighs and taut arms swell with lifelike vitality. Based on an increasing knowledge of skeletal structure and anatomical details, the sculptor has concentrated on portraying the body. Greek artists, from the very first efforts at monumental sculpture, were never interested in portrait busts, but instead were concerned with the depiction of the body. This does not imply that the head was secondary—far from it. It simply means that Greek artists were intent on portraying the whole person, especially the vibrantly healthy body the Greeks so admired.

The ancient Greeks also seemed to possess a unique visual sensibility. Many factors may account for this. Meticulous observation was basic to Greek science, itself an area in which the Greeks had no rivals. In medical practice as exemplified by Hippokrates, there was an emphasis on the accumulation of sensory information. The Greek gods were conceived in the images of men and women and were thus immediately accessible for artistic representation. Perhaps most important, however, is the fact that the Greeks were not subjected to views of reality imposed from above by either a divine-right monarch or an organized religion.

During the discussion of the *Anavyssos Kouros* (figure 7.9) it was pointed out that Greek sculptors portrayed the entire person, concentrating on the body, but without de-emphasizing the head. By deliberately selecting only the enchanting head of the kore figure that is sometimes called *La Delicata* (figure 7.10), it is clearly apparent that the creator of this masterful portrait of a beautiful woman wished to highlight her pensive, almost melancholy, mood. Also known as "the girl with the almond eyes," this work epitomizes the Archaic style at its best.

FIGURE 7.10 Kore (La Delicata; *detail*), ca. 500 B.C. *Marble with traces of paint. Akropolis Museum, Athens.*

FIGURE 7.11 *Sosias painter, cup (detail): "Akhilleus Bandaging Patrokles' Wound," ca. 500 B.C. Attic red-figure cup, ca. 7" high. Antikenmuseum Staatliche Museen Preussischer Kulturbesitz Berlin.*

Red Figure Pottery

Around 530 B.C. vase painters began working with a color scheme of red figures against a black background, the reverse of black-figure technique. The luminous new *red-figure* technique permitted secondary markings like hair, muscles, details of dress, and even discreet shadings. The two styles coexisted for thirty or forty years, but the red-figure technique, with its greater opportunities for delicacy and subtlety, became the dominant style of the Classical Period. In the red-figure cup by the Sosias painter (figure 7.11), we see the first example of eyes painted just the way they actually appear in profile. This significant advance marks a phase beyond the Egyptian convention of always depicting the eyes as they are viewed frontally. In the painting Akhilleus is intent upon tending the wound, while in a very human reaction, Patroklos has turned his head away as if he were not even a party to this unhappy event—or wishes he weren't. Below the platform are three palmettes, a decorative motif invented by the Greeks based on a stylized rendering of a palm leaf. Some basic differences between red-figure and black-figure technique become apparent when this painting is compared with that of Exekias (colorplate 11). It cannot be said that one of these works is better than another, only that different techniques lead to dissimilar styles. Black-figure painting is characteristic of the vigorous Archaic period, while red-figure vases typify the later Classical style.

Classical Period, 480–323 B.C.

Early Classical, 480–450 B.C.

The year 480 marked a critical turning point in the history of Athens. Invaded and humiliated by Xerxes' Persian forces, their city ravaged, and their culture in ruins, the Athenians and their allies struck back by destroying the Persian fleet at Salamis and defeating the army the following year. A resurgent Athens moved unerringly towards power, prosperity, and a legendary Golden Age epitomized by the confident Classical style.

The Severe Style

The *Kritios Boy* (figure 7.12), a prime example of the Severe style of early classicism, was created at about the same time as Aeschylus was gaining fame as a playwright. Somewhat like the innovations of Aeschylus, this statue represents a new principle in art. It is wearing an expression of composed, classical solemnity (compare this with the Archaic smile) and is truly a standing figure. Archaic sculptures were limited to a striding pose with an equal distribution of weight; here we have a formal composition with a fine balance of tense and relaxed muscles, the head turned slightly, one hip a bit elevated, and the weight on one leg with the other at rest. This is how any of us might stand in natural repose.

FIGURE 7.12 Kritios Boy, *481/480 B.C. marble, height 34". Akropolis Museum, Athens.*

FIGURE 7.13 Delphi Charioteer, *ca. 470 B.C. Bronze, height 71". Archeological Museum, Delphi.*

FIGURE 7.14 Delphi Charioteer, *rear view, detail.*

Also representing the Severe style is the *Delphi Charioteer* (figure 7.13), which was once part of a large composition of a chariot and four horses. Chariot races were entered by the owners of racing teams and driven by highly skilled charioteers, much like thoroughbred horses today are ridden by professional jockeys. Overlooking the disheveled, dusty condition of a charioteer after a grueling race, the artist idealizes a proud champion, with his chiton falling in fluted folds like those of a Doric column (see figure 7.21). Included, however, are such realistic details as a device to keep the chiton from billowing in the wind—a cord that passed over the shoulders, under the armpits, and crossed in back. The headband performed exactly the same function as a tennis player's sweatband (figure 7.14).

One of the finest original Greek bronzes, *Poseidon* (*Zeus* according to some; figure 7.15) stands majestically, prepared to hurl his trident (or thunderbolt). The figure is stridently asymmetrical: arms, legs, even the head, turn in different angles from the torso, which in turn shows the competing muscular strains and tensions. Unlike even the most naturalistic Archaic statues, this body has rippling muscles functioning beneath taut skin. The various concavities and convexities of the bronze surface reflect a shimmering light that further animates the figure. It matters little that if Poseidon's arms were lowered his hands would dangle at the knees; that the

■
FIGURE 7.15 Poseidon (Zeus?), *ca. 460 B.C. Bronze, height 82". National Archeological Museum, Athens.*

■
FIGURE 7.17 *Myron,* Discobolus (Discus Thrower), *reconstructed Roman marble copy of a bronze original of ca. 450 B.C. Height 60". Museo della Terme, Rome.*

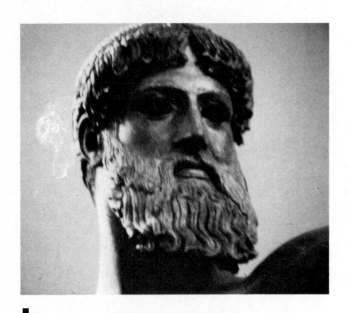

■
FIGURE 7.16 Poseidon (Zeus?), *detail.*

eyes are hollow sockets that were once filled with colored stones; or that the hair, beard, and eyebrows are highly stylized; the work exudes a kinetic energy never achieved in earlier sculptures. The idealism of Greek art—depicting people not as they were but as they should be—applied also to the gods (figure 7.16). Whether Poseidon the earthshaker or Zeus of the thunderbolt, this is how a god ought to look. Compare this regal demeanor with the idealized human faces of figures 7.13, 7.17, 7.18, and colorplate 12 and gauge the difference.

High Classical, 450–400 B.C.

The High Classical period (the Age of Perikles) was marked in part by the beginning of construction of the Akropolis, the early fame of Sophokles, and notable sculptures by Myron and Polykleitos. The *Discobolus (Discus Thrower;* figure 7.17) is intended to be viewed when standing to the left of the figure in order to become totally involved with the moment leading to explosive action. Though a celebrated classical statue, the figure follows Egyptian conventions. It is designed on a frontal plane with head and legs in profile and the upper torso turned towards the front. It is balanced by the arced arms and the head and left leg, a formal composition that displays the harmonious proportions characteristic of the classical style. With simplified anatomical details and a stylized pose, all is in readiness for the athlete to wheel about and hurl the discus. Excellence of form, which counted as half of the scoring, was as important as marking the distance of the throw, a procedure comparable to the scoring in modern competitive diving. An athlete could win the olive wreath with a second-place throw, provided he displayed a form comparable to that of the *Discobolus.* (See also the discussion of the Olympic Games beginning on page 215.)

The Riaci Bronze

The *Riaci* (ree-AH-chee) *Bronze* (colorplate 12), is one of two recently displayed (1981) Greek originals. Discovered together in 1972 near the coast of Italy, they were named after Riaci township in the southern province of Calabria. Statue A originally had a shield and a small sword; the eyes are now without pupils; and a tuft of hair is missing. Otherwise, this is a stunning representation of a youthful warrior in the prime of his vigorous life. Bronze is the primary material but the teeth are silver, the corneas of the eyes ivory and limestone, and the lips, nipples, and eyelashes made of copper. The pose is fascinating; the right turn of the head and the steady far-off gaze communicate strength and resolution. The thrown-back shoulders strikingly fix the warrior in space.

The creator of this splendid addition to the tiny treasure of original Greek art is unknown. Some scholars claim that the bronze is worthy of the great Pheidias of Athens (and it is) while others attribute it to the sculptor in Magna Graecia called Pythagoras. It could have been imported from Athens or made in Italy. Stylistically, the warrior stands somewhere between the Poseidon (figure 7.15) and the canon developed by Polykleitos (polly-KLY-toss) of Argos, who is known today only through Roman copies of his work. This copy of his *Doryphoros* (dory-FOR-os; figure 7.18) is of sufficiently high quality for us to see how it exemplified a "canon" (system of proportions), which became a model for several generations of artists. Displaying the powerful body of a finely conditioned athlete, the young man rests his full weight on the right leg with the left bent at the knee and his toes lightly touching the ground. With the head barely turned to the right and the right shoulder dropped slightly, the whole body can be traced as a long S curve from the feet to the head. At rest as no sculpted figure had ever been before, the composition is still dynamic, a balance of tension and relaxation throughout the entire body. Harmoniously proportioned and with a classic balance of artistic and natural form, this is the confident style of the Golden Age.

Architecture

Let us turn now to developments in architecture leading to the classical temples of the Age of Perikles. As discussed earlier, Greek temples had evolved into their canonical form during the early Archaic period (ca. 600). Fundamental to the temple canon is the architectural system of post and lintel (figure 7.19). After planting a post at all four corners of the space to be enclosed, the builder then placed a beam (lintel) on top of and across the posts. Roof beams (joists) were placed at regular intervals to link the opposite lintels, and were then covered with a roof. Spaces between the posts were filled,

FIGURE 7.18 *Polykleitos,* Doryphoros (Spear Bearer), *Roman marble copy after a bronze original of ca. 450–440* B.C. *Height 78". National Museum, Naples. Photo © Alinari/Art Resource.*

FIGURE 7.19 *Post and lintel system.*

FIGURE 7.20 *Typical Greek temple floor plan.*

FIGURE 7.21 *Typical Greek temple facade.*

as needed, with walls, windows, and doors. First employed in wood, then in brick, and eventually in stone construction, the post and lintel system was used for all major Greek buildings. The greater strength of arches and the arched vault (see Roman architecture, chapter 10) was known and used, but only for such minor works as the long arched corridor leading into the stadium at Nemea.

A typical temple floor plan (figure 7.20) shows a *cella,* a central room where the statue of the deity was placed. This basic core was provided with a columned porch at the front and, usually, one at the back, with the latter sometimes enclosed to function as a treasury. Large, important temples had exterior columns on all four sides forming a colonnade or peristyle.

The plan appears to be simple, but a diagram of a facade (figure 7.21) reveals a progression beyond the basic post and lintel. Because the Mediterranean area is subject to heavy winter rains, a sloping or saddle-back roof was developed to facilitate drainage. It was covered with terra-cotta or marble tiles, equipped with gutters and rain spouts, and adorned with decorative sculpture. The triangular space at each end, the *pediment,* was usually decorated with large-scale high reliefs or freestanding sculpture. Heavily ornamented pediments increased the weight of the superstructure and thus necessitated additional carefully spaced columns.

The Greeks constructed steps (usually three) on a stone foundation called a *stereobate* with the top level, the *stylobate,* forming the floor of the temple. (For the Greeks "three" was the perfect number because it represented a beginning, middle, and end.) From the stylobate rose columns (shafts with capitals) that supported the lintel, also called an *architrave.* The ends of the roof joists are *triglyphs* (TRY-glifs), a term derived from the three vertical grooves that had become a decorative stone adaptation of the natural grain of wood joist ends. The spaces between the triglyphs were filled by plain, painted, or relief rectangles called *metopes* (MET-o-pays).

The Doric Order

Determining the general mode of the basic temple plan was a problem that was brilliantly resolved with the inspired conception of three orders of columns, the classic Greek orders: Doric, Ionic, and Corinthian (figure 7.22). The first to be invented, the Doric order, is simple, solid, and serene. Placed directly upon the stylobate, the Doric column (shaft and capital) was about seven times as tall as its diameter, a ratio probably derived from the height of a man in relation to foot size. The column was fluted to provide visual depth and swelling in subtle convex curves (*entasis;* EN-ta-sis); it then rose to a capital (*echinus;* eh-KY-nus), or curved block under an *abacus* (AB-a-kus), which was a square block that joined the architrave. Surmounting the columns was a Doric frieze of alternating triglyphs and metopes. (For examples of Doric temples see figures 7.23, 7.40, and 7.41.)

The Ionic Order

The contrasting Ionic order, the second temple style to be developed, is lighter than the Doric and more graceful, with a slender shaft about eleven times its diameter (approximately a woman's height in proportion to the size of her foot). Its components are a tiered base, softer flutes separated by narrow bands of stone, and a delicate shaft that terminates in a capital with paired scrolls (volutes) capped by a minute but highly decorated abacus. Usually subdivided into three projecting bands, the Ionic architrave normally consists of a continuous sculptural frieze. (For Ionic temples see figures 7.33 and 7.35.)

The Corinthian Order

A variant of the Ionic, the Corinthian order, adored by the Romans, is considerably more decorative, even opulent. Taller and more slender than the Ionic, its column culminates in an inverted bell shape encrusted with stylized acanthus leaves, an ingenious transition from a circular shaft to a rectangular architrave. (See figure 7.52 for the only Corinthian temple in Greece.)

The columns are made up of stone sections or drums, like multiple layers of a cake. Roughed out in the quarry, the drums were transported to the site, fitted with metal pegs that had been coated with lead to resist corrosion, and stacked into columns. The assembled columns were then finished under the supervision of the architect.

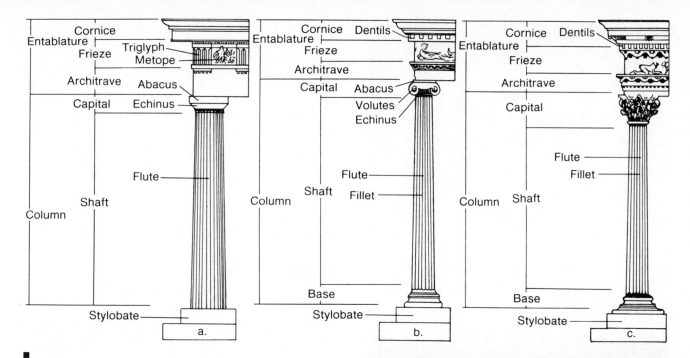

FIGURE 7.22 *Greek orders of columns: (a) Doric, (b) Ionic, and (c) Corinthian.*

With only one form and three modes of expression, Greek architecture might appear to be a rather limited achievement, but the attainment of perfection or near perfection is slow, tedious, and seldom achieved by *any* culture. For perfection of proportion and clarity of outline, subtlety of refinement, and visual appearance of solids and spaces in equilibrium, the Greek temple has never been excelled. Moreover, no two Dorian (or Ionian) temples are exactly alike; each is as distinctive and individualistic as the Greeks themselves.

The Akropolis

Most ancient Greek cities developed around an *akra* (high place), a fortified hilltop. As cities grew more prosperous and powerful, this people's high place (*akropolis*) became the center of religious and civic activity, suitably adorned with governmental buildings, libraries, and temples dedicated to the proprietary god or gods. According to legend the akropolis of Athens (figure 7.24), the burial place of the fabled hero-King Erechtheus, was the site where Poseidon and Athena contended for authority over the city.

Under the leadership of Perikles, the Athenians completed a building and art program on the akropolis surpassing in splendor and artistic quality anything the world had ever seen. It signified the beginning of the Golden Age, in about 450 B.C., when Pheidias was appointed overseer of all works on the akropolis. By 405 the Parthenon, Erechtheion, Propylaia, and Temple of Athena Nike had been built, and the brief period of glory

FIGURE 7.23 *Iktinus and Kallikrates, Parthenon (view from the northwest), ca. 447–432 B.C. Akropolis, Athens.*

FIGURE 7.24 *View from the west of the akropolis at Athens.*

FIGURE 7.25 *Model of the classical akropolis at Athens. American School of Classical Studies at Athens: Agora Excavations.*

FIGURE 7.26 *Stereobate and stylobate, north side of the Parthenon.*

FIGURE 7.27 *Schematic drawing of Parthenon refinements.*

was at an end. These four buildings can be identified in the model (figure 7.25): Temple of Athena Nike, tiny building on the right parapet above the stairs; Propylaia, at the top of the steps; Parthenon, largest building; and Erechtheion, two-part structure at the upper left near the wall. No other buildings have survived.

For a half century this small rocky plateau (ca. 1000′ long and 445′ wide) was a center of creative activity for the greatest painters, sculptors, and architects of the time, and one should not overlook the most skillful stonemasons in the Greek world. The ample funds of the Delian Treasury, which were entrusted to Athens for military preparedness, were lavished on an Athenian building project supposedly dedicated to the goddess Athena, but in reality devoted to proclaiming the power and glory of Athens.

The Parthenon

Built under the direction of architects Iktinus (ik-TIE-nus) and Kallikrates (ka-LIK-kra-teas), the temple of Athena Parthenos (Parthenon; figure. 7.26) was created as the crowning glory of the akropolis, complete with sculptural reliefs and a massive gold and ivory statue of Athena created by Pheidias. Although it is the largest Doric temple ever built on the Greek mainland, with refinements so subtle that the building symbolized the Periklean ideal of "beauty in simplicity," its basic plan was still that of the sixth-century archaic temple. Even though they invented nothing new, its architects clearly saw just how refined the temple form could be. Despite the great size (228′ × 101′ with 34′ columns) this was still a rectangular box surrounded by columns and surmounted by a triangular prism. A temple in which the Doric order achieved perfection, the Parthenon is so unified and harmonious that its immense size is belied by its lightly poised serenity.

That the building has virtually no straight lines or true right angles is at first surprising. By using slight deviations from mathematical regularity, presumably to correct optical distortions, the architects succeeded in creating a building that gave the appearance of mathematical precision. This bothered Plato, who could not reconcile the discrepancy between perfection and the illusion of perfection that was projected by the masterful design.

Thus the cella walls lean slightly inwards; the stylobate rises 4¼″ at the center of the 228′ sides (figure 7.26) and 2¾″ at the center of the other two sides. All columns lean inward about 2½″, except the corner columns, which lean diagonally, so much so that if they were extended, all four would meet at a point about a mile above the temple. Echoing the stylobate, the cornice, frieze, and architrave are all slightly higher in the center. The schematic drawing of some of the refinements (figure 7.27) seems strange indeed, but through exaggeration it reflects these subtleties.

Further adjustments are found in the corner columns, each of which is of greater diameter and about two feet closer to its neighbors than the other columns. It is probable that these deviations were adopted so that the corner columns, which are seen most directly against the sky, would seem more supportive. Practically all Doric buildings show some signs of "correction," for the Doric column always had a slight outward curve called the entasis. In early Doric temples the entasis looks like a bulge

FIGURE 7.28 *Reconstruction of east pediment of Parthenon, central section. Akropolis Museum, Athens.*

about a third of the way up the column; but with the entire 34′ Parthenon column, the deviation from a straight line is only 11/16″. Established as a convention long before, fluted Doric columns were not only visually attractive but they also made an optical correction; from a distance smooth-surfaced columns appear to be flat and without sufficient solidity and rigidity to perform support functions.

Adorned with some of the greatest marble carvings of antiquity, the Parthenon was virtually a visual encyclopedia of activities of the gods and of the Athenians themselves. A reconstruction of the east pediment (figure 7.28) illustrates the story of the miraculous birth of Athena, who has just emerged from the brow of Zeus. All the gods at the center are astir, but Dionysos (figure 7.29) is just awakening at the left corner as the sun god Apollo drives his chariot onto the scene. At the opposite end, three goddesses (figure 7.30) are about to hear the good tidings, as Artemis, the moon goddess, begins her nightly travels. Dionysos and the goddesses are freestanding; larger than life size; and carved in broad, clear planes and sharply delineated lines so that they could be seen from ground level. Whether they were carved by Pheidias or his assistants is of little concern. What is important is that these are masterpieces of monumentalized human form; graceful despite their amplitude; and animated, in the case of the goddesses, by garments that reveal as well as decorate the bodies.

A Parthenon metope depicting the *Combat between a Lapith and a Centaur* (figure 7.31) is a skillfully executed high relief symbolizing the ascendancy of human ideals over the bestial side of human nature. Detailed studies of the ninety-two outer metopes reveal consistent improvement in quality from the early, rather crude carvings to the exceptional work of later pieces, like the metope of figure 7.31. The stonemasons obviously benefitted from some kind of on-the-job training under the direction of Pheidias.

FIGURE 7.29 Dionysos, *from east pediment of Parthenon, ca. 438–432 B.C. British Museum, London. Reproduced by courtesy of the Trustees of the British Museum.*

FIGURE 7.30 *Three Goddesses: Hestia, Dione, Aphrodite, from east pediment of Parthenon, ca. 438–432 B.C. British Museum, London. Reproduced by courtesy of the Trustees of the British Museum.*

FIGURE 7.31 Combat between a Lapith and a Centaur, *metope from the Parthenon, ca. 447–443 B.C. Height 56". British Museum, London. Reproduced by courtesy of the Trustees of the British Museum.*

FIGURE 7.32 Horsemen, *from the north frieze of the Parthenon, ca. 440 B.C. Marble, ca. 42" high. British Museum, London. Reproduced by courtesy of the Trustees of the British Museum.*

The inner frieze, about 3¾′ in height and over 500′ in length, ran along the outer walls of the cella. This marble bas-relief[2] depicted the gods and Athenians in the Greater Panathenaea celebration that took place every four years. This contemporary scene portrays a procession carrying a peplos, woven for the occasion, to the

statue of Athena in the Parthenon. Apparently at the very moment that the procession is getting underway, the horsemen (figure 7.32) ready their mounts to escort the singing maidens to the temple. With its six hundred persons and countless horses, this scene depicts but one moment of activity; this is "simultaneous narration," a sculptural version of the classic unities of Greek drama. Probably the most interesting aspect of this frieze is the fact that Athenians, hundreds of them, are depicted, in idealized versions, on a temple frieze, something unthinkable in other cultures of the ancient world. Of the few surviving portrayals of mortal activity on a temple wall, all of them Greek, this is the most significant example. One has only to think of the dark and forbidden recesses of the Temple of Amon-Mut-Khonsu at Luxor (see figures 2.7 and 2.8) to understand some fundamental differences between the Egyptian and Greek civilizations.

The complex design of the Erechtheion (AIR-ek-thee-on; figure 7.33) probably results from two factors: an uneven building site and the legendary contest between Athena and Poseidon. With both gods competing for the guardianship of the city, Poseidon struck a rock on the akropolis with his trident and sea water, symbol of Athenian sea power, gushed forth. Athena then struck the ground with her spear and a full-grown olive tree appeared. Judging olives more important because they were so useful, the other Olympians awarded the city to Athena. The cautious Athenians dedicated shrines to both within the same temple, however, and to cover all bets, named the building after the mythical King Erechtheus who had supposedly lived on the site.

2. The degree of projection of the sculpture from the surface is described as high, medium, or *bas* (the French word for low). High relief is almost detached from the surface and a bas-relief (BA-ri-leef) is only slightly raised. Seen from ground level as a bas-relief, the upper portion of the Parthenon frieze actually projected farther from the surface. This was, of course, one more optical refinement.

The higher (eastern) level of this graceful Ionic temple was dedicated to Athena, while the lower level (right background) was the sanctuary of Poseidon. Three porticos, each of different dimensions and design, project from three sides. It is the south porch (figure 7.34) with its six caryatids (karry-AT-ids; female figures used as columns) that is best known. Only 10′ × 15′, the porch, which is actually a veranda, has an architrave supported by young women whose drapery suggests the fluting of columns. They are grouped as if in a procession toward the Parthenon, with three figures on one side slightly bending their right legs and those on the other side bending their left legs to give the appearance of life and animation. All columns suggest physical strain; despite the individual beauty of these figures, substituting a human form for a supporting column tends to place an undue burden on our imagination. One might characterize these caryatids as an excellent solution for a less than satisfactory idea. The caryatid to the right of the figure on the left corner is a copy of the figure Lord Elgin carried off to England (along with considerable booty from the Parthenon and other buildings) as part of a questionable attempt to "save" Greek art.[3] Compounding the irony, all of the figures have now been moved to a protected environment and replaced with fiberglass copies, including a copy of the copy. Air pollution, rather than the Turks or an English lord, is the latest and most deadly threat to the Athenian akropolis.

The Temple of Athena Nike

A classic example of architectural unity, the exquisite Temple of Athena Nike (figure 7.35) is a tiny building (17′9″ × 26′10″) of pentelic marble. Though architecture is usually defined as the art of enclosing space, Greek temples embody more than this. Each temple was designed as a series of receding planes from steps to columns to cella wall, with temple reliefs in comparable planes from surface to deepest recesses. Both a strongly defined form and a four-sided sculptural relief, the Greek temple is architectural but it is also a large sculptural composition. Rather than just enclosing space the temple also fills space, and none any better than the elegant temple of Nike, goddess of victory. Originally the temple housed a statue of the victory goddess with her wings clipped so that she could never leave Athens. Some twenty years after the completion of the building (in 404 B.C.) Athens fell to Sparta, never again to regain her political and military supremacy. Demolished by the Turks in the eighteenth century in order to build a fort, the

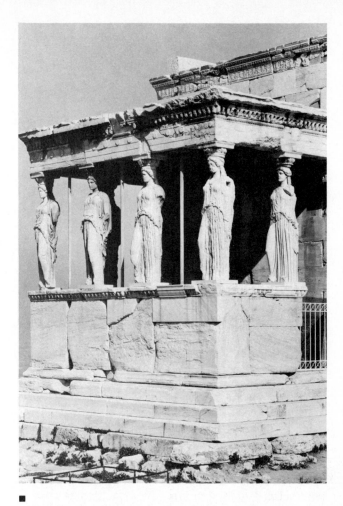

■

FIGURE 7.34 *Porch of the Maidens (view from the southwest), Erechtheion. Akropolis, Athens. Photo © Hirmer Fotoarchiv.*

Temple of Athena Nike was later reconstructed by retrieving the stone from the demolished fort. That the temple dedicated to the victory goddess could be reconstituted in something like its original form symbolizes the enduring quality of Athenian culture, which has survived invasions by Persians, Spartans, Romans, Venetians, Turks, Italians, and Germans.

The Classical style of the Golden Age, or Age of Perikles, was manifested not only in all the visual arts, and in literature, philosophy, music, drama, and dance but also in the finely balanced education and training of mind and body of Athenian citizens. Whenever the word *classical* is used, the basic reference point is Athens during the second half of the fifth century B.C., though the word may also be used to mean the best of its kind in any style.

---

3. See Theodore Vrettos' *A Shadow of Magnitude; The Acquisition of the Elgin Marbles* (1974) about which Lawrence Durrel wrote, "So thoroughly researched and energetically executed, this is the first portrait in depth of that ignoble monomaniac Lord Elgin who lives in history as the man who despoiled the Parthenon." The Greek government has repeatedly pressed for the return of the Elgin Marbles.

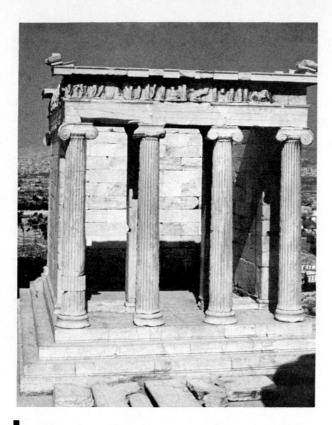

■ **FIGURE 7.35** *Kallikrates, Temple of Athena Nike, ca. 427–424* B.C. *Akropolis, Athens.*

Whether considering original artworks, Roman copies, or even their ruined temples, we can feel some of the maturity, poise, and confidence of the Golden Age. Consider, for example, the Temple of Poseidon (figure 7.36). Built to honor the god of the sea in grateful acknowledgement of the epochal victory at Salamis, the Doric temple is situated high on the promontory of Cape Sounion, where it replaced an earlier temple destroyed by the Persians. With 20′ columns that are considerably more slender than those of the Parthenon, the temple is poised lightly and elegantly, as if still awaiting the triumphant return of Theseus after the slaying of the dreaded Minotaur. Totally unlike ponderous Egyptian temples that attempt to fill desert landscapes, the Temple of Poseidon is more like a crown jewel placed, just so, on the tip of the hill. In *The Greek Way* Edith Hamilton[4] described temple placement:

> To the Greek architect the setting of his temple was all-important. He planned it, seeing it in clear outline against sea or sky, determining its size by its situation on plain hilltop or the wide plateau of an akropolis. It dominated the scene; indeed, it became through his genius the most important feature in it, but it was always a part of it. He did not think of it in and for itself, as just the building he was making; he conceived of it in relation to the hills and the seas and the arch of the sky.

4. New York: W. W. Norton, 1948, p. 304.

■ **FIGURE 7.36** *Temple of Poseidon, ca. 440* B.C., *Sounion.*

Vase Painters

Vase painters of this period were just as skilled as the architects and sculptors, and their best work can, in fact, be favorably compared with paintings by Renaissance artists. Though red-figure paintings were preferred by most artists (see figures 8.4, 8.5, and 8.6), some favored using a variety of colors on a white background in what is called the *white-ground* technique. Before being fired in the kiln, a white clay was added in the area to be decorated and the painting was done after firing. Though they were subject to fading because the color was not baked into the vase as in the red-figure technique, white-ground paintings are similar to easel paintings, but with the additional complication of working on curved surfaces. Some artists chose the permanency of red-figure painting, while others, like the Akhilleus Painter (figure 7.37), favored the color range of white-ground decorations. Though he did not sign his work, the distinctive style of the Akhilleus Painter has been recognized in over two hundred vase paintings. Here, sitting quietly on the sacred mountain of the muses, Polyhymnia, the muse of solemn hymn and religious dance, is reverently plucking her seven-string kithara. (See The Greek Muses in box 8.1.) Lightly decorated at top and bottom, the vase has nothing to draw our attention from the solitary figure with a lone bird at her feet. Through graceful line and harmonious composition we see a superb example of the Classical style.

■
FIGURE 7.38 Victory Untying Her Sandal, *from the parapet of the Temple of Athena Nike, ca. 410 B.C. Marble, height 42". Akropolis Museum, Athens.*

■
FIGURE 7.37 *Akhilleus Painter, white-ground lekythos (detail): "Muse on Mount Helicon," ca. 440–430 B.C. Height of vase 14½". Staatliche Antikensammlungen und Glyptothek, Munich.*

Sculpture

In the relief of *Victory Untying Her Sandal* (figure 7.38), we have a fine illustration of the celebrated wet drapery effect of Greek sculpture. Sculptors apparently dipped a filmy material in a starchlike substance, draped the female model, and arranged the folds for best artistic effect. Portrayed here is a rather awkward human action, but one accomplished so gracefully that the work is a marvel of softly flowing lines in a perfectly balanced design.

In a strikingly different portrait of Nike (figure 7.39), we see the goddess descending so rapidly from the sky that the startled eagle (lower left) has not yet made its escape. Wearing the diaphanous Ionic himation, Nike is moving so fast that the material covering her body is almost like a second skin. Originally balanced by a pair of large wings, the material billowing out behind is so skillfully carved that it appears to be undulating drapery rather than hard marble. Note also the exceptional skill that was used to create the illusion of an airborne figure not yet in contact with the ground. Discovered at Olympia in 1875, this is one of the all-too-scarce original marbles from the Periklean Age.

Doric Temples—Sicily

Two of the most sophisticated Doric temples of the Periklean age are found not in Greece but in Sicily, the southernmost portion of Magna Graecia. Both the Temple of Concord at Agrigento and the Temple of Segesta are in relatively good condition but for quite different reasons.

The prosperous Greek city of Akragas (ah-kra-GOSS; modern Agrigento) was built on a plateau overlooking the Mediterranean to the south. Because there was no akropolis, the citizens of Akragas (Gk., "high ground") built five Doric temples on the southern slope between the city and the sea. Lined up in a widely-spaced "avenue of temples," the structures provided a cohesive link between the city, the land, and the sea. For all who arrived by ship, the five temples were seen first, clearly identifying Akragas as a Greek city in what was still a foreign land. It can be said that the Greek gods were at home in Greece but they had to be imported into the very different environment of Italy and Sicily.

FIGURE 7.40   *Temple of Concord, ca. 425 B.C. Limestone, Agrigento, Sicily (ancient Akragas, Magna Graecia).*

FIGURE 7.39   *Paionios,* Nike, *ca. 421 B.C. Marble, height 76¾'' (85'' including base). Archeological Museum, Olympia.*

The Temple of Concord

The Temple of Concord (figure 7.40) was placed on a high spot midway between the city and the coastal plain. Concord is a hexastyle (six-column front) Doric temple that measures approximately 55′ × 129′. It has 23′ columns arranged in a 34-column peristyle (6 × 11). Like the Parthenon, it has rising stylobates and entablatures on both sides but, unlike the Parthenon, the six-column front is set in a straight line. The overall effect is a static front with longitudinal columns moving lightly down each side. When compared with the Parthenon, the most significant difference is the hexastyle facade. Six columns can, for most people, be taken in at a glance as a single unit. However, the eight-column front (octastyle facade) of the Parthenon (see figure 7.25) cannot be seen as a unit; for most observers the Parthenon insists upon a second or third look. The eye is forced to return to the building again and again as it tries to take it all in. Study the facade of Concord in figure 7.40 and compare that with the Parthenon. The latter appears to be restless and challenging; Concord reflects its name in its serenity, grace, and charm.

The Temple of Concord was, like all Greek temples, a sacred building, probably a sanctuary for Demeter, goddess of fertility, agriculture, and peace. Its sacred character notwithstanding, the temple escaped destruction only because it was converted into a Christian church

in A.D. 597. Greek religious architecture that in turn became sacred for Christians was always substantially altered. The alternative was the destruction meted out to all other sanctuaries.

Akragas was a very large Greek city (with a population of about 250,000) but Segesta was neither populous nor Greek. Why, then, did it have a large Greek theatre and one of the most interesting of all Doric temples? Located in the mountainous northwest, Segesta was within the orbit of Carthaginian influence, an influence that the city resisted for many years. Early in the sixth century B.C. Segesta adopted Greek writing and many of the Greek ways. Athens and Segesta even reached an agreement allowing marriage between the respective inhabitants.

The Temple of Segesta

The Temple of Segesta (figure 7.41) is a hexastyle Doric structure that measures about 76′ × 191′, making it considerably larger than Concord. The columns rise 32′ and are arranged in a 36-column peristyle (6 × 12). The temple is sometimes referred to as "anonymous"; no one knows which god it was intended to serve, only that the god was not Greek. The architect was probably Athenian (maybe even Iktinos) and certainly a knowledgeable and skillful master of the Classical style. Vincent Scully (see the Bibliography) refers to him as an "architectural Euripides."

Left in an unfinished condition for unknown reasons, the temple has no roof and there was no indication that an inner cella was ever planned. The columns are in

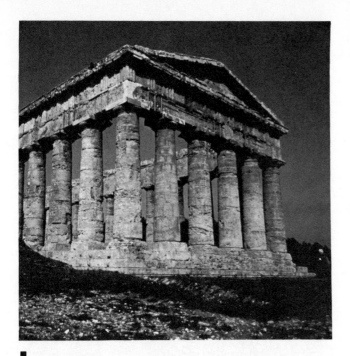

FIGURE 7.41 *Temple of Segesta, ca. 420s B.C. Limestone, Segesta, Sicily.*

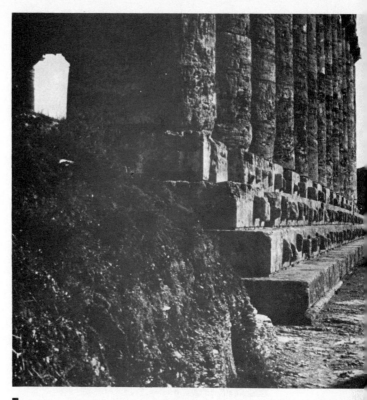

FIGURE 7.42 *Stylobate, Temple of Segesta.*

FIGURE 7.43 Stele of Hegesco, *ca. 400–390 B.C. Marble grave-relief, height 58½". National Archeological Museum, Athens.*

place awaiting the fluting that never took place. Particularly striking are the stone bosses on the stylobate and stereobate (figure 7.42) that were not chiseled off. These knobs facilitated the safe transport of heavy slabs from the quarry to this magnificent and very remote site.

As in Concord and the Parthenon, the longitudinal stylobate and entablature of Segesta arch upward but much more sharply than in the other two temples (figure 7.42). The straight, six-column front combined with the swift and tensile longitudinal arc give the building a strange and impressive energy. It is possible that the architect chose not to flute the columns after he saw them in place. Their solid mass contributes to the extraordinary power of the structure. It is possible, therefore, that the temple was deliberately left unfinished. That it was not destroyed by invading armies or zealous Christians was due solely to its isolation in the mountain wilderness of northwestern Sicily.

A comparison of the Temples of Concord and Segesta clearly reveals the range available to an imaginative architect. Both structures are easily classified as Doric by the elements identified in figure 7.22a (except for the lack of fluting in Segesta). The aesthetic impact, however, is remarkably different. Concord is serene; Segesta is restless. Concord is graceful; Segesta is massive and muscular. Concord was probably dedicated to the Greek goddess of peace. Segesta was intended for an unknown, non-Greek (meaning uncivilized) god. Concord could be transported to an appropriate site in Greece. Segesta is completely at home in the rugged mountains of Sicily.

A sculptured gravestone known as the *Stele* (STEE-lee) *of Hegesco* (figure 7.43) is civilized in the manner of the Temple of Concord. It shows a serving maid offering her seated mistress, the deceased who is commemorated, a casket of jewels. Common to Greek sculpture of the Classical Period is the serenity of facial expressions, whether the subjects are depicted as participating in a procession, a battle, or a meeting of the gods.

FIGURE 7.44 *Praxiteles,* Hermes with the Infant Dionysos. *Marble copy of probable bronze original of ca. 340 B.C., height 73". Archeological Museum, Olympia.*

FIGURE 7.45 *Praxiteles,* Aphrodite of Knidos. *Roman marble copy of marble original of ca. 350 B.C., height 80". Vatican Museums, Rome.*

Moreover, note that the heads of the standing servant and seated mistress are close to the same level; this same convention may also be noted in the Parthenon frieze (see figure 7.32) whether the participants are standing, sitting, or riding horses. This isocephalic (I-so-se-FALL-ik) convention, that is, the tradition of keeping all heads on approximately the same level, brings to Greek relief art of the Classical Period exceptional clarity; it is so subtly done that one's sense of rightness remains undisturbed.

With the defeat of Athens by Sparta in 404 B.C. the Golden Age came to an end. That both Sophokles and Euripides died at about the same time further marked the end of an era. Throughout the following century, until the death of Alexander in 323 B.C., the Classical tradition was maintained, though in a somewhat more theatrical manner. Greek artists prided themselves on adhering to the high standards of the preceding century; although Athens no longer ruled the seas, it was still the center of the artistic world.

Late Classical, 400–323 B.C.

The more pleasing and personal qualities of Late Classical sculpture and the superbly executed naturalism are due, in large part, to Praxiteles (prax-SIT-uh-leas) of Athens, the most celebrated of all ancient Greek sculptors. In his *Hermes with the Infant Dionysos* (figure 7.44) we see an example of the artist's exceptional skill in working marble. Praxiteles was apparently among the first to exploit the shimmering, translucent quality of marble.

There are no sharp angles; everything is smooth, rounded, polished. Compare, for example, the striking clarity of the *Doryphoros* (figure 7.18) with the softly sensuous treatment of the *Hermes.* Slimmer and certainly more relaxed, the *Hermes* looks positively decadent compared with the earnest Spear Bearer. Among today's experts the argument continues as to the correct attribution of the *Hermes.* Long regarded as the sole surviving original by Praxiteles, the current consensus is that this lovely sculpture is most likely a Hellenistic copy of what was possibly a bronze original. The head of the infant is proportionately too small and the rumpled drapery is inconsistent with the Late Classical style. The most telling discrepancy, however, is the marble bar that braces the hip of Hermes. Greek sculptors usually designed their works to be self-supporting, but a marble copy of an inherently strong bronze original would need to be braced. The ongoing controversy over the 2500-year-old work points up the cogent definition of culture as what remains after the society that created it has vanished.

Definitely a copy, and quite a good one, the *Aphrodite of Knidos* by Praxiteles (figure 7.45) is a revolutionary work. The single most popular statue in all antiquity, the *Aphrodite* was lavishly praised by the Roman historian Pliny (XXXVI, 20) as the finest statue in the world, so marvelous that it was placed in a shrine to be universally admired. (Pliny was equally enthusiastic about the Laokoön—figure 7.55—and called *it* the finest sculpture in the world.) Abandoning the traditional concept of a figure occupying a rectangular space, Praxiteles designed a slender goddess with sinuous lines rising all the

FIGURE 7.46 Boy from the Bay of Marathon, *ca. 340–300 B.C. Bronze, height 51". National Archeological Museum, Athens.*

way from her feet to the quizzical tilt of her head. The slight outward lean of the right leg increases the sensuous curvature of the right hip. Echoing the swelling curve of the hip, the left leg is flexed so that the thighs are pressed gently together with the knees nearly touching. From the knees—the narrowest part of the composition—the figure ascends in an hourglass configuration to the slightly startled reaction of a woman surprised in the act of bathing. In line, pose, proportion, and structure Praxiteles has created an incomparable idealization of femininity, the essence of womanhood. It should be noted that although nude males were portrayed in a variety of activities, Greek artists invariably depicted women in normal situations that justified nudity: bathing, making love, functioning as flute girls, or as hetairai.

Looking somewhat like a male version of the marble torso, the original bronze found in the Bay of Marathon (figure 7.46) was probably derived from the work of Praxiteles. The innate strength of bronze enabled the anonymous artist to dispense with visually irritating supports like the marble bar previously discussed (*Hermes* figure 7.44). The lightly poised figure, difficult to achieve in bronze but virtually impossible to reproduce in marble, is similar to the Hermes, especially in the modeling of the surfaces and the melting gaze of the eyes.

FIGURE 7.47 *Lysippos,* Apoxyomenos (Scraper). *Roman marble copy of a bronze original of ca. 330 B.C., height 6'9". Vatican Museums, Rome.*

Lysippos, who was sculptor for the court of Alexander the Great, was probably the most revolutionary artist of the Late Classical period. His *Apoxyomenos* (apox-e-o-MAY-nos) in figure 7.47 was as important for the fourth century as the *Doryphoros* of Polykleitos (figure 7.18) was for the fifth century; both works established new sculptural canons. Departing from the canon of Polykleitos, Lysippos introduced a new system of proportions in which the head was smaller, the body taller and more slender, and the limbs lithe and long. Using an S-shaped tool called a strigil, the athlete is scraping oil, dust, and sweat from his body, a standard procedure at the conclusion of athletic contests. Utilizing the space in front of the body, the extended arms break through the invisible barrier of the frontal plane, violating a convention dating back to the art of Egypt's Old Kingdom. There

FIGURE 7.48 The Dying Gaul. *Roman marble copy of bronze original from Pergamon, ca. 230–220 B.C. Life-size. Capitoline Museum, Rome.*

FIGURE 7.49 *Pythokritos of Rhodes,* Nike of Samothrace, *ca. 190 B.C. Marble, height 8'. The Louvre, Paris. © Renunion des Musees Nationaux.*

is a new sense of movement with trunk, head, and limbs turned in different directions; this is sculpture conceived, executed, and meant to be viewed in the round— all 360 degrees. As epitomized in the *Apoxyomenos,* these revolutionary ideas were not to be fully understood until the Italian Renaissance some seventeen centuries later.

Hellenistic Period, 323–30 B.C.

Symbolized by the death of Alexander, the long and enormously productive Classical age had come to an end. Artists were no longer concerned with idealized portraits and classical harmony, but instead became increasingly interested in actual appearances and in the infinite varieties of human nature and experience. In the midst of the rapid disintegration of the Alexandrian empire, the emphasis was upon basic survival in a world beset by constant sectional strife. Sometimes described as decadent, Hellenistic art did indeed include banalities, trivialities, pathos, and empty virtuosity. Greek genius was not yet exhausted, however, for the age also saw the production of exceptional works of art that were no less admirable than those of the classical era but were certainly different.

A Celtic tribe that ravaged Asia Minor until subdued by Attalos I of Pergamon, the Gauls were immortalized in the remarkable figure of *The Dying Gaul* (figure 7.48). Also known as the *Dying Trumpeter* because of the discarded battle trumpet in the right foreground, the hair, facial features, and ornamental collar about the neck realistically convey the idea of a Gallic tribesman. The figure, however, is in the heroic Greek tradition of the nude warrior; and the treatment of the vanquished barbarian is sympathetic, portraying a certain poignant nobility as the dying man braces his right arm against the ground in a futile effort to ward off an ignoble death.

The *Nike of Samothrace* (figure 7.49) is not only one of the most dramatic and compelling works ever created but a prime example of the continuing power of classical themes. Attributed to Pythokritos (py-THOCK-ri-toss) and erected in a sanctuary on Rhodes in honor of a naval victory over King Antiochus III of Syria, Victory is portrayed

■ **FIGURE 7.50** *Altar of Zeus, west front, from Pergamon, ca. 180 B.C. (restored). Berlin State Museums.*

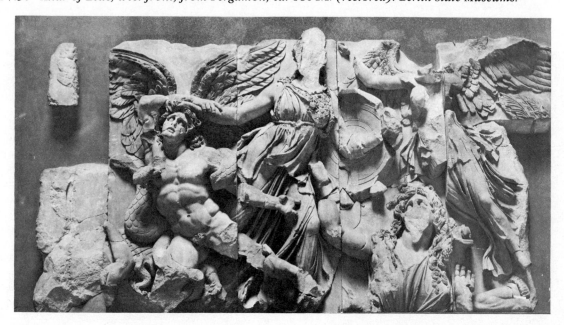

■ **FIGURE 7.51** The Battle of the Gods and Giants, *relief segment from the Altar of Zeus at Pergamon, ca. 180 B.C. Berlin State Museums.*

at the moment of alighting on the symbolic prow of a ship. With her great wings still extended, she is moving into a wind that becomes a tangible presence as it shapes the flowing draperies into deep diagonal folds, carrying our eyes restlessly over the entire surface. Victory, who is aptly characterized as poetry in motion, communicates both the immediacy of the moment and a feeling for ongoing action in a pervasive atmosphere of wind and sea.

One of the wonders of the ancient world, the great Altar of Zeus (figure 7.50), was built by the son and successor of Attalos I to commemorate his father's military victories. Even though it was designed as an Ionic structure for a site in Ionia, there is none of the delicacy of the classic Ionic style. With a base 100′ square, this truly monumental altar is intended to impress rather than inspire. The immense frieze around the base is over 400′ long and 7′–8′ high (figure 7.51). Using the traditional Greek device of portraying actual historical events in mythological terms, this is a highly emotional and dramatic work. Here is a world of giants, an exaggeration of physical and emotional force that, in its own way, accomplishes its goals fully as well as the classic Parthenon frieze (see figure 7.32). A comparison of the two friezes clearly defines the significant differences between the Classical and Hellenistic styles.

■
FIGURE 7.52 *Cossutius, Temple of the Olympian Zeus, ca. 174* B.C.–A.D. *131, Athens.*

■
FIGURE 7.53 *Signed by . . . Andros of Antioch on the Maeander,* Aphrodite of Melos, *ca. 120* B.C. *Marble, height 80″. The Louvre, Paris.*

As dramatic as the Altar of Zeus and of equally monumental proportions, Hellenistic public buildings stressed sheer size over classic restraint and harmonious proportions. Even in the scanty remains of the Temple of the Olympian Zeus (figure 7.52) one can detect some of the grandeur of a temple that originally had 104 columns over 56′ in height. Built in the Corinthian order and entirely of pentelic marble, the temple measured 130′ × 340′, as compared with the 101′ × 228′ dimensions of the Parthenon. Figure 7.52 shows the few remaining columns; it also reveals the full stylobate of the temple, clearly indicating its enormous size. In view of the Roman preference for the ornate Corinthian order, it is fitting that this architect was of Italic origin and that the grandiose project was completed by the Roman Emperor Hadrian.

The *Aphrodite of Melos* (figure 7.53), formerly known by her Roman name of *Venus de Milo* and once highly praised, is a fleshy counterpart of the three goddesses from the Parthenon pediment (see figure 7.30). She was once a fixture in pretentious Victorian parlors of the past century, usually cast in plaster and with a clock in her tummy. Drawing more attention than her body, the abundant fabric and heavy folds of her gown demonstrate the awkwardness of a clothes-falling-off-a-figure motif.

The bronze head from Delos (figure 7.54), originally part of a full-length statue, is a penetrating study of an apparently unhappy, fleshy-faced man who seems to be overwhelmed by doubt and anxiety. Though by no means limited to the Hellenistic age, this very private portrait seems to epitomize the predicament of helpless individuals in a chaotic and often violent world. A comparison of this face with that of the *Doryphoros* (see figure 7.18) sums it up; the Golden Age has receded to the distant past.

■
FIGURE 7.54 Portrait Head, *from Delos, ca. 80 B.C. Bronze, height 12¾". National Archeological Museum, Athens.*

The *Laokoön and His Sons* (lay-OK-o-on; figure 7.55) is an extravagantly dramatic version of the fate of the Trojan priest. Supposedly punished by Poseidon's sea serpents because he warned his people of the Trojan horse strategy, the three Trojans writhe and struggle, their faces distorted with terror. Despite his powerful muscles the priest is helpless before the power of the gods. When this work was discovered during the High Renaissance (in 1506), its striking virtuosity made an enormous impression on Michelangelo and other Renaissance artists. It is quite possible that the *Laokoön* was imported by the Romans because it represented an important episode in pre-Roman history. Supposedly forewarned of the fall of Troy by the punishment of the priest, Aeneas escaped from Troy to fulfill his destiny as the legendary founder of mighty Rome.

The Legacy of Greece

The Greeks of antiquity established the foundation for the development of Western art. During a cultural epoch of approximately a thousand years, they developed in many media a viable, complex art that changed constantly but generally in a rational and humanistic direction. Their achievements were by no means restricted to the sculpture, architecture, reliefs, and pottery and vase painting discussed in the limited space in this chapter. They also excelled in jewelry, coins, engraved gems, decorative metalwork, painting and mosaics, furniture, textiles, and glassware. When their contributions in philosophy, music, and the literary arts are added to this, we see a marvelously rounded culture. They established standards that serve as thesis or antithesis for contemporary judgments and achievements throughout our cultural life.

■
FIGURE 7.55 *Hagesandros, Polydoros, and Athenodoros of Rhodes,* Laokoön and His Sons, *1st century A.D. Marble, height 8'. Vatican Museums, Rome.*

A skeptical, resilient, and frequently cantankerous people, the Greeks respected excellence and despised mediocrity. Constantly seeking an understanding of the world and everything in it, they asked not only "Why?" but also "Why not?" And they expected sane, reasonable, and logical answers. There has never been anyone quite like them.

Exercises

1. Using several books from the bibliography, find some illustrations of geometric pottery and then draw a pot with your own design. Why did you choose these particular geometric motifs? How does your design compare with the Greek examples? In fact, since Greek vases were functional, why did they bother to decorate them? What does this tell us about the Greeks of even this early period?
2. Compare Greek vases of the three basic styles: geometric, black-figure, and red-figure. Which style do you find most appealing? Why?
3. When the *Anavyssos Kouros* and the *Kore from Chios* are compared with the *Kouros of Sounion* and the *Kore of Auxerre,* it is obvious that the Archaic style has evolved considerably. Identify the various changes and try to account for the degree and direction of the stylistic evolution. Where is the style going? To the *Doryphoros?* To the *Aphrodite of Knidos?* Can you relate these various art works to a view of reality generally held at the time of composition? For example, to what extent is the *Doryphoros* a "realistic" depiction? "Idealistic"? Why?

4. Consider the Classical style as described and illustrated in the text and then reflect on how you yourself use the term "classical" to describe things experienced in your own life. How are you using the term? How does this usage compare with that of the Greeks?

5. Select a piece of sculpture from each of the four major periods of Greek art. What do they have in common? How do they differ, one from another? What conclusions can you draw about the evolution of Greek styles? Which style is most appealing to you? Why?

6. Prepare a research project on "The Greek Architectural Influence in ———," specifying your own community. Which buildings are essentially Doric, or Ionic, or Corinthian? Which have elements of two or more orders and what are they? Are there any structures patterned after the Greek temple plan (such as the Parthenon) or are there modifications? Are there Greek facades stuck on other architectural styles?

The key to the project is the identification of Greek elements followed by an analysis of how these are used in conjunction with other architectural styles. Your project can culminate in a slide show, photo album, or perhaps a collection of drawings.

Summary

From the making of pottery during the transitional Geometric Period (900–750 B.C.) the Greeks greatly expanded their artistic output during the Archaic Period (750–480 B.C.). There was a marked evolution towards naturalism in their sculpture, particularly in the kore and kouros figures. Black-figure pottery dominated the period until red-figure vases were introduced late in the period (ca. 530 B.C.).

The Classical Period (480–323 B.C.) was the crowning glory of Greek excellence in art and architecture. Their magnificent sculpture includes the *Delphi Charioteer, Poseidon,* the *Discobolus,* the *Riaci Bronze,* the *Doryphoros,* the *Apoxyomenos,* and the works of Praxiteles. Their achievements in red-figure and white-ground vases have never been surpassed. Outstanding examples of the perfected temple include the Parthenon, the Erechtheion, and the temples of Athena Nike, Poseidon, Concord, and Segesta.

Sculptural masterworks of the Hellenistic Period (323–30 B.C.) include *The Dying Gaul, Nike of Samothrace,* the Altar of Zeus, and the *Laokoön.* Typical of the Hellenistic preference for large public buildings, the Temple of the Olympian Zeus was truly enormous.

Culture and Human Values

Though the Golden Age of Greece lasted only one generation, it left its mark on all subsequent Hellenic cultures, and most especially, upon Rome. The fragile balance between the freedom of the individual and the needs of the group could not be maintained but there still remained the ideals of Freedom, Beauty, Truth, and Justice. Though perhaps breached more often than honored, particularly during the Hellenistic Period, they still inspired those who placed these values above mere survival in the chaotic post-Alexandrian world.

Annotated Bibliography

Ashmole, Bernard. *Architect and Sculptor in Classical Greece.* New York: New York University Press, 1972. How sculpture and architecture were integrated in the Golden Age.

Bieber, Margarete. *The Sculpture of the Hellenistic Age.* New York: Hacker Art Books, 1980. Authoritative and well-illustrated.

Biers, William R. *The Archeology of Ancient Greece: An Introduction.* Ithaca: Cornell University Press, 1980. Major monuments plus minor objects found at archeological sites, showing that "stylistic development is to be seen in artifacts as well as in the major arts."

Carpenter, Rhys. *The Architects of the Parthenon.* Middlesex, England: Penguin Books, 1970. Intriguing theory about who built what and why.

Charbonneaux, Jean et al. *Grece Archaique (620–480 avant J. C.).* Paris: Gallimard, 1968. See also—in English—his *Classical Greek Art* (New York: Braziller, 1972) and his *Hellenistic Art* (New York: Braziller, 1973). All three works are in the series *The Arts of Mankind,* edited by Andre Malraux and Andre Parrot. Superb illustrations.

Hampe, Roland, and Simon, Erika. *The Birth of Greek Art: From the Mycenaean to the Archaic Period.* New York: Oxford University Press, 1981. Detailed and thorough.

Lawrence, A. W. *Greek Architecture.* Rev. ed. New York: The Viking Press, 1984. A comprehensive study.

Lullies, Reinhard, and Hirmer, Max. *Greek Sculpture.* New York: Henry N. Abrams, 1960. Includes 282 magnificent photographs by Hirmer.

MacKendrick, Paul. *The Greek Stones Speak: The Story of Archeology in Greek Lands.* 2d ed. New York: W. W. Norton & Company, 1983. Illustrated exploration of the important sites. For the nonspecialist.

Onians, John. *Art and Thought in the Hellenistic Age: The Greek World View 350–50 B.C.* London: Thames and Hudson, 1979. A rewarding interdisciplinary study.

Pollit, J. J. *The Ancient View of Greek Art: Criticism, History, and Terminology.* New Haven: Yale University Press, 1974. Illuminating observations on contemporary art by Greeks and Romans.

Ragghianti, Licia Collubi. *The Magnificent Heritage of Ancient Greece: 3,000 Years of Hellenic Art.* New York: Newsweek, 1979. A popular treatment with rich colorplates.

Richter, Gisela M. A. *Handbook of Greek Art.* 7th ed. New York: E. P. Dutton, 1980. Well illustrated and concise. Includes minor arts.

Robertson, Martin. *A History of Greek Art.* 2 vols. New York: Cambridge University Press, 1975. Detailed and interesting. Abridged edition available in paperback as *A Shorter History of Greek Art* (New York: Cambridge University Press, 1981).

Scully, Vincent. *The Earth, the Temple, and the Gods.* New Haven: Yale University Press, 1979. Fascinating study of the landscape of Greek sacred architecture.

8

The Greek Arts of Music, Poetry, Dance, and Theatre

Music

Music was a requisite for the good life in ancient Greece. The education of the young men of Athens was not complete without extensive instruction in the ethical qualities of music with approximately equal time devoted to the performance of music. Further, there must be instruction in gymnastics roughly equal to the time and effort expended on music. The question Glaucon posed for Sokrates was rhetorical: "After music our youth are to be educated by gymnastics?" For the record the Sokratic reply was a terse "Certainly." Music and gymnastics had to be evenly balanced to reach the goal of a sound mind in a healthy body. According to Plato, too much time in the gymnasium makes men "more brutal than they should be," while too much music making causes performers to be "softer than is good for them."

The original concept of the balanced regimen apparently originated with Pythagoras, who described an analogy between a vibrating, finely tuned string and the human mind and body. When the stretched string has the proper tension it will produce, when played, the exact musical tone that the performer requires. If stretched too fine, the string will break; if the tension is insufficient, the string will be dull and unresponsive. In other words, the mind (musical tone) and the body (tensed string) function best when they are completely in harmony with each other.

The Greek word for music (*mousike;* MOO-si-kay) means "of the Muses": the nine goddesses who presided over the arts, literature, and science (see box 8.1). "Music" was therefore an umbrella term, but music as we understand the word was prominent in everyday life. As an art form in its own right there were four aspects of music:

1. The arts of singing and of playing a musical instrument. The relationship of poetry and music was viewed as symbiotic; rarely did one art form appear without the other.

Box 8.1 *The Greek Muses*

The nine daughters of Zeus and Mnemosyne (nih-MOSS-uh-nee; goddess of memory) presided over literature, the arts, and science. Frequently called the "deities of graceful achievement," the Muses, under the leadership of Apollo, were the source of inspiration for all creative persons. In typically Greek fashion, their names were wonderfully descriptive of their particular function.

Calliope (kuh-LIE-uh-pea; "beautiful-voiced"), goddess of eloquence and epic poetry.

Clio (KLY-oh; "teller"), goddess of history.

Erato (air-uh-TOE; "loved"), goddess of love poetry.

Euterpe (you-TUR-pea; "charming"), goddess of lyric poetry and music.

Melpomene (mel-POM-uh-NEE; "the singing one"), goddess of tragedy.

Polyhymnia (polly-HIM-nee-uh; "abounding in songs"), goddess of singing, sacred poetry, and oratory.

Terpsichore (turp-SICK-uh-REE; "to delight in dance"), goddess of dance and choral song.

Thalia (tha-LEE-uh; "the blooming one"), goddess of comedy and pastoral poetry.

Urania (yoo-RAY-nee-uh; "the heavenly one"), goddess of astronomy.

TABLE 8.1 Greek Musical Instruments

Instrument	Lyre	Kithara	Aulos
Basic Form			
Tone Production	String instrument	String instrument	Wind instrument
Played	Plucking	Plucking	Blowing through double reed into twin pipes
Size	Small, hand-held	Larger than lyre, hand-held	Small, hand-held
Number of Strings or Air Columns	Usually seven strings	Usually eleven strings	Two pipes with up to eleven tone holes
Performance By	Amateurs (usually aristocrats)	Professional musicians	Professionals and amateurs
Function	Primarily to accompany solo songs	Accompany solo and group singing	Solo instrument and accompany group singing
Location	Home, school	Social and public gatherings	Plays, orgiastic religious ceremonies, elegies
Tone Quality	Light, delicate, serene	Louder than lyre but still delicate	Loud, nasal, penetrating
Ethos (Ethical Quality)	Intellectual, Dorian, Apollonian	Intellectual, Dorian, Apollonian	Emotional, Phrygian, Dionysian

2. Music in the educational process, that is, performing and listening to music as a vital part of the ethical training that inculcates virtue and "sobriety in the soul" (Plato). This is the *ethos* of music that figured so prominently in Greek philosophy.
3. The study of the scientific basis of music emphasizing acoustics and mathematics.
4. Music and mathematics as a key to understanding the harmony of the universe: the Pythagorean "music of the spheres."

All free Athenian men were involved in music performance, music listening, and music education. Plato, Aristotle, and other philosophers dealt with various aspects of music from the Muses to mathematics to metaphysics.

Musical Instruments

The principal instruments were the *lyre,* a larger version of the lyre called the *kithara,* and the *aulos* (see table 8.1). According to mythology the infant Hermes, son of Zeus, killed a turtle and strung gut strings across the hollow shell. That the strings were made from intestines of oxen stolen from his brother Apollo complicated the situation. Hermes craftily avoided further trouble by permitting Apollo to play his lyre. Thus the beginning of the legendary lyre and with it the lyre-playing tradition of the cult of Apollo (figure 8.1).

The seat of the Apollonian cult was the island of Delos and subsequently Delphi. The myths extol the virtues of the early musical life of the Greek mainland untouched by alien influences. Marvelous were the deeds of heroes and of divinely endowed musicians such as Orpheus, Amphion, Musaeus, and others, all with names connected with ancient tribes in the northern part of the mainland.

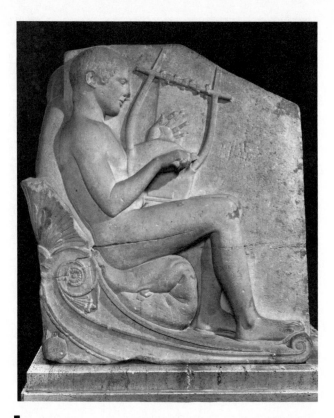

FIGURE 8.1 *Lyre Player "The Boston Throne" ca. 470–450 B.C. Three-sided marble relief, height 38". H. L. Pierce Fund. Courtesy, Museum of Fine Arts, Boston. The lyre was always played from a sitting position (also see figure 8.4).*

FIGURE 8.2 *Aulos Player of the Ludovisi Throne, ca. 460 B.C. Museo della Terme, Rome. One of the few female nudes from the Classical period, this lovely work is also notable for the relaxed and casual pose. Unlike the lyre, the aulos could be played standing or sitting.*

As the tribes migrated they carried their music with them. The Dorians moved as far south as Crete, the Aeolians settled in the eastern Aegean, and the Ionians moved from the west to the east central mainland and to Asia Minor.

The Lyre

The Ionians brought with them their music and their national instrument, the lyre. The influence of Oriental elements led to a synthesis of the two cultures which, in turn, led to the founding of Greek classical music, poetry, and dance. Mythology characteristically depicts the Ionian migration by relating how Orpheus accidentally dropped his lyre, which drifted eastward across the Aegean to the island of Lesbos.

The Aulos

The Near East produced the other national instrument, the reed pipe, or aulos (figure 8.2). The inventors of this pungent-toned instrument came from Phrygia in Asia Minor. The aulos was associated with the Phrygian mode[1] or scale and with the cult of Dionysos. The lyre became associated with the Dorian mode or scale and with the Apollonian cult.

There was a notable conflict between the cult of the two instruments. The lyre was not fully accepted in the East, possibly because its tone quality was too delicate when compared with the nasal quality of the aulos. Legend recounts the musical competition between Olen the Lycian on the lyre and Olympos the Phrygian on the aulos. The results of that contest were inconclusive, indicating that the competing instruments attained a state of parity. The whole of Greek musical culture reflected this kind of balance of power between the Apollonian lyre and the Dionysian aulos, that is, the intellect versus the passions.

The Musicians

The earliest musicians were apparently the blind singers who performed the Homeric epics. Greek legends abound with accounts of singers who foolishly persisted in challenging the gods. Thamyris was blinded by the muses because of his boasting; the blind singer Teiresias (cf. Sophokles's *Oedipus*) had suffered the same penalty by revealing things men should not know; Misenis lost a musical contest to the sea gods and was drowned in the Aegean. The satyr Marsyas was a spectacular loser. First, he picked up the aulos that Athena had discarded because she felt she looked undignified while playing it.

---

1. An approximation of the Phrygian mode can be made by playing the white notes on the piano from *d* to the next *d* above or below. The Dorian mode is found from *e* to *e* on the white notes.

■ **FIGURE 8.3** Apollo and Marsyas, *marble relief from Manitinea, ca. 400–350 B.C. Width, ca. 4'. From the workshop of Praxiteles. National Archeological Museum, Athens. Marsyas is on the right, frantically playing, while a slave waits patiently with a knife. Holding a kithara, Apollo sits serenely at the left, waiting to execute the satyr for his hubris.*

■ **FIGURE 8.4** *Orpheus Painter, red-figure krater (detail): "Orpheus Among the Thracians," ca. 440 B.C. Antikenmuseum Staatliche Museen Preussischer Kulturbesitz Berlin. The power of Orpheus's music obviously failed to charm the vulgar Thracians. They murdered him, which tends to confirm the Greek thesis that their music was too sophisticated for barbarians to appreciate.*

She had Marsyas beaten for his impudence. Failing to take the celestial hint, he then challenged Apollo to a playing contest, for which presumption he was flayed alive (figure 8.3).

The most famous singer-poet was Orpheus, reputedly the son of Apollo and Calliope. The powers attributed to Orpheus were staggering. In order to rescue Eurydice (you-RID-uh-sea), he enchanted the underworld with his lyre (figure 8.4). He cast spells on all aspects of nature, and he was credited with inventing poetic meter and even the alphabet. The last attribute may refer to the fact that the Greeks used an elaborate musical notation based on their alphabet.

The earliest historical figure to emerge from the legendary past personified by the mythical Olympos is the kithara-player, Terpander of Lesbos (ca. 675 B.C.). His musical powers were so great that he was ordered to Sparta by the Delphic Oracle to help quell dissension within the state. As the first known musician, Terpander is regarded as the founder of Greek classical music.

Terpander's successors competed in the Olympic Games (776 B.C.–A.D. 393) in poetry and music. They sang variations on the *nomos* (nomos = law), or sung strains using fundamental melodic and rhythmic phrases. In his *Laws,* Plato described distinct classes of songs, such as kitharodic nomes, hymns, dirges, paeans, and dithyrambs, including the information that each type of song had its own special rules that even precluded the interchange of poetic texts. Terpander was credited with increasing the sections of the kitharodic nomes to the hallowed number of seven (cf. the seven-stringed lyre, the seven gates of Thebes and the—at that time—seven muses).

Archilochos (are-ki-LOW-kos) of Paros, another seventh-century musician, advanced the art of lyric music— music sung to the lyre—by introducing rhythmic variety.

Much of his inspiration may have been drawn from folk song. Folk art was apparently widespread because literary sources mention a variety of work songs: songs for stamping barley, treading grapes, throwing pots, spinning wool; songs for watchmen, shepherds, drawers of water, and makers of rope.

The lyric works of the poet-musicians—Sappho, Alkaios, and Anakreon—were probably inspired by folk influences, as were many of the works performed at the great contests in Olympia and Delphi. Festival performances, however, were not limited to the lyre. At the Pythian Games at Delphi in 586 B.C., Sakadas of Argos won a celebrated victory with his *Nomos Pythikos* (*Pythian Nome*) for the aulos, depicting Apollo's triumph over the Python. While most nomes were written in praise of Apollo, the poet-musician Pindar won a measure of fame for odes written in praise of victorious athletes.

From the Homeric age until the decline of Greek civilization, the lyre was the preferred instrument for the performance of epic and lyric poetry. The reedy and colorful aulos was used to accompany elegies and dramatic choruses.

Poetry and Music

When the arts of poetry and music were combined, which was the usual practice, the text dominated the music. The instruments were always designated as participants. Thus *kitharodia* meant singing with the accompaniment of the kithara and *aulodia* meant singing with aulos accompaniment.

The principal musical-poetic type of composition was the *nomos,* which held a position analogous to the *epos* in literature. The nome was probably a melody originally, or perhaps a whole composition, but it later developed into a rather fixed style of words and music.

The nome is best understood by comparing it with architecture. A Doric temple, for example, is a kind of architectural nome. Architects were bound to a basic scheme and ornamentation called Doric but could assert their individuality by different organizations of the same elements. Refer back, for example, to the discussion in chapter 7 of the Temple of Concord (figure 7.40) and the Temple of Segesta (figures 7.41 and 7.42). Both temples are Doric but Concord is calm and serene while Segesta is burly and assertive. Similar extremes are possible in different pieces of music in the same nome.

The nome was usually associated with the name of one particular master but it was further developed, with certain restrictions, by other musicians without losing its basic melodic profile or rhythmic skeleton. The chief exponents of the nome from the mythic past were Olympos for the aulos nome and Terpander for the kithara nome.

Archilochos (fl. ca. 660 B.C.) must be added as the third major figure in Greek musical history. He instituted technical reforms that had far-reaching effects. Before his time, each note of the music was closely allied with the words. He added all sorts of embellishments that were improvised upon between songs. The musical accompaniment of the nomes followed the text, while instrumental solo playing now took place between the strophes (stanzas).

Archilochos even had the accompaniment play "dissenting" notes that were not in unison with the melody. These differing notes added considerable complexity to an already intricate musical style limited to three elements of music: melody, rhythm, and tone color. Harmony as we know it was never a part of Greek musical practice.

The profuse theoretical literature of classical antiquity did not deal with the laws of lyric poetry, that is, with rules about the metric structure of lyric verse. For the Greeks the union of lyric poetry and music was so complete that prosody and metrics did not belong to the domain of linguistics and poetry but rather formed part of the musical sciences practiced by the musician-poets.

Sappho

The illustrious musician-poet (or poet-musician) Sappho was born on the Aegean island of Lesbos around 630 B.C. and lived most of her long life there. At a time when Solon was legislating in Athens and Jeremiah was prophesying in Palestine, she was at the height of her fame and, moreover, fully aware of her reputation:

The Muses have made me happy
And worthy of the world's envy,
So that even beyond death
I shall be remembered.

Celebrated in both the Greek and Roman worlds, her poems were preserved until the third century A.D. by Alexandrian editors but were later almost totally destroyed along with other so-called pagan literature. The three surviving poems and numerous fragments remain to testify to the beauty of her lyric poetry, that is, poetry sung to the delicate sounds of the lyre.

Lead off, my lyre,
And we shall sing together.

■

FIGURE 8.5 *"Alkaios and Sappho with Lyres," detail of red-figure vase, ca. 450 B.C. Staatliche Antikensammlungen und Glyptothek, Munich. Standing as tall as her colleague, the poet Alkaios, Sappho is depicted as a poised and beautiful woman, fully the equal of a male poet-musician.*

Revolving mostly around Aphrodite, Sappho's themes focus on her passions and jealousies, but there are references to two brothers and to her daughter Kleïs. Though knowledge of her personal life is scanty, Sappho certainly enjoyed the social and domestic freedom of a society in which highly educated women mixed freely with men as their equals. Not confined to a haremlike existence like Ionian women or subject to a military discipline like the Dorians of Sparta, Aeolian women were devoted to the arts of beauty, especially poetry and music (figure 8.5).

In the following complete poem, Sappho appeals to Aphrodite to help her win the affections of a reluctant girl. Aphrodite's response is good-natured but a bit impatient; Sappho has made this kind of request before and she will certainly make it again. Moreover, as Aphrodite points out, the girl refuses your gifts today but you will refuse hers tomorrow.

God's wildering daughter deathless Aphródita,
A whittled perplexity your bright abstruse chair,
With heartbreak, lady, and breathlessness
Tame not my heart.

But come down to me, as you came before,
For if ever I cried, and you heard and came,
Come now, of all times, leaving
Your father's golden house

In that chariot pulled by sparrows reined and bitted,
Swift in their flying, a quick blur aquiver,
Beautiful, high. They drew you across steep air
Down to the black earth;

Fast they came, and you behind them, O
Hilarious heart, your face all laughter,
Asking, What troubles you this time, why again
Do you call me down?

Asking, In your wild heart, who now
Must you have? Who is she that persuasion
Fetch her, enlist her, and put her into bounden love?
Sappho, who does you wrong?

If she balks, I promise, soon she'll chase,
If she's turned from gifts, now she'll give them.
And if she does not love you, she will love,
Helpless, she will love.

Come, then, loose me from cruelties.
Give my tethered heart its full desire.
Fulfill, and, come, lock your shield with mine
Throughout the siege.

The next poem is also complete except for the last
four words added by the translator. The theme is jealousy, a recital of physical torments brought about by the
loved one's interest in conversing with a man. The emotions are strong but recollected in tranquility in carefully
chosen words. Translated into Latin by Catullus, this work
was praised by Plutarch as "a masterpiece among poems
of passionate love."

He seems to be a god, that man
Facing you, who leans to be close,
Smiles, and, alert and glad, listens
To your mellow voice

And quickens in love at your laughter.
That stings my breasts, jolts my heart
If I dare the shock of a glance.
I cannot speak,

My tongue sticks to my dry mouth,
Thin fire spreads beneath my skin,
My eyes cannot see and my aching ears
Roar in their labyrinths.

Chill sweat slides down my body,
I shake, I turn greener than grass.
I am neither living nor dead and cry
From the narrow between.

But endure, even (this grief of love.)

■

FIGURE 8.6 *"Young Girls Dancing Around the Altar,"
interior of red-figure bowl, ca. 450 B.C. The Hermitage,
Leningrad. Note the elegantly curved chair (a Greek
invention) on which the aulos player sits. The kithara
player stands at the altar, while the girls circle about in
a light and graceful dance. Note also the different hair
styles and the variety of dress design and decoration.*

The Art of Dance

The third art associated with music and poetry was that
of dance. In fact, the three arts were so mutually interconnected that it is difficult to consider any one of them
in isolation.

Human beings seem to have always enjoyed dance,
and few people appreciated dance more than the ancient
Greeks. Greek dance probably began as a form of worship, ritual, witchcraft, enchantment, and sex symbolism
in association with fertility rites. Plato believed that dance
was a natural expression of emotions and that it might
have grown out of the use of gestures to imitate words
and phrases.

All of our knowledge of steps and movements is
based on the figures on vases, on architectural friezes,
and, to some extent, on various writings referring to
dance. The dancing figures in Greek art display a variety
of design and gesture, but over many centuries certain
positions occur consistently. Arm movements were built
either upon a straight line of the arm from shoulder to
fingertip or upon the angularity of bending the arm at the
elbow to form a right angle. The designs could be somewhat curved by increasing the angle at the elbow, by
adding a curve at the waist, or both at the same time. The
basic design, however, was maintained. The straight lines
and curves were normally associated with light and delicate dances (figure 8.6). The angular designs were used
in strongly dramatic dances.

■ **FIGURE 8.7** *Theatre at Epidauros, ca. 350 B.C. Designed by Polykleitos the Younger. This view shows the great size (13,000 capacity) typical of Greek theatres. Nevertheless, actors and chorus could be understood even from the top row.*

Dionysian dances were invariably dramatic and frequently frenzied. Dancers sometimes wore the animal skins of the Dionysian cult: bull, fawn, goat, fox, and panther. For the wild mountain dances the dancers carried snakes. The dancers were called Maenads, Thyiades, Bacchantes, and Satyrs.

The four Dionysian festivals held every year influenced everyday Greek life as well as the arts and literature. These festivals included much dancing, sacrificial processions, banquets, choruses conducted by the poets, and most especially, performances of the tragedies and comedies.

Greek Theatre

Music played an important role in the theatre but the precise nature of that role is not clear. There is no question about the chorus; it performed vocal functions. On occasion, the individual actors sang their lines, and the aulos sounded at various times throughout the play. The aulos was the exclusive instrument for the theatre, never used except as a solo instrument and never replaced by the lyre.

Greek drama was, to a considerable degree, a musical experience and yet hardly comparable to an operatic production. In fact, nothing in our culture compares with the Greek amalgam of choric songs, spoken dialogues, solo songs, and aulos playing. Like other conventions of Greek tragedy—masks, stylized movement and speech, platform shoes—this unique form of theatre must be accepted on its own merits, which according to the Greeks themselves were quite sufficient.

Greek dramatic productions always utilized a circular or semicircular space in front of the stage on which the chorus danced. The theatre at Epidauros (figure 8.7) exemplifies the classical Greek theatre where the chorus sang and danced in the circular *orkhestra* (from *orkheisthai,* to dance).

Greek plays are no longer performed in their original versions because all of the music has been lost. Over a long period of time, those who copied and recopied the manuscripts began omitting the musical notation because they were unable to read it. As a consequence, the words were transmitted to future generations but the music is gone forever.

Choric passages were an integral part of the plays of Aeschylus and were almost as important throughout the plays of Sophokles and Euripides. Towards the end of classical antiquity, however, tragedies were often performed without the choral parts. The reasons for this diminution of a major musical element are not clear but could be attributed to a decline in musical expertise in the chorus or lack of audience sophistication or both.

The high point of Greek drama, musically speaking, occurred with the plays of Aeschylus. Sophokles was a dramatist with a strong sense of plot and action, while Aeschylus was a musician, a choral lyricist, who composed his words and his music as inseparable parts of the whole. His *Agamemnon* was considered in his time to be a consummate example of tragedy because the two elements of choral song and narrative speech were combined into a powerful artistic unity.

The Doctrine of Ethos

Music Education

Because music exerted a strong influence on the mood and spirits of the Greeks, the city-state assumed control of music education rather than leave such an important matter in the hands of performing artists. Sparta became the leader in this endeavor with Lycurgus ordering regular, supervised music education. No Spartan, regardless of age, sex, or rank, was to be excluded, and each was to do his or her part to further the moral, social, and political well-being of the state.

The songs to be sung must not offend the spirit of Sparta but rather praise the fatherland and lead to a sense of order, lawfulness, and dignity. The melodies should be in the Dorian mode because this evokes poise, temperance, and simplicity.

In Athens, the champion of music was Solon. All Athenian citizens received musical training until they were thirty, and all could be expected to sing on proper social, political, or religious occasions. Musical training was mandatory and universal but prohibited for slaves because it was considered a mark of nobility and of education reserved for free Athenians.

The primary role of music was a pedagogical one that implied the building of character and morals. The practice of music was therefore public rather than private, an affair of state rather than of the home. Every melody, rhythm, and instrument had its unique effect on the moral nature of man and therefore upon the morality of the state. Good music promoted the welfare of the state while bad music was harmful to the individual and to society.

Moral Imperatives

The emphasis upon moral imperatives led to the Greek doctrine of ethos, a doctrine that brought order into the domain of music. This doctrine was derived from the effect that music had upon the will. According to the philosophers, music influenced the will in three ways: (1) it could prompt action; (2) it could strengthen character just as, conversely, it could undermine mental health; and (3) it could suspend normal willpower and thus make the person unaware of his actions.

Plato's Writings

Plato was the most eloquent and powerful exponent of the doctrine of ethos. In the *Republic,* he recognized the balance of music and gymnastics in the education of free men, but he felt that music should precede and dominate gymnastics. Music first enables the soul, after which the soul should then build up the body.

Plato was, next to Aristoxenus, the greatest writer on music in antiquity. The philosopher saw an analogy between movements of the soul and musical progressions and therefore felt the aim of music must be more than mere amusement; the goal must be harmonic education and perfection of the soul.

In the *Republic* Plato included dance in gymnastics (in addition to wrestling) and poetry with music, with the latter two subject to state control (i.e., censorship). In advocating censorship of poetry and music, he implicitly acknowledged the power of these arts. Like all Athenian citizens, he had attended performances of tragedies by Aeschylus, Sophokles, and Euripides. One can imagine the waves of powerful emotions that swept over the 20,000 spectators, emotions so intense as to be almost palpable. No wonder Plato was so concerned about the role of poetry and music in educating the young to take pleasure in the right things.

In his *Laws,* his last work, Plato went beyond the *Republic,* adding a second function of poetry and music, that of recreation. In Book 2 of the *Laws,* he noted that music education had properly trained the emotions in childhood but that this was not enough; many rough spots in growing up disturbed the proper balance. There must be, he wrote, "festivals of the Muses, Apollo, and Dionysos" so that people might be "put right" by restoring the emotional balance. The restorative power of poetry and music appears to have much in common with Aristotle's theory of *katharsis* ("to purify"; see chapter 6).

Plato was convinced that the arts were important from the very beginning of life.

> Poetry, music, and the dance are then seen as the culmination of the gradual application of rhythm and harmony upon the random cries and uncoordinated movements of the human infant. These arts therefore have their roots deep in human nature.
>
> *Laws* 655b

He recommended the consistent practice of music by all generations. The entire male population was to be divided into choruses with a first chorus of boys, a second of men up to the age of thirty, and a third composed of men from thirty to sixty years of age.

The Dorian and Phrygian modes were considered by Plato and Aristotle to be morally superior to the other modes, but given a preference of both philosophers for rigor and austerity the Dorian might be considered superior because it was strong and dignified. Phrygian was ecstatic and religious and exerted a strong influence on the soul. Other modes were, respectively, piercing and suitable for lamentations or intimate and lascivious.

The two national instruments were naturally included in these ethical doctrines. The lyre was restrained and elegant and therefore proper for the performance of Dorian melodies. The aulos was strong and colorful and thus particularly suitable for the emotional intensity of Phrygian melodies.

In the final analysis, the doctrine of ethos, the lyre and the aulos, poetry, dance, drama, and music were all manifestations of the cults of Apollo and Dionysos. The Apollonian virtues of reason and rationality were balanced by the emotional drive of the Dionysian. As realists, the Greeks fully recognized the dualism, as they saw it, of the mind and body. As idealists, they preferred the dominance of the intellect over the passions.

Seikolos Song (A.D. 1st century)   Phrygian mode

Phrygian mode

As long as you live, be cheerful; let nothing grieve you. For life is short, and time claims its tribute.

Musical Example

Unfortunately no music has come down to us from the Periklean age. In fact, only a few scattered works and some fragments have survived even from Hellenistic times. The *Seikolis Song,* which was found engraved on a tombstone in Asia Minor, provides us with something akin to the sound of ancient Greek music.

Listening Example 1[2]

Greek Music

Anonymous, *Seikolos Song* (ca. A.D. 50)[3]

Time: :22

Exercises

1. List the four different functions of Greek music and briefly describe each. Does today's music—popular and classical—perform the same four functions? If not, what has changed? Why?
2. Explain what the Greeks—especially Plato and Aristotle—meant by the Doctrine of Ethos. Are there any modern parallels? Some people claim, for example, that hard rock (acid, punk) is "satanic" and/or that it will "corrupt the young." In the 1920s and 1930s, the accusations stated that jazz (swing, dance music) "corrupted the young." Have any of these charges been based on objective facts? Is the music (rock, jazz) to blame or something else? What?
3. Greek poetry, such as that of Sappho, was usually sung to the accompaniment of a musical instrument. From what we know of Greek music the accompaniment reflected the emotional content of the poetry. Does this procedure still apply today? Consider, for example, popular songs and songs from Broadway musicals. Are words (poetry) and music emotionally compatible, mutually reinforcing?

4. Consider the two basic forms of Greek dance—Apollonian and Dionysian. Are you familiar with any modern dances that are Dionysian? Apollonian? A bit of both? Identify the dances and describe the movements in terms that the Greeks might understand.
5. List the conventions of Greek theatre—masks, platform shoes, chorus, etc.—and explain how they worked in large outdoor theatres. Were Greek theatrical conventions unique? Consider, for example, the conventions of Shakespeare such as poetic dialogue and monologues. What are some of the conventions of modern theatre? Are there any plays that are wholly without conventions? Why or why not?

Summary

The Greeks yearned for reassurance that they lived in a rational and orderly universe in which there were certain eternal truths and, most important, an appropriate place for humanity. They based their rather unique realistic idealism quite heavily upon the multifarious approaches to music in terms of education, emotional communication, the ethical life, applied science, and metaphysics.

A proper balance of instruction in music and gymnastics provided the educational foundation for the citizens of ancient Greece. The study of music included the arts in general and music in particular, with special reference to its scientific basis (acoustics) and the comprehensive theory and tuning of music built on that basis. Music was also expected to further ethical instruction, which was designed to encourage rational behavior and intellectual control.

Through acoustics the Greeks determined the mathematical relationships of sounding bodies and built a theory resting on the conception of the unity and perfection of the vibrating string. This eventually led to the metaphysical concept of a universe that could be comprehended by the intellects of those philosophers who could go beyond the sensory data of the material world.

Music performance was allied with drama, dance, and especially poetry. Principal tone colors were the golden sounds of lyre or kithara (the instruments of Apollo) and the dark and pungent tone of the aulos (the instrument of Dionysos). Rhythm was almost entirely dependent on the rhythm and meter of poetry. Melody was developed to a fine art of subtle nuances. Harmony as such was unknown, but the melodic element has reigned supreme and unmatched by developments in Western music up to the present day.

---

2. A cassette is available with all of the listening examples from Volume 1 of this text.

3. T. Reinach, *La Musique Grecque.* 1926, p. 193.

The specialized art and craft of music notation achieved a notable degree of clarity and precision, almost all of which was lost during the centuries of copying and recopying Greek manuscripts. The precious little Greek music remaining can do no more than provide a tantalizing glimpse of the richness of Greek musical culture. Modern instruments distort beyond all recognition even this hint of past achievements. Only performances on lyre, kithara, and aulos in the original Greek tunings and in conjunction with poetry and drama can actually bring to life the glory that was Greece in the tonal art known as music.

Culture and Human Values

That the Greek state assumed full responsibility for music education is only one indication of the importance the Greeks attached to music. That it helped produce—when balanced with gymnastics—a sound mind in a healthy body was certainly the best way to enjoy life to the fullest. Ethical instruction through music was intended to help individuals take charge of their lives, to behave rationally and to maintain intellectual control. To be sure, music was always pleasurable; but, above all, it added its full share to the ideal of Beauty that was such a basic part of ideal Athenian life.

Annotated Bibliography

Music

Lippman, Edward A. *Musical Thought in Ancient Greece.* New York: Da Capo Press, 1975. Elucidates the theory behind the practice.

Rouget, Gilbert. *Music and Trance: A Theory of the Relations between Music and Possession.* Chicago: University of Chicago Press, 1985. A fascinating study of the effects of music and relevant to the Dionysian dimension in Greek musical culture.

Rowell, Lewis. *Thinking About Music: An Introduction to the Philosophy of Music.* Amherst: University of Massachusetts Press, 1983. Includes a concise survey of major contributions to the philosophy of music, beginning with the Greeks.

Schlesinger, K. *The Greek Aulos.* New York: Metheun, 1939. A study of the instrument bound up with Greek Tragedy.

Strunk, Oliver, ed. *Source Readings in Music History.* New York: W. W. North & Co., 1940. A collection of primary sources (in English), including selections from Plato, Aristotle, Aristoxenus, Cleonides, and others. The topics include music and the state, music education and the doctrine of ethos, and music theory.

Poetry

Barnstone, Willis, ed. and trans. *Greek Lyric Poetry.* New York: Schocken Books, 1972. A fine anthology that ranges from the seventh century B.C. to the Byzantine era.

Bowra, C. M. *Greek Lyric Poetry.* 2d ed. New York: Oxford University Press, 1961. By a noted classicist, this is regarded as the standard discussion of the topic.

Duban, Jeffrey M. *Ancient and Modern Images of Sappho: Translations and Studies in Archaic Greek Love Lyric.* Lanham, Md.: University Press of America, 1984. An illuminating focus on the great poet.

Webster, T. B. *Hellenistic Poetry and Art.* New York: Methuen, 1964. A survey of the connections between poetry and subjects treated in art.

Dance

Georgiades, Thrasybulos. *Greek Music, Verse, and Dance.* Reprint. New York: Da Capo Press, 1973. The interrelationships of music, poetry, and dance in Greek culture.

Sorell, Walter. *Dance in Its Time.* Garden City, N.Y.: Doubleday & Co., 1981. Dance in its cultural contexts throughout history.

Sparshott, Francis. *The Theory of the Arts.* Princeton: Princeton University Press, 1982. With implications for dance as well as the other arts, this work relates major theories of art to the "classical line" originating in Plato.

Theatre

Arnott, Peter D. *Greek Scenic Conventions in the Fifth Century B.C.* Reprint. Westport, Conn.: Greenwood Press, 1978. Dramatic conventions in the crucial century of their emergence.

Bieber, Margaret. *History of the Greek and Roman Theater.* rev. ed. Princeton: Princeton University Press, 1980. An indispensable account of all forms of theatrical performance in the ancient world.

Kitto, H. D. F. *Greek Tragedy: A Literary Study.* 3d ed., rev. New York: Methuen, 1966. A noted classicist explores the origins of tragedy.

Pickard-Cambridge, Arthur W. *The Dramatic Festivals of Athens.* 2d ed., rev. by J. Gould and D. M. Lewis. New York: Oxford University Press, 1968. An authoritative discussion of the theatre of Dionysos in its cultural context.

Walton, J. Michael. *Greek Theatre Practice.* Westport, Conn.: Greenwood Press, 1980. Greek drama as performed in the theatre.

ROME: THE INTERNATIONAL CULTURE

Golden Age

	Key Dates	People and Events	Literature	Art and Architecture	Religion, Science, Philosophy
600	**753** Founding of Rome (trad.)	**606–509** Etruscan period with Tarquin kings			
500	**509–27 Roman Republic**	**509** Tarquins overthrown			
400	**450** Romans colonize Italy			**ca. 500** *She-wolf of the Capital* (Etruscan)	
300	**343–290** Samnite wars; Rome dominant in Italy	**390** Gauls sack Rome	**Theocritus** 310?–250 poet		**Epicurus** ca. 342–270 **Zeno the Stoic** 335?–263?
200	**264–241** First Punic War with Carthage; Rome acquired Sicily, Corsica, Sardinia **218–201** Second Punic War; Rome rules western Mediterranean **214–146** Macedonian wars; Rome rules Greece **200–133** Conquest of Near East	**287** *Lex Hortensia* ends patrician-plebian conflict **216** Hannibal invades Italy; defeats Romans at Cannae **202** Scipio Africanus invades Africa	**Plautus** 254?–184 drama **Polybius** 205–133 history		
100 B.C.	**149–146** Third Punic War; Carthage destroyed	**146** Corinth destroyed	**Terence** 190?–159 drama **Cicero** 106–43 **Caesar** 102–44 *Commentaries*		
0	**88–82** Civil War: Sulla-Marius **80–43** Age of Cicero **60** First Triumvirate: Pompey, Crassus, Caesar **49** Caesar crosses Rubicon **44** Caesar assassinated by Brutus, Cassius, others **43** Second Triumvirate: Mark Antony, Lepidus, Octavian (Augustus) **42 B.C.–A.D. 17** Augustan Golden Age **31** Navel battle of Actium	**82–79** Sulla, dictator **73–71** Slave revolt; Spartacus **63** Cicero as consul **59** Caesar as consul **58–51** Caesar conquers Gaul **48–45** Caesar campaigns in Asia Minor, Egypt (Cleopatra), Spain **27 B.C.–A.D. 14** Reign of Caesar Augustus **4?** Birth of Christ	**Sallust** 86–34 history **Catullus** 84–54 poet **Virgil** 70–19 *Aeneid* **Horace** 65–8 *Odes* **Livy** 59 B.C.–A.D. 17 *History of Rome* **Ovid** 43 B.C.–A.D. 17 *Art of Love; Metamorphoses* **Seneca** 4 B.C.–A.D. 65 drama	**Vitruvius** ca. 50–ca. 10 *De Architectura* **ca. 50–** Villa of the Mysteries, Pompeii **27–** Roman Forum, *Ara Pacis*, Baths of Agrippa, Theatre of Marcellus **20** *Augustus of Primaporta* **20–10** Pont du Gard **19** Maison Carrée, Nimes	**Lucretius** ca. 95–55 *On the Nature of Things* (Epicureanism)
A.D. 100	**27 B.C.–A.D. 476 Roman Empire** **27 B.C.–A.D. 180** Pax Romana **A.D. 17–130** Silver Age **70** Titus destroyed Jerusalem and the Temple of Solomon **79** Mount Vesuvius destroyed Pompeii and Herculaneum **96–180** The "Good Emperors"	**14–37** Reign of Tiberius **37–41** Caligula **41–54** Claudius **54–68** Nero **69** Galba, Otho, Vitellius *Flavian Caesars* **69–79** Vespasian **79–81** Titus **81–96** Domitian *Antoninus Caesars* **96–98** Nerva **98–117** Trajan	**Petronius** d. 66 *Satyricon* **Pliny the Elder** 23–79 naturalist **Quintillian** 35–ca. 100 *Institutes of Oratory* **Lucan** 39–65 poet **Martial** 40–104 *Epigrams* **Plutarch** 46–120 history **Tacitus** 55–120 history **Juvenal** 60–140 *Satires* **Pliny the Younger** 62–114 writer **Suetonius**ca. ca. 70–160 *Lives of the Caesars*	**54** Roman Baths in England **70** *Herakles Discovering the Infant Telephos in Arcadia* **72–80** Colosseum **81** Arch of Titus	**d. 29?** Jesus Christ **d. 64?** Apostle Peter **d. 67?** Apostle Paul **Epictetus** ca. 60–110 Stoic philosopher, *Discourses*
200	**180–476** Decline and Fall	**117–138** Hadrian **138–161** Antoninus Pius **161–180** Marcus Aurelius **180–192** Commodus **193–211** Septimus Severus	**Lucian** ca. 117–180 Greek satirist **Apuleius** fl. 160 *Golden Ass*	**106–113** Column, Baths, and Forum of Trajan **118–125** Pantheon **135–139** Hadrian's Tomb and Villa **161–180** *Equestrian Statute of Marcus Aurelius*	**Marcus Aurelius** 121–180 *Meditations* **Ptolemy** fl. 126–151 astronomer **Galen** ca. 130–200 physician
300		**211–217** Caracalla **222–235** Alexander Severus **235–284** "Barracks Emperors" (25 of 26 murdered) **284–305** Diocletian		**ca. 212** Baths of Caracalla **298–306** Baths of Diocletian	**Plotinus** 205–270 Founder of Neo-Platonism
400	**313** Edict of Milan; freedom of worship **330** Constantine established Eastern capital in Constaninople **395** Theodosius proclaimed Christianity sole permitted state religion	**306–335** Constantine **353–361** Constantius **361–363** Julian **363–364** Jovian **364–378** Valens **379–395** Theodosius **395–403** Honorius		**312–315** Arch of Constantine **330** *Constantine the Great*	**St. Jerome** 340–420 **St. Ambrose** 340–397 **St. Augustine** 354–430

The Roman Empire "fell" in 410 with the sack of Rome by the Visigoths or in 476 when the last Roman emperor was deposed.

9

A Thousand Years of Rome

Roman Legends and Virtues

"So great a labor," wrote Virgil, "was it to found the Roman race." And it all began, according to legend, with Romulus and Remus, the twin sons of Mars, god of war, and of Rhea Silvia, daughter of King Numitor. It seems that Amulius, the wicked brother of Numitor, usurped the throne, forced his niece into service as a Vestal Virgin[1] and, to secure his rule against future claimants, ordered the infants placed in a flimsy basket and set adrift on the Tiber River. Rescued and suckled by a she-wolf, the ancient symbol of Rome, they were discovered by a shepherd couple and raised to vigorous manhood (figure 9.1). Upon learning their true identity, they demonstrated their straightforward Roman nature by immediately killing Amulius and restoring Numitor to the throne. Choosing to ignore an omen of birds that pointed to Romulus as the sole founder of Rome, they resolutely set off to fulfill their destiny: to establish a mighty city on the seven hills by the Tiber. The inevitable quarrel between Romulus, the serious twin, and the light-hearted Remus led to the death of the latter; one version of the story has Remus making fun of a wall constructed by Romulus and falling victim to his brother's self-righteous anger. Subsequently, Romulus gathered an army about him, supplied them with Sabine wives (the Rape of the Sabines), and, to make a long story short, founded Rome right on schedule in 753 B.C. And, much as Moses received the tablets of law on the mountain, he accepted the first constitution from the gods and completed his imperative by becoming the first king of the Romans.

Establishing the Roman Republic was but the first step; the Roman Empire had its own legendary beginning as related by Virgil in his epic poem the *Aeneid* (see Book VI of the *Aeneid* in this chapter). "It is the nature," boasted Ovid, "of a Roman to do and suffer bravely," and Aeneas was the prototype of the stoic Roman hero. After Troy fell to the Greeks under Agamemnon,

FIGURE 9.1 The Capitoline She-Wolf *depicts Romulus, Remus, and an Etruscan wolf on Capitoline Hill in Rome. The figures were created during the Renaissance, but the wolf is a copy of an Etruscan original. Completing the symbolic representation of the Eternal City, the Colosseum looms in the background, accompanied by an early Christian bell tower and modern lighting fixtures.*

---

1. Selected daughters of the best families served the goddess Vesta in chastity and obedience. Amulius undoubtedly forced Rhea Silvia into the arms of the goddess so that she would not bear a legitimate heir to the throne.

Aeneas and a loyal band of Trojan warriors escaped the debacle and sailed to the west to confront their destiny. After a mighty storm at sea they found themselves on the coast of North Africa, from whence they made their way to the nearby city of Carthage where Dido (DIE-doe), the queen, received them with full honors while promptly falling in love with Aeneas. As much as stern duty would permit, Aeneas responded in kind while always knowing that, sooner or later, he would have to abandon her in order to fulfill his sacred mission of founding Rome. A despairing Dido chose suicide and, while she lay on her funeral pyre, still hopeful of a last-ditch rescue, Aeneas sailed resolutely to Sicily and finally to the banks of the Tiber. There he fought and defeated Turnus; married Lavinia, the beautiful daughter of King Latinus; and dutifully established "first among cities, the home of gods, golden Rome" (Ausonius).

Rome was fated to be a city of warriors, and of grandeur and glory; the legends of Romulus and Remus and of Aeneas were actually self-fulfilling prophecies. Romulus was descended from the god of war and Aeneas was the progenitor of the stalwart city that would restore Trojan honor by conquering the wily Greeks of the wooden horse. Rome was nourished by the forces of nature, symbolized by the she-wolf, and elevated to maturity by the good people of the soil, the peasant couple who had reared the twins. Rome pursued her imperative by seizing the Sabine lands and women, and established her legitimacy with a god-given constitution.

The Romans saw themselves as destined for world leadership; as Cicero said, "We were born to unite with our fellowmen, and to join in community with the human race." They would triumph because they were a no-nonsense, practical people with the exemplary virtues of thrift, honesty, loyalty, and dedication to hard work. Little interested in abstractions or theory, they had two questions: "Does it work?" and "How can we get the job done?" As Remus discovered, the task of building an illustrious city was no laughing matter, and obligations to the city took precedence over everything else, even passion, a lesson that was lost on the ill-fated Queen of Carthage. Duty to the state, in the final analysis, was the noblest virtue of all.

Etruscan Influence

The legend of Aeneas was apparently based to a great extent on the Etruscans, the mysterious people who appeared in north central Italy during the ninth century B.C. Though the Etruscans used the Greek alphabet, their language was not an Indo-European dialect; according to the Greek historian Herodotos, they were an advanced culture from Asia Minor, a view modern historians have been unable to contradict. Leaving only partially deciphered inscriptions and no body of literature, their origins may never be known.

The Etruscans conquered most of central and northern Italy and ruled Rome itself during the sixth century B.C. From them Rome derived street plans for cities, the idea of the triumphal procession, divinations for foretelling the future, gladiatorial combat, and the masonry arch. But Rome did not accept all things Etruscan. Such Etruscan concerns as life after death,

elaborate tombs, and, most especially, a luxurious style of living did not suit sober Roman sensibilities. Moreover, the Romans were so outraged about the nearly equal status of Etruscan women that they accused them of gross promiscuity including copulating in the streets, a judgment that says more about self-righteous Roman males than about Etruscan morality.

Greek Influence

Rome came under Greek influence very early, in the eighth century B.C., when Greek colonies were established in southern Italy and Sicily in what the Romans called Magna Graecia. Syracuse, Naples, Paestum, Elea, the Pythagoreans of Krotona, the pleasure-loving Greeks of Sybaris—all were flourishing under the stern gaze of Rome. Throughout their long history the Romans were ambivalent about the Greeks. On one hand they were awed by a civilization so obviously superior, and yet there was hostility, for Greek culture amounted to a reversal of Roman values: literate, artistic, intellectual, sophisticated, delighting always in the pleasurable life, the good life. Roman enmity was not unexpected from an austere, rigid, and self-righteous society that stressed manly virtues, physical prowess, and duty to the state. From this point of view the Greeks were obviously effeminate and decadent.

The Republic, 509–27 B.C.

According to still another Roman tradition, the Republic began in 509 B.C. with the expulsion of the Etruscan king, Tarquin the Proud. In the absence of the deposed ruler the Romans were forced to devise a viable government. Never interested in abstractions or political theory, they pragmatically accepted the existing situation and made adjustments when they became necessary. It might be called the let's-try-it-this-way-and-see-if-it-stops-hurting theory of government. What existed after the hurried departure of Tarquin was an oligarchy (government by the few), and so this became the basis of the new state. The oligarchs, the land-owning aristocrats, established a republic with full citizenship reserved for the landowning class, the patricians (Latin, *pater,* father). The other ninety percent or so of the population, the plebeians (pluh-BEE-uns; Latin, *plebs,* the multitude), could neither hold office nor marry into the patrician class. They could make money, however, which meant that political adjustments were inevitable.

Patricians and Plebeians

The patrician class supplied the executive heads of state, two consuls who governed with full power for one year (except that each had veto power over the other). The consuls appointed patricians to life terms in the three-hundred-member Senate and were, of course, senators themselves. The other legislative body, the Centuriate Assembly, had less power than the Senate but it did elect the consuls and passed on laws submitted to it by the consuls or Senate. From among the exconsuls the Assembly elected two censors who determined eligibility for military service and ruled on the moral qualifications of Senate nominees.

■ **COLORPLATE 12** *Riaci Bronze (Statue A), ca. 460–450 B.C. Bronze, height 6'6''. Museo Nazionale di Reggio, Calabria, Italy.*

■ **COLORPLATE 11** *Exekias, Black-Figure Amphora with Akhilleus and Aias Playing Dice, ca. 530 B.C. Height 24''. Vatican Museums, Rome.*

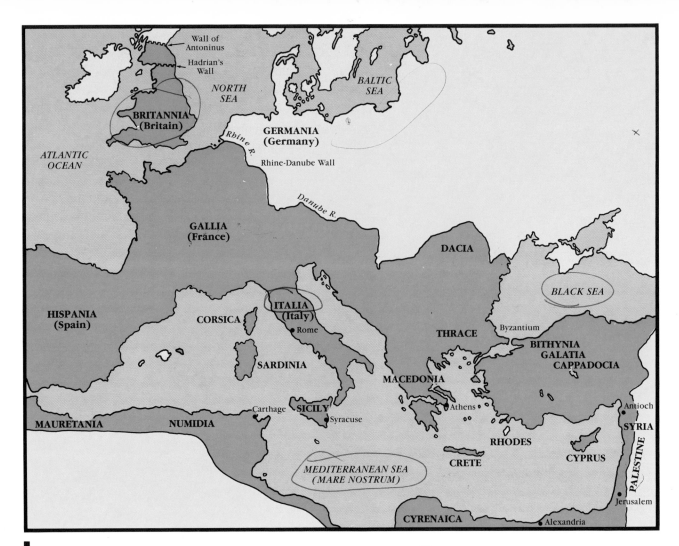

■
COLORMAP 5 *The Roman Empire in* A.D. *180.*

This map
for Test #3

COLORPLATE 13 *Giovanni Paolo Panini,* The Interior of the Pantheon. *Samuel H. Kress Collection, National Gallery of Art, Washington, D.C.*

COLORPLATE 17 Empress Theodora and Retinue, *ca. 547. Mosaic, San Vitale, Ravenna. Photo © American Archives of World Art, Inc.*

Consuls also served as commanders of the army, which meant that in time of war their mutual veto power could jeopardize the state. Of course the Romans invented another adjustment, a *dictator*, a supreme military commander who received his authority constitutionally and who relinquished it at the end of his six-month term. When Julius Caesar had himself voted dictator for life, his enemies had their worst fears confirmed.

The Roman oligarchy kept the plebeians in an intolerable situation; in effect they were minority stockholders in a closed corporation. Growing financial power, however, forced the Senate to create the new office of tribune, protector of the people. Later in the century (fifth century B.C.) plebeian forces accused the judges of abusing their power; there were no written laws and thus a made-to-order situation for the party in power. The Roman response was most uncharacteristic; the Senate decreed that the best legal code in existence should be studied, and accordingly sent a commission to Athens to observe the rational legal system of Solon, the notable law-giver. The commission returned to compose the Twelve Tables of Law, at which point Roman conservatism reasserted itself; the adopted laws were fully as harsh as the fierce legal code of Draco of nearly two centuries earlier, the very system the Greeks had thankfully discarded in favor of the humane reforms of Solon.

Economics and the Military

Accomplished Roman pragmatists never solved the problem of ownership of the land, a failure that had much to do with the demise of the Empire. From the beginning of the Republic absentee landlords controlled a large part of the agricultural market, leaving the working farmer, with his small acreage, struggling to make ends meet. Competition from estate holders plus drought and pestilence forced him into debt and, finally, into a slavery decreed by the severe Twelve Tables. Large estates grew larger, operating with lower overhead because they used war-booty slaves. The inexorable price for noncompetitive farms was bankruptcy. (There were strikingly similar dilemmas in the American South prior to the Civil War.) Even after reforms barring debt-slavery and attempts to redistribute the land, many farmers ended up as urban poor: landless and unemployed. Unable to work on the land their ancestors had farmed for centuries and unfit for employment in a city that relied on slave labor, they became part of the permanent welfare program. It is estimated that by the first century B.C. about eighty percent of Rome's population was either slave laborers or subsisting on "bread and circuses." The welfare program was a failure because, as Plutarch observed, "The man who first ruined the Roman people was he who first gave them treats and gratuities."

Roman talent for organization was most spectacularly evidenced by their awesome military power. Reducing the ponderous 8,000-man phalanx to 3,600 men armed with javelin and short Roman sword, they created a mobile striking force that could march twenty-four miles in five hours, each man carrying a sixty-pound pack. Steely discipline honor a war machine that gave no quarter and asked none.

It has been said that Rome inadvertently became an empire, much as England did in the nineteenth century, but this is doubtful, because Roman conquest clearly became an end in itself during Republican days. The point at which Rome set out to deliberately conquer the world was probably 146 B.C., the final year of the Punic Wars with Carthage (264–146 B.C.). The First Punic War began when Carthage, the powerful Phoenician colony in North Africa, attempted to expand its trading empire in eastern Sicily. Responding to the appeals of their Greek allies, Roman armies found themselves opposing the Carthaginian navy. Hurriedly building their first fighting fleet, the Romans managed to defeat Carthage even though ineptness cost them more ships than did enemy action.

Spain, which had resisted Roman domination for two centuries, became the Carthaginian base for the Second Punic War (218–201 B.C.). Stating that "we will either find a way or make one," the remarkable general Hannibal negotiated the Alps with his elephants and attacked Rome from the rear. Unable to compete with his brilliant tactics, Rome, in desperation, attacked his vulnerable homeland and thus ended Carthage's dominance of the western Mediterranean. The Third Punic War, however, was a different kind of conflict.

Marcus Porcius Cato (Cato the Elder, the Censor; 234–149 B.C.) was a senator, consul, censor, and writer and, even more importantly, one of the prime instigators of the final attack on Carthage. Renowned for his devotion to Roman ideals of simplicity, honesty, courage, ability to endure hardship, rigorous sexual morality, and loyalty to Rome and the family, Cato opposed luxury, cultivation of the arts, and extravagance in any form; he hated the Greeks. He believed all the children should be educated in the home and boasted of teaching his son reading, Roman law, and history, and training him in the arts of the javelin, riding, armoured combat, boxing, and swimming. Cato's maxim for slaves was that they should either be working or sleeping and they should be worked to death. Why not? Replacements were abundant and cheap.

Long since recovered from the Second Punic War but no longer a military threat to Rome, Carthage was another kind of target for Cato and other land-hungry Romans who lusted after her fertile soil and abundant harvests. After returning from a fact-finding mission to Carthage, Cato delivered an impassioned speech in the Senate about a resurgent foe that concluded, as did all subsequent speeches and writings, with a call to arms: "Delenda est Carthago!" (Carthage must be destroyed!). In 149 B.C. Rome launched an unprovoked attack upon an astonished and unprepared Carthage.

The conflict with Carthage was described by Rome as preventive warfare, but a more appropriate term would be armed robbery.[2] Carthage was not only captured but demolished and the area sown with salt. The men were

---

2. "From the Punic Wars on, [Rome's] internal history is that of a successful gang of cutthroats quarreling over the division of the swag." Basil Davenport, *The Portable Roman Reader* (Baltimore, Md.: Penguin Books, 1977), p. 7.

killed and the women and children sold into slavery, actions that prompted Tacitus to write, "they make a desert and call it peace." This was in 146 B.C., the fateful year in which another rapacious Roman army administered the same treatment to Corinth, the richest city in Greece. "To the victors belong the spoils" is Ovid's comment, but Seneca wrote: "We are mad, not only individually, but nationally. We check manslaughter and isolated murders; but what of war and the much vaunted crime of slaughtering whole peoples?"

Heading for Civil War

A new and very rich class of war-profiteering contractors, merchants, estate owners, province governors, and generals arose; they were known as *equites* (knights) because they could afford to buy equipment for the cavalry, the most expensive branch of the military. The city bulged with plunder, slaves, and increasing numbers of landless, jobless Romans. Reform was long overdue and, in the 130s and 120s, the patrician brothers Tiberius and Gaius Gracchus attempted to speak for the dispossessed. Although no one knew it then, it was the last opportunity the Senate would have to salvage the integrity of the state. The Senatorial response was to murder Tiberius and force Gaius into suicide, thus unwittingly setting the stage for one-man rule.

The first of the generals to seize power, Marius, won victories against North African and Celtic tribes, but his reorganization of the army was the critical change. The requirement that Roman citizens had to pay for their own equipment was abolished. With the state furnishing battle gear, full-time professional soldiers began replacing the citizen-soldiers who returned to their peacetime occupations between campaigns. With the beginning of Rome's war against King Mithridates in 88 B.C., Marius emerged from retirement to claim command. When the Senate chose Sulla instead, a bloody civil war ensued; ending in 84 B.C. with Sulla's conquest of Mithridates in Asia Minor. The arrogant and ruthless Pompey, a veteran of Sulla's campaigns, next rose to power and eventually formed a ruling triumvirate with Crassus and Julius Caesar.

The First Caesar

Gaius Julius Caesar (ca. 102–44 B.C.)[3] obviously viewed himself as the best-qualified man to rescue the foundering Republic. Not everyone agreed with him, then or now, because Caesar remains one of the most controversial figures in history. A man of enormous energy and even greater ambition, his mastery of power politics can be considered a textbook example on how to take over a state. He enjoyed spectacular success in war, politics, oratory, and statesmanship. Caesar's *Commentaries* on the Gallic campaigns were masterpieces of concise and lucid Latin and his social graces were remarkable. Cicero, who hated him, remarked that he would rather spend an evening conversing with Caesar than in any other way.

In tradition-minded Rome, family background was still important and Caesar had impressive credentials; the Julian *gens* (clan, family) was one of the oldest and most powerful in Rome. The patrician Caesar cast his lot, however, with the popular (democratic) party because he astutely saw the need to identify himself with those who opposed an entrenched and unpopular aristocracy. He passed rapidly through the usual offices, made dazzling orations, and, with a daring speech in defense of the legal rights of a treasonous conspirator, secured in one bold stroke the enmity of the Senate and the adulation of the people. He utilized a public office in Spain to add gloss to his growing reputation while also attempting to reduce some of his staggering debts which, it was said, resulted from his methodical program of paying huge bribes to the right people. He married his daughter to Pompey, the most successful general of the time, and completed an unbeatable combination by forming an alliance with Crassus, the richest man in Rome. The next step was by now inevitable: Caesar, Pompey, and Crassus became a ruling coalition called the First Triumvirate, a short-lived association, however, because, as Lucan pointed out, "It is a law of nature that every great man inevitably resents a partner in greatness."

Caesar's self-improvement program was not yet complete because political power in Rome was necessarily based on military power. He had himself appointed governor of the portion of Gaul that the Romans had conquered, forged a seemingly invincible army to conquer the rest of Gaul, and established his reputation as one of history's remarkable troop commanders. What Tacitus referred to as "the terror of the Roman name" was confirmed by Caesar's statement that, "It is the right of war for conquerors to treat those whom they have conquered according to their pleasure." Though his military prowess was only too apparent to the Gauls, Caesar needed strong support back in Rome. His inspired solution was the carefully composed *Commentaries on the Gallic Wars* (what would Latin classes do without Caesar?), which received wide distribution in Rome, becoming a veritable best-seller.

The Die Is Cast

By 49 B.C. Gaul was secured according to Caesar's pleasure, Crassus was dead in Parthia, Pompey had gone over to the Senate, and Caesar and his intensely loyal army were poised on the banks of the Rubicon in northern Italy. An apprehensive Senate reminded him of the standing order that all field commanders had to return to Rome without their troops whereupon Caesar, never known for indecisiveness, observed that "the die is cast," and invaded and conquered all of Italy in several weeks. Following his triumphant return to a wildly enthusiastic Rome (except the Senate and aristocracy, obviously), he won a war in Spain and then defeated his rival, Pompey, in Greece. He further solidified his power and filled his purse by campaigning in Egypt where he stabilized the reign of Cleopatra, Queen of Egypt (also fathering a child by her), and guaranteed almost the entire tax revenues of Egypt for himself. In four brief, brilliant years after crossing the Rubicon, Julius Caesar had triumphed in Italy, Spain, Greece, Syria, Egypt, and North Africa, strenghtening and consolidating the Empire as he went.

---

3. All Romans had three names: first name, family name, last name.

When he returned to Rome in 45 B.C. he was undisputed master of the Roman world and a legend in his, and our, time. Less than a year later, on the Ides of March, he died of multiple stab wounds on the Senate floor at the base of Pompey's statue. There were about sixty assassins.

The motives for murder ranged from genuinely patriotic concerns over constitutional violations to plain jealousy. Moreover, some of Caesar's reforms interfered with corrupt practices of the bloated aristocracy, providing additional incentive for murder. On the other hand the people, who supported Caesar throughout his meteoric career, regarded him as a martyr to the rapacity and greed of the aristocracy. A curious and puzzling fact about the whole affair is that Caesar was almost certainly aware of the conspiracy and yet did nothing to protect himself.

Caesar's will left three-quarters of an enormous fortune to his adopted grandnephew, Octavian, but Octavian's true legacy was the opportunity to acquire Rome itself. Though only eighteen when Caesar died (and unaware of the will), Octavian reacted like a veteran politician. He formed a Second Triumvirate with Mark Antony and Lepidus, brutally suppressed all dissent and used terror and the threat of death to raise some fighting money. To his everlasting discredit he failed to stop Mark Antony from having Cicero murdered. In Macedonia he avenged Caesar by defeating and driving to suicide two of his assassins, Brutus and Cassius. (Shakespeare has Brutus say, "Not that I loved Caesar less, but that I loved Rome more.") After Lepidus was dropped from the triumvirate Antony and Cleopatra tried to use Caesar's son in their own bid for the empire. After all the machinations and intrigue the final showdown was almost anticlimatic. In a naval battle off the northwest coast of Greece, near Actium, Octavian triumphed and the losers returned to Egypt to commit suicide.

The Empire, 27 B.C.—A.D. 476

Octavian (Caesar Augustus)

Though Octavian is considered the first emperor of Rome he was, in effect, the second, without most Romans even realizing that constitutional government had ended with Caesar. While prudently maintaining the appearance of restoring the Republic, Octavian orchestrated his power by redesigning the creaky governmental machinery to try to control the business of a vast empire. Careful to avoid the appellation of emperor, he did accept from the Senate the titles of Augustus (revered one) and *princeps* (first citizen). Although he ruled indirectly, he was just as much in control as any titled emperor.

Among many significant innovations, Augustus created a civil service based on merit, endowed a veterans pension fund from his own capital (secured by the taxes of Egypt), added a sales tax, rebuilt Rome ("I found Rome brick and left it marble"), created the first police and fire departments, overhauled the armed forces, and sponsored army construction of public works projects throughout the Empire. He adjusted the bureaucratic machinery of imperial Rome so it could continue to function under good, mediocre, or incompetent leadership. It survived even the tenures of murderous tyrants: Caligula, Nero, Commodus, and Caracalla.

■
FIGURE 9.2 *Roman coin, 17 B.C. Obverse: head of Augustus with the inscription "S.P.Q.R. IMP CAESARI." The reverse is characteristically Roman (more is better), featuring the emperor, Victory, and an elephant standing on a triumphal arch placed upon an aqueduct.*

Pax Romana

The *Pax Romana* (Roman peace) began with Caesar Augustus in 27 B.C. and ended with Marcus Aurelius in A.D. 180. (See colormap 5 of the Roman Empire in A.D. 180.) For over two centuries the Roman world was relatively peaceful because there were no major wars. The Western world was stable and orderly for the first time in history, and people felt quite safe in their homes and even when traveling over the roads and sea routes of the prosperous Empire. Roman coins (figure 9.2) replaced the "owls of Athena" (see figure 5.4) as the monetary standard of the ancient world. All was not rosy, however, because as Juvenal pointed out, "We are suffering the evils of a long peace. Luxury, more deadly than war, broods over the city, and avenges a conquered world."

Decline and Fall

After Marcus Aurelius, the position of emperor was usually decided by the army, with the legions supporting any general who would offer the largest benefits to the military. The problems all the emperors faced were very much the same: an increasing national debt because of military expense, a declining population in Italy, a growing disinclination to take public office in the cities outside Rome (the officers were held responsible for paying the cities' taxes to the central government, and with increasing rural poverty no one wanted to bankrupt himself by holding office), and growing rebellion on the borders of the Empire. A vast population movement from the north and east pushed Germanic, Gothic, and Vandal peoples west and south until they overran all of Italy and Spain.

The century of decline from Commodus to Diocletian (180–284) marked the beginning of the end even though the reforms of Diocletian temporarily halted the deterioration. The growth of Christianity posed an additional challenge to which Constantine responded with the Edict of Milan (313), granting freedom of worship throughout the Empire. Constantine also divided the Empire into west and east and located the capital of the Eastern Empire in the new city of Constantinople, built on the site of the old Greek colony of Byzantium. Theodosios made Christianity the official religion of the Empire, a decision that marked the beginning of vigorous

Christian persecution of other religions. As the barbarian invasions intensified, the western emperor Honorius (395–403) moved to Ravenna, leaving the Pope to defend Rome as best he could. Rome was sacked in 410 and again in 455; in 476 the first non-Roman occupied the throne of Caesar and the Roman Empire passed into history. The painfully protracted decline led Emerson to comment, "The barbarians who broke up the Roman Empire did not arrive a day too soon."

Rome's Achievements

know!

Law and Government

Rome's major and most enduring contribution to Western civilization was her legal system: the art and science of law. Administration of justice was an art, while science (jurisprudence) defined justice and injustice. There is no clearer evidence of Roman preference for facts as opposed to abstractions than in a body of law founded, as Cicero stated, "not on theory but on nature." Justice was a process rather than a concept, a way of dealing with practical problems in everyday life. "Law is nothing but a correct principle drawn from the inspiration of the gods, commanding what is honest and forbidding the contrary" (Cicero). Venality and rapacity were human characteristics the state had to control so that "the stronger might not in all things have their way" (Ovid). Bertrand Russell once stated that an ideal society, for him, would be one in which everyone was honest and he was the only thief. Roman law stood guard against the thief in all of us. Moreover, Roman law used its experience of empire to build up a body of international law based on a rational appraisal of consistent human behavior in a variable environment.

Modern research has shown that, contrary to popular belief, the Romans were not masters of the arts of governance; that their legal system worked need not imply, by inference, a government of comparable efficiency. Until the time of Caesar Augustus government was a chaotic mess of inefficiency and corruption caused not by a Republic trying to administer an empire but by time-honored inequities and improbabilities. Augustus did institute some reforms, but he followed the Roman habit of shuffling parts around when what he needed was a new engine. Diocletian (284–305) did design an efficient new system, but by this time it was like installing a new motor in a disintegrating vehicle.

Province management was a permanent problem because there was little governing; the governors were responsible primarily for sending money to Rome. Charging whatever taxes the traffic would bear and rendering "unto Caesar that which is Caesar's," they pocketed the rest. Moreover, the vaunted Roman toleration of provincial cultures was more pragmatic than magnanimous: don't do anything that will jeopardize the tax-potential of conquered territories. Except for Greece,[4] Rome treated all foreign cultures with equal indifference.

---

4. The love-hate relationship with Greece was largely involuntary. As Horace wrote, "Greece, taken captive, captured her savage conqueror, and carried her arts into clownish Latium."

■

FIGURE 9.3 *Main thoroughfare, Ostia Antica. Leading from Rome to its port city, this three-lane highway is a typical Roman road. Even when driving in Europe today a Roman route can be recognized by the way it rolls on and on without a curve.*

Science

Roman science dealt entirely with empirical data; theoretical science was something left to the Greeks. For example, Eratosthenes (air-uh-TOSS-thuh-neez), an Alexandrian Greek, used his reason, empirical data, and math to prove that the world was round. Pliny the Elder began with sensory evidence when he observed that the masts of ships approaching shore were visible before the hulls could be seen; from this he deduced that the world had a curved surface. Roman medical science benefitted when their organizational talent was combined with their passion for war to produce the field hospital, a predecessor of the general hospital

Public Projects

A fifty-thousand-mile network of paved roads linked Rome to all parts of the Empire. All roads did, in fact, lead to Rome. Originally designed as military roads, they carried the efficient postal service plus peripatetic Romans. Guidebooks, highway patrols, a stable every ten miles, and an inn every thirty miles made traveling easier and safer than at any other time prior to the late nineteenth century (figure 9.3). Skillful engineering also produced the aqueducts that supplied the huge amounts of

■ **FIGURE 9.4** *Great Bath, Roman bath complex, Bath, England, 54 A.D. Part of the finest group of Roman remains in England, this sumptuous pool is still fed by natural hot springs.*

■ **FIGURE 9.5** *Snack bar, Ostia Antica. Located across the street from a large apartment house, this cozy bar featured a common room adjoined by a roomy patio. Fast foods were undoubtedly one of the specialties.*

water needed for the luxurious public baths (figure 9.4) and for the many affluent households that used water for cooking and sanitary facilities. Only a few aqueducts remain, such as the one still servicing Segovia in Spain, and some of the plumbing—in the Pantheon, at Pompeii, and at Bath—still works. Almost everything else has vanished, like, for example, the vast irrigation system that watered productive farms in the northern Sahara.

As urbanization gradually supplanted Rome's early agrarian society, city building became a new specialty. Many residential units were five- and six-story apartment houses with such built-in services as nurseries, convenience markets, and neighborhood snack bars (figure 9.5). Rome and other large cities always had extensive forums that served as civic centers (suitable backdrops for Roman pomp and ceremony) and open-air markets comparable to our shopping malls. Rome was not, however, a neat and orderly city. Except for several thoroughfares there were no names for the fifty-four miles of streets nor any house numbers. (Sample conversation: "See Marius in the leather shop behind the Pantheon; he knows where your friend, Sepulvius, lives.") There was pollution ("cease to admire the smoke, wealth and noise of prosperous Rome."—Horace) and, as Sallust observed, corruption: "A city for sale and doomed to speedy destruction, if it finds a purchaser." City facilities always included public baths, but emperors who wished to improve their public image, which included most of those who stayed alive long enough, built elaborate facilities larger than several Grand Central Stations[5]; these hedonistic temples contained, in addition to the standard baths, indoor and outdoor swimming pools, gymnasiums, libraries, lounges, restaurants, bars, and numerous gardens. Sometimes included, apparently when in short supply in the community, were efficiently designed brothels. The center of each city featured a large amphitheatre, like the Colosseum, where the entertainment was highlighted by gladiatorial combat; wild animal hunts; naval battles; and an occasional gladiator, in a bid for freedom, single-handedly killing an elephant.

Rome's bequest to the Western world was a curious compound of justice under law, military conquest, the Latin language, and Greek culture. Implicit in the laws that recognized the constitutional rights of citizens was the germinal idea that laws required the consent of the governed. Military conquest, on the other hand, was a devastating legacy of which the world has no need. In particular, Horace's pious statement, *dolce et decorum est pro patria mori* (it is sweet and glorious to die for one's country), has been used time and time again to justify enormous crimes against humanity.

In the final analysis, law and Greek culture were Rome's finest contributions to Western civilization. More imitative than inventive, Rome had the great good sense to copy Greek culture. The Greek temple style was adopted, though mainly the ornate Corinthian order; Greek sculpture was copied so often that most of what we know of Greek work exists only as Roman copies. The work of Greek artists, serving Roman tastes, appeared in the frescoes, murals, and mosaics of their houses and public buildings. Greek slaves tutored Roman children in the Greek language and the classics: Homer, Hesiod, and the plays of Aeschylus, Sophokles, and Menander. Roman tourists made the obligatory pilgrimage to Greece to view the centuries-old wonders of the Akropolis and to consult the oracle at Delphi. Rome contributed the language, organization, and law upon which the Church of Rome and the Middle Ages were built; at the same time, Rome preserved and transmitted the Greek humanism, which inspired the Renaissance and edified the Age of Reason.

Roman Religions and Philosophy

Paganism

During the early days of the Republic, Roman religion encompassed household gods and earthly spirits appropriate to the simple life of a farmer. This traditional religion remained viable for those who clung to the land; the word *pagan* (literally, *countryman*) described those who adhered to the old religion of the city-state. Agrarian beliefs became inadequate, however, for urban life in an expanding empire, and the Romans again looked to Greece for suitable models. The Greek pantheon was adopted and given Roman names, albeit with somewhat different characteristics (see box 4.1 on page 56). For example, playfully amorous Aphrodite, who represented beauty and the pleasures of love, became Venus, the mother of Aeneas, bringer of good fortune and victory and protector of female chastity; Athena, the Greek goddess of wisdom and patroness of the arts, was transformed into Minerva, the goddess of learning and handicrafts; Poseidon, the powerful earthshaker and god of the sea, became, for the Romans, Neptune, the god of water.

> Jupiter, tho' called the best and the greatest, he was never, like Zeus, the supreme arbiter of the universe and the governor of the world. Zeus reigned from the heights of Mt. Olympus, Jupiter from a low and easily accessible hill. Zeus belonged to the shining space of the air, while Jupiter, as represented by the Romans, belonged to the earth as much as to the sky. Zeus was free. Jupiter was rigid. When we compare the two gods, we find we are comparing the imagination of the Greeks to the imagination of the Romans; they had almost nothing in common.[6]

The practical mind-set of the Romans also manifested itself in their religious practices. Dedicated pragmatist that he was, Ovid commented that "it is expedient that there should be gods, and as it is expedient, let us believe that they exist." In the interest of efficiency and the glory of the state, the Pantheon (from the Greek, meaning "of all gods") housed in one sumptuous structure the seven planetary gods (see figure 10.22). Patriotism was promoted by elevating the emperors, usually during their lifetime, to godly status. After Caesar Augustus, most emperors were deified by Senate action and emperor worship became the official religion of the Empire.[7] When the Emperor Vespasian was at the point of death, he wryly remarked, "Oh dear, I think I'm becoming a god."

Romanism

Emperor worship and the adopted gods of the Greek city-states gradually evolved into Romanism, the worship of the state. Seneca noted, "Religion is regarded by the common people as true, by the wise as false, and by the rulers as useful." The more personal spiritual needs of the common people, however, plus the diverse cultures

5. The New York landmark was modeled after Rome's Baths of Caracalla.

6. Robert Payne et al., *Horizon Book of Ancient Rome* (New York: American Heritage Publishing Company, 1966), p. 68.
7. Little interested in the religions of other cultures, Rome was deeply concerned over the Christians who refused to place the emperor above their God; this threatened the state and was therefore heretical.

within the Empire led to a variety of imported religious beliefs. Egypt contributed Isis, the wife of Osiris (figure 9.6) and mother of Horus, the dynamic goddess who raised her husband from the dead. Much more than Diana or Minerva, she appealed to Roman women because she was a giver of health, beauty, wisdom, and love and, moreover, she needed priestesses as well as priests. Cybele, the Great Mother goddess of Phrygia (in Asia Minor), turned up in Rome during the war with Hannibal. According to the legend she loved the glorious youth Attis, who like Osiris was raised from the dead (the rebirth motif was standard for fertility cults). Her frantic grief over his death and abandoned delirium at his rebirth were followed by his unfaithfulness, at which point she castrated him. All of this dramatic spectacle was echoed in the ecstatic and bloody (including self-castration) rites of Cybele's followers. Even the Romans were sometimes aghast at the orgies and blood baths and attempted to regulate the mayhem.

Mystery Religions and Mithraism

The Eleusian mysteries and Dionysian rites, both Greek mystery religions, had their Roman adherents, but the vows of silence of both sects have been frustratingly effective. Dionysian ritual celebrated the nonrational but the particulars are obscure. The Eleusian mysteries are particularly intriguing because it appears that the worshippers were able to overcome their fear of death. Eventually the ceremonies at Eleusis (near Athens) were suppressed by Christianity; any religion that could conquer humanity's deepest fear could not be permitted to exist. Imported from Persia was the resolutely virtuous worship of Mithras, the unconquered intermediary between Ahura-Mazda, lord of life and light, and Ahriman, lord of death and darkness. Mithras was the protector of humanity whose believers had to be courageous and morally pure. Soldiers were strongly attracted to this male-oriented religion, which in the third century A.D. was Christianity's greatest rival.

Astrology and Magic

Millions of believers looked to the stars as powerful deities on a par with Jupiter, Isis, and Cybele; astrology was the champion superstition of an age in which countless numbers preferred to believe the movements of heavenly bodies controlled their lives. Astrology, originating in Babylonia, had been known as early as Plato (he found it amusing) but it was not until Alexander's conquest of the Middle East that this persistent nonsense penetrated the Greek world and, ultimately, the entire Roman spectrum. The Eastern religions attracted different sectors of the populace but astrology fascinated all classes, from slaves to emperors. Greek skeptics asked how it was that people fated to die at different times all went down in the same shipwreck, or how one-twelfth of humankind could share the basic characteristics of a Capricorn, but these rational queries simply bored true believers. Augustus and Tiberius, never ones to take chances, banned astrologers from Rome, not to put a stop to larceny, but out of fear of rivals whose horoscopes might predict an enticing throne in the offing. Practitioners of magic also did a thriving business. Spells, incantations, charms, curses, and hexes were for sale to an endless procession of fervently gullible Romans. Fraud flourished on its customery grand scale.

■
FIGURE 9.6 *Priest of Serapis, ca. 170–180* A.D. *J. Paul Getty Museum, Santa Monica, California. The sacred bull in Egyptian religion, Serapis was ruler of the underworld and supposedly the incarnation of Osiris. The priest is identified by the diadem and rosette.*

Epicureanism

Epicureanism and Stoicism, two eminent Athenian schools of philosophy of the third century B.C., developed ethical systems that would assist indiviuals in feeling more secure in an unstable and hostile world. Materialistic and practical, both philosophies were suited to thoughtful, educated Romans who chose to face up to the problems of living an ethical life in a society plagued by dissension, vice, and corruption.

The philosophy of Epicurus (341–270 B.C., figure 9.7) was designed primarily to secure tranquility. He considered pleasure to be the ultimate good and adhered, with remarkable consistency, to the consequences of this view. "Pleasure," he said, "is the beginning and the end of the blessed life." And further, "I know not how I can conceive the good if I withdraw the pleasures of love and those of hearing and sight. The beginning and the root of all good is the pleasure of the stomach; even wisdom and culture must be referred to this." The pleasure of the mind is therefore the contemplation of the pleasures of the body. Sokrates and Plato would disagree of course, because of their insistence upon intellectual development as the chief good, but they did not have to contend with the unsettling problems of a violent age. For Epicurus one acquired virtue by "prudence in the pursuit of pleasure." Justice was not an abstract ideal as in Plato's *Republic* but a practical matter of acting so as not to cause fear and resentment in other people. Rather than a virtue in its own right, justice was essentially a defense mechanism against pain.

■

FIGURE 9.7 *Portrait bust of Epicurus. Roman marble copy, probably after a bronze original of ca. 275–250 B.C., life size, 15⅞" high. Rogers Fund, 1911. Metropolitan Museum of Art. This is one of the finest of many copies. The long face marked by time and poor health is obviously an actual likeness, but in the wrinkled brow and deep-set eyes we also see "the philosopher."*

Epicureanism was on a considerably higher level than mere hedonism, the pursuit of physical pleasures. All materialistic philosophies contain elements of hedonism but Epicurus advocated intellectual pleasures as superior to purely sensual pleasures. He preferred quiet pleasures to violent joys. Eat moderately for fear of indigestion; drink moderately for fear of the morning after; avoid politics, love, and other turmoil; do not present hostages to fortune by marrying and having children; above all live so as to avoid fear. For Epicurus the safest social pleasure was friendship. Holding public office was dangerous because a man multiplied envious enemies as he achieved power. "The wise man will try to live unnoticed so that he will have no enemies."

Epicurus identified two of the greatest sources of fear as religion and the dread of death. He preferred to believe that the gods, if they existed, did not interfere in human affairs and that the soul perished with the body. Religion was not a consolation but a threat; supernatural interference with nature seemed to him to be a source of terror because immortality denied the hope of being released from pain. Death was both extinction and liberation.

In his poem, *De Rerum Natura* (*On the Nature of Things*; included later in this chapter), the Latin poet and philosopher Lucretius (loo-KREE-shus; ca. 96–55 B.C.) explained the workings of the universe as seen by the Epicurean: a rational, materialistic interpretation of the ways in which all things came to be. The poet Horace (65–8 B.C.), known for his odes, exemplified Epicureanism in his life-style and recorded the ethical results

of the philosophy in his poetry. He advocated moderation in all things though he did warn against the inconvenience of poverty; above all, he said, avoid high positions because lightning strikes the tallest trees and highest mountains. A lively sense of humor was Horace's chief Epicurean pleasure. As a sophisticated man he recognized the foibles of his time, laughed at most of them, and unashamedly participated in a goodly number. As the creed of a cultivated minority, Epicureanism survived about six hundred years, though with diminishing vigor.

Stoicism

Stoicism was taught by Zeno the Stoic (335?–263? B.C.), a Phoenician who lived and taught in Athens. He believed totally in *common sense* which, in Greece, meant *materialism.* He trusted his senses and had no patience with metaphysical subtleties. When the skeptic asked Zeno what he meant by the real world the reply was, "I mean solid and material, like this table." "And God," asked the skeptic, "and the soul?" "Perfectly solid," answered Zeno, "more solid than the table." In response to further questioning Zeno added virtue and justice to his list of solid matter. Later Stoics like the Emperor Marcus Aurelius (A.D. 121–180) abandoned materialism but retained the ethical doctrines in virtually the same form. Stoicism was less Greek than any other doctrine because it was emotionally limited and somewhat fanatical. Moreover, its sober austerity contained religious elements the Greeks seemed unable to supply or endorse. In short, it had qualities that appealed to the Romans.

The main doctrines of Stoicism are concerned with cosmic determinism and human freedom. "There is no such thing as chance," said Zeno, "and the course of nature is determined by natural law." The natural world was originated by a Lawgiver, a supreme power called, variously, God or Zeus or Jupiter, who is the soul of the world. Each person has within a part of the Divine Fire. All things are part of a single system called Nature and the individual life is good when it is in harmony with nature. People are in harmony with nature, in one sense, because they cannot violate natural laws but in another, the stoic sense, a human life harmonizes with nature when the individual *will* is directed to ends that agree with nature. *Virtue,* therefore, is a *will* that is in agreement with nature. The wicked obey God's laws involuntarily, like a horse driven by a charioteer.

In an individual's life, virtue is the sole good; such things as health, happiness, possessions are of no account. Since virtue resides in the will, everything good or bad in a person's life depends entirely on that person. A person may be poor but virtuous; one can be sentenced to death, like Sokrates, who was looked upon as a patron saint by the Stoics. Other people may have power over externals; virtue, the only true good, is internal. All people can have perfect freedom to the degree that they free themselves from all mundane desires. The doctrine has a certain, non-Greek coldness; not only are bad passions condemned but all passions. The Stoic sage does not feel bereft when his wife and children die because his virtue is not disturbed. Friendship is all very well but don't let the misfortunes of your friend interfere with your detached calm. Participation in politics is permitted but helping other people does nothing for virtue.

Stoic doctrine does have some logical difficulties. If virtue is the only good then the divine Lawgiver must promote virtue; why, then, are there more sinners than saints? Also, how can injustice be wrong if, as Stoics liked to point out, it provided Stoics with more opportunities to endure and therefore more chances to be virtuous?

The Romans were acquainted with Stoicism mainly through the writings of Cicero, but the three most influential Roman Stoics were Seneca, Epictetus, and Marcus Aurelius: a minister, a slave, and an emperor, in that order. Seneca (ca. 3 B.C.–A.D. 65) was the teacher of Nero and also a multimillionaire, which casts some doubt on his reputation as a teacher and as a Stoic. Falsely accused of plotting Nero's assassination, he was ordered to commit suicide. His final words to his grieving family were, "Never mind, I leave you what is far more valuable than earthly riches, the example of a virtuous life."

Epictetus (ep-ik-TEE-tus; ca. A.D. 60–110) was a Greek and a slave though he did achieve his freedom. The Greek slave and Emperor Marcus Aurelius were in nearly complete agreement about the elements of Stoicism but their lives displayed some ironic contrasts. Marcus Aurelius was devoted to Stoic virtue, of which he had great need, since his reign was an endless procession of wars, insurrections, pestilence, and a few earthquakes. He was conscientious in his efforts but mainly unsuccessful and certainly frustrated. Out of political necessity he tried vainly to stamp out the Christian sect because their rejection of the state religion was an intolerable threat to the stability of the Empire. On the other hand, Epictetus lived a relatively short and uneventful life but his teaching had a profound effect on early Christianity. Consider, for example, the implications of the following:

On earth we are prisoners in an earthly body.
God is the Father of all men and we are all brothers.
Slaves are the equal of other men because all are alike in the eyes of God.
We must submit to God as a good citizen submits to the law.
The soldier swears to respect no man above Caesar but we are to respect ourselves first of all.
We must love our enemies.

Late Stoicism, in the philosophy of Epictetus and Marcus Aurelius, emphasized the idea of the brotherhood of all mankind; since the great intelligence (divine spark) is within each person, and each person is a necessary part of the rational scheme of things, then all men are brothers in the changing universe. Roman law interpreted this concept as all men being equal in the eyes of the law.

Neoplatonism

A third imported Greek philosophy was Neoplatonism, which became even more of a religion than did Stoicism. Its picture of an afterlife offered comfort to those Romans who enjoyed little satisfaction or self-fulfillment in their earthly existence. Based on Platonic doctrines, Neoplatonism came to Rome from the Academy founded by Plato, the still-flourishing Athenian school (until A.D. 529). The Neoplatonists began with the Platonic concept of Ideas as the true reality. Now, said the Neoplatonists,

people can never know ideas in their pure form. For example, we always know and appreciate beauty in some of its manifestations in a beautiful person, or beautiful landscape or picture, but we can never imagine pure beauty apart from any of any of these things. To use another example, we can never imagine pure mind; we can only approach a knowledge of the mind as we see people acting according to the dictates of their mind. We see only the manifestations of the mind, never the reality. By the same token, the true reality of Good (God or Pure Idea) is something people can never conceive of on earth. A person's goal, therefore, is to approach as near as possible to an understanding of reality while on earth so that they may, upon death, be fit to enter the City of Good and finally contemplate the True Reality. With Neoplatonism there is the beginning of an idea of salvation and eternal life for those who lived their earthly lives in contemplation and with a desire for true wisdom. The influence of these ideas on Christianity can scarcely be overemphasized, for it was St. Augustine (354–430), a Neoplatonist in his youth, who laid the foundation for the doctrine of the early Christian church in his monumental volume, *The City of God.*

Games and Contests in Greece and Rome

This chapter has referred to the differences between Greek and Roman cultures. Consider now the athletic contests in the ancient world as a way of highlighting the differences. The Olympic Games and gladiatorial combat were both athletic contests, though we might refer to the Olympics as "games" and call battling gladiators something quite different, which already tells us something significant about the Greeks and the Romans. First we shall describe the games the Greeks played and then take a look at the Roman versions. By comparing the radically different approaches to athletics (sports), the reader can draw some conclusions about the two cultures in question.

Olympic Games

The Greeks staged many festivals that featured contests in drama, music, poetry, and athletics, especially athletics. It seems that the cities of Sparta, Elis, and Pisa were always squabbling and, rather than settling their difficulties by the usual fractious methods, they decided upon a truce built around a footrace to determine superiority. This worked so well that by 776 B.C. almost the entire Hellenic world was involved in footracing and other contests at the sacred site of Olympia. In fact, 776 was felt to be so significant that the Greeks began dating their entire history from that date. The contests were held every four years (the Olympiad) and so 776 was the first Olympiad, 772 the second Olympiad, and so on through the three hundred and twentieth Olympiad in A.D. 392: 1,168 years of Greek history.

From the beginning the truce was the critical factor and it was unique to the Olympic Games. The conditions were simple: no one was to bear arms in Elis (the province of the games); all athletes and spectators were guaranteed safe access to Elis from anywhere in the Greek world; all fighting would cease throughout that world. It is now thought that the truce lasted for ten months and probably included travel time to and from the games. True to style, the Greeks pledged on their honor to abide by these rules. The one time that Sparta violated the truce the entire Greek-speaking world was called upon to witness their shame; there were no further violations.

Athletic contests were staged throughout Greece and the greatest of these was at Olympia, not just because of the caliber of competition but because Olympia symbolized peace, the only extended periods of peace in the ancient world. Sportsmanship and brotherhood were also basic components of the games. Cheating was simply not permitted even though the Greeks were realistic enough to require from each athlete an oath of fair play. The kinship of all Greeks was recognized and competition was therefore open to all of Greek descent regardless of rank, class, or the city from which they came. Brotherhood was national rather than universal, however, because barbarians (from the Greek world for foreigner) could not compete. The dominating spirit of the games was precisely the same as it was for all Greek culture: *Kalos k'agathos,* the beautiful and the good.

The best athletes in each city (selected by competition) started training exactly ten months before the festival; no one contestant had an unfair advantage. Because training was not permitted at the sacred site, final warm-ups were scheduled at Elis, after which everyone moved to Olympia for five days of competition dedicated to Zeus and Hera. Since the Olympiad was Greece's top event it had to be scheduled for both good weather and maximum attendance. Consequently, competition began on the third full moon of summer (in July or August), which placed the festivities after the grain and olive harvests and before the demands of fall planting. Adapting to the natural world was a consistent characteristic of Greek life.

The basic events of the games were footraces, primarily because all Greeks took great pride in their speed and stamina as runners.[8] The unit of distance was based on the length of the stadium at Olympia, which was about 200 yards. There were sprints of one-stade (200 yards), two-stade (400 yards), and so on up to distances of about three miles. There were no places (2d, 3rd) in the Olympics; there was one winner and everyone else was an also-ran. The prize, a simple olive wreath,[9] was the most sought after in Greece; though the leaves soon withered and fell, the winner's name was recorded in the roll of the Olympics and, ever after, his descendents would recall his name.

■

FIGURE 9.8 Runner at the Starting Point, Two Wrestlers, Javelin Thrower. *Bas-relief, marble, ca. 500 B.C., 12¼" × 26½". National Archeological Museum, Athens. Originally decorating the base of a kouros, this illustrates the bound hair and heavily muscled bodies of the athletes.*

The winner of a footrace in the modern Olympics is, as everyone knows, the first to break the tape, unless disqualified because of a foul. The Greeks were more sophisticated; in the judging the position of finish counted only fifty percent. The other half was evaluated independently by judges who searched for that something special: grace, poise, rhythm, what we might call, in one word, style.[10] As usual, the Greeks had a word for it: *arete* (ARE-uh-tay), which can be translated as skill, or stylish grace or, more precisely, diligence in the pursuit of excellence.[11] Besides the quality of *arete,* the games differed from the modern version in one other significant respect. Though the Greeks honored tradition they were not bound by the past, preferring instead to live enthusiastically in the present. They kept meticulous records of each Olympiad but they never recorded winning distances or times; athletes competed with each other, not with the past.

Except for chariot racing the ancient Olympic events are still a basic part of the modern Olympics: footracing, broad jump, discus, javelin, and boxing and wrestling (figure 9.8). The composite event, the pentathlon,[12] featured the kind of individual the Greeks especially admired, a well-rounded person who could do many things well. The Romans admired specialists; Greeks, generalists.

During the 1,169 years of the Olympic Games the high point was reached, not unexpectedly, during the Golden Age of Perikles. There was a slight decline in quality and integrity after that time, which accelerated rapidly beginning in 146 B.C., the year in which Carthage and Corinth were razed, the year in which the Romans

8. Cross-country running was, surprisingly, not one of the Olympic events. The marathon, based on the Marathon-to-Athens run of Pheidippides to announce the wondrous victory over the Persians, was introduced at the modern Olympics which began at Athens in 1896.
9. The other games of the sacred circuit awarded the laurel at Delphi (Pythian), pine at Corinth (Isthmian), and wild celery at Nemea (Nemean). The olive branch of the Olympic Games remains as a nearly universal symbol of peace.

10. Athletes competed in the nude so that judges could better evaluate their performance. It should also be noted that women were forbidden to attend the games under penalty of death, a prohibition based on religious reasons rather than the fact of nudity, which was not a problem for the Greeks, who looked upon their readiness to strip in public as one of the traits that separated them from barbarians.
11. Style is a factor in judging modern Olympic events like diving, gymnastics, and ice skating.
12. Five events: sprint, broad jump, wrestling and boxing, discus, and javelin. The decathlon (ten events) of the modern Olympics dropped the wrestling and boxing and added shot put, pole vault, high jump, 110-meter hurdles, and 100-, 400-, and 1500-meter races.

FIGURE 9.9 *Temple of Hera, ca. 600 B.C., Olympia. The column drums still lie where they were pushed over on orders of Theodosius or, as some would claim, toppled by an earthquake.*

took over Olympia. Typical of the Roman way was the behavior of Nero, who had himself declared winner of any event he entered; there was no one who could deny him. The games came to an end in A.D. 393, after the three hundred and twentieth Olympiad, when the Emperor Theodosios, in the name of Christianity, issued an edict forbidding the games because they "promoted the worship of heathen and false gods." No mention was made of the ancient truce when the emperor completed his work by ordering the destruction of the statues and temples. *Arete, kalos k'agathos* (skill, beauty, and goodness) vanished from the sacred groves of the peaceful river valley at Olympia (figure 9.9).

Roman Spectacles

Roman games were originally conceived and produced to honor the gods but, by the time of the Empire, private individuals were sponsoring extravagant spectacles honoring themselves, with just passing references to the gods. While the Romans had frequent athletic contests the public was far more entranced by the giant spectacles staged in the Colosseum and Circus Maximus (see figures 10.14, 10.15, and 10.16). When the Romans discussed the *ludi* (games, from which we get the word *ludicrous*), they referred specifically to five types of extravaganzas produced for immense arenas: chariot races, gladiatorial combat, wild animal hunts, naval battles, and mythological pantomimes. These *ludi* were not competitive in the Greek sense nor was there any concern for style or beauty. They were intended for the entertainment of vast crowds, and so we can credit the Romans with the invention of mass entertainment. As a part of the welfare program that also supplied food to the unemployed, the games were free. The familiar phrase "bread and circuses" aptly describes the Roman manner of controlling their constituency.

Most popular were the *ludi circenses* (games in a ring), the chariot races held at six racetracks in and about Rome. Racing was a frenzied and dangerous sport, if one can call driving four-horse chariots on a tight oval track that had only one rule—to the victor goes the spoils—a sport. The stakes were certainly high enough; the best drivers made a great deal of money and also enjoyed a status exceeding the combined charisma of a pro football star and a Grand Prix champion. There is no contemporary equivalent for a day at the races at the Circus Maximus in ancient Rome. Try to imagine an oval track 2,000 feet in circumference, four tense and tough racing teams (blues, greens, whites, reds) and 250,000 fanatical spectators who had millions riding on every race. Moreover, the races provided the ideal setting for the intrigues and assignations that were so much a part of Roman life (see Ovid's *The Art of Love* in "Literary Selections").

Gladiatorial combat calls for a more extensive discussion, not only because it was unique to Roman civilization but also because it was so characteristic of Roman values. There has been a tendency, probably dating back to Napoleon, to ascribe the Roman virtues of nobility, courage, and honesty to the austere days of the Republic, and thus blame the Empire for much of the brutality and decadence for which Rome is justly infamous. It was the Republic, however, that brutally destroyed Carthage and Corinth in 146 B.C. and it was the Republic that bred gladiatorial combat, beginning in 264 B.C.

The ritual of mortal combat always began with the ceremonial march of the gladiators into the arena and the famous words to the royal box: *Ave, Caesar, morituri te salutant* (Hail, Caesar, we who are about to die salute you). Then there was the drawing of lots and the inspection of arms. A typical match-up, to start the show, would be a gladiator of the Thracian type versus one of the *hoplomachi* fighting style. The Thracian wore a heavy helmet, had leather and metal covering much of his body, and carried a small shield and curved sword. The *hoplomachi* wore a heavy helmet, was nearly naked, and carried a large, oblong shield and a Roman sword. Bodies were guarded by a variety of clothing and armament, all designed to protect the combatant from disabling minor wounds. What the crowd wanted was a skillful, courageous, and relatively even fight; given this kind of battle, public sentiment tended towards a thumbs-up verdict for the loser, who could then fight another day. The *editor,* the sponsor of the day's games, had the final say, however, and the verdict could just as well be thumbs-down. The loser was then expected to display his superb training and discipline (he was also trained in how to die) by presenting his naked throat to his conqueror's sword. Anguish and gore enough it would seem, but the Romans further embellished the bloody scene with an actor dressed as a god and brandishing a white-hot staff, which he pressed into the flesh of the fallen man to make certain he was dead. The tattered body was then hooked behind a horse and dragged away and the entire arena sprayed with perfume, after which the crowd settled contentedly back for the next contest.

The next pair, perhaps a *retiarius* and a *secutor,* were always great crowd pleasers. Possessing neither helmet nor shield, the *retiarius* had a dagger in his belt, while one hand gripped a net and the other a trident. His opponent, the *secutor,* wore a helmet and carried a long rectangular shield and a sword plus the standard dagger in his belt. The *retiarius* had to be very mobile because the contest amounted to a swift runner attacking a human tank; the advantage usually lay with the tank. Although the two pairs described above appeared at most spectacles, there was also fighting from chariots, dwarf gladiators, female combatants, and whatever else could be concocted to stimulate the interest of the common people in the upper tiers. Staging these extravanganzas was so expensive that the government had to assume the responsibility for special schools, which in Rome alone trained and housed some two thousand gladiators. Amphitheatre combat was probably scheduled only several times a year; this kept expenses down, helped maintain a full complement of gladiators (about six hundred pairs fought in each production) and, most importantly, heightened expectations for the next spectacular event.

Other spectacles involved elaborately staged hunts, which featured an African jungle, for example, in the Colosseum with hunters and assorted lions and tigers stalking each other, though it is doubtful the starved, frightened creatures wanted anything more than a place to hide from their tormentors. Many thousands of wild animals were slaughtered in this manner, so many in fact, that whole species were annihilated. Fought in pools built for the occasion, naval battles were reenactments of famous engagements, bloody reminders of the power of Roman arms at sea. Finally, there were dramatic pantomimes based on familiar mythological plots and starring condemned criminals in their first and last performance.

Treated to mythology in action, audiences witnessed Herakles being consumed by flames, Dirce lashed to the horns of a maddened bull, Ikaros of the failing wings falling among wild beasts, and other edifying splendors. Roman efficiency was well-served; the mob was entertained and enlightened while, at the same time, justice was served.

The Roman games were so appallingly brutal that some apologists have tried to rationalize the whole bloody business into justifiable and necessary entertainment for restless and potentially dangerous mobs. Others have sought evidence that educated Romans disapproved of the institution; they have looked in vain, however, since Romans of every class and station attended and enjoyed the games. With the possible exception of Seneca and Pliny the Younger, we know of not a single Roman who ever voiced any concerns, humane or otherwise, about the events staged in the Colosseum. Death, in this ancient time, was not a significant consideration for those in power, particularly when the lower classes were doing the dying. Ironically, the one event that was vigorously denounced was the *sparsio,* the bonus episode that usually followed the final gladiatorial contest. While the upper class beat a hasty retreat, a machine with a rotating arm that hurled clay or wooden tablets in the general direction of the upper tiers was wheeled into the arena. Whatever was depicted on the tally was redeemable in kind: a water buffalo, ten pounds of ostrich feathers, an occasional elephant, two tickets in the lower tier for the next attraction, and so on. Horace spoke for the upper class when he wrote: "I hate the vulgar herd and hold it far."

It should be noted, in conclusion, that Roman spectacles were enthusiastically adopted throughout the Mediterranean world. Roman games, however, were never staged in Athens, Delphi, Delos, Epidauros, or, most especially, Olympia.

The Best of the Roman Ideal

Artistically and creatively, Rome reached its peak during the Golden Age of Caesar Augustus (see the Time Chart on p. 202). Augustus had won, at long last, the Civil War, bringing peace to an embattled Republic that had emerged from the chaos as the mighty Roman Empire. As he was rebuilding Rome, he turned his attention to a literary project much more important than erecting a city of gleaming marble—the fabulous history of the city that was destined to rule the world.

The Aeneid

Augustus selected Virgil as his poet of Roman greatness and commissioned him to write an epic poem celebrating the Augustan victory at Actium in 31 B.C. The emperor wanted to be depicted as the noble conqueror of the forces of darkness (led by Mark Antony and Cleopatra) and as the conqueror of Egypt, the richest agricultural land in the ancient world. What happened to the sponsored project was something not only unexpected but infinitely better than anything Augustus had envisioned: Virgil wrote the *Aeneid* (uh-NEE-id).

It was apparent to Virgil that much of the greatness of Athens resulted from the tradition provided by Homer's *Iliad* and *Odyssey*. Virgil knew these poems well and he deliberately patterned his epic upon them to give Rome the same kind of golden past that the Greeks had enjoyed, and to provide inspiration for the creation of great and noble works.

Books I–VI of the *Aeneid,* concerned with the wanderings of Aeneas (uh-NEE-us) after his escape from Troy, are based on the *Odyssey.* Books VII–XII are based on the *Iliad* and tell of war and death in Italy as Aeneas follows his destiny. Virgil's major innovation was not to undertake an adventure story but the tackling of a noble subject, the founding of an empire. For the Romans, reality was the State and the principle aim of all literature was to stir patriotism. The *Aeneid* is literature and it is also propaganda for a great nation. But what's the matter with propaganda for a good cause?

Virgil created Aeneas as both Homeric and Roman, ancient and modern, a contemporary of Akhilleus and Odysseus but also a true Augustan Roman. Clearly we can see Virgil thinking to himself: "Tomorrow we are going to start the old tradition of Roman greatness." Somehow the overthoughtful, rather pompous figure of Aeneas falls short of the glory-bound Akhilleus and Hektor, not to mention the wily Odysseus. In Aeneas, the Homeric hero is redefined as a man who can decide a whole civilization, who can write past, present, and future in himself and whose heroism consists in the fact that he can actually do this and others cannot. In no other person—real or fictional—are the superior qualities of the noble Roman better exemplified.

The hero is middle-aged but he has gained the wisdom that sometimes comes with maturity. Aeneas sees clearly that a kind of sadness underlies all heroic acts and that many things that people do result from choices that are forced upon them. Compared with Homer, Virgil loses much in dash; what he gains is a sad and chastened wisdom.

The poem recounts the legend of the founding of Rome by the Trojan hero Aeneas after the fall of Troy to Agamemnon and the Greeks. Aeneas, commanded by Jupiter and Aeneas's goddess mother, escaped from Troy with his aged father, his son Askanius (a-SKAY-nee-us; also called Ilus, and later Iulus to relate him to the Julian line of Caesars), and with the household gods that are to be the gods of the new city, Rome. The voyage is full of epic incident, storms at sea, battles, rather pleasant interludes, and the final war on Italian soil to conquer the kingdom of Latium and arrange for the marriage that will produce the Roman line.

Only two or three incidents need be mentioned to suggest the flavor of the epic. At the first of the book Aeneas, storm-tossed, landed on the shore near Carthage where he and his companions were made welcome by Dido, the queen of the city. As he recounted his adventures, Dido fell in love with him, and he with her. So satisfying was the affair that Aeneas lingered for a long time, while Dido tried to persuade him to settle there and make Carthage the city he was supposed to found.

Aeneas, prodded by his stoic sense of duty, knew that he must push on, and so one morning before daybreak he and his companions set sail. Aeneas as a person hated his decision, but he was honor-bound to make it; Dido was so devastated that she had a great funeral pyre built and committed suicide in the flames. One of the ironies of the poem lies in the meeting of the lovers in the underworld in Book VI (included in this chapter), when Aeneas tries to rekindle their love and she turns against him. Aeneas knew all there was to know about the founding of cities, but he understood little about the human heart.

Another of the little incidents occurs when the Trojans land on Sicily. The land is so beautiful that a number of Aeneas's group suggest that the city be founded there, but the hero knows that this is not the place, so he allows some of his party to stay while he again sails away to make war and cause death so that the city might be properly founded. Once again he realized the tragedy of his choice, but Duty, stern daughter of the voice of god, would not let him make the easy choice.

Many other events could be cited to illustrate the same point. Aeneas's chief adversary in Italy is a hero named Turnus, a thoroughly noble person; probably a better man than Aeneas. Turnus was patterned on the character of Hektor in the *Iliad.* Turnus must be destroyed, and Aeneas does it. Hektor, too, had to be killed. The difference is that Akhilleus, the youthful hero, fought his battle fiercely and killed his enemy in passion. Aeneas simply knew that the better man must be killed, and he did the job in full knowledge and for a greater good (the founding of the city of Rome) than would be accomplished by the saving of one good man.

Such is the tone of the whole poem except for some interludes, such as the funeral games for Ankhises when Virgil allows himself to relax and enjoy the deeds of physical strength and skill. The *Aeneid,* like the stoic philosophy, sees duty as the highest way of life, and the true Roman hero places duty above all other human values. Virgil wonderfully gave Rome its best and highest creed when, in the underworld, Ankhises told his son Aeneas:

Others will cast more tenderly in bronze
Their breathing figures, I can well believe,
And bring more lifelike portraits out of marble;
Argue more eloquently, use the pointer
To trace the paths of heaven accurately
And accurately foretell the rising stars.
Roman, remember by your strength to rule
Earth's peoples—for your arts are to be these:
To pacify, to impose the rule of law,
To spare the conquered, battle down the proud.

This was the highest of the Roman ideal. While it sacrificed much in the realm of human value, while it denigrated such qualities as imagination and joy, it furnished a noble code of conduct as long as the Romans adhered to it.

A Day in Ancient Rome

Marcellus wakes at dawn to the cheery sound of birds singing in the garden. His bedroom is sparsely furnished (wooden bed with mattress and spread, chamber pot) but elegantly decorated with frescoed walls and a mosaic floor. Since he slept in his underclothes (loin cloth and short tunic), his toilet is simple: slip on sandals and dash some water in his face. His breakfast is equally perfunctory: a bit of bread and some goat cheese. His valet helps him don his voluminous white linen toga, the necessary garment for a lawyer with official business before the Senate or, today, for pleading a case before the bar.

Stepping onto the porch bordering the inner courtyard Marcellus walks to his wife's bedchamber. There Lucretia is completing her morning ritual with the aid of her *ornatrix* (slave girl). Already her eyebrows are outlined with chalk, her eyelids shadowed with powdered antimony, her lips and cheeks colored with a lead-based rouge. At the moment her hair is being piled into a mountain of curls in the popular Flavian style, after which she will don her white linen *stola,* a tunic falling in graceful folds to her sandaled feet. This Roman matron, reflects Marcellus proudly, is also a very beautiful woman.

Leaving his luxurious marble house, Marcellus strolls toward the forum while listening to the increasing din rising from the nearby business district. Block after block of six-story brick apartment houses fill almost every available site. Ground floor shops line the street, their wares displayed in the crowded streets. Marcellus thinks grimly to himself how congested it would be if all vehicles were not banned during Rome's daylight hours. Noises assail his patrician ears: the babble of plebeian merchants, peddlars hawking their wares, blacksmiths hammering, carpenters sawing, stonecutters chiseling. Most everyone is clothed in a dark woolen tunic or cloak; not many can afford to clean white clothing. Everywhere there are snack bars where crowds of commoners stand around downing stews or pots of vegetables. Over in the ever-growing poor quarter the welfare cases are standing wearily in line waiting for their coarse bread, thin gruel, and—state holiday today!—free tickets to the gladiatorial games in the colosseum.

After his morning in court, which went very well, Marcellus starts home for lunch, noting the boys and girls reciting their daily lessons. Both sexes begin primary school at age seven to learn reading, writing, and arithmetic in Latin and Greek, the two languages of the empire. At age thirteen the boys will go on to secondary school to study advanced grammar, history, and the Greek and Latin literary classics. The girls will remain at home learning how to manage a household.

During a light lunch of bread, cheese, and fruit, Marcellus listens to Lucretia's account of her busy morning. The new slaves need much more instruction in shopping and cleaning, but the experienced kitchen staff is already preparing a sumptuous evening meal for their special guest.

Following a brief siesta Marcellus drops by his barber for a shave and then heads for the nearest of five public baths—all free and open to rich and poor alike—checks out the lecture hall (nothing scheduled today), and settles down in the library. The custom of reading aloud is particularly enjoyable when one reads some of the speeches of Cicero. After a workout with weights and a fast game of handball, he has a slave rub him with oil before he enters the steam room. A cold plunge completes the daily ritual.

By midafternoon he is home with his wife and both dress for the late afternoon dinner. Lucretia chooses a violet tunic, Marcellus a bright blue one. While waiting for his guest, a famous colleague and judge, he and his son Arminius discuss the approaching ceremony when Arminius will be robed in a white toga as the mark of a mature Roman male. The young man listens respectfully, for Marcellus is *paterfamilias,* the absolute lifetime head of the family.

Later, husband, wife, and honored guest enter the *triclinium* (dining room) where several benches surround a central low table. Propped up on pillows, the men lie on the benches while Lucretia sits on a stool. The hors d'oeuvres include sliced eggs, shrimp, and vegetables with herbs: olives, leeks, lettuce, and mint. They feast leisurely on no less than four meat dishes (beef, pork, fowl, fish) and drink diluted Roman wine. As usual, dessert consists of succulent fruits: apples, pears, peaches, plums. As they linger over the food a Greek slave reads to them from Virgil's "Eclogues." (Last night it was the ever-popular *Iliad.*) Another Greek slave strums the lyre and sings some popular lyrics as the two lawyers stroll in the garden and talk shop. It has been a very satisfying day.

Literary Selections

ON THE REPUBLIC

from Book VI, Scipio's Dream

Marcus Tullius Cicero (106–43 B.C.)

In both his political career and his writing Cicero is the perfect embodiment of the noble Roman statesman and cultured man of letters. Metaphysics and aesthetics are Greek concerns and of no interest for a patriot committed to the austere business of being a Roman. Rather, practicality and devotion to the state are his central concerns; these support a Rome whose destiny is to establish order and to civilize the world.

In his *On the Republic* (54–51 B.C.), Cicero follows Stoic teaching on promoting the welfare of the state, but adopts some details from Plato's *Republic*. Although patterned after Plato's *Myth of Er* (*Republic*, Book X), Cicero's *Scipio's Dream* is unequivocally Roman. Plato's myth is a vision of aspiration towards the state as an absolute ideal; Cicero uses a dream device to illustrate duty, honor, and patriotism, for as Scipio is told, "the noblest of pursuits . . . are those undertaken for the safety of your country."

The narrator is Scipio Africanus the Younger, the adopted grandson of Scipio Africanus the Elder, the general who defeated Hannibal at Carthage (Second Punic War, 218–201 B.C.). Scipio the Younger totally destroyed Carthage at the end of the Third Punic War (149–146 B.C.). In this essay he is an officer under the consul Manius Manilius, whom he later replaced. Widely read in the Middle Ages, this essay influenced both Chaucer and Dante; the geography and cosmology of the latter's *Hell* (see chapter 14) can be compared with Cicero's summary of the science of his day.

I served in Africa as military tribune of the Fourth Legion under Manius Manilius, as you know. When I arrived in that country my greatest desire was to meet King Masinissa, who had good reasons to be attached to my family. The old man embraced me tearfully when I called, and presently looked up to heaven and said, "I thank thee, sovereign sun, and ye lesser heavenly beings, that before I depart this life I behold in my realm and beneath my roof Publius Cornelius Scipio, whose very name refreshes my strength, so inseparable from my thought is the memory of that noble and invincible hero who first bore it." Then I questioned him about his kingdom, and he me about our commonwealth, and the day wore away with much conversation on both sides.

After I had been royally entertained we continued our conversation late into the night, the old man talking of nothing but Africanus and rehearsing his sayings as well as his deeds. When we parted to take our rest I fell into a deeper sleep than usual, for the hour was late and I was weary from travel. Because of our conversation, I suppose—our thoughts and utterances by day produce an effect in our sleep like that which Ennius speaks of with reference to Homer, of whom he used frequently to think and speak in his waking hours—Africanus appeared to me, in the shape that was familiar to me from his bust rather than from his own person. I shuddered when I recognized him, but he said: "Courage, Scipio, lay aside your dread and imprint my words on your memory. Do you see yonder city which I forced to submit to Rome but which is now stirring up the old hostilities and cannot remain at rest (from a lofty eminence bathed in brilliant starlight he pointed to Carthage), the city which you have come to attack, slightly more than a private? Within two years you shall be consul and overthrow it, and so win for yourself that which you now bear by inheritance. When you shall have destroyed Carthage, celebrated your triumph, been chosen censor, have traversed Egypt, Syria, Asia, and Greece as ambassador, you will be chosen consul a second time in your absence and will put an end to a great war by extirpating Numantia. But when you shall be borne into the capitol in your triumphal chariot, you shall find the government thrown into confusion by the machinations of my grandson; and here, Africanus, you must display to your country the lustre of your spirit, genius, and wisdom.

"But at this period I perceive that the path of your destiny is a doubtful one; for when your life has passed through seven times eight oblique journeys and returns of the sun; and when these two numbers (each of which is regarded as complete, one on one account and the other on another) shall, in their natural circuit, have brought you to the crisis of your fate, then will the whole state turn itself toward thee and thy glory; the senate, all virtuous men, our allies, and the Latins, shall look up to you. Upon your single person the preservation of your country will depend; and, in short, it is your part, as dictator, to settle the government, if you can but escape the impious hands of your kinsmen."—Here, when Laelius uttered an exclamation, and the rest groaned with great excitement, Scipio said, with a gentle smile, "I beg that you will not waken me out of my dream; listen a few moments and hear what followed.

"But that you may be more earnest in the defense of your country, know from me, that a certain place in heaven is assigned to all who have preserved, or assisted, or improved their country, where they are to enjoy an endless duration of happiness. For there is nothing which takes place on earth more acceptable to that Supreme Deity who governs all this world, than those councils and assemblies of men bound together by law, which are termed states; the governors and preservers of these go from hence, and hither do they return." Here, frightened as I was, not so much from the dread of death as of the treachery of my friends, I nevertheless asked him whether my father Paulus, and others, whom we thought to be dead, were yet alive? "To be sure they are alive (replied Africanus), for they have escaped from the fetters of the body as from a prison; that which is called life is really death. But behold your father Paulus approaching you."—No sooner did I see him than I poured forth a flood of tears; but he, embracing and kissing me, forbade me to weep. And when, having suppressed my tears, I regained the faculty of speech, I said: "Why, thou most sacred and excellent father, since this is life, as I hear Africanus affirm, why do I tarry on earth, and not hasten to come to you?"

"Not so, my son," he replied; "unless that God, whose temple is all this which you behold, shall free you from this imprisonment in the body, you can have no admission to this place; for men have been created under this condition, that they should keep that globe called earth which you see in the middle of this temple. And a soul has been supplied to them from those eternal fires which you call constellations and stars, and which, being globular and round, are animated with divine spirit, and complete their cycles and revolutions with amazing rapidity. Therefore you, my Publius, and all good men, must preserve your souls in the keeping of your bodies; nor are you, without the order of that Being who bestowed them upon you, to depart from mundane life, lest you seem to desert the duty assigned you by God. But, Scipio, like your grandfather here, like me who begot you, cherish justice and duty, a great obligation to parents and kin but greatest to your country. Such a life is the way to heaven and to this assembly of those who have already lived, and, released from the body, inhabit the place which you now see" (it was the circle of light which blazed most brightly among the other fires), "which you have learned from the Greeks to call the Milky Way." And as I looked on every side I saw other things transcendently glorious and wonderful. There were stars which we never see from the earth, and all were vast beyond what we have ever imagined. The least was that farthest from heaven and nearest the earth which shone with a borrowed light. The starry spheres were much larger than the earth; the earth itself looked so small as to make me ashamed of our empire, which was a mere point on its surface.

As I gazed more intently on earth, Africanus said: "How long will your mind be fixed on the ground? Do you not see what lofty regions you have entered? These are the nine circles, or rather spheres, by which all things are held together. One, the outermost, is the celestial; it contains all the rest and is itself the Supreme God, holding and embracing within itself the other spheres. In this are fixed those stars which ever roll in an unchanging course. Beneath it are seven other spheres which have a retrograde movement, opposite to that of the heavens. Of these, the globe which on earth you call Saturn, occupies one sphere. That shining body which you see next is called Jupiter, and is friendly and salutary to mankind. Next the lucid one, terrible to the earth, which you call Mars. The Sun holds the next place, almost under the middle region; he is the chief, the leader, and the director of the other luminaries; he is the soul and guide of the world, and of such immense bulk, that he illuminates and fills all other objects with his light. He is followed by the orbit of Venus, and that of Mercury, as attendants; and the Moon rolls in the lowest sphere, enlightened by the rays of the Sun. Below this there is nothing but what is mortal and transitory, excepting those souls which are given to the human race by the goodness of the gods. Whatever lies above the Moon is eternal. For the earth, which is the ninth sphere, and is placed in the center of the whole system, is immovable and below all the rest; and all bodies, by their natural gravitation, tend toward it."

When I had recovered from my amazement at these things I asked, "What is this sound so strong and sweet that fills my ears?" "This," he replied, "is the melody which, at intervals unequal, yet differing in exact proportions, is made by the impulse and motion of the spheres themselves, which, softening shriller by deeper tones, produce a diversity of regular harmonies. It is impossible that such prodigious movements should pass in silence; and nature teaches that the sounds which the spheres at one extremity utter must be sharp, and those on the other extremity must be grave; on which account that highest revolution of the star-studded heaven, whose motion is more rapid, is carried on with a sharp and quick sound; whereas this of the moon, which is situated the lowest and at the other extremity, moves with the gravest sound. For the earth, the ninth sphere, remaining motionless, abides invariably in the innermost position, occupying the central spot in the universe. But these eight revolutions, of which two, those of Mercury and Venus, are in unison, make seven distinct tones, with measured intervals between, and almost all things are arranged in sevens. Skilled men, copying this harmony with strings and voice, have opened for themselves a way back to this place, as have others who with excelling genius have cultivated divine sciences in human life. But the ears of men are deafened by being filled with this melody; you mortals have no duller sense than that of hearing. As where the Nile at the Falls of Catadupa pours down from lofty mountains, the people who live hard by lack the sense of hearing because of the cataract's roar, so this harmony of the whole universe in its intensely rapid movement is so loud that men's ears cannot take it in, even as you cannot look directly at the sun, your sense of sight being overwhelmed by its radiance." While I marveled at these things I was ever and anon turning my eyes back to earth, upon which Africanus resumed:

"I perceive that even now you are fixing your eyes on the habitation and abode of men, and if it seems to you diminutive, as it in fact is, keep your gaze fixed on these heavenly things and scorn the earthly. What fame can you obtain from the speech of men, what glory worth the seeking? You perceive that men dwell on but few and scanty portions of the earth, and that amid these spots, as it were, vast solitudes are interposed! As to those who inhabit the earth, not only are they so separated that no communication can circulate among them from the one to the other, but part lie upon one side, part upon another, and part are diametrically opposite to you, from whom you assuredly can expect no glory. You observe that the same earth is encircled and encompassed as it were by certain zones, of which the two that are most distant from one another and lie as it were toward the vortexes of the heavens in both directions, are rigid as you see with frost, while the middle and the largest zone is burned up with the heat of the sun. Two of these are habitable. The southern, whose inhabitants imprint their footsteps in an opposite direction to you, has no relation to your race. As to this other, lying toward the north, which you inhabit, observe what a small portion of it falls to your share; for all that part of the earth which is inhabited by you, which narrows toward the south and north but widens from east to west, is no other than a little island surrounded by that sea which on earth you call the Atlantic, sometimes the great sea, and sometimes the ocean; and yet with so grand a name, you see how diminutive it is! Now do you think it possible for your renown, or that of any one of us, to move from those cultivated and inhabited spots of ground, and pass beyond that Caucasus, or swim across yonder Ganges? What inhabitant of the other parts of the east, or of the extreme regions of the setting sun, of those tracts that run toward the south or toward the north, shall ever hear of your name? Now supposing them cut off, you see at once within what narrow limits your glory would fain expand itself. As to those who speak of you, how long will they speak?

"Let me even suppose that a future race of men shall be desirous of transmitting to their posterity your renown or mine, as they received it from their fathers; yet when we consider the convulsions and conflagrations that must necessarily happen at some definite period, we are unable to attain not only to an eternal, but even to a lasting fame. Now of what consequence is it to you to be talked of by those who are born after you, and not by those who were born before you, who certainly were as numerous and more virtuous; especially, as amongst the very men who are thus to celebrate our renown, not a single one can preserve the recollections of a single year? For mankind ordinarily measure their year by the revolution of the sun, that is of a single heavenly body. But when all the planets shall return to the same position which they once had, and bring back after a long rotation the same aspect of the entire heavens, then the year may be said to be truly completed; I do not venture to say how many ages of mankind will be contained within such a year. As of old the sun seemed to be eclipsed and blotted out when the soul of Romulus entered these regions, so when the sun shall be again eclipsed in the same part of his course and at the same period of the year and day, with all the constellations and stars recalled to the point from which they started on their revolutions, then count the year as brought to a close. But be assured that the twentieth part of such a year has not yet elapsed.

"Consequently, should you renounce hope of returning to this place where eminent and excellent men find their reward, of what worth is that human glory which can scarcely extend to a small part of a single year? If, then, you shall determine to look on high and contemplate this mansion and eternal abode, you will neither give yourself to the gossip of the vulgar nor place your hope of well-being on rewards that man can bestow. Virtue herself, by her own charms, should draw you to true honor. What others may say of you regard as their concern, not yours. They will doubtless talk about you, but what they say is limied to the narrow regions which you see; nor does talk of anyone last into eternity—it is buried with those who die, and lost in oblivion for those who come afterward."

When he had finished I said: "Truly, Africanus, if the path to heaven lies open to those who have deserved well of their country, though from my childhood I have ever trod in your and my father's footsteps without disgracing your glory, yet now, with so noble a prize set before me, I shall strive with much more diligence."

"Do so strive," replied he, "and do not consider yourself, but your body, to be mortal. For you are not the being which this corporeal figure evinces; but the soul of every man is the man, and not that form which may be delineated with a finger. Know also that you are a god, if a god is that which lives, perceives, remembers, foresees, and which rules, governs, and moves the body over which it is set, just as the Supreme God rules the universe. Just as the eternal God moves the universe, which is in part mortal, so does an everlasting soul move the corruptible body.

"That which is always in motion is eternal; but that which, while communicating motion to another, derives its own movement from some other source, must of necessity cease to live when this motion ends. Only what moves itself never ceases motion, for it is never deserted by itself; it is rather the source and first cause of motion in whatever else is moved. But the first cause has no beginning, for everything originates from the first cause; itself, from nothing. If it owed its origin to anything else, it would not be a first cause. If it has no beginning, it has no end. If a first cause is extinguished, it will neither be reborn from anything else, nor will it create anything else from itself, for everything must originate from a first cause. It follows that motion begins with that which is moved of itself, and that this can neither be born nor die—else the heavens must collapse and nature perish, possessing no force from which to receive the first impulse to motion.

"Since that which moves of itself is eternal, who can deny that the soul is endowed with this property? Whatever is moved by external impulse is soulless; whatever possesses soul is moved by an inner impulse of its own, for this is the peculiar nature and property of soul. And since soul is the only force that moves itself, it surely has no beginning and is immortal. Employ it, therefore, in the noblest of pursuits; the noblest are those undertaken for the safety of your country. If it is in these that your soul is diligently exercised, it will have a swifter flight to this, its proper home and permanent abode. Even swifter will be the flight if, while still imprisoned in the body, it shall peer forth, and, contemplating what lies beyond, detach itself as far as possible from the body. For the souls of those who have surrendered themselves to the pleasures of the body and have become their slaves, who are goaded to obedience by lust and violate the laws of gods and men—such souls, when they pass out of their bodies, hover close to earth, and do not return to this place till they have been tossed about for many ages."

He departed; I awoke from sleep.

Exercises

1. Scipio describes the earth's geography and the universe as seen in his dream. How close was he to current concepts of earth and the heavens?
2. What deeds qualify a person to go to Cicero's concept of "heaven"? What does this suggest about the focus of Roman values?
3. Compare and contrast the values as represented in Cicero's *On the Republic* and Plato's *Republic*. Specifically, how do the values of the Roman state differ from Plato's ideal *polis?*

THE WORLD BELOW

(THE AENEID, BOOK VI)

Virgil (Publius Virgilius Maro) (*70–19* B.C.)

Introduction

In the story of the journey of Aeneas (i-NEE-us), the Trojan hero has fled from Troy, and, after a great storm at sea caused by Juno, he and his people landed on the coast of North Africa. They made their way to Carthage, a land ruled by Queen Dido (DIE-doe). In her court he told the story of the last days of the Trojan War and of the fall of Troy. He told how he gathered a group around him including his aged father, Anchises (an-KI-sees), son Askanius (A-SKAY-nee-us), and the household gods and fled from the coast of Asia Minor. He also told of their subsequent wanderings and of the death of Anchises.

In the meantime Dido has fallen in love with Aeneas, and he, as much as his duty will allow, with her. Fearful of what might come of this, Aeneas and his band fled to Sicily, and Dido built a great funeral pyre and cast herself upon it. In Sicily, Aeneas left a good part of his group who were tired of wandering, and with a select band he pushed on to fulfill his destiny—the founding of the City of Rome. The group arrived in Italy after Palinurus (pal-uh-NOOR-us), the steersman, was lost overboard. Long before, Aeneas had been told that on his arrival he should consult the Kumean Sibyl (kyoo-MEE-an si-bil), a prophetess of Apollo, and that he should visit the underworld where he would meet the spirit of his father. This visit is presented here in full. After the visit, the little group sailed up the Tiber and established a village and fort. Engaging in war with the Italian hero Turnus, they finally vanquished him. Then Aeneas was ready to follow his destiny further by marrying Lavinia, daughter of King Latinus (la-TIE-nus), and establishing the Roman Empire.

The selection given here, the pivotal book of the entire poem, is patterned very closely after Homer. In Book XI of the *Odyssey* (see chapter 4) Odysseus descended to the underworld primarily to secure Teiresias's prophecy about what the future held for him. Homer took full advantage of the opportunity to introduce many notable figures from Greek history. Virgil used a similar device of presenting past, present, and future but in a significantly different way. Rather than the prophecies of a seer, the future in the *Aeneid* is graphically portrayed.

It is in Book VI that Aeneas finally and fully encounters the future—the Romans still to come—and accepts, once and for all, his Roman destiny. Just as interesting as his encounters with future Romans is his meeting with the ghost of Dido. Granted that his leaving of Dido in Carthage was unromantic, to put it mildly, he does not have an easy conscience about the abandonment. He even tries for a reconciliation in the underworld but Dido will, of course, never forgive him. Here is another example of stoic Roman heroism. The Roman hero must walk over others on the road to his destiny but the process (for the Roman) is always painful. (The greater pain of the "others" was not a consideration.) The hero must deny both past and present for he has chosen to live for the future. Events move well beyond his desires, leaving only an unpleasant choice. Aeneas is sorry for Dido and for himself as the agent of her destruction. During the three Punic Wars, Rome was indeed the cause of the ruin of Carthage but, in the larger sense, Rome's destiny was to rule the world and that of Carthage was to be conquered and destroyed. Given the general Roman view that the State was the ultimate reality, the manifest destiny of the empire can be viewed as the proper course of history. For the conquered peoples of the empire, there was another and totally different viewpoint: the so-called destiny of Roman world conquest was a self-fulfilling prophecy and one that in no way justified the merciless onslaught of the Roman legions.

The Roman view—in particular, Virgil's—was that the opponents of Roman destiny die as they must but their deaths are considered the necessary price of civilization, of Roman civilization. Despite the conflicting points of view, it is still a fact that the Roman peace (*Pax Romana*) lasted from the reign of Caesar Augustus to that of Marcus Aurelius, a period of two centuries in which there was no major war anywhere in the Roman world.

Since Dante used Virgil as his guide through Hell and Purgatory (see chapter 14), there is an obvious influence of Virgil on the *Divine Comedy.* So, the line of influence extends from the *Iliad* and *Odyssey* to the *Aeneid* and all the way to Dante in the final years of the Middle Ages.

The selection given below was translated by the noted poet and scholar Rolfe Humphries.

The Aeneid

Mourning for Palinurus, he drives the fleet
To Cumae's coast line; the prows are turned, the anchor
Let down, the beach is covered by the vessels.
Young in their eagerness for the land in the west,
They flash ashore; some seek the seeds of flame
Hidden in veins of flint, and others spoil
The woods of tinder, and show where water runs.
Aeneas, in devotion, seeks the heights
Where stands Apollo's temple, and the cave
Where the dread Sibyl dwells, Apollo's priestess,
With the great mind and heart, inspired revealer
Of things to come. They enter Diana's grove,
Pass underneath the roof of gold.
                    The story
Has it that Daedalus fled from Minos' kingdom[13]
Trusting himself to wings he made, and travelled
A course unknown to man, to the cold north,
Descending on this very summit; here,
Earth-bound again, he built a mighty temple,

---

13. Daedalus (DED-uh-lus) was a mythical artist and inventor. Imprisoned by King Minos of Crete, he constructed wings for himself and his son Icarus (IK-ar-us) and flew away. Icarus flew too near the sun and melted the wax wings. The other pieces of sculpture mentioned here show other incidents in Daedalus' life.

Paying Apollo homage, the dedication
Of the oarage of his wings. On the temple doors
He carved, in bronze, Androgeos' death, and the payment
Enforced on Cecrops' children, seven sons
For sacrifice each year: there stands the urn,
The lots are drawn—facing this, over the sea,
Rises the land of Crete: the scene portrays
Pasiphae in cruel love, the bull
She took to her by cunning, and their offspring,
The mongrel Minotaur, half man, half monster,
The proof of lust unspeakable; and the toil
Of the house is shown, the labyrinthine maze
Which no one could have solved, but Daedalus
Pitied a princess' love, loosened the tangle,
Gave her a skein to guide her way. His boy,
Icarus, might have been here, in the picture,
And almost was—his father had made the effort
Once, and once more and dropped his hands; he could
   not
Master his grief that much. The story held them;
They would have studied it longer, but Achates[14]
Came from his mission; with him came the priestess,
Deiphobe, daughter of Glaucus, who tends the temple
For Phoebus and Diana; she warned Aeneas:
"It is no such sights the time demands; far better
To offer sacrifice, seven chosen bullocks,
Seven chosen ewes, a herd without corruption."
They were prompt in their obedience, and the priestess
Summoned the Trojans to the lofty temple.
      The rock's vast side is hollowed into a cavern,
With a hundred mouths, a hundred open portals,
Whence voices rush, the answers of the Sibyl.
They had reached the threshold, and the virgin cried:
"It is time to seek the fates; the god is here,
The god is here, behold him." And as she spoke
Before the entrance, her countenance and color
Changed, and her hair tossed loose, and her heart was
   heaving,
Her bosom swollen with frenzy; she seemed taller,
Her voice not human at all, as the god's presence
Drew nearer, and took hold on her. "Aeneas,"
She cried, "Aeneas, are you praying?
Are you being swift in prayer? Until you are,
The house of the gods will not be moved, nor open
Its mighty portals." More than her speech, her silence
Made the Trojans cold with terror, and Aeneas
Prayed from the depth of his heart: "Phoebus Apollo,
Compassionate ever, slayer of Achilles
Through aim of Paris' arrow, helper and guide
Over the seas, over the lands, the deserts,
The shoals and quicksands, now at last we have come
To Italy, we hold the lands which fled us:
Grant that thus far, no farther, a Trojan fortune
Attend our wandering. And spare us now;
All of you, gods and goddesses, who hated
Troy in the past, and Trojan glory. I beg you,
Most holy prophetess, in who foreknowing
The future stands revealed, grant that the Trojans—
I ask with fate's permission—rest in Latium
Their wandering storm-tossed gods. I will build a temple,

In honor of Apollo and Diana,
Out of eternal marble, and ordain
Festivals in their honor, and for the Sibyl
A great shrine in our Kingdom, and I will place there
The lots and mystic oracles for my people
With chosen priests to tend them. Only, priestess,
This once, I pray you, chant the sacred verses
With your own lips; do not trust them to the leaves,[15]
The mockery of the rushing wind's disorder."
      But the priestess, not yet subject to Apollo,
Went reeling through the cavern, wild, and storming
To throw the god, who presses, like a rider,
With bit and bridle and weight, tames her wild spirit,
Shapes her to his control. The doors fly open,
The hundred doors, of their own will, fly open,
And through the air the answer comes:—"O Trojans,
At last the dangers of the sea are over;
That course is run, but grave ones are waiting
On land. The sons of Dardanus[16] will reach
The kingdom of Lavinia[17]—be easy
On that account—the sons of Dardanus, also,
Will wish they had not come there. War, I see,
Terrible war, and the river Tiber foaming
With streams of blood. There will be another Xanthus,
Another Simois,[18] and Greek encampment,
Even another Achilles, born in Latium,
Himself a goddess' son. And Juno further
Will always be there: you will beg for mercy,
Be poor, turn everywhere for help. A woman
Will be the cause once more of so much evil,
A foreign bride, receptive to the Trojans,
A foreign marriage. Do not yield to evil,
Attack, attack, more boldly even than fortune
Seems to permit. An offering of safety,—
Incredible!—will come from a Greek city."
      So, through the amplifiers of her cavern,
The hollow vaults, the Sibyl cast her warnings,
Riddles confused with truth; and Apollo rode her,
Reining her rage, and shaking her, and spurring
The fierceness of her heart. The frenzy dwindled,
A little, and her lips were still. Aeneas
Began:—"For me, no form of trouble, maiden,
Is new, or unexpected; all of this
I have known long since, lived in imagination.
One thing I ask: this is the gate of the kingdom,
So it is said, where Pluto reigns, the gloomy
Marsh where the water of Acheron[19] runs over.

---

15. The prophecies of this Cumaean Sibyl were usually written on leaves which the winds in the cave might scatter and confuse (v. Book III).

16. The mythical founder of Troy.

17. The daughter of the Italian King Latinus. Aeneas was later to marry her to establish his kingdom.

18. Rivers near Troy that ran with blood during the Trojan War.

19. This is the river (AK-uh-ron) that leads to Hades. Other rivers in the lower world are the Styx, which forms a boundary for the region, Cocytus (ko-SI-tus), the Phlegethon (FELG-uh-thon), which serves as a barrier between the mild punishments and the more severe.

---

14. Achates (a-KOT-eez) is a companion of Aeneas.

Teach me the way from her, open the portals
That I may go to my beloved father,
Stand in his presence, talk with him. I brought him,
Once, on these shoulders, through a thousand weapons
And following fire, and foemen. He shared with me
The road, the sea, the menaces of heaven,
Things that an old man should not bear; he bore them,
Tired as he was. And he it was who told me
To come to you in humbleness. I beg you
Pity the son, the father. You have power,
Great priestess, over all; it is not for nothing
Hecate[20] gave you this dominion over
Avernus' groves. If Orpheus could summon
Eurydice from the shadows with his music,
If Pollux could save his brother, coming, going,
Along this path,—why should I mention Theseus,
Why mention Hercules?[21] I, too, descended
From the line of Jupiter." He clasped the altar,
Making his prayer, and she made answer to him:
"Son of Anchises, born of godly lineage,
By night, by day, the portals of dark Dis[22]
Stand open: it is easy, the descending
Down to Avernus. But to climb again,
To trace the footsteps back to the air above,
There lies the task, the toil. A few, beloved
By Jupiter, descended from the gods,
A few, in whom exalting virtue burned,
Have been permitted. Around the central woods
The black Cocytus glides, a sullen river;
But if such love is in your heart, such longing
For double crossing of the Stygian lake,
For double sight of Tartarus, learn first
What must be done. In a dark tree there hides
A bough, all golden, leaf and pliant stem,
Sacred to Proserpine.[23] This all the grove
Protects, and shadows cover it with darkness.
Until this bough, this bloom of light, is found,
No one receives his passport to the darkness
Whose queen requires this tribute. In succession,
After the bough is plucked, another grows,
Gold-green with the same metal. Raise the eyes,
Look up, reach up the hand, and it will follow
With ease, if fate is calling; otherwise,
No power, no steel, can loose it. Furthermore,
(Alas, you do not know this!), one of your men
Lies on the shore, unburied, a pollution
To all the fleet, while you have come for counsel
Here to our threshold. Bury him with honor;
Black cattle slain in expiation for him
Must fall before you see the Stygian kingdoms,
The groves denied to living men."

20. Hecate (HEK-uh-tee) is a very powerful goddess who,
among many responsibilities, controlled the spirits of the dead.
Avernus is a very deep pool surrounded by gloomy woods. Its
depth and gloom inspired the idea that it led to the underworld.

21. All of these are the names of mythical heroes who had
descended into Hades and returned.

22. Dis is another name for the underworld.

23. Proserpine (pro-SUR-pi-nee), as wife of Pluto, is queen of
the underworld.

Aeneas,
With sadness in his eyes, and downcast heart,
Turned from the cave, and at his side Achates
Accompanied his anxious meditations.
They talked together: who could be the comrade
Named by the priestess, lying there unburied?
And they found him on dry sand; it was Misenus,[24]
Aeolus' son, none better with the trumpet
To make men burn for warfare. He had been
Great Hector's man-at-arms; he was good in battle
With spear as well as horn, and after Hector
had fallen to Achilles, he had followed
Aeneas, entering to meaner service.
Some foolishness came over him; he made
The ocean echo to the blare of his trumpet
That day, and challenged the sea-gods to a contest
In martial music, and Triton, jealous, caught him,
However unbelievable the story,
And held him down between the rocks, and drowned him
Under the foaming waves. His comrades mourned him,
Aeneas most of all, and in their sorrow
They carry out, in haste, the Sibyl's orders,
Construct the funeral altar, high as heaven,
They go to an old wood, and the pine-trees fall
Where wild beasts have their dens, and holm-oak rings
To the stroke of the axe, and oak and ash are riven
By the splitting wedge, and rowan-trees come rolling
Down the steep mountain-side. Aeneas helps them,
And cheers them on; studies the endless forest,
Takes thought, and prays: "If only we might see it,
That golden bough, here in the depth of the forest,
Bright on some tree. She told the truth, our priestess,
Too much, too bitter truth, about Misenus."
No sooner had he spoken than twin doves
Came flying down before him, and alighted
On the green ground. He knew his mother's birds,[25]
And made his prayer, rejoicing,—"Oh, be leaders,
Wherever the way, and guide me to the grove
Where the rich bough makes rich the shaded ground.
Help me, O goddess-mother!" And he paused,
Watching what sign they gave, what course they set.
The birds flew on a little, just ahead
Of the pursuing vision; when they came
To the jaws of dank Avernus, evil-smelling,
They rose aloft, then swooped down the bright air,
Perched on the double tree, where the off-color
Of gold was gleaming golden through the branches.
As mistletoe, in the cold winter, blossoms
With its strange foliage on an alien tree,
The yellow berry gilding the smooth branches,
Such was the vision of the gold in leaf
On the dark holm-oak, so the foil was rustling,
Rattling, almost, the bract in the soft wind
Stirring like metal. Aeneas broke it off
With eager grasp, and bore it to the Sibyl.
    Meanwhile, along the shore, the Trojans mourned,
Paying Misenus' dust the final honors.
A mighty pyre was raised, of pine and oak,
The sides hung with dark leaves, and somber cypress
Along the front, and gleaming arms above.

24. mi-SEEN-us.
25. Aeneas' mother was Venus.

Some made the water hot, and some made ready
Bronze caldrons, shimmering over fire, and others
Lave and anoint the body, and with weeping
Lay on the bier his limbs, and place above them
Familiar garments, crimson color; and some
Take up the heavy burden, a sad office,
And, as their fathers did, they kept their eyes
Averted, as they brought the torches nearer.
They burn gifts with him, bowls of oil, and viands,
And frankincense; and when the flame is quiet
And the ashes settle to earth, they wash the embers
With wine, and slake the thirsty dust. The bones
Are placed in a bronze urn by Corynaeus,
Who, with pure water, thrice around his comrades
Made lustral cleansing, shaking gentle dew
From the fruitful branch of olive; and they said
Hail and farewell! And over him Aeneas
Erects a mighty tomb, with the hero's arms,
His oar and trumpet, where the mountain rises
Memorial for ever, and named Misenus.

    These rites performed, he hastened to the Sibyl.
There was a cavern, yawning wide and deep,
Jagged, below the darkness of the trees.
Beside the darkness of the lake. No bird
Could fly above it safely, with the vapor
Pouring from the black gulf (the Greeks have named it
Avernus, or A-Ornos, meaning *birdless*),
And here the priestess for the slaughter set
Four bullocks, black ones, poured the holy wine
Between the horns, and plucked the topmost bristles
For the first offering to the sacred fire,
Calling on Hecate, a power in heaven,
A power in hell. Knives to the throat were driven,
The warm blood caught in bowls. Aeneas offered
A lamb, black-fleeced, to Night and her great sister,
A sterile heifer for the queen; for Dis
An altar in the night, and on the flames
The weight of heavy bulls, the fat oil pouring
Over the burning entrails. And at dawn,
Under their feet, earth seemed to shake and rumble,
The ridges move, and bitches bay in darkness,
As the presence neared. The Sibyl cried a warning,
"Keep off, keep off, whatever is unholy,
Depart from here! Courage, Aeneas; enter
The path, unsheathe the sword. The time is ready
For the brave heart." She strode out boldly, leading
Into the open cavern, and he followed.

    Gods of the world of spirit, silent shadows,
Chaos and Phlegethon, areas of silence,
Wide realms of dark, may it be right and proper
To tell what I have heard, this revelation
Of matters buried deep in earth and darkness!

    Vague forms in lonely darkness, they were going
Through void and shadow, through the empty realm
Like people in a forest, when the moonlight
Shifts with a baleful glimmer, and shadow covers
The sky, and all the colors turn to blackness.
At the first threshold, on the jaws of Orcus,
Grief and avenging Cares have set their couches,
And pale Diseases dwell, and sad Old Age,
Fear, evil-counselling Hunger, wretched Need,
Forms terrible to see, and Death, and Toil,
And Death's own brother, Sleep, and evil Joys,
Fantasies of the mind, and deadly War,
The Furies' iron chambers, Discord, raving,
Her snaky hair entwined in bloody bands.

An el-tree loomed there, shadowy and huge,
The aged boughs outspread, beneath whose leaves,
Men say, the false dreams cling, thousands on thousands.
And there are monsters in the dooryard, Centaurs,
Scyllas, of double shape, the beast of Lerna,
Hissing most horribly, Briareus,
The hundred-handed giant, a Chimaera
Whose armament is fire, Harpies, and Gorgons,
A triple-bodied giant. In sudden panic
Aeneas drew his sword, the edge held forward,
Ready to rush and flail, however blindly,
Save that his wise companion warned him, saying
They had no substance, they were only phantoms
Flitting about, illusions without body.

    From here, the road turns off to Acheron,
River of Hell; here, thick with muddy whirling,
Cocytus boils with sand. Charon[26] is here,
The guardian of these mingling waters, Charon,
Uncouth and filthy, on whose chin the hair
Is a tangled mat, whose eyes protrude, are burning,
Whose dirty cloak is knotted at the shoulder.
He poles a boat, tends to the sail, unaided,
Ferrying bodies in his rust-hued vessel.
Old, but a god's senility is awful
In its raw greenness. To the bank come thronging
Mothers and men, bodies of great-souled heroes,
There life-time over, boys, unwedded maidens,
Young men whose fathers saw their pyres burning,
Thick as the forest leaves that fall in autumn
With early frost, thick as the birds to landfall
From over the seas, when the chill of the year compels
    them.
To sunlight. There they stand, a host, imploring
To be taken over first. Their hands, in longing
Reach out for the farther shore. But the gloomy boatman
Makes choice among them, taking some, and keeping
Others far back from the stream's edge. Aeneas,
Wondering, asks the Sibyl, "Why the crowding?
What are the spirits seeking? What distinction
Brings some across the livid stream, while others
Stay on the farther bank?" She answers, briefly:
"Son of Anchises, this is the awful river,
The Styx,[27] by which the gods take oath; the boatman
Charon; those he takes with him are the buried,
Those he rejects, whose luck is out, the graveless.
It is not permitted him to take them over
The dreadful banks and hoarse-resounding waters
Till earth is cast upon their bones. They haunt
These shores a hundred restless years of waiting
Before they end postponement of the crossing."
Aeneas paused, in thoughtful mood, with pity
Over their lot's unevenness; and saw there,
Wanting the honor given the dead, and grieving,
Leucaspis, and Orontes, the Lycian captain,
Who had sailed from Troy across the stormy waters,
And drowned off Africa, with crew and vessel,

---

26. KARE-on.
27. STICKS.

And there was Palinurus, once his pilot,
Who, not so long ago, had been swept over,
Watching the stars on the journey north from Carthage.
The murk was thick; Aeneas hardly knew him,
Sorrowful in that darkness, but made question:
"What god, O Palinurus, took you from us?
Who drowned you in the deep? Tell me. Apollo
Never before was false, and yet he told me
You would be safe across the seas, and come
Unharmed to Italy; what kind of promise
Was this, to fool me with?" But Palinurus
Gave him assurance:—"It was no god who drowned me,
No falsehood on Apollo's part, my captain,
But as I clung to the tiller, holding fast
To keep the course, as I should do, I felt it
Wrenched from the ship, and I fell with it, headlong.
By those rough seas I swear, I had less fear
On my account than for the ship, with rudder
And helmsman overboard, to drift at the mercy
Of rising seas. Three nights I rode the waters,
Three nights of storm, and from the crest of a wave,
On the fourth morning, sighted Italy,
I was swiming to land, I had almost reached it, heavy
In soaking garments; my cramped finger struggled
To grasp the top of the rock, when barbarous people,
Ignorant men, mistaking me for booty,
Struck me with swords; waves hold me now, or winds
Roll me along the shore. By the light of heaven
The lovely air, I beg you, by your father,
Your hope of young Iulus,[28] bring me rescue
Out of these evils, my unconquered leader!
Cast over my body earth—you have the power—
Return to Velia's harbor,—or there may be
Some other way—your mother is a goddess,
Else how would you be crossing this great river,
This Stygian swamp?—help a poor fellow, take me
Over the water with you, give a dead man
At least a place to rest in." But the Sibyl
Broke in upon him sternly:—"Palinurus,
Whence comes this mad desire? No man, unburied,
May see the Stygian waters, or Cocytus,
The Furies' dreadful river; no man may come
Unbidden to this bank. Give up the hope
That fate is changed by praying, but hear this,
A little comfort in your harsh misfortune:
Those neighboring people will make expiation,
Driven by signs from heaven, through their cities
And through their countryside; they will build a tomb,
Thereto bring offerings yearly, and the place
Shall take is name from you, Cape Palinurus."
So he was comforted a little, finding
Some happiness in the promise.
                    And they went on,
Nearing the river, and from the stream the boatman
Beheld them across the silent forest, nearer,
Turning their footsteps toward the bank. He
    challenged:—

"Whoever you are, O man in armor, coming
In this direction, halt where you are, and tell me
The reason why you come. This is the region
Of shadows, and of Sleep and drowsy Night;
I am not allowed to carry living bodies
In the Stygian boat; and I must say I was sorry
I ever accepted Hercules and Theseus
And Pirithous, and rowed them over the lake,
Though they were sons of gods and great in courage.
One of them dared to drag the guard of Hell,
Enchained, from Pluto's throne, shaking in terror,
The others to snatch our queen from Pluto's chamber."
The Sibyl answered briefly: "No such cunning
Is plotted here; our weapons bring no danger.
Be undisturbed: the hell-hound in his cavern
May bark forever, to keep the bloodless shadows
Frightened away from trespass; Proserpine,
Untouched, in pureness guard her uncle's threshold.
Trojan Aeneas, a man renowned for goodness,
Renowned for nerve in battle, is descending
To the lowest shades; he comes to find his father.
If such devotion has no meaning to you,
Look on this branch at least, and recognize it!"
And with the word she drew from under her mantle
The golden bough; his swollen wrath subsided.
No more was said; he saw the bough, and marvelled
At the holy gift, so long unseen; came sculling
The dark-blue boat to the shore, and drove the spirits,
Lining the thwarts, ashore, and cleared the gangway,
And took Aeneas aboard; as that big man
Stepped in, the leaky skiff groaned under the weight,
And the strained seams let in the muddy water,
But they made the crossing safely, seer and soldier,
To the far margin, colorless and shapeless,
Grey sedge and dark-brown ooze. They heard the baying
Of Cerberus,[29] that great hound, in his cavern crouching,
Making the shore resound, as all three throats
Belled horribly; and serpents rose and bristled
Along the triple neck. The priestess threw him
A sop with honey and drugged meal; he opened
The ravenous throat, gulped, and subsided, filling
The den with his huge bulk. Aeneas, crossing
Passed on beyond the bank of the dread river
Whence none return.
              A wailing of thin voices[30]
Came to their ears, the souls of infants crying,
Those whom the day of darkness took from the breast
Before their share of living. And there were many
Whom some false sentence brought to death. Here
    Minos[31]
Judges them once gain; a silent jury
Reviews the evidence. And there are others,
Guilty of nothing, but who hated living,
The suicides. How gladly, now, they would suffer
Poverty, hardship, in the world of light!
But this is not permitted; they are bound
Nine times around by the black unlovely river;
Styx holds them fast.

---

28. This is Aeneas' son, also known as Askanius.

---

29. SIR·bur·us.

30. Here and about 190 lines later you might compare the sins and their punishments with the disposition Dante makes of the souls in Hell in Canto XI of the *Inferno.*

31. MI·nus.

They came to the Fields of Mourning,
So-called, where those whom cruel love had wasted
Hid in secluded pathways, under myrtle,
And even in death were anxious. Procris, Phaedra,
Eriphyle, displaying wounds her son
Had given her, Caeneus, Laodamia,
Caeneus, a young man once, and now again
A young man, after having been a woman.
And here, new come from her own wound, was Dido,[32]
Wandering in the wood. The Trojan hero,
Standing near by, saw her, or thought he saw her,
Dim in the shadows, like the slender crescent
Of moon when cloud drifts over. Weeping, he greets
      her:—
"Unhappy Dido, so they told me truly
That your own hand had brought you death. Was I—
Alas!—the cause? I swear by all the stars,
By the world above, by everything held sacred
Here under the earth, unwillingly, O queen,
I left your kingdom. But the gods' commands,
Driving me now through these foresaken places,
This utter night, compelled me on. I could not
Believe my loss would cause so great a sorrow.
Linger a moment, do not leave me; whither,
Whom, are you fleeing? I am permitted only
This last word with you."
      But the queen, unmoving
As flint or marble, turned away, her eyes
Fixed on the ground: the tears were vain, the words,
Meant to be soothing, foolish; she turned away,
His enemy forever, to the shadows
Where Sychaeus, her former husband, took her
With love for love, and sorrow for her sorrow.
And still Aeneas wept for her, being troubled
By the injustice of her doom; his pity
Followed her going.
      They went on. They came
To the farthest fields, whose tenants are the warriors,
Illustrious throng. Here Tydeus came to meet him,
Parthenopaeus came, and pale Adrastus,
A fighter's ghost, and many, many others,
Mourned in the world above, and doomed in battle,
Leaders of Troy, in long array; Aeneas
Sighed as he saw them: Medon; Polyboetes,
The priest of Ceres; Glaucus; and Idaeus
Still keeping arms and chariot; three brothers,
Antenor's sons; Thersilochus; a host
To right and left of him, and when they see him,
One sight is not enough; they crowd around him,
Linger, and ask the reasons for his coming.
But Agamemnon's men, the Greek battalions,
Seeing him there, and his arms in shadow gleaming,
Tremble in panic, turn to flee for refuge,
As once they used to, toward their ships, but where
Are the ships now? They try to shout, in terror;
But only a thin and piping treble issues
To mock their mouths, wide-open.
      One he knew
Was here, Deiphobus[33] a son of Priam,

With his whole body mangled, and his features
Cruelly slashed, and both hands cut, and ears
Torn from his temples, and his nostrils slit
By shameful wounds. Aeneas hardly knew him,
Shivering there, and doing his best to hide
His marks of punishment; unhailed, he hailed him:—
"Deiphobus, great warrior, son of Teucer,
Whose cruel punishment was this? Whose license
Abused you so? I heard, it seems a story
Of that last night, how you had fallen, weary
With killing Greeks at last; I built a tomb,
Although no body lay there, in your honor,
Three times I cried, aloud, over your spirit,
Where now your name and arms keep guard. I could not,
Leaving my country, find my friend, to give him
Proper interment in the earth he came from."
And Priam's son replied:—"Nothing, dear comrade,
Was left undone; the dead man's shade was given
All ceremony due. It was my own fortune
And a Spartan woman's[34] deadliness that sunk me
Under these evils; she it was who left me
These souvenirs. You know how falsely happy
We were on that last night; I need not tell you.
When that dread horse came leaping over our walls,
Pregnant with soldiery, she led the dancing,
A solemn rite, she called it, with Trojan women
Screaming their bacchanals; she raised the torches
High on the citadel; she called the Greeks.
Then—I was worn with trouble, drugged in slumber,
Resting in our ill-omened bridal chamber,
With sleep as deep and sweet as death upon me—
Then she, that paragon of helpmates, deftly
Moved all the weapons from the house; my sword,
Even, she stole from underneath my pillow,
Opened the door, and called in Menelaos,
Hoping, no doubt, to please her loving husband,
To win forgetfulness of her old sinning.
It is quickly told: they broke into the chamber,
The two of them, and with them, as accomplice,
Ulysses came, the crime-contriving bastard.
O gods, pay back the Greeks; grant the petition
If goodness asks for vengeance! But you, Aeneas,
A living man—what chance has brought you here?
Vagrant of ocean, god-inspired,—which are you?
What chance has worn you down, to come, in sadness,
To these confusing sunless dwelling-places?"
      While they were talking, Aurora's rosy car
Had halfway crossed the heaven; all their time
Might have been spent in converse, but the Sibyl
Hurried them forward:—"Night comes on, Aeneas;
We waste the hours with tears. We are at the cross-road,
Now; here we turn to the right, where the pathway leads
On to Elysium, under Pluto's ramparts.
Leftward to Tartarus, and retribution,
The terminal of the wicked, and their dungeon."

---

34. This is Helen of Troy. Virgil believes that she was married to
Deiphobus after Paris' death.

---

32. Dido, Queen of Carthage, filled with rage and guilt had
committed suicide when Aeneas sailed away from her city.

33. dee-IF-uh-bus.

Deiphobus left them, saying, "O great priestess,
Do not be angry with me; I am going;
I shall not fail the roll-call of the shadows.
Pride of our race, go on; may better fortune
Attend you!" and, upon the word, he vanished.
         As he looked back, Aeneas saw, to his left,
Wide walls beneath a cliff, a triple rampart,
A river running fire, Phlegethon's torrent,
Rocks roaring in its course, a gate, tremendous,
Pillars of adamant, a tower of iron,
Too strong for men, too strong for even gods
To batter down in warfare, and behind them
A Fury, sentinel in bloody garments,
Always on watch, by day, by night. He heard
Sobbing and groaning there, the crack of the lash,
The clank of iron, the sound of dragging shackles.
The noise was terrible; Aeneas halted,
Asking, "What forms of crime are these, O maiden?
What harrying punishment, what horrible outcry?"
She answered:—"O great leader of the Trojans,
I have never crossed that threshold of the wicked;
No pure soul is permitted entrance thither,
But Hecate, by whose order I was given
Charge of Avernus' groves, my guide, my teacher,
Told me how gods exact the toll of vengeance.
The monarch here, merciless Rhadamanthus,
Punishes guilt, and hears confession; he forces
Acknowledgment of crime; no man in the world,
No matter how cleverly he hides his evil,
No matter how much he smiles at his own slyness,
Can fend atonement off; the hour of death
Begins his sentence. Tisiphone, the Fury,
Leaps at the guilty with her scourge; her serpents
Are whips of menace as she calls her sisters.
Imagine the gates, on jarring hinge, rasp open,
You would see her in the doorway, a shape, a sentry,
Savage, implacable. Beyond, still fiercer,
The monstrous Hydra dwells; her fifty throats
Are black, and open wide, and Tartarus
Is black, and open wide, and it goes down
To darkness, sheer deep down, and twice the distance
That earth is from Olympus. At the bottom
The Titans crawl, Earth's oldest breed, hurled under
By thunderbolts; here lie the giant twins,
Aloeus' sons, who laid their hands on heaven
And tried to pull down Jove; Salmoneus here
Atones for high presumption,—it was he
Who aped Jove's noise and fire, wheeling his horses
Triumphant through his city in Elis, cheering
And shaking the torch, and claiming divine homage,
The arrogant fool, to think his brass was lightning,
His horny-footed horses beat out thunder!
Jove showed him what real thunder was, what lightning
Spoke from immortal cloud, what whirlwind fury
Came sweeping from the heaven to overtake him.
Here Tityos, Earth's giant son, lies sprawling
Over nine acres, with a monstrous vulture
Gnawing, with crooked beak, vitals and liver
That grow as they are eaten; eternal anguish,
Eternal feast. Over another hangs
A rock, about to fall; and there are tables
Set for a banquet, gold with royal splendor,
But if a hand goes out to touch the viands,
The Fury drives it back with fire and yelling.

Why name them all, Pirithous, the Lapiths,
Ixion? The roll of crime would take forever.
Whoever, in his lifetime, hated his brother,
Or struck his father down; whoever cheated
A client, or was miserly—how many
Of these there seem to be!—whoever went
To treasonable war, or broke a promise
Made to his lord, whoever perished, slain
Over adultery, all these, walled in,
Wait here their punishment. Seek not to know
Too much about their doom. The stone is rolled,
The wheel keeps turning; Theseus forever
Sits in dejection; Phlegyas, accursed,
Cries through the halls forever: *Being warned,
Learn justice; reverence the gods!* The man
Who sold his country is here in hell; the man
Who altered laws for money; and a father
Who knew his daughter's bed. All of them dared,
And more than dared, achieved, unspeakable
Ambitions. If I had a hundred tongues,
A hundred iron throats, I could not tell
The fullness of their crime and punishment."
And then she added:—"Come: resume the journey,
Fulfill the mission; let us hurry onward.
I see the walls the Cyclops made, the portals
Under the archway, where, the others tell us,
Our tribute must be set." They went together
Through the way's darkness, came to the doors, and
     halted,
And at the entrance Aeneas, having sprinkled
His body with fresh water, placed the bough
Golden before the threshold. The will of the goddess
Had been performed, the proper task completed.
         They came to happy places, the joyful dwelling,
The lovely greenery of the groves of the blessed.
Here ampler air invests the fields with light,
Rose-colored, with familiar stars and sun.
Some grapple on the grassy wrestling-ground
In exercise and sport, and some are dancing,
And others singing; in his trailing robe
Orpheus strums the lyre; the seven clear notes
Accompany the dance, the song. And heroes
Are there, great-souled, born in the happier years,
Ilus,[35] Assaracus; the city's founder,
Prince Dardanus. Far off, Aeneas wonders,
Seeing the phantom arms, the chariots,
The spears fixed in the ground, the chargers browsing,
Unharnessed, over the plain. Whatever, living,
The men delighted in, whatever pleasure
Was theirs in horse and chariot, still holds them
Here under the world. To right and left, they banquet
In the green meadows, and a joyful chorus
Rises through groves of laurel, whence the river
Runs to the upper world. The band of heroes
Dwell here, all those whose mortal wounds were suffered
In fighting for the fatherland; and poets,
The good, the pure, the worthy of Apollo;
Those who discovered truth and made life nobler;
Those who served others—all, with snowy fillets
Binding their temples, throng the lovely valley.
And these the Sibyl questioned, most of all
Musaeus,[36] for he towered above the center
Of that great throng:—"O happy souls, O poet,
Where does Anchises dwell? For him we come here,
For him we have traversed Erebus' great rivers."

---

35. These are all ancestors of Aeneas, all former kings of Troy.

36. A mythical poet and singer.

And he replied:—"It is all our home, the shady
Groves, and the streaming meadows, and the softness
Along the river-banks. No fixed abode
Is ours at all; but if it is your pleasure,
Cross over the ridge with me; I will guide you there
By easy going." And so Musaeus led them
And from the summit showed them fields, all shining,
And they went on over and down.
        Deep in a valley of green, father Anchises
Was watching, with deep earnestness, the spirits
Whose destiny was light, and counting them over,
All of his race to come, his dear descendants,
Their fates and fortunes and their work and ways,
And as he saw Aeneas coming toward him
Over the meadow, his hands reached out with yearning,
He was moved to tears, and called:—"At last, my son,—
Have you really come, at last? and the long road nothing
To a son who loves his father? Do I, truly,
See you, and hear your voice? I was thinking so,
I was hoping so, I was counting off the days,
And I was right about it. O my son!
What a long journey, over land and water,
Yours must have been! What buffeting of danger!
I feared, so much, the Libyan realm would hurt you."
And his son answered:—"It was your spirit, father,
Your sorrowful shade, so often met, that led me
To find these portals. The ships ride safe at anchor,
Safe in the Tuscan sea. Embrace me, father;
Let hand join hand in love; do not forsake me."
And as he spoke, the tears streamed down. Three times
He reached out toward him, and three times the image
Fled like the breath of the wind or a dream on wings.
        He saw, in a far valley, a separate grove
Where the woods stir and rustle, and a river,
The Lethe,[37] gliding past the peaceful places,
And tribes of people thronging, hovering over,
Innumerable as the bees in summer
Working the bright-hued flowers, and the shining
Of the white lilies, murmuring and humming.
Aeneas, filled with wonder, asks the reason
For what he does not know, who are the people
In such a host, and to what river coming?
Anchises answers:—"These are spirits, ready
Once more for life; they drink of Lethe's water
The soothing potion of forgetfulness.
I have longed, for long, to show them to you, name them,
Our children's children; Italy discovered,
So much the greater happiness, my son."
"But, O my father, is it thinkable
That souls would leave this blessedness, be willing
A second time to bear the sluggish body,
Trade Paradise for earth? Alas, poor wretches,
Why such a mad desire for light?" Anchises
Gives detailed answer: "First, my son, a spirit
Sustains all matter heaven and earth and ocean,
The moon, the stars; mind quickens mass, and moves it.
Hence comes the race of man, of beast, of winged
Creatures of air, of the strange shapes which ocean
Bears down below his mottled marble surface.
All these are blessed with energy from heaven;[38]
The seed of life is a spark of fire, but the body
A clod of earth, a clog, a mortal burden.

Hence humans fear, desire, grieve, and are joyful,
And even when life is over, all the evil
Ingrained so long, the adulterated mixture,
The plagues and pestilences of the body
Remain, persist. So there must be a cleansing,
By penalty, by punishment, by fire,
By sweep of wind, by water's absolution,
Before the guilt is gone. Each of us suffers
His own peculiar ghost. But the day comes
When we are sent through wide Elysium,
The Fields of the Blessed, a few of us, to linger
Until the turn of time, the wheel of ages,
Wears off the taint, and leaves the core of spirit
Pure sense, pure flame. A thousand years pass over
And the god calls the countless host to Lethe
Where memory is annulled, and souls are willing
Once more to enter into mortal bodies."
        The discourse ended; the father drew his son
And his companion toward the hum, the center
Of the full host; they came to rising ground
Where all the long array was visible,
Anchises watching, noting, every comer.
"Glory to come, my son, illustrious spirits
Of Dardan lineage, Italian offspring,
Heirs of our name, begetters of our future!
These I will name for you and tell our fortunes:
First, leaning on a headless spear, and standing
Nearest the light, that youth, the first to rise
To the world above, is Silvius; his name
Is Alban; in his veins Italian blood
Will run with Trojan; he will be the son
Of your late age; Lavinia will bear him,
A king and sire of kings; from him our race
Will rule in Alba Longa.[39] Near him, Procas,
A glory to the Trojan race; and Capys,
And Numitor, and Silvius Aeneas,
Resembling you in name, in arms, in goodness,
If ever he wins the Alban kingdom over.
What fine young men they are! What strength, what
      prowess!
The civic oak already shades their foreheads.
These will found cities, Gabii, Fidenae,
Nomentum; they will crown the hills with towers
Above Collatia, Inuus fortress, Bola,
Cora, all names to be, thus far ungiven.
        "And there will be a son of Mars; his mother
Is Ilia, and his name is Romulus,
Assaracus' descendant. On his helmet
See, even now, twin plumes; his father's honor
Confers distinction on him for the world.
Under his auspices Rome, that glorious city,
Will bound her power by earth, her pride by heaven,
Happy in hero sons, one wall surrounding
Her seven hills, even as Cybele, riding
Through Phrygian cities, wears her crown of towers,
Rejoicing in her offspring, and embracing
A hundred children of the gods, her children,
Celestials, all of them, at home in heaven.

---

39. One of the earliest of the Italian cities, near Rome.
Supposedly founded by Askanius.

---

37. LEE-thee.
38. You might compare this with Dante's ideas on the same
thing. See, for example, Purgatory, Cantos XVI and XVIII.

Turn the eyes now this way; behold the Romans,
Your very own. These are Iulus' children,
The race to come. One promise you have heard
Over and over: here is its fulfillment,
The son of a god, Augustus Caesar, founder
Of a new age of gold, in lands where Saturn
Ruled long ago; he will extend his empire
Beyond the Indies, beyond the normal measure
Of years and constellations, where high Atlas
Turns on his shoulders the star-studded world.
Maeotia[40] and the Caspian seas are trembling
As heaven's oracles predict his coming,
And all the seven mouths of Nile are troubled
Not even Hercules, in all his travels,
Covered so much of the world, from Erymanthus
To Lerna; nor did Bacchus, driving his tigers
From Nysa's summit. How can hesitation
Keep us from deeds to make our prowess greater?
What fear can block us from Ausonian land?

  "And who is that one yonder, wearing the olive,
Holding the sacrifice? I recognize him,
That white-haired king of Rome, who comes from Cures,
A poor land, to a mighty empire, giver
Of law to the young town. His name is Numa.
Near him is Tullus; he will rouse to arms
A race grown sluggish, little used to triumph.
Beyond him Ancus, even now too boastful,
Too fond of popular favor. And then the Tarquins,
And the avenger Brutus, proud of spirit,
Restorer of the balance. He shall be
First holder of the consular power; his children
Will stir up wars again, and he, for freedom
And her sweet sake, will call down judgment on them,
Unhappy, however future men may praise him,
In love of country and intense ambition.

  "There are the Decii,[41] and there the Drusi,
A little farther off, and stern Torquatus,
The man with the axe, and Camillus, the regainer
Of standards lost. And see those two, resplendent
In equal arms, harmonious friendly spirits
Now, in the shadow of night, but if they ever
Come to the world of light, alas, what warfare,
What battle-lines, what slaughter they will fashion,
Each for the other, one from Alpine ramparts
Descending, and the other ranged against him
With armies from the east, father and son
Through marriage, Pompey and Caesar. O my children,
Cast out the thoughts of war, and do not murder
The flower of our country. O my son,
Whose line descends from heaven, let the sword
Fall from the hand, be leader in forbearing!

  "Yonder is one who, victor over Corinth,
Will ride in triumph home, famous for carnage
Inflicted on the Greeks; near him another,
Destroyer of old Argus and Mycenae
Where Agamemnon ruled; he will strike down
A king descended from Achilles; Pydna
Shall be revenge for Pallas' ruined temple,
For Trojan ancestors. Who would pass over,

Without a word, Cossus, or noble Cato,
The Gracchi, or those thunderbolts of warfare,
The Scipios, Libya's ruin, or Fabricius
Mighty with little, or Serranus, ploughing
The humble furrow; My tale must hurry on:
I see the Fabii next, and their great Quintus
Who brought us back an empire by delaying.
Others, no doubt, will better mould the bronze[42]
To the semblance of soft breathing, draw, from marble,
The living countenance; and others plead
With greater eloquence, or learn to measure,
Better than we, the pathways of the heaven,
The risings of the stars: remember, Roman,
To rule the people under law, to establish
The way of peace, to battle down the haughty,
To spare the meek. Our fine arts, these, forever."

conquer rule justly

  Anchises paused a moment, and they marvelled,
And he went on:—"See, how Marcellus triumphs,
Glorious over all, with the great trophies
Won when he slew the captain of the Gauls,
Leader victorious over leading foeman.
When Rome is in great trouble and confusion
He will establish order, Gaul and Carthage
Go down before his sword, and triple trophies
Be given Romulus in dedication."

  There was a young man going with Marcellus,
Brilliant in shining armor, bright in beauty,
But sorrowful, with downcast eyes. Aeneas
Broke in, to ask his father: "Who is this youth
Attendant on the hero? A son of his?
One of his children's children? How the crowd
Murmurs and hums around him! what distinction,
What presence, in his person! But dark night
Hovers around his head with mournful shadow.
Who is he, father?" And Anchises answered:—
"Great sorrow for our people! O my son,
Ask not to know it. This one fate will only
Show to the world; he will not be permitted
Any long sojourn. Rome would be too mighty,
To great in the gods' sight, were this gift hers.
What lamentation will the field of Mars
Raise to the city! Tiber, gliding by
The new-built tomb, the funeral state, bear witness!
No youth from Trojan stock will ever raise
His ancestors so high in hope, no Roman
Be such a cause for pride. Alas for goodness,
Alas for old-time honor, and the arm
Invincible in war! Against him no one,
Whether on foot or foaming horse, would come
In battle and depart unscathed. Poor boy,
If you should break the cruel fates; if only—
You are to be Marcellus. Let me scatter
Lilies, or dark-red flowers, bringing honor
To my descendant's shade; let the gift be offered,
However vain the tribute."

  So through the whole wide realm they went together,
Anchises and his son; from the fields of air
Learning and teaching of the fame and glory,
The wars to come, the toils to face, or flee from,
Latinus' city and the Latin peoples,
The love of what would be.

---

40. These names merely signify that the empire will extend from
one end to the other of the known world.

41. These are the names of families who produced famous men
in Rome's history.

---

42. Probably these nine lines are a better expression of the best
of the Roman spirit than can be found in any other place.

There are two portals,
Twin gates of Sleep, one made of horn, where easy
Release is given true shades, the other gleaming
White ivory, whereby the false dreams issue
To the upper air. Aeneas and the Sibyl
Part from Anchises at the second portal.
He goes to the ships, again, rejoins his comrades,
Sails to Caieta's harbor, and the vessels
Rest on their mooring-lines.

Exercises

1. What exactly was Aeneas seeking in the lower world and why?
2. Consider the crimes that condemn people to the lower world. What, for the Romans, were the worst crimes? What do "state" and "duty" mean? What, for example, does "Learn justice; reverence the gods" really mean in practical Roman terms?
3. a. Consider the statement of Anchises on the Roman "arts": "To pacify, to impose the rule of law, to spare the conquered, battle down the proud." Is this political science? Why do the Romans consider governance an art form?
   b. Who creates better bronzes and marbles? Who is more fluent in rhetoric and knowledgeable in astronomy? Are the fine arts and science more or less important than Roman rule? Why?
4. Why did Virgil deliberately pattern his epic poem after the poetry of Homer? What did he hope to gain?

ECLOGUE IV

Virgil (Pubilius Virgilius Maro)

Virgil's *Fourth Eclogue* (EK-log, a pastoral or idyllic poem), known as the "Pollio" from the name of the friend to whom it was addressed and known also as "The Messianic Eclogue," was written in 40 B.C. to commemorate the birth of a child; but the identity of the child has eluded the scholars—there is no agreement among them. However, the high praise and the mystical allusions of the poet, strongly reminiscent of the very phrases of Isaiah in his prophecies of the Messiah, have connected the poem in the minds of many with the coming of the Christ. Early Christians found in the Eclogue corroboration of the biblical prophecies, and consequently thought of Virgil as a "virtuous Pagan," one to whom had been vouchsafed some gleams of the advent of Christ. Virgil's reputation as a good, even holy, man, grew as the Middle Ages remembered his poem; his reputation increased, in folklore, as a magician and seer—possibly because of his birthplace, where witchcraft, necomancy, and magic were always a matter of popular concern. So strong was his reputation as a foreteller of Christ's birth that Dante saw fit to make him his "guide, philosopher, and friend" in the *Divine Comedy;* he was led by Virgil as far as the pagan could take him, to the very entrance of the earthly Paradise.

The student would do well to refresh the memory with the verses of Isaiah, especially in Chapters vii, ix, and xi, that have to do with vines and briers, "unto us a child is born," the concord among living things, and the like. There is no evidence that Virgil was acquainted with the writings of the Hebrew prophet.

Pastoral[43] Muses of Sicily,
   now let us sing a loftier song;
   not all are pleased with country themes
      of orchard trees and lowly shrubs:
   if we sing in pastoral style,
      let it be a style still worthy of a consul's ear!

Now, even now, the last great age is coming in,
   foretold in the Cumaean Sybil's book;
The great cycle of the ages[44] starts anew,
   as from the beginning;
Astraea returns, the maiden Justice;
   the Golden Age of Saturn comes again;
   a new generation is sent us from high heaven.

Diana,—Lucina, Light-Bringer—chaste goddess,
   look favorably upon the coming birth,
   the child for whom the old bad Iron Race yields
      to a new Golden one, rising over all the world:
   your brother Apollo begins his reign.

Pollio,[45] in your term of office, even while you are consul,
   this Wonder of Time will begin his being;
   the majestic months commence their progress;
   under your leadership, Pollio,
   even if traces remain of our human guilt,
   new times will free earth from its abiding terror.

This child will live like a god;
   he will see gods and heroes mingling together,
   and himself will be seen of them a god and a hero;
   he will rule over a world made peaceful,
      with ancestral virtues.
For you, little child, the earth untilled
   will pour forth, as your first birthday-gifts,

---

43. "Pastoral"—it is interesting to note that the more sophisticated the civilization, the more urban and artificial the life of time, the greater the appeal of pastoral poetry, "the simple life," "back to nature." Virgil's age is a case in point; torn with the dissensions of civil strife and the growing importance of metropolitan Rome, the Italy of his day found satisfaction in "getting away from it all" thru the medium of the pastoral.

44. "The cycle of the ages"—it is unnecessary to go into the ancient (Etruscan?) notion that the world-cycle moved thru successive stages back to a point identical with the beginning; the "Platonic Year," when even the stars and planets would return to their position as at Creation. Suffice it to say, Virgil does have some sort of cycle of world history in mind; the Ages of Gold, Silver, Brass, and Iron, returning eventually to a new Golden Age.

45. "Pollio"—C. Asinus Pollio, Virgil's friend to whom the Eclogue is addressed, was a well-known public figure of the times; a general and adherent of Julius Caesar, he became consul in 40 B.C., and concluded the peace treaty between Octavian and Antony, known as the Treaty of Brundisium. It has been suggested (but not proved) that the child of the Eclogue may have been one of Pollio's sons.

her plants and herbs; twining ivy,
and valerian, and the arum lily,
  intermingling with the gay acanthus.

Of themselves the goats, untended, will return home,
  their udders swollen with milk;
  the herds will have no fear of mighty lions;
  your very cradle will run over with lovely flowers.
    The serpent will die, poison's treacherous plant
    will die;
    Oriental spice will spring up everywhere.

When you are old enough to read of great men,
  and the deeds of your fathers before you,
  when you understand the meaning of manliness,
  then will the harvest field turn yellow with volunteer
    grain,
  the reddening grape-cluster hang in the place of the
    profitless bramble,
  and tough old oaks will drip with honey-dew.

(Even then will linger some last vestiges
  of the wickedness of man;
  the lusting passion that delights
  to dare the sea with ships,
  to ring towns about with high walls,
  to scar the earth with furrows:
there will still be another Tiphys,[46]
  piloting a new Argo that carries its chosen heroes;
there will still be wars; once again
  some great Achilles will be sent against another
    Troy . . .)

But when the maturing years find you fully grown,
  then even the trader will abandon the sea;
  no pine-masted vessels will barter wares;
  instead, everywhere the whole earth
    will of itself yield all things needful.
  No more will the ground suffer the harrow,
    nor the vine the pruning-hook;
  the stalwart plowman will remove the yoke from his
    oxen.

Wool will not have to learn the deception of lying dyes,
  for the ram in the meadows will himself
  change the color of his fleece,
  sometimes to soft purple, like the murex,
  sometimes to saffron yellow;
  of its own volition
    crimson will clothe the grazing lamb.

"Run on, such times as these!"
  —thus say the Gray Sisters over their spindles,
  agreeing in the fixed decree of destiny.

Go on, little child, to great honors;
  your hour is at hand, dear offspring of divinity,
  great fulfillment of Jove.
  See, earth bows its vaulted weight,
    the lands, the expanse of the sea, even the deep
    heavens;
  see how everything rejoices in the time that is to be!

With you for my theme, Orpheus, singer of Thrace, could
  not overcome me,
  though he were helped by his mother Calliope;
  nor Linus,[47] however much comely Apollo, his father,
  assisted him;

even Pan, if Arcadia his homeland judged him with
  me,
  even Pan, with Arcadia judging, would admit himself beaten!

Begin, then, little boy, by greeting your mother with a
  smile;
  she has waited thru the long weariness of many
  months.
  Learn to smile, little child—[48]
  for one whom his parents have not smiled upon
  no god deems worthy of his table, nor goddess of
  her couch.

Exercises

1. Virgil envisions a time of peace, plenty, and
   unity with nature; Isaiah had a similar dream
   and others after him. Why does this vision keep
   recurring? What does this imply about the
   actual state of the world? Are these idealistic
   visions a waste of time and effort? Why or why
   not?

2. Is this poem a prophecy of the birth of Christ?
   What evidence seems to support this thesis? On
   the other hand, does the evidence seem to
   point to Caesar Augustus? Which view seems
   more probable?

ON THE NATURE OF THINGS

Titus Lucretius Carus (ca. 96–55 B.C.)

Nothing at all is known of Lucretius (Titus Lucretius
Carus) beyond the fact that he is credited with a poem
(excerpted below) extolling materialism and the philosophy of Epicurus, under whose disciples he probably
studied. This is the most complete exposition of the materialistic basis of Epicureanism as well as being one of
the world's outstanding poems.

In the following passage, Lucretius discusses the rise
of ambition, of republican forms of government, of religions, the discovery of metals, of garments, of agriculture, of singing and dancing, and finally of the total
development of luxurious civilization. Notice how carefully he suggests a materialistic origin for all of these
things.

At several points during the selection he makes general statements about the nature of men and of human
motives. Can you piece these together to discover Lucretius's basic thoughts about human nature and human
motives, and about the nature of the best life? From these
would you say that the author was essentially an optimist,
a pessimist, or something in between? Compare the ideas
with some of those expressed by Marcus Aurelius.

More and more every day men who excelled in intellect
and were of vigorous understanding, would kindly show
others how to exchange their former way of living for new
methods. Kings began to build towns and lay out a citadel
as a place of strength and of refuge for themselves, and

---

46. "Tiphys"—the pilot of the Argo: Jason and the Argonauts,
sailing after the Golden Fleece, suggest to the reader at once
adventurousness and cupidity, bravery and selfishness.
47. Orpheus, Linus, and Pan; the greatest singers of classical
antiquity.

48. The ending is apparently a mildly humorous good luck
charm: "Smile, baby, so that your parents will smile at you;
unwanted, unwelcome children are Bad Luck, but smiling,
happy, wanted ones are blessed."

divided cattle and lands and gave to each man in proportion to his personal beauty and strength and intellect; for beauty and vigorous strength were much esteemed. Afterwards wealth was discovered and gold found out, which soon robbed of their honors strong and beautiful alike, for men however valiant and beautiful of person generally follow in the train of the richer man. But were a man to order his life by the rules of true reason, a frugal subsistence joined to a contented mind is for him great riches; for never is there any lack of a little. But men desired to be famous and powerful, in order that their fortunes might rest on a firm foundation and they might be able by their wealth to lead a tranquil life; but in vain, since in their struggle to mount up to the highest dignities they rendered their path one full of danger; and even if they reach it, yet envy like a thunderbolt sometimes strikes and dashes men down from the highest point with ignominy into noisome Tartarus; since the highest summits and those elevated above the level of other things are mostly blasted by envy as by a thunderbolt, so that far better it is to obey in peace and quiet than to wish to rule with power supreme and be the master of kingdoms. Therefore let men wear themselves out to no purpose and sweat drops of blood, as they struggle on along the straight road of ambition, since they gather their knowledge from the mouths of others and follow after things from hearsay rather than the dictates of their own feelings; and this prevails not now nor will prevail by and by any more than it has prevailed before.

Kings therefore being slain, the old majesty of thrones and proud sceptres were overthrown and laid in the dust, and the glorious badge of the sovereign head bloodstained beneath the feet of the rabble mourned for its high prerogative; for that is greedily trampled on which before was too much dreaded. It would come then in the end to the lees of uttermost disorder, each man seeking for himself empire and sovereignty. Next a portion of them taught men to elect legal officers, and drew up codes, to induce men to obey the laws. For mankind, tired out with a life of brute force, lay exhausted from its feuds; and therefore the more readily it submitted of its own free will to laws and stringent codes. For as each one moved by anger took measures to avenge himself with more severity than is now permitted by equitable laws, for this reason men grew sick of a life of brute force. Thence fear of punishment mars the prizes of life; for violence and wrong enclose all who commit them in their meshes and do mostly recoil on him whom they began; and it is not easy for him who by his deeds transgresses the terms of the public peace to pass a tranquil and a peaceful existence. For though he eludes God and man, yet he cannot but feel a misgiving that his secret can be kept forever; seeing that many by speaking in their dreams or in the wanderings of disease have often we are told betrayed themselves and have disclosed their hidden deeds of evil and their sins.

And now what cause has spread over great nations the worship of the divinities of the gods and filled towns with altars and led to the performance of stated sacred rites, rites not in fashion on solemn occasions and in solemn places, from which even now is implanted in mortals a shuddering awe which raises new temples of the gods over the whole earth and prompts men to crowd them on festive days, all this is not so difficult to explain in words. Even then in sooth the races of mortal men would see in waking mind glorious forms, would see them in sleep of yet more marvellous size of body. To these then they would attribute sense, because they seemed to move their limbs and to utter lofty words suitable to their glorious aspects and surpassing powers. And they would give them life everlasting, because their face would appear before them and their form abide; yes, and yet without all this because they would not believe that beings possessed of such powers could lightly be overcome by any force. And they would believe them to be pre-eminent in bliss, because none of them was ever troubled with the fear of death, and because at the same time in sleep they would see them perform many miracles, yet feel on their part no fatigue from the effort. Again they would see the system of heaven and the different seasons of the years come round in regular succession, and could not find out by what cause this was done; therefore they would seek a refuge in handing over all things to the gods and supposing all things to be guided by their nod. And they placed in heaven the abodes and realms of the gods, because night and moon are seen to roll through heaven; moon, day and night, and night's austere constellations and night-wandering of the sky and flying bodies of flame, clouds, sun, rains, snow, winds, lightnings, hail, and rapid rumblings and loud threatful thunderclaps.

O hapless race of men, when that they charged the gods with such acts and coupled with them bitter wrath! What groanings did they then beget for themselves, what wounds for us, what tears for our children's children! No act is it of piety to be often seen with veiled head to turn to a stone and approach every altar and fall postrate on the ground and spread out the palms before the statues of the gods and sprinkle the altars with much blood of beasts and link vow on vow, but rather to be able to look on all things with a mind at peace. For when we turn our gaze on the heavenly quarters of the great upper world and ether fast above the glittering stars, and direct our thoughts to the courses of the sun and moon, then into our breasts burdened with other ills that fear as well begins to exalt its reawakened head, the fear that we may haply find the power of the gods to be unlimited, able to wheel the bright stars in their varied motion; for lack of power to solve the question troubles the mind with doubts, whether there was ever a birth-time of the world, and whether likewise there is to be any end; how far the walls of the world can endure this strain of restless motion; or whether gifted by the grace of gods with an everlasting existence they may glide on through a neverending tract of time and defy the strong powers of immeasurable ages. Again who is there whose mind does not shrink into itself with fear of the gods, whose limbs do not cower in terror, when the parched earth rocks with the appalling thunder-stroke and rattling runs through the great heaven? Do not people and nations quake, and proud monarchs shrink into themselves smitten with fear of the gods, lest for any foul transgression or overweening work the heavy time of reckoning has arrived at its fullness? When, too, the utmost fury of the headstrong wind passes over the sea and sweeps over its waters the commander of a fleet together with his mighty legions and elephants, does he not draw near with vows to seek the mercy of the gods and ask in prayer with fear and trembling a lull in the winds and propitious gales; but all in vain, since often caught up in the furious hurricane he is borne none the less to the shoals of death? So constantly does some hidden power trample on human grandeur and is seen to tread under its heel and make sport for itself of the renowned rods and cruel axes.[49]

---

49. A bundle of rods enclosing an axe was the emblem of magisterial authority at Rome.

Again when the whole earth rocks under their feet and towns tumble with the shock or doubtfully threaten to fall, what wonder that mortal men abase themselves and make over to the gods in things here on earth high prerogatives and marvelous powers, sufficient to govern all things?

To proceed, copper and gold and iron were discovered and at the same time weighty silver and the substance of lead, when fire with its heat had burnt up vast forests on the great hills, either by a discharge of heaven's lightning, or else because men waging with one another a forest-war had carried fire among the enemy in order to strike terror, or because drawn on by the goodness of the soil they would wish to clear rich fields, and bring the country into pasture, or else to destroy wild beasts and enrich themselves with the booty; for hunting with pitfall and with fire came into use before the practice of enclosing the lawn with nets and stirring it with dogs. Whatever the fact is, from whatever cause the heat of flame had swallowed up the forests with a frightful crackling from their very roots and had thoroughly baked the earth with fire, there would run from the boiling veins and collect into the hollows of the ground a stream of silver and gold, as well as of copper and lead. And when they saw these afterwards cool into lumps and glitter on the earth with a brilliant gleam, they would lift them up attracted by the bright and polished lustre, and they would see them to be moulded in a shape the same as the outline of the cavities in which each lay. Then it would strike them that these might be melted by heat and cast in any form or shape soever, and might by hammering out be brought to tapering points of any degree of sharpness and fineness, so as to furnish them with tools and enable them to cut the forests and hew timber and plane smooth the planks, and also to drill and pierce and bore, and they would set about these works just as much with silver and gold at first as with the overpowering strength of stout copper, but in vain, since their force would fail and give way and not be able like copper to stand the severe strain. At that time copper was in higher esteem and gold would be neglected on account of its uselessness, with its dull blunted edge; now copper lies neglected, gold has mounted up to the highest place of honor. Thus time as it goes round changes the seasons of things. That which was in esteem, falls at length into utter disrepute; and then another thing mounts up and issues out of its degraded state and every day is more and more coveted and blossoms forth high in honor when discovered and is in marvelous repute with men.

And now to find out by yourself in what way the nature of iron was discovered. Arms of old were hands, nails, and teeth, and stones and boughs broken off from the forest, and flame and fire, as soon as they had become known. Afterwards the force of iron and copper was discovered, and the use of copper was known before that of iron, as its nature is easier to work and it is found in greater quantity. With copper they would labor the soil of the earth, with copper stir up the billows of war and deal about the wide gaping wounds and seize cattle and lands; for everything defenseless and unarmed would readily yield to them with arms in hand. Then by slow steps the sword of iron gained ground and the make of the copper sickle became a by-word; and with iron they began to plough through the earth's soil, and the struggles of wavering war were rendered equal. . . .

A garment tied on the body was in use before a dress of woven stuff. Woven stuff comes after iron, because iron is needed for weaving a web; and in no other way can such finely polished things be made, as heddles and spindles, shuttles and ringing yarnbeams. And nature impelled men to work up the wool before womankind; for the male sex in general far excels the other in skill and is much more ingenious; until the rugged countrymen so upbraided them with it, that they were glad to give it over into the hands of the women and take their share in supporting hard toil, and in such hard work hardened body and hands.

But nature parent of things was herself the first model of sowing and first gave rise to grafting, since berries and acorns dripping from the trees would put forth in due season swarms of young shoots underneath; and hence also came the fashion of inserting grafts in their stocks and planting in the ground young saplings over the fields. Next they would try another and yet another kind of tillage for their loved piece of land and would see the earth better the wild fruits through genial fostering and kindly cultivation, and they would force the forests to recede every day higher and higher up the hillside and yield the ground below to tilth, in order to have on the uplands and plains, meadows, tanks, runnels, cornfields, and glad vineyards, and allow a gray-green strip of olives to run between and mark divisions, spreading itself over hillocks and valleys and plains; just as you now see richly dight with varied beauty all the ground which they lay out and plant with rows of sweet fruit-trees, and enclose all round with plantations of other goodly trees.

But imitating with the mouth the clear notes of birds was in use long before men were able to sing in tune smooth-running verses and give pleasure to the ear. And the whistlings of the zephyr through the hollows of reeds first taught peasants to blow into hollow stalks. Then step by step they learned sweet plaintive ditties, which the pipe pours forth pressed by the fingers of the players, heard through pathless woods and forests and lawns, through the unfrequented haunts of shepherds and abodes of unearthly calm. These things would soothe and gratify their minds when sated with food; for then all things of this kind are welcome. Often therefore stretched in groups on the soft grass beside a stream of water under the boughs of a high tree at no great cost they would pleasantly refresh their bodies, above all when the weather smiled and the seasons of the year painted the green grass with flowers. Then went round the jest, the tale, the peals of merry laughter; for the peasant muse was then in its glory; then frolick mirth would prompt to entwine head and shoulders with garlands plaited with flowers and leaves, and to advance in the dance out of step and move the limbs clumsily and with clumsy feet beat mother earth; which would occasion smiles and peals of merry laughter, because all these things then from their greater novelty and strangeness were in high repute, and the wakeful found a solace for want of sleep in this, in drawing out a variety of notes and going through tunes and running over the reeds with curving lip; whence even at the present day watchmen observe these traditions and have lately learned to keep the proper tune; and yet for all this receive not a jot more of enjoyment than erst the rugged race of sons of earth received. For that which we have in our hands, if we have known before nothing pleasanter, pleases above all and is thought to be the best;[50] and as a rule the later discovery of something better spoils the taste for the former things and changes the feelings in regard to all that has gone before. Thus began distaste for the acorn, thus were abandoned those sleeping places strawn with grass and enriched with leaves. The dress too of wild beasts' skin fell into neglect; though I can fancy that in those days it was found to arouse such jealousy that he who first wore it met his death by an ambuscado, and after all it was torn in pieces among them and drenched in blood, was utterly destroyed and could not be turned to any use. In those times therefore skins, now gold and purple plague men's lives with cares and wear them out with war. And in this methinks the greater blame rests with us; but us it harms not in the least to do without a robe of purple, spangled with gold and large figures, if only we have a dress of the people to protect us. Mankind therefore ever toils vainly and to no purpose wastes life in groundless cares, because sure enough they have not learnt what is the true end of getting and up to what point genuine pleasure goes on increasing: this by slow degrees has carried life out into the deep sea and stirred up from their lowest depths the mighty billows of war.

But those watchful guardians sun and moon traversing with their light all around the great revolving sphere of heaven taught men that the seasons of the year came round and that the system was carried on after a fixed plan and fixed order.

Already they would pass their life fenced about with strong towers, and the land, portioned out and marked off by boundaries, be tilled; the sea would be filled with ships scudding under sail; towns have auxiliaries and allies as stipulated by treaty, when poets began to consign the deeds of men to verse; and letters had not been invented long before. For this reason our age cannot look back to what has gone before, save where reason points out any traces.

Ships and tillage, walls, laws, roads, dress, and all such like things, all the prizes, all the elegancies too of life without exception, poems, pictures, and chiselling of fine-wrought statues, all these things practiced together with the acquired knowledge of the untiring mind taught men by slow degrees as they advanced on the way step by step. Thus time by degrees brings each several things forth before men's eyes and reason raises it up into the borders of light; for things must be brought to light one after the other and in due order in the different arts, until these have reached their highest point of development.

Exercises

1. According to Lucretius, what seem to be the positive traits in human nature? The negative traits? What do these characteristics tell us about Lucretius's point of view?
2. Based on the evidence in the poem, what seems to be Lucretius's conception of the good life?

---

50. Notice throughout this piece the philosophic generalizations which Lucretius makes. Try reading them together without the intervening descriptions and see if you can get a fairly complete picture of his philosophy.

POETRY

Catullus

Gaius Valerius Catullus (ca. 84–54 B.C.), the leading Latin lyric poet, composed his love poetry for the enchanting Clodia (Lesbia in the poems), wife of Quintus Metellus. She became the most notoriously faithless beauty in Rome, while Catullus struggled with a virulent passion for her that slowly shriveled to despair before subsiding into bitter maledictions. Poems 5, 51, 58, 72, and 75 testify to the stages of his infatuation. The first three stanzas of poem 51 are a partial translation by Catullus of a poem by Sappho, the seventh-century Greek poet from the island of Lesbos. Poems 1, 22, 40, and 42 are concerned with poets and poetry; poem 42 refers to the stubborn muse of poetry who frustrates the best of poets by failing to provide the requisite inspiration.

1

less noble poetry

Who do I give this neat little book to
all new and polished up and ready to go?
You, Cornelius, because you always thought
there was something to this stuff of mine,
and were the one man in Italy with guts enough
to lay out all history in a couple of pages,
a learned job, by god, and it took work.
So here's the book, for whatever it's worth
I want you to have it. And please, goddess,
see that it lasts for more than a lifetime.

5

Let's you and me live it up, my Lesbia,
and make some love, and let old cranks
go cheap talk their damn fool heads off.
Maybe suns can set and come back up again,
but once the brief light goes out on us
the night's one long sleep forever.
First give me a kiss, a thousand kisses,
then a hundred, and then a thousand more,
then another hundred, and another thousand,
and keep kissing and kissing me so many times
we get all mixed up and can't count anymore,
that way nobody can give us the evil eye
trying to figure how many kisses we've got.

sun will rise and set daily once man dies its over — life brief death long love compensate for short life

22

Take Suffenus, now you know the guy, Varus,
handsome, good talker, knows his way around,
well he writes poetry also, in big shipments.
I think he's got thousands, maybe millions
copied out, I don't mean in rough draft either:
fancy imperial stock, new rolls, new pegs,
thongs of red leather, sheepskin slip covers,
lines ruled, edges trimmed, the whole works.
Then you read them. Suddenly your suave and
sophisticated Suffenus turns into a goat milker,
a shit shoveler from the mountains. It's grim!
What's going on anyway? Here he is, sharp,
looks like he could slice you down in a word,
but the minute he starts fooling with poetry,
watch out, he's clumsier than a hick is clumsy.
And he's never happier than when writing a poem,
or more pleased, he thinks he's just wonderful!
Okay, it's true, we all do it, there's nobody
who isn't a Suffenus in one thing or another.
Everybody has a pack of faults on his shoulders,
if heads were on backwards we'd all see our own.

40

Lost your mind Ravidus, you poor ass,
landing smack into one of my poems like this?
Is some god getting you into trouble
because you didn't say your prayers right?
Or are you just out to get talked about?
What do you want? To be famous, never mind how?
Okay you will, and being that it's my girl you're after,
you're going to suffer for a long, long time.

42

Calling all syllables! Calling all syllables!
Let's go! I need all the help I can get!
Some filthy whore's playing games with me
and won't give me back my manuscripts with
your pals inside! Are you going to let her?
Who is she, you ask? Well go take a look,
she's over there shaking her ass all around
and flashing smiles like a Pomeranian bitch.
Ready? Okay, line up and let her have it!
'O foul adulteress, O lascivious witch,
give me back my notebooks, you dirty bitch!'
What? Up yours, you say? You slut, tramp,
you've sunk so low you look up to see down!
Still, we can't let her get away like this,
if all else fails, at least let's see whether
we can force a blush from the hard-faced beast.
Try again, fellas, good and loud this time!
'O FOUL ADULTERESS, O LASCIVIOUS WITCH,
GIVE ME BACK MY NOTEBOOKS, YOU DIRTY BITCH!'
No use. It won't work. Nothing moves her.
We've got to switch to different tactics,
almost anything will work better than this.
'O maiden so modest, O virgin so pure . . .'

51

To me, that man seems to be one of the gods,
or to tell the truth, even more than a god,
sitting there face to face with you, forever
looking, listening

to you laughing sweetly, while poor me, I take
one look at you and I'm all torn up inside,
Lesbia, there's nothing left of me. I can't
make a sound, my tongue's

stuck solid, hot little fire flashes go
flickering through my body, my ears begin
ringing around in my head, my eyes black out,
shrouded in darkness . . .

This soft life is no good for you. Catullus,
you wallow in it, you don't know when to stop.
A soft life's already been the ruin of both
great kings and cities.

58

Caelius, our Lesbia, that Lesbia,
the Lesbia Catullus once loved
more than himself and all he owns,
now works streets and back alleys
groping big-hearted sons of Remus.

72

Time was you said only Catullus could touch you,
that God in heaven couldn't have you before me.
I loved you then, not just as a guy does a girl,
but the way a father loves his sons and grandsons.

Now I know you, Lesbia, and if my passion grows,
you're also much cheaper to me and insignificant.
How's that? Because, hurt a man in love and he
lusts for you more, but the less he really cares.

75

My mind's sunk so low, Lesbia, because of you,
wrecked itself on your account so bad already,
I couldn't like you if you were the best of women,
or stop loving you, no matter what you do.

Exercises

1. Faced with writing an essay, have you ever had
   trouble beginning? As you undoubtedly know,
   this is called "writer's block." How well does
   poem 42 express your own frustration in trying
   to write? Does this poem make you more aware
   of Catullus as another human being like
   yourself? What does this say about the nature of
   poetry?
2. In poems 5, 51, 58, 72, and 75 Catullus seems to
   have mixed emotions about his Lesbia. What
   does he love about her? Hate about her? What *is*
   romantic love? Can it last?

ODES

Horace

Horace (Quintus Horatius Flaccus; 65–8 B.C.) specialized in writing odes. Given below are two odes in contemporary translations by M. A. Crane. The first is a wry
commentary about Pyrrha, his former mistress, while the
second ode is an expression of Horace's Epicurean philosophy.

1

On the bulletin board there's a picture of me
Luckily saved from disaster at sea
Donating my gear to the God of the Ocean.
Tonight, some boy smelling of after-shave lotion
Is making a play for you, Pyrrha, my fair,
Trying that innocent look with your hair.
His turn will come soon to complain of foul weather
If he thinks that after you're going together
You'll stay bland and easy as on this first date.
Until you up anchor, all dinghys look great!

2

The peace that the sailor seeks in the storm
And the rest that's the warrior's aim
Can't be purchased with wealth in any form
Nor, Grosphus, with power or fame.
The pauper who wants only what he can afford
Sleeps soundly. But he who would fly
To new fortunes, although he hastens abroad
Speedy vessels, sees his troubles stand by.
Fools nourish dreams of perfect joy;
I'll take less, having witnessed a hero
Die young and watched rotting old age destroy
Tithonus, reduced to a jibbering zero.
It may be *I* have just those things that *you* need
Amidst your horses, fine clothing, and cattle-
Subsidence, and joy from the poems I read,
And no jealous mob doing me battle.

Exercises

1. A "conceit" is an extended poetic comparison (metaphor) between two unlike things, applying the qualities of one to the other. In Ode 1 what conceit does Horace develop, and to whom or what is it applied?
2. According to the Epicurean philosophy expressed in Ode 2, what is necessary for happiness? Where do material possessions rate on the happiness scale? Why?

THE ART OF LOVE

Publius Ovidius Naso (43 B.C.–A.D. 17)

Ovid was the most popular poet of antiquity. His engaging versions of Greek and Roman myths, the *Metamorphoses,* is unique; no classic is easier or more pleasant to read. Included here is an excerpt from the *Art of Love,* a sophisticated guide to seduction, which also includes deft descriptions of everyday life in Rome. As you read Ovid's "manual" you might ask yourself if times or techniques have really changed.

This is a book for the man who needs instruction in
    loving.
    Let him read it and love, taught by the lines he has
    read.
Art is a thing one must learn, for the sailing, or rowing, of
    vessels,
    Also for driving a car: love must be guided by art.
Automedon excelled with the reins in the car of Achilles,
    Tiphys in Jason's craft, crafty with rudder and sail;
Thanks be to Venus, I too deserve the title of master,
    Master of Arts, I might say, versed in the precepts of
    love.
Love, to be sure, is wild and often inclined to resent me;
    Still, he is only a boy, tender and easily swayed.
When Achilles was young, Chiron could tame his wild
    spirit,
    Even could teach his hands how to move over a lyre.
He, who frightened his foes, and frightened his friends
    just as often,
    Dreaded one aged man, so all the ages believe.
He would reach out his hands, submissive and meek, for
    a lashing:
    Those were the violent hands Hector was later to
    know.
Chiron instructed Achilles, and I am Cupid's preceptor,
    Each of them savage and rough, each one a
    goddess's son.
Yet, in good time, as bulls accept the yoke and the
    ploughshare,
    As the wild horses submit, taking the bridle and bit,
So will Love yield to me, though he wounds my heart
    with his arrows,
    Whirls his torch in the air, showering sparks from the
    brand.
So much the worse for him: the more he pierces and
    burns me,
    I shall avenge all the more all of the wounds he has
    made.
I am no liar to claim that my art has come from Apollo,
    Nor am I taught my song by the voices of birds in the
    air,

Neither has Clio appeared at my side, with all of her
    sisters,
    While I was tending my flocks out in some
    countryside vale.
No: I have learned what I know from experience, take my
    word for it.
    It is the truth you will hear. Venus, give aid to my
    song!
Keep far away, stern looks and all of modesty's emblems,
    Headdresses worn by the pure, skirts hiding feet in
    their folds.
What is the theme of my song? A little pleasant
    indulgence.
    What is the theme of my song? Nothing that's very far
    wrong.
First, my raw recruit, my inexperienced soldier,
    Take some trouble to find the girl whom you really
    can love.
Next, when you see what you like your problem will be
    how to win her.
    Finally, strive to make sure mutual love will endure.
That's as far as I go, the territory I cover,
    Those are the limits I set: take them or leave them
    alone.
While you are footloose and free to play the field at your
    pleasure,
    Watch for the one you can tell, "I want no other but
    you!"
She is not going to come to you floating down from the
    heavens:
    For the right kind of a girl you must keep using your
    eyes.
Hunters know where to spread their nets for the stag in
    his covert,
    Hunters know where the boar gnashes his teeth in
    the glade.
Fowlers know brier and bush, and fishermen study the
    waters
    Baiting the hook for the cast just where the fish may
    be found.
So you too, in your hunt for material worthy of loving.
    First will have to find out where the game usually
    goes.
I will not tell you to sail searching far over the oceans,
    I will not tell you to plod any long wearisome road.
Perseus went far to find his dusky Indian maiden:
    That was a Grecian girl Paris took over the sea.
Rome has all you will need, so many beautiful lovelies
    You will be bound to say, "Here is the grace of the
    world!"
Gargara's richness of field. Methymna's abundance of
    vineyard.
    All the fish of the sea, all the birds in the leaves.
All the stars in the sky, are less than the girls Rome can
    offer;
    Venus is mother and queen here in the town of her
    son.
If you are fond of them young, you will find them here by
    the thousands,
    Maids in their teens, from whom you will have
    trouble to choose.
Maybe a bit more mature, a little bit wiser? Believe me.
    These will outnumber the first as they come trooping
    along.
Take your time, walk slow, when the sun approaches the
    lion.
    There are porticoes, marbled under the shade,

Pompey's Octavia's, or the one in Livia's honor.
　　Or the Danaids' own, tall on the Palatine hill.
Don't pass by the shrine of Adonis, sorrow to Venus,
　　Where, on the Sabbath day, Syrians worship, and
　　Jews.
Try the Memphian fane of the Heifer, shrouded in linen;
　　Isis makes many a girl willing as Io for Jove.
Even the courts of the law, the bustle and noise of the
　　forum.
　　(This may be hard to believe) listen to whispers of
　　love.
Hard by the marble shrine of Venus, the Appian fountain,
　　Where the water springs high in its rush to the air.
There, and more than once, your counsellor meets with
　　his betters,
　　All his forensic arts proving of little avail:
Others he might defend; himself he cannot; words fail
　　him,
　　Making objections in vain; Cupid says, *Overruled!*
Venus, whose temple is near, laughs at the mortified
　　creature,
　　Lawyer a moment ago, in need of a counsellor now.
Also, the theater's curve is a very good place for your
　　hunting,
　　More opportunity here, maybe, than anywhere else.
Here you may find one to love, or possibly only have fun
　　with,
　　Someone to take for a night, someone to have and to
　　hold.
Just as a column of ants keeps going and coming forever,
　　Bearing their burdens of grain, just as the flight of
　　the bees
Over the meadows and over the fields of the thyme and
　　the clover,
　　So do the women come, thronging the festival
　　games.
Elegant, smart, and so many my sense of judgment is
　　troubled.
　　Hither they come, to see; hither they come, to be
　　seen.
This is a place for the chase, not the chaste, and Romulus
　　knew it,
　　Started it all, in fact; think of the Sabine girls.
There were no awnings, then, over the benches of
　　marble,
　　There were no crimson flowers staining the
　　platform's floor,
Only the natural shade from the Palatine trees, and the
　　stage-set
　　Quite unadorned, and the folk sitting on steps of
　　sod,
Shading their foreheads with leaves, studying, watching
　　intently,
　　Each for the girl he would have, none of them saying
　　a word.
Then, while the Tuscan flute was sounding its primitive
　　measure,
　　While the dancer's foot thrice beat the primitive
　　ground,
While the people roared in uninhibited cheering,
　　Romulus gave the sign. They had been waiting. They
　　knew.
Up they leaped, and their noise was proof of their
　　vigorous spirit.
　　Never a virgin there was free from the lust of a hand.
Just as the timid doves fly from the swooping of eagles,
　　Just as the newest lamb tries to escape from the wolf,

So those girls, fearing men, went rushing in every
　　direction;
　　Every complexion, through fright, turning a different
　　hue.
Though their fear was the same, it took on different
　　guises;
　　Some of them tore their hair; some of them sat
　　stricken dumb.
One is silent in grief, another calls for her mother,
　　One shrieks out, one is still; one runs away, and one
　　stays.
So, they are all carried off, these girls, the booty of
　　husbands,
　　While, in many, their fear added endowments of
　　charm.
If one struggled too much, or refused to go with her
　　captor,
　　He'd pick her up from the ground, lift her aloft in
　　his arms,
Saying, "Why do you spoil your beautiful eyes with that
　　crying?
　　Wasn't your mother a wife? That's all I want you to
　　be."
Romulus, you knew the way to give rewards to your
　　soldiers!
　　Give me rewards such as these, I would enlist for the
　　wars.
So, to this very day, the theater keeps its tradition:
　　Danger is lurking there still, waiting for beautiful
　　girls.
Furthermore, don't overlook the meetings when horses
　　are running;
　　In the crowds at the track opportunity waits.
There is no need for a code of finger-signals or nodding.
　　Sit as close as you like; no one will stop you at all.
In fact, you will have to sit close—that's one of the rules,
　　at a race track.
　　Whether she likes it or not, contact is part of the
　　game.
Try to find something in common, to open the
　　conversation;
　　Don't care too much what you say, just so that every
　　one hears.
Ask her, "Whose colors are those?"—that's good for an
　　opening gambit.
　　Put your own bet down, fast, on whatever she plays.
Then, when the gods come along in procession, ivory,
　　golden,
　　Outcheer every young man, shouting for Venus, the
　　queen.
Often it happens that dust may fall on the blouse of the
　　lady.
　　If such dust should fall, carefully brush it away.
Even if there's no dust, brush off whatever there isn't.
　　Any excuse will do: why do you think you have
　　hands?
If her cloak hangs low, and the ground is getting it dirty,
　　Gather it up with care, lift it a little, so!
Maybe, by way of reward, and not without her indulgence,
　　You'll be able to see ankle or possibly knee.
Then look around and glare at the fellow who's sitting
　　behind you,
　　Don't let him crowd his knees into her delicate
　　spine.
Girls, as everyone knows, adore these little attentions:
　　Getting the cushion just right, that's in itself quite an
　　art;
Yes, and it takes a technique in making a fan of your
　　program
　　Or in fixing a stool under the feet of a girl.

Such is the chance of approach the race track can offer a
    lover.
        There is another good ground, the gladiatorial
        shows.
On that sorrowful sand Cupid has often contested,
        And the watcher of wounds often has had it himself.
While he is talking, or touching a hand, or studying
    entries,
        Asking which one is ahead after his bet has been
        laid.
Wounded himself, he groans to feel the shaft of the arrow;
        He is a victim himself, no more spectator, but show.
Parties are also fine, not only for food on the tables.
        Something more than the wine you will find there if
        you look.
Often Bacchus lies there at his ease, and bright-colored
    Cupid,
        Soft-armed Cupid, near by, coaxes with wheedling
        charm,
Finds that his thirsty wings are suddenly sprinkled with
    wine-drops,
        Stands in his place, weighed down, almost unable to
        move,
Shakes out his dripping plumes, to be sure, in all kinds of
    a hurry—
        This may hurt more than you think, getting a
        dousing from love.
Wine sets the spirit afire, and wine brings passionate
    ardor;
        When there is plenty of wine, sorrow and worry take
        wing,
Then the laughter comes, and even the poor man has
    plenty,
        Wrinkles and frowns depart, grief is gone from the
        heart,
Then simplicity comes, and the inhibitions are banished,
        Slyness dispelled by a grace all too rare in our day.
That is the time when the girls can capture the hearts of
    their young men:
        When you have Venus in wine, then you have fire in
        fire.
Don't, at any such time, put too much faith in the
    lamplight.
        Judgment of beauty can err, what with the wine and
        the dark.
In the full light of the day the judgment of Paris was
    given:
        That was the time when he said, "Venus, no doubt
        that you win."
Flaws are hidden at night, and every flaw is forgiven;
        When the cats are all gray, then are the women all
        fair.
Take the advice of the light when you're looking at linens
    or jewels;
        Looking at faces or forms, take the advice of the day.
Why should I mention them all, the gathering-places of
    women?
        They are as many—no, more than all the sands of the
        shore,
Baiae, for instance, or Bath (as the British barbarians call
    it),
        Where the waters steam sulphurous out of the
        ground.
        And the drops from the tree are called by her name,
        the myrrh.
Once in the shadowy vales, the wooded uplands of Ida,
        Roamed a snow-white bull, glory and pride of the
        herd.
There was one black spot between the horns of his
    forehead,
        That was his only mark, all of the rest white as milk.

All the heifers of Cnossus, and all the Cydonean heifers
        Wanted him riding their backs—that was their prayer
        and desire.
Pasiphae, the queen, desired this bull for her lover,
        Jealous, with hate in her heart for all the beautiful
        cows.
I sing of things well-known, and Crete can never deny
    them,
        Liar though Crete may be through all her hundreds
        of towns.
Pasiphae, I say, with hands not used to such labors,
        Gathered new leaves and young grass, holding them
        out to the beast,
Went where the heifers would go, and had no thought of
    her husband,
        Minos, the lord of Crete. (He, too, was horned, it
        appears.)
Ah, what good did it do to put on her costliest dresses?
        To such a lover as hers riches meant nothing at all.
Why take a mirror along, seeking the herds on the
    mountains?
        Why, in your foolishness, constantly tend to your
        hair?
Still, the mirror is right in telling you that you're no
    heifer,
        Not however you wish, can you grow horns on your
        brow.
Does not Minos suffice? Why seek an adulterous lover?
        If he must be deceived, then let it be with a man.
Leaving her bower, the queen goes to the glades and the
    woodlands,
        As the Bacchanals go when the Aonian calls.
Often she looked at a cow, and frowned with a jealous
    expression,
        "How in the world," she says, "can he find pleasure
        in her?
Look how she lumbers and leaps before him over the
    meadows,
        Nor do I doubt the damn fool thinks she's a beautiful
        sight."
Then she would order the beast, poor thing, to be led
        from the pasture,
        Put the yoke on her neck, set her to hauling the
        plough,
Or, on some pretense of sacrificial devotion,
        Have her struck down, and hold entrails in jubilant
        hands,
Pleasing the altars of gods with the slaughtered corpse of
    a rival,
        "Go now, and please our lord!" her benediction
        would be.
Sometimes she wished she had been Io, and sometimes
    Europa;
        One was a cow for a while, one carried off by a bull.
Finally had her way, devising a heifer of maple,
        So her Minotaur son proved the success of the sire.
Had Aerope abstained from her guilty love of Thyestes
        (Pleasing one man alone seems such a lesson to
        learn!)—
Never would Phoebus have turned his car from the town
    of Mycenae,
        Wheeling his steeds around, reining them back to
        the East.
Scylla, the daughter of Nisus, stole from the head of her
    father
        That one precious lock: now the hounds rage in her
        womb.
Agamemnon survived the wars and the violent oceans,
        Victim in his own halls, slain by a murderous wife.

Who has not mourned for the flames of Ephyrean Creusa
  Or the mother's hands, stained with the blood of her
  sons?
Phoenix, the son of Amyntor, weeping from eyes that
  were blinded,
  Theseus' dismembered son, torn by his horses in
  fright,
Phineus, blinding his sons, the victims of false accusation,
  Suffering in his turn torments of hunger and doom—
All of these crimes, every one, arose from the lust of a
  woman,
  Keener in their desire, fiercer, more wanton than
  ours.
So, you need have little doubt when it comes to winning
  them over;
  Out of the many there are, hardly a one will refuse.
If they say Yes, or say No, they're pleased with the
  invitation:
  Even suppose you guess wrong, it costs you nothing
  to try.
But why should you be wrong? Untried delights are a
  pleasure:
  Those which we do not own tempt with attraction
  and charm.
In the fields of our neighbor the grass forever is greener;
  Always the other man's herd offers the richer reward.
Take some trouble, at first, to make her handmaiden's
  acquaintance:
  She, more than any one else, really can lighten your
  way.
She must be one you can trust, if she knows of the tricks
  you are playing,
  Confidante. wise and discreet, high in her mistress'
  regard.
Spoil her by promising much, and spoil her by pleading a
  little,
  What you seek you will find, if she is willing you
  should.
She will choose the right time—a maid is as good as a
  doctor—
  When she is in the right mood, all the more ripe to
  be had.
When she is in the right mood, you will know it because
  she is happy,
  Like the flowers in the field, seeming to burst into
  bloom.
When the hearts are glad, and sorrow does not confine
  them,
  Then they are open wide, and Venus steals coaxingly
  in.
Troy, in her days of gloom, was well defended by armor;
  When she rejoiced, the horse entered with Greeks in
  its womb.
It is worth making a try when she's grieving because of a
  rival,
  Vengeance can quickly be hers if you're
  conveniently there.
While her maid is at work, combing her hair in the
  morning,
  Let her keep urging her on, let her add oars to the
  sail,

Let her say with a sigh, or the softest murmuring whisper,
  "I don't suppose, after all, there is a thing you can
  do,"
Then let her talk about you, and add some words of
  persuasion,
  Let her swear that she knows you must be dying of
  love.
Hurry! before the sails are furled and the breezes grown
  milder;
  Anger, like brittle ice, dies with a little delay.
"Do not think it would do any good to seduce the maid?"
  What a question!
  Any such notions involve, always, too much of a risk.
One gets up from the bed too anxious, another too lazy,
  One aids her mistress's cause, one wants you all for
  her own.
Maybe it works, maybe not: it might be amusing to try it,
  Still, my advice would be, let it completely alone.
I would not show you the way over steep and precipitous
  passes,
  No young man in my school ever will ride for a fall,
Yet, if she seems to please, while giving and taking your
  letters,
  By her figure and face, not by her service alone,
Go for the lady first, and let the servant come second;
  When you are making love, do not begin with the
  maid.
One final warning word: if you have any faith in my
  teaching,
  If my words are not swept over the sea by the gale,
Either succeed, or don't try—she never will be an
  informer,
  If she is guilty herself: how could she tattle on you?
Birds, with the lime on their wings, cannot take flight to
  the heavens,
  Boars cannot plunge to their dens, caught in the
  mesh of the net.
Don't let your fish get away after the bait has been taken:
  Press the attack, keep on; don't go away till you've
  won.
Then she can never betray you, because you were guilty
  together;
  All of her mistress's acts, all of her words you will
  know.
Do not give her away: if she knows you are keeping her
  secrets,
  She will be yours any time, knowing and willingly
  known.

Exercises

1. What characteristics of this excerpt make it
   clearly Roman rather than Greek?
2. With appropriate changes in names, clothing,
   places, and activities, is Ovid's description of
   the dating game a fairly accurate representation
   of today's practices? Have you used any of
   Ovid's strategies? Can you recommend any as
   being particularly effective?
3. Ovid recommends chariot races for his little
   games. What might today's equivalent be?

Epigrams

Martial

Martial (Marcus Valerius Martialis; ca. A.D. 40–104) wrote hundreds of epigrams, which are brief poems, often satiric, ending in a surprise twist or climax. His style can be described as terse, sardonic, sparse, ascerbic, sarcastic, witty, and, withal, strikingly and delightfully modern.

I, i

Here he is—the one you read,
the one you ask for—Martial,
recognized the world over
for his witty books of epigrams.
Learned reader, you've given him
(while he's still alive to enjoy it)
the glory poets rarely get
after they've turned to ashes.

I, xxxv

You take me to task for writing
poems that aren't as prissy
and prim as they might be, Cornelius.
Not the kind a schoolmaster
would read aloud in the classroom.
But my little books wouldn't satisfy
(anymore than husbands can
their wives) without a little sex.
Would you want me to write a wedding-song
without using the words that wedding-songs
always use? Would you cover up
Flora's nymphs with a lot of clothing
or let prostitutes hide their shamefulness
under ladies' robes? There's a rule
that merry songs can't be merry
unless they're a bit indecent.

So forget your prudishness, please,
and spare my jokes and my naughtiness,
and don't try to castrate my poems.
Nothing's worse than Priapus posing
as a eunuch of Cybele.

II, xxxvi

I don't say you should curl your hair,
but you could comb it.
I don't say your body should be oiled,
but you could take a bath.
You needn't have a eunuch's beard
or a jailbird's. I don't insist
upon too much manliness,
Pannychus, or too little.
As it is, your legs are hairy
and your chest is shaggy with bristles,
but your mind, Pannychus, is bald.

II, lxviii

Don't think me insolent, Olus,
for calling you by your name
nowadays instead of "Patron"
or "Master" as I used to do.
I've bought my freedman's cap
with everything I possessed.

A man needs patrons and masters
if he isn't master of himself
and covets the same things patrons
and masters covet. But once
he can get along without a slave,
he can get along without a master.

III, xxxviii

Tell me, what brings you to Rome
so self-confidently, Sextus?
What are you after, and what
do you expect to find there?
"First of all, I'll plead cases
more eloquently than Cicero
himself. There won't be anyone
in the three forums to touch me."
Atestinus and Civis
(you know them both) pled cases,
but neither one of them took in
enough to pay the rent.
"Well, if nothing comes of that,
I'll write poems. When you hear them,
you'll say they're Vergil's work."
You're crazy. Wherever you look
you'll see Ovids and Vergils—all of them
shivering in their thin cloaks.
"Then I'll cultivate rich men."
That sort of thing has supported
maybe three or four. The rest
of the crowd are pale with hunger.
"What *will* I do? Advise me.
I'm determined to live in Rome."
Well, Sextus, if you're honest,
you'll be lucky to stay alive.

IV, xlix

Believe me, Flaccus—anyone
who calls epigrams mere trifles
and frivolities doesn't understand
what they are. It's more frivolous,
really, when somebody writes
about Tereus' revolting dinner
or that undigestible meal
of yours, Thyestes, or Daedalus
fitting the meltable wings
to his son, or Polyphemus
grazing his Sicilian sheep.
That kind of windiness
won't be found in any of my poems.
My Muse doesn't puff herself up
with such tragic nonsense.
    "Still,
everybody praises that kind
of thing—admires it—worships it!"
Granted. They praise it, but
it's my kind of poem they read.

[handwritten margin annotations: "Lawyer knows Rome", "Poet", "Patron", "typical: live dishonest; die honest: die", "like short witty poems", "short lyric poetry not noble"]

V, xiii

I'll admit I'm poor, Callistratus,
and always have been. And yet
two Emperors gave me a knighthood
and I'm not altogether unknown,
and my reputation isn't bad.
I've got a great many readers
everywhere in the world who will say
"That's Martial," and recognition
such as few receive after they're dead
has come to me while I'm alive.
On the other hand, your house-roof
is supported by a hundred columns,
and your money-boxes contain
a freedman's wealth, and wide fields
near Syene on the River Nile
call you master, and Parma in Gaul
shears its countless flocks for you.
That's what we are, you and I.
But you can never be what I am,
while anyone at all can be like you.

V, lvi

You've been wondering and worrying
and asking me every day
whom you ought to hand over your son to
for instruction, Lupus. I warn you:
stay away from all those grammarians
and professors of rhetoric.
Don't let him have anything to do
with Cicero's writings, or Vergil's,
and let Tutilius, the author
and advocate, earn his reputation
somewhere else. If the boy writes poems,
disown the young versifier!
Does he want to learn to make money?
Then have him take lessons in harping
or fluting. Or if the young fellow's
not too bright, you can turn him into
a salesman or an architect.

VI, xiv

You keep insisting, Labierus,   *sarcastic*
that you know how to write fine poems.
Then why is it you're unwilling
to try? Knowing how to write
fine poems and never doing it!
What will power, Labierus!

VI, xxxi

You know your wife's playing around   *lover will*
with your physician, Charidemus,   *kill husband*
but you don't do anything about it.
My guess is you won't have to wait
for a fever to carry you off.

VIII, xii

Why don't I marry a rich wife?   *sexist*
Because I won't make my wife
my master. A wife should be
submissive to her husband, Priscus.
There's no other way to give men
an equal chance with their women.

XI, lxvi

You're a spy and a blackmailer,
a forger, a pimp, a pervert,
and a trainer of gladiators,
Vacerra. I can't understand
why you aren't rich.

On the Dedication of the Colosseum in Rome

Barbaric Egypt, boast no more
    The wonders of your pyramids!
Babylon, vaunt no longer now
    The gardens of Semiramis!
Let not the soft Ionians swell
    With pride for their great Artemis
Whose temple splendor long has been
    The claim and fame of Ephesus.
Let Delos hide its head in shame
    And say no more Apollo
Himself did rear the altar there
    (A claim both weak and hollow).
Let not the Carians wildly praise
    The wondrous, sculptured tomb
The Queen at Halicarnassus raised
    When Mausolus met his doom.
Let every wonder of the past
    Yield now to this great wonder.
Fame shall cling to this at last,
    Her applause as loud as thunder.

Exercises

1. Martial frequently ridicules the person named in the epigram. Who (or what) are his favorite targets?
2. a. Try to identify the timeless qualities in Martial's art. For example, substitute the name of some well-known public figures of today in several epigrams; make sure the shoe fits!
   b. Try rewriting several epigrams, altering as necessary, e.g., XI, lxvi

   You're a fink and a toady,
   a cheat, a liar, a thief,
   and a politician,
   (<u>add appropriate name</u>). I can't understand
   why you aren't rich.

DISCOURSES OF EPICTETUS, BOOK I, CHAPTER 1

Arrian (b. A.D. 108)

This lecture of Epictetus (ca. A.D. 60–110), as recorded by his student Arrian, together with the meditations of Marcus Aurelius (121–180), which follows, present the Stoic point of view. This philosophy assumes that the great *Logos* (Intelligence) pervades the entire world and directs all that happens. Therefore, as will be seen in the selections, it is essentially a stern philosophy of acceptance, duty, and brotherhood of all men.

On Things in Our Power and Things Not in Our Power

Of our faculties in general you will find that none can take cognizance of itself; none therefore has the power to approve or disapprove its own action. Our grammatical faculty for instance: how far can that take cognizance? Only so far as to distinguish expression. Our musical faculty? Only so far as to distinguish tune. Does any one of these then take cognizance of itself? By no means. If you are writing to your friend, when you want to know what words to write grammar will tell you; but whether you should write to your friend or should not write grammar will not tell you. And in the same way music will tell you about tunes, but whether at this precise moment you should sing and play the lyre or should not sing nor play the lyre it will not tell you. What will tell you then? That faculty which takes cognizance of itself and of all things else. What is this? The reasoning faculty: for this alone of the faculties we have received is created to comprehend even its own nature; that is to say, what it is and what it can do, and with what precious qualities it has come to us, and to comprehend all other faculties as well. For what else is it that tells us that gold is a goodly thing? For the gold does not tell us. Clearly it is the faculty which can deal with our impressions. What else is it which distinguishes the faculties of music, grammar, and the rest, testing their uses and pointing out the due seasons for their use? It is reason and nothing else.

The gods then, as was but right, put in our hands the one blessing that is best of all and master of all, that and nothing else, the power to deal rightly with our impressions, but everything else they did not put in our hands. Was it that they would not? For my part I think that if they could have entrusted us with those other powers as well they would have done so, but they were quite unable. Prisoners on the earth and in an earthly body and among earthly companions, how was it possible that we should not be hindered from the attainment of these powers by these external fetters?

But what says Zeus? 'Epictetus, if it were possible I would have made your body and your possessions (those trifles that you prize) free and untrammelled. But as things are—never forget this—this body is not yours, it is but a clever mixture of clay. But since I could not make it free, I gave you a portion in our divinity, this faculty of impulse to act and not to act, of will to get and will to avoid, in a word the faculty which can turn impressions to right use. If you pay heed to this, and put your affairs in its keeping, you will never suffer let nor hindrance, you will not groan, you will blame no man, you will flatter none. What then? Does all this seem but little to you?'

Heaven forbid!

'Are you content then?'

So surely as I hope for the gods' favour.

But, as things are, though we have it in our power to pay heed to one thing and to devote ourselves to one, yet instead of this we prefer to pay heed to many things and to be bound fast to many—our body, our property, brother and friend, child and slave. Inasmuch then as we are bound fast to many things, we are burdened by them and dragged down. That is why, if the weather is bad for sailing, we sit distracted and keep looking continually and ask, 'What wind is blowing?' 'The north wind.' What have we to do with that? 'When will the west wind blow?' When it so chooses, good sir, or when Aeolus chooses. For God made Aeolus the master of the winds, not you. What follows? We must make the best of those things that are in our power, and take the rest as nature gives it. What do you mean by 'nature'? I mean, God's will.

'What? Am I to be beheaded now, and I alone?'

Why? Would you have had all beheaded, to give you consolation? Will you not stretch out your neck as Lateranus did in Rome when Nero ordered his beheadal? For he stretched out his neck and took the blow, and when the blow dealt him was too weak he shrank up a little and then stretched it out again. Nay more, on a previous occasion, when Nero's freedman Epaphroditus came to him and asked him the cause of his offence, he answered, 'If I want to say anything, I will say it to your master.'

What then must a man have ready to help him in such emergencies? Surely this: he must ask himself, 'What is mine, and what is not mine? What may I do, what may I not do?'

I must die. But must I die groaning? I must be imprisoned. But must I whine as well? I must suffer exile. Can any one then hinder me from going with a smile, and a good courage, and at peace?

'Tell the secret!'

I refuse to tell, for this is in my power.

'But I will chain you.'

What say you, fellow? Chain me? My leg you will chain—yes, but my will—no, not even Zeus can conquer that.

'I will imprison you.'

My bit of a body, you mean.

'I will behead you.'

Why? When did I ever tell you that I was the only man in the world that could not be beheaded?

These are the thoughts that those who pursue philosophy should ponder, these are the lessons they should write down day by day, in these they should exercise themselves.

Thrasea used to say 'I had rather be killed to-day than exiled tomorrow.' What then did Rufus say to him? 'If you choose it as the harder, what is the meaning of your foolish choice? If as the easier, who has given you the easier? Will you not study to be content with what is given you?'

It was in this spirit that Agrippinus used to say—do you know what? 'I will not stand in my own way!' News was brought him, 'Your trial is on in the Senate!' 'Good luck to it, but the fifth hour is come'—this was the hour when he used to take his exercise and have a cold bath— 'let us go and take exercise.' When he had taken his exercise they came and told him, 'You are condemned.' 'Exile or death?' he asked. 'Exile.' 'And my property?' 'It is not confiscated.' 'Well then, let us go to Aricia and dine.'

Here you see the result of training as training should be, of the will to get and will to avoid, so disciplined that nothing can hinder or frustrate them. I must die, must I? If at once, then I am dying: if soon, I dine now, as it is time for dinner, and afterwards when the time comes I will die. And die how? As befits one who gives back what is not his own.

Exercises

1. What exactly are the "things not in our power?" What is the one thing that *is* under our control?
2. What is the proper stoic attitude toward those things we cannot control?

MEDITATIONS, BOOK II

Marcus Aurelius (121–180)

Begin the morning by saying to thyself, I shall meet with the busybody, the ungrateful, arrogant, deceitful, envious, unsocial. All these things happen to them by reason of their ignorance of what is good and evil. But I who have seen the nature of the good that it is beautiful, and of the bad that it is ugly, and the nature of him who does wrong, that it is akin to me, not only of the same blood or seed, but that it participates in the same intelligence and the same portion of the divinity, I can neither be injured by any of them, for no one can fix on me what is ugly, nor can I be angry with my kinsman, nor hate him. For we are made for cooperation, like feet, like hands, like eyelids, like the rows of the upper and lower teeth. To act against one another then is contrary to nature; and it is acting against one another to be vexed and to turn away.

2. Whatever this is that I am, it is a little flesh and breath, and the ruling part. Throw away thy books; no longer distract thyself: it is not allowed; but as if thou wast now dying, despise the flesh; it is blood and bones and a network, a contexture of nerves, veins, and arteries. See the breath also, what kind of a thing it is, air, and not always the same, but every moment sent out and again sucked in. The third then is the ruling part: consider thus: Thou art an old man; no longer let this be a slave, no longer be pulled by the strings like a puppet to unsocial movements, no longer be either dissatisfied with thy present lot, or shrink from the future.

5. Every moment think steadily as a Roman and a man to do what thou hast in hand with perfect and simple dignity, and feeling of affection, and freedom, and justice; and to give thyself relief from all other thoughts. And thou wilt give thyself relief, if thou doest every act of thy life as it were the last, laying aside all carelessness and passionate aversion from the commands of reason, and all hypocrisy, and self-love, and discontent with the portion which has been given to thee. Thou seest how few the things are, that which if a man lays hold of, he is able to live a life which flows in quiet, and is like the existence of the gods; for the gods on their part will require nothing more from him who observes these things.

9. This thou must always bear in mind, what is the nature of the whole, and what is my nature, and how this is related to that, and what kind of a part it is of what kind of a whole; and that there is no one who hinders thee from always doing and saying the things which are according to the nature of which thou art a part.

11. Since it is possible that thou mayest depart from life this very moment, regulate every act and thought accordingly. But to go away from among men, if there are gods, is not a thing to be afraid of, for the gods will not involve thee in evil; but if indeed they do not exist, or if they have no concern about human affairs, what is it to me to live in a universe devoid of gods or devoid of Providence? But in truth they do exist, and they do care for human things, and they have put all the means in man's power to enable him not to fall into real evils. And as to the rest, if there was anything evil, they would have provided for this also, that it should be altogether in a man's power not to fall into it. Now that which does not make a man worse, how can it make a man's life worse?

But neither through ignorance, nor having the knowledge, but not the power to guard against or correct these things, is it possible that the nature of the universe has overlooked them; nor is it possible that it has made so great a mistake, either through want of power or want of skill, that good and evil should happen indiscriminately to the good and the bad. But death certainly, and life, honour and dishonour, pain and pleasure, all these things equally happen to good men and bad, being things which make us neither better nor worse. Therefore they are neither good nor evil.

16. The soul of man does violence to itself, first of all, when it becomes an abscess and, as it were, a tumour on the universe, so far as it can. For to be vexed at anything which happens in a separation of ourselves from nature, in some part of which the natures of all other things are contained. In the next place, the soul does violence to itself when it turns away from any man, or even moves towards him with the intention of injuring, such as are the souls of those who are angry. In the third place, the soul does violence to itself when it is overpowered by pleasure or by pain. Fourthly, when it plays a part, and does or says anything insincerely and untruly. Fifthly, when it allows any act of its own and any movement to be without an aim, and does anything thoughtlessly and without considering what it is, it being right that even the smallest things be done with reference to an end; and the end of rational animals is to follow the reason and the law of the most ancient city and polity.

17. Of human life the time is a point, and the substance is in a flux, and the perception dull, and the composition of the whole body subject to putrefaction, and the soul a whirl, and fortune hard to divine, and fame a thing devoid of judgement. And, to say all in a word, everything which belongs to the body is a stream, and what belongs to the soul is a dream and vapour, and life is a warfare and a stranger's sojourn, and after-fame is oblivion. What then is that which is able to conduct a man? One thing and only one, philosophy. But this consists in keeping the daemon within a man free from violence and unharmed, superior to pains and pleasures, doing nothing without a purpose, nor yet falsely and with hypocrisy, not feeling the need of another man's doing or not doing anything; and besides, accepting all that happens, and all that is allotted, as coming from thence, wherever it is, from whence he himself came; and, finally, waiting for death with a cheerful mind, as being nothing else than a dissolution of the elements of which every living being is compounded. But if there is no harm to the elements themselves in each continually changing into another, why should a man have any apprehension about the change and dissolution of all the elements? For it is according to nature, and nothing is evil which is according to nature.

Exercises

1. Consider the "ruling part" of human nature; according to Marcus Aurelius, should it be reason, passion, conscience, tradition, authority, or revelation? Why?
2. According to the emperor, what is the proper way to face death?

AGAINST THE CITY OF ROME

Decimus Junius Juvenalis (ca. 60–140)

Juvenal (Decimus Junius Juvenalis) was the last and best of the remarkable Roman satirists. As a brilliant social critic who was scarred by abrasive poverty, he saw through the glass darkly. The bitter tone, merciless barbs, and blatant prejudices (against Greeks and the "inferior" sex) are directed against a Rome he despises because it has become foolish and wicked.

Troubled because my old friend is going, I still must
    commend him
For his decision to settle down in the ghost town of
    Cumae,[51]
Giving the Sibyl one citizen more. That's the gateway to
    Baiae
There, a pleasant shore, a delightful retreat, I'd prefer
Even a barren rock in that bay to the brawl of Subura.
Where have we ever seen a place so dismal and lonely
We'd not be better off there, than afraid, as we are here, of
    fires,
Roofs caving in, and the thousand risks of this terrible city
Where the poets recite all through the dog days of
    August?
While they are loading his goods on one little four-
    wheeled wagon,
Here he waits, by the old archways which the aqueducts
    moisten.
This is where Numa, by night, came to visit his goddess.
That once holy grove, its sacred spring, and its temple,
Now are let out to the Jews, if they have some straw and a
    basket.
Every tree, these days, has to pay rent to the people.
Kick the Muses out; the forest is swarming with beggers.
So we go down to Egeria's vale, with its modern
    improvements.
How much more close the presence would be, were there
    lawns by the water,
Turf to the curve of the pool, not this unnatural marble!
Umbricius has much on his mind. "Since there's no place
    in the city,"
He says, "For an honest man, and no reward for his
    labors,
Since I have less today than yesterday, since by tomorrow
That will have dwindled still more, I have made my
    decision. I'm going
To the place where, I've heard, Daedalus put off his
    wings,[52]
While my white hair is still new, my old age in the prime
    of its straightness,
While my fate spinner still has yarn on her spool, while
    I'm able
Still to support myself on two good legs, without
    crutches.
Rome, good-bye! Let the rest stay in the town if they want
    to,
Fellows like A, B, and C, who make black white at their
    pleasure,
Finding it easy to grab contracts for rivers and harbors,
Putting up temples, or cleaning out sewers, or hauling off
    corpses,
Or, if it comes to that, auctioning slaves in the market.
Once they used to be hornblowers, working the carneys;
Every wide place in the road knew their puffed-out
    cheeks and their squealing.
Now they give shows of their own. Thumbs up! Thumbs
    down! And the killers
Spare or slay, and then go back to concessions for private
    privies.
Nothing they won't take on. Why not?—since the
    kindness of Fortune
(Fortune is out for laughs) has exalted them out of the
    gutter
"What should I do in Rome? I am no good at lying.
If a book's bad, I can't praise it, or go around ordering
    copies.
I don't know the stars; I can't hire out as assassin
When some young man wants his father knocked off for a
    price; I have never
Studied the guts of frogs, and plenty of others know
    better
How to convey to a bride the gifts of the first man she
    cheats with.
I am no lookout for thieves, so I cannot expect a
    commission
On some governor's staff. I'm a useless corpse, or a
    cripple.
Who has a pull these days, except your yes men and
    stooges
With blackmail in their hearts, yet smart enough to keep
    silent?
No honest man feels in debt to those he admits to his
    secrets,
But your Verres must love the man who can tattle on
    Verres[53]
Any old time that he wants. Never let the gold of the
    Tagus,
Rolling under its shade, become so important, so
    precious
You have to lie awake, take bribes that you'll have to
    surrender,
Tossing in gloom, a threat to your mighty patron forever.
"Now let me speak of the race that our rich men dote on
    most fondly.
These I avoid like the plague, let's have no coyness about
    it.
Citizens, I can't stand a Greekized Rome. Yet what
    portion
Of the dregs of our town comes from Achaia only?
Into the Tiber pours the silt, the mud of Orontes,
Bringing its babble and brawl, its dissonant harps and its
    timbrels,
Bringing also the tarts who display their wares at the
    Circus.
Here's the place, if your taste is for hat-wearing whores,
    brightly colored!
What have they come to now, the simple souls from the
    country
Romulus used to know? They put on the *trechedipna*
(That might be called, in our tongue, their running-to-
    dinner outfit),

---

51. Cumae was the oldest Greek colony in Italy.

52. Daedalus, according to Virgil, ended his flight at Cumae.

53. Verres was the corrupt governor of Sicily against whom Cicero delivered his famous prosecution speeches. The name passed into the language as the emblem of rapacious administrators.

Pin in their *niketeria* (medals), and smell *ceromatic*
(Attar of wrestler). They come, trooping from Samos and
      Tralles,
Andros, wherever that is, Azusa and Cucamonga,
Bound for the Esquiline or the hill we have named for the
      vineyard,
Termites, into great halls where they hope, some day, to
      be tyrants.
Desperate nerve, quick wit, as ready in speech as Isacus,
Also a lot more long-winded. Look over there! See that
      fellow?
What do you take him for? He can be anybody he
      chooses,
Doctor of science or letters, a vet or a chiropractor,
Orator, painter, masseur, palmologist, tightrope walker.
If he is hungry enough, your little Greek stops at nothing.
Tell him to fly to the moon, and he runs right off for his
      space ship.
Who flew first? Some Moor, some Turk, some Croat, or
      some Slovene?
Not on your life, but a man from the very center of
      Athens.
"Should I not run away from these purple-wearing
      freeloaders?
Must I wait while they sign their names? Must their
      couches always be softer?
Stowaways, that's how they got here, in the plums and figs
      from Damascus.
I was here long before they were: my boyhood drank in
      the sky
Over the Aventine hill; I was nourished by Sabine olives.
Agh, what lackeys they are, what sycophants! See how
      they flatter
Some ignoramus's talk, or the looks of some horrible
      eyesore,
Saying some Ichabod Crane's long neck reminds them of
      muscles
Hercules strained when he lifted Antaeus aloft on his
      shoulders,
Praising some cackling voice that really sounds like a
      rooster's
When he's pecking a hen. We can praise the same objects
      that they do,
Only, they are believed. Does an actor do any better
Mimicking Thais, Alcestis, Doris without any clothes on?
It seems that a woman speaks, not a mask; the illusion is
      perfect
Down to the absence of bulge and the little cleft under
      the belly.[54]
Yet they win on praise at home, for all of their talent.
Why?—Because Greece is a stage, and every Greek is an
      actor.
Laugh, and he splits his sides; weep, and his tears flow in
      torrents
Though he's not sad; if you ask for a little more fire in the
      winter
He will put on his big coat; if you say 'I'm hot,' he starts
      sweating.
We are not equals at all; he always has the advantage,
Able, by night or day, to assume, from another's
      expression,
This or that look, prepared to throw up his hands, to
      cheer loudly
If his friend gives a good loud belch or doesn't piss
      crooked,

Or if a gurgle comes from his golden cup when inverted
Straight up over his nose—a good deep swig, and no
      heeltaps!
"Furthermore, nothing is safe from his lust, neither
      matron nor virgin,
Nor her affianced spouse, or the boy too young for the
      razor.
If he can't get at these, he would just as soon lay his
      friend's grandma.
(Anything, so he'll get in to knowing the family secrets!)
Since I'm discussing the Greeks, let's turn to their
      schools and professors,
The crimes of the hood and gown. Old Dr. Egnatius,
      informant,
Brought about the death of Barea, his friend and his
      pupil,
Born on that riverbank where the pinion of Pegasus
      landed.
No room here, none at all, for any respectable Roman
Where a Protogenes rules, or a Diphilus, or a
      Hermarchus,
Never sharing their friends—a racial characteristic!
Hands off! He puts a drop of his own, or his countryside's
      poison
Into his patron's ear, an ear which is only too willing
And I am kicked out of the house, and all my years of
      long service
Count for nothing. Nowhere does the loss of a client
      mean less.
"Let's not flatter ourselves. What's the use of our service?
What does a poor man gain by hurrying out in the
      nighttime,
All dressed up before dawn, when the praetor nags at his
      troopers
Bidding them hurry along to convey his respects to the
      ladies,
Barren, of course, like Albina, before any others can get
      there?
Sons of men freeborn give right of way to a rich man's
Slave; a crack, once or twice, at Calvina or Catiena
Costs an officer's pay, but if you like the face of some
      floozy
You hardly have money enough to make her climb down
      from her high chair.
Put on the stand, at Rome, a man with a record
      unblemished,
No more a perjurer than Numa was, or Metellus,
What will they question? His wealth, right away, and
      possibly, later,
(Only possibly, though) touch on his reputation.
'How many slaves does he feed? What's the extent of his
      acres?
How big are his platters? How many? What of his goblets
      and wine bowls?'
His word is as good as his bond—if he has enough bonds
      in his strongbox.
But a poor man's oath, even if sworn on all altars
All the way from here to the farthest Dodecanese island,
Has no standing in court. What has he to fear from the
      lightnings
Of the outraged gods? He has nothing to lose: they'll
      ignore him.
"If you're poor, you're a joke, on each and every occasion.
What a laugh, if your cloak is dirty or torn, if your toga
Seems a little bit soiled, if your shoe has a crack in the
      leather,
Or if more than one patch attests to more than one
      mending!

---

54. In Greek-style comedies women's roles were played by men.

Poverty's greatest curse, much worse than the fact of it, is that
It makes men objects of mirth, ridiculed, humbled, embarrassed.
'Out of the front-row seats!' they cry when you're out of money,
Yield your place to the sons of some pimp, the spawn of some cathouse,
Some slick auctioneer's brat, or the louts some trainer has fathered
Or the well-groomed boys whose sire is a gladiator.
Such is the law of place, decreed by the nitwitted Otho:
All the best seats are reserved for the classes who have the most money.
Who can marry a girl if he has less money than she does?
What poor man is an heir, or can hope to be? Which of them ever
Rates a political job, even the meanest and lowest?
Long before now, all poor Roman descendants of Romans
Ought to have marched out of town in one determined migration.
Men do not easily rise whose poverty hinders their merit.
Here it is harder than anywhere else: the lodgings are hovels,
Rents out of sight; your slaves take plenty to fill up their bellies
While you make do with a snack. You're ashamed of your earthenware dishes—
Ah, but that wouldn't be true if you lived content in the country,
Wearing a dark-blue cape, and the hood thrown back on your shoulders.
"In a great part of this land of Italy, might as well face it,
No one puts on a toga unless he is dead. On festival days
Where the theater rises, cut from green turf, and with great pomp
Old familiar plays are staged again, and a baby,
Safe in his mother's lap, is scared of the grotesque mask,
There you see all dressed alike, the balcony and the front rows,
Even His Honor content with a tunic of simple white.
Here, beyond our means, we have to be smart, and too often
Get our effects with too much, an elaborate wardrobe, on credit!
This is a common vice; we must keep up with the neighbors,
Poor as we are. I tell you, everything here costs you something.
How much to give Cossus the time of day, or receive from Veiento
One quick glance, with his mouth buttoned up for fear he might greet you?
One shaves his beard, another cuts off the locks of his boyfriend,
Offerings fill the house, but these, you find, you will pay for.
Put this in your pipe and smoke it—we have to pay tribute
Giving the slaves a bribe for the prospect of bribing their masters.
"Who, in Praeneste's cool, or the wooded Volsinian uplands,
Who, on Tivoli's heights, or a small town like Gabii, say,
Fears the collapse of his house? But Rome is supported on pipestems,
Matchsticks; it's cheaper, so, for the landlord to shore up his ruins,
Patch up the old cracked walls, and notify all the tenants
They can sleep secure, though the beams are in ruins above them.

No, the place to live is out there, where no cry of *Fire!*
Sounds the alarm of the night, with a neighbor yelling for water,
Moving his chattels and goods, and the whole third story is smoking.
This you'll never know: for if the ground floor is scared first,
You are the last to burn, up there where the eaves of the attic
Keep off the rain, and the doves are brooding over their nest eggs.
Codrus owned one bed, too small for a midget to sleep on,
Six little jugs he had, and a tankard adorning his sideboard,
Under whose marble (clay), a bust or a statue of Chiron,
Busted, lay on its side; an old locker held Greek books
Whose divinest lines were gnawed by the mice, those vandals.
Codrus had nothing, no doubt, and yet he succeeded, poor fellow,
Losing that nothing, his all. And this is the very last straw—
No one will help him out with a meal or lodging or shelter.
Stripped to the bone, begging for crusts, he still receives nothing.
"Yet if Asturicus' mansion burns down, what a frenzy of sorrow!
Mothers dishevel themselves, the leaders dress up in black,
Courts are adjourned. We groan at the fall of the city, we hate
The fire, and the fire still burns, and while it is burning,
Somebody rushes up to replace the loss of the marble,
Some one chips in toward a building fund, another gives statues,
Naked and shining white, some masterpiece of Euphranor
Or Polyclitus' chef d'oeuvre; and here's a fellow with bronzes
Sacred to Asian gods. Books, chests, a bust of Minerva,
A bushel of silver coins. *To him that hath shall be given!*
The Persian, childless, of course, the richest man in the smart set,
Now has better things, and more, than before the disaster.
How can we help but think he started the fire on purpose?
"Tear yourself from the games, and get a place in the country!
One little Latian town, like Sora, say, or Frusino,
Offers a choice of homes, at a price you pay here, in one year,
Renting some hole in the wall. Nice houses, too, with a garden,
Springs bubbling up from the grass, no need for windlass or bucket,
Plenty to water your flowers, if they need it, without any trouble.
Live there, fond of your hoe, an independent producer,
Willing and able to feed a hundred good vegetarians.
Isn't it something, to feel, wherever you are, how far off,
You are monarch? At least, lord of a single lizard.
"Here in town the sick die from insomnia mostly.
Undigested food, on a stomach burning with ulcers,
Brings on listlessness, but who can sleep in a flophouse?
Who but the rich can afford sleep and a garden apartment?

That's the source of infection. The wheels creak by on the narrow
Streets of the wards, the drivers squabble and brawl when they're stopped,
More than enough to frustrate the drowsiest son of a sea cow.
When his business calls, the crowd makes way, as the rich man,
Carried high in his car, rides over them, reading or writing,
Even taking a snooze, perhaps, for the motion's composing.
Still, he gets where he wants before we do; for all of our hurry
Traffic gets in our way, in front, around and behind us.
Somebody gives me a shove with an elbow, or two-by-four scantling.
One clunks my head with a beam, another cracks down with a beer keg.
Mud is thick on my shins, I am trampled by somebody's big feet.
Now what?—a soldier grinds his hobnails into my toes.
"Don't you see the mob rushing along to the handout?
There are a hundred guests, each one with his kitchen servant.
Even Samson himself could hardly carry those burdens,
Pots and pans some poor little slave tries to keep on his head, while he hurries
Hoping to keep the fire alive by the wind of his running.
Tunics, new-darned, are ripped to shreds; there's the flash of a fir beam
Huge on some great dray, and another carries a pine tree,
Nodding above our heads and threatening death to the people.
What will be left of the mob, if that cart of Ligurian marble
Breaks its axle down and dumps its load on these swarms?
Who will identify limbs or bones? The poor man's cadaver,
Crushed, disappears like his breath. And meanwhile, at home, his household
Washes the dishes, and puffs up the fire, with all kinds of a clatter
Over the smeared flesh-scrapers, the flasks of oil, and the towels.
So the boys rush around, while their late master is sitting,
Newly come to the bank of the Styx, afraid of the filthy
Ferryman there, since he has no fare, not even a copper
In his dead mouth to pay for the ride through the muddy whirlpool.
"Look at other things, the various dangers of nighttime.
How high it is to the cornice that breaks, and a chunk beats my brains out,
Or some slob heaves a jar, broken or cracked, from a window.
Bang! It comes down with a crash and proves its weight on the sidewalk.
You are a thoughtless fool, unmindful of sudden disaster,
If you don't make your will before you go out to have dinner.
There are as many deaths in the night as there are open windows
Where you pass by; if you're wise, you will pray, in your wretched devotions,
People may be content with no more than emptying slop jars.

"There your hell-raising drunk, who has had the bad luck to kill no one,
Tosses in restless rage, like Achilles mourning Patroclus,
Turns from his face to his back, can't sleep, for only a fracas
Gives him the proper sedation. But any of these young hoodlums,
All steamed up on wine, watches his step when the crimson
Cloak goes by, a lord, with a long, long line of attendants,
Torches and brazen lamps, warning him, *Keep your distance!*
Me, however, whose torch is the moon, or the feeblest candle
Fed by a sputtering wick, he absolutely despises.
Here is how it all starts, the fight, if you think it is fighting
When he throws all the punches, and all I do is absorb them.
He stops. He tells me to stop. I stop. I have to obey him.
What can you do when he's mad and bigger and stronger than you are?
'Where do you come from?' he cries, 'you wino, you bean-bloated bastard?
Off what shoemaker's dish have you fed on chopped leeks and boiled lamb-lip?
What? No answer? Speak up, or take a swift kick in the rear.
Tell me where you hang out—in some praying-house with the Jew-boys?'
If you try to talk back, or sneak away without speaking,
All the same thing: you're assaulted, and then put under a bail bond
For committing assault. This is a poor man's freedom.
Beaten, cut up by fists, he begs and implores his assailant,
Please, for a chance to go home with a few teeth left in his mouth.
"This is not all you must fear. Shut up your house or your store,
Bolts and padlocks and bars will never keep out all the burglars,
Or a holdup man will do you in with a switch blade.
If the guards are strong over Pontine marshes and pinewoods
Near Volturno, the scum of the swamps and the filth of the forest
Swirl into Rome, the great sewer, their sanctuary, their haven.
Furnaces blast and anvils groan with the chains we are forging:
What other use have we for iron and steel? There is danger
We will have little left for hoes and mattocks and ploughshares.
Happy the men of old, those primitive generations
Under the tribunes and kings, when Rome had only one jailhouse!
"There is more I could say, I could give you more of my reasons,
But the sun slants down, my oxen seem to be calling,
My man with the whip is impatient, I must be on my way.
So long! Don't forget me. Whenever you come to Aquino
Seeking relief from Rome, send for me. I'll come over
From my bay to your hills, hiking along in my thick boots
Toward your chilly fields. What's more, I promise to listen
If your satirical verse esteems me worthy the honor."

Exercises

1. The debate about the relative virtues of rural and urban life is as old as cities. What does Juvenal detest about Rome? What does he admire about the country or small-town life? Why do you think he chose to stay in Rome?
2. Twentieth-century cities have their share of problems. Which of these seem to be common to ancient Rome and modern cities?

Summary

The pragmatic Romans cherished their flawed institutions and their proclivity for war, plunder, and profits, but they did have the saving grace of being able to laugh at themselves. Enthusiastically adapting satire to Roman tastes, they lambasted all that they held dear: politics, material possessions, manners, and morals. The Romans were, in the final analysis, rational and civilized people, and nowhere is there clearer evidence of this than in their literature. No more given to profundities than their society, Roman writers were, collectively, sophisticated, worldly-wise, and sometimes jaded. They sought to entertain and to inform rather than to enlighten, and they accomplished this with great style and a kind of lusty elegance. The literature is consistently entertaining, often irreverent, frequently lewd; it certainly makes lovely reading.[55]

Culture and Human Values

The Greeks and the Romans were realists living in a world about which they had few illusions. However, the Greeks were also idealists who believed that people should (and could) be better than they were, that they could achieve freedom, beauty, truth, and justice.

Though not denying the desirability of these ideals, the Romans were thorough-going pragmatists. They rejected theory and precedent in favor of practical approaches and expediency. The meaning of a course of action lay in its observable consequences, the sum of which was its meaning. Serving the Roman state, for example, as a member of a Roman legion brought security, status, discipline, and a reasonable income. The sum of these benefits meant that soldiering was a good life and one that benefited first the state and then the individual. The state rather than the soldier was the true reality, a direct reversal of Greek values that placed the individual above the state. Duty, honor, and patriotism were Roman virtues as opposed to the Greek ideals of freedom, truth, and beauty.

Justice was a deep concern for both cultures but in very different ways. The Greeks pursued the theory of perfect justice in a perfectly ordered society. Roman justice was pragmatic, a process that dealt with practical problems in everyday life. Venality and greed were human characteristics that the state controlled so that the strong could not triumph over the weak. Roman law implied the consent of the governed and every citizen, regardless of class, had the right to "appeal to Caesar." Moreover, Roman law was international and based on a pragmatic appraisal of consistent human behavior and misbehavior regardless of the environment. Though we may admire the Greek ideal of justice, it is Roman law that has provided the basic framework of today's body of laws.

The state of balance of the culture-epoch theory was essentially maintained from the beginning of the Classical Period in Greece to the death of Marcus Aurelius, the sixth and last of the so-called good emperors (480 B.C.–A.D. 180). The ensuing decline and fall of Rome is a topic for later discussion.

Annotated Bibliography

General

Auguet, Roland. *Cruelty and Civilization: The Roman Games*. London: Allen and Unwin, Ltd., 1972. Excellent survey of a subject both fascinating and repulsive.

Bonner, Stanley F. *Education in Ancient Rome: From the Elder Cato to the Younger Pliny*. Berkeley: University of California Press, 1978. A standard survey that reveals the inroads of Greek influence.

Brantlinger, Patrick. *Bread and Circuses: Theories of Mass Culture as Social Decay*. Ithaca: Cornell University Press, 1985. The "decline and fall" motif from Greece and Rome to the present day.

Cary, Max, and Scullard, H. H. *A History of Rome*. New York: St. Martin's Press, 1975. One of finest short histories.

Casson, Lionel. *The Horizon Book of Daily Life in Ancient Rome*. New York: American Heritage, 1975. Outstanding series that also includes Ancient Egypt, the Middle Ages, Renaissance, and Victorian England.

Clark, M. L. *The Roman Mind: Studies in the History of Thought from Cicero to Marcus Aurelius*. New York: W. W. Norton & Company, 1968.

Gardiner, E. N. *Athletics in the Ancient World*. Chicago: University of Chicago Press, 1978. The single most useful source on interrelations of athletics and religion in Greece and Rome.

Gibbon, Edward. *The Decline and Fall of the Roman Empire*. In various editions, preferably a one-volume abridgement. The classic work from the Enlightenment point of view.

Graves, Robert. *I, Claudius* (1934). In various editions. Fascinating historical novel by the eminent classicist. See, too, the sequel: *Claudius the God*.

---

55. Though much too long for inclusion here, it is strongly recommended that you read the rest of the *Aeneid* and all of Ovid's *Metamorphoses*. Further, reading all of the latter's *Art of Love* (plus *Amores* and *Remedy of Love*) clearly reveals why Ovid was so important to the medieval troubadour-trouvère tradition (see chapter 16) and the Age of Chivalry.

Gruen, Eric S. *The Hellenistic World and the Coming of Rome.* Berkeley: University of California Press, 1984. An authoritative study on Roman expansion in the Hellenistic world.

———. *The Last Generation of the Roman Republic.* Berkeley: University of California Press, 1974. Focus on the crucial phases.

Hadas, Moses. *Imperial Rome.* New York: Time-Life Books, 1965. Excellent overview from the *Great Ages of Man* series.

Luck, Georg. *Arcana Mundi: Magic and the Occult in the Greek and Roman Worlds.* Baltimore: The Johns Hopkins University Press, 1985.

Nicolet, Claude. *The World of the Citizen in Republican Rome.* Berkeley: University of California Press, 1980. Probably the finest study of social and political life in the republic.

Ogilvie, R. M. *Early Rome and the Etruscans.* Atlantic Highlands, N. J.: Humanities Press, 1976. Probably the best study of this early period.

Petit, Paul. *Pax Romana.* Translated by James Willis. Berkeley: University of California Press, 1976. Excellent study of the Roman world order.

Rostovzeff, Mikhail. *Social and Economic History of the Roman Empire.* New York: Oxford University Press, 1957. The standard work.

Translations and Interpretations of Original Material

Translations of all Roman authors are available in the Loeb Classical Library series published by Harvard University Press. Excellent translations of standard works are also published by the Indiana University Press, Bloomington, Indiana. The following works are also recommended:

Davenport, Basil, ed. *The Portable Roman Reader.* New York: Viking Press, 1959. The best cross section of Roman literature in a single volume.

Graves, Robert. *Suetonius: The Lives of the Twelve Caesars.* Baltimore: Penguin Books, 1957. The author of *I, Claudius* is also a superb translator.

Hammond, N. G., and Scullard, H. H. *Oxford Classical Dictionary.* Oxford: Clarendon Press, 1970. The definitive reference work for Greek and Roman culture.

MacKendrick, Paul L., and Howe, Herbert M., eds. *Latin Literature.* Vol. 1 of *Classics in Translation.* Madison: University of Wisconsin Press, 1952. One of finest and most comprehensive collections.

Mulls, Barriss. *Epigrams from Martial: A Verse Translation.* Lafayette: Purdue University Press, 1969. Skillful contemporary translation.

Sesar, Carl. *Selected Poems of Catullus.* New York: Mason & Lipscomb, 1974. Idiomatic, profane, erotic, and scatalogical and, thus, very close to the style and spirit of the original.

Turner, Paul. *Plutarch's Lives.* Carbondale: Southern Illinois University Press, 1963. Good translation of a standard work.

10

Roman Art and Music: The Arts of Megalopolis

Etruscan Civilization

The Etruscans controlled northern Italy for about four hundred years and even ruled Rome for nearly a century. Their influence on Roman civilization was considerable but there was almost no mutual exchange; Rome did not impress the Etruscans. It was the arts of Greece that they admired: sculpture, painting, and vases, especially vases (most Greek pottery recovered to date has been found in Etruscan tombs).

As strong as the Greek influence was, the Etruscans did develop a distinctive kind of art. Provincial, sometimes homespun, with an occasional masterpiece, their work had an earthy vigor that impressed their Roman conquerors. In fact, we know more of Etruscan art than of their culture in general. With no literature and little

more than some massive stone walls remaining of their fortified hilltop cities, our scanty knowledge of Etruscan culture is based almost entirely on the contents of the thousands of tombs found throughout central Italy. Etruscan skill in making terra-cotta objects is exemplified by the funerary sculpture (figure 10.1) found in the *necropolis* (city of the dead) outside Cerveteri, northwest of Rome. A deceased couple is shown resting their left elbows on a couch as if they are attending a celestial banquet. The smooth bodies, braided hair, and archaic smiles in the Greek manner are typical of the Etruscan style, as is the display of mutual affection and the individualized features of the couple. The exact meaning of festive banquet scenes in tomb paintings and as depicted on numerous sarcophagi is unknown, but continuation of the good life after death may have been intended.

■ **FIGURE 10.1** *Etruscan sarcophagus, from Cerveteri, Italy, ca. 510 B.C. Painted terra-cotta, length ca. 79". Museo Nazionale della Villa Giulia, Rome.*

FIGURE 10.2 Chimera of Arezzo, *from Arezzo, ca. 380–360 B.C. Bronze, height 31". Museo Archeologico, Florence.*

The remarkable *chimera* (figure 10.2) is a masterful monster that radiates the vigor so characteristic of Etruscan art. In Greek mythology a chimera was usually a fire-breathing monster with the head of a lion, body of a goat, and a serpent for a tail. Here the head and tail fit the pattern, but the body is more "lion" than "goat" and the pattern down the backbone seems to be dragonlike. Compounding the four-footed hybrid is the head of a goat protruding from the back with the left horn caught in the fangs of the snake. (A mistake in reconstruction placed the snake's head too low; it should be raised higher so that it's fangs can intimidate observers.) There is no Greek influence here. The Greeks polished off the rough edges of their demons, but the Etruscans created a whole company of monsters that specialized in tormenting the dead in the underworld. This seems to reflect the Asiatic origins of the Etruscans, about which Herodotos was so positive.

Moreover, this creature has precedents that go back to Egyptian sphinxes (see figure 2.1) and the winged, man-faced bulls of Assyria (see figure 1.8).

Roman Arts, ca. 753 B.C.–A.D. 476

For the stern Romans, art was a corrupting influence that could undermine the moral fiber of the people, especially the citizen-soldiers of the republic. As late as the third century B.C., Rome was, according to Plutarch, a drab and dreary city full of battle trophies, barbarous weapons, triumphal monuments, and bloodstained hostages—a metropolis devoid of refinement and beauty. The penetration of Greek culture, especially Greek art, was a slow process that gathered momentum with Roman triumphs over Greek territories. During the conquest of the luxurious cities of Magna Graecia (southern Italy) in 212 B.C., for example, one general returned bearing Greek statues and paintings with which to adorn the city, while another general displayed gold and jewels, which according to the old guard was the only proper kind of booty. With the conquest of the Greek mainland in 146 B.C., a huge volume of confiscated artworks flooded the city, overwhelming the hostility of the die-hard conservatives and establishing Rome as the prime custodian of the Hellenic artistic tradition. Geared more to copying than creating, doing rather than theorizing, the native arts in Rome were produced by an army of anonymous artisans, with most efforts directed at a burgeoning mass market.

Though much of what we call Roman art is derived from Greek models and often created by Greek artists, the Romans did make some significant and original contributions with their realistic portrait busts, landscape painting, and, especially, their architecture. Justly famous for the monumental architecture of the imperial period, the Romans must also be credited with developing the "art" of civilized living. During the early days of the Republic, more attention was paid to the efficient design of military camps than to the urban planning of Rome and other growing cities of the rapidly expanding Republic. With the shift from a simple rural to an affluent urbanized society, the Romans had to come to grips with the problems of city planning. Taking their cue from Etruscan hill towns, they learned how to design and build the basic requirements for urban life: fortifications; streets; bridges; aqueducts; sewers; town houses; apartment houses; and recreational, shopping, and civic centers.

Pompeii

With no art and very little architecture remaining from the early centuries of the Republic, we will begin our study of the arts of Rome with Pompeii, which through an accident of history is the only surviving city of the Roman Republic. The eruption of Mount Vesuvius in A.D. 79 buried Pompeii under cinders and ashes that, in effect, preserved the city as a museum of Roman civilization. Probably founded in the sixth century B.C., Pompeii was inhabited by Italic Oscans and Samnites, plus some Greeks, until its conquest by Rome in about 80 B.C.

FIGURE 10.3 *Two sections, west colonnade of the forum, Pompeii. Vesuvius looms in the right background.*

City Plan

Containing the earliest extant amphitheatre and public baths, Pompeii was built in a modified Greek grid plan around the most important early forum outside Rome (figure 10.3). Reflecting Greek influence, the Doric colonnade with super-imposed Ionic columns was a device that was later extended to four levels in the design of the Colosseum (see figure 10.15). There are, in fact, so many different elements of Etruscan, Greek, and Italic contributions to Pompeiian decoration that it is impossible to precisely determine who did what. Measuring 125′ × 466′, the civic center, or forum, was bordered on the west and east by matching two-story colonnades, each 466 feet long and ending at arches that flanked the main city Temple of Jupiter, Juno, and Minerva. One arch and a portion of the temple base can be seen in the right background of figure 10.3. Combining religious, commercial, and civil functions, forums were found in every Roman city, reflecting Roman concerns for centralized authority and control.

Domestic Architecture

Because the city-center forum was always closed to vehicular traffic, the network of streets began at the perimeter and expanded outward to the suburbs. Much as old Italian towns are today, the streets nearer the forum were lined by shops, which were flanked by houses of shopkeepers and other citizens. The *domus*, single-family residence, was entered through a front doorway set in a windowless wall that guaranteed privacy and shut out city noise and dirt. An entrance hall led to the *atrium* (figure 10.4), a typical Italic-Roman design for larger houses and for the still more elaborate villas in the surrounding

FIGURE 10.4 *Atrium, House of the Vetti, Pompeii. Photo © Interdipress, Naples.*

FIGURE 10.5   *Bust of Julius Caesar, first century* B.C.
Marble, height 38". National Archeological Museum,
Naples.

FIGURE 10.6   Augustus of Primaporta, *ca. 20* B.C. *Marble,*
height 81". Vatican Museums, Rome.

FIGURE 10.7   *Three portrait busts of Caesar Augustus.*
British Museum, London. Reproduced by courtesy of the
Trustees of the British Museum.

countryside. A rectangular, windowless court that kept
out heat while admitting light and air, the atrium had an
inwardly sloping roof that drained rainwater into the pool
below, from which it was piped to a cistern. Surrounding
the central atrium were the kitchen, parlors, and other
rooms for everyday living. Beyond the atrium were the
bedrooms, with porches fronting on an open courtyard
surrounded by a peristyle of, in this case, Doric columns.
As was customary with Roman houses, the numerous
blank walls were either brightly painted or decorated with
murals like those on the two square columns and exterior bedroom walls in figure 10.4. The combination of
Roman atrium and Hellenistic Greek peristyle court,
which was adopted in the second century B.C., makes the
Roman house or villa an ideal design for hot Mediterranean summers.

Portrait Busts

Maintaining a strong sense of identity was a major concern for Roman families; they preserved collections of
exact portrait masks in wax of their ancestors. Recognizable portrayals were therefore required, accounting for
the long tradition of starkly realistic marble portrait busts
as represented, for example, by the bust of Julius Caesar
(figure 10.5). As the man responsible for the final demise
of the embattled Republic, Caesar is depicted as history
has revealed him to be: imperious, ruthless, a charis-
matic leader of men. With their no-nonsense approach
to reality, the Romans insisted upon an exactitude that
included every wart, pimple, line, and blemish. This bust
may have been done from life; if so, it is possible that
Caesar relished the portrait, particularly the commanding tilt of the head.

There are no blemishes on the commanding statue
of Caesar Augustus from the Imperial Villa at Primaporta
(figure 10.6). Idealized in the Greek manner, this is how
Augustus intended to be seen and to be remembered—
a noble ruler. Based on the *Doryphoros* (see figure 7.18),
with the commanding gesture probably derived from
Near Eastern art, this is an official portrait. With his likeness on Roman coins and with thousands of busts like
those in figure 10.7 distributed throughout the Empire,
Augustus created the imperial image of powerful Rome.

FIGURE 10.8 *Maison Carrée, ca. 19 B.C., Nîmes, France.*

Based on Virgil's tracing of his ancestry to Aeneas, founder of Rome, Augustus's divine origins are revealed here in the cupid and the dolphin, symbols of Venus, mother of Aeneas. Indicating the secular history, the statue's cloak has fallen low enough to reveal the relief sculpture on the armor detailing the emperor's road to power. The only realistic elements are the tactile illusions of leather, metal, and cloth that give the feeling of actuality prized by Romans but considered trite by Greeks. Becoming a stock device for depicting kings, emperors, and dictators, the commanding gesture will also be seen in the figure of Christ in the Royal Portal of Chartres Cathedral (see figure 15.31) and in Michelangelo's Christ of the *Last Judgment* in the Sistine Chapel. The *Augustus of Primaporta* is a superb example of a didactic art form, probably forever after destined to serve church and state.

Architecture

Though no intact Augustan temples remain in Rome, the remarkably well preserved temple nicknamed the Maison Carrée (marble house; figure 10.8) embodies the qualities advocated by the emperor. Unlike their Greek counterparts, Roman temples stand on high podiums and are entered from the front by a single flight of steps. The open form of the Greek temple, with a walkway and three steps on all four sides, has been converted to the closed form of buildings designed to enclose space. This temple uses the rich Corinthian order (figure 10.9) favored by most Roman architects and engaged columns attached to the cella walls in a decorative device from Republican days. A small building measuring 59' × 117' with 30' columns, the Maison Carrée became a prototype of temples honoring notable emperors, much as the Jefferson Memorial

FIGURE 10.9 *Corinthian capital. Sketch from Dover Publications, New York.*

in Washington memorializes an illustrious president. This building, in fact, inspired Thomas Jefferson to utilize the classic style of Rome in his neoclassic designs of the Virginia State Capitol, the University of Virginia, and his own home of Monticello.

The Roman Arch

Rome made a lasting contribution to the development of the rounded arch and vault as structural architectural principles. Used for centuries in Asia Minor and Greece for lesser works like gates, storage areas, corridors, and sewers, the arch was exploited by Roman engineers on a massive scale. They were concerned with spanning and enclosing space, and thus used arches to build bridges,

(a)

(b)

■ **FIGURE 10.10** *(a) Semicircular arch arcade (b) Semicircular arch vault.*

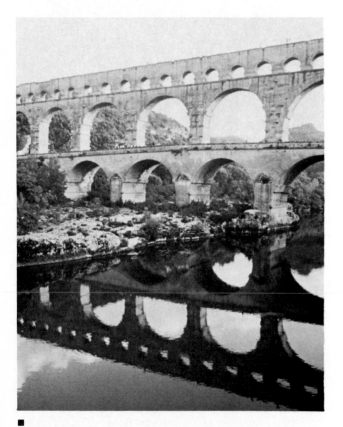

■ **FIGURE 10.11** *Pont du Gard, ca. 20–10 B.C., near Nîmes, France.*

aqueducts, baths, and basilicas, the secular structures necessary for the efficient operation of Roman cities. A semicircle of stone blocks, or bricks and mortar (figure 10.10), spanning spaces between piers or walls, the arch was better suited to the utilitarian needs of Roman engineering than the post and lintel system. Not intended to bridge large spaces, the lintel is the weaker portion of the system because it can support a limited amount of weight. To bear greater loads it must be enlarged, the columns moved closer together, or both. In the arch, the wedge-shaped blocks called *voussoirs* (voo-SWAHR) curve up to the keystone at the apex of the arch, giving strength and stability because of the mutually supporting pressures from pier to keystone. From the keystone the thrust is transmitted through the voussoirs down through the pier, or wall, to the ground. When the arches are side by side they form an arcade, as in the Pont du Gard (see figure 10.11). When extended longitudinally along its axis, the arch is called a barrel or tunnel vault, as in the Arch of Titus (see figure 10.19).

Aqueducts

Representing Roman engineering and power, aqueducts were a highly visible portion of the network of waterways and roadways that interconnected the empire. Built by Agrippa, a lieutenant under Augustus, the Pont du Gard (figure 10.11) is 180′ high and in its present condition about 900′ long. It carried water some twenty-five miles from the mountains, across the gorge of the Gard River, and into Nîmes. Spanning over 80′, each massive arch supports an arch of similar dimensions but with much less masonry, which in turn undergirds the watercourse itself. Supported by three small arches for each large one, the water flowed steadily down an approximate 1 percent grade, dropping about one foot every hundred feet. Using stones weighing up to six tons each and assembled without mortar, the bridge of the lowest arcade has been in continuous use for two thousand years.

Funerary Memorials

The best-preserved of all Roman funerary memorials, the so-called Mausoleum (figure 10.12) is actually a cenotaph that honors the dead but does not contain the remains. Erected in honor of two grandsons of Augustus who died in childhood, the three-stage structure has reliefs on the solid base and engaged Corinthian columns flanking the second-level arches. Statues of the two children are within the circular third level. The combination of reliefs, projecting cornices, squared-off arches, and rounded forms is eclectic rather than classical and illustrates how far removed Roman opulence is from Greek restraint.

Painting

In *Herakles Discovering the Infant Telephos in Arcadia* (figure 10.13) we see an example of the continuing interest in classical themes, which formed one of the bridges between Greek and Roman cultures. The powerful nude figure stands before a classically conceived woman representing the mythical Arcadia, where

FIGURE 10.13 Herakles Discovering the Infant Telephos in Arcadia, *wall painting from Herculaneum, ca.* A.D. *70, approximately 86″ × 74″. Roman copy of a Hellenistic painting of second century* B.C. *National Museum, Naples. Photo © Alinari/Art Resource.*

FIGURE 10.12 *Roman Mausoleum, ca.* A.D. *40, St.-Remy-du-Provence, France.*

everyone lived at peace with one another and with nature. The lion is painted in a vaguely impressionistic manner, while the doe in the left foreground is light, lovely, and graceful. The disparate figures look like they have been placed in a preexisting space with little concern for how they relate to each other or to the overall unity of the painting. In common with much Roman painting, the work does display, however, great technical skill in the manipulation of light, lines, and shapes, and in the illusion of three-dimensional space.

Greek Theory and Roman Practice

A comparison of the assemblage of visual images of the *Herakles* with the figure of the *Doryphoros* (see figure 7.18) illustrates some fundamental differences between Greek and Roman cultures. More concerned with practice than theory, the Romans itemized rather than conceptualized. The *Herakles* is a kind of visual catalog of a specific event: Herakles finding his son in Arcadia. The *Doryphoros* is not a specific person but a realization of the ideal athlete, the embodiment of a concept against

which individual athletes measured themselves. The Romans portrayed people as they were and the Greeks depicted them as they should be. The Romans were practical, the Greeks theoretical. It is no wonder that the Romans viewed the Greeks with awe, contempt, envy, and suspicion. The Romans accepted the world, with its imperfections as it was; the Greeks wanted something better. The quarreling Greek city-states were forcibly united by Alexander; Rome conquered the world.

That Greek culture was generally superior to any other was acknowledged by the Romans, and Greek literature, art, and architecture became basic strands in the fabric of Roman civilization. The empire was, in fact, administered in both languages—the Latin of the ruling Romans and the Greek of the conquered Hellenes. (Try to imagine Napoleon administering the French Empire in French *and* German.) Where the two cultures differed significantly was in sheer size. Athens of the Golden Age had a population of about 100,000; Imperial Rome had a much larger population and greater wealth. It also had the endless problems that plague large cities in any culture.

FIGURE 10.14 *Reconstruction of fourth-century Rome (detail) by I. Gismondi. Museum of Roman Civilization, Rome.*

FIGURE 10.15 *Colosseum, A.D. 72–80, 513' × 620' × 161' high, Rome.*

FIGURE 10.16 *Colosseum, Rome (aerial view).*

The Imperial City

Shown in figure 10.14 is part of the central section of a city with over fifty miles of streets, almost none with names, and a population in the second century A.D. of about 1,200,000. Much of the area shown was constructed by the Flavian emperors (A.D. 69–96); the monumental civic structures were completed by Nerva, Trajan, and Hadrian (A.D. 96–138).

In the far upper left of the model can be seen the Baths of Trajan; with a central complex of thermal rooms surrounded by thermal rooms further enclosed by peripheral rooms, this became the model for all subsequent imperial baths. Near the bottom of the model is the Circus Maximus, the primary stadium for chariot racing and the common meeting ground for all levels of Roman society (see the selection from Ovid on page 237). Achieving its final form in about 329 B.C. the stadium enclosed a race course measuring 220 yards × 650 yards. Seating about 250,000 spectators and operating a full racing program on 240 days of the year, the Circus Maximus could, with full houses, total about seventy million admissions a year. Thinking big was the Roman way.

Directly above the Circus Maximus are the Imperial Forums and the Claudius Aqueduct leading to the Palatine, highest of the seven hills of Rome and urban abode of the aristocracy.

The Colosseum

Seen at the upper left is the Colosseum, the single most representative building of the Roman Empire, then and now. Designed for the staging of battles between various combinations of animals and gladiators, the Colosseum seated about 50,000 spectators around an arena measuring 156' × 258'. With underground corridors for gladiators, animals, and technicians, and elaborate stage equipment for crowd-pleasing effects, the Colosseum was a complete entertainment center. Built on four levels, the exterior is unified by four super-imposed orders of columns (figure 10.15). Beginning with a simplification of the Doric column called Tuscan, the columns mount upwards through the Ionic and Corinthian orders to flat Corinthian piers called *pilasters.* Topping the wall are sockets for pennants and for a removable canvas covering that helped keep off the sun and rain. A key design unit in the exterior wall is the characteristic combination of a Roman arch flanked by a Greek order. Called the Roman arch order, the basic elements are a Roman arch set in a Greek post and lintel frame. Used in triumphal arches and other structures, this device was revived in the Italian Renaissance and can be seen today in neoclassic building facades in Europe and America.

Invented by the Romans as a derivation of Greek theatre design, the Colosseum is an amphitheatre (Gk., *amphi,* both; *theatron,* theatre). As the name indicates, this building is actually two theatres facing each other to form an oval-shaped bowl (figure 10.16). Brilliantly designed and executed, the Colosseum exemplifies the qualities the Roman architect Vitruvius (first century B.C.) considered basic for superior design: firmness, commodity, and delight. Structurally sound in its own day (firmness), the Colosseum functioned exceptionally well

■ **FIGURE 10.17** *Roman amphitheatre, first century* A.D.*; 21,000 capacity. Nîmes, France.*

as a grand arena with eighty portals for easy ingress and egress, comfortable seating, and unobstructed sightlines (commodity). Though not a prime Roman concern, it does have a quality of "delight," an aesthetic appeal that makes a work of art exalted and memorable.

Erected by the Flavian emperors, the Colosseum, also known as the Flavian Amphitheatre, was largely built by prisoners of the Jewish Wars, which had ended in A.D. 70 with the conquest of Jerusalem and the destruction of the Temple of Solomon. Dedicated by Titus in A.D. 80, the Colosseum opened with inaugural ceremonies that lasted 100 days and that were, according to contemporary accounts, very successful, costing the lives of some 9,000 wild animals and 2,000 gladiators.

The Colosseum was the largest Roman amphitheatre (see Martial's "On the Dedication of the Colosseum in Rome" on page 242), but its basic design was anything but innovative. Apparently the amphitheatre concept was first realized at Pompeii in about 80 B.C. and copied throughout the empire before finally appearing in Rome. The Roman procedure was to develop a workable design and then to increase the efficiency of later structures through improved engineering. Amphitheatres are still used today in Verona, Italy and in France at Arles and Nîmes (figure 10.17), testifying to the remarkable stability of Roman structural engineering. The amphitheatre at Verona is used for operatic productions but the one at Nîmes has many functions, from concerts to bullfights.

With stability restored after the murderous excesses of Caligula and Nero, the Flavian emperors (Vespasian, Titus, and Domitian, 69–96) presided over an even larger and richer empire. Despite attempts, especially by Vespasian, to return to the austerity of sober Republican days,

■ **FIGURE 10.18** Flavian Woman, *ca.* A.D. *80. Marble, life-size. J. Paul Getty Museum, Santa Monica, California.*

Flavian artists became highly proficient in the dynamic sculptural techniques of Praxiteles and the Hellenistic sculptors. Representative of the high fashion of the Flavian age, the portrait of a Flavian woman (figure 10.18) is notable both for the towering coiffure and for its relentless Roman realism. Undoubtedly a Flavian aristocrat, the lady is as homely as she is stylish.

FIGURE 10.19 *Arch of Titus, A.D. 81, Rome.*

FIGURE 10.20 *Column of Trajan, ca. A.D. 106–113. Marble, height 125′ with base, Rome.*

The Triumphal Arch

Julius Caesar contended that the only truly effective way of controlling conquered people was to execute every man, woman, and child. However, the practical Roman alternative to extermination was the conversion of prisoners of war into a tractable slave labor force. One of the most effective propaganda devices for impressing their bondage on the slaves was the triumphal arch, a symbolic representation of the yoke of oxen. In a ritualistic dramatization of Roman might, victorious generals marched their prisoners through hastily erected temporary arches to the accompaniment of Roman battle trumpets and drums. The overall effect was meant to be awesome and intimidating.

To commemorate his brother Titus's destruction of Jerusalem in A.D. 70, Domitian had a permanent version of the triumphal arch erected where the Via Sacra enters the Roman Forum (figure 10.19). (By the end of the empire there would be over sixty triumphal arches in Rome and many more throughout the empire.) Constructed of concrete with a marble facing, the Arch of Titus utilized a Roman arch order similar to that of the Colosseum. Massive piers with dual-engaged columns provided a post and lintel frame for a deep Roman arch vault (see figure 10.10). With a superstructure called the *attic* bearing the commemorative inscription, the walls of the vault were decorated with high reliefs depicting Titus's successful campaign against the Jews. Symbolizing a major Roman victory, the arch was also a graphic reminder for all slaves, especially the Jews who labored on the Colosseum, of the futility of opposing the might of Rome.

Trajan's Column

The assassination of Domitian in A.D. 96 ended the Flavian dynasty and ushered in the era of the so-called good emperors: Nerva, Trajan, Hadrian, Antoninus Pius, and Marcus Aurelius (96–180). The first non-Italian to occupy the throne, the brilliant Spanish general, Trajan, led Rome to the maximum expansion of her empire. Among the monuments commemorating his phenomenal successes is the Column of Trajan (figure 10.20), an unprecedented conception. Carved in low relief in 150 scenes, the 658′ frieze winds 23 times around the column as it narrates the highlights of Trajan's two campaigns into Dacia (modern Romania and Hungary). To "read" the story, it is necessary to walk around and around the column, but it soon becomes impossible to read it without binoculars. How and if this story was read in its entirety has never been satisfactorily explained. Perhaps there were special viewing balconies or perhaps slaves were stationed at the base of the monument delivering illuminating lectures and selling guidebooks.

Though the inspiration for this unusual monument is unknown, it is perhaps significant that it was placed between the Latin and Greek libraries of Trajan; the column is quite similar to library books of the time—*rotuli* (scrolls), which were wound on two spindles. The basic inspiration, however, is the "continuous narration" technique, which is so typically Roman, as opposed to Greek "simultaneous narration." The Greek unities of time, place, and action as observed in the Parthenon frieze (see figure 7.32) were apparently not suitable for the day-to-day world of empire building. Reflected in the Column

FIGURE 10.21 *Column of Trajan, detail. Photo © Alinari/Art Resource.*

FIGURE 10.22 *The Pantheon, ca.* A.D. *118–125, Rome. Photo © Alinari/Art Resource.*

of Trajan is Roman interest in biography and history; the basic unity is the focus on the leadership of Trajan while history is served by the unfolding scenes of campaigns. A detail from the bottom of the column (figure 10.21) depicts a river god, symbolizing the Danube, and landscapes as stylized stage sets. Artistic details are minimized, making the soliders the prime figures of the Roman conquest. Executed under the direction of a single artist, the frieze is a masterpiece of didactic art in the tradition of the *Augustus of Primaporta* (see figure 10.6). The column was originally topped by a statue of Trajan, which was destroyed during the Middle Ages; the figure now standing at the top is a sixteenth-century statue of St. Peter. The first pope of the Church of Rome is positioned over a visual record of two bloody Roman campaigns, symbolizing the Church's triumph over Rome.

Hadrian's Pantheon

Probably the best educated of all Roman emperors and certainly the most cosmopolitan, Hadrian (117–138) was more interested in improving the cultural life of the empire than in extending political frontiers. Indicating the extent of the Roman Empire at that time, Hadrian lived and worked in Britain, southern France, Spain, Morocco, Asia Minor, Greece, Tunisia, Greece (again), Syria, Palestine, and Egypt. He finally returned after ten years abroad to build Hadrian's Villa at Tivoli near Rome. A student of all things Greek, Hadrian was more concerned with supporting the intellectual life of Greece than with whatever took place in the mercantile environment of Rome. He did, however, strongly support the most advanced concepts of Roman architects in their designs of interior space.

One of the most revolutionary and authoritative structures ever built, the Pantheon (figure 10.22) has influenced the architecture of every age from ancient Rome to the present day. The inscription on the frieze, "M. AGRIPPA L. F. COS TERTIUM FECIT" (Marcus Agrippa, son of Lucius, consul for the third time, built this), does not refer to this building but to previous structures erected in 27–25 B.C. by Agrippa, son-in-law of Augustus.

Because the original buildings included baths and a temple called Pantheon (Gk., to all the gods), Hadrian, displaying his fine sense of Roman history, had the original inscription repeated on the new temple. With a portico 59′ high and measuring 143′ in the interior (diameter and height), the Pantheon is topped by one of the largest domes ever built. (St. Peter's dome is 140′ in diameter and that of Florence Cathedral averages 137½′.) Twenty feet thick at the outside edge, the poured concrete dome decreases to less than five feet at the center. Resting on eight enormous piers and providing interior lighting with a circular opening (*oculus*) that is nearly 30′ in diameter, the dome is coffered (indented panels) to decrease the weight without sacrificing structural strength. The water from rainstorms can be drained away in a matter of minutes by a plumbing system that still works. The Pantheon is the best preserved of all Roman buildings because it was converted into a Christian church early in the history of the Church of Rome.

The eight-column front of Corinthian capitals topping polished granite columns is, in effect, a Greek portico opening into a massive drum derived from the circular Greek tholos. One of the most astounding spatial accomplishments in architecture, the impressiveness of the interior is communicated better by the Panini painting (colorplate 13) than by any contemporary photograph. Originally painted blue, the hemisphere of concrete was highlighted with rosettes of gilded bronze set into each coffer. Softly colored columns alternate with marble panels, pilasters, and niches, forming a harmonious blend within a single, self-sufficient, uninterrupted space. Dedicated to the worship of the seven planetary gods, the Pantheon is a stunning human version of the sky itself, the Dome of Heaven.

The bronze head of Hadrian (colorplate 14), which wears a trim beard in the Greek manner, was probably created during the enlightened reign of that remarkable monarch. A combination of the staid portrait style of Republican tradition and the glamorous, more sensuous

FIGURE 10.23 Equestrian Statue of Marcus Aurelius, *ca.* A.D. *161–180. Bronze, over life size. Piazza del Campidoglio, Rome.*

FIGURE 10.24 Head of a Bearded Man, *ca.* A.D. *250. Marble, life size. J. Paul Getty Museum, Santa Monica, California.*

Hellenistic imperial style, the bust was found in the Thames River under London Bridge. That a masterful portrait of this most urbane of Roman rulers should be found in the outermost reaches of empire symbolizes the international culture of Rome. Writing during the reign of Trajan, the Greek biographer Plutarch remarked, "I am a citizen, not of Athens or of Greece, but of the world."

Marcus Aurelius

The last of the illustrious Antonine emperors,[1] Marcus Aurelius (161–180) was an unusual combination of distinguished general and Stoic philosopher. Most un-Roman in his detestation of war, he confined his military activities to defending the borders against barbarian incursions, particularly in the Balkans. It was on that distant frontier that the philosopher-king died in the performance of his stoic duty towards the state. As depicted in the only equestrian statue surviving from the ancient world (figure 10.23), the emperor wore a beard in the Greek style first adopted by Hadrian. With his right arm extended in the characteristic gesture of a general about to address his troops, the emperor is both commanding and resigned to the necessity of fulfilling his responsibilities. Vigorous and impatient, the high-spirited warhorse displays the artist's exceptional knowledge of equine anatomy. Originally the head of a conquered warrior was under the raised right hoof of the charger as a symbol of Roman dominance. That the imperial bronze survived at all was due to a case of mistaken identity; Christians mistook it for a depiction of the Emperor Constantine.

Rome in Decline

After the death of Marcus Aurelius in 180, the empire was in an almost continual state of disruption. Between 235 and 284 there were no less than 26 "barracks emperors" sponsored by various army factions. The accession of Diocletian in 284 replaced anarchy with a rigid despotism under which the Roman Senate lost the last vestige of its by then ephemeral powers. A time of agony and despair, the chaotic third century saw the flourishing of many mystery cults as people sought spiritual salvation in the midst of nihilism. Representative of the malaise of the time, the *Head of a Bearded Man* (figure 10.24) is a study in ambivalence: hopefulness coupled with despair, spiritual aspirations conflicting with the problem of sheer physical survival. It was the worst of times.

Constantine

Seizing power from his corulers, Constantine (312–337) represented the last effective authority in an empire doomed to destruction from external assaults and from internal corruption and decadence. Built to celebrate his

---

1. The very last Antonine was Commodus (180–192), the son of Marcus Aurelius. Anything but illustrious, he was corrupt, demented, and, ultimately, the victim of a household conspiracy.

■
FIGURE 10.25 *Arch of Constantine,* A.D. *312–315, Rome.*

assumption of sole imperial power, the Arch of Constantine (figure 10.25) was wholly dependent on its predecessors for its impressive appearance. In an attempt to recapture the glorious past, the three-arch design was copied from the Arch of Septimus Severus (ca. 203) in the Roman Forum, while the eight Corinthian columns are literally from the time of Domitian (81–96). The freestanding statues, with heads recarved to resemble Constantine, were lifted from monuments to Trajan, Hadrian, and Marcus Aurelius. Despite the borrowed design and transferred columns and statues, there is little trace of the Hellenic tradition. The inferior craftsmanship of the carved reliefs can be explained by a shortage of skilled artists; there had been no official relief sculpture in nearly a century. Despite the technical inadequacies, the shift from classical to a new Constantinian style appears, however, to have been deliberate. Compare, for example, the classical style of the *Augustus of Primaporta* (see figure 10.6) with the head of Constantine the Great (figure 10.26). In addition to the notable stylistic differences, it is clear that the latter is intended as a much more obvious symbol of imperial majesty *and* spiritual superiority. Part of a colossal statue enthroned in his basilica, the masterful modeling of the head demonstrates a total awareness of the Hellenistic tradition with the significant exception of the remarkably large eyes. Carved even with a marble fleck representing light reflecting from the cornea, these are not the eyes of a mere man; this is an exalted being, unique in authority and vision, with godlike eyes fixed upon infinity. Symbolizing sanctity and sometimes saintliness, oversized eyes become a convention in Early Christian and Byzantine art.

■
FIGURE 10.26 Constantine the Great, *ca.* A.D. *330.*
Marble, height 8'. Palazzo dei Conservatori, Rome.
Photo © Hirmer Fotoarchiv.

■
FIGURE 10.27 Diptych of Consul Boethius, *ca.* A.D. *487.*
Ivory miniature. Brescia Museum, Italy. Photo
© *Alinari/Art Resource.*

Though a miniature in fact and truly miniscule when compared with the head of Constantine, the *Diptych of Consul Boethius* (bow-E-thi-us; figure 10.27) is similar to the bust in that the artist has denied the physical reality of Boethius and emphasized instead his authority and spirit. Costume, body, and space are reduced to patterned lines that are more emotional than representational. One of the last Roman consuls and the author of *Consolation of Philosophy* (A.D. 524), the other-worldliness of Boethius can be compared to the physical reality of the *Augustus of Primaporta* (see figure 10.6). Both share the commanding arm gesture—a symbol of authority—but all else has changed. In the *Augustus* we see a man with supreme authority and in the *Boethius* there is depicted supreme authority that happens to be a man.

Exercises

1. Obviously the Romans admired Greek art as evidenced by so many copies; yet they were frequently uncomfortable with it. Why? Are there any parallels in American attitudes toward twentieth-century art?
2. Roman architecture was generally utilitarian (i.e., responding to public desires and expectations). Was propaganda for the state one of the functions? What do the size, mass, lines, and overall design of triumphal arches, amphitheatres, temples, baths, and the Circus Maximus tell us about the Roman Empire?
3. The style of Roman art shifted during Constantine's reign. Why? Describe the changes and speculate about the significance of the shift.
4. Edgar Allan Poe, the nineteenth-century American writer, wrote about "the glory that was Greece and the grandeur that was Rome." Explain how this statement may apply to the visual arts of the two civilizations.
5. How is the influence of Roman architecture evident in the history and culture of the United States? Consider, for example, our government buildings and athletic facilities.

Roman Music

No Roman music survives nor are there any extant musical documents or theoretical treatises. With nothing original to contribute, the Romans were content to use the brass instruments of the Etruscans and to adopt the whole of Greek musical culture. Though some musical instruments have survived, our knowledge of Roman music has been derived from sculptures, mosaics, wall paintings, and references to music by Cicero, Seneca, and Quintilian. According to the evidence, music was highly esteemed, particularly in association with poetry. Interested in the visual arts mainly as collectors, the patrician class left the messy business of painting and sculpting to artisans and slaves. Writing verse and singing to lute accompaniment was, however, a worthy pursuit for wealthy amateurs of both sexes. The arts of poetry and music added to the social graces of patricians and emperors alike. Hadrian wrote poetry in Latin and Greek and, like Antoninus Pius and the tyrant Caracalla, was an accomplished performer on the kithara and the hydraulis.[2] A kind of chamber instrument with clear and delicate tones, the effect of the hydraulis was described by Cicero as a "sensation as delectable to the ears as the most delicious fish to the palate."

2. Hydraulis (Gk., *hydor,* water; *aulos,* pipe) invented ca. 300 B.C. Of Near Eastern origin and improved on by the Greeks, this was actually a pipe organ. Air was pumped into an inverted bowl with air pressure controlled by the volume of water holding the bowl in place. Adding water increased the pressure of the air supplied to the pipes and thus the volume of sound. Though no instruments have survived, a precise clay model found in the ruins of Carthage has provided enough information for modern reconstructions.

Music of a public nature provided appropriate settings for acrobats, pantomime, popular theatre, dancing, chariot racing, gladiatorial combat, and the maneuvers of Roman troops. Commensurate with Roman ideas of grandeur, instruments were increased in number and size, particularly the trumpets and drums that relayed battle commands to the Roman legions. Quintilian, in fact, equated the brassy loudness of Roman trumpets with the supremacy of Roman arms. Audiences in amphitheatres were treated to musical spectacles featuring huge choral and instrumental groups that sometimes outnumbered the spectators. The limpid-toned hydraulis was converted to an advertising medium for the proclaiming of gladiatorial contests. Traveling on a large wagon and with vastly increased air pressure supplied by hordes of toiling slaves, the now strident tone had a reputed range of over three miles.[3]

Roman drama omitted the Greek choruses but used musical interludes throughout, all of which were composed by specialists rather than by the dramatists themselves, as had been the case with Greek drama. The aulos, called *tibia* in Latin, and the kithara were still employed much as they were in Greek plays and generally played by Greek musicians, who were usually more skilled than Roman musicians. Nero fancied himself an outstanding instrumentalist and had coins minted depicting him playing the kithara. He did not start the great fire that burned most of Rome in 64 nor, contrary to legend, did he "fiddle while Rome burned." He was blamed for the fire, however, and launched the first persecution of the new Christian sect to divert attention from himself.

Using a variety of drums plus trumpetlike instruments such as the buccina, lituus, and tuba, official bands were important components of military establishments throughout the empire. With their ceremonial music they effectively proclaimed the magnificence of the state, much as military bands have done in just about every culture since ancient times.

Summary

Roman achievements in architecture were notable and still act upon the modern world. The first to achieve mastery of enclosing space, Roman prototypes are visible today in grandiose train stations, monumental public buildings, and the ubiquitous football and soccer stadiums patterned after the Colosseum. In fact, one essential difference between the Astrodome and the Colosseum is that the latter had a removable canvas roof. With their superbly designed roads, bridges, and aqueducts, Roman engineers made essential contributions to civilizing and humanizing people that were fully as important as their monuments, buildings, and stadiums. Indeed, roads, bridges, and sewers may be as essential for the development of civilization as art, music, and literature.

Sculpture was as common in the Roman world as billboards are in the United States, but considerably more attractive. Streets, buildings, and homes were filled with portrait busts and freestanding statues or reliefs of the gods of all major and minor religions. Included were masterpieces confiscated from Greece and Egypt and mass-produced copies of Greek works of all periods. A compelling urge to create was characteristic of Greek artists, while the Romans were often content to copy. It was in portraiture and historical narrative that Roman artists excelled, precisely because they were copyists of the world as they saw it.

The little that is left of Roman painting was found mainly in the ruins of Pompeii and Herculaneum (see figure 10.13), which were buried by the eruption of Vesuvius in A.D. 79. Excavations beginning in the eighteenth century have revealed at least four major styles of painting. Whether this work was accomplished by Greek, Hellenistic, or Roman artists cannot be determined. Furthermore, later development of painting during the enlightened regimes of the Antonines may never be known. Deeply indebted to Greek developments in painting techniques, it is safe to assume that Roman painters produced works comparable to the Pantheon and the *Augustus of Primaporta*.

Culture and Human Values

The Romans were as pragmatic about their art and architecture as with most everything else in their lives. Does it do what it is supposed to do? was a more pertinent question than Is it beautiful? Portrait busts, for example, exactly recalled emperors, statesmen, and ancestors. Their function was to graphically represent a specific person, warts and all, with absolutely no doubt about the subject. The aesthetic quality was of no concern and indeed, rarely apropos.

Triumphal arches pose a similar problem. Designed to awe and intimidate Rome's conquered foes, they apparently fulfilled their function very well or else so many would not have been built. Historically interesting, they are not as artistically inspiring as other structures such as, for example, the amphitheatres.

In fact, roads, bridges, aqueducts, and amphitheatres are consistently more interesting than busts or arches. Why is this so? The answer, in a word, is engineering. An engineer is a problem solver and the Romans produced superb problem solvers. How do I cross the river? Build a bridge. How do I get fresh water daily? Construct an aqueduct. How do I get from here to there? Design a road.

Roman amphitheatres were designed to solve many problems: large capacity, easy ingress and quick exit, good sight lines, unobtrusive stage equipment, and so forth. The Colosseum is an outstanding example of Roman engineering at its best. All of its 50,000 spectators could easily see the arena, the structure could be cleared in five minutes, the sun/rain cover could be cranked into position in a few minutes and retracted just as quickly. After each contest perfume was sprayed throughout the amphitheatre through built-in ducts. Good architecture, according to the Roman architect Vitruvius, must have firmness, commodity, and delight. The Colosseum is remarkably successful on all counts thanks largely to its incredibly sophisticated engineering.

---

3. The association of the hydraulis with the so-called games in the arena, especially those with assorted lions and Christians, delayed for many centuries the introduction of the pipe organ into Christian services.

The main point about Roman pragmatism is that it usually worked, which means that, by definition, the Roman virtues of duty, honor, and love of country were true. When combined with Roman practicality and efficiency, the Roman virtues helped build the mightiest empire that the world had yet seen. Theories, concepts, ideas, and ideals may occupy a higher ground but Roman pragmatism made its civilization the dominant way of life in much of Europe, North Africa, and the Middle East.

Annotated Bibliography

Boethius, Axel, and Ward-Perkins, J. B. *Etruscan and Early Roman Architecture.* New York: Penguin Books, 1979. Comprehensive.

Brilliant, Richard. *Visual Narratives: Storytelling in Etruscan and Roman Art.* Ithaca: Cornell University Press, 1984. How narrative purpose can shape artistic conventions.

Brown, Frank E. *Cosa: The Making of a Roman Town.* Ann Arbor: University of Michigan Press, 1980. Case study of civic planning.

Grant, Michael. *The Art and Life of Pompeii and Herculaneum.* New York: Newsweek, 1979. A popular and picturesque account.

Hadas, Moses. *Imperial Rome.* Great Ages of Man Series. Alexandria, Va.: Time-Life Books, 1965. Popular account by a classical scholar.

Henig, Martin, editor. *A Handbook of Roman Art: A Comprehensive Survey of All the Arts of the Roman World.* Ithaca: Cornell University Press, 1983.

MacDonald, William L. *The Pantheon: Design, Meaning, and Progeny.* Cambridge: Harvard University Press, 1976.

Merrifield, Ralph. *London: City of the Romans.* Berkeley: University of California Press, 1983. A reconstruction of Roman London.

Nash, Ernest. *Pictorial Dictionary of Ancient Rome.* Two volumes. New York: Hacker Art Books, 1980. Illustrated guide to art and artifacts.

Sear, Frank. *Roman Architecture.* Ithaca: Cornell University Press, 1983. Comprehensive overview of a thousand years of Rome.

Smith, E. Baldwin. *Architectural Symbolism of Imperial Rome and the Middle Ages.* New York: Hacker Art Books, 1978. Makes the architecture comprehensible in terms of its political and religious significance.

Toynbee, Jocelyn M. *Animals in Roman Life and Art.* Ithaca: Cornell University Press, 1973. Animal motifs in Roman art.

UNIT 4
JUDAISM AND CHRISTIANITY

	Key Dates	People and Events	Religion	Philosophy and Theology	Art and Literature
1900	After 1900 Abraham and Israelites migrate from Ur to the Land of Canaan				
1600	**ca. 1600** Israelites follow Joseph into Egypt				
1300 1200	**1300/1200** Moses leads Children of Israel out of Egypt	**ca. 1230** Joshua takes Jericho			
1100	**ca. 1165–1050** Israelite armies battle Canaanites				
1000		**1020–1000** King Saul defeats Philistines			
900	**933–722** Kingdom of Israel **933–586** Kingdom of Judah	**1000–960** King David **960–933** King Solomon			
800			Prophet: Elijah		
700	**722** Assyria conquers Kingdom of Israel	**722–** "Lost tribes of Israel"	Prophets: Amos, Hosea, Isaiah I, Micah		
600			Jeremiah		
500	**586** Nebuchadnezzar II conquers Kingdom of Judah **539–322** Palestine vassal state of Persian Empire	**586–539** Babylonian captivity	Ezekiel Isaiah II		**ca. 550** Sacred writings in form somewhat like *Old Testament*
400					
300	**332–63** Palestine vassal state of Alexander and of Egypt				
200					
100 B.C.					*Old Testament* arranged in present form
0	**63** Palestine conquered by Rome, becomes protectorate **ca. 4 B.C.–A.D. 29** Jesus Christ	**37–4** Herod, king of Judea **27 B.C.–A.D. 14** Reign of Caesar Augustus		**Philo Judaeus** ca. 30 B.C.–A.D. 50 Hellenistic-Jewish philosopher	**Virgil** 70–19 *Eclogue IV*
A.D. 100	**50–300** Rise of papacy	**64** Persecution of Christians under Nero **70** Romans destroy Jerusalem and Temple; disperse Jews **93** Persecution of Christians under Domitian	Writing of *New Testament* (dates approx.) **55** Paul's epistles to Corinthians **60** Acts of Apostles Gospels **70** Mark **80–85** Matthew; Luke **93** Revelation **100–120** John	**Epictetus** ca. 60–110 Stoic philosopher, *Discourses*	
200	**180–476** Decline and fall of Rome	**111** Trajan classifies Christians as traitors	**d. 165?** Justin Martyr, *First Apology*	**Tertullian** ?160–240? Latin Father of Church **Origen** ?185–254? Father of Christian theology	
300		**250** Persecution of Christians under Decius	**ca. 200** *New Testament* becomes canonical Christian text	**Plotinus** 205–279 Founder of Neoplatonism	**ca. 250** Earliest known Christian church, Dura-Europos, Syria **ca. 250** *The Good Shepherd*, Catacombs of St. Calixtus, Rome
400	**300–** Growth of monasticism **313** Constantine's Edict of Milan legalizes Christianity throughout empire **325** First Council of Nicaea condemns Arian heresy **330** Constantine establishes new capital at Constantinople **375–500** Invasions of empire by barbarian tribes **395** Theodosius proclaims Christianity official and only religion of Rome	**302** Persecution of Christians under Diocletian **306–335** Reign of Constantine **314–335** Pope Sylvester I **379–395** Reign of Theodosius I; split empire into West and East; began persecution of non-Christians	**ca. 330–379** St. Basil; established rules for Greek church and Greek monasticism **374–397** St. Ambrose as Bishop of Milan	**St. Augustine** 354–430	**ca. 313–** Lateran Basilica, Rome **ca. 330–** Old St. Peter's **ca. 359** *Sarcophagus of Junius Bassus* **386–** Basilica of St. Paul's Outside-the-Walls **397** Augustine, *The Confessions*
500	**402** Ravenna new capital of Western Roman Empire **410; 455** Rome sacked by Visigoths and by Vandals **451** Attila the Hun defeated at the battle of Chalons **476** Last Roman emperor deposed **ca. 493–527** Theodoric and Ostrogothic Kingdom; capital at Ravenna	**400–600** Invasions of England by Angles and Saxons **440–461** Pope Leo I the Great; saves Rome from Attila the Hun **St. Benedict** 480–543	**ca. 400** Jerome, *Vulgate* (Latin Bible) **Augustine** 413–425 *City of God*	**Boethius** ca. 480–524? *The Consolation of Philosophy*	**425–450** Mausoleum of Galla Placidia, Ravenna **430** *Crucifixion*, Church of Santa Sabina, Rome **440–** Basilica of Santa Maria Maggiore, Rome

11

The Star and the Cross

It was pointed out in the preceding unit on Rome that life in the later years of the Empire was a matter of increasing disillusionment and pessimism. Epicureanism is grounded on pessimism; Stoicism is at best a resignation to the evil of the world; popular cults provided little abiding satisfaction. The discontent and dissatisfaction were not found only among thinkers and philosophers, but were shared by the common people. A Roman epitaph found rather frequently reveals the spirit of cynicism and disillusionment; it reads

I was not
I was
I am not
I do not care

One could scarcely go further in general world-weariness, yet the sentiment was not uncommon.

There were two conflicting tendencies during this period and earlier. One was the general disbelief in the old Olympian religion, and a cynical attitude toward emperor worship; the intellectual element in the population was skeptical about religion in general. The other was, contradictorily, the appeal of mystical cults and religions, usually of oriental origin: Mithraism, the worship of Isis, the cult of Cybele, and the like. However much scoffing or indifferent disregard there may have been at the upper level of society, the poor and uneducated were ready for the emotional appeal of any religiosity that softened their uncertainties and insecurities; there was a need for comfort and reassurance.

The genius of the Greeks was intellectual rather than moral or spiritual, and the Romans had little to add on the latter score to what they inherited from the Greeks. Both peoples had advocated the life lived according to reason. For a Plato, an Aristotle, a Cato, such a life could be worthy and satisfying, but not many men in any generation are of such caliber, and even those few are often felt to be wanting in human warmth. At best, the God whom Aristotle finds the sum of perfection is cold, distant, and aloof from human affairs: a noble concept, but again lacking warmth.

Reason, important as it is, has never been the only tool that human beings possess. Call it emotion, belief, faith—there is something that is not in the same category. No one will seriously give six good reasons why he or she loves the beloved, for love is not "reasonable." That is not to say that it is necessarily contrary to reason; it simply moves in another dimension. The "something" beyond reason may be considered the compulsion of a moral ideal or a yearning for spiritual satisfaction; it is more pronounced in some people than in others, but hardly ever totally absent in any individual. It is precisely such a range of human experience that the perhaps overly intellectualized philosophical traditions of Greece and Rome failed to satisfy.

While the Greek and Roman cultures were developing—cultures devoted to two forms of rationalism—a third and entirely different type of society had come into being in Palestine. A vast amount of pure intellectual power has gone into the development of Jewish doctrine, but the core of Judaism is faith, as faith is different from, though not opposed to reason. The Jewish religion itself, as it has had wider influence through Christianity, wove another strand into the great amalgam we call Western civilization.

The Chosen People

The Jews would have been just another set of Near Eastern tribes, small in number and lacking talent for art and invention, had it not been for their remarkable religion. Other civilizations have come and gone; Jews have maintained their culture essentially intact for four thousand years.

The Jews were first called Hebrews (from *Habiru* or *Ibri*; alien, outcast, nomad), a descriptive term used mostly by their enemies and still used today to designate the biblical Jews. However, long before the Bible was written these nomads of the desert had named themselves after the grandson of Abraham, a man originally called Jacob and subsequently named Israel. These, then, were the Israelites, the Children of Israel.

Early Jewish History

Sometime after 1900 B.C., the Israelites followed Abraham from the Sumerian city of Ur "of the Chaldees" into the lands northwest of the Euphrates river valley. Several generations later, nomads no longer, they moved west into the Land of Canaan—subsequently called Palestine after the Philistine inhabitants. Sometime after 1600 B.C., and probably prompted by famine, many Israelites followed Joseph into Egypt, where they prospered along with Joseph, who achieved a position of considerable importance. Time passed until there was a new Pharaoh "who did not know Joseph," according to the Bible. The Children of Israel were reduced to slavery but were finally delivered out of bondage by an Israelite with the Egyptian name of Moses. Leading his people out of Egypt and into Sinai (ca. 1300 B.C.), Moses gave them the concept of a single tribal god, Yahweh (later mistranslated as Jehovah), and a covenant with Yahweh based on their acceptance of the commandments that, according to the Book of Exodus, Moses had carried down the mountain.

Following the death of Moses, after about forty years "in the wilderness," the Promised Land "flowing with milk and honey" was taken by conquest, with the key city of Jericho falling to Joshua around 1230 B.C. By 1020 the twelve tribes had been unified and a monarchy forged with Saul as the first king. It was under Saul's leadership that the powerful and tenacious Philistines were finally subdued.

The height of Israelite political power was reached with the Twelve Tribes of Israel under King David (1000–960) and his son Solomon (960–933). After Solomon's death the accumulated resentment against his policies of forced labor and high taxes led to the secession of the ten northern tribes to form a separate Kingdom of Israel. The two southern tribes of Judah and Benjamin, though holding to the capital of Jerusalem, were left with the apparently weaker Kingdom of Judah.[1] (See the map: Palestine in 933 B.C.)

Israel did not survive long as a divided kingdom, falling to the Assyrians in 722. Following the standard Assyrian procedure, the kingdom was brutally ravaged and the Ten Tribes dispersed forever, to be known thereafter as the Lost Tribes of Israel. Judah managed to survive until 586, when it was conquered by Nebuchadnezzar II and most of its citizens sent into an exile known to history as the Babylonian Captivity (586–539 B.C.). The Persian conquest of Babylon freed the Jews, some of whom returned to Jerusalem where they eventually rebuilt the Temple of Solomon. No longer a commonwealth, they were politically subservient to three successive empires: the Persian (539–332); Alexander and the Ptolemies of Egypt (332–63); and the might of Rome, which proved fatal.

The Romans never did know what exactly to do with the Jews; nothing, in fact, seemed to work. After their conquest of Palestine in 63 B.C., they designated the country a Roman protectorate, a very special status.

Among other privileges, the Jews were excused from military service and permitted freedom of religion. This was not enough. In A.D. 66 the Jews launched what turned out to be their most disastrous rebellion against Rome. By A.D. 70, Jerusalem was totally destroyed and much of the population dead or driven from the land, a Diaspora (Dea-AS-po-ra; scattering) that was to last until the establishment of the State of Israel in A.D. 1948.

Four Unique Aspects of Judaism

The will to resist and to survive was based on their religion, Judaism,[2] four aspects of which were different from all other Near Eastern religions.

1. Monotheism: There was only one God and he came to be viewed as universal.
2. Covenant: God chose Israel to be his people and they accepted him as their God.
3. Graven images: Images of God or of any living thing were prohibited.
4. The name of God (Yahweh, meaning "he causes to be" or "the creator") was not to be taken "in vain," i.e., was not to be spoken.

Let us examine each of these concepts. Beginning with the Mosaic period in the Sinai, Yahweh was the primary God among many: "You shall have no other gods before me" (Exodus 20:3). This concept gradually evolved into a monotheism in which there was one Israelite God and, later, one universal God. The first people to insist upon monotheism, the Jews found this to be, throughout their history, their greatest source of strength.

The covenant was a religious bond that the Hebrews made of their own free will with Yahweh. Moses climbed the mountain and returned with knowledge of God's will—"commandments" inscribed on tablets of stone and subsequently amplified in the Torah. In a narrow sense the Torah consists of the first five books of the Bible, the so-called Pentateuch, or Books of Moses. Torah means Law but it also means "teaching" or "direction." In the broad modern sense, Torah refers to the total content of God's unending revelation to and through Israel.

The prohibition of graven images separated Judaism from all other religions, which represented their gods in a variety of ways. This stricture, designed to guard against idolatry, had the effect of nullifying any significant artistic development.

The injunction against using the Lord's name in vain emphasized a reverence unknown to other ancient religions.

In sum, Judaism was a People in covenant with God, a Book (the Hebrew Scriptures), a Way of Life, and a Hope grounded in Faith.

---

2. A term coined by Greek-speaking Jews to distinguish their religious way of life from that of the Hellenes. Though the term is late, the religion to which it refers goes back to the beginnings of Jewish spiritual life.

---

1. The residents of Judah (later called Judea) were thereafter known as Jews.

Prophecy

The Jewish prophets of the eighth to fifth centuries B.C. emerged from a tradition of augurs and seers who, as they did in other religions, sought to ascertain the divine will and to forecast the future through dreams, divinations, and induced ecstasy. Eventually these professionals were denounced as "false prophets" and replaced by a succession of preachers, mystics, moralists, and poets who felt themselves to be speaking for Yahweh. Prophets like Amos and Isaiah spoke as instruments of Yahweh's creative purpose in the lives of his people. Ethical considerations were primary and the predictive element secondary, an extension of ethical and religious tendencies into a foreseeable future. Stressing righteousness and justice, the prophets spoke and, more importantly, wrote as restorers and conservators of Israel's inspiring spiritual heritage. Not always accepted by various classes of society, they preached an uncompromising and lofty doctrine of ethical monotheism.

Amos

The first and perhaps most important of the notable eighth-century prophets, Amos preached against luxury, corruption, and selfishness, pointing the way to altruism and a higher form of religion.

¹¹Therefore because you trample upon the poor
    and take from him exactions of wheat,
you have built houses of hewn stone,
    but you shall not dwell in them;
you have planted pleasant vineyards,
    but you shall not drink their wine.
¹²For I know how many are your transgressions,
    and how great are your sins—
you who afflict the righteous, who take a bribe,
    and turn aside the needy in the gate.
¹³Therefore he who is prudent will keep silent in such a
        time;
    for it is an evil time.
¹⁴Seek good, and not evil,
    that you may live;
and so the LORD, the God of hosts, will be with you,
    as you have said.
¹⁵Hate evil, and love good,
    and establish justice in the gate;
it may be that the LORD, the God of hosts,
    will be gracious to the remnant of Joseph.

Amos 5:11–15

⁴"Woe to those who lie upon beds of ivory,
    and stretch themselves upon their couches,
and eat lambs from the flock,
    and calves from the midst of the stall;
⁵who sing idle songs to the sound of the harp,
    and like David invent for themselves instruments of
        music;
⁶who drink wine in bowls,
    and anoint themselves with the finest oils,
    but are not grieved over the ruin of Joseph!
⁷Therefore they shall now be the first of those to go into
        exile,
    and the revelry of those who stretch themselves shall
        pass away."

⁸The Lord GOD has sworn by himself
(says the LORD, the God of hosts):
"I abhor the pride of Jacob,
    and hate his strongholds;
    and I will deliver up the city and all that is in it."

Amos 6:4–8

Isaiah

Active around 740–700 B.C., Isaiah[3] was the prophet of faith, preaching an abiding trust in the providence of God. Also a prophet of doom like the other preachers, Isaiah saw that a purging was necessary in the interest of spiritual betterment in a kindlier and more loving world. He was among the first to picture a warless world under the benign rule of a Prince of Peace, a Messiah ("anointed one") descended from the House of David.

¹There shall come forth a shoot from the stump of Jesse,
    and a branch shall grow out of his roots.
²And the Spirit of the LORD shall rest upon him,
    the spirit of wisdom and understanding,
    the spirit of counsel and might,
    the spirit of knowledge and the fear of the LORD.
³And his delight shall be in the fear of the LORD.
He shall not judge by what his eyes see,
    or decide by what his ears hear;
⁴but with righteousness he shall judge the poor,
    and decide with equity for the meek of the earth;
and he shall smite the earth with the rod of his mouth,
    and with the breath of his lips he shall slay the
        wicked.
⁵Righteousness shall be the girdle of his waist,
    and faithfulness the girdle of his loins.
⁶The wolf shall dwell with the lamb,
    and the leopard shall lie down with the kid,
and the calf and the lion and the fatling together,
    and a little child shall lead them.
⁷The cow and the bear shall feed;
    their young shall lie down together;
    and the lion shall eat straw like the ox.
⁸The sucking child shall play over the hole of the asp,
    and the weaned child shall put his hand on the
        adder's den.
⁹They shall not hurt or destroy
    in all my holy mountain;
for the earth shall be full of the knowledge of the LORD
    as the waters cover the sea.

Isaiah 11:1–9

For unto us a child is born,
    to us a son is given;
and the government will be upon his shoulder,
    and his name will be called
"Wonderful Counselor, Mighty God,
Everlasting Father, Prince of Peace."

Isaiah 9:6

---

3. The Book of Isaiah contains prophecies attributed to Isaiah (chaps. 1–39) and those by an unknown prophet of the fifth century, known today as Second Isaiah (chaps. 40–66).

Ezekiel

During the Babylonian Captivity when his people were far from home, their city and Temple destroyed, Ezekiel preached the universality of the faith and of the personal relationship between the individual Jew and his God. God existed wherever the people were; the city and the Temple were not indispensable. Each person had the option of selecting good over evil or even turning from evil ways to a righteous life.

25"Yet you say, 'The way of the Lord is not just.' Hear now, O house of Israel: Is my way not just? Is it not your ways that are not just? 26When a righteous man turns away from his righteousness and commits iniquity, he shall die for it; for the iniquity which he has committed he shall die. 27Again, when a wicked man turns away from the wickedness he has committed and does what is lawful and right, he shall save his life. 28Because he considered and turned away from all the transgressions which he had committed, he shall surely live, he shall not die. 29Yet the house of Israel says, 'The way of the Lord is not just.' O house of Israel, are my ways not just? Is it not your ways that are not just?

30"Therefore I will judge you, O house of Israel, every one according to his ways, says the Lord GOD. Repent and turn from all your transgressions, lest iniquity be your ruin. 31Cast away from you all the transgressions which you have committed against me, and get yourselves a new heart and a new spirit! Why will you die, O house of Israel? 32For I have no pleasure in the death of any one, says the Lord GOD; so turn, and live."

Ezekiel 18:25–32

The Second Isaiah

The celebrated unknown prophet of the exile, known as Second Isaiah, was the great architect of Jewish ethical monotheism. Climaxing the prophetic movement, his ethical and religious insight set the sufferings of the Jews against a background of God's eventual redemption of the entire world. He saw the Jews as a people chosen to exemplify in their characters and lives the spiritual presence of the Lord. "A light to the nations" (Isaiah 42:1), their suffering had not been in vain. The world would say of Israel:

3He was despised and rejected by men;
   a man of sorrows, and acquainted with grief,
and as one from whom men hide their faces
   he was depised, and we esteemed him not.
4Surely he has borne our griefs
   and carried our sorrows,
yet we esteemed him stricken,
   smitten by God, and afflicted.
5But he was wounded for our transgressions,
   he was bruised for our iniquities;
upon him was the chastisement that made us whole,
   and with his stripes we are healed.
6All we like sheep have gone astray;
   we have turned every one to his own way;
and the LORD has laid on him
   the iniquity of us all.

Isaiah 53:3–6

They were to return to the New Jerusalem where the work of redemption would be a model for all the world.

1Comfort, comfort my people,
   says your God.
2Speak tenderly to Jerusalem,
   and cry to her
that her warfare is ended,
   that her iniquity is pardoned,
that she has received from the LORD'S hand
   double for all her sins.
3A voice cries:
   "In the wilderness prepare the way of the LORD,
   make straight in the desert a highway for our God.
4Every valley shall be lifted up,
   and every mountain and hill be made low;
the uneven ground shall become level,
   and the rough places a plain.
5And the glory of the LORD shall be revealed,
   and all flesh shall see it together,
   for the mouth of the LORD has spoken."
6A voice says, "Cry!"
   And I said, "What shall I cry?"
All flesh is grass,
   and all its beauty is like the flower of the field.
7The grass withers, the flower fades,
   when the breath of the LORD blows upon it;
   surely the people is grass.
8The grass withers, the flower fades;
   but the word of our God will stand for ever.
9Get you up to a high mountain,
   O Zion, herald of good tidings,
life up your voice with strength,
   O Jerusalem, herald of good tidings,
   lift it up, fear not;
say to the cities of Judah,
   "Behold your God!"

Isaiah 40:1–9

The profound insights of Second Isaiah strongly influenced later Judaism but were even more significant for early Christianity. His writings were studied and pondered by those who awaited the coming of the Messiah. In particular the story of the sufferings of Israel (see Isaiah 53:3–6 above) was so specific and individualized that later generations came to believe that he was speaking of a particular person, a Messiah who would redeem the world through his suffering. In Jesus of Nazareth the early Christians found that Messiah.

Some of the Teachings of Jesus

Jesus was born in the year we now call 4 B.C., or possibly 6 B.C.,[4] a time that was ripe for his message of hope and love. He preached for possibly three years, but in the two thousand years since that time—whether people have believed his teachings or not, whether they have acted upon them or not—men and women throughout what was once called "Christendom" have been hearing the teachings of Jesus. What are the cardinal points of his teaching? These: that One God (a Personal Spirit, not an abstract idea nor a principle) is not only the Creator, but also the loving Father of all humankind; that all people are consequently the children of God, and that as a result

---

4. The idea of denominating the years of the Christian era was introduced in A.D. 525 by Dionysius Exiguus; the B.C. sequence extending backwards from the birth of Christ was not added until the seventeenth century.

all men and women are brothers and sisters; that as children of God, human beings are capable of better lives than they lead; that their human inadequacies, imperfections, and shortcomings can be forgiven if they are repentant; that life is eternal, and death is not extinction; that "all the Law and the Prophets" hangs upon the joint commandment to "Love thy God, and thy neighbor as thyself"; and that the intention—the act of the personality—is of greater importance than the deed—the act of the person.

Not the least of the appeals of Christianity is the joy and hope that it carries with it because of its doctrine of Christ as Redeemer. Theologically, one of several explanations may be stated in this way: because of the sin of Adam, humankind as a whole carried with it the taint of original sin, a sort of moral disease. But God, loving all people, sought to redeem them. This was accomplished through the mystery of Incarnation in which God became man, taking to himself all of humankind's inherent guilt. Then, in Christ's death as a mortal, the guilt is atoned, and human beings are set free. The possibility of salvation and eternal life with God, from that moment on, lies before each person. In a world-weary and guilt-ridden time like that of the late Roman Empire, even as in our own time, such a possibility can bring hope and joy to the believer.

All of these teachings affect the world of here and now, for Christianity is a "social" religion; that is, its effects are seen in the daily acts of people in relation to other people. It is not essentially a religion in which the believers isolate themselves from others and seek individual salvation through private contemplation. It is a religion of involvement for most Christians. Love must prompt the worshipper to present acts of love, mercy, and compassion as evidence of an inward change. The act of the believer in Christ cannot wait upon another world. If three words could be used to sum up this teaching, those three, with their many implications, might be those Jesus addressed to Peter: "Feed my sheep."

Early Christianity

Jesus left no written record of his work nor are there any surviving accounts contemporary with his ministry. A collection of his sayings, written in Aramaic, disappeared before A.D. 60, and scholars are still debating some of the references to Jesus in the Dead Sea Scrolls. His life, character, and message inspired hope and joy but this, coupled with the absence of documentation, was not sufficient for a theology. By definition, Christian theology is a discipline concerned with God and God's relation to the world. It remained for the followers of Jesus to construct a systematic theology as a solid foundation for the propagation of the new faith.

Written accounts in Greek began to appear several decades after Christ's death: Saint Paul's epistles to the Corinthians (ca. A.D. 55); the Acts of the Apostles (ca. 60); the four Gospels telling the story of Jesus: Mark (ca. 70); Matthew and Luke (ca. 80–85); and John (ca. 100–120). By about A.D. 200 the texts were revised in Alexandria into a canonical Christian text.

Paul

An upper-class Jew of Orthodox parentage, Saint Paul (Saul of Tarsus) was first a persecutor of Christians and later one of the most ardent missionaries of the faith. A Hellenized Jew, Paul took the position that "there is neither Jew nor Greek" (Galatians 3:28). Contending at first with Paul, Saint Peter believed instead that the Christian message was intended only for Jews and converted Gentiles. Paul argued (and Peter later agreed) that the Law was no longer valid, even for Jews; it could only bring people to an understanding of their dependence on Christ in a new covenant with Christ the Saviour. Sweeping aside Jewish rituals and practices, Paul, the "apostle to the Gentiles," carried the message of salvation through faith in Christ throughout the eastern Mediterranean and into Rome itself.

An enthusiastic teacher, organizer, and administrator, Paul was neither a theologian nor a logician. He was convinced that Christian faith was not a matter of reasoning but rather an act of faith. Confirmed by his own conversion experience on the road to Damascus, Paul believed that faith was a gift of God. Christians had only to accept the discipline of the Church and to lead quiet, faithful, and firmly Christian lives.

Logos and John

A synthesis of Judaic, Greek, and Christian ideas, Christian theology developed separately from the work of the Apostle Paul. In his Prologue, which introduces the fourth Gospel, John states that:

> In the beginning was the Word, and the Word was with God, and the Word was God. He was in the beginning with God; all things were made through him, and without him was not anything made that was made. In him was life, and the life was the light of men. The light shines in the darkness, and the darkness has not overcome it.
>
> John 1:1–5

In the Greek of the New Testament, "word" is a translation of *logos*, a word as old as the Greek language. Introduced by Herakleitos in the fifth century B.C., logos was a principle of cosmic interpretation. Constantly changing, the cosmos was a total process of becoming controlled by an agency called logos. To avoid chaos, change had to conform to fixed patterns; logos was thus an intelligent and eternal agent that imposed an orderly process upon change.

Though the concept of logos is vague and unspecified in Plato and Aristotle, the Stoics took it from them but used logos to designate a divine element present in all men. It remained for Philo Judaeus of Alexandria (ca. 30 B.C.—A.D. 50) to go beyond the Stoics and to consciously construct a synthesis of Hebraic and Hellenic philosophy. Philo saw logos as a mediator between God and man and as a translation of the Hebrew word for "wisdom." As a personal agent of God in the creation of the world, logos was not identical with God but distinctly separate from him.

The Prologue of John is thus a creation story; Jesus is a divine being whose existence antedates the world itself. God's relation to this imperfect world was through the intervention of the logos; in Christ "the Word became flesh and dwelt among us, full of grace and truth" (John 1:14). It can be said that Herakleitos and Second Isaiah meet in John, representing two contrasting civilizations, which are synthesized into a Christian philosophy of history.[5]

The Impact of Christianity

Objective study of the historical Jesus and the facts about his life and death yields no clear-cut answers to some basic questions. Was he the Messiah, "Son of God," "son of man," a religious reformer, prophet, humanitarian, inspired teacher? Or was he, as his Jewish critics claim, a blasphemer and an imposter? Based on currently available sources there has been no final answer acceptable to everyone. The multiplicity of Christian beliefs (Catholic, Orthodox, varieties of Protestantism) testifies to the different interpretations of the evidence.

Nevertheless, the Christian emphasis on the importance of the human personality carries a religious sanction weightier than the speculations of the philosophers. The worth and dignity of the individual soul, and its responsibility to itself, has been a shaping influence in Western thought.

As discussed earlier, reality, for the Greeks, was the individual and for the Romans it was the state. What the two cultures had in common was their secular view of the world. Neither the Greeks nor the Romans rejected religion or religious beliefs. There were, in fact, several religions and many believers but religion did not have a central role in the classical world. The rise of Christianity caused a massive shift from a secular to a religious world view with God as the ultimate reality (see color map 7: Christianity in A.D. 500). The new view of reality caused major changes in values and value systems, which will be considered later in this volume.

It is small wonder that Christianity spread from an obscure, remote province of the Roman Empire to practically throughout the known world within the first century of its existence; its message of hope, joy, salvation, and a merciful and loving God in a world that knew only the sterner aspects of justice made its welcome assured. Encompassing the whole of life, and able to take to itself the good things of any civilization, Christianity could appropriate to itself the best of Greek thought, as well as the most notable product of Rome: its law and organization. With the passage of time, it produced such diverse offshoots as the elegance and beauty of Chartres Cathedral and the horror and brutality of the Inquisition; but its impact upon the Western world is fundamental.

---

5. See chap. 13 for subsequent developments in Christian theology.

Exercises

1. What were the significant events that occurred on the following dates (most of which are approximate)? 1900 B.C., 1300, 1230, 1000, 933, 586–539, 363–32, 63, 4 B.C., A.D. 64, 200, 313. What was going on in Egypt and Mesopotamia on or about these dates (through 63 B.C.)?
2. Four aspects of Judaism were different from all other Near Eastern religions. What were these and how did they differ from other religions?
3. How do the Old Testament prophets differ from a Greek seer such as Teiresias in *Oedipus the King?*
4. What were the basic teachings of Jesus and how did these differ from the Judaism of his time?
5. Trace the changing (evolving) meanings of the term *logos* from Herakleitos through its use in John 1:14.

Literary Selections

The Bible (Greek, Ta Biblia, The Books) has exercised a more profound and continuous influence upon Western civilization than has any other literary work. By its style alone, it has burnished the tongues of poets and writers from Chaucer to Shakespeare to Lincoln, and its ethical tenets have become basic to the codes and customs of Western culture. Of its two main divisions, the Old Testament (thirty-nine books in the King James Version) was written almost entirely in Hebrew (with a little Aramaic) from the eleventh to the second century B.C. The New Testament (twenty-seven books in the King James Version) was written in Greek from about A.D. 40 to 150.

Divided into three parts, the Hebrew Scripture (Old Testament) consists of the Law (Pentateuch or Torah), the Prophets, and the Hagiographa (Writings). The Book of Job is from the Hagiographa.

THE BOOK OF JOB

Because the Book of Job is not included in this text, the reader is referred to any version of the Bible that may be available.[6] The following comments and Exercises may be used in conjunction with your Old Testament reading about the incredible trials of Job.

The problem of human suffering, particularly the suffering of the innocent, the just, and the good, has confused humankind since the beginning of time, particularly when people believe in a just and benevolent God. The Book of Job, written sometime after the seventh century B.C., tackles this problem as few books do. The author is unknown (indeed there is a strong possibility that the prose, prologue, and epilogue were originally a unit, and that the poetic drama is an interpolation), and the hero, Job, may or may not have been a historical character. It seems probable that the book is addressed to all of Israel after one of the frequent persecutions of the Jews.

---

6. The translations included in this chapter are all from the American Revised Standard Version (RSV).

Perhaps the author is attempting to explain to his people the nature of their suffering. If one considers the final answer from a completely rational point of view—as the Greeks, the Romans, and twentieth-century Americans would—one is left unsatisfied, for the attempt to probe God's secrets with the unaided human mind has seldom brought satisfactory results. If the reader can somehow translate his or her questioning into the realm of faith and mystery, an intuitive understanding may be reached.

From verses 1–5 in chapter 1, we must accept the fact that Job is a completely good man, and totally loyal to God. Job's comforters hold to an old religious concept of a simple cause-and-effect relationship between God and man: if man is upright, God will reward him; if he is evil, God will punish him. The generation gap is quite apparent when the youth, Elihu, speaks in chapter 32 and begins to introduce a totally new idea of the nature of the God-man relationship, an idea that is developed as God speaks out of the whirlwind.

The reader should not expect a logical development of ideas up to chapter 32. Rather, Job's searing doubts are explored with ever-greater intensity, and the arguments for the old religious idea are reiterated by the three comforters. Although this is not a drama in the strict sense of the word, the reader should try to imagine the tone of voice of the speakers. Notice, for example, the timid way in which Eliphaz begins his argument in chapter 4 after sitting on the ground for seven days and seven nights, or how Bildad's argument in chapter 25 sputters to a quick conclusion. What is Elihu's tone after listening to the lengthy discussions of Job?

Exercises

1. The reader might question the role of Satan at the first of the book. As one of the children of God, what force does he represent? A force for evil, almost as powerful as God himself?
2. One of the central arguments of Job's comforters is that the wicked are always destroyed, while the good prosper. In chapter 21 Job answers this argument. What is the basis for the argument of the comforters? What is the basis for Job's final answer?
3. In all the discussion up to Elihu's outburst the four men are searching for something not understood in the governing of the world. Sometimes this takes the form of sinfulness, which Job does not recognize, sometimes a question about the ways of God in determining the course of the universe. Using this search for the "something not understood" as a key question, follow all of the speeches.
4. How does Elihu's rebuke to the three old men foreshadow the revelation given from God in the voice out of the whirlwind? Question very carefully God's answer to the problem that is faced in the book. What is He really saying?
5. Do you find the final rewarding of Job with the twofold return of everything that he has lost a satisfactory conclusion to the book?

6. This Hebrew book and the play *Oedipus the King* have much in common in that both represent the downfall of a good man through the intervention of God or gods. Do you see any difference in the spirit of the inquiry between the Hebrew and the Greek exploration of the problem?

PSALMS OF DAVID

The third part of the Hebrew Bible is a collection of late writings, including the Psalms, a hymnal (Psalter) reflecting the whole history of Jewish worship. The Psalmists sing Israel's praise of God the creator, intone their sorrow for national guilt and tribulations, and carol the songs of salvation. Following are two Psalms of salvation and glory.

24 The earth is the LORD'S and the fulness thereof,
the world and those who dwell therein;
for he has founded it upon the seas,
    and established it upon the rivers.
Who shall ascend the hill of the LORD?
    And who shall stand in his holy place?
He who has clean hands and a pure heart,
    who does not lift up his soul to what is false,
    and does not swear deceitfully.
He will receive blessing from the LORD,
    and vindication from the God of his salvation.
Such is the generation of those who seek him,
    who seek the face of the God of Jacob.   *Selah*
Lift up your heads, O gates!
    and be lifted up, O ancient doors!
    that the King of glory may come in.
Who is the King of glory?
    The LORD, strong and mighty,
    The LORD, mighty in battle!
Lift up your heads, O gates!
    and be lifted up, O ancient doors!
    that the King of glory may come in!
Who is this King of glory?
    The LORD of hosts,
    he is the King of glory!   *Selah*

150 Praise the LORD!
Praise God in his sanctuary;
    praise him in his mighty firmament!
Praise him for his mighty deeds;
    praise him according to his exceeding greatness!
Praise him with trumpet sound;
    praise him with lute and harp!
Praise him with timbrel and dance;
    praise him with strings and pipe!
Praise him with sounding cymbals;
    praise him with loud clashing cymbals!
Let everything that breathes praise the LORD!
Praise the LORD!

Apparently composed during the Babylonian Captivity (586–538 B.C.), Psalm 137 is a Lamentation. Though the condition of the Jews in Babylon was relatively favorable, the mourning is caused by the destruction of Jerusalem and by their own separation from the homeland. This magnificent poem was especially prominent in the worship services of American slaves, who viewed slavery as Babylonian or Egyptian captivity, an enforced exile from the African homeland.

137 By the waters of Babylon,
there we sat down and wept,
      when we remembered Zion.
On the willows there
      we hung up our lyres.
For there our captors
      required of us songs,
and our tormentors, mirth, saying,
      "Sing us one of the songs of Zion!"
How shall we sing the LORD'S song
      in a foreign land?
If I forget you, O Jerusalem,
      let my right hand wither!
Let my tongue cleave to the roof of my
            mouth,
      if I do not remember you,
if I do not set Jerusalem
      above my highest joy!
Remember, O LORD, against the E'domites
      the day of Jerusalem,
how they said, "Rase it, rase it!
      Down to its foundations!"
O daughter of Babylon, you devastator!
      Happy shall he be who requites you
      with what you have done to us!
Happy shall he be who takes your little
            ones
      and dashes them against the rock!

ECCLESIATES

From the Writings part of the Old Testament, Ecclesiastes (Greek, the preacher) is representative of pessimistic Oriental wisdom (teaching) literature. It dates from the third century B.C. and reflects some of the inroads of Greek civilization, but not enough to disturb the basic philosophy that all is vanity and that a young man should enjoy his youth.

3 For everything there is a season, and a time for every
      matter under heaven:
a time to be born, and a time to die;
a time to plant, and a time to pluck up what is planted;
a time to kill, and a time to heal;
a time to break down, and a time to build up;
a time to weep, and a time to laugh;
a time to mourn, and a time to dance;
a time to cast away stones, and a time to gather stones
      together;
a time to embrace, and a time to refrain from embracing;
a time to seek, and a time to lose;
a time to keep, and a time to cast away;
a time to rend, and a time to sew;
a time to keep silence, and a time to speak;
a time to love, and a time to hate;
a time for war, and a time for peace.
What gain has the worker from his toil?

I have seen the business that God has given to the sons of men to be busy with. He has made everything beautiful in its time; also he has put eternity into man's mind, yet so that he cannot find out what God has done from the beginning to the end. I know that there is nothing better for them than to be happy and enjoy themselves as long as they live; also that it is God's gift to man that every one should eat and drink and take pleasure in all his toil. I know that whatever God does endures for ever; nothing can be added to it, nor anything taken from it; God has made it so, in order that men should fear before him. That which is, already has been; that which is to be, already has been; and God seeks what has been driven away.

Moreover I saw under the sun that in the place of justice, even there was wickedness, and in the place of righteousness, even there was wickedness. I said in my heart, God will judge the righteous and the wicked, for he has appointed a time for every matter, and for every work. I said in my heart with regard to the sons of men that God is testing them to show them that they are but beasts. For the fate of the sons of men and the fate of beasts is the same; as one dies, so dies the other. They all have the same breath, and man has no advantage over the beasts; for all is vanity. All go to one place; all are from the dust, and all turn to dust again. Who knows whether the spirit of man goes upward and the spirit of the beast goes down to the earth? So I saw that there is nothing better than that a man should enjoy his work, for that is his lot; who can bring him to see what will be after him?

THE SERMON ON THE MOUNT

Matthew 5–7

The New Testament contains four sections: (1) the Gospels and Acts of the Apostles, (2) the Epistles of Paul, (3) the pastoral and general Epistles, and (4) the Book of Revelation. Mark's Gospel emphasizes the human aspect of Jesus, while Matthew and Luke include substantial additions dealing mainly with the birth and teaching of Jesus, including the Sermon on the Mount and the parables. The basic ethical teachings of Christ are presented in the Sermon on the Mount, in which the Mosaic Ten Commandments are compared with a new ethic. Beginning with the statement "You have heard that it was said to the men of old," Jesus takes each commandment in turn and contrasts it with his own commandment. As presented by Matthew, Jesus is the new Moses expounding a new Torah, which commands a higher righteousness than that found even in the best of Judaism.

Seeing the crowds, he went up on the mountain, and when he sat down his disciples came to him. And he opened his mouth and taught them, saying:

"Blessed are the poor in spirit, for theirs is the kingdom of heaven.

"Blessed are those who mourn, for they shall be comforted.

"Blessed are the meek, for they shall inherit the earth.

"Blessed are those who hunger and thirst for righteousness, for they shall be satisfied.

"Blessed are the merciful, for they shall obtain mercy.

"Blessed are the pure in heart, for they shall see God.

"Blessed are the peacemakers, for they shall be called sons of God.

"Blessed are those who are persecuted for righteousness' sake, for theirs is the kingdom of heaven.

"Blessed are you when men revile you and persecute you and utter all kinds of evil against you falsely on my account. Rejoice and be glad, for your reward is great in heaven, for so men persecuted the prophets who were before you.

"You are the salt of the earth; but if salt has lost its taste, how can its saltness be restored? It is no longer good for anything except to be thrown out and trodden under foot by men.

"You are the light of the world. A city set on a hill cannot be hid. Nor do men light a lamp and put it under a bushel, but on a stand, and it gives light to all in the house. Let your light so shine before men, that they may see your good works and give glory to your Father who is in heaven.

"Think not that I have come to abolish the law and the prophets; I have come not to abolish them but to fulfill them. For truly, I say to you, till heaven and earth pass away, not an iota, not a dot, will pass from the law until all is accomplished. Whoever then relaxes one of the least of these commandments and teaches men so, shall be called least in the kingdom of heaven; but he who does them and teaches them shall be called great in the kingdom of heaven. For I tell you, unless your righteousness exceeds that of the scribes and Pharisees, you will never enter the kingdom of heaven.

"You have heard that it was said to the men of old, 'You shall not kill; and whoever kills shall be liable to judgment.' But I say to you that every one who is angry with his brother shall be liable to judgment; whoever insults his brother shall be liable to the council, and whoever says, 'You fool!' shall be liable to the hell of fire. So if you are offering your gift at the altar, and there remember that your brother has something against you, leave your gift there before the altar and go; first be reconciled to your brother, and then come and offer your gift. Make friends quickly with your accuser, while you are going with him to court, lest your accuser hand you over to the judge, and the judge to the guard, and you be put in prison; truly, I say to you, you will never get out till you have paid the last penny.

"You have heard that it was said, 'You shall not commit adultery.' But I say to you that every one who looks at a woman lustfully has already committed adultery with her in his heart. If your right eye causes you to sin, pluck it out and throw it away; it is better that you lose one of your members than that your whole body be thrown into hell. And if your right hand causes you to sin, cut it off and throw it away; it is better that you lose one of your members than that your whole body go into hell.

"It was also said, 'Whoever divorces his wife, let him give her a certificate of divorce.' But I say to you that every one who divorces his wife, except on the ground of unchastity, makes her an adulteress; and whoever marries a divorced woman commits adultery.

"Again you have heard that it was said to the men of old, 'You shall not swear falsely, but shall perform to the Lord what you have sworn.' But I say to you, do not swear at all, either by heaven, for it is the throne of God, or by the earth, for it is his footstool, or by Jerusalem, for it is the city of the great King. And do not swear by your head, for you cannot make one hair white or black. Let what you say be simply 'Yes' or 'No'; anything more than this comes from evil.

"You have heard that it was said, 'An eye for an eye and a tooth for a tooth.' But I say to you, Do not resist one who is evil. But if any one strikes you on the right cheek, turn to him the other also; and if any one would sue you and take your coat, let him have your cloak as well; and if any one forces you to go one mile, go with him two miles. Give to him who begs from you, and do not refuse him who would borrow from you.

"You have heard that it was said, 'You shall love your neighbor and hate your enemy.' But I say to you, Love your enemies and pray for those who persecute you, so that you may be sons of your Father who is in heaven; for he makes his sun rise on the evil and on the good, and sends rain on the just and on the unjust. For if you love those who love you, what reward have you? Do not even the tax collectors do the same? And if you salute only your brethren, what more are you doing than others? Do not even the Gentiles do the same? You, therefore, must be perfect, as your heavenly Father is perfect.

"Beware of practicing your piety before men in order to be seen by them; for then you will have no reward from your Father who is in heaven.

"Thus, when you give alms, sound no trumpet before you, as the hypocrites do in the synagogues and in the streets, that they may be praised by men. Truly, I say to you, they have their reward. But when you give alms, do not let your left hand know what your right hand is doing, so that your alms may be in secret; and your Father who sees in secret will reward you.

"And when you pray, you must not be like the hypocrites; for they love to stand and pray in the synagogues and at the street corners, that they may be seen by men. Truly, I say to you, they have their reward. But when you pray, go into your room and shut the door and pray to your Father who is in secret; and your Father who sees in secret will reward you.

"And in praying do not heap up empty phrases as the Gentiles do; for they think that they will be heard for their many words. Do not be like them, for your Father knows what you need before you ask him. Pray then like this:

'Our Father who art in heaven,
Hallowed be they name.
Thy kingdom come,
Thy will be done,
    On earth as it is in heaven.
Give us this day our daily bread;
And forgive us our debts,
    As we also have forgiven our debtors;
And lead us not into temptation,
    But deliver us from evil.'

"For if you forgive men their trespasses, your heavenly Father also will forgive you; but if you do not forgive men their trespasses, neither will your Father forgive your trespasses.

"And when you fast, do not look dismal, like the hypocrites, for they disfigure their faces that their fasting may be seen by men. Truly, I say to you, they have their reward. But when you fast, anoint your head and wash your face, that your fasting may not be seen by men but by your Father who is in secret; and your Father who sees in secret will reward you.

"Do not lay up for yourselves treasures on earth, where moth and rust consume and where thieves break in and steal, but lay up for yourselves treasures in heaven, where neither moth nor rust consumes and where thieves do not break in and steal; for where your treasure is, there will your heart be also.

"The eye is the lamp of the body. So, if your eye is sound, your whole body will be full of light; but if your eye is not sound, your whole body will be full of darkness. If then the light in you is darkness, how great is the darkness!

"No one can serve two masters; for either he will hate the one and love the other, or he will be devoted to the one and despise the other. You cannot serve God and mammon.

"Therefore I tell you, do not be anxious about your life, what you shall eat or what you shall drink, nor about your body, what you shall put on. Is not life more than food, and the body more than the clothing? Look at the birds of the air: they neither sow nor reap nor gather into barns, and yet your heavenly Father feeds them. Are you not of more value than they? And which of you by being anxious can add one cubit to his span of life? And why be anxious about clothing? Consider the lilies of the field, how they grow; they neither toil nor spin; yet I tell you, even Solomon in all his glory was not arrayed like one of these. But if God so clothes the grass of the field, which today is alive and tomorrow is thrown into the oven, will he not much more clothe you, O men of little faith? Therefore do not be anxious, saying, 'What shall we eat?' or 'What shall we drink?' or 'What shall we wear?' For the Gentiles seek all these things; and your heavenly Father knows that you need them all. But seek first his kingdom and his righteousness, and all these things shall be yours as well.

"Therefore do not be anxious about tomorrow, for tomorrow will be anxious for itself. Let the day's own trouble be sufficient for the day.

"Judge not, that you be not judged. For with the judgment you pronounce you will be judged, and the measure you give will be the measure you get. Why do you see the speck that is in your brother's eye, but do not notice the log that is in your own eye? Or how can you say to your brother, 'Let me take the speck out of your eye,' when there is the log in your own eye? you hypocrite, first take the log out of your own eye, and then you will see clearly to take the speck out of your brother's eye.

"Do not give dogs what is holy; and do not throw your pearls before swine, lest they trample them underfoot and turn to attack you.

"Ask, and it will be given you; seek, and you will find; knock, and it will be opened to you. For every one who asks receives, and he who seeks finds, and to him who knocks it will be opened. Or what man of you, if his son asks him for a loaf, will give him a stone? Or if he asks for a fish, will give him a serpent? If you then, who are evil, know how to give good gifts to your children, how much more will your Father who is in heaven give good things to those who ask him? So whatever you wish that men would do to you, do so to them; for this is the law and the prophets.

"Enter by the narrow gate; for the gate is wide and the way is easy, that leads to destruction, and those who enter by it are many. For the gate is narrow and the way is hard, that leads to life, and those who find it are few.

"Beware of false prophets, who come to you in sheep's clothing but inwardly are ravenous wolves. You will know them by their fruits. Are grapes gathered from thorns, or figs from thistles? So, every sound tree bears good fruit, but the bad tree bears evil fruit. A sound tree cannot bear evil fruit, nor can a bad tree bear good fruit. Every tree that does not bear good fruit is cut down and thrown into the fire. Thus you will know them by their fruits.

"Not every one who says to me, 'Lord, Lord,' shall enter the kingdom of heaven, but he who does the will of my Father who is in heaven. On that day many will say to me, 'Lord, Lord, did we not prophesy in your name, and cast out demons in your name, and do many mighty works in your name?' And then will I declare to them, 'I never knew you; depart from me, you evil-doers.'

"Every one then who hears these words of mine and does them will be like a wise man who built his house upon the rock; and the rain fell, and the floods came, and the winds blew and beat upon that house, but it did not fall, because it had been founded on the rock. And everyone who hears these words of mine and does not do them will be like a foolish man who built his house upon the sand; and the rain fell, and the floods came, and the winds blew and beat against the house, and it fell; and great was the fall of it."

And when Jesus finished these sayings, the crowds were astonished at his teaching, for he taught them as one who had authority, and not as their scribes.

Exercises

1. It has been said that this Sermon represents the ethics of the Kingdom of Heaven. What sort of moral conduct is expected of citizens who claim to live under the rule of God? That is, what seems to be the general *spirit* of the behavior that Jesus teaches?
2. Jesus gave only three or four commands while Moses gave over 600 commandments. In what sense, therefore, does Jesus mean that he has "come to fulfill the law"? (Consider the entire message of the sermon.)

FROM FIRST CORINTHIANS

The Apostle Paul wrote his letters to the Corinthians during the years A.D. 54 to 56. Perhaps the most familiar of all his Epistles is chapter 13 of 1 Corinthians in which Paul speaks eloquently of the place of love in Christian living.

13 If I speak in the tongues of men and of angels, but have not love, I am a noisy gong or a clanging cymbal. And if I have prophetic powers, and understand all mysteries and all knowledge, and if I have all faith, so as to remove mountains, but have not love, I am nothing. If I give away all I have, and if I deliver my body to be burned, but have not love, I gain nothing.

Love is patient and kind; love is not jealous or boastful; it is not arrogant or rude. Love does not insist on its own way; it is not irritable or resentful; it does not rejoice at wrong, but rejoices in the right. Love bears all things, believes all things, hopes all things, endures all things.

Love never ends; as for prophecy, it will pass away; as for tongues, they will cease; as for knowledge, it will pass away. For our knowledge is imperfect and our prophecy is imperfect; but when the perfect comes, the imperfect will pass away. When I was a child, I spoke like a child, I thought like a child, I reasoned like a child; when I became a man, I gave up childish ways. For now we see in a mirror dimly, but then face to face. Now I know in part; then I shall understand fully, even as I have been fully understood. So faith, hope, love abide, these three; but the greatest of these is love.

Exercises

1. Is Paul's poetic message necessarily limited to Christians?
2. How and to what extent might it speak to Buddhists? Hindus? Muslims? Atheists?

FIVE PARABLES

I

(Matthew 18:23–35)

"Therefore the kingdom of heaven may be compared to a king who wished to settle accounts with his servants. When he began the reckoning, one was brought to him who owed him ten thousand talents; and as he could not pay, his lord ordered him to be sold, with his wife and children and all that he had, and payment to be made. So the servant fell on his knees, imploring him, 'Lord, have patience with me, and I will pay you everything.' And out of pity for him the lord of that servant released him and forgave him the debt. But that same servant, as he went out, came upon one of his fellow servants who owed him a hundred denarii; and seizing him by the throat he said, 'Pay what you owe.' So his fellow servant fell down and besought him, 'Have patience with me, and I will pay you.' He refused and went and put him in prison till he should pay the debt. When his fellow servants saw what had taken place, they were greatly distressed, and they went and reported to their lord all that had taken place. Then his lord summoned him and said to him, 'You wicked servant! I forgave you all that debt because you besought me; and should not you have had mercy on your fellow servant, as I had mercy on you?' And in anger his lord delivered him to the jailers, till he should pay all his debt. So also my heavenly Father will do to every one of you, if you do not forgive your brother from your heart."

II

(Matthew 20:1–16)

"For the kingdom of heaven is like a householder who went out early in the morning to hire laborers for his vineyard. After agreeing with the laborers for a denarius a day, he sent them into his vineyard. And going out about the third hour he saw others standing idle in the market place; and to them he said, 'You go into the vineyard too, and whatever is right I will give you.' So they went. Going out again about the sixth hour and the ninth hour, he did the same. And about the eleventh hour he went out and found others standing; and he said to them, 'Why do you stand here idle all day?' They said to him, 'Because no one has hired us.' He said to them, 'You go into the vineyard too.' And when evening came, the owner of the vineyard said to his steward, 'Call the laborers and pay them their wages, beginning with the last, up to the first.'

And when those hired about the eleventh hour came, each of them received a denarius. Now when the first came, they thought they would receive more; but each of them also received a denarius. And on receiving it they grumbled at the householder, saying, 'These last worked only one hour, and you have made them equal to us who have borne the burden of the day and the scorching heat.' But he replied to one of them, 'Friend, I am doing you no wrong; did you not agree with me for a denarius? Take what belongs to you, and go; I choose to give to this last as I give to you. Am I not allowed to do what I choose with what belongs to me? Or do you begrudge my generosity?' So the last will be first, and the first last."

III

(Luke 10:30–37)

"A man was going down from Jerusalem to Jericho and he fell among robbers, who stripped him and beat him, and departed, leaving him half-dead. Now by chance a priest was going down that road; and when he saw him he passed by on the other side. So likewise a Levite, when he came to the place and saw him, passed by on the other side. But a Samaritan, as he journeyed, came to where he was; and when he saw him, he had compassion, and went to him and bound up his wounds, pouring on oil and wine; then he set him on his own beast and brought him to an inn, and took care of him. And the next day he took out two denarii and gave them to the innkeeper, saying, 'Take care of him; and whatever more you spend, I will repay you when I come back.' Which of these three, do you think, proved neighbor to the man who fell among the robbers?" He said, "The one who showed mercy on him." And Jesus said to him, "Go and do likewise."

IV

(Luke 15:11–32)

"There was a man who had two sons; and the younger of them said to his father, 'Father, give me the share of property that falls to me.' And he divided his living between them. Not many days later, the younger son gathered all he had and took his journey into a far country, and there he squandered his property in loose living. And when he had spent everything, a great famine arose in that country, and he began to be in want. So he went and joined himself to one of the citizens of that country, who sent him into his fields to feed swine. And he would gladly have fed on the pods that the swine ate; and no one gave him anything. But when he came to himself he said, 'How many of my father's hired servants have bread enough and to spare, but I perish here with hunger! I will arise and go to my father, and I will say to him, "Father, I have sinned against heaven and before you; I am no longer worthy to be called your son; treat me as one of your hired servants." ' And he arose and came to his father. But while he was yet at a distance, his father saw him and had compassion, and ran and embraced him and kissed him. And the son said to him, 'Father, I have sinned against heaven and before you; I am no longer worthy to be called your son.' But the father said to his servants, 'Bring quickly the best robe, and put it on him; and put a ring on his hand, and shoes on his feet; and bring the fatted calf and kill it, and let us eat and make merry; for this my son was dead, and is alive again; he was lost, and is found.' And they began to make merry.

Now his elder son was in the field; and as he came and drew near to the house, he heard music and dancing. And he called one of the servants and asked what this meant. And he said to him, 'Your brother has come, and your father has killed the fatted calf, because he has received him safe and sound.' But he was angry and refused to go in. His father came out and entreated him, but he answered his father, 'Lo, these many years I have served you, and I never disobeyed your command; yet you never gave me a kid, that I might make merry with my friends. But when this son of yours came, who has devoured your living with harlots, you killed for him the fatted calf!' And he said to him, 'Son, you are always with me, and all that is mine is yours. It was fitting to make merry and be glad, for this your brother was dead, and is alive; he was lost, and is found.' "

V

(Matthew 25:14–30)

"For it [the Kingdom of Heaven] will be as when a man going on a journey called his servants and entrusted to them his property; to one he gave five talents, to another two, to another one, to each according to his ability. Then he went away. He who had received the five talents went at once and traded with them; and he made five talents more. So too, he who had the two talents made two talents more. But he who had received the one talent, went and dug in the ground and hid his master's money. Now after a long time the master of those servants came and settled accounts with them. And he who had received the five talents came forward, bringing five talents more, saying, 'Master, you delivered to me five talents; here I have made five talents more.' His master said him, 'Well done, good and faithful servant; you have been faithful over a little, I will set you over much; enter into the joy of your master.' And he also who had the two talents came forward, saying, 'Master, you delivered to me two talents; here I have made two talents more.' His master said to him, 'Well done, good and faithful servant; you have been faithful over a little, I will set you over much; enter into the joy of your master.' He also who had received the one talent came forward, saying, 'Master, I knew you to be a hard man, reaping where you did not sow, and gathering where you did not winnow; so I was afraid, and I went and hid your talent in the ground. Here you have what is yours.' But his master answered him 'You wicked and slothful servant! You knew that I reap where I have not sowed, and gather where I have not winnowed? Then you ought to have invested my money with the bankers, and at my coming I should have received what was my own with interest. So take the talent from him, and give it to him who has the ten talents. For to every one who has will more be given, and he will have abundance; but from him who has not, even what he has will be taken away. And cast the worthless servant into the outer darkness; there men will weep and gnash their teeth.' "

Exercises

The East has always been fond of teaching by parable, the brief narrative that by comparison provides a way of getting at a truth. It is not quite like an algebraic problem, to be solved by substituting terms: "x = y," "a = b," and the like. It is rather a way of stimulating the imagination, of getting at the point by *insight*. Jesus was following an ancient, well-established tradition in teaching by parables. These stories must be understood on an exceedingly literal level; they mean what they say; but they do not stop there—the mind goes on to seize upon the inherent likenesses, the points to be compared. Here are some questions over the parables in the text.

1. "The Wicked Servant." What prompted the action of the servant's lord, at the beginning and at the end? What is the specific fault of the servant? What was the point that Jesus was trying to convey?
2. "The Vineyard." Imagine a disciple of Plato, who wrote the whole treatise of the *Republic* in order to consider the question "What is Justice?", commenting upon this story. In two or three sentences, what would his opinion be? Imagine a disciple of Jesus trying to answer, again in two or three sentences. Where is the point of departure between the two?
3. "The Good Samaritan." Why does Jesus make a *Samaritan* the subject of his tale? In trying to modernize it, what word would you pick instead? (On second thought—better *not* answer that question!) What fault or shortcoming among his contemporaries was Jesus pointing out?
4. "The Prodigal Son." It is always tempting to feel a great deal of sympathy for the elder brother in this story. When you do so (or when you side with the workers in the vineyard who had worked all day), what *basis* of judgment are you using? How does this measuring rod of what is just differ from that of Jesus?
5. "The Talents." Which of the other parables is this most like? As a story it is harsh and forbidding; how would you answer the argument that it does not portray a merciful and loving God?

REVELATION

For several centuries before and after Christ, there flourished a distinctive writing known as apocalypse or revelation. Apocalyptic thought was based on the Jewish eschatological[7] view of history. A portion of the Book of Daniel is an apocalypse, and Paul included several apocalyptic verses in 2 Thessalonians. The last book of the Bible, called Revelation or Apocalypse of John, is the only full apocalypse in the New Testament. Writing to seven beseiged churches around A.D. 93 during Domitian's savage persecution of Christians, John of Patmos declares, in visionary terms, the ultimate triumph over the empire and his perception of a new heaven, a new earth,

---

7. Eschatology (Gk., *eschatos,* furthest) is a branch of theology dealing with the last things, such as death, judgment, resurrection, and immortality.

FIGURE 11.1 The Fourth Horseman of the Apocalypse, *Angers Tapestries, Angers Castle, France. Height ca. 8'. Woven by Nicolas Bataillel in 1375/80 in Paris, this is the oldest known French tapestry.*

and a new Jerusalem after all souls have been raised from the dead for the Last Judgment. In the early Church there was a widespread belief that the Second Coming of Christ was imminent.

In the following selection, Christ opens four of the seven seals, releasing the Four Horsemen of the Apocalypse: Conquest, War, Famine, and Death (figure 11.1).

6 Now I saw when the Lamb opened one of the seven seals, and I heard one of the four living creatures say, as with a voice of thunder, "Come!" ²And I saw, and behold, a white horse, and its rider had a bow; and a crown was given to him, and he went out conquering and to conquer. ³When he opened the second seal, I heard the second living creature say, "Come!" ⁴And out came another horse, bright red; its rider was permitted to take peace from the earth, so that men should slay one another; and he was given a great sword. ⁵When he opened the third seal, I heard the third living creature say, "Come!" And I saw, and behold, a black horse, and its rider had a balance in his hand; ⁶and I heard what seemed to be a voice in the midst of the four living creatures saying, "A quart of wheat for a denarius, and three quarts of barley for a denarius, but do not harm oil and wine!"

⁷When he opened the fourth seal, I heard the voice of the fourth living creature say, "Come!" ⁸And I saw, and behold, a pale horse, and its rider's name was Death, and Hades followed him; and they were given power over a fourth of the earth, to kill with sword and with famine and with pestilence and by wild beasts of the earth.

Revelation 6:1–8

Following the Last Judgment, John presents a golden vision of the world to come.

21 Then I saw a new heaven and a new earth; for the first heaven and the first earth had passed away, and the sea was no more. ²And I saw the holy city, new Jerusalem, coming down out of heaven from God, prepared as a bride adorned for her husband; ³and I heard a great voice from the throne saying, "Behold, the dwelling of God is with men. He will dwell with them, and they shall be his people, and God himself will be with them; ⁴he will wipe away every tear from their eyes, and death shall be no more, neither shall there be mourning nor crying nor pain any more, for the former things have passed away."

Revelation 21:1–4

Summary

The Graeco-Roman secular world was gradually superseded by two strains of religion, first by Judaism and later by Christianity. The basic strength of the Jews was their religion, the first montheistic religion of the Western world. Judaism was, briefly stated, a people who had a covenant with God, a book (the Hebrew Scriptures), a way of life, and a hope based on faith. This is what sustained them through conquests by Assyrians, Babylonians, Persians, Alexander, and the Romans. They were without a homeland from the Diaspora (scattering) in A.D. 66 until the reestablishment of the state of Israel in 1948.

The strongest impact upon Rome was that of Christianity, a new faith derived partly from Judaism and based on the teachings of Jesus, who was recognized by Christians as the Messiah. With its doctrine of Christ as the Redeemer, Christianity was a religion of joy and hope, particularly in the weary, guilt-ridden days of the late Roman Empire.

Culture and Human Values

The rise of Rome caused a shift from the Greek view of the individual as the ultimate reality to one in which reality was the state. With the decline of the empire and the rise of Christianity the view of reality shifted once again. God became the ultimate reality and the goal of all Christians was to join Him in the Heavenly Kingdom.

The advent of Christianity also caused a major change in values. Prudence, temperance, fortitude, and justice were accepted as the four cardinal virtues (as earlier identified by Plato and the Stoics) to which were added the Christian (theological) virtues of faith, hope, and love. Justice was administered as best they could by courts of justice in the City of Man but only God the Father could dispense infallible justice in the City of God.

Annotated Bibliography

Judaism: General History and Culture

Albright, William F. *From the Stone Age to Christianity.* Baltimore: Johns Hopkins Press, 1957. A standard work that traces the rise of monotheism.

Beltz, Walter. *God and the Gods.* Translated by Peter Heinegg. New York: Penguin Books, 1983. Relates biblical stories to religious traditions of surrounding cultures.

Bright, John. *A History of Israel.* Philadelphia: Westminister Press, 1972. Excellent survey by a noted biblical scholar.

Encyclopaedia Judaica. The indispensable reference work on all things Jewish.

Kenyon, Kathleen. *Archaeology in the Holy Land.* New York: Frederick A. Praeger, 1960. Interesting study of one of the richest archaeological areas in the world.

Miller, Madeleine S., and Miller, J. Lane. *Harper's Encyclopedia of Bible Life.* New York: Harper & Row, 1978. Solid information on everyday life and culture in the biblical period.

Orlinsky, H. M. *Ancient Israel.* Ithaca: Cornell University Press, 1960. The best brief introduction.

Scholem, G. G. *The Messianic Idea in Judaism.* London: Allen & Unwin, 1971. The nature of Jewish expectations concerning the Messiah.

Christianity: General History and Culture

Cohn, Haim. *The Trial and Death of Jesus.* New York: Harper and Row, 1971. Assembles the historical evidence to reconstruct Jewish and Roman legal procedures.

Johnson, Paul. *A History of Christianity.* New York: Atheneum, 1976. A detailed survey from the Apostolic and Patriarchal Ages to the present.

McCasland, S. Vernon. *The Pioneer of Our Faith: A New Life of Jesus.* New York: McGraw-Hill Book Company, 1964. Placing Jesus firmly in his Jewish roots, a modern Christian scholar analyzes how he understood himself and his teachings.

Meeks, Wayne A. *The First Urban Christians: The Social World of the Apostle Paul.* New Haven: Yale University Press, 1983. What it was like to be an ordinary Christian in the Roman Empire.

Papini, Giovanni. *Life of Christ.* Translated by Dorothy Canfield Fisher. New York: Harcourt, Brace, & World, 1951. A vivid, powerful biography by a foremost Italian man of letters.

Pelikan, Jaroslav. *Jesus Through the Centuries: His Place in the History of Culture.* New Haven: Yale University Press, 1985. A stimulating, informative, and illustrated study of the changing role of Christ in cultural movements of Western civilization.

Wilken, Robert L. *The Christians as the Romans Saw Them.* New Haven: Yale University Press, 1985. A fascinating account of the Christian movement from a non-Christian perspective.

Translations and Expositions of the Bible

Bruce, F. F. *The English Bible: A History of Translations from the Earliest English Versions to the New English Bible.* New York: Oxford University Press, 1961.

Frye, Northrop. *The Great Code: The Bible and Literature.* New York: Harcourt, Brace, Jovanovich, 1982. A renowned critic examines the continuing significance of the Bible as the single most important influence in the imaginative tradition of Western art and literature.

Gastor, Theodor H. *The Dead Sea Scrolls.* Garden City, N.Y.: Anchor Books, 1976. Assesses the significance for biblical studies of this modern find of ancient manuscripts.

Glatzer, Nahum, ed. *The Dimensions of Job: A Study and Selected Readings.* New York: Schocken Books, 1969. A collection of critical and scholarly discussions of this religious and literary masterpiece.

Jeremias, J. *The Parables of Jesus.* New York: Charles Scribner's Sons, 1963. A study of Jesus' use of the ancient Jewish teaching form.

Laymon, Charles M., ed. *The Interpreter's One-Volume Commentary on the Bible.* New York: Abingdon Press, 1971. The most authoritative one-volume reference work with scholarly introductions and commentary on each book, including the Apocrypha.

May, Herbert G., and Metzger, Bruce M., eds. *The Oxford Annotated Bible.* New York: Oxford University Press, 1962. The Revised Standard Version with introductions, notes, articles, and maps.

Pritchard, J. B., ed. *Ancient Near Eastern Texts Relating to the Old Testament.* Princeton, N. J.: Princeton University Press,1955. Mesopotamian and Egyptian documents that exhibit provocative parallels with biblical texts.

Stendahl, K. *The Bible and the Role of Women.* Philadelphia: Fortress Press, 1966.

12

The Beginnings of Christian Art

The first two centuries of Christianity had little need for art in any form. Meeting in small groups in private homes, early Christians conducted simple services centered around the Eucharist, the consecrated bread and wine commemorating Christ's sacrifice on the cross. Dating from about 250 the earliest known church building is a Greek peristyle house in Dura-Europos, Syria. Suitable for a congregation of no more than sixty, this was a private home converted to liturgical use though it possessed neither decorations nor architectural distinction. There is, in fact, no surviving Christian art from the first two centuries and very little from the third century, and that almost entirely from the catacombs of Rome.[1]

Roman Catacombs

Initially and during most of the first two centuries, Christians were buried in regular Roman cemeteries. Rejecting cremation (the usual procedure for the lower classes) because of their belief in the Resurrection, Christians continued burying their dead in surface cemeteries except in the outskirts of Rome, Naples, and Syracuse, where porous stone (tufa) was easily excavated for subterranean tombs. During the late second century Christian communities became increasingly interested in separate burial areas where they could, in privacy, perform rites for the dead and also safeguard the tombs. Because Roman law permitted no burials within city limits, Christian families or groups bought land on hillsides alongside the major highways leading into Rome, sites that already contained the funerary monuments of wealthy Roman families. Utilizing surface buildings and subterranean passages, these cemeteries were ideally suited to Christian concerns for seclusion and security.

At no time, however, were the catacombs exclusively Christian nor were they used as secret meeting places; Roman officials knew the location and extent of the burial grounds. There were, after all, some thirty-eight subterranean cemeteries outside Rome in which were interred about four million bodies.

The Roman catacombs had up to five subterranean levels with superimposed niches for sarcophagi eight to ten deep in each passage. Each cemetery included small chapels for burial and commemorative services. In the chapels and sometimes over the burial niches are found the earliest examples of Christian figurative art. Executed by artisans working by lamplight in a dark, dank, and undoubtedly malodorous environment, the representations were generally simple and often hastily executed. However, neither the client nor the artist was preoccupied with aesthetics; Christians were mainly interested in conveying a message or a prayer that would be understood by the Christian community and, above all, by God.

The Orant

The most common representation in the catacombs was the *orant* (OR-an; from the Latin word for *praying;* figure 12.1), a figure presented in full frontality, standing with arms raised in prayer or supplication. The orant can symbolize the soul of the deceased praying for salvation or it can reflect the Hellenistic view, a personification in human form of abstract ideas like resurrection or salvation.

---

1. See the Time Chart on page 268 for an overview of the development of Christianity and of Christian art.

FIGURE 12.1 Orant, *ca.* A.D. *300. Catacombs of St. Priscilla, Rome. Photo © Hirmer Fotoarchiv.*

FIGURE 12.2 The Good Shepherd, *ca.* A.D. *250. Ceiling painting, Catacombs of St. Callixtus, Rome. Photo © Hirmer Fotoarchiv.*

The Good Shepherd

The figure of Jesus as *The Good Shepherd* (figure 12.2), a commonly used representation of Christ throughout the centuries, appears frequently in catacomb frescoes. As might be expected, the Good Shepherd motif can be found in most cultures in which sheepherding is an important occupation. There is, for example, the *Calf-Bearer* (see figure 7.5) of Archaic Greek sculpture and, in the Hebraic tradition, David the shepherd boy, giant-killer, psalmist, and king. Christ as the Good Shepherd is a symbol of the guardian of the faithful of his church; further, Jesus was a descendent of the David who tended sheep in Palestine.

Christian Symbols

Artistic representation of the concepts inherent in the new religion caused difficulties never dreamed of by Egyptian, Greek, and Roman artists. The Greeks, for example, had created the gods in their own image, thus making the divinities instantly available for artistic representation: Zeus with a thunderbolt symbolizing the power principle; Poseidon with his trident; Aphrodite as the Goddess of Love, and so forth. How, then, was the Christian artist to depict such abstractions as the Trinity, the Holy Spirit, salvation, redemption, the Eucharist, immortality? In time, artists worked out a variety of solutions using biblical stories, parables, and symbols. The idea of immortality, for example, could be represented through biblical scenes of salvation: Moses leading his people out of Egypt; Jonah released from the whale; Daniel escaping from the lion's den; Lazarus rising from his tomb. The anchor came to represent hope, the dove was peace or the Holy Spirit, and the palm meant victory through martyrdom. Symbolizing Christ is the Khi-Rho (KYE-ro) monogram, which superimposes the first two letters of Christ's name (Khristos) in Greek: ☧ . The first and last letters of the Greek alphabet, Alpha (**A**) and Omega (Ω), symbolize infinity as in Christ's statement, "I am Alpha and Omega, the Beginning and the End." Multiple meanings are found in the symbol of the fish: (1) the Last Supper; (2) Christian evangelism as represented in Christ's exhortation to his fishermen disciples to be "fishers of men"; and (3) an anagram upon a Greek phrase, the initial letters of which form the Greek word *ikhthys,* or *fish* (figure 12.3).

The one event that was not symbolized in catacombs paintings was the Crucifixion. The most ignoble and horrible method of Roman execution, crucifixion was reserved for criminals judged guilty of foul and heinous acts; Christ was crucified by the Romans as an "enemy of the state," treason being the worst of all crimes. For early Christians, the simple geometric form of the cross was all that was needed to symbolize Christ's sacrifice. Perhaps the earliest extant crucifixion scene produced for a public place is a small, wooden, low-relief panel on one of the doors of the Church of Santa Sabina (figure 12.4). Set amidst a door rich with elaborately carved panels this, the simplest panel, appears to be a deliberate attempt to tone down the horror of the crucifixion.

FIGURE 12.3 Greek anagram:

$$
\begin{array}{l}
\mathrm{I}\eta\sigma o\upsilon\varsigma \\
\mathrm{X}\rho\iota\sigma\tau o\varsigma \\
\Theta\varepsilon o\upsilon \\
\text{'}\Upsilon\iota o\varsigma \\
\Sigma\omega\tau\eta\rho
\end{array}
$$

FIGURE 12.3 *Anagram as derived from the Greek for "Jesus Christ, the Son of God, Savior."*

FIGURE 12.4 Crucifixion, *from the west door of the Church of Santa Sabina, ca.* A.D. *430, Rome. Wood, 11″ × 15¾″. Photo © Hirmer Fotoarchiv.*

Christian Sculpture

Early Christians also refrained from producing sculpture in the round, especially life-size figures. God's commandment to Moses that "Thou shall not make unto thee any graven images" remained basic to Christianity though religious conservatives chose to interpret this injunction literally. The recognition by the early church fathers of the didactic and educational value of art was summed up by Pope Gregory the Great (rules 590–604): "Pictures are used in the church in order that those who are ignorant of letters may, merely by looking at the walls, read there what they were unable to read in books." Supplementing this realistic position was the theological argument that since Jesus was "made flesh and dwelt among us," he had a human likeness and nature that could be represented in art. Conservatives were nevertheless suspicious of freestanding statues because they associated these with the gods of other religions, which is the main reason why there was very little monumental sculpture between the fourth and tenth centuries.

Two very rare three-dimensional sculptures do survive from fourth-century Rome. Classical in pose and reminiscent of the catacomb painting in figure 12.2, the *Good Shepherd* (figure 12.5) is as carefully detailed as the finest Hellenistic genre sculpture. Stylistically it still relates to the *Calf-Bearer* (see figure 7.5) that was created about a thousand years earlier.

The statue of *Christ Enthroned* (figure 12.6) depicts Christ as a young, clean-shaven philosopher or emperor. Features, clothing, and gestures are classical, as is the smooth, idealized face. Not accepted until the Byzantine era, though certainly the universal image today, the concept of a bearded Christ was probably Syrian in origin. Because this was art of the spirit rather than the flesh, literal depiction was not the goal; this is Christ the symbol, the Son of God. Just as the image of Christ is venerated as if it were the person, so too can a cross or relic be venerated. Nevertheless, the existence of these two sculptures is unusual and might even be construed as images from another religion if very similar figures did not also appear on innumerable early Christian sarcophagi.

FIGURE 12.5 Good Shepherd, *ca.* A.D. *350. Marble, height 39″. Vatican Museums, Rome. Photo © Hirmer Fotoarchiv.*

By the middle of the third century important church leaders were entombed in stone sarcophagi, but the practice was not widely accepted until Christianity was legalized in the fourth century. Drawing on both classical sources and catacomb paintings, the superb *Jonah Sarcophagus* (figure 12.7) depicts the Jonah story in a continuous narration, a series of successive episodes in which Jonah appears three times and the strangely serpentine "whale" twice. (In Jonah 1:17, this is "a great fish.") Reading from left to right: Jonah is cast naked into a swirling sea by the sailors and heads directly into the mouth of the waiting whale; after the confused whale disgorges Jonah, the latter ends up sleeping nude under a protective arbor of gourds. Noah appears in a miniscule box floating on the sea to the right of the second whale, while in the upper left-hand corner Jesus addresses a tiny mummy standing in front of a tomb, thus paralleling the raising of Lazarus with the Noah and Jonah stories. Though using biblical material to communicate the idea of salvation, the artist was clearly influenced by classical sculptors.

By the middle of the fourth century, sarcophagi began to emphasize New Testament scenes, as evidenced in the *Sarcophagus of Junius Bassus* (figure 12.8). The front panel, illustrated here, is divided into ten reliefs on two levels. The top level includes: (1) the Sacrifice of Isaac, (2) the Arrest of St. Peter, (3) Christ Enthroned between St. Peter and St. Paul, and (4–5) Christ before Pilate. The bottom level shows: (1) the Misery of Job, (2) Adam and Eve after the Fall, (3) Christ's Entry into Jerusalem, (4) Daniel in the Lion's Den, and (5) St. Paul Led to His Martyrdom. Many interpretations are possible for a series this complex: The sacrifice of Isaac is in response to God's command, as is the testing of Job; Daniel, Abraham, and Job represent salvation; the fall of Adam and Eve represents the condition of humanity that is redeemed by Christ's sacrifice; the triumphal entry into Jerusalem signals the eternal triumph of

■
FIGURE 12.6 Christ Enthroned, *ca.* A.D. *350–360.*
Marble, smaller than life size. National Museum, Rome.
Photo © Hirmer Fotoarchiv.

■
FIGURE 12.7 The Jonah Sarcophagus, *late third century* A.D. *Lateran Museum, Rome. Photo © Hirmer Fotoarchiv.*

■ **FIGURE 12.8** The Sarcophagus of Junius Bassus, *ca.* A.D. *359. Marble, 46½″ × 96″, St. Peter's, Rome. Photo © Hirmer Fotoarchiv.*

the Resurrected Christ, depicted directly above. The implications are endless. All of the Old and New Testament figures look like Romans of the time and, indeed, the central top panel shows the Roman sky god Caelus holding up the firmament on which Christ is resting his feet.

The Age of Constantine

Christianity made its great leap forward after Constantine proclaimed freedom of religion in the Edict of Milan:

> When we, Constantine Augustus and Licinius Augustus, met so happily at Milan, and considered together all that concerned the interest and security of the State, we decided . . . to grant to Christians and to everybody the free power to follow the religion of their choice, in order that all that is divine in the heavens may be favorable and propitious towards us and towards all who are placed under our authority.
> From a rescript issued at Nicomedia by Licinius, June 13, 313.[2]

Though it came soon after the two most severe and methodical persecutions of Christians, by Decius in 249–251 and by Diocletian in 303–305, this declaration of religious freedom found organized Christianity ready to build churches and otherwise assume a prominent role in the empire.

■ **FIGURE 12.9** *Roman basilica, Volubilis, Morocco, third century* A.D.

Basilicas

For centuries the Romans had constructed basilicas, large buildings that served as meeting halls, mercantile centers, halls of justice, and the like. The basilica was a prototype of the kind of large, dignified structure Christians needed for worship services. For example, the basilica at Volubilis (figure 12.9) originally had five aisles and four rows of arcades like the one pictured here. Serving as a hall of justice for a large Roman colony, the building has the usual Roman arches with Corinthian pilasters punctuating the heavy columns.

None of the great basilica-type churches erected in Constantine's Rome have survived as such. Old St. Peter's was replaced by the present church, and hardly anything original remains of St. John Lateran after numerous restorations. St. Paul's Outside the Walls was destroyed

2. Laotantius, *De mortibus persecutorum,* xlviii. Constantine did not assume sole leadership of the empire until 324, when he had Licinius, his coregent, executed.

FIGURE 12.10   *Interior, St. Paul's Outside the Walls, begun 386 A.D., Rome. Etching by Giambattista Piranesi, 1749.*

FIGURE 12.11   *Schematic floor plan of St. Paul's, Rome.*

by fire in 1823 and faithfully reconstructed in 1854, insofar as that was possible. However, the etching by Piranesi (figure 12.10) is of the original church and clearly illustrates a basic design used for nearly all Western churches throughout the entire medieval period. The secular basilica was usually entered from its longitudinal sides, but Christians shifted the entrances to a shorter side, usually the western end, thus orienting the building along a longitudinal axis. The interior space was divided into a large area called the *nave,* because it seemed to symbolize a ship (*navis,* the ship of souls), flanked by two aisles on each side (see figure 12.11). The nave joins a secondary space, the *transept,* which is placed at right angles to the nave proper and forms an interior Latin cross. Later churches would lengthen the transept so that even the exterior walls assumed a cruciform shape, the most characteristic church design in Western Christendom. Behind the transept is a semicircular space called an *apse* (aps) in which the altar is placed on a raised platform. The nave was covered with an A-shaped truss roof; at a level well below the nave roof the aisles were covered by lean-to-truss roofs so that the clerestory,

FIGURE 12.12 Christ Teaching the Apostles in the Heavenly Jerusalem, *mosaic in the apse of Santa Pudenziana, ca. A.D. 401–407, Rome. Photo © Hirmer Fotoarchiv.*

or clearstory, windows could be set in the upper nave wall to illuminate the interior. Corinthian columns connected a nave arcade above which was the *triforium,* usually painted or covered with mosaics; above that was the clerestory area with alabaster windows. Aesthetically, the basilica interior is complex and stimulating, for there is no single point from which one can comprehend the space. The strong rhythm of the nave arcade seems to march inexorably towards the eastern end and the triumphal arch that frames the ultimate focus of the design: the high altar where the sacraments are celebrated.

An obvious choice for Christian use, the basilica had imperial associations that suited the triumph of Christianity and a spacious interior that could accommodate thousands of worshippers; Old St. Peter's was said to have a capacity of 40,000. In addition to the interior space, large churches like St. Paul's and Old St. Peter's were fronted by an open courtyard called an *atrium,* which was surrounded on three sides by a covered arcade called an *ambulatory,* or walkway. On the fourth side of the atrium was a porch, or *narthex,* that led to the front doors of the church. Adapted from Roman house plans (see figure 10.4), the atrium was later moved to the south side of monastic churches to become the medieval cloister. Traversing the entire complex from the ambulatory into the arcaded courtyard (atrium), going through the narthex, entering the church proper, and walking down the nave to the altar is curiously suggestive of the layout of Egyptian temples (see figure 2.8).

Christian Mosaics

With a deliberately plain exterior of brick or rubble construction, Christian churches reserved glorious interiors—embellished structural materials, marble panels, paintings, and mosaics—for their congregations. Very little of early Christian mural painting has survived, and what remains is not as striking as the incredibly beautiful mosaics. As created by Hellenistic and Roman artists, mosaics were composed of small bits of marble called *tesserae* (TES-ser-ay). Almost always designed as floor mosaics, artists incorporated subtle gradations of color into designs, some of which were reproductions of existing paintings. Early Christian mosaics were, on the other hand, unprecedented. Designed entirely as wall or ceiling decorations, the tesserae were made of bits of glass cubes that had a wide range of color and intensity, including transparent pieces backed with glittering gold leaf. With shiny, irregular glass faces, the tesserae were set into plaster at slightly varying angles, turning a flat wall surface into a shimmering screen of color. Depicting Christ enthroned and raised above the Apostles, the much renovated mosaic of Santa Pudenziana (figure 12.12), asserts Christ's authority and, by implication, the institutional authority of the church. In the background are buildings representing the Heavenly Jerusalem, while in the sky are winged symbols of the four evangelists: the lion of St. Mark, the ox of St. Luke, the eagle of St. John, and the winged man of St. Matthew. Of uncertain origin

FIGURE 12.13 Abraham and the Celestial Visitors, *mosaic from the second quarter of the fifth century, Church of Santa Maria Maggiore, Rome. Photo © Alinari/Art Resource.*

FIGURE 12.14 The Good Shepherd, *mosaic; Mausoleum of Galla Placidia, ca. 425–450, Ravenna, Italy. Photo © Hirmer Fotoarchiv.*

but widely employed by this time,[3] these evangelical images continued throughout Christian iconography. Not meant to be read as a historical event, this scene is an essay on salvation as assured by Christ's death on the cross, of which we have been informed by the evangelists, and which is available through the church, the representative of God on earth.

What is believed to be the oldest cycle of evangelical and biblical mosaics is found in the fifth-century church of Santa Maria Maggiore in Rome. One scene depicts, on two levels, the encounter of Abraham with the

three celestial visitors at Mamre and his subsequent vision of the Trinity (figure 12.13). On the lower level Sarah prepares food, which Abraham then sets before the three young men, whose celestial status is marked by halos. On the upper level Abraham bows before his visitors, who now appear in a vision; this time the central figure of Christ is completely surrounded by an oval field of light called an *aureole* (OR-e-ol). This manner of representing the Holy Trinity was common in the West into the Gothic period and even in today's Byzantine world.

Ravenna and the Byzantine World

Serving briefly as an imperial city for the Romans, Ostrogoths, and the Byzantine Empire, provincial Ravenna was, when compared with Rome, a most unlikely capital. Located south of Venice in the midst of extensive swamps, the port of Ravenna did provide the Western emperors with an easily defensible site and, perhaps more importantly, a low profile compared with the once mighty city of Rome, now the natural target of every barbarian invader. Becoming the capital of the West under Honorius in 404, Ravenna fell to Odoacer in 476 but emerged as the capital of Theodoric's Ostrogothic Kingdom (489–526), and concluded its royal career as the Western capital of Justinian's Byzantine Empire (527–565). Modern Ravenna contains notable artworks from all three imperial periods.

The mausoleum that Empress Galla Placidia, half sister of Honorius, built for members of her family contains some of the best-preserved and splendid mosaics of the fifth century. Set in a *lunette* (lew-NET), a semicircular wall of a vaulted room, the mosaic of *The Good Shepherd* (figure 12.14) depicts a majestic Christ watching over six attentive sheep, who balance him in pyramid formations of three on each side, thus symbolizing the Trinitarian doctrine. The regal pose spirals upwards from the right hand feeding a sheep to the left hand, which grasps a knob-ended cross signifying the earthly death of the King of Kings. In the Hellenic tradition of classical painting, the forms are positioned in a real space and give the illusion of having three-dimensional bulk. Particularly notable is the rocky landscape, which though increasingly stylized remained in the repertoire of landscape painting throughout the Byzantine tradition and into the late medieval style of such painters as Giotto. Often overlooked are the funnel-shaped tubes along the lower border that represent footlights illuminating a liturgical tableau.

Theodoric, King of the Ostrogoths, built some notable churches in Ravenna. Originally dedicated by Theodoric to "Our Lord Jesus Christ" to serve his Arian sect, the Church of Sant' Apollinare Nuovo (figure 12.15) was later renamed by the Orthodox church after Apollinarus, a disciple of St. Peter and the patron saint of Ravenna. Though the teaching of Arius of Alexandria (ca. 256–336) was condemned by the 325 Council of Nicea over which Constantine presided, many Germanic tribes like the Ostrogoths persisted in the Arian heresy. Briefly, the Arians held to the rationalistic belief that since Christ was created by God the Father, he must be subordinate and not of the same divine substance as his creator. Jesus was therefore the highest of created beings but human

---

3. Revelation 4:6–8 describes these same symbols as "four living creatures" that apparently represent the whole of creation: wild and domesticated animals, birds, and humankind. How they came to symbolize the evangelists is not known.

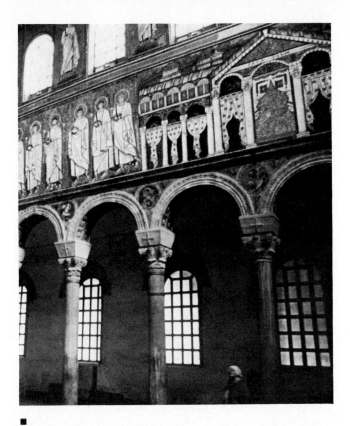

■
FIGURE 12.15 *Interior, Church of Sant' Apollinare Nuovo, ca. 493–526, Ravenna.*

■
FIGURE 12.16 *San Vitale, ca. 526–547, Ravenna. Photo © Hirmer Fotoarchiv.*

rather than divine. The orthodox Byzantine view was that Christ, as the Word Incarnate, was of single substance with the Father and thus wholly divine. The popes of the Western church held to a middle ground: the Word was made flesh, and so Christ was both divine and human and a full member of the Holy Trinity. Reflecting the controversy between Arianism and Byzantine orthodoxy, the mosaics of Sant' Apollinare Nuovo are arranged in three levels. Created by Roman artists for Theodoric, the top band includes scenes from the life of Christ, while the figures between the clerestory windows represent Old Testament patriarchs and prophets. After the Byzantine conquest of Ravenna, Bishop Angellus ordered the lowest band removed, presumably because Arian beliefs were depicted. These were replaced with Byzantine-style saints in procession, women on the north wall and men on the south (figure 12.15). The nave itself has an arcade of columns with ornate capitals topped by blocks from which spring the semicircular arches. With only one side aisle and no transepts, the plan is that of a small and unpretentious basilica, which further highlights the splendid mosaics.

Marking the true beginning of the Byzantine style, the reign of Justinian (527–565) was notable for artistic production and for the Justinian Legal Code, plus the dubious distinction of closing, after a thousand years, Plato's Academy in Athens. Operating from his capitals of Constantinople in the East and Ravenna in the West, Justinian was both an emperor in the Roman tradition and an Oriental potentate in what was to later become the Byzantine Empire. Except for some architecture in Constantinople, most Byzantine art created prior to 1402 can

be found in Ravenna. The rape of Constantinople by the Fourth Crusade (1204) destroyed most of the art and much of the city, which was not retaken from the Latins until 1261.

San Vitale

The most "Byzantine" of the many religious buildings in Ravenna is the octagonal domed church of San Vitale (figure 12.16), a prototype of the central-plan churches that were to dominate the world of Orthodox Christianity just as the basilica plan prevailed throughout Western Christendom. The brick exterior is a complex and subtle interplay of angular patterns around a central core, marred only by the addition of a Renaissance doorway. The interior is a veritable jewel box (colorplate 15), with walls of polychromed marble, pierced marble screens, hundreds of decorative and pictorial mosaics, marble floor mosaics, and numerous carved alabaster columns. San Vitale is an octagonal structure surmounted by an octagonal drum on which the circular dome rests. The transition from the octagonal drum to the round dome was accomplished by using *squinches,* stone lintels placed diagonally across corners formed by the octagonal walls (figure 12.17). Topping the aisle that surrounds the nave is a vaulted triforium gallery reserved for women, as was customary for Orthodox Christianity. Compact and intimate, San Vitale functioned for the imperial court somewhat like a diminutive, luxurious theatre.

FIGURE 12.17 *Supporting a dome with (a) Squinches (b) Pendentives.*

FIGURE 12.18 Christ Pantocrater, *dome mosaic, ca. 532, Church of St. Irene, Constantinople (Istanbul).*

Facing the altar from opposite sides are the two justly celebrated mosaics of Emperor Justinian (colorplate 16) and Empress Theodora (colorplate 17). Though extensively reconstructed, these ceremonial works are still the best extant examples of early Byzantine mosaics. Illustrating the new ideal of the Byzantine style, the figures are tall and slim with small feet, solemn faces, and large oval eyes. Frozen in time without a hint of movement, the grave figures are depicted in full frontality, highly stylized, but nevertheless revealing individual differences. Flanked by twelve companions suggesting the twelve Apostles, Justinian stands in the exact center holding the offering of bread for the mass. He is crowned with both the imperial diadem and a halo, representative of the unity of the spiritual force of the church and of the temporal power of the state. At Justinian's left is Bishop Maximianus, who was responsible for the completion of San Vitale and whose importance is signified by the label over his head. The composition of the work delineates the threefold structure of the empire: the six soldiers represent the army, the three staff members the state, and the three clergymen the church. One of the soldiers holds a shield with the Chrismon insignia that symbolizes not only the name of Christ but allegorically becomes a combination of the cross and shepherd's crook, indicating Christ's death and his pastoral mission.

Unlike the emperor, Theodora is depicted in a more specific setting, probably the narthex of San Vitale. About to pass through a doorway to which she is beckoned by an attendant, she is carrying the offering of wine in a gold chalice encrusted with precious stones. With her huge diadem, ropes of pearls, and luxurious ceremonial gown in royal purple, Theodora is portrayed as the strong-willed, intelligent, and beautiful empress history has revealed her to be, and considerably removed from her early career as circus performer and courtesan. Pictured on her gown are the Magi bringing their offerings to the infant Jesus, suggesting a parallel with her gift-bearing activity. Both mosaics achieve some of their clarity by conforming to the Greek isocephalic convention of placing all heads on about the same level.

The City of Constantine

Dedicated by Constantine in 330 as "New Rome," Constantinople, as the city quickly came to be known, was the sumptuous center of Byzantine civilization for over a thousand years. Typical of central-plan churches, St. Irene was only one of Justinian's many building projects for the imperial city. Contrasting with the extended longitudinal axis of the basilica plan, central-plan churches are built around a vertical axis which extends from the floor to the ceiling mosaic of the central dome. Figure 12.18 illustrates the psychological impact of the head of Christ as the ultimate focus of the vertical axis, and symbolizes the total dominance of the Orthodox faith under the aegis of the emperor who built the churches and appointed the patriarch of Constantinople.

Justinian's building program for Constantinople began in 532 as a matter of necessity. It was in that year that the Blues and Greens, rival chariot-racing factions, had combined in a powerful revolt against the autocratic rule of Justinian and Theodora. Before the imperial troops put down the revolution by slaughtering about 30,000 people, most of the public buildings had been destroyed, including the Constantinian Basilica of Hagia Sophia (HA-jeh SO-fee-ah; Church of Holy Wisdom).

Disdaining the usual procedure of selecting an architect for a building project, Justinian appointed the noted mathematician Anthemius of Tralles to design the new Hagia Sophia. Assisted by Isodorus of Miletos and possibly Justinian himself, Anthemius invented a revolutionary new design unlike anything in either the Roman or Byzantine world (figure 12.19). Combining the longitudinal axis of the basilica plan with the domed structure of a central plan, abutted on east and west by half domes, the new Hagia Sophia was a beautiful and inspiring building, truly a majestic architectural achievement. No wonder Justinian is said to have exclaimed as he rode up to the church for its consecration, "O Solomon, I have excelled thee!"

Hagia Sophia

The interior of Hagia Sophia is breathtaking (figure 12.20). The dome seems to float on light, as it rests upon a tightly spaced ring of forty windows. The entire interior is, in fact, flooded with light from hundreds of windows in the thin, shell-like walls. Adding to the magical effect of all this light were thousands of tesserae that were set into the walls, but later covered with plaster and paint when the Turks converted the building into a mosque. With an interior measuring 240′ × 270′, crowned by a dome 112′ in diameter and extending to 184′ above the pavement, this is one of the largest space enclosures achieved prior to this century. At the corners of a 100′ square area under the dome are 70′ piers that support massive arches. They in turn are connected by *pendentives* (pen-DEN-tivs), which effect the trasnsition from the basic square to the circular rim of the dome. Best described as concave spherical triangles, two of the four pendentives can be seen in figure 12.20 (see also figure 12.17). A more graceful transition from a square base to a round dome than squinches, pendentives also facilitate the covering of more floor space. Their origin remains unknown and their use on the monumental scale of Hagia Sophia is unprecedented. Henceforth used in most Byzantine architecture, pendentives became standard structural devices from the Renaissance to the present day.

As sometimes happens with highly original buildings, there were some technical problems, the most serious being the collapse of the dome twenty-one years after its completion. The present higher-arched dome solved that problem. Byzantium never produced another structure to equal Hagia Sophia. Though it inspired similar designs that can be seen all over Istanbul, it remains unique—the first and best of its kind. First a church and then a mosque, Hagia Sophia is now a museum.

The Iconoclastic Controversy

Brutally termininating the first Byzantine Golden Age, the Iconoclastic Controversy lasted off and on, mostly on, from 726 to 843. Issuing an imperial decree forbidding idolatry, Leo III ordered the destruction of all images of Christ, saints, prophets, and the like. Representations of all sorts, including mosaics in Hagia Sophia, were destroyed along with the entire legacy of pictorial art of Justinian's age, except in Byzantine Italy and on Mount Sinai. Iconoclasts (image-destroyers) mutilated, blinded, tortured, and sometimes executed those who tried to protect sacred images. Ostensibly a religious issue based on the biblical commandment forbidding graven images, the controversy was essentially a conflict between Church and State. The monastic movement had achieved great wealth and power and won considerable respect from the faithful, much to the consternation of the emperors; furthermore, monasteries were diverting revenue from the state and paying little or no taxes. As principal repositories for sacred images, monasteries were attacked, sometimes confiscated, and their resident monks executed, without, however, stamping out the image-worshipping monks (iconodules) in the West. A later Empress Theodora allowed images again in 843, but the

FIGURE 12.19 *Anthemius of Tralles and Isodorus of Miletos, Hagia Sophia, 532–537, Constantinople (Istanbul). Photo © Hirmer Fotoarchiv.*

FIGURE 12.20 *Interior of Hagia Sophia, Constantinople (Istanbul). Photo © Hirmer Fotoarchiv.*

FIGURE 12.21 *Aerial view of St. Mark's Cathedral, begun 1063, Venice. Photo © Alinari/Art Resource.*

FIGURE 12.22 Crucifixion, *mosaic. ca. 1100, Monastery Church, Daphne, Greece. Photo © Alinari/ Art Resource.*

Western and Eastern branches of Christianity were already launched on a parting of the ways, which led, in 1054, to a schism that has yet to be healed. Though the extent of the loss of priceless artworks can never be known, the disaster was not total. The controversy did help to spark a renewed interest in secular art and Late Classical motifs, setting the stage for the Second Byzantine Golden Age of ca. 900–1100.

The Second Golden Age

The largest and most profusely decorated church of the Second Golden Age, St. Mark's of Venice is also the most ambitious structure outside the empire. St. Mark's differs from Hagia Sophia in that the Greek cross form is clearly visible from within and that in addition to the central dome, each arm of the cross is capped by a full dome. From the exterior and especially from the air (figure 12.21), St. Mark's, with each of its five domes encased in wood covered by gilt copper sheathing and topped by ornate lanterns, is the splendid showcase the Republic of Venice intended it to be. As required by law, every ship's captain had to return to Venice with something of value for construction or decoration of the cathedral. Because of the law, many treasures from the 1204 sack of Constantinople found their way to Venice. Despite Romanesque and Gothic elements, the Greek cross plan, multiple domes, strong interior lighting, and glittering mosaics make St. Mark's a Byzantine masterpiece.

After the victory of the iconophiles (image-lovers) in 843, Byzantine painting and mosaics began to blend the otherworldly beauty of Justinian's time with a renewed interest in classical Greek art. Perhaps the finest examples of art of the Second Golden Age are to be found in the monastery church at Daphne, Greece. In the *Crucifixion* mosaic (figure 12.22), there are no Apostles, soldiers, or thieves, only the grief-stricken Mary looking up at Christ and John gazing on in sorrow. The suffering is intense but restrained, reflecting an adaptation of classical Greek sculptural elements to the linear Byzantine style. The skull at the base of the cross represents Golgotha, the "place of the skull." Symbolizing the sacraments of the Eucharist and Baptism, the blood spilling from Christ's side also nourishes the flowers, which represent a new life in Christ. Controlled and compassionate, this is not a historical representation but a humanized portrayal of the Passion of Jesus Christ, his ultimate sacrifice for all of humankind.

The Byzantine style spread throughout the Balkans, Russia, and as far west as Sicily. Strongly influencing some of the Western art of the Middle Ages, it flourished in Eastern Europe for centuries beyond the demise of the Byzantine empire in 1453.

Exercises

1. Explain what is meant by *squinch* and *pendentive*. What purpose did they serve? How and why did they differ?
2. Latin, Greek, Celtic, Maltese, Cross of Lorraine—the cross has many variations. Identify ten different forms and draw them, giving the name of each. Identify the area where each is used and add any special meaning that each form may have.
3. Many animals, birds, flowers, and objects function as symbols in Christian art. What is symbolized by the dove, rose, fish, anchor, lion, peacock, ox, eagle, lily, cup, lamb? What are some of the symbols for salvation, communion, immortality, and peace? Are any of these symbols of pre-Christian or nonChristian origin? Which?
4. Draw floor plans of hypothetical basilica-plan and central-plan churches and identify the areas. Which churches in your community are basilica plan? Central plan? Is there a relationship between certain churches and particular branches of Christianity (Catholic, Greek Orthodox, Baptist, etc.)?
5. Compare the Parthenon, Pantheon, and Hagia Sophia in terms of purpose, size, and style. Rate each building for firmness, commodity, and delight.
6. What exactly is didactic art? Give some examples from early Christianity and some from current magazines and newspapers.
7. How much Christian symbolism do you encounter in everyday life? List, explain, and evaluate religious symbolism as contrasted with governmental (political) symbolism.

Summary

The simple services of the early Christian congregations had no need for art. There were, moreover, two negative factors: (1) the Judaic prohibition of graven images and (2) a basic dislike—even fear—of classical art. However, the explosive growth of the church in the fourth century called for more and more churches, resulting in a need to instruct masses of new converts in the tenets of the faith. The Bible was basic, of course, but artists significantly broadened religious instruction by developing symbols for Christian themes that they used in murals, mosaics, and relief sculptures. By the time of Pope Gregory the Great (590–604) the Church was actively supporting the production of Christian art with careful attention to its didactic function.

As the classical age receded further into the past, there was less and less concern with representational art. For the new faith, physical reality was not as important as authority and spirit. Except for the basilica architectural plan, the early Christians rejected virtually the whole of classical culture from styles to ideals. In its place they introduced different sources of inspiration, thereby changing the entire nature of art.

The Byzantine Empire was a phase of the Roman Empire, beginning with Constantine's transfer of his capital to Constantinople in A.D. 330. The stream of culture was unbroken from the Hellenistic Age through the ascendancy of Rome to Byzantium itself. The main ingredient of that culture was Greek but the Christian synthesis included Oriental elements. In its original form, Christianity was, of course, an Eastern religion. Also Eastern was the absolutism of the emperor, who claimed that his power came directly from God. Eastern features of Byzantium's highly developed art included its abstract nature, its deliberate two-dimensionality, brilliant colors, and elaborate ornamentation.

One of the great triumphs of Byzantine art was the construction of Hagia Sophia, a magnificent conception that was to influence both Christian and Islamic architecture, especially the latter. A more direct influence on Western art were the mosaics and churches of Ravenna during its glory days as capital of the Western empire. Many of the sacred buildings were built in the Eastern style and most of the pictorial art was created by artisans from Constantinople.

The two basic styles of church architecture were developed during these early centuries. From Rome came the basilica form with a long central hall or nave, one or two side aisles, and usually ending with a half dome at the far end. Byzantium contributed the central-plan building, usually in the shape of a Greek cross, with a central dome over the intersection of the arms of the cross.

The ancient prohibition of graven images returned with a vengeance during the Iconoclastic Controversy (726–843) that ended Byzantium's First Golden Age. The next major shock was the Great Schism of 1054 that led to the continuing separation of the Eastern Orthodox churches from the Church of Rome. Inspired by the Second Golden Age (ca. 900–1100), St. Mark's of Venice was constructed as the most elaborate church outside the Byzantine empire. Byzantine art flourished for centuries after the demise of the empire in 1453 and is still a force today.

Culture and Human Values

During its long decline, Rome presided over a world growing increasingly chaotic; the barbarian invasions that contributed to its death throes only added to the confusion. The waning of a strong central authority left a power vacuum that was gradually filled by the Christian Church. The final step in the organization of the Church was to establish a firm leadership that could assure unity of practice and purpose, and resolve any issue that divided the bishops. For a variety of reasons the Bishop of Rome reserved for himself a place of primary importance in the Christian world. By the fifth century the Roman bishop was calling himself the pope (Latin, *papa,* father), an absolute monarch who possessed the "keys of the kingdom" as the "vicar of Christ" here on earth. Though acknowledged as the Father of the Church in the West, the pope was not regarded as supreme in the East, leading eventually to a schism in 1054 that split the Latin and Greek churches. It was at this time that the pope excommunicated the patriach of Constantinople and the patriarch excommunicated the pope.

The administrative authority of the church hierarchy was paralleled by the development of Biblical authority. The bishops, in fact, used their authority to decide what the Scriptures would and would not include. These determinations were completed near the end of the fourth century, at which time the pope declared Jerome's Latin translation as the standard text—which it still is today for the Church of Rome.

Christian art was concerned, of course, with the spiritual world view of the young church but the dominant concept was authority in any form, from church doctrine to the Bible, the bishops, the pope, Jesus, and God the Father. Representational art of the classical world was rejected; instead, people were depicted in terms of their authority—what they represented rather than how they might look.

There were other values that artists tried to depict, particularly the seven virtues of justice, faith, hope, love, fortitude, temperance, and prudence. The seven deadly sins of pride, envy, anger, avarice, dejection, gluttony, and lust were, supposedly, unfit subjects for art; nevertheless, these attitudes or activities were occasionally graphically depicted as examples of what *not* to do.

Christian values dominated Western culture for the next thousand years or so. In varying degrees, they retain their importance today for those who adhere to one of a variety of Christian beliefs.

Annotated Bibliography

Beckwith, John. *Early Christian and Byzantine Art.* Pelican History of Art Series. New York: Penguin Books, 1980. A good introduction in a fine series.

Demus, Otto. *Byzantine Mozaic Decoration: Aspects of Monumental Art in Byzantium.* New Rochelle, N.Y.: Aristide E. Caratzas, Publishers, 1976. An illuminating study of a long tradition.

Ferguson, George. *Signs and Symbols in Christian Art.* New York: Oxford University Press, 1966. Clear explanations of the conventional motifs.

Grabor, Andre. *Christian Iconography: A Study of Its Origins.* Princeton: Princeton University Press, 1980. A detailed study by one of the top scholars in the field.

Hulme, F. Howard. *Symbolism in Christian Art.* Atlantic Highlands, N.J.: Humanities Press, 1971. A classic study of the subject.

Mango, Cyril. *Art of the Byzantine Empire.* Englewood Cliffs, N.J.: Prentice-Hall, 1972. A wide-ranging survey.

———. *Byzantine Architecture.* History of World Architecture Series. New York: Harry N. Abrams, 1976. Excellent study in a consistently good series.

THE AGE OF FAITH

	Key Dates	People and Events	Art, Architecture, Literature	Religion	Philosophy, Science, Education
500	**527–565** First Byzantine Golden Age	**527–565** Reign of Emperor Justinian **529** Justinian closes Plato's Academy **533** Legal Code of Justinian **590–604** Pope Gregory the Great; established political power, codified liturgy and chant **597** St. Augustine's mission to England	**ca. 500** Early materials of *Ring of the Nibelung* **ca. 526–547** San Vitale, Ravenna **ca. 530–539** Church of Sant' Apollinare in Classe, Ravenna **532–537** Hagia Sophia, Constantinople (Istanbul)	**ca. 529** Benedictine Order founded by St. Benedict at Monte Cassino **Mohammed** 570–630	**ca. 500** Origin of Seven Liberal Arts
600	**600–800** Irish Golden Age	**622–732** Islamic conquest of Middle East, western Asia, north Africa, Portugal, and Spain	**ca. 698–721** *Lindisfarne Gospels*	**622** Mohammed's flight from Mecca (The Hegira) **630** Mohammed captures Mecca	
700	**750–900** Carolingian Period	**732** Battle of Poitiers; Muslim expansion checked by Charles Martel **751–** Pepin, King of the Franks **768–814** Reign of Charlemagne (Carolingian Empire)	**ca. 740** *Beowulf* **ca. 760–820** *Book of Kells* **785–990** Mosque of Cordoba **792–805** Palatine Chapel of Charlemagne, Aachen		**781** Charlemagne's Palace School established. Beginning of Carolingian Renaissance
800	**800–1100** Development of Feudalism	**800** Charlemagne crowned Holy Roman Emperor by Pope Leo III **ca. 820** Beginning of Viking raids on England and France, later on Italy and Sicily	**806** Germigny des Pres		
900	**900–1100** Second Byzantine Golden Age	**955** Invading Magyars stopped by German King Otto **987** Foundation of French monarchy by Hugh Capet		**ca. 900** Conversion of Kievan Russia to Orthodox Christianity	
1000	**1000–1200** Romanesque Period	**ca. 1000** Viking Leif Eriksson reached North America (?) **1042–1066** Edward the Confessor, Anglo-Saxon king **1061–1091** Norman conquest of Sicily **1066** Norman conquest of England by William the Conqueror	**ca. 1000** *Song of Roland* written down **1004–1218** St. Benoit-sur-Loire **1017–** Mont St. Michel **1037–1067** Abbey of Jumièges **1056–** Westminster Abbey **1063–1272** Pisa Cathedral **1064** St. Etienne, Caen **ca. 1070–1080** Bayeux Tapestry **1080–** Tower of London **1080–1120** St. Sernin, Toulouse	**1054** Separation of Eastern and Western churches **1095** First Crusade preached by Pope Urban II **1096–1291** Period of major crusades	**ca. 1000–1100** Battle of Universals (Realist-Nominalist controversy) **Abelard** 1079–1142 philosopher and theologian
1100	**1140–1200** Early Gothic Period	**Eleanor of Aquitaine** 1122–1204 (m. Louis VII of France and Henry II of England) **1152–1190** Reign of Frederick Barbarosa, Emperor of Holy Roman Empire **1154–1189** Reign of Henry II, first Angevin king of England **1189–1199** Reign of Richard the Lion-Heart	**ca. 1104–1132** Ste. Madeleine, Vezelay **1140–1144** Gothic choir, St. Denis, near Paris **ca. 1160** *Tristan et Iseult* written down **1163–1250** Notre Dame, Paris **1174–** Canterbury Cathedral **fl. 1183** Perotin, composer, Notre Dame, Paris **1194–1260** Chartres Cathedral	**1147–1149** Second Crusade **St. Francis of Assisi** 1182–1226 *Little Flowers of St. Francis* **1198–1216** Pope Innocent III; apex of church political and ecclesiastical power	**ca. 1150** Complete works of Aristotle become available from Islam; founding of Univ. of Paris **ca. 1163** Founding of Oxford Univ.
1200	**1200–1300** High Gothic Period	**1215** King John signs Magna Carta **1220–1250** Reign of Frederick II, Holy Roman Emperor; royal vs. papal power **1226–1270** Reign of Louis IX of France (St. Louis) **1295** Model Parliament of Edward I (Angevin), England	**ca. 1200** *Ring of the Nibelung* written down **ca. 1220–1288** Notre Dame, Amiens **ca. 1225–** Beauvais Cathedral **Adam de la Halle** ca. 1237–1288 composer **Cimabue** 1240–1302 painter **Ste. Chapelle** 1245–1248 Paris **Duccio** ca. 1255–1319 painter **Dante Alighieri** 1265–1321 **Giotto** ca. 1266–1336 painter **Philippe de Vitry** 1291–1361 (Ars Nova in music)	**1210** St. Francis founded Franciscan order	**Roger Bacon** ca. 1214–1294 scientist **Thomas Aquinas** ca. 1225–1274 scholastic philosopher **William of Occam** ca. 1270–1347 nominalist philosopher
1300	**1300–1500s** Late Gothic Period; International Style	**1322–1328** Charles IV, last of Capetian kings of France **1328–1350** Philip VI, first Valois king of France **1337–1453** Hundred Years' War: England vs. France **1347–1349** Black Death sweeps through Europe **1377–1399** Richard II, last Angevin king of England **1399–1413** Henry IV, House of Lancaster, England	***Petrarch** 1304–1374 ***Boccaccio** 1313–1375 *The Decameron* ***Chaucer** 1340–1400 *The Canterbury Tales* **1354–1427** Alhambra, Granada ***Gentile da Fabriano** 1370–1427 painter ***Brunelleschi** 1377–1446 Florentine architect ***Fra Angelico** 1387–1455 painter	**1305–1376** Papacy at Avignon ("Babylonian Captivity") **1378–1417** Great Schism of the Church of Rome	
1400	**1453** Constantinople falls to Ottoman Turks; end of Eastern Roman Empire		**ca. 1485** *Everyman*		**ca. 1400** Arabs transmit compass and astrolabe to Europe

*These artists and writers represent the Early Renaissance, clearly indicating that a new movement arises as the previous era fades away.

13

Building Medieval Walls

The so-called Middle Ages extended for approximately a thousand years from about A.D. 410 to around 1400. Furthermore, they divide themselves sharply at about the year 1000, for reasons that will become apparent. This long period constitutes an amalgamation of various cultures—some features of the Arabic and Muslim, the Eastern civilization that had its source in Byzantium (Constantinople), and principally the crude northern way of life of Germany and the Scandinavian countries—into the old Graeco-Roman institutions. As such, the gestation of the Middle Ages constitutes an almost new start for Western culture, with only a memory of past glories, with written records that lay dormant for centuries, and with the Roman Church as foci of centralizing forces. The rather glorious medieval culture, which reached maturity during the twelfth and thirteenth centuries, represents a fusion of seemingly contradictory ways of life, and of opposition in ways of feeling and thought. Once again we can witness a testimony to the toughness of the human spirit, which lives, survives, changes itself, and finally triumphs over darkness and confusion, expressing itself in magnificent symbols of new growth.

We have already said that Rome "fell" sometime in the fifth century—the arbitrary dates of 410 or 476 do not make much difference. It should be remarked, however, that the average Roman citizen living at the time did not know that Rome had fallen. Life went on much as it had before; life got tougher and tougher, but the government and the Emperor, whether he be Italian or Ostrogoth, were still there. For example, the philosopher Boethius (Bo-EE-thi-us; ca. 475–524), who wrote the famous *Consolation of Philosophy* during the last year of his life, held the office of Roman consul about fifty years after the final "official" date for the fall of Rome.

As a matter of fact, the power of Rome dwindled until it was virtually nonexistent. For centuries the Roman legions had been replaced by barbarian mercenaries, and Rome, unable to defend its borders, either pulled back the soldiers who had been stationed on the extreme boundaries of the Empire or allowed them to become integrated with the local peoples. An ever-increasing number of tribesmen were settled in Italy when the original Italian peoples deserted the land. The capital of the Empire was moved, once to Milan and later to Ravenna, and under the Emperor Constantine the Empire was split into an eastern and a western section, with a growing sense of independence in each area. The "fall" was simply a slow disintegration of power, not a sudden cataclysm. But as civil control failed, the Church gained in strength until it became the great unifying power in Western civilization. The development of this power needs to be considered.

The Early Church

Christianity had its source in the teachings of Christ, but it became an institutionalized church largely through the efforts of two men. The first of these was the apostle Paul, who traveled widely and kept up a very active correspondence with the communities of Christians throughout the Roman world. Largely through his efforts, the various congregations in the important cities were held together. After his work, a centralized doctrine and a widely accepted institution for the preservation and the propagation of the faith was still lacking. This last task was accomplished in large measure by St. Augustine (354–430).

Augustine, the Searcher

Augustine was a North African who was very well educated in the arts of logic and dialectic in his native town of Thagaste and in Carthage. The chief Christianizing influence on the young man was his mother, Monica, who admonished him and prayed for him so much that she must have been a real millstone around the neck of the passionate and high-spirited young man. Always a searcher for a firm belief, Augustine first became a Manichaean, an austere religion founded by a third-century Persian named Mani. The central core of the religion was a strong dualistic belief (derived in part from Zoroastrianism; see chapter 1) in a power of good and a power of evil conflicting in the world and in people. The teaching was very ascetic with the "elect" or "perfect" leading an austere life and practicing strict celibacy, thus assuring immediate happiness after death. Augustine's logical mind could not, however, accept all of this doctrine—particularly celibacy—and later, in Rome, he became a sceptic, a believer in nothing, not even his own existence.

His Conversion to Christianity

Finally he began reading some of the Neoplatonists (see chapter 9) and was strongly influenced by them, so much so that he regarded his Neoplatonic period as the crucial stepping-stone to his acceptance of Christianity, for his doctrine incorporated much of Neoplatonism (minus Greek rationalism). This was in Milan, where he was serving as a municipally appointed teacher (his students in Carthage had been too unruly for him to put up with; the students in Rome were better behaved but they seldom paid their tuition), where his Christian mother, Monica, had joined him, and where he heard the impressive preaching of Bishop Ambrose, a critical influence on his eventual conversion to Christianity. After experiencing his famous mystical experience in the garden (as recounted in his noted autobiography, *The Confessions*), he was baptized in 387 by St. Ambrose. Although he preferred to lead a contemplative life, his later duties as Bishop of Hippo forced him into vigorous activity as a powerful advocate of the Roman Church against the Manichaeans, the Arians and, especially, against the Donatist heresy, which he energetically persecuted.

Fighting Heresies

The Arian and Donatist heresies represented practical and philosophical problems of the early Christian church, problems that were still of great concern to Augustine and his contemporaries. Roman persecution of Christians after A.D. 303 forced many priests to collaborate with authorities by handing over sacred texts. After Constantine's edicts of toleration in 311 and 313, these "handers-over" (*traditores*) resumed their roles as priests only to be challenged by Donatus, bishop of Carthage. Donatus advocated punishing weak, collaborationist priests by declaring their administration of the sacraments invalid, a politically dangerous position because it gave believers opportunities to judge which priests were dispensing valid sacraments. Because of the political nature of the controversy, Constantine utilized his imperial prerogative by ruling that once a priest has been properly ordained, his administration of the sacraments remains valid even though his actions may become reprehensible. The problems of dissent and violence over the Donatist heresy continued to plague North Africa even after Augustine's tenure as Bishop of Hippo.

Heresy also involved such philosophical principles as Arianism, named after Arius, an Alexandrian priest who maintained that God the Son could not be precisely of the *same* essence as God the Father because the begetter must be somehow superior to, as well as necessarily earlier in time than, the begotten. This view threatened to diminish the divinity of Christ and to break up the Holy Trinity, as emphasized by Arius's bitter opponent, Athanasius, bishop of Alexandria. Disdaining logic and espousing mystery, Athanasius and his followers exhorted Christians to simply accept on faith that the Trinity of Father, Son, and Holy Ghost was both equal and contemporary. Unable to settle the quarrel, in 325 Constantine called the first meeting to involve the whole church, an ecumenical council (Greek, *oikoumene,* the inhabited world). Meeting at Nicaea, across the straits from Constantinople, the assembled bishops backed Athanasius's view, resulting in the famous Nicene Creed ("We believe in one God"), which was issued by Constantine with all the force of an imperial decree.

Augustine was not only a theologian but also a very busy administrator as Bishop of Hippo and propagandist for the Roman Church. In this respect he was faced with the problem of the efficacy of the sacraments when performed by priests who belonged to heretical sects or who led impure lives. His judgment in the matter was that the efficacy of the sacraments (it must be remembered that only through the sacraments did one find salvation) lay in the office of the priesthood, not in the man who performed them. The basis for this decision rested in the argument that if the benefit of the sacraments lay in the quality of the man who performed them, then people themselves would be placed in judgment of God's grace. The promulgation of this doctrine did much to establish the concept of the infallibility of the Church, since its power was inherent within its offices. This power, it was argued, descended directly from the apostles, who were the original bishops of the Church. From them it passed to other bishops, and from the bishops to the priests through the "laying on of hands." Through this act, the power to administer the sacraments was given and could not be revoked.

Augustine's Theology

When considering Augustine as a philosopher and theologian we are confronted with the vast number of books written about the whole body of his thought. Here we shall give an overview of his ideas about the nature of God, of the creation, of free will, his philosophy of history, and the infallibility of the Church, for these beliefs provide the backbone for European civilization up to the late Middle Ages.

Earlier in our study we made the point that a culture is based upon the idea of Reality that is held by that culture. According to Augustine, God was the only reality, who created the world out of nothingness. This God was a mystic being, not an intellectual principle as was the case with the Neoplatonists, so that knowledge of God and life in him was available to all human beings, whether they were philosophers or not. Although Augustine regarded his own early philosophic speculations as stepping-stones to belief, he felt that his conversion came about through the grace of God, not through human efforts, and that this grace is available to all people. For Augustine and all believers throughout the Middle Ages, union with God is the only true goal and the only true happiness for people, all of which takes place in the hereafter.

The process of creation-from-nothingness took place because of two aspects of the mind of God, roughly corresponding to the Platonic essences, but with significant differences. One such aspect corresponds to the eternal truths, such as the truth that the sum of the angles of a triangle always equals 180°. Such truths, existing before creation and after the destruction of the world, constitute the basic patterns and harmonies of the universe. Another aspect of God's mind consists of the "seminal (or seed) reasons" for created things. These are the patterns that acquire physical substance and form the visible things of the world: the visible people, trees, earth, and the myriad things that are apparent to our senses. These sense-apparent things exist in time; they rise, disintegrate, and pass away, and because of their transitory nature are the least important of God's creations.

Implicit in the last statement is Augustine's dualistic concept of time. He believed in a direct flow of time in which humanity's activities (never repeating themselves in spiral or circular patterns) moved upward toward eventual perfection, toward the godlike. The flow of time and all the changes that occur within it are characteristic of the temporal world. God, however, with all the attributes of his mind, dwells in eternity, which is really a timeless instant. In this realm past and future have no meaning; all is present.

In this way, Augustine reconciled the problem of God's foreknowledge of all events and humanity's free will. He asserted that people had free will even though God knew every event that would take place. How does one avoid fatalism and the idea of predestination if all of a person's actions are known in advance? The answer is that God's seeing all things as present-time allows for foreknowledge in what *we* call time, yet the "seeing" of things does not influence them. All events are simultaneous for God, and thus he can know them without influencing them. A person's vision is shackled by past, present, and an inscrutable future, but in the temporal world there is complete free will.

In his attitude toward the body and the whole world of matter, Augustine was somewhat ambivalent. If this world is God's creation then it must be good. On the other hand, being overly concerned with the acquisition of worldly goods can turn a person away from God, and that is of course sinful. The matter of bodily pleasures was especially disturbing. Before his conversion, Augustine had lived a lusty life of fleshly pleasures; his proclivities were dramatized in his famous prayer: "O Lord, make me chaste, but not yet." He shifted to the other extreme after his conversion and condemned sexual pleasure (music was included in this censure because, like the sex act, it kept the mind from contemplating God).

His view of the material world was strongly influenced by Platonic doctrine, but not entirely. He believed that the physical things of the world are all passing away and changing. For example, in *The City of God* he makes the point that in Rome in 410 many people lost all of their worldly possessions, yet Christians remained happy since their "possessions" were in their spirit and could not be taken away. The conclusion is that a concern with worldly things is a concern with nothing, since these things are ephemeral. The only vital concern is with the things of the spirit, which have their existence in the realm of eternity. This type of thought is not completely dualistic in that it does not despise the flesh and the things of the world, yet it tends in that direction. Many later Christian thinkers were to turn completely against the world and the flesh, asserting even more strongly than Plato and Augustine that these things were traps for the mind and the spirit of humanity. Much of the puritanical thought of our time comes from this basic reasoning.

Augustine, in the first complete formulation of a Christian philosophy of history, viewed the story of humanity as a conflict between two cities. (He used the word *city* as we might use the word *community* in such a phrase as the "business community.") One of these was the City of God, the other the City of Man. In the beginning, when time was created, he stated, everything belonged to the good city, yet with the revolt of the angels and Satan's expulsion from heaven, the other city came into being. From that time until the birth of Christ, almost all of humanity belonged to the Earthly City. Only a few Hebrews who had faith in the coming of a Savior belonged to the City of God. With Christ's coming for the redemption of mortals, and with the formation of the Church, the membership in the two cities was more sharply divided, since all members of the City of God were also members of the Church. This, he was careful to assert, did not work conversely—all members of the Church were not necessarily members of God's City. The end of history will come with the Last Judgment and the final and complete separation of the two cities. The saved will be reclothed in their perfect bodies and take their place with God; the damned will undergo eternal torture with Satan. Since the members of the good city are already known to God, we find here the basis for the doctrine of the elect, a tenet that was to be completely enunciated by Calvin after the Reformation.

This philosophy of history has at least one other important consequence. If the original members of the City of God are to be found only among the Hebrews, they alone knew truth. Thus all other learning, that of the Greeks, for example, is falsehood and is not to be studied. The loss of the Graeco-Roman heritage had an incalculable effect on the course of Western civilization.

The Authority of the Church in Rome

Sometime after the death of Augustine final authority of the Church in Rome was achieved, for the bishops of Rome had asserted their supremacy over the other bishops. The argument for this was that St. Peter had founded the Church in Rome, and that he was Christ's spiritual successor. Biblical authority was given for this claim from Christ's words concerning Peter, "Upon this rock (*petras*) will I build my church." Leo, Bishop of Rome from 440 to 461, first made this claim to ecclesiastical authority, and Pope Gregory the Great, slightly more than a century later, was such an able diplomat and churchman that the primacy of the pope became universally accepted for the Western Church.

These were the moves that established a body of doctrine of the Church, a strong and revered institution that was able to maintain its authority throughout the troubled and confused years of the early Middle Ages as the only source of order throughout all of Europe. Very early on the Church was divided into two branches: the regular clergy (from the Latin *regula* or *rule*) composed of the monks and those who retreated from the active life, and the secular clergy, the pope, the bishops, and parish priests who lived among the people and sought to lead them to a better life. During the time of the decline of the Roman authority, a very great number of men, particularly among the intellectual class, retreated from the world to live and work in the communal life of monasteries leading the contemplative existence. This is not an unusual phenomenon during any time of cultural upheaval, including our own.

Feudalism and Manorialism

Following the withdrawal of Roman military and governmental stability, the people of western Europe had to find ways by which they could govern themselves with some semblance of justice, and by which they could make a living. The governmental system, feudalism, did not develop fully until the tenth century, but it can be described here as the slowly evolving political system of the Middle Ages. Manorialism, the economic arrangement by which the people made a living, actually had its beginnings during late Roman times when the peasants were forced to stay on the land and became serfs. Furthermore, the two systems, at the lowest level—the demesne, or land-holding of a single knight—are so intertwined that they are scarcely distinguishable.

In its essence, feudalism is simply an arrangement by which the whole territory of the former empire was divided up into small enough units so that a single man could rule each one. It also created a fighting society, since the lords constantly raided adjoining territories, and all of them were subject to the forays of the northern tribes from Germany and Scandinavia.

In what had once been the civilized Roman Empire, we find a number of kings who lacked both the money and the power to hold their kingdoms together. These rulers proceeded to split up their kingdoms among the nobility, the highest ranking of which were the barons. The barons accepted the land from the king, and in return swore allegiance to him and agreed to furnish a certain number of fighting men when the kingdom was attacked. Thus a baron became a *vassal* of the king. But since the barons also lacked power to administer their lands, they took vassals under them, further subdividing the land. This successive division of land continued down to the knight, who owned one estate or demesne consisting of a village and the rather extensive farmlands surrounding it. Each member of the nobility was thus a despotic ruler over the land that he actually controlled, subject only to the oaths of loyalty he swore to the lord immediately over him. One knight could control his one small village and the farms that surrounded it and provide some form of rough justice for the inhabitants.

The manorial system was simply the totality of the life within one of these villages. Here, unless he was away at war, resided the lord in his manor house. A priest took care of the spiritual needs of the community, and the church and parish house usually occupied the center of the village. In addition to these buildings, one usually found a community bake-oven, a winepress, and a mill for grinding grain. The farming land (one can assume that an average demesne comprised about a thousand acres) was divided into three main sections, two of which were planted each year and the third left fallow. The lord retained about half of the land (the best part) as his personal property (though it was farmed by his serfs), the priest was given a small parcel ("God's acre"), a section was retained as common woodland, and another as a common meadow. Each serf was given certain strips of land in each of the three fields—each strip was usually an eighth of a mile in length and about seventeen feet wide.[1] The serf and his family were "attached" to the land, that is, they could not leave, but neither could they be turned away. The serf gave a certain portion of his produce to the lord and was also obligated to work a certain number of days on the lord's land. The lord, in his turn, was obliged to protect his villagers and to provide justice, though he was the only judge in the case of disputes, and his word was final.

The manorial system gives us a picture of a poverty-stricken and almost totally isolated life. All of the bare necessities were provided within the single manor, and the serf scarcely ever traveled beyond it. No news of the world came in except when the lord returned from a war, or when an occasional itinerant peddler came through. Formal education was unknown; illiteracy was standard for the serfs and for many of the lords. Life on the manor was an endless round of hard work, birth, marriage, and death, with some time off for religious holidays (see "A Day on a Medieval Manor" in this chapter). Life was maintained at a minimal level behind medieval walls, which shut out hostile forces but which also, figuratively speaking, kept out ideas that might disturb the rigid order enforced by the church and the barons (figure 13.1). It is little wonder that people regarded the world as a vale of tears and that they lived in hopeful anticipation of a glorious afterlife in heaven.

The Rise of Islam

Western Christianity, Byzantium, and Islam had a common heritage—Graeco–Roman civilization—but the three cultures generally preferred emphasizing their differences. During the Early Middle Ages the West, the most primitive and backward civilization, accused the Muslims of being "infidels" and saw Byzantium as "decadent" and "treacherous." In fact, Eastern and Western Christianity and Islam were monotheistic faiths with their roots buried deep in Judaism. However reluctant, medieval Europe had much to learn from Islam and Byzantium and, in time, it was strongly influenced by its neighbors as it evolved a unique synthesis of classical, Christian, and Germanic traditions.

For over twelve centuries the relationships between Islam and Christianity have ranged from distrust and fear to open warfare; the Muslim conquest of Spain and invasion of France, the Crusades, and the Christian reconquest of Spain are only a few of the major conflicts. However, alienation and hostility between the two cultures was and is caused more by politics and economics than by ideology. Centuries ago the problems involved Muslim control of Palestine and trade routes to the Far East. Today those problems include Palestine, trade, oil, and Israel.

■

FIGURE 13.1 *Aigues-Mortes, France. Located on the Mediterranean coast, this perfectly preserved medieval town was founded as a staging area and supply base for the crusades. Medieval walls were a common denominator throughout Europe. Photo © Ray Delvert.*

Islam was the last of the great monotheistic religions but it made up for lost time with the breathtaking speed of its expansion. Beginning in the Arabian Peninsula in 622, the militant faith, in little more than a century, spread east to the borders of China and west to North Africa and the Iberian Peninsula, an area greater than Rome at its height.

Pre-Islamic Arabia was a hot, dry, barren, and backward land inhabited mainly by nomadic Bedouin tribesmen who worshipped trees, stones, and pieces of wood that were supposedly inhabited by supernatural powers. Human virtues, by their standards, were courage, manliness, loyalty, and generosity. The chief Arabian city was prosperous Mecca, the hub of the lucrative caravan trade and site of Arabia's holiest shrine known as the Kaaba. Chief deity of the city was Allah, creator of the universe but still just one of some three hundred gods.

Mohammed

Mohammed (also spelled Muhammad or Mahomet) was born in this bustling city in about 570. After supporting himself by tending sheep and then as a merchant, he became an agent for an older businesswoman and later married her. It was undoubtedly on his business trips for her that he came into contact with Judaism and Christianity. At about age forty he began his practice of retiring to a mountain cave to meditate. Here he received certain spiritual insights that he later compared with "the breaking of dawn." He had visions of an angel and then of a giant Archangel Gabriel. After a second revelation ordering him to "rise and warn" the people, Mohammed began preaching in Mecca in 613. His ministry angered the wealthy and powerful Meccans, and he fled for his life (the Hegira) to the city of Yathrib (later called Medina, "City of the Prophet"). This was in 622, which became the first year of the new faith.

---

1. Replacing the scratch plow, a new kind of plow was invented (late seventh century) which was equipped with a vertical knife to cut the furrow, a horizontal plowshare to slice under the sod, and a moldboard to turn it over. Pulled by eight oxen (communally owned), it attacked the land with such violence that cross-plowing was unnecessary and fields tended to be shaped in long strips. Found nowhere else in the world (for centuries to come), this plow marked the beginning of a technological revolution that would change the European from nature's partner to an exploiter of natural resources, leading to today's ecological problems.

■

MAP 13.1 *Expansion of Islam 622 to ca. 750.*

Main Articles of Faith

The main *articles* of that faith are a belief in:

1. Allah, who is the only God.
2. the angels (Gabriel and others).
3. the Prophets (Mohammed, Abraham, Noah, Moses, and Jesus).
4. the sacred books (Old and New Testaments, Psalms of David, and the Koran).
5. the Qadar (God's plan for the collective benefit of all humankind).
6. Resurrection on the Day of Judgement.

The minimum requirement for the religious *duties* of Muslims is called the Five Pillars of Faith:

1. "There is no God but Allah, and Mohammed is his prophet." This is the *Shahadah,* which Muslims believe implies all six articles given above. A fundamental part of the religion, this creed needs only to be uttered for any person to be accepted as a Muslim.
2. The obligation of the five daily prayers (dawn, midday, midafternoon, sunset, and nightfall).
3. Giving to the poor (once voluntary, this is now an assessment).
4. Fasting during the month of Ramadan, the ninth month of the Muslim lunar calendar. This marks the month in which Allah gave the Koran to Gabriel for revelation to Mohammed.
5. Pilgrimage to Mecca. Though many cannot do this, millions have done so for the experience of mingling as an equal with all other believers and for the sense of the unity of all Islam.

In the early stages of Islam, a sixth duty was required for all able-bodied men: to fight in the *jihad* (holy war). Each caliph ("successor" to Mohammed) felt obligated to reduce the infidel "territory of war" by armed conquest in the name of Allah. With the exception of Spain, all territories that were converted by the sword remain Muslim to this day (see the map: Expansion of Islam).

The Koran

Islam is based on the Shahadah, the Koran, which embodies all of Mohammed's teachings, and the Hadith (traditions), a collection of the Prophet's sayings and decisions (some of which are apocryphal). All the believer has to do is submit to the will of Allah. The Arabic word for submission is *Islam,* the faith; he who submits is a "Muslim," a believer. Submitting unreservedly to an all-powerful God, believers make up a religious community that follows the Koran's detailed rules for every aspect of daily life. Compiled from the writings of the Prophet some twenty years after his death in 632, the Koran is the only authority, the last word in theology, law, and all social institutions. By far the most important textbook in Muslim universities, the Koran may never be translated; the faith has one language and that language is Arabic.

Islamic civilization reached its high point during the tenth century as a kind of Middle Eastern renaissance. Though culturally backward, Arabs contributed little more than the language, which proved to be a decisive factor. The language of the Koran is the great unifier of the faith, just as Latin used to be the common language of the Church of Rome. The Arabic form of writing was

■ **FIGURE 13.2** *Mohammed Ago ibn Abd al-Muin, Mosque of Sultan Ahmet I (far right), 1609–1616, Istanbul, Turkey. The Hagia Sophia is at the far left. Aerial view.*

also important, leading, in Islamic art, to the development of an infinite variety of abstract ornament and a remarkable system of linear abstraction that is uniquely Islamic.

Islamic Culture

Islamic culture was a synthesis of Greek, Syrian, Persian, and Indian traditions, but Islam digested as well as borrowed. There was hardly a field of human endeavor that was not enriched. Significant advances were made in medicine, astronomy, navigation, and mathematics. Apparently it was from the Hindus that they appropriated "Arabic" numerals, the zero, and algebra. Omar Khayyam, the Persian astronomer and poet of the *Rubaiyat,* devised a remarkably accurate calendar. Philosophers studied Plato and Aristotle, translating them from Syriac (Syrian scholars had earlier translated the Greek) into Arabic. Trade routes were opened clear to China so that material goods and immaterial ideas flowed freely through the Islamic world. Learning flourished in Islam with great universities at Cairo and Toledo. The art of gracious living was finely developed, particularly in the luxurious cities of Baghdad and Cordoba. While Western Europe was slogging along in the mud, a high culture flourished in the lands of the mosques, the riches of which would not be known until after the Crusades began.

One of the distinctive features of this culture was its art and, especially, its architecture. National styles of the pre-Islamic era made important contributions but Muslim artistic achievements were not of a particular people or country. Unified and shaped by religion, Islamic art was one of the glories of an entire civilization.

The Mosque

Islam provided direct access to God through prayer; there was no liturgy, sacraments, or priestly class and, thus, no need for a special kind of architecture. Praying could be done literally anywhere and Mohammed did indeed teach and pray everywhere including his own home. Paradoxically, a religion that had no architectural requirements developed a mosque design that remained essentially the same throughout the vast Muslim empire.

The open court mosque was derived from encampment mosques of the conquering Muslim armies. The "army mosque" was an open field with a ditch and a rustic prayer shelter on the *kibla* side—the wall facing Mecca. Permanent mosques utilized the basic idea of a large open court enclosed on three sides by covered arcades with a roofed prayer hall on the kibla side. (The arcades provided areas shaded from the torrid desert sun.) Inside the hall a central niche, the *mihrah,* was added to the kibla wall. To the right of the mihrah was the *minibar,* or pulpit, for readings from the Koran and the Friday sermon. A characteristic feature from the earliest days, the *sahn,* a pool for ritual ablutions, was located in the courtyard. Though *muezzins* (mu-EZ-ins; criers) could call the faithful to prayer from any high place, *minarets* or tall, slender towers quickly became standard features of the overall mosque design.

The Mosque of Sultan Ahmet I (figure 13.2) was apparently designed by a student of Koca Sinan, Turkey's greatest architect. The original prayer hall of early Islamic architecture has been enlarged into the domed mosque, the finest architectural achievement of the Ottoman Turks. Minarets are placed at the four corners of the mosque and at the two corners of the arcade. There was no mandatory number of minarets; the sole stipulation was that no mosque may have seven minarets like the Great Mosque in Mecca.

■ **FIGURE 13.3** *Interior, Mosque of Sultan Ahmet I.*

■ **FIGURE 13.4** *Ceiling, Mosque of Sultan Ahmet I.*

The interior of a mosque (figure 13.3) clearly illustrates the "dissolution of matter" that was so fundamental to the Islamic style. In the mosque everyone must have the feeling of being equal in the face of Allah. Further, there must be a feeling of eternity for all true believers and a disregard for earthly existence. Highly ornamented surfaces help to disguise and "dissolve" matter. Solid walls are, in effect, camouflaged with tiles and plaster decorated with arabesques and endlessly repetitive designs that are referred to as "infinite patterns." The intent is to provide a feeling of infinity or eternity.

Featuring a highly complex series of intersecting arcs and semicircles, the ceiling (figure 13.4) is a veritable fairyland of Arabic script, elaborate medallions, radiating spokes, and flowering chains. Again, the kaleidoscope of geometry and decoration gives the illusion of ethereal lightness. The exterior (figure 13.2) is notable for its piled up masses of heavy masonry with multiple cupolas and topped by a massive central dome. Inside, the decoration has dissociated the appearance of wall and column from actual function. The result is like gazing into a magnificent flower garden. Also known as the Blue Mosque because of the rich blue in the stained glass windows, the Mosque of Ahmet I has one of the most enchanting interiors in Istanbul, a city full of impressive mosques.

At the top of figure 13.2 is the Hagia Sophia, the incredible sixth-century church (now a museum) constructed by Justinian (see chapter 12). A comparison of the mosque with the former church reveals the inspiration for Ottoman Turk central-domed mosques. The higher dome and lack of interior decoration give the interior of Hagia Sophia a much different feeling from that of the Blue Mosque. They do represent two very different religious views. At the left in figure 13.2 is the site of the Roman Hippodrome where the chariot races were staged. The lower column is the Column of Serpents that the Romans took from the Temple of Apollo at Delphi. The upper column is the Obelisk of Theodosius that the Emperor had moved to Constantinople from the Temple of Karnak. In turn, Istanbul has been a Greek, Roman, Christian, and Muslim city.

The Great Mosque

Begun by Caliph Abd al-Rahman in the eighth century, the mosque of the caliphs of Cordoba (figure 13.5) is so large that a sixteenth-century Christian church was built in its midst. With no axis and thus no focus, the forest of columns—856 in all—symbolizes the worshippers who are as individual as the columns but who are all united in common prayer, part of the great community of believers. The striped arches are a Muslim invention but the columns were recycled, having been taken from Roman and Christian buildings. In common with mosques throughout the Muslim world, the Great Mosque has no sculpture and no figurative decoration. There is no prohibition against the painting of pictures or the representation of living forms in Islam and no mention of figurative art in the Koran. Mosques, however, never have any figurative art lest there be a misinterpretation of idolotry; idolotry was expressly prohibited.

The doorway of the Great Mosque (figure 13.6) emphasizes the characteristic horseshoe arch of Mozarabic (Spanish Christian) design. Lavishly embellished with mosaics and abstract reliefs, the overall style is best described as Moorish, a synthesis of North African and Spanish styles. One of the glories of Muslim Spain, the Great Mosque was only one of the wonders of Cordoba, itself the most illustrious center of art and learning in all of Europe until its conquest by Christians in 1236.

The Alhambra

The ponderous exterior of the palace of the caliphs of Granada, the Alhambra, shields an inner architectural fairyland resonating to the liquid murmer of running water. Because of its desert origins, Islam pictures Hell and Paradise as extensions of the natural environment; Hell is an arid and flaming inferno while Paradise is like an oasis: cool, wet, and lush. Drawing unlimited water from the snows of the Sierra Nevadas, the caliphs built an earthly paradise: delicate, intimate, cooled and soothed by playful fountains and the channels of water coursing throughout the palace, the embodiment of what an Arabian Nights setting should be. The main units of the palace are patios framed by architecture. The Court of Myrtles (figure 13.7) is essentially a reflecting pool patio with the illusion of floating columns and arches. Multi-colored tiles and plaster casements are decorated with elegant infinite patterns.

Another of the patios is the famous Court of Lions (figure 13.8), a kind of reverse image of the Court of Myrtles. Here the water runs through the court in slender ribbons, tying the unit together in an intimate arrangement. Fittingly, this is the area reserved exclusively for the ruler, his harem, his family, and the servants. Guarded by sculptures of stylized lions, the fountain adds its bubbling sounds to the flowing waters of a fantastic courtyard of delicate columns and arches decorated with tiles and stucco. Lacy arabesques and airy stuccoed ceilings contribute to what is actually a lucid, rhythmic design.

■
FIGURE 13.5 *Interior, The Great Mosque, 785–990, Cordoba, Spain. Now the Cathedral of Cordoba.*

■
FIGURE 13.6 *Portal, Great Mosque, Cordoba.*

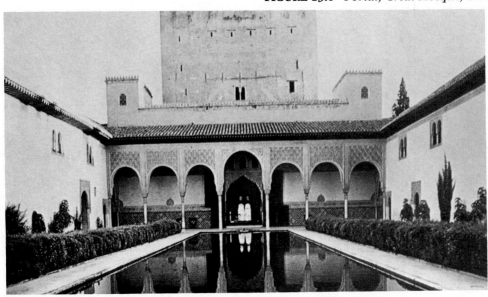

■
FIGURE 13.7 *Court of Myrtles, 1354–1391. The Alhambra, Granada, Spain.*

FIGURE 13.8 *Court of Lions, The Alhambra.*

FIGURE 13.9 *Abencerrajes Gallery, The Alhambra. Interior view looking up into the cupola.*

Not a single column is both perfectly tapered and precisely vertical, thus symbolizing the imperfections of earthly existence. In other words, even this manufactured Eden is but a defective version of the heavenly paradise to come.

The Alhambra contains some of the most elaborate stalactite vaults in all of Islam (figure 13.9). The Islamic practice of dissolving solid walls and ceilings has evolved into a fantastic array of stucco stalactites dangling from a huge honeycomb. The star-shaped cupola appears to be lightly floating atop the rhythmic in-and-out undulation of the circle of windows. The last notable structure built in Moorish Spain, the Alhambra fell to Ferdinand and Isabella in the eventful year of 1492.

Charlemagne and the Carolingian Renaissance

The expansion of Islam into France was halted by Charles Martel (688?–741), "mayor of the palace" of the Frankish kingdom of the House of Pepin. Chief official of the kingdom, Charles Martel ("the Hammer") was the first of the Carolingian line (after *Carolus,* Latin for Charles). Facing the Moors (also called Saracens) at Poitiers in western France, he used his tightly knit cavalry to drive the enemy back to Spain. Because this was the most northern Muslim penetration of Europe, the Battle of Poitiers of 732 came to be known as a landmark in European history.

Pepin the Short (ruled 751–768), son of Charles Martel, declared himself King of the Franks and further consolidated his kingdom, which was subsequently inherited by his son Charlemagne (Charles the Great, ruled 768–814). The most important political and humanistic period of the early Middle Ages, the reign of Charlemagne lit the first bright spark in the so-called Dark Ages of Western culture. Charlemagne sponsored a Carolingian Renaissance that proved that the light of civilization had not been entirely extinguished.

First, Charlemagne set about to expand and solidify the kingdom of the Franks, fighting the Muslims in Spain, the Norsemen up to the border of Denmark, and the Germanic Lombards in Italy. The Battle of Roncevaux in 778 in which Charles's knight, Count Roland, was ambushed and killed furnished the kernel for the great cycle of songs and stories relating to the exploits of Charles. In return for this warring activity against the pagans, and as a shrewd political move, the Pope crowned Charles as "Emperor of the Romans" on Christmas day in the year 800.

A Learning Revival

Important as these political events are, they cannot be our main concern. The significant factor here is that Charles had a great respect for learning and brought scholars from all Europe to his court at Aachen (Aix-la-Chapelle). The architecture of this court itself is a landmark in Western culture, for Charles had been to Ravenna where he had seen the magnificent architecture and the gleaming mosaics, the ideas for which had come directly from Byzantium. The chapel at Aachen is modeled after the Church of San Vitale in Ravenna, and it was responsible for introducing Eastern ideas of beauty and Roman stone construction to the Western world (figure 12.16, colorplate 15, and figure 15.3).

Most important of all in this revival of learning was the establishment of the Palace (or Palatine) School. To direct it, Charles imported the English scholar Alcuin from the cathedral school at York, and in addition to teaching and directing the school itself, Alcuin collected a considerable number of manuscripts of ancient learning and revived the monastic practice of copying manuscripts, both for the palace library and for distribution to other seats of learning. The Palatine School did not generate much original thought, but it was the first center of scholarship since the collapse of classical civilization and thus very important in terms of later intellectual development.

On the map labels:
NORTH SEA, IRELAND, ENGLAND, London, ATLANTIC OCEAN, BALTIC SEA, SLAVS, SAXONIA, Cologne, AUSTRASIA, Elbe R., Oder R., POLES, Paris, Seine R., NEUSTRIA, Rhine R., Regensburg, Loire R., Tours, AQUITAINE, Garonne R., BURGUNDY, Drave R., AVARS, PROVENCE, Danube R., BULGARS, KINGDOM OF ASTURIAS, Duero R., SPANISH MARCH, BLACK SEA, Tagus R., Toledo, CALIPHATE OF CORDOVA, Cordova, BALEARIC ISLANDS, SPANISH, ITALY, Rome, ADRIATIC SEA, SERBS, Constantinople, CORSICA, SARDINIA, DUCHY OF BENEVENTO, Guadalquivir R., MEDITERRANEAN SEA, SICILY, BYZANTINE EMPIRE, CRETE, CYPRUS, CALIPHATE OF BAGDAD UNDER THE ABBASIDS

Scale of Miles 0 500

The Empire of Charlemagne, 814 A.D.

Tributary peoples

MAP 13.2 *The Empire of Charlemagne in 814.*

Under Charles, northern Italy, some of northern Spain, all of France, and western and southern Germany were united under one ruler, though Charles made no attempt to impose a single law code on the diverse people (see map: The Empire of Charlemagne in 814). He did, however, have all of his counties inspected regularly to see that the lands were well governed and that justice was administered. Further than that he strengthened the power of the Church, since he forcibly Christianized all of the pagans whom he conquered. One consequence of his being crowned as emperor by the pope lay in the development of the idea that the Church was superior to all secular authority, an idea that was to give all sorts of trouble in later centuries.

After Charlemagne's death in 814, and the short rule of his ineffective son Louis the Pious, his empire was divided among his three grandsons, none of whom was able to continue the tradition that each had inherited. The empire rapidly fell apart, particularly under the invasions of the Norsemen, the Vikings, who ravaged all of Europe and even sailed to the continent that was later to be named America.

The Assimilation of Cultures

Earlier in this chapter it was pointed out that the most important development during the early Middle Ages was the digestion of several very different and opposed cultures. No one can deny that the old classic tradition of

Greece and Rome had run its full course and that it was no longer fruitful. If life was to become meaningful, new ideas, new ways of life, new blood needed to be transfused into the cultural body. The dark period from the fifth to the tenth centuries, full of fear, doubt, confusion, and strife, was the result of these clashing cultures. From the vantage point of not having to live in those times, this can now be seen as a period of transition leading to a new culture.

In the main, Byzantine and Muslim cultures remained as storehouses that would be drawn upon by European civilization in the later Middle Ages. Except for a brief conquest of Italy and North Africa under the Eastern emperor Justinian and the influence we have already noted during the rule of Charlemagne, Byzantium was chiefly important as a bastion against Eastern infringement upon Europe by the Persians, and by the Slavic and Magyar peoples who settled in what is now Hungary, the Balkans, and southern Russia. These peoples were Christianized and civilized chiefly by missionaries from the Eastern Catholic Church. Another and rather unusual influence of the East came through the Christianizing of Ireland according to the Eastern ritual. For a time at least, Ireland enjoyed a higher and more enlightened culture than did the rest of Europe, and subtle influences of this civilization reached the mainland, mostly in the form of Irish missionaries.

A Day on a Medieval Manor

The dawning sun glistens on the manor castle with its thick stone walls, conical roofs, crocketed eaves, tall chimneys, and weather vanes. It is autumn in southern France in the Year of Our Lord 1149. The lord of the castle, Sir Henri Duval, throws off the embroidered spread and linen covers as he climbs out of his feather-mattress bed. Pulling a silk tunic over his head he steps into breeches with thigh-high stockings and curled-toe shoes. Buckling on scabbard and sword, he hangs a pendant cross about his neck. Tossing a short cape (which doubles as a hood) over his shoulders, he mounts the winding stairs to the tower to scan the horizon for approaching peril—though times are now more peaceful (and prosperous) than his father ever knew.

Descending to the manor chapel, Henri attends mass with his personal priest before he meets with his steward (bailiff) to review the accounts of his serfs. Maybe he should increase the small fees the peasants pay to use the manor ovens, water mill, wine press, individual field strips, common pasture, and kindling from his woods.

It is now mid-morning and time for the big meal of the day. The large dining hall, painted bright green, is adorned with banners, armor, weapons, and hanging tapestries that help keep out the drafts. The stone floor is covered with small rushes and boughs, not to mention the hounds sleeping near the central hearth. The room is crowded with tables for Henri's host of retainers. A knight himself, Henri is in turn vassal to a baron, who has given him this fief in return for his sworn allegiance and his provision of twenty men-at-arms, fully trained and equipped, to fight for the baron. In addition to the troops there are the ladies in waiting, household servants, priest, steward, entertainers, and all the children. Joining his wife, Marie, at the head table, Henri admires her elegant velvet gown and the pink silk scarf imported from the Holy Land. Eggs, black bread, cheese, and roast pork are eaten with the fingers from pewterware, and washed down with wine and beer while the troubadour plays his lute and sings songs of chivalry and courtly love.

After the meal Marie oversees the making of butter and cheese and then checks on the bakery, laundry, winery, and brewery. Then she will turn to the clothes-making industry: spinning, knitting, weaving, and embroidering. As mistress of the castle her authority equals that of the lord.

The lord himself gratefully rides away from the castle bustle, passing the wooden stables, storehouses, outhouses, and servants' quarters. When the manor was last attacked, he muses, all the serfs were crowded inside the fortified walls along with a veritable zoo of cattle, pigs, chickens, and dogs. Now the serfs are busily harvesting grapes. Dressed in coarse blouses and trousers, wool jackets, and boots, they empty their baskets into an oxcart holding two huge tubs brimming with the luscious purple harvest.

Better to be a lord than a serf, Henri mutters to himself as he rides past another field where cereal grain had been harvested last summer. Later in the fall the peasants will work together to harvest the lord's fields and their own strips of land. And then it will be time to plow the fallow field. Since the invention of the horse collar more horses than ponderous oxen are used to pull the heavy plows and harrows. New technology certainly increases farm efficiency.

Near the fields are the peasant dwellings—miserable hovels made of wattle (braided twigs) and mud with bare earth floors that were usually cold and damp. Beds are made of coarse fern branches called bracken. The diet is equally grim. Fruit is rare and the meager vegetables usually limited to onions, turnips, cabbages, and leeks. These are boiled in water to make a thin soup. They have, the peasants say, two-course meals: a gruel much like porridge and a porridge much like gruel. Meat is so rare that it usually takes a holy-day festival to bring forth a chicken or a scrawny pig. However, the lord does invite everyone to the castle on a feast day or two each year.

Beyond the common pasture, where peasant livestock are grazing, is the manor's deep forest. There Sir Henri hunts grouse, thrush, pigeons, and small game, both for sport and for the castle larder, but only for the castle. Peasants who poached were promptly punished.

Henri returns home by late afternoon to change his clothes and join Marie in the dining room, where supper is not nearly as interesting as the upcoming jousting tournament. Knights will ride in from near and far and show off their fighting prowess before adoring women of all ages. While the warriors hone their skills the boys will receive their lessons in the art of war. Who needs priestly lessons in reading and writing when you can wear shining armor and ride a prancing white horse?

After a game of chess with his steward, the master retires, leaving the securing of the castle to his lady in her customary role as keeper of the keys. She breezes through her nightly routine: quick inventory of wine bottles, banking the hearth fires, instructions for tomorrow's menus and chores. As she sinks into sleep, Marie wonders if her husband realizes that she works much harder than he does. Probably not.

As discussed previously, the single strongest influence on Western culture was Islamic religion and culture. That influence was twofold: Islam as a powerful cultural force in its own right and Islam as a storehouse of classical civilization.

A Cultural Blend

By far the greatest cultural fusion in the early Middle Ages was that of the Celto-Germanic peoples of the north with the Graeco-Romans of the south. We have already become well acquainted with the balanced and intellectual culture of the Greeks and Romans, whose horizontal-linear architecture and predictable designs in art and architecture give a clue, at least, to their reposeful, rational character. We have already seen, too, that many of the northern people had come into the Roman Empire either by invitation, infiltration, or military conquest. But these people were vastly different in basic character from the Romans. Their architectural line was energetic, vertical, and angular; their decorations were twisted and unpredictable. Just about the time of the removal of Roman authority, we witness a great folk-wandering of these peoples, with tribes from the east pressing upon the Germanic tribes, and they, in turn, moving outward both as colonizers and as warlike raiders through all of the continent of Europe. This restless movement of peoples was to continue for centuries, with an inevitable clash and subsequent fusion of the two cultures.

The Norsemen

The basic social organization of these northern peoples was the *comitatus*, which was the banding together of a group of fighting men under the leadership of a warrior chieftain. The men pledged their loyalty and their strength to the chief, and he, in turn, promised to give them rewards from captured plunder. Thus in the early Germanic poem of *Beowulf*, both the hero and another leader, Hrothgar, are frequently called "ringgivers" from their roles as leaders distributing gold to their fighting men. Once the comitatus was formed, it had only one function: to fight, to capture, and to plunder. The dragonships of the Norsemen were frequent and fearful visitors in England and all Europe.

But there is another aspect to these people that is revealed in their religion. The contemporary philosopher Lewis Mumford has spoken of the Graeco-Romans as "pessimistic of the body and optimistic for the soul," and of the Celto-Germanic peoples as "optimistic of the body but pessimistic for the spirit." The distinction is a valid one. The classic and Christian southern peoples regarded life here on earth only as a short period of pain and sorrow to be followed, they hoped, by a joyous afterlife in heaven. The Celto-Germanics ate greatly, drank deeply, raped widely, but were ultimately pessimistic about the afterlife. Theirs was perhaps the only religion that pictures the ultimate defeat of the "good" gods by the forces of evil and darkness.

The Norsemen worshipped a group of anthropomorphic "good" gods who lived in a celestial residence called Valhalla. Wotan was the king of the gods; the most active, certainly, was Thor, the thunder god. Baldur represented the idea of beauty, springtime, and warmth; Loki was the trickster. Even in the heavenly abode the pessimistic nature of these gods appears, for, through a trick of Loki's, Baldur was slain. For the fighting men on earth, an afterlife among the gods was promised, but far different from any heaven conceived of by Christians, Muslims, or Jews. If a warrior was killed in battle, semidivine maidens (the Valkyrie) swooped over the battlefield to take him to Valhalla. Here the hero simply continued his earthly life of fighting, eating, and drinking.

For the gods and heroes, however, an awful fate was predicted, for Valhalla was surrounded by the land of the giant Jotuns, probably representing the cold and the darkness of the northern climate. The gods and the Jotuns were engaged in constant small warfare and trickery, but in the Norse religion, the future held a great battle between the two forces, with the Jotuns winning and bringing about the downfall of the gods. Thus the ultimate and total pessimism of the spirit of the Scandinavian-Germanic people.

Boethius

The difference between the Graeco-Roman and the Celto-Germanic personalities has been suggested earlier with a comparison between the structural line and the type of ornamentation that each found beautiful and that, therefore, may give a clue to the differences in character. A comparison between the type of literature each culture produced may strengthen our awareness of the clash of cultures. No better example of the Graeco-Roman literature of the very early Middle Ages can be found than Boethius's *Consolation of Philosophy*. Boethius, one remembers, was a Roman consul, serving under the Roman emperor (actually an ostrogoth) Theodoric. The *Consolation* was written in the year 524 while he was languishing in prison awaiting death after being accused by his emperor of treason.

Boethius gives his work the form of a highly rational dialogue between himself as a man who is deeply distressed by his fate in the world, and a vision of philosophy as a stately woman. The dialogue is interspersed with poetical passages that serve to sum up the previous discussion and form a bridge into their next topic. The subjects for discussion range from the nature of fortune and chance, of happiness, the existence of evil, of free will, and the paradox of humanity's free will and an all-knowing God. In reading the whole discussion, one is reminded of a Sokratic dialogue, and indeed Boethius draws heavily on Platonic thought. While the ideas themselves are not new, the reader is constantly aware of a classic coolness and dignified withdrawal from the passions of life. Perhaps a brief quotation may make this clear. The excerpt is drawn from book III, prose X. Philosophy speaks first:

> "But it has been conceded that the highest Good is happiness?"
>
> "Yes," I said.
>
> "Therefore," she said, "it must be confessed that God is Happiness itself."
>
> "I cannot gainsay what you premised before," said I, "and I perceive that this follows necessarily from those premises."
>
> "Look, then," she said, "whether the same proposition is not proved more strongly by the following argument: there cannot be two different highest Goods. For it is clear that where there are two different goods the one cannot be the other; wherefore neither one can be the perfect Good while each is wanting to the other. And that which is not perfect is manifestly not the highest; therefore, if two things are the highest Good, they can by no means be different. Further, we have concluded that both God and happiness are the highest Good; therefore the highest Deity must be identical with the highest happiness."
>
> "No conclusion," said I, "could be truer in fact or stronger in theory or worthier of God."
>
> "Over and above this," she said, "let me give you a corollary such as geometricians are wont to do when they wish to derive a deduction from the propositions they have demonstrated. Since men become happy by attaining happiness, and happiness is identical with divinity, it is plain that they become happy by attaining divinity. And as men become just by attaining justice and wise by attaining widom, so by the same reasoning they become godlike by attaining divinity. Every happy man, then, is God-like; but, while there is nothing to prevent as many men as possible for being God-like, only one is God by nature: men are God-like by participation."[2]

Northern Hero Epics

Nothing could be more urbane, civilized, classic, or rational than the discussion cited above. To become aware of the difference in spirit between this and the Celto-Germanic personality, one may look briefly at two of the hero-epics from the northern people. *Beowulf* and the *Nibelungenlied* will serve as examples. The very sound of the harsh lines, much smoothed and rounded in modern English translation, reveals something of the lusty vigor of the people. Consider, for example, the alliteration of crashing consonants in the line, "Bit his bone-frame, drank blood from his veins." This is a far cry from the epics of Greece and Rome in its very tone.

---

2. Boethius, *The Consolation of Philosophy*, edited by James J. Buchanan (New York: Frederick Ungar Publishing Co., 1957), 31–32.

Beowulf

The story of Beowulf is almost equally harsh. It tells of Beowulf, a warrior from the south of Sweden who went to the court of his uncle in Denmark. There he slew a monster, Grendel, who had been devastating the uncle's kingdom. As a trophy of the fight, Beowulf brought home the arm and shoulder of the monster as it had been wrenched from the giant's torso. Following the victory, a great banquet was held in the hero's honor. Having eaten and drunk until they could hold no more, Beowulf and his men lay down on the floor of the banquet hall, their war gear hanging by them, for the night's rest. But when all was quiet, Grendel's mother entered the hall, killed some of the men, and took the bloody arm and shoulder of her son back to the home she had beneath the waters of a dismal fen.

On the next morning Beowulf set out and tracked Grendel's mother to the shore of a swamp. Fearlessly he donned his armor and plunged into the water, down to the opening of the cave. Here he grappled with the hag-monster and finally killed her with a weapon forged by the giants of old. (See the Literary Selections.)

The last episode of the poem tells of Beowulf's last days when, as king or chief of his Swedish tribe, his own land was threatened by a dragon. As a warrior hero and leader, he went forth, killed the dragon, and was mortally wounded himself. The poem ends with his funeral pyre as a Viking chieftain, and the construction of his tomb as a monument that would serve as a landmark for Viking ships at sea.

Beowulf was never tender, never kind, never sympathetic. When his friends were slain in battle or in the great hall of Heorot, he never wept for them or extolled their virtues. Rather, he swore vengeance and went forth to do it. He was the mighty warrior, the great adventurer. Such was the Germanic hero.

Song of the Niblungs

Another example is at once older and younger; it is the German tale called the *Nibelungenlied,* or *Song of the Niblungs.* It was not written down in its present form until the 1200s, but its materials hark back to the days of Attila the Hun, in the fifth century. The Scandinavian version of the tale is known as the *Volsunga saga;* Wagner freely adapted the tale in his four music-dramas, *The Ring of the Nibelung.*

The epic is concerned with the hero Siegfried, who loved Kriemhild, sister of the Burgundian king, Gunther. In order to win her, Siegfried promised his help in Gunther's wooing of Brunhild, the warlike queen of a distant country. By magical means Siegfried assisted him in the feats of strength that won her. On their wedding night, Brunhild tied Gunther up in knots, and hung him behind the door; again it was Siegfried who came to the rescue, and on the second night, wrapped in his cloak of invisibility, wrestled with her and subdued her, without Brunhild's being aware that her adversary was Siegfried, not Gunther. How he took from her then a ring and a girdle, giving them to Kriemhild; how the two queens quarreled; how Kriemhild, in haughty anger, revealed the trick of Brunhild's conquest; and how Brunhild plotted revenge, is quickly recounted. The climax of the first part is the treacherous murder of Siegfried by Hagen, the loyal henchman of Gunther, and the villain of the piece. The last half of the story concerns Kriemhild's revenge against the Burgundians. Married, after many years, to Etzel (Attila), King of the Huns, she invited the Burgundians to visit her, and there follows a general massacre in which they are all slain, including Kriemhild.

One sees in these epics the warrior's world of the first half of the medieval period, its spirit of adventure, courage, bravery, harshness, and blood.

Perhaps these examples can help one to visualize the difference between the character of the two peoples who encountered each other during the early Middle Ages. So important was it that Dorothy Sayers in her introduction to the translation of the *Divine Comedy* attributes the origin of the two great political factions that tore Italy apart in late medieval times, the Guelfs and the Ghibellines, to this cultural difference. She contends that the Ghibellines represented the descendants of the northern stock with all of their vigorous energy, and that the Guelfs were essentially the native Italian land-owning, placid southern people.

Be that as it may, by the tenth century the two cultures achieved a physical amalgamation. Many of the northerners had moved to the south, had become Christianized, and had given up some of their savage ways. The Anglos and Saxons settled in England, other Norsemen took over the great province of Normandy in France. Throughout all of Europe the Germanic people settled and took land, so that the northern chieftain moved into the already evolving feudal system, becoming a baron or a count, a duke or a knight, holding land from his suzerain and granting fiefs to those under him. It was still a warlike society, the difference being chiefly in its fairly settled nature. The leader gave up his wooden hall for a castle built of stone. The highest virtue became a mutual loyalty between the lord and his vassals.

Song of Roland

The *Song of Roland* furnishes a good example of this new civilization. This minor epic was written in French at about the time of the first crusade (the 1090s), but the written version simply records a hero-story that had been sung and recited concerning the events that happened (legendarily) three centuries before in the days of Charlemagne. The persons of the story are Franks, the Germanic conquerors who gave their name to France; the central figure is Roland, the emperor's nephew. The central event of the poem is the ambush by Saracens of the rear guard of Charlemagne's army in the passes of the Pyrenees at Roncevaux. (During the Middle Ages, Christians called all Muslims Saracens regardless of nationality. These Saracens were actually Moors from Spain.)

The ambush was arranged by Roland's treacherous kinsman Ganelon, who was inspired by envy and revenge. Roland and his companion, Oliver, together with the militant Archbishop Turpin, are the last survivors of the Frankish host; they too are killed, facing overwhelming odds. One of the best-known episodes is that of Roland's refusal to blow his ivory horn (oliphant), despite the urging of Oliver, to recall Charlemagne's host before the battle begins. When he realizes that he and his Franks are doomed, he does at last blow three mighty blasts that Charlemagne hears, thirty leagues away, and the Emperor returns to rout the Saracens and avenge the death of Roland and his companions. The epic concludes with the trial and punishment of Ganelon.

It is a truly feudal poem, full of the vigorous, active, restless spirit of the northern warrior. Roland is the man-at-arms, the warrior, unsoftened by the chivalry of later knighthood; he is a splendid barbarian, courageous in the face of overwhelming odds, loyal to his friends, utterly devoted to God, his spiritual overlord, and to Charlemagne, his temporal one. He is blood brother to his earlier northern kinsman, Beowulf; both heroes represent the all-out, do-or-die, go-for-broke spirit of the heroic age.

There are many magnificent scenes: the pathetic one in which the wounded Oliver, dazed and blinded by blood, strikes his best friend Roland, and the two are immediately reconciled; the striking one in which Roland tries to shatter his sword, "Durendal," against a rock lest its hilt, which is a reliquary with sacred relics in it, fall into pagan hands. Let us read only one, the one hundred and seventy-sixth stanza, or "laisse," of the poem:

And now Count Roland,   lying beneath a pine,
Has turned his face   to look toward pagan Spain;
And he begins   remembering these things:
The many lands   his valor won the king,
Sweet France, his home,   the men of his own line,
And Charlemagne   who raised him in his house—   *2380*
The memories   make him shed tears and sigh.
But not forgetting   how close he is to death,
He prays that God   forgive him all his sins:
"O my true Father,   O Thou who never lied,
Thou who delivered   Lazarus from the grave,
Who rescued Daniel   out of the lions' den,
Keep now my soul   from every peril safe,
Forgive the sins   that I have done in life."
Roland, in homage,   offers his glove to God.
Saint Gabriel comes   and takes it from his hand.   *2390*
His head sinks down   to rest upon his arm;
Hands clasped in prayer,   the count has met his end.
God sends from heaven   the angel Cherubin,
Holy Saint Michael   who saves us from the sea,
And with these two   the Angel Gabriel flies.
Count Roland's soul   they bring to Paradise.

The similarities and differences between this story and that of *Beowulf* are immediately apparent. *Roland*, with its heavy Christian overlay, is much more "civilized" than the early epic. But it is still a very masculine, savagely militaristic poem, extolling the glories of war, of bravery, and of loyalty. Not least interesting in the poem is the role of the Archbishop Turpin, who is a great Church leader, at least in title. Throughout the battle, however, he ranges through the ranks of fighting men, wielding his great mace (at this time it was illegal for a churchman to wield a sword) and breaking heads with the best of them. We see here a new role of the Church, with churchmen active in feudal society, holding great areas of land, and as much concerned with battle and secular affairs as with the religious life. The final act of Roland reveals much of the spirit of the time, for his offer of his glove to God is the very act of pledging loyalty to a feudal lord. Roland, always a vassal of Charlemagne, has now accepted a new suzerain in God, and the acceptance of the glove signifies God's approval of Roland as a vassal in the celestial feudal system.

Exercises

1. In your own words explain how Augustine could believe that people have free will but that God knows the future.
2. Explain how each heresy—Arian and Donatist—differed from the official position (doctrine) of the Church of Rome. Why didn't the church permit several versions of doctrine? What did the church do to eliminate these heresies? Can violence against heretics be justified? Why or why not?
3. Describe the key features of a medieval manor. How does this differ from a contemporary American farm community?
4. Review, in your own words, the basic articles and duties of Islam and explain what they mean. Compare these with Roman Catholicism and with some specific Protestant church. What are the critical differences between the three religions? How does Islam compare with Judaism?
5. Explain how and why Islam expanded so rapidly. Can violence in the name of religion be justified? Have Christians ever waged holy wars?
6. What, exactly, was the Carolingian Renaissance? Why would a semiliterate king promote a cultural revival?

7. In practical terms, how did a Germanic *comitatus* work? Was this similar to the feudal system? Why didn't these northern people have manors?
8. Contrast the vision of the hereafter of the Norse religion with the Graeco–Roman tradition and then compare both with medieval Christianity. What are the key differences? What do the differences say about the three cultures?

Literary Selections

Beowulf's Fight with Grendel's Dam from BEOWULF

The oldest of English epics, *Beowulf* probably dates from early in the eighth century. Written by an unknown author of exceptional talent, the poem is a brilliant example of the masculine code, the embodiment of the heroic tradition.[3] In the brief excerpt given below (see page 312 for a synopsis of the plot), Beowulf tracks Grendel's hag-mother to her cave in the depths of a swamp where he battles her to the death. The modern translation in alliterative verse is by Charles W. Kennedy; the line numbers are from Klaeber's Old English text.

> Beowulf spoke, the son of Ecgtheow:
> 'Sorrow not, brave one! Better for man
> To avenge a friend than much to mourn.
> All men must die; let him who may
> Win glory ere death. That guerdon is best
> For a noble man when his name survives him.
> Then let us rise up, O ward of the realm,
> And haste us forth to behold the track
> Of Grendel's dam. And I give you pledge
> She shall not in safety escape to cover,
> To earthy cavern, or forest fastness,
> Or gulf of ocean, go where she may.
> This day with patience endure the burden
> Of every woe, as I know you will.'
> Up sprang the ancient, gave thanks to God
> For the heartening words the hero had spoken.
>
> Quickly a horse was bridled for Hrothgar,
> A mettlesome charger with braided mane;
> In royal splendor the king rode forth
> Mid the trampling tread of a troop of shieldmen.
> The tracks lay clear where the fiend had fared
> Over plain and bottom and woodland path,
> Through murky moorland making her way
> With the lifeless body, the best of thanes
> Who of old with Hrothgar had guarded the hall.
> By a narrow path the king pressed on
>
> [1384–1408]
>
> Through rocky upland and rugged ravine,
> A lonely journey, past looming headlands,
> The lair of monster and lurking troll.

---

3. The warrior code of *Beowulf* should be compared with the courtly code of the age of chivalry in chapter 14 (*The Art of Courtly Love, Morte Darthur*) and in chapter 16 (troubadour-trouvère tradition).

Tried retainers, a trusty few,
Advanced with Hrothgar to view the ground.
Sudden they came on a dismal covert
Of trees that hung over hoary stone,
Over churning water and blood-stained wave.
Then for the Danes was the woe the deeper,
The sorrow sharper for Scylding earls,
When they first caught sight, on the rocky sea-cliff,
Of slaughtered Æschere's severed head.
The water boiled in a bloody swirling
With seething gore as the spearmen gazed.
The trumpet sounded a martial strain;
The shield-troop halted. Their eyes beheld
The swimming forms of strange sea-dragons,
Dim serpent shapes in the watery depths,
Sea-beasts sunning on headland slopes;
Snakelike monsters that oft at sunrise
On evil errands scour the sea.
Startled by tumult and trumpet's blare,
Enraged and savage, they swam away;
But one the lord of the Geats brought low,
Stripped of his sea-strength, despoiled of life,
As the bitter bow-bolt pierced his heart.
His watery-speed grew slower, and ceased,
And he floated, caught in the clutch of death.
Then they hauled him in with sharp-hooked boar-spears,
By sheer strength grappled and dragged him ashore,
A wondrous wave-beast; and all the array

[1409–1440]

Gathered to gaze at the grisly guest.
    Beowulf donned his armor for battle,
Heeded not danger; the hand-braided byrny,
Broad of shoulder and richly bedecked,
Must stand the ordeal of the watery depths.
Well could that corselet defend the frame
Lest hostile thrust should pierce to the heart.
Or blows of battle beat down the life.
A gleaming helmet guarded his head
As he planned his plunge to the depths of the pool
Through the heaving waters—a helm adorned
With lavish inlay and lordly chains,
Ancient work of the weapon-smith
Skillfully fashioned, beset with the boar,
That no blade of battle might bite it through.
Not the least or the worst of his war-equipment
Was the sword the herald of Hrothgar loaned
In his hour of need—Hrunting its name—
An ancient heirloom, trusty and tried;
Its blade was iron, with etched design,
Tempered in blood of many a battle.
Never in fight had it failed the hand
That drew it daring the perils of war,
The rush of the foe. Not the first time then
That its edge must venture on valiant deeds.
But Ecglaf's stalwart son was unmindful
Of words he had spoken while heated with wine,
When he loaned the blade to a better swordsman.
He himself dared not hazard his life
In deeds of note in the watery depths;
And thereby he forfeited honor and fame.

[1440–1471]

Not so with that other undaunted spirit
After he donned his armor for battle.

Beowulf spoke, the son of Ecgtheow:
'O gracious ruler, gold-giver to men,
As I now set forth to attempt this feat,
Great son of Healfdene, hold well in mind
The solemn pledge we plighted of old,
That if doing your service I meet my death
You will mark my fall with a father's love.
Protect my kinsmen, my trusty comrades,
If battle take me. And all the treasure
You have heaped on me bestow upon Hygelac,
Hrothgar beloved! The lord of the Geats,
The son of Hrethel, shall see the proof,
Shall know as he gazes on jewels and gold,
That I found an unsparing dispenser of bounty,
And joyed, while I lived, in his generous gifts.
Give back to Unferth the ancient blade,
The sword-edge splendid with curving scrolls,
For either with Hrunting I'll reap rich harvest
Of glorious deeds, or death shall take me.'
    After these words the prince of the Weders
Awaited no answer, but turned to the task,
Straightway plunged in the swirling pool.
Nigh unto a day he endured the depths
Ere he first had view of the vast sea-bottom.
Soon she found, who had haunted the flood,
A ravening hag, for a hundred half-years,
Greedy and grim, that a man was groping
In daring search through the sea-troll's home.
Swift she grappled and grasped the warrior

[1471–1501]

With horrid grip, but could work no harm,
No hurt to his body; the ring-locked byrny
Cloaked his life from her clutching claw;
Nor could she tear through the tempered mail
With her savage fingers. The she-wolf bore
The ring-prince down through the watery depths
To her den at the bottom; nor could Beowulf draw
His blade for battle, though brave his mood.
Many a sea-beast, strange sea-monsters,
Tasked him hard with their menacing tusks,
Broke his byrny and smote him sore.
    Then he found himself in a fearsome hall
Where water came not to work him hurt,
But the flood was stayed by the sheltering roof.
There in the glow of firelight gleaming
The hero had view of the huge sea-troll.
He swung his war-sword with all his strength,
Withheld not the blow, and the savage blade
Sang on her head its hymn of hate.
But the bold one found that the battle-flasher
Would bite no longer, nor harm her life.
The sword-edge failed at his sorest need.
Often of old with ease it had suffered
The clash of battle, cleaving the helm,
The fated warrior's woven mail.
That time was first for the treasured blade
That its glory failed in the press of the fray.

But fixed of purpose and firm of mood
Hygelac's earl was mindful of honor;
In wrath, undaunted, he dashed to earth
The jewelled sword with its scrolled design,

[1502–1532]

The blade of steel; staked all on strength,
On the might of his hand, as a man must do
Who thinks to win in the welter of battle
Enduring glory; he fears not death.
The Geat-prince joyed in the straining struggle,
Stalwart-hearted and stirred to wrath,
Gripped the shoulder of Grendel's dam
And headlong hurled the hag to the ground.
But she quickly clutched him and drew him close,
Countered the onset with savage claw.
The warrior staggered, for all his strength,
Dismayed and shaken and borne to earth.
She knelt upon him and drew her dagger,
With broad bright blade, to avenge her son,
Her only issue. But the corselet's steel
Shielded his breast and sheltered his life
Withstanding entrance of point and edge.
    Then the prince of the Geats would have gone his
        journey,
The son of Ecgtheow, under the ground;
But his sturdy breast-net, his battle-corselet,
Gave him succor, and holy God,
The Lord all-wise, awarded the mastery;
Heaven's Ruler gave right decree.
    Swift the hero sprang to his feet;
Saw mid the war-gear a stately sword,
An ancient war-brand of biting edge,
Choicest of weapons worthy and strong,
The work of giants, a warrior's joy,
So heavy no hand but his own could hold it,
Bear to battle or wield in war.

[1533–1562]

Then the Scylding warrior, savage and grim,
Seized the ring-hilt and swung the sword,
Struck with fury, despairing of life,
Thrust at the throat, broke through the bone-rings;
The stout blade stabbed through her fated flesh.
She sank in death; the sword was bloody;
The hero joyed in the work of his hand.
The gleaming radiance shimmered and shone
As the candle of heaven shines clear from the sky.
Wrathful and resolute Hygelac's thane
Surveyed the span of the spacious hall;
Grimly gripping the hilted sword
With upraised weapon he turned to the wall.
The blade had failed not the battle-prince;
A full requital he firmly planned
For all the injury Grendel had done
In numberless raids on the Danish race,

When he slew the hearth-companions of Hrothgar,
Devoured fifteen of the Danish folk
Clasped in slumber, and carried away
As many more spearmen, a hideous spoil.
All this the stout-heart had stern requited;
And there before him bereft of life
He saw the broken body of Grendel
Stilled in battle, and stretched in death,
As the struggle in Heorot smote him down.
The corpse sprang wide as he struck the blow,
The hard sword-stroke that severed the head.
    Then the tried retainers, who there with Hrothgar
Watched the face of the foaming pool,
Saw that the churning reaches were reddened,

[1563–1593]

The eddying surges stained with blood.
And the gray, old spearmen spoke of the hero,
Having no hope he would ever return
Crowned with triumph and cheered with spoil.
Many were sure that the savage sea-wolf
Had slain their leader. At last came noon.
The stalward Scyldings forsook the headland;
Their proud gold-giver departed home.
But the Geats sat grieving and sick in spirit,
Stared at the water with longing eyes,
Having no hope they would ever behold
Their gracious leader and lord again.
    Then the great sword, eaten with blood of battle,
Began to soften and waste away
In iron icicles, wonder of wonders,
Melting away most like to ice
When the Father looses the fetters of frost,
Slackens the bondage that binds the wave,
Strong in power of times and seasons;
He is true God! Of the goodly treasures
From the sea-cave Beowulf took but two,
The monster's head and the precious hilt
Blazing with gems; but the blade had melted,
The sword dissolved, in the deadly heat,
The venomous blood of the fallen fiend.

Exercises

1. Literary heroes generally symbolize the virtues
   that a culture values. Consider the heroic
   Beowulf and then describe the traits that
   Germanic culture prized.
2. In American culture, movie heroes frequently
   exemplify the virtues that Americans, at a given
   time, prize. What do the following popular
   heroes tell us (during their popularity) about
   American values—John Wayne, Clint Eastwood,
   Rocky, Rambo?

EVERYMAN

Medieval drama began in the tenth century as liturgical drama (discussed in detail in chapter 16), out of which grew plays in the vernacular called mysteries or mystery plays (a corruption of the Latin *ministerium,* service). Performed by trade guilds, mystery plays were cycles depicting the history of humanity from damnation to redemption. The various guilds enacted episodes associated with their own craft; thus, the shipwright's guild was responsible for the building of the ark, the water drawers for Noah's flood, the goldsmiths for the story of the magi, and so on.

Performed outdoors from dawn to dusk on "pageants" (L. *paginae*), wagons consisting of roofed platforms on wheels, the plays used scanty scenery but often elaborate costumes. Cycles like, for example, *The Second Shepherd's Play* included a large repertoire of acting conventions, comic elaboration, and considerable opportunity for improvisation. During the sixteenth century the plays became more and more secular, with increasing elements of comedy and outright buffoonery until, during the reign of Elizabeth I, they were suppressed. By this time they had been superseded by the plays of Marlowe and Shakespeare.

On the continent miracle plays dealt with miracles worked by the saints; in England the word was interchangeable with mystery. A completely separate category, but developing along with mystery plays, the morality play was a single work rather than a cycle. Mystery plays dramatized biblical events to show their relevance to everyday life; morality plays were more directly didactic, enacting the conflict between good and evil, the constant struggle within each person between virtue and vice.

The contest was presented as an allegory with virtues and vices personified: Patience vs. Anger, Pride vs. Humility, and so forth. A key element was penance, the recognition and confession of sin to the priest followed by absolution, on condition of the performance of assigned penances. One of the primary themes of *Everyman* is the necessity of penitence for sin before death within the discipline of the church.

Everyman was written about 1485 and may be a translation of a Dutch play on the same theme or possibly the Dutch play was a translation from the English. The most famous of its type, *Everyman* is not a battle between opposites but rather a somber stripping of wordly goods from a man, concentrating on his increasing isolation as he descends into the grave. Only Good Deeds is left as a mediator between him and Judgment. *Everyman* is a moral allegory of preparation for death, a solemn statement of the human predicament, and, no less important, an exposition of church doctrine.

■

FIGURE 13.10 *Morality play performed in York Cathedral. Woodcut, from The Bettmann Archive.*

CHARACTERS:

Messenger	Knowledge
God (Adonai)	Confession
Death	Beauty
Everyman	Strength
Fellowship	Discretion
Kindred	Five-Wits
Cousin	Angel
Goods	Doctor
Good-Deeds	

HERE BEGINNETH A TREATISE HOW THE HIGH FATHER OF HEAVEN SENDETH DEATH TO SUMMON EVERY CREATURE TO COME AND GIVE ACCOUNT OF THEIR LIVES IN THIS WORLD AND IS IN MANNER OF A MORAL PLAY.

Messenger: I pray you all give your audience,
And hear this matter with reverence,
By figure a moral play—
The *Summoning of Everyman* called it is,
That of our lives and ending shows
How transitory we be all day.

Everyman → represents mankind called to die

This matter is wondrous precious,
But the intent of it is more gracious,
And sweet to bear away.
The story saith,—Man, in the beginning,
Look well, and take good heed to the ending,
Be you never so gay!
Ye think sin in the beginning full sweet,
Which in the end causeth thy soul to weep,
When the body lieth in clay.
Here shall you see how *Fellowship* and *Jollity*,
Both *Strength, Pleasure,* and *Beauty,*
Will fade from thee as flower in May.
For ye shall hear, how our heaven king
Calleth *Everyman* to a general reckoning:
Give audience, and hear what he doth say.
God: I perceive here in my majesty,
How that all creatures be to me unkind,
Living without dread in wordly prosperity:
Of ghostly sight the people be so blind,
Drowned in sin, they know me not for their God:
In worldly riches is all their mind,
They fear not my right wiseness, the sharp rod:
My law that I shewed, when I for them died,
They forget clean, and shedding of my blood red:
I hanged between two, it cannot be denied:
To get them life I suffered to be dead:
I healed their feet, with thorns hurt was my head:
I could do no more than I did truly,
And now I see the people do clean forsake me,
They use the seven deadly sins damnable;
As pride, covetise, wrath, and lechery,
Now in the world be made commendable;
And thus they leave of angels the heavenly company;
Everyman liveth so after his own pleasure,
And yet of their life they be nothing sure:
I see the more that I them forbear
The worse they be from year to year;
All that liveth appaireth[4] fast,
Therefore I will in all the haste
Having a reckoning of Everyman's person
For and I leave the people thus alone
In their life and wicked tempests,
Verily they will become much worse than beasts;
For now one would by envy another up eat;
Charity they all do clean forget.
I hoped well that Everyman
In my glory should make his mansion,
And thereto I had them all elect;
But now I see, like traitors deject,
They thank me not for the pleasure that I to them meant
Nor yet for their being that I them have lent;
I proffered the people great multitude of mercy,
And few there be that asketh it heartily;
They be so combered with worldly riches,
That needs of them I must do justice,
On Everyman living without fear.
Where art thou, Death, thou mighty messenger?

---

4. Is impaired.

Death: Almighty God, I am here at your will,
Your commandment to fulfil.
God: Go thou to Everyman,
And show him in my name
A pilgrimage he must on him take,
Which he in no wise may escape;
And that he bring with him a sure reckoning
Without delay or any tarrying.
Death: Lord, I will in the world go run over all,
And cruelly outsearch both great and small;
Every man will I beset that liveth beastly
Out of God's laws, and dreadeth not folly:
He that loveth riches I will strike with my dart,
His sight to blind, and from heaven to depart,
Except that alms be his good friend,
In hell for to dwell, world without end.
Lo, yonder I see Everyman walking;
Full little he thinketh on my coming;
His mind is on fleshly lusts and his treasure,
And great pain it shall cause him to endure
Before the Lord Heaven King.
Everyman, stand still; whither art thou going
Thus gaily? Hast my Maker forgot?
Everyman: Why askst thou?
Wouldest thou wete?[5]
Death: Yea, sir, I will show you;
In great haste I am sent to thee
From God out of his majesty.
Everyman: What, sent to me?
Death: Yea, certainly.
Though thou have forget him here,
He thinketh on thee in the heavenly sphere,
As, or we depart, thou shalt know.
Everyman: What desireth God of me?
Death: That shall I show thee;
A reckoning he will needs have
Without any longer respite.
Everyman: To give a reckoning longer leisure I crave;
This blind matter troubleth my wit.
Death: On thee thou must take a long journey:
Therefore thy book of count with thee thou bring;
For turn again thou can not by no way,
And look thou be sure of thy reckoning:
For before God thou shalt answer, and show
Thy many bad deeds and good but a few;
How thou hast spent thy life, and in what wise,
Before the chief lord of paradise.
Have ado that we were in that way,
For, wete thou well, thou shalt make none attournay.[6]
Everyman: Full unready I am such reckoning to give.
I know thee not: what messenger art thou?
Death: I am Death, that no man dreadeth.
For every man I rest and no man spareth;
        For it is God's commandment
That all to me should be obedient.
Everyman: O Death, thou comest when I had thee
        least in mind,
In thy power it lieth me to save,
Yet of my good will I give thee, if ye will be kind,
Yea, a thousand pound shalt thou have,
And defer this matter till another day.

---

5. Know.
6. Mediator.

Death: Everyman, it may not be by no way;
I set not by gold, silver, nor riches,
Ne by pope, emperor, king, duke, ne princes.
For and I would receive gifts great,
All the world I might get;
But my custom is clean contrary.
I give thee no respite: come hence, and not tarry.
Everyman: Alas, shall I have no longer respite?
I may say Death giveth no warning:
To think on thee, it maketh my heart sick,
For all unready is my book of reckoning.
But twelve year and I might have abiding,
My counting book I would make so clear,
That my reckoning I should not need to fear.
Wherefore, Death, I pray thee, for God's mercy,
Spare me till I be provided of remedy.
Death: Thee availeth not to cry, weep, and pray:
But haste thee lightly that you were gone the journey.
And prove thy friends if thou can.
For, wete thou well, the tide abideth no man,
And in the world each living creature
For Adam's sin must die of nature.
Everyman: Death, if I should this pilgrimage take,
And my reckoning surely make,
Show me, for saint charity,
Should I not come again shortly?
Death: No, Everyman; and thou be once there,
Thou mayst never more come here,
Trust me verily.
Everyman: O gracious God, in the high seat celestial,
Have mercy on me in this most need;
Shall I have no company from this vale terrestrial
Of mine acquaintance that way me to lead?
Death: Yea, if any be so hardy,
That would go with thee and bear thee company.
Hie thee that you were gone to God's magnificence,
Thy reckoning to give before his presence.
What, weenest thou thy life is given thee,
And thy worldly goods also?
Everyman: I had wend so, verily.
Death: Nay, nay; it was but lent thee;
For as soon as thou art go,
Another awhile shall have it, and then go therefro
Even as thou has done.
Everyman, thou art mad; thou hast thy wits five,
And here on earth will not amend thy life,
For suddenly I do come.
Everyman: O wretched caitiff, whither shall I flee,
That I might scape this endless sorrow!
Now, gentle Death, spare me till to-morrow,
That I may amend me
With good advisement.
Death: Nay, thereto I will not consent,
Nor no man will I respite,
But to the heart suddenly I shall smite
Without any advisement.
And now out of thy sight I will me nie;
See thou make thee ready shortly,
For thou mayst say this is the day
That no man living may scape away.

[handwritten margin note: O.K. to bring friend]

Everyman: Alas, I may well weep with sighs deep;
Now have I no manner of company
To help me in my journey, and me to keep;
And also my writing is full unready.
How shall I do now for to excuse me?
I would to God I had never be gete![7]
To my soul a full great profit it had be;
For now I fear pains huge and great.
The time passeth; Lord, help that all wrought;
For though I mourn it availeth nought.
The day passeth, and is almost a-go;
I wot not well what for to do.
To whom were I best my complaint to make?
What, and I to Fellowship thereof spake,
And showed him of this sudden chance?
For in him is all mine affiance;
We have in the world so many a day
Be on good friends in sport and play.
I see him yonder, certainly;
I trust that he will bear me company;
Therefore to him will I speak to ease my sorrow.
Well met, good Fellowship, and good morrow!
Fellowship: Everyman, good morrow by this day.
Sir, why lookest thou so piteously?
If any thing be amiss, I pray thee, me say,
That I may help to remedy.
Everyman: Yea, good Fellowship, yea.
I am in great jeopardy.
Fellowship: My true friend, show to me your mind;
I will not forsake thee, unto my life's end,
In the way of good company.
Everyman: That was well spoken, and lovingly.
Fellowship: Sir, I must needs know your heaviness;
I have pity to see you in any distress;
If any have ye wronged he shall revenged be,
Though I on the ground be slain for thee—
Though that I know before that I should die.
Everyman: Verily, Fellowship, gramercy.
Fellowship: Tush! by thy thanks I set not a straw;
Show me your grief, and say no more.
Everyman: If my heart should to you break,
And then you to turn your mind from me,
And would not me comfort, when you hear me speak,
Then should I ten times sorrier be.
Fellowship: Sir, I say as I will do in deed.
Everyman: Then be you a good friend at need:
I have found you true here before.
Fellowship: And so ye shall evermore;
For, in faith, and thou go to Hell,
I will not forsake thee by the way!
Everyman: Ye speak like a good friend; I believe you
    well;
I shall deserve it, and I may.

[handwritten margin note: Asks to go w/ friends]

---

7. Been gotten, been born.

Fellowship: I speak of no deserving, by this day.
For he that will say and nothing do
Is not worthy with good company to go;
Therefore show me the grief of your mind,
As to your friend most loving and kind.
Everyman: I shall show you how it is;
Commanded I am to go a journey,
A long way, hard and dangerous,
And give a strait count without delay
Before the high judge Adonai.[8]
Wherefore I pray you, bear me company,
As ye have promised, in this journey.
Fellowship: That is matter indeed! Promise is duty,
But, and I should take such a voyage on me,
I know it well, it should be to my pain:
Also it make me afeard, certain.
But let us take counsel here as well as we can,
For your words would fear a strong man.
Everyman: Why, ye said, If I had need,
Ye would me never forsake, quick nor dead,
Though it were to hell truly.
Fellowship: So I said, certainly,
But such pleasures be set aside, thee sooth to say:
And also, if we took such a journey,
When should we come again?
Everyman: Nay, never again till the day of doom.
Fellowship: In faith, then will not I come there!
Who hath you these tidings brought?
Everyman: Indeed, Death was with me here.
Fellowship: Now, by God that all hath bought,
If Death were the messenger,
For no man that is living today
I will not go that loath journey—
Not for the father that begat me!
Everyman: Ye promised other wise, pardie.
Fellowship: I wot well I say so truly
And yet if thou wilt eat, and drink, and make good cheer,
Or haunt to women, the lusty company,
I would not forsake you, while the day is clear,
Trust me verily!
Everyman: Yea, thereto ye would be ready;
To go to mirth, solace, and play
Your mind will sooner apply
Than to bear me company in my long journey.
Fellowship: Now, in good faith, I will not that way.
But and thou wilt murder, or any man kill,
In that I will help thee with a good will!
Everyman: O that is a simple advice indeed!
Gentle fellow, help me in my necessity;
We have loved long, and now I need,
And now, gentle Fellowship, remember me.
Fellowship: Whether ye have loved me or no,
By Saint John, I will not with thee go.
Everyman: Yet I pray thee, take the labour, and do so
    much for me
To bring me forward, for saint charity,
And comfort me till I come without the town.

---

8. God.

Fellowship: Nay, and thou would give me a new gown,
I will not a foot with thee go;
But and you had tarried I would not have left thee so.
And as now, God speed thee in thy journey,
For from thee I will depart as fast as I may.
Everyman: Whither away, Fellowship? Will you forsake
    me?
Fellowship: Yea, by my fay, to God I betake thee.
Everyman: Farewell, good Fellowship; for this my
    heart is sore;
Adieu for ever, I shall see thee no more.
Fellowship: In faith, Everyman, farewell not at the end;
For you I will remember that parting is mourning.
Everyman: Alack! shall we thus depart indeed?
Our Lady, help, without any more comfort,
Lo, Fellowship forsaketh me in my most need:
For help in this world whither shall I resort?
Fellowship herebefore with me would merry make;
And now little sorrow for me doth he take.
It is said, in prosperity men friends may find,
Which in adversity be full unkind.
Now whither for succour shall I flee,
Sith that Fellowship hath forsaken me?
To my kinsmen I will truly,
Praying them to help me in my necessity:
I believe that they will do so,
For kind will creep where it may not go,
Where be ye now, my friends and kinsmen?
Kindred: Here be we now at your commandment
Cousin, I pray you show us your intent
In any wise, and not spare.
Cousin: Yea, Everyman, and to us declare
If ye be disposed to go any whither,
For wete you well, we will live and die together.
Kindred: In wealth and woe we will with you hold,
For over his kin a man may be bold.
Everyman: Gramercy, my friends and kinsmen kind.
Now shall I show you the grief of my mind:
I was commanded by a messenger,
That is an high king's chief officer;
He bade me go a pilgrimage to my pain,
And I know well I shall never come again;
Also I must give a reckoning straight,
For I have a great enemy, that hath me in wait,
Which intendeth me for to hinder.
Kindred: What account is that which ye must render?
That would I know.
Everyman: Of all my works I must show
How I have lived and my days spent;
Also of ill deeds, that I have used
In my time, sith life was me lent;
And of all virtues that I have refused.
Therefore I pray you go thither with me,
To help to make mine account, for saint charity.
Cousin: What, to go thither? Is that the matter?
Nay, Everyman, I had liefer fast bread and water
All this five year and more.
Everyman: Alas, that ever I was bore![9]
For now shall I never be merry
If that you forsake me.

family relatives

---

9. Born.

Kindred: Ah, sir; what, ye be a merry man!
Take good heart to you, and make no moan.
But one thing I warn you, by Saint Anne,
As for me, ye shall go alone.
Everyman: My Cousin, will you not with me go?
Cousin: No, by our Lady; I have the cramp in my toe.
Trust not to me, for, so God me speed,
I will deceive you in your most need.
Kindred: It availeth not us to tice.
Ye shall have my maid with all my heart;
She loveth to go to feasts, there to be nice,
And to dance, and abroad to start:
I will give her leave to help you in that journey,
If that you and she may agree.
Everyman: Now show me the very effect of your mind.
Will you go with me, or abide behind?
Kindred: Abide behind? Yea, that I will and I may!
Therefore farewell until another day.
Everyman: How should I be merry or glad?
For fair promises to me make,
But when I have most need, they me forsake.
I am deceived; that maketh me sad.
Cousin: Cousin Everyman, farewell now,
For verily I will not go with you;
Also of mine own an unready reckoning
I have to account; therefore I make tarrying.
Now, God keep thee, for now I go.

relatives)

Everyman: Ah, Jesus, is all come hereto?
Lo, fair words maketh fools feign;
They promise and nothing will do certain.
My kinsmen promised me faithfully
For to abide with me steadfastly,
And now fast away do they flee:
Even so Fellowship promised me.
What friend were best me of to provide?
I lose my time here longer to abide.
Yet in my mind a thing there is:—
All my life I have loved riches;
If that my goods now help me might,
He would make my heart full light.
I will speak to him in this distress.—
Where art thou, my Goods and riches?
Goods: Who calleth me? Everyman? What haste thou
hast!
I lie here in corners, trussed and piled so high,
And in chests I am locked so fast,
Also sacked in bags, thou mayst see with thine eye,
I cannot stir; in packs low I lie,
What would ye have, lightly me say.

worldly wealth

Everyman: Come hither, Good, in all the haste thou
may,
For of counsel I must desire thee.
Goods: Sir, and ye in the world have trouble or adversity,
That can I help you to remedy shortly.
Everyman: It is another disease that grieveth me;
In this world it is not, I tell thee so.
I am sent for another way to go,
To give a straight account general
Before the highest Jupiter of all;
And all my life I have had joy and pleasure in thee.
Therefore I pray thee go with me,
For, peradventure, thou mayst before God Almighty
My reckoning help to clean and purify;
For it is said ever among,
That money maketh all right that is wrong.

Goods: Nay, Everyman, I sing another song,
I follow no man in such voyages;
For and I went with thee
Thou shouldst fare much the worse for me;
For because on me thou did set thy mind,
Thy reckoning I have made blotted and blind
That thine account thou cannot make truly;
And that has thou for the love of me.
Everyman: That would grieve me full sore,
When I should come to that fearful answer.
Up, let us go thither together.
Goods: Nay, not so, I am too brittle, I may not endure;
I will follow no man one foot, be ye sure.
Everyman: Alas, I have thee loved, and had great
pleasure
All my life-days on good and treasure.
Goods: That is to thy damnation without lesing,
For my love is contrary to the love everlasting
But if thou had me loved moderately during,
As, to the poor give part of me,
Then shouldst thou not in this dolour be,
Nor in this great sorrow and care.
Everyman: Lo, now was I deceived or I was ware,
And all I may wyte[10] my spending of time.
Goods: What, weenest thou that I am thine?
Everyman: I had wend so.
Goods: Nay, Everyman, I say no;
As for a while I was lent thee,
A season thou hast had me in prosperity;
My condition is man's soul to kill;
If I save one, a thousand I do spill;
Weenest thou that I will follow thee?
Nay, from this world, not verily.
Everyman: I had wend otherwise.
Goods: Therefore to thy soul Good is a thief;
For when thou art dead, this is my guise
Another to deceive in the same wise
As I have done thee, and all to his soul's reprief.
Everyman: O false Good, cursed thou be!
Thou traitor to God, that has deceived me,
And caught me in thy snare.
Goods: Marry, thou brought thyself in care,
Whereof I am glad,
I must needs laugh, I cannot be sad.
Everyman: Ah, Good, thou has had long my heartly
love;
I gave thee that which should be the Lord's above.
But wilt thou not go with me in deed?
I pray thee truth to say.
Goods: No, so God me speed,
Therefore farewell, and have good day.
Everyman: O, to whom shall I make moan
For to go with me in that heavy journey?
First Fellowship said he would with me gone;
His words were very pleasant and gay,
But afterward he left me alone.
Then spake I to my kinsmen all in despair,
And also they gave me words fair,
They lacked no fair speaking,
But all forsake me in the ending.
Then went I to my Goods that I loved best,
In hope to have comfort, but there had I least:
For my Goods sharply did me tell
That he bringeth many into hell.

---

10. Blame.

Then of myself I was ashamed,
And so I am worthy to be blamed;
Thus may I well myself hate,
Of whom shall I now counsel take?
I think that I shall never speed
Till that I go to my Good-Deed,
But alas, she is so weak,
That she can neither go nor speak,
Yet will I venture on her now.—
My Good-Deeds, where be you?

Good-Deeds: Here I lie cold on the ground; [*I Kindness to others*]
Thy sins hath me sore bound,
That I cannot stir.

Everyman: O, Good-Deeds, I stand in fear;
I must you pray of counsel,
For help now should come right well.

Good-Deeds: Everyman, I have understanding
That ye be summoned account to make
Before Messias, of Jerusalem King;
And you by me[11] that journey what[12] you will I take.

Everyman: Therefore I come to you, my moan to make;
I pray you, that ye will go with me.

Good-Deeds: I would full fain, but I cannot stand verily.

Everyman: Why, is there anything on you fall?

Good-Deeds: Yea, sir, I may thank you of all;
If ye had perfectly cheered me,
Your book of account now full ready had be.
Look, the books of your works and deeds eke;
Oh, see how they lie under the feet,
To your soul's heaviness.

Everyman: Our Lord Jesus, help me!
For one letter here I can not see.

Good-Deeds: There is a blind reckoning in time of
distress!

Everyman: Good-Deeds, I pray you, help me in this
need,
Or else I am for ever damned indeed;
Therefore help me to make reckoning
Before the redeemer of all thing,
That king is, and was, and ever shall.

Good-Deeds: Everyman, I am sorry of your fall,
And fain would I help you, and I were able.

Everyman: Good-Deeds, your counsel I pray you give
me.

Good-Deeds: That shall I do verily;
Though that on my feet I may not go,
I have a sister, that shall with you also,
Called Knowledge, which shall with you abide,
To help you to make that dreadful reckoning.

Knowledge: Everyman, I will go with thee, and be thy
guide,
In thy most need to go by thy side.

Everyman: In good condition I am now in every thing,
And am wholly content with this good thing;
Thanked be God my Creator.

Good-Deeds: And when he hath brought thee there,
Where thou shalt heal thee of thy smart,
Then go you with your reckoning and your Good-Deeds
together
For to make you joyful at heart
Before the blessed Trinity.

11. If you go by me.
12. With.

Everyman: My Good-Deeds, gramercy;
I am well content, certainly,
With your words sweet.

Knowledge: Now go we together lovingly,
To Confession, that cleansing river.

Everyman: For joy I weep; I would we were there;
But, I pray you, give me cognition
Where dwelleth that holy man, Confession.

Knowledge: In the house of salvation:
We shall find him in that place,
That shall us comfort by God's grace.
Lo, this is Confession: kneel down and ask mercy,
For he is in good conceit with God almighty.

Everyman: O glorious fountain that all uncleanness
doth clarify,
Wash from me the spots of vices unclean,
That on me no sin may be seen;
I come with Knowledge for my redemption,
Repent with hearty and full contrition;
For I am commanded a pilgrimage to take,
And great accounts before God to make.
Now, I pray you, Shrift, mother of salvation,
Help my good deeds for my piteous exclamation.

Confession: I know your sorrow well, Everyman;
Because with Knowledge ye come to me,
I will you comfort as well as I can,
And a precious jewel I will give thee,
Called penance, wise voider of adversity;
Therewith shall your body chastised be,
With abstinence and perseverance in God's service:
Here shall you receive that scourge of me,
Which is penance strong, that ye must endure,
To remember thy Savior was scourged for thee
With sharp scourges, and suffered it patiently;
So must thou, or thou scape that painful pilgrimage;
Knowledge, keep him in this voyage,
And by that time Good-Deeds will be with thee.
But in any wise, be sure of mercy,
For your time draweth fast, and ye will saved be;
Ask God mercy, and he will grant truly,
When with the scourge of penance man doth him bind,
The oil of forgiveness then shall he find.

Everyman: Thanked be God for his gracious work!
For now I will my penance begin;
This hath rejoiced and lighted my heart,
Though the knots be painful and hard within.

Knowledge: Everyman, look your penance that ye fulfil,
What pain that ever it to you be,
And Knowledge shall give you counsel at will,
How your accounts ye shall make clearly.

Everyman: O eternal God, O heavenly figure,
O way of rightwiseness, O goodly vision,
Which descended down in a virgin pure
Because he would Everyman redeem,
Which Adam forfeited by his disobedience:
O blessed Godhead, elect and high-divine,
Forgive my grievous offence;
Here I cry thee mercy in this presence.
O ghostly treasure, O ransomer and redeemer
Of all the world, hope and conductor,
Mirror of joy, and founder of mercy,
Which illumineth heaven and earth thereby,
Here my clamorous complaint, though it late be;
Receive my prayers; unworthy in this heavy life,
Though I be, a sinner most abominable,
Yet let my name be written in Moses' table;
O Mary, pray to the Maker of all thing,
Me for to help at my ending,
And save me from the power of my enemy,
For Death assaileth me strongly;

And, Lady, that I may be means of thy prayer
Of your Son's glory to be partaker,
By the means of his passion I it crave,
I beseech you, help my soul to save.—
Knowledge, give me the scourge of penance;
My flesh therewith shall give a quittance:
I will now begin, if God give me grace.
Knowledge: Everyman, God give you time and space:
Thus I bequeath you in the hands of our Saviour,
Thus may you make your reckoning sure.
Everyman: In the name of the Holy Trinity,
My body sore punished shall be:
Take this, body, for the sin of the flesh;
Also thou delightest to go gay and fresh,
And in the way of damnation thou did me bring;
Therefore suffer now strokes and punishing.
Now of penance I will wade the water clear,
To save me from purgatory, that sharp fire.
Good-Deeds: I thank God, now I can walk and go;
And am delivered of my sickness and woe.
Therefore with Everyman I will go, and not spare;
His good works I will help him to declare.
Knowledge: Now, Everyman, be merry and glad;
Your Good-Deeds cometh now; ye may not be sad;
Now is your Good-Deeds whole and sound,
Going upright upon the ground.
Everyman: My heart is light, and shall be evermore;
Now will I smite faster than I did before.
Good-Deeds: Everyman, pilgrim, my special friend,
Blessed be thou without end;
For thee is prepared the eternal glory.
Ye have me made whole and sound,
Therefore I will bide by thee in every stound.[13]
Everyman: Welcome, my Good-Deeds; now I hear thy voice,
I weep for very sweetness of love.
Knowledge: Be no more sad, but ever rejoice,
God seeth thy living in his throne above;
Put on this garment to thy behove,
Which is wet with your tears,
Or else before God you may it miss,
When you to your journey's end come shall.
Everyman: Gentle Knowledge, what do you it call?
Knowledge: It is a garment of sorrow:
From pain it will you borrow;
Contrition it is,
That getteth forgiveness;
It pleaseth God passing well.
Good-Deeds: Everyman, will you wear it for your heal?
Everyman: Now blessed be Jesu, Mary's Son!
For now have I on true contrition.
And let us go now without tarrying;
Good-Deeds, have we clear our reckoning?
Good-Deeds: Yea, indeed I have it here.
Everyman: Then I trust we need not fear;
Now, friends, let us not part in twain.
Knowledge: Nay, Everyman, that will we not, certain.
Good-Deeds: Yet must thou lead with thee
Three persons of great might.
Everyman: Who should they be?
Good-Deeds: Discretion and Strength they hight,
And thy Beauty may not abide behind.
Knowledge: Also ye must call to mind
Your Five-wits as for your counsellors.
Good-Deeds: You must have them ready at all hours.
Everyman: How shall I get hither?

Knowledge: You must call them all together,
And they will hear you incontinent.
Everyman: My friends, come hither and be present,
Discretion, Strength, my Five-wits, and Beauty.
Beauty: Here at your will we be all ready.
What will ye that we should do?
Good-Deeds: That ye would with Everyman go,
And help him in his pilgrimage,
Advise you, will ye with him or not in that voyage?
Strength: We will bring him all thither,
To his help and comfort, ye may believe me.
Discretion: So will we go with him all together.
Everyman: Almighty God, loved thou be,
I give thee laud that I have hither brought
Strength, Discretion, Beauty, and Five-wits; lack I nought;
And my Good-Deeds, with Knowledge clear,
All be in my company at my will here;
I desire no more to my business.
Strength: And I, Strength, will by you stand in distress,
Though thou would in battle fight on the ground.
Five-Wits: And though it were through the world round,
We will not depart for sweet nor sour.
Beauty: No more will I unto death's hour,
Whatsoever thereof befall.
Discretion: Everyman, advise you first of all;
Go with a good advisement and deliberation;
We all give you virtuous monition
That all shall be well.
Everyman: My friends, hearken what I will tell:
I pray God reward you in his heavenly sphere.
Now hearken, all that be here
For I will make my testament
Here before you all present.
In alms half my good I will give with my hands twain
In the way of charity, with good intent,
And the other half still shall remain
In quiet to be returned there it ought to be.
This I do in despite of the fiend of hell
To go quite out of his peril
Ever after and this day.
Knowledge: Everyman, hearken what I say;
Go to priesthood, I you advise,
And receive of him in any wise
The holy sacrament and ointment together;
Then shortly see ye turn again hither;
We will all abide you here.
Five-Wits: Yea, Everyman, hie you that ye ready were,
There is no emperor, king, duke, ne baron,
That of God hath commission,
As hath the least priest in the world being;
For of the blessed sacraments pure and benign,
He beareth the keys and thereof hath the cure
For man's redemption, it is ever sure;
Which God for our soul's medicine
Gave us out of his heart with great pine;
Here in this transitory life, for thee and me
The blessed sacraments seven there be.
Baptism, confirmation, with priesthood good,
And the sacrament of God's precious flesh and blood,
Marriage, the holy extreme unction, and penance;
These seven be good to have in remembrance,
Gracious sacraments of high divinity.
Everyman: Fain would I receive that holy body
And meekly to my ghostly father I will go.

---

13. Season.

Five-Wits: Everyman, that is the best that ye can do:
God will you to salvation bring,
For priesthood exceedeth all other thing;
To us Holy Scripture they do teach,
And converteth man from sin heaven to reach;
God hath to them more power given,
Than to any angel that is in heaven;
With five words he may consecrate
God's body in flesh and blood to make,
And handleth his maker between his hands;
The priest bindeth and unbindeth all bands,
Both in earth and in heaven;
Thou ministers all the sacraments seven;
Though we kissed thy feet thou were worthy;
Thou art surgeon that cureth sin deadly:
No remedy we find under God
But all only priesthood.
Everyman, God gave priests that dignity,
And setteth them in his stead among us to be;
Thus be they above angels in degree.
Knowledge: If priests be good it is so surely;
But when Jesus hanged on the cross with great smart
There he gave, out of his blessed heart,
The same sacrament in great torment:
He sold them not to us, that Lord Omnipotent.
Therefore Saint Peter the apostle doth say
That Jesu's curse hath all they
Which God their Saviour do buy or sell,
Or they for any money do take or tell.
Sinful priests giveth the sinners example bad;
Their children sitteth by other men's fires, I have heard;
And some haunteth women's company,
With unclean life, as lusts of lechery:
These be with sin made blind.
Five-Wits: I trust to God no such may we find;
Therefore let us priesthood honour,
And follow their doctrine for our souls' succour;
We be their sheep, and they shepherds be
By whom we all be kept in surety.
Peace, for yonder I see Everyman come,
Which hath made true satisfaction.
Good-Deeds: Methinketh it is he indeed.
Everyman: Now Jesu be our alder speed.[14]
I have received the sacrament for my redemption,
And then mine extreme unction:
Blessed be all they that counselled me to take it!
And now, friends, let us go without longer respite;
I thank God that ye have tarried so long.
Now set each of you on this rod your hand,
And shortly follow me:
I go before, there I would be; God be our guide.
Strength: Everyman, we will not from you go,
Till ye have gone this voyage long.
Discretion: I, Discretion, will bide by you also.
Knowledge: And though this pilgrimage be never so
    strong,
I will never part you fro:
Everyman, I will be as sure by thee
As ever I did by Judas Maccabee.
Everyman: Alas, I am so faint I may not stand,
My limbs under me do fold;
Friends, let us not turn again to this land,
Not for all the world's gold,
For into this cave must I creep
And turn to the earth and there to sleep.

---

14. Speed in help of all.

Beauty: What, into this grave? Alas!
Everyman: Yea, there shall you consume more and less.
Beauty: And what, should I smother here?
Everyman: Yea, by my faith, and never more appear.
In this world live no more we shall,
But in heaven before the highest Lord of all.
Beauty: I cross out all this; adieu by Saint John;
I take my cap in my lap and am gone.
Everyman: What, Beauty, whither will ye?
Beauty: Peace, I am deaf; I look not behind me,
Not and thou would give me all the gold in thy chest.
Everyman: Alas, whereto may I trust?
Beauty goeth fast away hie;
She promised with me to live and die.
Strength: Everyman, I will thee also forsake and deny;
Thy game liketh me not at all.
Everyman: Why, then ye will forsake me all.
Sweet Strength, tarry a little space.
Strength: Nay, sir, by the rood of grace
Though thou weep till thy heart brast.
Everyman: Ye would ever bide by me, ye said.
Strength: Yea, I have you far enough conveyed;
Ye be old enough, I understand,
Your pilgrimage to take on hand;
I repent me that I hither came.
Everyman: Strength, you to displease I am to blame;
Will you break promise that is debt?
Strength: In faith, I care not;
Thou art but a fool to complain,
You spend your speech and waste your brain;
Go thrust thee into the ground.
Everyman: I had wend surer I should you have found.
He that trusteth in his Strength
She him deceiveth at the length.
Both Strength and Beauty forsaketh me,
Yet they promised me fair and lovingly.
Discretion: Everyman, I will after Strength be gone,
As for me I will leave you alone.
Everyman: Why, Discretion, will ye forsake me?
Discretion: Yea, in faith, I will go from thee,
For when Strength goeth before
I follow after evermore.
Everyman: Yet I pray thee, for the love of the Trinity,
Look in my grave once piteously.
Discretion: Nay, so nigh will I not come.
Farewell, every one!
Everyman: O all thing faileth, save God alone;
Beauty, Strength, and Discretion;
For when Death bloweth his blast,
They all run from me full fast.
Five-Wits: Everyman, my leave now of thee I take;
I will follow the other, for here I thee forsake.
Everyman: Alas! then may I wail and weep,
For I took you for my best friend.
Five-Wits: I will no longer thee keep;
Now farewell, and there an end.
Everyman: O Jesu, help, all hath forsaken me!
Good-Deeds: Nay, Everyman, I will bide with thee,
I will not forsake thee indeed;
Thou shalt find me a good friend at need.
Everyman: Gramercy, Good-Deeds; now may I true
    friends see;
They have forsaken me every one;
I loved them better than my Good-Deeds alone.
Knowledge, will ye forsake me also?
Knowledge: Yea, Everyman, when ye to death do go:
But not yet for no manner of danger.
Everyman: Gramercy, Knowledge, with all my heart.
Knowledge: Nay, yet I will not from hence depart,
Till I see where ye shall be come.

Everyman: Methinketh, alas, that I must be gone
To make my reckoning and my debts pay,
For I see my time is nigh spent away.
Take example, all ye that this do hear or see,
How they that I loved best do forsake me,
Except my Good-Deeds that bideth truly.

Good-Deeds: All earthly things is but vanity:
Beauty, Strength, and Discretion, do man forsake,
Foolish friends and kinsmen, that fair spake,
All fleeth save Good-Deeds, and that am I.

Everyman: Have mercy on me, God most mighty;
And stand by me, thou Mother and Maid, holy Mary.

Good-Deeds: Fear not, I will speak for thee.

Everyman: Here I cry God mercy.

Good-Deeds: Short our end, and minish our pain;
Let us go and never come again.

Everyman: Into thy hands, Lord, my soul I commend;
Receive it, Lord, that it be not lost;
As thou me boughtest, so me defend,
And save me from the fiend's boast,
That I may appear with that blessed host
That shall be saved at the day of doom.
In manus tuas—of might's most
For ever—*commendo spiritum meum.*[15]

Knowledge: Now hath he suffered that we all shall
endure;
The Good-Deeds shall make all sure.
Now hath he made ending;
Methinketh that I hear angels sing
And make great joy and melody,
Where Everyman's soul received shall be.

Angel: Come, excellent elect spouse to Jesu:
Hereabove thou shalt go
Because of thy singular virtue:
Now the soul is taken the body fro;
Thy reckoning is crystal-clear.
Now shalt thou into the heavenly sphere,
Unto the which all ye shall come
That liveth well before the day of doom.

Doctor: This moral men may have in mind;
Ye hearers, take it of worth, old and young,
And forsake pride, for he deceiveth you in the end,
And remember Beauty, Five-wits, Strength, and
Discretion,
They all at the last do Everyman forsake,
Save his Good-Deeds, there doth he take.
But beware, and they be small
Before God, he hath not help at all.
None excuse may be there for Everyman:
Alas, how shall he do then?
For after death amends may no man make,
For then mercy and pity do him forsake.
If his reckoning be not clear when he do come,
God will say—*ite maledicti in ignem aeternum.*[16]
And he that hath his account whole and sound,
High in heaven he shall be crowned;
Unto which place God brings us all thither
That we may live body and soul together.
Thereto help the Trinity,
Amen, say ye, for saint Charity.
THUS ENDETH THIS MORALL PLAY OF EVERYMAN.

15. Into your hands I commend my spirit.
16. Be damned to the eternal fire.

Exercises

1. Arrange Fellowship, Goods, Knowledge, and the rest of the personified entities in your own rank order of values. How does your system compare with the implied order in *Everyman?*
2. In your own words explain what the "moral" is in the morality play.

AUCASSIN AND NICOLETTE

Contrasting sharply with *Everyman,* the *chant-fable* of *Aucassin and Nicolette*[17] points up the conflicts in medieval life represented by the somber morality play and the charming fable of the young lovers. One smiles with pleasure at the sensuous description of Nicolette, or the piling up of ludicrous incidents: Aucassin riding forth to battle like every stereotype of the medieval knight, only to forget what he should be doing, and ending as a captive; or again, falling off his horse and dislocating his shoulder. Meanwhile Nicolette hides behind a bush and waits until he drags himself most painfully into her little bower before she gives him comfort and love that is more potent than penicillin. One could list many incidents, or call attention to the gracefulness of the verse as opposed to the earnest tone and sober rhythms of *Everyman.* The *chant-fable* not only speaks of the joy of life, it *is* that joy. The two as a side-by-side contrast ask the question, "Which way is this civilization to go?"

Who will deign to hear the song,
Solace of a captive's wrong,
Telling how two children met,
Aucassin and Nicolette;
How by grievous pains distraught,
Noble deeds the varlet wrought
For his love, and her bright face!
Sweet my rhyme, and full of grace,
Fair my tale, and debonair.
He who lists—though full of care,
Sore astonied, much amazed,
All cast down, by men mispraised,
Sick in body, sick in soul,
Hearing, shall be glad and whole,
So sweet the tale.
Now they say and tell and relate:

How the Count Bougars of Valence made war on Count Garin of Beaucaire, war so great, so wonderful, and so mortal, that never dawned the day but that he was at the gates and walls and barriers of the town, with a hundred knights and ten thousand men-at-arms, on foot and on horse. So he burned the Count's land, and spoiled his heritage, and dealt death to this men. The Count Garin of Beaucaire was full of years, and frail; he had long outworn his day. He had no heir, neither son nor daughter, save one only varlet, and he was such as I will tell you. Aucassin was the name of the lad. Fair he was,

17. The names are pronounced oh-kah-SAN and ni-koh-LET.

and pleasant to look upon, tall and shapely of body in every whit of him. His hair was golden, and curled in little rings about his head; he had grey and dancing eyes, a clear, oval face, a nose high and comely, and he was so gracious in all good graces that nought in him was found to blame, but good alone. But love, that high prince, so utterly had cast him down, that he cared not to become knight, neither to bear arms, nor to tilt at tourneys, nor yet to do aught that it became his name to do.

His father and his mother spake him thus, "Son, don now thy mail, mount thy horse, keep thy land, and render aid to thy men. Should they see thee amongst them, the better will the men-at-arms defend their bodies and their substance, thy fief[18] and mine."

"Father," said Aucassin, "why speakest thou in such fashion to me? May God give me nothing of my desire if I become knight, or mount to horse, or thrust into the press to strike other or be smitten down, save only that thou give me Nicolette, my sweet friend, whom I love so well."

"Son," answered the father, "this may not be. Put Nicolette from mind. For Nicolette is but a captive maid, come hither from a far country, and the Viscount of this town bought her with money from the Saracens, and set her in this place. He hath nourished and baptized her, and held her at the font. On a near day he will give her to some young bachelor, who will gain her bread in all honor. With this what has thou to do? Ask for a wife, and I will find thee the daughter of a king, or a count. Were he the richest man in France, his daughter shalt thou have, if so thou wilt."

"Faith, my father," said Aucassin, "what honor of this world would not Nicolette, my very sweet friend, most richly become! Were she Empress of Byzantium or of Allemaigne, or Queen of France, or England, low enough would be her degree, so noble is she, so courteous and debonair, and gracious in all good graces."

Now is sung:

Aucassin was of Beaucaire,
Of the mighty castle there,
But his heart was ever set
On his fair friend, Nicolette.
Small he heeds his father's blame,
Or the harsh words of his dame:
"Fool, to weep the livelong day,
Nicolette trips light and gay.
Scouring she from far Carthage,
Bought of Paynims for a wage.
Since a wife beseems thee good,
Take a wife of wholesome blood."
"Mother, nought for this I care,
Nicolette is debonair;
Slim the body, fair the face,
Make my heart a lighted place;
Love has set her as my peer,
      Too sweet, my dear."

Now they say and tell and relate:

When the Court Garin of Beaucaire found that in nowise could he withdraw Aucassin his son from the love of Nicolette, he sought out the Viscount of the town, who was his man, and spake him thus, "Sir Count, send Nicolette your godchild straightly from this place. Cursed be the land wherefrom she was carried to this realm; for because of her I lose Aucassin, who will not become

knight, nor do aught that it becometh knight to do. Know well that, were she once within my power, I would hurry her to the fire; and look well to yourself for you stand in utmost peril and fear."

"Sire," answered the Viscount, "this lies heavy upon me, that ever Aucassin goes and he comes seeking speech with my ward. I have bought her with my money, and nourished and baptized her, and held her at the font. Moreover, I am fain to give her to some young bachelor, who will gain her bread in all honor. With this Aucassin your son had nought to do. But since this is your will and your pleasure, I will send her to so far a country that nevermore shall he see her with his eyes."

"Walk warily," replied the Count Garin, "for great evil easily may fall to you of this." So they went their ways.

Now the Viscount was a very rich man, and had a rich palace standing within a garden. In a certain chamber of an upper floor he set Nicolette in ward, with an old woman to bear her company, and to watch; and he put there bread and meat and wine and all things for their need. Then he placed a seal upon the door, so that none might enter in, nor issue forth, save only that there was a window looking on the garden, strictly close, whereby they breathed a little fresh air.

Now is sung:

Nicolette is prisoned fast,
In a vaulted chamber cast,
Shaped and carven wondrous well,
Painted as by miracle.
At the marble casement stayed
On her elbow leaned the maid;
Golden showed her golden hair,
Softly curved her eyebrows rare,
Fair her face, and brightly flushed,
Sweeter maiden never blushed.
In the garden from her room
She might watch the roses bloom,
Hear the birds made tender moan;
Then she knew herself alone.
" 'Lack, great pity 'tis to place
Maid in such an evil case.
Aucassin, my liege, my squire,
Friend, and dear, and heart's desire,
Since thou dost not hate me quite,
Men have done me foul despite,
Sealed me in this vaulted room,
Thrust me to this bitter doom.
But by God, Our Lady's Son,
Soon will I from here begone.
      So it be won.' "

Now they say and tell and relate:

Nicolette was prisoned in the chamber, as you have heard and known. The cry and the haro[19] went through all the land that Nicolette was stolen away. Some said that she had fled the country, and some that the Count Garin of Beaucaire had done her to death. Whatever man may have rejoiced, Aucassin had no joy therein, so he sought out the Viscount of the town and spake him thus, "Sir Viscount, what have you done with Nicolette, my very sweet friend, the thing that most I love in all the world? Have you borne her off, or hidden her from my sight? Be sure that should I die hereof, my blood will be required of you, as is most just, for I am slain of your two hands; since you steal from me the thing that most I love in all the world."

18. Fief—the demesne of the Count.

19. Protest against injustice.

"Fair sire," answered the Viscount, "put this from mind. Nicolette is a captive maid whom I brought here from a far country. For her price I trafficked with the Saracens, and I have bred and baptized her, and held her at the font. I have nourished her duly, and on a day will give her to some young bachelor who will gain her bread in honorable fashion. With this you have nought to do; but only to wed the daughter of some count or king. Beyond this, what profit would you have, had you become her lover, and taken her to your bed? Little enough would be your gain therefrom, for your soul would lie tormented in Hell all the days of all time, so that to Paradise never should you win."

"In Paradise what have I to do? I care not to enter, but only to have Nicolette, my very sweet friend, whom I love so dearly well. For into Paradise go none but such people as I will tell you of. There go those aged priests, and those old cripples, and the maimed, who all day long and all night cough before the altars, and in the crypts beneath the churches; those who go in worn old mantles and old tattered habits; who are naked, and barefoot, and full of sores; who are dying of hunger and of thirst, of cold and of wretchedness. Such as these enter in Paradise, and with them have I nought to do. But in Hell will I go. For to Hell go the fair clerks and the fair knights who are slain in the tourney and the great wars, and the stout archer and the loyal man. With them will I go. And there go the fair and courteous ladies, who have friends, two or three, together with their wedded lords. And there pass the gold and the silver, the ermine and all rich furs, harpers and minstrels, and the happy of the world. With these will I go, so only that I have Nicolette, my very sweet friend, by my side."

"Truly," cried the Viscount, "you talk idly, for never shall you see her more; yea, and if perchance you spoke together, and your father heard thereof, he would burn both me and her in one fire and yourself might well have every fear."

"This lies heavy upon me," answered Aucassin. Thus he parted from the Viscount making great sorrow.

Now is sung:

Aucassin departed thus
Sad at heart and dolorous;
Gone is she, his fairest friend,
None may comfort give or mend,
None by counsel make good end.
To the palace turned he home,
Climbed the stair, and sought his room.
In the chamber all alone
Bitterly he made his moan,
Presently began to weep
For the love he might not keep.
"Nicolette, so gent, so sweet,
Fair the faring of thy feet,
Fair thy laughter, sweet thy speech,
Fair our playing each with each,
Fair thy clasping, fair thy kiss,
Yet it endeth all in this.
Since from me my love is ta'en
I misdoubt that I am slain;
        Sister, sweet friend."

Now they say and tell and relate:

Whilst Aucassin was in the chamber lamenting Nicolette, his friend, the Count Bougars of Valence, wishful to end the war, pressed on his quarrel, and setting his pikemen and horsemen in array, drew near the castle to take it by storm. Then the cry arose and the tumult; and the knights and the men-at-arms took their weapons, and hastened to the gates and the walls to defend the castle, and the burgesses climbed to the battlements, flinging quarrels[20] and sharpened darts upon the foe. Whilst the siege was so loud and perilous, the Count Garin of Beaucaire sought the chamber where Aucassin lay mourning, assotted upon[21] Nicolette, his very sweet friend, whom he loved so well.

"Ha, son," cried he, "craven art thou and shamed, that seest thy best and fairest castle so hardly beset. Know well that if thou lose it, thou art a naked man. Son, arm thyself lightly, mount the horse, keep thy land, aid thy men, hurtle into the press. Thou needest not to strike together, neither to be smitten down, but if they see thee amongst them, the better will they defend their goods and their bodies, thy land and mine; and thou art so stout and strong that very easily thou canst do this thing, as is but right."

"Father," answered Aucassin, "what sayest thou now? May God give me naught that I require of Him if I become a knight, or mount to horse, or thrust into the press to strike knight or to be smitten down, save only thou givest me Nicolette, my sweet friend, whom I love so well!"

"Son," replied the father, "this can never be. Rather will I suffer to lose my heritage, and go bare of all, than that thou shouldst have her, either as woman or as dame."

So he turned without farewell; but when Aucassin saw him part, he stayed him, saying, "Father, come now; I will make a true bargain with thee."

"What bargain, fair son?"

"I will arm me, and thrust into the press on such bargain as this: that if God bring me again safe and sound, thou wilt let me look on Nicolette, my sweet friend, so long that I may have with her two words or three, and kiss her only one time."

"I pledge my word to this," said the father. Of this covenant had Aucassin much joy.

Now is sung:

Aucassin the more was fain
Of the kiss he sought to gain,
Rather than his coffers hold
A hundred thousand marks of gold.
At the call his squire drew near,
Armed him fast in battle gear;
Shirt and hauberk donned the lad,
Laced the helmet on his head,
Girt his golden-hilted sword—
Came the war-horse at his word—
Gripped the buckler and the lance,
At the stirrups cast a glance;
Then, most brave from plume to heel,
Pricked the charger with the steel,
Called to mind his absent dear,
Passed the gateway without fear
        Straight to the fight.

Now they say and tell and relate:

Aucassin was armed and horsed as you have heard. God, how bravely showed the shield about his neck, the helmet on his head, and the fringes of the baldric upon his left thigh! The lad was tall and strong, slender and comely to look upon; and the steed he bestrode was great and speedy, and fiercely had he charged clear of the gate.

---

20. Square-headed crossbow-bolt.
21. Infatuated with.

Now think not that he sought spoil of oxen and cattle, nor to smite others and himself escape. Nay, but of all this he took no heed. Another was with him; and he thought so dearly upon Nicolette, his fair friend, that the reins fell from his hand, and he struck never a blow. Then the charger, yet smarting from the spur, bore him into the battle, amidst the thickest of the foe, so that hands were laid upon him from every side, and he was made prisoner. Thus they spoiled him of shield and lance, and forthwith led him from the field a captive, questioning amongst themselves by what death he should be slain.

When Aucassin marked their words, "Ha, God!" cried he. "Sweet Creature, these are my mortal foes who lead me captive, and who soon will smite off my head; and when my head is smitten, never again may I have fair speech with Nicolette, my sweet friend, whom I hold so dear. Yet have I a good sword; and my horse is yet unblown. Now if I defend me not for her sake, may God keep her never, should she love me still!" The varlet was hardy and stout, and the charger he bestrode was right fierce. He plucked forth his sword, and smote suddenly on the right hand and on the left, cutting sheer through nasal and headpiece, gauntlet and arm, making such ruin around him as the wild boar deals when brought to bay by hounds in the wood, until he had struck down ten knights, and hurt seven more, and won clear of the *melee,* and rode back at utmost speed, sword in hand.

The Count Bougars of Valence heard tell that his men were about to hang Aucassin, his foe, in shameful wise, so he hastened to the sight; and Aucassin passed him not by. His sword was yet in hand, and struck the Count so fiercely upon the helm that the headpiece was cleft and shattered upon the head. So bewildered was he by the stroke that he tumbled to the ground, and Aucassin stretched forth his hand, and took him, and led him captive by the nasal of the helmet, and delivered him to his father. "Father," said Aucassin, "behold the foe who wrought such war and mischief upon you! Twenty years hath this war endured, and none was there to bring it to an end."

"Fair son," replied his father, "better are such deeds as this than foolish dreams!"

"Father," returned Aucassin, "preach me no preachings; but carry out our bargain."

"Ha! What bargain, fair son?"

"How now, father, hast thou returned from the market? By my head, I will remember—whosoever may forget—so close is it to my heart! Didst thou not bargain with me, when I armed me and fared into the press, that if God brought me again safe and sound, thou wouldst grant me sight of Nicolette, my sweet friend, so long that I might have with her two words or three, and kiss her once? Such was the bargain; so be thou honest dealer."

"I!" cried the father. "God aid me never, should I keep such terms. Were she here, I would set her in the flames; and thou thyself might well have every fear."

"Is this the very end?" said Aucassin.

"So help me God," said his father, "yea!"

"Certès," said Aucassin, "grey hairs go ill with a lying tongue."

"Count of Valence," said Aucassin, "thou art my prisoner?"

"Sire," answered the Count, "it is verily and truly so."

"Give me thy hand," said Aucassin.

"Sire, as you wish!" So each took the other's hand.

"Plight me thy faith," said Aucassin, "that so long as thou drawest breath, never shall pass a day but thou shalt deal with my father in shameful fashion, either in goods or in person, if so thou canst."

"Sire, for God's love make me not a jest, but name me a price for my ransom. Whether you ask gold or silver, steed or palfrey, pelt or fur, hawk or hound, it shall be paid."

"What!" said Aucassin; "art thou not my prisoner?"

"Truly, sire," said the Count Bougars.

"God aid me never," quoth Aucassin, "but I send thy head flying, save thou plight me such faith as I said."

"In God's name," cried he, "I plight such affiance as seems most meet to thee." He pledged his troth; so Aucassin set him upon a horse, and brought him into a place of surety, himself riding by his side.

Now is sung:

When Count Garin knew his son
Aucassin still loved but one,
That his heart was ever set
Fondly on fond Nicolette,
Straight a prison he hath found,
Paved with marble, walled around,
Where in vault beneath the earth
Aucassin made little mirth,
But with wailing filled his cell
In such wise as now I tell
"Nicolette, white lily-flow'r,
Sweetest lady found in bow'r,
Sweet as grape that brimmeth up
Sweetness in the spiced cup,
On a day this chanced to you:
Out of Limousin there drew
One, a pilgrim, sore adread—
Lay in pain upon his bed,
Tossed, and took with fear his breath,
Very dolent, near to death—
Then you entered, pure and white,
Softly to the sick man's sight,
Raised the train that swept adown,
Raised the ermine-bordered gown
Raised the smock, and bared to him,
Daintily, each lovely limb.
Then a wondrous thing befell.
Straight he rose up, sound and well,
Left his bed, took cross in hand,
Sought again his own dear land.
Lily-flow'r, so white, so sweet,
Fair the faring of thy feet,
Fair thy laughter, fair thy speech,
Fair our playing each with each!
Sweet thy kisses, soft thy touch!
All must love thee overmuch.
'Tis for thee that I am thrown
In this vaulted cell alone;
'Tis for thee that I attend
Death, that comes to make an end—
For thee, sweet friend!

Now they say and tell and relate:

Aucassin was set in prison as you have heard tell, and Nicolette for her part was shut in the chamber. It was in the time of summer heat, in the month of May, when the days are warm, long and clear, and the night still and serene. Nicolette lay one night sleepless on her bed, and watched the moon shine brightly through the casement, and listened to the nightingale plain in the garden. Then she bethought her of Aucassin, her friend, whom she loved so well. She called also to mind the Count Garin of Beaucaire, her mortal foe, and feared greatly to remain, lest her hiding-place should be told to him, and she be put to death in some shameful fashion. She made certain that the old woman who held her in ward was sound asleep. So she rose, and wrapped herself in a very fair silk mantle, the best she had, and taking the sheets from her bed and the towels of her bath, knotted them together to make so long a rope as she was able, tied it about a pillar of the window, and slipped down into the garden. Then she took her skirt in both hands, the one before, and the other behind, and kilted her lightly against the dew which lay thickly upon the grass, and so passed through the garden. Her hair was golden, with little lovelocks; her eyes blue and laughing; her face most dainty to see, with lips more vermeil than ever was rose or cherry in the time of summer heat; her teeth white and small; her breasts so firm that they showed beneath her vesture like two rounded nuts. So frail was she about the girdle that your two hands could have spanned her, and the daisies that she brake with her feet in passing showed altogether black against her instep and her flesh, so white was the fair young maiden.

She came to the postern, and unbarring the gate, issued forth upon the street of Beaucaire, taking heed to keep within the shadows, for the moon shone very bright, and thus she fared until she chanced upon the tower where her lover was prisoned. The tower was buttressed with pieces of wood in many places, and Nicolette hid herself amongst the pillars, wrapped close in her mantle. She set her face to a crevice of the tower, which was old and ruinous, and there she heard Aucassin weeping within, making great sorrow for the sweet friend whom he held so dear; and when she had hearkened awhile, she began to speak.

Now is sung:

Nicolette, so bright of face,
Leaned within this buttressed place,
Heard her lover weep within,
Marked the woe of Aucassin.
Then in words her thought she told:
"Aucassin, fond heart and bold,
What avails thine heart should ache
For a Paynim maiden's sake?
Ne'er may she become thy mate,
Since we prove thy father's hate,
Since thy kinsfolk hate me too;
What is left for me to do?
Nothing, but to seek the strand,
Pass o'er sea to some far land."
Shore she then one golden tress,
Thrust it in her love's duress;
Aucassin hath seen the gold
Shining bright in that dark hold,
Took the lock at her behest,
Kissed and placed it in his breast;
Then once more his eyes were wet
    For Nicolette.

Now they say and tell and relate:

When Aucassin heard Nicolette say that she would fare into another country, he was filled with anger. "Fair sweet friend," said he, "this be far from thee, for then wouldst thou have slain me. And the first man who saw thee, if so he might, would take thee forthwith and carry thee to his bed, and make thee his leman. Be sure that if thou wert found in any man's bed, save it be mine, I should not need a dagger to pierce my heart and slay me. Certes, no; wait would I not for a knife; but on the first

wall or the nearest stone would I cast myself, and beat out my brains altogether. Better to die so foul a death as this than know thee to be in any man's bed, save mine."

"Aucassin," said she, "I doubt that thou lovest me less than thy words; and that my love is fonder than thine."

"Alack," cried Aucassin, "fair sweet friend, how can it be that thy love should be so great? Woman can not love man, as man loves woman; for woman's love is in the glance of her eye, and the blossom of her breast, and the tip of the toe of her foot; but the love of man is set deep in the hold of his heart, from whence it can not be torn away."

Whilst Aucassin and Nicolette were thus at odds together, the town watch entered the street, bearing naked swords beneath their mantles, for Count Garin had charged them strictly, once she were taken, to put her to death. The warder from his post upon the tower marked their approach, and as they drew near, heard them speaking of Nicolette, menacing her with death.

"God," said he, "it is great pity that so fair a damsel should be slain, and a rich alms should I give if I could warn her privily, and so she escape the snare; for of her death Aucassin, my liege, were dead already, and truly this were a piteous case."

Now is sung:

Brave the warder, full of guile,
Straight he sought some cunning wile:
Sought and found a song betime,
Raised this sweet and pleasant rhyme.
"Lady of the loyal mind,
Slender, gracious, very kind,
Gleaming head and golden hair,
Laughing lips and eyes of vair!
Easy, Lady, 'tis to tell
Two have speech who love full well.
Yet in peril are they met,
Set the snare, and spread the net.
Lo, the hunters draw this way,
Cloaked, with privy knives, to slay.
Ere the huntsmen spy the chase[22]
Let the quarry haste apace
    And keep her well."

Now they say and tell and relate:

"Ah," said Nicolette, "may the soul of thy father and of thy mother find sweetest rest, since in so fair and courteous a manner hast thou warned me. So God please, I will indeed keep myself close, and may He keep me too."

She drew the folds of her cloak about her, and crouched in the darkness of the pillars till the watch had passed beyond; then she bade farewell to Aucassin, and bent her steps to the castle wall. The wall was very ruinous, and mended with timber, so she climbed the fence, and went her way till she found herself between wall and moat. Gazing below, she saw the fosse was very deep and perilous, and the maid had great fear.

"Ah, God," cried she, "sweet Creature, should I fall, my neck must be broken; and if I stay, tomorrow shall I be taken, and men will burn my body in a fire. Yet were it better to die, now, in this place, than to be made a show tomorrow in the market."

---

22. Quarry.

She crossed her brow, and let herself slide down into the moat, and when she reached the bottom, her fair feet and pretty hands, which had never learned that they could be hurt, were so bruised and wounded that the blood came from them in places a many; yet knew she neither ill nor dolor because of the mightiness of her fear. But if with pain she had entered in, still more it cost her to issue forth. She called to mind that it were death to tarry, and by chance found there a stake of sharpened wood, which those within the keep had flung forth in their defense of the tower. With this she cut herself a foothold, one step above the other, till with extreme labor she climbed forth from the moat. Now the forest lay but the distance of two bolts from a crossbow, and ran some thirty leagues in length and breadth; moreover, within were many wild beasts and serpents. She feared these greatly, lest they should do her a mischief; but presently she remembered that should men lay hands upon her, they would lead her back to the city to burn her at the fire.

Now is sung:

Nicolette the fair, the fond,
Climbed the fosse and won beyond;
There she kneeled her, and implored
Very help of Christ the Lord.
"Father, King of majesty,
Where to turn I know not, I.
So, within the woodland gloom
Wolf and boar and lion roam,
Fearful things, with rav'ning maw,
Rending tusk and tooth and claw.
Yet, if all adread I stay,
Men will come at break of day,
Treat me to their heart's desire,
Burn my body in the fire.
But by God's dear majesty
Such a death I will not die;
Since I die, ah, better then
Trust the boar than trust to men.
Since all's evil, men and beast,
       Choose I the least."

Now they say and tell and relate:

Nicolette made great sorrow in such manner as you have heard. She commended herself to God's keeping, and fared on until she entered the forest. She kept upon the fringes of the woodland, for dread of the wild beasts and reptiles; and hiding herself within some thick bush, sleep overtook her, and she slept fast until six hours of the morn, when shepherds and herdsmen came from the city to lead their flocks to pasture between the wood and the river. The shepherds sat by a clear, sweet spring, which bubbled forth on the outskirts of the greenwood, and spreading a cloak upon the grass, set bread thereon. Whilst they ate together, Nicolette awoke at the song of the birds and the laughter, and hastened to the well.

"Fair children," said she, "God have you in His keeping."

"God bless you also," answered one who was more fluent of tongue than his companions.

"Fair child," said she, "do you know Aucassin, the son of Count Garin of this realm?"

"Yes, we know him well."

"So God keep you, pretty boy," said she, "as you tell him that within this wood there is a fair quarry for his hunting; and if he may take her, he would not part with one of her members for a hundred golden marks, nor for five hundred, nay, nor for aught that man can give."

Then looking upon her steadfastly, their hearts were troubled, the maid was so beautiful. "Will I tell him?" cried he who was readier of words than his companions. "Woe to him who speaks of it ever, or tells Aucassin what you say. You speak not truth but faery, for in all this forest there is no beast neither stag, nor lion, nor boar—one of whose legs would be worth two pence, or three at very best, and you talk of five hundred marks of gold! Woe betide him who believes your story, or shall spread it abroad! You are a fay, and no fit company for such as us; so pass upon your road."

"Ah, fair child," answered she, "yet you will do as I pray; for this beast is the only medicine that may heal Aucassin of his hurt. And I have here five sous in my purse; take them, and give him my message. For within three days must he hunt this chase and if within three days he find not the quarry, never may he cure him of his wound."

"By my faith," cried he, "we will take the money and if he comes this way, will give him your message; but certainly we will not go and look for him."

"As God pleases!" answered she. So she bade farewell to the shepherds, and went her way.

Now is sung:

Nicolette, as you heard tell,
Bade the shepherd lads farewell;
Through deep woodlands warily
Fared she 'neath the leafy tree,
Till the grass-grown way she trod
Brought her to a forest road,
Whence, like fingers on a hand,
Forked sev'n paths throughout the land.
There she called to heart her love,
There bethought her she would prove
Whether true her lover's vows.
Plucked she then young sapling boughs,
Grasses, leaves that branches yield,
Oak shoots, lilies of the field—
Built a lodge with frond and flow'r—
Fairest mason, fairest bow'r!
Swore then, by the truth of God,
Should her lover come that road,
Nor for love of her who made
Dream a little in its shade,
'Spite his oath, no true love, he
       Nor fond heart, she!

Now they say and tell and relate:

Nicolette builded the lodge, as you have heard; very pretty it was and very dainty, and well furnished, both outside and in, with a tapestry of flowers and of leaves. Then she withdrew herself a little way from the bower, and hid within a thicket to spy what Aucassin would do. And the cry and the haro went through all the realm that Nicolette was lost; some had it that she was stolen away, and others that Court Garin had done her to death. Whoever had joy thereof, Aucassin had little pleasure. His father, Court Garin, brought him out of his prison, and sent letters to the lords and ladies of those parts bidding them to a very rich feast, so that Aucassin, his son, might cease to dote. When the feast was at its merriest, Aucassin leaned against the musicians' gallery, sad and all discomforted. No laugh had he for any jest, since she whom most he loved was not amongst the ladies set in hall.

A certain knight marked his grief, and coming presently to him, said, "Aucassin, of such fever as yours, I, too, have been sick. I can give you good counsel, if you are willing to listen."

"Sir knight," said Aucassin, "great thanks! Good counsel, above all things, I would hear."

"Get to horse," said he; "take your pleasure in the woodland amongst flowers and bracken and the songs of the birds. Perchance (who knows?) you may hear some word of which you will be glad."

"Sir knight," answered Aucassin, "great thanks! This will I do." He left the hall privily, and went downstairs to the stable where was his horse. He caused the charger to be saddled and bridled, then put foot in stirrup, mounted, and left the castle, riding till he entered the forest, and so by adventure came upon the well whereby the shepherd lads were sitting; and it was then about three hours after noon. They had spread a cloak upon the grass, and were eating their bread, with great mirth and jollity.

Now is sung:

Round about the well were set
Martin, Robin, Esmeret—
Jolly shepherds, gaily met—
Frulin, Jack, and Aubriet.
Laughed the one, "God keep in ward
Aucassin, our brave young lord—
Keep besides the damsel fair,
Blue of eye and gold of hair,
Gave us wherewithal to buy
Cate and sheath-knife presently,
Horn and quarter-staff and fruit,
Shepherd's pipe and country flute;
    God make him well!"

Now they say and tell and relate:

When Aucassin marked the song of the herdboys he called to heart Nicolette, his very sweet friend, whom he held so dear. He thought she must have passed that way, so he struck his horse with the spurs and came quickly to the shepherds.

"Fair children, God keep you!"

"God bless you!" replied he who was readier of tongue than his fellows.

"Fair children," said he, "tell over again the song that you told but now."

"We will not tell it," answered he who was more fluent of speech than the others. "Sorrow be his who sings it to you, fair sir!"

"Fair children," returned Aucassin, "do you not know me?"

"Oh, yes; we know that you are Aucassin, our young lord. But we are not your men; we belong to the Count."

"Fair children, sing me the song once more, I pray you!"

"By the Wounded Heart, what fine words! Why should I sing for you if I have no wish to do so? Why, the richest man in all the land—saving the presence of Count Garin—would not dare to drive my sheep and oxen and cows from out his wheatfield or his pasture, for fear of losing his eyes! Wherefore, then, should I sing for you if I have no wish to do so?"

"God keep you, fair children; yet you will do this thing for me. Take ten sous that I have in my purse."

"Sire, we will take the money; but I will not sing for you, since I have sworn not to do so. But I will tell it in plain prose, if such be your pleasure."

"As God pleases!" answered Aucassin. "Better the tale in prose than no story at all!"

"Sire, we were in this glade between six and nine of the morn, and were breaking our bread by the well, just as we are doing now, when a girl came by, the loveliest thing in all the world, so fair that we doubted her a fay,

and she brimmed our wood with light. She gave us money, and made a bargain with us that if you came here we would tell you that you must hunt in this forest; for in it is such a quarry that if you may take her you would not part with one of her members for five hundred silver marks, nor for aught that man can give. For in the quest is so sweet a salve that if you take her you shall be cured of your wound; and within three days must the chase be taken, for if she be not found by then, never will you see her more. Now go to your hunting if you will, and if you will not, let it go; for truly have I carried out my bargain with her."

"Fair children," cried Aucassin, "enough have you spoken; and may God set me on her track!"

Now is sung:

Aucassin's fond heart was moved
When this hidden word he proved
Sent him by the maid he loved.
Straight his charger he bestrode,
Bade farewell, and swiftly rode
Deep within the forest dim,
Saying o'er and o'er to him:
"Nicolette, so sweet, so good,
'Tis for you I search this wood—
Antler'd stag nor boar I chase—
Hot I follow on your trace.
Slender shape and deep blue eyes,
Dainty laughter, low replies,
Fledge the arrow in my heart.
Ah, to find you—ne'er to part!
Pray God give so fair an end,
    Sister, sweet friend!"

Now they say and tell and relate:

Aucassin rode through the wood in search of Nicolette, and the charger went right speedily. Do not think that the spines and the thorns were pitiful to him. Truly, it was not so; for his raiment was so torn that the least tattered of his garments could scarcely hold to his body, and the blood ran from his arms and legs and flanks in forty places, or at least in thirty, so that you could have followed after him by the blood which he left upon the grass. But he thought so fondly of Nicolette, his sweet friend, that he felt neither ill nor dolor. Thus all day long he searched the forest in his fashion, but might learn no news of her, and when it drew towards dusk, he commenced to weep because he had heard nothing. He rode at adventure down an old grass-grown road, and looking before him, saw a young man standing, such as I will tell you. Tall he was, and marvelously ugly and hideous. His head was big and blacker than smoked meat; the palm of your hand could easily have gone between his two eyes; he had very large cheeks and a monstrous flat nose with great nostrils; lips redder than uncooked flesh; teeth yellow and foul; he was shod with shoes and gaiters of bull's hide, bound about the leg with ropes to well above the knee; upon his back was a rough cloak; and he stood leaning on a huge club. Aucassin urged his steed towards him, but was all afeared when he saw him as he was.

"Fair brother, God keep you."

"God bless you too," said he.

"As God keeps you, what do you here?"

"What is that to you?" said he.

"Truly, naught," answered Aucassin. "I asked with no wish to do you wrong."

"And you, for what cause do you weep?" asked the other, "and make such heavy sorrow? Certainly, were I so rich a man as you are, not the whole world should make me shed a tear."

"Do you know me, then?" said Aucassin.

"Yes, well I know you to be Aucassin, the son of the Count, and if you will tell me why you weep, well, then I will tell what I do here."

"Certes," said Aucassin, "I will tell you with all my heart. I came this morning to hunt in the forest, and with a white grey-hound, the swiftest in the whole world. I have lost him, and that is why I weep."

"Hear him," cried he, "by the Sacred Heart, and you make all this lamentation for a filthy dog! Sorrow be his who shall esteem you more. Why, there is not a man of substance in these parts who would not give you ten or fifteen or twenty hounds—if so your father wishes—and be right glad to make you the gift. But for my part I have full reason to weep and cry aloud."

"And what is your grief, brother?"

"Sire, I will tell you. I was hired by a rich farmer to drive his plough, with a yoke of four oxen. Now three days ago, by great mischance, I lost the best of my bullocks, Roget, the very best ox in the plough. I have been looking for him ever since, and have neither eaten nor drunk for three days; since I dare not go back to the town, because men would put me into prison, as I have no money to pay for my loss. Of all the riches of the world I have nought but the rags upon my back. My poor old mother, too, who had nothing but one worn-out mattress, why, they have taken that from under her, and left her lying on the naked straw. That hurts me more than my own trouble. For money comes and money goes; if I have lost today, why, I may win tomorrow; and I will pay for my ox when pay I can. Not for this will I wring my hands. And you—you weep aloud for a filthy cur. Sorrow take him who shall esteem you more."

"Certes, thou art a true comforter, fair brother, and blessed may you be. What is the worth of your bullock?"

"Sire, the villein demands twenty sous for his ox. I can not beat the price down by a single farthing."

"Hold out your hand," said Aucassin, "take these twenty sous which I have in my purse, and pay for your ox."

"Sire," answered the hind, "many thanks, and God grant you find that for which you seek."

So they parted from each other, and Aucassin rode upon his way. The night was beautiful and still, and so he fared along the forest path until he came to the seven crossroads where Nicolette had builded her bower. Very pretty it was, and very dainty, and well furnished both outside and in, ceiling and floor, with arras and carpet of freshly plucked flowers; no sweeter habitation could man desire to see. When Aucassin came upon it, he reined back his horse sharply, and the moonbeams fell within the lodge.

"Dear God," cried Aucassin, "here was Nicolette, my sweet friend, and this has she builded with her fair white hands. For the sweetness of the house and for love of her, now will I dismount, and here will I refresh me this night."

He withdrew his foot from the stirrup, and the charger was tall and high. He dreamed so deeply on Nicolette, his very sweet friend, that he fell heavily upon a great stone, and his shoulder came from its socket. He knew himself to be grievously wounded, but he forced him to do all that he was able, and fastened his horse

with the other hand to a thorn. Then he turned on his side, and crawled as best he might into the lodge. Looking through a crevice of the bower, he saw the stars shining in the sky, and one brighter than all the others, so he began to repeat—

Now is sung:

Little Star I gaze upon
Sweetly drawing to the moon.
In such golden haunt is set
Love, and bright-haired Nicolette.
God hath taken from our war
Beauty, like a shining star.
Ah, to reach her, though I fell
From her Heaven to my Hell!
Who were worthy such a thing,
Were he emperor or king?
Still you shine, oh perfect Star,
    Beyond, afar.

Now they say and tell and relate:

When Nicolette heard Aucassin speak these words, she hastened to him from where she was hidden near by. She entered in the bower, and clasping her arms about his neck, kissed and embraced him straitly. "Fair sweet friend, very glad am I to find you."

"And you, fair sweet friend, glad am I to meet." So they kissed, and held each other fast, and their joy was lovely to see.

"Ah, sweet friend," cried Aucassin, "it was but now that I was in grievous pain with my shoulder, but since I hold you close I feel neither sorrow nor wound."

Nicolette searched his hurt, and perceived that the shoulder was out of joint. She handled it so deftly with her white hands and used such skillful surgery, that by the grace of God (who loveth all true lovers) the shoulder came back to its place. Then she plucked flowers, and fresh grass and green leafage, and bound them tightly about the setting with the hem torn from her shift, and he was altogether healed.

"Aucassin," said she, "Fair sweet friend, let us take thought together as to what must be done. If your father beats the wood tomorrow, and men take me, whatever may chance to you, certainly I shall be slain."

"Certes, fair sweet friend, the sorer grief would be mine. But so I may help, never shall you come to his hands." So he mounted to horse, and setting his love before him, held her fast in his arms, kissing her as he rode, and thus they came forth to the open fields.

Now is sung:

Aucassin, that loving squire,
Dainty fair to heart's desire,
Rode from out the forest dim
Clasping her he loved to him.
Placed upon the saddlebow
There he kissed her, chin and brow,
There embraced her, mouth and eyes.
But she spake him, sweetly wise:
"Love, a term to dalliance;
Since for us no home in France
See we Rome or far Byzance?"
"Sweet my love, all's one to me,
Dale or woodland, earth or sea;
Nothing care I where we ride
So I hold you at my side."

So, enlaced, the lovers went,
Skirting town and battlement,
Rocky scaur,[23] and quiet lawn;
Till one morning, with the dawn,
Broke the cliffs down to the shore,
Loud they heard the surges roar,
　　Stood by the sea.

(From this point Aucassin and Nicolette were separated. After some adventures Aucassin returned to his home where he became Court of Beaucaire. Nicolette was taken to Carthage where she was recognized as the king's daughter and was to be married to a Moorish Prince. She ran away, however, and made her way to Beaucaire disguised as a minstrel.)

Now is sung:

Neath the keep of strong Beaucaire
On a day of summer fair,
At his pleasure, Aucassin
Sat with baron, friend and kin.
Then upon the scent of flow'rs,
Song of birds, and golden hours,
Full of beauty, love, regret,
Stole the dream of Nicolette,
Came the tenderness of years;
So he drew apart in tears.
Then there entered to his eyes
Nicolette, in minstrel guise,
Touched the viol with the bow,
Sang as I will let you know.
"Lords and ladies, list to me,
High and low, of what degree;
Now I sing, for your delight,
Aucassin, that loyal knight,
And his fond friend, Nicolette.
Such the love betwixt them set
When his kinsfolk sought her head,
Fast he followed where she fled.
From their refuge in the keep
Paynims bore them o'er the deep.
Nought of him I know to end.
But for Nicolette, his friend,
Dear she is, desirable,
For her father loves her well;
Famous Carthage owns him king,
Where she has sweet cherishing.
Now, as lord he seeks for her,
Sultan, Caliph, proud Emir.
But the maid of these will none,
For she loves a dansellon,
Aucassin, who plighted troth.
Sworn has she some pretty oath
Ne'er shall she be wife or bride,
Never lie at baron's side
　　Be he denied."

Now they say and tell and relate:

When Aucassin heard Nicolette sing in this fashion, he was glad at heart; so he drew her aside, and asked, "Fair sweet friend," said Aucassin, "know you nought of this Nicolette, whose ballad you have sung?"

"Sire, truly, yea; well I know her for the most loyal of creatures, and as the most winning and modest of maidens born. She is daughter to the King of Carthage, who took her when Aucassin also was taken, and brought her to the city of Carthage, till he knew for certain that she was his child, whereat he rejoiced greatly. Any day he would give her for husband one of the highest kings in all Spain; but rather would she be hanged or burned than take him, however rich he be."

"Ah, fair sweet friend," cried the Count Aucassin, "if you would return to that country and persuade her to have speech with me here, I would give you of my riches more than you would dare to ask of me or to take. Know that for love of her I choose not to have a wife, however proud her race, but I stand and wait; for never will there be wife of mine if it be not she, and if I knew where to find her I should not need to grope blindly for her thus."

"Sire," answered she, "if you will do these things, I will go and seek her for your sake, and for hers too; because to me she is very dear."

He pledged his word, and caused her to be given twenty pounds. So she bade him farewell, and he was weeping for the sweetness of Nicolette. And when she saw his tears, "Sire," said she, "take it not so much to heart; in so short a space will I bring her to this town, and you shall see her with your eyes."

When Aucassin knew this, he rejoiced greatly. So she parted from him, and fared in the town to the house of the Viscountess, for the Viscount, her godfather, was dead. There she lodged, and opened her mind fully to the lady on all the business; and the Viscountess recalled the past, and knew well that it was Nicolette whom she had cherished. So she caused the bath to be heated, and made her take her ease for fully eight days. Then Nicolette sought an herb that was called celandine, and washed herself therewith, and became so fair as she had never been before. She arrayed her in a rich silken gown from the lady's goodly store, and seated herself in the chamber on a rich stuff of broidered sendal; then she whispered the dame, and begged her to fetch Aucassin, her friend. This she did. When she reached the palace, lo, Aucassin in tears, making great sorrow for the long tarrying of Nicolette, his friend; and the lady called to him, and said, "Aucassin, behave not so wildly; but come with me, and I will show you that thing you love best in all the world; for Nicolette, your sweet friend, is here from a far country to seek her love." So Aucassin was glad at heart.

Now is sung:

When he learned that in Beaucaire
Lodged his lady, sweet and fair,
Aucassin arose, and came
To her hostel, with the dame;
Entered in, and passed straightway
To the chamber where she lay.
When she saw him, Nicolette
Had such joy as never yet;
Sprang she lightly to her feet,
Swiftly came with welcome meet.
When he saw her, Aucassin
Oped both arms, and drew her in,
Clasped her close in fond embrace,
Kissed her eyes and kissed her face.

---

23. Isolated cliff.

In such greeting sped the night,
Till, at dawning of the light,
Aucassin, with pomp most rare,
Crowned her Countess of Beaucaire.
Such delight these lovers met,
Aucassin and Nicolette,
Length of days and joy did win,
Nicolette and Aucassin;
Endeth song and tale I tell
    With marriage bell.

Exercises

1. The coexistence of morality plays and romances seems to indicate some contradictions between church teachings and actual life. For instance, what differences in attitudes about the body are found in these two works? Are there similar contradictions in our own society?
2. What was "love" in the Middle Ages? What did these two lovers see in each other? On what was their mutual attraction based? Are today's concepts about attraction and love somewhat different? Considerably different? Account for the differences.

Summary

It is almost symbolic that the people of the early Middle Ages built walls around their villages—wooden palisades in the early days, later, with feudalism, the walls were constructed of stone and the lord's house and the whole village became a fortified enclave. The total way of life at the time paralleled those confining fortifications, because early medieval people built battlements of equal strength around their minds.

The universe was based on the Church of Rome, which allowed no questioning of its tenets or of its actions. Further, the Church, through a contraction of the Augustinian doctrine, took a very dim view of all worldly pleasure and carefully restrained any questioning of the physical world. Science as we know it was lost completely, so that the natural world was a closed book, to be interpreted only as a vague shadow of the intention and mind of God. Life here and now was viewed as a brief and transitory journey through a dismal land, with true life and true happiness coming only after death. Furthermore, as is particularly apparent in the morality play of *Everyman* (see the Literary Selections), the only way to reach the blissful afterlife lay in the faithful acceptance of the doctrines and the sacraments of the Church.

The economic system of manorialism bound the greatest part of the population to the thousand acres or so of the manor itself. They could not escape; the few who traveled any distance at all had to have special permission. In fact, the average serf never strayed as much as one mile from the demesne. Food, clothing, and meager physical comforts were limited to what the manor could produce. Not even the mind could escape the narrow confines; reading was almost unknown because there was so little literacy (not even all of the clergy could read and write). Illiteracy and minimal travel meant also that news of the outside world almost never penetrated the closed miniworld of the manor.

The political system of feudalism was equally narrowing. Justice lay entirely in the hands of the feudal lord or, more often, his deputy. Except for the specific obligations of serf to lord and vassal to suzerain, which were generally known and accepted, the law was made up on the spot, and the individual never knew what to expect.

About the only contact that feudal society had with the outside world were the bloody confrontations with the barbarian Norsemen or Magyars, or with the Muslims. Not until the middle of the Middle Ages (ca. 1000) would the Norsemen and Magyars be absorbed by Christian societies and the advanced culture of Islam be acknowledged, studied, and drawn into the evolving Western synthesis. Western civilization would not in fact be what it is today without the vital infusion of Islamic culture.

The narrow confines of Church, manorialism, and feudalism provided the walls that closed in upon the human spirit. Creativity and freedom of thought were almost unknown. But, with the withdrawal of Roman protection and with all the dangers from bands of marauders, these walls provided protection for the individual. If ordinary serfs could not live well, they could at least live safely.

Perhaps Elinor Wylie's twentieth-century poem "Sanctuary" expresses the same problem:

This is the bricklayer; hear the thud
Of his heavy load dumped down on stone,
His lustrous bricks are brighter than blood,
His smoking mortar whiter than bone.

Set each sharp-edged, fire-bitten brick
Straight by the plumb-line's shivering length;
Make my marvelous wall so thick
Dead nor living may shake its strength.

Full as a crystal cup with drink
Is my cell with dreams, and quiet, and cool . . .
Stop, old man! You must leave a chink;
How can I breathe? *You can't, you fool!*

But the human spirit is never content with mere security. Particularly with gaining of a little freedom as it did in the tenth century, it clamors more and more for expansion. The seeds that were to germinate and eventually break down medieval walls were already planted. Some of the directions for that growth may be indicated.

First, the human spirit has never long been content to *not* examine the world around it. The varied forms of the world, its beauties, and reason for being demand attention. Both art and science express this quest for an exploration of the world of the senses.

Second, the two personality types of Europe, the rational Graeco-Roman and the emotional and energetic Germanic lived side by side but not in unison by the year 1000.

Some form of synthesis between these two personality types, almost exactly opposite each other, needed to be found.

Third, a problem limited largely to politics: the question of supremacy of church or state demanded settlement. At a time when the secular power was so weak as to be almost nonexistent, the Church could and did assert its authority over kings and lords. But with the growth of the powers of the world a struggle was inevitable, a bitter conflict of church and state that has been waged all over the Western world and which is still not fully resolved.

Fourth, and perhaps most important, people demand and need joy in the present life, but this was sternly denied by the Church. A desire for immediate physical and intellectual pleasure in life now would necessarily conflict with the doctrine that life here was nothing, the afterlife was everything. The pull of life as opposed to the Church-dictated pull of death was bound to tear the human personality apart until some synthesis could be effected.

These are the latent problems one sees at the end of the early Middle Ages. Their solutions will be dealt with in subsequent chapters.

Culture and Human Values

It is very difficult to look back on the early Middle Ages and really understand life in the walled bastions, castles, enclaves, and towns. There is a natural tendency to view these medieval inhabitants as shut off from the outside world by what amount to prison walls. That outside world, however, was dangerous. Brigands roamed the countryside, not to mention occasional marauding armies of rival lords. The sheltering walls meant security and safety with hardly anyone giving much thought to anything beyond eating, working, sleeping, and just plain surviving.

Inside the walls people were protected and controlled, and life went on. The Church promised salvation for the faithful, a glorious existence in the afterlife. A sparse and meager existence in this harsh world would be more than made up for by eternal life in the paradise to come. Strict adherence to the Church's teaching of the Scriptures and to Church doctrine—plus avoidance of sin—virtually assured admission to that eternal bliss.

The virtues and vices as defined by the Church can also be considered from another point of view, as pointed out by scholars of the early Middle Ages. This was a chaotic time in which the Church was the only absolute authority. Scholars have suggested that the virtues (and forbidden vices) also served to reinforce the power and authority of the Church. The first and foremost value was obedience to authority. After this, the seven virtues of justice, faith, hope, love, fortitude, temperance, and prudence would contribute to the dominance of Rome. The forbidden sins of pride, envy, anger, avarice, dejection, gluttony, and lust would help guard against any temptation to tinker with the status quo. Whatever the interpretation, life during these difficult times was bleak and dismal for most of the population, and was to remain so for centuries.

Annotated Bibliography

General

Aland, Kurt. *A History of Christianity: From the Beginnings to the Threshold of the Reformation.* Philadelphia: Fortress Press, 1985. A fine study utilizing the latest scholarship.

Barber, Richard. *A Penguin Guide to Medieval Europe.* New York: Penguin Books, 1984. A helpful handbook on life and culture from Charlemagne to the Renaissance.

Bishop, Morris. *The Middle Ages.* Magnolia, Mass.: Peter Smith Publisher, 1983. A graceful and witty account of the thousand years between Rome and the Renaissance.

Duby, Georges. *The Three Orders: Feudal Society Imagined.* Translated by Arthur Goldhammer. Chicago: University of Chicago Press, 1980. A brilliant reconstruction of the structure of medieval social classes by a noted scholar.

Gies, Joseph, and Gies, Frances. *Life in a Medieval Castle.* New York: Harper & Row, Publishers, 1979. Everyday life in a castle.

Grant, Michael. *Dawn of the Middle Ages:* A.D. *476–816.* New York: McGraw-Hill Book Co., 1981. Traces the transition from the fall of Rome.

Strayer, J. R. *Western Europe in the Middle Ages.* Glenview, Ill.: Scott, Foresman and Co., 1982. Perhaps the best short introduction to political and cultural history.

Literature

Brentano, Robert, ed. *The Early Middle Ages: 500–1000.* New York: Macmillan Publishing Co., 1964. Perhaps the best short anthology of Western Christian sources.

Jackson, William T. *The Literature of the Middle Ages.* New York: Columbia University Press, 1960. A richly illustrated synthesis of the backgrounds, attitudes, devices, and motifs of medieval literature.

Oates, Whitney J., ed. *Basic Writings of Saint Augustine,* 2 vols. New York: Random House, 1948. Special attention is directed to *The Enchiridion: On Faith, Hope, and Love.* In this remarkable treatise, Augustine has given a compact yet complete expression to his whole position on faith, hope, and love.

Terry, Patricia. *The Song of Roland.* Indianapolis: Bobbs-Merrill Educational Publishing, 1965. Generally considered the best available translation and the one used in this chapter.

Trapp, J. B., ed. *Medieval English Literature.* New York: Oxford University Press, 1973. Fine anthology that includes *Beowulf, Sir Gawain and the Green Knight,* Chaucer, and other classics.

14

The Late Middle Ages: Expansion and Synthesis

A New Century

It is impossible to pinpoint any particular reason for the liberation of a whole social structure, but as we look back over the centuries, we know that it happened in eleventh-century Europe.[1] Perhaps not the least of the reasons was a release from a sense of doom; the end of the world had been predicted for the year 1000 and the prediction was widely believed by the peasantry. One must imagine the wonder of a whole culture when people woke up on New Year's morning of the year 1001, pinched themselves, and found that they were still alive in the flesh, and felt the pangs of hunger, not for spiritual food, but for a very physical breakfast. Such a reprieve may have been one of the causative factors in the general awakening of Europe. The people were still in the Middle Ages; God was still the accepted Reality, but what a difference was soon to be discovered in the lives and the thoughts of men and women!

The difference expresses itself in various ways. One can notice a change from the masculine code of feudalism to the feminine code of chivalry, closely associated with the rising Cult of the Virgin, which became the dominant popular religious force in late medieval times. Another factor to be considered is the rise of cities. The Crusades, still another leavening influence, brought about an increasing knowledge of the relatively luxurious life of Islamic culture. Within the new cities we also witness the revival of humanistic learning with the rise of the great universities. Last to be mentioned, though perhaps basic to the whole movement, was the philosophic ferment about the nature of reality itself, which culminated in the "Battle of Universals" in philosophic circles.

The Rise of Cities

Historians attribute the rise of cities to a number of causes, all of which were probably significant. One reason lay in the increase of land available for agriculture because of the drainage of swamps, for it must be remembered that cities need agriculture to supply food. The needs of the great nobility for central fighting forces gave another impetus to the gathering of people, for as wars became bigger and landholdings wider, the barons needed men in a central place who could be mobilized immediately. Perhaps the most important force in the development of cities was the rise of trade and commerce (though one who asks for the causative force in this development cannot find a specific answer except that it happened). At any rate, the itinerant peddler, traveling from manor to manor, had been known throughout the early Middle Ages. Sometime about the eleventh century this trade became somewhat stabilized as the peddlers-become-merchants set up stalls under the protection of the great churches or abbeys, and the Church law that governed the place insured peaceful transactions. This brought about another change. If trade were to flourish, the old barter system was no longer adequate, and money was reintroduced to Europe. The nobility was quick to seize upon this change and to foster it. For centuries they had collected their feudal dues in produce and goods, but money offered them much greater freedom in carrying on their activities. They were willing, therefore, to grant charters to the cities, giving them varying degrees of freedom from feudal responsibilities in return for tax money. Thus did the towns grow, and whatever the immediate forces that made them flourish, their development was but a symptom of a general stirring of the human spirit.

Throughout Europe the word went around, "City air is free air," for in free cities the custom was established that a serf who could maintain his residence for a year and a day became a free man. The more adventurous and intelligent serfs flocked to the city. Here men of common interests—interests centered in their trades—formed themselves into guilds to regulate the quality and price of their goods and to provide insurance and a measure of social life for the members and their families. As these guilds—first craft guilds, later merchant guilds—became wealthy, the grand guildhalls flanked the cathedral to form a quadrangle about the open marketplace; this central grouping became the characteristic feature of medieval towns and cities.

---

1. See the Time Chart on page 300 for an overview of the Middle Ages.

■
MAP 14.1 *The Major Crusades.*

The Crusades

For a variety of reasons, the Crusades were a major force for change. Preached by Pope Urban II in 1095, the First Crusade captured Jerusalem in 1099, becoming the only successful venture in a series of Crusades lasting into the Renaissance—and that success was only temporary (see the map: The Major Crusades). The intent of the Crusades was to take the Holy Land from its Muslim inhabitants so that Christian shrines might become more accessible for pilgrims from the West. Generally speaking, the West saw the Crusades as holy wars to wrest biblical lands from infidels; Muslims viewed the Crusades as unprovoked wars of aggression by infidels who were barbarians to boot. The repercussions have yet to end.

The long-lasting effects of the invasions of the Middle East did, however, include significant positive aspects. Though Europe had already encountered Islamic culture in Sicily and Spain, the crusaders entered the heart of this rich civilization causing, eventually, sweeping changes in virtually every aspect of European life. The luxurious booty carted home by the soldiers, as is the ancient custom of all soldiers, contributed to the rising expectations for a better life. First imported as luxuries, food (sugar, saffron, rice, citrus, melon) and manufactured goods (silk, damask, muslin, cotton) quickly became necessities. More important than food and textiles,

however, was the rich reservoir of Islamic science, medicine, and mathematics and the carefully tended heritage of ancient Greece. The way was still long and tortuous but semibarbaric Europe began, finally, to develop the arts of civilized living.

Feminine Influence: A Move from Feudalism to Chivalry

One of the most interesting transformations was that from feudalism to chivalry, a movement from a masculine to a feminine code of behavior. Feudalism, according to the historian Henry Adams, was the code of men-at-arms. With the later Middle Ages, however, especially in France, women assumed a more prominent role in matters of taste and manners. Men were away from home for great stretches of time, trading, fighting, and crusading. In their absence their wives had opportunities to expand their limited roles by introducing poetry and music to the courts and elevating the standards of behavior, dress, and manners. If we must have one name to fix this movement in our memory, Adams gives us that of the remarkable Eleanor of Aquitaine (1122–1204), Queen of France and then of England. Insisting on accompanying her husband, King Louis VII of France, on the Second Crusade in 1147, Eleanor was especially impressed by the so-phistication of Constantinople, and undoubtedly incorporated elements of Byzantine and Muslim culture into her already extensive education. Along with her daughter, Marie of Champagne, and granddaughter, Blanche of Castile, Eleanor established Courts of Love that were to write legal-sounding codes of etiquette. Epic tales of bloody battles and mighty heroes were replaced by lyrical love songs composed and performed by aristocratic troubadours and trouvères (figure 14.1; see also chapter 16). This change may be seen in the contrast between Roland's lament over the fallen Franks at Roncevaux, representative of the ideals of feudalism, and the lament over the dead Lancelot, representative of the chivalrous knight. Roland, surveying the field of death where lie his comrades in arms, says:

> Lords and barons, now may God have mercy upon you, and grant Paradise to all your souls that you may rest among the blessed flowers. Man never saw better men of arms that ye were. Long and well, year in and year out, have you served me, and many wide lands have ye won for the glory of Charles. Was it to such an end that he nourished you? O France, fair land, today art thou made desolate by rude slaughter. Ye Frankish barons, I see you die through me, yet I can do naught to save and defend you. May God, who knows no lie, aid you!

Yet when Lancelot, the almost perfect knight of chivalry, lies dead, we hear the following lament:

> Thou wert the courtliest knight that ever bare shield, and thou wert the truest friend to thy lover that ever bestrode horse, and thou wert the truest lover among sinful men that ever loved woman, and thou wert the kindest man that ever struck with sword, and thou wert the goodliest person that ever came among the crowd of knights, and thou wert the meekest man and the gentlest that ever are in hall among ladies, and thou wert the sternest knight to thy mortal foe that ever put spear in breast.

From this we see the transformation from a fighting code to a courtly and courteous one. Both are found in the lament over Lancelot, but the virtues of mildness, of love, and of humility always stand before the virtues of strength or the recognition of human weakness.

Given the vagaries of human nature, the elaborate codes of courtly love were undoubtedly violated about as often as they were observed, there being few Lancelots in this world. They assisted nevertheless in the long process of civilizing barbaric Europe.

The Church of Our Lady

Closely allied to the evolution of chivalry was the development of beauty and warmth within the Church. As has already been pointed out, the official doctrine of the Church was a vast intellectual monument. It centered in

FIGURE 14.1 *"Music and Her Attendants" from Boethius, De Arithmetica, Biblioteca Nazionale, Naples. Holding a portable pipe organ, the elegant lady who symbolizes the civilized art of courtly music is surrounded by an ensemble of female court musicians. In the circle at the top King David plays a psaltery, the instrument named after the Psalms (Psaltery) of David.*

the Trinity—the Father, the Son, and the Holy Ghost—a Three who were always One, administering the rigid justice found in the development of doctrine from the time of Augustine. For sinful people, justice is the last thing to be desired, and medieval men and women, guilt-ridden by the absolutism of the time, were convinced that they were sinful. They sought not justice, but mercy, turning to the Virgin, the highest of the Saints, the Queen of Heaven. She was the essence of purity, an idealized version of love, warmth, and beauty. A manifestation of the polarized medieval view of women, the Cult of the Virgin venerated one woman, pure in body and soul, possessor of all the womanly virtues. Her diametric opposite was Eve the temptress, the "fallen" woman who had been beguiled by Satan, a concept that was to have disastrous consequences in later centuries, including our own.

The Virgin was nevertheless the loving Mother who could mercifully intercede for the faithful, and it was to her that the great cathedrals were dedicated. Indeed, in

France one asks not how to get to the cathedral, but how to get to Notre Dame, the church of "Our Lady." The two are almost synonymous. As Adams points out:

> The measure of this devotion [to the Virgin], which proves to any religious American mind, beyond possible cavil, its serious and practical reality, is the money it cost. According to statistics, in the single century between 1170 and 1270, the French built 80 cathedrals and nearly five hundred churches of the cathedral class, which would have cost, according to an estimate made in 1840, more than five thousand millions to replace. Five thousand million francs is a thousand million dollars,[2] and this covered only the great churches of a single century. . . . The share of this capital which was—if one may use a commercial figure—invested in the Virgin cannot be fixed . . . but in a spiritual and artistic sense, it was almost the whole. . . .
>
> Expenditure like this rests invariably on an economic idea. . . . In the thirteenth [century] they trusted their money to the Queen of Heaven— because of their belief in her power to repay it with interest in the life to come.

Therein lay the power of the Virgin in bringing human understanding and human sympathy into the cold philosophic structure of Church doctrine. While the philosophers wrangled about the nature of the universal substance, the common people found comfort and a release of pent-up energies in the addition of a Person with human sympathy and warmth to the austere Trinity. Such faith reveals itself in the great body of stories of the mysteries of the Virgin, one of the most widely known and touching of which is "Our Lady's Juggler," given on page 349.

Scholasticism

Most important of all in terms of a basic way of life were the continual attacks and modifications of the doctrine of the Church itself, for the Church insisted upon absolute authority. In spite of his early philosophic gropings, St. Augustine had finally said, "I believe in order that I may know." Thus *faith* in the Scripture and the writings of the early churchmen and total submission to these sources was the first necessity for Christian life. Knowledge came second, and if at any point the doctrine seemed contrary to reason or inexplicable by it, the doctrine was to be believed and intellect was to be denied.

Upon this basis was built the great structure of Christian Scholasticism, the way of thought of the late Middle Ages. Most simply, Scholasticism can be explained in this way: If a thinker had any question for which he wanted an answer, he went first to the Bible and the writings of the Church Fathers to discover all the passages that pertained to his subject. This was his only source for basic data; experimentation in the world of his senses was not permitted. Then, as a second step, he used Aristotelian logic to work on his source material. Such

logic is built upon the three-part syllogism: a major premise, *all men are mortal;* a minor premise, *Sokrates is a man;* a conclusion, *therefore Sokrates is mortal.* Then this conclusion can be used as a major or minor premise in further syllogisms until the thinker reaches an answer to his problems.[3]

The Conflict: Faith and Reason

As early as the ninth century the conflict between faith and reason had been pointed up by John Scotus Erigena, who insisted that both reason and the Scriptures had come from God, and that there could be no conflict between them. After his time, the Church's stand on faith alone had been reaffirmed, particularly by Anselm of Canterbury in the eleventh century.

This reaffirmation was not to stand unchallenged for long. In the late eleventh century a philosophic conflict broke out that was called the Battle of Universals. The "battle" involved a lengthy philosophic dispute, greatly simplified here, about the nature of reality. Twentieth-century students may view this as a dry wrangle between a number of ivory-towered philosophers, but it was not. In the first place it has been pointed out that the idea of reality that is held at any time determines the nature of civilization, and that a change in this idea will bring about a change in the way people think and live. We are dealing with thinkers as important to their time as Einstein and Freud have been to ours. Second, the philosophers were important Churchmen, and since the Church was the central institution of the time, any change in its position would and did have a very great effect on life itself. True, the peasant on the farm or the craftsman in his shop neither knew nor cared about the Battle of Universals, but the men concerned in it were the men who made and moved society as a whole.

The Realist Position

To see the nature of this "battle" we may remember that one of the strongest foundations of Church doctrine was a Christian adaption of the Neoplatonist belief that reality was permanent, unchanging, without any body or material substance, existing in the mind of God. This position sprang from Plato's belief in essences (forms, ideas) as the ultimate reality. Thus body and substance, all physical things subject to change were only illusory shadows,

---

2. This is the money values of 1840. If we multiplied the figure by fifty, it would still be low for the late twentieth century.

---

3. Modern students tend to scoff at this type of reasoning until they remember that *every* culture sets similar limits to its thought process. For example, in the early twentieth century, the searcher for truth drew the basic material for investigation from the world of the senses (one was not encouraged to go outside of this realm) and then used the scientific method to refine the raw data and find answers to the questions. The type of knowledge found through the use of this technique of research is totally different from that found in the Middle Ages, but the limitations are equally severe. A God-centered society results from one method; a completely materialistic society comes from the other.

imperfect copies, of the Idea (see Plato's "Allegory of the Cave" for a full explanation). According to this accepted doctrine, the human body was to be disregarded and a study of the physical world wasted time that should be spent seeking eternal truths. This Neoplatonic, Augustinian doctrine was accepted up to the eleventh century, by the "Establishment" and became known as the *Realist* position.

The Nominalist Position

The philosopher Roscellinus first challenged this doctrine and established what was called the *Nominalist* position, very close to the belief of most people today. He said that physical things were the only reality. For example, each sense-apparent tree is real and as far as trees are concerned, no higher reality exists. The question then arises, "How can we know the 'idea' tree?" Certainly we know these insubstantial ideas, for we can speak of trees, or people, or elephants, or justice when no specific one is present to our senses. Roscellinus answered that these "ideas" were only names (hence the word *Nominalist*), and that we form the idea as a generalization only after experience with a great number of individual things. We experience, he said, specific examples of elms, pines, palms, and all kinds of trees. In our mind we then generalize and form the "idea" tree so that we can talk about the species—and understand each other—in the middle of the ocean, with no specific tree within a thousand miles.

The two positions in the battle were thus established, as opposite as any two opposites can be. William of Champeaux stoutly defended the Realist position, the standard doctrine of the Church. If he should fail, the Church itself would be in danger, and indeed it was.

The Conceptualist Position

A middle position was suggested by the brilliant thinker Peter Abelard, probably the most popular teacher in the early University of Paris. (Abelard is shown as a hero for the twentieth century as well as a brilliant thinker of the eleventh and twelfth centuries in the contemporary play *Abelard and Heloise.*) Abelard had studied with both Roscellinus and William of Champeaux and knew their arguments thoroughly and, as a matter of interest, he defeated William in a public debate on the nature of the universals. (Henry Adams in *Mont-St. Michel and Chartres* gives an imaginary debate between the two, which is not too difficult to follow.) Abelard's compromise became known as the *Conceptualist* position, and anticipates an Aristotelian view of the problem even before the whole body of Aristotle's works was known to Europe. The Conceptualist view can be stated rather quickly, for it will become much better developed with the work of St. Thomas a century or so later. Briefly, Abelard held that the *idea* is *real,* but that it does not exist either before a particular physical thing or after it. That is, reality as idea exists only in the physical, sense-apparent object.

Abelard's intellectual daring was condemned by the Church, but the Battle of Universals was debated without conclusion for a century. The Realist, the Nominalist, and the Conceptualist positions remained at loggerheads and were a sore point in Church doctrine until the great synthesis, which was to be made by St. Thomas, who established what was to become the official dogma of the Church.

Abelard not only developed one of the sides in the Battle of Universals, but he threw another bombshell into the religious thought of the time when he published his book *Sic et non* (Yes and No). One remembers that the source of all knowledge at the time lay in the Scriptures and the writings of the early commentators on the Bible, the Church Fathers. In *Sic et non,* Abelard proposed a number of important religious questions, then in opposite columns set down what the Fathers had written on the subject. In doing so, he demonstrated that one could find contradictory answers in this body of writings. If this body was the source of knowledge, and if contradictions existed within it, as Abelard clearly showed, how wrong must conclusions be that were based on this writing. The whole way of thought of Scholasticism was threatened if its original source of knowledge was self-contradictory, and all answers to questions that had been derived by the method must be suspect.

Aristotle Rediscovered

Still another fire broke out in the structure of the Church with the rediscovery of all of Aristotle's works in the last part of the twelfth century. Because his logic had been universally used as the method of thinking, Aristotle, though a pagan, was perhaps the most venerated name among all of the world's philosophers throughout the early Middle Ages, but only his work on logic was known to the philosophers of the time. About the year 1200 almost the entire corpus of his works was brought into Europe through a curious process. Aristotle had written in Greek, Syrian scholars had translated him into Syriac, then Arabic writers had converted those translations into Arabic. Finally, through the Muslims in Spain, the body of thought was discovered, turned into medieval Latin, and made available to all of Europe. The discovery of this trove of scientific knowledge posed several touchy questions, but the most important was that it revealed that Aristotle had developed considerable knowledge of the world by investigating and classifying *physical* things. The Church had stood against any studies of the physical world, yet here was a man more revered by scholars than were most of the saints, who had developed his knowledge by such investigation. The impact was about as great as if we discovered that one of our most revered scientists received his knowledge and made his discoveries by consulting a witch doctor. What was the Church to do?

The first reaction was to ban the newly discovered works entirely, and in 1210 and for the next few years we have records of the books being banned at the University of Paris. The discovery of the books was sufficiently well known, however, that they could not so conveniently be done away with. The next step was the publication of "authorized" versions from which all of Aristotle's ideas that were directly contradictory to Church doctrine had been expurgated. Since the minds of the scholars were hungry for new material, this step did not work either, and finally the entire body of knowledge was made available to the scholars of the late Middle Ages.

The Church had preached complete otherworldliness and disdained earthly knowledge except as it seemed to be a symbol or testimony of scriptural knowledge and heavenly life. Yet these books revealed that the most revered mind of the Middle Ages had dissected animals to discover similarities and differences between species; had classified plants according to their structure. Thus another problem was presented, demanding synthesis if the Church were to maintain its authority.

The Universities

The rise of the universities is the last of the symptoms of new life we will consider here. Actually their origin is very obscure, for we have little knowledge of them until their formal charters were issued. In Christian Europe (as different from Muslim Spain) the University of Salerno, which specialized in medicine, was probably the earliest, for we have records of its existence in the middle of the eleventh century, yet situated in southern Italy, it had little influence on the general dawn of culture. The University of Bologna with its great law school was given a formal grant of rights in 1158; the University of Paris was granted a royal charter in 1200 and a Papal license in 1231. Oxford was formed in the twelfth century when a group of teachers and students seceded from Paris, and Cambridge came into being somewhat later when a dissident group left Oxford. The growth was so rapid that by the end of the Middle Ages we find eighty universities scattered throughout Europe. The actual founding dates for the universities are of relatively little importance, since it is probable that schools had existed in connection with cathedrals and abbeys where the universities were founded at least a century before formal charters were granted; this, at least, was the case with the University of Paris, which had a long history as the Cathedral School of Notre Dame before it was licensed as a university. Nor did the schools have a smooth course throughout; the occasion for the Papal license of the University of Paris in 1231 was the reopening of the University that had been closed for two years following a riot between students and the city authorities. Few things are new under the sun!

Universitas

The word *universitas* is Latin for a corporation such as a trade guild. When teachers (or students) joined together as a legal body, a university came into existence. Operating under the protection of a charter granted usually by the pope or a king, universities were generally freed from local jurisdiction, though they could not avoid "town and gown" conflicts that seem to be endemic to university communities. Their operation paralleled that of craft guilds, with guild masters (professors) awarding qualifying certificates (degrees) to apprentices (students), who were working to become masters in the teaching corporation (university). Graduation of the apprentices marked their "commencement" as certified teachers.

Offering instruction in all recognized fields of knowledge, the University of Paris was the leading institution of the time, with faculties of medicine, law, theology, and liberal arts. As a prerequisite for professional courses, the liberal arts curriculum followed the seven liberal arts pattern of monastic schools: trivium (grammar, rhetoric, logic) and quadrivium (arithmetic, geometry, astronomy, and music, plus the works of Aristotle). In today's terms the subjects of the trivium were humanistic and those of the quadrivium mathematical.

Initial studies were devoted to the trivium (including analyses of works of philosophy, literature, and history) but with no prescribed hours or units of credit. Achievement was measured solely by comprehensive oral examinations, after which the bachelor of arts (B.A.) degree was awarded as the necessary prerequisite for studying the quadrivium. Passing the second set of examinations certified the student as a master of arts (M.A.), and thus qualified to teach the liberal arts curriculum. The higher degrees of doctor (in law, medicine, and theology) were also teaching degrees, with the doctor of philosophy (Ph.D.) added later for advanced study in the liberal arts. Usually based upon four years of study beyond the M.A., doctorates were awarded after passing another set of rigorous examinations and successfully defending a "thesis," or proposition, before a faculty board. The comparative few who survived this ordeal were granted not only a doctorate but also the opportunity to put on a banquet for the examiners.

Though some women had been admitted to Plato's Academy and some Hellenistic scholars were women, medieval universities were operated solely by and for the masculine sex. The medieval assumption that women had no need for formal education resulted, of course, in an incalculable loss of the brain power of half the human race, a cultural deprivation still not entirely rectified.

As guilds of teachers and scholars, universities at first had no campus and no buildings. With classes meeting wherever rooms could be found, usually in churches, early regulations specified charges for room and board, the price of books (usually rented because manuscripts were expensive), the minimum number of classes students had to attend to be "official" (usually two a week), and the number of lectures and their length that a professor had to give to collect his fees. Students could fine professors for absences or for lecturing too long and, by not attending his classes, cost him a portion of his fees.

Collegium

The *collegium* (L., community, society) was a residence hall that private benefactors began providing for students who were too poor to pay room and board. Robert de Sorbon, royal chaplain to Louis IX, endowed a hall in 1257 called the College de Sorbonne, now the college of arts and sciences of the University of Paris.

This was a new group of people who had been unknown in the early Middle Ages. They were eager for all sorts of knowledge and questing for experience. Their motto may well have been Abelard's famous teaching, "for by doubting we come to inquiry, by inquiry we discover the truth." These people would not tolerate a culture that walled itself in by authority and allowed no questioning of that authority. Here, as in most areas of life in the late Middle Ages, we see life bursting out at the seams.

At the end of the preceding chapter we saw that medieval men and women had sheltered themselves within the narrow walls of the authoritarian church and of feudalism and manorialism. These provided a measure of physical and psychological safety but little room in which to grow. With the rise of cities and the increasing intellectual ferment in the universities, we see the breeching of medieval walls in the search for knowledge of the physical world. Contacts with Muslim and Byzantine cultures and the civilizing effects of chivalry and the courts of love indicated that life here on this earth could be made immeasurably better. In the ferment of city life and in the idea-ferment of the universities all established modes of existence were called into question, a questioning that is revealed in the literature of the time.

Life's Questions as Seen in Literature

In the preceding chapter the morality play *Everyman* and the French chante-fable *Aucassin and Nicolette* were presented. *Everyman,* to review briefly, faced either eternal damnation or eternal bliss; there is no middle ground and the fear of death hangs like a pall over all of life. *Aucassin and Nicolette,* on the other hand, speaks not only of the joy of life but *is* itself that joy. As a side-by-side contrast the question is reiterated: "Which way is this civilization to go?"

Chaucer, in his "Prolog" to *The Canterbury Tales,* illustrates this problem, though his tone and outlook are essentially realistic. While he is not seeking to illustrate anything, while he is trying only to describe an assortment of people with their too human weakness, he poses the problem nevertheless. The basic nature of the gathering of the pilgrims is a case in point. The pilgrimage to the Shrine of St. Thomas is, or should be, a religious exercise. Yet these people, or some of them at any rate, seem to be there for an extended picnic and nothing else. In the characters, again, we see the division of personality. On the one hand we have the poor and virtuous Parson; on the other we see the Friar, the Summoner, and the Pardoner, who are devoted entirely to the gratification of the flesh, and all of whom exploit their religious affiliation to make these gratifications possible.

In some instances, we see the city men, the new class of merchants, lawyers, doctors, and guildsmen. Their aim is profit and they will achieve their purpose regardless of any nice concerns about religion. They partake of the upsurging spirit that denies the balance of the old Graeco-Roman tradition. Chaucer draws no moral from this collection of people, nor does he attempt to state a problem with the exactness of a mathematician or a social worker. What does the reader make of this collection of medieval men and women?

Nowhere is the spiritual conflict of the time better illustrated than in the student songs, for the universities themselves were products of the new and stirring life. The pulls upon the personality are particularly evident in one of the student creeds in which the dying goliard burlesques the creed of the Church. With almost savage vigor he takes each word of the Church's creed and turns it to a flaunting of his vices. Then the student faces the final moment. Centuries of religious tradition combined with dread of the unknown cause him to cry out in anguish as he commits his soul to God.

The Medieval Synthesis

The conflicts in the late Middle Ages were between new secular ways of thinking and living that challenged the older religious and mystic ways. Where was the art that could bring these together in a new synthesis? Where were the people who could define new relationships between human beings and the universe, human beings and God, the individual person and society as a whole? Where could be found artists to suggest new purposes for life since the old were so sorely challenged?

Philosophy: St. Thomas Aquinas

It would seem that this new synthesis came about in three places. In philosophy, it was St. Thomas Aquinas who built a new philosophic structure that could accommodate the divergent points of view. In art, the medieval Gothic cathedral furnished a synthesis at the point when the artist's skill and the function came together. Chartres Cathedral is the prime example of such a structure. In literature, the new balance was suggested by Dante Alighieri in *The Divine Comedy.* Let us look briefly at the ways in which the synthesis was achieved in these three forms.

It cannot be our purpose here to go into detail in a discussion of the doctrines of St. Thomas. Rather, we shall show how he reconciled some of the contradictions of the time. In discussing Thomas's thought, one can scarcely avoid using the symbol of the equilateral triangle as a representation of the individual person, of the nation, and of the universe, for all of his ideas seem to shape themselves around that symbol. It was no accident that this is also the symbol of the Trinity of God; it may have been accident that it is also a shape that suggests both stability and upward motion. In its visual form it unifies the energy of the Celto-Germanic spirit with the desire for stability of the Graeco-Roman world.

Central Doctrine

In Thomas's unification of Aristotelian thought with that of the Church, he accepted the central Aristotelian doctrine, similar to that of the Conceptualists. This doctrine was that matter and form (or idea) cannot exist separately. Matter, he said, had only potentiality—that is, the possibility of being itself—until it was entered into by the idea of the thing. Then it became that thing. For example, "clay" is not "brick," nor is there "brick" without "clay"; but when "clay," which has only potentiality by itself, is joined with the form or idea of "brick," then the "brick" exists. Next, he said, lower forms of existence are only matter in the formation of higher forms. And everything, he said, was moving, changing, growing, turning into something else. This movement is the movement toward perfection, which is God. Thus the First Mover, God, does not move things from behind, but is the purpose toward which all things are moving. Since things must desire the thing toward which they move, then the motive force is the love of God.

This argument involves the most important of Thomas's proofs of the existence of God. (He proposed five such proofs, bearing out his belief that all things accepted by faith could be proved by reason.) His most famous proof is that of motion. Very briefly stated, this proof proceeds in this way: We see motion. If there is motion, there must be a mover. If we think backward, for example, I roll a stone; something causes me to move to roll it; but something causes the mover which moves me, etc.; we have an endless and infinite series of movers. On the other hand, consider the first mover as a force that attracts rather than pushes from behind. Then we can come to a first "attracting force" (like a magnet), which sets all other things in motion. This First Mover, or if you will, the Unmoved Mover, is God, pulling all things toward himself.

Form and Matter

Furthermore, in the idea that both *form* and *matter* are necessary for reality, Thomas brought together the conflicting arguments in the Battle of Universals. Here we may consider the question of whether form (or Idea) has existence *before,* or only *in* a specific thing, and whether it exists *after* the specific has vanished. All three, said Thomas. The Idea exists (as potentiality) before the thing; it exists in the thing, and in its continuing progress upward, it exists after the particular thing. Thus, borrowing heavily from the Conceptualist view, he brought the three positions into harmony.

It was with the doctrine of lower and higher forms, all in motion toward perfection, that Thomas brought together the conflict between the growing desire of people for natural knowledge and the doctrine of the Church that such knowledge was a study of nothingness, for, said Thomas, the highest human studies are philosophy and law. He considered philosophy as a study of the humanly knowable laws for the discipline of the spirit, and law, of course, as the study of the rules for the governing of our physical nature. Both, according to the Aristotelian concept of reality, are necessary and equal. To reach a knowledge of these subjects, a study of all forms and all matter is necessary. It is in this way that people attain their highest human perfection—through knowledge.

Then, he continued, there is another realm of knowledge, complementary to philosophy. This is theology, which has its source in God. It cannot be understood through natural learning, but only by revelation. The two, however, are not opposed to each other. Rather, a knowledge of philosophy leads to the possibility of receiving revelation and revelation presupposes a knowledge of philosophy. Finally, he said that true knowledge, the union with the divine science, came only after death.

Thomas's Plan of Education

The Separate, Equal Roles of Church and State

It was the duty of people, therefore, during their lifetimes to acquire as much natural knowledge as possible that they might be fit to receive the final revelation of God after their death.

The settlement of the opposition of Church and State came with a justification of feudalism on the basis of the lower forms constantly seeking the higher. However, in the governing of people he believed Church and State equal, with both the king and the pope receiving their power directly from God. It was the duty of the king to administer God's laws for the physical nature of human beings; of the pope and the Church to administer the law for the spirit of humankind. This solution, which justified the status quo, ran contrary to the secular spirit of the time and the growing nationalism. Thomas's argument would not stand for long against the moving social and political forces.

The pull of life and death, perhaps the greatest question of all, was solved by St. Thomas, first with the Aristotelian doctrine of matter and form existing only when they were together and in each other. With this, and with Thomas's insistence that natural knowledge, gained through the use of human senses, was necessary for the perfection of the human being, he banished the dualism that had existed since the time of Augustine and the idea of the City of God. Hereafter, both body and soul were necessary for earthly perfection, the one as important as the other.

Thus it was that the Middle Ages, in this final great synthesis, opened the way for people to begin to develop themselves, just as the cities were expanding beyond their encircling walls. Science was expanding, too, with scientific research conducted both within and without the universities. Winding down, at long last, was the antagonism between Church and State because of a growing realization that the State was a necessary form of order leading to the highest order—that of the kingdom of God. This philosophical synthesis was all well and good for the increasing numbers of intellectuals but what about the common people?

The Cathedral: "Bible in Stone"

The cathedral was central—literally and symbolically—in the everyday lives of the people. Standing tall at the center of the city, it represented the best of the two worlds, the sacred and the secular. Cathedral and civic center, church of Our Lady and theatre, school, court, concert hall, and general meeting place, the Gothic cathedral was a three-dimensional synthesis of Church and State and of aspirations both spiritual and worldly.

The thrust of the Gothic cathedral was always strongly upward (see figures 15.30, 15.32, and 15.36). Standing before it, the beholder's gaze, impelled by the dynamic pointed arches, moved up its great towers until the spire was reached with its sharp finger pointing toward heaven. Partly because of its architectural sculpture, the cathedral has been called a "Bible in stone." Much of its art is indeed didactic, but a Gothic cathedral is much more than the sum of its parts. It is power and glory and spiritually personified. The richly colored light filtered through the stained glass windows, the gliding sound of Gregorian chant, the musky aroma of incense, the pageantry of the celebration of the mass—all these added beauty, majesty, and joy to the lives of the people. Even the task of building these cathedrals, a grand communal effort shared alike by nobility, wealthy burghers, and common people, provided a creative outlet for every participant. In a very real sense, the cathedral belonged equally to all who built it and all who used it (see colorplate 23).

The Tower

Among the thousands of symbols connected with the Gothic cathedral, one significance of the tower deserves mention. The lower, heavy square tower represented earthly life. The spire signified human aspiration toward the divine. And finally, the elevation of the eye from the last point of physical stone toward the sky suggested union with God. The architect of the south tower at Chartres (see figure 15.38) had the right idea when he created a transition between the square tower and the octagonal spire that is almost imperceptible. In a truly Thomistic sense, the things of this world blend perfectly with those of the next; the physical and the spiritual are united. The transition triumphs both as architecture and as symbol of the best thought of the time.

In one other aspect the cathedral was the symbol of the synthesis of the Middle Ages, for it was here that the Cult of the Virgin reached its height. The sudden flowering of this cult may be ascribed to the sense of sin that obsessed the people, convinced as they were of their moral deformity from Adam, and of their weakness to withstand the pulls of the world around them. For them, the justice of the Trinity was a thing to flee from, and they fell back upon the mercy of the Mother. Miracles were needed to insure their salvation and a whole body of literature has grown up to tell of the miracles wrought by the Gracious Lady. Mary provided comfort, solace, and understanding for nobility and common people alike. Thus people could believe that a juggler doing his act for her amusement was as important as the learned friar writing scholarly books according to the formulas of Scholasticism.

Dante's *Divine Comedy:* An Intellectual Vision

The cathedral symbolized one medieval synthesis and the work of Thomas Aquinas still another. In the realm of literature the *Commedia* (*Divine Comedy*) of Dante can be seen as a third kind of synthesis.

A particularly important aspect of the *Commedia* was the removal of restrictions that in earlier centuries had been imposed upon people. The goal and final purpose of human beings was still the attainment of heaven and the bliss of that afterlife, but people were left free to achieve this goal through their own power and through the discipline of their own will. Dante's God was no accountant; rather, he was perfect wisdom, which in Dante's mind was almost synonymous with love. The purpose and goal of humankind, like the enteleche of Aristotle, was perfect union with this God. For Dante, this heavenly state is the true home of humankind, which must ever be earned anew because of Adam's fall from grace. Furthermore, people, while they are alive, cannot know the wisdom or order or love of God; for salvation, the final union was still a matter of God's grace rather than a result of human effort. It was as if God's wisdom were a different category of wisdom from that of human beings, one to which people may aspire, but to which they can be admitted only by the will of God.

While people may not achieve union with God through their own efforts, they may prepare themselves for it by gaining the maturity that accompanies earthly wisdom. This mature nature is called innocence by Dante, by which he meant the happy state of Adam and Eve before the fall. It is for this reason that Dante places the Garden of Eden, the Earthly Paradise, at the top of the mountain of Purgatory. It is here that men and women, after having attained their full maturity, the totality of human wisdom, may await the act of God that will transport them into the category beyond.

Mystery plays represented an emotional approach to God, while morality plays like *Everyman* were didactic. Dante's vision, on the other hand, was intellectual. For him human beings were part of God's rational order, which was love; so it was through the pull of the love of God that individual human beings, exercising their own free will, ascended the ladder of love. The choice was made on earth and that choice, expressed in faith and good works, determined the destiny of each person in the afterlife.

Sin: Loss of Freedom

What were the choices? Since the way of God is discipline and orderliness, the way of Satan is disorder and lack of proportion. God himself is perfect freedom, and the way toward him is the constant increase of one's personal freedom. Essential sin is the loss of freedom. This idea can be illustrated with the simple example of smoking—or any other harmful addiction.

At first—in relation to cigarettes—the individual is ignorant, knowing neither the pleasures nor the harms of smoking. So, for one reason or another, the person tries one. *The act in itself is not sinful,* nor are subsequent experiences with smoking. The person always says, "I can quit any time." And, for a time, that is true. A time comes, however, when given a choice of smoking or not smoking, true addicts will always choose to smoke; they have lost the power to say no, and if cigarettes are denied, they will end up climbing the wall. Thus they have sacrificed one aspect of their freedom of choice, and this, for Dante, is sin. Godlike freedom is the ability to say yes, no, or any of the choices between. Sin is loss of that ability, and in Dante's Hell we see that the degree of sin is measured by the extent to which the person consciously twists a body or an intellect away from free choice. The person who loses hope of making free choices is destined for Hell, and the inscription Dante envisions over the mouth of Hell, "Abandon hope, all ye that enter here," is an expression of the state the condemned ones have reached. In their choice, they have abandoned all hope and desire to be anything or anywhere else. The punishments Dante saw for the souls in Hell are symbolic of the nature they have made for themselves. With the body removed, in other words, we see them exactly as they have made themselves to be. Step by descending step we traverse the cone of Hell, in each lower depth viewing the souls who are deeper and deeper in sin. Step by descending step we see these souls deprived of more and more freedom, until at the very bottom of the pit we find Satan, the greatest sinner of all, deprived of movement, frozen, as he is, in ice. So is he bound by his sins.

Purgatory

Emerging with Dante at the base of the mountain of Purgatory, we find another picture. Here are the souls who have erred, who have somehow strayed in their earthly lives from the path of wisdom. The difference is that these people still have hope; they aspire toward their own true selves and toward God. Their labors are difficult as they expiate their sin, but through all the labor they are joyous, for they know that the end will be full wisdom and maturity, the Garden of Eden, and the state of Earthly Paradise. It is of utmost importance to realize that each soul decides for itself when it is completely purged of any sin and is ready to move upward to another cornice of the mountain. The decision is never made by an angel or any other outside force. So free of envy are all the souls on the mountain that they chant *Gloria in excelsis* in unison when an individual moves upward.

This is explicitly stated when Dante and Virgil, toiling up the mountain, encounter the spirit of the Latin poet Statius, who has just moved from a lower cornice to a higher one. The occasion is so momentous that the whole mountain has shaken, and all the souls have shouted the *Gloria*. It is of great importance to note that while the soul moves upward through its own free choice, it disciplines itself so that the movement is never made until it feels that the stain of former sin is completely removed (see the seventh through the thirteenth quoted lines).

> Below that point, there may be small or ample
> tremors; but here above, I know not why,
> no wind concealed in earth has ever caused
>   a tremor; for it only trembles here
> when some soul feels it's cleansed, so that it rises
> or stirs to climb on high; and that shout follows.
>   The will alone is proof of purity
> and, fully free, surprises soul into
> a change of dwelling place—effectively.
>   Soul had the will to climb before, but that
> will was opposed by longing to do penance
> (as once, to sin), instilled by divine justice.
>   And I, who have lain in this suffering
> five hundred years and more, just now have felt
> my free will for a better threshold: thus,
>   you heard the earthquake and the pious spirits
> throughout the mountain as they praised the Lord—
> and may He send them speedily upward."
>   So did he speak to us; and just as joy
> is greater when we quench a greater thirst,
> the joy he brought cannot be told in words.

Heaven

Finally in Heaven, and guided by Beatrice, Dante receives instruction in theology, the science of God. It is here that he sees the perfect order of the whole universe, both of humans and of angels. He sees the Church and its officers as the guardians of the human spirit and he sees the kings' importance to God, for they maintain temporal order on earth. Here, too, he finds freedom, as opposed to the ever-increasing bondage he witnessed in Hell, for in Heaven, though the souls are symbolically assigned to different spheres as a result of their different capacities for joy and love, yet they are actually free to pass through all the spheres and to approach the throne of God itself. There is no bondage here. In the final Cantos of the *Paradise,* Dante comes as close as any human being can to communicating the mystic union of the soul with God as actual living experience.

What Is Dante Saying to Us?

Is this only a poem of death or does Dante have something to say for living people? We believe that he has much to say to us. He says that people must make their choice, for which they have their own wills. If they choose wisely, they will choose a life of order and discipline. Throughout their life, they will gain knowledge, for that and its resultant wisdom will make them free. Finally, he tells us, our studies should turn to philosophy and law, the fields of knowledge that represent the best possible concepts of order on earth; the former disciplines and instructs the spirit, the latter has the same function in our temporal dealings with each other. This life will be one that is joyously led, and leads to the final realization of the true self when, by the will of God, the soul is united with the perfect wisdom.

These ideas, too, are stated clearly in Canto 27 of the *Purgatory* with Virgil's farwell to Dante. The mountain has been climbed and we have reached the point of perfect *human* wisdom. Since Virgil was a pagan, he can go no farther, and the "fair eyes" of Beatrice will guide Dante farther on his way. Incidentally, the "temporary fire" referred to is that of Purgatory; the "eternal" is that of Hell. Further, a miter is the hat worn by a bishop; the crown is a king's hat. Thus from this point onward, Dante, through his free choices, has complete control over both his spiritual and physical natures, in accordance with his own and St. Thomas's philosophy.

> My will on will to climb above was such
> that at each step I took I felt the force
> within my wings was growing for the flight.
>   When all the staircase lay beneath us and
> we'd reached the highest step, then Virgil set
> his eyes insistently on me and said:
>   "My son, you've seen the temporary fire
> and the eternal fire; you have reached the place past
> which my powers cannot see.
>   I've brought you here through intellect and art;
> from now on, let your pleasure be your guide;
> you're past the steep and past the narrow paths.
>   Look at the sun that shines upon your brow;
> look at the grasses, flowers, and the shrubs born here,
> spontaneously, of the earth.

> Among them, you can rest or walk until
> the coming of the glad and lovely eyes—
> those eyes that, weeping, sent me to your side.
>   Await no further word or sign from me:
> your will is free, erect, and whole—to act
> against that will would be to err: therefore
> I crown and miter you over yourself."

What has Dante brought together here? In the first place, he envisions a life at once balanced and aspiring. These are the Gothic and classic elements of the Middle Ages. He brings together the desire for broad worldly knowledge and religion, for his poem itself is scientific according to the science of his time, and he counsels the widest possible earthly knowledge as a necessary condition for heavenly bliss. He brings together the pulls of life and death, for his concept of the full life is one that is joyous and in which people use their full powers, yet use them as they aspire to the greatest possible happiness and freedom both now and in the hereafter. Finally, he unites the rival claims of pope and king as he sees each working God's will and God's order on earth, each in his own way and in his own place.

This is the final answer of the Middle Ages to the great question of the search for freedom. It started with the building of walls, for people needed their protection. It has progressed through the stage where they found their walls no longer necessary for protection and found them cramping in the human desire for the good life. It emerges in a great synthesis in which human nature is free, by nature divine, but in which human beings have freedom of choice. The *Commedia* unites body and soul in the process of discipline—one individuals must choose for themselves, a discipline that must occur in the present life. This discipline, in its order, produces freedom here and prepares the spirit for freedom in the afterlife. Particularly in the cathedrals and in the *Commedia* we see the artist at work, proposing new answers to the great questions of humankind. It is upon these answers that the institutions are to be reshaped, and upon them that a new pattern for existence is to be built.

Human Freedom

What was the nature of human freedom within this new design? The period of synthesis during the late Middle Ages was brief. Dante lived from 1265 to 1321. St. Thomas lived from 1225 to 1274. Chartres dates from the thirteenth century. Yet by the beginning of the fifteenth century, the Renaissance had burst upon Europe. The forces that had challenged the old walls of life that had been built during the early Middle Ages were too strong to be held in check, and the secular spirit was to go ahead to new triumphs. But in those 200 years, we can witness a new freedom toward which many world-weary people of the twentieth century look back with longing. It is worthy of at least a brief examination.

The single and fundamental characteristic of medieval freedom lies in the sense of unity that provided strict rules for all types of human behavior, and yet furnished complete individual freedom to create within those rules. This seems to be a paradox, a contradiction. At least it can be seen as a most delicate balance between individual aspiration and endeavor and community solidarity, which offers stability.

Perhaps better than anywhere else, this balance can be seen in the art of the late Middle Ages. Consider, for example, the cathedral. Its pattern was extremely strict. It had to be oriented with the altar toward the east. It had to be cruciform. Each part of the structure carried some symbolic meaning, so that the symbols had to be exactly treated. All this was a part of the strict rule that governed art and life in the period of balance.

Yet consider the freedom of the individual within this rule. The stonecarver was free to do as he wanted. If he wanted to carve little fat angels or animals he had seen or imagined, that was his decision. One sees much of this type of work on the miserere seats in the choir stall. Here a woodcarver thought that it would be fun to carve a pig playing a fiddle. No sooner thought of than started! Or somewhere else, the carver wished to caricature a fat burgher of the town. He could do it because he was a free man, working within the limits of the grand design. These were no machine-made units to be put up as they came from the factory. They were the work of free and independent craftsmen.

This same freedom, within strict limits, is found in all spheres of activity during the late Middle Ages. For example, the craftsman necessarily belonged to his guild. It was the association that regulated the quality of his work, the price that could be charged, and many other things. Beyond that, the guild served as an insurance and burial society for its members, a social group, and a dramatic society, since the mystery and miracle plays that amused and inspired the city-dwellers were functions of the guild. The guild-hall was not only a place of business, but was also a social center where banquets, weddings, and balls were held. The guild also very strictly regulated the membership within itself and established stringent rules for the training of the craftsmen. All these point to the strict communal regulation of the individual.

But within those limits, the member of a guild, the shoemaker, let us say, was absolutely free. He had his own shop, which was part of his home. He did his work only on order, so that when there was no business, he could lock up and take the members of his family, together with the apprentices and journeymen in his shop, and go for an outing in the country. Furthermore, and one suspects that this is the important aspect of the whole system, each pair of shoes was an individual creation. The pride of craft and of creation entered into all of the work done, and the master craftsman developed a sense of pride in each item of his work. The very fact that he did the whole job, from heel to toe, from sole to the very top of the uppers, gave him a sense of responsibility and of pride.

The story of "Our Lady's Juggler" reveals the same type of freedom within religion. The Catholic creed was strict, and its rules were absolute. But within them people were free. There was sufficient opportunity for individual practice of the religious observances to satisfy each person. Dante's idea of freedom as participation in the wisdom, the order, and the love of God are of great importance here. The person who was not free was the one who, by his or her own choices, had become inhuman in outward form and in nature. The order of God, however, was of sufficient latitude that people could make a comfortable life within it. In addition to this, there was the one provision of the Christian scheme of things that has always been a source of strength for that faith. This was the idea that a mistake does not mean inevitable damnation. Such an error may need purging, but it is only when one comes to a conscious desire for the way of evil that one is damned.

The concept of freedom in this period of balance in the Middle Ages, then, was one in which all the forces of the culture grouped themselves around the individual to provide support. Yet they did not hamper freedom, individuality, or creativity as long as he or she stayed within the rules of that culture.

This balance, like all others we have seen, was too delicate to last. Within a brief time, the secular forces we saw born during the Middle Ages were to triumph, breaking down the new designs that had been made by St. Thomas, by the architects of the great cathedrals, and by Dante. The fundamental beliefs of the culture were to change in a new epoch, which we call the Renaissance.

Exercises

1. Imagine growing up on a medieval manor and then moving to the city. What opportunities might come your way? What new temptations? What new problems? Which aspects of rural life might you miss?
2. What do medieval guilds and modern unions have in common? How do they differ? Why do they differ?
3. Given the European point of view, what were the positive aspects of the Crusades? Negative aspects? Now try asking these two questions from the Muslim point of view.
4. Are the virtues espoused by Courts of Love "feminine" or might they be called "civilized"? Are there *any* purely masculine or feminine virtues?
5. Are you a Realist, Nominalist, Conceptualist, or none of the above? Why?
6. Where, in your course of study, are the subjects of the trivium and quadrivium? To what extent do your studies differ from the medieval curriculum? Is every difference necessarily better?
7. The Virgin Mary and Eve, the Temptress, represented two extremes of medieval womanhood. What are the extremes today? What is the female ideal of womanhood? The male ideal? Can the values of both sexes be synthesized into a single image?

SONGS AND POEMS OF THE WANDERING SCHOLARS

The pull of life was strong in the time when new ideas were breaking down the old medieval walls. And students (even those who were to become learned clergymen) were much the same in those days as they are now.

GAUDEAMUS IGITUR

Let us live, then, and be glad
　　While young life's before us!
After youthful pastime had,
After old age, hard and sad,
　　Earth will slumber o'er us.

Where are they who in this world
　　Ere we kept, were keeping?
Go ye to the gods above;
Go to hell; inquire thereof;
　　They are not; they are sleeping.

Brief is life, and brevity
　　Briefly shall be ended;
Death comes like a whirlwind strong,
Bears us with his blast along;
　　None shall be defended.

Live this university,
　　Men that learning nourish;
Live each member of the same,
Long live all that bear its name,
　　Let them ever flourish!

Live the commonwealth also,
　　And the men that guide it!
Live our town in strength and health,
Founders, patrons, by whose wealth
　　We are here provided!

Live all gods! A health to you,
　　Melting maids and beauteous;
Live the wives and women too,
Gentle, loving, tender, true,
　　Good, industrious, duteous!

Perish cares that pule and pine!
　　Perish envious blamers!
Die the Devil, thine and mine!
Die the starch-neck Philistine!
　　Scoffers and defamers!

LAURIGER HORATIUS

Horace with your laurel crowned,
Truly have you spoken:
Time, a-rush with leap and bound,
Devours and leaves us broken.

Where are now the flagons, full
Of sweet wine, honey-clear?
Where the smiles and shoves and frowns
Of blushing maiden dear?

Swift the young grape grows and swells;
So do comely lasses!
Lo, on the poet's head, the snows
Of the Time that passes!

What's the good of lasting fame,
If people think it sinful
Here and now to kiss a dame
And drink a jolly skinful!

A GOLIARD'S CREED

A *goliard* is dying; the priest sent for in haste speaks comfortable words; have comfort, good son; let him but recite his Credo.[4]

That I will, Sir, and hear me now.

Credo—in dice I well believe,
That got me often bit and sup,
And many a time hath had me drunk,
And many a time delivered me
From every stich and every penny.

In Deum—never with my will
Gave Him a thought nor ever will.
The other day I took a shirt
From a ribald and I diced it,
And lost, and never gave it back.
If I die, he can have mine.
Put it in writing, 'tis my will,
I would not like it were forgot.

Patrem—at St. Denis in France,
Good sir, I had a father once,

Omnipotentem in his having,
Money and horses and fine wearing,
And by the dice that thieveth all things
I lost and gamed it all away. . . .

Creatorem who made all
I've denied—He has His will
Of me now, I know I'm dying,
Nothing here but bone and hide.

Coeli—of Heaven ever think?
Nay, but the wine that I could drink.

Et terrae—there was all my joy. . . .
(The burlesque recitation goes on to the final phrase)

Et corporis—the body's lust
I do perform. Sir Priest, I chafe
At thinking of that other life.
I tell you 'tis not worth a straw.
And I would pray to the Lord God
That He will in no kind of way

Resurrectionem make of me,
So long as I may drench the place
With good wine where I'll be laid
And so pray I of all my friends
That if I can't, themselves will do't,
And leave me a full pot of wine
Which I may to the Judgment bring.

Vitam aeternam wilt Thou give,
O Lord God? wilt Thou forgive
All my evil, well I know it,

Amen. Priest, I now am through with't.
Through with life. Death hath its pain.
Too much. . . . too much. . . . This agony. . . .
I'm dying, I to God commend you.
I ask it of you—Pray for me."

---

4. The Creed being recited is as follows: I believe (credo) in God (in Deum) the Father (Patrem), Omnipotent (Omnipotentem), the Creator (Creatorem) of heaven (coeli) and earth (et terrae) . . . and in the resurrection (et . . . resurrectionem) of the body (corporis) and life everlasting (vitam aeternam). Amen.

1. Prominent in these songs is the theme of *carpe diem* (''seize the day,''—eat, drink, and be merry for tomorrow we may die). Is this theme present in any of today's songs?
2. These students were certainly aware of the Church's teaching about virtue and sin. How, then, do you account for their attitudes about sex, drinking, gambling, stealing, and other vices?

OUR LADY'S JUGGLER

In this simple story one can see the hold and the charm of the Cult of the Virgin, especially for the simple people for whom chivalry and philosophy had no meaning (figure 14.2)

In the days of King Louis there lived a poor juggler by the name of Barnabas, a native of Compiegne, who wandered from city to city performing tricks of skill and prowess.

On fair days he would lay down in the public square a worn and aged carpet, and after having attracted a group of children and idlers by certain amusing remarks which he had learned from an old juggler, and which he invariably repeated in the same fashion without altering a word, he would assume the strangest postures and balance a pewter plate on the tip of his nose. At first the crowd regarded him with indifference, but when, with his hands and head on the ground he threw into the air and caught with his feet six copper balls that glittered in the sunlight, or when, throwing himself back until his neck touched his heels, he assumed the form of a perfect wheel and in that position juggled with twelve knives, he elicited a murmur of admiration from his audience, and small coins rained on his carpet.

Still, Barnabas of Compiegne, like most of those who exist by their accomplishments, had a hard time making a living. Earning his bread by the sweat of his brow, he bore rather more than his share of those miseries we are all heir to through the fault of our Father Adam.

Besides, he was unable to work as much as he would have liked, for in order to exhibit his wonderful talents, he required—like the trees—the warmth of the sun and the heat of the day. In winter time he was no more than a tree stripped of its leaves, in fact, half-dead. The frozen earth was too hard for the juggler. Like the cicada mentioned by Marie de France, he suffered during the bad season from hunger and cold. But, since he had a simple heart, he suffered in silence.

He had never thought much about the origin of wealth nor about the inequality of human conditions. He firmly believed that if this world was evil the next could not but be good, and this faith upheld him. He was not like the clever fellows who sell their souls to the devil; he never took the name of God in vain; he lived the life of an honest man, and though he had no wife of his own, he did not covet his neighbor's, for woman is the enemy of strong men, as we learn by the story of Samson which is written in the Scriptures.

■

FIGURE 14.2 *''King David Playing Harp under the Inspiration of the Holy Ghost, while One Attendant Juggles and Others Play the Rebec, Trumpet and Oliphant.'' British Museum, London, eleventh century, English. Reproduced by the courtesy of the Trustees of the British Museum. This curious juxtaposition of David the Psalm Singer with common people juggling and playing musical instruments was a standard medieval practice. At the lower right the ivory oliphant is like the one Roland blew (too late) to summon Charlemagne to his rescue. Of Arab origin, the rebec was an early precursor of the violin (see Chapter 16).*

Verily, his mind was not turned in the direction of carnal desire, and it caused him far greater pain to renounce drinking than to forgo the pleasure of women. For, though he was not a drunkard, he enjoyed drinking when the weather was warm. He was a good man, fearing God, and devout in his adoration of the Holy Virgin. When he went into a church he never failed to kneel before the image of the Mother of God and to address her with his prayer:

''My Lady, watch over my life until it shall please God that I die, and when I am dead, see that I have the joys of Paradise.''

One evening, after a day of rain, as he walked sad and bent with his juggling balls under his arm and his knives wrapped up in his old carpet seeking some barn where he might go supperless to bed, he saw a monk going in his direction, and respectfully saluted him. As they were both walking at the same pace, they fell into conversation.

"Friend," said the monk, "how does it happen that you are dressed all in green? Are you perchance going to play the part of the fool in some mystery?"[5]

"No, indeed, father," said Barnabas. "My name is Barnabas, and my business is that of juggler. It would be the finest calling in the world if I could eat every day."

"Friend Barnabas," answered the monk, "be careful what you say. There is no finer calling than the monastic. The priest celebrates the praise of God, the Virgin, and the saints; the life of a monk is a perpetual hymn to the Lord."

And Barnabas replied: "Father, I confess I spoke like an ignorant man. My estate cannot be compared to yours, and though there may be some merit in dancing and balancing a stick with a denier[6] on top of it on the end of your nose, it is in no wise comparable to your merit. Father, I wish I might, like you, sing the Office every day, especially the Office of the Very Holy Virgin, to whom I am specially and piously devoted. I would willingly give up the art by which I am known from Soissons to Beauvais, in more than six hundred cities and villages, in order to enter the monastic life."

The monk was touched by the simplicity of the juggler, and as he was not lacking in discernment, he recognized in Barnabas one of those well-disposed men of whom Our Lord has said, "Let peace be with them on earth." And he made answer therefore:

"Friend Barnabas, come with me and I will see that you enter the monastery of which I am the Prior. He who led Mary the Egyptian through the desert put me across your path in order that I might lead you to salvation."

Thus did Barnabas become a monk. In the monastery which he entered, the monks celebrated most magnificently the Cult of the Holy Virgin, each of them bringing to her service all the knowledge and skill which God had given him.

The Prior, for his part, wrote books, setting forth, according to the rules of scholasticism, all the virtues of the Mother of God. Brother Maurice copied these treatises with a cunning hand on pages of parchment, while Brother Alexandre decorated them with delicate miniatures representing the Queen of Heaven seated on the throne of Solomon, with four lions on guard at the foot of it. Around her head, which was encircled by a halo, flew seven doves, the seven gifts of the Holy Spirit: fear, piety, knowledge, power, judgment, intelligence, and wisdom. With her were six golden-haired virgins: Humility, Prudence, Retirement, Respect, Virginity, and Obedience. At her feet two little figures, shining white and quite naked, stood in suppliant attitudes. They were souls imploring, not in vain, Her all-powerful intercession for their salvation. On another page Brother Alexandre depicted Eve in the presence of Mary, that one might see at the same time sin and its redemption, woman humiliated, and the Virgin exalted. Among the other much prized pictures in his book were the Well of Living Waters, the Fountain, the Lily, the Moon, the Sun, and the Closed Garden, of which much is said in the Canticle; the Gate of Heaven and the City of God. These were all images of the Virgin.

Brother Marbode, too, was one of the cherished children of Mary. He was ever busy cutting images of stone, so that his beard, his eyebrows, and his hair were white with the dust, and his eyes perpetually swollen and full of tears. But he was a hardy and a happy man in his old age, and there was no doubt that the Queen of Paradise watched over the declining days of Her child. Marbode represented Her seated in a pulpit, her forehead encircled by a halo, with an orb of pearls. He was at great pains to make the folds of Her robe cover the feet of Her of whom the prophet has said, "My beloved is like a closed garden."

At times he represented Her as a graceful child, and Her image seemed to say, "Lord, Thou art My Lord!"

There were also in the monastery poets who composed prose writings in Latin and hymns in honor of the Most Gracious Virgin Mary; there was, indeed, one among them—a Picard—who translated the Miracles of Our Lady into rimed verses in the vulgar tongue.

Perceiving so great a competition in praise and so fine a harvest of good works, Barnabas fell to lamenting his ignorance and simplicity.

"Alas!" he sighed as he walked by himself one day in the little garden shaded by the monastery wall, "I am so unhappy because I cannot, like my brothers, give worthy praise to the Holy Mother of God to whom I have consecrated all the love in my heart. Alas, I am a stupid fellow, without art, and for your service, Madame, I have no edifying sermons, no fine treatises nicely prepared according to the rules, no beautiful paintings, no cunningly carved statues, and no verses counted off by feet and marching in measure! Alas, I have nothing."

Thus did he lament and abandon himself to his misery.

One evening when the monks were talking together by way of diversion, he heard one of them tell of a monk who could not recite anything but the *Ave Maria*. He was scorned for his ignorance, but after he died there sprang from his mouth five roses, in honor of the five letters in the name Maria. Thus was his holiness made manifest.

In listening to this story, Barnabas was conscious once more of the Virgin's beneficence, but he was not consoled by the example of the happy miracle, for his heart was full of zeal and he wanted to celebrate the glory of his Lady in Heaven.

He sought for a way in which to do this, but in vain, and each day brought him greater sorrow, until one morning he sprang joyously from his cot and ran to the chapel, where he remained alone for more than an hour. He returned thither again after dinner, and from that day onward he would go into the chapel every day the moment it was deserted, passing the greater part of the time which the other monks dedicated to the pursuit of the liberal arts and the sciences. He was no longer sad and he sighed no more. But such singular conduct aroused the curiosity of the other monks, and they asked themselves why Brother Barnabas retired alone so often, and the Prior, whose business it was to know everything that his monks were doing, determined to observe Barnabas. One day, therefore, when Barnabas was alone in the chapel, the Prior entered in company with two of the oldest brothers, in order to watch, through the bars of the door, what was going on within.

---

5. Mystery—one of the religious dramas of the time.

6. Denier—a small coin.

They saw Barnabas before the image of the Holy Virgin, his head on the floor and his feet in the air, juggling with six copper balls and twelve knives. In honor of the Holy Virgin he was performing the tricks which had in former days brought him the greatest fame. Not understanding that he was thus putting his best talents at the service of the Holy Virgin, the aged brothers cried out against such sacrilege. The Prior knew that Barnabas had a simple soul, but he believed that the man had lost his wits. All three set about to remove Barnabas from the chapel, when they saw the Virgin slowly descend from the altar and, with a fold of her blue mantle, wipe the sweat that streamed over the juggler's forehead.

Then the Prior, bowing his head down to the marble floor, repeated these words:

"Blessed are the pure in heart, for they shall see God."

"Amen," echoed the brothers, bowing down to the floor.

THE PROLOG TO THE CANTERBURY TALES

Geoffrey Chaucer (1340?–1400)

Chaucer was exceptionally well read for his time, learned in French, Italian, and Latin literature. Having visited Italy, where he acquired a fair knowledge of Italian, he knew the works of Dante but was more influenced by the writings of Boccaccio, especially the *Decameron*. Though he may have been influenced by earlier collections of stories like the *Decameron* and Ovid's *Metamorphoses* (which he also knew well), Chaucer invented the scheme of a pilgrimage as a device to frame his stories and develop the interplay of his characters.

The following excerpt from the "Prolog" (lines 1–18) is given in the original Middle English (*Beowulf* is in Old English), the language in use from early in the twelfth century until late in the fifteenth century, when it was superseded by Early Modern English. For the modern reader, the prime difficulty with Middle English is in the spelling, which can be described as a phonetic system. Therefore, the flavor and some of the meaning of Chaucer's language can be best appreciated by reading these lines aloud, pronouncing each syllable distinctly and with gusto. This version is based on the Hengwrt Manuscript.

Whan that Aprille with his shoures soot
The droghte of Marche hath perced to the roote,
And bathed every veyne in swich licour,
Of which vertu engendred is the flour;
When Zephyrus eek with his swete breeth
Inspired hath in every holt and heeth
The tendre croppes, and the yonge sonne
Hath in the Ram his halfe cours yronne,
And smale fowles maken melodye,
That slepen al the night with open yë,
(So priketh hem Nature in hir corages):
That longen folk to goon on pilgrimages,
(And palmeres for to seken straunge strondes)
To ferne halwes, couthe in sondry londes;
And specially, from every shires ende
Of Engelond, to Caunterbury they wende,
The holy blisful martyr for to seke,
That hem hath holpen, whan that they were seke.

■ **FIGURE 14.3** Pilgrim *from the Ellesmere Manuscript of Chaucer's* Canterbury Tales, *ca. 1410. Courtesy of The Henry E. Huntington Library and Art Gallery, San Marino, Calif.*

Following now is the complete "Prolog," translated into modern English by Leslie Dae Lindou. Here we are introduced to a fascinating cast of characters representing a panorama of life in the late Middle Ages. Note the shrewdness of Chaucer's descriptions, deft touches that reveal the personality of each individual.

When April with its sweet and welcome showers
The drought of March has pierced, and to the flowers
And every vein of growing things has sent
Life-giving moisture, wholesome nourishment;
When Zephyr,[7] too, has with his own sweet breath
Revived again in every wood and heath
The tender shoots, and when the northering sun
Has half his course into the Ram[8] now run,
And little song-birds make their melody
That sleep all thru the night with open eye
—So Nature urges them with her commands—
Then people long to go in pilgrim bands,
And palmers[9] once again to seek far strands
And distant shrines, well known in many lands:
Especially, from every county's end
Of England, Canterbury-ward they wend,
The holy blessed martyr[10] there to seek
Who was their help when they were ill or weak.

---

7. Zephyr—the west wind: here, the life-giving breath of Spring.

8. Ram—the third sign of the zodiac, which the sun enters ca. March 12 and leaves ca. April 11 to enter Taurus. Chaucer is only saying that April is well advanced; the date is about April 18.

9. Palmers—pilgrims who had visited the Holy Lands bore palms as token of their pilgrimage.

10. Martyr—Thomas à Becket, murdered in the cathedral at Canterbury in 1170, was canonized in 1173. His shrine was the great national shrine, and many stories of miraculous cures were told of it.

The Late Middle Ages: Expansion and Synthesis **351**

It happened in that season, on a day,
In Southwerk at the Tabard as I lay,
Ready my pilgrimage to undertake
To Canterbury, for my own soul's sake,
At night there came into that hostelry
Some nine-and-twenty in a company
Of various folk, who came by chance to fall
Into one group, and pilgrims were they all;
To Canterbury they all planned to ride.
The chambers and the stables there were wide,
And we were lodged in comfort, with the best.
And very soon—the sun now gone to rest—
So had I spoken with them, every one,
That I was of their fellowship anon,
And planned with them quite early to arise
To take our way, as I shall you advise:

    —Nevertheless, while I have time and space,
Before I further in this story pace,
It seems to me both sensible and sound
To tell you in detail of all I found
About each one, just as it seemed to me,
And what they were, and what was their degree,
And tell what kind of costume they were in;
And at a knight, then, will I first begin.

Knight

A knight there was, a worthy man,
Who from the time when that he first began
To ride on quests, had well loved chivalry,
Truth and honor, freedom and courtesy.
Full worthy was this man in his lord's war,
And therein had he ridden—none so far—
Thru Christendom, and heathen lands no less,
Always honored for his worthiness.
At Alexandria was he when it was won;
Many a time he had the board begun[11]
Above all other guests, in distant Prussia;
In Latvia[12] he fought, again in Russia,
No Christian man so oft, of his degree.
Against the Moors in Spain he fought, and he
In Africa and Asia Minor warred
Against the infidel; his mighty sword
Found service all about the Inland Sea;
At any noble action, there he'd be.
At mortal battles had he been—fifteen;
And for the faith he fought, at Tramyssene,
In tourney thrice, and each time slew his foe.
And this same worthy knight had been also
At one time with the lord of Palatye
Against another heathen land—Turkey;
And every time he held the topmost prize.
And yet, with all his courage, he was wise—
His conduct, meek as that of any maid.
No villainy had this man ever said
In all his life to any sort of wight,
He was a true, a perfect, gentle knight.

---

11. He sat in the seat of honor, at the head of the table: a mark of distinction and worth.

12. Probably he had fought in Latvia or Lithuania, with the Order of Teutonic Knights. Chaucer lists by name other scenes of the Knights's exploits: the main point is, they were associated with fighting for the faith rather than for gain. The Knight is very nearly the ideal knight of chivalry.

    —But, to tell you briefly his array,
His horse was good, but certainly not gay;
He wore a fustian garment (a gypoun)
All rust-and-armor stained (his haubergeon),
For he had just completed the last stage
Of travel, and at once made pilgrimage.

Squire

With him was his son, a fine young Squire,
A lover and a lusty bachelor,
With locks as curly as if I laid in press;
Near twenty years of age he was, I guess.
His stature was of ordinary length,
But agile, and revealing a great strength.
And he had ridden in the cavalry
In Flanders, in Artois, and Picardy,
And born him well, within his life's short space,
In hope that he might win his lady's grace.
Fancily clad in fashion's newest whim,
—One thought of flowering fields, on seeing him!—
Singing he was, or whistling, all the day:
He was as fresh as is the month of May.
His gown was short, with sleeves both long and wide;
He knew just how to sit a horse and ride,
To make up songs, and fit the words aright,
To joust, and dance, and draw, and even write.
So hot he loved (at least, so goes the tale)
He slept o'nights less than the nightingale!
Courteous was he, meek, in service able,
And carved before his father at the table.

Yeoman

A yeoman had he—no other servants, tho,
As at that time; it pleased him to ride so—
And he was clad in coat and hood of green.
A sheaf of peacock arrows, bright and keen,
Under his belt he carried, gay but grim;
(He well knew how to keep his gear in trim—
His arrow never drooped with feathers low)
And in his hand he bore a mighty bow.
His head was cropped; his face the sun had burned;
Of woodcraft, every subtle trick he'd learned.
Upon his arm a bracer gay he wore
And by his side a sword and buckler bore,
And on the other side, a dagger gay,
As sharp as point of spear, well sheathed away.
A Christopher medal gleamed upon his breast;
His horn's green sling was hung across his chest.
He must have been a forester, I guess.

Prioress

There was also a nun, a Prioress,
Whose smile was sweetly simple, but coy;[13]
Her greatest oath was but by good St. Loy;
And she was known as Madam Eglantine.
Full well she sang the services divine
Intoning thru her nose right properly.
And French she spoke, both well and carefully,
But Stratford-fashion, if the truth be told;
Parisian French she knew not—hers was old.
Her table-manners were well taught, withal;
She never from her lips let morsels fall,

---

13. In Chaucer's text the word meant "bashful" or "modest."

Nor wet her fingers in the sauce too deep;
She knew just how to lift her food, to keep
A single drop from falling on her breast.
In etiquette she found the greatest zest.
Her upper lip she always wiped so clean
That in her cup there never could be seen
A speck of grease, when she had drunk her fill;
Fine manners at the table were her will.
And truly she was fond of harmless sport,
Pleasant, friendly, and of good report;
She took great pains the court to imitate,
Her manner formal, an affair of state;
For she would have men do her reverence.
But now, to tell about her moral sense,
So kindly was she and so piteous,
She wept, if ever that she saw a mouse
Caught in a trap, if it were dead, or bled.
Some little dogs she had, and these she fed
With roasted meat, or milk and good white bread.
But sore she wept if one of them were dead,
Or if men hit one with a stick, to smart;
And all for her was conscience, tender heart.
Becomingly her wimple fell in pleat;
As blue as glass her eyes, her nose right neat;
Her mouth was very small, and soft, and red;
But certainly she had a fine forehead;
It was almost a span in breadth, I'd say—
She was not under-sized, in any way!
Quite stylish was the cloak the lady wore;
About her arm small coral beads she bore,
And they were interspersed with gauds[14] of green,
And therefrom hung a brooch of golden sheen,
Whereon was written first a crowned "A,"
And after, "Amor Vincit Omnia."
She had another nun, for company,
Who was her chaplain; and her priests were three.

Monk

A monk there was—th' administrative sort—
Outrider,—hunting was his favorite sport—
A manly man, to be an abbott able.
Full many a fancy horse he had in stable,
And when he rode, men could his bridle hear
Jingling in the whistling wind as clear
And just as loud as does the chapel bell
Where this good lord was Keeper of the Cell.
The rule of Maurus or St. Benedict[15]
This monk considered old and over-strict.
He'd rather let the old things go their way.
And follow fashions of a newer day.
For texts he didn't give a well-plucked hen
That say that hunters are not holy men,
Nor that a monk, who leaves his cloister's bounds
Is like a fish that's out of water—zounds!
—Why shouldn't monks go out of cloister?
Texts like that aren't worth an oyster!
And I said his views were good thereon.
Why should he study till his wits were gone
Upon a book in cloister, like a clerk,
Or labor with his hands, always at work,

As old St. Austin[16] bids? What good is served?
Let Austin have his work to him reserved!
And so this monk his hunting much preferred.
Greyhounds had he, swift as any bird;
In riding, and in hunting of the hare,
Was his delight—and for no cost he'd spare.
I saw his sleeves were fur-trimmed at the hand,
Expensively, the finest in the land;
And, to fasten up his hood beneath his chin.
He had a rich, elaborate, golden pin;
A love-knot in the larger end there was.
His head was bald, and shone as bright as glass;
As if anointed shone his ruddy face.
He was a lord right fat, and in good case.
His eyes were staring, rolling in his head,
Gleaming like the furnace-fires red.
His boots were supple, and his horse was great;
Now certainly, he was a fine prelate!
He was not pale as some poor starveling ghost.
A fat swan loved he best of any roast.
His palfrey was as brown as any berry.

Friar

A friar there was, a wanton man and merry;
A Limiter,[17] a most impressive one;
Indeed in all four orders there was none
Who knew so much of small talk, fine language;
And he had made right many a marriage
Of young girls at his own expense and hire;
A pillar of his order was this friar!
Familiar and full well beloved was he
With franklins[18] over all in his county,
For as confessor he had won renown
Far more than curates had in their possession
—His order licensed him to hear confession.
His hearing of confession was a pleasure,
His absolution always within measure;
The penance he imposed was never stern—
If something for himself he'd thereby earn!
For when to his poor order gifts were given,
It must be sign the givers were well shriven;
For such gifts, said this friar for his part,
Show clearly that a man is changed at heart.
For many men are hardened, it appears,
So that they find no outlet thru their tears;
Instead of tears and useless weeping, then,
The silver that they give will save such men.
He always kept his tippet[19] stuffed with knives
And pins to give to young attractive wives.
Certainly he had a merry note;
He knew well how to sing, and play a rote,[20]
At song-fests he would win the prize outright.
As any lily flower his neck was white.
And like a champion wrestler he was strong.

---

14. Gauds—the large Paternoster beads marking off the sections of a rosary.

15. St. Benedict and his diciple Maurus, founders of the Benedictine Order; St. Benedict established the famous monastery at Monte Cassino in 529.

16. St. Augustine, Bishop of Hippo, was a great proponent of labor as part of the monastic life.

17. A "Limiter" was a friar licensed to beg within a definite ("limited") region.

18. Franklins were landholders of free, but not of noble, birth; they ranked below the gentry.

19. Tippet—a long scarf; a handy substitute for pockets.

20. Rote—a stringed instrument, sometimes played with a bow, sometimes with a fixed wheel like a hurdy-gurdy. (See figure 16.3.)

All the taverns, as he went along,
And every hostler, and barmaid, he knew,
Better than outcasts and the beggar-crew;
Because, to such a worthy man as he,
It was not fitting, you will all agree,
To have acquaintance with such worthless wretches;
Such contact brings no profit, nothing fetches. . . .
There is no gain in dealing with *canaille*,[21]
But with rich men, of social station high.
And thus, whenever profit would arise,
This friar was humble, courteous, and wise.
So virtuous a man was nowhere found;
And what a beggar, as he made his round!
Why, if a widow had no shoe to show,
So pleasant was his "In principio . . ."[22]
He'd have the widow's mite, before he went!
His income always went beyond his rent.
And he could play around like any whelp;
On love-days[23] he knew how to be of help.
He was not like a needy monk or scholar,
Threadbare, shabby, down to his last dollar;
But he was like a great man or a pope.
Of finest woolen was his semicope,[24]
That rounded like a bell out of its mold.
He lisped a little, if the truth be told,
To make his speech sound sweeter on his tongue;
And in his harping, after he had sung,
His twinkling eyes shone in his head as bright
As do the stars on cold and frosty night.
This worthy Limiter was called Hubert.

Merchant

The merchant, next:—with forked beard, and girt
In livery, high on his horse he sat,
Upon his head a Flemish beaver hat;
His boots were clasped up in the latest mode;
He spoke in serious fashion as he rode,
Referring always to his gains in gold.
He wished, he said, to have the sea patrolled
From Middleburgh across to Orewell.[25]
A money-changer, he could buy or sell;
This worthy man knew how his wits to set;
No one ever knew he was in debt,
So well he managed all the deals he made,
His sales and bargains, and his tricks of trade.
He was a worthy man, in every way;
But what his name, I never heard men say!

---

21. Canaille—riff-raff, rabble.

22. "In principio. . ."—the beginning of the Last Gospel. These verses were thought to have supernatural powers, and were used as greeting, blessing, and the like.

23. "Love-days" were days set aside for settlement of disputes by arbitration; the clergy were often the judges.

24. A short cape or cloak.

25. The port of Middleburgh, just off the coast of Netherlands, was just opposite the English port of Harwich (then called "Orewell"). The merchant was probably engaged (among other things!) in the wool trade, and desired protection for his shipping.

Clerk

A clerk of Oxford rode with us also,
Who turned to logic-study long ago;
His horse was lean and skinny as a rake,
And he was not so fat, I'll undertake!
But hollow-looking, hungry evermore;
Quite threadbare were the shabby clothes he wore,
For he had found as yet no benefice,
Nor was so worldly as to hold office.
For he had rather have, at his bed's head,
A score of books, all bound in black or red,
Of Aristotle and philosophy
Than rich robes, fiddle, or gay psaltery.
And yet philosophy, if truth be told,
Had brought him in but very little gold,
But all that willing friends to him had lent
On books and learning eagerly he spent;
When friends helped with his schooling, then for those
He'd pray in earnest, for their souls' repose.
Of study he took every care and heed;
Not a word he spoke more than was need;
Then what he said was formal, reverent,
Short and to the point, of high intent;
Pertaining unto virtue was his speech;
And gladly would he learn, and gladly teach.

Sergeant-at-law

A sergeant of the law, who used to go
Full many a time to St. Paul's portico,[26]
There was also, of richest excellence;
Discreet he was and of great reverence.
—At least he seemed so, for his words were wise.
He often sat as justice in assize,[27]
By full commission or in his own right.
His learning and his fame were more than slight,
So he had fees, and robes, abundantly.
Nowhere a greater purchaser[28] than he.
Provisions of the law so well he knew
That none could quibble with the deeds he drew.
But no one does as much as this man does—
And yet, he seemed much busier than he was . . .
From William's day[29] he knew each court decision
In every case, by heart, and with precision.
His documents were drawn up so that none
Could find a fault or loop-hole—not a one;
The Statutes he'd recite, and all by rote.
He rode quite simply in a medley coat,
Girt with a belt of striped silk. No more
I have to tell of what this Sergeant wore.

Franklin

With him a franklin rode, whose beard was white
As any daisy, and his face was bright
And ruddy: sanguine, one would call the man.
He loved a wine-sop as the day began.

---

26. The porch of St. Paul's Cathedral was a traditional meeting-place for lawyers.

27. Assize: session of the court.

28. Purchaser—a buyer of land. Does Chaucer imply that the Sergeant is desirous of becoming a landed gentleman, or that he is a land-speculator?

29. The Sergeant knew the law clear back to the conquest—the statutes of William the Conqueror.

He liked to live in comfort and in joy;
Truly, he was Epicurus' boy,
Who stoutly held that comfort—that is, pleasure—
Was of happiness the only measure.
A householder, and a great, was he;
He was St. Julian[30] in his own country.
His bread and ale were uniformly fine;
No man was better stocked than he with wine;
Baked meats were never lacking at his place—
Both fish and flesh—or he'd have felt disgrace!
It snowed in his house both of meat and drink,
Of every good thing that a man can think.
According to the season of the year,
So changed his food, and all his table-cheer;
Fat partridges he kept on his preserve,
And fishponds stocked, his table well to serve.
Woe to the cook, unless his sauce were fine,
And sharp and tasty, and the meal on time!
His covered table was not put away
But stood in readiness the live-long day.
At session,[31] he was lord—no man stood higher—
And many a time he served as Knight-of-Shire.
He wore a knife, and purse—made all of silk—,
Hung from his girdle, white as morning milk.
He'd served as sheriff, and county auditor;
Nowhere was a more worthy vavasour.[32]

The Five Tradesmen

A haberdasher, and a carpenter,
A weaver, dyer, and an arras-maker,
—All these were clad in the same livery
Of one great dignified fraternity;
All fresh and new the gear they wore, it seemed;
Not with brass their knives and trimmings gleamed,
But silver, and fine work in every part;
Their belts and purses were in style, and smart.
Important citizens, enough, were all
These men, to sit on dais in guild-hall,
And anyone of them, it's safe to state,
Was wise enough to be a magistrate;
They certainly had goods enough, and rent;
And, I'm sure, their wives would give assent,
For otherwise they would have been in blame;
It's good to hear a "Madam" with one's name,
And lead the way at church, and to be seen
With mantle borne, as royal as a queen!

Cook

A cook was in their party, to prepare
Their favorite dishes, foods both rich and rare:
Chickens, marrow-bones, and tarts well-flavored.
Many a draught of London ale he'd savored.
He knew how to roast, boil, broil, and fry,
Make soups and sauces hot, and bake a pie.
A pity was it, so it seemed to me,
That on his shin an ulcerous sore had he.
His blanc-mange[33] would be rated with the best.

Shipman

A shipman was there, living far to west
—For all I know he came from Dartmouth town.
He rode as best he could a nag: his gown
Of falding[34] rough hung clear down to his knee;
A dagger hanging on a lace had he
About his neck, beneath his arm and down.
Hot summer suns had made his hue all brown;
A boon companion was this salty tar.
He'd helped himself to many a good wine jar
From Bordeaux, while below his owners slept.
Fine scruple was a thing he never kept.
In sea-fights, if he got the upper hand,
By water he sent them home to every land.
But no man, in his skill to reckon tides,
His streams, his chance and all besides,
His harbors, and his moons, and navigation;
From Hull to Carthage had his reputation.
Bold he was, but wise, in undertaking;
Many a tempest set his beard to shaking!
And he knew all the havens as they were
From Gotland to the Cape of Finisterre,[35]
And every creek in Brittany and Spain.
His barge was called the good ship "Madeleine."

Physician

A doctor of physic, known both far and near,
Was with us; nowhere could you find his peer,
In surgery or physic; what is more,
Well-grounded in astrology's deep lore,
He treated patients for the better part
By horoscope and such-like magic art.
For he knew how to forecast, by his spell,
The ascendant planets that would make them well.
He knew the cause of every malady,
Whether of cold or hot or moist or dry,[36]
Where engendered, from what humor traced;
He was a doctor of much skill and taste.
The cause once known, and of the source once sure,
He quickly brought the sick man to his cure.
And he had ready his apothecaries
To send him potent drugs and lectuaries[37]
For each assisted other, gold to gain;
Their friendship was no new one, that is plain!
—This doctor knew old Esculapius,
The Greek Deiscorides, and ancient Rufus,
Hippocrates, Galen, Hali the Saracen,
Serapion, and Rhazes, Avicen,
Averroes, Bernard, Constantine,
Gatesden, Gilbert, John the Damascene.[38]
And in his diet temperate was he;
It was not full of superfluity,
But wholesome, one of healthful nourishment.

---

30. St. Julian is the patron saint of hospitality.

31. These were probably sessions of the Justices of the Peace, not the big assizes.

32. Vavasour—a substantial landholder.

33. Not like the modern pudding, but a compound of minced capon, almonds, cream, sugar, and flour!

---

34. Falding—coarse woolen cloth with shaggy nap.

35. That is, from Sweden to the western tip of France.

36. The reference is to the theory of the "bodily humors," or fluids, and their effect on the health and temperament of the person.

37. Lectuaries—more properly, electuaries. Medicine in a sticky or sirupy base, originally meant to be "licked up" by the patient!

38. This impressive list is to indicate that the doctor was thoroughly versed in all the medical authorities, ancient and "modern." It seems curious to a modern reader to find among his qualifications that he is an excellent astrologer.

Bible-study was not this man's bent.
He dressed in costly colors, red and blue,
With taffeta and silken linings, too;
And yet he was a man to hate expense.
He kept what he had earned in pestilence;
And since, in physic, gold's a cordial, he
Found gold was what he loved especially!

Wife of Bath

A goodwife came from Bath, that ancient city,
But she was rather deaf; and that's a pity.
Her skill in making cloth, I hear, was such
That, as they say, she wove "to beat the Dutch."[39]
In all the parish never a woman came
To offering before this worthy dame—
But if there did, so much enraged was she
That she lost all her Christian charity!
Her kerchiefs were of finest weave, and dear;
They must have weighed a full ten pounds, or near,
That on a Sunday covered up her head.
Her hose[40] were fancy-fine, of scarlet red,
And tightly tied, her shoes were soft and new.
Her face was bold, and fair, and red of hue.
She was a worthy woman all her life;
To husbands five this woman had been wife,
Not counting other company in youth;
There's no need now to speak of that, in truth!
Three times to Jerusalem she'd been;
Full many a distant stream her feet were in . . .
To Rome she'd been, and gone to far Boulogne,
In Spain to Santiago, to Cologne;
She knew a lot of wandering by the way.
Gap-toothed this goodwife was, the truth to say.
Easily her ambling horse she sat,
With flowing wimple—on her head a hat
As broad as is a buckler or a shield;
A foot-mantle left her ample hips concealed;
And on her feet she wore well-sharpened spurs.
The gift of laughter and of fun was hers.
Love's remedies she knew, and not by chance;
She knew first-hand the art of that old dance.

Parson

A good religious man went on this ride,
A parish priest, who served the countryside;
Poor in money, rich in holy work,
A very learned scholar was this clerk.
The gospel of Our Lord he strove to preach,
And tried his poor parishioners to teach.
Benign he was, hard-working, diligent,
In adverse seasons patiently content,
As he had proved on more than one occasion.
He did not threaten excommunication
When poor folk could not pay their tithes; instead,
The little that he had he'd share, his bread
As well as money, with a cheerful heart.
Contentment with a little was his art.
Tho wide his parish, houses far asunder,
He'd not neglect, in spite of rain or thunder,
The afflicted in mind, body, or estate,
The farthest in his parish, small or great;
Staff in hand, he'd visit them, on foot.

This fine example to his flock he put,
That first he acted; afterward he taught.
From out the Gospel these words he had caught.
This figure he had added thereunto:
"If fine gold rust, what shall poor iron do?"
For if the priest be foul, in whom we trust,
No wonder if the ignorant people rust;
A sham it is, and brings the priest to mock—
A shitty shepherd, tending a clean flock!
Rather should a priest example give,
By his clean living, how his sheep should live.
He never set his benefice to hire
And left his sheep encumbered in the mire,
Running up to London, to St. Paul's,
Singing paid requiems within those walls;
Nor in some brotherhood withdrew, alone;
But caring for his flock he stayed at home,
So that no wolf his helpless sheep might harry;
He was a shepherd, not a mercenary.
A virtuous man and holy was he, then,
Not arrogant in scolding sinful men,
Not haughty in his speech, or too divine,
But prudent in his teaching and benign.
To draw the folk to heaven by kindliness
And good example was his business.
But then, if any one were obstinate,
Whoever he was, of high or low estate,
He's scold him sharply, raise a mighty row;
Nowhere was there a better priest, I vow.
No hankering after pomp and reverence,
No putting on of airs, and no pretence;
The lore of Christ and His apostles true
He taught; but what he preached, he'd do.

Plowman

With him there was a plowman, his own brother,
Who'd loaded many a cart with dung; no other
Was a worker good and true as he,
Living in peace and perfect charity.
God he loved best, with his entire soul,
At all times, whether he knew joy or dole;
And next, as Christ commands, he loved his neighbor.
For he would thresh, or ditch, or dig, and labor
For Jesus' sake, without a thot of pay,
To help poor folk, if in his power it lay.
Cheerfully, in full, his tithes he paid
Both on his goods, and what by work he made.
In tabard clad, he rode an old gray mare.
—(A miller and a reeve was also there,
A summoner, also, and a pardoner,
A manciple and I—that's all there were.)

Miller

The miller was a big and hefty lout,
Brawny, burly, big of bone, and stout.
Against all comers, as events turned out,
He won the ram[41] at every wrestling-bout,
Stocky, broad-shouldered, in build a battering-ram,
There was no door he couldn't tear from jamb
Or break it, running at it with his head.
His beard like any sow or fox was red,
And broad as any spade, and cut off short,
Right atop his nose he had a wart;
In it stood a little tuft of hairs,
Red as the bristles in an old sow's ears.

---

39. Chaucer says "She passed hem of Ypres and of Gaunt"—the Low Countries were famous for textiles.

40. Not stockings, but gaiters or leggings.

41. The customary wrestling prize.

As for his nostrils, they were black and wide;
A sword and buckler bore he by his side.
His big mouth like a furnace needed stoking:
He was a jesting clown whose bawdy joking
Mostly ran to sin: it wasn't nice.
From the grain he ground he'd steal—and then toll thrice;
Good millers have a golden thumb, it's said . . .
A white coat, and a blue hood on his head,
He wore; and with his bagpipe's merry sound
He cheered us as we started, outward-bound.

Manciple

There was a manicple[42] from the Inns of Court[43]
To whom all purchasers could well resort
To learn to buy supplies in large amount;
For whether he bought by cash, or on account,
He watched his dealings with so close an eye
That he came out ahead in every try.
Now is it not indeed by God's own grace
That he, uneducated, could outface
His masters—that heap of learned men?
His employers numbered three times ten,
Legal experts, with good sense endowed:
—There must have been a dozen in the crowd
Worthy to be stewards of rent or land
Of any lord in England, to help him stand
Within his income, if he only would,
In honor, out of debt, all to the good,
Or help him live as sparsely as desired:
Why, they could help a county, as required,
In any kind of case that might befall:—
And yet this manciple could beat them all.

Reeve

The reeve, a scrawny, peevish man was he;
His beard was shaved as close as close could be;
His hair was shorn off short around his ears,
His top docked like a priest's, so it appears.
His legs were very long and very lean,
Thin as a stick; no calf could there be seen.
He managed well the granary and bin;
No auditor could get ahead of him.
And he could estimate, by drought and rain,
The yield he could expect of seed and grain.
His lord's sheep, cows, and other stock,
The swine and horses, and the poultry-flock,
Were wholly in his hands to manage well,
And on his oath the reckoning to tell,
Ever since his lord reached twenty years.
No man could ever find him in arrears.
There was no agent, shepherd, hired hand,
Whose tricks he didn't know or understand;
They feared him, everyone, as they feared death.
His dwelling place stood fair upon the heath,
But sheltered was his place with green trees' shade.
Far better bargains than his lord he made;
Richly he had feathered his own nest.
He knew the way to please his master best,
By giving him, or lending, his own goods,
And getting not mere thanks, but coats and hoods.
In youth, he'd learned a trade—he was a wright;
In carpentry he was a skillful wight.

---

42. Steward, or purchasing agent.
43. The lodgings of the lawyers.

This reeve's good horse rode at an easy trot;
A dapple-gray he was; his name was Scot.
His long surcoat of Persian blue was made,
And by his side he bore a rusty blade.
Of Norfolk was this reeve of whom I tell,
From just outside a town called Baldeswell.
He tucked up all his garments like a friar,
And rode the hindmost: Such was his desire.

Summoner

A summoner[44] was there with us in that place,
Who had a fire-red cherubic face,
All pimply, full of whelks; his eyes were narrow,
And he was hot and lecherous as a sparrow,
With black and scabby brows, and scanty beard:
His was the sort of face that children feared.
There was no mercury nor brimstone, salve
Of tartar, lead, or borax, that could have
The strength to rid him of the lumps and knobs
Disfiguring his face in ugly gobs;
These acneous pimples covered both his cheeks.
And he was fond of garlic, onions, leeks;
He loved to drink strong wine, as red as blood;
Then spoke and cried as one demented would.
And having drunk his wine, and feeling gay,
Then not a word but Latin would he say.
—He knew a few expressions—two or three—
That he had picked up, out of some decree—
No wonder, for he heard it every day:
And everybody knows that even a jay
Can learn to call out "Wat!" as well as the Pope!
But when he tried with other things to cope,
His slender stock of learning would give out:
"Questio quid juris!"[45] he would shout.
He was a noble rascal, and a kind;
A better fellow would be hard to find.
He would arrange it, for a quart of wine,
For a friend of his to keep a concubine
The whole year thru, and never get in trouble;
Oh, he was very good at dealings double!
And if he liked a person whom he saw,
He'd teach that person not to stand in awe
Nor fear, for what he did, the archdeacon's curse—
Why, does a man's soul live within his purse?
Yet purse alone can suffer penalty:
"Purse is the archdeacon's hell," said he.
(But well I know he lied in saying so;
Such curses ought the guilty men forego.
As absolution saves, so curses slay;
From all *Significavits*,[46] stay away!)
And at his mercy, in his tender charge,
Were young folks of the diocese at large;
He knew their secrets; they were easily led.
He had set a garland on his head
So large it would have served for an ale-stake.[47]
A buckler he had made him of a cake.

---

44. Process-server or bailiff for the ecclesiastical court, usually presided over by the archdeacon.
45. "The question is, what part of the law applies?"—a lawyer's technicality.
46. *Significavit*—the opening word in a summons to appear before the ecclesiastical court.
47. Ale was advertised by a bunch of greens, hanging on a stake or pole above the door.

Pardoner

With him a noble-pardoner rode, his pal
And peer (his patron-house was Ronceval),[48]
Who straight from Rome had come—or so said he—
And loud he sang, "Come hither, love, to me!"
The summoner added, in the bass, a ground:
No trumpet had one half so loud a sound.
The pardoner had yellow hair, like wax,
That hung as limp as does a bunch of flax;
Stringily his locks hung from his head,
So that his shoulders were all overspread.
But thin it lay, in hanks there, one by one.
No hood he wore; he left it off, for fun,
Trussed up in his bag. It seemed to him
That thus he rode in fashion's latest whim,
Uncovered—save for cap—his head all bare.
Staring eyes he had, just like a hare.
A vernicle he'd sewed upon his cap.
His wallet lay before him, in his lap,
Brimful of pardons, hot from Rome, please note!
Small the voice he had, just like a goat.
He had no beard: nor ever would, in truth:
As it were fresh-shaved, his face was smooth;
I think he was a gelding—or a mare.
But of his trade, from Berwyck clear to Ware
Was never such a pardoner as this lad!
In his bag a pillow-case he had
Which—so he claimed—was once Our Lady's veil—
He said he had a fragment of the sail
That once St. Peter used, in days of yore,
Before Our Lord gave him new work, ashore!
He had a cross of latten,[49] set with stones,
And in a glass jar carried some pig's bones.
But with these silly "relics," when he spied
Some simple priest out in the country-side,
On such a day more money would he win
Than in two months the parson could fetch in;
And thus, with flattery and lying mock,
He'd fool the priest and all his simple flock.
But give the devil his due; for, when all's past,
In church he was a great ecclesiast;
Well knew he how to read a Bible story,
But especially well he sang the offertory;
For well he knew that when the song was sung,
He then would preach, and sharpen up his tongue,
To win their money from the gullible crowd;
That's why he sang so merrily and loud.
Now I've told you briefly, clause by clause,
The state, the number and array and cause
In which assembled was this company
In Southwerk at this noble hostelry
That's called the Tabard Inn, right near the Bell.

---

48. A London hospital.
49. Cheap metal.

Exercises

1. The pilgrims can be classified into several groups: the chivalric class, the money class, the corrupt clergy, the sincere clergy, the simple commoners. Name the pilgrims who belong to each group and describe the general traits of each class.
2. Compare this society with our own. What are the differences? The similarities?

The Reeve's Tale from THE CANTERBURY TALES

Chaucer

Just as Chaucer gave a very wide view of the population of the people of the late Middle Ages in his Prolog, in the stories that they tell during the pilgrimage, he presents many of the types of literature of the time. "The Reeve's Tale," like the preceding "Miller's Tale," is a *fabliau,* a type of boisterous and bawdy story popular at the time and, in fact, most any other time. A manager on a large country estate, Oswald the Reeve is shrewd, cunning, and bad tempered. In his early days he was a carpenter, which explains why he became incensed by the Miller's version of a foolish old carpenter who was cuckolded by his young and lively wife. Furthermore, the Reeve was old and, as he said in his Prologue (not given here), is now like everyone else who "knows that when a man no longer has the ability to do a certain thing, he spends his time talking about it." Prodded by the Host to cease his sermonizing, the Reeve begins his story, warning that his language will be just as rough as that used by the Miller. Not surprisingly, the foolish victim of the Reeve's tale is a miller. The modern English translation is by Neville Coghill.

At Trumpington, not far from Cambridge town,
   A bridge goes over where the brook runs down
And by that brook there stands a mill as well.
And it's God's truth that I am going to tell.
   There was a miller lived there many a day
As proud as any peacock and as gay;
He could play bag-pipes too, fish, mend his gear,
And turn a lathe, and wrestle, and poach deer.
And at his belt he carried a long blade,
Trenchant it was as any sword that's made,
And in his pouch a jolly little knife.
No one dared touch him, peril of his life.
He had a Sheffield dagger in his hose.
Round was his face and puggish was his nose;
Bald as an ape he was. To speak more fully,
He was a thorough-going market bully
Whom none dared lay a hand on or come near
Without him swearing that they'd buy it dear.
   He was a thief as well of corn and meal,
And sly at that; his habit was to steal.
Simpkin the Swagger he was called in scorn.
He had a wife and she was nobly born;
Her father was the parson of the town;
A dowery of brass dishes he put down
In order to have Simpkin his relation.

The nuns had given her an education.
Simpkin would take no woman, so he said,
Unless she were a virgin and well-bred,
To save the honour of his yeoman stock;
And she was proud, pert as a magpie cock.
　　　It was a proper sight to see the pair
On holidays, what with him strutting there
In front of her, his hood about his head,
And she behind him all decked out in red,
Like Simpkin's hose, for scarlet-red he had 'em.
No one dared call her anything but 'Madam',
And there was no one bold enough to try
A bit of fun with her or wink an eye,
Unless indeed he wanted Sim the Swagger
To murder him with cutlass, knife or dagger,
For jealous folk are dangerous, you know,
At least they want their wives to think them so.
And then her birth was smirched to say the least;
Being the daughter of a celibate priest
She must maintain her dignity, of which
She had as much as water in a ditch.
She was a sneering woman and she thought
That ladies should respect her, so they ought,
What with her well-connected family,
And education in a nunnery.
　　　They had a daughter too between them both,
She was a girl of twenty summers' growth;
But that was all except a child they had
Still in the cradle, but a proper lad.
The wench was plump, well-grown enough to pass,
With a snub nose and eyes as grey as glass;
Her rump was broad, her breasts were round and high;
She'd very pretty hair, I will not lie.
The parson of the town, for she was fair,
Intended to appoint the girl as heir
To all his property in house and land
And he was stiff with suitors to her hand.
He purposed to bestow her if he could
Where blood and ancient lineage made it good.
For Holy Church's goods should be expended
On Holy Church's blood, so well-descended,
And holy blood should have what's proper to it
Though Holy Church should be devoured to do it.
　　　This miller levied toll beyond a doubt
On wheat and malt from all the land about,
Particularly from a large-sized College
In Cambridge, Solar Hall. 'Twas common knowledge
They sent their wheat and malt to him to grind it.
Happened one day the man who ought to mind it,
The college manciple, lay sick in bed,
And some reported him as good as dead.
On hearing which the miller robbed him more
A hundred times than he had robbed before;
For up till then he's only robbed politely,
But now he stole outrageously, forthrightly.
　　　The Warden scolded hard and made a scene,
But there! The miller didn't give a bean,
Blustered it out and swore it wasn't so.
　　　Two poor young Bible-clerks or students, though,
Lived in this College (that of which I spoke).
Headstrong they were and eager for a joke
And simply for the chance of sport and play
They went and plagued the Warden night and day
Just for a little leave to spend the morn
Watching the miller grind their meal and corn,
And each was ready to engage his neck
The miller couldn't rob them half a peck
Of corn by trickery, nor yet by force;
And in the end he gave them leave of course.

One was called John and Alan was the other,
Both born in the same village, name of Strother,
Far in the north, I cannot tell you where.
　　　Alan collected all his gear with care,
Loaded his corn upon a horse he had,
And off he went with John the other lad,
Each with his sword and buckler by his side.
John knew the way—he didn't need a guide—
Reaches the mill and down the sack he flings.
　　　Alan spoke first: 'Well, Simon, lad, how's things?
And how's your canny daughter and your wife?'
Says Simpkin, 'Welcome, Alan! Odds my life,
It's John as well! What are you up to here?'
'By God,' said John. 'Needs-must has got no peer,
And it behoves a man that has nie servant
To work, as say the learned and observant.
Wor[50] Manciple is like enough to dee,
Such aches and torments in his teeth has he;
So Alan here and I have brought wor sack
Of corn for grinding and to bring it back.
Help us get home as quickly as ye can.'
'It shall be done,' said he, 'as I'm a man.
What'll you do while I've the job in hand?'
'By God,' said John, 'I have a mind to stand
Right by the hopper here and watch the corn
As it gans in. Never since I was born
Saw I a hopper wagging to and fro.'
　　　Alan spoke up: 'Eh, John, and will ye so?
Then I shall stand below a short way off
And watch the meal come down into the trough;
I need no more than that by way of sport,
For John, in faith, I'm one of the same sort
And diven't knaa nowt of milling, same as ye.'
　　　The miller smiled at their simplicity
And though, 'It's just a trick, what they're about
They think that nobody can catch them out,
But by the Lord I'll blear their eyes a bit
For all their fine philosophy and wit.
The more they try to do me on the deal,
When the time comes, the more I mean to steal.
Instead of flour they shall be given bran.
"The greatest scholar is not the wisest man",
As the wolf said in answer to the mare.
Them and their precious learning! Much I care.'
　　　And when he saw his chance he sidled out
Into the yard behind and looked about
Without their noticing until at last
He found their horse where they had made him fast
Under an arbour just behind the mill.
　　　Up to the horse he goes with quiet skill
And strips the bridle off him there and then.
And when the horse was loose, off to the fen
Through thick and thin, and whinneying 'Weehee!'
He raced to join the wild mares running free.
　　　The miller then went back, and did not say
A word of this, but passed the time of day
With John and Alan till their corn was ground;
And when the meal was fairly sacked and bound,
John wandered out and found their horse was gone.
'Good Lord! Help! Help! Come quickly!' shouted John,
'Wor horse is lost, Alan! The devil's in it!
God's bones, man, use your legs! Come out this minute!
Lord save us all, the Warden's palfrey's lost.'

---

50. *Wor* means 'our.' John is speaking the north of England dialect.

Alan forgot his meal and corn and cost,
Abandoning frugality and care.
'What's that?' he shouted, 'Palfrey? Which way? Where?'
    The miller's wife ran clucking like a hen
Towards them, saying, 'Gone off to the fen
To the wild mares as fast as he can go.
Curse on the clumsy hand that tied him so!
Should have known better how to knit the reins.'
John said, 'Bad luck to it. Alan, for Christ's pains,
Put down your sword, man; so will I; let's gan!
We'll rin him like a roe together, man!
God's precious heart! He cannot scape up all!
Why didn't you put the palfrey in the stall?
You must be daft, bad luck to you! Haway!'
And off ran John and Alan in dismay,
Towards the fen as fast as they could go.
    And when the miller saw that this was so,
A good half-bushel of their flour he took
And gave it over to his wife to cook.
'I think,' he said, 'these lads have had a fright.
I'll pluck their beards. Yes. Let 'em read and write,
But none the less a miller is their match.
Look at them now! Like children playing catch.
Won't be an easy job to get him, though!'
    These foolish Bible-clerks ran to and fro
And shouted, 'Woa, lad, stand! . . . Look out behind!
Whistle him up . . . I've got him . . . watch it . . . *mind!*'
But to be brief, it wasn't until night
They caught the palfrey, hunt him as they might
Over the fens, he ran away so fast;
But in a ditch they captured him at last.
    Weary and wet, like cattle in the rain,
Came foolish John and Alan back again.
Said John, 'Alas the day that I was born!
We've earned nowt here but mockery and scorn.
Wor corn is stolen and they'll call us fools,
Warden and all wor meäts in the Schools,
And most of all the miller. What a day!'
    So back they went, John grousing all the way,
Towards the mill and put the horse in byre.
They found the miller sitting by the fire,
For it was night, too late for going home,
And, for the love of God, they begged a room
For shelter and they proffered him their penny.
'A room?' the miller said. 'There isn't any.
There's this, such as it is; we'll share it then.
My house is small, but you are learned men
And by your arguments can make a place
Twenty foot broad as infinite as space.
Take a look round and see if it will do,
Or make it bigger with your parley-voo.'
'Well, Simon, you must have your little joke
And, by St. Cuthbert, that was fairly spoke!
Well, people have a proverb to remind them
To bring their own, or take things as they find them,'
Said John. 'Dear host, do get us out the cup;
A little meat and drink would cheer us up.
We'll give ye the full payment, on my word.
No empty-handed man can catch a bird;
See, here's the silver, ready to be spent.'

Down into Trumpington the daughter went
For bread and ale; the miller cooked a goose,
And tied their horse up lest it should get loose
Again, and in his chamber made a bed
With clean white sheets and blankets fairly spread,
Ten foot from his, upon a sort of shelf,
His daughter had a bed all by herself
Quite close in the same room; they were to lie
All side by side, no help for it, and why?
Because there was no other in the house.
    They supped and talked and had a fine carouse
And drank a lot of ale, the very best.
Midnight or thereabout they went to rest.
    Properly pasted was this miller's head,
Pale-drunk he was, he's passed the stage of red;
Hiccupping through his nose he talked and trolled
As if he'd asthma or a heavy cold.
To bed he goes, his wife and he together;
She was as jolly as a jay in feather,
Having well wet her whistle from the ladle.
And by her bed she planted down the cradle
To rock the baby or to give it sup.
    When what was in the crock had been drunk up,
To bed went daughter too, and thereupon
To bed went Alan and to bed went John.
That was the lot; no sleeping-draught was needed.
The miller had taken so much booze unheeded,
He snorted like a cart-horse in his sleep
And vented other noises, loud and deep.
His wife joined in the chorus hot and strong;
Two furlongs off you might have heard their song.
The wench was snoring too, for company.
    Alan the clerk in all this melody
Gave John a poke and said, 'Are ye awake?
Did ye ever hear sich sang for guidness sake?
There's family prayers for ye among they noddies!
Wild fire come doon and burn them up, the bodies!
Who ever heard a canny thing like that?
The devil take their souls for what they're at!
All this lang neet I shall na get nie rest.
    'But never ye mind, all shall be for the best;
I tell ye, John, as sure as I'm a man,
I'm going to have that wench there, if I can!
The law grants easement when things gan amiss,
For, John, there is a law that gans like this:
"If in one point a person be aggrieved,
Then in another he shall be relieved."
    'Wor corn is stolen, nivvor doubt of that;
Ill-luck has followed us in all we're at,
And since no compensation has been offered
Against wor loss, I'll take the easement proffered.
God's soul, it shall be so indeed, none other?'
    John whispered back to him, 'Be careful brother,
The miller is a torble man for slaughter;
If he should wake and find ye with his daughter
He might do injury to you and me.'
'Injury? Him! I coont him nat a flea!'
    Alan rose up; towards the wench he crept.
The wench lay flat upon her back and slept,
And ere she saw him, he had drawn so nigh
It was too late for her to give a cry.
To put it briefly, they were soon as one.
Now, Alan, play! For I will speak of John.
    John lay there still for quite a little while,
Complaining and lamenting in this style:
'A bloody joke . . . Lord, what a chance to miss!
I shall be made a monkey of for this!

My meät has got some comfort for his harms,
He has the miller's daughter in his arms;
He took his chance and now his needs are sped,
I'm but a sack of rubbish here in bed.
And when this jape is told in time to come
They'll say I was a softie and a bum!
I'll get up too and take what chance I may,
For God helps those that help theirsels, they say.'
　　　He rises, steals towards the cradle, lifts it,
And stepping softly back again, he shifts it
And lays it by his bed upon the floor.
　　　The miller's wife soon after ceased to snore,
Began to wake, rose up, and left the room,
And coming back she groped about in gloom,
Missing the cradle John had snatched away.
'Lord, Lord,' she said, 'I nearly went astray
And got into the student's bed. . . . How dreadful!
There would have been foul doings. What a bed-ful!'
　　　At last she gropes to where the cradle stands,
And so by fumbling upwards with her hands
She found the bed and thinking nought but good,
Since she was certain where the cradle stood,
Yet knew not where she was, for it was dark,
She well and fairly crept in with the clerk,
Then lay quite still and tried to go to sleep.
John waited for a while, then gave a leap
And thrust himself upon this worthy wife.
It was the merriest fit in all her life,
For John went deep and thrust away like mad.
It was a jolly life for either lad
Till the third morning cock began to sing.
　　　Alan grew tired as dawn began to spring;
He had been hard at work the long, long night.
'Bye-bye,' he said, 'sweed Molly. . . . Are ye a'right?
The day has come, I cannot linger here,
But ever mair in life and death, my dear,
I am your own true clerk, or strike me deid!'
'Good-bye, my sweet,' she whispered, 'take good
　　　heed . . .
But first I'll tell you something, that I will!
When you are riding homewards past the mill
By the main entrance-door, a bit behind it,
There's the half-bushel cake—you're sure to find it—
And it was made out of the very meal
You brought to grind and I helped father steal. . . .
And, dearest heart, God have you in his keeping!'
And with that word she almost burst out weeping.
　　　Alan got up and thought, 'Dawn's coming on,
Better get back and creep in beside John.'
But there he found the cradle in his way.
'By God,' he thought, 'I nearly went astray!
My heed is tottering with my work to-neet,
That'll be why I cannot gan areet!
This cradle tells me I have lost my tether;
You must be miller and his wife together.
　　　And back he went, groping his weary way
And reached the bed in which the miller lay,
And thinking it was John upon the bed
He slid in by the miller's side instead,
Grabbing his neck, and with no more ado
Said, 'Shake yourself, wake up, you pig's-head, you!
For Christ's soul, listen! O such noble games
As I have had! I tell you, by St. James,
Three times the neet, from midnight into morn,
The miller's daughter helped me grind my corn
While you've been lying in your cowardly way . . .
'You scoundrel!' said the miller, 'What d'you say?
You beast! You treacherous blackguard! Filthy rat!

God's dignity! I'll murder you for that!
How dare you be so bold as to fling mud
Upon my daughter, come of noble blood?'
　　　He grabbed at Alan by his Adam's apple,
And Alan grabbed him back in furious grapple
And clenched his fist and bashed him on the nose.
Down miller's breast a bloody river flows
Onto the floor, his nose and mouth all broke;
They wallowed like two porkers in a poke,
And up and down and up again they go
Until the miller tripped and stubbed his toe,
Spun round and fell down backwards on his wife.
　　　She had heard nothing of this foolish strife,
For she had fallen asleep with John the clerk,
Weary from all their labours in the dark.
The miller's fall started her out of sleep.
'Help!' she screamed. 'Holly cross of Bromeholme keep
Us! Lord! Into thy hands! To Thee I call!
Simon, wake up! The devil's among us all!
My heart is bursting, help! I'm nearly dead,
One's on my stomach, and another's on my head.
Help, Simpkin, help! These nasty clerks are fighting!'
　　　Up started John, he needed no inciting,
And groped about the chamber to and fro
To find a stick; she too was on the go
And, knowing the corners better than them all,
Was first to find one leaning by the wall;
And by a little shaft of shimmering light
That shone in through a hole—the moon was bright—
Although the room was almost black as pitch
She saw them fight, not knowing which was which;
But there was something white that caught her eye
On seeing which she peered and gave a cry,
Thinking it was the night-cap of the clerk,
　　　Raising her stick, she crept up in the dark
And, hoping to hit Alan, it was her fate
To smite the miller on his shining pate,
And down he went, shouting, 'O God, I'm dying!'
　　　The clerks then beat him well and left him lying
And throwing on their clothes they took their horse
And their ground meal and off they went, of course,
And as they passed the mill they took the cake
Made of their meal the girl was told to bake.
　　　And thus the bumptious miller was well beaten
And done out of the supper they had eaten,
And done out of the money that was due
For grinding Alan's corn, who beat him too.
His wife was plumbed, so was his daughter. Look!
That comes of being a miller and a crook!
　　　I heard this proverb when I was a kid,
'Do evil and be done by as you did.'
Tricksters will get a tricking, so say I;
And God that sits in majesty on high
Bring all this company, great and small, to Glory!
Thus I've paid out the Miller with my story!

Exercises

1. What seems to be the attitude (Chaucer's? society's?) towards "clerks" (students who will become clergy)?
2. Compare the tone of this tale with the morally elevating *Everyman*. What does this tell you about fourteenth-century England?

THE ART OF COURTLY LOVE

Andreas Capellanus (fl. 1174–1186)

Countess Marie of Champagne established a Court of Love at Troyes where Andreas was probably chaplain to the court, or so he claimed. Andreas was an accomplished writer whose treatise on love provides us with a vivid and probably accurate picture of courtly life. Specifically, Andreas intended his manual as a portrayal of the Poitiers court of Marie's mother, Queen Eleanor of Aquitaine, as it was between 1170 and 1174.

Undoubtedly written by direction of Countess Marie, the manual is a codification of the etiquette of love. Andreas combines quotations from classic Latin writers (mainly Ovid) and the spirit of lyric love poetry by troubadours like Bernart de Ventadorn (see chapter 16) with his own observation of actual practices, producing a unique work known throughout Europe in a variety of translations.

Book One: Introduction to the Treatise on Love

We must first consider what love is, whence it gets its name, what the effect of love is, between what persons love may exist, how it may be acquired, retained, increased, decreased, and ended, what are the signs that one's love is returned, and what one of the lovers ought to do if the other is unfaithful.

Chapter I. What Love Is

Love is a certain inborn suffering derived from the sight of and excessive meditation upon the beauty of the opposite sex, which causes each one to wish above all things the embraces of the other and by common desire to carry out all of love's precepts in the other's embrace.

That love is suffering is easy to see, for before the love becomes equally balanced on both sides there is no torment greater, since the lover is always in fear that his love may not gain its desire and that he is wasting his efforts. He fears, too, that rumors of it may get abroad, and he fears everything that might harm it in any way, for before things are perfected a slight disturbance often spoils them. If he is a poor man, he also fears that the woman may scorn his poverty; if he is ugly, he fears that she may despise his lack of beauty or may give her love to a more handsome man; if he is rich, he fears that his parsimony in the past may stand in his way. To tell the truth, no one can number the fears of one single lover.[51] This kind of love, then, is a suffering which is felt by only one of the persons and may be called "single love." But even after both are in love the fears that arise are just as great, for each of the lovers fears that what he has acquired with so much effort may be lost through the effort of someone else, which is certainly much worse for a man than if, having no hope, he sees that his efforts are accomplishing nothing, for it is worse to lose the things you are seeking than to be deprived of a gain you merely hope for. The lover fears, too, that he may offend his loved one in some way; indeed he fears so many things that it would be difficult to tell them.

That this suffering is inborn I shall show you clearly, because if you look at the truth and distinguish carefully you will see that it does not arise out of any action; only from the reflection of the mind upon what it sees does this suffering come. For when a man sees some woman fit for love and shaped according to his taste, he begins at once to lust after her in his heart; then the more he thinks about her the more he burns with love, until he comes to a fuller meditation. Presently he begins to think about the fashioning of the woman and to differentiate her limbs, to think about what she does, and to pry into the secrets of her body, and he desires to put each part of it to the fullest use.[52] Then after he has come to this complete meditation, love cannot hold the reins; but he proceeds at once to action; straightway he strives to get a helper and to find an intermediary. He begins to plan how he may find favor with her, and he begins to seek a place and a time opportune for talking; he looks upon a brief hour as a very long year, because he cannot do anything fast enough to suit his eager mind. It is well known that many things happen to him in this manner. This inborn suffering comes, therefore, from seeing and meditating. Not every kind of meditation can be the cause of love, an excessive one is required; for a restrained thought does not, as a rule, return to the mind, and so love cannot arise from it.

In Chapter VIII (Book Two), Andreas presents the Rules of Love as the climax of a properly romantic mission. It seems that a knight of Britain cannot win the love of "a certain British lady" until he has brought her the hawk sitting on a golden perch in King Arthur's court. And, he is told,

> you can't get this hawk that you are seeking unless you prove, by a combat in Arthur's palace, that you enjoy the love of a more beautiful lady than any man at Arthur's court has; you can't even enter the palace until you show the guards the hawk's gauntlet, and you can't get this gauntlet except by overcoming two mighty knights in a double combat.

After defeating the pugnacious keeper of a golden bridge, the Briton then vanquishes a giant and rides on to Camelot where he manfully accomplishes the assigned tasks. While seizing the hawk he discovers a written parchment and is told that "This is the parchment on which are written the rules of love which the King of Love . . . pronounced for lovers. You should take it with you and make these rules known to lovers."

These are the rules.

    I. Marriage is no real excuse for not loving.
    II. He who is not jealous cannot love.
    III. No one can be bound by a double love.
    IV. It is well known that love is always increasing or decreasing.
    V. That which a lover takes against the will of his beloved has no relish.
    VI. Boys do not love until they arrive at the age of maturity.
    VII. When one lover dies, a widowhood of two years is required of the survivor.
    VIII. No one should be deprived of love without the very best of reasons.

---

51. Ovid *Art of Love* II. 517 ff.

52. Compare Ovid *Metamorphoses* VI. 490–93.

IX. No one can love unless he is impelled by the persuasion of love.

X. Love is always a stranger in the home of avarice.

XI. It is not proper to love any woman whom one would be ashamed to seek to marry.

XII. A true lover does not desire to embrace in love anyone except his beloved.

XIII. When made public love rarely endures.

XIV. The easy attainment of love makes it of little value; difficulty of attainment makes it prized.

XV. Every lover regularly turns pale in the present of his beloved.

XVI. When a lover suddenly catches sight of his beloved his heart palpitates.

XVII. A new love puts to flight an old one.[53]

XVIII. Good character alone makes any man worthy of love.

XIX. If love diminishes, it quickly fails and rarely revives.

XX. A man in love is always apprehensive.

XXI. Real jealousy always increases the feeling of love.

XXII. Jealousy, and therefore love, are increased when one suspects his beloved.

XXIII. He whom the thought of love vexes eats and sleeps very little.

XXIV. Every act of a lover ends in the thought of his beloved.

XXV. A true lover considers nothing good except what he thinks will please his beloved.

XXVI. Love can deny nothing to love.

XXVII. A lover can never have enough of the solaces of his beloved.

XXVIII. A slight presumption causes a lover to suspect his beloved.

XXIX. A man who is vexed by too much passion usually does not love.

XXX. A true lover is constantly and without intermission possessed by the thought of his beloved.

XXXI. Nothing forbids one woman being loved by two men or one man by two women.

These rules, as I have said, the Briton brought back with him on behalf of the King of Love to the lady for whose sake he endured so many perils when he brought her back the hawk. When she was convinced of the complete faithfulness of this knight and understood better how boldly he had striven, she rewarded him with her love. Then she called together a court of a great many ladies and knights and laid before them these rules of Love, and bade every lover keep them faithfully under threat of punishment by the King of Love. These laws the whole court received in their entirety and promised forever to obey in order to avoid punishment by Love. Every person who had been summoned and had come to the court took home a written copy of the rules and gave them out to all lovers in all parts of the world.

---

53. Compare Cicero, *Tusculan Disputations* IV. XXXV.

Exercises

1. As the selection indicates, many characteristics of romantic love were developed during the Middle Ages. Considering the definition and rules in the text, which concepts are still basic to romantic love?

2. What has changed? Can you explain the changes?

MORTE DARTHUR

Sir Thomas Malory (ca. 1410–1471)

Arthur, the representative of goodness and order, is killed by the forces of evil and disorder but, either in his own person or as a later English king, he shall return. He is the "once and future king," lord of Camelot, England, and the world, the embodiment of the noble virtues of chivalry. No discussion of the medieval world would be complete without some of the romance of King Arthur, his Knights of the Round Table, and Camelot, the original Court of Love.

The Sword in the Stone

Then the queen Igraine drew daily near her time when the child Arthur should be born, and it fell, within half a year, that king Uther asked her by the faith she owed unto him, who was father to her child? Then was she sore abashed to give an answer. "Fear you not," said the king; "but tell me the truth, and I shall love you the better by that faith of my body." "Sir," said she, "I shall tell you the truth. The same night that my lord was dead, that hour of his death, there came unto my castle of Tintagil a man like my lord in speech and countenance, and two knights with him in likeness of his two knights, Brastias and Jordains; and so I received him as I ought to do my lord; and that same night, as I shall answer unto God, the child was begotten." "That is truth," said the king, "as you say, for it was I myself that came in his likeness; and therefore, fear you not, for I am father to the child." And there he told her all the cause how it was by Merlin's counsel. Then the queen made great joy when she knew who was the father of her child. Soon came Merlin unto the king, and said, "Sir you must provide you for the nourishing of your child." "As thou wilt," said the king, "be it." "Well," said Merlin, "I know a lord of yours, in this land, that is a passing true man, and faithful, and he shall have the nourishing of your child; his name is Sir Ector, and he is a lord of fair livelihood, in many parts of England and Wales. And this lord, Sir Ector, let him be sent for, for to come and speak with you, and desire him yourself, as he loveth you, that he will put his own child to nourishing to another woman, and that his wife nourish yours; and when the child is born, let it be delivered unto me, at yonder postern, unchristened." As Merlin had devised, so it was done. And when Sir Ector was come, he made affiance to the king for to nourish the child, like as the king desired; and there the king granted Sir Ector great rewards. Then when the queen was delivered, the king commanded two knights and two ladies to take the child, bound in rich cloth of gold, "And deliver him to what poor man you meet at the postern gate of the castle." So the child was delivered unto Merlin, and so he bore it forth unto Sir Ector, and made a holy man to christen him, and named him Arthur; and so Sir Ector's wife nourished him with her own breasts.

Then within two years king Uther fell sick of a great malady; and in the meanwhile his enemies usurped upon him, and did a great battle upon his men, and slew many of his people. "Sir," said Merlin, "you may not lie so as you do, for you must to the field, though you ride in a horse-litter; for you shall never have the better of your enemies but if your person be there, and then shall you have the victory." So it was done as Merlin had devised, and they carried the king forth in a horse-litter, with a great horse towards his enemies. And at St. Alban's there met with the king a great host of the north; and that day Sir Ulfius and Sir Brastias did great deeds of arms, and king Uther's men overcame the northern battle, and slew much people, and put the remnant to flight; and then the king returned to London, and made great joy of his victory. And within a while after he was passing sore sick, so that three days and three nights he was speechless, wherefore all the barons made great sorrow, and asked Merlin what counsel were best? "There is none other remedy," said Merlin, "But God will have his will; but look ye that all his barons be before him to-morrow, and God and I shall make him to speak." So on the morrow all the barons, with Merlin, came before the king; then Merlin said aloud unto king Uther, "Sir, shall your son Arthur be king after your days of this realm, with all the appurtenances?" Then Utherpendragon turned him and said, in hearing of them all, "I give him God's blessing and mine, and bid him pray for my soul, and righteously and worshipfully that he claim the crown upon forfeiture of my blessing." And therewith he yielded up the ghost. And then he was interred as belonged unto a king; wherefore Igraine, the queen, made great sorrow, and all the barons. Then stood the realm in great jeopardy a long while, for every lord that was mighty of men made him strong, and many weened to have been king. Then Merlin went to the Archbishop of Canterbury, and counselled him to send for all the lords of the realm, and all the gentlemen of arms, that they should come to London before Christmas, upon pain of cursing; and for this cause, that as Jesus was born on that night, that He would of His great mercy show some miracle as He was come to be king of all mankind, for to show some miracle who should be rightwise king of this realm. So the archbishop, by the advice of Merlin, sent for all the lords and gentlemen of arms, that they should come by Christmas even to London; and many of them made them clean of their lives, that their prayer might be the more acceptable to God. So in the greatest church of London (whether it were Paul's or not the French book maketh no mention) all the estates and lords were long or it was day in the church for to pray. And when matins and the first mass was done, there was seen in the churchyard, against the high altar, a great stone, four-square, like to a marble stone, and in the midst thereof was an anvil of

steel, a foot of height, and therein stuck a fair sword, naked by the point, and letters of gold were written about the sword that said thus: "Whoso pulleth out this sword of this stone and anvil is rightwise king born of England." Then the people marvelled and told it to the archbishop. "I command you," said the archbishop, "that you keep you within your church; and pray unto God still that no man touch the sword till the high mass be all done." So when all the masses were done, all the estates went for to behold the stone and the sword, and when they saw the scripture, some assayed, such as would have been king; but none might stir the sword, nor move it. "He is not yet here," said the archbishop, "that shall achieve the sword, but doubt not God will make him to be known. "But this is my counsel," said the archbishop "that we let purvey ten knights, men of good fame, and they to keep this sword." And so it was ordained, and then there was made a cry, that every man should assay that would for to win the sword. And, upon new year's day, the barons let make a joust and tournament, that all knights that would joust and tourney there might play; and all this was ordained for to keep the lords together, and the commons, for the archbishop trusted that God would make him known that should win the sword. So, upon new year's day, when the service was done, the barons rode to the field, some to joust, and some to tourney. And so it happened that Sir Ector, that had great livelihood about London, rode to the jousts, and with him rode Sir Kaye, his son, and young Arthur, that was his nourished brother; and Sir Kaye was made knight at Allhallowmas afore. So as they rode towards the jousts, Sir Kaye had lost his sword, for he had left it at his father's lodging; and so he prayed young Arthur to ride for his sword. "I will with a good will," said Arthur, and rode fast after the sword; and when he came home, the lady and all were gone out to see the jousting. Then was Arthur wrath, and said to himself, "I will ride to the churchyard and take the sword with me that sticketh in the stone, for my brother, Sir Kaye, shall not be without a sword this day." And so, when he came to the churchyard, Arthur alighted, and tied his horse to the stile, and so went to the tent, and found no knights there, for they were all at the jousting; and so he handled the sword by the handles, and lightly and fiercely he pulled it out of the stone, and took his horse, and rode his way till he came to his brother, Sir Kaye, and delivered him the sword. And, as soon as Sir Kaye saw the sword, he wist well that it was the sword of the stone; and so he rode to his father, Sir Ector, and said, "Sir, lo! here is the sword of the stone; wherefore I must be king of this land." When Sir Ector beheld the sword, he returned again, and came to the church, and there they alighted all three, and went into the church; and anon he made Sir Kaye to swear upon a book how he came to that sword. "Sir," said Sir Kaye, "by my brother, Arthur, for he brought it to me." "How gat you this sword?" said Sir Ector to Arthur. "Sir, I will tell you; when I came home for my brother's sword I found nobody at home for to deliver me his sword; and so I thought my brother, Sir Kaye, should not be swordless, and so I came thither eagerly, and pulled it out of the stone without any pain." "Found ye any knights about this sword?" said Sir Ector. "Nay," said Arthur. "Now," said Sir Ector to Arthur, "I understand that you must be king of this land." "Wherefore I?" said Arthur, "and for what cause?" "Sir," said Sir Ector, "for God will have it so; for there should never no man have drawn out this sword, but he that shall be rightwise king to this land. Now, let me see whether ye can put the sword there as it was, and pull it out again." "That is no mastery," said Arthur; and so he put it in the stone. Therewith Sir Ector assayed to pull out the sword, and failed.

IV.

"Now assay you," said Sir Ector to Sir Kaye. And anon he pulled at the sword with all his might, but it would not be. "Now shall ye assay," said Sir Ector to Arthur. "With a good will," said Arthur, and pulled it out easily. And therewithal Sir Ector kneeled down to the earth, and Sir Kaye also. "Alas!" said Arthur, "mine own dear father, and my brother, why kneel you to me?" "Nay, nay, my lord Arthur, it is not so. I was never your father, nor of your blood, but I wot well that you are of an higher blood than I weened you were?" And then Sir Ector told him all how he was betaken him to nourish and by whose commandment, and by Merlin's deliverance. Then Arthur made great moan when he understood that Sir Ector was not his father. "Sir," said Sir Ector unto Arthur, "will you be my good and gracious lord when you are king?" "Else were I to blame," said Arthur, "for you are the man in the world that I am most beholden unto, and my good lady and mother, your wife, that, as well as her own, hath fostered and kept me; and, if ever it be God's will that I be king, as you say, ye shall desire of me what I may do, and I shall not fail you; God forbid I should fail you." "Sir," said Sir Ector, "I will ask no more of you but that you will make my son, your fostered brother, Sir Kaye, seneschal of all your lands." "That shall be done, sir," said Arthur, "and more by the faith of my body, and that never man shall have that office but he while that he and I live." Therewithal they went unto the archbishop, and told him how the sword was achieved, and by whom. And, upon the twelfth day, all the barons came thither for to assay to take the sword who that would assay. But there before them all there might none take it out but only Arthur, wherefore there were many great lords wrath, and said, "It was great shame unto them all and the realm, to be governed with a boy of no high blood born." And so they fell out at that time that it was put off til Candlemas, and then all the barons should meet there again. But always the ten knights were ordained for to watch the sword both day and night; and so they set a pavilion over the stone and the sword, and five always watched. And at Candlemas many more great lords came thither for to have won the sword, but none of them might prevail; and right as Arthur did at Christmas he did at Candlemas, and pulled out the sword easily, whereof the barons were sore aggrieved, and put it in delay till the high feast of Easter; and, as Arthur sped before, so did he at Easter; and yet there were some of the great lords had indignation that Arthur should be their king, and put it off in delay till the feast of Pentecost. Then the Archbishop of Canterbury, by Merlin's providence, let purvey of the best knights that might be gotten, and such knights as King Uttherpendragon loved best, and most trusted in his days; and such knights were put about Arthur, as Sir Boudwine, of Britain; Sir Kaye, Sir Ulfias, and Sir Brastias; all these, with many others, were always about Arthur, day and night, till the feast of Pentecost.

V.

And, at the feast of Pentecost, all manner of men assayed for to pull at the sword that would assay; and none might prevail but Arthur, and he pulled it out before all the lords and commons that were there; wherefore all the commons cried at once, "We will have Arthur unto our king, we will put him no more in delay, for we all see that it is God's will that he shall be our king, and who that holdeth against it we will slay him," and therewithal they all kneeled down all at once, and cried Arthur mercy because they had delayed him so long. And Arthur forgave it them, and took the sword between both his hands, and offered it to the altar, where the archbishop was, and was made knight of the best man that was there. And so anon was the coronation made, and there was he sworn to the lords and commons for to be a true king, to stand with true justice from thenceforth all the days of his life; and then he made all the lords that held off the crown, to come in and do him service as they ought to do. And many complaints were made unto King Arthur, of great wrongs that were done since the death of King Uttherpendragon, of many lands that were bereaved of lords, knights, ladies, and gentlemen; wherefore King Arthur made the lands for to be rendered again unto them that owed them. When this was done, that the king had established all the countries about London, then he did make Sir Kaye seneschal of England, and Sir Boudwine, of Britain, was made constable, and Sir Ulfias was made chamberlain, and Sir Brastias was made warden, for to wait upon the north from Trent forward; for it was that time, for the most part, enemy unto the king. But within few years after, King Arthur won all the north. Scotland, and all that were under their obeisance; also a part of Wales held against King Arthur, but he overcame them all, as he did the remnant, and all through the noble prowess of himself and his knights of the Round Table.

The Book of the Queen's Maying

I.

And thus it passed on from Candlemas until after Easter, that the month of May was come, when every lusty heart beginneth to blossom, and to bring-forth fruit. For, like as herbs and trees bring forth fruit, and flourish in May, in likewise every lusty heart, that is in any manner a lover, springeth and flourisheth in lusty deeds; for it giveth unto all lovers courage that lusty month of May in some thing, for to constrain him in some manner of thing; more in that month than in any other month, for divers causes; for then all herbs and trees renew a man and woman. And, in likewise, lovers call again to their mind old gentleness and old service, and many kind deeds that were forgotten by negligence. For, like as winter rasure doth always rase and deface green summer; so fareth it by unstable love in a man, and in woman, for in many persons there is no stability. For we may see all day a little blast of winter's rasure, anon we shall deface and put away true love for little or naught, that cost much thing; this is no wisdom no stability, but is feebleness of nature, and great disworship, whosoever useth this. Therefore, like as May month flowereth and flourisheth in many gardens, so in likewise let every man of worship flourish his heart in this world; first unto God, and next unto the joy of them that he promiseth his faith unto. For there was never worshipful woman, but they loved one better than another. And worship in arms may never be defiled. But first, reserve the honour unto God; and secondly, the quarrel must come of thy lady; and such love I call virtuous love. But now-a-days men cannot love, may not endure by reason; for where they be soon accorded, and hasty heat soon cooleth; right so fareth love now-a-days, soon hot, soon cold. This is no stability, but the old love was not so. Men and women could love together seven years, and no lusts were between them; and then was love, truth and faithfulness. And so in likewise was love used in King Arthur's days; wherefore, I liken love now-a-days unto summer and winter: for, like as the one is hot and the other cold, so fareth love now-a-days. Therefore, all ye that be lovers, call unto your remembrance the month of May, like as did Queen Guenever, for whom I make here a little mention, that while she lived she was a true lover, and there she had a good end.

II.

Now it befell in the month of lusty May that Queen Guenever called unto her knights of the Round Table, and she gave them warning, that early in the morning she should ride a-maying into woods and fields beside Westminster; "and I warn you that there be none of you but that he be well horsed, and that ye all be clothed in green; and I shall bring with me ten ladies, and every knight shall have a lady behind him, and every knight shall have a squire and two yeomen, and I will that ye and all be well horsed." So they made them ready in the freshest manner, and these were the names of the knights: Sir Kaye, Sir Agravaine, Sir Brandiles, Sir Sagramore, Sir Donidas, Sir Ozanna, Sir Ladinas, Sir Persuant, Sir Ironside, and Sir Pelleas. And those ten knights made them ready in the most freshest manner to ride with the Queen. So on the morrow they took their horses and rode a-maying with the Queen in great joy and delight; and the Queen purposed to have been again with the King at the furthest by ten of the clock, and so was her purpose at that time. Then there was a knight, the which hight Sir Meliagraunce, and he was son unto King Bagdemagus; and this knight had at that time a castle of the gift of King Arthur, within seven miles of Westminster. And this knight, Sir Meliagraunce, loved passing well Queen Guenever, and so he had done long and many years; and he had laid long in wait for to steal away the Queen, but evermore he forbear, because of Sir Launcelot du Lake, for in nowise he would meddle with the Queen if Sir Launcelot were in her company, or else and he were near hand her; and that time there was such a custom, that the Queen rode never without a great fellowship of men of arms about her; and there were many good knights, and the most part were young men that would have worship, and they were called the Queen's knights, and never in no battle, tournament, or jousts, they never bear none of them no manner of knowledge of their own arms, but plain white shields, and thereby they were called the Queen's knights. And then when it happened any of them to be of great worship by his noble deeds, then at the next high feast of Pentecost, if there were any slain or dead, as there was no year that failed but some were dead, then was there chosen in their stead that were dead the most men of worship, that were called the Queen's knights. And thus they came up all first, or they were renowned men of worship, both Sir Launcelot and all the remnant of them. But this knight, Sir Meliagraunce, had fulwell espied the Queen and her purpose, and how Sir Launcelot was not with her, and how she had no men of arms with her, but the ten knights all arrayed in green for maying. Then he purveyed him twenty men of arms, and a hundred archers to destroy the Queen and her knights, for he thought that time was the best season to take the Queen.

III.

So as the Queen had mayed and all her knights, all were bedecked with herbs and flowers, in the best manner and freshest. Right so came out of a wood Sir Meliagraunce, with eight score men armed, as they should fight in battle of arrest, and bade the Queen and her knights abide, for mauger there heads they should abide. "Traitor knight,"

said Queen Guenever, "what thinkest thou to do? wilt thou shame thyself? Bethink thee how thou art a king's son, and knight of the Round Table, and thou to be about for to dishonour the noble king that made thee knight; thou shamest the high order of knighthood and thyself! and me, I let the wit, shalt thou never shame, for I had rather cut my throat in twain, rather than thou shouldst dishonour me." "As for all this language," said Sir Meliagraunce, "be it as it may, for wit ye well, madam, that I have loved you many years, and never or now could I get you at such advantage as I do now, and therefore I will take you as I find you." Then spake the ten knights all with one voice, and said, "Sir Maliagraunce, wit ye well ye are about to jeopard your worship to dishonour, also ye cast for to jeopard our persons; howbeit we be unarmed, ye have us at a great advantage; for it seemeth by you that ye have laid watch on us; but rather than ye should put the Queen to shame and us all, we had as leave to depart from our lives, for and if we otherwise did we were shamed for ever." Then Sir Meliagraunce said, "Dress you as well as you can, and keep the Queen." Then the ten knigths of the Round Table drew their swords, and the others let run at them with their spears; and the ten knights manly abode them, and smote away their spears, that no spear did them harm. Then they lashed together with their swords, and anon Sir Kay, Sir Griflet, Sir Agravaine, Sir Dodinas, and Sir Ozanna were smitten to the earth with grimly wounds. Then Sir Brandiles and Sir Persuant, Sir Ironside and Sir Pelleas, fought long, and they were full sore wounded; for these knights, or ever they were laid to the ground, slew forty men of the best of them. So when the Queen saw her knights thus dolefully wounded, and needs must be slain at the last, then for pity and sorrows she cried and said, "Sir Meliagraunce, slay not my knights, and I will go with thee upon this convenant, that thou save them, and suffer them to be no more hurt; with this, that they be led with me wheresoever thou leadest me, for I will rather slay myself than I go with thee, unless that these, my noble knights, may be in presence." "Madam," said Sir Meliagraunce, "For your sake they shall be led with you into my castle, with that ye will be ruled and ride with me."

The Queen Guenever prayed the four knights to leave their fight, and she and they would not depart. "Madam," said Sir Pelleas, "we will do as ye do; for as for me, I take no force of my life nor death." For Sir Pelleas gave such buffets there, that no armour might hold them.

IV.

Then by the Queen's command they left battle, and dressed the wounded knights on horseback, some sitting and some athward, that it was pity to behold them. And then Sir Meliagraunce charged the Queen and all the knights, that none of her fellowship should depart from her; for full sore he dreaded Sir Launcelot du Lake, lest he should have any knowledge. All this espied the Queen, and privily she called unto her a child of her chamber, which was swiftly horsed, to whom she said, "Go thou, when thou seest thy time, and bear this ring unto Sir Launcelot du Lake, and pray him as he loveth me that he will come and see me, and that he rescue me if ever he will have joy of me, and spare not thou thy horse," said the Queen, "neither for water nor yet for land." And so the child espied his time, and lightly he mounted upon his horse, and smote him with his spurs, and so departed from there as fast as ever his horse might run. And when Sir Meliagraunce saw the child so flee, he understood well it was by the Queen's command, for to warn Sir Launcelot. Then they that were best horsed chased him, and shot at him; but the child went from them all. And then Sir Meliagraunce said unto Queen Guenever, "Madam, ye be about to betray me; but I shall ordain for Sir Launcelot, that he shall not lightly come at you." And then he rode with her and they all to his castle, in all the haste that they might; and by the way Sir Meliagraunce laid in an ambushment the best archers that he might get in his country, to the number of thirty, for to wait upon Sir Launcelot, charging them, that if they saw such a manner of knight come by the way upon a white horse, in anywise to slay his horse; but in no manner of wise not to have to do with him bodily, for he is overhard to be overcome. So this was done, and they were come to his castle; but in nowise the Queen would never let none of the ten knights and her ladies be out of her sight, but alway they were in her presence; for that Sir Meliagraunce durst make no masteries for dread of Sir Launcelot, inasmuch as he deemed that he had warning. So when the child was departed from the fellowship of Sir Meliagraunce, within a while he came to Westminster, and anon he found Sir Launcelot; and when he had told his message, and delivered him the Queen's ring, "Alas!" said Sir Launcelot, "now am I ashamed for ever only that I may rescue that noble lady from dishonour." Then eagerly he asked his armour, and ever the child told Sir Launcelot how the ten knights fought marvellously, and how Sir Pelleas, Sir Ironside, Sir Brandiles, and Sir Persuant of Inde fought strongly, but mainly Sir Pelleas; for there was none might withstand him, and how they all fought till at the last they were laid to the earth. And then the Queen made appointment for to save their lives, and went with Sir Meliagraunce. "Alas!" said Sir Launcelot, "that that most noble knight should be destroyed; I had rather," said Sir Launcelot, "than all the realm of France, that I had been there well armed." So when Sir Launcelot was all armed and upon his horse, he prayed the child of the Queen's chamber for to warn Sir Lavaine how suddenly he was departed, and for what cause; and pray him that, as he loveth me, that he will hie him fast after me, and that he stint not till that he come to me unto the castle whereas Sir Meliagraunce abideth or dwelleth. "For there," said Sir Launcelot, "shall he hear of me, if I be a man living! and rescue the queen, and the ten knights, the which full traitorously have been taken, that shall I prove upon his head, and all them that holdeth with him."

V.

Then Sir Launcelot rode as fast as he might, and then he took the water at Westminster bridge, and made his horse for to swim over the Thames to Lambeth. And then within a while he came to the place whereas the ten knights had fought with Sir Meliagraunce. And then Sir Launcelot followed the trace until he came unto a wood, and there was a straight way, and therein the thirty archers bade Sir Launcelot to turn again and follow no longer the trace. "What command have ye thereto," siad Sir Launcelot, "to cause me, that am a knight of the Round Table, to leave my right way?" "This way shalt thou leave, or else thou shalt go it upon thy feet; for wit thou well, thy horse shall be slain." "That is little mastery," said Sir Launcelot, "for to slay my horse; but as for myself, when my horse is slain, I give right nought for you, not and ye were five hundred more." So then they shot Sir Launcelot's horse, and smote him with many arrows. And then Sir Launcelot avoided his horse and went on foot; but there were so many ditches and hedges between them and him, that he might not meddle with one of them. "Alas! for shame," said Sir Launcelot, "that ever one knight should betray

another knight; but it is an old saying, 'A good man is never in danger but when he is in danger of a coward.' " Then Sir Launcelot went awhile on foot, and then was he foul cumbered with his armour, shield, and spear, and all that belonged to him; wit ye well he was full sore annoyed, and full loth he was to leave any thing that belonged unto him, for he dread right sore the treason of Sir Meliagraunce. And then by fortune there came by a chariot, the which came thither for to fetch wood. "Tell me, carter," said Sir Launcelot, "what shall I give thee for to suffer me to leap into the chariot, and that thou bring me unto a castle within these two miles." "Thou shalt not come within my chariot," said the carter; "for I am sent for to fetch wood for my lord, Sir Meliagraunce." "With him would I fain speak," said Sir Launcelot. "Thou shalt not go with me," said the carter. Then Sir Launcelot leapt to him, and gave him such a buffet, that he fell to the ground stark dead. Then the other carter, his fellow, was afraid, and thought to have gone the same way, and then he cried and said, "Fair lord, save my life, and I will bring you where you will." "Then I charge thee," said Sir Launcelot, "that thou drive me and this chariot even unto Sir Meliagraunce Castle." "Leap up into the chariot," said the carter, "and ye shall be there anon." So the carter drove forth as fast as he could; and Sir Launcelot's horse followed the chariot with more than forty arrows broad and rough in him. And more than an hour and a half Queen Guenever was in a bye window waiting with her ladies, and espied an armed knight standing in a chariot, "See, madam" said a lady, "whereas rideth in a chariot a goodly armed knight; I suppose that he rideth to hanging." "Where?" said the Queen. And then the Queen espied by his shield that he was there himself, Sir Launcelot du Lake. And then she was aware where came his horse after that chariot. "Alas!" said the Queen, "now I see well and prove, that well is him that hath a trusty friend. Ah! most noble knight." said Queen Guenever, "I see well that thou hast been hard bestead, when thou ridest in a cart," Then she rebuked that lady that likened him to ride in a chariot to hanging. "It was foul mouthed," said the Queen, "and evil likened, so for to liken the most noble knight in the world in such a shameful death. Oh! Jesu, defend him and keep him," said the Queen, "from all mischievous end." By this was Sir Launcelot come unto the gate of the castle, and he descended down, and cried, that all the castle rang of it: "Where art thou, false traitor, Sir Meliagraunce, and knight of the Round Table? Now come forth here, thou false traitor knight, thou and thy fellowship with thee, for here I am, Sir Launcelot du Lake; I shall fight with thee." And therewithal he bear the gate wide open upon the porter, and smote him under his ear with his gauntlet, that his neck brake asunder.

VI.

So when Sir Meliagraunce heard that Sir Launcelot was come, he ran to the Queen, and fell upon his knees, and said, "Mercy, madam! now I put me wholly in your grace." "What aileth you now?" said Queen Guenever: "forsooth, ye might well wit that some good knight would revenge me, though my lord King Arthur wist not of this your work." "Madam," said Sir Meliagraunce, "all that is done amiss on my part shall be amended, right as yourself will devise, and wholly I put me in your grace." "What would ye that I did?" said the Queen. "I would no more," said Sir Meliagraunce, "but that ye would take into your own hands, and that ye will rule my lord, Sir Launcelot; and such cheer as may be made him in this poor castle ye shall have until to-morrow. And then may ye and all your knights and ladies return to Westminster, and my body, and all that I have, shall I put into your rule." "Ye say well," said the Queen; "and better is peace than always war; and the less strife is made, the more is my worship." Then the Queen and her fair ladies went down unto the knight, Sir Launcelot, which stood wroth out of measure in the inner court for to abide battle, and ever he said, "Thou traitor knight, come forth here!" Then the Queen came unto him, and said, "Sir Launcelot, why be ye so moved?" "Ah! madam," said Sir Launcelot, "wherefore ask ye me that question? Me seemeth," said Sir Launcelot, "ye ought to be more displeased that I am, for ye have the hurt and the dishonour; for wit ye well, madam, my hurt is but little for the killing of a mare's son, but the despite grieveth me much more than all my hurt." "Truly," said Queen Guenever, "ye say truth: but heartily I thank you," said the Queen, "but ye must come in with me peaceably, for all things is put in my hands, and all that is evil shall be for the best, for the knight full sore repenteth him for the misadventure that is befallen him." "Madam," said Sir Launcelot, "sith it is so that ye are accorded with him: as for me, I may not be against it, howbeit Sir Meliagraunce hath done full shamefully to me and full cowardly. Madam," said Sir Launcelot, "if I had wist that ye would have been so soon accorded with him, I would not have made such haste to you." "Why say you so?" said the Queen: "do you forethink yourself of your good deeds? Wit ye well," said the Queen, "I accorded never unto him for favour, nor love that I have unto him, but for to lay down every shameful noise." "Madam," said Sir Launcelot, "Ye understand full well that I was never willing nor glad of shameful slander nor noise; and there is neither king, queen, nor knight that beareth life, except my lord King Arthur and you, madam, that should let me, but that I should make Sir Meliagraunce's heart full cold or I depart from hence." "That wot I well," said the Queen, "but what will ye more; ye shall have all things ruled as ye like to have it." "Madam," said Sir Launcelot, "so that ye be pleased, I care not; as for my part, ye shall full soon please." Right so the Queen took Sir Launcelot by the bare hand, for he had put off his gauntlet, and so she went with him to her chamber. And then she commanded him to be unarmed; and then Sir Launcelot asked where the ten knights were, that were sore wounded. So she showed them unto Sir Launcelot, and there they made great joy of his coming; and Sir Launcelot made great dole for their hurts, and bewailed them greatly. And there Sir Launcelot told them how cowardly and traitorously Sir Meliagraunce had set archers to slay his horse, and how he was fain to put himself in a chariot. Thus they complained the one unto the other: and full fain they would have been revenged, but they appeased themselves because of the Queen. Then Sir Launcelot was called many a day after Le Chevalier du Chariot, and did many deeds, and great adventures he had.

And so leave we off this tale of Chevalier du Chariot, and return we unto our tale. So Sir Launcelot had great cheer with the Queen; and then Sir Launcelot made a promise with the Queen, that the same night he should come into a window, outward into a garden, and that window was barred with iron. And there Sir Launcelot promised to meet her, when all folks were asleep. So then came Sir Lavaine driving to the gate crying, "Where is my lord, Sir Launcelot du Lake?" Then was he forthwith sent for, and when Sir Lavaine saw Sir Launcelot he said, "My lord, I found well how ye were hard bestead, for I have found your horse, the which was slain with arrows." "As for that," said Sir Launcelot, "I pray you, Sir Lavaine, speak ye of other matters, and let this pass; and we shall right it another time, when we best may."

VII.

Then the knights that were wounded were searched, and soft salves were laid to their wounds, and so it passed on till supper time; and all the cheer that might be made them, there it was showed unto the Queen and her knights. Then, when season was, they went to their chamber: but in no wise the Queen would not suffer the wounded knights to be from her, but that they were laid within draughts, upon beds and pillows, that she herself might see to them, that they lacked nothing. So when Sir Launcelot was in his chamber, that was assigned unto him, he called unto him Sir Lavaine, and told him, that that night he must go speak with his lady, Dame Guenever. "Sir," said Sir Lavaine, "let me go with you, and it please you, for I dread me sore of the treason of Sir Meliagraunce." "Nay," said Sir Launcelot, "I thank you; I will have no person with me at this time." And then Sir Launcelot took his sword in his hand, and privily went unto a place whereas he had espied a ladder beforehand, and that he took under his arm, and bear it through the garden, and set it up in a window, and there anon the Queen was ready to meet him; and then they made either to other their complaints of divers things: and then Sir Launcelot wished that he might come in. "Wit ye well," said the Queen, "I would as fain as ye that ye might come in." "Would ye, madam," said Sir Launcelot, "with your heart that I were with you?" "Yea, truly," said the Queen. "Now shall I prove my might," said Sir Launcelot, "for the love of you." And then he set his hand upon the bars of iron, and pulled at them with such a great might, that he break them clean out of the stone walls; and therewithal one of the bars of iron cut the brawn of Sir Launcelot's hand throughout to the bone, and then he leapt into the chamber to the Queen. "Make ye no noise," said the Queen, "for my wounded knights lie here fast by me." And so, to pass forth upon this tale, Sir Launcelot took no force of his hurt hand, but took his pleasure and his liking until it was in the dawning of the day; and wit ye well he slept not, but watched. And when he saw the time that he might tarry no longer he took his leave and departed at the window, and put it together as well he might again, and so departed unto his own chamber; and there he told Sir Lavaine how he was hurt. Then Sir Lavaine dressed his hand and staunched it, and put upon it a glove, that it should not be espied; and so the Queen lay long in her bed, until it was nine of the clock. Then Sir Meliagraunce went to the Queen's chamber, and found her ladies there ready clothed. "Jesu, mercy!" said Sir Meliagraunce, "what aileth you, madam, that ye sleep thus long?" And so forthwithal he opened the curtains for to behold her; and then was he ware where she lay, and all the sheet and pillow was all bloody, with the blood of Sir Launcelot's hurt hand: and when Sir Meliagraunce espied that blood, then he deemed in himself that she was false unto the King, and that some of the wounded knights had been with her all that night. "Ah! madam," said Sir Meliagraunce, "Now I have found you false traitoress unto my lord, King Arthur; for now I prove it well, that it was not for nought ye laid these wounded knights within the bounds of your chamber. Therefore I will accuse you of treason before my liege lord, King Arthur, and now I have proved you, madam, with a shameful deed, and that they be all false, or some of them, and that I will make good; for a wounded knight this night hath been with you." "That is false," said the Queen, "and that I report me to them all." Then, when the ten knights heard Sir Meliagraunce's words, they spake all with one voice, and said to Sir Meliagraunce, "Thou sayeth falsely, and wrongfully puttest upon us such a deed; and that we will make good, any of us, choose which thou list of us, when we are whole of our wounds." "Ye shall not," said Sir Meliagraunce, "say nay, with proud language: for here ye may all see," said Sir Meliagraunce, "that by the Queen this night a wounded knight hath lain." Then were they all ashamed when they saw the blood. And wit ye well that Sir Meliagraunce was passing glad that he had the Queen at such advantage, for he deemed that should hide his treason. So in this rumour came in Sir Launcelot, and found them all at a great array.

VIII.

"Aha! what array is this?" said Sir Launcelot. Then Sir Meliagraunce told him what he had found, and showed him the Queen's bed. "Truly," said Sir Launcelot, "ye did not your part, nor knightly, to touch a queen's bed, the while it was drawn, and she lying therein. For I dare say, and make good, that my lord King Arthur himself would not have displaced her curtains, she being within her bed, unless that it had pleased him to have lain down by her; and therefore have ye done unworshipfully and shamefully to yourself." "I wot not what you mean," said Sir Meliagraunce: "but well I am sure there hath one of her wounded knights lain with her this night; and therefore I will prove it, by my hands, that she is a traitoress unto my lord, King Arthur." "Beware what ye do," said Sir Launcelot, "for and ye say so, that he will prove it, it shall be taken at your hands." "My lord, Sir Launcelot," said Sir Meliagraunce, "be you aware also what ye do; for though ye are never so good a knight, as wot ye well that ye are renowned the best knight of the world, yet should ye be advised to do battle in a wrong quarrel. For God will have a stroke in every battle that is done." "As for that," said Sir Launcelot, "God is to be dreaded. But as to that I say nay plainly, that this night there was none of these ten wounded knights with my lady, Queen Guenever, and that will I prove with my hands, that ye say untruly in that now." "Hold!" said Sir Meliagraunce, "here is my glove, that she is a traitoress unto my lord, King Arthur." "And I receive your glove," said Sir Launcelot. And so they were sealed with their signets, and delivered to the ten knights. "Upon what day shall we do battle together?" said Sir Launcelot. "This day eight days," said Sir Meliagraunce, "in the field beside Westminster." "I am agreed," said Sir Launcelot. "But now," said Meliagraunce, "sith it is that we must do battle together, I beseech you, as ye are a noble knight, await me with no treason, nor no villainy, in the meanwhile." "Nor none for you, so God me help," said Sir Launcelot: "ye shall right well wit I was never of these conditions, for I report me unto all knights that ever knew me, I used never no treason; nor I loved never to be in the fellowship of no man that used treason." "Then let us go to dinner," said Sir Meliagraunce, "and after dinner ye and the Queen, and ye all, may ride unto Westminster." "I will well," said Sir Launcelot. And then Sir Meliagraunce said unto Sir Launcelot, "Please it you to see the features of this castle?" "With a good will," said Sir Launcelot. And then they went together from chamber to chamber: for Sir Launcelot dreaded no perils. For ever a man of worship and of prowess dreadeth always perils

least; for they ween that every man is as they be; but always he that dealeth with treason putteth a man oft in great danger. So it befell Sir Launcelot that no peril dreaded. And, as he went with Sir Meliagraunce, he trod on a trap, and the board rolled, and therewith Sir Launcelot fell down more than ten fathoms into a cave, upon straw. And then Sir Meliagraunce departed, and made semblance as though he had no wist where he was. And when Sir Launcelot was thus missed, they marvelled where he was become; and then Queen Guenever, and many of them, deemed that he had departed, as he was wont to do suddenly. For Sir Meliagraunce made suddenly to put out of the way Sir Launcelot's horse, that they might all understand that Sir Launcelot was departed suddenly. So it past forth until after dinner, and then Sir Lavaine would not stint until that he had ordained horse-litters for the wounded knights, that they might be laid in them; and so with the Queen, and them all, both ladies and gentlewomen, and many other went to Westminster. And the knights told unto King Arthur how Sir Meliagraunce had appealed the Queen of high treason; and how Sir Launcelot had received the glove of him, and this day eight days they shall do battle together afore you. "By my head," said King Arthur, "I am afraid that Sir Meliagraunce hath taken upon him a great charge: but where is Sir Launcelot?" said the King. "Sir," said they all, "we wit not where he is; but we deem he is ridden to some adventures, as he is oftentimes wont to do, for he hath Sir Lavaine's horse." "Let him be," said the King; "he will be found, unless he be trapped with some treason."

IX.

Now return we unto Sir Launcelot, lying within that cave, in great pain. And every day there came a lady and brought him his meat and his drink, and wooed him to have his love; and ever the noble knight, Sir Launcelot, said her nay. "Sir Launcelot," said she, "ye are not wise, for ye may never come out of this prison, but if ye have my help; and also your lady, Queen Guenever, shall be burnt in your default, unless that you be there at the day of battle." "God defend it," said Sir Launcelot, "That she should be burnt in my default; and if that be so," said Sir Launcelot, "that I may not be there, it shall be well understood, of both the King and of the Queen, and with all men of worship, that I am dead, or sick, or else in prison; for all men that know me will say for me, that I am in some evil case, if I be not there that day: and well I wot there is some good knight, either of my blood, or else some other that loveth me, that will take my quarrel in hand; and, therefore," said Sir Launcelot, "wit ye well that ye shall not fear me: and if there were no more women in this land but you, I would not have your love." "Then art thou shamed and destroyed for ever," said the lady. "As for world's shame," said Sir Launcelot, "Jesu defend me; and as for my distress, it is welcome whatsoever it be that God sendeth me." So she came unto Sir Launcelot that same day that the battle should be, and said to him, "Sir Launcelot, me thinketh ye are too strong hearted; but wouldest thou kiss me once, I would deliver thee and thine armour, and the best horse that is within Sir Meliagraunce's stable." "As for to kiss you," said Sir Launcelot, "I may do that and lose no worship; and wit you well, and I understand there was any disworship for to kiss you, I would not do it." Then he kissed her, and then she gat him, and brought him to his armour. And when he was armed she brought him to a stable, whereas stood twelve good coursers, and bade him choose the best. Then Sir Launcelot looked upon a white courser which liked him best; and anon he commanded the keeper fast to saddle him with the best saddle of war that was there: and so it was done as he commanded. Then gat he his spear in his hand, and his sword by his side, and commended the lady to God, and said, "Lady, for this good deed I shall do you service, if ever it be in my power."

X.

Now leave we Sir Launcelot galloping all that he might, and speak we of Queen Guenever that was brought to a fire to have been burnt; for Sir Meliagraunce was sure him thought that Sir Launcelot should not be at that battle; and, therefore, he ever cried upon King Arthur for to do him justice, or else for to bring forth Sir Launcelot. Then was the King and all the court full sore abashed and shamed, that the Queen should be burnt in the default of Sir Launcelot. "My good lord, King Arthur," said Sir Lavaine, "ye may right well understand that it is not well with my lord, Sir Launcelot, for and he were alive, so that he be not sick or in prison, wit ye well that he would be here, for never heard ye that ever he failed his part for whom he should do battle; and, therefore, now," said Sir Lavaine, "my lord, King Arthur, I beseech you give me license to do battle here this day for my lord and master, and for to save my lady, the Queen." "Gramercy, gentle knight, Sir Lavaine," said King Arthur, "for I dare say what Sir Meliagraunce putteth upon my lady, Queen Guenever, is wrong; for I have spoken with all the ten wounded knights, and there is not one of them, and he were whole, and able to do battle, but that he would prove upon Sir Meliagraunce's body that it is false that he putteth upon the Queen." "So shall I," said Sir Lavaine, "in defending my lord, Sir Launcelot, and ye will give me leave." "Now I give you leave," said King Arthur, "and do your best; for I dare well say there is some treason done to Sir Launcelot." Then was Sir Lavaine horsed, and suddenly at the list's end he rode to perform this battle. And right as the heralds should cry, "*Laissez les aller,*" right so came in Sir Launcelot, driving with all the force of his horse. And so King Arthur cried, "Go and abide." Then was Sir Launcelot called before King Arthur on horseback, and there he told openly before the King, and all them that were present, how Sir Meliagraunce had served him first and last. And when the King and the Queen and all the lords knew of the treason of Sir Meliagraunce, they were all ashamed on his behalf. And then was Queen Guenever sent for, and set by the King in great trust of her champion. And so then there was no more to say, but Sir Launcelot and Sir Meliagraunce dressed them unto battle, and took their spears, and so they came together as thunder, and there Sir Launcelot bore him down quite over his horse's croup: and then Sir Launcelot alighted and dressed his shield on his shoulder, with his sword in his hand: and Sir Meliagraunce in the same wise dressed him unto Sir Launcelot. And there they smote many strokes together; and at the last Sir Launcelot smote him

such a buffet upon the helm, that he fell on the one side to the ground, and then he cried upon him aloud, "Most noble knight, Sir Launcelot du Lake, I pray you save my life, for I yield me unto you; and I beseech you, as ye be a knight and fellow of the Round Table, slay me not, for I yield me as an overcome knight; and, whether I shall live or die, I put me in the King's hands and yours." Then Sir Launcelot wist not what to do, for he had rather than all the good of the world he might have been revenged upon Sir Meliagraunce. And then Sir Launcelot looked towards Queen Guenever if he might espy, by any sign or countenance, what he should have done: and then the Queen wagged her head upon Sir Launcelot, as though she should say, slay him. Full well knew Sir Launcelot by the wagging of the head, that she would have him dead. Then Sir Launcelot bade him "arise for shame, and perform that battle to the uttermost." "Nay," said Sir Meliagraunce, "I will never arise until that ye take me as yielden and recreant." "I shall proffer you large proffers," said Sir Launcelot; "that is to say, I shall unarm my head, and the left quarter of my body, all that may be unarmed, and I shall let bind my left hand behind me, so that it shall not help me; and right so I shall do battle with you." When Sir Meliagraunce heard that, he started up on his legs, and said on high, "My lord, King Arthur, take heed to this proffer, for I will take it, and let him be disarmed and bound according unto his proffer." "What say ye," said King Arthur unto Sir Launcelot; "will ye abide by your proffer?" "Yea, my lord," said Sir Launcelot, "I will never go from that I have once said." Then the knights' porters of the field disarmed Sir Launcelot, first his head, and after his left arm, and his left side; and then they bound his left arm behind his back, without shield or any thing, and then were they put together. Wit ye well, there was many a lady and knight marvelled that Sir Launcelot would jeopard himself in such wise. Then Sir Meliagraunce came with his sword all on high, and Sir Launcelot showed him openly his bare head, and the bare left side; and when he weened to have smitten him upon the head, then lightly he avoided the left leg and the left side, and put his right hand and his sword to that stroke, and so put it aside with great sleight; then with great force, Sir Launcelot smote him upon the helmet such a buffet, that the stroke carved the head in two parts. Then there was no more to do, but he was drawn out of the field; and, at the instance of the knights of the Round Table, the King suffered him to be buried, and the mention made upon him, and for what cause he was slain. And then the King and the Queen made much of Sir Launcelot, and more he was cherished than ever he was before.

Exercises

1. The stories of King Arthur and the knights of the round table were immensely popular in fourteenth-century England and France. What values do they suggest that may explain some of their popularity?
2. As a Broadway musical and Hollywood movie, *Camelot* has been very popular in our own time. Are the tales of Arthur and Camelot popular in our day for the same reasons? If there are differences, what are they and how might they be explained?

THE DIVINE COMEDY

Dante Alighieri (1265–1321)

At the outset, let us agree that reading the *Commedia* is no easy task. Dante himself recognized this when, in writing to a friend and patron, he said:

> The meaning of this work is not simple . . . for we obtain one meaning from the letter of it, and another from that which the letter signifies; and the first is called *literal,* but the other *allegorical* or *mystical.* . . .
>
> The subject of the whole work, then, taken in the literal sense is "the state of the soul after death straightforwardly affirmed," for the development of the whole work hinges on and about that. But, if, indeed, the work is taken *allegorically,* its subject is: "Man, as by good or ill deserts, in the exercise of his free choice, he becomes liable to rewarding or punishing justice."

On two scores, the rewards of reading the *Commedia* justify the effort. First, it represents the finest statement of the medieval synthesis that we have; it is comparable to Chartres Cathedral or the *Summa Theologica* of St. Thomas. Second, and more important, it presents one of the half-dozen very great insights into the nature and meaning of human life in all of literature or art. It is meaningful to us in the twentieth century not only as a splendid historical document, but as living literature.

Its form represents as tight a discipline as we know in literature, for it takes its shape around the number three. It is written in *terza rima,* a form preserved in the translations taken from the Hell and Paradise as excerpts from those sections are given here. It is written in three great sections: Hell, Purgatory, and Heaven (figure 14.3). Within the first of these sections we find one introductory canto, followed by thirty-three more cantos, and in each of the following sections thirty-three cantos are to be found. The sum is the number one hundred, the perfect and complete number.

Insofar as its meaning is concerned, the poem will speak for itself. We must understand, however, that Dante accepts the idea that all of nature is in motion, following the laws, the love, and the wisdom of God. Of all the orders of being, humans alone have both free will and the potentiality of turning from the way of God. With free will comes the responsibility of choosing and accepting the consequences of choice. People cannot logically argue that they are innocent victims at the mercy of heredity or environment. With the gift of intellect and free will, each person must assume the full weight of making choices, and must, as well, accept the idea that the choices are important and that they do make a difference for others, and most particularly for oneself.

Considered by many scholars as the best available version, the verse translation is by poet and scholar Allen Mandelbaum.

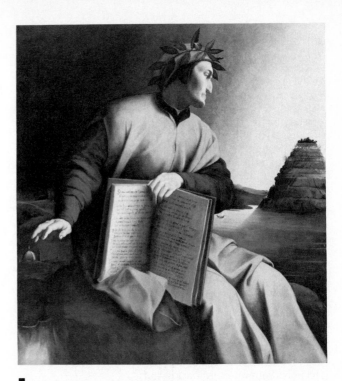

FIGURE 14.4 *Florentine school,* Allegorical Portrait of Dante, *ca. 1575–1585, 50″ × 47¼″. Samuel H. Kress Collection. National Gallery of Art, Washington, D.C. On the open book are inscribed the first forty-eight lines of Canto XXV of* Paradise *in which Dante yearns to return from exile to be honored by the Florentines. In the right background is the mountain of Purgatory, behind which is the divine glow of Paradise. With his right hand over the dome of Florence Cathedral, the poet tries to protect his beloved city from the flames of Hell.*

Hell

Canto I

The Story

The voyager-narrator astray by night in a dark forest. Morning and the sunlit hill. Three beasts that impede his ascent. The encounter with Virgil, who offers his guidance and an alternative path through two of the three realms the voyager must visit.

When I had journeyed half of our life's way,
I found myself within a shadowed forest,
for I had lost the path that does not stray.
    Ah, it is hard to speak of what it was,   4
that savage forest, dense and difficult,
which even in recall renews my fear:
    so bitter—death is hardly more severe!   7
But to retell the good discovered there,
I'll also tell the other things I saw.

I cannot clearly say how I had entered   10
the wood; I was so full of sleep just at
the point where I abandoned the true path.

But when I'd reached the bottom of a hill—   13
it rose along the boundary of the valley
that had harassed my heart with so much fear—

I looked on high and saw its shoulders clothed   16
already by the rays of that same planet
which serves to lead men straight along all roads.

At this my fear was somewhat quieted;   19
for through the night of sorrow I had spent,
the lake within my heart felt terror present.

And just as he who, with exhausted breath,   22
having escaped from sea to shore, turns back
to watch the dangerous waters he has quit,

so did my spirit, still a fugitive,   25
turn back to look intently at the pass
that never has let any man survive.

I let my tired body rest awhile.   28
Moving again, I tried the lonely slope—
my firm foot always was the one below.

And almost where the hillside starts to rise—   31
look there!—a leopard, very quick and lithe,
a leopard covered with a spotted hide.

He did not disappear from sight, but stayed;   34
indeed, he so impeded my ascent
that I had often to turn back again.

The time was the beginning of the morning;   37
the sun was rising now in fellowship
with the same stars that had escorted it

when Divine Love first moved those things of beauty;   40
so that the hour and the gentle season
gave me good cause for hopefulness on seeing

that beast before me with his speckled skin;   43
but hope was hardly able to prevent
the fear I felt when I beheld a lion.

His head held high and ravenous with hunger—   46
even the air around him seemed to shudder—
this lion seemed to make his way against me.

And then a she-wolf showed herself; she seemed   49
to carry every craving in her leanness;
she had already brought despair to many.

The very sight of her so weighted me   52
with fearfulness that I abandoned hope
of ever climbing up that mountain slope.

Even as he who glories while he gains   55
will, when the time has come to tally loss,
lament with every thought and turn despondent,

so was I when I faced that restless beast,   58
which, even as she stalked me, step by step
had thrust me back to where the sun is speechless.

While I retreated down to lower ground,   61
before my eyes there suddenly appeared
one who seemed faint because of the long silence.

When I saw him in that vast wilderness,   64
"Have pity on me," were the words I cried,
"whatever you may be—a shade, a man."

He answered me: "Not man; I once was man.   67
Both of my parents came from Lombardy,
and both claimed Mantua as native city.

And I was born, though late, *sub Julio,*   70
and lived in Rome under the good Augustus—
the season of the false and lying gods.

I was a poet, and I sang the righteous   73
son of Anchises who had come from Troy
when flames destroyed the pride of Ilium.

But why do you return to wretchedness?   76
Why not climb up the mountain of delight,
the origin and cause of every joy?"

"And are you then that Virgil, you the fountain   79
that freely pours so rich a stream of speech?"
I answered him with shame upon my brow.

"O light and honor of all other poets,   82
may my long study and the intense love
that made me search your volume serve me now.

You are my master and my author, you—   85
the only one from whom my writing drew
the noble style for which I have been honored.

You see the beast that made me turn aside;   88
help me, o famous sage, to stand against her,
for she has made my blood and pulses shudder."

"It is another path that you must take,"   91
he answered when he saw my tearfulness,
"if you would leave this savage wilderness;

the beast that is the cause of your outcry   94
allows no man to pass along her track,
but blocks him even to the point of death;

her nature is so squalid, so malicious   97
that she can never sate her greedy will;
when she has fed, she's hungrier than ever.

She mates with many living souls and shall   100
yet mate with many more, until the Greyhound
arrives, inflicting painful death on her.

That Hound will never feed on land or pewter,   103
but find his fare in wisdom, love, and virtue;
his place of birth shall be between two felts.

He will restore low-lying Italy   106
for which the maid Camilla died of wounds,
and Nisus, Turnus, and Euryalus.

And he will hunt that beast through every city   109
until he thrusts her back again to Hell,
from which she was first sent above by envy.

Therefore, I think and judge it best for you   112
to follow me, and I shall guide you, taking
you from this place through an eternal place,

where you shall hear the howls of desperation   115
and see the ancient spirits in their pain,
as each of them laments his second death;

and you shall see those souls who are content   118
within the fire, for they hope to reach—
whenever that may be—the blessed people.

If you would then ascend as high as these,   121
a soul more worthy than I am will guide you;
I'll leave you in her care when I depart,

because that Emperor who reigns above,   124
since I have been rebellious to His law,
will not allow me entry to His city.

He governs everywhere, but rules from there;   127
there is His city, His high capital:
o happy those He chooses to be there!"

And I replied: "O poet—by that God   130
whom you had never come to know—I beg you,
that I may flee this evil and worse evils.

to lead me to the place of which you spoke,   133
that I may see the gateway of Saint Peter
and those whom you describe as sorrowful."

Then he set out, and I moved on behind him.   136

Canto II

The Story

The following evening. Invocation to the Muses. The narrator's questioning of his worthiness to visit the deathless world. Virgil's comforting explanation that he has been sent to help Dante by three Ladies of Heaven. The voyager heartened. Their setting out.

Canto III

The Story

The inscription above the Gate of Hell. The ante-Inferno, where the shades of those who lived without praise and without blame now intermingle with the neutral angels. He who made the great refusal. The River Acheron. Charon. Dante's loss of his senses as the earth trembles.

THROUGH ME THE WAY INTO THE SUFFERING CITY,
THROUGH ME THE WAY TO THE ETERNAL PAIN,
THROUGH ME THE WAY THAT RUNS AMONG THE LOST.

JUSTICE URGED ON MY HIGH ARTIFICER;   4
MY MAKER WAS DIVINE AUTHORITY,
THE HIGHEST WISDOM, AND THE PRIMAL LOVE.

BEFORE ME NOTHING BUT ETERNAL THINGS   7
WERE MADE, AND IN ENDURE ETERNALLY.
ABANDON EVERY HOPE, WHO ENTER HERE.

These words—their aspect was obscure—I read   10
inscribed above a gateway, and I said:
"Master, their meaning is difficult for me."

And he to me, as one who comprehends: 13
"Here one must leave behind all hesitation;
here every cowardice must meet its death.

For we have reached the place of which I spoke,   16
where you will see the miserable people,
those who have lost the good of the intellect."

And when, with gladness in his face, he placed   19
his hand upon my own, to comfort me,
he drew me in among the hidden things.

Here sighs and lamentations and loud cries   22
were echoing across the starless air,
so that, as soon as I set out, I wept.

Strange utterances, horrible pronouncements,   25
accents of anger, words of suffering,
and voices shrill and faint, and beating hands—

all went to make a tumult that will whirl   28
forever through that turbid, timeless air,
like sand that eddies when a whirlwind swirls.

And I—my head oppressed by horror—said: 31
"Master, what is it that I hear? Who are
those people so defeated by their pain?"

And he to me: "This miserable way   34
is taken by the sorry souls of those
who lived without disgrace and without praise.

They now commingle with the coward angels,   37
the company of those who were not rebels
nor faithful to their God, but stood apart.

The heavens, that their beauty not be lessened,   40
have cast them out, nor will deep Hell receive them—
even the wicked cannot glory in them."

And I: "What is it, master, that oppresses   43
these souls, compelling them to wail so loud?"
He answered: "I shall tell you in few words.

Those who are here can place no hope in death,   46
and their blind life is so abject that they
are envious of every other fate.

The world will let no fame of theirs endure;   49

both justice and compassion must disdain them;
let us not talk of them, but look and pass."

And I, looking more closely, saw a banner   52
that, as it wheeled about, raced on—so quick
that any respite seemed unsuited to it.

Behind that banner trailed so long a file   55
of people—I should never have believed
that death could have unmade so many souls.

After I had identified a few,   58
I saw and recognized the shade of him
who made, through cowardice, the great refusal.

At once I understood with certainty: 61
this company contained the cowardly,
hateful to God and to His enemies.

These wretched ones, who never were alive,   64
went naked and were stung again, again
by horseflies and by wasps that circled them.

The insects streaked their faces with their blood,   67
which, mingled with their tears, fell at their feet,
where it was gathered up by sickening worms.

And then, looking beyond them, I could see   70
a crowd along the bank of a great river;
at which I said: "Allow me now to know

who are these people—master—and what law   73
has made them seem so eager for the crossing,
as I can see despite the feeble light."

And he to me: "When we have stopped along   76
the melancholy shore of Acheron,
then all these matters will be plain to you."

At that, with eyes ashamed, downcast, and fearing   79
that what I said had given him offense,
I did not speak until we reached the river.

And here, advancing toward us, in a boat,   82
an aged man—his hair was white with years—
was shouting: "Woe to you, corrupted souls!

Forget your hope of ever seeing Heaven: 85
I come to lead you to the other shore,
to the eternal dark, to fire and frost.

And you approaching there, you living soul,   88
keep well away from these—they are the dead."
But when he saw I made no move to go,

he said: "Another way and other harbors—   91
not here—will bring you passage to your shore:
a lighter craft will have to carry you."

My guide then: "Charon, don't torment yourself: 94
our passage has been willed above, where One
can do what He has willed; and ask no more."

Now silence fell upon the wooly cheeks   97
of Charon, pilot of the livid marsh,
whose eyes were ringed about with wheels of flame.

But all those spirits, naked and exhausted,   100
had lost their color, and they gnashed their teeth
as soon as they heard Charon's cruel words;

they execrated God and their own parents   103
and humankind, and then the place and time
of their conception's seed and of their birth.

Then they forgathered, huddled in one throng,   106
weeping aloud along that wretched shore
which waits for all who have no fear of God.

The demon Charon, with his eyes like embers,   109
by signaling to them, has all embark;
his oar strikes anyone who stretches out.

As, in the autumn, leaves detach themselves,   112
first one and then the other, till the bough
sees all its fallen garments on the ground,

similarly, the evil seed of Adam   115
descended from the shoreline one by one,
when signaled, as a falcon—called—will come.

So do they move across the darkened waters; 118
even before they reach the farther shore,
new ranks already gather on this bank.

"My son," the gracious master said to me, 121
"Those who have died beneath the wrath of God,
all these assemble here from every country;

and they are eager for the river crossing 124
because celestial justice spurs them on,
so that their fear is turned into desire.

No good soul ever takes its passage here; 127
therefore, if Charon has complained of you,
by now you can be sure what his words mean."

And after this was said, the darkened plain 130
quaked so tremendously—the memory
of terror then, bathes me in sweat again.

A whirlwind burst out of the tear-drenched earth, 133
a wind that crackled with a bloodred light,
a light that overcame all of my senses;

and like a man whom sleep has seized, I fell. 136

Canto IV

The Story

Dante's awakening to the First Circle, or Limbo,
inhabited by those who were worthy but lived before
Christianity and/or without baptism. The welcoming of
Virgil and Dante by Homer, Horace, Ovid, Lucan. The
catalogue of other great-hearted spirits in the noble castle
of Limbo.

The heavy sleep within my head was smashed
by an enormous thunderclap, so that
I started up as one whom force awakens;

I stood erect and turned my rested eyes 4
from side to side, and I stared steadily
to learn what place it was surrounding me.

In truth I found myself upon the brink 7
of an abyss, the melancholy valley
containing thundering, unending wailings.

That valley, dark and deep and filled with mist, 10
is such that, though I gazed into its pit,
I was unable to discern a thing.

"Let us descend into the blind world now," 13
the poet, who was deathly pale, began;
"I shall go first and you will follow me."

But I, who'd seen the change in his complexion, 16
said: "How shall I go on if you are frightened,
you who have always helped dispel my doubts?"

And he to me: "The anguish of the people 19
whose place is here below, has touched my face
with the compassion you mistake for fear.

Let us go on, the way that waits is long." 22
So he set out, and so he had me enter
on that first circle girdling the abyss.

Here, for as much as hearing could discover, 25
there was no outcry louder than the sighs
that caused the everlasting air to tremble.

The sighs arose from sorrow without torments, 28
out of the crowds—the many multitudes—
of infants and of women and of men.

The kindly master said: "Do you not ask 31
who are these spirits whom you see before you?
I'd have you know, before you go ahead,

they did not sin; and yet, though they have merits, 34
that's not enough, because they lacked baptism,
the portal of the faith that you embrace.

And if they lived before Christianity, 37
they did not worship God in fitting ways;
and of such spirits I myself am one.

For these defects, and for no other evil, 40
we now are lost and punished just with this:
we have no hope and yet we live in longing."

Great sorrow seized my heart on hearing him, 43
for I had seen some estimable men
among the souls suspended in that limbo.

"Tell me, my master, tell me, lord," I then 46
began because I wanted to be certain
of that belief which vanquishes all errors,

"did any ever go—by his own merit 49
or others'—from this place toward blessedness?"
And he, who understood my covert speech,

replied: "I was new-entered on this state 52
when I beheld a Great Lord enter here;
the crown he wore, a sign of victory.

He carried off the shade of our first father, 55
of his son Abel, and the shade of Noah,
of Moses, the obedient legislator,

of father Abraham, David the king, 58
of Israel, his father, and his sons,
and Rachel, she for whom he worked so long,

and many others—and He made them blessed; 61
and I should have you know that, before them,
there were no human souls that had been saved."

We did not stay our steps although he spoke; 64
we still continued onward through the wood—
the wood, I say, where many spirits thronged.

Our path had not gone far beyond the point 67
where I had slept, when I beheld a fire
win out against a hemisphere of shadows.

We still were at a little distance from it, 70
but not so far I could not see in part
that honorable men possessed that place.

"O you who honor art and science both, 73
who are these souls whose dignity has kept
their way of being, separate from the rest?"

And he to me: "The honor of their name, 76
which echoes up above within your life,
gains Heaven's grace, and that advances them."

Meanwhile there was a voice that I could hear: 79
"Pay honor to the estimable poet;
his shadow, which had left us, now returns."

After that voice was done, when there was silence, 82
I saw four giant shades approaching us;
in aspect, they were neither sad nor joyous.

My kindly master then began by saying: 85
"Look well at him who holds that sword in hand,
who moves before the other three as lord.

That shade is Homer, the consummate poet; 88
the other one is Horace, satirist;
the third is Ovid, and the last is Lucan.

Because each of these spirts shares with me 91
the name called out before by the lone voice,
they welcome me—and, doing that, do well."

And so I saw that splendid school assembled, 94
led by the lord of song incomparable,
who like an eagle soars above the rest.

Soon after they had talked awhile together, 97
they turned to me, saluting cordially;
and having witnessed this, my master smiled;

and even greater honor then was mine, 100
for they invited me to join their ranks—
I was the sixth among such intellects.

So did we move along and toward the light, 103
talking of things about which silence here
is just as seemly as our speech was there.

We reached the base of an exalted castle,   106
encircled seven times by towering walls,
defended all around by a fair stream.

We forded this as if upon hard ground;   109
I entered seven portals with these sages;
we reached a meadow of green flowering plants.

The people here had eyes both grave and slow;   112
their features carried great authority;
they spoke infrequently, with gentle voices.

We drew aside to one part of the meadow,   115
an open place both high and filled with light,
and we could see all those who were assembled.

Facing me there, on the enameled green,   118
great-hearted souls were shown to me and I
still glory in my having witnessed them.

I saw Electra with her many comrades,   121
among whom I knew Hektor and Aeneas,
and Caesar, in his armor, falcon-eyed.

I saw Camilla and Penthesilea   124
and, on the other side, saw King Latinus,
who sat beside Lavinia, his daughter.

I saw that Brutus who drove Tarquin out,   127
Lucretia, Julia, Marcia, and Cornelia,
and, solitary, set apart, Saladin.

When I had raised my eyes a little higher,   130
I saw the master of the men who know,
seated in philosophic family.

There all look up to him, all do him honor: 133
there I beheld both Sokrates and Plato,
closest to him, in front of all the rest;

Democritus, who ascribes the world to chance,   136
Diogenes, Empedocles, and Zeno,
and Thales, Anaxagoras, Heraklitos;

I saw the good collector of medicinals,   139
I mean Dioscorides; and I saw Orpheus,
and Tully, Linus, moral Seneca;

and Euclid the geometer, and Ptolemy,   142
Hippokrates and Galen, Avicenna,
Averroës, of the great Commentary.

I cannot here describe them all in full;   145
my ample theme impels me onward so:
what's told is often less than the event.

The company of six divides in two;   148
my knowing guide leads me another way,
beyond the quiet, into trembling air.

And I have reached a part where no thing gleams.   151

Canto V

The Story

*The Second Circle, where the Lustful are forever buffeted
by violent storm. Minos. The catalogue of carnal sinners.
Francesca da Rimini and her brother-in-law, Paolo
Malatesta. Francesca's tale of their love and death, at
which Dante faints.*

So I descended from the first enclosure
down to the second cirlce, that which girdles
less space but grief more great, that goads to weeping.

There dreadful Minos stands, gnashing his teeth: 4
examining the sins of those who enter,
he judges and assigns as his tail twines.

I mean that when the spirit born to evil   7
appears before him, it confesses all;
and he, the connoisseur of sin, can tell

the depth in Hell appropriate to it;   10
as many times as Minos wraps his tail
around himself, that marks the sinner's level.

Always there is a crowd that stands before him: 13
each soul in turn advances toward that judgment;
they speak and hear, then they are cast below.

Arresting his extraordinary task,   16
Minos, as soon as he had seen me, said:
"O you who reach this house of suffering,

be careful how you enter, whom you trust;   19
the gate is wide, but do not be deceived!"
To which my guide replied: "But why protest?

Do not attempt to block his fated path: 22
our passage has been willed above, where One
can do what He has willed; and ask no more."

Now notes of desperation have begun   25
to overtake my hearing; now I come
where mighty lamentation beats against me.

I reached a place where every light is muted,   28
which bellows like the sea beneath a tempest,
when it is battered by opposing winds.

The hellish hurricane, which never rests,   31
drives on the spirits with its violence:
wheeling and pounding, it harasses them.

When they come up against the ruined slope,   34
then there are cries and wailing and lament,
and there they curse the force of the divine.

I learned that those who undergo this torment   37
are damned because they sinned within the flesh,
subjecting reason to the rule of lust.

And as, in the cold season, starlings' wings   40
bear them along in broad and crowded ranks,
so does that blast bear on the guilty spirits:

now here, now there, now down, now up, it drives
them.   43
There is no hope that ever comforts them—
no hope for rest and none for lesser pain.

And just as cranes in flight will chant their lays,   46
arraying their long file across the air,
so did the shades I saw approaching, borne

by that assailing wind, lament and moan;   49
so that I asked him: "Master, who are those
who suffer punishment in this dark air?"

"The first of those about whose history   52
you want to know," my master then told me,
"once ruled as empress over many nations.

Her vice of lust became so customary   55
that she made license licit in her laws
to free her from the scandal she had caused.

She is Semíramis, of whom we read   58
that she was Ninus' wife and his successor:
she held the land the Sultan now commands.

That other spirit killed herself for love,   61
and she betrayed the ashes of Sychaeus;
the wanton Cleopatra follows next.

See Helen, for whose sake so many years   64
of evil had to pass; see great Achilles,
who finally met love—in his last battle.

See Paris, Tristan . . ."—and he pointed out   67
and named to me more than a thousand shades
departed from our life because of love.

No sooner had I heard my teacher name   70
the ancient ladies and the knights, than pity
seized me, and I was like a man astray.

My first words: "Poet, I should willingly   73
speak with those two who go together there
and seem so lightly carried by the wind."

And he to me: "You'll see when they draw closer   76
to us, and then you may appeal to them
by that love which impels them. They will come."

No sooner had the wind bent them toward us 79
than I urged on my voice: "O battered souls,
if One does not forbid it, speak with us."

Even as doves when summoned by desire, 82
borne forward by their will, move through the air
with wings uplifted, still, to their sweet nest,

those spirits left the ranks where Dido suffers, 85
approaching us through the malignant air;
so powerful had been my loving cry.

"O living being, gracious and benign, 88
who through the darkened air have come to visit
our souls that stained the world with blood, if He

who rules the universe were friend to us, 91
then we should pray to Him to give you peace,
for you have pitied our atrocious state.

Whatever pleases you to hear and speak 94
will please us, too, to hear and speak with you,
now while the wind is silent, in this place.

The land where I was born lies on that shore 97
to which the Po together with the waters
that follow it descends to final rest.

Love, that can quickly seize the gentle heart, 100
took hold of him because of the fair body
taken from me—how that was done still wounds me.

Love, that releases no beloved from loving, 103
took hold of me so strongly through his beauty
that, as you see, it has not left me yet.

Love led the two of us unto one death. 106
Caïna waits for him who took our life."
These words were borne across from them to us.

When I had listened to those injured souls, 109
I bent my head and held it low until
the poet asked of me: "What are you thinking?"

When I replied, my words began: "Alas, 112
how many gentle thoughts, how deep a longing,
had led them to the agonizing pass!"

Then I addressed my speech again to them, 115
and I began: "Francesca, your afflications
move me to tears of sorrow and of pity.

But tell me, in the time of gentle sighs, 118
with what and in what way did Love allow you
to recognize your still uncertain longings?"

And she to me: "There is no greater sorrow 121
than thinking back upon a happy time
in misery—and this your teacher knows.

Yet if you long so much to understand 124
the first root of our love, then I shall tell
my tale to you as one who weeps and speaks.

One day, to pass the time away, we read 127
of Launcelot—how love had overcome him.
We were alone, and we suspected nothing.

And time and time again that reading led 130
our eyes to meet, and made our faces pale,
and yet one point alone defeated us.

When we had read how the desired smile 133
was kissed by one who was so true a lover,
this one, who never shall be parted from me,

while all his body trembled, kissed my mouth. 136
A Gallehault indeed, that book and he
who wrote it, too; that day we read no more."

And while one spirit said these words to me, 139
the other wept, so that—because of pity—
I fainted, as if I had met my death.

And then I fell as a dead body falls. 142

Cantos VI–XI

The Story

Dante finds the Gluttonous in the Third Circle, where they are flailed by cold and filthy rain. In the Fourth Circle the Avaricious and the Prodigal endlessly roll weights in circles while, in the Fifth Circle, the Wrathful and Sullen are tormented by the River Styx. The two poets are rowed across the Styx to the City of Dis but cannot enter without divine intervention. The Furies appear and threaten to unloose Medusa. Dante is frightened but a Heavenly Messenger appears to open the city gates. They go into the Sixth Circle where they see the burning tombs of the Heretics.

Canto XII

The Story

The Seventh Circle, First Ring: the Violent against their Neighbors. The Minotaur. The Centaurs, led by Chiron, who assigns Nessus to guide Dante and Virgil across the boiling river of blood (Phlegethon). In that river, Tyrants and Murderers, immersed, watched over by the Centaurs.

The place that we had reached for our descent
along the bank was alpine; what reclined
upon that bank would, too, repel all eyes.

Just like the toppled mass of rock that struck— 4
because of earthquake or eroded props—
the Adige on its flank, this side of Trent,

where from the mountain top from which it thrust 7
down to the plain, the rock is shattered so
that it permits a path for those above:

such was the passage down to that ravine. 10
And at the edge above the cracked abyss,
there lay outstretched the infamy of Crete,

conceived within the counterfeited cow; 13
and, catching sight of us, he bit himself
like one whom fury devastates within.

Turning to him, my sage cried out: "Perhaps 16
you think this is the Duke of Athens here,
who, in the world above, brought you your death.

Be off, you beast; this man who comes has not 19
been tutored by your sister; all he wants
in coming here is to observe your torments."

Just as the bull that breaks loose from its halter 22
the moment it receives the fatal stroke,
and cannot run but plunges back and forth,

so did I see the Minotaur respond; 25
and my alert guide cried: "Run toward the pass;
it's better to descend while he's berserk."

And so we made our way across that heap 28
of stones, which often moved beneath my feet
because my weight was somewhat strange for them.

While climbing down, I thought. He said: "You wonder, 31
perhaps, about that fallen mass, watched over
by the inhuman rage I have just quenched.

Now I would have you know: the other time 34
that I descended into lower Hell,
this mass of boulders had not yet collapsed;

but if I reason rightly, it was just 37
before the coming of the One who took
from Dis the highest circle's splendid spoils

that, on all sides, the steep and filthy valley 40
had trembled so, I thought the universe
felt love (by which, as some believe, the world

has often been converted into chaos);   43
and at that moment, here as well as elsewhere,
these ancient boulders toppled, in this way.

But fix your eyes below, upon the valley,   46
for now we near the stream of blood, where those
who injure others violently, boil."

O blind cupidity and insane anger,   49
which goad us on so much in our short life,
then steep us in such grief eternally!

I saw a broad ditch bent into an arc   52
so that it could embrace all of that plain,
precisely as my guide had said before;

between it and the base of the embankment   55
raced files of Centaurs who were armed with arrows,
as, in the world above, they used to hunt.

On seeing us descend, they all reined in;   58
and, after they had chosen bows and shafts,
three of their number moved out from their ranks;

and still far off, one cried: "What punishment   61
do you approach as you descend the slope?
But speak from there; if not, I draw my bow."

My master told him: "We shall make reply   64
only to Chiron, when we reach his side;
your hasty will has never served you well."

Then he nudged me and said: "That one is Nessus,   67
who died because of lovely Deianira
and of himself wrought vengeance for himself.

And in the middle, gazing at his chest,   70
is mighty Chiron, tutor of Achilles;
the third is Pholus, he who was so frenzied.

And many thousands wheel around the moat,   73
their arrows aimed at any soul that thrusts
above the blood more than its guilt allots."

By now we had drawn near those agile beasts;   76
Chiron drew out an arrow; with the notch,
he parted his beard back upon his jaws.

When he'd uncovered his enormous mouth,   79
he said to his companions: "Have you noticed
how he who walks behind moves what he touches?

Dead souls are not accustomed to do that."   82
And my good guide—now near the Centaur's chest,
the place where his two natures met—replied:

"He is indeed alive, and so alone   85
it falls to me to show him the dark valley.
Necessity has brought him here, not pleasure.

For she who gave me this new task was one   88
who had just come from singing halleluiah:
he is no robber; I am not a thief.

But by the Power that permits my steps   91
to journey on so wild a path, give us
one of your band, to serve as our companion;

and let him show us where to ford the ditch,   94
and let him bear this man upon his back,
for he's no spirit who can fly through air."

Then Chiron wheeled about and right and said   97
to Nessus: "Then, return and be their guide;
if other troops disturb you, fend them off."

Now, with our faithful escort, we advanced   100
along the bloodred, boiling ditch's banks,
beside the piercing cries of those who boiled.

I saw some who were sunk up to their brows,   103
and that huge Centaur said: "These are the tyrants
who plunged their hands in blood and plundering.

Here they lament their ruthless crimes; here are   106
both Alexander and the fierce Dionysius,
who brought such years of grief to Sicily.

That brow with hair so black is Ezzelino;   109
that other there, the blonde one, is Obizzo
of Este, he who was indeed undone,

within the world above, by his own stepson."   112

Then I turned to the poet, and he said:
"Now let him be your first guide, me your second."

A little farther on, the Centaur stopped   115
above a group that seemed to rise above
the boiling blood as far up as their throats.

He pointed out one shade, alone, apart,   118
and said: "Within God's bosom, he impaled
the heart that still drips blood upon the Thames."

Then I caught sight of some who kept their heads   121
and even their full chests above the tide;
among them—many whom I recognized.

And so the blood grew always shallower   124
until it only scorched the feet; and here
we found a place where we could ford the ditch.

"Just as you see that, on this side, the brook   127
continually thins," the Centaur said,
"so I should have you know the rivulet,

along the other side, will slowly deepen   130
its bed, until it reaches once again
the depth where tyranny must make lament.

And there divine justice torments Atilla,   133
he who was such a scourge upon the earth,
and Pyrrhus, Sextus; to eternity

it milks the tears that boiling brook unlocks   136
from Rinier of Corneto, Rinier Pazzo,
those two who waged such war upon the highroads."

Then he turned round and crossed the ford again.   139

Cantos XIII–XVII

The Story

In the Second Ring of the Seventh Circle they find the Violent against Themselves (Suicides) or against their Possessions (Squanderers). The Suicides are transformed into strange trees and the Squanderers are hounded by bitches. The Violent against God (Blasphemers, Sodomites) are, respectively, supine on fiery sands and reeling under rains of fire. Three Florentines tell Dante of the decadence of Florence. In the Third Ring are the Violent against Nature and Art (Userers), each seated beneath a fiery rain with purses around the neck.

Canto XVIII

The Story

The Eighth Circle, called Malebolge ("Evil-Pouches"), with its Ten Pouches, where "ordinary" fraud is punished. The First Pouch, with Panders and Seducers scourged by horned demons. Venedico Caccianemico. Jason. The Second Pouch, with Flatterers immersed in excrement. Alessio Interminei. Thais.

There is a place in Hell called Malebolge,
made all of stone the color of crude iron,
as is the wall that makes its way around it.

Right in the middle of this evil field   4
is an abyss, a broad and yawning pit,
whose structure I shall tell in its due place.

The belt, then, that extends between the pit   7
and that hard, steep wall's base is circular;
its bottom has been split into ten valleys.

Just as, where moat on moat surrounds a castle   10
in order to keep guard upon the walls,
the ground they occupy will form a pattern,

so did the valleys here form a design;   13
and as such fortresses have bridges running
right from their thresholds toward the outer bank,

so here, across the banks and ditches, ridges   16
ran from the base of that rock wall until
the pit that cuts them short and joins them all.

This was the place in which we found ourselves   19
when Geryon had put us down; the poet
held to the left, and I walked at his back.

Upon the right I saw new misery,   22
I saw new tortures and new torturers,
filling the first of Malebolge's moats.

Along its bottom, naked sinners moved,   25
to our side of the middle, facing us;
beyond that, they moved with us, but more quickly—

as, in the year of Jubilee, the Romans,   28
confronted by great crowds, contrived a plan
that let the people pass across the bridge,

for to one side went all who had their eyes   31
upon the Castle, heading toward St. Peter's,
and to the other, those who faced the Mount.

Both left and right, along the somber rock,   34
I saw horned demons with enormous whips,
who lashed those spirits cruelly from behind.

Ah, how their first strokes made those sinners lift   37
their heels! Indeed no sinner waited for
a second stroke to fall—or for a third.

And as I moved ahead, my eyes met those   40
of someone else, and suddenly I said:
"I was not spared the sight of him before."

And so I stayed my steps, to study him;   43
my gentle guide had stopped together with me
and gave me leave to take a few steps back.

That scourged soul thought that he could hide himself   46
by lowering his face; it helped him little,
for I said: "You, who cast your eyes upon

the ground, if these your features are not false,   49
must be Venèdico Caccianemico;
but what brings you to sauces so piquant?"

And he to me: "I speak unwillingly;   52
but your plain speech, that brings the memory
of the old world to me, is what compels me;

For it was I who led Ghisolabella   55
to do as the Marquis would have her do—
however they retell that filthy tale.

I'm not the only Bolognese who weeps here;   58
indeed, this place is so crammed full of us
that not so many tongues have learned to say

sipa between the Sàvena and Reno;   61
if you want faith and testament of that,
just call to mind our avaricious hearts."

And as he spoke, a demon cudgeled him   64
with his horsewhip and cried: "Be off, you pimp,
there are no women here for you to trick."

I joined my escort once again; and then   67
with but few steps, we came upon a place
where, from the bank, a rocky ridge ran out.

We climbed quite easily along that height;   70
and turning right upon its jagged back,
we took our leave of those eternal circlings.

When we had reached the point where that ridge opens   73
below to leave a passage for the lashed,
my guide said: "Stay, and make sure that the sight

of still more ill-born spirits strikes your eyes,   76
for you have not yet seen their faces, since
they have been moving in our own direction."

From the old bridge we looked down at the ranks   79
of those approaching from the other side;
they too were driven onward by the lash.

And my good master, though I had not asked,   82
urged me: "Look at that mighty one who comes
and does not seem to shed a tear of pain:

how he still keeps the image of a king!   85
That shade is Jason, who with heart and head
deprived the men of Colchis of their ram.

He made a landfall on the isle of Lemnos   88
after its women, bold and pitiless,
had given all their island males to death.

With polished words and love signs he took in   91
Hypsipyle, the girl whose own deception
had earlier deceived the other women.

And he abandoned her, alone and pregnant;   94
such guilt condemns him to such punishment; and for
Medea, too, revenge is taken.

With him go those who cheated so: this is   97
enough for you to know of that first valley
and of the souls it clamps within its jaws."

We were already where the narrow path   100
reaches and intersects the second bank
and serves as shoulder for another bridge.

We heard the people whine in the next pouch   103
and heard them as they snorted with their snouts;
we heard them use their palms to beat themselves.

And exhalations, rising from below,   106
stuck to the banks, encrusting them with mold,
and so waged war against both eyes and nose.

The bottom is so deep, we found no spot   109
to see it from, except by climbing up
the arch until the bridge's highest point.

This was the place we reached; the ditch beneath   112
held people plunged in excrement that seemed
as if it had been poured from human privies.

And while my eyes searched that abysmal sight,   115
I saw one with a head so smeared with shit,
one could not see if he were lay or cleric.

He howled: "Why do you stare more greedily   118
at me than at the others who are filthy?"
And I: "Because, if I remember right,

I have seen you before, with your hair dry;   121
and so I eye you more than all: you are
Alessio Interminei of Lucca."

The he continued, pounding on his pate: 124
"I am plunged here because of flatteries—
of which my tongue had such sufficiency."

At which my guide advised me: "See you thrust   127
your head a little farther to the front,
so that your eyes can clearly glimpse the face

of that besmirched, bedraggled harridan   130
who scratches at herself with shit-filled nails,
and now she crouches, now she stands upright.

That is Thaïs, the harlot who returned   133
her lover's question, 'Are you very grateful
to me?' by saying, 'Yes, enormously.' "

And now our sight has had its fill of this."   136

Cantos XIX–XXXIII

The Story

The Simonists are in the Eighth Circle (including Pope Nicholas III), as are the Diviners, Astrologers, and Magicians, each of the latter with their heads turned backwards. Further on in the same circle they see Swindlers plunged in boiling pitch, Hypocrites clothed in lead cloaks, Thieves bitten by serpents, and the Fraudulent Counselors (including Ulysses and Diomedes) clothed in eternal flames. The Sowers of Scandal and Schism (including Mohammed and Ali), Alchemists plagued by scabs, Counterfeiters, and Liars occupy the remainder of the circle. The poets pass to the final circle, the Ninth, and gaze down into the central pit of Hell. Two giants lower them to the icy floor, where they see Traitors to their Kin and Traitors against their Guests.

Canto XXXIV

The Story

The Ninth Circle, Fourth Ring, called Judecca, where Traitors against their Benefactors are fully covered by ice. Dis, or Lucifer, emperor of that kingdom, his three mouths rending Judas, Brutus, and Cassius. Descent of Virgil and Dante down Lucifer's body to the other, southern hemisphere. Their vision of the stars.

"*Vexilla regis prodeunt inferni*
toward us; and therefore keep your eyes ahead,"
my master said, "to see if you can spy him."
      Just as, when night falls on our hemisphere   4
or when a heavy fog is blowing thick,
a windmill seems to wheel when seen far off,
      so then I seemed to see that sort of structure.   7
And next, because the wind was strong, I shrank
behind my guide; there was no other shelter.
      And now—with fear I set it down in meter—   10
I was where all the shades were fully covered
but visible as wisps of straw in glass.
      There some lie flat and others stand erect,   13
one on his head, and one upon his soles;
and some bend face to feet, just like a bow.
      But after we had made our way ahead,   16
my master felt he now should have me see
that creature who was once a handsome presence;
      he stepped aside and made me stop, and said: 19
"Look! Here is Dis, and this the place where you
will have to arm yourself with fortitude."
      O reader, do not ask of me how I   22
grew faint and frozen then—I cannot write it:
all words would fall far short of what it was.
      I did not die, and I was not alive;   25
think for yourself, if you have any wit,
what I became, deprived of life and death.
      The emperor of the despondent kingdom   28
so towered from the ice, up from midchest,
that I match better with a giant's breadth
      than giants match the measure of his arms;   31
now you can gauge the size of all of him
if it is in proportion to such parts.
      If he was once as handsome as he now   34
is ugly and, despite that, raised his brows
against his Maker, one can understand
      how every sorrow has its source in him!   37

I marveled when I saw that, on his head,
he had three faces: one—in front—bloodred;
      and then another two that, just above   40
the midpoint of each shoulder, joined the first;
and at the crown, all three were reattached;
      the right looked somewhat yellow, somewhat white;   43
the left in its appearance was like those
who come from where the Nile, descending, flows.
      Beneath each face of his, two wings spread out,   46
as broad as suited so immense a bird:
I've never seen a ship with sails so wide.
      They had no feathers, but were fashioned like   49
a bat's; and he was agitating them,
so that three winds made their way out from him—
      and all Cocytus froze before those winds.   52
He wept out of six eyes; and down three chins,
tears gushed together with a bloody froth.
      Within each mouth—he used it like a grinder—   55
with gnashing teeth he tore to bits a sinner,
so that he brought much pain to three at once.
      The forward sinner found that biting nothing   58
when matched against the clawing, for at times
his back was stripped completely of its hide.
      "That soul up there who has to suffer most,"   61
my master said: "Judas Iscariot—
his head inside, he jerks his legs without.
      Of those two others, with their heads beneath,   64
the one who hangs from that black snout is Brutus—
see how he writhes and does not say a word!
      That other, who seems so robust, is Cassius.   67
But night is come again, and it is time
for us to leave; we have seen everything."
      Just as he asked, I clasped him round the neck;   70
and he watched for the chance of time and place,
and when the wings were open wide enough,
      he took fast hold upon the shaggy flanks   73
and then descended, down from tuft to tuft,
between the tangled hair and icy crusts.
      When we had reached the point at which the thigh   76
revolves, just at the swelling of the hip,
my guide, with heavy strain and rugged work,
      reversed his head to where his legs had been   79
and grappled on the hair, as one who climbs—
I thought that we were going back to Hell.
      "Hold tight," my master said—he panted like   82
a man exhausted—"it is by such stairs
that we must take our leave of so much evil."
      Then he slipped through a crevice in a rock   85
and placed me on the edge of it, to sit;
that done, he climbed toward me with steady steps.
      I raised my eyes, believing I should see   88
the half of Lucifer that I had left;
instead I saw him with his legs turned up;
      and if I then became perplexed, do let   91
the ignorant be judges—those who can
not understand what point I had just crossed.
      "Get up," my master said, "be on your feet: 94
the way is long, the path is difficult;
the sun's already back to middle tierce."
      It was no palace hall, the place in which   97
we found ourselves, but with its rough-hewn floor
and scanty light, a dungeon built by nature.
      "Before I free myself from this abyss,   100
master," I said when I had stood up straight,
"tell me enough to see I don't mistake:
      Where is the ice? And how is he so placed   103
head downward? Tell me, too, how has the sun
in so few hours gone from night to morning?"

And he to me: "You still believe you are 106
north of the center, where I grasped the hair
of the damned worm who pierces through the world.

And you were there as long as I descended; 109
but when I turned, that's when you passed the point
to which, from every part, all weights are drawn.

And now you stand beneath the hemisphere 112
opposing that which cloaks the great dry lands
and underneath whose zenith died the Man

whose birth and life were sinless in this world. 115
Your feet are placed upon a little sphere
that forms the other face of the Judecca.

Here it is morning when it's evening there; 118
and he whose hair has served us as a ladder
is still fixed, even as he was before.

This was the side on which he fell from Heaven; 121
for fear of him, the land that once loomed here
made of the sea a veil and rose into

our hemisphere; and that land which appears 124
upon this side—perhaps to flee from him—
left here this hollow space and hurried upward."

There is a place below, the limit of 127
that cave, its farthest point from Beelzebub,
a place one cannot see: it is discovered

by ear—there is a sounding stream that flows 130
along the hollow of a rock eroded
by winding waters and the slope is easy.

My guide and I came on that hidden road 133
to make our way back into the bright world;
and with no care for any rest, we climbed—

he first, I following—until I saw, 136
through a round opening, some of those things
of beauty Heaven bears. It was from there

that we emerged, to see—once more—the stars. 139

Dante's Ultimate Vision

Dante has ascended the Mountain of Purgatory and, led by Beatrice, has moved through the spheres of the heavens, where he has been instructed in the nature of God's order for the universe; in his own spirit he has experienced this love, order, and wisdom. Finally they have reached the Empyrean, beyond the last sphere of the heavens, which is the place of God and of souls who have experienced the joy of salvation. Here St. Bernard, the special devotee of the Virgin, becomes Dante's guide.

Paradise

Canto XXXIII

The Story

Still the Tenth Heaven: the Empyrean. Prayer of St. Bernard to the Virgin. Her acknowledgment of his prayer. Dante sees the Eternal Light. The three circles of the Trinity. The mystery of the Incarnation. The flashing light that fulfills Dante's vision. His desire and will at one with Love.

"Virgin mother, daughter of your Son,
more humble and sublime than any creature,
fixed goal decreed from all eternity,

you are the one who gave to human nature 4
so much nobility that its Creator
did not disdain His being made its creature.

That love whose warmth allowed this flower to bloom 7
within the everlasting peace—was love
rekindled in your womb; for us above,

you are the noonday torch of charity, 10
and there below, on earth, among the mortals,
you are a living spring of hope. Lady,

you are so high, you can so intercede, 13
that he who would have grace but does not seek
your aid, may long to fly but has no wings.

Your loving-kindness does not only answer 16
the one who asks, but it is often ready
to answer freely long before the asking.

In you compassion is, in you is pity, 19
in you is generosity, in you
is every goodness found in any creature.

This man—who from the deepest hollow in 22
the universe, up to this height, has seen
the lives of spirits, one by one—now pleads

with you, through grace, to grant him so much virtue 25
that he may lift his vision higher still—
may lift it toward the ultimate salvation.

And I, who never burned for my own vision 28
more than I burn for his, do offer you
all of my prayers—and pray that they may not

fall short—that, with your prayers, you may disperse 31
all of the clouds of his mortality
so that the Highest Joy be his to see.

This, too, O Queen, who can do what you would, 34
I ask of you: that after such a vision,
his sentiments preserve their perseverance.

May your protection curb his mortal passions. 37
See Beatrice—how many saints with her!
They join my prayers! They clasp their hands to you!"

The eyes that are revered and loved by God, 40
now fixed upon the supplicant, showed us
how welcome such devotions are to her;

then her eyes turned to the Eternal Light— 43
there, do not think that any creature's eye
can find its way as clearly as her sight.

And I, who now was nearing Him who is 46
the end of all desires, as I ought,
lifted my longing to its ardent limit.

Bernard was signaling—he smiled—to me 49
to turn my eyes on high; but I already
was doing what he wanted me to do,

because my sight, becoming pure, was able 52
to penetrate the ray of Light more deeply—
That Light, sublime, which in Itself is true.

From that point on, what I could see was greater 55
than speech can show: at such a sight, it fails—
and memory fails when faced with such excess.

As one who sees within a dream, and, later, 58
the passion that had been imprinted stays,
but nothing of the rest returns to mind,

such am I, for my vision almost fades 61
completely, yet it still distills within
my heart the sweetness that was born of it.

So is the snow, beneath the sun, unsealed; 64
and so, on the light leaves, beneath the wind,
the oracles the Sibyl wrote were lost.

O Highest Light, You, raised so far above 67
the minds of mortals, to my memory
give back something of Your epiphany,

and make my tongue so powerful that I   70
may leave to people of the future one
gleam of the glory that is Yours, for by
　　returning somewhat to my memory   73
and echoing awhile within these lines,
Your victory will be more understood.

　　The living ray that I endured was so   76
acute that I believe I should have gone
astray had my eyes turned away from it.

　　I can recall that I, because of this,   79
was bolder in sustaining it until
my vision reached the Infinite Goodness.

　　O grace abounding, through which I presumed   82
to set my eyes on the Eternal Light
so long that I spent all my sight on it!

　　In its profundity I saw—ingathered   85
and bound by love into one single volume—
what, in the universe, seems separate, scattered:

　　substances, accidents, and dispositions   88
as if conjoined—in such a way that what
I tell is only rudimentary.

　　I think I saw the universal shape   91
which that knot takes; for, speaking this, I feel
a joy that is more ample. That one moment

　　brings more forgetfulness to me than twenty-   94
five centuries have brought to the endeavor
that startled Neptune with the Argo's shadow!

　　So was my mind—completely rapt, intent,   97
steadfast, and motionless—gazing; and it
grew ever more enkindled as it watched.

　　Whoever sees that Light is soon made such   100
that it would be impossible for him
to set that Light aside for other sight;

　　because the good, the object of the will,   103
is fully gathered in that Light; outside
that Light, what there is perfect is defective.

　　What little I recall is to be told,   106
from this point on, in words more weak than those
of one whose infant tongue still bathes at the breast.

　　And not because more than one simple semblance   109
was in the Living Light at which I gazed—
for It is always what It was before—

　　but through my sight, which as I gazed grew stronger,
　　　　112
that sole appearance, even as I altered,
seemed to be changing. In the deep and bright

　　essence of that exalted Light, three circles   115
appeared to me; they had three different colors,
but all of them were of the same dimension;

　　one circle seemed reflected by the second,   118
as rainbow is by rainbow, and the third
seemed fire breathed equally by those two circles.

　　How incomplete is speech, how weak, when set   121
against my thought! And this, to what I saw
is such—to call it little is too much.

　　Eternal Light, You only dwell within   124
Yourself, and only You know You; Self-knowing,
Self-known, You love and smile upon Yourself!

　　That circle—which, begotten so, appeared   127
in You as light reflected—when my eyes
had watched it with attention for some time,

　　within itself and colored like itself,   130
to me seemed painted with our effigy,
so that my sight was set on it completely.

　　As the geometer intently seeks
to square the circle, but he cannot reach,
through thought on thought, the principle he needs,

　　so I searched that strange sight: I wished to see   136
the way in which our human effigy
suited the circle and found place in it—

　　and my own wings were far too weak for that.   139
But then my mind was struck by light that flashed
and, with this light, received what it had asked.

　　Here force failed my high fantasy; but my   142
desire and will were moved already—like
a wheel revolving uniformly—by

　　the Love that moves the sun and the other stars.   145

Exercises

One way to better understand Dante's Hell is to convert his allegorical meanings into modern terms. Following are just a few examples:

1. What is actually meant by the "shadowed forest"?
2. What might the leopard, lion, and she-wolf stand for? Consider these clues. Cantos III–VIII describe sins of incontinence such as lust, gluttony, and hoarding (leopard). Cantos IX–XXVII cover sins of violence such as heresy and suicide (lion). The remaining cantos are about sins of malicious fraud such as pandering, seducing, thieving, and treason (wolf).
3. Translate the inscription above the Gate of Hell into modern English.

Summary

The eleventh century marked the beginning of a new era that culminated in the Gothic style of the High Middle Ages. Cities began to grow and develop as manorialism gradually faded away. International trade began not long after the first Crusader entered Jerusalem in 1099. Even more importantly, contact with the civilized Middle East tapped the reservoir of Islamic science, medicine, and mathematics plus the carefully preserved culture of ancient Greece.

　　Partly because of the increasing influence of important women, feudalism began to give way to the more civilized code of chivalry. Hundreds of magnificent churches were erected, many of them in honor of Our Lady (Notre Dame).

　　Though scholasticism was the dominant mode of Christian thought, its tenets were challenged by the Battle of Universals that marked the beginning of the conflict between faith and reason. The rediscovery of the complete works of Aristotle also challenged the theologians. Further, the proliferation of medieval universities led inevitably to intellectual challenges of the monolithic Church.

　　In philosophy, the synthesis of the High Middle Ages was made by St. Thomas Aquinas, who merged Christian and Aristotelian thought. Called a "Bible in stone," the Gothic cathedral represented the synthesis in three-dimensional form. Dante's *Divine Comedy* delineated the options available to humankind. The goal was still heaven but people were free to pursue it under their own power and through the discipline of their own will.

　　Illustrating some of the themes of the period were selections from Goliard songs, "Our Lady's Juggler," and selections from Chaucer's *Canterbury Tales* and Dante's *Divine Comedy*.

Culture and Human Values

God was still the ultimate reality for the High Middle Ages but there was a shift in attitudes and values in the ever-growing educated class. Church doctrine that had been accepted for centuries was increasingly questioned. This is not to say that there was any widespread unrest, for the educated population was still too small—and most of them were clergymen.

In looking back on the volatile fourteenth century, one can perceive the early stirrings that would lead to the Renaissance, the Reformation, and the modern world. Call it 20–20 hindsight, but the necessary ingredients were there: the rise of science; the growing universities; the rise of humanism in Italy; the rediscovery of Aristotle followed by the whole of ancient Greek culture as preserved in the Islamic world.

The Gothic Age was at its zenith in the fourteenth century but, on April 8, 1341, Petrarch was crowned in Rome with a laurel wreath as the first poet laureate of modern times. The first rays of the Renaissance were already filtering through the medieval haze and the world would never again be the same.

Annotated Bibliography

General

Barber, Richard. *The Knight and Chivalry.* New York: Harper & Row Publishers, 1982. An overview of a fascinating subject.

Bishop, Morris. *St. Francis of Assisi.* Boston: Little, Brown & Co., 1977. A popular account of a popular saint.

Bynum, Caroline Walker. *Jesus as Mother: Studies in the Spirituality of the High Middle Ages.* Berkeley: University of California Press, 1984. The title essay explores the significance of feminine imagery.

Duby, Georges. *The Chivalrous Society.* Translated by Cynthia Postan. Berkeley: University of California Press, 1978. Wide-ranging essays by a noted scholar.

Durrell, Lawrence. *Pope Joan.* New York: Penguin Books, 1974. The persistent legend of the Joan who became Pope John engagingly retold by a reknowned novelist.

Gies, Frances. *Joan of Arc: The Legend and the Reality.* New York: Harper & Row Publishers, 1981.

———, and Gies, Joseph. *Life in a Medieval City.* New York: Harper & Row Publishers, 1981. An engaging popular account with a focus on thirteenth century Troyes.

Gies, Joseph, and Gies, Frances. *Women in the Middle Ages.* New York: Barnes & Noble, 1980. The status and roles of women.

Gimpel, Jean. *The Medieval Machine: The Industrial Revolution of the Middle Ages.* New York: Penguin Books, 1977. Significant technological developments in late medieval times.

Heller, Julek, and Headon, Deirdre. *Knights.* New York: Schocken Books, 1982. Rich illustrations capture the romance of legendary knights: Lancelot, Galahad, Tristan, Roland.

Howarth, David. *1066: The Year of Conquest.* New York: Penguin Books, 1981. Masterful and exciting recreation of the Norman invasion of England.

Lopez, Robert. *The Commercial Revolution of the Middle Ages: 950–1350.* New York: Cambridge University Press, 1976. Explores another area for which the Middle Ages has received insufficient credit.

Mayer, Hans Eberhard. *The Crusades.* Translated by John Gillingham. New York: Oxford University Press, 1972. The idealism, realism, and barbarism of the crusades in what is acclaimed as the best one-volume survey.

Power, Eileen, and Postan, M. *Medieval Women.* New York: Cambridge University Press, 1976. Among the more informative books on the role of women in this period.

Tuchman, Barbara. *A Distant Mirror: The Calamitous Fourteenth Century.* New York: Alfred A. Knoph, 1978. A beautifully written evocation of what fourteenth century life was like. However, the author's thesis that this period was as disastrous as our own century is not convincing.

Translations and Studies of Original Material

Anderson, William. *Dante the Maker.* Boston: Routledge & Kegan Paul, Ltd., 1980. Fine study of all his works.

Clark, Mary T., ed. *An Aquinas Reader.* Garden City, N.Y.: Doubleday & Co., 1972. A good selection from the works of the great theologian.

Gray, Douglas, ed. *The Oxford Book of Late Medieval Verse and Prose.* New York: Oxford University Press, 1985. The period from Chaucer's death to Henry VIII.

Hyman, Arthur, and Walsh, James J. *Philosophy in the Middle Ages: The Christian, Islamic, and Jewish Traditions.* Indianapolis: Hackett Publishing Company, 1983. Includes a fair representation of the important Jewish and Islamic thinkers.

Kibler, William, ed. and trans. *Chretien de Troyes: Lancelot, or the Knight of the Cart.* New York: Garland Publishing, 1981. A fine translation of one of the greatest medieval romances.

Loomis, Laura H., and Loomis, Roger S., eds. *Medieval Romances.* New York: Random House, 1965. The best of the genre.

Radice, Betty, trans. *The Letters of Abelard and Heloise.* New York: Penguin Books, 1976. The correspondence of the most famous love affair of the Middle Ages.

Richards, Earl Jeffrey, trans. *The Book of the City of Ladies* by Christine de Pizan. New York: Persea Books, 1982. First published in 1405, this is a delightful book by a remarkable writer who produced ten other prose works and ten volumes of verse. Christine was an articulate and angry (but courteous) feminist.

Wilhelm, James J., and Laila Zamuelis Gross, eds. *The Romance of Arthur: An Anthology.* Arthurian material in modern translation.

15

The Medieval Synthesis in Art

The giants of medieval art are comparable to Dante and Chaucer but very few of their names have come down to us. For one thing, the creation rather than the creator was much more important in the God-centered world of the Middle Ages; the cathedral dedicated to Our Lady and built for the greater glory of God far transcended the identity of the master builder who supervised its construction. Moreover, individual personalities were generally submerged in the groups of artists who labored on such cooperative projects as illuminated manuscripts (Book of Kells), tapestries (Angers), stained glass windows (Sainte Chapelle), architectural sculpture (Ste-Madeleine, Vézelay), and especially, the majestic Romanesque and Gothic cathedrals that rose all over Europe (Mont St. Michel and Chartres).

Significant, high-quality art was produced throughout medieval Europe. The complexity of that art and the sheer length of the era make it necessary (and prudent) to divide this chapter into the following periods or styles (all dates approximate):

600–800	Hiberno–Saxon Period
750–900	Carolingian Art
1000–1150/1200	Romanesque Period
1140–1200	Early Gothic Period
1200–1300	High Gothic Period
	Gothic Style outside France
1300–1500s	Late Gothic Period

Hiberno-Saxon Period, ca. 600–800

Though never part of the Roman Empire, Ireland was known by the Latin name *Hibernia,* which later became *Ivernin* in Old Celtic and then *Erin* in Old Irish. Occupied by Celts and Christianized by St. Patrick of Gaul, Ireland was cut off from the continent by the Anglo-Saxon conquest of England. This isolation led to the development of a unique form of Christian monasticism patterned after the solitary hermits of Egypt rather than the urbanized Roman version of Christianity. Founding monasteries in the countryside, Irish monks emphasized a strict ascetic discipline and, unlike the desert saints, a deep devotion to scholarship. Preempting the power of the bishops, Irish monasteries sponsored a remarkable missionary program in England and western Europe which resulted in a spiritual and cultural dominance fittingly called the Irish Golden Age of ca. 600–800.[1]

Manuscripts were produced in abundance to supplement these missionary activities, especially numerous copies of the Bible, all elaborately decorated to signify the supreme importance of the sacred texts. Displaying little interest in the figurative art of Roman Christianity, monks synthesized Celtic and Germanic elements to produce a richly decorated art based on geometric designs and organic abstractions derived from plant and animal forms. Created at a monastery on the island of Lindisfarne off the east coast of England, the *Lindisfarne Gospels* is a superb example of Hiberno-Saxon decorative art. As meticulous as printed electronic circuitry, the "Cross Page" (figure 15.1) is a miniature maze of writhing shapes and mirror-image effects highlighted by intertwined dragons and serpents. The Celtic cross spans a page bursting with energy and vitality. With details so fine that they are best studied with a magnifying glass, one wonders how this work was accomplished.

---

1. See the time chart on page 300 for an overview of the Middle Ages.

The "X–P (khi-rho) Page" (colorplate 18) is lovely testimony to the masterful use of color to enhance but not compete with either the linear composition or the importance of the gospel text.

The last of the remarkable Hiberno-Saxon illuminated manuscripts, the *Book of Kells* is also the most elaborately decorated. Reduced to the Greek letters XPI (khri), the name of Christ dominates a page swirling with animal and abstract interlaces and geometric decoration (figure 15.2). Whorls within circles within larger circles dazzle the eye, but closer study reveals two human faces and, on the left vertical of the X, three human figures depicted from the waist up. Near the bottom and to the right of the same vertical is a playful genre scene featuring two cats and four mice.

Hiberno-Saxon manuscripts typify the early period of intricate and painstaking northern craftsmanship, which included weaving, ivory and stone carving, jewelry, and stained glass, a tradition that led to spectacular achievements in the Gothic age and, eventually, to machine design and the industrial revolution. An important factor in the development of northern crafts may have been climate, for these are mainly indoor activities that could be carried on regardless of the inclement weather of long, dark winters.

Carolingian Art, ca. 750–900

Ruling from 768 to 814 as a Frankish king, Charlemagne saw himself as a successor to the Caesars of Rome, a concept that was reinforced in 800 when the pope crowned him Emperor of the Holy Roman Empire. To his capital at Aachen, Germany, he brought scholars, artists, and craftsmen to help revive classical antiquity. Short-lived but vital for later developments, the Carolingian Renaissance utilized Celtic-Germanic and Mediterranean traditions to produce a Carolingian art that combined classic forms with Christian symbols and subject matter.

Societies tend to develop an architecture based on the availability of building materials, and at that time the vast forests of northern Europe provided an endless supply of wood for the timber-frame construction of private and public buildings. Charlemagne, however, wanted impressive palaces and churches built in the Roman manner, and to do that he had to import southern principles of building in stone. Because there were no local stonemasons, he undoubtedly imported southern masons to work on his buildings and to instruct northern craftsmen, a procedure culminating in the expert stonework of Romanesque and Gothic cathedrals.

One of the few buildings to survive intact from the age of Charlemagne, the chapel of his palace at Aachen (figure 15.3) is an impressive example of northern stone construction. Designed by Odo of Metz, the first known northern architect, the chapel is modeled after San Vitale (see colorplate 15), which so impressed Charlemagne during a visit to Ravenna. A revision of San Vitale and not a copy, the chapel is simpler in style but still patterned after the Byzantine central plan. The central octagon is formed by arcades resting on heavy piers. Above this there are tall arches and within them are two levels of decorative columns. As might be expected during the early period of stone construction, the columns and most of

FIGURE 15.3   *Odo of Metz, Palatine Chapel of Charlemagne, 792–805, Aachen, Germany.*

FIGURE 15.4   *Germigny des Près, view from the east, 806.*

FIGURE 15.5   *Interior, Germigny des Près.*

the capitals were taken from existing Roman buildings. One would suspect that Charlemagne preferred using columns of the Caesars for his personal chapel.

One of the oldest churches in France, Germigny des Près (figure 15.4) was erected by Theodolphus, a friend of Charlemagne, and by the emperor's Armenian architect. Taller than the usual Byzantine church, this brick building is topped by a square tower that is capped with a peaked tile roof. Despite destructive attacks by Viking invaders, later called Northmen, and then Normans, the mosaic and much of the structure was preserved and then restored in the nineteenth century. The interior features heavy semicircular arches with a focus from the central altar, which is modern, to the mosaic in the apse (figure 15.5). Brought back by Charlemagne from Theodoric's palace in Ravenna and composed of 130,000 glass cubes, this is the only Byzantine mosaic in France.

The "Saint Mark" from the *Gospel Book of Archbishop Ebbo of Reims,* which was painted shortly after Charlemagne's death, derives from a classic model (figure 15.6). The Hiberno-Saxon influence is discernible in the draperies swirling about the torso in lines as dynamic as those in an Irish manuscript. Rather than a scholar writing a book, Mark is a man inspired by divine guidance, a transmitter of the sacred text. This follows the ancient view that poets, like Homer for example, are divinely inspired and possess superhuman powers.

Influenced possibly by Byzantine decorative arts, Carolingian book covers were made of precious metals and richly ornamented with jewels. Created during the waning influence of the Carolingian dynasty, the "Crucifixion Cover" of the *Lindau Gospels* is of gold, with the figures of Christ and angels delineated in graceful, sinuous lines (colorplate 19). Outlining the golden Greek

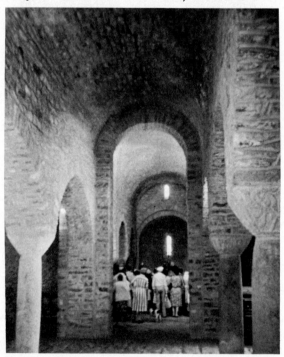

■ FIGURE 15.6 *"St. Mark" from the* Gospel Book of Archbishop Ebbo of Reims, *816–835. Municipal Library, Epernay, France. Photo © Giraudon/Art Resource.*

■ FIGURE 15.7 *Interior, St. Martin du Canigou, eleventh century, near Vernet-les-Bains, France.*

cross in gold beads, semiprecious and precious stones, the artist has reinforced the cross motif with jeweled crosses in the four panels and all around the border. Major stones are set away from the gold surface so that reflected light can add to their brilliance. There can be no doubt of the importance of the text within this cover.

After the remarkable reign of Charlemagne (768–814) the Holy Roman Empire declined in power and influence. Nevertheless, the revival of Greek and Roman learning sparked a synthesis of classical civilization and Celtic-Germanic culture, elements of which are still discernible in modern Europe and America.

Romanesque Period, ca. 1000–1150/1200

By about 1000 A.D. virtually all of Europe had been Christianized. After centuries of ferocious attacks, the barbaric Vikings, Magyars, and Slavs had finally been converted to Christianity and assimilated by their victims. Stupendous building programs began all over Europe to replace damaged structures and to construct new churches and monasteries. During the eleventh century the Cluniac Order alone built nearly a thousand monastic churches; every hamlet, village, town, and city had at least one new church. Inevitably architecture and architectural sculpture became the dominant art forms of this vigorous new age.

Vaulted Churches

Located high in the French Pyrenees, the tiny monastic church of St. Martin du Canigou is one of the earliest structures with a complete barrel vault of cut stone (figure 15.7). Vaulted stone roofs became the rule for Romanesque churches in place of the wooden truss roofs of earlier buildings; whether accidental or caused by hostile invaders, fire was a constant danger. Stone roofs relieved that difficulty but brought about another: how to support the heavy roof. The solution included thick walls supported by evenly spaced columns alternating with massive piers and connected by semicircular arches. Dimly lit because large windows weaken supporting walls, Romanesque churches are characteristically heavy and solid, giving a feeling of protective walls shutting out a hostile world. Intended for the exclusive use of the religious community, the monastic church shielded the monks from all outside influences.

Christians had been making pilgrimages to scenes of Christ's life since the third century and, during Charlemagne's reign, in ever-increasing numbers. By the tenth century it was commonly believed that viewing sacred relics of Christ and the Saints secured God's pardon for sins, a belief encouraged by pilgrimage churches housing sacred relics. Featuring the relics of St. Benedict, which were supposedly rescued from Monte Cassino,[2] the Abbey of Fleury (now St.-Benoit-sur-Loire) became one of the prime destinations for organized parties of pilgrims

---

2. The saint's remains were lost in the ruins of Monte Cassino during its destruction by the Lombard invasion of 577.

FIGURE 15.8 *St.-Benoit-sur-Loire, 1004–1218, near Sully-sur-Loire. View from the southeast.*

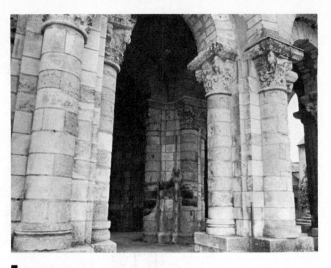

■ **FIGURE 15.9** *Capitals and piers, west porch, St.-Benoit-sur-Loire.*

■ **FIGURE 15.10** *"Flight to Egypt" capital, St.-Benoit-sur-Loire.*

(figure 15.8). Rebuilt after brutal Viking raids of the ninth century, the abbey church, with its belfry-topped porch and noble crossing tower, rests in the lush French countryside like a ship in a calm sea. Ornamented by the largest surviving group of carved capitals, many of them Corinthian, the porch is supported by early examples of compound piers (figure 15.9). Just as strong as the solid masonry piers of St. Martin du Canigou (see figure 15.7), the clustered columns around a central core became basic to mature Romanesque architecture.

Prime examples of early architectural sculpture, the lavishly carved capitals are among the glories of St.-Benoit-sur-Loire and harbingers of a sculptural renaissance that climaxed in the Gothic Age (figure 15.10). The "Flight to Egypt" features Joseph carrying a palm frond and leading the donkey carrying the Virgin and Child. On the left is the star and an angel slaying a dragon, as described in chapter 12 of the Revelation. Not nearly as naive as it might first appear, the carving relates the flight from Herod in unmistakable terms for the illiterate peasantry.

Illustrating the increasing height of Romanesque vaulting, the choir of St.-Benoit-sur-Loire features a barrel vault with ornamental ribs (figure 15.11). The clerestory windows, which admit considerable light for a Romanesque church, are set above a blind arcade that decorates the upper wall. Adorned only with architectural details, the masonry walls are supported by majestic columns connected by Roman arches. The interiors of French Romanesque and Gothic churches are always restrained, depending for their effect on a unity of basic design and discreet architectural embellishment without recourse to mosaics, murals, frescoes, or other extraneous decorations. The result is a rational design of awesome power.

Most but not all pilgrimage churches were monastic. A major stop on the pilgrimage road from Italy and Provence to Spain's Santiago de Compostela, the church of St. Sernin is a superb example of the Burgundian Romanesque style. The semicircular barrel vault is punctuated by nonstructural transverse arches evenly distributed down the nave (figure 15.12). Constructed on the module of the crossing square under the tower, the size of each compartment between the columns, called a *bay*, is exactly half the size of the crossing square (figure 15.13). On the side aisles each square is one-quarter of the module. The compound columns are two stories high with arches supporting a gallery that runs above the side aisles and that was probably used by some of the pilgrim throngs. Minus the triumphal arch of Early Christian churches, the evenly spaced columns and identically sized bays lead inexorably down the nave to the focal point of the altar. St. Sernin is a classic example of French Romanesque design, unified and lucid.

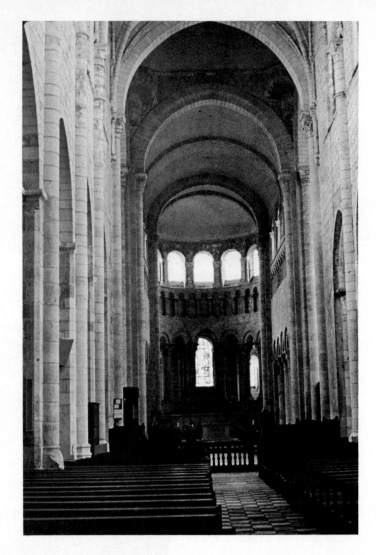

■
FIGURE 15.11 *Choir, looking east, St.-Benoit-sur-Loire.*

■
FIGURE 15.12 *Collegiate Church of St. Sernin, ca. 1080–1120. Toulouse, France. Photo courtesy of French Government Tourist Office.*

■
FIGURE 15.13 *Plan of St. Sernin (after Kenneth John Conant).*

Now one of the most imposing ruins in France, the Abbey of Jumièges was founded in the seventh century and destroyed by Vikings in the ninth. It was reconsecrated in 1067 in the presence of William the Conqueror, a descendent of the Viking marauders (figure 15.14). With its 141' twin towers and outward-thrusting porch, Jumièges represents the impressive Norman style that was to decisively influence Gothic architecture. The present state of Jumièges typifies the fate of French monasteries after the 1789 Revolution. After the monks were dispersed, the abbey was auctioned off in 1793 to a timber merchant who quarried and sold many of the stones. The ruins now belong to the nation.

Begun shortly before the Conqueror sailed for England, St. Etienne was under the personal protection of King William (figure 15.15). The characteristic twin towers of Norman achitecture reach 295' with the aid of spires that were a Gothic addition. The seven towers are a vigorous contribution to the design as well as symbols of the Holy Trinity plus the Four Evangelists. With the Conqueror's tomb before the high altar, St. Etienne still stands as the royal church of the Norman king.

The Bayeux Tapestry

Probably designed by a woman and embroidered on linen by Saxon women, the Bayeux Tapestry is the most precise medieval document which has survived intact, providing daily life scenes and details of clothes, customs, and weapons. In fifty-eight scenes, the rivalry between King Harold of England and William of Normandy is depicted, culminating in the Battle of Hastings (figure 15.16). In this episode the English, identified by their mustaches, are beginning to succumb to the superior numbers of the French. The tripartite design features an

■
FIGURE 15.14 *West facade, Abbey of Jumièges, 1037– 1067, on the lower Seine near Rouen, France.*

■
FIGURE 15.15 *St. Étienne (Abbaye aux Hommes), 1064–1135, Caen, France. View from the southeast.*

■ FIGURE 15.16 *"The Battle Rages," detail from Bayeux Tapestry, ca. 1070–1080. Wool embroidery on linen. Height ca. 20″, entire length 231′. Town Hall, Bayeux, with special authorization of the Village of Bayeux.*

■ FIGURE 15.17 Mission of the Apostles, *tympanum of the central portal of the narthex, ca. 1120–1132, Ste.-Madeleine, Vézelay, France.*

ornamental band above the violent battle scene and a lower band depicting the casualties. Despite the stylized design, the details are brutally realistic; warriors and horses have died in agony.

The abbey church of Ste.-Madeleine in the village of Vézelay is intimately associated with another kind of warfare: holy war. Originally scheduled for Vézelay, Pope Urban II preached the First Crusade from Clermont in 1095, calling on all Christians to free the Holy Land from the Saracens. In 1146 Vézelay was the site for St. Bernard's Second Crusade and, in 1190, King Richard the

Lion-Hearted of England and King Phillip Augustus of France departed from Vézelay on the Third Crusade, a disastrous failure, as was every Crusade from the Second in 1146 to the Eighth in 1291. Intended to support and define the Crusades as a second mission to convert the heathen, the *Mission of the Apostles* tympanum at Vézelay (figure 15.17) exemplifies the revived relationship of architecture and sculpture in the Romanesque style. Set between the arch and lintel, the tympanum is a compendium of sermons calling on the faithful to emulate the Apostles: save or condemn, preach the gospel, heal the sick, and drive out devils. Following the old convention of relating the size of a figure to its importance, Christ dominates the composition, poised in an almond-shaped frame wearing swirling draperies patterned after Hiberno-Saxon manuscripts. On both sides the Apostles are rising from their seats to commence their evangelical mission. On the archivolts, the relief bands that frame the tympanum, and above the lintel are the benighted people of the world, who in their diseased, crippled, or animalistic condition await the enlightenment. Under the ornamented top archivolt is an inner band of zodiac signs, the seasons, and monthly labors, signifying the year-round Christian mission. In its original condition, complete with bright colors and gold embellishment, the impact of this dynamic work must have been even greater.

Ste.-Madeleine

One of the most distinctive of all Romanesque interiors, the nave of Ste.-Madeleine (figure 15.18) is high, about 90′, with unusual transverse arches of black and white stone, probably inspired by such Islamic buildings as the Great Mosque in Cordoba (see figure 13.5). The tunnel, or barrel, vault was no longer used because of its inherent drawback: an unbroken series of arches pressed back to back can be lighted or opened only on the opposite ends. Any and every opening in the supporting

FIGURE 15.18 *Nave, Ste.-Madeleine, ca. 1104–1132, Vezelay, France.*

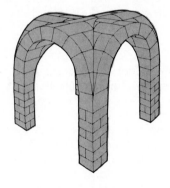

FIGURE 15.19 *Schematic drawing of a cross-vault.*

FIGURE 15.20 *Trumeau figure of "The Prophet," Abbey Church of St. Pierre, ca. 1125–1130, Moissac. Photo © Giraudon/Art Resource.*

wall weakens the entire structure. One of the earliest French churches to abandon the barrel vault, Ste.-Madeleine's uses a vault that is intersected at right angles by another vault to form a "groin" or "cross" vault (figure 15.19). Note that at this high level the groined vaults of Vézelay permit considerable illumination from the clerestory windows. Close study of the interior also reveals that the architect used groin vaults that were too heavy for the exterior wall, vaults so massive that the upper walls are pushed outwards. External flying buttresses (see an example of the principle in figure 15.28 had to be added to balance the thrust of the vaults, thus stabilizing this lovely nave.

An outstanding example of architectural sculpture, the strange other-worldly figure of a prophet, possibly Jeremiah, appears on the trumeau, or supporting pier, of a portal of the Abbey Church of St. Pierre at Moissac (MWA-zak; figure 15.20). The attenuated shape, the long and slender legs, and delicate lines recall Hiberno-Saxon manuscripts. Seemingly too slight to support the mass of masonry, the gentle prophet expresses a spiritual tension and nervous vigor similar to an El Greco painting of four centuries later.

The medieval love of embellishment ranged from manuscripts to stone, including priests' vestments and such ceremonial objects as crosses, chalices, incense burners, candlesticks, and reliquaries. A casket containing a sacred object, a reliquary was invariably made of precious materials and highly decorated. The silver Rhenish reliquary in the shape of a head (colorplate 20) is quite restrained for the period, particularly in the classical details of the hair. Embossed and incised silver figures of the twelve Apostles surround the base of what the twentieth century would label a three-dimensional composite work or "combine." In the twelfth century it was not even regarded as sculpture but as a reliquary, pure and simple.

FIGURE 15.21 *Busketus, Pisa Cathedral and Campanile, 1063–1272.*

FIGURE 15.22 *Pisa Cathedral with Baptistery.*

The linear style of the Ste.-Madeleine tympanum (see figure 15.17) and "The Prophet" (see figure 15.20) are also prominent in the *Psalter of St. Swithin* (color-plate 21). In both manuscript scenes elegant arabesques gracefully outline the figures, thus emphasizing the grotesque faces of the brutal soldiers in comparison to the resigned passivity of Christ. Beauty and horror are effectively combined to convey a powerful spiritual message.

Tuscan Romanesque

The basic Romanesque style of Roman arches and stone vaults supported by compound columns and heavy walls spread throughout western Europe, always displaying, however, certain variations depending on regional conventions and traditions. Adhering closely to the basilica plan of Early Christian churches, the buildings of Tuscany also evidenced an increased interest in classical art, a heritage that had never been totally forgotten. The most distinguished complex in the Tuscan Romanesque style is the cathedral group at Pisa (figure 15.21). Constructed of readily available white marble, the cathedral resembles an Early Christian basilica, but with Romanesque characteristics: the dome over the crossing; the superimposed arcades on the west front; the blind arches encircling the entire building. The extended transepts with an apse at each end add to the poise and serenity of the design, which makes the famous Leaning Tower, the campanile, all the more striking. Begun in 1174 by Bonanno Pisano on an unstable foundation, the tower began to tilt well before its completion in 1350. Adjusted slightly to the left, the three upper sections were supposed to compensate for the rightward incline. Over 14′ off the perpendicular, the tower, whose bells haven't rung in years, is still moving. Engineering schemes to save the structure are complicated by the stipulation that the tower be stabilized without, however, correcting the tilt of one of Italy's prime tourist attractions.

The view from the top of the campanile clearly shows the cruciform plan of the cathedral with its clerestory windows and upper level of blind arcades (figure 15.22). The massive baptistery, topped with a dome 115′ in diameter, was built between 1153 and 1278 and later embellished at the upper level with Gothic details, the only discordant note in a grand design.

Mont St. Michel

In all its manifestations, Romanesque art finds its unity in architecture; the church is the Fortress of God where the apocalyptic vision is ever called to mind. Exemplifying this concept, the Abbey of Mont St. Michel in the Sea of Peril (figure 15.23), rises in awesome majesty off the coast of France. Begun about 1020 by Abbot Hildebert and Richard II of Normandy, grandfather of William the Conqueror, the building program covered five centuries as abbot succeeded abbot and crusade followed crusade. Mont St. Michel summarizes medieval architecture, a glorious mixture of Norman, Norman Romanesque and Early, High, and Late Gothic styles.

Early Gothic Period, ca. 1140–1200

Erected usually in the countryside as part of monastic communities, Romanesque churches were built by and for "regular" clergy, those who lived under the rule *(regula)* of a religious order. The rise of the great cities of Europe was paralleled by the development of the new Gothic style. Staffed by the "secular" clergy, priests who lived "in the world" *(in saecula),* Gothic churches were urban establishments designed to serve city parishes. Each city's glory and chief community center, the Gothic cathedral was not only the seat *(ex cathedra)* of the bishop but a theatre, classroom, concert hall, court, and general meeting place.

FIGURE 15.23 *Mont St. Michel, ca. 1017–1144; 1211–1521. Aerial view.*

Gothic Vaulting

Though the basic structural elements of Gothic architecture were developed and used during the Romanesque period, it remained for an unknown architectural genius to put it all together at St. Denis, just north of Paris (figure 15.24). Carried out under Abbot Suger who left a detailed account of his administration (1122–1151), the designer supported the weight of the vaults with pointed arches, which are more stable than semicircular arches. The arch principle is one of mutual support; the two halves lean against each other so that the force (gravity) that would cause either to fall actually holds them in place. But, the flatter the arch the greater the lateral thrust at the springline, that is, the outward push where the arch turns upward (figure 15.25). The lateral thrust is significantly reduced when the pointed arch is used because the springline is angled more nearly downward. Hence, the more pointed the arch the less the tendency to push its supporting pier outwards, thus reducing the need for massive supports.

The rounded arch has a fixed diameter because it is always half of a circle. Since it has no unalterable diameter, the pointed arch can rise to almost any height and span any space (figure 15.26). In the illustration the first rounded arch spans the short side, the second the long side, and the third the diagonal, necessitating piers of different heights. With their identical height, pointed arches simplify the engineering and improve the aesthetic effect with slender columns topped by capitals at a uniform height.

The Gothic vaulting and piers of identical height can be seen at St. Denis (see figure 15.24). The piers on the right have less masonry to support than the main piers to the left, and are thus considerably slimmer. Still appearing bulky from the back, the primary piers are less massive than Romanesque columns, particularly when viewed from the choir, where the clustered columns now rise gracefully to the high ceiling.

FIGURE 15.24 *Choir and ambulatory, Abbey Church of St. Denis, 1140–1144.*

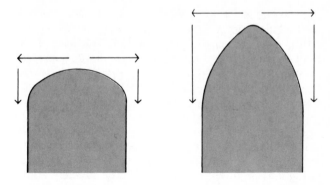

FIGURE 15.25 *Schematic drawings of Romanesque and Gothic arch thrusts.*

■ FIGURE 15.26 *(a) Cross vault of semicircular arches over an oblong bay; (b) Cross vault of pointed arches over an oblong bay.*

■ FIGURE 15.27 *West facade, Notre Dame, Paris. Plan, 1163–1250; facade, ca. 1200–1250. Photo © Museum of Notre Dame de Paris.*

The most striking difference at St. Denis is the marked increase in light. In figure 15.24 one can see, on all three levels, stained glass windows that function as light converters, transforming the interior into a hazy luminosity of shifting colors. The windows are subdivided first by mullions (carved stone posts), by stone tracery to form still smaller glass panels, and by thin lead strips to hold in place the individual pieces of colored glass. The light penetrating the stained glass provides a polychromatic effect, making the glass transparent, while the stone and metal dividers become opaque black lines separating and highlighting the colors. The mystical coloration of Gothic interiors represents the philosophical idea of light as a Neoplatonic form of ultimate beauty, an earthly manifestation of the divine light of the heavenly kingdom.

■ FIGURE 15.28 *Apse with flying buttresses, Notre Dame, Paris.*

On June 11, 1144, Abbot Suger proudly presided at the dedication of the choir of St. Denis in the company of hundreds of priests and laymen, five archbishops, and Louis VII of France and his Queen, Eleanor of Aquitaine. This was a truly momentous occasion, sparking a veritable frenzy of Gothic construction in the Ile de France, the region surrounding Paris. The cathedral at Chartres was begun in 1142, even before the formal dedication at St. Denis, Laon in 1160, Notre Dame of Paris in 1163, Bourges in 1185, and Chartres again in 1194 after a catastrophic fire. These cathedrals, all major enterprises, were followed by hundreds of other churches in a vast building program that, in a single century, included every major city in northern Europe.

Notre Dame

The imposing facade of Notre Dame (figure 15.27) has been justly admired for over seven centuries as a masterpiece of rational design. Solidly buttressed at the corners, the facade rises effortlessly in three levels on which sculptural embellishment is subordinate to the architecture. Unlike the projecting porches of later Gothic cathedrals, the three portals are recessed from the frontal plane and topped by a row of carved saints. The rose window centerpiece is flanked by smaller roses over double windows, above which there is a line of lacy pointed arches. With their subtly embellished cornices and elongated windows, the square towers complete the design with restraint and dignity. This majestic west front is a fitting symbol for the ascendancy of Paris as the cultural and intellectual center of Europe.

The view of the east end of Notre Dame (figure 15.28) displays in no uncertain terms that critical component of Gothic design, the flying buttress. Springing from heavy piers, two sets of arches curve upwards to

North Porch

West

1. Narthex
2. Nave
3. Bay
4. Aisle
5. Crossing

6. Transept
7. Choir
8. Apse
9. Radiating Chapel

East

South Porch

FIGURE 15.29 *Hypothetical cruciform floor plan of a church.*

support the piers of the exterior walls, providing the counterbalancing force needed to stabilize the structure. It is the flying buttress principle that enabled architects to utilize the curtain walls of stone pierced by numerous stained glass windows. Also visible in figure 15.27 is the Late Gothic flèche, the slender spire that rises above the crossing. Flying buttresses represent an exposed engineering which provides both the needed physical support and the psychological assurance that the building is totally solid and safe, as indeed it is.

The floor plan of Notre Dame was a long rectangle with a rounded eastern end, but most Romanesque and Gothic churches were designed in the shape of a Latin cross (cruciform floor plan). Figure 15.29 is a simplified plan illustrating the basic outline. The terminology for the various parts of the church is standard and applies to all cruciform designs. The "orientation" of the plan is also standard; worshippers enter through a west door and walk towards Jerusalem in the east (Orient). In this plan there are six bays (sections between columns) in the nave and three in each arm of the transept.

High Gothic Period, ca. 1200–1300

After a disastrous fire in the village of Chartres in 1194, which left intact only the Early Gothic facade of the still unfinished cathedral, the rebuilding of Chartres Cathedral commenced immediately and moved rapidly, with the basic structure completed by 1220. The idea that Gothic cathedrals took decades or even centuries to build is erroneous and probably based on the fact that these buildings were never fully completed; there was always something to be added or elaborated.

Chartres Cathedral

The first masterpiece of the mature period, Chartres Cathedral has been called the Queen of Cathedrals, the epitome of Gothic architecture (figure 15.30). Typically High Gothic but unique to Chartres, the south (right) tower begins with a square base that evolves smoothly into the octagonal shape of the fourth level. From here the graceful spire soars to a height of 344', the characteristic "finger pointing to God" of the Gothic age. The elaborate north tower, which was not completed until well into the Northern Renaissance, lacks the effortless verticality of the south tower. Verticality was a hallmark of Gothic; cities competed in unspoken contests to erect cathedrals with the highest vaults and the tallest towers. An inspiring House of God was also a symbol of civic achievement. With a facade 157' wide and measuring 427' in length, Chartres Cathedral is as prominent a landmark today as when it was built, thanks in part to modern zoning ordinances that control building heights throughout the village.

Incorporated into the facade when the cathedral was rebuilt, the Royal Portal (western doorways) of the earlier church emphasizes the Last Judgment theme of Romanesque portals but with significant differences (figure 15.31). Rather than the harsh Damnation of the Last Judgment, the theme is now the Second Coming with its promise of salvation. No longer is there the inventive freedom of the Romanesque; all is unified and controlled. The outer frame is provided by the twenty-four elders of the Apocalypse on the archivolts and the lower

■
FIGURE 15.30 *West facade, Chartres Cathedral, ca. 1142–1507.*

■
FIGURE 15.31 *Central doorway, Royal Portal, ca. 1140–1150, Chartres Cathedral. Photo © Hirmer Fotoarchiv.*

row of twelve Apostles. Surrounded by symbols of the four Evangelists, the now benign figure of Christ raises an arm in benediction in the manner of Caesar Augustus (see figure 10.6). Beneath the tympanum are the jamb figures, a wholly new idea in architectural sculpture. Conceived and carved in the round, the figures were very likely fashioned after live models rather than copied from manuscripts, a further indication of the emerging this-worldly spirit of the age.

The most significant manifestation of the new age was the dedication of the cathedrals themselves. Named after apostles and saints in previous eras, the new churches were almost invariably dedicated to Our Lady *(Notre Dame).* Mary was Queen of Heaven, interceding

for her faithful who, sinners all, wanted mercy, not justice. This was the Cult of the Virgin Mary, the spiritual counterpart of the vastly enhanced status of women. The masculine Romanesque was the age of feudalism and conflict; the more feminized Gothic was the Age of Chivalry, as derived from courts of love sponsored by powerful women like Eleanor of Aquitaine, Queen of France and then of England. With the development of cathedral schools such as those at Paris and Chartres, Mary was viewed much like Athena, as patroness of arts and science. The right doorway of the Chartres Royal Portal (not illustrated) includes portraits of Aristotle, Cicero, Euclid, Ptolemy, Pythagoras and symbols of the Seven Liberal Arts. The Gothic cathedral represents the medieval synthesis of spiritual and secular life at its best.

COLORPLATE 18 *Bishop Eadfrith (?), "X-P Page," Lindisfarne Gospels. British Library, London. Reproduced by permission of the British Library.*

COLORPLATE 25 *Duccio,* The Calling of the Apostles Peter and Andrew, *ca. 1308. Tempera on wood, 17⅛" × 18⅛". Samuel H. Kress Collection. National Gallery of Art, Washington, D.C.*

COLORPLATE 26 *Simone Martini,* Annunciation, *1333. Tempera on wood 8'8" × 10'. (Saints in side panels by Lippo Memmi.) Uffizi Gallery, Florence. Photo © Scala/Art Resource.*

FIGURE 15.32 *Choir, Notre Dame of Chartres.*

FIGURE 15.33 *Floor plan (after Dehio) of Notre Dame of Chartres.*

Featuring a nave 53′ in width, the most spacious of all Gothic naves, the interior of Notre Dame of Chartres is 130′ in length and 122′ high, the loftiest vault of its day (figure 15.32). At the rounded end of the choir are the tall pointed arches of the arcade and the triforium gallery of the second level, culminating in the lofty and luminous stained glass windows. At the sides of the illustration can be seen two of the four enormous piers which frame the crossing and which are carved as clustered columns to minimize their bulk. Columns clustered around a central core have the same diameter as a solid pier, but their appearance gives the illusion of lightness and grace.

Chartres has six bays in the nave and two in the transepts, a single aisle in the nave and a double aisle in the apse (figure 15.33). Figure 15.34a depicts a full bay (center) and the three levels of the nave wall. The diagram of the vaulting (figure 15.34b) gives some idea of the complexity of the exterior support system.

One of the chief glories of Gothic interiors is the kaleidoscopic color cascading from the mighty stained glass windows. Retaining most of its original windows, Chartres is a treasure house of the art, with clerestory windows 44′ high, all in all some 20,000 square feet of medieval glass. Located at the south end of the transepts, the southern rose is like a gigantic multicolored jewel set above the five figurative lancet windows (colorplate 22). Because it is a southern exposure window, the predominance of color leans towards the warm part of the spectrum from roses to oranges to reds. Its counterpart,

the northern rose (not illustrated), transmits the cooler colors, especially many hues of blue. Contrary to what one might expect, direct sunlight on any of the southern windows upsets the chromatic balance of the interior. All of the windows were designed to function best under the even light of the generally grey skies of northern France, enabling the warm and cool colors to effect a balance of color tones. Surpassing anything up to that time, the craftsmanship and sheer beauty of Gothic stained glass remain incomparable.

As usually seen by tourists, a Gothic cathedral is an enormous empty building, very impressive but more like a museum than a church. Despite the awesome scale of the interior, the cathedral is not at all intimidating in the manner of, say, Egyptian temples. Rather, the church is built for people and when functioning as intended, the interior comes vibrantly alive as an inspirational setting for public worship. Colorplate 23 illustrates an actual high mass in a nave nearly filled with worshippers. A superb example of the Norman High Gothic style, Coutances has a characteristically unadorned and harmonious interior that derives its whole effect from the architecture. Not even the modern dress of the congregation or the speakers on the columns can detract from the timelessness of the setting; the scene is very nearly the same as it has been for over seven centuries.

Vaulting

Rose
Windows

Clerestory

Lancet
Windows

Triforium Gallery

Nave Arcade

Flying Buttresses

Buttress

(a)   (b)

FIGURE 15.34 *(a) Section of nave wall; (b) diagram of vaulting, Notre Dame of Chartres. Drawings by Goubert.*

FIGURE 15.35 *West facade, Notre Dame of Amiens, ca. 1220–1288.*

Other French Cathedrals

Designed originally by one of the first known master builders, Robert de Luzarches, the Cathedral of Notre Dame of Amiens marks the culmination of the best ideas of the French Gothic style. Modeled after that of Notre Dame in Paris, the west front (figure 15.35) is not as controlled and majestic as its model. Its grandeur, however, is overwhelming. Looking like one gigantic and intricate work of sculpture, the facade is dominated by its incomparable portals. The imposing entrances thrusting outward from the facade proclaim the interior in unmistakable terms; the central portal announces the lofty nave and the two flanking doorways the side aisles. In other words, the inner structure is foretold by the exterior design.

Patterned after Chartres, the nave of Amiens is even more integrated, soaring in one breathtaking sweep to 144′ above the pavement (figure 15.36). Unfortunately minus its stained glass, the interior is still the culmination of the High Gothic style: lofty arcades with slender columns rising to the ribbed vaults. Once thought to have functioned as structural supports for the ceiling, the ribs are actually decorative extensions of columns carrying the design to the pinnacle of the ceiling, which with its groined vaults is completely self-supporting (figure 15.37).

FIGURE 15.36 *Nave, Notre Dame of Amiens.*

(a)   (b)

FIGURE 15.37 *Robert de Luzarches. (a) Plan and (b) vaulting, Notre Dame of Amiens.*

Completed in less than thirty-three months for Louis IX of France, later St. Louis, Sainte Chapelle (figure 15.38) is today a small chapel set in the midst of the Palais de Justice. With virtually no stone walls the structure is a set of piers supporting walls of stained glass. Topped by a spire reaching 246′ into the sky, the upper chapel, with its 49′ windows, rests on a lower level intended for the use of servants. With almost 7,000 square feet of glass containing 1,134 scenes the upper chapel is a jewelbox of color dominated by brilliant reds and luminous blues (figure 15.39). Because there are no side aisles, there are no flying buttresses to impede the penetration of light into a building whose walls are about 75 percent glass. Rivaling Chartres in the extent and quality of its original glass, Sainte Chapelle managed to survive the Revolution; damaged and neglected, it became a storage area for old government files. Restored in the nineteenth century to an approximation of its original condition, the remarkable fact is that its basic structure is so flawless, so perfectly engineered that it survived completely intact for seven centuries.

FIGURE 15.38 *Sainte Chapelle, 1245–1248, Paris. View from northeast.*

FIGURE 15.39 *Interior, upper chapel, Sainte Chapelle.*

FIGURE 15.40 *Choir of Beauvais Cathedral, France. Aerial view. Begun ca. 1225. Photo © Ray Delvert.*

With the cathedral at Beauvais, the competition to build the highest vault came to a crashing end (figure 15.40). Reaching the incredible height of 157′, the vaulting was a wonderment to all until its collapse in 1284; only the apse was left standing. Rebuilt over a period of forty years, the choir remains today as a testimonial both to Gothic vertical aspirations and the waning of enthusiasm for building enormously expensive churches; the money ran out along with the spirit. Though commonly thought that "tortured stone" could not withstand the lofty vaults of Beauvais, modern engineering research[3] points to a design flaw in an exterior pier, the deterioration of which was not detected. The collapse of 1284 ironically confirmed the nature of Gothic engineering in which the stability of the vaulting depends on the proper functioning of all components. When the single pier failed due to undetected weathering, all the choir vaults came tumbling down. The apse remained standing simply because it was structurally independent. Interestingly enough, the design flaw was corrected during the rebuilding program, meaning that the entire cathedral could then have been completed as originally planned. Today one can look at the choir section and only wonder at what might have been at Beauvais.

Gothic Style outside France

By the second half of the thirteenth century the Gothic style had been accepted throughout Europe, though Italy was less than enthusiastic. Regional variations gave each area its own brand of Gothic. Taking to Gothic as if they had invented it, the English built in the style from the twelfth to the nineteenth centuries. Drawing directly upon the Ile de France style, the English utilized clearly recognizable Gothic characteristics in a manner just as distinctly non-French. The clean lines of French verticality were abandoned at the outset in favor of a multiplicity of verticals topped by veritable forests of ribs that almost obscured the groined vaults, as evidenced in Canterbury Cathedral (figure 15.41). The nave is not seen as a majestic succession of bays but rather as a steady procession of supports and arches. Because the ribs arch up from the triforium, the clerestory windows are not as prominent in the design as in the French style nor is the stained glass comparable in workmanship or design. A comparison of the interior of Canterbury with the interiors of Chartres (figure 15.32) and Amiens (figure 15.36) reveals just how drastic the difference is, which the French are only too willing to point out. The English, on the other hand, view French interiors as cold and impersonal, while English Gothic is warmly intimate, hospitable, and comfortable. Different styles suit different people.

The Italians took up the Gothic style slowly and with many reservations; they were, after all, the ones who had labeled the new style as a barbaric creation of the Goths of the north. Distinctly unclassical, a Gothic cathedral is restless, unsettled, always incomplete, whereas a classical temple is at rest, serenely complete. Nevertheless,

---

3. Robert Mark, *Experiments in Gothic Structure* (Cambridge, Mass.: MIT Press, 1982), pp. 58–77.

FIGURE 15.41 *Nave, Canterbury Cathedral, begun 1174.*

the Gothic spirit was on the move in Italy, becoming part of the classical and Romanesque traditions. For all its Gothic elements, the Cathedral of Siena (figure 15.42) has square doorways, triangular pediments, and a balanced design reminiscent of the classical and Romanesque traditions. There is a Gothic rose window minus stained glass plus Gothic towers, lacy blind arches, and the three portals. Most of the statuary has been liberated from its architectural bondage and the tympanums feature colorful mosaics. Faced with multicolored marble, the facade is an ensemble of Gothic elements mixed with Tuscan Romanesque, all in all a notable example of Italian reaction to the Gothic spirit.

Whatever its regional variations, the Gothic cathedral epitomizes the explosive creativity and intellectual boldness of the Gothic age. Never completely finished, a process rather than an end product, it stood at the center of the storm of changes that would sweep away the medieval synthesis. It represents both the triumphant climax of the Age of Faith and the end of the Middle Ages.

Late Gothic Period, ca. 1300–1500s

An integral part of Gothic architecture, stained glass windows and relief sculpture served the pictorial purposes once provided by mosaics, murals, and frescoes. Virtually nonexistent in the Gothic north, large-scale paintings were still done in Italy, which had maintained its contact with Byzantium. It was Italian painters who synthesized Byzantine and Gothic styles to create new procedures crucial to the future development of Western painting.

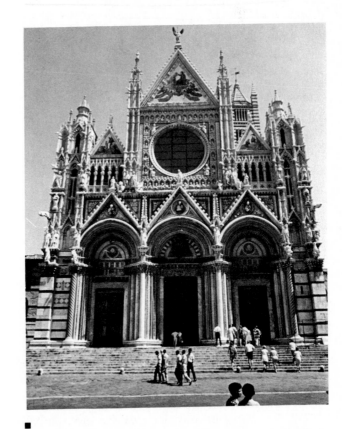

FIGURE 15.42 *Giovanni Pisano, Facade, Cathedral of Siena, begun ca. 1285.*

Cimabue

Renowned for his skill as a fresco and tempera painter , the Florentine Cimabue (chee-ma-BOO-uh; 1240?–1302) introduced features that were incorporated into the developing Italian style. His *Madonna Enthroned* (figure 15.43) illustrates the new characteristics of strong, forceful figures in an atmosphere of complete serenity. The human scale of the lower figures emphasizes the towering dignity of the Madonna as she holds the mature-looking child. Distinguished from Byzantine icons by its much greater size, the gable shape and solid throne are also Gothic in origin as is the general verticality. The rigid, angular draperies and rather flat body of the Madonna are from the Byzantine tradition, but the softer lines of the angels' faces and their lightly hung draperies were inspired by works from contemporary Constantinople.

Giotto

Cimabue's naturalistic, monumentally scaled work had a profound influence on his purported pupil Giotto (JOT-toe; ca. 1267–1337), the acknowledged "father of Western painting." Giotto was a one-man revolution in art, who established the illusionary qualities of space, bulk, movement, and human expression, all features of most pictorial art for the next six centuries. His indebtedness to Cimabue is obvious in his *Madonna Enthroned* (figure 15.44), but there are significant changes that make it not necessarily better but certainly different. Giotto abandoned the Byzantine tradition and patterned his work after Western models, undoubtedly French cathedral statues. His solid human forms occupy a three-dimensional space surrounded by an architectural framework. His *Madonna Enthroned* is highlighted by the protruding knee of the Madonna, showing that there is a tangible body underneath the robe, a figure of monumental substance. When compared with Cimabue's angels, we see that Giotto's angels, especially the kneeling ones, are placed firmly at the same level on which the base of the Gothic throne rests. The ethereal, floating quality of Byzantine painting has been abandoned in favor of the illusion of tangible space occupied by three-dimensional figures.

Giotto's reputation, already imposing in his own time, rests mainly on his frescoes, most notably the biblical scenes in the Arena Chapel, which are among the most celebrated in the whole history of art. In his *Lamentation* (colorplate 24) the artist has composed a scene in the manner of a Greek tragedy. The mourning tableau is placed in the foreground so that the picture space is at eye level, making us participants in the tragedy, our involvement heightened by the wonderfully expressive backs of the two anonymous mourners. Grief is individualized, with each participant mourning according to his

FIGURE 15.43 *Cimabue,* Madonna Enthroned, *ca. 1280–1290. Panel, 12'7½'' × 7'4''. Uffizi Gallery, Florence. Photo © Alinari/Art Resource.*

or her personality. The emotional range is vast, from the controlled intensity of the earth-bound figures to the tortured grief of the writhing angels. Giotto's achievements are summarized in this one powerful work: the creation of subtle illusions of tactile qualities; existence and movement in space; a deep psychological understanding of subject and viewer; and the establishment of a continuity of space between viewer and painting. To all of these achievements he brought a profound sense of humanity's awareness of human emotions and of their place in the world. Difficult as it is to realize today, Giotto's contemporaries saw these works as the ultimate reality, so "real" that you could walk into them. We can give proper credit to this view by comparing Giotto's work with that of his contemporaries and by remembering also that reality, or the illusion of reality, changes from epoch to epoch.

---

4. Fresco paintings are made on fresh wet plaster with pigments suspended in water; tempera uses pigments mixed with egg yolk and applied, usually, to a panel. Because the drying time for both techniques is very fast, corrections are virtually impossible without redoing entire areas. Therefore, artists had to work rapidly and with precision.

FIGURE 15.44 *Giotto,* Madonna Enthroned, *ca. 1310.
Tempera on panel, 10'8" × 6'8". Uffizi Gallery,
Florence. Photo © Alinari/Art Resource.*

FIGURE 15.45. *Duccio,* Rucellai Madonna, *1285.
Tempera on wood, 14'9" × 9'6". Uffizi Gallery,
Florence. Photo © Alinari/Art Resource.*

Two Artists from Siena

From Siena came two artists whose work was unlike that
of either Cimabue or Giotto but who were instrumental
in establishing the International Style, the first international movement in Western art. Duccio (DOOT-cho; ca.
1255–1319) painted Byzantine-type faces except for the
eyes, but in a style comparable to northern Gothic manuscripts and ivories. The most elegant painter of his time,
his *Rucellai Madonna* (figure 15.45) is highly decorative, with sinuous folds of background drapery and a remarkable delicacy of line for so large a work. Contrasting
with the Byzantine-style flatness of the Madonna, the
kneeling angels are portrayed much more in the round,
combining the Hellenistic-Roman naturalistic tradition
with that of French architectural sculpture. This one work
is a virtual encyclopedia of the International Style synthesis of Mediterranean and northern cultures.

In his *The Calling of the Apostles Peter and Andrew*
(colorplate 25), Duccio depicts a world of golden sky
and translucent greenish sea where the commanding but
elegant figure of Christ beckons gently to the slightly
puzzled fishermen. It is a lovely creation, the world of
Duccio, and this is the style the popes at Avignon and
the northern kings and queens admired and called upon
their artists to emulate.

Serving the pope's court in Avignon, Duccio's pupil
Simone Martini (1284–1344) combined the grace of the
Sienese school with the exquisite refinement of Late
Gothic architecture. His *Annunciation* (colorplate 26)
epitomizes the courtly style. Completely Gothic, the
frame is replete with *crockets,* or ornamental leaves and
flowers, and *finials,* or carved spires; signifying eternity,
the gold-leaf background is Byzantine. Delineated in
graceful curved-lines, the Angel Gabriel kneels before
the Virgin to proclaim "Hail Mary, full of grace. . . ." As
the words travel literally from his lips she draws back in
apprehension, her body arranged in an elaborate S-curve
and covered by a rich blue robe. Between the two figures
is an elegant vase containing white lilies symbolic of
Mary's purity. As delicately executed as fine jewelry, the
artistic conception is aristocratic and courtly, comparable
to the polished sonnets of Petrarch, who also served the
papal court at Avignon.

With its combined Classical/Byzantine/Gothic attributes, the International Style was promulgated
throughout the religious and secular courts of Europe. It
found an enthusiastic response wherever wealthy clients
prized grace, delicacy, and refinement in art, music, manners, and dress. Aesthetic pleasure was the goal, not spiritual enlightenment.

Exercises

1. What exactly was the purpose of "pilgrimage churches"? How were they supported? Would merchants want a pilgrimage church in their town?

2. Explain the differences between barrel and groined vaults.

3. Explain the differences between Romanesque and Gothic architecture. Then explain why Gothic developed as an urban art form when Romanesque was essentially a rural style.

4. Literally and symbolically, Gothic churches were at the center of city life. What does the average American city have at its center? Your city?

5. Medieval churches were very expensive but many hundreds of them were built, indicating that they were highly valued by society. Which of the following are most valued by our society?

Museums	Sports facilities
Airports	Scientific facilities
Office buildings	Nuclear power
Educational buildings	plants
Military bases	Other

   What does this tell us about American values?

6. Scholars still argue about which building is better (greater, more beautiful, more inspired): the Parthenon or Chartres Cathedral. Pick one and defend your choice.

7. Identify the influence of medieval art and architecture in your community.

Summary

A curious backwater during Roman times, Christianized Ireland launched missionary activities that led to a golden age highlighted by the production of exquisite manuscripts in the Hiberno-Saxon style. Establishing a tradition of meticulous northern craftsmanship, the *Lindisfarne Gospels* and *Book of Kells* were among the first and best of a long history of illuminated manuscripts.

Charlemagne seized the opportune moment to create the Holy Roman Empire and launch the Carolingian Renaissance. Importing technology and stonemasons from the Mediterranean area, he set in motion the forces that would produce the Romanesque style and climax in the Gothic Age.

The year A.D. 1000 marked the Christianization of virtually all of Europe and the launching of a vast building program of monasteries and churches. Inspired by Roman models, builders constructed stone-vaulted churches such as the pilgrimage chuches of St.-Benoit-sur-Loire, St. Sernin, and Ste.-Madeleine. Notable among the numerous monasteries built during the period were Jumièges and Mont St. Michel.

Inspired by the revolutionary design of the choir of St. Denis, French master builders erected some of the most sublime buildings ever conceived by humankind, most notably the Gothic cathedrals of Chartres and Amiens.

Though relatively immune to Gothic architecture, Italian artists synthesized Classical, Byzantine, and Gothic elements to create the first International Style in art. A medieval man like Dante and his friend and fellow Florentine Giotto carried medieval art to its final consummation. Indeed, Dante's work marks the end of the Middle Ages and sets the stage for the Renaissance.

Culture and Human Values

Of the many significant artistic achievements of the Middle Ages, the Gothic cathedral would have to rank as the crowning glory. These incredible structures represented, simultaneously, great engineering, breathtaking architecture, reverent settings for Christian worship, and notable symbols of civic pride. The Church ranked pride with the seven deadly sins but pride—a sense of one's own dignity and value—was a vital factor in artistic achievement, not to mention how it stimulated the competitive drives in economics, business, and trade. The striving for excellence was matched by the vying for position, profit, or prizes.

Deriving pleasure and satisfaction from one's own work and achievements was not the only factor in the dynamics of the age, but it was a powerful force. Similarly, the achievements of the ancient Greeks were due in large measure to their strong sense of self-worth and passion for excellence.

Annotated Bibliography

Adams, Henry. *Mont-Saint-Michel and Chartres.* Reprint. Marietta, Ga.: Lanlin Corp., 1978. A classic work of 19th century criticism.

Brown, Peter, ed. *The Book of Kells: A Selection from the Irish Medieval Manuscripts.* New York: Alfred A. Knopf, 1980. Reproductions from one of the world's most beautiful books.

Calkins, Robert. *Illuminated Books of the Middle Ages.* Ithaca, N.Y.: Cornell University Press, 1983. Includes exquisite colorplates.

Demus, Otto. *The Mosaics of San Marco in Venice.* Chicago: University of Chicago Press, 1984. A four-volume set with hundreds of illustrations of glorious mosaics, recently restored.

Duby, Georges. *The Art of the Cathedrals: Art and Society, 980–1420.* Translated by Eleanor Levieux and Barbara Thompson. Chicago: University of Chicago Press, 1981. Changing attitudes as reflected by art and architecture.

Facillon, Henri. *The Art of the West in the Middle Ages.* Translated by Donald King. Landmarks in Art History Series. Ithaca, N.Y.: Cornell University Press, 1980. Excellent study in two volumes.

Gimpel, Jean. *The Cathedral Builders.* Translated by Teresa Waugh. New York: Harper & Row Publishers, 1984. Copiously illustrated study of many dimensions of ecclesiastical architecture from 1050 to 1350, when 80 major cathedrals and 500 large churches were built in France.

Macaulay, David. *Castle.* Boston: Houghton Mifflin Co., 1982. Traces, with wonderful pen-and-ink illustrations, the planning and building of a Welsh fortress and village.

———. *Cathedral: The Story of Its Construction.* Boston: Houghton Mifflin Co., 1981. A fascinating account of the building of a French Gothic cathedral from hewing down half a forest to placing the last sheet of lead on the spire.

Male, Emile. *Art and Artists in the Middle Ages.* Translated by Sylvia Lowe. Redding Ridge, Conn.: Black Swan Books, Ltd., 1981. Fine illustrations with a text by a noted French art historian.

———. *Chartres.* New York: Harper & Row Publishers, 1984. An aesthetic analysis in the tradition of Henry Adams's classic book.

Smart, Alastair. *The Dawn of Italian Painting, 1250–1400.* Ithaca, N.Y.: Cornell University Press, 1978. Late medieval developments leading toward the Renaissance.

16

Medieval Music: Sacred and Secular

The bountiful storehouse of medieval music marks the first great era of Western music, and yet little of this large repertory is heard by modern audiences. An inseparable part of everyday life, medieval music served the needs of the society: ballads to preserve tales and legends; songs of love and beauty; dances and popular tunes to celebrate the joys of life; dirges and lamentations to express the sorrows; sacred music for praise and worship. This is not the musical art of today's concert halls, but recordings of much of this rich heritage are available in authentic versions.

There is a large body of sacred music but comparatively little secular music prior to the fourteenth century. In common with other nonliterate societies, secular music was passed along to later generations through oral tradition. Music of the church, on the other hand, had a status comparable to the high social position of clerics. As part of the province of the literate and the learned, music was preserved in written form as a link to the eternal. However, the sheer mass of sacred music and

secular music (after the thirteenth century) has to be indicative of a comparable amount of secular music, a folk art that was rarely taken seriously and seldom written down. The survival of nearly 1,700 troubadour-trouvère melodies (discussed later in this chapter) attests to the importance of secular music in medieval life.

Sacred Music

The oldest type of music is *monophonic,* or a single melodic line with no other parts or accompaniment. The liturgical (officially authorized) music of the Church of Rome is monophonic in a style called Gregorian chant, or plainsong.

Gregorian Chant

According to legend, Pope Gregory the Great (ruled 590–604; figure 16.1) ordered a body of liturgical music organized, priests trained in singing the music, and a

FIGURE 16.1 *"King David as Organist (left) and Pope Gregory the Great," 1241, from Codex Lat. 17403, Bayerische Staatsbibliothek, Munich. Traditionally attributed to David, the Psalms formed a large part of the Gregorian repertory. Inspired by the dove of the Holy Spirit and holding a monochord, Gregory is depicted in his legendary role as codifier of liturgical chant.*

common liturgy disseminated throughout the Western church. He did reorganize the church, but the chant that bears his name reached its final form during and shortly after the reign of Charlemagne (ruled 768–814). Consisting today of nearly 3,000 melodies, Gregorian chant is a priceless collection of subtle and sophisticated melodies.

Gregorian chant is monophonic, *a cappella* (unaccompanied), and sung by male voices (solo and chorus) in Latin in the musical modes defined by the church. The texts determine the note values and musical accents; the rhythm of the music follows the rhythm of the words. There is no steady pulsation or beat, no division into regular accents as there would be in a march or waltz. The undulating melodies flow smoothly, resonating through the cavernous stone churches, weaving a web of sound, and evoking in the worshippers feelings of awe and reverence.

Like secular music, Gregorian chant existed for centuries as an oral tradition. The precise musical notation of the ancient Greeks had been lost, and it was not until the eighth century that a new notational system began to evolve. Symbols for musical pitches, called *neumes,* were at first imprecise as to the actual pitch indicated, leading the monk Guido of Arezzo (ca. 990–1050) to remark that, "In our times, of all men, singers are the most foolish." Blaming the lack of precise musical notation for "losing time enough in singing to have learned thoroughly both sacred and secular letters," Guido invented

a four-line musical staff on which neumes could symbolize precise pitches (figure 16.2). Because of its limited range, chant is still scored on a four-line staff. In the following example the upper staff gives the neumes in Gregorian notation, below which the same melody is scored on the modern five-line staff. The clef sign (upper left) in Gregorian notation is C; the standard staff uses a G clef. In both notations, the letter-names of the notes are F–G–E–D–F–A–G–A–G, etc.

Many Gregorian melodies were adapted from Jewish Synagogue chant, especially the Alleluias (Hebrew, *Hallelujah,* praise ye the Lord). The seventh item of the mass (see table 16.1), Alleluias are characteristically *melismatic,* with many notes sung to one syllable. Following is the beginning of an Alleluia from the mass for Epiphany (visit of the Magi). The long and expressive melisma on the final syllable led eventually to innovations in texts and music called *tropes* and *sequences* (see below).

Al - le - - lu - ia.

Listening Example 2

Gregorian Chant

Alleluia, Vidimus stellam
(codified 590–604; excerpt)[1]

Time: 1:00

Gregorian chant

Solo   Chorus

Al - le - lu __ ia ___   Al -le - lu __

ia _____

■ **FIGURE 16.2** *Guido d'Arezzo, twelfth century manuscript, State Library, Vienna. Seated at the left, Guido is demonstrating on a monochord the two-octave scale (A–B–C–D–E–F–G, etc.), which was converted to neumes and placed on the staff.*

1. Simple musical notation is used on a modest scale throughout this text; these are guides to listening just as literary quotes are guides to reading. See the Appendix, "Music Listening and Notation," for the basic principles of reading music.

The Mass

The two basic types of Catholic services are the Mass and the Daily Hours of Divine Services, usually called Office Hours. The latter are celebrated eight times daily in religious communities such as monasteries. The Mass, also celebrated daily, is the principal service of the church. Essentially an elaborate reenactment of the Lord's Supper, the central theme is the consecration of the bread and the wine and the partaking of these elements by the congregation. Everything else in the service is either preparation for Communion (the Eucharist, Gk., thanksgiving) or a postscript to this commemorative act.

In a *low* Mass, the words are quietly enunciated by the priest in a low (speaking) voice in front of a silent congregation. In a *high* Mass, the service is recited and sung in a high (singing) voice using either Gregorian chant or a combination of chant and other music.

The Mass consists of the *proper,* in which the texts vary according to the liturgical calendar, and the *ordinary,* which uses the same texts throughout the church year. Both proper and ordinary have texts that are recited or chanted by the celebrants (clergy) or sung by the choir.

The complete Mass is outlined in table 16.1 (italics indicate the sung portions of the text). Although modernization of the Mass permits the incorporation of indigenous modern language, increased layman participation, and congregational singing, the essential structure remains unchanged.

TABLE 16.1   The Mass

Ordinary (same text)	Proper (changing texts)
	1. *Introit*
2. *Kyrie*	
3. *Gloria*	
	4. Oratio (prayers, collect)
	5. Epistle
	6. Gradual
	7. *Alleluia* (or *Tract* during Lent)
	8. Gospel
9. *Credo*	
	10. *Offertory*
	11. Secret
	12. Preface
13. *Sanctus*	
14. Canon	
15. *Agnus Dei*	
	16. *Communion*
	17. Postcommunion
18. *Ite missa est* (or *Benedicamus Domino*)	

Tropes

A *trope* (Latin, *tropus,* figure of speech) is a textual addition to an authorized text, an interpolation in the chant. Sentences or even whole poems were inserted between words of the original text. Sometimes, added words were fitted to preexisting notes; at other times both words and music were injected together into the established text. For example, the chant *Kyrie eleison* (Lord have mercy upon us), with an interpolated trope, would read: Lord, *omnipotent Father, God, Creator of all,* have mercy upon us.

The practice of troping could have resulted from boredom, a desire for creativity, an inability to remember the notes, or varying combinations of all three. The authorized texts had not only remained the same for generations but many of them, particularly the texts of the ordinary, were sung countless times. Thus a need for some variety may have been one of the motivating factors.

More positively, troping permitted exercises in creativity that could enliven the unvarying liturgical music. Of course one wonders, in this connection, how often creative acts are the direct result of trying to cope with monotonous repetition.

A third reason for troping may have been utilitarian. Troping originated during the time (ca. 700) when the musical liturgy was still learned by rote. Many chants had long *melismas,* that is, extended series of notes on a single syllable. (Note: The Alleluia used above as an illustration of chant has an extended melisma on the last syllable.) Attempting to remember all these melismas must have been very trying for singers who already had a large amount of liturgical music crammed into their heads. Textual additions that supplied a syllable for each note of the melisma provided additional reference points for all singers. Tropes, therefore, must have been well received by medieval choirs.

Indeed, tropes became so popular that they threatened to engulf the authorized texts. It was perhaps inevitable that the Council of Trent (1545–1563) finally abolished all tropes.

Sequences

The oldest form of trope was the last syllable, the 'ia' (ja) of the Alleluia (again see the example of the Alleluia given above). Many Alleluias, because of their Oriental origin, ended with an exotic and elaborate melisma on the final syllable. New poetry was added to this melisma and then, in time, the last section was detached from the Alleluia to become a separate composition called a *sequence*—that which follows. After separation had been accomplished, composers felt at liberty to alter the melody line.

The sequence is of special interest because it signaled the beginnings of musical composition for its own sake, a new development that was to lead to the works of composers such as Palestrina, Beethoven, and Stravinsky. The composition of sequences was a first step away from the rigidity of a prescribed musical repertoire. Composers began to explore ever more musical innovations and thus to breech and, ultimately, to break down medieval walls.

A large repertoire of sequences threatened for a time to dominate traditional Gregorian chant. The Council of Trent also tried to abolish sequences, but met with such opposition that four sequences were permitted to remain in the repertoire. Following is the oldest of the surviving sequences, the so-called Easter Sequence by Wipo (Weepo; ca. 1024–1050), chaplain of Emperor Henry III. This melody also served as the basis for a Lutheran Easter chorale, "Christ Lay in the Bonds of Death," with text by Martin Luther.

Listening Example 3

Sequence

Wipo, "Victimae paschali laudes" (11th century)

Time: 1:30

Wipo

Vi - cti - mae pa - scha - li lau - des im - mo-lent Chri-sti - a - ni. etc.
(Let Christians dedicate their praises to the Easter victim.)

Liturgical Drama

Religious ceremonies, such as the Mass, extend themselves into the realm of the theatre. The dramatic reenactment of the Last Supper in the Mass led, in time, to the development of medieval drama. The impulse was somewhat similar to that which saw classical Greek drama evolve from the cult of Dionysus. There were notable differences, however; Greek tragedy dealt with ethical choices made under stress. The common people of the Middle Ages were not nearly as literate as the Greeks. They were more concerned with representations of the Nativity, the Shepherds, the Three Wise Men, and other specific events connected with their religion.

The actors were, in the beginning, priests of the Church and the plays episodes from the life of Christ, particularly the Christmas and Easter stories. During the liturgy, priests interpolated paraphrased dialogues from the Gospels, frequently using tropes. But these miniature dramas were too brief and too abstract for the unlettered congregation. Gradually the actors (clergy) enlarged the Scriptures by using Latin for the formal sections and the vernacular for the dialogues. Eventually whole plays were performed in the native language, which in the early plays was French.

Early liturgical dramas were enacted by the clergy in front of the altar. As the vernacular elements were added, the performances were moved to the church portal and the acting parts taken by laymen who, in time, formed confraternities of actors.

Liturgical dramas were mainly musical plays relying for their effects on singing and on a rich variety of accompanying instruments. Of the dozens of instruments available, favorites included the organ, harp, lyre, horn, trumpet, recorder, rebec (precursor of viols and then violins), drums, and other percussion instruments (figure 16.3).

■
FIGURE 16.3 *From the* Hortus Deliciarum *by the Abbess Herrad van Landsberg, late twelfth century. Formerly in the town library of Strasbourg, the manuscript was destroyed in the 1870 war. Hanging at the right is a rebec, a bowed string instrument of Arab origin. The female performer holds a harp while, at the left, there hangs a wheel-lyre (organistrum). This instrument has three strings set in motion by a revolving wheel operated by a hand crank, and is an ancestor of the hurdy-gurdy.*

The following opening dialogue (sung in Latin) is from *The Play of the Three Kings*, which dates from the late eleventh century. Some of the melodies were borrowed from plainsong, but considerable music was undoubtedly composed for the occasion. This recorded performance is a cappella, but instruments could have been added to underscore the Oriental origins of the Magi.

Listening Example 4

Time: 1:00

Liturgical Drama

"Infantem Vidimus" (11th–12th century; excerpt)

Shepherds
Infantem vidimus.
(We have seen the Infant.)
Boys
Qui sunt hi, quos stella ducit nos adeuntes, inaudita ferentes?
(Who are those whom the star leads, approaching us and bearing strange things?)
Magi
Nos sumus quos cernites reges Tharsis et Arabum et Saba, dona offerentes Christo Reginato Domino.
(We are those whom you see—the kings of Tharsis, Arabia, and Saba, offering gifts to Christ the King, the new-born Lord.)

Song of the Ass [2]

Time: 20

O-ri-en-tis par-ti-bus Ad-ven-ta-vit a-si-nus Pulcher et
(Out from lands of Orient Was the ass divinely sent. Strong and

Coda

for - ti - si - mus Sar-ci-nis ap-ti-si-mus, Hez, Sir As-ne, hez.
very fair was he, Bearing burdens gallantly. Heigh, Sir Ass, oh heigh!)

Conductus

The *conductus* was a processional used to "conduct" important characters on and off the stage. One of the most familiar of these was the "Song of the Ass," which was often used to describe Mary's flight into Egypt riding on a donkey. This song is shown as it was used in the twelfth-century *Play of Daniel*. Accompanying the Virgin as she rides into the church on a donkey, the conductus, as befits its function as processional music, is *metrical*. It has four beats to each measure in the manner of a solemn march. Only one of the seven verses is given here.

After the thirteenth century, liturgical drama developed into mystery plays (from Latin, *ministerium,* service) performed entirely in the vernacular under secular sponsorship. Using music only for processions, fanfares, and dances, these dramatic portrayals of biblical stories (life of Jesus, the Creation, and so forth) eventually evolved into European drama.

Secular Music

Goliards

The goliards of the tenth through thirteenth centuries were wandering students, vagabonds, defrocked priests, minstrels, rascals, artists, and dreamers. They were generally disenchanted with established values and entrenched institutions. They professed to take their name from a "Bishop Golias," whom they claimed as a patron—a very tolerant patron.

Their songs cover many subjects: love songs, drinking songs, spring songs, songs moral and immoral. Their songs were generally light-hearted and frequently obscene and, apparently, so was their conduct.

Though little of their music is extant, considerable poetry has survived. A thirteenth-century manuscript has been published under the title *Carmina Burana.* Selections from this collection have been set to music by the contemporary German composer Carl Orff. (See volume 2.)

A sampling of the opening lines from poetry in the *Carmina Burana* indicates some basic themes.

"Were the world all mine from the sea to the Rhine, I would gladly forsake it all if the Queen of England were in my arms"
"In rage and bitterness I talk to myself"
"I am the Abbot of Cluny, and I spend my time with drinkers"
"When we are in the tavern we don't care who has died"
"The God of Love flies everywhere"
"When a boy and a girl are alone together"
"Sweetest boy I give myself completely to you"

(Note: Three goliard poems are printed on page 348.)

The vigorous conduct of the goliards and their assault upon established values inevitably led to conflicts with the Church. The movement died out, not because of clerical opposition, but because of the rise of the great medieval universities that replaced wandering students with resident ones.

Jongleurs

The *jongleurs* of France (and the *Gauklers,* their German counterparts) were generally not as educated as the goliards. Appearing first during the ninth century, these wandering men—and women—were seldom composers but always entertainers. They played music and sang songs that others had written, did tricks with trained animals, and, in general, helped enliven weddings and other special events. Although some of them were sufficiently talented to be socially acceptable, many were disreputable as far as a despairing clergy was concerned.

Their repertoire included *chansons de geste,* epic chronicles of the valorous deeds of heroes like Charlemagne and Roland. Because the melodies consisted of easily remembered tunes, there was no real need to notate the music and thus very little of it has survived. In a twelfth-century manuscript of the *Chanson de Roland* there are sketches that were apparently used to sing of the exploits of Roland and his horn. The *chant-fable,* part prose and part verse, was similar to the *chanson de geste* but with a slightly different form. The best-known chant-fable is *Aucassin et Nicolette* (see page 325).

---

2. G. M. Dreves, *Analecta hymnica* xx, 217, 257; H. C. Greene, *Speculum vi.*

Troubadours and Trouvères

Coinciding with the flowering of the age of chivalry, the troubadours of Provence and their later followers in northern France, the trouvères, produced the finest repertoire of lyric song of the Middle Ages. Educated aristocrats, both men and women, composed love poetry in the tradition of Ovid, whose love poems and *Art of Love* (see chapter 9) were undoubtedly known to the cultured nobles of the south of France. The repertoire is large (2,600 troubadour poems, ca. 300 melodies; 4,000 trouvère poems, 1,400 melodies) and covers many subjects: the Crusades, travel, adventure, but mostly romantic love. Despite the relative paucity of surviving melodies, all of the poems were meant to be sung. According to the troubadour Folquet of Marseilles (ca. 1155–1231), "A verse without music is a mill without water."

The earliest known troubadour, Duke William IX of Aquitaine (1071–1126), was a crusader, poet, and performer, whose lusty life and romantic pursuits are reflected in his poetry, of which eleven poems but only one melody have survived. The boldly masculine attitude in the following poem is comparable to Ovid's most aggressive style.

TROUBADOUR SONG

Duke William IX of Aquitaine

1. Friends, I'll write a poem that will do:
   But it'll be full of fun
   And not much sense.
   A grab-bag all about love
   And joy and youth.
2. A man's a fool if he doesn't get it
   Or deep down inside won't try
   To learn.
   It's very hard to escape from love
   Once you find you like it.
3. I've got two pretty good fillies in my corral:
   They're ready for any combat—
   They're tough.
   But I can't keep 'em both together:
   Don't get along.
4. If I could tame 'em the way I want,
   I wouldn't have to change
   This set-up,
   For I'd be the best-mounted man
   In all this world.
5. One's the fastest filly up in the hills,
   And she's been fierce and wild
   A long, long time.
   In fact, she's been so fierce and wild,
   Can't stick her in my pen.
6. The other was born here—Confolens way—
   And I never saw a better mare,
   I swear
   But she won't change her wild, wild ways
   For silver or gold.
7. I gave to her master a feeding colt;
   But I kept myself a share
   In the bargain too:
   If he'll keep her one whole year,
   I will a hundred or more.
8. Knights, your advice in this affair!
   I was never so troubled by
   Any business before.
   Which of these nags should I keep:
   Miss Agnes? Miss Arsen?
9. I've got the castle at Gimel under thumb,
   And over at Nieul I strut
   For all the folks to see.
   Both castles are sworn and pledged by oath:
   They belong to *me!*

Considerably more subtle, the next poem is designed to create a romantic, seductive atmosphere.

TROUBADOUR SONG

Duke William IX of Aquitaine

1. I'm going to write a brandnew song
   Before the wind and rain start blowing.
   My lady tries and tests me
   To see the way I love her.
   Yet despite the trials that beset me,
   I'd never break loose from her chain.
2. No, I put myself in her bondage,
   Let her write me into her charter.
   And don't think that I'm a drunkard
   If I love my good lady thus,
   For without her I couldn't live.
   I'm so hungry for her love.
3. O, she's whiter than any ivory statue.
   How could I worship any other?
   But if I don't get reinforcements soon
   To help me win my lady's love,
   By the head of St. George, I'll die!—
   Unless we kiss in bower or bed.
4. Pretty lady, what good does it do you
   To cloister up your love?
   Do you want to end up a nun?
   Listen: I love you so much
   I'm afraid that grief will jab me
   If your wrongs don't become the rights I beg.
5. What good will it do if I'm a monk
   And don't come begging round your door?
   Lady, the whole world's joy could be ours,
   If we'd just love each other.
   Over there at my friend Daurostre's
   I'm sending this song to be welcomed and sung.
6. Because of her I shake and tremble,
   Since I love her with the finest love.
   I don't think there's been a woman like her
   In the whole grand line of Lord Adam.

William's son governed the duchy for a few years, followed by his granddaughter, the celebrated Eleanor of Aquitaine (1122–1204), who established a Court of Love in Poitiers and later in Normandy and possibly England. Eleanor sponsored several troubadours and trouvères, the most notable of which was Bernart de Ventadorn (d. 1195). Dante conferred the title of master singer on Arnaut Daniel and consigned another troubadour, Bertran de Born, to Hell but modern critics have ceded the palm to the poet-musician from Ventadorn as the finest lyric poet of the age.

Forty poems, eighteen with music, by Bernart de Ventadorn are known today. Lively, witty, and eminently singable, the subject is always the same: love rewarded, unrequited, noble, sacred, or profane, but always love. In the following *canso* (love song; *chanson* in northern France) the first of six verses is given in both Provençal, the language of the troubadors, and in English.

Listening Example 5

Troubadour Canso

Bernart de Ventadorn, "Be m'an perdut"[3]
(12th century; excerpt)

Time: :50

Bernart de Ventadorn (d. 1195)

Musical theme

Be ma'an perdut lai enves Ventadorn tuih meo amic,
(I am indeed lost from the region of Ventadorn/ To all my friends,
pois ma domna no m'ama; et es be dreihz que jamais lai no torn
for my lady loves me not; With reason I turn not back again,
c'a des estai vas me salvatj' egrama.
For she is bitter and ill-disposed toward me.
Veus per quem fai semblan irat emorn;
See why she turns a dark and angry countenance to me;
car en s'amor me deleih e'm sojorn!
Because I take joy and pleasure in loving her!
ni de ren als no's rancura ni's clama.
Nor has she ought else with which to charge me.)

After her divorce from the king of France, Eleanor married, in 1152, Henry II, Duke of Normandy and, later, king of England. The next poem implies that Bernart has followed her Court of Love to England and that the haughty highborn lady is either Eleanor herself or a member of her court. Even without the music, the singable quality of the poetry is quite evident.

---

3. C. Appel, *Bernart von Ventadorn* (Halle, 1915), Plate ix (citing Milan manuscript *Chansonnier* G, folio 14). The form is AAB.

LANCAN VEI PER MEI LA LANDA

Bernart de Ventadorn

1. Whenever I see amid the plain
   The leaves are drifting down from trees
   Before the cold's expansion,
   And the gentle time's in hiding,
It's good for my song to be heard,
For I've held back more than two years
   And it's right to make amends.
2. It's hard for me to serve that woman
   Who shows me only her haughty side,
   For if my heart dares make a plea,
   She won't reply with a single word.
Truly this fool desire is killing me:
I follow the lovely form of Love,
   Not seeing Love won't attend me.
3. She's mastered cheating, trickery,
   So that always I think she loves me.
   Ah, sweetly she deceives me,
   As her pretty face confounds me!
Lady, you're gaining absolutely nothing:
In fact, I'm sure it's toward your loss
   That you treat your man so badly.
4. God, Who nurtures all the world,
   Put it in her heart to take me,
   For I don't want to eat any food
   And of nothing good I have plenty.
Toward the beautiful one, I'm humble,
And I render her rightful homage:
   She can keep me, she can sell me.
5. Evil she is if she doesn't call me
   To come where she undresses alone
   So that I can wait at her bidding
   Beside the bed, along the edge,
Where I can pull off her close-fitting shoes
Down on my knees, my head bent down:
   If only she'll offer me her foot.
6. This verse has been filled to the brim
   Without a single word that will tumble,
   Beyond the land of the Normans,
   Here across the wild, deep sea.
   [Apparently England.]
And though I'm kept far from Milordess,
She draws me toward her like a magnet:
   God, keep that beauty ever safe!
7. If the English king and the Norman duke
   Will it, I'll see her soon
   Before the winter overtakes us.
8. For the king I remain an English-Norman,
   And if there were no Lady Magnet,
   I'd stay here till after Christmas.

A number of female troubadours have been identified, including Azalais of Porcairagues, Maria of Ventadorn, Lombarda, and the Countess Garsenda of Provence. The most notable poet-musician, whose work is comparable to that of any troubadour, was the Countess of Dia (present day Die), who lived in the Drôme valley in southern France during the twelfth century. Known as Beatritz, her voice is as distinctive as that of Sappho (see chapter 8). In the following dialogue song the lady sweeps aside male rationalizations and exacts a pledge of loyalty, devotion, and a love that was to be shared equally.

TROUBADOUR SONG

Beatritz, Countess of Dia

1. Friend, I stand in great distress
   Because of you, and in great pain;
   And I think you don't care one bit
   About the ills that I'm enduring;
   And so, why set yourself as my lover
   Since to me you bequeath all the woe?
   Why can't we share it equally?

2. Lady, love goes about his job
   As he chains two friends together
   So the ills they have and the lightness too
   Are felt by each—in his fashion.
   And I think—and I'm no gabber—
   That all this deepdown, heartstruck woe
   I have in full on my side too.

3. Friend, if you had just one fourth
   Of this aching that afflicts me now,
   I'm sure you'd see my burden of pain;
   But little you care about my grief,
   Since you know I can't break free;
   But to you it's all the same
   Whether good or bad possess me.

4. Lady, because these glozing spies,
   Who have robbed me of my sense and breath,
   Are our most vicious warriors,
   I'm stopping: not because desire dwindles.
   No, I can't be near, for their vicious brays
   Have hedged us in for a deadly game.
   And we can't sport through frolicsome days.

5. Friend, I offer you no thanks
   Because my damnation is not the bit
   That checks those visits I yearn for so.
   And if you set yourself as watchman
   Against my slander without my request,
   Then I'll have to think you're more "true-blue"
   Than those loyal Knights of the Hospital.

6. Lady, my fear is most extreme
   (I'll lose your gold, and you mere sand)
   If through the talk of these scandalmongers
   Our love will turn itself to naught.
   And so I've got to stay on guard
   More than you—by St. Martial I swear!—
   For you're the thing that matters most.

7. Friend, I know you're changeable
   In the way you handle your love,
   And I think that as a chevalier
   You're one of that shifting kind;
   And I'm justified in blaming you,
   For I'm sure other things are on your mind,
   Since I'm no longer the thought that's there.

8. Lady, I'll never carry again
   My falcon, never hunt with a hawk,
   If, now that you've given me joy entire,
   I started chasing another girl.
   No, I'm not that kind of shyster:
   It's envy makes those two-faced talk.
   They make up tales and paint me vile.

9. Friend, should I accept your word
   So that I can hold you forever true?

10. Lady, from now on you'll have me true,
    For I'll never think of another.

More direct than most of the poetry of her male counterparts, the following song leaves no doubt about the lady's fiery passion. The slighting reference to the husband may have amused the Count, for this is after all a fictional account of a woman who has much in common with the Wife of Bath in Chaucer's *Canterbury Tales*.

TROUBADOUR SONG

Beatritz, Countess of Dia

1. I've suffered great distress
   From a knight whom I once owned.
   Now, for all time, be it known:
   I loved him—yes, to excess.
       His jilting I've regretted,
   Yet his love I never really returned.
   Now for my sin I can only burn:
       Dressed, or in my bed.

2. O, if I had that knight to caress
   Naked all night in my arms,
   He'd be ravished by the charm
   Of using, for cushion, my breast.
       His love I more deeply prize
   Than Floris did Blancheflor's.
   Take that love, my core,
       My sense, my life, my eyes!

3. Lovely lover, gracious, kind,
   When will I overcome your fight?
   O, if I could lie with you one night!
   Feel those loving lips on mine!
       Listen, one thing sets me afire:
   Here in my husband's place I want *you*,
   If you'll just keep your promise true:
       Give me everything I desire.

By the middle of the twelfth century, troubadour influences had spread to northern France where notable trouvères included Blondel de Nesles (b. ca. 1155), minstrel to Richard the Lionhearted (ruled 1189–1199 and himself a trouvère); Thibaut IV, King of Navarre (1201–1253); and Adam de la Halle (ca. 1240–1287). Like troubadour cansos, trouvère chansons were monophonic with accompaniment an option depending on available instruments. The following *virelai* is a trouvère form that begins with a refrain that repeats after each verse. Composed by an unknown trouvère, this is a superb example of the sophisticated style of northern France.

Listening Example 6

Trouvère Virelai

"Or la truix"[4] (12th–13th century; excerpt)

Time: :45

Musical theme

Or la truix trop durete, voir, voir! A ceu k'elle est simplete.
(I find it hard to woo her, indeed! Because she is so simple.
Trop por outrecuidiés me taius, cant je cudoie estre certains
Much too presumptuous did I act, e'en though it seem'd I was so sure
de ceu ke n'averaides mois, oix, oix! C'est ceu ke plus me blece.
of that which I shan't have so soon, alas! 'Tis mostly that which hurts me.
Or la truix trop durete, voir, voir! A ceu k'elle est simplete.
I find it hard to woo her, indeed! Because she is so simple.)

In 1208 Pope Innocent III preached a crusade against the Albigensian heresy (latter-day Manicheans; see St. Augustine), stating that the church must "use against heretics the spiritual sword of excommunication, and if this does not prove effective, use the material sword." Exploiting the Albigensian Crusade as an excuse to plunder the south of France, nobles and the French Crown totally destroyed the high culture that had fostered the troubadour tradition, chivalry, and the Courts of Love.

Minnesingers and Meistersingers

The *minnesinger* (Ger., *minne*, love) of Germanic literature flourished during the twelfth and thirteenth centuries. Despite the title of "love singer" these poet-musicians were strongly influenced by Christianity and sang spiritual songs of sadness, of tears, and of thoughts of death. The *minnesong* was, in effect, a reconciliation of Christian elements with erotic-secular literature of the troubadour-trouvère tradition.

Meistersingers (master singers) were "prize" singers of the fourteenth through sixteenth centuries. The art of the minnesinger was transformed into a guild of singers who practiced the art and craft of writing and singing songs much as cabinetmakers practiced the art of woodworking. The best-known meistersinger was Hans Sachs, the protagonist of Richard Wagner's opera *Die Meistersinger von Nürnberg.*

---

4. Bodleian Oxford, Douce 308, folio 226 and 237. The form is ABAA.

Polyphonic Music

The high point of medieval music was the development of polyphony. Polyphony (*Gk., poly-phonos*, many voices) is a style of music in which two or more melodies are played and/or sung together. "Row, Row, Row Your Boat," when sung as a round, is an example of one kind of polyphonic music in which the same melody is sung at different times. "Jesu, Joy of Man's Desiring" by J. S. Bach combines three different melodies.

Related to polyphonic music is a style that evolved several centuries later and is called homophonic (Gk., *homo-phonos*, same voice). Homophonic music consists of a single melody plus accompaniment or, to put it another way, melody and harmony. For example, "The Star Spangled Banner" and "The Battle Hymn of the Republic" are homophonic.

Polyphonic and homophonic are the two aspects of multivoiced music. Neither style exists in a pure form. Music that emphasizes two or more melodies of roughly equal importance is termed polyphonic. Homophonic music emphasizes a predominant melody line accompanied by harmony. The two styles may be illustrated as follows:

Non-Western music (Middle and Far East and Africa) never developed polyphonic or homophonic styles of music. Polyphony was spontaneous rather than planned, the result of accidental conjunctions of melodies rather than a premeditated polyphonic practice such as that developed by Western culture.

Polyphony and harmony (homophony) in Western culture are therefore unique in the world of music. Without the development of polyphonic music during the Middle Ages no subsequent expansion of musical styles could have taken place: no Bach, Beethoven, Beatles, Bob Dylan, or Rolling Stones; no blues, ragtime, jazz, country-western, rock, or pop.

Medieval polyphonic music originally drew on the rich treasury of monophonic chants. Early attempts at multiple melodies were quite literal: another voice was added at a fixed interval from the original chant (*parallel organum*). Later, in *free organum,* the two voices generally moved in contrary motion, that is, when one voice went up the other would go down. Still later, in *melismatic organum,* one voice moved slowly on prolonged notes (the original chant) while the other traced elaborate melismas.

Listening Example 7

Early Polyphony: Organum (900–1150)

Parallel: "Rex caeli, Domine"[5]

Time: 2:45

Unison Start ⎡——— Fixed Interval ———⎤ Unison Cadence

Etc.

Rex cae - li Do - mi - ne ma - ris un - di - so - ni.

Free: Trope, "Agnus Dei"[6]

Trope

Etc.

Qui ————————

Melismatic: "Benedicamo Domino"[7]

Etc.

Be - - ne -

Cantus Firmus

Eventually the chant melody was consistently placed in the lowest voice and referred to as the *cantus firmus* (fixed song). The chant was identified by quoting the initial phrase of the Latin text. The cantus firmus was also called the tenor (Latin, *tenere,* to hold) because it held (retained) the original chant.

All polyphonic compositions of the medieval period used a cantus firmus, usually assigned to the tenor, as a basis for writing music. The practice of using authorized liturgical music (plainsong) as a foundation for composing original music is comparable to basing a sermon on a scriptural quotation. Both procedures quote an approved source as the prerequisite for what was essentially an exercise in creativity.

Polyphonic writing developed rapidly during the twelfth century due, in part, to the invention of rhythmic notation by composers of the School of Music associated with the Cathedral of Notre Dame in Paris. The Paris composers wanted the larger sound of more voices for the cavernous nave of Notre Dame. They began writing three- and four-part compositions after they discovered how to synchronize the different voices, how to keep the singers moving together to the right notes at the right time. This Notre Dame notation (now called rhythmic modes) was based on the poetic modes such as iambic, dactylic, trochaic, and so forth. These were patterns of long and short sounds that were transformed into musical notation. The remarkable thing about rhythmic notation was that "it represented the first symbolic manipulation of measured time—time independent of motion and detached from the environment."[8] The Notre Dame composers were the first to discover how to measure time.

Following is a three-part organum by Perotin, probably the foremost composer of the Notre Dame School. The beginning measures are given in musical notation so that the two voice parts plus instrumental line can be seen as well as heard. The music is now "measured" with a time signature and bar lines separating the measures. Any of the melodies can be sung, whistled, or played on an instrument. The complexity of polyphony results from the simultaneity of, in this case, rather uncomplicated melody lines.

5. M. Gerbert, *Scriptores,* St. Blaise, 1784, Vol. I, p. 167.

6. Besseler, *Die Musik das Mitteralters,* Potsdam, 1931, p. 95.

7. F. Ludwig, *Handbuch der Musikgeschichte,* Frankfurt am Main, 1924, p. 148.

8. Szamosi, Geza. "The Origin of Time: How Medieval Musicians Invented the Fourth Dimension." *The Sciences* 26 (September/October 1986):33–37.

Listening Example 8

Three-Part Organum

Perotin (12th century), "Alleluya" (Nativitas) (excerpt)[9]

Time: 1:30

The *motet,* one of the most important forms of sacred music, was developed in the thirteenth century. In the following example, the text indicates only the source of the borrowed plainsong because an instrument was now used for the cantus firmus. Immediately above the tenor is a composed line with its own set of words, hence the name *motetus* (Fr., *le mot,* the word). The top voice also had its own set of words, which could be a different poem or even a different language. Increasing secularization led to motets, such as the one illustrated, with variations on the same love song sung in French by the *Triplum* and *Motetus.* Titles of early motets were given by indicating the beginning words of all three texts. The opening measures of notation again illustrate the uncomplicated nature of the individual melodies.

Listening Example 9

Motet

Anonymous, "En non Diu! Quant voi; Eius in Oriente" (13th century excerpt)[10]

Time: 1:03

The earliest extant piece in six parts is the "Reading Rota," a double round found at Reading Abbey and set to a Middle English text: "Sumer Is Icumen In." The top melody is sung by four voices as a four-part round. One voice begins alone, the second voice begins when the first has gotten to the *, and so on. At the same time the lower two voices sing a two-part round to the words "sing cuccu."

Listening Example 10

Double Round

Anonymous, "Sumer Is Icumen In" (ca. 1240; excerpt)

Time: 1:38

Sum - er is i - cum - en in____ Lhud - e sing cuc - cu

Sing cuc - cu nu,____ Sing cuc - cu

Sing cuc - cu   Sing cuc - cu

---

9. Y. Rokseth, *Polyphonies du XIIIe siecle* (Paris, 1935).

10. Y. Rokseth, *Polyphonies du XIIIe siecle* (Paris, 1935).

Polyphonic Mass

Musical styles developed very rapidly during the Gothic period (thirteenth and fourteenth centuries) and some composers acquired international reputations. Paradoxically, composers came to be known by name while many of the great master builders of Gothic cathedrals remained anonymous. Guillaume de Machaut, equally proficient as poet and as a composer of both sacred and secular music, was the most acclaimed of the gifted artists of the late Middle Ages (figure 16.4). He was the first to write a polyphonic setting of all five movements of the ordinary of the Mass, a practice that was subsequently followed by every major composer through the sixteenth century and by many composers up to the present day.

The following portion of the *Agnus Dei* is sung by the upper three voices and accompanied by an instrument on the *contratenor* part, as indicated by the absence of text. The tenor, now the next lowest voice, still sings the cantus firmus. The polyphonic Mass, as distinguished from a motet, uses the Latin text of the monophonic chant. The beginning of the movement is notated in an open score (one staff for each part) so that the more complex movement of the melodies can be compared with the examples previously given of an organum and a motet.

FIGURE 16.4 *"Machaut Receiving Honors of Royalty and Clergy." Miniature by the Master of Bocqueteaux. Biblioteque Nazionale, Paris. This first known portrait of a Western composer is indicative both of Machaut's reputation and the status of a creative artist in Gothic France.*

Listening Example 11

Polyphonic Mass

Guillaume de Machaut (ca. 1300–1377), "Agnus Dei" (excerpt), *Mass of Notre Dame* (1364)[11]

Time: 1:30

Medieval Dance

Sacred Dance

Dancing as a glorification of God was widely accepted in early Christian communities. Especially popular was the "Hymn of Jesus," a round dance (or ring dance) with twelve dancers representing the twelve disciples and the twelve signs of the zodiac. The idea of zodiac dancing in order to restore order to the cosmos can be traced as far back as the ancient Egyptians. However, the most direct influence probably stemmed from the Pythagorean concept of the music of the spheres. This ring dance was also called the Ring Dance of Angels or, simply, Angel Dance.

The *tripudium* dated from early Christianity and was one of the few dance steps to survive into the medieval period. A tripudium was a three-step dance with two steps forward and one step backward. The dance symbolized both the Holy Trinity and, probably, the concept of two (spiritual) steps forward and one (human frailty) step backwards. Beginning as a solemn processional dance, the tripudium later evolved into a lively hopping dance that is still performed in modern Luxembourg in honor of a medieval saint.

"The Way of Jerusalem" was a stately dance that symbolized a pilgrimage to the Holy City. The dance was executed on the design of a labyrinth inlaid in the floor of the church nave. A leader was chosen whose function it was to determine the pace and the steps that matched the pattern of the floor tiles. This was a slow, spiraling dance that coordinated the dance steps with an accompanying chant. In order to make it all the way to Jerusalem, the leader had to arrive at the center of the labyrinth at the precise moment that the final syllable of the chant was sung. The dance was usually performed on a labyrinth modeled after the Cretan version in the palace of King Minos at Knossos. The labyrinth at the Cathedral of Chartres dates from the twelfth century and is forty feet in diameter.

11. H. Besseler, *Die Musik des Mittelalters und der Renaissance* (Bucken, *Handbuch der Musikwissenschaft*), Potsdam, 1931, p. 149.

The Dance of Death (*Danse Macabre*) was a phenomenon that appeared during the plague (Black Death), an epidemic that began in Constantinople in 1347 and ravaged all of Europe. The pestilence was virulent and, at the time, inexplicable. An explanation was nevertheless forthcoming: God was punishing the wicked for their sins. The universal hysteria generated by the plague was fanned by the preaching of the Church, which called upon the sinners to repent.

The peasants, especially, suffering from plague, war, and famine, responded with repentance based on fear: fear of eternal damnation, of the plague, of the dancing ghouls from the graveyard who sought the living for the dance of death. The living, in turn, executed the dance in propitiation of their sins and in hopes of forestalling the Angel of Death.

Choreomania, a kind of dance mania, probably first appeared in England in the twelfth century. It was characterized by group psychosis and frenzied, even demented dancing. During the plague of the Black Death flagellants danced, sang, and vigorously lashed themselves in order to avert the wrath of God. Some participants died while dancing; others were mentally and/or physically crippled for the rest of their lives.

In 1374 a great dance epidemic broke out in most of Europe. Contemporary accounts of this manic behavior were medically farfetched but graphically descriptive of the pervasiveness of this kind of mass hysteria. *Choreomania* has been attributed to many causes, including psychotic reactions to the problems of war, famine, plague, and fear of death.

Secular Dance

Little is known of dancing in the early Middle Ages, but by the eighth or ninth centuries social dancing was a universal activity enjoyed by all persons at all levels of society. The frequent fairs and festivals, with the attendant vigorous dancing, enabled the peasantry to temporarily forget their otherwise bleak and meager existence. Their dances ranged from solo or lusty round dances to gaily executed couple dances.

The milkmaid's dance was an integral part of the May festival, a rite of spring that began on May 29th with a milking festival followed by games and dancing around the fertility symbol of the Maypole. Involving flirtatious milkmaids, garlands of flowers, and virile male pursuit, the milkmaid's dance appears to have been a kind of blindman's buff set to music.

The country dance (round dance) has been a popular folk form in virtually every society. The lustiness of peasant country dancing is legendary, an exuberance that was tamed by the feudal lords and ladies to become the more genteel contre dance. In the contre dance, there was gradual entrance of couple after couple, which led to a round dance followed by couple dances, all somewhat in the manner of ballroom dancing.

The estampie (Provencal, *estamper*, to stamp) was the most popular dance of the Gothic Age and also one of the oldest forms of instrumental music. Originally a gay open-air dance, it eventually became more compact and, by the fifteenth century was performed indoors. Although it probably began as a round dance, it was the most popular couple dance of the age.

The music for the estampie was in 3/4 time and consisted of short, rotating phrases that were repeated many times during the course of the dance. To begin the dance, couples stood side by side in a semicircle. The first part of the dance began with both starting on the same foot with a step, close, step, close to first position with heels together. The movements were first to the right, then backward, then forward, then backward once more, and then begin the pattern all over again.

Following is a two-part estampie with the parts labeled simply as Cantus Superior (C.S.) and Cantus Inferior (C.I.). They were to be played by any available instruments. An approximation of the medieval dancing mood can be attained by executing the steps of the estampie to an accompaniment of any two or more different instruments. Percussion instruments such as drum, tambourine, bells, and triangle can and should be added. Liveliness of spirit is far more important than precise execution of dance steps and music.

Listening Example 12

Estampie

Anonymous, Estampie: "Instrumental Dance" (13th century; excerpt)[12]

Time: 1:00
13th century

Table 16.2, *Development of Medieval Music,* is an outline and summary of the major developments in music during the Middle Ages. Dotted lines indicate either prior development leading up to a specific musical instrument or, as with monasticism, the waning influence of that way of life. Arrows indicate continuing development or, as with the connection between feudalism and chivalry, one developing out of the other.

---

12. Wooldridge, *Early English Harmony,* London, 1897, pl. 19.

TABLE 16.2 Development of Medieval Music

	600	700	800	900	1000	1100	1200	1300	1400
Stylistic Periods	Romanesque ———				High Romanesque ———		Early Gothic ———		Late Gothic ———
General Periods	Monasticism ———		Feudalism ———			Crusades ·········			
						Age of Chivalry ····			
Musical Periods	Early Middle Ages ———					School of St. Martial ———	School of N. Dame ———	Ars Antiqua ———	Ars nova
Musical Styles **Monophonic Music**									
Sacred	Gregorian Chant ———			Sequences, Tropes ———					
					Liturgical Drama (Conductus) ———				
Secular				Goliards ———					
				Jongleurs ———					
						Troubadours ———			
							Trouvères ———		
							Minnesingers ———		
									Meistersingers
Polyphonic Music				Organum ———			Motet ———		
									Mass ———
Instrumental Music **Dances**						Estampie (Ductia) ———			
Musical Instruments						Flageolet ·········			Recorder
						(Drum) Tabor ———			
	(aulos) ·········					Shawm ———			
	? ·········					Bagpipe ———			
						Trumpet ———			
						Lute ———			
	(kithara) ·········					Gittern ———			
					Rabab ———	Rebec ———			
								Vielle ———	

The compositional school of Notre Dame was indebted to the School of St. Martial for the latter's development of organum. The Ars Antiqua (Old Art) and Ars Nova (New Art) were theoretical labels for old and new styles of music. Guillaume de Machaut was recognized in his own time as a composer of new music, that is, modern music.

The listing of musical instruments provides only a cross section of the many that were available. Other instruments that could have been listed include the psaltery, harp, rotta (Celtic lyre), fiddle, horn, and a large variety of percussion instruments.

Exercises

1. Hearing an authentic performance of music that has been sung for a thousand years or more is an experience worth pursuing. Find, if you can, a vocal group in your area that sings Gregorian chant. This choir might be in a Catholic church or monastery or in a college music department. The latter group is usually called a Collegium Musicum, a chorus that performs medieval music.

2. How does a Protestant service (Presbyterian, Methodist, Episcopalian, and so on) differ from the Catholic mass? (Note: The several denominations also differ considerably from each other.) What do the mass and various forms of Protestant services have in common?

3. What, if anything, do rock lyrics have in common with troubadour songs? You might want to look up additional troubadour songs for better comparisons.

Summary/Culture and Human Values

The history of medieval music is much more than the study of the musical practices of a cultural period. Music of any era, in the playing and the singing, reflects and expresses the hopes, aspirations, frustrations, and despairs of people of all classes and stations in life. Music is still the nearest equivalent to an international language that humanity has yet devised.

Medieval music, when properly performed, can convey to us the *sound* of an era. It can bring alive the vast panorama of medieval life from Gregorian chant to liturgical drama, from troubadour love songs to peasant dances.

The sound of the music has a correlation with the architectural styles of the period. Gregorian chant, for example, was intended for participating worshippers rather than a listening audience. It is, therefore, more effective and persuasive inside the cloistered security of of the monastery with its narrow windows, heavy walls, and pervasive quietude.

Polyphonic music, on the other hand, was performance oriented. The greatly expanded interior space of Romanesque churches was a proper area for the new multivoiced style. The arching melodies of organum complemented the rounded arches and high vaulting of the large Romanesque churches.

The dynamic, asymmetrical, complex mass of interacting tension of stone structure, pointed arches, and soaring vaults that is the Gothic cathedral has its aural counterpart in the dynamic, asymmetrical, complex, and tension-packed art that is Gothic polyphonic music. That the first polyphonic mass was written for performance in the Cathedral of Notre Dame in Paris is more than coincidental. Guillaume de Machaut wrote music, whether consciously or unconsciously, to completely fill the interior of that great cathedral with vigorous and brilliant sound.

Annotated Bibliography

Collins, Fletcher, Jr. *The Production of Medieval Church Music–Drama.* Charlottesville: The University Press of Virginia, 1972. Both historical and practical.

Drinker, Sophie. *Music and Women: The Story of Women in Their Relation to Music.* New York: Coward McCann, 1948, reprinted 1980. Influential women in music, art, poetry, and politics from the ancient world to the modern era.

Harksen, Sibylle. *Women in the Middle Ages.* New York: Abner Schram, 1975. From anonymous women in everyday life to those in art, music, professions, and positions of power.

Liber Usualis. Tournai, Belgium: Desclee & Cie, 1952. The complete liturgical music (Gregorian chant) of the Roman Catholic church.

Strunk, Oliver. *Source Readings in Music History from Classical Antiquity through the Romantic Era.* New York: W. W. Norton & Company, 1950. Useful primary material about music excerpted from the writings of Clement of Alexander, St. Basil, St. Jerome, St. Augustine, Boethius, Cassiodorus, Odo of Cluny, Guido of Arezzo, and others.

Whigham, Peter, ed. *The Music of the Troubadours.* Santa Barbara: Ross–Erikson, 1979. Good collection of words and music.

Wilhelm, James J. *Seven Troubadours: The Creators of Modern Verse.* University Park: The Pennsylvania State University Press, 1970. Engaging study of some fascinating troubadours.

Appendix
Music Listening and Notation

Music listening is always enriched by a knowledge of basic facts such as those outlined herein. This appendix should, ideally, be studied for content and also used, along with the glossary, as often as necessary in conjunction with the chapters on music.

Characteristics of Musical Sounds

Musical tones are sounds of definite pitch and duration, as distinct from noises and other less definite sounds. Musical tones have the four characteristics of *pitch, intensity, tone color,* and *duration,* which may be described as follows:

Pitch   The location of musical sound from low to high or high to low.
Intensity   Relative degree of softness or loudness.
Tone Color   The quality of a sound that distinguishes it from other musical sounds of the same pitch and intensity; for example, the different tone quality of a flute as contrasted with a clarinet. Also called *timbre.*
Duration   The length of time a tone is audible.

The Four Elements of Music

Rhythm, melody, harmony, and *tone color* are the essential elements of music. Composers and performers are concerned with each, while for the listener, they are experienced as a web of sound that makes it difficult to single out any one element. Each can, however, be considered in isolation as a guide to understanding.

Rhythm

Though little is known about prehistoric music, the earliest music was probably the beating out of rhythms long before the existence of either melody or speech. There is rhythm in the universe: our heartbeat, alternating day and night, the progression of the seasons, waves crashing on a beach. Manufactured rhythm can be heard in train wheels clicking on rails, a Ping-Pong game, or the clacking castanets of a Spanish dancer.

Essentially, rhythm is the organization of musical time, that is, everything that takes place in terms of sound and silence, accent and nonaccent, tension and relaxation. Rhythm can also be defined as the "melody of a monotone"; music can be recognized just by hearing its rhythm. For example, tapping out the rhythmic patterns of "Dixie" can bring that familiar melody to mind.

Rhythm is the name of the whole and is not to be confused with *beat,* which results from a certain regularity of the rhythmic patterns. Beat, or pulse, can be compared with the heartbeat or the pulse rate. The beat will usually be steady but it may temporarily speed up or slow down. It may be *explicit* (the uniform thump of a bass drum in a marching band) or *implicit* (resulting from combinations of rhythmic patterns). As soon as one duration follows another, there will be rhythm but not necessarily beat. Certain types of music (such as Gregorian chant) do not produce the regular pulsation called beat.

When beats are produced by the music in a repeating pattern of accents, the result is *meter. Metered* music is *measured* music, with groupings of two, three, or four beats (or combinations of these) in each *measure,* or *bar.*

Time Signatures

When there is a regular pattern of accented and unaccented beats, it is customary to use a *time signature* in which the upper figure indicates the number of beats in a measure and the lower figure (though not in every case), the unit of beat; that is, the note value the composer has selected to symbolize one beat. For example:

2 = two beats per measure (duple meter)
4 = ♩ unit of beat (quarter note receives one beat)

3 = three beats per measure (triple meter)
8 = ♪ unit of beat (eighth note receives one beat)

Melody and Harmony

A melody is a horizontal organization of pitches or, simply, a succession of musical tones. Harmony is a vertical organization of pitches in which two or more tones are sounded together. The following example illustrates melody on the upper staff and harmony on the lower staff.

Old Folks at Home

Tone Color

Sometimes called timbre (TAM-ber), tone color is to music what color is to the painter. It is tone color that enables us to distinguish between a flute, a clarinet, and an oboe. A soprano voice is higher in pitch than a bass voice, but the tone color is also different. Through experience, everyone has learned to recognize the unique colors of many instruments. Further study leads to finer discriminations between similar instruments such as violin and viola, oboe and English horn, and so on. Composers select instruments for expressive purposes based largely on their coloration, whether singly or in combination. The full sound of a Beethoven symphony differs from a work by Richard Strauss, for example, because Strauss uses a wider range of instrumental colors.

Musical Literacy

The most abstract of the arts, music is sound moving in time. Factual information about music certainly helps the listener, but all the facts in the world can only assist the listening process; information about music can never replace the sound of music. One extremely useful method of instruction is to present major themes and ideas in musical notation, a practice common to virtually all books on music listening.

A practical approach to intelligent listening must include some instruction in musical literacy sufficient to read a single line of music. This is a simple process that can be quickly learned by young children and can be taught to an adult in a few minutes. The strangely prevalent folklore about musical notation being "too hard" or "too technical" has no foundation in fact, and probably refers to reading music as a performer, which is a very different matter that need not concern us here. As basic to music as the ABC's of written language but easier to understand, musical notation is an indispensable guide for music listeners. Learning to read music well enough to figure out a single line of music and to plunk it out on a piano is simply basic musical literacy.

Educated listeners quickly learn to enjoy picking out musical themes. This turns abstract sounds into tangible tunes, thus giving the listener an opportunity to preview the themes so that they can be anticipated in the music. Equally valuable is the repetition of themes after the listening experience. To summarize, picking out melodies is an aid to understanding, a helpful preview of music to be listened to, and a reminder of music already heard.

Approach the following material not with apprehension but with anticipation. Master the principles of musical notation with the positive attitude that this will materially assist not only in a better understanding of the music in this text but also lead, in time, to a lifetime of pleasurable listening.

Musical Notation

Pitch

The essential elements of our notational system were devised some ten centuries ago and subsequently altered and augmented to become a reasonably efficient means of communicating the composer's intentions to listener and performer. The system is based on the first seven letters of the alphabet and can best be illustrated by using a segment of the piano keyboard. The pitches range from low to high, from A through G in a repeating A–G pattern.

In order to know which of the eight A's available on the piano is the intended note, the following is necessary:

1. Use a musical *staff* of five lines and four spaces.

2. Use a symbol for a musical pitch, i.e., *note*. o

3. Place the notes on the lines or in the spaces of the staff.

4. Indicate by means of a *clef sign* the *names* of the notes.

Clef (French, *key*) implies that the key to precise placement of the notes is the establishment of the letter name of *one* of the lines or spaces of the staff. There are two clefs in common use. Both are ornamental symbols derived from the letters G and F. The solid lines are the present clef signs and the dotted lines their original form:

The clefs are placed on the staff to indicate the location of the letters they represent. The lower portion of the G clef curls around the second line to fix the location of G; the two dots of the F clef are placed above and below the fourth line to show that this is the F line.

Once the five-line staff has received its pitch designation of G or F, the *staff* is subsequently identified as a *treble* or a *bass staff*.

Treble Staff

Bass Staff

Not all melodies are composed so that they can be played on the white notes only of the piano. Sometimes another *key,* or different set of pitches, is used as demonstrated in the following examples:

Joy to the World

Key of C

In the second version the *key signature* indicates that all of the F's and C's have been raised a half step to the next closest note. A symbol called a sharp (♯) indicates raised notes. Key signatures can include up to seven sharps or flats.

Joy to the World

Key of D

The other common symbol that changes a note is the *flat* (♭), which lowers a note a half step to the next closest note. Following is the same melody written in the key of B♭. As indicated by the key signature, all the B's and E's have been lowered to B♭ and E♭.

Joy to the World

Key of B♭

You will note that the staff given above has an added short line, a *ledger line,* used to accommodate the last two notes.

A piano keyboard has *white* keys and *black* keys, with the black keys grouped in alternating sets of two and three. The white note, or key, immediately to the left of the two black keys is always C. There are eight C's; the C closest to the center is *middle C.* It is from this C that you can locate the notes of the themes.

Middle C   Middle C

Below is a guide to the *chromatic scale,* which is all of the black and white keys in one octave.

Chromatic Scale

Duration

The notation of the length of time of musical sounds (and silences) was developed in conjunction, more or less, with the notation of pitch. The modern *note-value* system consists of fractional parts of a whole unit, or *whole note* (𝅝), expressed in mathematical terms as 1/1. A *half note* (𝅗𝅥) is one-half the whole unit, or 1/2; a *quarter note* (𝅘𝅥) is one-quarter the unit, or 1/4; and so forth.

The *name* of the note value indicates the *number* of notes in the whole-note unit. There are four quarter notes (4 × 1/4 = 1/1), eight eighth notes (8 × 1/8 = 1/1), etc.

With note values smaller than the whole note, the relationships remain constant. There are two quarter notes in a half note (2 × 1/4 = 1/2), two eighth notes in a quarter note (2 × 1/8 = 1/4), etc.

Rhythmic notation is both relative and fixed. The duration of a whole note is dependent on the tempo (speed) and notation of music. It may have a duration of one second, eight seconds, or something in between. The interior relationships, however, never vary.

A whole note has the same duration as two half notes, four quarter notes, and so forth. The mathematical relationship is fixed and precise. See the table below for an outline of the system.

Table 3.1. Note and Rest Values

Note Value	Symbol
Whole note (basic unit)	𝅝
Half note	𝅗𝅥
Quarter note	𝅘𝅥
Eighth note	𝅘𝅥𝅮
Sixteenth note	𝅘𝅥𝅯

Rest Value	Symbol
Whole (note) rest	▬
Half rest	▬
Quarter rest	𝄽
Eighth rest	𝄾
Sixteenth rest	𝄿

Voices and Instruments

Choral ensembles are usually divided into four voice parts ranging from high to low: soprano and alto (women) and tenor and bass (men).

Instruments of the symphony orchestra and other ensembles are grouped by family, from highest pitch to lowest:

Strings	Woodwinds	Brass	Percussion
violin	piccolo	trumpet	snare drum
viola	flute	(and cornet)	timpani
cello	oboe	French horn	bass drum
bass	clarinet	trombone	cymbals
	bassoon	tuba	many others

Keyboard instruments include piano, harpsichord, and organ. The piano, originally called pianoforte, is based on the principle of hammers striking the strings; the harpsichord has a mechanism that plucks the strings. Built with two or more keyboards called manuals, organs either use forced air to activate the pipes or some version of an electronic reproduction of sound.

Musical Texture

The words for the three kinds of musical texture are derived from Greek and are virtually self-explanatory:

Monophonic (one sound)
Homophonic (same sound)
Polyphonic (many sounds)

Monophonic music has a single unaccompanied melody line. Much of the world's music is monophonic, including Chinese and Hindu music and, in Western civilizations, Gregorian chant and troubadour songs. Homophonic music has a principal melodic line accompanied by harmony, sometimes referred to as chordal accompaniment. While it is relatively unknown outside Western culture, homophonic comprises the bulk of our music including nearly all popular music. Polyphonic music has two or more melodies sounding simultaneously. Familiar rounds like "Three Blind Mice" and "Row, Row, Row Your Boat" are polyphonic, as is most Renaissance music. The music of baroque composers such as Bach, Handel, and many others is basically polyphonic.

Musical Form

Briefly stated, form in music is a balance of unity and variety. Too much unity becomes boring, while excessive variety leads to fragmentation and even chaos. Understanding form in music is a high priority for educated listeners. As Robert Schumann remarked, "Only when the form is quite clear to you will the spirit become clear to you."

The smallest unit of form is the *motive,* which to be intelligible must have at least two notes plus an identifiable rhythmic pattern. The principle motive in the first movement of Beethoven's Fifth Symphony has two different pitches in a four-note rhythmic pattern:

A musical phrase is a coherent group of notes roughly comparable to a literary phrase and having about the same function. Two related phrases form a *period,* in the manner of a literary sentence. In the period illustrated below, note that the first phrase has a transitional ending called a *half cadence,* while the second phrase ends solidly with a *full cadence.* Note also the extreme unity; the first three measures of both phrases are identical.

In large works the musical periods are used in various combinations to expand the material into sections comparable to paragraphs, and these are then combined to make still larger units.

Musical structure can be comprehended only *after* the music has arrived at wherever the composer intends it to go. Look again at "Ode to Joy." You can "see" its form only because the music is notated, which is why learning some notation is so important. When the music is played, your ear follows the line to the half cadence, which is then heard as a statement that demands completion. As the second phrase begins, there is aural recognition of its relationship to the first phrase. When the second phrase concludes with a gratifying full cadence, there is a kind of flashback to the memory of the first phrase. In other words, the conclusion of the second phrase is satisfying because it completes the thought of

the still-remembered first phrase. The music conforms to its own inner logic; that is, the second phrase is a logical consequence of the first.

As a general rule, most music is constructed around two different but logically related (inner logic) musical ideas. We can call one idea *A* and the other *B.* One common musical form is two-part (binary), or simply A–B. An even more common form is three-part (ternary), or A–B–A. In two-part form the composer makes a musical statement (A), which is followed by a new section (B), which is sufficiently different to provide variety but not so different as to destroy the balance. The following hymn tune is a complete composition in two-part form, with two phrases in each section. Section B has the same rhythm as Section A, but the melody is a kind of inversion of the melody in A. The inner logic is maintained through the similarities.

The following complete hymn tune has a form related to two-part form: A–A^1–B, called A, A prime, B. Part A is followed by another A that is varied going into the cadence. Part B is properly different but related to A and A^1 by the similarity of measures 2, 6, and 10. In terms of measures, the structure of the piece can be diagrammed as:

Three-part form operates on the principle of closing with the melody that began the piece, a rounding off of the material: A–B–A. The following example can be analyzed as A–A^1–B–A^1 and diagrammed as:

$$\begin{array}{cccc} A & A^1 & B & A^1 \\ 4+4 & 4+4 & 4+4 & 4+4. \end{array}$$

This is the thirty-two-measure form most commonly used for popular songs.

There are, of course, other variants of AB and ABA forms as well as several other structures. However, the examples given illustrate the principle of a balance between unity and variety, of which unity is paramount. Perhaps because it is rather amorphous, music, more than any other art, emphasizes repetition, restating the material again and again, but mixing with enough variety to maintain interest. The forms illustrated can also be heard in the larger context of longer compositions. For example, "In the Gloaming" has 32 measures in a basic ABA form; a large symphonic work could have, say, 200 measures and be diagrammed as follows:

A	B	A	*or*	A	B	A¹	*or*	A	B	A¹
aba	aba	aba		aba¹	aba	aba¹		aa¹ba	aba	aa¹ba¹

The Listening Experience

Listening to music begins with the question, What do you hear? This is an objective question that has nothing whatever to do with a story you may imagine the music is telling, random associations the music happens to trigger, or any meaning that may be attributed to the music. For the educated listener the procedure is to objectively identify the sounds you hear, to determine how the sounds are produced, and to try to determine how the sounds are organized.

Composers do not pour out notes as if emptying a glass of water on a tabletop. They arrange their sounds in a sort of container in a manner that molds the container to the material it holds. Learning to comprehend the musical structure leads inevitably to the ability to *anticipate* the next melody, cadence, section, or whatever. Being able to anticipate what is to happen next means that you are tuned in to the web of sound, listening along with the pace of the music. Almost everyone has already acquired the ability to follow the progress of popular music and to anticipate what comes next in favorite recordings. As stated before, the larger world of classical music is only a step beyond the listening expertise of most individuals.

Glossary

Pronunciation: Approximations are given where necessary. The syllables are to be read as English words and with the capital letters accented.

Abbreviations: L., Latin; F., French; G., German; Gk., Greek; I., Italian; v., Vide (see).

Asterisks: An asterisk preceding a word or phrase indicates that a definition and/or illustration can be found under that heading.

A

Abacus　The flat slab on top of a *capital.

Academy　Originally derived from the *Akademeia,* the grove in which Plato taught his seminars.

Acanthus　A plant whose thick leaves are reproduced in stylized form on *Corinthian capitals. (See figure 10.9.)

A cappella　(ah ka-PELL-ah; L.) Originally unaccompanied music sung "in the chapel." Term now applies to choral music without instrumental accompaniment.

Acoustics　The science of sound.

Aerial perspective　*See* Perspective.

Aesthetic　Concerned with a sensitivity to the pleasurable and the beautiful; the opposite of anaesthetic.

Aesthetics　The study or philosophy of beauty; theory of the fine arts and human responses.

Agnosticism　(Gk., *agnostos,* unknowing) The impossibility of obtaining knowledge of certain subjects; assertion that people cannot obtain knowledge of God.

Agnus Dei　(L., Lamb of God) Last item of the *Ordinary of the *Mass.

Agora　In ancient Greece, a marketplace/public square.

Allegory　A literary mode with a literal level of meanings plus a set of meanings above and beyond themselves. This second level may be religious, social, political, or philosophical, e.g., *The Faerie Queen* by Spenser is an allegory about Christian virtues.

Alleluia　Latinization for the Hebrew *Halleluyah* ("praise ye the Lord"). Third item of the *Proper of the *Mass.

Altarpiece　A painted (or sculptured) panel placed behind an altar.

Ambulatory　A passageway around the *apse of a church. (See figure 15.24.)

Amphora　Greek vase, usually quite large, with two handles and used to store food staples. (See colorplate 11.)

Apocalypse　Prophetic revelation; the Book of Revelation in the New Testament.

A posteriori　(a-pos-TEER-e-or-e; L., following after) Reasoning from observed facts to conclusions; inductive; empirical.

A priori　(a-pree-OAR-e) Reasoning from general propositions to particular conclusions; deductive; nonempirical.

Apse　A recess, usually semicircular, in the east wall of a Christian church or, in a Roman *basilica, at the wall opposite to the general entrance way.

Arabesque　Literally Arab-like. Elaborate designs of intertwined flowers, foliage, and geometric patterns used in Islamic architecture.

Arcade　A series of connected *arches resting on columns. (See figure 10.10.)

Arch　A curved structure (semicircular or pointed) spanning a space, usually made of wedge-shaped blocks. Known to the Greeks, who preferred a *post and lintel system, but exploited by the Romans.

Archetype　(Gk. *arche,* first: *typos,* form) The original pattern of forms of which things in this world are copies.

Architrave　The lowest part of an *entablature, a horizontal beam or *lintel directly above the *capital. (See figure 7.23.)

Aria　(I., AHR-yah; F., air) Solo song (sometimes duet) in *operas, *oratorios, *cantatas.

Ars antiqua　(L., old art) Music of the late twelfth and thirteenth centuries.

Ars nova　(L., new art) Music of the fourteenth century. Outstanding composers were Machaut (France) and Landini (Italy).

Art Nouveau　A style of architecture, crafts, and design of the 1890s and a bit later characterized by curvilinear patterns. Examples include Tiffany lamps and the work of Beardsley and Klimt.

Art song Song intending an artistic combination of words and music, as distinct from popular song or folk song.

Atheism (G., *a*, no; *theos,* god) The belief that there is no God; also means "not theistic" when applied to those who do not believe in a personal God.

Atrium The court of a Roman house, roofless, and near the entrance. Also the open, colonnaded court attached to the front of early Christian churches. (See figure 10.4.)

Aulos (OW-los) A shrill sounding oboelike instrument associated with the Dionysian rites of the ancient Greeks. Double-reed instrument normally played in pairs by one performer. (See figure 8.2.)

Avant-guard (a-vahn-GARD) A French term meaning, literally, advanced guard, and used to designate innovators and experimentalists in the various arts.

B

Baldachino (ball-da-KEEN-o) A canopy over a tomb or altar of which the most famous is that over the tomb of St. Peter in St. Peter's in Rome; designed by Bernini.

Ballad (L., *ballare,* to dance) Originally a dancing song. A narrative song, usually folk song but term also applied to popular songs.

Ballade Medieval *trouvère song. In the nineteenth and twentieth centuries dramatic piano pieces, frequently inspired by romantic poetry.

Balustrade A railing plus a supporting row of posts.

Banjo *Guitar family instrument, probably introduced into Africa by Arab traders and brought to America on the slave ships. The body consists of a shallow, hollow metal drum with a drumhead on top and open at the bottom. It has four or more strings and is played with fingers or plectrum.

Barrel vault v. Vault.

Basilica In Roman architecture, a rectangular public building used for business or as a tribunal. (See figure 12.9.) Christian churches that use a *cruciform plan are patterned after Roman basilicas. Though basilica is an architectural style, the Roman church calls a church a basilica if it contains the bones of a saint.

Bay In Romanesque and Gothic churches the area between the columns.

Behaviorism School of psychology that restricts both animal and human psychology to the study of behavior; stress on the role of the environment and on conditioned responses to exterior stimuli.

Blank verse Unrhymed *iambic pentameter* (v. meter) in the English language, much used in Elizabethan drama.

Bourgeoisie The middle class; in Marxist theory the capitalist class, which is opposed to the proletariat, the lower or industrial working class.

Buttress Exterior support used to counter the lateral thrust of an *arch or *vault. A *pier buttress* is a solid mass of masonry added to the wall; a *flying buttress* is typically a pier standing away from the wall and from which an arch "flies" from the pier to connect with the wall at the point of outward thrust. (See figure 15.28.)

C

Cadence Term in music applied to the concluding portion of a phrase (temporary cadence) or composition (permanent cadence).

Campanile Italian for bell tower, usually freestanding. The Leaning Tower of Pisa is a campanile. (See figure 15.21.)

Canon (Gk., law, rule) 1. A body of principles, rules, standards, or norms. 2. In art and architecture, a criterion for establishing proportion, measure, or scale. 3. In music, in which a melody is imitated strictly and in its entirety by another voice. Canons that have no specified way to end but keep going around are called "rounds," for example, "Three Blind Mice."

Canso A *troubadour song in "bar form," for example, A-A-B.

Cantata (I., *cantare,* to sing) A "sung" piece as opposed to a "sound" (instrumental) piece, for example, sonata. The term is now generally used for secular or sacred choral works with orchestral accompaniment, which are on a smaller scale than *oratorios.

Cantilever A self-supporting projection that needs no exterior bracing; e.g., a balcony or porch can be cantilevered.

Cantus firmus (L., fixed song) A preexisting melody used as the foundation for a *polyphonic composition. *Plainsong melodies were used for this purpose, but other sources included secular songs, Lutheran *chorales, and *scales. Any preexisting melody may serve as a cantus firmus.

Capital The top or crown of a column.

Cartoon A full-size preliminary drawing for a pictorial work, usually a large work such as a *mural, *fresco, or *tapestry. Also a humorous drawing.

Caryatid (care-ee-AT-id) A female figure that functions as a supporting *column; male figures that function in a like manner are called *atlantes* (at-LAN-tees; plural of Atlas). (See figure 7.35.)

Catharsis (Gk., *katharsis,* purge, purify) Purification, purging of emotions effected by tragedy (Aristotle).

Cella The enclosed chamber in a classical temple that contained the cult statue of the god or goddess after whom the temple was named.

Chamber music Term now restricted to instrumental music written for a limited number of players in which there is only one player to each part, as opposed to orchestral music, which has two or more players to some parts, for example, sixteen players on the first violin part. True chamber music emphasizes ensemble rather than solo playing.

Chanson (F., song) A major part of the *troubadour-*trouvère tradition, dating from the eleventh through the fourteenth centuries. Generic term for the general song production to a French text.

Chevet (sheh-VAY; F., pillow) The eastern end of a church, including *choir, *ambulatory, and *apse.

Chiaroscuro (kee-AR-oh-SKOOR-oh; I., light-dark) In the visual arts the use of gradations of light and dark to represent natural light and shadows.

Chinoiserie (she-nwaz-eh-REE; F.) Chinese motifs as decorative elements for craft objects, screens, wallpaper, and furniture; prominent in eighteenth-century rococo style.

Choir That part of the church where the singers and clergy are normally accommodated; usually between the *transept and the *apse; also called chancel. (See figure 15.29.)

Chorale A *hymn tune of the German Protestant (Lutheran) church.

Chord In music the simultaneous sounding of three or more tones.

Chromatic (Gk., *chroma,* color) The use of notes that are foreign to the musical *scale and have to be indicated by a sharp, flat, natural, etc. The *chromatic scale* is involved in these alterations. It consists of twelve tones to an octave, each a semitone apart.

Cire perdue (seer pair-DUE; F., lost wax) A metal casting method in which the original figure is modeled in wax and encased in a mold; as the mold is baked the wax melts and runs out, after which the molten metal is poured into the mold.

Clavichord The earliest type of stringed keyboard instrument (twelfth century). Probably developed from the *monochord. It is a 2′ × 4′ oblong box with a keyboard of about three octaves. The strings run parallel to the keyboard, as opposed to harpsichords and pianos, in which the strings run at right angles to the keyboard. The keys are struck from below by metal tangents fastened to the opposite ends of elongated keys. The tone is light and delicate but very expressive because the performer can control the loudness of each note. It was sometimes called a "table *clavier" because it was portable.

Clavier Generic term for any instrument of the stringed keyboard family: clavichord, harpsichord, and piano.

Clef (F., key) In music a symbol placed on the staff to indicate the pitches of the lines and spaces. There are three clefs in use today: G, F, and C. The G clef is used to indicate that the note on the second line is G (treble clef). The F clef is usually used to indicate that F is on the fourth line (bass clef).

Treble Clef

Bass Clef

Clerestory In a *basilica or church, the second level, the wall that rises above the roof of the other parts and has numerous windows.

Cloister An inner court bounded by covered walks; a standard feature of monastery architecture.

Collage (F., pasting) Paper and other materials pasted on a two-dimensional surface.

Colonnade A series of spaced *columns, usually connected by *lintels. (See figure 12.10.)

Column A vertical support, usually circular, which has a base (except in *Doric style), shaft, and *capital. (See figure 7.23.)

Comedy A play or other literary work in which all ends well, properly, or happily. Opposite of *tragedy.

Concerto (con-CHAIR-toe; I.) A musical work for one or more solo voices with orchestral accompaniment.

Contrapposto (I., set against). Figural sculpture in which parts of the body (usually hips and legs, arms and shoulders) are set against each other along a central axis, setting up an alternation of tension and relaxation.

Corinthian The most ornate style of Greek architecture, little used by the Greeks but preferred by the Romans; tall, slender, channeled *columns topped by an elaborate *capital decorated with stylized *acanthus leaves. (See figure 10.9.)

Cornice The horizontal, projecting member crowning an *entablature.

Cosmology Philosophic study of the origin and nature of the universe.

Couplet In poetry two successive rhymed lines in the same meter.

Credo (L., I believe) Third item of the *Ordinary of the *Mass.

Crocket In Gothic architecture an ornamental device shaped like a curling leaf and placed on the outer angles of *gables and pinnacles. (See colorplate 26.)

Crossing In a church, the space formed by the interception of the *nave and the *transepts.

Cruciform The floor plan of a church in the shape of a *Latin cross. (See figure 15.29.)

Cupola A rounded roof or ceiling; a small *dome.

D

Daguerrotype After L. J. M. Daguerre (1789–1851) the inventor. Photograph made on a silver-coated glass plate.

Determinism (L., *de* + *terminus,* end) The doctrine that all events are conditioned by their causes and that people are mechanical expressions of heredity and environment; in short, we are at the mercy of blind, unknowing natural laws; the universe could not care less.

Deus ex machina (DAY-oos ex ma-KEE-na; L.) In Greek and Roman drama a deity who was brought in by stage machinery to resolve a difficult situation; any unexpected or bizarre device or event introduced to untangle a plot.

Dialectic Associated with Plato as the art of debate by question and answer. Also dialectical reasoning using *syllogisms (Aristotle) or, according to Hegel, the distinctive characteristic of speculative thought.

Dome A hemispherical vault; may be viewed as an *arch rotated on its vertical axis.

Doric The oldest of Greek temple styles, characterized by sturdy *columns with no base and an unornamented cushionlike *capital. (See figure 7.23.)

Drum The circular sections that make up the shaft of a *column; also the circular wall on which a *dome is placed. (See figure 7.22.)

Drums Percussion musical instruments having a skin stretched over one or both ends of a frame.

Dualism In *metaphysics, a theory that admits two independent substances, e.g., Plato's dualism of the sensible and intelligible worlds, Cartesian dualism of thinking and extended subjects, Kant's dualism of the noumenal and the phenomenal.

E

Elegy   A meditative poem dealing with the idea of death.

Elevation   The vertical arrangements of the elements of an architectural design; a vertical projection.

Empiricism   A proposition that the sole source of knowledge is experience, that no knowledge is possible independent of experience.

Engaged column   A nonfunctional form projecting from the surface of a wall; used for visual articulation. (See figure 10.8.)

Engraving   The process of using a sharp instrument to cut a design into a metal plate, usually copper; also the print that is made from the plate after ink has been added.

Entablature   The part of a building of *post and lintel construction between the *capitals and the roof. In classical architecture this includes the *architrave, *frieze, and *cornice. (See figure 7.22.)

Entasis   (EN-ta-sis) A slight convex swelling in the shaft of a *column.

Epic   A lengthy narrative poem dealing with protagonists of heroic proportions and issues of universal significance, e.g., Homer's *Iliad*.

Epicurean   One who believes that pleasure, especially that of the mind, is the highest good.

Epistemology   A branch of philosophy that studies the origin, validity, and processes of knowledge.

Eschatology   (Gk., *ta eschata,* death) That part of theology dealing with last things: death, judgment, heaven, hell.

Estampie   (es-TAHM-pea) A dance form popular during the twelfth to fourteenth centuries. Consists of a series of repeated sections, for example, aa, bb, cc, etc.

Etching   A kind of *engraving in which the design is incised into a wax-covered metal plate, after which the exposed metal is etched by a corrosive acid; the print made from the plate is also called an etching.

Ethos   In ancient Greek music the "ethical" character attributed to the various modes. The Dorian was considered strong and manly; the Phrygian, ecstatic and passionate; the Lydian, feminine, decadent, and lascivious; the Mixolydian, mournful and gloomy.

Euphemism   An innocuous term substituted for one considered to be offensive or socially unacceptable, e.g., "passing away" for "dying."

F

Facade   One of the exterior walls of a building, usually the one containing the main entrance.

Fenestration   The arrangement of windows or other openings in the walls of a building.

Fiddle   Colloquialism for the violin. Also used to designate the bowed ancestors of the violin, particularly the medieval instrument used to accompany dances.

Finial   In Gothic architecture an ornament fitted to the peak of an *arch; any ornamental terminating point, such as the screw-top of a lamp. (See colorplate 26.)

Flamboyant   Late Gothic architecture of the fifteenth or sixteenth centuries, which featured wavy lines and flamelike forms.

Flèche   (flesh; F., arrow) In architecture a slender spire above the intersection of the *nave and *transepts. (See figure 15.28.)

Flute   A *woodwind instrument made of wood (originally), silver, gold, or preferably platinum. It is essentially a straight pipe with keys, is held horizontally and played by blowing across a mouthpiece.

Fluting   The vertical grooves, usually semicircular, in the shaft of a *column or *pilaster.

Foot   A metrical unit in poetry such as the iamb   /. Also see meter.

Foreshortening   Creating the illusion in painting or drawing that the subject is projecting out of or into the frontal plane of a two-dimensional surface.

Free Verse   A verse that uses parallelism and sound effects rather than *meter and rhyme.

Fresco   (I., fresh) Painting on plaster, usually wet plaster on which the colors are painted, sinking in as the plaster dries and the fresco becomes part of the wall.

Frieze   In architecture, a decorated horizontal band, often embellished with carved figures and molding; the portion of an *entablature between the *architrave and the *cornice above. (See figure 7.22.)

Fugue   *Polyphonic musical composition in which a single theme is developed by the different musical voices in succession. A favorite style of Baroque composers like Bach and Handel.

G

Gable   In architecture the triangular section at the end of a pitched roof, frequently with a window below.

Genre   (ZHAN-re) In the pictorial arts, a depiction of scenes of everyday life. In literature, the type of work—epic, novel, and so on.

Goliards   Wandering scholars of the tenth through the thirteenth centuries: students, young ecclesiastics, dreamers, and the disenchanted.

Gospels   In the Bible, New Testament accounts (Matthew, Mark, Luke, and John) of the life and teachings of Christ.

Gouache   (goo-AHSH; F.) Watercolor made opaque by adding zinc white.

Graphic arts   Visual arts that are linear in character: drawing, engraving, printing, printmaking, typographic, and advertising design.

Greek cross   A cross in which the four arms are of equal length.

Gregorian chant   v. Plainsong.

Groin   In architecture the edge (groin) formed by the intersection of two *vaults. (See figures 15.18 and 15.19.)

Guitar   A plucked string instrument with a flat body and six strings (modern guitar). Brought into Europe during the Middle Ages by the Moorish conquest of Spain.

H

Harpsichord   Actually a harp turned on its side and played by means of quills or leather tongues operated by a keyboard. It was the most common keyboard instrument of the sixteenth to eighteenth centuries and is again being built today in increasing numbers.

Hatching   A series of closely spaced parallel lines in a drawing or print giving the effect of shading.

Hedonism   The doctrine that pleasure or pleasant consciousness are intrinsically good; that pleasure is the proper—and the actual—motive for every choice.

Heroic couplet   Two successive lines of rhymed iambic pentameter, e.g., Pope's *Essay on Man*.

Hieratic   (HYE-uh-RAT-ik) Of or used by priests; priestly.

Hieroglyphics   Symbols or pictures standing for a word, syllable, or sound; writing system of ancient Egyptians.

Homophonic   (Gk., same sound) Music in which a single melodic line is supported by chords or other subordinate material (percussion instruments).

Hubris   (HU-bris) *Tragic flaw,* i.e., excessive pride or arrogance that injures other people (not physically) and brings about the downfall of the person with the flaw.

Hue   The name of a color. The chief colors of the spectrum are: red, yellow, blue (primary); green, orange, violet (secondary).

Hydraulis   Ancient Greek *pipe organ, probably invented in the Middle East 300–200 B.C. Air for the pipes was provided by hydraulic pressure and the pipes activated by a keyboard. Originally the tone was delicate and clear, but the Romans converted it into a noisy outdoor instrument by a large increase in air pressure.

Hymn   A poem of praise. Usually, but not necessarily, sacred. The music accompanying a hymn is called the hymn tune.

I

Icon   (EYE-kon; Gk., image) Two-dimensional representation of a holy person; in the Greek church a panel painting of a sacred personage. (See figure 12.22.)

Iconography   Visual imagery used to convey concepts in the visual arts; the study of symbolic meanings in the pictorial arts.

Illumination   Decorative illustrations or designs, associated primarily with medieval illuminated manuscripts.

Impasto   (I., paste) A painting style in which the pigment is laid on thickly, as in many of van Gogh's paintings.

Intaglio   (in-TAL-yo) A graphic technique in which the design is incised; used on seals, gems, and dies for coins and also for the kinds of printing and printmaking that have a depressed ink-bearing surface.

Ionic   A style of Greek classical architecture using slender, *fluted *columns and *capitals decorated with scrolls and *volutes. (See figure 7.22.)

Isocepholy   (I-so-SEPH-uh-ly) In the visual arts a convention that arranges figures so that the heads are at the same height. (See figure 7.44.)

J

Jamb figure   Sculpted figure flanking the portal of a Gothic church. (See figure 15.31.)

Jihad   Muslim holy war; a Muslim crusade against unbelievers.

Jongleur   (zhon-GLEUR) French professional musicians (minstrels) of the twelfth and thirteenth centuries who served the *troubadours and *trouvères.

K

Keystone   The central wedge-shaped stone in an *arch; the last stone put in place and which makes the arch stable. (See figure 15.26.)

Kibla   The point towards which Muslims turn when praying, towards Mecca.

Kithara   (KITH-a-ra) The principal stringed instrument of the ancient Greeks. Essentially a larger version of the *lyre, it has a U-shaped form and usually seven to eleven strings running vertically from the cross arm down to the sound box at the base of the instrument. The legendary instrument of Apollo. (See figure 8.3.)

Kyrie eleison   (Gk., Lord have mercy) The first item of the *Ordinary of the *Mass.

L

Lantern   In architecture a small decorative structure that crowns a *dome or roof.

Latin cross   A cross in which the vertical member is longer than the horizontal arm it bisects.

Libretto   (I., little book) The text or words of an *opera, *oratorio, or other extended choral work.

Lied, Lieder   (leet, LEE-der; G., song, songs). Term usually applied to the German romantic *art songs of Schubert, Schumann, Brahms, Wolf, and others. Also used for medieval songs, that is, *minnesinger and *meistersinger.

Lintel   In architecture a horizontal crosspiece over an open space, which carries the weight of some of the superstructure. (See figure 7.20.)

Lithography   A printmaking process that uses a polished stone (or metal plate) on which the design is drawn with a crayon or greasy ink. Ink is chemically attracted only to the lines of the drawing, with a print made by applying paper to the inked stone.

Liturgical   Pertaining to public worship, specifically to the organized worship patterns of the Christian churches.

Liturgical drama   Twelfth- and thirteenth-century enactments of biblical stories, frequently with music. Developed into the "mystery plays" of the fourteenth through sixteenth centuries.

Lituus   (L.) Bronze trumpet used by the Roman armies. Shaped like the letter J.

Lost wax process   v. *cire perdue*.

Lute   Plucked stringed instrument with a pear-shaped body and a fingerboard with frets. It had eleven strings tuned to six notes (five sets of double strings plus a single string for the highest note). It was the most popular instrument of the sixteenth century and was used into the eighteenth century. Lutes are again being made, mainly for present-day performances of Renaissance music.

Lyre   (or Lyra) Ancient Greek instrument, a simpler form of the *kithara. The sound box was often made of a tortoise shell. Used mainly by amateurs. The larger kithara was used by professional musicians. (See figure 8.1.)

Lyric   Poetry sung to the accompaniment of a *lyre (Greek); *troubadour and *trouvère poetry intended to be sung; short poems with musical elements. (See figure 8.4.)

M

Madrigal   Name of uncertain origin that refers to fourteenth-century vocal music or, usually, to the popular sixteenth-century type. Renaissance madrigals were free-form vocal pieces (usually set to love lyrics) in a *polyphonic style with intermixed *homophonic sections. Flemish, Italian, and English composers brought the madrigal to a high level of expressiveness in word painting and imagery. Madrigals were sometimes accompanied but mostly *a cappella.

Mass   The central service of public worship of some Christian churches, principally the Roman Catholic church. The musical portions are indicated below.

Ordinary (Same Text)	Proper (Text Varies by the Liturgical Calendar)
Kyrie Eleison	Introit
Gloria in Excelsis Deo	Gradual
Credo in Unum Deum	Alleluia
Sanctus	Offertory
Agnus Dei	Communion

Materialism   The doctrine that the only reality is matter; that the universe is not governed by intelligence or purpose but only by mechanical cause and effect.

Meistersinger   (G., mastersinger) The highest level in the music-poetry guilds of Germany in the fifteenth and sixteenth centuries. Succeeding the earlier *minnesinger tradition the guilds held song schools and awarded prizes, with top prizes for creating new songs going to the "mastersingers."

Melisma   A melodic unit sung to one syllable; *plainsong has frequent *melismatic* passages.

Metaphor   A form of figurative language that compares dissimilar objects (e.g., publicity is a two-edged sword).

Metaphysics   Philosophic inquiry into the ultimate and fundamental reality; "the science of being as such."

Meter   In music a grouping of beats into patterns of two, three, or four beats or combinations thereof; in English poetry the basic rhythmic pattern of stressed (—) and unstressed (‿) syllables. Metrical patterns include: *iambic* (‿ —), *trochaic* (— ‿), *anapestic* (‿ ‿ —), and *dactylic* (— ‿ ‿).

Metope   (MET-o-pay) In classical architecture the panel between two *triglyphs in a *Doric *frieze; may be plain or carved. The Parthenon metopes are all carved.

Minaret   A tall, slender tower attached to a Muslim mosque from which a muezzin calls the faithful to prayer.

Minnesinger   (G., from *minne,* love) German poet-musicians of noble birth of the thirteenth to fifteenth centuries (leading to the *meistersingers) who were influenced by the *troubadour-trouvère tradition of the age of chivalry. They composed *monophonic songs, usually in *bar form.

Minstrel   v. Jongleur.

Modes, rhythmic   A thirteenth-century system of music rhythmic notation based on the patterns of poetic meter. Rhythmic modes give the characteristic flavor to thirteenth-century *organum and *motets because of the constant repetition of the same rhythmic patterns. All modes were performed in so-called "perfect" meter, that is, triple.

Rhythmic Mode	Poetic Meter	Accent Pattern	Performed
I	Trochaic	— ‿	♩ ♫♩ ♪
II	Iambic	‿ —	♫♩ ♫♩
III	Dactylic	— ‿ ‿	♩. ♫♪
IV	Anapaestic	‿ ‿ —	♫♩ ♩.
V	Spondiac	— —	♩. ♩.
VI	Tribrachic	‿ ‿ ‿	♫♫ ♫♫

Monism   (Gk., *mones,* single) The philosophical position that there is but one fundamental reality. The classical advocate of extreme monism was Parmenides of Elea; Spinoza is a modern exponent.

Monochord   A device consisting of a single string stretched over a soundboard with a movable bridge. Used to demonstrate the laws of acoustics, especially the relationships between intervals and string lengths and the tuning of *scales. (See figure 16.2.)

Monophonic   (Gk., one sound) A single line of music without accompaniment or additional parts, as in *plainsong, *troubadour-trouvère-minnesinger songs, and some *folk songs, hollers, street cries, and blues.

Montage   (moan-TAHZH) A composition made of existing photographs, paintings, or drawings; in cinematography the effects achieved by superimposing images or using rapid sequences.

Mosaic   The technique of embedding bits of stone, colored glass, or marble in wet concrete to make designs or pictures for walls or floors. To achieve a complex interplay of light and shadows, the bits are set in the holding material with minute differences in the angles, as in the mosaics of San Vitale in Ravenna. (See colorplates 16 and 17.)

Motet   (from F., *mot,* word) The most important form of early *polyphonic music (ca. thirteenth to seventeenth centuries).
   1. *Medieval motet* (thirteenth-fourteenth centuries). Usually 3 parts (triplum, motetus, tenor). The tenor "holds" to a *cantus firmus and the upper two voices sing different texts (sacred and/or secular).
   2. *Renaissance motet* (fifteenth-sixteenth centuries). A four- or five-part composition, *a cappella, generally *polyphonic, with a single Latin text. A serious vocal piece intended for use in sacred services.
      There are also Baroque motets (by J. S. Bach) for mixed chorus and orchestra (German text) and some Romantic motets (Brahms), again in the *a cappella style.

Mullion   A vertical member that divides a window into sections; also used to support the glass in stained-glass windows.

Mural   A painting on a wall; a *fresco is a type of mural.

Myth   Stories explaining natural phenomena, customs, institutions, religious beliefs, and so forth of a people. Usually concerned with the supernatural, gods, goddesses, heroic exploits, and the like.

N

Narthex   A porch or vestibule of a church through which one passes to enter the *nave.

Naturalism   The view that the universe requires no supernatural cause or government, that it is self-existent, self-explanatory, self-operating, and self-directing, that the universe is purposeless, deterministic, and only incidentally productive of man. In relation to literature sometimes defined as "realism on all fours." The dominant traits of literary naturalism are biological determinism (people are what they must be because of their genes) and environmental determinism (people are what they are because of where they were nurtured).

Nave   The main central space of a church running from the entrance to the *crossing of the *transepts; typically flanked by one or two side aisles. Name derived from *naval* because the barrel *vault ceiling has the appearance of the inside hull of a ship.

Nomos, Nome   (Gk., law, rule) In the Homeric tradition in ancient Greece the term is used to refer to the traditional phrases and melodies singers used to recite the *epics and *odes.

Notre Dame school   The composers of the twelfth- and thirteenth-century cathedral school at Notre Dame de Paris, most notably Leonin and Perotin. The Notre Dame school invented rhythmic notation for *polyphonic music.

O

Oboe   (from F., "high wind," that is, high-pitched instrument) A double-reed, soprano-range instrument with a conical bore (slightly expanding diameter from reed to bell). It has a nasal but mellow and poignant tone.

Odalisque   (oh-de-LISK) French word for a harem slave or concubine but used more broadly to refer to a reclining female figure, a favorite subject of painters like Ingres and Matisse.

Ode   A formal lyric on a usually dignified theme, in exalted language, e.g., works by Horace.

Office hours   In the Roman Catholic church the services (usually observed only in monastic churches) that take place eight times a day (every three hours): Matins, Lauds, Prime, Terce, Sext, None, Vespers, and Compline. Musically the important services are Matins, Vespers, and Compline.

Ontology   (Gk., *on,* being + *logos,* logic) Philosophic inquiry into the ultimate nature of things, what it means to be.

Opera   (from I., *opera in musica,* work in music) A play in which the text is generally sung throughout to the accompaniment of an orchestra. Modern opera had its beginnings in Florence in the late sixteenth century when some musicians, poets, and scholars attempted a revival of Greek drama, which they assumed to have been sung throughout.

Oratorio   A musical setting of a religious or epic theme for performance by soloists, chorus, and orchestra in a church or concert hall. Originally (early seventeenth century) they were similar to operas (sacred operas) with staging, costumes, and scenery. They are now usually presented in concert form, for example, *The Messiah,* by G. F. Handel.

Orchestra   (from Gk., *orcheisthai,* to dance) In ancient Greek theatres the circular or semicircular space in front of the stage used by the chorus; group of instrumentalists performing ensemble music, e.g., symphony orchestra.

Ordinary of the Mass   v. Mass.

Organ, Pipe organ   An instrument (see Hydraulis) of ancient origin consisting of from two to seven keyboards (manuals) and a set of pedals (usually thirty-two notes) for the feet.

Organum   (OR-ga-num; L.) The name given to the earliest types of *polyphonic music. Beginning with about the ninth century, organum was first strict, then parallel, free (contrary motion), and *melismatic. See (in the text) the section on medieval music for description and illustrations of the stages of organum.

P

Pantheism (Gk., *pan,* all, + *theos,* god) As a religious concept, the doctrine that God is immanent in all things.

Pediment In classic architecture a triangular space at the end of a building framed by the *cornice and the ends of the sloping roof (*raking cornices). (See figure 7.21.)

Pendentive In architecture a concave triangular piece of masonry, four of which form a transition from a square base to support the circular rim of a *dome. (See figure 12.17.)

Percussion Instruments that are played by striking, shaking, scraping, etc.

Peristyle A series *of columns that surround the exterior of a building or the interior of a court, e.g., the Parthenon has a peristyle. (See figure 7.23.)

Perspective The illusion of a three-dimensional world on a two-dimensional surface. *Linear perspective* uses lines of projection converging on a vanishing point and with objects appearing smaller the further from the viewer. *Aerial (atmospheric) perspective* uses diminished color intensity and blurred contours for objects apparently deeper in space.

Pier A mass of masonry, usually large, used to support *arches or *lintels; more massive than a *column and with a shape other than circular. (See figure 15.9.)

Pietà (pyay-TA; I., pity, compassion) Representations of the Virgin mourning the body of her Son.

Pilaster A flat vertical column projecting from the wall of a building; usually furnished with a base and *capital in the manner of an *engaged column, which is rounded rather than rectangular like the pilaster.

Plainsong The term generally used for the large body of nonmetrical, *monophonic, *liturgical music of the Roman Catholic church. Also called Gregorian chant.

Polyphony (po-LIF-o-nee) *Polyphonic* (pol-ly-PHON-ik) "Many-voiced" music, that is, melodic interest in two or more simultaneous melodic lines. Examples of polyphonic music would be *canons and *rounds.

Positivism Philosophic inquiry limited to problems open to scientific investigation. Traditional subjects such as *aesthetics and *metaphysics are dismissed as "meaningless" because their content cannot be subjected to verification.

Post and lintel A structural system in which vertical supports or columns support horizontal beams. The lintel can span only a relatively short space because the weight of the superstructure centers on the mid-point of the horizontal beam. In a structural system using *arches the thrust is distributed to the *columns supporting the bases of the arches, thus allowing for a greater span. The lintel is also called an *architrave. (See figure 7.19.)

Pragmatism (Gk., *pragma,* things done) Philosophic doctrine that the meaning of a proposition or course of action lies in its observable consequences and that its meaning is the sum of its consequences. In everyday life the favoring of practical means over theory; if something works, it's good; if not, it's bad.

Primary colors The *hues of red, yellow, and blue with which the colors of the spectrum can be produced. Primary colors cannot be produced by mixing.

Program music Music intended to depict ideas, scenes, or other extramusical concepts.

Proper of the Mass v. Mass.

Proscenium (Gk., *pro,* before; *skene,* stage) In traditional theatres the framework of the stage opening.

Psalm A sacred song, poem, or *hymn; the songs in the Old Testament book of The Psalms.

Psalter Vernacular name for the book of The Psalms. v. Psalm.

Psaltery Ancient or medieval instrument consisting of a flat soundboard over which a number of strings are stretched. A psaltery is plucked with the fingers. A similar instrument, the dulcimer, is played by striking the strings with hammers. The *harpsichord is a keyed psaltery. (See figure 14.1.)

Putto (I., plural *putti,* boy) The cherubs in Italian Renaissance painting and in rococo painting of the eighteenth century.

Q

Quatrain A stanza of four lines, either rhymed or unrhymed.

R

Raking cornice The end (*cornice) on the sloping sides of a triangular *pediment.

Rebec A small bowed medieval string instrument adapted from the Arabian *rebab.* It was one of the instruments from which the violin developed during the sixteenth century. (See figure 16.3.)

Recorder A straight, end-blown *flute, as distinct from the modern side-blown (transverse) flute. It was used from the Middle Ages until the eighteenth century and has been revived in the twentieth century.

Refrain Recurring section of text (and usually music), e.g., verse-refrain.

Relief In sculpture, carvings projecting from a background that is a part of the whole. Reliefs may be high (almost disengaged from the background) or low (*bas relief,* slightly raised above the background).

Reliquary (F., remains) A receptacle for storing or displaying holy relics. (See colorplate 20.)

Round In music a commonly used name for a circle *canon. At the conclusion of a melody the singer returns to the beginning, repeating the melody as often as desired. Examples: "Brother James," "Dona Nobis Pacem," and "Row, Row, Row Your Boat."

S

Sanctuary   A sacred or holy place set aside for the worship of a god or gods; a place of refuge or protection.

Sanctus   (L., Holy) The fourth item in the *Ordinary of the *Mass.

Sarcophagus   A stone coffin.

Satire   An indictment of human foibles using humor as a weapon, e.g., the relatively mild satires of Horace and the bitter ones of Juvenal.

Scale   (L., ladder) The tonal material of music arranged in a series of rising or falling pitches. Because of the variety in the world's music there are many different scales. The basic scale of European music is the diatonic scale (C-D-E-F-G-A-B-C), i.e., the white keys of the piano. This arrangement of tones is also called a major scale or, more properly, a C major scale.

Scholasticism   The philosophy and method of medieval theologians in which speculation was separated from observation and practice, revelation was regarded as both the norm and an aid to reason, reason respected authority, and scientific inquiry was controlled by theology.

Secondary colors   Those *hues located between the *primary hues on a traditional color wheel: orange, green, and violet.

Sequence   A type of chant developed in the early Middle Ages in which a freely poetic text was added to the long *melisma at the end of the *Alleluias. Subsequently separated from the Alleluias, the sequences became independent syllabic chants. The composition of many original sequences finally led to the banning of all but five sequences by the Council of Trent (1545–1563).

Sfumato   (sfoo-MAH-toe) A hazy, smoky blending of color tones in a painting to create ambiguities of line and shape, as in Leonardo's *Mona Lisa.*

Simile   A comparison between two quite different things, usually using "like" or "as."

Sonnet   A fourteen-line poem in iambic pentameter. Petrarch, the fourteenth-century Italian poet, used a rhyming scheme of *abbaabba* followed by *cde cde* or variants thereof. Shakespeare used a rhyming scheme of *abab cdcd efef gg,* or four *quatrains followed by a *rhymed couplet.

Squinch   In architecture a device to effect a transition from a polygonal base to a circular *dome. (See figure 12.17 and accompanying explanation.)

Stele   (STEE-lee) A carved slab of stone or pillar used especially by the Greeks as a grave marker. (See figure 7.44.)

Still life   In pictorial arts inanimate objects used as subject matter.

Stylobate   The third of three steps of a Greek temple on which the *columns rest; essentially the platform on which the *cella and *peristyle are erected. (See figure 7.28.)

Syllogism   A form of deductive reasoning consisting of a major premise, minor premise, and a conclusion. Example: all men are mortal; Sokrates is a man; therefore Sokrates is mortal.

T

Teleology   (Gk., *telos,* end, completion) The theory of purpose, ends, goals, final cause; opposite of materialism.

Tempera   A painting technique using pigment suspended in egg yolk.

Tenor   (L., *tenere,* to hold) (1) Originally the part that "held" the melody on which early sacred *polyphonic music was based. (2) The highest male voice (S A T B). (3) Prefix to the name of an instrument, for example, tenor saxophone.

Terra-cotta   (I., baked earth) A baked clay used in ceramics and sculptures; a reddish color.

Tesserae   (TESS-er-ee) Bits of stone and colored glass used in *mosaics.

Thrust   The outward force caused by the weight and design of an *arch or *vault, a thrust that must be countered by a *buttress. (See figure 15.26.)

Tragedy   A serious play or other literary work with an unhappy or disastrous ending caused, in Greek drama, by *hubris on the part of the protagonist.

Transcendental   Beyond the realm of the senses; rising above common thought or ideas; exalted.

Transept   That part of a *cruciform-plan church whose axis intersects at right angles the long axis of the cross running from the entrance through the *nave to the *apse; the cross-arm of the cross.

Triforium   In a Gothic cathedral, the gallery between the *nave arcades and the *clerestory; the triforium gallery opens on the nave with an *arcade. (See figure 15.34.)

Triglyph   Projecting block with vertical channels that alternates with *metopes in a *Dorian *frieze of a Greek temple. The ends of the marble beams are stylized versions of the wooden beams used in early temples.

Trompe-l'oeil   (trohmp LUH-yuh; F.) Illusionistic painting designed to convince the observer that what is seen is an actual three-dimensional object rather than a two-dimensional surface; literally, "eye fooling."

Trope   Additional text and/or music added to a preexisting *plainsong. The earliest tropes were *sequences. Troping became so widespread that it was banned by the Council of Trent. *Liturgical drama was a direct outgrowth of the trope.

Troubadour   Poet-musicians, mostly of aristocratic birth, of southern France (Provence) who, during the period ca. 1100–1300, cultivated the arts of poetry and music in chivalrous service to romantic love. Their music was *monophonic in style and popular in flavor but exerted considerable influence on the development of *polyphonic music.

Trouvère   Poet-musicians of central and northern France from ca. 1150–1300. Their music developed from the *troubadours and showed the same general characteristics except for the change in language from that of the south (Provençal) to the medieval forerunner of modern French.

Trumeau   A pillar or column placed in the center of a portal to help support the *lintel. (See figure 15.20.)

Tympanum   The space, usually elaborately carved, enclosed by the *lintel and *arch of a doorway; also, the space within the horizontal and *raking cornices of a *pediment. (See figure 15.17.)

V

Vanishing point   In linear *perspective the point at which parallel lines converge on the horizon.

Vault   A masonry ceiling constructed on the principle of the *arch. A *barrel vault* is an uninterrupted series of arches amounting to a very deep arch. (See figure 15.7.)

Virelai   A form of medieval French poetry with a *refrain before and after each stanza. Virelais were used by *trouvères and exploited during the Gothic period by Machaut and others.

Virginal   A *harpsichord used mainly in England and supposedly played by young ladies. The shape was frequently rectangular. When built in the standard two-keyboard form it was called a "pair of virginals."

Volute   The spiral scrolls of an *Ionian *capital.

Voussoir   (voo-SWAHR; F.) The wedge-shaped blocks of stone used to construct *arches and *vaults.

W

Woodcut   A wood block that has been carved so that the design stands out slightly from the block, comparable to printing type.

Z

Ziggurat   A temple tower of the ancient Mesopotamians.

Credits

Index

All B.C. dates are specified. Titles of works are set in *italics* with the artist/ creator's name in parentheses. Page numbers of black-and-white illustrations are in **boldface** type; colorplates are designated by colorplate number. See the Glossary for definitions of technical terms.

A